Continued on inside back cover

Intermediate Accounting

REVISED SIXTH EDITION

Intermediate Accounting

A. N. MOSICH, Ph.D., C.P.A.

Ernst & Whinney Professor of Accounting
University of Southern California

McGraw-Hill Book Company

New York | St. Louis | San Francisco | Auckland | Bogotá | Caracas
Colorado Springs | Hamburg | Lisbon | London | Madrid | Mexico | Milan
Montreal | New Delhi | Oklahoma City | Panama | Paris | San Juan
São Paulo | Singapore | Sydney | Tokyo | Toronto

**Intermediate
Accounting**

1 2 3 4 5 6 7 8 9 0   VNHVNH   8 9 4 3 2 1 0 9

ISBN 0-07-041855-1

This book was set in Times Roman by York Graphic Services, Inc.
The editors were Robert D. Lynch and Larry Goldberg;
the designer was Nicholas Krenitsky;
the production supervisor was Janelle S. Travers.
The drawings were done by York Graphic Services, Inc.
The cover photograph was taken by DeMarco/Tomaccio.
Von Hoffmann Press, Inc., was printer and binder.

Library of Congress Cataloging-in-Publication Data

Mosich, A. N.
   Intermediate accounting.

   Includes index.
   1. Accounting.   I. Title.
HF5635.M8754 1988   657'.044   88–27140
ISBN 0-07-041855-1

Contents

Preface

The revised sixth edition of *Intermediate Accounting* is designed for use in an intermediate-level financial accounting course following the introductory course in financial accounting. The book may be used in a two-semester or a three-semester course, or in a single course at the graduate level. The emphasis throughout is on underlying concepts and on analysis of the problems that arise in the application of the concepts to financial accounting. Appropriate attention is given to the use of accounting information as a basis for decisions by management, stockholders, creditors, and other users of financial statements.

The revised sixth edition reflects the dramatic changes that have been occurring in the development and application of accounting principles, with special attention to the pronouncements and exposure drafts of the Financial Accounting Standards Board and the Securities and Exchange Commission. In particular, the new FASB requirements in the areas of accounting for income taxes, statement of cash flows, and accounting for the effects of price change have been incorporated.

Features of This Edition

Four chapters have been significantly updated to include relevant pronouncements by accounting rule-making bodies. These pronouncements have been incorporated in this new edition in a manner that we consider pedagogically sound. Discussion of the economic consequences of new accounting principles has been expanded, and many illustrations have been added or strengthened.

For the sixth edition we prepared a new chapter, "Revenue and Expense Recognition; Income Measurement and Reporting,'' following the introductory chapters on accounting principles and information processing. We consider the concepts involved in the recognition of revenue and expenses (including gains and losses) as providing a useful foundation for much of the discussion in subsequent chapters dealing with the measurement of assets and liabilities. Because we place this new chapter early in the text (Chapter 3), our illustrations of revenue recognition situations are designed to cover the important concepts without unnecessary complexities. In this new chapter we cover revenue and expense recognition issues for service industries as well as for trading and manufacturing enterprises. Because revenue and expenses are the primary determinants of net income, we conclude with a discussion of income measurement concepts and special problems accountants face in the reporting of income.

The subject matter in Chapter 3 made it possible for us to present the discussion of financial statements in a single chapter (Chapter 4), thus maintaining this edition at 25 chapters. Chapter 4 also includes a section on ''Additional Disclosures,'' with special emphasis on reports filed with the Securities and Exchange Commission and annual reports issued to shareholders by publicly owned corporations.

Many additional topics have been incorporated in this edition. These include, for example, a discussion of standards overload, ''Big GAAP,'' and ''Little GAAP''; double-extension and link-chain techniques for estimating inventories under dollar-value lifo; depreciation for income tax purposes under the Accelerated Cost Recovery System (ACRS); unrealized intercompany profits in the application of the equity method of accounting for investments in equity securities; zero-coupon and deep-discount bonds; extinguishment of bonds through debt-equity swaps and in-substance defeasance; induced conversion of convertible debt (*FASB Statement No. 84*); contingent stock warrants issued to customers and junior stock issued to employees; effective yield test for determining common stock equivalency of convertible securities (*FASB Statement No. 85*); reporting a change in the reporting entity as a result of pooling-type business combinations; and the statement of changes in financial position on the cash concept that highlights operating, investing, and financing activities.

The financial section of the annual report of Walt Disney Productions is included in an Appendix at the end of Chapter 4, and reference is made to it in many of the subsequent chapters. The tables of present values and future amounts are included in an Appendix at the end of Chapter 5.

This edition also features innovative use of color to facilitate the learning process. The number of exercises and problems has been expanded significantly in many of the chapters. We have made a strong effort to cover all new topics added in the revised sixth edition in the questions, exercises, cases, and problems. The first exercise in each chapter consists of a series of multiple-choice questions, many adapted from recent Uniform CPA Examinations.

Organization of Subject Matter

We have organized the book in six parts to give focus to the subject matter and to provide a psychological benefit to students by making the contents more digestible. This arrangement should facilitate for instructors the planning and presentation of the subject matter and make it easier for students to learn and retain the concepts and procedures presented. A description of the contents of the six parts follows.

Part 1: Basic Concepts and Financial Statements (Chapters 1–5). The first part includes an overview of accounting principles and professional practice, a concise summary of the accounting process, recognition of revenue and expenses, financial statements and additional disclosures, and the application of present and future value concepts to financial accounting measurements. Chapter 1 places in perspective the development and application of accounting principles. The student is introduced to the issue of "standards overload" and to the debate between supporters of a single body of accounting standards and the advocates of "Little GAAP" and "Big GAAP." Increased emphasis is given to the objectives of financial statements, to the conceptual framework project of the FASB, to the economic consequences of accounting principles, and to the role of the SEC in stressing timely and relevant disclosure and in protecting investors. The review of basic data-collecting processes in Chapter 2 reinforces the student's understanding of fundamental recording, classifying, and summarizing procedures. This chapter includes a new section on the type of analysis required for the preparation of correcting entries. The background developed in the first two chapters leads to a consideration in Chapter 3 of the revenue and expense recognition principles on which income measurement is based. Special problems in income reporting also are included in this chapter; financial statements and additional disclosures are covered in Chapter 4.

The discussion in these early chapters (and throughout the book) is not limited to a description of acceptable practices. We believe it is important at this stage in accounting education to encourage students to evaluate accounting principles critically and to make them aware of the conflicts and shortcomings that exist in the traditional structure of accounting theory. At the same time, it is important to provide students with an analytical foundation for making this evaluation and to stress that many controversial areas in financial accounting frequently revolve around the economic consequences of accounting principles. To this end, the critical evaluation of accounting concepts is correlated with the *Statements* of the Financial Accounting Standards Board, the *Opinions* and *Statements* of the Accounting Principles Board, and the *Financial Reporting Releases* and *Staff Accounting Bulletins* of the Securities and Exchange Commission.

The first four chapters of the book constitute an overview of the accounting process and financial statements and are designed to provide a gradual transition from the introductory course in financial accounting to the more rigorous level of analysis in subsequent chapters of this book.

The final chapter in Part 1 addresses the concepts of present and future values of cash flows. The early introduction of this material enables us to make appropriate use of present and future value concepts for receivables and liabilities, for the acquisition of plant assets, for investments in bonds and promissory notes, for amortization of bond discount and premium, and for pension plans and leases.

Part 2: Working Capital (Chapters 6–10). The second part of the book addresses the accounting for cash and short-term investments, receivables, inventories, current liabilities, and contingencies. The discussion and illustrations of accounting for investments in short-term securities have been expanded and made more efficient. The components of electronic banking are described with the purpose of introducing students to computer-induced changes in handling cash transactions.

The section on the use of receivables to accelerate cash inflows has been expanded and updated to conform to the requirements of *FASB Statement No. 77,* ''Reporting by Transferors for Transfers of Receivables with Recourse.'' The discussion and illustrations of accounting for notes receivable have been extensively revised.

The two chapters on inventories have been expanded and updated. For example, the double-extension and link-chain techniques of applying the dollar-value lifo method have been added, and the section on accounting for construction-type contracts has been rewritten. Included is a discussion of input and output measures of degree of performance on contracts and an evaluation of accounting practices for construction-type contracts. Accounting for contingencies, notes payable, and other current liabilities has been reorganized and improved, and a new tabular summary of different types of contingencies has been provided.

Part 3: Long-Term Assets and Liabilities (Chapters 11–15). This part includes chapters on plant assets and depreciation, intangible assets, long-term investments, and long-term liabilities. New material is included relative to accelerated depreciation computations and the use of ACRS for income tax purposes. Coverage of natural resources and depletion has been expanded to include a discussion of the successful efforts and full cost methods of accounting by oil and gas enterprises.

The chapter on long-term investments includes an expanded treatment of the equity method of accounting for equity securities. Among new topics are: unrealized intercompany profits, retroactive application of the equity method of accounting, market value method of accounting for the conversion by investors of bonds to common stock, and long-term receivables.

We have attempted to sharpen the relationship of long-term investments to long-term debt. Accounting for zero-coupon bonds, debt-equity swaps, in-substance defeasance of debt, and restructured debt has either been added or significantly expanded. The illustration of the type of analysis required for a refunding decision (a financial management topic) has been deleted from the current edition.

Part 4: Stockholders' Equity (Chapters 16–18). The coverage of accounting topics unique to corporations is again presented in three chapters. The first chapter includes the accounting for the traditional issues relating to paid-in capital, retained earnings, and dividends. In the second chapter, we have significantly revised the discussion of stock warrants, convertible securities, and employee capital accumulation plans. New sections have been added on contingent stock warrants to customers, market value method of accounting by the issuer for the conversion of bonds to common stock, induced conversion of convertible bonds, accounting for terminated stock options, and accounting for junior stock. The accounting for employee stock ownership plans (ESOP) is now illustrated with journal entries and the coverage of stock option plans has been updated and made more cohesive.

Part 4 concludes with consideration of accounting for treasury stock and earnings per share. These two subjects are combined in this chapter for two reasons—to achieve a better balance of learning modules in this part of the textbook and to emphasize the importance of treasury stock transactions and the ''treasury stock method'' for outstanding stock options and stock warrants in the computation of primary and fully diluted earnings per share. Developments in the areas of ''hostile corporate takeovers,'' ''greenmail'' payments to corporate ''raiders,'' ''tender offers'' for large amounts of outstanding capital stock, and the ''effective yield'' method to test the common stock equivalency of convertible securities are incorporated in this chapter.

Part 5: More Complex Accounting Topics (Chapters 19–22). The chapters in this part are grouped together because they address some of the more specialized and challenging financial accounting topics. Separate chapters are devoted to the accounting for employee pension plans, leases, and income taxes. Chapter 19 fully incorporates *FASB Statement No. 87,* ''Employers' Accounting for Pension Plans.'' The final chapter includes three topics—changes in accounting principles and estimates, correction of accounting errors, and the preparation of financial statements from fragmentary accounting records.

Among the improvements we have made in this part are the following: (1) substantial rewrite and expansion of discussion of defined benefit pension plans; (2) presentation of differing views on nature of pension liabilities; (3) expanded amortization and funding tables to illustrate more typical measurement of pension expense; (4) new illustration of accounting for a legal obligation for unfunded past service cost; (5) expanded coverage of accounting for sales-type leases and addition of discussion of the effect of investment tax credits retained by lessors; (6) more complete discussion of income taxes for interim periods and the new *FASB Statement No. 96;* and (7) a new section illustrating a change in the reporting entity.

Part 6: Analytical Procedures and Statements (Chapters 23–25). The final part consists of three chapters on special financial statements (statements of cash flow, constant-purchasing power and current-cost financial statements), the new *FASB Statement No. 89,* and the analysis and interpretation of financial statements. Special emphasis is given to the impact of inflation on financial statements and on business decisions. The chapter on the statement of cash flow has been thoroughly revised. Emphasis is given to the new reporting requirements of *FASB Statement No. 95* and to a new statement format that highlights operating, investing, and financing activities of business enterprises.

Features Carried Forward from Prior Edition

A continuing feature of this edition is the accompanying *Test Bank* (formerly called *Examination Questions*) with test material arranged on a chapter-by-chapter basis. This booklet contains true or false and multiple-choice questions and numerous short problems for each chapter. It should be a most useful source for instructors who prepare their own examinations and emphasize specific chapters or topics. Answers for the questions and short problems are provided in the booklet.

An especially useful supplement carried forward from the prior edition is a *Study Guide* prepared by the authors and designed to help students measure their progress by immediate feedback. The Guide contains an outline of the most important points for each chapter, plus a variety of objective questions and short exercises. Answers to the questions and short exercises appear at the end of each chapter of the Guide to help students evaluate their understanding of the topics covered in the text. The Appendix of the *Study Guide* includes check figures for selected exercises in the text.

The *Instructor's Manual,* written by Prof. Talmadge C. Tillman, Jr., of California State University, Long Beach, again has been prepared for use with the revised sixth edition of *Intermediate Accounting.* It is available at no cost to instructors. The *Manual* includes for each chapter a description of all available assignment materials (problems, cases, exercises, and review questions), suggested assignments, objectives of the chapter and suggested teaching approach, review of the subject matter of the chapter, selected multiple-choice questions from recent CPA Examinations, and a suggested list of supplementary readings.

Also continued from the prior edition is a two-volume set of partially filled-in working papers, a comprehensive package of transparencies for problem solutions, and (inside the text covers) a list of check figures for problems.

Questions, Exercises, Cases, and Problems

An expanded amount of learning and assignment material is provided at the end of each chapter. This material is divided into four groups—questions, exercises, cases, and problems.

The questions are intended for use by students as a self-testing and review device to measure their comprehension of key points in each chapter. Many of the questions are provocative, which makes them suitable for written assignments and class discussion.

Exercises generally cover a specific point or topic and do not require extensive computations. Instructors may use the exercises for homework assignments, for class discussion, and for examination purposes. We have class-tested all exercises included in this edition.

Cases generally require analytical reasoning but involve little or no quantitative data. In these cases, students are required to analyze business situations, to apply accounting principles, and to propose a course of action. However, they are not required to prepare lengthy working papers or otherwise to manipulate accounting data on an extensive scale. The cases also have been class-tested and are an effective means of encouraging students to take positions in the evaluation of controversial accounting issues. A number of the cases have been adapted from Uniform CPA Examinations. The cases and questions are especially recommended as a means of sharpening students' skills in communicating accounting concepts and in weighing the merits of opposing arguments.

Many of the problems are new, and most of the problems carried over from the preceding edition have been updated and revised. Special attention has been given to the inclusion of an adequate number of short problems in each chapter. The problems range in difficulty from easy to strong. Most of the problems in the Accounting Theory and Accounting Practice sections of recent Uniform CPA Examinations that are appropriate to intermediate accounting are included, although many have been considerably modified. In addition, several problems in each chapter are designed especially to demonstrate the concepts presented in the theoretical discussion included in the chapter. (Problems adapted from the Uniform CPA Examination are not identified in the text because we have selected such problems solely for their "learning value" and because many of them have been altered to conform to the contents of the chapter and to subsequent changes in accounting principles. However, we identify the problems adapted from the Uniform CPA Examination in the *Instructor's Manual.*)

Helping Students to Achieve Proficiency in Solving Professional Level Problems

A feature of this edition is the inclusion of a large number of short problems closely correlated with the text material. The gradation in difficulty is carefully tailored to aid the student in a smooth progression from introductory accounting to a professional level of achievement.

A List of Key Figures is provided for problems. The purpose of the list is to aid students in verifying problem solutions and in discovering errors. The list appears on the inside covers of the book.

Two sets of partially filled-in working papers are available. One set is designed for problems in Chapters 1 through 13, and one set for problems in Chapters 14 through 25. On these working papers, the company names, problem numbers, numerous headings, and some preliminary data (such as trial balances) have been entered to save student time and to facilitate rapid review by the instructor. Use of partially filled-in working papers permits assignment of a larger variety of problems and reduces student frustration in deciding on appropriate solution format.

Transparencies of Problem Solutions

Transparencies are available for most problems, to be used by instructors who wish to display in a classroom complete solutions to problems. For longer, more complex problems, the transparencies are an effective means of showing desired organization and format of solutions. Transparencies have not been prepared for some short or easy problems.

Computer-Assisted Practice Set

Accompanying the revised sixth edition of *Intermediate Accounting* is *American Aircraft Sales Corporation,* a computer-assisted practice set that includes computer instructions, computer controls, and a solution. It is essentially a comprehensive problem incorporating many of the concepts in the first half of the text and requires the recording of transactions and the preparation of financial statements.

Contributions by Others

The material for the revised sixth edition was prepared by Charles J. Davis of California State University—Sacramento. Without his help, this edition would not have come out as timely, up-to-date, and as comprehensive as it is. His assistance was invaluable and much appreciated. A special thanks goes to Bruce Bublitz, University of Kansas, and Walter A. Parker, Central Connecticut State, for their additional contribution in reviewing the revised material for this edition.

The many instructors and students who have used previous editions of this book have contributed to the improvements in this edition. Their suggestions for modification of certain problems and alterations of certain sections of the text material have been most valuable. We would like to again acknowledge the advice received in the revision for the sixth edition from Profs. Wayne Bremser, Villanova University; Jane E. Campbell, Ohio State University; Myrtle Clark, University of Kentucky; Darrel Davis, University of Northern Iowa; Susan Harrison, Webster University, Leiden, The Netherlands; Richard Kochanek, University of Connecticut, Storrs; John Lacey, University of Southern California; George Lazar, Owens Technical College; Yu Ku Li, State University of New York at Brockport; Judy McClean, Moorehead State University; Robert Pommerich, Loras College; Mary Stone, University of Alabama, Birmingham; and Paul Zatko, Owens Technical College.

We are especially indebted to Profs. Joseph F. Guy of Georgia State University and Walter A. Parker of Central Connecticut State College for their superb review of the sixth edition end-of-chapter problem material for accuracy and clarity.

We wish to acknowledge the attention given to this revised sixth edition and its many supplements by the editorial staff of McGraw-Hill, especially Robert D. Lynch and Larry Goldberg.

Our sincere appreciation goes to the American Institute of Certified Public Accountants for giving us permission to quote from many of its pronouncements and to adapt questions and problems from the Uniform CPA Examinations. All quotations and adaptations from the Uniform CPA Examinations are copyrighted by the American Institute of Certified Public Accountants.

We also are grateful to the Financial Accounting Standards Board for granting us permission to quote from its *Statements, Discussion Memoranda, Interpretations,* and *Exposure Drafts.* All quotations used are copyrighted by the Financial Accounting Standards Board, High Ridge Park, Stamford, Connecticut 06905, U.S.A., and are reprinted with permission. Copies of the copyrighted documents are available from the Financial Accounting Standards Board.

Finally, we thank Walt Disney Productions for permitting us to include excerpts from its annual report in this edition.

A. N. Mosich

Basic Concepts and Financial Statements

1

Accounting principles evolve in a constantly changing business and economic environment. A conceptual framework of financial accounting and reporting is essential for the development of internally consistent accounting principles and reporting practices. Business transactions and events result in inflows and outflows of resources for a business enterprise. These resource flows are measured and summarized to facilitate the preparation of financial statements—the income statement, the balance sheet, the statement of cash flows, and the statement of stockholders' equity.

The measurement of assets and liabilities is closely related to the measurement of revenue and expenses. Increases in assets result from revenue realization, and expense recognition is accompanied by a decrease in assets and an increase in liabilities. The measurement process in financial accounting frequently involves compound interest fundamentals discussed in the final chapter of this part.

This initial part establishes the theme and general framework for the subsequent sections of the textbook.

Accounting Principles and Professional Practice

1 THE ENVIRONMENT OF ACCOUNTING

Fair presentation of financial affairs is the essence of accounting theory and practice. With the increasing size and complexity of United States business enterprises and the increasing economic role of government, the responsibility placed on accountants is greater today than ever before. If accountants are to meet this challenge, they must have a logical and consistent body of accounting theory to guide them. This theoretical structure must be realistic in terms of the economic environment and must be designed to meet the needs of users of financial statements.

Financial statements and reports prepared by accountants are vital to the successful working of society. Economists, investors, business executives, labor leaders, bankers, and government officials all rely on these financial statements and reports as fair and meaningful summaries of day-to-day business transactions. In addition, these groups are making increased use of accounting information as a basis for forecasting future economic trends. Accountants are being challenged to go beyond the timely reporting and interpretation of past events and to aid in the creation of useful forecasts of future operations. Consequently, accountants and the theoretical principles they use are at the center of financial and economic activities in the United States.

Users of Accounting Information

The basic assumptions that underlie current accounting practice have evolved over many years in response to the needs of various users of accounting information. The users of accounting information may be divided into two broad groups: *internal users* and *external users.*

Internal users include all the management personnel of a business enterprise who use accounting information either for planning and controlling current operations or for formulating long-range plans and making major business decisions. The term *managerial accounting* relates to internal measurements and reporting; it includes the development of detailed current information helpful to all levels of management in decision making designed to achieve the goals of the enterprise.

External users of accounting information include stockholders, bondholders, potential investors, bankers and other creditors, financial analysts, economists, labor unions, and numerous government agencies. The field of *financial accounting* is directly related to external reporting because it provides investors and other outsiders with the financial information they need for decision making.

In this book we are primarily concerned with financial accounting; therefore, we emphasize the accounting principles and reporting standards that produce timely and informative financial statements. The increasing importance of financial accounting rests on the premise that the public has a right to know whether large business enterprises are functioning efficiently and in harmony with the broad goals of society.

Organizations and Laws Affecting Financial Accounting

Certain professional organizations, governmental agencies, and legislative acts have been extremely influential in shaping the development of the existing body of financial accounting theory. Among the most important of these have been the American Institute of Certified Public Accountants, the Financial Accounting Standards Board, the American Accounting Association, and the Securities and Exchange Commission. Other organizations and laws that have influenced the development of accounting principles are the New York Stock Exchange, the National Association of Accountants, the Financial Executives Institute, the Cost Accounting Standards Board, the Institute of Internal Auditors, the Federal Government Accountants Association, and the whole complex of federal, state, and local income tax laws.

Awareness of the roles of these institutional forces is helpful in gaining an understanding of current accounting principles and practices. Efforts to improve existing principles of accounting will have a better chance of success if they are made with full recognition of the needs of the various groups that use accounting information.

American Institute of Certified Public Accountants (AICPA)   The American Institute of Certified Public Accountants is the professional organization of practicing certified public accountants. As a professional organization, the AICPA has been concerned with developing standards of professional practice for its members. The AICPA publishes the *Journal of Accountancy* monthly as a forum for accountants. Beginning in the early 1930s, the AICPA, in concert with the newly created Securities and Exchange Commission, began to develop standards of financial accounting and reporting. From 1939 to 1959, the AICPA published a series of *Accounting Research Bulletins* dealing with a wide variety of accounting and reporting issues.

Accounting Principles Board (APB)   In 1959 the AICPA undertook a more comprehensive program of research into the problems of financial accounting and reporting. The Accounting Principles Board was established with the responsibility of formulating financial accounting and reporting principles based on underlying research. The APB consisted of 21 (later 18) part-time members who served without pay.

The APB issued two separate series of publications. The more influential series consisted of the 31 *Opinions of the Accounting Principles Board,* issued between 1959 and 1973. Prior to 1964, pronouncements by the AICPA were not binding on practicing Certified Public Accountants (CPAs). However, in 1964, the AICPA began requiring that departures from *APB Opinions* be disclosed either in notes to the financial statements or in the audit reports of AICPA members in their capacity as independent auditors. CPAs could not give their approval to financial statements that deviated from *APB Opinions,* unless they wanted to assume the considerable personal risk and burden of proof of defending the ''unauthorized practices.'' Few business enterprises or auditors were anxious to assume the burden of defending financial statements that differed from *APB Opinions;* thus, this action gave a new strength and authority to *Opinions* of the APB.

Accounting Standards Division   Following the creation of the Financial Accounting Standards Board (described in the next section), the AICPA established an Accounting Standards Division to influence the development of accounting standards. The Accounting Standards Executive Committee (AcSEC) of the Accounting Standards Division issues *Statements of Position* to propose revisions of AICPA-published *Industry Audit Guides* and *Accounting Guides.* These *Statements of Position* do not establish enforceable accounting standards; however, members of the AICPA must justify departures from practices recommended in the *Statements.* In addition, the Accounting Standards Division prepares *Issues Papers* to develop financial accounting and reporting issues that the division believes should be considered by the Financial Accounting Standards Board.

Financial Accounting Standards Board (FASB)   The Financial Accounting Standards Board was established in 1972 to develop financial accounting standards for business enterprises and nonprofit organizations. This independent body consisted of seven full-time members and a large supporting staff.

Lending support and counsel to the FASB are the Financial Accounting Foundation, which appoints members of the FASB and raises funds for its operations, the Financial Accounting Standards Advisory Council, a Screening Committee on

Emerging Problems, and numerous Task Forces consisting of financial executives, accounting educators, lawyers, and CPAs.

CPAs are not the only persons concerned with financial accounting and reporting. Consequently, the articles of incorporation creating the FASB required that only four members shall be CPAs from public accounting practice; the other three members must be highly qualified in financial accounting and reporting but need not be CPAs. An individual appointed to the FASB must sever all connections with other organizations to avoid any suggestion of *conflict of interest.* Briefly stated, the public accounting profession is now engaged in a strenuous effort to improve the quality of financial accounting and reporting through an independent rule-making body that includes representatives from outside the field of public accounting.

The FASB is authorized to issue *Statements of Financial Accounting Standards,* as well as *Interpretations* and *Technical Bulletins,* to guide individuals and organizations in preparing and auditing financial statements. Before a formal *Statement* is drafted, the FASB frequently issues a *Discussion Memorandum* that identifies and analyzes the issues to be considered. Public hearings then are held on the issues identified in the *Discussion Memorandum.* Next, an *Exposure Draft* of the proposed statement is circulated. These procedures are designed to encourage the widest participation possible by all interested parties before a new financial accounting standard is issued. As of the beginning of 1985 the FASB had issued 82 *Statements.* Those *Statements* dealing with the subject matter of Intermediate Accounting have been incorporated in this book to the maximum extent possible.

American Accounting Association (AAA) The American Accounting Association, an organization of accounting educators and practitioners, has played an important role in the development of accounting principles. The activities of the AAA have emphasized the development of a theoretical foundation for accounting rather than the application of the theory to practical situations. The AAA encourages accounting research and continuous appraisal of accounting concepts through committee reports and the publication of a quarterly journal, *The Accounting Review.*

Securities and Exchange Commission (SEC) The Securities and Exchange Commission was established in 1934 by Congress to regulate the interstate issuance of securities to the public and the trading of securities listed on stock exchanges and over the counter. The SEC has broad authority to prescribe accounting principles, forms to be filed, and information to be disclosed by business enterprises subject to its regulation. Although the SEC has the authority to prescribe accounting principles, it generally has relied on the private sector (FASB and AICPA) to perform this function. However, the SEC has exerted strong influence on the development of accounting principles and reporting practices. SEC actions have included: (1) continual review (and occasional rejection) of financial statements; (2) issuance of *Regulation S-X,* which prescribes detailed accounting and financial reporting requirements; (3) publication of numerous *Financial Reporting Releases* and *Staff Accounting Bulletins;* and (4) prodding the private sector to develop or revise certain financial accounting and reporting practices.

A corporation planning to issue securities interstate to the public must prepare a *prospectus* and have it reviewed by the SEC. The prospectus contains detailed information about the corporation's products, competition, and management, as well as financial statements. Corporations that are under the jurisdiction of the SEC must file voluminous documents, including an annual report (*Form 10-K*) that includes information not presented in the annual report to shareholders, and a quarterly report (*Form 10-Q*). The financial statements included in the annual report filed with the SEC must be audited by independent CPAs; the financial information included in the quarterly reports need not be audited but must be reviewed by independent CPAs.

The primary concern of the SEC is *disclosure* of all relevant and material facts about the financial affairs of publicly owned business enterprises. In recent years, the SEC has become more active in its role as the watchdog for investors. The chief accountants of the SEC have pushed to expand the quality as well as the quantity of information disclosed to the public. The SEC has been primarily responsible for expansion of disclosure into such areas as inventory profits caused by inflation, replacement costs of inventories and plant assets, unusual risks and uncertainties, and replacements of independent auditors. Particular emphasis has been placed by the SEC on the concept of *continuous disclosure* of *relevant* information on a *timely basis* so that the information is of maximum value to investors. Accordingly, the SEC has required independent auditors to review quarterly financial reports and also has encouraged business enterprises to issue financial forecasts.

Cost Accounting Standards Board (CASB) Although our interest in this book is focused on financial accounting rather than managerial or cost accounting, our listing of organizations that have contributed importantly to improved accounting practices must include the federal Cost Accounting Standards Board, which was active from 1971 to 1980. The primary goal of the CASB was to issue standards that achieved more uniformity in cost accounting practices among business enterprises working on government contracts. Because almost every large industrial enterprise has government contracts, the issuance of standards by the CASB had considerable impact on financial statements and measurement of contract costs.

Income Tax Laws The enactment of the federal income tax law in 1913 and the subsequent amendments and legal interpretations comprising the present tax law have been perhaps the most important forces on the development of applied accounting procedures, as distinguished from accounting theory. Managers of business enterprises have attempted to lessen the impact of taxes on the enterprises. The result has been the adoption of accounting procedures that conform to generally accepted accounting principles and at the same time minimize taxable income.

The Internal Revenue Code has been developed with the interests of the federal government as its focal point, which means that Congress has been more concerned with public policy objectives than with the development of accounting theory. The acceptance of certain tax regulations as the basis for financial accounting has resulted in the adoption of procedures that accelerate the recognition of expenses or postpone the recognition of revenue. In Chapter 21 we consider some of the reporting problems created by these differences, and throughout this book reference is made to income tax regulations and their impact on accounting practice. However, we must keep in mind that this book is concerned with the principles and procedures of financial accounting, not of income taxation.

Attest Function of CPAs

A conflict of interest may exist between a business enterprise preparing financial statements and some of the users of those statements. For example, an enterprise applying for a bank loan may tend to be overly optimistic in portraying its financial position. Similarly, a corporation planning to raise cash by issuing common stock to the public has an incentive to overstate its reported net income. To protect the users of financial statements against a natural bias or outright misrepresentation, it is important to have independent professional accountants (auditors) examine the financial statements (and supporting evidence) prepared by the accounting staff of an enterprise. The auditors then have a basis for expressing their professional opinion on the financial statements. This **attest function** is the primary role of Certified Public Accountants. To attest to financial statements means to vouch for their validity. Performance of the attest function requires the existence of an independent public accounting profession.

Because of the public interest in **audited financial statements,** each state recognizes public accounting as a profession and issues the certificate of Certified Public Accountant to those who demonstrate through written examinations and the satisfaction of educational and experience requirements their competence to enter the public accounting profession.

CONCEPTUAL FRAMEWORK
FOR FINANCIAL ACCOUNTING AND REPORTING

One of the initial projects of the Financial Accounting Standards Board was a study designed to identify the "broad qualitative standards for financial reporting." After extensive work on the project, the FASB decided to expand the scope of the project to include the entire conceptual framework of financial accounting and reporting, including objectives, qualitative characteristics, and the needs of users of accounting information. The purpose of the conceptual framework project was to provide a sound and consistent basis for the development of financial accounting standards. The diagram on page 11 depicts the elements of a conceptual framework for financial accounting and reporting.[1]

The *fundamentals of accounting and reporting* are the basic concepts underlying the measurement and disclosure of business transactions and events. For example, fundamentals might include the definitions of an accounting entity, assets, liabilities, net income, revenue, and expenses. *Accounting and reporting standards* represent general solutions to financial accounting problems, and *interpretations* clarify the accounting and reporting standards as an aid to their application in

---

[1]*FASB Discussion Memorandum,* "Conceptual Framework for Accounting and Reporting," FASB (Stamford: 1974), p. 15.

Elements of a
conceptual framework
for financial accounting
and reporting

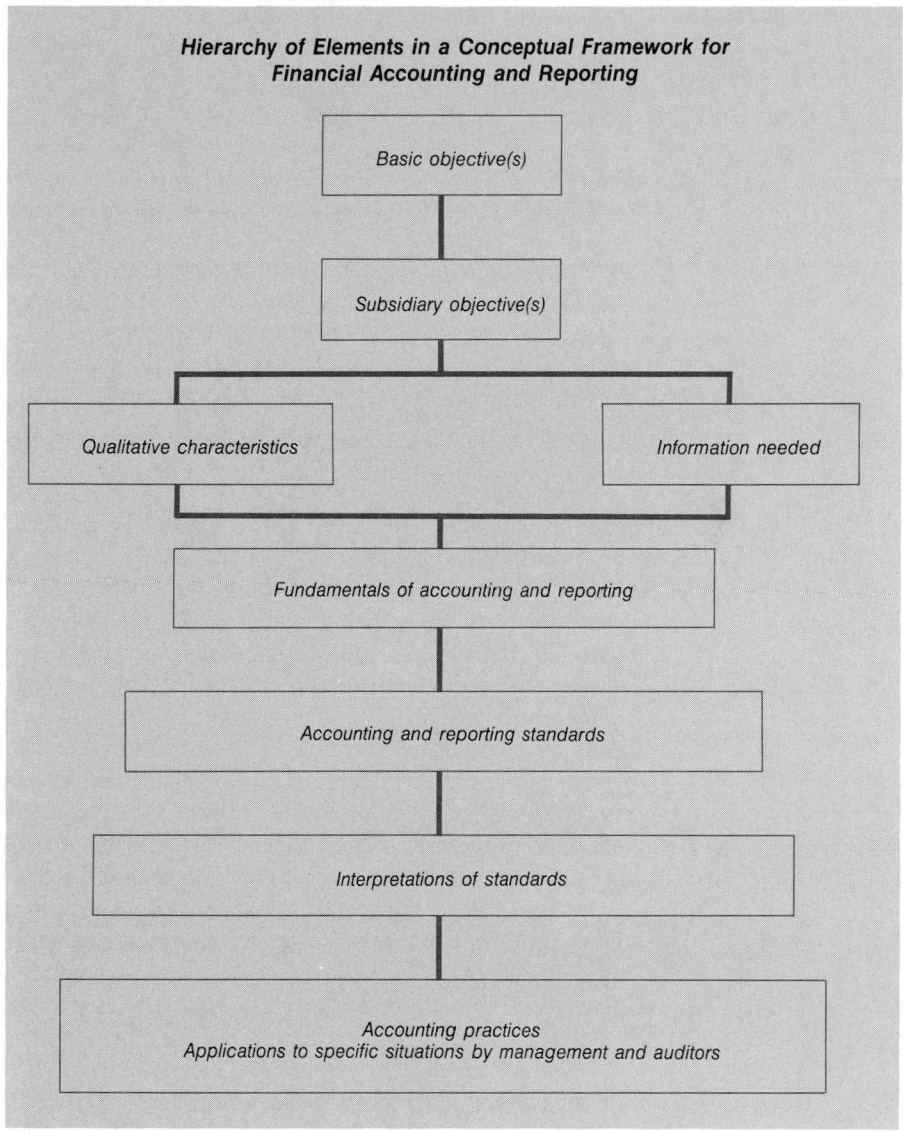

Hierarchy of Elements in a Conceptual Framework for Financial Accounting and Reporting

Basic objective(s)

Subsidiary objective(s)

Qualitative characteristics

Information needed

Fundamentals of accounting and reporting

Accounting and reporting standards

Interpretations of standards

Accounting practices
Applications to specific situations by management and auditors

accounting practices. ***Accounting practices*** are the means used by managements and independent auditors to achieve the objectives of financial statements and financial reporting.

The expanded conceptual framework project undertaken by the Financial Accounting Standards Board has resulted in the publication of the following relating to business enterprises:

Statement of Financial Accounting Concepts No. 1, "Objectives of Financial Reporting by Business Enterprises"

Statement of Financial Accounting Concepts No. 2, "Qualitative Characteristics of Accounting Information"

Statement of Financial Accounting Concepts No. 3, "Elements of Financial Statements of Business Enterprises"

Statement of Financial Accounting Concepts No. 5, "Recognition and Measurement in Financial Statements of Business Enterprises"

Statements of Financial Accounting Concepts, unlike *Statements of Financial Accounting Standards,* do not establish generally accepted accounting principles. Instead, they establish the objectives and concepts that the FASB will use to establish financial accounting and reporting standards. In the following sections we consider the components of the conceptual framework project applicable to business enterprises.

Objectives of Financial Reporting and Financial Statements

The objectives of financial reporting and financial statements are derived from the needs of the external users of accounting information. Financial statements intended to serve all external users often are called *general-purpose financial statements.* Stating the objectives of financial statements would be simpler if all external users had the same needs and interests, but they do not. For example, a banker considering the granting of a 90-day loan is primarily interested in the short-run debt-paying ability of the business enterprise, whereas the long-term investor in common stock is more concerned with earning capacity, potential growth in earnings per share, and the ability of the enterprise to survive as a going concern.

Because general-purpose financial statements serve a variety of users, the needs of some users receive more emphasis than the needs of others. In present-day accounting practice the needs of the potential investor or creditor are subordinated to those who have already invested resources in the enterprise. This emphasis leads management of the enterprise to stress the uses made of the resources entrusted to it. A deep concern over reporting on management's role as custodian of resources may be one reason for the adherence to historical cost despite substantial changes in the general price level in recent years. This tradition may also explain, in part, the omission from the financial statements of *social costs,* which may be increasingly important to a society becoming more aware of the need for preserving the quality of its environment.

In recent years the environment in which business enterprises operate has been changing at a rapid pace. Changes in the economic, political, and social structure of society cause changes in the informational needs of users of financial statements. Higher standards of measurement and reporting, along with a significant expansion of the amount of information disclosed, have been foremost among the new needs of users of financial statements.

The Financial Accounting Standards Board issued *Statement of Financial Accounting Concepts No. 1,* "Objectives of Financial Reporting by Business Enterprises," to establish the objectives of general-purpose external financial reporting by business enterprises.[2] The objectives established by the FASB were as follows:[3]

1 Financial reporting should provide information that is useful to present and potential investors and creditors and other users in making rational investment, credit, and similar decisions. The information should be comprehensible to those who have a reasonable understanding of business and economic activities and are willing to study the information with reasonable diligence.

2 Financial reporting should provide information to help present and potential investors and creditors and other users in assessing the amounts, timing, and uncertainty of prospective cash receipts from dividends or interest and the proceeds from the sale, redemption, or maturity of securities or loans. The prospects for those cash receipts are affected by an enterprise's ability to generate enough cash to meet its obligations when due and its other cash operating needs, to reinvest in operations, and to pay cash dividends and may also be affected by perceptions of investors and creditors generally about that ability, which affect market prices of the enterprise's securities. . . .

3 Financial reporting should provide information about the economic resources of an enterprise, the claims to those resources, . . . and the effects of transactions, events, and circumstances that change resources and claims to those resources.

4 Financial reporting should provide information about an enterprise's financial performance during a period. Investors and creditors often use information about the past to help in assessing the prospects of an enterprise. . . .

5 The primary focus of financial reporting is information about an enterprise's performance provided by measures of earnings and its components.

6 Financial reporting should provide information about how an enterprise obtains and spends cash, about its borrowing and repayment of borrowing, about its capital transactions, including cash dividends and other distributions of enterprise resources to owners, and about other factors that may affect an enterprise's liquidity or solvency.

7 Financial reporting should provide information about how management of an enterprise has discharged its stewardship responsibility to owners (stockholders) for the use of enterprise resources entrusted to it.

8 Financial reporting should provide information that is useful to managers and directors in making decisions. . . .

Summarizing, the Financial Accounting Standards Board identified eight objectives of financial reporting, all of which focused on providing information

---

[2]*Statement of Financial Accounting Concepts No. 1,* "Objectives of Financial Reporting by Business Enterprises," FASB (Stamford: 1978), p. 1.
[3]*Statement of Financial Accounting Concepts No. 2,* "Qualitative Characteristics of Accounting Information," FASB (Stamford: 1980), pp. 9–10.

needed by current and prospective investors and creditors of a business enterprise in their decision making. The primary emphasis was placed on information regarding the enterprise's earnings.

Qualitative Characteristics of Accounting Information

The Financial Accounting Standards Board issued *Statement of Financial Accounting Concepts No. 2,* ''Qualitative Characteristics of Accounting Information,'' to examine the characteristics of accounting information that make it useful.[4] Thus, the FASB identified *usefulness for decision making* as the most important qualitative characteristic of accounting information.[5] To be useful, accounting information must be *understandable* to users (decision makers). The FASB summarized the qualitative characteristics in the diagram below:[6]

Qualitative characteristics of accounting information

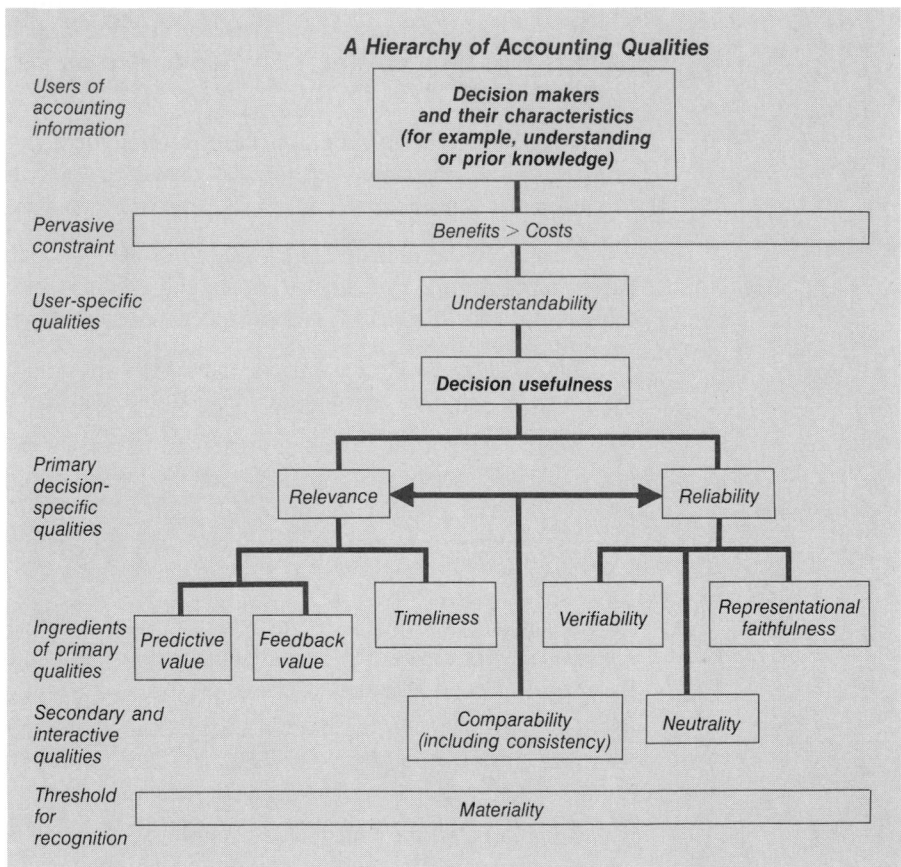

[4]Ibid., p. 1.
[5]Ibid., pp. 13–14.
[6]Ibid., p. 15.

The diagram identifies *relevance* and *reliability* as the two primary qualities of useful accounting information, with related ingredients of each primary quality also set forth. *Comparability* (including *consistency*) and *neutrality* are identified as secondary qualities of useful accounting information, and the concepts of *cost-benefit considerations* and *materiality* are recognized as constraints. In the following pages, we discuss the qualities set forth in this diagram.

Cost-Benefit Considerations   In recent years, the demands of many users of financial statements and other financial information have appeared insatiable to accountants. There has been an explosive growth in the amount of information disclosed in the annual reports of publicly owned corporations, and the cost of producing such information is substantial. The Financial Accounting Standards Board recognized the impact of cost-benefit considerations as follows:[7]

> Before a decision is made to develop a standard, the Board needs to satisfy itself that the matter to be ruled on represents a significant problem and that a standard that is promulgated will not impose costs on the many for the benefit of a few. If the proposal passes that first test, a second test may subsequently be useful. There are usually alternative ways of handling an issue. Is one of them less costly and only slightly less effective? Even if absolute magnitudes cannot be attached to costs and benefits, a comparison between alternatives may yet be possible and useful.

Relevance   Relevant accounting information may make a difference in a decision by helping investors, creditors, and other users to evaluate past, present, and future events (*predictive value*) or to confirm or correct expectations (*feedback value*).[8] For example, information concerning past dividends declared by a corporation enables investors to predict the prospects of dividends in future years; information on net income for the first three quarters of a fiscal year enables investors to evaluate a prior estimate of net income for the entire fiscal year.

Accounting information generally is not relevant unless it is *timely,* that is, unless it is available to decision makers before it becomes too dated to influence the decision.[9] The availability of computers has enabled accountants to make great strides in providing timely information to decision makers.

Reliability   Accounting information is reliable if it is reasonably free from error and bias and faithfully represents what it purports to present.[10] To be reliable, information must be *verifiable* and must have *representational faithfulness,* or *validity.*[11] Supporting documents showing the details of completed ''arm's-length'' transactions provide clear evidence that may be verified. To *verify* means to prove

---

[7]Ibid., p. 58.
[8]Ibid., pp. xv, xvi.
[9]Ibid., p. 25.
[10]Ibid., p. xvi.
[11]Ibid., p. 26.

something to be true by examination of evidence of underlying facts. If accounting information is free from bias, the same conclusions would be reached by different accountants working independently and following the same measurement techniques. In most cases, *actual costs* provide the most reliable data capable of being independently verified.

However, financial statements are not completely factual; *estimates* on such matters as the economic life of plant assets, the net realizable value of inventories, and the collectibility of accounts receivable are inherent in the accounting process. The reliability quality calls for accountants to adhere as closely as possible to *objectively verifiable evidence.* The alternative approach would be to establish accounting values through unrestricted use of appraisal reports, estimates of future events, and expressions of opinion. Such an approach to accounting, although often helpful in providing more relevant data, makes it more difficult for CPAs to perform independent verifications of financial statements. Today, accountants recognize that a trade-off exists between *relevance* and *reliability* of data used in the preparation of financial statements. In recent years, the Securities and Exchange Commission consistently has favored relevance as the more useful criterion. For example, the SEC has encouraged the issuance of financial forecasts and has required the disclosure of replacement cost data (both based on estimates), on the grounds that such information is useful to investors in making decisions to acquire, sell, or retain corporate securities.

Conservatism   Although not a qualitative characteristic of accounting information, *conservatism* is a concept that may be discussed in connection with reliability. Many accounting measurements do not have a single "correct answer"; a choice must be made among alternative assumptions under conditions of uncertainty. The concept of conservatism holds that when reasonable support exists for alternative accounting methods and for different measurement techniques, accountants should select the method or technique with the least favorable effect on net income and financial position in the current accounting period.

Conservatism generally is regarded as a powerful influence stressing caution against the danger of overstating earnings or financial position. However, many business enterprises are not in favor of conservative accounting policies. Enterprises planning to issue securities to the public naturally try to project an image of superior management and increasing earnings. An enterprise that reports increased earnings year after year gains the reputation of being a "growth company"; financial analysts refer to its common stock as a "glamor issue"; and the market price of its common stock often rises to a high multiple of earnings per share. Once such a reputation is established, an enterprise finds it easier to raise needed capital through the issuance of additional securities or through bank loans. Attracting management talent also is easier. Executive compensation tends to increase both in salaries and through stock option and pension plans. All these pleasant *economic consequences* of a reputation for increasing earnings give enterprise management a powerful incentive to choose accounting policies that maximize current net income.

However, enterprises must be alert to the possible adverse economic consequences of following unconservative accounting policies. The issue we are raising relates to the *quality of reported earnings.* The earnings of an enterprise using unconservative accounting policies are viewed as being of lower quality, and its common stock will tend to trade at a low price-earnings ratio. Small business enterprises that do not seek capital from the public and do not report their earnings to anyone other than income tax authorities have an incentive to choose acceptable accounting policies that hold income to the lowest level that may be justified.

Ideally, accountants should make estimates and select accounting policies that neither overstate nor understate the current net income and financial position of a business enterprise. The concept of conservatism should not be distorted to the point of deliberate understatement; however, the judicious use of conservatism in accounting may help to prevent the catastrophes that have befallen many investors and employees when enterprises with excessively optimistic accounting policies suddenly reached the limit of credibility and collapsed.

Comparability and Consistency Comparability of the financial statements of a business enterprise from one accounting period to the next is essential if favorable and unfavorable trends in the enterprise are to be identified. If the financial statements for the current accounting period show larger earnings than for the preceding period, the user assumes that operations have been more profitable. However, if a material change in an accounting principle has occurred, the reported increase in earnings could have been caused solely by the accounting change, rather than by any improvement in the underlying business activity. Consistent application of accounting principles for a business enterprise from one accounting period to the next is needed in order that the financial statements of successive periods will be comparable.

The consistency principle does not mean that a particular method of accounting, once adopted, should not be changed. Accounting principles and methods change in response to changes in the environment of accounting. When an accounting change is desirable, it should be made, together with disclosure of the change and its effect in dollar amounts on the reported net income of the accounting period in which the change is made. *APB Opinion No. 20,* "Accounting Changes," stated that:[12]

> The presumption that an entity should not change an accounting principle may be overcome only if the enterprise justifies the use of an alternative acceptable accounting principle on the basis that it is preferable. . . .

> The nature of and justification for a change in accounting principle and its effect on income should be disclosed. . . . The justification for the change should explain why the newly adopted accounting principle is preferable.

Comparability among financial statements of business enterprises in the same industry also is a useful quality. However, differences in the operating policies among such enterprises result in the adoption of various accounting practices in such areas as valuation of inventories and depreciation of plant assets. Thus, comparability of financial statements of enterprises in the same industry is difficult to achieve.

---

[12]*APB Opinion No. 20,* "Accounting Changes," AICPA (New York: 1971), p. 391.

Neutrality   The Financial Accounting Standards Board defined the quality of *neutrality* as the absence in reported information of bias intended to attain a predetermined result or to induce a particular mode of behavior.[13] Because of the many users of general-purpose financial statements, freedom from bias is essential. For example, financial statements designed solely to influence the actions of investors could be damaging to the needs of creditors, another major user group for financial statements.

Materiality   Disclosure is necessary in financial statements or in notes to the financial statements only for *material* matters. The meaning of materiality in an accounting context is a state of *relative importance.* Items that are trifling in amount need not be treated in strict accordance with accounting theory but rather should be handled in the most economical manner. For example, most business enterprises establish a minimum dollar amount in considering whether an expenditure should be recorded as a depreciable plant asset. In theory, the cost of a new pencil sharpener should be capitalized and depreciated over its economic life. As a practical matter, the expense of making such allocations of cost would exceed the cost of the pencil sharpener and would represent an unjustifiably wasteful accounting policy.

That which is material for one business enterprise may not be for another. For a small enterprise, an uninsured loss, say $50,000, might be considered as material; for a large enterprise it would not be material. In deciding on the materiality of an item in terms of financial statement disclosure, accountants should consider whether knowledge of the item would be likely to influence the decisions of users of financial statements.

Qualitative standards should be considered in judging the materiality of an item as well as its dollar amount. For example, a transaction between a business enterprise and its president is not at arm's length and suggests a possible conflict of interest. Disclosure of the transaction is appropriate, even though disclosure of such a transaction between independent parties would not be required.

In discussing quantitative measures of materiality, the Financial Accounting Standards Board made the following statement:[14]

> The Board's present position is that no general standards of materiality could be formulated to take into account all the considerations that enter into an experienced human judgment. However, that position is not intended to imply either that the Board may not in the future review that conclusion or that quantitative guidance on materiality of specific items may not appropriately be written into the Board's standards from time to time. That has been done on occasion already (for example, in the Statement on financial reporting by segments of a business enterprise), and the Board recognizes that quantitative materiality guidance is sometimes needed. . . . However, whenever the Board or any other authoritative body imposes materiality rules, it is substituting generalized collective judgments for specific individual judgments, and there is no reason to suppose that the collective judgments are always superior.

---

[13]*Statement of Financial Accounting Concepts No. 2,* p. xvi.
[14]Ibid., p. 53.

Elements of Financial Statements of Business Enterprises

In *Statement of Financial Accounting Concepts No. 3,* "Elements of Financial Statements of Business Enterprises," the Financial Accounting Standards Board identified ten interrelated elements (building blocks) of financial statements: Assets, liabilities, equity, investments by owners, distributions to owners, comprehensive income, revenues, expenses, gains, and losses. These elements were defined by the FASB as follows:[15]

Assets are probable future economic benefits obtained or controlled by a particular entity as a result of past transactions or events.

Liabilities are probable future sacrifices of economic benefits arising from present obligations of a particular entity to transfer assets or provide services to other entities in the future as a result of past transactions or events.

Equity is the residual interest in the assets of an entity that remains after deducting its liabilities. In a business enterprise, the equity is the ownership interest.

Investments by owners are increases in net assets of a particular enterprise resulting from transfers to it from other entities of something of value to obtain or increase ownership interests (or equity) in it. Assets are most commonly received as investments by owners, but that which is received may also include services or satisfaction or conversion of liabilities of the enterprise.

Distributions to owners are decreases in net assets of a particular enterprise resulting from transferring assets, rendering services, or incurring liabilities by the enterprise to owners. Distributions to owners decrease ownership interests (or equity) in an enterprise.

Comprehensive income is the change in equity (net assets) of an entity during a period from transactions and other events and circumstances from nonowner sources. It includes all changes in equity during a period except those resulting from investments by owners and distributions to owners.

Revenues are inflows or other enhancements of assets of an entity or settlements of its liabilities (or a combination of both) during a period from delivering or producing goods, rendering services, or other activities that constitute the entity's ongoing major or central operations.

Expenses are outflows or other using up of assets or incurrences of liabilities (or a combination of both) during a period from delivering or producing goods, rendering services, or carrying out other activities that constitute the entity's ongoing major or central operations.

Gains are increases in equity (net assets) from peripheral or incidental transactions of an entity and from all other transactions and other events and circumstances affecting the entity during a period except those that result from revenues or investments by owners.

---

[15]*Statement of Financial Accounting Concepts No. 3,* "Elements of Financial Statements of Business Enterprises," FASB (Stamford: 1980), pp. xi–xii.

Losses are decreases in equity (net assets) from peripheral or incidental transactions of an entity and from all other transactions and other events and circumstances affecting the entity during a period except those that result from expenses or distributions to owners.

Except for "comprehensive income," the foregoing elements are similar to the traditional concepts of components of financial statements. The FASB deliberately used the term *comprehensive income* rather than *earnings* to broaden the scope of measurements of the operating results of business enterprises.[16]

To allay fears that the foregoing definitions of elements of financial statements might suggest a radical change in financial reporting, the FASB stated:[17]

> The Board expects most assets and liabilities in present practice to continue to qualify as assets or liabilities under the definitions in this Statement. The Board emphasizes that the definitions neither require nor presage upheavals in present practice, although they may in due time lead to some evolutionary changes in practice or at least in the ways certain items are viewed. They should be especially helpful in understanding the content of financial statements and in analyzing and resolving new financial accounting issues as they arise.

Recognition and Measurement in Financial Statements of Business Enterprises

The Financial Accounting Standards Board essentially completed the conceptual framework project by issuing *Statement of Financial Accounting Concepts No. 5,* "Recognition and Measurement in Financial Statements of Business Enterprises." In that *Statement,* the FASB provided guidance on what information is to be included in financial statements and the timing of its inclusion (*recognition*) and on the quantification of the information (*measurement*). Among the provisions of the *Statement* are the following:[18]

1   A full set of financial statements for an accounting period should show financial position at the end of the period and earnings, comprehensive income, cash flows, and investments by and distributions to owners for the period. Disclosure is not a substitute for items that should be recognized in financial statements.

2   *Earnings* is similar to *net income* for an accounting period; however, it excludes certain items currently included in net income, such as the cumulative effect of a change in accounting principle. *Comprehensive income* is not the same as *earnings* because comprehensive income includes such items as changes in the market value of noncurrent marketable equity securities and gains or losses from holding nonmonetary assets during a period of changing current costs.

---

[16]Ibid., p. 28.
[17]Ibid., p. xiii.
[18]*Statement of Financial Accounting Concepts No. 5,* "Recognition and Measurement in Financial Statements of Business Enterprises," FASB (Stamford: 1984), pp. vii–ix.

3 The use of different attributes, such as historical cost, current cost, current fair value, and net realizable value, which is a feature of current measurement techniques in financial accounting, is expected to continue. Information based on current prices should be recognized if it meets the qualitative characteristics of relevance and reliability and meets the cost-benefits test.

Evaluation of Conceptual Framework Project

The Financial Accounting Standards Board labored more than 10 years on the conceptual framework project. The four *Statements of Financial Accounting Concepts* described in the preceding sections provide the FASB with a foundation for future *Statements of Financial Accounting Standards*. For example, the definitions provided by the FASB in *Statement of Financial Accounting Concepts No. 3* (see pages 19–20) have been used extensively in recent publications of the FASB dealing with proposed changes in accounting for pensions.

One wonders, however, whether the output of the conceptual framework project was cost effective in terms of the substantial time, effort, and cost devoted to it. A close study of the four *Statements of Financial Accounting Concepts* outlined in the preceding sections discloses nothing revolutionary or even significantly different from present financial accounting concepts. The concept of *comprehensive income,* for example, had roots in the "all-inclusive income statement" theory in effect many years ago. Perhaps the most significant impact of the conceptual framework has been an increased emphasis on *cash flows* as a measure of a business enterprise's performance during an accounting period. Time will tell whether the benefits provided by the conceptual framework project in terms of a cohesive body of financial accounting theory were worth the energies devoted to the project.

GENERALLY ACCEPTED ACCOUNTING PRINCIPLES (GAAP)

The term *generally accepted accounting principles* has long been used in financial accounting. This term also is used by CPAs in their audit reports to indicate whether the business enterprise being audited has prepared its financial statements in an acceptable manner, so that they may be compared with the prior year's statements and to some extent with the statements of other enterprises. The principles of accounting are not rooted in the laws of nature as are the physical sciences. Therefore, *accounting principles must be developed in relation to the stated objectives of financial reporting and financial statements.*

Although a body of generally accepted accounting principles has long been recognized, no complete official list of such principles exists. The most authoritative sources of generally accepted accounting principles in recent years have been the *Statements* issued by the FASB, the *Opinions* issued by the APB, the *Accounting Research Bulletins* issued by the AICPA Committee on Accounting Procedure, and *Financial Reporting Releases* issued by the SEC. Besides these sources, there are other pronouncements, many of which are identified in preceding sections of this chapter, that provided information on generally accepted accounting principles. One writer has conceived a "House of GAAP" to summarize the various sources of generally accepted accounting principles, as follows:[19]

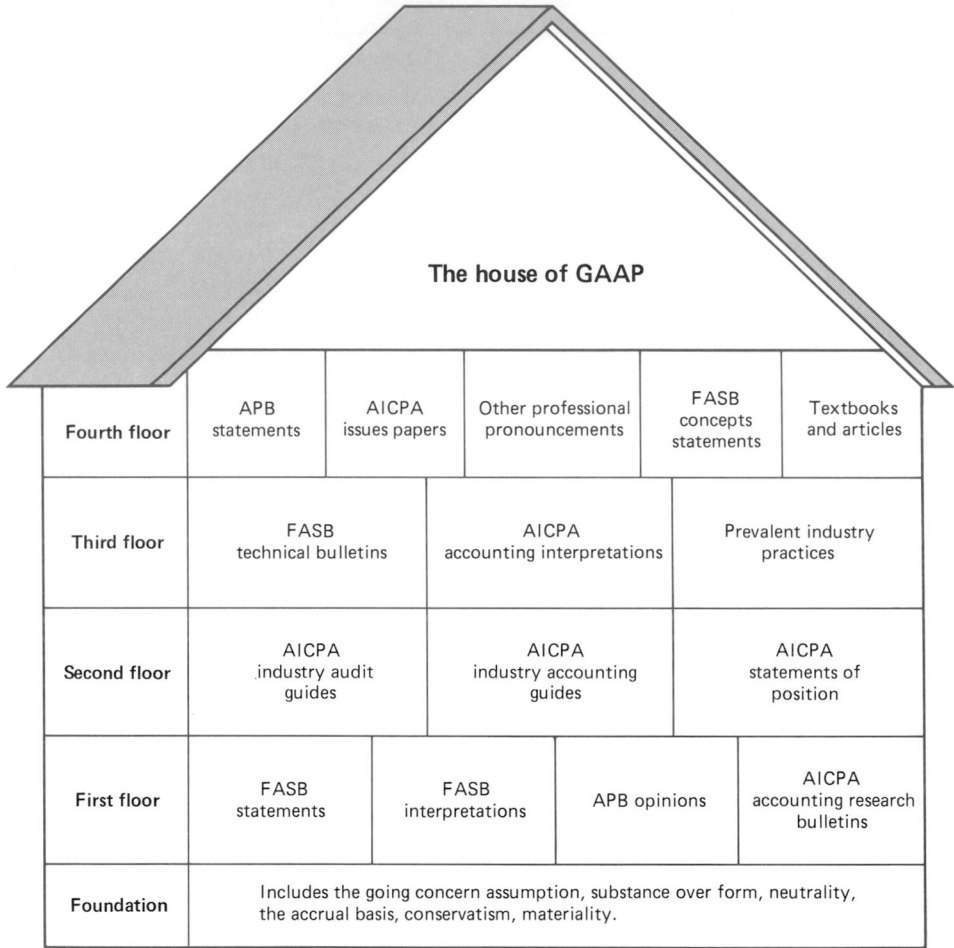

The house of GAAP

Fourth floor	APB statements	AICPA issues papers	Other professional pronouncements	FASB concepts statements	Textbooks and articles
Third floor	FASB technical bulletins		AICPA accounting interpretations		Prevalent industry practices
Second floor	AICPA industry audit guides		AICPA industry accounting guides		AICPA statements of position
First floor	FASB statements	FASB interpretations	APB opinions		AICPA accounting research bulletins
Foundation	Includes the going concern assumption, substance over form, neutrality, the accrual basis, conservatism, materiality.				

In the following sections we discuss a number of fundamental accounting principles and concepts included in the "foundation" of the "House of GAAP." These principles and concepts are broad in nature and have been developed by accountants in an effort to meet the needs of the users of financial statements. In subsequent chapters we consider the application of these broad principles and concepts to specific accounting and reporting issues.

Business Entity Principle

Because economic activity is carried on by various legal and economic entities, accounting results are summarized in terms of these entities. Accountants deal pri-

---

[19]Steven Rubin, "The House of GAAP," *Journal of Accountancy* (June 1984), p. 123.

marily with three general kinds of business entities: single proprietorships, partnerships, and corporations. Regardless of the form of organization, the business affairs of the entity are distinguished from those of its owners. We see the effect of this principle when accounting income is measured as it accrues to the entity, not when it is distributed to owners. Similarly, an obligation of the entity to owners is treated as a liability, despite the fact that the owners owe a portion of the debt to themselves.

Accountants sometimes find it useful to prepare financial statements for economic entities that do not coincide with legal entities. For example, *consolidated financial statements* often are prepared for an economic entity that includes several corporate entities operating under common control exercised through common stock ownership. In contrast, separate financial statements may be prepared for divisions or segments of a large corporation.

Continuity or Going-Concern Principle

The *continuity* or *going-concern principle* means that accountants assume that a business entity will continue to exist indefinitely. In deciding how to report various items in financial statements, accountants often are faced with this issue: ''Shall we assume that the business enterprise (entity) will continue to operate, or shall we assume that the enterprise will be terminated in the near future?'' The most probable situation for enterprises in general is that they will continue to operate for an indefinite period of time, and this is one of the most fundamental assumptions underlying financial accounting.

To illustrate the significance of the continuity principle, consider the possibility that if an enterprise ceased operations, certain liabilities would mature immediately and require a payment in excess of their carrying amount. Productive assets such as machinery might have to be sold at a substantial loss. The assumption of continued existence provides the logical basis for recording probable future economic benefits as assets and probable future outlays as liabilities.

The continuity principle implies not permanence of existence but simply that a business enterprise will continue in existence long enough to carry out present plans and meet contractual commitments. This principle affects the classification of assets and liabilities in a balance sheet. Because it is assumed that assets will be used and obligations paid in the normal course of operation, no attempt is made to classify assets and liabilities in terms of their ultimate disposition or legal priority in case of liquidation.

There are times when the going-concern principle gives way to evidence that an enterprise has a limited life or intends to terminate operations. In such cases, accountants prepare financial statements under the assumption of a *quitting concern* rather than a going concern.

Revenue Realization Principle

Revenue may be defined as the value of goods and services that a business enterprise transfers to its customers.[20] Thus, revenue is the principal factor responsible

---

[20]A more formalized definition of *revenues*, developed by the FASB, appears on page 19.

for increases in the net assets of a business enterprise apart from investments by owners. For a specific accounting period, revenue equals the inflow of cash and receivables from sales made during that period. For a single transaction, revenue equals the value of assets (cash and accounts receivable) received from the customer.

Any definition of revenue immediately raises questions as to timing—the essence of the *revenue realization principle.* At what point or points during the creation of marketable products or services should revenue be recorded? What is the *critical event* that indicates revenue has been realized and justifies recording a change in net assets by replacing the carrying amount of assets such as inventories with a higher valuation representing their current fair value? Ideally, because each step in the process of producing and distributing goods is essential to earning revenue, the accounting *recognition* of revenue should be continuous rather than being linked to a single critical event. However, as a practical matter, reliable evidence is needed to support the recognition of revenue, and for most business enterprises that evidence lies in an arm's-length transaction in which title to goods passes to the customer. Thus, the revenue realization principle dictates that assets such as inventories be carried *at cost* until appreciation in value is realized through sale. The reasoning underlying this practice is explained in Chapter 3.

Valuation Principle

Realization, which is a key principle in income measurement, also forms the basis for distinguishing methods of valuation used in the reporting of assets and liabilities in a balance sheet.

A general class of assets called *monetary assets* usually is carried in the balance sheet at amounts closely approximating current value. Examples are cash, certificates of deposit, investments in bonds, and receivables; all these represent current purchasing power. Promissory notes receivable and notes payable that are noninterest-bearing, or that have an unrealistically low rate of interest, are not to be valued at face amount, but at their present value. *Present value* is determined by discounting all future payments on a promissory note at the current fair rate of interest. This requirement for discounting receivables and payables to their present value applies principally to notes; it is not applicable to receivables and payables arising from transactions with customers or suppliers that are due within one year or less.

Another broad category of assets, termed *nonmonetary assets* or *productive resources,* is reported in the balance sheet at *cost.* Inventories and prepayments are examples of short-term productive resources that will be realized (used) at an early date. Buildings, equipment, patents, and investments in affiliated companies are examples of long-term productive resources that will be realized over a number of accounting periods. Until realization occurs, productive resources are measured and reported in the balance sheet at historical costs; after realization, valuations of the monetary assets received in exchange for productive assets generally approximate current fair value. These valuation principles govern the accounting for assets.

How should cost be measured when nonmonetary assets or services are acquired in noncash transactions? For example, land may be acquired in exchange for a corporation's own common stock. Cost then is defined as the cash equivalent (current fair value) of the land acquired or the cash equivalent of the common stock issued, *whichever is more clearly evident.* If the common stock is listed on a stock exchange and is widely traded, the market price of the common stock may be stronger and more reliable evidence of the cost of the land than is an appraisal of the land.

Because a liability is an obligation to convey assets or perform services, the appropriate valuation of liabilities in a balance sheet is in terms of the cash (or cash equivalent) necessary to discharge the obligation on the balance sheet date. If payment is to be made later, liabilities are measured at the present discounted value (determined by use of the current fair rate of interest) of the future payments necessary to discharge the obligation. In the double-entry system of accounting, the present value of a long-term debt at the time it is incurred determines the cash proceeds of the borrowing or the cost of the asset received in exchange. As the maturity of a debt approaches, its carrying amount may change, and this change is a part of the computation of the interest expense on the debt. This topic is considered in Chapter 15.

Matching Principle

The *matching principle* means that after the revenue (accomplishment) for an accounting period has been determined, the costs (effort) associated with this revenue must be deducted from revenue to measure net income. The term *matching* refers to the close relationship that exists between certain costs and the revenue recognized as a result of incurring those costs.

Expenses may be defined as the cost of goods or services used to obtain revenue.[21] The matching of a business enterprise's expenses (or expired costs) with its revenue for an accounting period is the primary activity in the measurement of the results of the enterprise's operations for that period. For example, expenditures for advertising attract customers and generate sales. The outlay for the advertising is one of the expenses to be deducted from the revenue of an accounting period. Similarly, the recognition of doubtful accounts expense illustrates the importance of the accounting period in the matching of expenses and revenue. Doubtful accounts expense is caused by selling goods or services on credit to customers who fail to pay their bills. To match this expense with the related revenue, the expense must be recorded and deducted from revenue in the accounting period in which the sales are made and recorded, even though the receivables are not determined to be uncollectible until the following period. The use of estimates is necessary in this and in many other situations in order to implement the matching principle.

Monetary Principle

The *monetary principle* means that accountants assume money to be a useful *standard measuring unit* for reporting the effects of business transactions. Money is used as the common denominator throughout the accounting process. Some of the information necessary to give a comprehensive picture of a business enterprise is difficult or impossible to quantify and express in money or other units of measurement. Examples are the competence, health, and morale of management and employees,

---

[21]A more formalized definition of *expenses,* developed by the FASB, appears on page 19.

and the effect of the operations of the enterprise on the natural environment. However, if information is to be included in financial statements, it must be expressed in monetary terms. If such measurement is not practicable, a possible alternative method of communication is to use notes to the financial statements.

In the United States the monetary unit is the dollar. To meet the test of being a useful unit of measurement, the dollar ideally should be of unchanging value. For many years the rate of price-level change in the United States was not considered to be significant enough to cast serious doubt on the usefulness of the dollar as a measuring unit. However, in many recent years, the continuing and relatively rapid inflation has reduced significantly the "value of a dollar" and has made the monetary principle one of the most controversial elements of generally accepted accounting principles. By the "value of a dollar" we usually mean the *quantity of goods and services* that the dollar will command in exchange. What kind of common denominator will enable us to measure the physical quantities of all the diverse goods and services that the dollar will buy?

The statistical solution to this question is a *price index.* An index number is a somewhat imperfect device for measuring changes in the weighted-average price of a representative sample of goods and services between two points in time. Despite their shortcomings, price indexes covering broad categories of goods and services are useful tools for measuring changes in the value of the dollar.

The monetary principle is reflected in a balance sheet by valuations of nonmonetary assets and stockholders' equity expressed in dollars of different time periods, that is, *nominal dollars* having different purchasing power (if the general price level changed).

If the monetary assumption were changed, and balance sheets were expressed in *constant purchasing power,* the two categories most affected would be nonmonetary (productive) assets (plant assets and inventories) and owners' equity. Monetary assets and most liabilities are stated at approximately their current fair values, and thus are expressed in constant purchasing power. However, the accounting valuation of nonmonetary assets is a mixture of historical costs. Similarly, paid-in capital and retained earnings in the stockholders' equity section of a balance sheet are expressed in nominal dollars that may have lost much of their significance because of changes in the general price level.

To illustrate this point, consider the case of Shan Company, which has been in business for 10 years, during which period the general price level has risen steadily. A balance sheet (in highly condensed and somewhat unorthodox form) for Shan is shown on page 27, expressed in both "nominal dollars" and "constant purchasing power." Compare the amounts under each approach.

Note the upward revision of nonmonetary assets and stockholders' equity when they are expressed in "constant purchasing power." The decline in retained earnings expressed in constant purchasing power (from $100,000 to $60,000) occurs because the cost of goods sold, depreciation, and amortization of intangible assets are larger when they are expressed in constant purchasing power during a period of inflation. The "unrealized purchasing power gain" ($140,000) is more complex. It results from the fact that nonmonetary assets were financed in part by debt. Creditors are entitled to a repayment of only a fixed number of dollars. Thus, when nonmonetary assets are restated in terms of an increased amount of constant pur-

SHAN COMPANY
Balance Sheet
December 31, Year 10

Assets	Nominal dollars (monetary assumption)	Constant purchasing power (revised assumption)
Monetary assets (cash, investments in debt securities, and receivables—stated in fixed number of dollars)	$200,000	$200,000
Nonmonetary assets (inventories, plant assets, and intangible assets)	400,000	700,000
Total assets	$600,000	$900,000
Liabilities & Stockholders' Equity		
Liabilities (stated in fixed number of dollars)	$300,000	$300,000
Stockholders' equity:		
Common stock	$200,000	$400,000
Retained earnings	100,000	60,000
Unrealized purchasing power gain..........................		140,000
Total stockholders' equity	300,000	600,000
Total liabilities & stockholders' equity	$600,000	$900,000

chasing power, Shan gains at the expense of its creditors. Bear in mind that this illustration does not use current fair values for assets, but historical costs adjusted for the change in the general price level.

Financial reporting in terms of constant purchasing power has been tried in a few countries where price inflation has been extreme. In the United States, supplementary constant-purchasing power data in annual reports to shareholders have attracted considerable attention. However, it appears unlikely that the monetary principle will be abandoned completely in primary financial statements, barring a greater change in the value of the dollar than the United States thus far has experienced. The procedures for converting nominal-dollar financial statements to constant purchasing power are discussed in Chapter 25.

Disclosure Principle

The *disclosure principle* requires that financial statements be complete in the sense of including all information necessary to users of the statements. If the omission of certain information would cause the financial statements to be misleading, disclosure of such information is essential. The disclosure principle does not require the listing of precise dollar amounts. In the published financial statements of most large companies, all amounts are rounded to the nearest thousand dollars. For example, if the general ledger has a balance for accounts receivable of $45,778,501.50 and a related allowance for doubtful accounts of $500,000.00, the balance sheet would show accounts receivable (net) at $45,279. In reading this amount, one must bear in mind that five digits have been omitted.

Published financial statements include detailed notes that are considered to be an integral part of the statements. However, disclosures in the notes should supplement the information in the body of the financial statements and should not be used to correct improper presentation of information in the body of the statements.

Typical examples of information often disclosed in notes to financial statements include the following: a summary of significant accounting policies, related party transactions, descriptions of stock option and pension plans, status of litigation in which the business enterprise is a party, amount and nature of loss contingencies and commitments, and terms and status of proposed business combinations.

The concept of disclosure applies not only to transactions and events that have occurred during the accounting period covered by the financial statements, but also to material *subsequent events* that occur after the balance sheet date but before the financial statements are released. Such events are disclosed in a note to the financial statements.

Standards Overload and Economic Consequences of Accounting Standards

The foregoing discussion has concerned fundamental principles and concepts that comprise the "foundation" of the "House of GAAP" illustrated on page 22. In the chapters that follow we discuss and illustrate a number of the more detailed accounting principles contained in *Statements* of the Financial Accounting Standards Board and other pronouncements that constitute the "first floor" of the "House of GAAP." These pronouncements have proliferated in recent years, as indicated in the following tabulation:

Accounting Research Bulletins   issued by AICPA
Committee on Accounting Procedure (1939–1959). *51*

Opinions   issued by AICPA Accounting Principles Board (1959–1973) . . .   *31*

Statements of Financial Accounting Standards   issued by FASB
(1973–January 1985). *82*

Standards Overload   As indicated by the foregoing tabulation, the frequency of issuances of pronouncements on accounting principles has increased from an average of less than three a year by the two AICPA organizations to an average of more than nine a year by the FASB. This rapid acceleration in pronouncements on accounting principles has resulted in a *standards overload*. In a 1983 report, the AICPA's Special Committee on Accounting Standards Overload reached the following conclusion:[22]

---

[22]*Report of the Special Committee on Accounting Standards Overload,* AICPA (New York: 1983), p. 1.

We find that the following factors have contributed to accounting standards overload:

(1) Too many standards

(2) Standards that are too detailed

(3) An inability to be selective in the application of standards

(4) Failure to provide sufficiently for differences between public and nonpublic entities, annual and interim financial statements, and large and small enterprises

(5) Requirements for excessive disclosures and complex measurements

The recommendations of the Special Committee included the following:[23]

We conclude that the FASB is the appropriate body to take effective action, both in the short-term and the long-term, to provide relief from accounting standards overload and recommend that—

(1) The FASB promptly reconsider and act on certain accounting standards that are widely perceived to be unnecessarily burdensome and costly, particularly for small nonpublic entities.

(2) In reconsidering existing standards and in developing new standards, the FASB's objective should be to simplify standards by avoiding complex and detailed rules for all entities to the extent feasible.

(3) To the extent that simplicity and flexibility are not feasible, the FASB should explicitly and specifically consider the information needs of the users of the financial statements of small nonpublic entities and the costs and benefits of developing the information with the objective of providing, within the framework of a unified set of generally accepted accounting principles, differential disclosure alternatives . . . as well as differential measurement alternatives for such entities.

The reaction of many accountants to the Special Committee's recommendations has been negative. While recognizing the existence of the standards overload and the difficulties posed by it, these accountants fear that adoption of the Special Committee's recommendations might lead to a "Big GAAP" and "Little GAAP" state of affairs for financial accounting, with one set of generally accepted accounting principles applicable to large publicly owned business enterprises and another set applicable to small, nonpublic enterprises. The existence of two sets of generally accepted accounting principles is unacceptable to many accountants.

The FASB has been slow to respond to the recommendations of the AICPA's Special Committee. For example, in reviewing the accounting standards for leases (one of the areas criticized in the Special Committee's report), the FASB concluded

---

[23]Ibid., pp. 3–4.

that it would not place the topic on its agenda for possible new standards development. Instead, the FASB undertook to simplify the language of the accounting standards for *lessees.* This topic is discussed in Chapter 20.

Economic Consequences of Accounting Standards   Another area of concern to accountants with respect to generally accepted accounting principles has been the unforeseen economic consequences of accounting standards when they have been applied in practice. In several cases, either the AICPA (through the Accounting Principles Board) or the Financial Accounting Standards Board has been forced to modify or to repeal a pronouncement on generally accepted accounting principles shortly after its issuance. One example was the repeal of a requirement that a portion of the proceeds of a convertible bonds issuance be allocated to the conversion feature of the bonds (see Chapter 15 for a detailed discussion of this topic). Another example was the radical change in the accounting for adjustments resulting from the translation of financial statements of a business enterprise's foreign subsidiary, investee, or branch to U.S. dollars. In both instances, accounting standards that many accountants believed were based on sound accounting theory were repealed and replaced by less desirable accounting standards because business enterprises that were required to apply the original standards found that their application resulted in financial statement presentations that were alleged *not to be in accord with economic realities.* Such incidents raise apprehensions among many accountants that sound theoretical principles are being abandoned in the establishment of accounting standards because of allegations of unfavorable economic consequences resulting from application of the standards.

The problems caused by standards overload and economic consequences of accounting standards are not easily resolved. As financial activities of business enterprises become increasingly complex, it becomes more difficult for the Financial Accounting Standards Board to establish accounting standards for measuring and reporting such activities. Thus, the establishment of generally accepted accounting principles in the future promises to be more difficult than ever before.

CASH FLOWS AND INCOME MEASUREMENT

Accountants assume that a business enterprise has continuous existence. Therefore, they record the prospect of future cash inflows as an increase in assets and as revenue whenever they have reliable evidence of the amount of the future cash receipt. Cash inflows often occur before an enterprise has performed its part of a contract. In this case, an increase in assets is recorded, but a liability is recognized instead of revenue. The liability indicates an obligation on the part of the enterprise to perform in accordance with the contract. When performance is completed, the revenue is recognized. Thus, cash inflows are closely related to revenue realization; however, the assumptions underlying the timing of revenue realization do not always permit cash inflows and revenue to be recorded in the same accounting period.

Similarly, cash outflows are closely related to expenses of a business enterprise; however, cash outflows and expenses may not be recorded in the same accounting period. For example, enterprises frequently acquire for cash in one period assets that will be productive over several future periods, and assets that are productive only during the current period often are acquired in exchange for a promise to pay cash in a future period.

Information concerning cash flows during an accounting period is valuable in judging the ability of the business enterprise to pay its debts, to pay regular dividends, to finance replacements of productive assets, and to expand its scope of operations. However, the increase or decrease in cash during a period is not useful in evaluating an enterprise's operating performance, because cash receipts and payments are not representative of the economic activities carried on in specific periods.

Accrual Basis of Accounting

The *accrual basis of accounting* is assumed throughout this book. Revenue is recognized when realized and expenses are recognized when incurred, without regard to the time of cash receipt or payment. The focus of the accrual basis of accounting is on the realization of revenue, the incurrence of costs, and the matching of revenue realized with costs expired (expenses). Adopting the assumption that revenue is recognized when realization occurs and the related assumption that costs contributing to the realization of this revenue may be traced through the earning process requires the use of an *accrual-deferral system* of accounting.

The need for frequent measurement of the past performance of a business enterprise as the basis for decisions about the future has obliged accountants to adopt the accrual basis of accounting. Under the accrual basis, the accounting records are adjusted periodically to ensure that all assets and liabilities (and thus revenue and expenses) are correctly stated.

Cash Basis of Accounting

Under the *cash basis of accounting,* revenue is recorded only when cash is received and expenses are recorded only when cash is paid. The determination of income thus rests on the *collection* of revenue and the *payment* of expenses, rather than on the *realization* of revenue and the *incurring* of expenses. Use of the cash basis of accounting is not compatible with the matching principle described earlier in this chapter. Consequently, financial statements prepared under the cash basis of accounting do not present the financial position or operating results of an enterprise in conformity with generally accepted accounting principles.

A strict cash basis of accounting seldom is found in practice, but a *modified cash basis* (a mixed cash-accrual basis) may be used for income tax purposes. Under the modified cash basis of accounting, taxpayers who acquire property having an economic life of more than one year may not deduct the entire cost in the year of acquisition. They must treat the cost as an asset to be depreciated over its economic life. Expenses such as rent or advertising paid in advance also are regarded as assets and are deductible only in the year or years to which they apply. Expenses paid after the year in which incurred are deductible only in the year paid. Revenue is reported for income tax purposes in the year received. However, in any business enterprise in which the purchase, production, or sale of merchandise is a significant factor, these transactions must be reported on an accrual basis. For example, when merchandise is sold on credit, the revenue must be recognized immediately. The cost of goods sold must reflect purchases on credit and inventories on hand, whether paid for or not. Thus, for a merchandising enterprise the revenue from sales, the cost of goods sold, and the gross profit on sales will be the same under the accrual basis of accounting as under the modified cash basis of accounting.

Illustration   The difference between the cash basis and accrual basis of accounting is illustrated below for Tina Carson, a practicing CPA, who maintains accounting records on a cash basis. During Year 10, Carson collected $150,000 from her clients and paid $80,000 for operating expenses, resulting in a cash-basis net income of $70,000. Carson's fees receivable, accrued liabilities, and short-term prepayments on January 1 and on December 31, Year 10, were as follows:

Accrual-basis items of business enterprise that uses cash basis of accounting

	Jan. 1, Year 10	Dec. 31, Year 10
Fees receivable	$18,200	$37,000
Accrued liabilities	6,200	4,000
Short-term prepayments....................	3,500	2,500

A working paper showing the necessary adjustments to restate Carson's income statement from the cash basis of accounting to the accrual basis of accounting is illustrated on page 33.

Because the revenue from fees under the cash basis does not include the fees receivable on December 31, which were realized in Year 10, this amount is added to the cash collected in the restatement of revenue from fees to the accrual basis of accounting. Because fees receivable on January 1 were realized in Year 9 and collected in Year 10, this amount is subtracted from cash collections in the restatement of revenue from fees to the accrual basis of accounting.

The adjustments to restate operating expenses from the cash basis of accounting to the accrual basis of accounting are explained below:

(1)   The amount of accrued liabilities on December 31, Year 10, represents expenses incurred in Year 10 that will be paid in Year 11, and the amount of short-term prepayments on January 1, Year 10, represents services paid for in Year 9 that were consumed in Year 10. Therefore, both amounts are *added* to the amount of cash paid to restate the operating expenses for Year 10 to the accrual basis of accounting.

(2)   The amount of accrued liabilities on January 1, Year 10, represents expenses of Year 9 paid for in Year 10, and the amount of short-term prepayments on December 31, Year 10, represents cash outlays in Year 10 for services that will be consumed in Year 11. Therefore, both amounts are *deducted* from the amount of cash paid to restate the operating expenses for Year 10 to the accrual basis of accounting.

REVIEW QUESTIONS

1   Identify the organizations or legislative acts that have been primarily responsible for the development of accounting principles and practices in the United States.

TINA CARSON, CPA
Working Paper to Restate Income Statement from Cash Basis to Accrual Basis of Accounting
For Year Ended December 31, Year 10

	Income statement under cash basis of accounting	Adjustments to restate to accrual basis of accounting		Income statement under accrual basis of accounting
		Add	Deduct	
Revenue from fees received in cash	$150,000			
Add: Fees receivable, Dec. 31, Year 10		$37,000		$168,800
Less: Fees receivable, Jan. 1, Year 10			$18,200	
Operating expenses paid in cash	80,000			
Add: Accrued liabilities, Dec. 31, Year 10		4,000		
Short-term prepayments, Jan. 1, Year 10		3,500		78,800
Less: Accrued liabilities, Jan. 1, Year 10			6,200	
Short-term prepayments, Dec. 31, Year 10			2,500	
Net income under cash basis of accounting	$ 70,000			
Net income under accrual basis of accounting				$ 90,000

What is the relationship between each of these organizations or acts and certified public accountants?

2 Identify the following as being governmental organizations or part of the private sector of the economy: Financial Accounting Standards Board, Securities and Exchange Commission, New York Stock Exchange, American Accounting Association.

3 Describe the procedures followed by the Financial Accounting Standards Board in the development of a new financial accounting standard.

4 Briefly describe the Financial Accounting Standards Board's conceptual framework project for financial accounting and reporting.

5 What are four publications of the Financial Accounting Standards Board issued as parts of the conceptual framework project?

6   Briefly describe three objectives of financial reporting identified by the Financial Accounting Standards Board.

7   What is the most important qualitative characteristic of accounting information, according to the Financial Accounting Standards Board?

8   The two primary qualities of accounting information identified by the Financial Accour..ng Standards Board are *relevance* and *reliability.* Are these qualities as likely to be present in a forecast of future earnings as in an income statement? Explain.

9   Is *conservatism* a qualitative characteristic of accounting information? Explain.

10   Briefly summarize the position of the Financial Accounting Standards Board on *materiality* as an influencing factor on the quality of accounting information.

11   What is *comprehensive income* as defined by the Financial Accounting Standards Board?

12   What is the Financial Accounting Standards Board's position on the use of different attributes such as historical cost and current cost in the measurement techniques used in financial accounting?

13   Are generally accepted accounting principles applicable to both financial accounting and managerial accounting? Explain.

14   What is meant by the *continuity* or *going-concern principle* of accounting? How does it affect the valuation of assets? When is this principle not applicable?

15   Define the *revenue realization principle.* How is this principle related to the *valuation principle* and the *matching principle?*

16   Wembley Corporation acquired land in exchange for 50,000 shares of its $5 par common stock. How is the valuation principle of accounting applied in recording this transaction?

17   The *monetary principle* assumes that money is a useful standard measuring unit for reporting the effects of business transactions. State and explain two major criticisms or limitations of this accounting principle.

18   Hardy Corporation has total assets of $136,542,816.22. The balances of Hardy's Accounts Receivable and Allowance for Doubtful Accounts ledger accounts on December 31, Year 6, were $4,118,263.81 and $92,774.18, respectively. How may accounts receivable be presented in Hardy's December 31, Year 6, balance sheet under the *disclosure principle?* Explain.

19   Some accountants believe that reaction to the *standards overload* might lead to a "Big GAAP" and "Little GAAP" state of affairs. What is meant by those two terms?

20   What is a potential danger of giving too much weight to the *economic consequences* of proposed accounting standards?

21 Distinguish between the *cash basis of accounting* and the *accrual basis of accounting.* Do financial statements prepared under either method present the financial position and operating results of a business enterprise in conformity with generally accepted accounting principles?

EXERCISES

Ex. 1-1 Select the best answer for each of the following multiple-choice questions:

1 The valuation of a promise to receive cash in the future at present value in the financial statements of a business enterprise is valid because of the accounting principle or concept of:
a Entity   **b** Materiality   **c** Going concern   **d** Neutrality

2 Which of the following is disclosed in the Summary of Significant Accounting Policies note to the financial statements?
a Amount of rent expense
b Maturity dates of long-term debt
c Methods of amortizing intangible assets
d Composition of plant assets

3 The imputation of interest for certain assets and liabilities is based primarily on the accounting principle or concept of:
a Valuation   **b** Conservatism   **c** Consistency   **d** Stable monetary unit

4 Which of the following is considered a pervasive constraint by *Statement of Financial Accounting Concepts No. 2,* ''Qualitative Characteristics of Accounting Information''?
a Benefits/costs   **b** Conservatism   **c** Timeliness   **d** Verifiability

5 According to *Statement of Financial Accounting Concepts No. 2,* ''Qualitative Characteristics of Accounting Information,'' relevance and reliability are the two primary qualities that make accounting information useful for decision making. Is predictive value an ingredient of:

	Relevance?	*Reliability?*
a	No	No
b	No	Yes
c	Yes	Yes
d	Yes	No

6 Under *Statement of Financial Accounting Concepts No. 2,* ''Qualitative Characteristics of Accounting Information,'' which of the following is an ingredient of the primary quality of *reliability?*
a Understandability   **b** Verifiability   **c** Predictive value   **d** Materiality

7 The entire premium for a three-year insurance policy expiring on December 31, Year 3, was paid on January 2, Year 1. If the payment was debited to the Unexpired Insurance ledger account, how is each of the following ledger account balances affected in Year 3?

	Unexpired Insurance	Insurance Expense
a	No change	Increase
b	No change	No change
c	Decrease	No change
d	Decrease	Increase

8   Under *Statement of Financial Accounting Concepts No. 2,* "Qualitative Characteristics of Accounting Information," *timeliness* is an ingredient of the primary quality of:

a Reliability   **b** Relevance   **c** Verifiability   **d** Representational faithfulness

9   Under *Statement of Financial Accounting Concepts No. 3,* "Elements of Financial Statements of Business Enterprises," does *comprehensive income* include changes in owners' equity resulting from:

	Investments by owners?	Distributions to owners?
a	No	No
b	No	Yes
c	Yes	No
d	Yes	Yes

Ex. 1-2   Norm Company debits all insurance premium payments to the Unexpired Insurance ledger account and prepares adjusting entries at the end of each month to recognize expired insurance premiums as an expense. Balances of the affected ledger accounts were as follows for Year 6:

Unexpired Insurance:

Jan. 1, Year 6	$150,000
Dec. 31, Year 6	175,000
Insurance Expense, Dec. 31, Year 6	625,000

Compute the total insurance premiums paid by Norm Company during Year 6.

Ex. 1-3   Lemo Corporation owns a small building with offices that it rents under contracts calling for payments either monthly or yearly in advance. However, some tenants are delinquent in their rent payments. During Year 2, Lemo received $20,000 from tenants. Lemo's ledger account balances for Year 2 included the following:

	Jan. 1, Year 2	Dec. 31, Year 2
Rent Receivable	$2,400	$3,100
Unearned Rent.............................	8,000	6,000

Compute Lemo Corporation's rent revenue for Year 2 under the accrual basis of accounting.

Ex. 1-4   Gilbert Company assigns some of its patents to other business enterprises under licensing contracts. Under some licenses, advance royalties are received; under other licenses, royalties are paid within 60 days after each license year ends. During Year 5, Gilbert received royalty checks of $200,000. Gilbert's ledger account balances for Year 5 included the following:

	Jan. 1, Year 5	Dec. 31, Year 5
Royalties Receivable	$90,000	$85,000
Unearned Royalties	60,000	40,000

Compute Gilbert Company's royalties revenue for Year 5 under the accrual basis of accounting.

Ex. 1-5 Cash paid by Langley Corporation for operating expenses during the month of October, Year 6, totaled $16,480. Short-term prepayments and accrued liabilities were as follows:

	Oct. 1, Year 6	Oct. 31, Year 6
Short-term prepayments	$1,240	$1,690
Accrued liabilities	2,570	1,820

Compute Langley Corporation's operating expenses for the month of October, Year 6, under the accrual basis of accounting.

Ex. 1-6 Identify each of the following phrases as being associated with the cash basis of accounting or the accrual basis of accounting:

a Revenue recognized at time of collection
b Individual income tax returns
c Business enterprise with a material amount of inventories
d Minimum amount of record keeping
e Generally accepted accounting principles
f Postponement of recognition of revenue
g Flexibility in recognition of expenses
h Emphasis on consistency and matching in the measurement of net income
i Sophisticated accounting system
j Small service enterprise with accounting records limited to information required for income tax purposes

Ex. 1-7 The general-purpose financial statements of Matt Corporation contain the following item and note to the financial statements:

Inventories $1,760,000

Note 1: Summary of Significant Accounting Policies *Inventories are valued at the lower of cost or market; cost is determined on the first-in, first-out basis.*

Discuss the appropriateness of the foregoing in relation to the disclosure principle of accounting.

Ex. 1-8 Crocus Company uses the accrual basis of accounting. It reported advertising expense for Year 7 of $35,460. Prepaid advertising at the end of Year 7 amounted to $4,820, and cash paid for advertising during Year 7 amounted to $36,680. There was no advertising payable at either the beginning or the end of Year 7.

Compute the amount of Crocus Company's prepaid advertising at the beginning of Year 7.

Ex. 1-9   The financial statements of Weir Company include the items shown below, together with the related notes to the financial statements.

Cash *(Note 1)* . . . . $ 96,500

Accounts receivable *(Note 2)*   210,300

Note 1: *The amount reported as cash includes four checking accounts, two petty cash funds, and one change fund.*

Note 2: *Accounts receivable include $48,400, representing the selling price of merchandise shipped on consignment and held for sale by consignees acting as agents. It is anticipated that this merchandise will be sold within six months and that none of it will have to be returned to the warehouse.*

Discuss the appropriateness of *Note 1* and *Note 2* to Weir Company's financial statements as a means of carrying out the disclosure principle and the objectives of general-purpose financial statements.

CASES

Case 1-1   Generally accepted accounting principles require the use of accruals and deferrals in the determination of net income.

Instructions

a How does the accrual basis of accounting affect the measurement of net income? Include a discussion of what constitutes an accrual and a deferral, and give examples of each.

b Contrast the accrual basis of accounting with the cash basis of accounting.

Case 1-2   During the first class meeting in an accounting course, Professor Logan asked three students to explain the nature of revenue and expenses as related to the preparation of financial statements for business enterprises. Carl Lucas stated that revenue and expenses reflect changes in the owners' equity of a business enterprise. Lois Chu stated that Carl was wrong and explained that revenue represents inflows of assets and expenses represent outflows of assets. Morris Dean responded as follows: "Revenue and expenses are those items that determine net income," Professor Logan took the position that each student was on the right track, but that none had presented an entirely satisfactory explanation.

Instructions

Evaluate Professor Logan's response and describe the nature of revenue and expenses as these terms are used in financial accounting.

Case 1-3   The board of directors of DuPre Corporation is debating whether to adopt the straight-line method of depreciation or an accelerated depreciation method. Some directors are primarily interested in reporting steadily increasing earnings; others argue that the best way to achieve a favorable "accounting image" in the financial community is to adopt conservative accounting policies.

Instructions

Explain whether the conservative effect of accelerated depreciation on net income and financial position will be realized for only a few years or whether it will continue indefinitely to result in the reporting of lower earnings and a lower valuation of plant assets.

Case 1-4   A financial newspaper carried an advertisement of a small manufacturing enterprise being offered for sale by its owner. The advertisement emphasized the unusual profitability of the enterprise. Assume that you were interested in acquiring a business of this type and you therefore contacted the owner, Laura Griffin, who stated that Griffin Company in its first year of operations had realized net income of $95,000. You inquired whether the accrual basis of accounting had been used to determine the net income, and Griffin replied as follows:

> "We use a mixed cash-accrual basis of accounting, just as many other small companies do. As you probably know, a strict cash basis is not satisfactory, but a modified or mixed cash-accrual basis is acceptable for income tax purposes and meets our other needs. For example, our purchases of merchandise are recorded only when cash payments are made. Our sales are recorded immediately, whether on a cash or a credit basis. We do not guess about doubtful accounts receivable in advance, but we do not hesitate to write off any receivable that proves to be uncollectible. We took a physical inventory at year-end and entered it in the accounting records. We did not record any depreciation on equipment because equipment was acquired by issuance of long-term promissory notes. No journal entry will be made for these transactions until cash payments are made. We find this system gives us better results than a strict cash basis of accounting and requires less work than the accrual basis of accounting."

Instructions

Evaluate point by point the statement made by Laura Griffin. Do you regard Griffin Company's system as conforming with the usual standards of a "modified cash basis" of accounting? Is the net income of $95,000 during the first year of operations a valid measurement? Explain.

Case 1-5   In a discussion of the concept of conservatism as an influence on financial accounting and reporting, Alice Wu argued that conservatism often is used as a means of understating net income of the current accounting period and the financial position at the end of the period. George Case defended conservatism on the grounds that accountants frequently have to make choices among alternative assumptions under conditions of uncertainty and that making such choices on a conservative basis would help avoid dangerous overstatements of net income that could injure both investors and certified public accountants.

Wu and Case considered the five following situations but were unable to reach agreement on the proper accounting treatment for any of them.

(1) A business enterprise has expended $125,000 (which is 5% of its annual sales) for research and development in an effort to develop new commercial products. No specific products have emerged from this research, but management believes that the research, if continued, eventually will lead to important new products. Furthermore, management believes that its existing products will lose

their market appeal in a few years and that the enterprise must have new products to survive. Wu favors including the $125,000 in the balance sheet as an intangible asset, Deferred Research and Development Costs; Case favors treating the $125,000 as expense of the current year.

(2) After occupying an old building on leased land for 17 years of a 20-year operating lease, the lessee enterprise constructed a new frame building, because the old building was unsatisfactory and the lessor refused to make repairs. Improvements on the land will revert to the lessor at the end of the lease term. There is a possibility, but no assurance, that the lessor will agree to renew the lease. Wu favors capitalizing the cost of the building; Case favors writing off the cost of the building as expense of the current year.

(3) The products sold by a manufacturing enterprise are guaranteed for a period of one year. Wu favors the recognition of warranty expense only as claims are presented for repair or replacement of products; Case favors the recognition of warranty expense and crediting a liability for an estimated amount in the year of sale.

(4) The inventory of a retailing enterprise contains a large quantity of item K for which demand has largely disappeared. Wu wants to include item K as an asset in the balance sheet on the grounds that the item is not subject to deterioration and customer demand for it may revive; Case favors writing off the cost of this item.

(5) Credit terms of a retailing enterprise are 30 days. Case favors writing off a large receivable six months past due from a customer who went to Europe for an extended stay and cannot be located; Wu is opposed because the customer has been delinquent before and later paid in full.

Instructions

For each of the five situations, state your position on the proposed action and explain the reasoning underlying your position.

Case 1-6   Spivak Corporation owns several office buildings and rents space to tenants. One of these office buildings was acquired at a cost of $750,000 and has been depreciated for five years on a straight-line basis. Residual value is zero. The carrying amount, net of accumulated depreciation, will be $680,000 at the end of the current year.

At the time the building was acquired, Spivak Corporation had borrowed $750,000 from Curtis Evan, one of the founders of Spivak and presently a director and major stockholder. The promissory note payable issued for the loan made no mention of interest but called for repayment of $1,000,000 five years from the date of the note. In a directors' meeting near the end of the current year, Evan stated that, because of rising price levels, he considered the office building to be worth more than it had cost. Evan offered to accept the office building in full settlement of the $1,000,000 promissory note, which was about to mature.

During a discussion of the offer by the board of directors, the following opinions were expressed:

Director Jacobs: "If we give up the building in settlement of the $1,000,000 note payable, we shall increase our earnings this year by $250,000, and we shall have to correct our prior years' earnings by eliminating all depreciation on the building, because this transaction provides reliable evidence that the building has not depreciated. My understanding of generally accepted accounting principles is that our treatment of the transaction must use the reliable evidence provided by Evan's offer.''

Director Winton: ''In my opinion we could accept the offer and not have to recognize any gain. Spivak will not receive cash, receivables, or any other asset, so there is no gain involved. The revenue realization principle states that there must be an inflow of cash or receivables in order to have revenue.''

Director Toby: ''Spivak received only $750,000 when it issued the note payable, and it has not paid or recorded any interest. Now we shall give up an asset that cost $750,000 to discharge a recorded liability of the same amount, so this is a perfect example of the matching principle, and no gain or loss is involved.''

Instructions

a Evaluate the opinions expressed by each of the three directors, giving attention to the references made to accounting principles. Use a separate paragraph or paragraphs to evaluate each director's position and indicate what accounting principles are involved.

b Explain how the proposed transaction should be accounted for by Spivak Corporation. Indicate the accounting principle or principles you consider to be applicable. Include in your answer whether interest and depreciation should be recognized and the amount of the gain or loss, if any, that would result from acceptance of Curtis Evan's offer.

c In the financial statements prepared immediately after completion of the exchange with Curtis Evan, is it necessary to make any disclosure of this transaction apart from the usual accounting for disposal of a building? Explain.

d Assuming that Spivak Corporation accepts Curtis Evan's offer, prepare a journal entry to record the transaction. Assume that depreciation expense has been recorded for the current year and that the accounting records have not been closed. No interest expense has been recorded on the promissory note payable. Assume also that the journal entry made at the time the note payable was issued consisted of a debit to Cash for $750,000, a debit to Discount on Notes Payable for $250,000, and a credit to Notes Payable for $1,000,000. *Suggestion:* The interest expense applicable to prior years may be debited to Retained Earnings (Prior Period Adjustment). Assume that the interest expense applicable to the current year is $55,000.

PROBLEMS

1-1 Haig Corporation was organized by Howard Haig and Richard Haig for the purpose of operating a hardware store. Each invested $60,000 cash, and each received 3,000 shares of $1 par common stock. Howard Haig also loaned $50,000 to Haig Corporation and received a two-year, 12% promissory note. Haig Corporation then issued 3,600 shares of its common stock in exchange for land and a building. The land had a current fair value of $30,000.

Merchandise costing $70,000 was purchased on credit, and a sales representative was employed to begin work the following week at a weekly salary of $500.

Haig Corporation plans to use the periodic inventory system. Office supplies and office equipment were acquired for $15,000. The office supplies were valued at $2,600 and the office equipment at $12,400.

Instructions

a What cost should be recorded for the land and the building acquired in exchange for Haig Corporation's common stock? Explain the reasoning underlying your answer.

b Prepare journal entries for the foregoing transactions of Haig Corporation.

c After one year of operations, Haig Corporation had a strong working capital position, but retained earnings amounted to only $20,000. Under these circumstances, would it be proper for Haig Corporation to pay the $50,000 note payable to Howard Haig? Explain.

1-2 Carl Will and George Burr formed Will-Burr Corporation to operate a charter fishing boat. Each invested $54,000 cash, for which each received 6,000 shares of $1 par common stock. Will-Burr Corporation also issued 2,400 shares of common stock to acquire a used boat. Wilma Todd, the former owner of the boat, had pledged it as collateral for a $50,000 bank loan, and this $50,000 liability was assumed by Will-Burr Corporation in the contract for acquisition of the boat.

Wilma Todd's accounting records showed that the original cost of the boat was $150,000 and that she had recorded depreciation expense of $90,000 by the straight-line method.

Will-Burr Corporation acquired fishing equipment for $12,800 and supplies for $1,500. A crew member was hired to begin work the following week at a weekly salary of $550.

Instructions

a What effect, if any, does the amount of recorded depreciation and the depreciation method used by Wilma Todd have on the depreciation program to be used for the boat by Will-Burr Corporation? Explain the reasoning underlying your answer.

b What cost should be recorded for the boat acquired in exchange for 2,400 shares of Will-Burr Corporation common stock? Explain.

c Prepare journal entries to record the transactions completed by Will-Burr Corporation.

1-3 Plumm Company is a successful enterprise that is expanding rapidly. On May 1, Year 5, additional manufacturing facilities were acquired from the Towne & Bates Partnership, which was terminating operations because of a dispute between the partners. The property had been advertised for sale at a price of $950,000. Bates asserted that the land alone was worth that much and that the building was insured for $500,000, its cost of construction.

Plumm acquired the property by issuing to the partnership 60,000 shares of its $5 par common stock and agreed to assume a $250,000 mortgage note payable on the property.

Prior to the acquisition, Plumm hired a firm of industrial engineers to appraise the building. The report from this firm set forth a current fair value for the building of $480,000. The common stock of Plumm is listed on a stock exchange and was trading on May 1, Year 5, at a price of $12 a share.

Shortly after acquiring the property from the Towne & Bates Partnership, Plumm received a letter from a large corporation offering to acquire the property from Plumm for $1,000,000.

Instructions

a Prepare a journal entry to record the transaction of Plumm Company.

b Explain the reasoning underlying your answer to part **a.**

1-4 Gill Corporation issues promissory notes frequently in borrowing from various sources. Some of the notes provide for payment of interest in advance; others do not. (For the purposes of this problem, you need not challenge the propriety of prepaid interest.) Gill uses the accrual basis of accounting. Interest expense under the accrual basis for Year 3 was $19,600. Information relating to prepaid interest and to interest payable on two successive balance sheet dates appears below:

	Dec. 31, Year 2	Dec. 31, Year 3
Prepaid interest	$1,800	$ 400
Interest payable	1,700	2,200

Gill owns several buildings that it rents to tenants. Some tenants pay rent in advance; others do not. The amount of cash collected from the tenants during Year 3 was $56,400. The following information relates to rent receivable and unearned rent on two successive balance sheet dates:

	Dec. 31, Year 2	Dec. 31, Year 3
Rent receivable	$6,400	$5,000
Unearned rent	3,600	2,800

Instructions

a Compute the amount of cash paid by Gill Corporation for interest during Year 3.

b Compute the amount of Gill Corporation's rent revenue for Year 3, under the accrual basis of accounting.

1-5 Lido Company uses the accrual basis of accounting. Lido owns buildings that it rents to tenants. Rent collected in cash during Year 5 amounted to $108,400. The amounts of rent receivable and of unearned rent on two successive balance sheet dates were as follows:

	Dec. 31, Year 4	Dec. 31, Year 5
Rent receivable	$3,600	$4,900
Unearned rent	4,400	1,640

Lido advertises its merchandise through television, radio, and newspapers. Some of the advertising is paid in advance and some is paid on receipt of invoices. Advertising expense under the accrual basis of accounting for Year 5 was $64,200.

The amounts of prepaid advertising and advertising payable at the beginning and at the end of Year 5 were as follows:

	Jan. 1, Year 5	Dec. 31, Year 5
Prepaid advertising	$5,360	$6,400
Advertising payable	7,840	2,930

Instructions

a Compute the amount of rent revenue that should appear in Lido Company's income statement for Year 5, under the accrual basis of accounting.

b Compute the amount of cash paid by Lido Company for advertising during Year 5.

1-6 A summary of operating results for Perez Company for Year 2 is presented below:

Cash collected from customers......................................	$466,000
Cash paid to merchandise suppliers	268,200
Cash paid for operating expenses	79,400

The following data were taken from comparative balance sheets prepared on the accrual basis of accounting:

	Dec. 31, Year 1	Dec. 31, Year 2
Accounts receivable	$52,400	$48,600
Inventories	75,000	72,100
Short-term prepayments...................................	4,100	9,500
Accounts payable (merchandise suppliers)	32,000	37,400
Accrued liabilities	2,800	3,200
Accumulated depreciation (there were no disposals of plant assets during Year 2)	50,000	74,000

Instructions

Prepare income statements for Perez Company for Year 2, under (**a**) the accrual basis of accounting, and (**b**) the modified cash basis of accounting whereby operating expenses (other than depreciation) are computed on the cash basis. Perez's income is taxed at 45%. Show supporting computations.

1-7 The information listed below was obtained from the comparative balance sheets of Merk Company for Year 4:

	Year 4	
	Jan. 1	Dec. 31
Accounts receivable	$ 77,500	$ 84,200
Inventories	110,000	125,000
Short-term prepayments...................................	6,200	1,700
Accounts payable (merchandise suppliers)	49,500	38,000
Operating expenses payable	3,200	1,900
Accumulated depreciation (there were no disposals of plant assets during Year 4)	66,000	100,000

A summary of cash receipts and payments for Year 4 follows:

Cash collected from customers	*$723,500*
Cash paid to merchandise suppliers	*440,000*
Cash paid for operating expenses	*122,800*

Instructions

Prepare income statements for Merk Company for Year 4, under (**a**) the accrual basis of accounting, and (**b**) the modified cash basis of accounting whereby operating expenses (excluding depreciation) are computed on the cash basis. Merk's income is taxed at 45%. Show supporting computations.

Information Processing and the Accounting Cycle

2

Accounting has been called the "language of business" because it is a method of communicating business information. As with other languages, it is undergoing continuous change in an attempt to develop better means of communicating.

The *accounting process* consists of three major parts: (1) the recording of transactions during an accounting period, (2) the summarizing of information at the end of the period, and (3) the preparation of financial statements.

During an accounting period business transactions and events are recorded as they occur, and at the end of each period the accounting records are summarized in order to prepare financial statements. After an unadjusted trial balance is prepared, adjusting entries are required to bring the accounting records up-to-date. Some adjustments must be made to the recorded data for changes that have occurred since the transactions were recorded; other adjustments are needed for events that have not been recorded but affect the financial position and operating results of the business enterprise. Examples of these unrecorded events are depreciation and other expirations of asset services, the accrual of expenses such as salaries and various taxes, and the accrual of revenue such as rent and interest.

When the accounting records have been made as complete, accurate, and up-to-date as possible, accountants prepare financial statements reflecting the financial position and the results of operations. An important measure of the success of the accounting process is the responsiveness of financial reporting to the needs of the users of accounting information.

RECORDING BUSINESS TRANSACTIONS AND EVENTS

If the accounting process is to provide the users of accounting information with reliable, timely reports, transactions during an accounting period must be interpreted in conformity with generally accepted accounting principles and recorded promptly and accurately. *Business transactions* and other *events* cause changes in the assets, liabilities, or owners' equity of a business enterprise. Transactions and events may be classified into two broad groups: (1) *external transactions and events,* or those between the business enterprise and another party, and (2) *internal events,* such as the expiration or transfer of costs within the enterprise, the recording of depreciation of plant assets, the recognition of obsolescence in inventories, the transfer of production costs from the goods in process inventory to the finished goods inventory, and the recognition of estimated doubtful accounts expense.

Supporting Documents

A *supporting document* (sometimes called a *business paper* or a *voucher*) is the first record prepared for a transaction. Such documents show the date, amount, and nature of the transaction, and the parties involved. Entries in the various journals are prepared from supporting documents; for example, sales invoices support entries in the sales journal. The original copy of a sales invoice is sent to the customer, who uses it as a basis for recording the purchase; a duplicate copy is retained by the seller as evidence of the sale. Some supporting documents may never leave the business enterprise, as, for example, cash register tapes, receiving reports, time reports, journal vouchers, and minutes of directors' meetings.

Any verification of financial statements or accounting records is likely to include tests in which summary amounts are traced to the supporting documents. The practice of identifying each type of document with serial numbers and accounting for all numbers in the series helps prevent the omission of transactions because of missing documents. Proper design and use of supporting documents is an important element in the system of internal controls, regardless of whether the enterprise uses a manual accounting system or a computerized system.

Computerized Data Processing

The increasing use of computers by business enterprises, governmental units, and other organizations has changed significantly the methods of recording, summarizing, and classifying accounting information. The computer not only processes data with incredible speed and a high degree of accuracy, but also permits the classification and summarization of data in more forms and at lower cost than has been possible with manual systems.

The input data for a computer generally are on punched cards or tapes, created as a by-product when business papers such as invoices and checks are prepared. The computer output, also on cards or tapes, is read by printers that can produce various reports and financial statements.

In business enterprises that use computers, the recording, classifying, and summarizing steps used in creating accounting information may be combined into one process. With an ***on-line, real-time computer system,*** the recording of a business transaction causes instantaneous updating of all relevant files. You have probably encountered these on-line, real-time (OLRT) systems at airline ticket offices and in savings and loan associations. At most banks and savings and loan associations, a teller can update a depositor's account immediately by recording the deposit or withdrawal on a computer terminal. It is not difficult to envision a computer-based system that produces daily a set of financial statements or special reports updated to include all transactions to date and also provides the current amounts for such items as interest, depreciation, and labor costs.

Although the traditional forms of journals and ledgers are not essential to the processing of accounting information by computers, the concepts implicit in these records also are used in a computerized system. Furthermore, the output of the computers may be designed to provide information in a form similar to traditional journals and ledgers.

Because our primary focus in this book is on accounting principles and financial statements rather than on accounting systems, we rely on manual recording methods as the simplest and clearest means of illustrating the application of accounting principles to business transactions and events.

Double-Entry System

The standard accounting model for accumulating data in a business enterprise consists of the ***double-entry system*** based on the basic accounting equation. As the name implies, the ***journal entry*** made for each transaction is composed of two parts: one or more debits and one or more credits. All journal entries are made within the framework of the basic ***accounting equation*** (assets = liabilities + owners' equity). Each transaction must be analyzed in terms of its effects on the elements of this equation. The advantages of the double-entry system include built-in controls that automatically call attention to many types of errors and offer assurance that once assets are recorded, they will not be forgotten or overlooked. Management's responsibility for the custody of assets thus is strengthened by the inherent discipline of the double-entry system. The self-balancing nature of this system facilitates the preparation of a complete set of financial statements as frequently as desired.

The double-entry system is in practically universal use; it takes its name from the fact that equal debit and credit entries are made for every transaction or event. The terms ***debit*** and ***credit*** may be related to the basic accounting equation (A = L + OE) in the following way:

Changes in balance sheet accounts

Assets accounts	=	*Liability + Owners' Equity accounts*
Increases are recorded by debits		*Increases are recorded by credits*
Decreases are recorded by credits		*Decreases are recorded by debits*

Assets and liabilities are the two independent variables in the above equation; the dependent variable, owners' equity, is derived from the valuation assigned to assets and liabilities. One source of change in the owners' equity is the change in the *net assets* (assets minus liabilities) as a result of operations, measured by two classes of ledger accounts—revenue and expenses. *Revenue* accounts measure the inflow of assets resulting from the production and distribution of goods and services to customers. *Expense* accounts measure the outflow of assets necessary to produce and distribute these goods and services. The change in the net assets as a result of these two flows is reflected in the owners' equity. Revenue and expense accounts are subject to the same rules of debit and credit as applied to assets, liabilities, and owners' equity accounts. The application of the rules of debit and credit for revenue and expenses is summarized below:

Changes in income statement accounts

Expense accounts	Revenue accounts
Increases are recorded by debits	Increases are recorded by credits
Decreases are recorded by credits	Decreases are recorded by debits

As the terms *debit* and *credit* are used in accounting, they have no meaning except as a directive for recording data in ledger accounts. Debit refers to the left side of a ledger account, and credit refers to the right side.

Accounting Period

The normal accounting period is one year, beginning on a specific day and ending 12 months later. A *calendar-year* accounting period ends on December 31; all other 12-month periods are known as *fiscal years.* Business enterprises frequently adopt fiscal years that end when operations are at a low point in order to simplify year-end procedures and facilitate a better measurement of financial position and the results of operations. Such an accounting period is referred to as a *natural business year* because it conforms to the natural annual cycle of the enterprise. For example, the fiscal year of Walt Disney Productions, whose financial statements are illustrated in the Appendix to Chapter 4, is October 1 through September 30, the end of the natural business year of Disney's theme parks.

Reports issued for shorter periods, such as one quarter of the year or one month, are called *interim reports.* Interim reports of the operating results of publicly owned corporations are needed to assist investors in reaching decisions to buy, hold, or sell securities. Traditionally, interim reports have not been audited by certified public accountants. At present, however, independent accountants frequently review their clients' interim reports to assure consistency with the annual financial statements.[1]

---

[1]For a discussion of the special measurement problems relating to interim financial reports, see *APB Opinion No. 28,* "Interim Financial Reporting," AICPA (New York: 1973).

Accounting Cycle

The *accounting cycle* is a complete sequence of accounting procedures that are repeated in the same order during each accounting period. The cycle in a traditional manual system (and with modifications in a computerized system) includes the following steps:

1   Recording business transactions and events in the journals

2   Classifying data by posting from the journals to the ledger

3   Summarizing data from the ledger in an unadjusted trial balance (first pair of columns in the work sheet)

4   Adjusting, correcting, and updating recorded data; completion of the work sheet

5   Summarizing adjusted and corrected work sheet data in the form of financial statements

6   Closing the accounting records (nominal accounts) to summarize the operations of the accounting period

7   Preparation of a post-closing trial balance

8   Reversing certain adjusting entries to facilitate the recording process in the subsequent accounting period[2]

When these steps are completed, the cycle begins again for the next accounting period. A brief explanation of journals, the ledger, and the various steps of the accounting cycle is presented in the following sections.

Journals

The information shown in business papers is recorded in chronological order in the appropriate journals. Because a journal is organized chronologically by transactions and events, we may say that the unit of organization for a journal is the individual transaction or event. Although a small business enterprise conceivably could record all transactions and events in a single journal (the general journal), this approach seldom is used. When numerous transactions of the same nature occur (such as transactions involving the receipt of cash), *special journals* may be used as a more efficient means of recording and summarizing such recurring transactions.

The journalizing process requires the analysis of business transactions and events in terms of debits and credits to the ledger accounts they affect: (1) assets, (2) liabilities, (3) owners' equity, (4) revenue, and (5) expenses. To portray business transactions and events in a journal entry, we must identify and classify each important element of a transaction or event.

---

[2]This is an optional step, as explained on pages 65–67.

A growing business enterprise usually designs its accounting system to handle efficiently the increasing volume of transactions. One purpose of the accounting system is to facilitate the summarization of a large volume of transactions into meaningful totals for various uses. The basic accounting problems for large and small enterprises are quite similar; however, the procedures adopted for accumulating accounting data may differ.

Every business enterprise, regardless of its size, has certain established routines that are basic to the collection of accounting data. For example, documents are used to initiate transactions or to report their occurrence. As the complexity of the enterprise increases, methods such as the preparation of several copies of these documents may be required, and various types of billing machines, mechanical registers, and preprinted forms may be used. In this way the time lag between the initiation of a transaction and its ultimate disposition may be shortened. Obviously, as the volume of similar transactions increases, the degree of automation possible in handling the data increases.

The great majority of business transactions are of four types, and for that reason most of the data may be recorded by the use of special multicolumn journals and a general journal. The four most commonly used special journals are: *sales journal, voucher register* (or purchases journal), *cash receipts journal,* and *cash payments journal.* The primary types of transactions or events and the journals in which these are recorded are:

Type of transaction or event	Journal
Sales of merchandise on credit	Sales journal (S)
Purchases of merchandise, supplies, etc., on credit	Voucher register (VR) (or purchases journal PJ)
Receipts of cash	Cash receipts journal (CR)
Payments of cash	Cash payments journal (CP)
Other transactions or events	General journal (J)

Types of transactions recorded in each journal

A set of five journals, similar to those listed above, is adequate for the transactions of most small business enterprises. The general journal is necessary, regardless of the special journals involved, to record unusual and nonrepetitive transactions and events and also to record adjusting and closing entries at the end of the accounting period.

The following journals for Merchandise Mart, Inc., are presented as an illustration of one possible form for each journal. The columnar headings are dictated by the needs of each business enterprise. Merchandise Mart, Inc., uses special journals to facilitate the recording of transactions involving sales, purchases (the periodic inventory system is used), cash receipts, and cash payments. Subsidiary ledgers are used for accounts receivable and vouchers (accounts) payable.

Sales Journal   The partial sales journal used by Merchandise Mart, Inc., is illustrated on page 53.

	Sales Journal			Page 50
Date	**Customer**	**Inv. No.**	**Ref.**	**Amount**
Year 10				
Jan. 2	Emily Taylor	1001	√	690
3	R. O. Black	1002	√	850
3	Dan Crane	1003	√	1,050
28	D. A. Adams	1025	√	600
29	Jack Urbanks	1026	√	1,215
				42,460
				(7) (115)
				Dr, A/R
				Cr, Sales

The procedure for recording sales requires that all credit sales be entered at the gross amount in the sales journal and all cash sales in the cash receipts journal (see page 54). There is no need for a breakdown of sales by products or departments, and the accounts receivable ledger is posted from the sales journal. When the individual accounts are posted, a check mark (√) is placed beside the amount in the sales journal. The total of the one money column is posted monthly as a debit to the Accounts Receivable ledger account (ledger account No. 7) and a credit to the Sales ledger account (ledger account No. 115). All credit sales have terms of 2/10, n/30.

Cash Receipts Journal   All cash receipts are recorded by Merchandise Mart, Inc., in the cash receipts journal (see page 54) from a detailed list of checks received by mail, a report of daily cash sales, store cash collections, and other cash sources. If a credit customer takes the cash discount offered, it is recorded at the time cash is received. The customers' accounts are posted daily from the cash receipts journal. The individual ledger accounts are posted weekly from the Other Ledger Accounts columns, and the column totals are posted monthly, except for the Other Ledger Accounts columns for which totals are not posted (***not pos.***).

Voucher Register   Merchandise Mart, Inc., has found that control over cash payments is improved by use of a voucher register. The voucher register serves both as a subsidiary ledger for vouchers payable and as a purchases journal. Purchases of merchandise are recorded net of cash discounts offered, and all cash discounts are taken.

A good system of internal controls requires that all checks be supported by a voucher. At the time a voucher is paid, the check number is entered in the appropriate column of the voucher register. Any vouchers entered in the register without check numbers are unpaid and constitute the liability to vendors at that time. Note in the voucher register on page 54 that voucher No. 1500 has not been paid and that

Cash Receipts Journal

Date	Explanation	Cash	Sales discounts	Debits — Other ledger accounts: Account	Ref.	Amount	Credits — Accounts receivable: ✓	Amount	Sales	Credits — Other ledger accounts: Account	Ref.	Amount
Year 10												
Jan. 2	1st Union Bank	10,000								Notes Payable	71	10,000
5	D. A. Adams	833	17				✓	850				
6	Cash sales	452							452			
11	Dan Crane	1,029	21				✓	1,050				
31	Cash sales	800							800			
		46,807	256			1,240		31,780	3,423			13,100
		(1)	(117)			(not pos.)		(7)	(115)			(not pos.)

Voucher Register

Date	Payee	Explanation	Paid by Ck. No.	Vou. No.	Credit — Vouchers payable	Debits — Purchases	Freight-in	Salaries expense	Debits — Other ledger accounts: Account	Ref.	Amount
Year 10											
Jan. 2	Adams Supply Co.	Merchandise		1500	8,000	8,000					
2	Bross Trucking, Inc.	Freight-in	1001	1501	50		50				
5	1st Union Bank	Paid note and interest	1002	1502	4,040				{ Notes Payable	71	4,000 }
									{ Interest Expense	170	40 }
30	Media Services	Advertising		1597	2,000				Advertising Exp.	165	2,000
31	Ace Company	Merchandise		1598	900	900					
					48,720	25,680	980	8,220			13,840
					(70)	(104)	(105)	(72)			(not pos.)

voucher No. 1501 was paid by check No. 1001. The totals of the special columns are posted monthly, and the individual ledger accounts in the Other Ledger Accounts columns are posted at least once a month. The total liability represented by unpaid vouchers may include vouchers from the preceding month.

Cash Payments Journal The requirement that all checks be supported by a voucher means that only one column is needed in the cash payments journal of Merchandise Mart, Inc., illustrated below:

Cash Payments Journal				Page 60
Date	Payee	Voucher No.	Check No.	Amount
Year 10				
Jan. 5	Bross Trucking, Inc.	1501	1001	50
5	1st Union Bank	1502	1002	4,040
31	Dart Brothers	1593	1090	570
				42,690
				(70) (1)
				Dr, V/P
				Cr, Cash

The total of the one column is posted to Vouchers Payable (ledger account No. 70) as a debit and to Cash (ledger account No. 1) as a credit. Recording the payment in the subsidiary ledger for vouchers payable (the voucher register) is done by entering the check number in the voucher register. The totals of the cash payments journal are posted monthly.

General Journal The general journal is used to record all transactions and events that do not involve ledger accounts represented in the four special journals and for adjusting, closing, reversing, and correcting entries. The majority of transactions normally will be recorded in the special journals. A partial page of the general journal for Merchandise Mart, Inc., is illustrated below:

General Journal				Page 70
Date	Account titles and explanations	LP	Debit	Credit
Year 10				
Jan. 24	Allowance for Doubtful Accounts	8	150	
	Accounts Receivable—Tyrone Kong	7/√		150
	To write off uncollectible account receivable.			

The posting instructions for the illustrated entry in the general journal are: (1) Post the debits and credits to the accounts in the ledger indicated by the ledger account numbers in the ledger page (LP) column (the debit is posted to ledger account No. 8 and the credit is posted to ledger account No. 7); and (2) post the $150 credit to the accounts receivable subsidiary ledger in the account of Tyrone Kong. The check mark indicates that the posting to the subsidiary ledger has been completed.

Ledger

We have indicated how the information contained in business papers is analyzed and expressed in terms of debits and credits by entries in the journals. Next is the step of transferring this information to ledger accounts. This transfer process is called *posting,* which means that each debit and credit amount in the journals is entered in the appropriate ledger account.

A *ledger* consists of a number of accounts. Each ledger account represents stored information about a particular asset, liability, owners' equity, revenue, or expense. As previously indicated, the transaction is the unit of organization for the journal; similarly, the ledger account is the unit of organization for the ledger. When computers are used, accounting information may be stored on magnetic tapes or discs rather than on the pages of a traditional ledger. However, the printed form of ledger page is most convenient for our illustrations and analyses and is still used by many small- and medium-size business enterprises.

Ledger accounts often are classified as *nominal* (temporary) and *real* (permanent) accounts. The nominal (revenue and expense) accounts are closed at the end of each accounting period by transferring their balances to other accounts. The real (balance sheet) accounts remain open and normally show a balance after the accounting records are closed. During an accounting period, a balance sheet account or an income statement account may contain both real and nominal portions. Such accounts are known as *mixed accounts.* For example, the Unexpired Insurance ledger account may include both unexpired insurance premiums and expired premiums before the end-of-period adjusting entries are made. When the time arrives for preparation of financial statements, the nominal and real portions of a mixed account are separated by end-of-period adjusting entries. Thus, the nominal portion in the Unexpired Insurance account is transferred to Insurance Expense.

Two forms of the ledger account for Accounts Receivable are illustrated below and on page 57 for Merchandise Mart, Inc. Note that the balance of $23,212 on

"T" form of ledger account

			Accounts Receivable				**Ledger Account No. 7**	
Date	**Explanation**	**Ref.**	**Amount**	**Date**	**Explanation**	**Ref.**	**Amount**	
Year 10				Year 10				
Jan. 1	Balance		12,682	Jan. 24		J70	150	
31		S50	42,460	31		CR42	31,780	
				31	Balance		23,212	
			55,142				55,142	
Feb. 1	Balance		23,212					

Running
balance
form of
ledger
account

	Accounts Receivable				Ledger Account No. 7
Date	**Explanation**	**Ref.**	**Debit**	**Credit**	**Balance**
Year 10					
Jan. 1	Balance				12,682 dr
24		J70		150	12,532 dr
31		S50	42,460		54,992 dr
31		CR42		31,780	23,212 dr

January 31, Year 10, is the same as in the unadjusted trial balance on page 58. The three entries to the Accounts Receivable ledger account were posted from the journals illustrated on pages 53–55.

In many cases greater detail is desired for a particular ledger account, and a *subsidiary ledger* is set up to contain the details supporting the main or *controlling account*. For example, the controlling account, Accounts Receivable, is adequate for general purposes; however, in order to facilitate the preparation of monthly statements to customers, it is desirable to have each customer's purchases and payments separately classified. In such situations a subsidiary ledger is established to provide the desired information. At all times, the total of the subsidiary ledger account balances should agree with the balance of the related controlling account in the ledger.

In addition to the use of a controlling account and subsidiary ledger for accounts receivable, other common examples of this concept include:

A Vouchers Payable controlling account supported by a voucher register (illustrated on page 54)

A Buildings controlling account supported by a subsidiary ledger that shows the individual buildings owned

A Common Stock controlling account supported by a stockholders' ledger

Separate subsidiary ledgers not only provide the detailed information needed for certain purposes, but also strengthen internal controls by bringing to light most kinds of errors in the recording of business transactions and events.

Trial Balance

At the end of each accounting period an *unadjusted trial balance* of the ledger is prepared (usually in the first pair of columns of the work sheet) to determine that the mechanics of the recording and posting operations have been carried out accurately. The unadjusted trial balance consists of a listing of all ledger accounts and their balances; it provides evidence that an equality of debits and credits exists in the general ledger. The unadjusted trial balance on page 58 summarizes the account balances in the ledger of Merchandise Mart, Inc., on January 31, Year 10.

Trial balance at end
of first month of
fiscal year

MERCHANDISE MART, INC.
Unadjusted Trial Balance
January 31, Year 10

	Debit	Credit
Cash	$ 15,454	
Accounts receivable	23,212	
Allowance for doubtful accounts		$ 850
Inventory (Jan. 1, Year 10)	47,860	
Unexpired insurance	200	
Land	45,000	
Building	80,000	
Accumulated depreciation of building		10,000
Equipment	16,000	
Accumulated depreciation of equipment		4,000
Notes payable—current		15,000
Vouchers payable		17,000
Common stock, $10 par		75,000
Paid-in capital in excess of par		55,000
Retained earnings (Jan. 1, Year 10)		49,207
Sales		45,883
Sales discounts	256	
Purchases	25,680	
Freight-in	980	
Salaries expense	8,220	
Advertising expense	4,620	
Delivery expense	2,180	
Property taxes expense	1,220	
Interest expense	80	
Miscellaneous expenses	978	
Totals	$271,940	$271,940

Note that the dollar amounts of certain revenue and expense accounts in the trial balance for Merchandise Mart, Inc., may be traced to the five journals on pages 53–55. For example, the amount of sales consists of credit sales from the sales journal plus cash sales from the cash receipts journal ($42,460 + $3,423 = $45,883); the amount of sales discounts ($256) appears in the cash receipts journal; and the amounts for purchases, freight-in, and salaries expense appear in separate columns of the voucher register.

Trial balances of the subsidiary ledgers also may be prepared to prove that the totals of their balances agree with the balances in the related controlling accounts in the general ledger. These trial balances also may be used for other purposes; for example, a copy of the accounts receivable trial balance (page 59) may be sent to the credit department for use in following up collections and as a basis for setting future credit policy.

List of claims from
customers

MERCHANDISE MART, INC.
Accounts Receivable Trial Balance
January 31, Year 10

D. A. Adams..	$ 1,500
R. O. Black...	3,410
Other accounts (not listed here to avoid unnecessary detail)	18,302
Balance of Accounts Receivable controlling account (ledger account No. 7)...	$23,212

The number of accounts, type of financial statements, and other aspects of the accounting system are designed to meet the needs of a particular business enterprise; the preceding examples illustrate the type of accounting system used by many small and medium-size enterprises.

ADJUSTING ENTRIES

Financial reporting on an annual, quarterly, or monthly basis requires accountants to summarize the operations of a business enterprise for a specific time period. The two types of end-of-period adjusting entries are those (1) to apportion *prepayments* of expenses and revenue, and (2) to record *accrued* expenses and revenue. Transactions that were recorded during an accounting period in balance sheet or income statement ledger accounts may affect two or more periods, and an end-of-period adjustment may be needed. Some financial events not recognized on a day-to-day basis must be recorded through *adjusting entries* at the end of the period *to bring the accounting records up to date.* If one should choose to record depreciation expense daily or to accrue interest expense daily, no adjustment for depreciation or interest expense would be needed at the end of the accounting period.

Note that every adjusting entry affects both a balance sheet account and an income statement account. This characteristic of adjusting entries reflects their dual purpose: (1) to measure all assets and liabilities accurately, and (2) to measure net income correctly by matching expired costs (expenses) with realized revenue.

In illustrating the wide variety of adjusting entries, it is helpful to classify them into the following groups:

Apportionment of recorded costs

Apportionment of recorded revenue

Accrual of unrecorded expenses

Accrual of unrecorded revenue

Valuation of certain assets and liabilities, for example accounts receivable

Apportionment of Recorded Costs

Costs that will benefit more than one accounting period frequently are incurred. These costs must be apportioned between periods in a manner that approximates the usefulness derived from the goods and services in the realization of revenue; this apportionment process is a necessary step under the matching principle to determine net income of each period. Recording periodic depreciation expense as shown below is an example of a cost-apportionment adjusting entry:

Journal entry for depreciation

Depreciation Expense......................................	12,000	
Accumulated Depreciation of Building		12,000
To record depreciation expense for one year.		

The periodic depreciation expense is considered a cost of production or a period expense to be deducted from revenue, depending on the nature of services derived from the asset. In the balance sheet, accumulated depreciation is deducted from the cost of plant assets.

Cost apportionment also is involved in accounting for all types of prepayments. However, the adjusting entry will vary depending on the accounting procedure followed in recording the original transaction. To illustrate, assume that office supplies are acquired during the accounting period at a cost of $5,000. At the end of the period a physical inventory reveals that supplies on hand cost $550. At the time the supplies were acquired, the $5,000 may have been debited to an asset account or an expense account. The required adjusting entry for each approach is illustrated below:

Prepayment Debited to Asset Account   The adjusting entry required is to transfer the *expired* portion of the cost to an *expense* account as illustrated below:

Adjusting entry reduces asset ledger account

	Inventory of Office Supplies		Office Supplies Expense	
Balance, Dec. 31	5,000			
Adjusting entry		4,450	4,450	

Prepayment Debited to Expense Account   The adjusting entry required is to transfer the *unexpired* portion of the cost to an *asset* account as illustrated below:

Adjusting entry establishes asset ledger account

	Inventory of Office Supplies		Office Supplies Expense	
Balance, Dec. 31			5,000	
Adjusting entry	550			550

Under either approach, the final result is the same: There is an asset of $550 and an expense of $4,450. In both cases the amount of the unexpired cost was determined, and an adjusting entry was necessary to make the ledger account balances agree with the information available.

Apportionment of Recorded Revenue

When a business enterprise receives payment for goods and services before the goods are delivered or the services are performed, a liability exists until performance takes place. If cash is received, the original transaction may be recorded by a credit to either a liability account or a revenue account. For example, assume that customers paid $500,000 for magazine subscriptions during the current accounting period; however, $75,000 represented payments for magazines to be delivered in subsequent periods. The adjusting entries for each of the two methods of recording cash receipts are:

Liability Account Credited on Receipt of Cash   The required adjusting entry to record the *earned* revenue for the period appears below:

Adjusting entry reduces liability ledger account

	Unearned Subscriptions		*Subscriptions Revenue*	
Balance, Dec. 31		*500,000*		
Adjusting entry	*425,000*			*425,000*

Revenue Account Credited on Receipt of Cash   The required adjusting entry to transfer the *unearned* revenue to a liability account is shown below:

Adjusting entry establishes liability ledger account

	Unearned Subscriptions		*Subscriptions Revenue*	
Balance, Dec. 31				*500,000*
Adjusting entry		*75,000*	*75,000*	

Under either approach, the adjusted amount of the liability is $75,000, and the adjusted amount of the revenue is $425,000.

Accrual of Unrecorded Expenses

The incurring of certain expenses is related to the passage of time. These expenses generally are not recorded until payment is made, unless the end of an accounting period comes before the required date of payment. Interest and salaries are typical of the expenses that accrue with the passage of time and are recorded only when paid, except when the end of a period occurs between the time the expense was incurred and the payment is due. In order to measure expenses accurately for a period, an adjusting entry is necessary to record the accrued expense and the corresponding liability. For example, assume that interest of $18,000 on a $400,000 note payable is paid on March 1 and September 1 of each year. If expenses and liabilities are to be reported accurately on December 31, the following year-end adjusting entry is required:

Journal entry to record
accrued expense

Interest Expense   12,000
    Interest Payable   12,000
To record the interest accrued on a 9%, $400,000 note for
four months to Dec. 31.

Accrual of Unrecorded Revenue

Revenue that has been realized but not recorded must be recognized at the end of an accounting period. For example, revenue that is realized on assets leased to others or on interest-bearing loans seldom is recognized until the cash is received, except at the end of a period. In order to measure accurately the results of operations under the matching principle, revenue is recognized in the period earned. For example assume that rent totaling $625 that has been realized but not collected for the month of December has not been recorded. The following adjusting entry on December 31 is required to measure assets and revenue accurately:

Journal entry to record
accrued revenue

Rent Receivable   625
    Rent Revenue......................................   625
To record rent revenue earned during December.

Valuation of Accounts Receivable

A policy of making sales on credit almost inevitably results in some accounts receivable that are uncollectible. To achieve a satisfactory matching of revenue and expenses, the estimated expense arising from sales on credit should be recorded in the accounting period in which sales occur. This estimate of probable expense from the granting of credit requires an end-of-period adjusting entry to revise the valuation originally assigned to accounts receivable. For example, if doubtful accounts expense is estimated at $2,500, the following adjusting entry is made:

Journal entry to record
doubtful accounts
expense

Doubtful Accounts Expense   2,500
    Allowance for Doubtful Accounts.....................   2,500
To record doubtful accounts expense.

The Doubtful Accounts Expense ledger account generally is reported as an operating expense in the income statement. Some accountants prefer to deduct it directly from sales to measure net sales, because no revenue is realized if accounts receivable are not collected. The credit balance of the allowance account is deducted from accounts receivable in the balance sheet to state accounts receivable at net realizable value.

The Work Sheet and Financial Statements

Adjusting entries initially are prepared in a work sheet, and adjusted account balances then are summarized in columns designed to facilitate the preparation of financial statements. A work sheet for a merchandising enterprise is illustrated on pages 70–71, and a work sheet for a manufacturing enterprise is illustrated on pages 76–77. Complete financial statements are illustrated in Chapter 4.

CLOSING PROCEDURES

Closing Revenue and Expense Accounts

Revenue and expense ledger accounts are closed at the end of each accounting period by transferring the balances of these ledger accounts to a summary ledger account, Income Summary. Revenue and expense accounts are extensions of owners' equity and are used to measure periodic net income. Once this information has been summarized, the revenue and expense accounts have served their purpose, and the net increase or decrease in owners' equity is transferred to an appropriate owners' equity ledger account. Thus, the closing of the revenue and expense accounts keeps separate the operating results of each period.

If we assume that a Subsciptions Revenue ledger account after adjustment has a credit balance of $425,000, the closing entry is:

Journal entry to close revenue ledger account

Subscriptions Revenue	425,000	
Income Summary....................................		425,000
To close the Subscriptions Revenue ledger account.		

The balance of the Subscriptions Revenue ledger account is now zero. Temporarily, the Income Summary account has a credit balance of $425,000. All other revenue accounts are closed similarly.

To close an expense ledger account, one must transfer its debit balance to the left side of the Income Summary account. The following journal entry to close a Salaries Expense account with a debit balance of $61,625 is illustrative of this phase of the closing process:

Journal entry to close expense ledger account

Income Summary...	61,625	
Salaries Expense		61,625
To close the Salaries Expense ledger account.		

The Salaries Expense account now has a zero balance, and the credit balance in the Income Summary account is reduced by the debit for salaries expense in the amount of $61,625. All other expense accounts are closed similarly. When there are numerous revenue and expense accounts, all may be closed in one journal entry as illustrated on page 74 for Merchandising Company.

Closing Inventories and Related Ledger Accounts

When the *periodic inventory system* is used, the journal entry to establish the cost of goods sold and the ending inventory balance for the accounting period may be viewed as an adjusting entry; however, because there may be little need for a ledger account for cost of goods sold, the adjusting and closing entries for inventories may be combined. This procedure is accomplished by closing the beginning inventory, ending inventory, purchases, and all related ledger accounts to the Income Summary account. At this point, the balance in the Income Summary account represents the cost of goods sold for the period. To illustrate, assume the following for Year 10: January 1 inventory, $80,000; purchases, $275,000; freight-in, $40,000; purchases returns and allowances, $2,500; December 31 inventory, including applicable freight-in, $60,000. The journal entry to close the accounts and to record the ending inventory is as follows:

Closing entry for inventories and purchases	*Inventory (Dec. 31, Year 10)* *60,000*	
	Purchases Returns and Allowances *2,500*	
	Income Summary *332,500*	
	Inventory (Jan. 1, Year 10)	*80,000*
	Purchases	*275,000*
	Freight-in	*40,000*
	To close beginning inventory and net purchases for the period, and to record ending inventory.	

Some merchandising enterprises prefer to use a separate ledger account, Cost of Goods Sold, to summarize the merchandising accounts when the periodic inventory system is used. The journal entry (which may be viewed as an adjusting entry) ***reflecting cost of goods sold in a separate ledger account*** follows:

Alternative: Record cost of goods sold in ledger account	*Inventory (Dec. 31, Year 10)* *60,000*	
	Purchases Returns and Allowances *2,500*	
	Cost of Goods Sold *332,500*	
	Inventory (Jan. 1, Year 10)	*80,000*
	Purchases	*275,000*
	Freight-in	*40,000*
	To record ending inventory and cost of goods sold for the period.	

When the perpetual inventory system is used, Cost of Goods Sold is debited and Inventory is credited during an accounting period as sales are made. An adjusting entry may be required if the carrying amount of inventory differs from the amount determined by physical count. At the end of the period, Cost of Goods Sold is closed to Income Summary, along with all other revenue and expense accounts.

Closing the Income Summary Account

After all revenue and expenses (including the cost of goods sold) have been closed, the balance of the Income Summary ledger account indicates the net income or net loss for the year. A credit balance in the Income Summary account indicates a profitable year and an increase in owners' equity; a debit balance indicates a net loss and a decrease in owners' equity. The Income Summary account is closed by transferring its balance to the Retained Earnings account.

REVERSING ENTRIES

After the accounting records have been adjusted and closed at the end of an accounting period, reversing entries *may be made* on the first day of the next period. The purpose of the reversing entries is to simplify the recording of routine transactions by disposing of the accrued items (assets and liabilities) that were entered in balance sheet accounts through adjusting entries. A reversing entry, as the name implies, *is the exact reverse of an adjusting entry.* It consists of the same ledger accounts and dollar amounts as the adjusting entry, but the debits and credits are reversed, and the date is the beginning of the next period.

For example, assume that on July 31, Year 1, Clark Company borrowed $200,000 at 12% on a long-term note with interest of $6,000 payable every three months. The first payment of interest was made on October 31, Year 1; the next interest payment is due on January 31, Year 2. Clark is on a calendar-year basis. Before the accounting records are closed on December 31, Year 1, an adjusting entry must be made debiting Interest Expense and crediting Interest Payable for $4,000, the amount of interest for November and December. If no reversing entry is made on January 1, Year 2, the next quarterly interest payment of $6,000 on January 31, Year 2, will be recorded by a debit of $4,000 to Interest Payable, a debit of $2,000 to Interest Expense, and a credit of $6,000 to Cash. However, assume that on January 1, Year 2, the following reversing entry is made:

Reversing entry for
accrued expense

Year 2			
Jan. 1	Interest Payable	4,000	
	Interest Expense		4,000
	To reverse interest accrual made on Dec. 31, Year 1.		

This reversing entry has eliminated the liability account Interest Payable and has caused the Interest Expense account to have a $4,000 credit balance. Consequently, the cash payment of three months' interest on January 31 will not need to be apportioned. The January 31 entry will consist of a debit to Interest Expense for $6,000 and a credit to Cash for $6,000. In other words, the interest payment on January 31 (by reason of the reversing entry) may be recorded in the same manner as the three other quarterly interest payments during the year. After the January 31 interest payment has been recorded, the Interest Expense ledger account for Year 2 will contain a debit of $6,000 and a credit of $4,000, which produce a net debit balance of $2,000 representing interest expense for the month of January, Year 2.

An argument for reversing entries is apparent from this example. Employees with limited knowledge of accounting may be instructed to follow a standard procedure for recording all recurring transactions such as receipts and payments of cash.

The reversing entries, as well as the year-end adjusting entries, are recorded in the general journal by an accountant who understands the concept involved.

General Guidelines for Reversing Entries

When a *policy of using reversing entries is adopted,* the following general rules are followed:

1   When an adjusting entry affects an asset or a liability account that normally is not used during an accounting period, *a reversing entry is required.* Thus, adjustments to accrue revenue and expenses are reversed because asset and liability accounts such as Rent Receivable and Interest Payable are not used in the normal course of accounting during a period. Similarly, if payments for insurance and supplies during a period are recorded in expense accounts, or if revenue received in advance during a period is recorded in revenue accounts, the adjusting entries would have to be reversed because asset and liability accounts normally not used during the period would be affected by the adjusting entries.

2   When an adjusting entry adjusts an asset or liability account that normally is used to record transactions during a period, *no reversing entry is required.* Thus, if acquisitions of supplies and other short-term prepayments during a period are recorded in asset accounts, or if revenue received in advance is recorded in liability accounts, the adjusting entries would bring *existing asset and liability balances up to date,* and no reversing entry would be required. For the same reason, adjusting entries for depreciation and doubtful accounts expense, for example, are not reversed.

Previously, we suggested that reversing certain adjusting entries is an *optional procedure* designed to simplify recording of recurring transactions. Another way of stating this is that reversing entries are never required as long as adjusting entries bring existing asset and liability accounts up to date.

To illustrate three alternative approaches for adjusting and reversing entries, let us return to the Clark Company example on page 65. Use of any of the three approaches illustrated on page 67 results in a balance of $24,000 in Interest Expense and a balance of $4,000 in Interest Payable *at the end of Year 2.*

Note that no adjusting entry was required under alternative **3** because the amount of interest payable at the end of Year 2 was the same as it was at the end of Year 1. If the accrued interest at the end of Year 2 was other than $4,000, an adjusting entry would be required to Interest Payable, with a corresponding debit or credit to Interest Expense.

CORRECTING ENTRIES

Correcting entries are not considered adjusting entries because their function is to correct errors of omission or commission. For example, the failure to record a

Each alternative approach produces identical results

Alternative 1	Alternative 2	Alternative 3
No reversing entry; $4,000 of first interest payment in Year 2 is debited to the Interest Payable account	Reversing entry (R) is made; all interest payments in Year 2 are recorded in the Interest Expense account	No reversing entry; all interest payments in Year 2 are recorded in the Interest Expense account

Interest Expense

Alternative 1		Alternative 2		Alternative 3	
(a) 20,000		(a) 24,000	(R) 4,000	(a) 24,000	
(b) 4,000		(b) 4,000			
Bal. 24,000		Bal. 24,000			

Interest Payable

Alternative 1		Alternative 2		Alternative 3	
(a) 4,000	Bal. 4,000	(R) 4,000	Bal. 4,000		Bal. 4,000
	(b) 4,000		(b) 4,000		
	Bal. 4,000		Bal. 4,000		

(a) Payments of interest in Year 2; Cash account is credited for $24,000.
(b) Adjusting entry, Dec. 31, Year 2.
(R) Reversing entry, Jan. 1, Year 2.

transaction would be rectified by a journal entry as it should have been originally; the improper recording of a transaction requires a journal entry to ensure that ledger accounts are stated properly. When an error is made in one accounting period but discovered in a subsequent period, the effect of the error on the net income of the earlier periods is closed to the Retained Earnings ledger account. When an error is discovered in the period in which the error occurs, but before the accounting records are closed, revenue and expense accounts may require correction and the Retained Earnings account generally is not affected.

For example, assume that the following two errors were made in Year 1 and were discovered at the end of the accounting period when the work sheet for the year ended December 31, Year 1, was being prepared:

1   A purchase of merchandise for $500 cash was erroneously recorded by a debit of $50 to the Supplies Expense ledger account and a credit of $50 to Cash.

2   An acquisition of equipment for cash of $4,000 on April 1, Year 1, was recorded as a purchase of merchandise. The equipment had an economic life of 10 years with no residual value, and was depreciated by the straight-line method for nine months in Year 1.

An analysis of the two errors to determine the appropriate correcting entries follows:

Incorrect journal entry as recorded	Correct journal entry that should have been made	Required correcting entry
1 Supplies Exp. 50	Purchases 500	Purchases 500
Cash 50	Cash 500	Supplies Exp. 50
		Cash 450
2 Purchases 4,000	Equipment 4,000	Equipment 4,000
Cash 4,000	Depr. Expense . . 300*	Depr. Expense 300
	Cash 4,000	Purchases 4,000
	Accum. Depr.	Accum. Depr. . . . .
	of Equipment 300	of Equipment 300
	*$4,000 × 0.10 × ¾ = $300.	

A complete discussion of accounting errors and correcting entries appears in Chapter 22.

WORK SHEET

Accountants use many forms of work sheets and working papers. ***An end-of-period work sheet*** is a critical part of the accounting cycle. In this chapter we are concerned only with the end-of-period work sheet, and we shall refer to it simply as the ***work sheet.*** The work sheet is a columnar working paper designed to facilitate the organization and arrangement of accounting data at the end of an accounting period. A major function of the work sheet is to uncover errors that otherwise might be entered in the accounting records. Accountants prepare a work sheet as an informal record strictly for their own purposes; a work sheet does not replace any financial statement and is never presented as the end result of the accountants' work. The work sheet is a tool that permits adjusting and closing entries and financial statements to be prepared informally before any part of this work is formalized.

The work sheet may be thought of as a ''testing ground'' on which the ledger accounts are adjusted, balanced, and arranged in the general form of financial statements. The satisfactory completion of the work sheet provides considerable assurance that all end-of-period accounting procedures have been brought together properly. The finished work sheet then serves as the source for the preparation of financial statements and for the recording and posting of the adjusting and closing entries.

Illustration of Work Sheet for a Merchandising Enterprise

A commonly used form of work sheet with appropriate headings is illustrated on pages 70–71 for Merchandising Company for Year 4. The work-sheet heading contains the name of the company, the title (work sheet), and the period of time covered. The body of this work sheet contains six pairs of money columns, each pair consisting of a debit and credit column. The procedures required in the preparation of the work sheet *when the periodic inventory system is used* are described below:

1 Enter the ledger account titles and balances on the work sheet, using the first two money columns—the Unadjusted Trial Balance. Time and effort may be saved by arranging the ledger accounts (both in the ledger and in the trial balance) in the order in which they will appear in the financial statements. Frequently, several adjustments will affect a single ledger account; consequently, several lines should be left blank following such an account to facilitate listing the adjustments.

2 Enter the adjustments in the Adjustments columns. Adjusting entries always should be entered in the work sheet before they are journalized. One of the functions of the work sheet is to establish the correctness of the adjusting entries. The information used as the basis for the adjustments illustrated in the work sheet for Merchandising Company is stated below:

(a) The short-term investments consist of government bonds on which accrued interest amounts to $33 on December 31, Year 4.

(b) The accounts receivable arising from sales during Year 4 that are expected to be uncollectible are estimated to be ½% of gross sales.

(c) Accounts receivable totaling $520 are considered to be uncollectible, and the credit manager has authorized the write-off of these accounts.

(d) The balances in the Short-Term Prepayments ledger account are as follows:

	Jan. 1, Year 4	Dec. 31, Year 4
Unexpired insurance	$ 750	$ 450
Inventory of supplies	600	700
Prepaid rent	150	400
Totals	$1,500	$1,550

All cash payments for these items during Year 4 were recorded in expense accounts. Merchandising Company *does not reverse any adjusting entries.*

(e) The furniture and fixtures are estimated to have an economic life of 10 years, with no residual value at the end of that time.

(f) Accrued interest on the notes payable amounts to $40 on December 31, Year 4.

(g) Salaries accrued since the last payday total $818 on December 31, Year 4.

(h) The inventory on December 31, Year 4, is $28,900, and income taxes expense for the year ended December 31, Year 4, is estimated at $370.

After adjustments (a) through (h) are entered in the work sheet, the Adjustments columns must be totaled (footed) to prove the equality of the debits and credits. Without this proof of arithmetical accuracy, errors are likely to be carried forward in the remaining columns of the work sheet.

3 Determine the new account balances and enter these in the Adjusted Trial Balance columns. The purpose of this step is to prove the accuracy of the work of combining the adjustments and the original balances. The Adjusted Trial Balance columns often are omitted from the work sheet, especially if adjustments are few.

MERCHANDISING COMPANY
Work Sheet
For Year Ended December 31, Year 4

	Unadjusted trial balance		Adjustments		Adjusted trial balance		Income statement		Retained earnings statement		Balance sheet	
	Debit	Credit	Debit	Credit	Debit	Credit	Debit	Credit	Debit	Credit	Debit	Credit
Cash	8,650				8,650						8,650	
Short-term investments	2,000				2,000						2,000	
Accounts receivable	15,700			(c) 520	15,180						15,180	
Allowance for doubtful accounts		800	(c) 520	(b) 875		1,155						1,155
Inventory (periodic system)	28,000				28,000		28,000	28,900			28,900	
Short-term prepayments	1,500		(d) 50		1,550						1,550	
Furniture and fixtures	6,000				6,000						6,000	
Accumulated depreciation		1,800		(e) 600		2,400						2,400
Notes payable—current		4,000				4,000						4,000
Accounts payable		10,000				10,000						10,000
Common stock, $1 par		40,000				40,000						40,000
Retained earnings (Jan. 1, Year 4)		3,170				3,170				3,170		
Dividends	1,500				1,500				1,500			
Sales		175,000				175,000		175,000				
Sales returns and allowances	2,500				2,500		2,500					

Account	Trial Balance Dr	Trial Balance Cr	Adjustments Dr	Adjustments Cr	Adjusted Trial Balance Dr	Adjusted Trial Balance Cr	Income Statement Dr	Income Statement Cr	Retained Earnings Statement Dr	Retained Earnings Statement Cr	Balance Sheet Dr	Balance Sheet Cr
Sales discounts	3,150				3,150		3,150					
Purchases	128,000				128,000		128,000					
Purchases returns and allowances		3,000				3,000		3,000				
Salaries expense	22,500		(g) 818		23,318		23,318					
Rent expense	5,050			(d) 250	4,800		4,800					
Advertising expense	9,000				9,000		9,000					
Janitorial expense	1,500				1,500		1,500					
Miscellaneous expenses	2,000			(d) 100	1,900		1,900					
Interest expense	120		(f) 40		160		160					
Property taxes expense	600				600		600					
Interest receivable			(a) 33		33						33	
Interest revenue				(a) 33		33		33				
Doubtful accounts expense			(b) 875		875		875					
Insurance expense			(d) 300		300		300					
Depreciation expense			(e) 600		600		600					
Interest payable				(f) 40		40						40
Salaries payable				(g) 818		818						818
Income taxes expense			(h) 370		370		370					
Income taxes payable				(h) 370		370						370
Net income							3,530			3,530		
Retained earnings (Dec. 31, Year 4)									5,030	1,500		5,030
Totals	237,770	237,770	3,606	3,606	239,986	239,986	206,933	206,933	5,030	5,030	62,313	62,313

4   Extend each balance from the adjusted trial balance (or from the first four columns) to the Income Statement, Retained Earnings Statement, or Balance Sheet columns. *Note that the beginning inventory of $28,000 is entered in the Income Statement debit column.*

5   *Enter the ending inventory in the Income Statement credit column and the Balance Sheet debit column.* This procedure in effect deducts the ending inventory from the total goods available for sale to leave the costs comprising the cost of goods sold for the year in the Income Statement columns.

6   Total (foot) the Income Statement columns. The balancing amount is the net income or loss for the year. The difference of $1,860 between the credit and debit columns in this illustration represents net income, and is entered in the debit column of the Income Statement and in the credit column of the Retained Earnings Statement.

7   Balance the Retained Earnings Statement columns and enter the difference in the debit column of the Retained Earnings Statement and in the credit column of the Balance Sheet. This adjusts the retained earnings balance for changes during the year (net income and dividends).

8   Total the Balance Sheet columns. Considerable assurance of the arithmetical accuracy of the year-end procedures is provided if these two columns balance.

Although the work sheet proves the mathematical accuracy of what has been done, it does not prove that some adjustments have not been omitted or that the amounts used in making the adjustments were correct.

Work Sheet and Year-End Procedures   The work sheet is the source of the formal adjusting entries. Once the adjusting entries are entered in the work sheet, the identical information is recorded in the general journal and the ledger. The adjusting journal entries for Merchandising Company on December 31, Year 4, are illustrated below and on page 73.

Adjusting entries at end of period

MERCHANDISING COMPANY
Adjusting Entries
December 31, Year 4

(a) Interest Receivable	*33*	
Interest Revenue		*33*
To accrue interest on short-term investments.		
(b) Doubtful Accounts Expense	*875*	
Allowance for Doubtful Accounts		*875*
To increase allowance for doubtful accounts by ½% of		
gross sales ($175,000 × 0.005 = $875).		

(c) Allowance for Doubtful Accounts   520
       Accounts Receivable   520
    To write off uncollectible accounts.

(d) Short-Term Prepayments   50
    Insurance Expense   300
       Rent Expense   250
       Miscellaneous Expenses   100
    To adjust Short-Term Prepayments ledger account to
    year-end balance.

(e) Depreciation Expense   600
       Accumulated Depreciation   600
    To record depreciation at 10% of cost of furniture
    and fixtures ($6,000 × 0.10 = $600).

(f) Interest Expense   40
       Interest Payable   40
    To accrue interest on notes payable.

(g) Salaries Expense   818
       Salaries Payable   818
    To accrue unpaid salaries.

(h) Income Taxes Expense   370
       Income Taxes Payable   370
    To record estimated income tax liability.

The data in the Income Statement columns of the work sheet also may be used to prepare the closing entries. When a work sheet is prepared, the closing process generally is summarized in a series of closing entries as illustrated below and on page 74 for Merchandising Company:

Closing entries at
end of period

MERCHANDISING COMPANY
Closing Entries
December 31, Year 4

Inventory (Dec. 31, Year 4)   28,900
Purchases Returns and Allowances   3,000
Income Summary   124,100
       Inventory (Jan. 1, Year 4)   28,000
       Purchases   128,000
To close beginning inventory and net purchases for Year 4,
and to record ending inventory.

Sales	175,000	
Interest Revenue	33	
Sales Returns and Allowances		2,500
Sales Discounts		3,150
Salaries Expense		23,318
Rent Expense		4,800
Advertising Expense		9,000
Janitorial Expense		1,500
Miscellaneous Expenses		1,900
Interest Expense		160
Property Taxes Expense		600
Doubtful Accounts Expense		875
Insurance Expense		300
Depreciation Expense		600
Income Taxes Expense		370
Income Summary		125,960
To close revenue and expense accounts.		
Income Summary	1,860	
Retained Earnings		1,860
To close Income Summary account.		
Retained Earnings	1,500	
Dividends		1,500
To close Dividends account.		

Post-Closing Trial Balance

After the closing entries have been posted and the nominal accounts closed, a post-closing trial balance is prepared to make certain that the debit and credit balances in the open ledger accounts are equal. The trial balance may be prepared on an adding machine tape or by computer, or it may be prepared more formally as illustrated below and on page 75 for Merchandising Company:

MERCHANDISING COMPANY
Post-Closing Trial Balance
December 31, Year 4

	Debit	Credit
Cash	$ 8,650	
Short-term investments	2,000	
Interest receivable	33	
Accounts receivable	15,180	
Allowance for doubtful accounts		$1,155
Inventory	28,900	
Short-term prepayments	1,550	

(continued)

Furniture and fixtures	6,000	
Accumulated depreciation.............................		2,400
Notes payable—current		4,000
Interest payable		40
Accounts payable		10,000
Salaries payable		818
Income taxes payable		370
Common stock, $1 par.....................................		40,000
Retained earnings		3,530
Totals	$32,313	$62,313

Note that the balances in the foregoing post-closing trial balance are identical to those in the balance sheet columns of the work sheet on pages 70–71.

Illustration of Work Sheet for a Manufacturing Enterprise

The procedures for preparing a work sheet for a manufacturing enterprise are similar to those used for a merchandising enterprise. The addition of a pair of columns to summarize the manufacturing operation is the major difference. These columns allow for one more step in the classification of the data. The adjusted trial balance, which is an optional step, is omitted from this illustration.

The following data are the basis for the adjusting entries included in the work sheet for Cole Manufacturing Company for the year ended December 31, Year 4, on pages 76–77.

(a) Doubtful accounts expense for Year 4 is estimated to be $3,000.

(b) A three-year insurance policy was acquired on July 1, Year 3, at a cost of $1,800. The insurance expense is allocated to other factory costs and other general expenses in a 4:1 ratio.

(c) The wages accrued since the last pay period are direct labor, $1,800 and indirect labor, $950. The officers, office staff, and sales staff are paid on the last day of each month.

(d) Interest of $1,125 has accrued on notes payable.

(e) Depreciation expense for the plant assets is computed by the straight-line method based on the following information:

Asset	Estimated economic life, years	Estimated residual value	Cost allocation, % Factory	Cost allocation, % General
Building	40	$ –0–	80	20
Machinery and equipment	10	–0–	100	–0–
Furniture and fixtures	20	2,000	10	90

(f) The power bill for December has not been received as of December 31, Year 4. Based on past experience, the cost applicable to December is estimated to be $1,450. All heat, light, and power costs relate to the factory.

COLE MANUFACTURING COMPANY
Work Sheet
For Year Ended December 31, Year 4

	Unadjusted trial balance		Adjustments		Manufacturing		Income statement		Retained earnings statement		Balance sheet	
	Debit	Credit	Debit	Credit	Debit	Credit	Debit	Credit	Debit	Credit	Debit	Credit
Cash	32,000										32,000	
Accounts receivable	70,000										70,000	
Allowance for doubtful accounts		1,200		(a) 3,000								4,200
Inventories (Jan. 1, Year 4):												
Finished goods	48,000						48,000	41,500			41,500	
Goods in process	21,000				21,000	26,350					26,350	
Raw material	16,000				16,000	12,650					12,650	
Unexpired insurance	1,500			(b) 600							900	
Land	72,000										72,000	
Buildings	150,000										150,000	
Accum. depr. of buildings		45,000		(e) 3,750								48,750
Machinery and equipment	130,000										130,000	
Accum. depr. of mach. and equip.		52,000		(e)13,000								65,000
Furniture and fixtures	10,000										10,000	
Accum. depr. of furn. and fixtures		3,000		(e) 400								3,400
Notes payable—current		75,000										75,000
Accounts payable		41,300		(f) 1,450								42,750
Common stock, $10 par		100,000										100,000
Paid-in capital in excess of par		100,000										100,000
Retained earnings (Jan. 1, Year 4)		88,875								88,875		
Dividends	6,000								6,000			
Sales		633,600						633,600				
Sales returns and allowances	3,600						3,600					
Raw material purchases	125,000				125,000							
Purchases returns and allowances		4,000				4,000						

Worksheet (manufacturing company). The column-group headings are torn off at the top of the page; the six double-ruled column pairs are shown here as successive Dr/Cr columns.

Account	Dr	Cr	Dr	Cr	Dr	Cr	Dr	Cr	Dr	Cr	Dr	Cr
Freight-in	3,500				3,500							
Direct labor costs	192,500		(c) 1,800		194,300							
Indirect labor costs	72,600		(c) 950		73,550							
Heat, light, and power	12,300		(f) 1,450		13,750							
Other factory costs	15,000		(b) 480	(g) 850	14,630							
Advertising expense	35,000						35,000					
Sales salaries expense	42,000						42,000					
Delivery expense	8,000						8,000					
Administrative salaries expense	50,000						50,000					
Office salaries expense	20,000						20,000					
Telephone and telegraph expense	1,800						1,800					
Other general expenses	2,800		(b) 120				2,920					
Interest expense	3,375		(d) 1,125				4,500					
Doubtful accounts expense			(a) 3,000				3,000					
Wages payable				(c) 2,750								2,750
Interest payable				(d) 1,125								1,125
Depreciation of bldg. (factory)			(e) 3,000		3,000							
Depreciation of bldg. (general)			(e) 750				750					
Depreciation of mach. and equip. (factory)			(e) 13,000		13,000							
Depreciation of furn. and fix. (factory)			(e) 40		40							
Depreciation of furn. and fix. (general)			(e) 360				360					
Inventory of factory supplies			(g) 850								850	
Income taxes expense			(h) 3,500				3,500					
Income taxes payable				(h) 3,500								3,500
Cost of finished goods manufactured						434,770	434,770					
Net income							16,900			16,900		
Retained earnings (Dec. 31, Year 4)									99,775			99,775
Totals	1,143,975	1,143,975	30,425	30,425	477,770	477,770	675,100	675,100	105,775	105,775	546,250	546,250

(g) An inventory of factory supplies on December 31, Year 4, indicates that supplies costing $850 are on hand.

(h) The income taxes expense for Year 4 is estimated at $3,500.

(i) Inventories on December 31, Year 4, are as follows:

Finished goods	$41,500
Goods in process	26,350
Raw material	12,650

Work Sheet and Year-End Procedures   The journal entries for closing the manufacturing ledger accounts, for adjusting the inventory balances, for closing the revenue and expense accounts, and for closing the Dividends account are illustrated below and on page 79, for Cole Manufacturing Company.

Closing entries for manufacturing enterprise

COLE MANUFACTURING COMPANY
Closing Entries
December 31, Year 4

Raw Material Inventory (Dec. 31, Year 4)	12,650	
Goods in Process Inventory (Dec. 31, Year 4)	26,350	
Purchases Returns and Allowances	4,000	
Cost of Finished Goods Manufactured	434,770	
Raw Material Inventory (Jan. 1, Year 4)		16,000
Goods in Process Inventory (Jan. 1, Year 4)		21,000
Raw Material Purchases		125,000
Freight-in		3,500
Direct Labor Costs		194,300
Indirect Labor Costs		73,550
Heat, Light, and Power		13,750
Other Factory Costs		14,630
Depreciation of Buildings		3,000
Depreciation of Machinery and Equipment		13,000
Depreciation of Furniture and Fixtures		40
To record cost of finished goods manufactured and ending inventories of raw material and goods in process.		
Finished Goods Inventory (Dec. 31, Year 4)	41,500	
Cost of Goods Sold	441,270	
Cost of Finished Goods Manufactured		434,770
Finished Goods Inventory (Jan. 1, Year 4)		48,000
To record ending finished goods inventory and cost of goods sold.		

Sales	633,600	
Cost of Goods Sold		441,270
Sales Returns and Allowances		3,600
Advertising Expense		35,000
Sales Salaries Expense		42,000
Delivery Expense		8,000
Administrative Salaries Expense		50,000
Office Salaries Expense		20,000
Telephone and Telegraph Expense		1,800
Other General Expenses		2,920
Interest Expense		4,500
Doubtful Accounts Expense		3,000
Depreciation of Buildings		750
Depreciation of Furniture and Fixtures		360
Income Taxes Expense		3,500
Income Summary		16,900
To close revenue and expense accounts.		
Income Summary	16,900	
Retained Earnings		16,900
To close Income Summary account.		
Retained Earnings	6,000	
Dividends		6,000
To close Dividends account.		

Statement of Cost of Finished Goods Manufactured

The cost of goods completed during an accounting period is summarized in a statement of cost of finished goods manufactured. The information for this statement, illustrated on page 80 for Cole Manufacturing Company, is taken from the Manufacturing columns of the work sheet on pages 76–77.

Uses and Limitations of Accounting Information

The ultimate objective of accounting is the *use* of accounting information, through analysis and interpretation, as a basis for business decisions. Information derived from accounting records serves business executives in controlling current operations and in planning future business activities. Financial statements afford outsiders a means of analyzing the financial position and results of operations of business enterprises in which they have an interest. These financial statements essentially reflect past business transactions and events. The past is often the key to the future, however, and for this reason accounting information is highly valued by decision makers, both inside and outside the enterprise.

A statement of production costs for an accounting period

COLE MANUFACTURING COMPANY
Statement of Cost of Finished Goods Manufactured
For Year Ended December 31, Year 4

Goods in process inventory (Jan. 1, Year 4)............		$ 21,000
Raw material used:		
Raw material inventory (Jan. 1, Year 4)	$ 16,000	
Raw material purchases (net)	124,500	
Cost of raw material available for use	$140,500	
Less: Raw material inventory (Dec. 31, Year 4)	12,650	
Cost of raw material used	$127,850	
Direct labor costs	194,300	
Factory overhead costs (see work sheet for details)	117,970	
Total manufacturing costs		440,120
Total cost of goods in process during Year 4............		$461,120
Less: Goods in process inventory (Dec. 31, Year 4)		26,350
Cost of finished goods manufactured...................		$434,770

Among the main objectives of this book are: (1) to examine the basic accounting principles and their effectiveness as the underlying assumptions of accounting, (2) to explore the rules and conventions of accounting, and (3) to consider the possible uses of accounting information once it is accumulated. However, we must be aware of the fact that accounting is justified only because the information accumulated is useful and that such information often is limited because many factors that are not measurable in terms of money have been omitted. Examples include the human resources of a business enterprise and the economic environment in which the enterprise operates. Furthermore, continuing inflation has made the dollar an imperfect tool for measurement of accounting information. But even in the absence of inflation, it should be recognized that many business transactions and events are complex and inconclusive at the time they are recorded (pension costs and loss contingencies, for example). Thus, it may not be realistic to expect financial statements to achieve a higher level of certainty than the transactions and events that they reflect.

REVIEW QUESTIONS

1   Describe the *accounting cycle* and list the sequence of procedures involved in the accounting cycle.

2   State in concise form the *rules of debits and credits* for the five basic types of ledger accounts.

3   Describe the function of *journals.*

4   What is the function of a *ledger?*

5   Explain the advantage of using *controlling accounts* and *subsidiary ledgers.*

6   What is the purpose of an *unadjusted trial balance?* Does it provide proof that there have been no errors in the recording, classifying, and summarizing of business transactions?

7   How are the *temporary* or *nominal ledger accounts* (revenue and expense accounts) related to the basic accounting equation, A = L + OE?

8   What is the objective of using *special journals?*

9   With the advent of electronic computers, the cost of data-processing equipment and the complexity of operations increased significantly. What economies are available to the user to offset the added costs of converting to and using this type of equipment?

10   What are *adjusting entries* and why are they necessary?

11   Why is it necessary to prepare adjusting entries to change the carrying amount of accounts receivable when the journal entries for receivables usually are made only on objective evidence of credit sales and cash collections?

12   Prepare adjusting entries on June 30, Year 6, indicated by the following information:

a Accrued wages total $3,000.

b The estimate of doubtful accounts expense is $2,000, and the allowance for doubtful accounts has a zero balance.

13   What are *closing entries?* Why are they made? What ledger accounts are closed?

14   You are given the following information about the merchandise ledger accounts of Foxx Company and are asked to prepare a single journal entry to adjust the Inventory account and close the relevant accounts to the Cost of Goods Sold account:

Inventory (Jan. 1, Year 10, ledger account balance)	$ 44,000
Purchases	276,400
Purchases returns and allowances	1,700
Purchases discounts	3,800
Freight-in	4,800
Handling and storage costs	26,800
Inventory (Dec. 31, Year 10, physical count; valued at net invoice	
cost plus freight-in, handling, and storage costs)	46,200

15   What are *reversing entries,* and under what circumstances are they most commonly used?

16   Which of the following adjusting entries (explanations omitted) would be reversed when a business enterprise adopts a policy of preparing reversing entries? For each entry, indicate your reasons for reversing or not reversing.

a Unearned Subscriptions Revenue	10,000	
Subscriptions Revenue		10,000

| **b** Inventory of Office Supplies .... | 5,000 | |
| Office Supplies Expense .... | | 5,000 |

| **c** Interest Expense .... | 300 | |
| Interest Payable................................. | | 300 |

| **d** Depreciation Expense .... | 8,000 | |
| Accumulated Depreciation .... | | 8,000 |

17   What is the purpose of a *work sheet,* and what benefits may be derived from using it?

18   List three limitations of accounting information.

EXERCISES

Ex. 2-1   Select the best answer for each of the following multiple-choice questions:

1   The accounting cycle for a business enterprise includes all the following procedures except:
a Closing the accounting records
b Classifying data by posting to ledger accounts
c Preparation of supporting documents for a business transaction
d Adjusting, correcting, and updating recorded data

2   The premium on a three-year insurance policy expiring on December 31, Year 3, was paid on January 2, Year 1. Assuming that the original payment was recorded in an asset ledger account, how would each of the following be affected in Year 3?

	Assets	**Expenses**
a	No change	Increase
b	No change	No change
c	Decrease	No change
d	Decrease	Increase

3   A business enterprise uses the periodic inventory system and uses a closing entry to record the ending inventory (December 31). If the ending inventory is $56,200 and the beginning inventory (January 1) was $42,300, the correct closing entry (explanation omitted) is:

| **a** Income Summary .... | 56,200 | |
| Inventory (Dec. 31) .... | | 56,200 |

| **b** Inventory (Jan. 1) .... | 42,300 | |
| Inventory (Dec. 31) .... | | 42,300 |

| **c** Inventory (Dec. 31) .... | 56,200 | |
| Income Summary .... | | 56,200 |

| **d** Inventory (Dec. 31) .... | 13,900 | |
| Inventory (Jan. 1) .... | | 13,900 |

4   Chamber Company credits unearned fees received to an Unearned Fees Revenue liability account. On December 31, Year 2, before end-of-year adjusting entries, the credit balance in the Unearned Fees Revenue ledger account was $6,312. The credit balance in this account should be $4,286 on December 31, Year 2. The appropriate December 31, Year 2, adjusting entry (explanation omitted) is:

a Unearned Fees Revenue   2,026
      Fees Revenue   2,026

b Cash..   4,286
      Unearned Fees Revenue   4,286

c Fees Revenue   4,286
      Unearned Fees Revenue   4,286

d None of the foregoing

Ex. 2-2   Total manufacturing costs for Latest Products, Inc., for Year 3, were $642,700. The cost of finished goods manufactured in Year 3 was $655,500.

Compute the amount of the goods in process inventory of Latest Products, Inc., on December 31, Year 3, assuming that the goods in process inventory on January 1, Year 3, was $62,000.

Ex. 2-3   The balance in the Accounts Receivable controlling account (Ledger Account No. 8) on January 1, Year 2, was $146,220. In January, sales on credit from the sales journal (page 22) were $109,800, and cash collections from the cash receipts journal (page 11) were $120,000 after sales discounts of $1,800. Accounts receivable of $2,200 were written off as uncollectible in the general journal (page 30) on January 22, and a provision of $1,460 for doubtful accounts was recorded on January 31.

Reproduce the ledger account (three-column form) for the Accounts Receivable controlling account for the month of January, Year 2.

Ex. 2-4   For Year 5, the gross profit on sales of Oxnard Company was $102,000; the cost of finished goods manufactured was $340,000; the beginning inventories of goods in process and finished goods were $28,000 and $45,000, respectively; and the ending inventories of goods in process and finished goods were $38,000 and $63,500, respectively.

Compute the amount of Oxnard Company's sales for Year 5.

Ex. 2-5   During the month ended December 31, Year 3, Hope Company completed the following transactions:

Dec. 6   Acquired office supplies for cash of $12,000. The acquisition was recorded in the Office Supplies Expense ledger account. The December 1 balance of the Inventory of Office Supplies ledger account was $1,000; the inventory of office supplies on December 31, Year 3, was $2,500.

    7   Borrowed $20,000 from National Bank on a 90-day, 12% promissory note. Hope Company computes interest on a 360-day year.

Prepare (*a*) journal entries to record the transactions described above, and (*b*) adjusting entries on December 31, Year 3, for each transaction. (Omit explanations.) Hope Company does not use reversing entries.

Ex. 2-6   Among the items requiring adjusting entries for Horizon Company on January 31, Year 2, were the following:

a Office supplies used, $64,290. Acquisitions of office supplies were recorded in the Inventory of Office Supplies ledger account.

b Rent revenue received in advance, $16,200. Advance rent received from lessees is credited to the Rent Revenue ledger account.

c Interest accrued on a 60-day, 18%, $60,000 note payable dated January 16, Year 2. Horizon uses a 360-day year to compute interest.

d Royalty revenue accrued from licensing a patent, $6,200.

e Doubtful accounts expense, $82,800. The credit balance, before adjustment, in the allowance account was $64,600.

Prepare adjusting entries on January 31, Year 2, for each item described above. (Omit explanations.) Horizon Company uses reversing entries.

Ex. 2-7   The account balances below are taken from the ledger of Paradise Company:

	May 1	May 31
Accounts receivable	$20,000	$28,500
Inventories	50,000	48,000
Accounts payable (suppliers of merchandise)	30,000	21,600
Retained earnings	28,000	40,400
Dividends declared and paid		12,900

Cash collections from customers in May were $106,000, and net purchases of merchandise were $65,000. No allowance for doubtful accounts is used, and no accounts receivable were written off. The only entries in the Retained Earnings ledger account were to close the Income Summary and Dividends ledger accounts.

Compute the following for Paradise Company for the month of May:

a Total net sales

b Cost of goods sold

c Amount of cash paid to suppliers of merchandise

d Net income

e Total expenses (other than cost of goods sold)

Ex. 2-8   The information below for Pinehurst Company provides a basis for making all necessary adjusting entries on December 31, Year 5, the end of Pinehurst's first fiscal year:

a On June 1, Year 5, borrowed $60,000 by issuing a 9% mortgage note payable that required interest to be paid quarterly, beginning September 1, Year 5.

b On October 1, Year 5, paid $2,700 for three years of insurance coverage commencing on that date. The Unexpired Insurance ledger account was debited.

c On November 1, Year 5, credited a nominal account when $4,800 in rent revenue was received from a tenant. This amount represented six months' rent paid in advance.

d On May 1, Year 5, acquired bonds with a face amount of $20,000 and an annual interest rate of 12% at face amount as an investment. Interest on the bonds is paid on April 1 and October 1.

e On December 31, Year 5, after an aging of accounts receivable, estimated that probable uncollectible accounts would total $4,000. The Allowance for Doubtful Accounts ledger account had an unadjusted credit balance of $900.

Prepare adjusting entries for Pinehurst Company on December 31, Year 5. Include in the explanation portion of each entry any computations required to prepare the adjusting entry.

Ex. 2-9 Selected ledger account balances of Lobo Company before and after the December 31 adjusting entries are listed below:

	Before adjustment	*After adjustment*
a *Allowance for doubtful accounts*	*$ 2,000 credit*	*$ 5,500 credit*
b *Accumulated depreciation*	*14,000 credit*	*16,000 credit*
c *Sales salaries expense*	*24,200 debit*	*24,650 debit*
d *Income taxes payable*	*3,700 credit*	*6,250 credit*
e *Interest revenue*	*6,500 credit*	*6,585 credit*
f *Royalty revenue*	*5,000 credit*	*5,800 credit*

Prepare the adjusting journal entries that were made by Lobo Company for each ledger account on December 31.

Ex. 2-10 Rainbow Company's accounting records provide the following information concerning certain ledger account balances and changes in the balances during Year 5:

a Accounts receivable: Jan. 1 balance, $15,000; Dec. 31 balance, $20,500; uncollectible accounts written off during the year, $4,100; accounts receivable collected during the year, $56,000. (Record sales on credit.)

b Allowance for doubtful accounts: Jan. 1 balance, $1,500; Dec 31 balance, $2,200; adjusting entry increasing allowance on Dec. 31, $4,800. (Record write-off of uncollectible accounts receivable.)

c Inventory of office supplies: Jan. 1 balance, $1,600; Dec. 31 balance, $1,450; office supplies expense for the year, $9,500. (Record acquisition of office supplies.)

d Equipment: Jan. 1 balance, $20,500; Dec. 31 balance, $18,000; equipment costing $8,000 was sold during the year. (Record acquisition of equipment.)

e Accounts payable: Jan. 1 balance, $9,000; Dec. 31 balance, $11,500; purchases of merchandise on credit for the year, $48,000. (Record payments to suppliers.)

Transaction information is missing from each of the above. Prepare Rainbow Company's journal entry to record the missing information (indicated in the parenthetical instructions) for each ledger account.

Ex. 2-11 The accounting policies of Gina Publications, Inc., require that subscriptions received from customers be credited to Subscriptions Revenue when received. Acquisitions of supplies are regularly debited to Supplies Expense at time of acquisition. The post-closing trial balance on December 31, Year 5, includes the following ledger accounts:

	Debit	Credit
Accounts receivable	$ 24,000	
Allowance for doubtful accounts		$ 2,200
Inventory of supplies.	1,710	
Equipment	135,500	
Accumulated depreciation of equipment		48,000
Notes payable		20,000
Interest payable		350
Wages payable		1,230
Unearned subscriptions revenue		2,940

Assuming that Gina Publications, Inc., follows a policy of reversing the adjusting entries that set up new balance sheet accounts, prepare the appropriate reversing entries on January 1, Year 6.

Ex. 2-12 The following transactions were completed in January (the first month of operations) by Lane's Markets:

(1) Sales on credit totaled $13,000. Terms, 2/10, n/60.
(2) Cash sales amounted to $24,000.
(3) Purchases of merchandise totaled $50,000.
(4) Payments of $28,600 were made to creditors in full settlement of purchase invoices totaling $29,000.
(5) Accounts receivable in the amount of $10,000 were collected; one-half of these collections were made before the expiration of the 10-day discount period.
(6) P. Lane, the owner, withdrew merchandise for personal use. This merchandise had a cost of $3,000 and had been marked to sell for $3,900. Lane also withdrew $500 cash during January.
(7) Inventory of goods on hand at the end of January was $23,000.
(8) Operating expenses for the month totaled $15,500.

Compute the net income or net loss of Lane's Markets for the month of January. Show supporting computations.

Ex. 2-13 During the review of the accounting records and the preparation of year-end adjusting entries for Sunburst Company, you discover the following errors:

a The perpetual inventory amount in the accounting records was overstated by $4,750 as a result of errors in pricing merchandise sold.

b Office equipment acquired for $10,500 was recorded in the Equipment Maintenance ledger account. The adjusting entry for depreciation expense has not been recorded.

c A payment to a supplier in the amount of $1,210 was debited to the Accounts Receivable ledger account.

d A sale on credit for $419 was recorded in the sales journal at $491. The correct amount of $419 was received from the customer and was recorded in the cash receipts journal.

e When 1,000 shares of $10 par common stock were issued for $42,000, the entire amount was credited to Common Stock in the cash receipts journal.

Prepare a correcting entry for each error described above. (Omit explanations.)

Ex. 2-14 All but one of the ledger accounts of Arnold's Store, a single proprietorship owned by J. Arnold, appear in the following list on December 31, Year 1:

Accounts receivable (net)	$17,500
Accounts payable	21,000
Accrued liabilities	1,300
Cash...	8,500
Inventory	15,000
Notes payable	18,000
Plant assets (net)	41,000
Short-term prepayments	500

On January 1, Year 1, Arnold's equity in the proprietorship amounted to $27,000. In Year 1, Arnold withdrew $8,400 cash and made an additional investment of $5,000 of plant assets that had been part of another business enterprise owned by Arnold.

Compute the net income or net loss of Arnold's Store for Year 1, and show supporting computations. (Hint: First prepare a trial balance to find the balance of the missing ledger account.)

CASES

Case 2-1 Sharon Bebout, accountant for Arcadia Paint Store, Inc., has not recorded conventional closing entries for 10 years. Instead, she recorded the following journal entry annually and posted only the credit to the Retained Earnings account in the ledger:

Revenue and Expenses (not posted)	xxx	
Dividends (not posted).............................		xxx
Retained Earnings		xxx

In the ledger, Bebout skipped two lines to distinguish clearly the revenue and expenses for each year. For example, the Sales ledger account for the two most recent years appears as follows:

Sales Ledger Account No. 80

Date	Explanation	Ref.	Debit	Credit	Balance
Year 9					
Dec. 31		S 48		741,200	741,200 cr
31		CR52		192,888	934,088 cr
Year 10					
Dec. 31		S 53		780,100	780,100 cr
31		CR58		219,600	999,700 cr

When a staff accountant working for Arcadia Paint Store's auditors objected to Bebout's closing procedure, she responded: "You should not object unless you can show me that the financial statements are in any way deficient. All assets, liabilities, stockholders' equity, revenue, and expense balances are 100% correct under my procedure. My only objective has been to be efficient and accurate; I wanted to dispense with the meaningless ritual of journalizing and posting closing entries to nominal accounts at the end of each year."

Instructions

Evaluate Sharon Bebout's response to the staff accountant.

Case 2-2 On January 2, Year 5, Paul Falk established a single proprietorship, Falk's Nursery. He signed a three-year lease on a store building at a monthly rent of $300 and made the first monthly payment on January 2, Year 5. Also on that date, Falk acquired store equipment for $10,000 and purchased merchandise for $16,000. The store equipment had an estimated economic life of 10 years with no residual value. Falk made no other investment in the enterprise.

Both Falk and his wife worked in the enterprise; they had no employees. From time to time the Falks withdrew cash from the enterprise to meet their personal needs. Because the Falks had no prior business experience, they chose to minimize record keeping. The only records maintained were a checkbook, which was reconciled monthly with the bank statement, a file folder of unpaid purchase invoices, and another file folder of uncollected sales invoices for a few customers.

On December 31, Year 6, Falk carried out the following procedures in an effort to see how the proprietorship stood after two years of operations:

(1) Took a physical inventory of merchandise and priced the items, using invoice prices of recent purchases. This procedure indicated a total cost for the inventory of $45,000.

(2) Reconciled the December 31 bank statement with the checkbook and found the correct cash balance to be $7,200.

(3) Added the unpaid purchase invoices in the file, which showed a total liability to suppliers of $22,700.

(4) Added the uncollected sales invoices and found that the total amount receivable from customers was $4,200.

(5) Computed the withdrawals of cash for personal needs during the two-year period at $20,000.

Instructions

a Prepare a balance sheet for Falk's Nursery (a single proprietorship) on December 31, year 6. (Disregard income taxes, including the fact that apparently no personal income tax return was prepared to reflect Falk's tax liability for the first year of operations.)

b Explain to Falk the advantages of a double-entry accounting system as compared with his present set of accounting records. Could the same information obtainable from a double-entry system be obtained from his present system?

c What conclusions may be reached about Falk's operations for the first two years?

Case 2-3   Carmen Garcia began her working career in the accounting department of Mod Company. Although Garcia had never taken a formal course of study in accounting, she gradually developed a thorough knowledge of Mod's accounting system, and eventually she was promoted to the position of chief accountant.

While attending a meeting of accountants, Garcia was puzzled by a statement made in a group discussion. The statement was: "Reversing entries are frequently helpful; however, they are not essential to the record-keeping function." Garcia was concerned because reversing entries had been used regularly by Mod Company, and she had always considered them an essential part of the accounting cycle.

Instructions

a Explain why reversing entries are not essential but why they may be helpful. Your answer should include an explanation as to when reversing entries are appropriate and when they should not be used.

b Using the data below, demonstrate with journal entries how reversing entries may be used or ignored. The accounting policy is to debit the Supplies Expense ledger account for all supplies acquired. The cost of supplies on hand on December 31, Year 4, was determined by count to be $1,150. The balance in the Inventory of Supplies ledger account was zero. The following adjusting entry was made:

Inventory of Supplies	*1,150*	
Supplies Expense		*1,150*
To record inventory of supplies on Dec. 31, Year 4.		

During Year 5, supplies were acquired at a cost of $17,500 and debited to Supplies Expense. The inventory of supplies on December 31, Year 5, was $850.

PROBLEMS

2-1   The Income Statement columns in the work sheet for Billy Jack, Inc., for the year ended September 30, Year 2, are reproduced below:

	Debit	*Credit*
Inventory (periodic system)	*$ 75,800*	*$ 94,200*
Sales		*875,000*
Sales returns and allowances	*10,800*	
Sales discounts	*12,500*	
Purchases	*588,000*	
Purchases returns and allowances		*15,000*
Purchases discounts		*10,200*
Salaries expense	*82,500*	
Rent expense	*24,000*	
Advertising and promotion expense	*52,100*	
Other operating expenses	*38,700*	
Income taxes expense	*26,750*	
Net income	*83,250*	
Totals	*$994,400*	*$994,400*

Instructions

Prepare closing entries for Billy Jack, Inc., on September 30, Year 2, similar to those illustrated on pages 73–74.

2-2 Verena Company uses the periodic inventory system. Selected transactions and adjustments for Year 2 are listed below:

(1) Sales on credit totaled $44,120.

(2) A building and a tract of land were acquired at a cost of $300,000. The current fair value of the land was estimated at $90,000. One-fifth of the acquisition cost was paid in cash, and a 10% mortgage note payable was issued for the balance.

(3) Merchandise costing $24,200 was purchased, subject to a cash discount of 2% if paid within 10 days. (Record invoice at net amount.)

(4) Freight charges of $495 related to merchandise purchased were paid.

(5) Uncollectible accounts receivable of $515 were written off. Verena uses an allowance for doubtful accounts and makes provisions for doubtful accounts at the end of each year.

(6) The invoice for the purchase in item (3) was paid in full within the discount period.

(7) Cash collections on customers' accounts totaled $27,400, after sales discounts of $350.

(8) Equipment on which accumulated depreciation amounted to $3,000 was sold for $500 cash; the cost of the equipment was $5,000.

(9) A cash dividend of $0.25 a share on 100,000 shares of outstanding common stock was declared and paid. (Prepare separate journal entries for the declaration and the payment.)

(10) 20,000 shares of $10 par common stock were issued for $14 a share.

(11) Defective merchandise purchased on credit for $650 (net amount) was returned for full credit.

(12) An expense account was debited when supplies were acquired. The Inventory of Supplies ledger account had an unadjusted balance of $750, but the inventory of supplies at the end of Year 2 was $950.

(13) The building acquired in item (2) was used in operations for nine months during Year 2. The building had an economic life of 25 years and no residual value. Depreciation was computed by the straight-line method.

Instructions

Prepare journal entries for Verena Company to record the foregoing transactions and adjustments for Year 2.

2-3 Marlboro Corporation uses the perpetual inventory system. A selected list of transactions and adjustments for Year 8 is presented below and on page 91.

(1) Sales on credit totaled $40,500; the cost of the goods was $27,500.

(2) Marlboro acquired land and a building at a total cost of $310,000. One-tenth of the acquisition cost was paid in cash, and a mortgage note payable was

issued for the balance. The building had an estimated current fair value of $192,000.

(3) Merchandise costing $29,500 was purchased. The invoice amount was subject to a 2% cash discount if paid within 10 days. Marlboro records purchases invoices at the net amount.

(4) Marlboro paid $850 for freight charges on merchandise purchased. Freight charges are recorded in a separate ledger account.

(5) Accounts receivable of $350 were written off as uncollectible. Marlboro maintains an allowance for doubtful accounts and makes a provision for doubtful accounts expense at the end of each year.

(6) The invoice for the purchase of merchandise in item (3) was paid within the discount period.

(7) Cash collections on customers' accounts amounted to $39,880. No sales discounts were allowed.

(8) Cash of $4,000 was received from disposal of equipment. The cost of the equipment was $20,000, and the accumulated depreciation was $17,500.

(9) A cash dividend of $0.50 a share on 80,000 shares of common stock was declared and paid. (Prepare separate journal entries for the declaration and the payment.)

(10) Defective merchandise was returned to a supplier for full credit. The merchandise had been purchased on credit for $750 (net).

(11) Marlboro issued 10,000 shares of its $5 par common stock and received cash of $9 a share.

(12) A customer's check for $180, received and deposited by Marlboro, was returned by the bank marked "NSF" (not sufficient funds).

(13) The building acquired in item (2) was used in operations for 10 months during Year 8. The building had an economic life of 40 years and no residual value. Depreciation was computed by the straight-line method.

Instructions

Prepare journal entries for Marlboro Corporation to record the foregoing transactions and adjustments for Year 8.

2-4 Tom Manufacturing Company uses the periodic inventory system. Its adjusted trial balance on December 31, Year 2, follows:

TOM MANUFACTURING COMPANY
Adjusted Trial Balance
December 31, Year 2

	Debit	Credit
Cash	$ 35,100	
Accounts receivable (net)	62,000	
Inventories (Jan. 1, Year 2):		
Finished goods	40,000	
Goods in process	20,000	
Raw material	25,000	

(continued)

Short-term prepayments	2,000	
Plant assets (net)	254,400	
Accounts payable		$ 48,500
Income taxes payable		40,000
Common stock, $1 par		100,000
Paid-in capital in excess of par		150,000
Retained earnings (Jan. 1, Year 2)		82,000
Dividends	44,000	
Sales (net)		980,000
Raw material purchases (net)	210,000	
Direct labor costs	220,000	
Factory overhead costs	190,000	
Selling expenses	130,000	
General and administrative expenses	122,000	
Income taxes expense	46,000	
Totals	$1,400,500	$1,400,500

Inventories on December 31, Year 2, were as follows:

Finished goods	$ 45,000
Goods in process	25,000
Raw material	32,500

Instructions

a Prepare closing entries for Tom Manufacturing Company on December 31, Year 2, similar to those illustrated on pages 78–79.

b Prepare a statement of cost of finished goods manufactured for Tom Manufacturing Company for the year ended December 31, Year 2. (See page 80.)

2-5   Dawn Merchandising Company has adopted a policy of not reversing any adjusting entries. All receipts and payments relating to revenue and expenses are recorded in nominal accounts, and the accruals and deferrals established at the end of the preceding year are adjusted to reflect current balances. The following unadjusted trial balance was prepared by Dawn Merchandising's accountant in the first pair of columns of the work sheet for the year ended October 31, Year 10:

DAWN MERCHANDISING COMPANY
Unadjusted Trial Balance
October 31, Year 10

	Debit	Credit
Cash	$ 49,000	
Accounts receivable	32,000	
Allowance for doubtful accounts		$ 200
Inventory (Nov. 1, Year 9)	47,000	
Inventory of advertising supplies	3,000	
Land	264,000	
Building	210,000	

(continued)

Accumulated depreciation of building		45,800
Equipment	252,000	
Accumulated depreciation of equipment		62,700
Notes payable		180,000
Accounts payable		45,000
Unearned rent revenue		3,200
Interest payable		4,000
Salaries payable		2,200
Bonds payable, 9%		100,000
Common stock, $5 stated value..................		200,000
Retained earnings (Nov. 1, Year 9)		88,800
Dividends	8,000	
Sales		830,000
Rent revenue		18,600
Purchases	480,000	
Salaries expense	56,500	
Selling expenses	122,500	
General expenses	41,000	
Interest expense	15,500	
Totals	$1,580,500	$1,580,500

Additional Information

(1) Aging of accounts receivable indicates that an allowance for doubtful accounts in the amount of $960 is required on October 31, Year 10.
(2) Inventory of advertising supplies is $1,850 on October 31, Year 10.
(3) The estimated economic life of the building is 30 years, and the residual value is zero. The estimated economic life of the equipment is 20 years, and the residual value is $12,000. (Use the straight-line method of depreciation.)
(4) Unearned rent revenue is $2,700 on October 31, Year 10.
(5) Interest payable is $6,400 on October 31, Year 10.
(6) Salaries payable amount to $1,200 on October 31, Year 10.
(7) The physical inventory on October 31, Year 10, is $35,000. (Prepare an adjusting entry to record cost of goods sold in a separate ledger account.)
(8) Income taxes expense for the year ended October 31, Year 10, is estimated at $32,000.

Instructions

Prepare Dawn Merchandising Company's October 31, Year 10, adjusting entries for each item above. Record expenses in specific ledger accounts, such as Doubtful Accounts Expense, Advertising Supplies Expense, Depreciation Expense of Building, etc.

2-6   Listed on page 94 are the adjusted ledger account balances of Rockingham Company on January 31, Year 3, except for retained earnings, which is the January 1, Year 3, balance. There are no assets or liabilities other than those listed. The Dividends account represents the amount declared and paid during January, Year 3.

Accounts payable.	$111,000
Accounts receivable.	96,000
Accumulated depreciation	222,000
Cash.	100,000
Common stock, $10 par	660,000
Dividends	24,000
Inventories.	192,000
Plant assets	870,000
Retained earnings (Jan. 1, Year 3).	231,000

Instructions

a Compute the net income of Rockingham Company for January, Year 3, by preparing a balance sheet on January 31, Year 3, that includes details showing the beginning balance, increases and decreases, and the ending balance of retained earnings.

b What was the amount of total sales for January, Year 3, assuming that the accounts receivable totaled $108,000 on January 1, Year 3, and that $480,000 was received on customers' accounts and from cash sales during January, Year 3?

c Determine the cost of goods sold for January, Year 3, assuming that inventories on January 1, Year 3, were $174,000 and that purchases of merchandise totaled $330,000 in January, Year 3.

d Compute the total of all other expenses for January, Year 3.

e Determine the total cash paid for merchandise purchases during January, Year 3, assuming that the January 31, Year 3, balance of accounts payable was $114,000 and that purchases (all on credit) amounted to $330,000 during January, Year 3.

2-7 Subsidiary ledgers and related controlling accounts are maintained by Robin Company for accounts receivable and accounts payable. On December 31, Year 9, the two subsidiary ledgers were summarized as follows:

ROBIN COMPANY
Accounts Receivable Trial Balance
December 31, Year 9

Paul Davis	$ 2,000
Ed Fairly.	6,000
Ken Iverson (credit balance).	(750)
Dolores Kiley.	13,500
Balance of controlling account.	$20,750

ROBIN COMPANY
Accounts Payable Trial Balance
December 31, Year 9

Joann Edwards	$ 588
John Gates (debit balance).	(570)
Julie Loomis	8,050
David Parks.	2,330
Balance of controlling account.	$10,398

Robin Company offers credit terms of 2/10, n/30 to all customer and records all sales at gross prices. Purchases of merchandise are recorded net of purchases discounts because it is Robin's policy to take all purchases discounts available. When Robin fails to take the discount offered by suppliers, the Purchases Discounts Lost ledger account is debited.

Robin carried customers' credit balances as an offset against debit balances, and suppliers' debit balances as an offset against credit balances in the subsidiary ledgers. These balances are reclassified for reporting purposes to reflect customers' credit balances as liabilities and suppliers' debit balances as assets.

Transactions for January, Year 10, were as follows:

(1) A check for $13,230 was received from Kiley in full settlement of her account within the discount period.
(2) Purchases from Edwards totaled $11,000, terms 2/10, n/30. (Record net of purchases discounts.)
(3) Payment to Loomis of $8,050 was made within the discount period.
(4) Sales to Iverson were $23,000, terms 2/10, n/30.
(5) Cash of $4,500 was received from Davis, including a $2,500 advance payment.
(6) Payment of $11,380 was made to Edwards in settlement of the account payable. Because of an oversight, the payment was not made until after the discount period had lapsed on the December invoice for $600.
(7) Purchases from Edwards totaled $13,200, terms 2/10, n/30.
(8) Cash of $3,920 was received from Fairly in partial payment of his account balance. The discount was allowed on this portion of the account balance, because cash was received within the discount period.
(9) Parks was paid $4,130, which represented payment of the balance due within the discount period and an $1,800 partial advance payment on a new order.
(10) Purchases from Loomis totaled $5,000, terms 2/10, n/30.

Instructions

a Enter the December 31, Year 9, balances and the foregoing transactions of Robin Company directly in the appropriate accounts in both the general ledger and the subsidiary ledgers for accounts receivable and accounts payable. You need not maintain ledger accounts for Cash, Purchases, or Sales. (Because this problem does not include journals or monthly totals, each transaction should be entered individually in a general ledger controlling account as well as in a subsidiary ledger account. The three-column ledger account form is recommended.)

b Prove the accuracy of Robin Company's accounting records by preparing trial balances of the subsidiary ledgers on January 31, Year 10, and by determining that the totals agree with the balances of the respective controlling accounts on that date.

c Which accounts with customers and suppliers should be reclassified in Robin Company's balance sheet on January 31, Year 10? Explain how such accounts should be presented in the balance sheet.

2-8 Suyanto Corporation adjusts and closes its accounting records at the end of each calendar year. The information presented on page 96 provides the basis for making the adjusting entries on December 31, Year 5.

(1) On July 1, Year 5, Suyanto received $7,260 of rent revenue covering a one-year period beginning with the date of receipt. The Rent Revenue ledger account was credited.

(2) Unexpired Insurance was debited on September 1, Year 5, when Suyanto paid a $2,700 premium for a three-year insurance policy effective on that date.

(3) Suyanto borrowed $90,000 on March 1, Year 5, by issuing a three-year, 10% mortgage note payable, with interest payable quarterly. Interest payments were made on May 31, August 31, and November 30 of Year 5.

(4) Bonds with a face amount of $20,000 and an interest rate of 12% were acquired at face amount as an investment on April 1. Interest payment dates are April 1 and October 1.

(5) The building occupied by Suyanto has a cost of $96,000. Estimated economic life is 20 years, with no residual value. Straight-line method of depreciation is used.

(6) An aging of the accounts receivable on December 31 indicated $4,100 to be a reasonable estimate of doubtful accounts. On that date the allowance for doubtful accounts had a *debit* balance of $260.

(7) Office Supplies Expense was debited on July 1, Year 5, when $2,200 was paid for office supplies. On December 31, Year 5, office supplies of $1,195 were on hand.

(8) A contract was signed on December 20, Year 5, requiring Suyanto to deliver merchandise to Plainville Company on January 29, Year 6. The contract price was $14,500 and the estimated cost of the merchandise to be delivered was $9,000.

Instructions

a Prepare adjusting entries for Suyanto Corporation on December 31, Year 5. Include in the explanation portion of each journal entry any computations used to determine the amount of the adjustment.

b Prepare reversing entries for Suyanto Corporation on January 1, Year 6, assuming that Suyanto follows a policy of reversing the adjusting entries that include a balance sheet ledger account normally not used during the accounting period.

2-9 Trijono Hardware Company uses the periodic inventory system and maintains its accounting records on a calendar-year basis. The unadjusted trial balance below and on page 97 was prepared from the general ledger on December 31, Year 3, and no adjusting entries had been made.

TRIJONO HARDWARE COMPANY
Unadjusted Trial Balance
December 31, Year 3

	Debit	Credit
Cash	$ 8,000	
Accounts receivable	40,000	
Inventory (Dec. 31, Year 2)	23,000	
Land	80,000	

(continued)

Building	200,000	
Accumulated depreciation of building		$ 42,000
Equipment	240,000	
Accumulated depreciation of equipment		59,500
Accounts payable		38,000
Interest payable		–0–
Salaries payable		–0–
Bonds payable, 12%		100,000
Common stock, $2 par............................		200,000
Retained earnings (Dec. 31, Year 2)		75,200
Dividends	25,000	
Sales		806,000
Purchases	479,500	
Salaries expense	55,200	
Selling expenses	120,000	
General and administrative expenses................	40,000	
Interest expense	10,000	
Totals	$1,320,700	$1,320,700

Reversing entries were made on January 1, Year 3, for interest payable and salaries payable that had been recorded by adjusting entries on December 31, Year 2.

Additional Information

(1) Trijono has decided, after an aging and analysis of accounts receivable, to establish an allowance for doubtful accounts of $3,000.

(2) The building and equipment are depreciated on the straight-line basis. The economic life of the building is 40 years and the residual value is zero; the economic life of the equipment is 15 years and the residual value is $15,000.

(3) Interest on the bonds payable is paid on May 1 and November 1.

(4) Salaries earned by employees but unpaid on December 31 amount to $6,000.

(5) Income taxes are estimated to be $17,000.

(6) The physical inventory on December 31, Year 3, was $28,000.

Instructions

a Prepare a 12-column work sheet for Trijono Hardware Company on December 31, Year 3, to adjust the ledger accounts and classify the balances as to income statement, retained earnings statement, and balance sheet. (Include columns for an adjusted trial balance.)

b Use the work sheet as a source for preparation of closing entries for Trijono Hardware Company on December 31, Year 3. (Adjusting entries are not required; do not record cost of goods sold in a separate ledger account.)

c Prepare reversing entries for Trijono Hardware Company dated January 1, Year 4, with respect to salaries payable and to interest payable, for which adjustments were made on December 31, Year 3.

2-10   The unadjusted trial balance below was prepared from the ledger of Rex Manufacturing Corporation on December 31, Year 10. Rex used reversing entries on January 1 of each year to reverse wages payable and interest payable.

REX MANUFACTURING CORPORATION
Unadjusted Trial Balance
December 31, Year 10

	Debit	Credit
Cash	$ 14,050	
Accounts receivable	80,000	
Allowance for doubtful accounts		$ 200
Inventories (Jan. 1, Year 10):		
Raw material.....................................	12,000	
Goods in process	56,000	
Finished goods	80,000	
Short-term prepayments...........................	9,000	
Land	50,000	
Building	457,000	
Accumulated depreciation of building		54,800
Machinery and equipment.........................	400,000	
Accumulated depreciation of machinery and		
equipment		120,000
Accounts payable		70,000
Wages payable		–0–
Interest payable		–0–
Bonds payable, 12%		200,000
Common stock, $10 par		400,000
Paid-in capital in excess of par		170,000
Retained earnings (Jan. 1, Year 10)		56,025
Dividends	15,000	
Sales (net)		992,000
Raw material purchases	310,000	
Direct labor costs	292,900	
Factory overhead costs	120,000	
Selling expenses	95,000	
General and administrative expenses.................	52,000	
Interest expense	20,075	
Totals	$2,063,025	$2,063,025

Additional Information

(1) The allowance for doubtful accounts should be increased to a balance equal to 6% of accounts receivable.

(2) Short-term prepayments at the beginning and end of Year 10 are as follows (insurance is an administrative expense):

	Jan. 1 Year 10	Dec. 31 Year 10
Unexpired insurance (two years remaining on Jan. 1)	$3,600	$1,800
Factory supplies	5,400	7,000
Totals	$9,000	$8,800

(3) Invoices for raw material included in the ending inventory but not recorded in the accounting records total $12,000.

(4) The straight-line method of depreciation is used to allocate the cost of plant assets. Other relevant data are presented below:

	Estimated economic life, years	Estimated residual value	Percentage allocated to	
			Factory	Administration
Building	50	$7,000	70	30
Machinery and equip- ment	10	5%	80	20

(5) Interest payments to bondholders are made semiannually on May 1 and November 1.

(6) The factory power bill for December, Year 10, $3,200, has not been recorded.

(7) Direct factory wages incurred but not paid on December 31, Year 10, total $1,800.

(8) Income taxes are estimated at $4,700 for Year 10.

(9) The ending inventories on December 31 are: Raw material, $18,000; goods in process, $53,000; and finished goods, $75,000.

Instructions

a Prepare a work sheet for Rex Manufacturing Corporation on December 31, Year 10, to adjust the accounts and classify the data as to manufacturing costs, income statement, retained earnings statement, and balance sheet. Do not include columns for an adjusted trial balance.

b Prepare Rex Manufacturing Corporation's closing entries on December 31, Year 10, to adjust the inventory accounts and to record the cost of finished goods manufactured and the cost of goods sold. You need not close any accounts to Income Summary.

c Prepare reversing entries for Rex Manufacturing Corporation as of January 1, Year 11, relating to wages payable and interest payable.

2-11 The post-closing trial balance for Steve Shirt Company on June 30, Year 5, is shown on page 100.

STEVE SHIRT COMPANY
Post-Closing Trial Balance
June 30, Year 5

	Debit	Credit
Cash	$ 26,200	
Accounts receivable	32,600	
Allowance for doubtful accounts		$ 1,100
Inventory	54,950	
Unexpired insurance	600	
Store fixtures	38,400	
Accumulated depreciation of store fixtures		13,800
Vouchers payable		18,300
Income taxes payable		6,100
Wages payable		1,300
Common stock, no-par value, 2,000 shares issued and outstanding		70,000
Retained earnings		42,150
Totals	$152,750	$152,750

Transactions recorded in the journals for the month of July, Year 5, are summarized below (to avoid unnecessary detail, all expenses are recorded in a single Operating Expenses ledger account):

Sales Journal (S): Debit to Accounts Receivable and credit to Sales $82,100

Cash Receipts Journal (CR):

Debits:	Cash	$88,800
	Sales Discounts	1,200
Credits:	Accounts Receivable	$70,000
	Common Stock (110 shares)	5,000
	Sales	15,000

Voucher Register (V):

Debits:	Purchases	$45,200
	Freight-in	900
	Operating Expenses	13,800
Credits:	Vouchers Payable	$59,200
	Purchases Discounts	700

Cash Payments Journal (CP): Debit to Vouchers Payable and credit to Cash $68,200

General Journal (J):

Debits:	Allowance for Doubtful Accounts	$ 200
	Notes Receivable	5,000
	Accumulated Depreciation of Store Fixtures	150
Credits:	Accounts Receivable	$ 5,200
	Store Fixtures	150

Additional Information

(1) Aging of accounts receivable indicates that an allowance for doubtful accounts of $1,250 is required on July 31, Year 5.
(2) Depreciation expense for the month of July, Year 5, is $850.
(3) Unexpired insurance amounts to $520 on July 31, Year 5.
(4) Wages payable amount to $800 on July 31, Year 5.
(5) Interest receivable is $40 on July 31, Year 5.
(6) Income taxes expense for July, Year 5, is estimated at $10,000.
(7) A physical inventory indicates that merchandise costing $51,000 is on hand on July 31, Year 5.

Instructions

a Post Steve Shirt Company's June 30, Year 5, balances and all transactions for July, Year 5, from the journals to ledger accounts.

b Prepare an unadjusted trial balance for Steve Shirt Company on July 31, Year 5, in the first pair of columns of a 12-column work sheet that includes an adjusted trial balance.

c Enter the adjustments in the work sheet and complete the work sheet.

d Record Steve Shirt Company's adjusting and closing entries on July 31, Year 5, in the general journal and post these entries to the ledger. (Reversing entries are not used.)

e Prepare Steve Shirt Company's income statement for the month of July, Year 5, and balance sheet on July 31, Year 5. (Disregard earnings per share.)

f Prepare a post-closing trial balance for Steve Shirt Company on July 31, Year 5.

Revenue and Expense Recognition; Income Measurement and Reporting

3

The measurement of periodic income of a business enterprise is perhaps the foremost objective of the accounting process. The concept of *income* (or *net income*) is elusive, and the art of accounting probably never will progress to the point where ''income'' is defined to everyone's satisfaction. Accountants measure income for an accounting period by matching expired costs with realized revenue under a system of accrual accounting. This process requires workable standards for the recognition of revenue, expenses, gains, and losses applicable to each period. The Financial Accounting Standards Board described *accrual accounting* as follows:[1]

[1]*Statement of Financial Accounting Concepts No. 3*, ''Elements of Financial Statements of Business Enterprises,'' FASB (Stamford: 1980), pp. 41–42.

Accrual accounting uses accrual, deferral, and allocation procedures whose goal is to relate revenues, expenses, gains, and losses to periods to reflect an enterprise's performance during a period instead of merely listing its cash receipts and outlays. Thus, recognition of revenues, expenses, gains, and losses and the related increments or decrements in assets and liabilities—including matching of costs and revenues, allocation, and amortization—is the essence of using accrual accounting to measure performance of business enterprises. The goal of accrual accounting for a business enterprise is to account in the periods in which they occur for the effects of transactions and other events and circumstances, to the extent that those financial effects are recognizable and measurable.

Our attention in this chapter focuses on the role of accrual accounting in the measurement and reporting of business income; the various forms of income statements are illustrated in Chapter 4.

RECOGNITION OF REVENUE

The concept of *revenue* originated in ancient times from the simple barter transactions involving goods and services between individuals. As societies matured and business organizations evolved, it was necessary to identify events and transactions that resulted in inflows of economic resources from customers (revenue) and to measure the value of such inflows in terms of a uniform standard of measurement such as money. In today's more complex and uncertain business environment, accountants are faced with the same two tasks relating to revenue—to determine *when revenue is realized* and the *dollar amount at which it is recognized* in the accounting records. Because of new and frequently complex ways of structuring business transactions, and because of the many new products and services developed in recent years, revenue recognition has become one of the most challenging problems in financial accounting.

The objective of any business enterprise is to generate income that will provide owners with a return on their investment. The major source of income for most enterprises is from its operations—the process of generating revenue by providing goods and services to outsiders. Operations involve the incurring of costs and expenses, and unless a satisfactory level of revenue is generated a loss or a low level of income will result, no matter how carefully costs and expenses are controlled. Consequently, the meaning of *revenue* and the criteria for its recognition are important not only to accountants but also to the enterprise and to the users of its financial statements.

Definition of Terms

Before undertaking the discussion of revenue recognition, a brief description of the following terms may be helpful:

Revenue   The Financial Accounting Standards Board has defined *revenue* as the inflow or other enhancement of assets of a business enterprise or settlements of its liabilities (or a combination of both) during an accounting period from delivering or producing goods, rendering services, or other activities that constitute the enterprise's ongoing major or central operations.[2] Revenue generally results in increases in cash and receivables. Examples of revenue items include sales, fees, gate receipts, interest, dividends, rents, and royalties.

Realization   A common definition of *realization* is the process of converting non-cash assets to cash or claims to cash. In the measurement of revenue, *realization* generally means that a measurable transaction (such as a sale) or an event (such as the rendering of services) has been completed or is sufficiently finalized to warrant the recording of earned revenue in the accounting records. The selection of the *critical event* indicating that revenue has been realized (earned) is the foundation of the revenue realization principle.

Revenue Recognition   The process of formally recording revenue in the accounting records is called *revenue recognition.* Before revenue is recognized it must be realized (or realizable) and measurable with sufficient reliability; thus, only realized and measurable revenue appears in a business enterprise's income statement.

Earning Process   The profit-directed activities of a business enterprise through which revenue is earned is known as the *earning process;* such activities may include purchasing, manufacturing, selling, rendering services, delivering and servicing products sold, allowing others to use enterprise resources, etc.

Conceptual Foundations of Revenue Recognition

Revenue is the measurable value of goods and services that a business enterprise transfers to its customers and clients, and realization refers to the *timing of revenue recognition.* A practical working rule is needed to signal that revenue has been earned as a result of the enterprise's profit-directed activities. Each step in the earning process is essential to the earning of revenue. Ideally, the recognition of revenue should be *continuous* rather than being tied to a *single critical event* (such as the completion of a sale transaction) in the revenue-generating activities of the enterprise. In fact, increases in the value of the goods and services (output) produced by the enterprise take place continuously throughout the earning process. However, because continuous valuation of the output is not practical, alternative procedures must be found to measure these increases as objectively as possible in order to measure realized revenue.

Revenue Realization Conditions   When a business enterprise acquires asset services, accountants assume an *even exchange* of values; that is, that no gain or loss occurs at the time of acquisition. An arm's-length *exchange price* is viewed as the best evidence of value received at the time a cost is incurred. When accountants trace the flow of costs internally, the assumption of an even exchange continues to control accounting procedures. For example, the allocation of material, direct labor, and factory overhead costs to inventories is limited to the actual costs incurred, and the fact that there may be increases in the value of the output beyond the costs added

---

[2]Ibid., pp. 31–32.

is ignored. However, somewhere along the line reliable evidence will arise that the value of the output is greater (or possibly less) than the costs incurred in producing the output. When such evidence becomes conclusive, the value of the output is measured and revenue emerges. Thus, revenue is recognized in financial accounting at a specific stage of the earning process, generally when the following three *revenue realization conditions* are met:

1   Sufficient *reliable evidence* exists to *measure* the market value of the output; such evidence generally is provided by an *exchange transaction* between independent parties. The *economic substance* of the transaction indicates that an exchange has occurred; mere *legal form* of an exchange does not support revenue realization.

2   The *earning process* (in essence the creation of goods and services) *is complete or virtually complete,* and all necessary costs have been incurred or may be estimated with reasonable accuracy.

3   *Collection* of the claims from customers and clients who have purchased goods and services *is reasonably assured.*

Many of today's revenue-generating transactions are complex and involve considerable uncertainty. Consequently, the implementation of the revenue realization principle is hardly a routine matter. Accountants must exercise professional judgment in the evaluation of the economic substance of a revenue-generating transaction and the evidence supporting it. In the sale of a product, for example, the seller must transfer all or substantially all risks of owning the product to the purchaser. Accountants must be especially careful not to recognize revenue prematurely or when a substantive exchange transaction is not present. Transactions between *related parties* and transactions without economic substance are not a source of realized revenue. A thorough understanding of the earning process and the costs involved in realizing revenue is essential before revenue is recognized. Finally, recognition of revenue is not appropriate when a relatively high probability exists that the claims from customers and clients will not be collected.

The Role of Evidence, Estimates, and Professional Judgment   In Chapter 2 we state that changes in assets and liabilities, and related changes in revenue and expenses, result either from *external transactions and events* or from *internal events.* Acquisitions of asset services, hiring and paying employees, sales of goods and services, borrowing funds, and issuing shares of capital stock are examples of market transactions between a business enterprise and outsiders. Such transactions stem from express or implied contracts and generally represent exchanges between independent parties at arm's-length prices supported by *external evidence.*

Internal events, such as accruals of revenue and cost allocations, leave a less distinct trail of *internal evidence.* In such revenue and expense recognition situations accountants face some difficult problems. For example, the amounts spent for material, labor, and other services may be measured objectively; however, the continuous transformation of these cost inputs into more valuable outputs is an internal process that requires estimates based on subjective judgment. In tracing the effect of this process and portraying it in terms of dollars, accountants do not have objective external evidence supporting market transactions as a basis for measurement and recording.

Whether revenue and expenses are recognized based on external or internal evidence, accountants nevertheless rely on *estimates* and *professional judgment* in making many revenue and expense recognition decisions. However, generally accepted accounting principles provide few guidelines for making estimates and for exercising professional judgment in specific revenue and expense recognition situations. As you study the topics in this chapter, remember that accounting is an *art*, not a *science*.

Pressures for Speeding Up Revenue Recognition In an effort to enhance their ability to attract capital, some companies are tempted to recognize revenue at the earliest possible stage in the earning process. Instances of fictitious sales and sales to related parties lacking economic substance have been attributed to middle management personnel anxious to meet sales quotas and earnings performance goals set by top management. Although income may be overstated by deferral of costs as well as by premature recognition of revenue, the latter probably provides more opportunities for creative interpretations of accounting principles, a practice known as "cooking the books."

Because of the emergence of many innovative sales and sales financing arrangements in recent years, revenue recognition practices for the sale of products frequently occupy center stage in some widely discussed cases of income manipulation. Today, accountants face a more difficult problem than ever before in determining when a "sale" has taken place and when a "service" has been substantially performed. In the following sections we discuss and illustrate the various stages of the earning process at which revenue may be recognized.

Revenue Recognized at Time of Sale and Delivery

In actual business situations, the most widely accepted evidence of revenue realization is the sale and delivery of a product or the performance of a service. There is little question about the reliability of evidence, because an arm's-length transaction has taken place that transfers title and possession of a product in return for cash or the expectation to receive cash. The transaction determines both the *time* at which to recognize revenue and the *amount* at which to record it.

One may question why accountants choose so late a stage in the earning process to recognize revenue and thus net income. The answer comes in two parts: (1) At any point prior to sale, the expected selling price of a product and the ability to sell it at a profit may be so uncertain that they do not constitute sufficient evidence to justify an upward valuation of the product, and (2) for most business enterprises the actual sale of a product is the most important step—the critical event—in the earning process. Until a sale is made and the product is delivered to and accepted by the customer, the future stream of revenue is both uncertain and unearned.

Shipments of goods on consignment do not constitute sales. In a *consignment*, goods are transferred to another party (the *consignee*), who acts as an agent for the owner of the goods (the *consignor*). Title to the goods remains with the owner until the agent sells the goods to ultimate consumers, at which time a sales transaction takes place and revenue is recognized by the consignor.

Revenue Recognition When Right of Return Exists   Even when a sale occurs, the recognition of revenue may be delayed because of unusual terms surrounding the sales transaction. For example, in the recorded music and book publishing industries it is common practice to give retail stores the *right to return* products sold and delivered to them if they cannot resell these products. When such a right of return exists, the seller continues to be exposed to the usual risks of ownership, and revenue is recognized on the date of sale only if *all of the following conditions are met:*[3]

1   The seller's price to the buyer is substantially fixed or determinable on the date of sale.

2   The buyer has paid the seller, or is obligated to pay the seller and the obligation is not contingent on resale of the product.

3   The buyer's obligation to the seller would not be changed in the event of theft or physical destruction or damage of the product.

4   The buyer acquiring the product for resale has economic substance apart from that provided by the seller.

5   The seller does not have significant obligations for future performance to bring about resale of the product by the buyer.

6   The amount of future returns can be reasonably estimated.

If these conditions are met and sales are recorded, provision for any costs or losses that may be expected in connection with any returns is made on the date of sale. The sales and cost of goods sold in the income statement exclude the portion for which returns are expected, and the allowance for estimated returns is deducted from trade accounts receivable in the balance sheet. Transactions for which revenue recognition is postponed are recorded as sales when the return privilege expires.

Sales on Installment Plan   A sale of goods or services on the installment plan generally provides for a cash down payment and a series of additional monthly payments. Because payments extend over a long period, the seller customarily charges interest and carrying charges on the unpaid balance of installment receivables. Revenue from installment sales is recorded in the same manner as from regular sales, unless the collection of the installment receivables is not assured and there is no reasonable basis for estimating the probability of collection. If the accrual basis of accounting is not considered appropriate, an alternative method of revenue recognition such as the installment method or the cost recovery method (discussed on pages 113–115), must be used.

Thus, even though the completion of a sale has been widely accepted as a prerequisite to the recognition of revenue, the preceding discussion indicates that "sale and delivery" and "revenue recognition" are not necessarily synonymous. In

[3]*FASB Statement No. 48,* "Revenue Recognition When Right of Return Exists," FASB (Stamford: 1981), pp. 2–3. See also: *FASB Statement No. 49,* "Accounting for Product Financing Arrangements," FASB (Stamford: 1981), pp. 1–5.

some situations, accountants may record revenue at other stages of the earning process, such as *before* or *after* delivery of the product. These and other revenue recognition situations are discussed in the following sections.

Revenue Recognition Before Delivery

We have seen that revenue must be realized before it is recognized in the accounting records. Generally, realization does not occur unless a sale has taken place. However, in some cases revenue is considered realized before the product is delivered to customers because a sale and a significant portion of the earning process, that is, performance by the seller, have taken place. Although performance by the seller is not completed, the amount of the partial performance may be both economically relevant and measurable. Under such circumstances, the postponement of revenue recognition until delivery of the product would be overly conservative and would assign the entire profit on the sale to the accounting period in which delivery is made. This may result in a shifting of income among periods and produce misleading financial statements.

Thus, accountants are faced with a perplexing question: When a sale occurs but is not considered to result in revenue realization, at what stage in the productive (earning) process might revenue be recognized? Possible answers to this question are: (1) prior to production, (2) during production, (3) on completion of production, and (4) at some other stage based, for example, on production, accretion, discovery, receipt of orders from customers, or billing of customers. These approaches to revenue recognition are discussed below.

Prior to Production An agreement to enter in an exchange of property rights on a future date is a *contract to sell,* not a *contract of sale* in which property rights are exchanged between a seller and a purchaser. Neither a contract to sell nor a contract of sale without performance by the seller is a transaction that signals the realization of revenue.

Contracts to sell and contracts of sale in advance of production are common in many industries. For example, motion pictures, agricultural products, fashion goods, recorded music, and computer products may be ''presold'' for future delivery, perhaps months in advance of actual production. Such transactions should be entered in the accounting records in memorandum form, or not at all, unless a deposit is received by the seller. When a deposit is received, it is carried in a liability ledger account until the sale is completed and the goods are delivered to the purchaser, at which time a sale is recorded and revenue emerges.

Magazine subscriptions, insurance premiums, rents, and fees for most services may be received in advance of production or performance of the goods or services. Amounts received by the sellers of such goods or services represent deferred revenue (a liability) until delivery or performance takes place.

During Production When revenue is generated from a large project such as the construction of a dam or a bridge, for example, that requires two or more years to complete, production is the major element in the earning process. The contract for such a project generally specifies a fixed price, and completion of the ''sale'' is dependent only on the satisfactory performance by the contractor. If the revenue on such a contract were to be recognized only on completion of the project, a distorted pattern of net income may result for the years the project was in progress. A better matching of effort (costs incurred) and accomplishment (the portion of the contract price considered realized) is achieved by using the *percentage-of-completion method* of accounting for construction-type contracts.

Under the percentage-of-completion method of accounting for construction-type contracts, revenue is recognized based on the amount of work (production) completed each year. Costs incurred each year are deducted from realized contract revenue to measure the gross profit earned in that year. The portion of the contract completed generally is measured by comparing the costs incurred to date with the total estimated costs of completing the contract. Thus, use of the percentage-of-completion method for revenue recognition is appropriate only when the actual costs incurred may be measured with reasonable precision and the estimate of the additional costs required to complete the contract is reasonably reliable.

To illustrate the percentage-of-completion method of revenue recognition for construction-type contracts, assume that in Year 1 Mori Company contracted to construct a dam for a fixed price of $10 million. In Year 1, Mori incurred costs of $2.2 million and expects to incur additional costs of $6.6 million to complete the contract. Mori's income statement for Year 1 includes the following contract revenue, costs, and gross profit relating to this contract:

Income statement amounts for first year of construction-type contract under percentage-of-completion method

Contract revenue ($10,000,000 × $2.2/$8.8)	*$2,500,000*
Less: Costs incurred	*2,200,000*
Gross profit	*$ 300,000*

At the end of Year 1, total costs to complete the contract are estimated at $8.8 million ($2.2 + $6.6 = $8.8). Thus, the percentage of completion to date is 25% ($2.2 ÷ $8.8 = 0.25), and 25% of the contract price of $10 million is recognized as contract revenue.

In Year 2, Mori incurred costs of $5 million on the contract, for a total to date of $7.2 million ($2.2 + $5.0 = $7.2), and it estimates that additional costs of $1.8 million will be incurred in Year 3 to complete the contract. Thus, at the end of Year 2 the total costs are estimated at $9 million ($7.2 + $1.8 = $9.0). Based on this information, Mori's income statement for Year 2 includes the following amounts:

Income statement amounts for second year of construction-type contract under percentage-of-completion method

Contract revenue [($10,000,000 × $7.2/$9.0) −$2,500,000	
recognized in Year 1]	*$5,500,000*
Less: Costs incurred	*5,000,000*
Gross profit	*$ 500,000*

At the end of Year 2, evidence indicates that total costs on the contract will be $9 million, a $0.2 million increase from the $8.8 million estimated at the end of Year 1. Costs of $7.2 million have been incurred through the end of Year 2, indicating that the project is 80% ($7.2 ÷ $9.0 = 0.80) completed. Therefore, 80% or $8 million of the contract price of $10 million is considered realized in the first two years, and because $2.5 million of contract revenue had been previously recognized in Year 1, only $5.5 million ($8.0 − $2.5 = $5.5) of contract revenue is recognized in Year 2.

In Year 3, Mori completed the contract by incurring additional costs of $1.75 million (compared with the earlier estimate of $1.8 million). Therefore, Mori's income statement for Year 3 includes the following amounts:

Income statement amounts for third year of construction-type contract under percentage-of-completion method

Contract revenue ($10,000,000—$8,000,000 recognized in Years 1 and 2)	$2,000,000
Less: Costs incurred	1,750,000
Gross profit	$ 250,000

Accounting for construction-type contracts is discussed in detail in Chapter 9; therefore, we purposely have limited our discussion to the use of the percentage-of-completion method for the recognition of contract revenue based on production. Discussion of the completed-contract method of accounting, progress billings to customers, treatment of projected losses, journal entries, and financial statement issues related to construction-type contracts is deferred to Chapter 9.

On Completion of Production   In some instances the recognition of revenue is delayed until production is completed, even though a contract of sale had occurred earlier. For construction-type contracts in which the use of the percentage-of-completion method is not appropriate, revenue is recognized when the project is essentially completed, under the *completed-contract method*. If the entire revenue is recognized on completion of production, any remaining "touch-up" costs should be accrued to achieve a proper matching of costs and revenue.

When special-order goods are produced to rigid customer specifications, or when customers request that delivery of goods be delayed for their convenience, title generally passes to customers as soon as such goods are produced. In such circumstances, revenue appropriately is recognized on completion of production.

Other Methods   In unusual circumstances, it may be argued that revenue is realized before delivery of the product because the economic wealth of the seller has increased. Although this line of reasoning may have some conceptual merit, accountants generally have rejected the notion that revenue accrues before performance by the seller is essentially complete or in absence of an arm's-length sales transaction. Such an approach would violate the revenue realization conditions discussed earlier in this chapter. Some additional methods that have been proposed, and generally rejected, for the realization of revenue prior to delivery of the product are the following:

1   *Production*   This method is similar to the completed-contract method used for construction-type contracts, except that a *sales transaction is absent*. In the mining and refining of precious metals, or in the manufacture of other products that have a ready market at assured prices, the completion of production may be viewed as a source of realized revenue.

2   Accretion Revenue may be considered realized as certain products, such as agricultural commodities, increase in value through the various stages from planting to harvesting. This method also has been proposed for livestock, timber, and cultured products such as fish and mushrooms. Under accrual accounting, ''accretion'' in value does not fit the definition of revenue; *it is a potential source of revenue*.

3   Discovery It is occasionally suggested that revenue results from the discovery of valuable deposits of ore or crude oil by business enterprises engaged in extractive industries. As in the case of accretion, ''discovery'' does not result in realized revenue because there is no sales transaction to provide reliable evidence for the measurement of revenue.

4   Receipt of Order Some business enterprises in the book publishing, mail-order, and computer hardware industries, for example, record sales at the time orders from customers are received. This method of revenue recognition may be appropriate in rare cases when firm orders are accompanied by substantial and nonreturnable cash deposits or when legal title to the products ordered passes to purchasers when orders are received. For financial accounting, receipt of an order seldom is viewed as a ''critical event,'' signalling the realization of revenue.

5   Billing A variation of the receipt-of-order method is to record sales when customers are billed, which may precede shipments to customers by several weeks. If the amount of such prematurely recorded sales are not material at the end of an accounting period, there is no serious distortion of revenue and net income; however, there is no theoretical support for use of the billing date to recognize revenue. Even though the billing generally is based on an existing sales contract, it is not a ''critical event,'' and the sales transaction is not considered completed.

The recognition of revenue prior to delivery generally is viewed as a departure from the revenue realization principle. Recognition of revenue on construction-type contracts under the percentage-of-completion method or on completion of ''special-order'' goods has considerable theoretical and practical support. In such cases a sale has occurred but delivery has not. Therefore, in the absence of a sales transaction, arguments supporting revenue recognition based on production, accretion, or discovery generally are rejected by accountants.

Revenue Recognition After Delivery

As stated in the preceding section, the most widely accepted evidence of revenue realization is the sale and delivery of products or the performance of services. However, in the case of product sales, revenue recognition may be delayed until some stage in the earning process subsequent to sale and delivery because the sale and delivery may not provide sufficient evidence of revenue realization. In such instances revenue may be recorded under the installment method, the cost recovery method, or some other method based on cash collections. These methods are discussed in the following sections.

Installment Method Business enterprises that sell goods on the installment plan may use the *installment method* of accounting only when accrual accounting is not considered appropriate. The installment method is widely used for income tax purposes because it postpones the payment of income taxes until installment receivables are collected. However, the installment method is not acceptable for financial accounting unless considerable doubt exists as to the collectibility of the receivables and a reasonable estimate of doubtful accounts expense cannot be made.[4]

Under the installment method, the seller recognizes gross profit on sales in proportion to the cash collected. If the rate of gross profit on installment sales is 40%, each dollar of cash collected on the installment receivables represents 40 cents of gross profit and 60 cents of cost recovery. For example, assume that Galeria Sales Company sold merchandise on the installment plan for $400,000 in Year 1, and that the cost of the merchandise sold was $240,000, or 60% of selling price. The terms of a typical sale required a down payment and 24 equal monthly payments. The cash collected, recovery of cost, and realized gross profit on these sales for Galeria Sales Company are summarized below:

Analysis of cash collected on installment receivables

Year	Cash collected (A)	Recovery of cost, 60% (B)	Realized gross profit, 40% (A − B)
1	$180,000	$108,000	$ 72,000
2	150,000	90,000	60,000
3	70,000	42,000	28,000
Totals	$400,000	$240,000	$160,000

Galeria Sales Company uses the perpetual inventory system, and adopted the installment method because it could not make a reasonable estimate of the collectibility of the installment receivables. Deferred interest and carrying charges on the installment receivables are disregarded for purposes of this illustration, and we have assumed that Galeria Sales eventually collected all receivables from these sales.

The journal entries during the three-year period for Galeria Sales Company under the installment method of accounting are presented on page 114.

Installment receivables from revenue transactions are included among current assets in the balance sheet. The balance in the Deferred Gross Profit (Year 1 Installment Sales) ledger account may be deducted from the receivables as a valuation account or included among current liabilities as a deferred revenue item. Reporting the deferred gross profit as a valuation account is preferred by the authors because it is more in concert with the reason for use of the installment method—absence of reasonable assurance that the full amount of the receivables will be collected.

Under the procedures illustrated above, the entire revenue and cost of goods sold are included in the income statement in the year installment sales are made, and the unrealized gross profit of $88,000 ($220,000 × 0.40 = $88,000) applicable to installment receivables outstanding at the end of Year 1 is deferred (deducted from

[4]*APB Opinion No. 10,* "Omnibus Opinion—1966," AICPA (New York: 1966) p. 149.

GALERIA SALES COMPANY
Journal Entries—Installment Method of Accounting
For Years 1, 2, and 3

Ledger accounts and explanation of transactions	Year 1		Year 2		Year 3	
	Debit	Credit	Debit	Credit	Debit	Credit
Installment Receivables	400,000					
Cost of Installment Sales	240,000					
Installment Sales		400,000				
Inventories		240,000				
To record installment sales and cost of installment sales.						
Installment Sales	400,000					
Cost of Installment Sales ...		240,000				
Deferred Gross Profit						
(Year 1 Installment Sales) .		160,000				
To record deferred gross profit at end of Year 1.						
Cash	180,000		150,000		70,000	
Installment Receivables		180,000		150,000		70,000
To record cash collections.						
Deferred Gross Profit (Year 1 Installment Sales)	72,000		60,000		28,000	
Realized Gross Profit on						
Installment Sales		72,000		60,000		28,000
To record realized gross profit on installment sales at 40% of cash collections.						

total gross profit) and is recognized in Year 2 and Year 3 as the receivables are collected. In the income statements for Year 2 and Year 3, the gross profit realized from Year 1 installment sales is added to each year's gross profit from regular sales.

An alternative procedure suggested by some accountants is to record revenue and cost of goods sold only as the installment receivables are collected. This approach would produce the following results for Galeria Sales Company:

	Year 1	Year 2	Year 3
Installment sales	$180,000	$150,000	$ 70,000
Cost of goods sold (60%)	108,000	90,000	42,000
Gross profit on sales (40%)	$ 72,000	$ 60,000	$ 28,000

If this approach is used, no ledger account for deferred gross profit is required, because the difference between the deferred portion of installment sales and the deferred cost of goods sold represents the amount of gross profit deferred.

Application of the installment method is complicated by variations in the gross profit rates from year to year, repossessions of goods sold on the installment plan, uncollectible installment receivables, interest and carrying charges on the receivables, and trade-in allowances. These issues are covered in *Modern Advanced Accounting* of this series; our purpose here is to focus attention on the revenue recognition aspect of the installment method of accounting.

Cost Recovery and Deposit Methods   The *cost recovery* and *deposit* methods may be used to account for revenue transactions when the terms of such transactions are ambiguous or the financial position of customers is so unstable as to make it virtually impossible to evaluate the collectibility of the related receivables. Under the *cost recovery method,* no profit is recognized until the cost of the products sold is fully recovered. In the period of sale, the cost of the products is deducted from sales (net of the deferred gross profit) in the income statement. The deferred gross profit also is deducted from the related receivables in the balance sheet. Collections of principal reduce the receivables, and any collections of interest are credited to the deferred gross profit ledger account. Deferred gross profit subsequently recognized as earned is presented as a separate item of revenue in the income statement.

A situation in which the cost recovery method may be appropriate is in the sale of recreational land. Such sales often are made to individuals who make only nominal down payments, have poor credit standing, and are able to cancel the sale at any time without penalty, other than the loss of the payments already made. In many states a seller has no legal right to take any action against customers other than to repossess the land. Because the seller has performed but the customer's ability to carry out the terms of the sale are very much in doubt in such cases, use of the cost recovery method of revenue recognition would be appropriate.

When a sales transaction is for any reason incomplete, performance by either the seller or the purchaser has not taken place. Even though the parties fully intend to consummate a sale, certain contingencies may have to be resolved before a sale is completed. Such contingencies may include the obtaining of permits or financing. Any cash received by the seller in such a ''potential sale'' is a deposit from customers rather than revenue. Thus, under the *deposit method,* cash received from customers is a liability (advances from customers) until the sale is completed. On completion of the sale, the liability is transferred to a revenue account, consistent with an appropriate revenue recognition method, for example, the accrual method, the installment method, or the cost recovery method.

Cash Collection Method   The recognition of revenue may be delayed beyond the point of sale until additional evidence confirms the sales transaction. For example, a significant degree of uncertainty may exist as to the collectibility of receivables resulting from revenue transactions, or a sales transaction may be lacking in economic substance and therefore may offer inadequate evidence of revenue realization. Under these circumstances revenue is recognized as cash is collected, and costs incurred are either recognized as expenses or deferred, as considered appropriate in a specific situation.

An extreme application of this test of revenue realization is the *cash basis of accounting* described in Chapter 1. In its most unrefined state, the cash basis of accounting calls for the recognition of revenue only when cash is received and for the recognition of expenses only when cash is paid. As previously pointed out, revenue recognition under the *installment* and *cost recovery* methods of accounting is based to a considerable extent on the timing of cash receipts.

Other Revenue Recognition Situations

New industries and new ways of structuring business transactions have focused public attention on numerous instances of "managed" and "manipulated" earnings, frequently as a result of creative approaches to the recognition of revenue. Financial statements issued by companies engaged in leasing, real estate development, banking, franchising, motion picture distribution, network television programming, and the assembly of computers and mobile homes frequently have been viewed as misleading because of the revenue recognition practices adopted by these companies. Because of the apparent obsession with growth in earnings on the part of corporate managements and investors, and because creativity is a pervasive human trait, it is likely that more examples of "cute accounting" in the area of revenue measurement and recognition will surface in the future.

The topics discussed in this section address a few additional revenue recognition situations encountered by accountants in today's business world.

Revenue from Service Transactions   Despite the large growth in service industries in the United States, the accounting for service transactions has received relatively little attention. Enterprises operating in service industries sell services, perform acts, agree to perform certain acts on a later date, or permit their resources to be used by others. Collectively these revenue-generating activities are called *service transactions*. Examples of service enterprises include advertising and other types of agencies, computer services organizations, entertainment enterprises, banks, public accounting and law firms, hospitals, stock and real estate brokerage firms, and leasing and franchising enterprises. For the most part service enterprises are small and privately owned; however, some are quite large and are publicly owned.

Generally, revenue is recognized from a service transaction when the provider has performed. *Performance* consists of the completion of a specified act or acts, or occurs with the passage of time. The following four methods of revenue recognition for service transactions have been suggested:[5]

1   *Specific-Performance Method*   This method is similar to the sales method of revenue recognition for product sales and is appropriate when a service transaction consists of a single act; revenue is recognized at the time the act is performed. Examples of single acts include all types of entertainment performances, the sale of real property for a commission, and placement of a candidate on a job by an employment agency.

---

[5]The discussion in this section is based on *Invitation to Comment,* "Accounting for Certain Service Transactions," FASB (Stamford: 1978).

2 *Completed-Performance Method* This method is similar to the completed-contract method of revenue recognition for construction-type contracts. It is used when the amount of services to be performed in the *last of a series of acts is so significant* in relation to the entire service transaction that performance is not deemed to have occurred until the final act is completed. For example, an enterprise hired to move household furniture may pack, load, store, and deliver the furniture to its destination, but the act of delivery is so significant that the recognition of revenue is deferred until delivery is essentially completed.

3 *Proportional-Performance Method* This method is used when a service transaction consists of (*a*) a specified number of similar acts, (*b*) a specified number of dissimilar acts, or (*c*) an unspecified number of similar acts with a fixed period for performance. The implementation of this method requires considerable judgment to determine the appropriate pattern of revenue recognition. Examples in which this method may be used are: A mortgage banker's processing monthly mortgage payments (specific number of similar acts); a correspondence school's preparation and mailing of lessons, grading of completed lessons, administration of examinations, and grading of examinations (specified number of dissimilar acts); and health clubs' sale of three-year memberships for unlimited use of its facilities (unspecified number of similar acts with a fixed period for performance).

When the number of similar acts is specified, an equal amount of revenue is recognized for each act expected to be performed; when the number of acts is specified but the acts are dissimilar, revenue is recognized based on the ratio of the direct costs incurred to the total estimated direct costs of the entire transaction; when the number of similar acts is unspecified and the period of performance is fixed, revenue is recognized ratably over the period of performance, unless evidence indicates that another method is more consistent with the observable pattern of performance.

4 *Cash-Collection Method* Revenue should be recognized only as cash is collected when considerable doubt exists that the revenue will be collected. This method is similar to the installment and cost recovery methods of revenue recognition for sales of goods on the installment plan.

A wide range of revenue recognition practices for service transactions has been used in the past, but more precise standards currently are being developed by the Financial Accounting Standards Board. The recognition of expenses for service transactions is discussed on pages 125–126.

Revenue from Franchise Sales In the early years of the franchising industry it was common practice for a *franchisor* to recognize revenue at the time it sold a *franchise* (the exclusive right to engage in a business, such as a fast-foods outlet, in a specific geographic location) to a *franchisee.* In some cases the contract of sale required the franchisor to assist the franchisee to locate a site, train a work staff, commence operations, and provide consulting and other services for a specified number of years. In return, the franchisor generally received cash and promissory notes from the franchisee as an *initial franchise fee.* The collectibility of the promissory notes in most cases was dependent on the business success of the franchisee.

Earnings of franchisors rose rapidly as they sold new franchises because the promissory notes and the franchise fee revenue were recorded at the face amount of the notes. This abuse of the revenue realization principle was curtailed when long-term notes receivable were required to be recorded at the discounted present value computed by use of an appropriate current rate of interest rather than at face amount.

Although the discounting of the promissory notes reduced the opportunities for the *front-ending of income,* it did not answer the question of when the franchise fee revenue should be recognized. The main objectives in accounting for franchising contracts are: (1) to determine the point in the earning process when the franchise fee revenue is realized, (2) to measure the amount of franchise fee revenue to be recognized, and (3) to evaluate the collectibility of the promissory notes representing the unpaid portion of the franchise fee. Depending on the contractual provisions and circumstances surrounding the sale of a franchise, the initial franchise fee may be recognized as cash is received, ratably over the term of the franchise contract, or at the inception of the franchise contract. The principles for the recognition of franchise fee revenue are stated in *FASB Statement No. 45,* ''Accounting for Franchise Fee Revenue,'' as follows:[6]

> Franchise fee revenue from an individual franchise sale ordinarily shall be recognized, with an appropriate provision for estimated uncollectible amounts, when all material services or conditions relating to the sale have been substantially performed or satisfied by the franchisor. Substantial performance for the franchisor means that (a) the franchisor has no remaining obligation or intent—by agreement, trade practice, or law—to refund any cash received or forgive any unpaid notes or receivables; (b) substantially all of the *initial services* of the franchisor required by the franchise agreement have been performed; and (c) no other material conditions or obligations related to the determination of substantial performance exist. . . . The commencement of operations by the franchisee shall be presumed to be the earliest point at which substantial performance has occurred, unless it can be demonstrated that substantial performance of all obligations, including services rendered voluntarily, has occurred before that time.
>
> Installment or cost recovery accounting methods shall be used to account for franchise fee revenue only in those exceptional cases when revenue is collectible over an extended period and no reasonable basis exists for estimating collectibility.

To illustrate the accounting for one possible form of a franchise sale, assume the following:

(1) On January 2, Year 1, Burito King, Inc., sold a franchise to El Paso Company for an initial fee of $100,000, payable $20,000 down and $40,000 on December 31, Year 1, and on December 31, Year 2. Two promissory notes with a face amount of $40,000 each were issued by El Paso to Burito King.

---

[6]*FASB Statement No. 45,* ''Accounting for Franchise Fee Revenue,'' FASB (Stamford: 1981), pp. 2–3.

(2) The current fair rate of interest on January 2, Year 1, was 12%, and the present value of the two notes discounted at 12% was $67,602 ($40,000 ÷ 1.12 = $35,714; $35,714 ÷ 1.12 = $31,888; $35,714 + $31,888 = $67,602). Burito King considers the notes to be fully collectible.

(3) Burito King will provide substantial services to El Paso in opening the franchise and in operating it during the initial year. The cash down payment is not refundable; however, the additional payment of $40,000 on December 31, Year 1, will be paid by El Paso only if the franchise is opened or nearly ready to be opened on that date, and the final payment of $40,000 on December 31, Year 2, will be paid only if the franchise is operating profitably on that date. Burito King appropriately considers the value of the services and other consideration transferred to El Paso on January 2, Year 1, to be worth at least $20,000. The value of services provided by Burito King in Year 1 and Year 2 is approximately equal each year.

(4) The franchise was opened by El Paso in December of Year 1, and was operating profitably on December 31, Year 2; El Paso paid $40,000 to Burito King on each of these dates.

The journal entries for Burito King, Inc., to record the foregoing transactions are as follows:

BURITO KING, INC.
Journal Entries for Year 1 and Year 2

Year 1

Jan. 2

Cash	20,000	
Notes Receivable	80,000	
Franchise Fee Revenue		20,000
Discount on Notes Receivable		
($80,000 − $67,602)		12,398
Deferred Franchise Fee Revenue		67,602
To record sale of franchise to El Paso Company.		

Dec. 31

Cash	40,000	
Discount on Notes Receivable		
[($80,000 − $12,398) × 0.12)]	8,112	
Deferred Franchise Fee Revenue		
($67,602 ÷ 2)	33,801	
Notes Receivable		40,000
Interest Revenue		8,112
Franchise Fee Revenue		33,801
To record collection of note receivable from El Paso Company, and to recognize realized interest and franchise fee revenue.		

Year 2

Dec. 31 Cash 40,000
         Discount on Notes Receivable
           ($12,398 − $8,112) 4,286
         Deferred Franchise Fee Revenue 33,801
               Notes Receivable 40,000
               Interest Revenue 4,286
               Franchise Fee Revenue 33,801
         To record collection of note receivable from El
         Paso Company, and to recognize realized
         interest and franchise fee revenue.

Because cash of $20,000 was received and the current fair value of the promissory note is $67,602, the amount of franchise fee revenue to be recognized as services are provided by Burito King, Inc., over the two-year period is $87,602 ($20,000 + $67,602 = $87,602). Of this amount, $20,000 is considered realized on the date the franchise is sold, and the balance of $67,602 is considered realized equally in Year 1 and Year 2 because equal amounts of services were provided in each year. The discount on notes receivable is recognized as interest revenue, computed at 12% of the carrying amount (face amount less discount) of the notes at the beginning of each year. If the notes were initially recorded at face amount, interest revenue would be understated by $12,398 and franchise fee revenue would be overstated by the same amount over the two-year period; however, the amount of total revenue in each year would differ because franchise fee revenue and interest revenue are recognized in different patterns.

Revenue from Sales-Type Leases   When a lease contract meets the criteria of a *sales-type lease,* the lease is recorded by the *lessor* as a sale, and the entire consideration received is recognized as revenue at the time the lease becomes effective. The consideration received generally consists of the present value of the monthly payments to be made by the *lessee* over the term of the lease.

As stated earlier, a lease contract is an example of a service transaction; yet in a sales-type lease the entire revenue and gross profit are recognized by the lessor despite the fact that the services from the leased asset are provided to the lessee over many years. Critics of accounting for sales-type leases argue that accountants give more weight to the *form* of the transaction than to its *economic substance.* For example, a sales-type lease may be recorded as a sale based on provisions in the lease contract transferring ownership of the leased asset to the lessee at the end of the lease term or giving the lessee an option to acquire the asset at a bargain price. In addition, the collectibility of the lease receivables recorded by the lessor must be reasonably assured, and the lease term must cover at least 75% of the economic life of the leased asset. The criticism of accounting for sales-type leases revolves around the logic of recording a sale today for a transaction that transfers ownership of the asset (already considered "sold") to the lessee perhaps ten or more years from now, or gives the lessee an option to acquire the asset (already recorded as a "sale" by the lessor) at some future date. The ability of accountants (or anyone else) to estimate the collectibility of long-term receivables and the economic lives of assets, often subject to rapid technological obsolescence, also has been questioned.

In framing the accounting principles for sales-type leases, the Financial Accounting Standards Board effectively eliminated some unacceptable accounting practices for leasing transactions. But as one writer stated, "No matter how many rules the accountants write, a smart fellow can find a way to bend them to his advantage."[7] We have discussed sales-type leases at this point not only because of their relevance to revenue recognition but also because they involve some interesting theoretical issues. A complete discussion of accounting for leases is presented in Chapter 20.

Savings and Cost Offsets Are Not Revenue

Purchases discounts and other cost savings should not be confused with revenue. Discounts available on purchases of merchandise or supplies are reductions in the cost of the assets purchased, not revenue. *Cost savings* are potential outflows of cash that a business enterprise is able to avoid, not sources of revenue. For example, suppose that a machine may be acquired either for $1,000 cash or for $1,200 on the installment plan. If the acquirer chooses the installment plan, it has acquired two types of asset services—the machine for $1,000 and the option of deferring payment for $200; if the acquirer chooses to pay cash, the $200 of avoided interest is not revenue but a cost saving.

Revenue from the sale of a by-product (or scrap) often is recorded as a reduction of the cost of the main product. The main product and the by-product emerge from a single process; thus, a portion of total manufacturing costs applies to the by-product. However, because the sales value of the by-product generally is small, an allocation of the manufacturing costs would not be "cost-efficient." Therefore, the revenue from the sale of the by-product is recorded as an *offset* to the cost of the main product. Similarly, when a plant asset is exchanged for another similar asset on terms that indicate a gain (a form of revenue) on the exchange, the gain is not considered realized but is deducted from the cost of the asset acquired.

Recognition of Gains

In financial accounting, *gains* may be defined as increases in a business enterprise's owners' equity from incidental transactions and from all other transactions and other events and circumstances except those that result from revenue or investments by owners. Gains from the disposal of assets or the extinguishment of debt generally are recognized in the accounting period in which the related transaction is considered to have resulted in the completion of the earning process. The recognition of gains must pass a more severe test than the recognition of losses because of the influence of the concept of conservatism. Except in the case of a current portfolio of marketable equity securities, gains must be "realized" (generally in the form of cash) before they are recognized; losses that are reasonably measurable are recognized even though they may not be substantiated by an arm's-length exchange transaction.

---

[7]*Forbes*, "You Better Believe," July 30, 1984, p. 112.

The recognition and income statement presentation of extraordinary gains and gains from disposals of business segments are covered in another section of this chapter. Other types of gains are discussed in subsequent chapters.

RECOGNITION OF EXPENSES

In the preceding pages our focus has been on the recognition of revenue, including gains. Similar issues arise in connection with the recognition of expenses and losses.

Expenses are outflows or other using up of assets or incurrences of liabilities during an accounting period from the sale of goods or the rendering of services. Initially, costs are incurred to acquire assets, and as assets are consumed or as the costs expire with the passage of time they become expenses.

Losses are decreases in a business enterprise's owners' equity from incidental transactions and other events and circumstances, except those that result from expenses or distributions to owners. Losses result when assets are consumed, costs expire, or liabilities are incurred without producing any discernible benefit for either the current or any future accounting period; thus, losses are never deferred because they have no future service potential.

Expenses and losses generally are recognized in the accounting records when a business enterprise's "economic benefits are consumed in revenue-earning activities or otherwise or . . . if it becomes evident that previously recognized future economic benefits of assets have been reduced or eliminated, or that liabilities have been incurred without associated economic benefits."[8]

In the measurement of net income the principles underlying the recognition of expenses and losses are as important as the principles for the recognition of revenue and gains. Before we outline the principles of expense recognition, a general discussion of the flow of costs in the operations of a business enterprise may facilitate our discussion.

The Flow of Costs

Ideally, all costs should be associated with some physical product or service. If all resources of a business enterprise are devoted to the production and sale of a single product, this approach may be reasonable, because all costs would be accumulated in inventory until the product is sold. However, even in a single-product case it is apparent that some costs are more directly related to the product than are others. The costs of direct material, direct labor, and some variable factory overhead, for example, may be traced to the product because the relationship between effort and accomplishment is relatively clear. At the other extreme, selling and administrative expenses are productive, but the relationship between effort and accomplishment is far more nebulous. In most cases it is virtually impossible to allocate these costs to specific products and accounting periods with any degree of precision. When we turn to the more realistic setting of an enterprise producing not one but many prod-

---

[8]*Statement of Financial Accounting Concepts No. 5,* "Recognition and Measurement in Financial Statements of Business Enterprises," FASB (Stamford: 1984), p. xi.

ucts and services, the difficulty of cost allocation increases. As a result, accountants must make reasonable assumptions for the allocation of costs to products and periods. It is not surprising that opinions as to what is "reasonable" in specific cases will differ.

Product and Period Costs   In the measurement of income for a manufacturing enterprise, certain *product costs* are traced to physical output and are accumulated in inventories until evidence of revenue realization is available. For example, the costs of direct material and labor used to manufacture a product *attach* to, and may be identified directly with, a unit of inventory. For a trading enterprise, product costs relate solely to the cost of goods acquired for resale; for an enterprise engaged in the sale of services, initial direct costs and direct costs (described on page 125) are analogous to product costs.

Other costs, called *period costs,* are considered expenses of the accounting period in which they occur. Period costs, such as advertising and sales salaries, generally are not related to production and are *expensed* (deducted from revenue immediately), because the benefits are received in the same period the costs are incurred.

Making a theoretical distinction between product costs and period costs may be easier than the practical application of the concept. To illustrate this problem, consider the cost of goods purchased by a merchandising enterprise. There are certain costs directly related to the purchase, such as the invoice cost of the product and freight-in. There are other indirect costs of purchasing, handling, storage, and display. The salary of a purchasing agent is an example, and decisions on the treatment of such costs are likely to differ among enterprises and often are resolved on the grounds of expediency. However, if the costs are material in amount, different practices may lead to significantly different net income amounts.

In addition to the distinction between product costs and period costs, another issue arises when identical goods are acquired at different prices. As the goods are sold, decisions must be made as to which costs are to be assigned to the goods sold. The decision to assume a first-in, first-out, a last-in, first-out, or a weighted-average flow of costs is somewhat arbitrary, but important, because different assumptions may produce materially different amounts of net income.

Expired Costs   Certain asset services, such as machinery and intangible assets, are acquired in advance of their use. For example, when a business enterprise acquires machinery, it acquires productive services. Some portion of the services will be used during the current accounting period; other portions will not be used for several periods. Accountants are faced with the problem of determining whether the cost of expired services is a product cost or a period cost. In addition, they are confronted with an even more perplexing question: How much of the asset services has been used during the current period, and what is the cost of the services used? In the case of material or merchandise, there is at least a physical flow of goods to indicate the changes that are taking place. In contrast, productive assets such as machinery exhibit little change in their physical condition as they provide services.

The expiration of the services of some productive assets is a function of time. If a three-year premium is paid for an insurance policy, the service acquired is three years of freedom from certain risks. It seems reasonable to assume that one-third of the cost of acquiring this service is used up in each of the three years. If the productive asset is an office building, the service acquired is floor space that may be rented to tenants. The value of the space in a new office building is greater than that of an older building, and thus the value of the services obtained from the building is greater in the early years. These facts should be considered in measuring the periodic cost (depreciation) of the building services used. Reliable evidence of the value of services used year by year is difficult to obtain. Furthermore, the economic life of the building is indefinite, and its residual value, if any, is not known. Therefore, any solution adopted for the measurement of periodic depreciation is highly subjective.

Principles of Expense Recognition

The expenses incurred by a business enterprise during an accounting period may be classified in the following three groups:[9]

1   Costs directly associated with revenue recognized in the period

2   Costs associated with the period on a basis other than a direct relationship with revenue

3   Costs that cannot reasonably be associated with any other period

The principles that provide accountants with guidelines for the recognition of expenses are: *associating cause and effect, systematic and rational allocation,* and *immediate recognition.*[10] These expense recognition principles are explained below.

Associating Cause and Effect   Costs may be recognized as expenses based on a presumed direct association with specific revenue. Costs that appear to be related to specific revenue are recognized as expenses concurrently with the recognition of the related revenue. Examples of costs related to specific revenue include the direct costs of goods sold or services provided, sales commissions, and direct costs incurred in relation to construction-type contracts. Accountants make assumptions regarding cost flows and the manner in which costs attach to products as they move through the productive process. For example, production costs may be considered to attach to products based on an association with a physical measure of activity such as labor hours or machine hours.

Systematic and Rational Allocation   If a direct means is not available to associate cause and effect, costs may be recognized as expenses based on an orderly allocation to the accounting periods in which the costs *appear to expire* and presumably provide benefits. This approach involves assumptions as to the pattern of benefits and as to the relationship between costs and benefits received, because neither can

---

[9]*Statement of the Accounting Principles Board No. 4,* ''Basic Concepts and Accounting Principles Underlying Financial Statements of Business Enterprises,'' AICPA (New York: 1970), p. 61.
[10]Ibid.

be objectively measured. The allocation bases selected should be perceived as ''reasonable'' and should be applied systematically. Examples of costs that are recognized as expenses under this principle are depreciation of plant assets, amortization of intangible assets, and allocated amounts of property taxes and insurance.

Immediate Recognition Expenses are recognized in the current accounting period when (1) costs incurred in the current period are not expected to provide any future benefit, (2) costs deferred as assets in earlier periods no longer provide benefits, and (3) allocation of costs to revenue or to accounting periods is impractical or is considered to serve no useful purpose. This principle requires research and development costs, general and administrative costs, and amounts paid to settle litigation to be recognized as expenses in the period they are incurred. Costs deferred in earlier periods that have lost their service potential (such as obsolete plant assets or worthless intangible assets) are written off as soon as the loss becomes evident and measurable.

Application of these expense recognition principles requires costs to be associated, if possible, with revenue on the basis of cause and effect; if such an association is not practical, a systematic and rational allocation of the costs is attempted; if neither of these procedures is feasible, costs are expensed as incurred or as soon as expiration of the service potential of the costs becomes evident.

Expense Recognition for Service Transactions[11]

Generally, costs are recognized as expenses in the accounting period in which the associated revenue is recognized, and costs not expected to be recovered are not deferred. In the application of this general principle to service transactions, costs may be classified in three categories as follows:

1 *Initial direct costs* are directly associated with negotiating and closing service contracts. Such costs include commissions, legal fees, costs of credit investigations, document processing fees, and a portion of any salespersons' compensation applicable to a specific service transaction. Initial direct costs do not include any portion of indirect operating expenses such as rent or supervisory and administrative salaries.

2 *Direct costs* are costs that have a clearly beneficial or causal relationship to the services performed for a specific customer or a group of customers, for example, labor and parts included in service contracts.

3 *Indirect costs* are all other costs not included in the first two categories. Such costs include selling expenses, general and administrative expenses (including doubtful accounts expense), and any costs incurred in negotiating service contracts that are not consummated. Indirect costs are recorded immediately as expenses, regardless of the method used to recognize revenue.

When revenue from service transactions is recognized under the *specific-performance method* or under the *completed-performance method,* initial direct costs

---

[11]Based on *Invitation to Comment,* ''Accounting for Certain Service Transactions,'' FASB (Stamford: 1978).

and direct costs are recognized as expenses in the accounting period that the related revenue is recognized; such costs incurred before revenue is recognized are deferred and recognized as expenses at the time the related revenue is recognized in the accounting records.

When the *proportional-performance method* of revenue recognition is used for service transactions, initial direct costs are recognized as expenses in the same manner as revenue is recognized. However, direct costs are expensed as incurred, because a close correlation generally exists between the amount of performance and the amount of direct costs incurred.

Under the *cash-collection method* of revenue recognition for service transactions, both initial direct costs and direct costs are recorded immediately as expenses because of the substantial uncertainty surrounding the collectibility of the claims from customers or clients.

Recognition of Losses

Under the accrual basis of accounting, losses are recognized in the accounting periods in which they occur as a result of transactions and other events and circumstances. Losses resulting from the disposal of assets or the retirement of debt are readily recognizable and measurable. Losses resulting from events and circumstances such as casualties, contingencies, declines in the market value of inventories and short-term investments in marketable securities, and impairments in the value of plant assets and long-term investments pose more difficult recognition problems. The current standards governing the recognition of losses resulting from events and circumstances are not highly developed and are not consistent with the standards for the recognition of gains. For example, losses from holding short-term investments in marketable equity securities are recognized, but holding gains are not. Recoveries of such losses are recognized as gains in subsequent periods, but similar recoveries of losses from write-downs of plant assets or long-term investments are not recognized as gains.

As stated earlier, the standards for the recognition of losses are less severe than the standards for the recognition of gains. For example, a loss from an exchange of a plant asset for a similar asset is recognized but a gain is not, because it is not considered realized. The recognition and income statement presentation of extraordinary losses and losses from disposals of business segments are covered in another section of this chapter; discussion of the recognition of specific types of losses (such as those resulting from contingencies and impairments in the value of plant assets and long-term investments) appear in other chapters of this book.

INCOME MEASUREMENT AND REPORTING

The concept of accounting income poses a double challenge for accountants—its *measurement* and the *reporting of its components in the income statement.* Generally accepted accounting principles rest on a foundation of historical costs and measurable evidence provided by business transactions and events, that is, the accrual basis of accounting. Accountants have considered and rejected both the *cash-basis concept* and the *economic concept* of income measurement. Yet some critics of accrual-basis income fret that such income portrays neither cash flows nor the change in a business enterprise's economic wealth. Thus, because both cash-basis income and economic income have serious shortcomings and are fundamentally incompatible, accountants have adopted the accrual basis of accounting as a reasonable approach to income measurement.

Probably no single concept of income would satisfactorily meet the widely divergent needs of various groups of users of financial statements. Perhaps some of these groups expect accountants to *measure the unmeasurable.* Some groups admit that income must *reflect past results* and at the same time they insist that income must be *predictive of future earnings performance.* In a rapidly changing and highly competitive business environment, income measurement is a complex process. In such an environment, the income for one accounting period probably predicts the income of the next period as accurately as today's score of a baseball game predicts the results of tomorrow's game between the same two teams. Furthermore, income tax laws, the effects of extraordinary items, disposals of business segments, changes in accounting principles, and the inclusion of earnings per share of common stock in the income statement further complicate the task of income measurement and reporting. These issues are discussed in the remaining pages of this chapter.

Income and the Objectives of Financial Reporting

Among the objectives of financial reporting identified by the Financial Accounting Standards Board that relate most directly to income measurement and reporting are the following:[12]

1   The primary focus of financial reporting is information about earnings and its components.

2   Information about enterprise earnings based on accrual accounting generally provides a better indication of an enterprise's present and continuing ability to generate favorable cash flows than information limited to the financial effects of cash receipts and payments.

3   Financial reporting is expected to provide information about an enterprise's financial performance during a period and about how management of an enterprise has discharged its stewardship responsibility to owners.

4   Investors, creditors, and others may use reported earnings . . . in various ways to assess the prospects for cash flows. They may wish, for example, to evaluate managements' performance, estimate "earning power," predict future earnings, assess risk, or to confirm . . . or reject earlier predictions or assessments. . . .

The highly condensed income statements issued by most publicly owned corporations probably are not achieving these objectives. In the opinion of the Financial Accounting Standards Board, better information on earnings would help users

---

[12]*Statement of Financial Accounting Concepts No. 1,* "Objectives of Financial Reporting by Business Enterprises," FASB (Stamford: 1978), p. ix.

of financial statements with their main need—the assessment of future earnings and cash flows.[13] Among the criticisms of the traditional income statement (illustrated in Chapter 4) are the following:

1   It does not provide enough information about past earnings to help users assess future earnings.

2   It does not require the separate disclosure of the effects of some unusual transactions and other events and circumstances.

3   It does not explain sufficiently the economic changes affecting the relationship between recurring revenue and expenses.

4   It places excessive emphasis on a single earnings amount, such as net income or earnings per share of common stock.

Improvements in the measurement and reporting of income are needed if income statements are to be of maximum value to users in predicting, comparing, and evaluating the earning power of business enterprises. For example, the earning of income consists of *earnings cycles* that may be *completed, incomplete,* or *prospective;* it may be useful to segregate "precisely measured results" from "estimated results." The basis of estimates might be explained so that users would be able to interpret the reported results in line with their own judgment and experience. Also, it may be useful to report the possible effects of changes in values of assets and liabilities on reported net income and to segregate expenses between fixed and variable components to help users predict cash flows and the possible effects of changes in volume of activity on future levels of net income.

The Complexity of Income Measurement

To illustrate the complexity of defining accounting income, let us assume that newly organized Pinecrest, Inc., acquired a tract of land to develop 500 lots for a residential community. The acquisition of the land required a small down payment that used up most of Pinecrest's available cash. Some of the land was level, some rolling, and some extremely steep. A golf course, riding stables, tennis courts, and a lake were to be constructed. Colorful sales brochures were prepared showing the attractiveness of the community after completion.

Residential lots were to be offered for sale by Pinecrest, Inc., with a down payment of only 3% of the selling price. Assume that 100 lots were sold with an average down payment of $400 received, along with long-term receivables calling for monthly payments of $175. How much income, if any, did Pinecrest earn when it sold the first 100 lots? The answer to this question is dependent on the answers to these related questions: How should revenue and expenses be measured? What is the value of the long-term receivables? How many of the 100 purchasers actually will make the monthly payments? What will it cost to develop roads, sewers, a lake, riding stables, and other recreational facilities? How many lots will be sold, and at

---

[13]*FASB Discussion Memorandum,* "An Analysis of Issues Relating to Reporting Earnings," FASB (Stamford: 1979), p. 1.

what prices and terms? How should the total cost of the tract be allocated among the level lots, hillside lots, and lakefront lots?

Despite all the efforts to develop concise accounting principles, a wide range of answers may be given to the question of how much income, if any, was earned by Pinecrest, Inc., from the sale of the first 100 lots. We might even question whether "sales" really took place, or whether Pinecrest was a "going concern" capable of carrying out its commitments. Assuming that Pinecrest did carry the project to a successful completion, the income (or loss) from the project then may be measured as the amount of revenue received from customers less all costs and expenses of acquiring, developing, and selling the land. However, the objective of timeliness in financial reporting requires *periodic measurement of net income* long before the project is completed. This example of a land developer illustrates some of the practical difficulties faced by accountants in the measurement of accounting income.

The Meaning of Income

In a very general sense, the objective in measuring income is to determine by how much a business enterprise has become "better off" during some period of time as a result of its operations. Economists define *income* as the maximum amount of assets that the enterprise could distribute to its owners during an accounting period and still be as well off at the end of that period as it was at the beginning. The key words in this definition are in the phrase "as well off." Anyone who studies the concept of income will soon discover that controversies over the meaning and measurement of income center on the problem of determining what the financial position of an enterprise is on a specific date, whether its position has improved or worsened during a specified period of time, and by how much.

Lifetime Income of a Business Enterprise Let us begin with a relatively simple income measurement problem. If we were asked to measure the *lifetime income* of a business enterprise at the time it was being liquidated, we could probably agree on the following computation:

Total proceeds received on liquidation of enterprise..................	$ 800,000
Add: Amounts withdrawn by owners during life of enterprise..........	300,000
Less: Amount of cash invested by owners...........................	(600,000)
Lifetime income of enterprise	$ 500,000

Lifetime income of a business enterprise

If we ignore the time value of money and effects of inflation, lifetime income of a business enterprise is easy to measure. The reason is that at the beginning and end of the life of any enterprise, the value of its net assets may be measured with reasonable accuracy. The investments by owners and the proceeds received on liquidation usually are definite amounts of cash or other assets. However, at any stage prior to final liquidation, the *net assets* of an enterprise constitute a complex set of economic resources, whose collective value depends largely on their future earning power. In theory, the only direct way to determine how "well off" an enterprise is on a specific date is to compute the present value of its future net cash inflows. This is known as the process of *direct valuation*.

Periodic Income of a Business Enterprise   Accountants readily concede their inability to determine at periodic time intervals the *direct value* of the net assets of a business enterprise. For this they should not be criticized for undue caution or modesty; they merely are being realistic about their limitations. Thus, in measuring how "well off" an enterprise is on a specific date in order to measure *periodic net income,* accountants record only those changes in financial position that may be substantiated by reasonably reliable evidence.

As stated earlier, revenue increases assets or decreases liabilities as a result of an enterprise's providing goods and services to customers and clients; expenses decrease assets or increase liabilities in the enterprise's process of generating revenue. Thus, in the process of measuring assets and liabilities, accountants are at the same time measuring income. Income emerges if the *effort* (expenses) to generate revenue is less than the *accomplishment* (revenue) of that effort; a loss emerges if the effort exceeds the accomplishment.

The Impact of Changing Prices   We have seen how revenue and expense recognition procedures affect the measurement of income. Now let us look briefly at an accounting principle that is equally fundamental—the assumption that the dollar is a *stable monetary unit* for measuring the effects of business transactions and events.

Assume that in Year 1 a business enterprise invests $80 to manufacture a product that is expected to sell for $120. The cost of producing an identical product has risen to $130 in Year 2, and because demand is strong the enterprise is able to sell the product for $180 at the end of Year 2. During Year 2, the *general price level* throughout the economy rose by 10%. The gross profit on the sale of the product might be measured in three ways as illustrated on page 131.

The *nominal-dollar* gross profit (method **1**) reflects the entire difference between revenue realized and historical cost, without regard to differences in the purchasing power of the dollar. Under method **2,** the effect of changes in *specific prices* is isolated, and the fact that one-half of nominal-dollar gross profit is attributed to rising replacement cost is disclosed. The difference between the actual cost of a product and its replacement cost at the time it is sold is known as *inventory profit.* Under method **3,** the measuring unit has been changed to *constant purchasing power;* both costs and revenue are stated in end-of-Year 2 purchasing power; thus, the gross profit in constant (end of Year 2) purchasing power is only $92, because the enterprise must now recover $88 to be as "well off" in terms of purchasing power as it was when it invested $80 in the product in Year 1.

During a period of *inflation* (an increase in the general price level), a clear understanding of the limitations of the dollar as a unit of measurement is required to interpret accounting income and financial statements meaningfully. Supplementary measurement of net income in constant purchasing power is considered in Chapter 25.

Three ways to
compute gross
profit on sale
of a product

1 *Nominal-dollar gross profit*

Revenue realized.. $180

Less: Actual cost incurred in Year 1.....................................   80

Nominal-dollar gross profit $100

2 *Nominal-dollar gross profit, with price gain isolated*

Revenue realized.. $180

Less: Replacement cost on date of sale   130

Operating margin .... $ 50

Add: Price gain or ***inventory profit*** *(the difference between replacement
cost of $130 on date of sale and actual cost of $80)*   50

Nominal-dollar gross profit *(operating margin and price gain)*............ $100

3 *Constant-purchasing power gross profit*

Revenue realized.. $180

Less: Actual cost in constant (end of Year 2) purchasing power
($80 × 1.10)   88

Gross profit in constant (end of Year 2) purchasing power .... $ 92

Special Problems in the Measurement and Reporting of Income

The measurement and reporting of income has become complex as a result of requirements for the allocation of income taxes, disposals of discontinued business segments, extraordinary items, changes in accounting principles and estimates, and the reporting of earnings per share data in the income statement. These topics are discussed briefly in the following sections.

Income Tax Allocation   Income taxes frequently constitute the largest single expense for many profitable corporations. ***Taxable income*** is a legal concept that is related to ***accounting income,*** but there are significant differences that may cause a corporation's taxable income for a specific year to differ materially from the pre-tax accounting income reported in its income statement. In addition, the total amount of income taxes expense (or credit) included in the income statement must be assigned to any nonoperating sources of income or loss. Accountants have developed extensive ***income tax allocation procedures*** to deal with these issues. At this point only the general nature of income tax allocation in the income statement is considered, with attention focused on the presentation of the income tax effects on continuing and discontinued operations, extraordinary items, and the cumulative effect of changes in accounting principles.

   Interperiod tax allocation is the process of apportioning income taxes among two or more accounting periods because of ***temporary differences*** in the recognition of revenue and expenses. Temporary differences result when revenue or expense items appear in the income statement either ***before*** or ***after*** they appear in the income tax return. By means of interperiod tax allocation, the income taxes expense in the income statement is related to the pre-tax income or loss reported in the income statement rather than on the amount of income or loss reported in the income tax return. Thus, income taxes are allocated among accounting periods as are other expenses.

In contrast, ***intraperiod tax allocation*** is the process of apportioning income taxes of a single accounting period among the different sources of income or loss that are presented separately in the income statement. These include (1) income or loss from continuing operations, (2) income or loss from discontinued operations, (3) extraordinary items, and (4) cumulative effects of changes in accounting principles. Similarly, the correction of a material error relating to earlier accounting periods is recorded as a ***prior period adjustment*** in the Retained Earnings ledger account, net of the related income tax effect. Interperiod and intraperiod allocations of income taxes are required by ***FASB Statement No. 96,*** "Accounting for Income Taxes." [14]

To illustrate the basic principles of interperiod and intraperiod allocation of income taxes, assume the following data for Irving Company for the year ended December 31, Year 5 (a tax rate of 45% applies to all items):

	Pre-tax amounts	Income tax effects
Interperiod and intraperiod income tax effects		
Income from continuing operations	$ 800,000	$ 360,000
Loss from operations of discontinued business segment (there was no gain or loss on the disposal)	(600,000)	(270,000)
Extraordinary item (gain)	300,000	135,000
Additional depreciation claimed in income tax return	(100,000)	(45,000)
Taxable income and income taxes payable for Year 5	$ 400,000	$ 180,000

Irving Company elected to take the additional depreciation of $100,000 in its income tax return for Year 5 in order to postpone the payment of $45,000 of income taxes. This is an example of interperiod allocation of income taxes; the other three income tax effects are examples of intraperiod allocation of income taxes. The various sources of income and loss are reported by Irving in the bottom portion of its income statement as follows:

Net-of-tax effects in income statement	
Income from continuing operations (after income taxes expense of $360,000; amount of income taxes payable currently is $180,000)	$ 440,000
Loss from operations of discontinued business segment, net of income tax credit of $270,000	(330,000)
Income before extraordinary item	$ 110,000
Extraordinary item (gain), net of income tax effect of $135,000	165,000
Net income	$ 275,000

---

[14]*FASB Statement No. 96,* "Accounting for Income Taxes," FASB (Stamford: 1987).

It is important to note that the income from continuing operations, the loss from discontinued operations, and the extraordinary item of Irving Company are reported in its income statement net of the related income tax effect. Similarly, any cumulative effect of a change in accounting principle would be reported in the income statement net of the related income tax effect, and any prior period adjustment would be reported in the statement of retained earnings (or the statement of stockholders' equity) net of the related income tax effect. A complete discussion of accounting for income taxes appears in Chapter 21.

Disposal of a Business Segment   A *business segment* is a component of a business enterprise whose activities represent a separate major line of business or class of customer.[15] A business segment may be a subsidiary or a division. However, the sale of a group of assets, the sale of part of a line of business, or the relocation of operations do not constitute disposals of business segments. The assets and operating results of the disposed segment must be clearly identifiable from the other assets and operations of the enterprise.

An income statement is more useful when the effects of material and unusual events and transactions are reported separately from the results of the continuing operations of a business enterprise. Therefore, the operating results of a *discontinued business segment* for the current accounting period and any gain or loss on the disposal of the segment are reported separately in the income statement, net of the related income tax effects. Such separate reporting makes successive income statements more comparable and enables users of financial statements to make better estimates of the enterprise's future earnings.

The accounting for the disposal of a business segment is relatively simple when the decision to discontinue a segment and the actual disposal occur in the same accounting period. When the disposal of the segment is expected to be completed in a subsequent accounting period, estimated results of operating the discontinued segment in the subsequent period *are included in the computation of the gain or loss on the disposal.* An estimated loss is included in the income statement of the period in which the decision to eliminate the segment is made; an estimated gain is reported in the subsequent period when the disposal takes place.

The income statement for the accounting period in which a business segment is discontinued includes the revenue and expenses from continuing operations only. The operating income (or loss) from the discontinued segment for the current period and the gain or loss on the disposal of the segment are reported, net of tax effects, in the income statement below the income (or loss) from continuing operations. The revenue generated by the discontinued segment prior to disposal is disclosed in a note to the financial statements. The presentation in the income statement of a loss from operations of a discontinued business segment and a gain on the disposal of the segment is illustrated below:

---

[15]*APB Opinion No. 30,* "Reporting the Results of Operations—Reporting the Effects of Disposal of a Segment of a Business, and Extraordinary, Unusual and Infrequently Occurring Events and Transactions," AICPA (New York: 1973), pp. 560–561.

Income from continuing operations before income taxes .		$2,800,000
Income taxes expense (amount of income taxes payable currently is $900,000)		1,260,000
Income from continuing operations		$1,540,000
Discontinued operations:		
Loss from operations of discontinued business segment, net of income tax credit of $450,000	$(550,000)	
Gain on disposal of discontinued business segment, net of income tax effect of $90,000	110,000	(440,000)
Net income (or income before extraordinary item and cumulative effect of change in accounting principle, if any)		$1,100,000

Other aspects of accounting for the disposal of a business segment are covered in *Modern Advanced Accounting* of this series.

Extraordinary Items   A troublesome area in the preparation of income statements is the measurement and reporting of unusual and extraordinary gains and losses. General agreement exists that an unusual gain or loss, *if material in amount,* should be disclosed in the income statement and presented as an *extraordinary item* only when the event or transaction giving rise to the gain or loss is of *unusual nature* and *infrequent occurrence,* or when specifically required by a rule-making body. The general standard for identifying extraordinary items is stated in *APB Opinion No. 30,* ''Reporting the Results of Operations—. . . ,'' as follows:[16]

Extraordinary items are events and transactions that are distinguished by their unusual nature and by the infrequency of their occurrence. Thus, *both* of the following criteria should be met to classify an event or transaction as an extraordinary item:

a *Unusual nature*—the underlying event or transaction should possess a high degree of abnormality and be of a type clearly unrelated to, or only incidentally related to, the ordinary and typical activities of the entity, taking into account the environment in which the entity operates.

b *Infrequency of occurrence*—the underlying event or transaction should be of a type that would not reasonably be expected to recur in the foreseeable future, taking into account the environment in which the entity operates.

To be considered unusual in nature, the event or transaction resulting in a gain or loss should be abnormal and unrelated to the ordinary and typical activities of an

---

[16]Ibid, pp. 564–565.

entity. The scope of operations, lines of business, operating policies, and environment in which an entity operates are considered in applying this criterion. The environment in which an entity operates includes such factors as the characteristics of its industry and the geographic location and the degree of government regulation of its activities.

If an event or transaction is not reasonably expected to take place in the foreseeable future, it is considered to occur infrequently. The past experience of an entity may be a helpful guide in determining the frequency of an event or transaction. Thus, according to *APB Opinion No. 30,* only *unusual* and *infrequent* events and transactions produce extraordinary items. However, this qualitative standard may be difficult to apply in practice, and differences of opinion exist in identifying extraordinary items. An event or transaction may be classified as "extraordinary" by one entity and as "normal" by another. Some examples of the classification of *material* gains and losses are listed below:

Material gains and losses that are or are not extraordinary items		
	Examples of extraordinary items	**Examples of items that are not extraordinary**
	1 *Loss from major casualties (such as earthquakes or severe hailstorms in localities where such events are infrequent)*	1 *Write-down or write-off of receivables, inventories, plant assets, or intangible assets*
	2 *Loss from prohibition under newly enacted law or regulation*	2 *Gain or loss from exchange or translation of foreign currencies (including major devaluation or revaluation)*
	3 *Loss from expropriation of assets by a foreign country*	3 *Gain or loss on disposal of a business segment*
	4 *Gain or loss on disposal of **only** holding of common stock or land that had been owned for many years*	4 *Gain or loss on disposal or abandonment of plant assets, investments, or intangible assets*
	5 *Gain or loss on extinguishment of debt*	5 *Loss from a labor strike or effect of adjustments of accruals on a construction-type contract*
	6 *Gain on restructuring of troubled debt*	6 *Cumulative effect of a change in accounting principle*
	7 *Write-off of interstate operating rights by a motor carrier*	7 *Prior period adjustment*

The reporting of the first four items as "extraordinary" is required by *APB Opinion No. 30;* the reporting of the remaining four items as "extraordinary" is required by other official pronouncements, primarily to avoid distortion of recurring income in the income statement. The presentation of an extraordinary item, including the per-share effect, in the income statement is illustrated below:

Presentation of an
extraordinary item in
income statement

Income before income taxes and extraordinary item	$600,000
Income taxes expense (amount of income taxes payable currently is $171,000)	270,000
Income before extraordinary item	$330,000
Extraordinary item (loss), net of income tax credit of $99,000	121,000
Net income	$209,000
Earnings per share of common stock:	
Income before extraordinary item	$ 3.30
Extraordinary item (loss)	(1.21)
Net income	$ 2.09

The gain or loss resulting from an event or transaction that is either unusual in nature or infrequent in occurrence, *but not both,* is included in the determination of income before extraordinary item. The nature and effect on net income of each such event or transaction is disclosed, either in the income statement or in notes to the financial statements.

Accounting Changes We stated earlier that a consistent application of accounting principles and methods over a number of years increases the usefulness of financial statements. However, management of a business enterprise may justify a change in accounting principles on grounds that it is *preferable.*[17] There are three types of accounting changes: (1) change in accounting principle, (2) change in accounting estimate, and (3) change in reporting entity.

A *change in accounting principle* (such as a change in the method of computing depreciation) generally requires the inclusion of the *cumulative effect* of a change to a new principle in net income of the accounting period in which the change is made.[18] Such a change requires the restatement of assets or liabilities as of the beginning of the current period to the amounts that would have existed if the newly adopted principle had been used in prior periods. The related debit or credit, reflecting the cumulative effect of the change on earnings of prior periods, is reported in the income statement net of income taxes following any extraordinary items. A few changes in accounting principle (such as a change from the last-in, first-out method to the first-in, first-out method of inventory pricing) are reported by a restatement of the financial statements of prior periods if the effect of the change is material.

A *change in accounting estimate* (such as the reduction of the original estimate of a 10-year economic life for a computer to a 7-year life) affects only the current and future years' financial statements; thus, no correcting journal entry is necessary. The carrying amount of the computer on the effective date of the change in economic life is allocated to the remaining years of economic life.

---

[17]*APB Opinion No. 20,* "Accounting Changes," AICPA (New York: 1971), p. 391.
[18]Ibid., pp. 391–392.

A *change in reporting entity* occurs when the group of business enterprises comprising the reporting entity changes (such as a business combination of two or more companies accounted for as a pooling of interests). A complete discussion of accounting changes appears in Chapter 22.

Earnings per Share of Common Stock   The amount of earnings per share of common stock for an accounting period is computed by dividing the net income available to common stockholders by the weighted-average number of shares of common stock and potentially dilutive *common stock equivalents* outstanding during the period. The purpose is to show earning power on a per-share basis to enable investors to relate the market price of a share of common stock to the income per share of common stock.

However, when a corporation has stock warrants, stock options, convertible bonds, or convertible preferred stock outstanding, presentation of a *single* earnings-per-share amount in the income statement would be misleading. In such cases, a *dual presentation* of *primary earnings per share* and *fully diluted earnings per share* is required in the income statement.[19] Fully diluted earnings per share is computed to reflect the maximum potential dilution from the *assumed exercise* of stock warrants and stock options and the *assumed conversion* of any outstanding convertible securities. In addition, when the income statement includes the disposal of a business segment, an extraordinary item, or a cumulative effect of a change in accounting principle, the effects of these items on both primary and fully diluted earnings per share also are included. An example of the dual presentation of earnings per share in a comparative income statement that includes extraordinary items and a cumulative effect of a change in accounting principle follows:

Dual presentation of earnings per share

	Year 2	Year 1
Earnings per share of common stock:		
Primary:		
Income before extraordinary item and cumulative		
effect of change in accounting principle	$5.50	$4.32
Extraordinary item—gain or (loss)	(0.88)	1.08
Cumulative effect of change in accounting principle	1.65	
Net income	$6.27	$5.40
Fully diluted:		
Income before extraordinary item and cumulative		
effect of change in accounting principle	$5.00	$4.00
Extraordinary item—gain or (loss)	(0.80)	1.00
Cumulative effect of change in accounting principle	1.50	
Net income	$5.70	$5.00

Procedures for the computation of earnings per share are discussed in Chapter 18.

---

[19]*APB Opinion No. 15,* "Earnings per Share," AICPA (New York: 1969), pp. 221–222.

Significance of Income Measurement and Reporting

Income reporting is probably the most significant aspect of financial accounting because of the economic consequences it has for a business enterprise, its owners and creditors, and its potential owners and creditors. Net income is the lifeblood of any enterprise organized to earn a return on the capital invested by its owners. The ability of an enterprise to compete effectively in its industry, and thus to prosper and survive, depends on its ability to generate income. Profitable operations represent the major source of cash and working capital, and it is unusual for a profitable enterprise to encounter difficulty making timely payments on its debt or to raise capital for expansion purposes.

Income measurement has to be based on sound principles of revenue and expense recognition to be of maximum value to management and other users of financial statements. The quality of a business enterprise's earnings depends to a large extent on the revenue and expense recognition practices it uses. A reputation of reporting **high quality earnings** is a valuable asset to an enterprise. However, income measurement is only one side of the coin; the other is income reporting. The reporting of income must be timely and the sources of income (from continuing and discontinued operations, for example) must be presented in a meaningful and consistent manner. Nonrecurring sources of income or loss are "nonrepeatable" and are not considered as significant as the recurring sources.

A continuing challenge for accountants is to report the components of income in a manner that enhances the predictive value of the income statement. Users of financial statements face a different challenge—to interpret the significance of the reported income in the clear light of a highly complex and inflationary business environment.

REVIEW QUESTIONS

1   What is the goal of **accrual accounting** for a business enterprise as perceived by the Financial Accounting Standards Board?

2   Describe two tasks accountants face relative to revenue. Why is the recognition of revenue so important in today's business environment?

3   Define each of the following terms:
a *Revenue*
b *Realization*
c *Revenue recognition*
d *Earning process*

4   Do you support the argument that the recognition of revenue should be based on **continuous activity** rather than on a **single critical event?**

5   Briefly describe the three **revenue realization conditions.**

6   Why does the implementation of the revenue realization principle pose significant challenges to financial accountants?

7   Briefly describe the importance of evidence, estimates, and professional judgment and experience in the process of recognizing revenue and expenses in the accounting records.

8   Business executives of publicly owned companies are at times under pressure to speed up revenue recognition. What is the possible explanation for this?

9   Assuming that revenue generally is recognized at the time of sale, what revenue-recognition problems are encountered in connection with each of the following:
a *Consignment* of goods to retail merchants
b Sale in which customer is given the *right to return* the goods purchased within 90 days of purchase
c Sale of goods on the *installment plan*

10   When a sale of goods is not considered to result in revenue realization, at what other stages of the productive (earning) process prior to delivery of goods to customers might revenue be recognized?

11   **a** Under what circumstances might revenue be recognized after the delivery of goods to customers?
b Describe the *installment method, cost recovery method,* and *deposit method* of revenue recognition for the sale of goods.

12   **a** Define *service enterprises* and *service transactions.*
b List and briefly describe four methods that may be used to recognize revenue for service transactions.

13   **a** What is meant by the expression "front-ending of income" in connection with the accounting of initial franchise fees received by a franchisor?
b Evaluate the following note to financial statements that appeared in the annual report of Collins Foods International, Inc.:

The Company recognizes initial franchise fees as income on the date the restaurant is opened, at which time the Company has substantially performed its obligations relating to such fees. Service fees (royalties) from franchise agreements are taken into income on an accrual basis as the fees are earned and become due from the franchisee.

14   What possible objections might be made to the recognition of revenue on the date that the contract for a sales-type lease becomes effective?

15   Distinguish between (**a**) *revenue* and *cost savings,* (**b**) *expenses* and *losses,* and (**c**) *product costs* and *period costs.*

16   **a** List the three groups in which the expenses of an accounting period may be classified.
b Describe the three principles of expense recognition.

17   **a** Define *initial direct costs, direct costs,* and *indirect costs* incurred by a service enterprise.
b How are the costs listed in **a** recognized under the *specific-performance, completed-performance, proportional-performance,* and *collection* methods of revenue recognition for service transactions?

18   "Big Mo" Nikola owns and operates a commercial tuna boat, the "Conte Blanco." His fiscal year ends on January 31. On January 10, Year 3, Nikola presold

400 tons of yellowfin tuna at $800 a ton to Pacific Packing Corporation. The tuna presold represented the expected catch of the initial Year 3 fishing trip to Central America by the "Conte Blanco." Because he felt that the success of the initial trip was "reasonably assured," Nikola asked his accountant to record the presale in his accounting records on January 10, Year 3. Nikola also asked his accountant to record the estimated costs and expenses of the initial Year 3 fishing trip as deductions from the $320,000 (400 × $800 = $320,000) revenue recorded. The costs and expenses were estimated at $250,000, including "shares" to be distributed to the 12-member crew of the "Conte Blanco."

Do you agree with Nikola's proposed accounting for the presale of the 400 tons of tuna? Explain.

19   If earnings reports were to meet better the objectives of financial statements, what changes would you recommend in the content of income statements of publicly owned companies?

20   If 10 accountants were asked to measure the **lifetime income** of a business enterprise and to assume no change in the purchasing power of the dollar, they probably would agree within narrow limits on this long-run income measurement. The same 10 accountants might vary over a wide range in their measurement of the same enterprise's **net income for an accounting period.** Why?

21   Define each of the following terms:
a *Nominal dollars*
b *Constant purchasing power*
c *General price level*
d *Specific price level*
e *Inventory profit*

22   Explain the meaning of **intraperiod tax allocation** and **interperiod tax allocation,** and explain how these procedures improve the usefulness of an income statement.

23   How are the results of a business segment reported in the income statement for the accounting period in which the segment is discontinued? Is the loss or gain on the disposal of a business segment reported as an extraordinary item in the income statement? Explain.

24   Describe the criteria for **extraordinary items** as set forth in **APB Opinion No. 30,** "Reporting the Results of Operations—. . . ."

25   Describe how the effect of a **change in accounting principle** and the effect of a **change in accounting estimate** are reported in an income statement.

26   What is the purpose of reporting **earnings per share** of common stock in an income statement? Under what circumstances is a **dual presentation** of earnings per share of common stock required in the income statement?

27   How is each of the following material losses reported in the income statement of a business enterprise?
a Loss incurred from shutdown of plant during a strike by employees.
b Loss from the abandonment of obsolete equipment.

c Loss sustained as a result of damage caused to the main warehouse by a tornado (tornadoes are unusual and infrequent in the geographic area where the enterprise is located).

d Loss incurred on the disposal of a professional football team (the business enterprise is a manufacturer of furniture).

28   An article in a business magazine described examples of falsified accounting records designed "to make the operating results of publicly owned companies look better." Some of the examples involved overstatements of inventories and premature recording of sales by executives in middle-management ranks whose salaries were based on earnings and who were under pressure from top management to report steady increases in net income.

What assurances do users of financial statements have that the statements of publicly owned companies are not based on falsified accounting records?

29   A few years ago, banking regulators adopted a rule that affected income measurement by U.S. banks. The rule required loans to Argentina to be classified by banks as "non-accrual" if the interest payments on the loans were more than 90 days overdue. No interest was permitted to be accrued on such loans, and any interest previously accrued was required to be deducted from current revenue.

How did the rule adopted by the banking regulators relate to accrual accounting and to the revenue realization principle?

EXERCISES

Ex. 3-1   Select the best answer for each of the following multiple-choice questions:

1   Under generally accepted accounting principles, net income is measured:
a By applying a value-added concept
b By using a transactions approach and matching costs and revenue
c As a change in the current fair value of owners' equity
d As a change in the purchasing power of owners' equity

2   Realization of revenue refers to:
a The timing of its recognition in the accounting records
b The knowledge that it has been earned
c Its receipt in the form of cash
d Its recognition in an adjusting entry at the end of an accounting period

3   Which of the following is the most widely accepted evidence of revenue realization by a manufacturing enterprise?
a The process of production of products
b The completion of production of products
c The sale and delivery of products to customers
d The receipt of cash from the sale of finished products

4   The determination of the periodic income of a business enterprise depends on the measurement of its economic resources and obligations and changes in them as these changes occur. This pertains to:
a Disclosure   **b** Accrual accounting   **c** Materiality   **d** The matching principle

5   Which of the following is not a basis for the immediate recognition of a cost as an expense of the current accounting period?

a The cost provides no discernible future benefit

b The cost recorded in a prior accounting period no longer produces discernible benefits

c The income tax savings under the immediate write-off method exceed the savings obtained by allocating the cost to several accounting periods

d Allocation of the cost on the basis of association with revenue or among several accounting periods is considered to serve no useful purpose

6   When costs may be reasonably associated with specific revenue but not with specific products, the costs should be:

a Charged to expense in the period incurred

b Allocated to specific products based on the best estimate of the production processing time

c Expensed in the period in which the related revenue is recognized

d Capitalized and then amortized over a period not to exceed 60 months

7   An event or transaction is considered to occur infrequently, and thus possibly to qualify as an extraordinary item, if it:

a Is not reasonably expected to take place in the near future

b Is of unusual nature

c Has not taken place for more than five years

d Is judged to be of infrequent occurrence by management of the reporting business enterprise

8   A loss from the disposal of a business segment is reported separately as a component of net income:

a After cumulative effect of a change in accounting principle and before extraordinary items

b Before cumulative effect of a change in accounting principle and after extraordinary items

c After extraordinary items and cumulative effect of a change in accounting principle

d Before extraordinary items and cumulative effect of a change in accounting principle

9   Marks Company had the following ledger account balances for the year ended December 31, Year 5:

Interest expense	$123,000
Loss on disposal of long-term investments	80,000
Write-down of plant assets to estimated current fair value	60,000
Loss on disposal of a business segment	50,000

In its income statement for Year 5, how much should Marks Company report as total extraordinary items?

a $50,000   **b** $80,000   **c** $110,000   **d** $140,000   **e** Some other amount

10   Treiger Construction Company has consistently used the percentage-of-completion method of accounting for its construction-type contracts. During Year 4,

Treiger started work on a $3 million construction contract that was completed in Year 5. The accounting records include the following information:

	Year 4	Year 5
Progress billings to customers	$ 950,000	$2,050,000
Costs incurred	900,000	1,820,000
Collections from customers	800,000	2,110,000
Estimated cost to complete contract..................	1,800,000	

How much contract revenue should Treiger Construction Company have recognized in Year 4?

a $800,000 **c** $950,000   **e** Some other amount
b $900,000 **d** $1,000,000

Ex. 3-2 Carmen Company began operations on January 2, Year 1, and a substantial part of its sales were made on the installment plan. For financial accounting, Carmen recognized revenue from all sales under the accrual method. However, in its income tax returns, Carmen reported revenue from installment sales under the installment method. Information concerning gross profit from installment sales under each method follows:

	Accrual method	Installment method
Year 1...	$500,000	$250,000
Year 2...	750,000	400,000

Assume that the effective income tax rate for both years was 40%, and there were no other timing differences.

Compute the amount of Carmen Company's deferred income tax credits on December 31, Year 2.

Ex. 3-3 Network Company sells office equipment service contracts agreeing to service equipment for a two-year period. Cash receipts from contracts are credited to unearned service contract revenue, and service contract costs are debited to service contract expense as incurred. Revenue from service contracts is recognized as earned over the term of the contracts. Additional information for the year ended December 31, Year 3, follows:

Unearned service contract revenue, Jan. 1, Year 3	$600,000
Unearned service contract revenue, Dec. 31, Year 3	720,000
Cash receipts from service contracts sold	980,000
Service contract expense	520,000

Compute the service contract revenue that Network Company should recognize for the year ended December 31, Year 3.

Ex. 3-4 Lovelace Company pays its outside salespersons base monthly salaries, plus a 3% commission on net sales. Sales commissions are computed and paid on a monthly basis (in the month following the month of sale), and the base salaries are treated as advances against commissions for this purpose. However, if the base salaries for salespersons exceed their sales commissions earned for a month, such excess is not charged back to them. Information for the month of June for the three salespersons in the Eastern Region follows:

Salesperson	Base salaries	Net sales
A	$ 3,250	$ 90,000
B	3,500	260,000
C	4,200	350,000
	$10,950	$700,000

Compute the sales commissions expense for the Eastern Region of Lovelace Company for the month of June.

Ex. 3-5 Briefly explain whether each of the following transactions should be classified as a disposal of a business segment in the preparation of an income statement:

a A sale by a diversified company of a major division that represents the company's only activity in the chemical industry.

b A sale by a communications company of all its television stations, representing 28% of the company's revenue and 35% of its net income.

c A sale by a United States company of a gold mining subsidiary in India. The subsidiary represents the company's only business activity in India, but the company continues to operate gold and silver mines in seven countries around the world.

d A sale of all assets related to the production of suits by a garment manufacturer to concentrate on the production of other lines of garments.

Ex. 3-6 For each of the following events and transactions, state whether Carr Company realized revenue or a gain. Give reasons in support of your conclusions.

a Gift certificates that may be exchanged by the holder for merchandise in a subsequent accounting period were sold for cash of $200.

b Land acquired for $45,000 two years ago has a current fair value of $65,000.

c A new factory building was constructed by Carr's employees at a cost of $190,000. Bids of $205,000 and $210,000 from independent contractors were rejected.

d Securities with a current market value of $17,650 were received from a customer in settlement of a trade account receivable of $16,500 that was more than a year past due.

e Merchandise with a cost of $480 was sold under a 24-month installment contract for a 10% down payment of $60. Title to the merchandise was to remain with Carr until all installment payments had been collected.

f Land held for investment is planted in tomatoes. If the crop is harvested successfully and demand remains strong, cash receipts are expected to exceed expenses by $20,000. The crop growth is halfway to maturity at this time.

g Services are rendered to a customer, and a check drawn on a small out-of-state bank is received from the customer.

Ex. 3-7 Cowan Company declared and paid cash dividends of $12,500 during Year 5. Cowan's accounting records show that changes in ledger account balances for the year ended December 31, Year 5, were as follows:

	Increase or (decrease)
Cash	$ 40,000
Trade accounts receivable (net)	(2,000)
Inventories	15,000
Buildings (net)	30,000
Equipment (net)	18,000
Notes payable	50,000
Trade accounts payable	(15,000)
Common stock, $5 par	30,000
Additional paid-in capital	10,000
Retained earnings	?

The only journal entries to the Retained Earnings ledger account were for dividends and net income.

Compute Cowan Company's net income for the year ended December 31, Year 5.

Ex. 3-8 Jeffrey Corporation is subject to a 45% tax rate on all sources of income. Information for the year ended December 31, Year 2, follows:

Income from continuing operations before income taxes	$600,000
Income taxes payable ($22,500 of income taxes expense is deferred because depreciation in the income tax return exceeds depreciation expense in the income statement)	315,000
Extraordinary item (gain before income tax effect)	300,000
Loss from operations and disposal of discontinued business segment	150,000
Dividends declared	165,000

a Prepare a partial income statement for Jeffrey Corporation for the year ended December 31, Year 2, with appropriate allocation of income taxes. Disregard earnings per share.

b Reconcile Jeffrey's income taxes expense of $270,000 ($600,000 × 0.45 = $270,000) applicable to continuing operations with the $315,000 income taxes payable for Year 2.

Ex. 3-9 On November 10, Year 2, Painting Contractors, Inc., commenced a $25,000 contract to sandblast and paint several buildings for a real estate investor. The direct costs of the contract (including subcontracting for the sandblasting, paint, and salaries of workers) were estimated at $20,000 on December 31, Year 2. The contract consisted of a large number of dissimilar acts. Through December 31, Year 2, the contract costs incurred amount to $14,000 and the acts performed to date amount to at least 80% of the total acts to be performed by Painting Contractors.

Compute three possible amounts of gross profit that Painting Contractors, Inc., might recognize for the year ended December 31, Year 2, on the foregoing contract.

Ex. 3-10 The following information for Odds & Ends, Inc., relates to sales on the installment plan:

| | December 31, | | |
	Year 3	Year 2	Year 1
Installment receivables—Year 1	$ 10,000	$20,000	$60,000
Installment receivables—Year 2	40,000	80,000	
Installment receivables—Year 3	280,000		
Installment sales	400,000		
Gross profit on installment sales	60%	55%	52%

Odds & Ends, Inc., uses the installment method of accounting because it is unable to make a reasonable estimate of the collectibility of installment receivables.

Compute the amount of realized gross profit that Odds & Ends, Inc., recognizes for the year ended December 31, Year 3, under the installment method.

Ex. 3-11   Slowe Construction Company uses the percentage-of-completion method of accounting for its construction-type contracts. The costs incurred and estimated additional costs to complete a $5 million fixed-price contract over a four-year period are summarized below:

Year ended Dec. 31,	Cumulative costs incurred to date	Estimated costs to complete contract	Total cost of contract
Year 1	$ 500,000	$3,500,000	$4,000,000
Year 2	2,100,000	2,100,000	4,200,000
Year 3	3,870,000	430,000	4,300,000
Year 4	4,250,000	none	4,250,000

Compute the contract revenue realized by Slowe Construction Company in each of the four years under the percentage-of-completion method.

Ex. 3-12   On January 5, Year 1, Fast-Fry Corporation sold a franchise to Horizon Enterprises for $20,000 cash. The initial franchise fee was nonreturnable; however, Fast-Fry agreed to help Horizon open the franchise and provide services for two years after the franchise opened. Horizon opened the franchise on October 1, Year 1. A reasonable estimate of the services Fast-Fry agreed to provide to Horizon follows:

In connection with opening of franchise	40%
For first 12 months of operations...	36%
For next 12 months of operations	24%

Compute the amount of the initial franchise fee revenue that Fast-Fry Corporation should recognize each year ended December 31, Year 1, Year 2, and Year 3.

Ex. 3-13   Orasco Company was organized on March 1, Year 1, and was sold for cash by its three stockholders on August 20, Year 10. Orasco's activities during its lifetime are summarized below and on page 147.

Proceeds from issuance of common stock in Year 1	$ 200,000
Proceeds from issuance of preferred stock in Year 4..................	50,000
Cost of treasury stock acquired in Year 8	19,800
Net income	845,200
Dividends declared and paid	590,000

Proceeds from sale of Orasco on Aug. 20, Year 10..................	1,050,000
Income taxes paid on gain on sale of Orasco.......................	150,000
Cash distributed on Dec. 31, Year 10, to stockholders after sale	
of Orasco...	900,000

Compute the lifetime income of Orasco Company.

Ex. 3-14 At the end of Year 5, Lash Corporation manufactured a machine at a cost of $10,000 with a selling price of $15,000. The cost of manufacturing an identical machine was estimated at $12,000 on December 31, Year 6, on which date the machine was sold for $18,750. The general price level rose by 15% in Year 6.

Compute the gross profit for Lash Corporation on the sale of the machine under each of the following procedures:

a Nominal-dollar gross profit

b Nominal-dollar gross profit, with price gain isolated

c Constant-purchasing power (end of Year 6 purchasing power) gross profit

Ex. 3-15 Indicate which of the following gains and losses that are material in amount are reported as extraordinary items in the income statement:

(1) Loss from earthquake in a city where earthquakes are extremely infrequent

(2) Write-off of receivables, inventories, plant assets, and intangible assets

(3) Loss from prohibition under new law passed by the United States Congress

(4) Gain or loss from the revaluation of foreign currencies

(5) Loss from expropriation of assets by a foreign country

(6) Gain or loss on disposal of a business segment

(7) Gain or loss on disposal of investment in common stock that had been owned for 30 years

(8) Gain or loss on disposal of plant assets

(9) Gain or loss on extinguishment of long-term debt

(10) Loss from a prolonged labor strike

(11) Realization of income tax benefit from an operating loss carryforward

(12) Cumulative effect (gain or loss) of a change in accounting principle

(13) Gain on restructuring of troubled debt

(14) Prior period adjustment resulting from material error in the financial statements of earlier years

(15) Write-off by a motor carrier of its interstate operating rights

Ex. 3-16 The income statements of Duall Corporation for the latest two years include the following:

	Year 10	Year 9
Income before extraordinary item and cumulative effect		
of change in accounting principle......................	$3,600,000	$4,200,000
Extraordinary item—gain or (loss), net of income tax effects	(720,000)	900,000
Cumulative effect of change in accounting principle,		
net of income tax effect...............................	1,800,000	
Net income	$4,680,000	$5,100,000

For both years, Duall had 500,000 shares of common stock outstanding for the computation of primary earnings per share and 600,000 for the computation of fully diluted earnings per share. Only common stock has been issued by Duall.

Show how primary and fully diluted earnings per share are presented in Duall Corporation's comparative income statements for Year 9 and Year 10.

CASES

Case 3-1 In a contract for the licensing of a new motion picture to network television, the producer of the motion picture generally recognizes revenue on commencement of the license period and when all the following conditions have been met:

(1) The sale price (license fee) for the motion picture is known.
(2) The cost of the motion picture is known or is reasonably determinable.
(3) Collectibility of the license fee is reasonably assured.
(4) The motion picture has been accepted by the licensee in accordance with the conditions of the licensing contract.
(5) The motion picture is available for delivery to the licensee on a date to be specified by the licensee.

Instructions

Evaluate the rationale of this revenue recognition standard for the licensing of a new motion picture for television viewing. Your discussion should be related to the three revenue realization conditions listed on page 106.

Case 3-2 At the beginning of Year 10, Richard Nye, owner and operator of a large farm, had no inventories on hand. During Year 10, Nye produced 8,000 bushels of soybeans, 10,000 bushels of barley, and 16,000 bushels of rye, and sold one-half of each of his crops at the following prices: soybeans $8 a bushel, barley $4.25 a bushel, rye $3 a bushel. Nye followed the daily price quotations of these commodities closely, and at the end of Year 10, he noted that the market prices for the commodities were as follows: soybeans $8.50 a bushel, barley $4.50 a bushel, and rye $3.20 a bushel.

The expenses incurred in operating the farm during Year 10 totaled $75,200, including depreciation of buildings and equipment. Nye estimates that his cost of selling and delivering the crops is $1 a bushel. The selling and delivering costs applicable to the crops sold were included in operating expenses for Year 10.

Instructions

a Prepare an income statement for Richard Nye for the year ended December 31, Year 10. Explain the principle of revenue realization employed in your measurement of income and, in particular, the basis you used in assigning a valuation to the commodities on hand on December 31, Year 10.

b In measuring income before income taxes for Year 10, what consideration did you give to the possibility that the market price of the commodities might change between the end of Year 10 and the time Richard Nye finally sells them?

c What is the essential difference between the problem of measuring income for Richard Nye and measuring income for a manufacturer of farm machinery?

Case 3-3 Six different business enterprises recognized the following items in their accounting records during Year 2:

(1) A gain of $3.9 million was recorded by Soledad Company from the extinguishment of bonds payable that were trading in the open market at a substantial discount because of the weak financial position of Soledad and high effective interest rates.

(2) An out-of-court settlement of litigation resulted in a payment by Exeter Corporation of $2 million to plaintiffs. The legal action was initiated two years ago.

(3) A pre-tax loss of $4 million resulted from the disposal of a chemical division (a business segment) operated by Grocery Chain Co. In the year of disposal, the chemical division had sales of $10 million and operating expenses of $12 million. The income tax rate is 45%, and the income (after income taxes) from continuing operations is $8.2 million.

(4) A loss of $6 million was recorded by XY, Inc., from write-offs of trade receivables and inventories caused by a severe business recession.

(5) A loss of $8 million was recorded by Apparel Mfg. Co. from the sale of all assets used in the manufacture of sweaters.

(6) Diversified Enterprises, Inc., sold a block of common stock from its portfolio of long-term investments. This was the first sale from its portfolio and resulted in a material gain of $4.5 million before income taxes.

Instructions

Indicate how each of the items above should be reported in the respective business enterprises' income statements for Year 2. Give a brief explanation for each item.

Case 3-4 The financial statements of World Publishing Company are presented to the board of directors for review after completion of the annual audit. Karen Young, a director, asks why the income statement is based on the assumption that an equal proportion of the revenue is earned with the publication of each issue of World Publishing's magazine. She feels that the "critical event" in the process of earning revenue in the magazine business is the cash sale of the subscription. She says that she does not understand why—other than for the smoothing of income—most of the revenue should not be recognized in the month of sale.

Instructions

a List three accepted methods for recognizing revenue and indicate the conditions under which the use of each method would be appropriate. Do not limit your listing to the methods for the recognition of revenue by magazine publishing enterprises.

b Discuss the propriety of timing the recognition of revenue in World Publishing Company's accounting records with:

(1) The cash sale of the magazine subscription

(2) The publication of the magazine each month

(3) Both events, by recognizing a portion of the revenue with the cash sale of the magazine subscription and a portion of the revenue with the publication of the magazine each month

Case 3-5   Creative Agency handles advertising for clients under contracts requiring that Creative Agency develop advertising copy and layouts and place ads in various media (television, radio, newspapers, etc.). Creative Agency charges a commission of 18% of the media cost as its fee and makes advance billings to its clients of estimated media cost plus its 18% commission. Later adjustments of these advance billings usually are minor. Both the billings and receipt of cash from these billings often occur before the period in which the advertising appears in the media.

In devising a system for measuring income, Creative Agency considered the following possible points at which revenue and expenses might be recognized and income measured: (1) At the time of the advance billing; (2) when payment is received from clients; (3) in the month in which the advertising appears in the media; (4) when the invoice for advertising is received from the media.

Creative Agency chose (1) above as the point at which it would recognize revenue and income, on the grounds that it has a contract with clients for specified advertising, and thus revenue and income are earned when billed. At the time of billing, Creative Agency records the accounts receivable from clients, the estimated liability to the media, and its 18% commission. Also at this time, Creative Agency records an expense and a liability for the estimated expenses related to the client's billing. Adjusting entries are made to record actual cost and revenue amounts when billings are received from media, when actual expenses are determined, and when final billings invoices are sent to clients.

Instructions

Discuss each of the four points at which Creative Agency might recognize revenue and income, and state your opinion as to the proper basis for accounting for revenue and income in this case. If you disagree with the method followed by Creative Agency, explain the basis for your disagreement and why you support an alternative point for revenue recognition.

Case 3-6   On May 1, Year 1, Axel Corporation signed a contract with Westside Company under which Westside agreed to (1) construct an office building on land owned by Axel, (2) accept responsibility for arranging financing for the project and finding tenants, and (3) manage the property for 10 years. The annual income from the project, after debt service, was to be divided equally between Axel and Westside. Westside was to accept its share of future income as full payment for its services in construction, obtaining financing, and managing the project.

By April 30, Year 2, the project was nearly completed, and tenants had signed leases to occupy 90% of the available space at annual rentals aggregating $3,300,000. It was estimated that, after operating expenses and debt service, the annual income would amount to $950,000. The owners of Westside believed that the economic benefit derived from the contract with Axel should be reflected in its financial statements for the fiscal year ended April 30, Year 2. Consequently, the owners of Westside requested their accountant to record revenue in an amount equal to the commercial value of the services Westside had rendered to Axel during the year, to record this amount in accounts receivable, and to deduct all expenditures incurred to date by Westside from the revenue recognized.

Instructions

a Explain the main difference between the economic concept of income as perceived by the management of Westside Company and the measurement of net income under generally accepted accounting principles.

b Discuss the factors to be considered in determining when revenue has been realized for the purpose of accounting measurement of net income.

c Is the belief of Westside Company's management in accord with generally accepted accounting principles for the recognition of revenue and expense for the year ended April 30, Year 2? Support your opinion by discussing the application to this case of the factors to be considered for asset measurement and revenue and expense recognition.

PROBLEMS

3-1 Sonrisa Company was organized in Year 1 to sell merchandise on the installment plan and on regular 30-day open accounts. Sonrisa's activities for Year 5 are summarized below:

Regular sales on credit	$ 720,000
Installment sales	1,200,000
Cost of regular sales	406,000
Cost of installment sales	780,000
Operating expenses (all paid in Year 5)	354,000
Collections on regular sales	620,000
Collections on installment sales	450,000

Sonrisa uses the perpetual inventory system. Income taxes and interest and carrying charges on the installment accounts receivable are to be disregarded in this problem.

Instructions

a Prepare journal entries for Sonrisa Company to record all transactions and adjustments for Year 5, assuming that Sonrisa uses the accrual basis of accounting. Closing entries are not required.

b Prepare journal entries for Sonrisa Company to record all transactions for Year 5 (including the closing entry to establish the deferred gross profit and the adjusting entry to record the realized gross profit on installment sales). Assume that Sonrisa uses the installment method of accounting because the collectibility of installment accounts receivable cannot be reasonably estimated. Other closing entries are not required.

3-2 Sergio Corporation had 200,000 shares of common stock outstanding throughout Year 5. During Year 5, Sergio sold a segment of its business. Sergio's results of operations for the year ended December 31, Year 5, are summarized as follows:

	Continuing operations	Discontinued business segment
Sales (net of returns, allowances, and discounts)	$10,600,000	$2,900,000
Costs and expenses	9,200,000	2,500,000
Gain on disposal of discontinued business segment, before income tax effect		800,000
Extraordinary item (gain), before income tax effect	880,000	
Cumulative effect of change in accounting principle (debit balance), net of income tax credit of $163,636	200,000	

The income tax rate for Sergio is 45%, and no potentially dilutive securities were outstanding.

Instructions

Prepare a partial income statement for Sergio Corporation for the year ended December 31, Year 5, starting with "income from continuing operations before income taxes." Include earnings per share data and disregard notes to the financial statements.

3-3   Gussman Company is engaged in the manufacture of auto parts. Several years ago it acquired a small bank, which has been operated at a loss since it was acquired. In Year 9, the board of directors of Gussman sold the bank for $5,100,000. Gussman's results of operations for the year ended December 31, Year 9, are summarized below:

	Auto parts	Bank
Revenue (net)	$26,000,000	$6,500,000
Costs and expenses	21,200,000	7,700,000
Loss on disposal of bank, before income tax effect		400,000
Extraordinary item (loss), before income tax effect	800,000	
Cumulative effect of change in accounting principle (credit balance), net of income tax effect of $675,000 .		825,000

The extraordinary item is deductible for income tax purposes. The income tax rate for Gussman is 45%. There were 400,000 shares of common stock (the only capital stock issued) outstanding during Year 9. No potentially dilutive securities were outstanding.

Instructions

Prepare a partial income statement for Gussman Company for the year ended December 31, Year 9, starting with "income from continuing operations before income taxes." Include earnings per share data and disregard notes to the financial statements.

3-4   Rosa Wong started a single proprietorship on July 1, Year 3, by investing $60,000 cash and plant assets with a current fair value of $100,000. A few days later, Francis Wong was admitted as partner for an investment of $120,000 cash. The partners adopted the name "Gentle Care" for their business enterprise. The balance sheet of Gentle Care on June 30, Year 11, follows:

GENTLE CARE
Balance Sheet
June 30, Year 11

Assets		Liabilities & Partners' Capital	
Cash	$ 85,980	Trade accounts payable . .	$ 52,940
Trade accounts receivable		Mortgage note payable . . .	100,000
(net)	57,820	Rosa Wong, capital	292,060
Inventories	64,200	Francis Wong, capital	155,000
Plant assets (net)	392,000	Total liabilities &	
Total assets	$600,000	partners' capital	$600,000

The partners disagreed over business policies and decided to liquidate the partnership, effective June 30, Year 11. Inventories were sold for $50,000 and plant assets for $560,000. Trade accounts receivable of $24,000 were collected, $32,000 were sold (without recourse) for $25,000, and $1,820 were written off as uncollectible. All liabilities were paid, including $400 of interest on the mortgage note payable not accrued at the time of the June 30, Year 11, balance sheet. During the life of Gentle Care, Rosa Wong and Francis Wong had withdrawn $300,000 and $196,000, respectively.

Instructions

a Compute the lifetime income of Gentle Care on the basis of the foregoing information. (Reminder: A partnership is not a taxable entity.)

b Explain whether there are any areas of uncertainty in your determination of the lifetime income of Gentle Care.

3-5 Bolero Construction Corporation is engaged in the construction of small-boat harbors in the State of Texas. During the first two years of its operations, Bolero completed three contracts and had two contracts in progress. Information relating to these contracts is summarized below:

Contract and fixed price	Costs	Year 2	Year 1
A—$100,000	Incurred		$82,000*
B—$150,000	Incurred	$ 84,000*	40,000
	Estimated to complete		80,000
C—$130,000	Incurred	78,500*	20,000
	Estimated to complete		80,000
D—$255,000	Incurred	82,000	
	Estimated to complete	123,000	
E—$500,000	Incurred	210,000	
	Estimated to complete	210,000	

*Completed during year.

Instructions

Compute the realized gross profit on contract revenue for each year for Bolero Construction Corporation under the following methods of accounting for construction-type contracts:

a Percentage-of-completion
b Completed-contract

3-6 On January 2, Year 1, Grove Corporation sold an idle machine to Anne Company for $350,000. On that date the machine had a cost of $600,000 and accumulated depreciation of $350,000 in Grove's accounting records. Under the contract, Anne paid $50,000 cash on January 2, Year 1, and signed a $300,000 promissory note bearing interest at the current fair rate of 10%. The promissory note was payable in installments of $50,000, $100,000, and $150,000 on January 2, Year 2, Year 3, and Year 4, respectively. The promissory note was not secured by any collateral. Grove appropriately accounted for the sale of the idle machine under the cost recovery method because there was no reasonable basis for estimating the collectibility of the promissory note. Anne made late payments on the note and interest as follows:

Date of payment	Principal	Interest
July 1, Year 2	$ 50,000	$ 45,000
December 31, Year 3	100,000	37,500
April 1, Year 5	150,000	18,750
Totals	$300,000	$101,250

Instructions

a Prepare journal entries to record the foregoing transactions in the accounting records of Grove Corporation under the cost recovery method of accounting. Record the unrealized gain in a Deferred Gain on Disposal of Machinery ledger account and any unrealized interest in a Deferred Interest Revenue ledger account. Assume that the gain on disposal of machinery is recovered before any interest revenue is recognized. Journal entries are required on the following dates:

(1) January 2, Year 1
(2) July 1, Year 2
(3) December 31, Year 3
(4) April 1, Year 5

b Show how the promissory note receivable, deferred gross profit on the disposal of machinery, and deferred interest revenue are presented in Grove Corporation's balance sheet on December 31, Year 3.

3-7 In Year 1, Jeannie Bowman opened an "exclusive" exercise-diet studio in Minneapolis. After profitable operations for nearly three years, Bowman organized a separate company, EXDI, Inc., on January 2, Year 4, to sell and service franchises in several large cities. Each franchise was sold for $50,000, payable $14,000 down and $12,000 a year for three years starting one year following sale. No other payments were required from franchisees.

EXDI, Inc., was obligated to provide considerable services to franchisees in opening and operating their studios for the first three years, including the preparation of promotional brochures, accounting systems, and training of employees. The down payment of $14,000 was designed to cover the initial direct costs of the franchise contract and for the right to use the name "EXDI Studios." The three payments of $12,000 each were for annual services provided to the franchisee.

The fair rate of interest during Year 4 was 15% a year; thus, the present value of the three promissory notes of $12,000 each received from a franchisee was approximately $27,396 on the date a franchise is sold. However, the accountant for EXDI, Inc., recorded each franchise contract by debits to Cash and Notes Receivable for $14,000 and $36,000, respectively, and a credit to Franchise Revenue for $50,000. The notes were considered fully collectible.

Sales of franchises by EXDI, Inc., during Year 4 were as follows:

Date	Number of franchises sold
April 1	5
May 1	8
July 1	6
September 30	4
October 30	10
Total	33

Operating expenses paid and accrued in selling the franchises and providing services to franchisees amounted to $271,800 for Year 4.

Instructions

a Compute the income before income taxes for EXDI, Inc., for the year ended December 31, Year 4, under the accounting procedure adopted by its accountant.

b Evaluate the accounting procedure used by EXDI, Inc., for the sale of franchises and compute its income before income taxes that you consider to be in accordance with generally accepted accounting principles. Round all computations to the nearest dollar.

3-8 The unadjusted trial balance of Selca Corporation included the following ledger account balances on March 31, Year 10:

Inventories (perpetual system)	$1,550,000
Deferred costs of unsuccessful contract proposals	19,500
Sales (regular and installment)	6,500,000
Cost of goods sold (regular and installment)	5,200,000
Contract revenue	500,000
Costs incurred on contracts	420,000
Purchases discounts revenue	40,000

Additional Information

(1) Sales included $75,000, representing a shipment of goods on consignment to Milna Company. The cost of these goods was $51,000 and was included in cost of goods sold. Accounts receivable included $75,000 from Milna because none of the goods had been sold.

(2) Sales also included $40,000, the estimated selling price of a special shipment of slow-moving goods to Diskonte, Inc. The $35,000 cost of these goods was included in cost of goods sold. Diskonte had the right to return 100% of these goods and to adjust the purchase price based on its ability to sell the goods and to obtain reasonable prices on the sales. Diskonte had not sold any goods included in this shipment.

(3) Installment sales included $100,000, of which $40,000 had been collected through March 31, Year 10. Because the collectibility of the balance was not reasonably assured, the installment method of accounting was used for this portion of installment sales. The gross profit rate on this installment sale was 32%. [Debit Deferred Gross Profit (to be offset from gross profit on sales in the income statement) and credit Deferred Gross Profit (to be offset from installment receivables in the balance sheet).]

(4) Sales included a deposit of $15,000 received from a customer who was considering a large order for the purchase of goods from Selca. No cost of goods sold was recorded.

(5) Inventories and sales included $10,000, the estimated value of old products discovered in the factory cellar that had not been opened for at least 10 years.

(6) Selca used the completed-performance method of revenue realization for its various service contracts, and it recognized contract revenue at the time the contracts were completed; however, all costs relating to contracts in progress had been recorded in the Costs Incurred on Contracts ledger account. You concluded that a contract for $30,000, on which 60% of the costs had been incurred, should be accounted for under the proportional-performance method of revenue recognition. An appropriate amount was debited to Accounts Receivable (not billed).

(7) Initial direct costs and direct costs in the amount of $15,880 related to contracts in progress for which revenue would be recognized under the completed-performance method (Debit Costs of Contracts in Progress).

(8) Selca had deferred certain costs of unsuccessful contract proposals and planned to charge these costs against several outstanding proposals that were expected to result in significant service contracts.

(9) Purchases discounts were recorded as revenue when invoices were paid within the discount period. Of the purchases discounts recorded, 15% relate to inventories on hand on March 31, Year 10, and 85% related to Cost of Goods Sold (regular and installment). The controller concluded that purchases discounts are cost offsets, not revenue.

Instructions

a For each ledger account listed in the partial trial balance for Selca Corporation, compute the correct amount based on the information given in items (1) through (9).

b Prepare journal entries to correct or adjust the accounting records of Selca Corporation on March 31, Year 10, for each item (1) through (9).

3-9 Lobo, Inc., sells restaurant franchises to independent operators (franchisees) under a standard contract that includes the following terms:

(1) Franchisee pays an initial fee of $40,000, of which 25% is payable at the time the contract is signed and $10,000 is payable at the end of each of the three subsequent years. The franchisee signs three noninterest-bearing promissory notes of $10,000 each for the balance payable to the franchisor. The initial $10,000 collected by the franchisor is to be refunded and the promissory notes canceled if the franchisee fails to open the restaurant for any reason within one year.

(2) Franchisor agrees to (a) assist the franchisee in selecting the location for the restaurant, (b) negotiate the lease for the land, (c) obtain financing and assist with building design, (d) supervise construction, (e) establish appropriate accounting records, and (f) provide advice relating to employee training, quality control, and advertising for three years starting on the date that the restaurant franchise is sold.

(3) In addition to the initial franchise fee, franchisee is required to pay a royalty of 2% of sales to Lobo for menu planning, recipe innovations, and option to purchase food and supplies from Lobo at discount prices. This fee is payable on January 31 each year.

The management of Lobo estimates that the value of the services rendered to the franchisee at the time the restaurant is opened amounts to at least $10,000. The services relating to employee training, quality control, and advertising are considered significant and are expected to be provided by Lobo ratably over the three-year period. During the 30 months that Lobo has been selling franchises, all franchisees have opened their restaurants on schedule and have made timely payments on the promissory notes and the 2% royalty.

The credit rating of the franchisees would enable them to borrow at the current annual interest rate of 15%. The present value of the three $10,000 promissory notes discounted at 15% is $22,832.

Instructions

a Given the nature of the standard contract with franchisees, how should revenue be recognized by Lobo, Inc.? Discuss the question of revenue recognition for the initial franchise fee, the 2% royalty based on sales, and interest revenue.

b Assume that Lobo, Inc., sold a franchise to Macon Company on December 31, Year 5, that Macon opened its restaurant on July 30, Year 6, and that sales for the restaurant were $480,000 for the year ended December 31, Year 6. Prepare journal entries for Lobo to record:

(1) The sale of the franchise on December 31, Year 5 (record the promissory notes receivable at present value)

(2) Recognition of franchise fee revenue on July 30, Year 6

(3) Recognition of interest revenue on December 31, Year 6

(4) Receipt of the second payment of $10,000 from Macon on December 31, Year 6, including recognition of franchise fee revenue on the straight-line basis

(5) Accrual of the 2% royalty on December 31, Year 6

3-10 Reseda Sales Outlet sells off-brand merchandise for cash and on the installment plan. Information for the first three years of its operations is summarized below:

	Year 3	Year 2	Year 1
Cash sales	$500,000	$400,000	$300,000
Installment sales	300,000	250,000	200,000
Collections on installment receivables from sales made in:			
Year 1	50,000	85,000	60,000
Year 2	120,000	80,000	
Year 3	100,000		
Cost of goods sold:			
Cash sales	350,000	290,000	205,000
Installment sales	186,000	150,000	130,000
Operating expenses	208,500	181,000	172,000
Gross profit percentages on installment sales .	38%	40%	35%

For purposes of this problem, interest and carrying charges on installment receivables, doubtful accounts expense, and income taxes are disregarded.

Instructions

Compute the net income of Reseda Sales Outlet for each of the three years under each of the following methods of accounting for installment sales (use one column for each year):

a Accrual basis of accounting

b Installment method (deduct unrealized gross profit on current year's installment sales from the total gross profit on all sales for that year, and add realized gross profit on installment sales of prior years to the total gross profit on all sales to compute realized gross profit for each year).

Financial Statements and Additional Disclosures

4

In the previous two chapters we have stressed that the measurement of the resources and obligations of a business enterprise is fundamental to the accounting process. The ongoing recording of transactions and events and the preparation of end-of-period adjusting entries may be described as a process of measuring assets and liabilities. If assets and liabilities are measured correctly, it should be apparent that revenue, expenses, and total owners' equity also are measured correctly. However, the measurement of assets and liabilities is not an easy process, and the result of this process is summarized in *general-purpose financial statements* that provide decision makers with useful information. A set of general-purpose financial statements is the foundation of the financial reporting and disclosure system and includes an income statement, a balance sheet, a statement of cash flows, a statement of retained earnings (or a statement of stockholders' equity when changes in paid-in capital occur during an accounting period), notes to the financial statements, data for interim periods and industry segments, and other supplementary disclosures.

The form and the content of financial statements have received considerable attention from accountants for many years. The heading of each financial statement includes the name of the business enterprise, the title of the statement, and the date or dates of the statement (or the period covered by the statement, such as "For Three Months Ended March 31, 1986"). The title should include any qualifying or descriptive words such as "consolidated," "comparative," or "condensed." When financial statements are not audited by independent accountants, the word "Unaudited" appears in the face of each financial statement. The manner of presenting information in the financial statements is discussed in this chapter.

The contents of a business enterprise's financial statements, including the supplementary disclosures, have *significant economic consequences* on the enterprise, its owners, its creditors, and all other parties who have an economic stake in its financial strength and profitability. Financial statements that are relevant, complete, objective, timely, and understandable are perceived by users to be *credible.* Credibility in financial reporting is an essential prerequisite to a healthy and efficient economic system.

A considerable amount of additional disclosures by publicly owned companies is required by rule-making bodies, notably the Financial Accounting Standards Board and the Securities and Exchange Commission. Such disclosures are intended to supplement the basic financial statements and may be included in notes to the financial statements, in other sections of the annual report to shareholders, or in reports filed with the Securities and Exchange Commission.

INCOME STATEMENT

In Chapter 3 we emphasize that the task of measuring revenue, expenses, gains, and losses is formidable. Also, the presentation of these items in the income statement has been more than a routine process for accountants. A formal income statement consists of more than an itemized list of revenue, expenses, gains, and losses. Attention must be given to such issues as the system of classification, the amount of detail that is appropriate, the order of presentation, the relationship among the various components of net income, and the titles used to describe the *line items* in the income statement.

A traditional income statement may not be as useful to management as statements showing income by products, departments, or divisions. Managers obviously are interested in detailed accounting and statistical data that shed light on the contribution of the various segments of a business enterprise to its overall success. Such information also might be useful to outsiders, but the information appearing in income statements issued to the public usually is highly condensed. More detailed income statements may be submitted to credit grantors and others having a special interest in the enterprise.

Some income statements may be quite complex. For example, if an enterprise sells a business segment, recognizes an extraordinary gain or loss, or implements a change in accounting principle that requires recognition of the cumulative effect of the change, the bottom portion of the income statement is expanded considerably. Also, *earnings per share data* are presented in the income statement of publicly owned companies, and this may be quite cumbersome when both *primary* and *fully diluted* earnings per share amounts are reported.

Alternative Forms of the Income Statement

The choice between the *multiple-step* form and the *single-step* form of income statement is an unsettled question. In the multiple-step form (illustrated below for Model Corporation) various intermediate amounts, such as gross profit on sales, income from operations, and income before income taxes, are presented as separate *line items*. The single-step form (illustrated on page 162) presents all revenue in one

Multiple-step form of
income statement

MODEL CORPORATION
Income Statement
For Year Ended December 31, Year 5
(In thousands of dollars)

Sales (net of discounts, returns, and allowances) . . .			$18,108
Cost of goods sold:			
Inventories Jan. 1, Year 5		$ 1,000	
Purchases (net of discounts, returns, and			
allowances)	$10,302		
Freight-in	1,266	11,568	
Cost of goods available for sale		$12,568	
Less: Inventories Dec. 31, Year 5		580	
Cost of goods sold			11,988
Gross profit on sales			$ 6,120
Operating expenses:			
Selling expenses:			
Sales salaries	$ 1,260		
Advertising and promotion	880		
Building occupancy (including depreciation			
and property taxes on building)	420		
Other	80	$ 2,640	
General and administrative expenses:			
Salaries	$ 1,160		
Property taxes	308		
Depreciation of equipment	80		
Other	72	1,620	
Total operating expenses			4,260
Income from operations			$ 1,860
Other revenue (expenses):			
Investment income		$ 420	
Gain on disposal of equipment		50	
Interest expense		(230)	240
Income before income taxes			$ 2,100
Income taxes expense (including $20 deferred) . .			1,043
Net income			$ 1,057
Earnings per share of common stock			$ 1.25

Single-step form of
income statement

MODEL CORPORATION
Income Statement
For Year Ended December 31, Year 5
(In thousands of dollars)

Revenue:		
Net sales		$18,108
Investment income		420
Gain on disposal of equipment		50
Total revenue		$18,578
Costs and expenses:		
Cost of goods sold	$11,988	
Selling expenses	2,640	
General and administrative expenses	1,620	
Interest expense	230	
Income taxes expense (including $20 deferred)	1,043	
Total costs and expenses		17,521
Net income		$ 1,057
Earnings per share of common stock		$ 1.25

category, all costs and expenses in another, and derives net income as the final amount. This form is widely used by publicly owned companies in their annual reports to shareholders.[1]

Those who favor the multiple-step form argue that there are several significant subtotals on the road to net income. The *gross profit on sales* indicates the markup on the merchandise sold that is available to cover operating expenses. The distinction between operating and nonoperating revenue and expenses permits the showing of *income from operations* as a measure of operating results. The *income before income taxes* reflects pre-tax earnings and emphasizes the special nature of income taxes expense.

Proponents of the single-step form maintain that net income emerges as the overall amount by which a business enterprise is better off after taking into account all revenue and all costs and expenses incurred in producing that revenue. They object to the implication of the multiple-step form that there is a priority of cost recovery; that is, that cost of goods sold is recovered first, then operating expenses, then other expenses, and finally income taxes. The multiple-step form also implies relationships that do not exist. For example, showing investment income as other revenue below income from operations implies that such income is realized without cost; yet some general and administrative expenses are incurred to produce investment income.

---

[1]Of the 600 companies included in *Accounting Trends & Techniques,* 38th ed. (1984), 314 used the single-step form and 286 used the multiple-step form.

The sequence of listing of expenses and the amount of detail shown in income statements vary considerably. The multiple-step form is more likely to be found in more detailed income statements prepared for the use of management, bankers, and other creditors. Most published income statements appear in single-step form and almost always are presented in *comparative form* for three years, similar to the one illustrated for Comcorp, Inc., on page 164 (see also page 220). Financial statements prepared in comparative form highlight trends and changes, and emphasize the fact that financial statements for a single accounting period are only a small part of the continuous history of a business enterprise.

Classification of Revenue

As stated in Chapter 3, the major source of revenue for most business enterprises is the production and sale of goods and services. Examples of secondary sources are dividends, royalties, interest, rents, investment income from affiliated companies, and gains on the disposal of assets. An objective of reporting revenue in an income statement is to disclose the major sources of revenue and to separate primary from miscellaneous sources. For example, some enterprises report revenue from government contracts separately from revenue from nongovernment sources, which enables the user to form some opinion of future prospects in the light of projected governmental expenditures.

Revenue *offsets* should be distinguished from expenses; they are deducted from gross revenue in the income statement. Such items as sales discounts and sales returns and allowances are not expenses, but rather revenue that is never realized.

Classification of Costs and Expenses

Costs and expenses are classified in the income statement to help users understand the operating cost relationships of the business enterprise. Classification may be according to the nature of expenses (*natural classification*), business functions (*functional classification*), areas of responsibility, or any other useful basis.

In many published income statements, costs and expenses are reported in single-step form, classified according to the *nature* of expenses, that is, in categories that reflect the kind of resources used during the accounting period. Examples of such categories include merchandise and supplies, salaries and fringe benefits, purchased services, depreciation, property taxes, interest, and income taxes.

The multiple-step income statement for Model Corporation on page 161 illustrates a classification of expenses into five categories on a *functional basis:* (1) cost of goods sold, (2) selling expenses, (3) general and administrative expenses, (4) other expenses, and (5) income taxes expense. In income statements prepared for different levels of management, the usefulness of the functional classification system may be improved by identifying additional functions. For example, material handling, production scheduling, assembly, inspection, and packing are examples of manufacturing subfunctions.

Illustration of Comprehensive Income Statement

The presentation of the results of discontinued operations, extraordinary items, cumulative effect of a change in accounting principle, and earnings per share data

Comprehensive
illustration of income
statements in
comparative form

COMCORP, INC.
Income Statements
For Years Ended December 31, Year 3, Year 2, and Year 1
(In thousands of dollars, except per-share data)

	Year 3	Year 2	Year 1
Net sales and other revenue...................	$85,360	$75,750	$67,800
Costs and expenses *(Note 1)*	65,880	60,390	55,500
Income from continuing operations before income taxes	$19,480	$15,360	$12,300
Income taxes expense (including $1,200 deferred each year)	9,350	7,370	6,400
Income from continuing operations	$10,130	$ 7,990	$ 5,900
Discontinued operations *(Note 2):*			
Income from operations of discontinued business segment, net of income tax effect of $383 in Year 3, $442 in Year 2, and $82 in Year 1	410	470	100
Loss on disposal of discontinued business segment, net of income tax effect of $1,880..	(2,040)		
Income before extraordinary item and cumulative effect of change in accounting principle.....................................	$ 8,500	$ 8,460	$ 6,000
Extraordinary item (gain), net of income tax effect of $493 *(Note 3)*......................		1,224	
Cumulative effect of change in accounting principle, net of income tax effect of $1,150 *(Note 4)*	1,250		
Net income	$ 9,750	$ 9,684	$ 6,000
Earnings per share of common stock:			
Income from continuing operations	$ 2.03	$ 1.60	$ 1.18
Income from operations of discontinued business segment	0.08	0.10	0.02
Loss on disposal of discontinued business segment..................................	(0.41)		
Income before extraordinary item and cumulative effect of change in accounting principle.....................................	$ 1.70	$ 1.70	$ 1.20
Extraordinary item (gain)		0.24	
Cumulative effect of change in accounting principle...................................	0.25		
Net income	$ 1.95	$ 1.94	$ 1.20

(continued)

Note 1: *Costs and expenses for Year 3 include $675,000 loss on disposal of plant assets.*

Note 2: *In October, Year 3, the company decided to dispose of its retailing segment that had consisted of 20 outlets in localities adjacent to its principal customers. Two of the outlets were closed in October, and the remaining 18 were sold prior to December 31, Year 3. Charges resulting directly from the decision to dispose of this business segment, principally termination costs on long-term leases, severance pay, and losses on disposal of assets related to the segment, less reduction in income taxes of $1,880,000, are reported separately from the results of continuing operations. The income statements for Year 1 and Year 2 have been reclassified to give effect to this presentation. Net sales of the discontinued business segment were $6,600,000 in Year 1, $7,590,000 in Year 2, and $9,200,000 in Year 3.*

Note 3: *During Year 2, the company received settlement from a state government for condemnation of land held for future expansion. The related gain, less income taxes of $493,000, is reported as an extraordinary item.*

Note 4: *Depreciation of plant assets is computed by the straight-line method in Year 3. Depreciation of plant assets in prior years was computed by the sum-of-the-years'-digits method. The new method of depreciation was adopted to be consistent with the practices of the company's industry, and has been applied retroactively to assets acquired in prior years. The effect of the change in Year 3 was to increase income before extraordinary item by $100,000 (or $0.02 per share). The adjustment of $1,250,000 (after reduction for income taxes of $1,150,000) to apply retroactively the new method is included in net income of Year 3 as a cumulative effect of change in accounting principle.*

in the income statement is illustrated (with the related notes) on pages 164–165 for Comcorp, Inc. Observe that in Year 3, for example, the operating income of the discontinued business segment is added to, and the loss on disposal of the discontinued business segment is deducted from, the "income from continuing operations" to determine the "income before extraordinary item and cumulative effect of change in accounting principle" of $8,500,000. After the cumulative effect of change in accounting principle of $1,250,000 is added to this amount, the net income of $9,750,000 is reported as a "bottom line" item. Note also the extensive detail of the earnings-per-share data included in the income statement of Comcorp, Inc., despite the fact that a *dual presentation* of earnings per share (*primary* and *fully diluted*) was not required.

STATEMENT OF RETAINED EARNINGS

A statement of retained earnings or a statement of stockholders' equity is included with every set of financial statements; however, neither is considered a basic financial statement. Changing concepts of financial reporting in recent years have firmly established the all-inclusive income statement, thus tending to shorten and simplify the statement of retained earnings (or the retained earnings section of the statement of stockholders' equity). Also significant has been the trend away from the use of appropriations of retained earnings. Consequently, the typical statement of retained earnings includes the beginning balance of retained earnings, the net income for the accounting period as an addition (or the net loss as a deduction), and the dividends declared (both cash and stock) as deductions, and concludes with the ending balance of retained earnings. Disclosure of cash dividends per share also is made in the statement of retained earnings. In addition, the beginning balance of retained earnings may be restated as a result of either a *prior period adjustment* or the effect on prior years' net income resulting from certain types of changes in accounting principles.

█████████████ ## Prior Period Adjustments

In contrast to extraordinary items described in Chapter 3, *prior period adjustments* are excluded from the determination of net income and are reported, *net of the income tax effect,* in the statement of retained earnings. Prior period adjustments are defined by the Financial Accounting Standards Board as follows:[2]

> . . . all items of profit and loss recognized during a period, including accruals of estimated losses from loss contingencies, shall be included in the determination of net income for that period.
>
> Items of profit and loss related to the following shall be accounted for and reported as prior period adjustments and excluded from the determination of net income for the current period:
>
> **a** Correction of an error in the financial statements of a prior period and
>
> **b** Adjustments that result from realization of income tax benefits of pre-acquisition operating loss carryforwards of purchased subsidiaries.

Material errors in the financial statements might include arithmetical mistakes, the misuse or omissions of information, mistakes in the application of accounting principles, and failure to interpret properly the accounting aspects of transactions. Another example of a correction of an error is a change from an accounting principle that is not generally accepted to one that is.

The adjustments from realization of income tax benefits of pre-acquisition operating loss carryforwards of purchased subsidiaries relate to the reduction in goodwill amortization of prior periods, because the tax benefits are recorded as a credit to previously recorded goodwill.

In the financial statements for the current accounting period, a prior period adjustment is reported as a correction to the beginning balance of retained earnings. When a correction of an error is made as a prior period adjustment, the issuance of comparative financial statements requires the restatement of prior periods' financial statements to reflect the correction.

Alternative Forms of Statement of Retained Earnings

The basic format of a statement of retained earnings that includes a prior period adjustment is illustrated on page 167 for Model Corporation. Model did not prepare a statement of stockholders' equity because there were no changes in any component of paid-in capital. The related income statement (multiple-step form) for Model appears on page 161; the related balance sheet and statement of changes in financial position are presented on pages 179–180 and on page 182, respectively.

As with other financial statements, the statement of retained earnings generally is presented in *comparative form* showing data for two or more years. Some companies combine the income statement with the statement of retained earnings. Such a presentation has the advantage of displaying in one statement any prior period adjustments and extraordinary items, thus reducing the possibility that any of these items will be overlooked. One minor objection to this form is that the net income or

---

[2]*FASB Statement No. 16,* "Prior Period Adjustments," FASB (Stamford: 1977), p. 5.

Statement of retained
earnings with a prior
period adjustment

MODEL CORPORATION
Statement of Retained Earnings
For Year Ended December 31, Year 5
(In thousands of dollars)

Retained earnings, beginning of year, as originally reported ..		$2,800
Less: Prior period adjustment (correction of error), net		
of income tax effect of $240		360
Retained earnings, beginning of year, as restated		$2,440
Add: Net income		1,057
Subtotal		$3,497
Less: Cash dividends on preferred stock ($6.00 a share).....	$ 57	
Cash dividends on common stock ($0.50 a share)	400	457
Retained earnings, end of year		$3,040

net loss appears in the middle of the statement. An example of **combined statements
of income and retained earnings** in comparative form for two years is shown
below:

Combined statements
of income and retained
earnings in comparative
form

RED COMPANY
Combined Statements of Income and Retained Earnings
For Year Ended December 31, Year 2 and Year 1

	Year 2	Year 1
Net sales	$1,295,100	$1,260,300
Less: Costs and expenses	1,014,000	1,021,600
Income before income taxes	$ 281,100	$ 238,700
Income taxes expense	142,100	126,900
Net income	$ 139,000	$ 111,800
Retained earnings, beginning of year................	403,800	377,800
Subtotals	$ 542,800	$ 489,600
Less: Cash dividends—$1.75 and $1.72 a share,		
respectively......................................	87,500	86,000
Retained earnings, end of year	$ 455,300	$ 403,600
Earnings per share of common stock................	$ 2.78	$ 2.24

An analysis of the changes in retained earnings may be presented as a part of
a statement of stockholders' equity as illustrated on page 181.

BALANCE SHEET

A **balance sheet** (or **statement of financial position**) presents the financial position
of a business enterprise on a specific date. A balance sheet provides a historical

summary of the following elements as defined by the Financial Accounting Standards Board:[3]

Assets are probable future economic benefits obtained or controlled by a particular entity as a result of past transactions or events.

Liabilities are probable future sacrifices of economic benefits arising from present obligations of a particular entity to transfer assets or provide services to other entities in the future as a result of past transactions or events.

Equity is the residual interest in the assets of an entity that remains after deducting its liabilities. In a business enterprise, the equity is the ownership interest.

A balance sheet is basically a historical statement, because it shows the cumulative effect of past transactions and events. Generally, it is described as a detailed expression of the basic accounting equation:

Assets = Liabilities + Owners' Equity

The theoretical concept of an asset may be related to the discussion of revenue and expenses in Chapter 3. Assets are costs that have not been deducted from revenue; they represent *expected future economic benefits*. However, the rights to assets have been acquired by a business enterprise as a result of past transactions. If no future economic benefit is expected from a cost incurred by the enterprise, the cost in question is not an asset and should not be included in the balance sheet.

Liabilities also result from past transactions; they are obligations that require settlement in the future, either by the transfer of assets or by the performance of services.

Implicit in these concepts of the nature of assets and liabilities is the meaning of owners' equity as the *residual equity* in the assets of a business enterprise.

Uses and Limitations of the Balance Sheet

At one time the balance sheet was considered the primary end product of accounting. However, experience pounded home the economic lesson that earning power is the prime determinant of the value of a business enterprise, and users of financial statements gradually placed more emphasis on the income statement. Today the balance sheet is recapturing much of the status it once had, because users of financial statements have come to realize that the income statement neither includes the economic resources and debt of an enterprise nor measures the enterprise's ability to raise sufficient capital for continued growth. Therefore, investors and creditors are placing more emphasis on an enterprise's current and acid test ratios, debt to equity ratio, and rates of return on assets and stockholders' equity. After recent experiences with "credit crunches," business recessions, high levels of interest rates, and inflation, enterprises are giving more attention to their balance sheets. In recent years, the accounting profession has taken significant actions to make the balance

---

[3]*Statement of Financial Accounting Concepts No. 3,* "Elements of Financial Statements of Business Enterprises," FASB (Stamford: 1980), p. xi.

sheet more relevant and useful for decision makers. These actions have included a movement toward disclosure of the effects of inflation, immediate expensing of most research and development costs, mandatory amortization of goodwill, and the reporting of certain long-term leases as acquisitions of plant assets.

A balance sheet in *comparative form* provides valuable information to creditors, stockholders, management, prospective investors, and the public. Individuals with the ability to interpret comparative balance sheets may learn much as to the short-run solvency of a business enterprise, favorable or unfavorable trends in liquidity, commitments that must be met in the future, and the relative positions of creditors and stockholders.

In an ideal balance sheet, the list of assets and liabilities would be all-inclusive, and each would be reported at its current fair value. As a result, the residual equity (assets minus liabilities) would reflect meaningful ''net worth'' of a business enterprise. The major *limitation* of the traditional balance sheet lies in the inability of accountants to measure the ''current fair value'' of an enterprise's net assets. The inability of accountants (or anyone else) to foresee future economic events necessitates the preparation of balance sheets on a different basis. Indirect methods of valuation must be used to measure certain assets and liabilities in the balance sheet. Furthermore, accountants are unable to identify and provide a valuation for many factors that have a material effect on the financial position of an enterprise. The quality, morale, and character of management and other personnel, the market position of an enterprise and the reputation of its products, the growth potential implicit in the nature and diversity of its operations—all these are subjective and intangible factors of great importance in the evaluation of the financial position of an enterprise. None of these factors is reported directly in the dollars-and-cents framework of the accounting process that leads to a balance sheet.

Some critics, in discussing the merits of various accounting principles and procedures, take the position that because the balance sheet does not reflect ''current fair value'' it does not matter what amounts appear in it. There is a serious defect in such thinking. To imply that *meaningful* income statements may be prepared as an adjunct to *meaningless* balance sheets shows a failure to understand the relationship between these two financial statements. A consistently applied set of principles for the measurement of assets and liabilities is a prerequisite to a meaningful measurement of net income.

Balance Sheet Classification

The classifications, group headings, and number of items on a balance sheet vary considerably depending on the size of the enterprise, the nature of its operations, and whether the financial statements are intended for wide distribution or for the use of a few owners and creditors. As an example of the diversity encountered in published financial statements, public utility companies usually place plant assets at the top of the balance sheet, followed by current assets. They also may use such fuzzy group headings as ''Assets and Other Debits,'' along with ''Liabilities and Other Credits.'' Financial institutions generally do not use the current/noncurrent classification for assets and liabilities. The consolidated balance sheet of Walt Disney Productions in the Appendix at the end of this chapter (p. 222) is not classified, for reasons set forth in Note 1 on page 228 under ''Principles of Consolidation.''

As a generalization subject to many exceptions, the following classification of balance sheet items is suggested as representative:

Assets
  Current assets
  Investments (held for control or not readily marketable)
  Plant assets
  Intangible assets
  Other noncurrent assets (including deferred charges)

Liabilities
  Current liabilities
  Long-term debt (including deferred income tax credits and deferred revenue)

Stockholders' equity
  Capital stock (preferred and common stock)
  Additional paid-in capital
  Retained earnings

This classification reflects the three elements of the basic accounting equation. In practice, it is not unusual to find a fourth category placed between liabilities and stockholders' equity (often with the caption ''Reserves'' or ''Deferred Credits''), to include items such as deferred income tax credits, unamortized investment tax credits, and minority interest in net assets of subsidiaries.

Working Capital

The **working capital** of a business enterprise is the excess of current assets over current liabilities. This amount always has been of considerable interest to credit grantors as a measure of short-run **solvency**—the ability to finance current operations and to pay obligations as they mature. The amounts of current assets and current liabilities, and the relationship between them (the **current ratio**), are widely quoted in financial circles and often are incorporated in contracts between an enterprise and its creditors and preferred stockholders. Most such contracts do not define working capital but simply state that it ''shall be determined in accordance with generally accepted accounting principles.'' Thus, a generally accepted and consistent basis is needed for determining which items are included in, and which are excluded from, the current assets and current liabilities sections of the balance sheet.

Current Assets   As a practical matter, it is easy to grasp the conceptual difference between a current asset and a noncurrent asset. However, the boundary between these two categories is hazy, and defining an exact boundary is not an easy task.

   Five general types of assets generally are included in the current assets classification:

1   *Cash*   Money in any form—cash and checks awaiting deposit, balances in checking accounts, and expendable cash funds.

2   *Secondary cash resources*   Various short-term investments that are readily marketable. Any such resources whose availability for current use is restricted by contract are excluded.

3   *Short-term receivables*   Trade accounts receivable (including installment receivables collected during the enterprise's operating cycle) and notes receivable with short-term maturities.

4   *Inventories*   Material, supplies, goods in process, finished goods. This category includes items held for sale in the ordinary course of operations, items in process of production, and items that will be consumed in the production of goods or services. Goods held on consignment from others are not included because title is not held to such goods.

5   *Short-term prepayments*   The cost of various services, such as insurance, taxes, and rent, that have been paid for in advance of use. Short-term prepayments sometimes are referred to as *prepaid expenses.*

There is little question about including cash, secondary cash resources, and short-term receivables in the current assets category. As might be expected, the troublesome area is the distinction between short-term and long-term investments in productive assets. The test usually applied in distinguishing current from noncurrent productive assets is whether the investment in these assets will be realized within the operating cycle or one year, whichever is the longer period.

The term *operating cycle* refers to the circulation of items within the current asset category. In a typical business enterprise, cash is invested in material, supplies, labor, and overhead costs, and these costs are traced through and assigned to inventories. Inventories eventually are realized by conversion to trade receivables, and trade receivables in turn are collected and once more become cash. The average period of time between the investment in goods and services and the conversion to cash is the length of the operating cycle of an enterprise. In most cases this is a matter of days or months, but in some industries, the operating cycle may extend beyond one year. Thus, *the conventional time test for current assets is realization within one year or the operating cycle, whichever is longer.*

There are some theoretical flaws in the application of the time test. In a realistic sense, all asset services that will be used to produce revenue during the immediately succeeding operating cycle or accounting period will be realized and converted to liquid assets. A portion of the cost of plant assets will be realized in the same sense, as will be the investment in material. For example, it may be argued that standing timber that will be used to manufacture plywood in the next operating cycle has as good a claim to inclusion among current assets as the inventory of glue that will bind the layers of wood. Thus, the attempt to distinguish between assets that are consumed physically and assets that yield services gradually through use has some stumbling blocks in its way. These conceptual niceties generally are disregarded in the reporting of current assets in a balance sheet.

In any system of classification, there are troublesome items that do not fit neatly in designated niches. For example, if money is borrowed for the express purpose of constructing plant assets, it may be argued that its inclusion in working capital is misleading. If fire insurance is acquired covering a three-year period, a question may be raised about the logical consistency of including the full amount of unexpired insurance as a current asset.

In resolving these difficulties, accountants find themselves at odds with a neat, logical statement of the characteristics that distinguish current assets. They may explain their difficulties as an inevitable conflict between theory and practice, but the result is that the distinction between current and noncurrent assets often is based more on rules-of-thumb than on precise definitions.

Current Liabilities   The distinction between current and noncurrent is easier to make for liabilities than for assets. Generally, current liabilities are obligations whose liquidation is expected to require the use of current assets or the creation of other current liabilities. Three main classes of current liabilities fall within this definition:

1   *Obligations for the acquisition of goods and services that have entered the operating cycle.* These include trade payables (including notes and accounts payable to suppliers) and accrued liabilities such as wages, commissions, income taxes, property taxes, etc.

2   *Other debts that may be expected to require payment within the operating cycle or one year.* This includes short-term notes payable to banks and the currently maturing portions of long-term debt.

3   *Collections received in advance of the delivery of goods or the performance of services.* These advances often are described as "deferred revenue," but it is the obligation to furnish the goods or services or to refund the payment that requires them to be classified in the current liabilities section of the balance sheet.

Some liabilities that will be paid shortly after the balance sheet date are excluded from current liabilities, because of the requirement that a current liability must involve the use of current assets or the issuance of new short-term debt for its extinction. Examples are (1) obligations due at an early date that will be retired by the issuance of new long-term debt, for example, bonds that will be refunded or a loan secured by the cash surrender value of life insurance policies (the amount of cash that would be received if the policies were canceled) that will be renewed, and (2) obligations that will be paid from a fund included among noncurrent assets, for example, a life insurance policy loan that will be liquidated by offset against the cash surrender value of the policy, or by deduction from the proceeds of the life insurance policy at maturity.

Noncurrent Resources and Obligations

Noncurrent Assets   The definition of current assets determines by exclusion those assets that are reported as noncurrent. There are four categories of noncurrent assets:

1   *Long-term funds, investments, and receivables*   Many long-term commitments of funds do not qualify as secondary cash resources. Investments in the common stock of investees made for the purpose of influence or control are included in this category. Also included are noncurrent receivables (such as long-term advances to affiliated companies), the cash surrender value of life insurance policies, and funds established for such purposes as the payment of pensions, retirement of preferred stock, or repayment of long-term debt. Assets such as land held for speculative purposes and future plant sites also are included in this category.

2 *Long-term tangible resources used in operations* The distinguishing characteristics of assets in this category are that they are tangible (have physical substance) and are held for productive use in business operations. Land, natural resources subject to depletion, buildings, equipment, machines, tools, leased assets under capital leases, leasehold improvements, and plant assets under construction are included. Long-term prepayments for the use of physical assets, such as leaseholds, easements, or rights of way, also may be included in this category, though some accountants group these in the next category.

3 *Long-term intangible resources* Long-term property rights of an intangible nature may be of greater importance to a business enterprise than its tangible assets. Examples of such assets are patents, goodwill, trademarks, copyrights, organization costs, and franchises. However, under generally accepted accounting principles most of these items are recorded as assets only when an expenditure has been made to acquire an intangible property right from outsiders. For example, internally developed goodwill is not recorded as an asset; instead, the costs incurred in building such goodwill are recognized currently as expenses. Similarly, all research and development costs, except those that are reimbursable, are recognized as expenses.

4 *Other noncurrent assets* Most published balance sheets include a category titled "Other Assets," "Other Noncurrent Assets," or "Deferred Charges." Included in this category are items such as plant assets no longer used in operations and held for disposal, costs incurred in the issuance of long-term debt, deferred start-up and moving costs, and any other noncurrent asset that is not included in one of the first three categories.

Contingent Assets Assets, as well as liabilities, may be contingent. A contingent asset is a property right whose existence is conditional on the happening of some future event (*gain contingency*). Generally, it is not appropriate to include contingent assets in the accounting records, because to do so would violate the principles of revenue realization and reliability. There is a lack of reliable evidence that an asset exists or that the earning process has been completed. However, the disclosure of the existence of contingencies that may result in material gains (and assets) is useful.[4] An example of such disclosure follows: ". . . the company has an income tax loss carryforward of $15,200,000 that may be deducted from future taxable income. . . ."

Noncurrent Liabilities A noncurrent liability is an obligation that will not require the use of current assets or the issuance of short-term debt within the next year or operating cycle, whichever is longer. There is some question whether there is any

---

[4]*FASB Statement No. 5,* "Accounting for Contingencies," FASB (Stamford: 1975), p. 8.

useful basis for subclassification within this category. In general practice, a distinction may be drawn between the following two classes:

1 *Long-term debt based on security issues or related contractual arrangements* Included in this category are notes and bonds, reported net of any unamortized discount and including any unamortized premium. The distinguishing characteristic is that there is a borrowing transaction supported by a contractual obligation to pay principal and interest.

2 *Other noncurrent liabilities* As the word ''other'' implies, this includes all long-term liabilities that do not belong in the first category. An amount received in advance on a long-term commitment to furnish goods or services is an example. Any portion of such advances that will be realized during the succeeding accounting period is reported as a current liability. Other examples are long-term advances from affiliated companies, noncurrent amounts payable under pension plans, liabilities under capital leases, deferred revenue, and deferred income tax credits.

Contingent Liabilities Liabilities that ***may*** or ***may not*** come into existence as a result of transactions or events that ***have not yet been finalized*** usually are not reported in dollar amounts in the balance sheet. Not only is the evidence with respect to such liabilities too vague to be called objective, but the events (***loss contingencies***) necessary to bring the liabilities into existence have not yet been completed. Such ***contingent liabilities*** are disclosed, usually by means of a note to the financial statements. Some examples of contingent liabilities are obligations to reimburse banks in case of default by the maker of discounted notes receivable, pending lawsuits that may result in the payment of damages, and possible additional income tax assessments.

Management would be imprudent to provide dollar estimates on anticipated unfavorable results from pending lawsuits, because such disclosure might be viewed as an admission of the merits of the opposing case. However, if the item is material, disclosure in general terms is essential.

A common error is the failure to distinguish between contingent liabilities and obligations that exist but are not definite as to amount, due date, or both. These obligations are called ***estimated liabilities.*** There are varying degrees of uncertainty about liabilities; some may be estimated with a high degree of accuracy; others may be subject to no more than an informed guess. The liability for income taxes or the amounts payable to employees under pension plans are examples of estimated liabilities that may be measured with reasonable precision on the basis of tentative income tax returns and other data. In contrast, it is difficult to estimate the cost of making good on potential product warranty claims. When such liabilities exist, they are estimated and included in the balance sheet.

Contra-Asset and Contra-Liability Ledger Accounts Some assets and liabilities are reported in two amounts as a convenient means of disclosing more information about these items than would be afforded by a net valuation. For example, trade accounts receivable are reported as the difference between the gross amount due from customers and an allowance for doubtful accounts. Similarly, bond discount is shown as a deduction from the face amount of bonds payable. The general criterion for determining whether to display a balance sheet item in one amount or two is the degree of usefulness of the added information. The amount of doubtful accounts receivable provides information about the expected collection experience on trade accounts receivable, and the amount of accumulated depreciation of plant assets provides information about depreciation policy and the age of plant assets. The disclosure may be made as a separate valuation ledger account or by a parenthetical notation.

The use of valuation ledger accounts should be distinguished from an actual *offsetting* of assets and liabilities. When valuation accounts are used, the amount deducted from an asset is not a liability, and the amount deducted from a liability is not an asset. Offsetting assets and liabilities is improper, because it implies an association between the two that seldom exists. For example, if a business enterprise voluntarily accumulates a fund to pay a long-term debt when it matures, the intention may be revoked before the debt is paid. Thus, the fund is reported as an asset and the debt as a liability until payment is made.

Owners' Equity

The owners' equity in a business enterprise is the residual interest in assets, after liabilities have been deducted. The amount of owners' equity thus is directly dependent on the values assigned to assets and liabilities. When owners invest assets in an enterprise, the valuation placed on assets determines the amount added to owners' equity. When operating results are summarized, the increase in net assets determines the amount of net income added to the owners' equity. This point is worth noting, because accountants sometimes are tempted to reverse this process and assume that if an amount (for example, the par or stated value of common stock) is associated with an element of ownership, there must be an asset to match.

Because of the legal differences between incorporated and nonincorporated business enterprises, there are variations in the balance sheet presentation of owners' equity for such organizations.

Single Proprietorships and Partnerships The owners' equity in single proprietorships and partnerships usually is reported in the balance sheet as a single amount

ALLEN & BATES PARTNERSHIP Statement of Partners' Capital For Year Ended June 30, Year 3			
	Allen	*Bates*	*Combined*
Partners' capital, beginning of year	$25,000	$34,000	$59,000
Add: Net income	12,600	18,200	30,800
Subtotals	$37,600	$52,200	$89,800
Less: Drawings	15,000	10,000	25,000
Partners' capital, end of year	$22,600	$42,200	$64,800

for each owner. There is no reason why the amount of capital invested by each owner should not be shown separately from the reinvested earnings, but because there is no legal restriction on the amounts proprietors or partners may withdraw from the enterprise, such information is less significant than in the case of corporations. Contractual arrangements among partners governing investments, drawings, and the division of net income or loss require that each partner's equity be determined accurately and reported in the balance sheet. A sample statement of partners' capital is illustrated on page 175.

The combined capital of $64,800 is reported as owners' equity in the balance sheet for Allen & Bates Partnership.

Corporations   The presentation of stockholders' equity in the balance sheet of a corporation is influenced strongly by legal considerations. As a result, there are a number of classifications (particularly in the "invested capital" section) that have no particular accounting significance. Below is an outline of the main sections of owners' equity for corporations:

1   *Invested capital*
a *Stated capital.* The amount assigned to shares of capital stock (preferred and common) outstanding as par or stated value is known as *legal capital* or *stated capital* of a corporation. This amount usually appears under the headings of *preferred stock* and *common stock.* For each class of stock, the amount of par or stated value per share, the number of shares authorized, issued, outstanding, and in the treasury, and any dividend or liquidating preference is disclosed in the balance sheet or in a note to the financial statements.
b *Additional paid-in capital.* This category includes all sources of invested capital in excess of stated (legal) capital. The terms *paid-in capital in excess of par* and *paid-in capital in excess of stated value* may be used to designate amounts invested by stockholders that exceed the par or stated value of each class of issued capital stock.

Additional paid-in capital may include both positive and negative amounts. For example, if a corporation receives less than par or stated value for its common stock, the contra-stockholders' equity ledger account Discount on Common Stock appears in this section of the balance sheet. Positive items include any amount in excess of par or stated value arising from the issuance of common stock, the reissuance of treasury stock at more than cost, donations of assets to the corporation (donated capital), or transfers from retained earnings through distributions of stock dividends. Similarly, the cost of *treasury stock* (a debit balance) is a contra-stockholders' equity item.

2   *Increase in stockholders' equity through the retention of earnings*
a *Retained earnings.* Net income of past accounting periods that has not been distributed to stockholders as dividends falls in this category. The term *retained earnings* is used far more widely than any other to describe this part of stockholders' equity. Alternative terms are *income retained for use in business* and *earnings reinvested in the business.* The term *earned surplus,* although still used by a few corporations, is obsolete.

b *Appropriated retained earnings.* A corporate board of directors sometimes may wish to indicate that a portion of retained earnings has been appropriated. A formal segregation of retained earnings is a means of disclosing that future dividend payments are restricted, either because of legal or contractual agreements or by management intent. The use of appropriations of retained earnings as a means of disclosure has almost disappeared; other more effective means of indicating the restriction of retained earnings are available, principally the use of a note to the financial statements.

3 *Unrealized appreciation in value of plant assets; and unrealized loss in value of long-term investments* In unusual cases a business enterprise may report unrealized appreciation or decline in the value of its assets in the balance sheet to disclose a material discrepancy between carrying amount and current fair value. This procedure is an *exception* to the accounting principle that only realized increases in asset values are entered in the accounting records. The offsetting increase or decrease in owners' equity is shown separately and designated as ''unrealized appraisal capital'' (an increase) or as ''unrealized loss in value of long-term investments in marketable equity securities'' (a decrease).

Use of Term "Reserve"

In the past the term *''reserve''* was used by accountants in a number of different and somewhat misleading ways. A reserve, in nonaccounting usage, usually is thought of as something held for a specific purpose, often for emergencies. This connotation leads to misinterpretation when the word ''reserve'' is included in the title of an asset valuation or estimated liability account. Currently, the trend is to avoid the use of the word ''reserve,'' although some business enterprises continue to use it in the assets and liabilities sections of the balance sheet.

The term ''reserve,'' when used to describe an appropriation of retained earnings, is acceptable, although its use continues to decline. A Reserve for Plant Expansion is more likely to be misunderstood than Retained Earnings Appropriated for Plant Expansion. If used at all, the term ''reserve'' should appear only in the stockholders' equity section of the balance sheet. Because its purpose is to indicate a restriction of retained earnings, the nature of the restriction may be set forth more clearly in a note to the financial statements than by an appropriation of retained earnings.

Standards of Disclosure

Accountants apply the disclosure principle as a basis for resolving a number of questions that arise in the preparation of balance sheets.

Account Titles In providing titles for ledger accounts, considerable leeway is permissible, in deference to convenience and economy of space. The persons involved in the accounting function understand the nature of the item; thus, short account titles are a matter of convenience. However, in the preparation of financial statements, users of the information must be kept in mind, and a clearly worded description of each item is desirable. For example, the title ''Accounts Receivable'' may be stated in the balance sheet as ''Amounts Due from Customers.'' In the choice between brevity and clarity, the latter should prevail in the preparation of financial statements. Of course, several ledger account balances may be combined into a single financial statement item, such as "inventories."

Basis of Valuation   Informed users of financial statements are presumed to be familiar with the general principles applicable to the valuation of assets and liabilities. However, variations in accounting procedures often produce balance sheet amounts whose significance is difficult to interpret unless the procedure used is disclosed. For example, the choice of first-in, first-out or last-in, first-out cost in inventory valuation results in materially different amounts for inventories during periods of inflation. The disclosure principle requires that the basis of valuation be indicated in the caption of all balance sheet items or in a note to the financial statements entitled "Summary of Significant Accounting Policies," unless it is obvious (as in the case of cash, for example).

Notes to the Financial Statements   Explanatory comments and supplementary disclosure are made in "Notes to financial statements." The notes may cover many pages of an annual report and include a complete description of significant accounting policies. For such matters as stock option plans, pension plans, leases, and business combinations, the only reasonable way to provide an adequate explanation is by use of notes. Additional discussion of notes to financial statements appears on page 186.

Supporting Exhibits   If the detail involved in a section of the balance sheet interferes with a concise presentation, it may be desirable to summarize the item in the balance sheet and show the detail in a supporting exhibit. For example, inventories may be reported in a single amount, and the detailed amounts of material, goods in process, goods on consignment, and finished goods presented in a separate exhibit. Business enterprises frequently show total long-term debt as a single amount and include a supporting exhibit in which the details are furnished (see Note 5 on page 230, for example). Thus, for users of financial statements who want only "highlight" information, the balance sheet provides it in concise form; users who want more detailed information will find it in the notes to the financial statements and supporting exhibits.

Form of the Balance Sheet

Fairly standard ways of presenting balance sheet information have been developed, but there is no universal form. The objectives are *clarity* and *adequate disclosure of all pertinent and material facts;* there are various ways of meeting these objectives, and experimentation should be encouraged. The arrangement of the major sections of the balance sheet also may vary. We shall describe the basic features of three forms of the balance sheet: *account form, report form,* and *financial position form.* Within the framework of these three forms a number of variations are possible. In a recent survey of 600 companies, 302 used the account form, 294 used the report form, and only 4 used the financial position form.[5]

---

[5]*Accounting Trends & Techniques,* 38th ed., AICPA (New York: 1984), p. 105.

MODEL CORPORATION
Balance Sheet
December 31, Year 5
(In thousands of dollars)

Assets

Current assets:

Cash		$ 485
Short-term investments (at cost, market value $220)		210
Notes and interest receivable		125
Trade accounts receivable	$1,162	
Less: Allowance for doubtful accounts....................	50	1,112
Inventories (at lower of average cost or market)		580
Short-term prepayments................................		60
Total current assets		$ 2,572

Investments:

Common stock of affiliated companies (at equity)..........	$1,250	
Fund for retirement of preferred stock	60	
Land held for future expansion	100	
Cash surrender value of life insurance policies	50	1,460

Plant assets:

	Cost	Accumulated depreciation	Carrying amount	
Land	$ 3,015		$3,015	
Buildings	10,950	$5,992	4,958	
Equipment	8,430	2,720	5,710	
Totals	$22,395	$8,712		13,683

Intangible assets (net of amortization):

Goodwill..	$1,105	
Patents...	105	1,210
Other noncurrent assets: plant assets held for disposal		45
Total assets		$18,970

Account Form A balance sheet for Model Corporation in account form appears above and on page 180. The distinguishing characteristic of this form is that all assets are listed on the left-hand side and liabilities and stockholders' equity are "balanced" against them on the right-hand side. This balance sheet includes typical accounts in each classification and follows current standards of disclosure and terminology. The appropriate degree of condensation in the balance sheet depends on the needs of users. Notes relating to the balance sheet are omitted from this illustration. An example of notes to the financial statements of Walt Disney Productions is included in the Appendix at the end of this chapter (pages 228–233).

Report Form The report form of balance sheet differs from the account form only in that the liabilities and stockholders' equity sections are listed below, rather than to the right of, the assets section.

Liabilities & Stockholders' Equity

Current liabilities:

Trade notes and accounts payable		$ 460
Income taxes payable		200
Dividends payable		125
Advances from customers		50
Retirement benefits payable currently		40
Accrued liabilities		30
Total current liabilities		$ 905

Long-term debt:

10% bonds payable, due Dec. 31, Year 15	$ 4,000	
Less: Discount on bonds payable	20	
Net bonds payable	$ 3,980	
Retirement benefits payable in future years	250	
Deferred income tax credits	300	
Total long-term debt		4,530
Total liabilities		$ 5,435

Stockholders' equity:

6% cumulative, convertible preferred stock, $100 par, callable at $105 a share, authorized 10,000 shares, issued and outstanding 9,500 shares	$ 950	
Common stock, no par, stated value $5, authorized 1,000,000 shares, issued and outstanding 800,000 shares	4,000	
Additional paid-in capital	5,545	
Total paid-in capital	$10,495	
Retained earnings	3,040	
Total stockholders' equity		13,535
Total liabilities & stockholders' equity		$18,970

Financial Position Form   Both the account form and the report form of the balance sheet express the basic accounting equation *Assets = Liabilities + Owners' Equity.* However, a few enterprises prefer to use a format that emphasizes working capital; this usually carries the title Statement of Financial Position rather than Balance Sheet. This is a *vertical* format in which current liabilities are deducted from current assets to derive working capital. Other assets then are added and other liabilities are deducted, leaving a residual amount as stockholders' equity.

The balance sheet for Model Corporation on page 179 and above is as of a specific date, December 31, Year 5. However, comparative amounts for the previous year are presented in almost every published balance sheet. Such *comparative balance sheets* for Walt Disney Productions are illustrated on page 222 of the Appendix at the end of this chapter.

STATEMENT OF STOCKHOLDERS' EQUITY

As stated on page 165, a statement of retained earnings explains the changes that have occurred in retained earnings during an accounting period. However, changes requiring disclosure also may occur in other components of stockholders' equity, that is, paid-in capital. In such circumstances, a *statement of stockholders' equity,* such as the one illustrated below for Pogo Corporation, also includes an analysis of the changes in retained earnings:

POGO CORPORATION
Statement of Stockholders' Equity
For Years Ended December 31, Year 2 and Year 3
(In thousands)

	Common stock, $10 par		Additional paid-in capital	Retained earnings	Total
	Number of shares	Amount			
Balances, Jan. 1, Year 2	1,250	$12,500	$137,858	$306,535	$456,893
Net income, Year 2				68,066	68,066
Cash dividends ($11 a share)				(13,750)	(13,750)
Balances, Dec. 31, Year 2	1,250	$12,500	$137,858	$360,851	$511,209
Net income, Year 3				79,685	79,685
Cash dividends ($16 a share)				(31,200)	(31,200)
Issuance of common stock	283	2,830	24,332		27,162
Conversion of bonds payable to common stock	417	4,170	30,315		34,485
50% stock dividend distributed	975	9,750		(9,750)	
Balances, Dec. 31, Year 3	2,925	$29,250	$192,505	$399,586	$621,341

STATEMENT OF CASH FLOWS

Along with an income statement and a balance sheet, a *statement of cash flows* is included in annual reports to shareholders of publicly owned companies and is covered by the auditors' opinion. The objectives of this statement are (1) to summarize the financing, operating, and investing activities of a business enterprise during an accounting period, including the amount of cash and cash equivalents obtained from operations, and (2) to complete the disclosure of changes in financial position during an accounting period that are not readily apparent in comparative balance sheets.

The statement of cash flows discloses transactions that affect cash directly, as well as significant investing and financing transactions that do not affect cash. For

MODEL CORPORATION
Statement of Cash Flows
For Year Ended December 31, Year 5
(in thousands of dollars)

Cash flows from operating activities

Net income $1,057

Items reconciling net income to net cash flow from operations:

Depreciation expense	186
Amortization of goodwill, patents, and bond discount	64
Retirement benefits payable in future years	40
Increase in deferred taxes..................................	20
Equity in income of subsidiaries	(110)
Increase in short-term investments	(60)
Increase in notes and interest receivable	(125)
Increase in trade accounts receivable	(312)
Decrease in inventories	420
Increase in short-term prepayments	(40)
Decrease in trade notes and payables	(330)
Decrease in income taxes payable	(150)
Decrease in advances from customers	(88)
Decrease in accrued liabilities	(50)
Increase in retirement benefits payable currently	5

Net cash provided by operating activities .... $ 527

Cash flows from investing activities

Disposal of equipment	$ 100
Increase in cash surrender value of life insurance	(10)
Acquisition of patents	(120)

Net cash used by investing activities .... $ (30)

Cash flows from financing activities

Issuance of preferred stock	$ 250
Dividends paid on preferred and common stock...............	(432)
Increase in fund for retirement of preferred stock	(30)

Net cash used by financing activities .... $(212)

Net increase in cash and cash equivalents	$ 285
Cash and cash equivalents at beginning of year	200
Cash and cash equivalents at end of year	$ 485

Supplemental schedule of noncash investing and financing activities

Acquisition of land in exchange for bonds payable .... $ 323

Disclosure of accounting policy

For purposes of reporting cash flows, cash and cash equivalents include cash on hand, amounts due from banks, and federal funds sold.

example, the issuance of bonds for land is disclosed in a schedule to the statement. Cash equivalents include debt securities with a maturity of three months or less.

A complete discussion of the statement of changes in cash flows is found in Chapter 23. In this chapter we illustrate the statement without further explanation. The statement of cash flows for Model Corporation appears on page 182. The related financial statements for Model Corporation appear in this chapter (income statement, page 164; statement of retained earnings, page 167; and balance sheet, pages 179–180). Note that the statement of cash flows is prepared in three sections: (1) *operating cash flows,* (2) *investing cash flows,* and (3) *financing cash flows.* A statement of cash flows for Walt Disney Productions appear in comparative form on page 224 in the Appendix at the end of this chapter.

ADDITIONAL DISCLOSURES

Publicly owned corporations play a dominant role in today's business environment. These corporations are managed by professional executives who are employed by the stockholders. Corporate managements are responsible for issuing periodic reports to stockholders to inform them of the corporation's operating and financial activities. Management's major means for communicating information to stockholders consist of the *annual report, quarterly reports of earnings,* and *news releases* of significant events and transactions.

The annual report of a corporation includes a complete set of financial statements prepared by management and examined by independent accountants. Management and the board of directors are responsible for the financial statements and for the selection of auditors who issue an opinion on the statements. The following excerpts from the annual report of General Motors Corporation describe the roles of management and independent accountants with respect to financial statements:

Management is responsible for financial statements

The following financial statements of General Motors Corporation and consolidated subsidiaries were prepared by the management which is responsible for their integrity and objectivity. The statements have been prepared in conformity with generally accepted accounting principles and, as such, include amounts based on judgments of management. . . .

Deloitte Haskins & Sells, independent certified public accountants, are engaged to examine the financial statements of General Motors Corporation and its subsidiaries and issue reports thereon. Their examination is conducted in accordance with generally accepted auditing standards which comprehend a review of internal accounting controls and a test of transactions. . . .

The Board of Directors, through the Audit Committee (composed entirely of non-employe Directors), is responsible for assuring that management fulfills its responsibilities in the preparation of the financial statements. The Commit-

tee selects the independent public accountants annually in advance of the Annual Meeting of Stockholders and submits the selection for ratification at the
Meeting. . . . To ensure complete independence, Deloitte Haskins & Sells
have full and free access to meet with the Committee, without management
representatives present, to discuss the results of their examination, the adequacy of internal accounting controls, and the quality of the financial reporting.

The Securities and Exchange Commission has a mandate from the U.S. Congress to prescribe accounting and disclosure standards for companies that issue
securities to the public. However, the SEC generally has relied on the private sector
(the Financial Accounting Standards Board and the American Institute of Certified
Public Accountants) to develop accounting principles and auditing standards. Thus,
the official pronouncements issued by these bodies provide the accounting and
disclosure guidelines for management and the auditing standards for independent
accountants. As stated in Chapter 1 (page 9), the SEC is primarily concerned with
timely and *continuous disclosure* of *relevant information* relating to the operating
and financial activities of publicly owned companies. Some results of the efforts by
the SEC and other rule-making bodies in improving the quality of disclosure to
stockholders and other users of financial information are discussed in the remainder
of this chapter.

Reports Filed with Securities and Exchange Commission

Before a company issues securities to the public it must file with the SEC a *registration statement* (*prospectus*), which includes current financial statements and detailed information about the company's management, products and markets, research and development, competition, and practically every facet of its operations.
In addition, companies subject to the SEC reporting requirements file the following
periodic reports with the Commission:

1   *Form 10-K*—an annual report filed within 90 days following the end of the
reporting company's fiscal year; it includes a considerable amount of information
not provided in the annual report to shareholders, and it *incorporates by reference*
information presented in the annual report to shareholders.

2   *Form 10-Q*—a quarterly report filed within 45 days after the end of each of the
first three quarters of the reporting company's fiscal year (a report for the fourth
quarter is not required). The *Form 10-Q* information is more extensive than that
provided in the interim reports issued to the public and mailed to shareholders.

3   *Form 8-K*—a report filed within 15 days following the occurrence of
(a) change in control of the reporting company, *(b)* major acquisition or disposal of

assets, *(c)* bankruptcy or receivership of the company, *(d)* change of independent auditors, or *(e)* any other event the company considers important to its shareholders.

4   *Proxy statement*—a document filed by a company soliciting proxies for its annual shareholders' meeting. The *proxy statement* includes a complete description of matters to be voted on and a complete set of financial statements when required (for example, in a proposed exchange of securities in a business combination).

Annual Reports to Shareholders

The annual report is the primary medium of publicly owned companies for communicating relevant information to its shareholders. Such information generally includes a summary of comparative financial highlights for the most recent years and a letter to the shareholders from the president (or from the chairman of the board and the president) in the first section of the annual report. The next section generally includes a description of the company's products and any important corporate developments, followed by the financial statements, other financial data, and a list of corporate officers and directors. At this point of our discussion, we are primarily concerned with the contents of the financial statements and other financial data section of the annual report, which generally consists of the following:

1   Two-year audited balance sheets and three-year audited statements of income and changes in financial position.

2   Five-year selected financial data such as sales, income (or loss) from continuing operations (including per-share amounts), total assets, amounts of long-term debt and redeemable preferred stock, cash dividends per share of common stock, and any additional items that enhance understanding and highlight trends in financial condition and results of operations (see page 237 in the Appendix).

3   Management's discussion and analysis of the company's financial condition and results of operations, including liquidity, capital resources, favorable or unfavorable trends, significant events or uncertainties, causes of material changes in the financial statements, narrative discussion of the impact of inflation and changing prices, and (as an optional item) projections or other forward-looking information (see pages 219–226, and 234–235 in the Appendix).

4   A summary of interim financial information for each quarter of the fiscal year (see page 236 in the Appendix).

5   Selected three-year data relating to industry segments, foreign and domestic operations, and export sales (see page 233 in the Appendix).

Notes to the Financial Statements   As stated in Chapter 1, the disclosure principle requires that financial statements include all significant information needed by users of the statements. If the omission of certain information would cause the financial statements to be misleading, disclosure of such information is essential. The financial statements included in annual reports to shareholders are accompanied by detailed notes to the statements. However, disclosure in notes is used *to supplement* the information in the body of the financial statements, *not to correct or justify improper presentations* in the statements.

Some examples of information often disclosed in notes to the financial statements included in annual reports of publicly owned companies include the following:

1   A summary of significant accounting policies.

2   Description of stock option, pension, and employee stock ownership plans.

3   Litigation in which the company is a party, loss and gain contingencies, and unusual commitments.

4   Terms of proposed business combinations and a description of any unusual events or transactions, such as *related party transactions* (for example, transactions between the company and its affiliated companies, officers, or directors).

5   The amounts of depreciation expense and research and development costs.

6   An analysis of the composition of income taxes expense, including a reconciliation of the company's effective income tax rate with the statutory federal income tax rate.

7   Detailed description or summary of receivables, inventories, investments, plant assets, intangible assets, borrowing arrangements with banks, long-term debt, and stockholders' equity.

This partial list of the type of information that may be disclosed in notes to the financial statements suggests that such notes may be both numerous and complex. With the growing complexity of business and the pressure for "full and complete disclosure," managements and independent accountants face a constant challenge to provide *sufficient information in concise form* in notes to the financial statements. Because of its relevance to topics covered throughout this book, the summary of significant accounting policies (usually presented as the first note to the financial statements) deserves special attention.

Summary of Significant Accounting Policies   In 1972, the Accounting Principles Board concluded that:[6]

> . . . information about the accounting policies adopted by a reporting entity is essential for financial statement users. When financial statements are issued purporting to present fairly financial position, changes in financial position,

---

[6]*APB Opinion No. 22,* "Disclosures of Accounting Policies," AICPA (New York: 1972), p. 434.

and results of operations in accordance with generally accepted accounting principles, a description of all significant accounting policies of the reporting entity should be included as an integral part of the financial statements.

This requirement does not apply to interim financial reports, unless the reporting entity has changed its accounting policies since the end of the preceding fiscal year. The disclosure includes a description of the accounting principles used, the methods of applying those principles, and judgments as to the appropriateness of principles relating to revenue recognition and cost allocations among accounting periods. It is particularly important to describe those principles and methods that (1) are peculiar to the industry in which the reporting company operates, (2) have been selected from other acceptable alternatives, or (3) represent unusual or "creative" applications of generally accepted accounting principles.

Examples of disclosures by a business enterprise in a separate section (or note) titled "Summary of Significant Accounting Policies" include the following:

1   Basis for preparation of consolidated financial statements (principles of consolidation).

2   Method or methods used to compute depreciation, depletion, and amortization.

3   Inventory pricing.

4   Methods of revenue recognition (especially when right of return exists and for revenue from construction-type contracts, installment sales, franchising contracts, and leasing activities).

5   Any changes in accounting principles during the most recent accounting period.

In the final analysis, the accounting principles used in the preparation of financial statements determine to a large extent the integrity and accuracy of financial statements and the "quality of reported earnings." Consequently, the description of accounting policies in the annual report is viewed by many users of financial statements as the key element of the disclosure system of publicly owned companies. The Summary of Significant Accounting Policies of Walt Disney Productions is on pages 228–229 of the Appendix at the end of this chapter.

Subsequent Events   The objective of providing users of financial statements with "full and complete disclosure" cannot be achieved without considering material events and transactions that occur after the balance sheet date but before the financial statements are issued.[7] Such *subsequent events* may require either an *adjustment* of amounts included in the financial statements or simply *disclosure* in a note to the financial statements.

Adjustment of amounts included in the financial statements is required as a result of subsequent events that provide evidence with respect to *conditions that existed on the balance sheet date* and materially affect the financial statements.

---

[7]*Statement on Auditing Standards No. 1* (New York: AICPA, 1973), pp. 123–124.

Information that becomes available prior to the issuance of the financial statements should be used by management and independent accountants to measure assets, liabilities, revenue, and expenses reported in the statements. For example, the filing for bankruptcy by a major customer shortly after the balance sheet date resulting in a material uncollectible trade receivable would be indicative of conditions existing on that date; thus, this evidence is used to measure the carrying amount of trade receivables and the amount of doubtful accounts expense included in the financial statements.

Disclosure in a note to the financial statements is appropriate when subsequent events provide evidence with respect to *conditions that did not exist on the balance sheet date*. For example, a material write-off of trade receivables as a result of a major catastrophe, such as an earthquake after the balance sheet date, is not indicative of a condition that existed on that date. Therefore, the financial statements would not be adjusted, but the amount of the write-off would be disclosed in a note to the statements. Other examples of subsequent events that *do not require adjustment* of the financial statements, *but require disclosure,* are listed below:

1   Issuance of material amounts of bonds or capital stock.

2   Acquisition or disposal of significant amounts of assets, including those resulting from business combinations.

3   Material net realized and net unrealized gains and losses on marketable equity securities held for investment purposes.

4   Filing or settlement of important litigation.

5   Material decline in the replacement cost of inventories not indicative of conditions existing on the balance sheet date.

6   Casualty losses and any other events that may have a material financial impact on the reporting company.

Supplementary Information in Annual Reports

Three special types of supplementary disclosures are discussed and illustrated in the final section of this chapter: (1) interim reports of earnings, (2) segment reporting, and (3) prospective financial statements and forecasts. The first two are required by the SEC, and the third one is optional. Information relating to inflation and changing prices also must be disclosed by certain large publicly owned companies. This topic is described and illustrated in Chapter 25.

Interim Reports of Earnings   Interim financial information generally is issued quarterly by publicly owned companies and may include current data on financial position, results of operations, and changes in financial position. However, interim financial reports issued to stockholders seldom include a complete set of financial statements. Although practices differ somewhat, most publicly owned companies issue only highly condensed *interim reports of earnings,* such as the one for Arlington Corporation illustrated at the top of page 189.

Publicly owned companies are required to issue *quarterly reports* to their sharcholders, to the SEC, and to the stock exchanges that list their securities. Such

Interim report of
earnings

ARLINGTON CORPORATION
Income Statements (Unaudited)
(In thousands—except per-share amounts)

	For three months ended		For nine months ended	
	Sept. 30, Year 2	Sept. 30, Year 1	Sept. 30, Year 2	Sept. 30, Year 1
Revenue	$1,238,600	$1,184,100	$3,973,900	$3,428,900
Costs and expenses	1,221,300	1,145,500	3,876,200	3,319,200
Income before income taxes	$ 17,300	$ 38,600	$ 97,700	$ 109,700
Income taxes expense	4,100	18,500	39,100	52,800
Net income	$ 13,200	$ 20,100	$ 58,600	$ 56,900
Earnings per common share:				
Primary	$ 0.64	$ 1.30	$ 3.25	$ 3.60
Fully diluted	$ 0.62	$ 1.23	$ 3.20	$ 3.40
Dividends per common share	$ 0.40	$ 0.30	$ 1.20	$ 0.90
Average number of common shares outstanding	17,600	15,800	17,600	15,700

Note: Shares outstanding and per-share data have been restated for the 3 for 1 split in Year 1.

reports are prepared in accordance with standards set forth in *APB Opinion No. 28,*
"Interim Financial Reporting."[8] An audit of interim reports of earnings is not
currently required. However, auditors generally perform a *limited review* of interim
financial information and convey their findings in a report addressed to the company, its board of directors, or its stockholders. The auditor's report on interim

---

[8]*APB Opinion No. 28,* "Interim Financial Reporting," AICPA (New York: 1973).

Summary of interim
financial information
included in annual
report

Interim Financial Information (Unaudited)
(In thousands, except per-share amounts)

Quarters ended	Net sales	Gross profit	Net income	Earnings per share
Year 5				
Dec. 31	$ 271,450	$103,640	$ 29,760	$0.53
Sept. 30	268,000	94,400	29,500	0.53
June 30	271,000	92,700	26,000	0.47
March 31	249,000	80,860	21,300	0.40
Totals	$1,059,450	$371,600	$106,560	$1.93
Year 4				
Dec. 31	$ 218,740	$ 78,110	$ 21,050	$0.40
Sept. 30	204,000	70,790	23,300	0.45
June 30	214,000	72,290	23,700	0.46
March 31	219,000	77,440	24,100	0.47
Totals	$ 855,740	$298,630	$ 92,150	$1.78

financial information does not include any expressions of assurance concerning the information, and each page of the interim financial information should be clearly marked as "unaudited."[9]

In addition to the issuance of quarterly reports of earnings for each of the first three quarters of a fiscal year, publicly owned corporations are required to include a summary of interim financial information for *each* quarter of a fiscal year in various filings with the SEC and in their annual reports. An example of such information included in an annual report is illustrated on pages 189 and 236.

Interim reports of earnings, including the measurement of interim revenue and expenses, are discussed in more detail in *Modern Advanced Accounting* of this series.

Segment Reporting   Many large and highly *diversified* business enterprises sell products and services to distinct groups of customers in various geographic areas. Disclosure of information relating to product lines, major customers, export sales, and operations in foreign countries is required by the Financial Accounting Standards Board and the Securities and Exchange Commission in order to enable investors to evaluate the activities, growth potential, profitability, and business risks of diversified enterprises. If a diversified enterprise were to report only aggregate results of operations, investors would not be able to assess meaningfully its future growth in revenue and earnings.

In reporting supplementary information relating to *industry segments* or *lines of business,* a business enterprise (1) identifies the products and services from which it derives revenue, (2) combines the products and services into meaningful industry segments, and (3) identifies the *reportable industry segments,* that is, those segments that are *significant* with respect to the enterprise as a whole. To be considered significant, and thus reportable, an industry segment generally must have 10% or more of the enterprise's total revenue, operating income, or identifiable assets. Examples of the information that is disclosed for each reportable industry segment include revenue, income or loss before income taxes, depreciation and amortization expense, identifiable assets, and capital expenditures. The disclosure of such information in a recent annual report to shareholders is illustrated on page 191.

Prospective Financial Statements and Forecasts   One of the objectives of financial statements is to provide information useful for the predictive process. The public accounting profession and the Securities and Exchange Commission have sought to find a satisfactory basis for the preparation and issuance of *prospective financial statements* and *forecasts,* including the expected results of future operations. Virtually every large business enterprise prepares forecasts of future operations as a means of defining goals and measuring performance. The problem is how to make such information available to the investing public yet avoid the danger of misleading investors.

---

[9]*Statement on Auditing Standards No. 24,* "Review of Interim Financial Information," AICPA (New York: 1979), p. 8.

Industry segment data included in annual report

	Year 3	Year 2	Year 1
		(In millions of dollars)	
Revenues:			
Industrial	$1,059.3	$1,058.6	$1,203.7
Aviation and electronics	1,035.1	898.3	865.2
Specialty metals	605.8	639.4	870.0
Consumer	278.8	267.5	298.7
Sales	$2,979.0	$2,863.8	$3,237.6
Insurance and finance	1,222.3	1,176.0	1,104.4
Totals	$4,201.3	$4,039.8	$4,342.0
Income before income taxes:			
Industrial	$ 106.3	$ 147.8	$ 216.2
Aviation and electronics	122.8	112.1	112.5
Specialty metals	55.1	74.3	147.5
Consumer	34.3	35.4	40.9
Total operating profit	$ 318.5	$ 369.6	$ 517.1
Corporate expenses	(33.7)	(28.1)	(29.6)
Interest expense	(29.7)	(31.6)	(26.3)
Interest and dividend revenue	78.1	65.8	49.4
Totals	$ 333.2	$ 375.7	$ 510.6
Depreciation and amortization expense:			
Industrial	$ 40.9	$ 45.5	$ 42.4
Aviation and electronics	25.5	20.9	17.8
Specialty metals	26.1	23.8	21.4
Consumer	2.4	2.8	2.8
Corporate	7.3	7.2	6.4
Totals	$ 102.2	$ 100.2	$ 90.8
Identifiable assets:			
Industrial	$ 356.5	$ 319.8	$ 353.8
Aviation and electronics	240.4	224.5	196.6
Specialty metals	241.5	252.6	281.0
Consumer	66.5	63.2	71.5
Totals for industry segments	$ 904.9	$ 860.1	$ 902.9
Investments in unconsolidated subsidiaries	2,097.2	1,677.4	1,504.7
Corporate	850.1	753.2	496.9
Totals	$3,852.2	$3,290.7	$2,904.5
Capital expenditures:			
Industrial	$ 14.1	$ 57.2	$ 48.6
Aviation and electronics	37.8	36.5	29.5
Specialty metals	16.9	29.6	34.0
Consumer	1.8	2.1	2.9
Corporate	5.2	7.4	18.0
Totals	$ 75.8	$ 132.8	$ 133.0

FIVE-YEAR FORECAST

We have included in this annual report a sales forecast for each of our major product lines and operating groups for 1988.

While we recognize that long-term forecasts are subject to many variables and uncertainties, our experience has been that our success is determined more by our own activities than by the performance of any industry or the economy in general. In addition, the balance and diversity of our products and markets have been such that a shortfall in expected performance in one area has been largely offset by higher than anticipated growth in another.

Although variations may occur in the forecast for any individual product line, we have a relatively high level of confidence that our overall five-year growth forecast is achievable.

ASSUMPTIONS USED IN FORECAST

1. Average 2-3 percent annual real growth in GNP.
2. Average inflation 5-7 percent.
3. Present tax structure to continue.
4. No change in currency exchange rates.
5. No acquisitions.
6. No additional financing.
7. Dividend payout ratio 20 percent.
8. Four percent after-tax return on investment of excess cash.
9. No exercise of stock options.

FIVE-YEAR CASH FLOW FORECAST

(In Thousands)	**1984-1988**
Net Income	$ 850,000
Depreciation	280,000
	1,130,000
Working Capital	(230,000)
Note Payments	(280,000)
Capital Expenditures	(260,000)
Dividends	(170,000)
Net Cash Change	190,000
Beginning Cash, 1-1-84	210,000
Cash, 12-31-88	$ 400,000

SALES GROWTH BY PRODUCTS

(In Thousands)

	Sales Forecast		Actual Sales		
	5-Year Growth Rate 1984-1988	1988	5-Year Growth Rate 1979-1983	1983	1978
Products for the Home and Family	14%	$1,225,000	16%	$ 638,000	$308,000
Products for Industry	16%	875,000	9%	421,000	278,000
Total Sales	15%	$2,100,000	13%	$1,059,000	$586,000

SALES GROWTH BY SPECIFIC MARKETS AND PRODUCTS[1] [2]

	Forecast		Actual			
	5-Year Growth Rate 1984-1988	1988	5-Year Growth Rate 1979-1983	1983	1978
				(In Thousands)	
Masco Faucet Sales[3]	15%	$490,000	9 %	$243,000	$155,000
Faucet Industry Sales–Units	7%	35,000	(5)%	25,000	32,000
Masco Market Share–Units	2%	38%	5 %	34%	27%
Housing Completions	4%	1,700	(4)%	1,400	1,700
Independent Cold Extrusion Industry Sales	13%	$580,000	1 %	$310,000	$290,000
Masco Cold Extrusion Sales[3]	14%	$170,000	5 %	$ 88,000	$ 70,000
Truck Production	7%	3,400	(8)%	2,400	3,700
Auto Production	4%	8,200	(6)%	6,800	9,200
Masco Auto Parts Sales	13%	$210,000	8 %	$113,000	$ 76,000

(1) Excludes foreign sales.   (2) Industry data Masco estimates.   (3) Includes foreign sales.

At one time the SEC proposed to require companies making earnings forecasts to meet detailed reporting standards but eventually withdrew its proposal. The SEC currently encourages but does not require public companies to file financial forecasts with the Commission. To encourage publicly owned companies to issue financial forecasts, the SEC developed a "Safe-Harbor Rule for Projections." The *safe-harbor rule* protects issuers of erroneous financial forecasts from liability if the forecasts were prepared in good faith and on a reasonable basis. Currently, very few companies issue prospective financial statements and forecasts to the public. However, many companies issue such statements and forecasts to lenders, underwriters, and prospective investors in connection with raising of capital.

In 1975, the Accounting Standards Division of the AICPA issued *Statement of Position 75-4* "as a guide for CPAs in the preparation of financial forecasts for clients."[10] The AICPA suggested that financial forecasts generally should include at least the following information: (1) sales or gross revenue, (2) gross profit, (3) income taxes expense, (4) net income, (5) gain or loss on disposal of a business segment, (6) extraordinary items, (7) earnings per share, and (8) significant anticipated changes in financial position. Subsequently, the AICPA prepared a *Guide for a Review of Financial Forecasts,* which neither requires nor recommends the preparation or review of financial forecasts.

An example of a five-year forecast included in the *1983 Annual Report* of Masco Corporation appears on page 192 and above.

---

[10]*Statement of Position 75-4,* "Presentation and Disclosure of Financial Forecasts," AICPA (New York: 1975).

REVIEW QUESTIONS

1 What are the components of a set of *general-purpose financial statements?*

2 What is generally included in the heading of a financial statement?

3 Explain the differences between the *single-step* form and the *multiple-step* form of the income statement. Are earnings per share amounts included in both forms of the income statement?

4 Distinguish between *functional* and *natural* classifications of costs and expenses in the income statement. What are the advantages of the functional classification of expenses in an income statement prepared for use by management?

5 Define *prior period adjustments* and indicate how these are reported in financial statements.

6 What is the major advantage of a combined statement of income and retained earnings? What disadvantages are there in such a statement?

7 List four significant limitations of a balance sheet prepared at the end of a single accounting period as a source of information for use by investors.

8 Dennis Oba is a member of the American Institute of Certified Public Accountants. In auditing the financial statements of Newport Corporation, Oba found that Newport applied an accounting principle with which he agrees but which has not been accepted either by the Securities and Exchange Commission or by the Financial Accounting Standards Board. Assuming that the difference in treatment has a material effect on the financial statements of Newport, what are the alternatives facing Oba in formulating an opinion on the financial statements of Newport?

9 **a** How is the definition of a *current liability* related to the definition of *current assets?*
b Explain the term *operating cycle* and its significance to the classification of assets and liabilities as current or noncurrent.
c Indicate circumstances under which liabilities payable within a few months after the balance sheet date might be excluded from current liabilities.

10 What is the distinction between an *estimated liability* and a *loss contingency?* Give an example of each.

11 Helwig Corporation issued $100 million face amount of 13% bonds, receiving proceeds of $98 million. The bonds are callable at any time at 105. An argument has arisen over the proper valuation of these bonds in Helwig's balance sheet. One official supports $98 million; another argues for maturity value, $100 million; a third argues that $105 million is the proper amount because the bonds may be called at any time. What accounting principle should govern the decision? Which position do you support, and why?

12 The term *reserve* has been used alternatively by business enterprises to describe a contra-asset ledger account, an estimated liability, and an appropriation of retained earnings. Why are these uses of the term *reserve* in ledger account titles objectionable? In which of the three uses is the term least misleading?

13 A balance sheet may be prepared in different forms. List these forms and indicate which one is most widely used.

14 What is the function of a *statement of stockholders' equity?*

15 Briefly state the objectives of a *statement of cash flows.*

16 Is the independent accounting firm engaged to audit the financial statements primarily responsible for financial statements included in the annual report to shareholders? Explain.

17 List and briefly describe four periodic reports that publicly owned companies file with the Securities and Exchange Commission.

18 What, generally, are the contents of the annual report to shareholders issued by a publicly owned company?

19 List some examples of information often disclosed in notes to the financial statements included in annual reports to shareholders of publicly owned companies.

20 Describe the type of disclosures that are made in a note to the financial statements entitled ''Summary of Significant Accounting Policies.''

21 Identify two types of *subsequent events* and indicate how each type should be accounted for in the financial statements or disclosed in a note to the statements.

22 What is the usual form of *interim reports of earnings?* Are such reports audited by independent accountants?

23 **a** What is the reason for disclosure of information relating to *industry segments* of a diversified business enterprise?
    b What is a *reportable industry segment* and what information is disclosed for such a segment?

24 In what ways are *financial forecasts* useful to investors in making investment decisions?

EXERCISES

Ex. 4-1 Select the best answer for each of the following multiple-choice questions:
1 The preparation of notes to the financial statements complies with the:
a Business entity principle
b Continuity principle
c Matching principle
d Disclosure principle

2 When a business enterprise receives a deposit from a customer to protect itself against nonpayment for future services, the deposit is classified by the enterprise as:
a Revenue
b A liability

c Part of the allowance for doubtful accounts

d A deferred credit deducted from trade accounts receivable

3   The circulation of items within the current asset category of the balance sheet is termed the:

a Accounting cycle

b Current cycle

c Operating cycle

d Working capital cycle

4   Unamortized discount on bonds payable is presented in the balance sheet as:

a Other noncurrent asset

b A deduction from the face amount of bonds payable

c Short-term prepayment (current asset)

d Part of stockholders' equity

5   Generally, which of the following is excluded from current liabilities in the balance sheet?

a Currently maturing portions of long-term debt

b Income taxes payable

c Life insurance policy loan payable that is regularly renewed on maturity

d None of the foregoing

6   Which of the following is disclosed in the balance sheet for each class of capital stock?

a Par or stated value per share

b Number of shares issued

c Number of shares outstanding

d Any dividends or liquidating preference

e All of the foregoing

7   The following expenses and loss were among those incurred by Kerr Company during Year 2:

Accounting and legal fees	$160,000
Interest	60,000
Loss on disposal of office equipment	25,000
Rent for office space	200,000

One-quarter of the rented premises is occupied by the sales department. How much of the items listed above is included in Kerr's general and administrative expenses for Year 2?

a $310,000   **b** $335,000   **c** $360,000   **d** $370,000   **e** Some other amount

8   Steve Company's working capital on December 31, Year 9, was $5,000,000. The following additional information pertains to Steve for Year 10:

Working capital provided from operations	$ 850,000
Capital expenditures	1,500,000
Short-term borrowings	500,000
Long-term borrowings	1,000,000

Payments on short-term borrowings	250,000
Payments on long-term borrowings.	300,000
Proceeds from issuance of common stock	700,000
Dividends declared on common stock	400,000

How much was Steve Company's working capital on December 31, Year 10?
a $5,350,000   **b** $5,600,000   **c** $5,750,000   **d** $6,000,000
e Some other amount

Ex. 4-2 Following are selected ledger account balances for Dinko Corporation for the year ended June 30, Year 10:

Inventories:			Selling expenses.	$52,800
June 30, Year 9	$ 35,600		General and administrative	
June 30, Year 10	27,200		expenses	32,400
Sales	374,000		Interest revenue	1,800
Sales returns and			Dividend revenue	4,000
allowances	6,480		Interest expense	1,000
Sales discounts.	5,360		Income taxes expense	22,000
Purchases	218,200		Retained earnings:	
Freight-in	25,320		June 30, Year 9.	80,000
Purchases discounts	4,840		June 30, Year 10	88,000
Purchases returns	7,320			

From the foregoing information, compute the following for Dinko Corporation for the year ended June 30, Year 10:
a Total net revenue
b Total costs and expenses (including cost of goods sold)
c Net income
d Dividends declared

Ex. 4-3 For the year ended December 31, Year 2, Soledad Company had general and administrative expenses of 10% of sales (or 20% of cost of goods sold). Selling expenses equaled 20% of sales. Beginning inventories were $100,000, and purchases amounted to 55% of sales. Income before income taxes of 40% was $80,000.
     Prepare Soledad Company's income statement for the year ended December 31, Year 2. (Show supporting computations.) *Suggestion:* (1) Compute the cost of goods sold as a percentage of sales by using the information relating general and administrative expenses to cost of goods sold *and* to sales; (2) prepare an income statement in percentages, including all items from sales to income before income taxes, with sales representing 100%; and (3) prepare an income statement in dollars, using the dollar amounts given and deriving the other dollar amounts from the percentage relationships.

Ex. 4-4 Selected information for Canyon Company for the year ended December 31, Year 5, follows:

Total assets	$2,255,000
Total liabilities	600,000

Preferred stock, $10 par	100,000
Common stock, $1 par...	300,000
Additional paid-in capital...	600,000
Prior period adjustment—overstatement of net income in Year 4 as a	
result of an accounting error, net of income tax effect of $57,600	70,400
Net income	175,000
Dividends declared on common stock ($0.20 a share)	60,000
Dividends declared on preferred stock ($1.50 a share)..............	15,000

Prepare Canyon Company's statement of retained earnings for the year ended December 31, Year 5.

Ex. 4-5 Edmund Corporation had inventories at the beginning and end of Year 3 as follows:

	Jan. 1	Dec. 31
Raw material..	$22,000	$30,000
Goods in process	40,000	48,000
Finished goods	25,000	18,000
Totals	$87,000	$96,000

During Year 3, the following costs and expenses were incurred by Edmund:

Raw material purchased...	$300,000
Direct labor...	120,000
Indirect factory labor	60,000
Property taxes and depreciation of factory building...................	20,000
Property taxes and depreciation of salesroom and office...............	15,000
Sales salaries...	40,000
Office salaries	24,000
Utilities (60% applicable to factory, 20% to salesroom, and	
20% to office)	60,000

Compute Edmund Corporation's cost of goods sold for the year ended December 31, Year 3.

Ex. 4-6 Prepare a skeleton balance sheet as of March 31, Year 5, for Bozajian Company (a hypothetical corporation) in account form, showing only major classifications (approximately ten group headings).

Ex. 4-7 The balance sheet of Pocono Company contains the following group headings:

A Current assets
B Investments and restricted funds
C Plant assets
D Intangible assets
E Other noncurrent assets (including deferred charges)

F Current liabilities
G Long-term debt
H Deferred credits
I Invested capital
J Retained earnings

For each of the 20 items listed below indicate the preferable balance sheet classification for Pocono Company by using the appropriate letter from the listing above. Place parentheses around the letter if the item is *subtracted* from other items in that classification.

1 Accrued interest on bonds payable
2 Convertible preferred stock
3 Mortgage note payable (outstanding for 12 years; due in two months)
4 Land held for price appreciation
5 Payroll account at Bank of Coe
6 Patents
7 Discount on bonds payable
8 Unexpired insurance
9 Deferred cost of moving home office (including employees) from Texas to Ohio
10 Leasehold improvements
11 Allowance for doubtful accounts
12 Cash surrender value of life insurance policies
13 Premium on bonds payable
14 Accumulated depreciation
15 Additional paid-in capital
16 Short-term prepayments
17 Machinery retired from use and held for disposal
18 Accrued payroll
19 Investment in common stock of IBM Corporation (100 shares at cost)
20 Advance payments from customers

Ex. 4-8 You have been requested to assist the accountant of Polo Corporation to prepare a balance sheet. The outline presented below represents the various classifications suggested by the accountant; classification ''L'' has been added for items to be excluded from the balance sheet. (You are not asked to approve or disapprove the various classifications set forth below.)

A Current assets
B Investments and restricted funds
C Plant assets
D Intangible assets
E Other noncurrent assets (including deferred charges)
F Current liabilities
G Long-term debt (including deferred credits)
H Preferred stock
I Common stock
J Additional paid-in capital
K Retained earnings
L Items excluded from the balance sheet or reported in notes to the financial statements

Using the letters representing the various balance sheet classifications, identify each of the following 20 items according to the preferred balance sheet presentation for Polo Corporation. If an item is an offsetting or valuation ledger account, place parentheses around the letter.

1 Dividend payable (on Polo Corporation's preferred stock)
2 Plant assets under construction
3 Goodwill
4 Bond issue costs
5 Land (held for possible future building site)
6 Merchandise (held by Polo Corporation on consignment)
7 Stock dividend to be distributed (on Polo Corporation's common stock)
8 Inventory of office supplies

   9 Sinking fund (First National Bank, Trustee)

10 Reserve for retirement of preferred stock

11 Installment accounts receivable (average collection period 18 months)

12 Paid-in capital in excess of par: preferred stock

13 Advances to officers (indefinite repayment date, noninterest-bearing)

14 Unredeemed merchandise coupons issued to customers

15 Shares of preferred stock held in treasury (at cost)

16 Small tools used in factory

17 Contingent liability from notes receivable discounted at Kong Bank

18 Allowance to reduce inventories to lower of cost or market

19 Common stock subscriptions receivable (considered currently collectible)

20 Common stock subscribed (Polo Corporation's common stock)

Ex. 4-9 The stockholders' equity of Valentine Corporation on June 30, Year 2, was as follows:

Common stock, $10 par	$ 200,000
Additional paid-in capital	225,000
Retained earnings	610,000
Total stockholders' equity	$1,035,000

The transactions affecting stockholders' equity for the year ended June 30, Year 3, were:

(1) An additional 7,500 shares of common stock were issued on May 1, Year 3 at $30 a share.

(2) Dividends declared June 2, Year 3, amounted to $100,000.

(3) Net income amounted to $195,000.

   Prepare a statement of stockholders' equity for Valentine Corporation for the year ended June 30, Year 3.

Ex. 4-10 From the following list of ledger account balances for Naughton Company, compute (**a**) the amount of working capital, and (**b**) the equity (book value) per share of common stock:

Investment in affiliated companies (at equity)	$100,000
Cash surrender value of life insurance policies	10,000
Organization costs	5,000
Interest receivable	2,000
Reserve for loss contingencies (recorded by a debit to Retained Earnings)	50,000
Retained earnings—unappropriated	170,000
Common stock, $5 par	400,000
Additional paid-in capital	200,000
Deferred income tax credits	40,000
Cost of (construction) contracts in progress (for customers)	150,000
Bond sinking fund	80,000
Liability under product warranty	6,000

Creditors' accounts with debit balances	4,500
Plant assets (net)	.426,500
Other current assets	198,000
Other current liabilities	108,000

Ex. 4-11 Listed below are selected ledger account balances of Glendale Company on December 31, Year 10:

Advances from customers	$ 15,000
Unused equipment held for sale	25,600
Bond sinking fund	260,000
Bonds payable (11% interest)	750,000
Discount on bonds payable	15,500
Installment notes payable (13% interest, due $150,000 a year)	600,000
Accrued payroll	72,000
Cash surrender value of life insurance policies	42,100
Unamortized bond issue costs	21,100
Advances to suppliers (12% interest, no due date)	100,000

Prepare the Investments and Long-Term Debt sections of Glendale Company's balance sheet on December 31, Year 10.

Ex. 4-12 The December 31, Year 5, balance sheet and other data for Bren Corporation are presented below. These are the only items in Bren's balance sheet. Amounts indicated by a question mark (?) may be computed from the other data given.

BREN CORPORATION
Balance Sheet
December 31, Year 5

Assets

Cash	$ 25,000
Trade accounts receivable (net)	?
Inventories	?
Plant assets (net)	294,000
Total assets	$432,000

Liabilities & Stockholders' Equity

Trade accounts payable	$?
Income taxes payable (current)	25,000
Long-term debt	?
Common stock, $1 par	300,000
Retained earnings (deficit)	?
Total liabilities & stockholders' equity	$432,000

Additional Information

Current ratio, Dec. 31, Year 5	1.5 to 1
Total liabilities divided by total stockholders' equity, Dec. 31, Year 5	0.8 to 1

Turnover of ending inventories (based on sales) for Year 5	15 times
Turnover of ending inventories (based on cost of goods sold) for Year 5	10.5 times
Gross profit on sales for Year 5	$315,000

Compute the amount of each of the following for Bren Corporation on December 31, Year 5:

a Inventories

b Trade accounts receivable (net)

c Trade accounts payable

d Retained earnings (deficit)

e Long-term debt

CASES

Case 4-1   The combined statements of income and retained earnings shown below were prepared by Modern Fabrics, Inc., a retail enterprise that makes most of its sales on credit. Accounts receivable are aged at the end of each accounting period, and the allowance for doubtful accounts is adjusted to an amount required to value receivables at estimated net collectible amount (net realizable value).

MODERN FABRICS, INC.
Combined Statements of Income and Retained Earnings
For Years Ended December 31, Year 5 and Year 4

	Year 5	Year 4
Revenue:		
Sales, including sales taxes collected	$ 876,900	$ 782,500
Less: Returns, allowances, and sales discounts	18,800	16,200
Net sales	$ 858,100	$ 766,300
Dividends, interest, and purchases discounts	30,250	18,300
Recoveries of receivables written off in prior years . . .	11,800	3,000
Total revenue	$ 900,150	$ 787,600
Costs and expenses:		
Cost of goods sold, including sales taxes collected . . .	$ 415,900	$ 332,200
Salaries and related payroll expenses	60,500	62,100
Rent	19,100	19,100
Freight-in and freight-out	3,400	2,900
Doubtful accounts expense	24,000	26,000
Total costs and expenses	$ 522,900	$ 442,300
Income before extraordinary items	$ 377,250	$ 345,300
Extraordinary items, before income tax effects:		
Loss on discontinued styles *(Note 1)*	(124,000)	(4,800)
Loss on sale of short-term investments *(Note 2)*	(52,050)	
Loss on sale of vacant warehouse *(Note 3)*	(17,950)	
Net income	$ 183,250	$ 340,500
Retained earnings, beginning of year	312,700	163,100
Subtotals	$ 495,950	$ 503,600

(continued)

Less: Income taxes expense	(100,000)	(170,000)
Cash dividends	(41,900)	(20,900)
Retained earnings, end of year	$ 354,050	$ 312,700
Earnings per share of common stock.................	$ 1.83	$ 3.41

Note 1: Changes in customer preferences resulted in a loss on the disposal of discontinued styles.
Note 2: A short-term investment was sold at a loss, with no income tax effect.
Note 3: A vacant warehouse and adjacent land were sold at a loss.

Instructions

Identify and discuss any deficiencies in classification and disclosure in the combined statements of income and retained earnings of Modern Fabrics, Inc. Explain why you consider these treatments to be deficiencies and what you consider to be the proper treatment of the items. Do not discuss form and terminology, and do not prepare revised combined statements of income and retained earnings.

Case 4-2 The complete set of financial statements issued by Caldera Corporation for the year ended August 31, Year 5, follows:

CALDERA CORPORATION
Combined Statement of Income and Retained Earnings
For Year Ended August 31, Year 5

Sales (net of $850,000 sales returns and allowances) ..		$10,700,000
Cost of goods sold		8,700,000
Gross profit on sales		$ 2,000,000
Operating expenses:		
Selling expenses	$1,500,000	
General and administrative expenses..............	940,000	2,440,000
Operating loss		$ (440,000)
Interest expense		(150,000)
Net loss		$ (590,000)
Retained earnings, beginning of year................		1,700,000
Subtotal		$ 1,110,000
Dividends declared:		
Cash—$1 a share	$ 40,000	
Common stock—6%	24,000	64,000
Retained earnings, end of year		$ 1,046,000
Average market price of common stock during the year		$ 15

CALDERA CORPORATION
Balance Sheet
August 31, Year 5

Assets

Cash	$ 104,000
Securities, at cost, which approximates market value ..	54,000
Trade accounts receivable (net of $65,000 allowance) .	917,000
Inventories (at cost)	775,000

(continued)

Plant assets	$3,200,000	
Less: Accumulated depreciation	1,475,000	1,725,000
Prepayments and other assets.		125,000
Total assets		$3,700,000

Liabilities & Stockholders' Equity

Trade accounts payable		$ 222,000
Miscellaneous liabilities		62,000
Bank loans and long-term debt		1,580,000
Total liabilities		$1,864,000
Common stock, $10 par (authorized 100,000 shares,		
issued and outstanding 42,400 shares)	$ 424,000	
Additional paid-in capital	366,000	
Retained earnings	1,046,000	1,836,000
Total liabilities & stockholders' equity		$3,700,000

Instructions

Identify and discuss any deficiencies and omissions in Caldera Corporation's financial statements for the year ended August 31, Year 5. Consider each deficiency or omission separately, and do not consider the cumulative effect of the deficiencies and omissions. There are no arithmetical errors in the financial statements. Assume that Caldera is not required to report constant purchasing-power or current-cost data.

Case 4-3   Kelvin Chen, a consulting engineer, developed and patented a device for measuring temperatures encountered in space travel. He offered to sell the patent to Dymo Company. A contract was signed under which Dymo acquired the patent and gave Chen in exchange $500,000 cash and a promissory note for $500,000. The note provided for payment only in shares of common stock of Dymo at the rate of 4,000 shares of $25 par common stock a year for each of the next five years.

   The accountant for Dymo included $100,000 among the current liabilities, labeled Note Payable in Common Stock, and $400,000 among the long-term liabilities similarly labeled. The accountant attached a note to the financial statements explaining the terms of the contract with Chen.

   The president of Dymo, who was about to present Dymo's financial statements to a bank in support of a loan application, objected to this treatment, contending that Dymo's liabilities were overstated. The accountant replied that liabilities were obligations to convey something of value, and that Dymo's common stock had a ''par value'' of $25 a share.

Instructions

a Discuss the appropriate treatment of the note payable in common stock in Dymo Company's balance sheet, giving reasons for your conclusions.

b Suppose that under the terms of the note, Kelvin Chen had the option of accepting each year $100,000 cash or 4,000 shares of common stock. Would this change your answer? Why?

Case 4-4   Doris Tang owns a resort located on an excellent fishing lake. Her busy season begins May 15 and extends through mid-fall. During the winter she engaged a contractor to build a boathouse for $50,000. The contract called for completion by May 15, because the resort was completely reserved for the week of May 15 to 22, the opening week of the fishing season. Because the completion date was so important to Tang, she specified in the contract that if the construction were not completed by May 15 the price would be adjusted downward by a penalty of $400 a day, until completed.

The construction was not completed until June 9, at which time Tang paid the contractor $40,000, deducting $400 for each of the 25 days of delay. Tang is convinced that she lost goodwill because her facilities were inadequate and that several of her guests reduced their stay because the boathouse was still under construction.

In her balance sheet prepared on September 30, the end of her fiscal year, Tang included the boathouse at $50,000. Included in her revenue was an item "Penalty payments received in lieu of lost revenue, $10,000."

The auditor who examined Tang's balance sheet objected to this treatment and insisted that the boathouse be recorded at its actual cost, $40,000. Tang stated that she could not understand the logic of this position. "Accounting principles are out of tune with reality," she complained. "What if the contract had been 125 days late and the boathouse had cost me nothing; would you record in my balance sheet that I had no asset? I lost at least $400 a day in revenue because of the construction delay."

Instructions

At what amount should the boathouse be reported in Doris Tang's balance sheet on September 30? (You may disregard any question of depreciation from June 9 to September 30.) Explain your position in terms of generally accepted accounting principles.

PROBLEMS

4-1   The following information was compiled from the accounting records of Zee Corporation as a basis for preparation of an income statement for the year ended June 30, Year 3:

Inventories, July 1, Year 2	$ 496,300
Inventories, June 30, Year 3	542,700
Purchases returns and allowances	65,200
Common stock, $10 par (no change during year)	200,000
Sales	4,231,200
Sales returns and allowances	44,100
Depreciation expense (75% selling; 25% general and administrative)	220,000
Gain on disposal of equipment	13,500
Rent revenue	15,360
Purchases	3,100,850

Freight-in	123,400
Selling expenses:	
Salaries and wages	301,010
Purchased services.	72,150
Supplies.	66,050
General and administrative expenses:	
Salaries and wages	420,200
Purchased services.	62,800
Supplies.	101,100

Assume that Zee Corporation's income tax rate is 45% and that any loss for Year 3 may be carried back to obtain a refund of income taxes paid in prior years.

Instructions

a Prepare a multiple-step income statement for Zee Corporation for the year ended June 30, Year 3. Include earnings or loss per share in the income statement.

b Prepare a single-step income statement for Zee Corporation for the year ended June 30, Year 3, under a functional classification of expenses. Include earnings or loss per share in the income statement.

4-2 Eric's, Inc., is a merchandising enterprise with $5 par common stock, of which 100,000 shares were outstanding throughout the year ended April 30, Year 10. In addition to its merchandising activities, Eric's obtains rent revenue of $28,324 a year for a part of its building leased to Western Wood Company.

The following information is available concerning the merchandising activities of Eric's for the year ended April 30, Year 10:

Inventories, April 30, Year 10 (a decrease of $54,264 during the year). .	$ 100,944
Purchases of merchandise (of which $11,224 was returned).	737,696
Freight-in	63,504
Sales (of which $21,696 was returned by customers)	1,584,768
Selling expenses (salaries and wages, $122,340; purchased services,	
$31,248; supplies, $10,224)	163,812
General and administrative expenses (salaries and wages, $100,688;	
purchased services, $38,048; supplies, $14,832)	153,568
Depreciation expense (75% selling; 25% general and administrative) . . .	67,840

In addition to these operating revenue and expenses, Eric's, Inc., incurred interest expense of $11,936 and declared dividends of $50,000. Income taxes expense was $154,000.

Instructions

a Prepare a multiple-step income statement for Eric's, Inc., for the year ended April 30, Year 10. Include earnings per share (rounded to the nearest cent) in the statement.

b Prepare a single-step income statement for Eric's, Inc., for the year ended April 30, Year 10, classifying expenses on a natural basis (for example, merchandise and supplies, salaries and wages, purchased services, depreciation, interest, and income taxes) rather than a functional basis. Include earnings per share (rounded to the nearest cent) in the income statement.

4-3 The following data were taken from the accounting records of Sunrise Company for the year ended December 31, Year 5. Income taxes for Year 5 applicable to ordinary income were $72,600. Income taxes applicable to the extraordinary gain were $10,500. Income tax credit applicable to the extraordinary loss was $28,500. Sunrise had 10,000 shares of common stock outstanding throughout Year 5.

Cost of goods sold	$1,020,000
Depreciation expense	30,000
Cash dividends declared	45,000
Extraordinary gain, before income tax effect	35,000
Insurance expense	7,000
Sales	1,500,000
Extraordinary loss, before income tax credit	60,000
Salaries expense	195,000
Retained earnings, Jan. 1, Year 5	1,666,200
Other operating expenses	62,400

Instructions

Prepare a combined statement of income and retained earnings for Sunrise Company for the year ended December 31, Year 5. Use the single-step form for the revenue and expenses part of the statement, and provide earnings per share (rounded to the nearest cent) in the income statement.

4-4 The following ledger account balances (listed in random order) are available for Medov-Lance Company on December 31, Year 5, after the accounts were closed:

Income taxes payable (current)	$ 41,625
Cash surrender value of life insurance policies	10,800
Trade accounts receivable (net of $10,000 advances from customers)	92,000
Allowance for doubtful accounts	5,800
Cash on hand	800
Cash in First National Bank of Bakersfield	44,025
Cash in Bank of Fresno	26,000
Short-term prepayments	3,500
Retained earnings	222,300
Current portion of 10% note payable	20,000
Long-term portion of 10% note payable (excluding current portion of $20,000)	230,000
Trade accounts payable	220,000
Inventories, at first-in, first-out cost	332,600
Short-term investments, at cost (market value, $58,500)	56,800
Buildings and equipment	300,000
Accumulated depreciation of buildings and equipment	109,600
Additional paid-in capital	105,200
Organization costs	16,000

Common stock, $1 par, authorized 250,000 shares	*110,000*
Long-term advance to affiliated companies	*50,000*
Patents (net of accumulated amortization of $18,950)	*32,000*
Land	*100,000*

Instructions

Prepare a classified balance sheet for Medov-Lance Company on December 31, Year 5, in report form. Use two money columns with rulings as necessary under subtotals. Notes to the financial statements are not required.

4-5   The following memorandum contains information concerning the financial position of Valley Commuter Co. on December 31, Year 10:

> Our plant assets consist of aircraft and other flight equipment acquired at a cost of $10,880,000, on which we have recorded depreciation of $2,431,200 to date. In addition, we have one other aircraft that has been withdrawn from use and has been offered for sale. The carrying amount of this aircraft is $750,000, and we are currently negotiating for its sale at a price of $600,000. The negotiations for this sale soon will be completed; therefore, we have recognized a loss of $150,000.
>
> When we acquired Commerce Parcel Service we paid $550,000 for goodwill, of which $348,000 has been amortized since acquisition.
>
> We have cash in checking accounts amounting to $380,600, and certificates of deposit for $801,600, including accrued interest at 15% a year. The controlling ledger account for trade accounts receivable shows a debit balance of $1,660,000, but this total includes a credit balance of $120,000 from a customer who made an advance payment. The allowance for doubtful accounts amounts to $44,400. Our inventories are carried at weighted-average cost, and amount to $91,200. Short-term prepayments amount to $42,000. The cash surrender value of life insurance policies naming the company as beneficiary amounts to $147,600.
>
> Among our liabilities are $3,000,000 in 8% long-term notes payable, of which $300,000 is due in Year 11. Trade accounts payable total $780,000, accrued liabilities $100,000, and income taxes payable $385,200.
>
> We have 5 million shares of $1 par common stock authorized, of which 1,440,000 shares were issued at a price of $5 a share. Our reinvested earnings total $864,200.

Instructions

Use the above information to prepare a balance sheet for Valley Commuter Co. on December 31, Year 10, in report form. Use two money columns, with rulings as necessary under subtotals. Notes to the financial statements are not required.

4-6   A condensed income statement prepared by Leventhal Corporation for the year ended March 31, Year 2, follows:

LEVENTHAL CORPORATION
Income Statement
For Year Ended March 31, Year 2

Sales (net)		$900,000
Costs and expenses:		
Cost of goods sold	$620,000	
Depreciation	28,000	
Amortization of intangible assets	7,000	
Other operating expenses	112,000	
Income taxes (including deferred income taxes of		
$10,000)	45,000	812,000
Net income		$ 88,000
Earnings per share of common stock		$ 4.40

Additional Information

(1) Dividends of $50,000 were declared and paid.

(2) Equipment of $40,000 was acquired in exchange for common stock.

(3) Equipment was sold for $14,500, its carrying amount.

(4) The common stock was split 2 for 1.

(5) Long-term investments were acquired for $60,000 cash.

(6) Treasury stock (common) was acquired for $8,500 cash.

(7) Cash received as proceeds from long-term borrowing was $100,000.

(8) The working capital at the beginning of the year was $425,400; working capital at the end of the year was $554,400. Cash at the beginning of the year was $120,000. Cash at the end of the year was $150,000.

Instructions

Prepare a statement of cash flows for Leventhal Corporation for the year ended March 31, Year 2. Use the form illustrated on page 182.

4-7 The following information was available for Clark Corporation on December 31, Year 8:

Sales...	$1,847,500
Extraordinary item (gain), net of income tax effect of $180,000.........	220,000
Prior period adjustment (debit balance, after applicable income tax	
credit of $90,000)	110,000
Dividends declared..	240,000
Purchases..	1,392,000
Purchases discounts..	20,000
Inventories, Jan. 1, Year 8.....................................	146,000
Income taxes applicable to ordinary income	117,000
Selling expenses	100,000
General and administrative expenses.............................	96,000

Inventories, Dec. 31, Year 8	152,000
Sales returns and allowances.......................................	25,500
Cumulative effect on prior years' net income of change in accounting principle (credit balance, net of income tax effect of $40,500)	49,500

The retained earnings on January 1, Year 8, were originally reported at $1,888,400. There were 100,000 shares of common stock outstanding throughout Year 8.

Instructions

a Prepare a multiple-step income statement for Clark Corporation, including earnings per share, for the year ended December 31, Year 8.

b Prepare a statement of retained earnings for Clark Corporation for the year ended December 31, Year 8.

4-8   Paradise Corporation had 200,000 shares of common stock outstanding throughout Year 4. Selected information on December 31, Year 4, is presented below:

Retained earnings, Jan. 1, Year 4...................................	$2,444,100
Inventories, Jan. 1, Year 4..	192,500
Extraordinary item (gain), net of income tax effect of $32,000..........	96,000
Purchases (continuing operations)	1,510,000
Sales (continuing operations)......................................	2,195,000
Royalties revenue	24,100
Inventories, Dec. 31, Year 4	208,000
Selling expenses (continuing operations)	120,400
Sales returns, allowances, and discounts	25,100
Purchases returns, allowances, and discounts	23,450
Dividends declared ($0.88 a share)	176,000
Gain on disposal of equipment used in continuing operations..........	27,500
Income taxes applicable to results from continuing operations	192,500
General and administrative expenses (continuing operations)	197,550
Prior period adjustment: decrease in retained earnings on Jan. 1, Year 4, as a result of correction of error, net of income tax effect of $81,500...	117,000
Loss from disposal and operations during Year 4 of discontinued business segment (includes all revenue and expenses of discontinued segment for Year 4 and income tax credit of $62,000)	84,000

Instructions

a Prepare an income statement for Paradise Corporation for the year ended December 31, Year 4. The results from continuing operations should be in single-step form. (A number of account balances may be combined to obtain summary amounts to appear in the single-step form for the income statement.) Include earnings per share (rounded to the nearest cent) in the income statement.

b Prepare a statement of retained earnings for Paradise Corporation for the year ended December 31, Year 4.

4-9 The condensed balance sheet of Tech Research, Inc., on June 30, Year 4, is presented below:

TECH RESEARCH, INC.
Condensed Balance Sheet
June 30, Year 4

Assets		Liabilities & Stockholders' Equity	
Current assets	$1,500,000	Current liabilities	$ 560,000
Noncurrent assets (net)	6,860,000	Long-term debt	2,500,000
		Paid-in capital	3,800,000
		Retained earnings	1,500,000
		Total liabilities &	
Total assets	$8,360,000	stockholders' equity ...	$8,360,000

Comments taken from an auditor's notes, describing certain components of the balance sheet, are listed below. Some of these comments indicate that the accountant for Tech Research, Inc., has handled certain items improperly.

(1) Included in long-term debt is a loan payable of $250,000 due on April 30, Year 5.

(2) A $125,000 dividend to be distributed in the form of Tech Research's common stock is included in current liabilities.

(3) Included in current liabilities is a loss contingency of $50,000 for possible lawsuits that may be filed. This amount was recorded by a debit to Retained Earnings.

(4) Included in current assets is $90,000 in cash surrender value of life insurance policies on the lives of Tech Research's officers. Included in long-term debt is an $80,000 loan made against this cash surrender value. Tech Research intends to renew this borrowing annually on the maturity date of the loan.

(5) Discount on long-term debt of $161,500 is included in noncurrent assets.

(6) Included in long-term debt is a $500,000 appropriation of retained earnings for retirement of preferred stock.

(7) Tech Research acquired 11,000 shares of its outstanding common stock for $400,000. This amount is equal to the par value of the common stock and is included in noncurrent assets.

(8) Rent received in advance, $74,800, is included in retained earnings.

(9) A cash dividend of $80,000 declared on June 15, Year 4, and payable on July 22, Year 4, has not been recorded.

(10) A fully depreciated plant asset was sold for $40,000, and the proceeds were credited to the Equipment ledger account.

(11) Deposits of $25,000 made with suppliers for goods ordered have been netted against the balance in the accounts payable controlling ledger account.

(12) An investment in the common stock of a supplier is included in current assets at a cost of $800,000.

(13) Research and development costs of $417,500, incurred in developing new products, have been debited to expense. The new products are expected to be successful revenue producers for at least three years.

Instructions

a List the dollar amounts of each of the six categories of the June 30, Year 4, balance sheet of Tech Research, Inc., on the first line of a six-column working paper. On separate lines below show the effect of any necessary corrections to the accountant's amounts as a result of the information contained in the auditor's notes. Identify each correction with the related number above. Show as an end result the corrected balance sheet data on June 30, Year 4. If the information contained in any of the auditor's notes does not indicate an improper treatment, explain briefly why no adjustment is necessary in each case. Disregard income taxes.

b Would your appraisal of Tech Research's financial position on June 30, Year 4, be changed as a result of the revised data? Explain.

4-10 The controller of Breeze Corporation must prepare a statement of working capital on June 30, Year 3. The purpose of this statement is to demonstrate that Breeze's working capital exceeds $750,000, the amount Breeze agreed to maintain under terms of a loan contract. The statement below was prepared by the assistant to the controller from information obtained from Breeze's accounting records:

BREEZE CORPORATION
Statement of Working Capital
June 30, Year 3

Current assets:		
Cash on hand and in banks		$ 157,500
Notes and securities		480,000
Receivables		542,500
Inventories and prepayments		562,300
Total current assets		$1,742,300
Current liabilities:		
Notes and accounts payable	$411,530	
Payroll taxes and pensions payable	495,000	
Reserve for loss contingencies	200,000	
Total current liabilities		1,106,530
Working capital......................................		$ 635,770

The controller, after some investigation, made the following notes relative to the items included in the foregoing statement of working capital:

(1) *Notes and securities.* Includes $280,000 of notes receivable, of which $100,000 has been discounted at a bank. Also, $250,000 face amount of U.S. Treasury notes (current market value $236,000) acquired for $216,000, on which

$8,500 of interest has accrued since the last interest date. Breeze holds $84,000 in five-year notes receivable from a subsidiary company, on which $5,200 of interest is accrued on June 30 and is payable annually.

(2) *Receivables.* A single controlling account is used for receivables. The balance of the controlling account, $542,500, includes trade accounts receivable of $394,040, a current receivable from a subsidiary company of $40,000, current advances to employees of $28,460, and an installment note receivable of $80,000 received in payment for the sale of a warehouse, due in four installments of $20,000 a year; accrued interest on this note on June 30 was $4,800. Certain customers have credit balances in their accounts, totaling $35,000, because they have made advances prior to the shipment of merchandise ordered. Of the trade accounts receivable, $12,000 are worthless and should be written off; it is estimated that $20,000 of the remaining trade accounts receivable will prove uncollectible.

(3) *Inventories and prepayments.* The inventory of merchandise on June 30 on a last-in, first-out cost basis amounted to $320,750; its current replacement cost is estimated to be $471,000. Included in the $562,300 balance is $98,000 of equipment that is rented to customers and $19,750 of merchandise on order for delivery in six months, the full cost of which is included in trade accounts payable. Also included in the $562,300 balance are short-term prepayments of $94,800 and $29,000 representing a defalcation loss, of which $25,000 is expected to be recovered from an insurance company.

(4) *Current liabilities.* Current trade accounts payable amount to $261,530 and Breeze owes $150,000 on a 90-day note payable to the bank, on which unrecorded interest of $900 has accrued. Amounts withheld from employees for various payroll taxes amount to $70,000; Breeze's required contribution of $28,700 for such taxes has not been recorded. A provision for employee pensions amounts to $425,000, of which $51,500 will be paid in the coming fiscal year. The ''reserve for loss contingencies'' was set up to provide for *possible* losses that may result from the obsolescence of plant assets. The reserve was established by a debit to Retained Earnings.

Instructions

a On the basis of the foregoing information, prepare a corrected statement of working capital for Breeze Corporation on June 30, Year 3. List current assets in detail, followed by current liabilities. Provide supporting computations to show how specific items were determined.

b Is Breeze Corporation complying with the terms of the loan contract as to the maintenance of working capital?

c Compute Breeze Corporation's current ratio on June 30, Year 3.

4-11 The alphabetical list of account balances (before the Income Summary and Dividends ledger accounts were closed) taken from the ledger of Westmont Company on December 31, Year 2, follows:

Accounts payable	$ 743,400
Accounts receivable	1,016,000
Accumulated depreciation of buildings	1,104,000
Accumulated depreciation of leased equipment	220,000

Additional paid-in capital	295,000
Allowance for doubtful accounts	36,000
Buildings	3,951,800
Cash	164,100
Cash surrender value of life insurance policies	115,000
Common stock, $50 par, authorized 100,000 shares	2,500,000
Dividends: common stock	125,000
Dividends: preferred stock	45,500
Goodwill (net)	62,400
Income summary (credit balance)	208,000
Income taxes payable	92,600
Insurance claim receivable (approved by insurance company)	250,000
Inventories, at lower of first-in, first-out cost or market	1,146,000
Issue costs on note payable	10,000
Land	800,000
Leased equipment under capital leases	1,400,000
Liability under capital leases (including current portion of $120,000)	1,050,000
Note payable, 9%, due Oct. 1, Year 10	1,000,000
Preferred stock, 7%, $100 par, authorized 10,000 shares	650,000
Premium on note payable	30,000
Retained earnings, Jan. 1, Year 2	1,344,800
Short-term investments (market value $205,000)	200,000
Unearned rent	12,000

Instructions

a Prepare a classified balance sheet for Westmont Company on December 31, Year 2.

b Prepare a statement of retained earnings for Westmont Company for the year ended December 31, Year 2.

4-12   In the following trial balance for Chan Corporation, all amounts have been properly adjusted, except income taxes expense and related accounts:

CHAN CORPORATION
Trial Balance
December 31, Year 5

	Debit	Credit
Cash	$ 360,000	
Trade accounts receivable (net)	1,300,000	
Inventories	2,700,000	
Buildings and equipment	11,250,000	
Accumulated depreciation of buildings and equipment		$ 2,875,000
Land	1,750,000	
Notes payable (due in Year 6)		500,000
Trade accounts payable		1,200,000
Income taxes payable		125,000

(continued)

Deferred income tax credits		410,000
Bonds payable (due in Year 14)		2,900,000
Common stock, $2 par (no change during year)		1,000,000
Additional paid-in capital		4,200,000
Retained earnings, Jan. 1, Year 5		3,000,000
Dividends	550,000	
Net sales (continuing operations)		10,940,000
Net sales (Disco Division)		1,900,000
Cost of goods sold (continuing operations)	7,100,000	
Cost of goods sold (Disco Division)	1,000,000	
Operating expenses (continuing operations)	2,000,000	
Operating expenses (Disco Division)	440,000	
Interest expense (continuing operations)	210,000	
Gain on disposal of equipment		60,000
Loss on disposal of Disco Division	200,000	
Gain on retirement of bonds payable		250,000
Income taxes expense	500,000	
Totals	$29,360,000	$29,360,000

Additional Information

(1) Income taxes expense in the adjusted trial balance consisted of the following:

Estimated payments made in Year 5...............................	$375,000
Add: Estimated amount accrued on Dec. 31, Year 5	125,000
Total debited to Income Taxes Expense ledger account	$500,000

The recorded income taxes expense does not properly reflect current or deferred income taxes expense or intraperiod income tax allocation.

(2) The effective income tax rate for Chan is 40%. Its taxable income for Year 5 was $2,000,000 (pretax income per accounting records of $2,200,000, less additional depreciation of $200,000 claimed for income tax purposes).

(3) On September 30, Year 5, Chan sold its Disco Division for $3,800,000. The carrying amount of the Disco Division was $4,000,000 on that date. For financial accounting, this was a disposal of a business segment.

(4) On June 30, Year 5, Chan extinguished $1,000,000 carrying amount of its bonds payable for $750,000. The gain on the extinguishment of bonds payable is taxable at a rate of 40% and is an extraordinary item.

Instructions

a Prepare an income statement for Chan Corporation in multiple-step form for the year ended December 31, Year 5, including earnings per share, rounded to the nearest cent. Allocate income taxes as required by generally accepted accounting principles and disregard notes to the financial statements.

b Prepare a statement of retained earnings for Chan Corporation for the year ended December 31, Year 5.

c Prepare a balance sheet in report form for Chan Corporation as of December 31, Year 5.

4-13 In January, Year 11, Paramount Company was seeking a short-term loan to finance a seasonal buildup of inventories and to pay a maturing installment on its serial bonds payable. Anthony Manos, the loan officer of Coe National Bank, reviewed the loan application from Paramount. Included in the file was the following balance sheet prepared by an inexperienced accountant employed by Paramount:

PARAMOUNT COMPANY
Balance Sheet
December 31, Year 10

Assets		Equities	
Cash..................	$ 78,700	Payable to suppliers........	$ 186,000
Trade receivables	294,300	Miscellaneous accrued ex-	
Inventories..............	376,200	penses	23,800
Land, buildings, and		Reserve for current income	
equipment............	940,000	taxes....................	50,000
Marketable securities	98,600	Serial bonds payable, 9%...	450,000
Prepaid expenses.......	18,400	Reserve for depreciation	420,000
Notes receivable	43,000	Reserve for bad debts......	11,800
Patents (net)............	75,000	Reserve for product warranty	10,900
Discount on bonds		Common stock.............	225,000
payable	22,500	Preferred stock.............	206,000
Organization costs (net)..	35,000	Earned surplus.............	398,200
Total assets...........	$1,981,700	Total equities............	$1,981,700

After some study of this balance sheet, Manos decided to ask Paramount to have its financial statements audited by a firm of independent accountants. During the audit, the following additional information was accumulated:

(1) Cash included demand deposits of $59,000, cash change funds of $800, and an IOU signed by Paramount's president for $18,900. (The IOU was collected on January 10, Year 11.)

(2) The balance of trade receivables consisted of the following:

Trade accounts receivable	$331,500
Advances to employees for expenses, to be covered by expense reports	
submitted monthly	12,800
Claim for insurance recovery on damages to equipment	35,000
Less: Customers' deposits on goods ordered.........................	(85,000)
Total trade receivables	$294,300

(3) Approximately $14,700 of trade accounts receivable were uncollectible.

(4) The cost of land owned by Paramount was $40,000, of buildings $750,800, and of equipment $299,200. The carrying amount of the buildings had been reduced by $150,000, representing an 11% mortgage note due on June 30, Year 15, on which interest of $8,250 was accrued but unrecorded on December 31, Year 10. The interest on the mortgage note was payable annually on June 30. Accumulated depreciation was as follows: buildings, $240,000; equipment, $180,000.

(5) Marketable securities consisted of the following:

	Cost	Market value
U.S. Treasury bonds	$20,000	$20,800
Second mortgage promissory note receivable from Rue		
Company, a supplier	66,390	?
Cash surrender value of life insurance policies	10,000	10,000
Accrued interest:		

		Cost	Market value
U.S. Treasury bonds	$ 250		
Second mortgage promissory note			
receivable from Rue Company	1,960	2,210	2,210
Total cost of marketable securities		$98,600	

(6) The inventories listed below were valued at lower of weighted-average cost or market:

Raw material.	$207,380
Goods in process	17,530
Finished goods.	151,290
Total inventories	$376,200

(7) Notes receivable were short-term and were acquired in exchange for trade accounts receivable; unrecorded accrued interest on December 31, Year 10, was $900. It was estimated that $2,400 of the trade notes receivable would prove uncollectible.

(8) In Year 9, Paramount issued $500,000 of 9% serial bonds maturing in annual installments of $50,000. Of the total, $50,000, plus unrecorded accrued interest of $40,500, is due on January 1, Year 11. The bond discount had been correctly amortized in Year 10: the amount of discount applicable to the current portion of serial bonds payable was $500.

(9) The reserve for product warranty represented the amount of the estimated obligation to service Paramount's products for a period of six months following sale.

(10) Common stock consisted of 15,000 shares of $10 par stock issued at $15 a share; preferred stock consisted of 2,000 shares of 10%, $100 par stock issued at $103 a share, callable at 105 a share. A total of 50,000 shares of each class of stock was authorized to be issued.

(11) Paramount is a defendant in a lawsuit with a potential loss that exceeds the insurance coverage. Paramount's attorney is of the opinion that the outcome of the litigation probably will not have a material effect on Paramount's financial position and results of operations.

Instructions

Prepare a revised balance sheet on December 31, Year 10, with improved terminology for Paramount Company, using the information accumulated during the audit. Prepare a separate supporting exhibit for the computation of the revised balance of retained earnings. Make adequate disclosure of the status of litigation against Paramount.

APPENDIX: FINANCIAL REVIEW AND FINANCIAL STATEMENTS FOR WALT DISNEY PRODUCTIONS

WALT DISNEY PRODUCTIONS AND SUBSIDIARIES

FINANCIAL REVIEW
(In thousands, except per share data)

OPERATIONS

Revenues and Earnings

Revenues for the Company increased by 27% in 1984 to almost
$1.7 billion. Net income totaled $97.8 million in 1984, an
increase of 5% from the $93.2 million earned in 1983. Earnings
per share increased to $2.73, computed on a higher average
number of shares outstanding, compared to $2.70 in the
previous year.

	1984	Change	1983	Change	1982
Revenues	$1,655,977	+27%	$1,307,357	+27%	$1,030,250
Operating income	291,033	+32%	220,375	+10%	200,116
Net income	97,844	+ 5%	93,160	− 7%	100,093
Per share	$2.73		$2.70		$3.01

A turnaround in the filmed entertainment segment together
with the inclusion of the new community development
segment provided higher revenues and operating income in
1984. The increase in operating income was partially offset by
higher corporate expenses and the impact of unusual charges
and a change in accounting. Operating results and
management's financial analysis of operations are discussed by
business segment in the forepart of this report.

Before unusual charges and a change in accounting
(discussed later), net income for 1984 increased 16% to $107.8
million, or $3.01 per share. Due to the unusual charges, the
Company reported a loss of $64.0 million in the fourth quarter.
Before the unusual charges, net income for the quarter was
$22.1 million, or $.65 per share, compared to $24.5 million, or
$.70 per share a year ago.

Corporate Expenses (Income)

	1984	Change	1983	Change	1982
General and administrative	$59,570	+68%	$35,554	+15%	$30,957
Percent of revenues	4%		3%		3%

The Company incurred almost $20 million in nonrecurring
general and administrative expenses in 1984 consisting
primarily of costs associated with the Arvida acquisition, a
termination fee and other expenses associated with the
terminated acquisition of Gibson Greetings, Inc. and costs
associated with changes in executive management. On June 5,
1984, the Company entered into an agreement to acquire
Gibson Greetings, Inc. This agreement was terminated on
August 17, 1984 and the Company became obligated to pay
Gibson $7.5 million plus certain expenses.

In addition, normal increases were experienced in labor,
materials and outside services, which were partially offset by
the recognition of a $5 million pretax capital gain from the
exchange of a parcel of land adjacent to Disneyland.

	1984	Change	1983	Change	1982
Design projects abandoned	$7,032	−4%	$7,295	+42%	$5,147

At the close of each fiscal quarter, management regularly
evaluates projects in the concept and design stages which have
been in progress for varying periods of time. Those which are
determined to have no future use are abandoned and charged
to expense. In connection with the separate review and
evaluation for the fiscal year 1984 with new management,
additional abandonments were identified and recorded based

upon newly defined corporate strategies (see Unusual Charges
below).

	1984	Change	1983	Change	1982
Interest expense (income) — net	$41,738	+197%	$14,066	+195%	$(14,781)

The Company incurred interest costs of $75.8 million in
1984 resulting from indebtedness averaging $625 million at an
average interest rate of 12%. Of that amount, $32.1 million was
capitalized to qualifying assets. Total interest costs incurred in
1983 and 1982 were $43.3 and $24.4 million, respectively, of
which $25.4 and $24.4 million were capitalized. Interest
income included above was $2.0, $3.8 and $14.8 in 1984, 1983
and 1982, respectively. Management anticipates that the
Company will continue to incur substantial interest costs for

REVENUES AND OPERATING INCOME
(In Millions of Dollars)

REVENUES

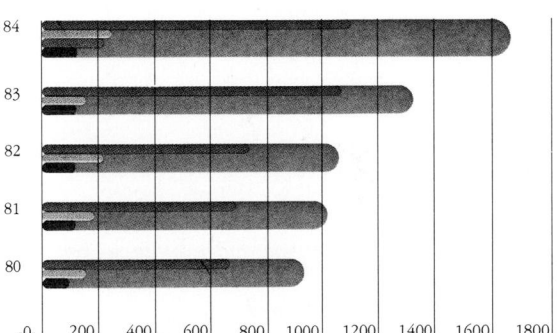

OPERATING INCOME

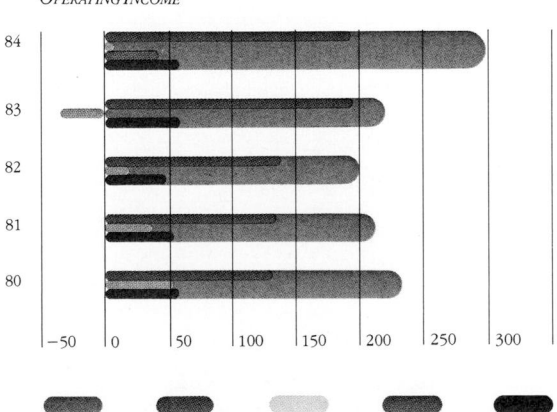

Total | Entertainment and Recreation | Filmed Entertainment | Community Development | Consumer Products

WALT DISNEY PRODUCTIONS AND SUBSIDIARIES

CONSOLIDATED STATEMENT OF INCOME
(In thousands, except per share data)

Year ended September 30	1984	1983	1982
Revenues			
Entertainment and recreation	$1,097,359	$1,031,202	$ 725,610
Filmed entertainment	244,552	165,458	202,102
Community development	204,384		
Consumer products	109,682	110,697	102,538
	1,655,977	1,307,357	1,030,250
Costs and Expenses			
Entertainment and recreation	904,664	834,324	592,965
Filmed entertainment	242,303	198,843	182,463
Community development	162,158		
Consumer products	55,819	53,815	54,706
	1,364,944	1,086,982	830,134
Income (Loss) Before Corporate Expenses and			
Unusual Charges			
Entertainment and recreation	192,695	196,878	132,645
Filmed entertainment	2,249	(33,385)	19,639
Community development	42,226		
Consumer products	53,863	56,882	47,832
	291,033	220,375	200,116
Corporate Expenses (Income)			
General and administrative	59,570	35,554	30,957
Design projects abandoned	7,032	7,295	5,147
Interest expense (income) — net	41,738	14,066	(14,781)
	108,340	56,915	21,323
Income Before Unusual Charges, Taxes on Income and			
Accounting Change	182,693	163,460	178,793
Unusual charges	165,960		
Income Before Taxes on Income and Accounting Change	16,733	163,460	178,793
Taxes on income (benefit)	(5,000)	70,300	78,700
Income Before Accounting Change	21,733	93,160	100,093
Cumulative effect of change in accounting for			
investment tax credits	76,111		
Net Income	$ 97,844	$ 93,160	$ 100,093
Earnings per Share			
Income before accounting change	$0.61	$2.70	$3.01
Cumulative effect of change in accounting	2.12		
	$2.73	$2.70	$3.01
Average number of common and common			
equivalent shares outstanding	35,849	34,481	33,225

WALT DISNEY PRODUCTIONS AND SUBSIDIARIES

the next several years while maintaining a significant level of debt. The amount of future interest to be capitalized may be less if the qualifying capital expenditures decrease in relation to total indebtedness.

Unusual Charges
In conjunction with an analysis and evaluation by new management of certain Company assets and of various options for growth in relation to newly defined corporate strategies and emerging business opportunities, the Company recorded unusual charges of approximately $166 million in the fourth quarter of fiscal 1984. Based on management's assessment of the redirection of the Company's filmed entertainment business, a provision of $112 million was made for adjusting the carrying values of several motion picture and television properties in release, in production and under development. As a result of management's decision to limit to pre-Epcot Center levels further annual investments in the existing theme parks, various design and development projects were determined to have no future use and were written down by $40 million. Costs of about $14 million resulting from other restructuring measures were also included in the unusual charges.

Taxes on Income (Benefit)

	1984	Change	1983	Change	1982
Taxes on income (benefit)	$(5,000)	−107%	$70,300	−11%	$78,700
Effective income tax rate	(30%)		43%		44%

The Company has realized a tax benefit in 1984 due principally to the impact of the unusual charges provided for in the fourth quarter and available tax credits. The effective income tax rate before the unusual charges was 41%, an improvement from 1983 attributable to tax benefits realizable from the Arvida operations. Generally, the difference between the U.S. federal income tax rate of 46% and the Company's effective income tax rate is primarily due to benefits received from investment tax credits. The Company recorded estimated claims for refundable income taxes of $60, $70 and $41 million at fiscal year ends 1984, 1983, and 1982, respectively; these refunds primarily resulted from investment tax credits and excess of tax over book depreciation relating to Epcot Center.

Change in Accounting
To conform to predominant industry practice, the Company in the fourth quarter of 1984 changed its accounting for investment tax credits to the flow-through method from the deferral method. The flow-through method reduces income taxes by the full amount of the allowable investment tax credits in the year the credits arise. The Company was required to record the change effective October 1, 1983; it resulted in the realization of $76 million of previously deferred tax credits as an increase to net income in the first fiscal quarter of 1984.

FINANCIAL POSITION

The Balance Sheet
The Company has changed its balance sheet to a nonclassified presentation, which does not distinguish between current and noncurrent assets and liabilities. Management believes that a nonclassified balance sheet provides a more meaningful presentation of real estate inventories, film production costs and entertainment attractions consistent with the business cycles of the Company's operations.

The Company's total assets have more than doubled over the last five years to $2.7 billion, representing an 18% average annual growth rate.

	1984	Change	1983	Change	1982
Total assets	$2,739,443	+15%	$2,381,195	+13%	$2,102,816

The increase in total assets during the past five years reflects the investment in Epcot Center, which opened September, 1982, and the acquisition of Arvida Corporation in fiscal 1984. Arvida's principal assets are real estate inventories, as set forth on the balance sheet, consisting of undeveloped land, community development work in progress and completed projects which have not yet been sold.

Borrowings have increased during 1984 due primarily to the $215 million of Arvida debt assumed upon the acquisition of Arvida and the $328 million for the repurchase of the Company's common stock from Reliance Insurance Company.

	1984	Change	1983	Change	1982
Borrowings	$861,909	+144%	$352,575	+12%	$315,000
Percent of total assets	31%		15%		15%

The Company has available through May, 1987 an unsecured revolving line of credit of up to $1.3 billion for general

TOTAL ASSETS, STOCKHOLDERS EQUITY AND BORROWINGS
(In Millions of Dollars)

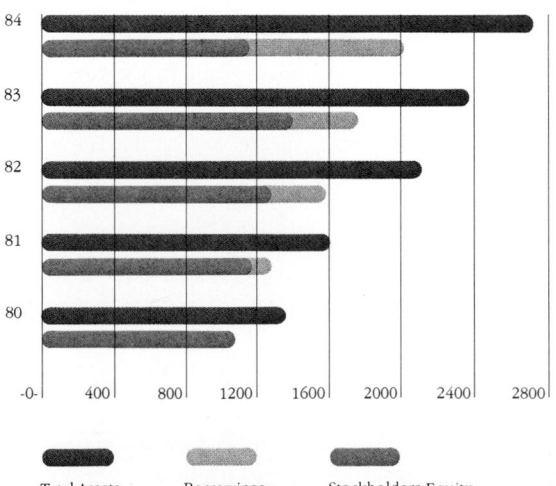

Total Assets   Borrowings   Stockholders Equity

WALT DISNEY PRODUCTIONS AND SUBSIDIARIES

CONSOLIDATED BALANCE SHEET
(In thousands)

September 30	1984	1983*
Assets		
Cash ($8,800 restricted in 1984)	$ 35,346	$ 18,055
Accounts and notes receivable, net of allowances	172,762	104,746
Taxes on income refundable	60,000	70,000
Merchandise inventories	83,467	77,945
Film production costs	102,462	127,010
Real estate inventories	229,424	
Entertainment attractions and other property, at cost		
Attractions, buildings and equipment	2,413,985	2,251,297
Less accumulated depreciation	(600,156)	(504,365)
	1,813,829	1,746,932
Construction and design projects in progress	94,710	108,190
Land	28,807	16,687
	1,937,346	1,871,809
Other assets	118,636	111,630
	$2,739,443	$2,381,195
Liabilities and Stockholders Equity		
Accounts payable, payroll and other accrued liabilities	$ 239,992	$ 182,709
Taxes on income payable	24,145	13,982
Borrowings	861,909	352,575
Unearned deposits and advances	178,907	109,556
Deferred taxes on income	279,005	321,845
Commitments and contingencies		
Stockholders equity		
Preferred shares, no par		
Authorized — 5,000 shares, none issued		
Common shares, no par		
Authorized — 75,000 shares		
Issued and outstanding — 33,729 and 34,509 shares	359,988	661,934
Retained earnings	795,497	738,594
	1,155,485	1,400,528
	$2,739,443	$2,381,195

*Restated to conform to nonclassified presentation.

WALT DISNEY PRODUCTIONS AND SUBSIDIARIES

corporate purposes. The line is available to support commercial paper borrowings and intermediate notes. As of September 30, 1984, the Company had outstanding $250 million under the line and $200 million of commercial paper.

The Company, through its Arvida subsidiary, has a real estate term loan of $132 million due in varying amounts through December, 1991 and a revolving line of credit of up to $50 million, of which $26 million was outstanding at September 30, 1984. The Company also has a term loan denominated in Japanese yen, due in equal amounts through February, 1993, of which $53 million was outstanding at September 30, 1984.

At September 30, 1984, the Company had outstanding two Eurodollar offerings, $100 million at 15.75% due in September, 1986 and $75 million at 12.50% due in March, 1989. On October 17, 1984, the Company called for the redemption of the $100 million 15.75% Eurodollar notes as of November 30, 1984.

The ratio of debt to total capitalization (stockholders equity plus borrowings) was 43% at September 30, 1984 compared to 20% at September 30, 1983 and 1982.

	1984	Change	1983	Change	1982
Stockholders equity	$1,155,485	−17%	$1,400,528	+10%	$1,274,784
Per share	$34.26		$40.58	+ 6%	$38.22
Percent of total assets	42%		59%		61%

The decrease in stockholders equity is attributable to the repurchase of 4.2 million common shares of the Company's stock from Reliance in June, 1984 for a total cost of $328 million. Also in June, the Company exchanged 3.3 million of its common shares for all of the outstanding shares of Arvida, which had a book value at January 1, 1984, the effective date of the acquisition, of $21.8 million.

Return on average stockholders equity was 7.7% in 1984.

The Company announced subsequent to year end that the Board of Directors authorized a stock repurchase program under which the Company may purchase, from time to time, up to 3.5 million shares of the Company's outstanding common stock.

Commitments and Contingencies

The Company has pension plans covering substantially all of its domestic employees not covered by union or industry pension plans. The plans are funded by Company and, where applicable, employee payments to trusts administered by several banks. Net assets available for benefits as of the date of the latest actuarial valuation were $73 million. The actuarial present value of accumulated plan benefits, using assumed rates of return ranging from 9½% to 12%, was $72 million.

The Company is a defendant in various routine litigation incident to the conduct of its business, including actions asserting claims under federal anti-trust laws regarding motion picture distributors. In addition, a number of lawsuits have been filed during 1984 alleging, among other things, breaches of fiduciary duties by members of the Company's Board of Directors in connection with the acquisition of Arvida and the repurchase of its stock from Reliance; plaintiffs are seeking, among other things, rescission of the two transactions. In the opinion of management and counsel, the Company will not suffer any material monetary liability by reason thereof.

CHANGES IN FINANCIAL POSITION

Cash Provided by Operations

One of the most important goals of management is the effective utilization of cash generated from the Company's operating businesses. Cash provided by operations has increased by 126% over the last five years and by 23% to $414 million in 1984.

	1984	Change	1983	Change	1982
Cash provided by operations	$414,036	+23%	$337,356	+23%	$274,782

Cash provided by operations was $316.2 million greater than reported net income of $97.8 million. This difference was principally due to (i) depreciation, amortization, unusual charges and other expenses charged to income which did not require current cash outlays, that were partially offset by the change in accounting for investment tax credits which did not provide cash in the current fiscal year and (ii) income tax refunds received in 1984 relating to prior years.

Cash requirements for dividends and investing activities exceeded cash provided by operations in 1984 by $309.2 million ($147.3 million — 1983) due principally to the repurchase of common stock from Reliance. This deficiency in cash from internal sources, as well as reductions in existing borrowings, was financed primarily by borrowings under the Company's unsecured revolving line of credit and the issuance of commercial paper.

PRINCIPAL SOURCES AND USES OF CASH
(In Millions of Dollars)

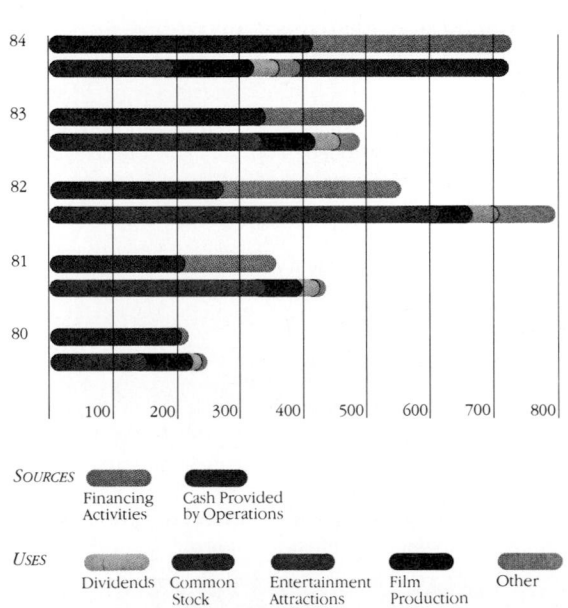

WALT DISNEY PRODUCTIONS AND SUBSIDIARIES

CONSOLIDATED STATEMENT
OF CHANGES IN FINANCIAL POSITION*
(In thousands)

Year ended September 30	1984	1983	1982
*Cash provided by operations before taxes on income**	$364,024	$308,369	$309,431
Taxes received (paid) on income — net	50,012	28,987	(34,649)
Cash provided by operations	414,036	337,356	274,782
Cash dividends	40,941	41,100	39,742
	373,095	296,256	235,040
Investing activities			
Common stock repurchase	327,679		
Entertainment attractions and other property, net of related payables	194,142	333,738	614,416
Film production and programming costs	127,595	83,750	52,295
Funding of pension program restructuring	24,338		
Rights to the Walt Disney name		(3,640)	40,000
Epcot Center and The Disney Channel preopening and start-up costs		18,253	19,170
Other	8,542	11,406	26,881
	682,296	443,507	752,762
	(309,201)	(147,251)	(517,722)
Financing activities			
Borrowings	421,119	137,500	205,000
Reduction of borrowings	(126,593)	(99,925)	
Participation fees, net of related receivables	6,892	11,169	23,867
Common stock offering		70,883	
Common stock issued (returned) to acquire rights to the Walt Disney name		(3,640)	46,200
Other	11,835	35,667	2,030
	313,253	151,654	277,097
Increase (decrease) in cash	4,052	4,403	(240,625)
Cash, beginning of year (including $13,239 for Arvida in 1984)	31,294	13,652	254,277
Cash, end of year	$ 35,346	$ 18,055	$ 13,652

*The difference between income before taxes on income and accounting change as shown on the Consolidated Statement of Income and cash provided by operations before taxes on income is explained as follows:

Income before taxes on income and accounting change	$ 16,733	$163,460	$178,793
Charges to income not requiring cash outlays:			
Depreciation	106,607	90,184	41,917
Amortization of film production and programming costs	54,134	65,575	64,868
Unusual charges	152,760		
Other	13,860	15,526	9,950
Changes in:			
Accounts and notes receivable	(15,507)	(25,863)	1,077
Merchandise inventories	(2,774)	(11,228)	(6,944)
Real estate inventories	6,465		
Accounts payable, payroll and other accrued liabilities	30,925	13,294	15,178
Other	821	(2,579)	4,592
	347,291	144,909	130,638
Cash provided by operations before taxes on income	$364,024	$308,369	$309,431

*The title of the statement of cash flows before *FASB Statement No. 95*.

WALT DISNEY PRODUCTIONS AND SUBSIDIARIES

Dividends

It is the Company's policy to consider periodic dividend increases to its stockholders consistent with earnings growth and its need for funds to support future growth. Total cash dividends in 1984 represent 42% of net income for the year, down from 44% a year ago. At its current annual rate of $1.20 per share, cash dividends have grown annually by 21% over the last five years.

	1984	Change	1983	Change	1982
Cash dividends	$40,941	—	$41,100	+3%	$39,742
Percent of net income	42%		44%		40%
Per share	$1.20		$1.20		$1.20

Investing Activities

The most significant investing activity in 1984 was the $328 million repurchase on June 11, 1984 of 4.2 million shares of Disney common stock from Reliance for $70.83 per share and estimated out-of-pocket expenses incurred by Reliance in connection with its actual and contemplated purchases of Disney shares relating to its proposed tender offer.

The Company continues to invest in the future through its capital improvements program. Over the past five years, the Company has invested over $1.6 billion in entertainment attractions and other property and almost $400 million in film production and programming for a total of more than $2.0 billion. These investments are intended to expand services and operating capability in the Company's entertainment and recreation businesses and to increase the capacity to expand its filmed entertainment businesses. The consumer product businesses have and will continue to benefit from this expansion of product.

In fiscal 1984, expenditures continued on several projects at Disneyland and Walt Disney World, including the Moroccan and Seas pavilions at Epcot Center. Additions to film production and programming include production activity on "The Black Cauldron" and other live-action features, as well as a variety of original programming for The Disney Channel.

	1984	Change	1983	Change	1982
Additions to entertainment attractions and other property	$182,051	−37%	$291,202	−55%	$648,765
Additions to film production and programming costs	127,936	+51%	84,518	+62%	52,295

The Company currently anticipates that expenditures during fiscal 1985 will approximate $170 million for entertainment attractions and other property, $115 million for theatrical and television production and $35 million in programming for The Disney Channel.

Management reviews the Company's capital program at least quarterly and revises the anticipated capital additions for the fiscal year, as appropriate. In addition, some interest costs will be capitalized, the amounts being dependent upon the extent of borrowings, the associated rates of interest incurred, and the amount of qualifying asset costs incurred during the year.

Financing Activities

The Company has developed financing strategies and various financing arrangements to cover projected financing needs over the next two to three years. These strategies give the Company the flexibility it needs during a period of major investing activities and interest rate fluctuations. The Company has received credit ratings of A-1 and P-1 for its commercial paper from two of the major rating agencies.

As mentioned earlier, the Company's cash requirements exceeded cash provided by operations by $309.2 million and $147.3 million in 1984 and 1983, respectively. The Company financed these shortfalls at an average cost of new borrowings of 12% in 1984, up from 10% in 1983.

In March, 1984, the Company negotiated a new credit agreement with Bank of America and a group of 15 other banks, raising the total line of credit from $400 million to $1.3 billion. The proceeds of the borrowings may be used by the Company to back commercial paper borrowings and intermediate notes, for general corporate purposes or to make acquisitions. In May, 1987, any amounts outstanding under this revolving line may be converted into a four-year term loan. The Company is required to meet certain financial covenants, including net worth and capitalization ratio requirements.

In September, 1984, the Company authorized the issuance of 12.50% notes relative to a new Eurodollar offering totalling $150 million. The proceeds from this offering were received on October 2, 1984. The notes will mature on October 1, 1987 and are not redeemable prior to maturity. Also subsequent to year end, the Company replaced the $250 million outstanding under the line with privately-placed commercial paper borrowings at lower interest rates.

NET INCOME AND CASH DIVIDENDS PER SHARE

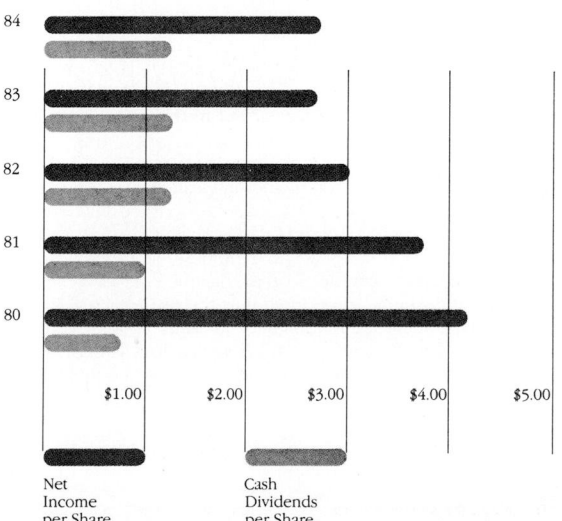

Net Income per Share   Cash Dividends per Share

Inflation and Changing Prices

In recognition of the need to provide readers of financial statements with information to assist them in assessing the impact of inflation, the Financial Accounting Standards Board requires supplementary income computations.

By adjusting the historical cost financial information for changes that have occurred in the general purchasing power of the dollar (referred to as the constant dollar method, which is measured by the Consumer Price Index for all Urban Consumers), the Company's net income is significantly reduced from net income reported in the primary financial statements due to additional theoretical depreciation which has been adjusted for inflation. However, the Company does not believe that this hypothetical calculation has much relevance to its operations. The Company believes that cash provided by operations adjusted for changing prices provides a more meaningful insight into the impact of inflation because it excludes non-cash charges such as depreciation. Cash provided by operations has increased at an annual average rate of 13% when expressed in average 1984 dollars compared to an annual rate of 21% as reflected in the primary financial statements.

Elsewhere in this report, the Company discusses its continuing program of investing in the future through its capital improvements program, which is intended to maintain and/or increase its productive capability. However, the Company is not confronted with a problem of replacing very old and worn out capital assets as a result of carefully planned and comprehensive refurbishing programs. When adjusted for the effects of changing prices, the Company has invested almost $2.2 billion in productive assets over the last five years compared to approximately $2.0 billion as reflected in the primary financial statements. To the extent that these expenditures are replacing existing assets, it is presumed that the costs in 1984 dollars are significantly higher than the costs of the original assets.

Foreign Currency Translation

The Company may realize a gain or loss on foreign currency transactions that reflects a change in rates of exchange between the time revenues are earned and the time they are converted to U.S. dollars. As the U.S. dollar strengthens in relation to a foreign currency, the foreign monies have less value, and conversely, when the dollar weakens the foreign monies have more value, when converted to the dollar. Such transaction gains and losses are included in income and are not material. In translating assets and liabilities that are recorded or denominated in currencies other than the U.S. dollar and are not part of a hedging arrangement, the resulting gains or losses are also included in income. Such gains or losses are not material due to the Company's relatively low foreign investment in inventories and property, plant and equipment.

The Company has hedged long term borrowings involving Japanese yen by designating the royalty revenues from Tokyo Disneyland to service interest and principal payments for such indebtedness, thus offsetting the effects of fluctuations in the exchange rate.

Foreign currency fluctuations from year-to-year can have a significant impact on the Company's earnings. The magnitude of currency changes have been significant during the past year as the U.S. dollar has strengthened against virtually all foreign currencies. Had currency rates remained constant year-to-year, it is estimated that revenues would have been over $23 million greater in 1984.

Stock Transfer Agent
Walt Disney Productions

Registrar
First Interstate Bank of California, Los Angeles

Stock Exchanges
The Common Stock of the Company is listed for trading on the New York, Pacific and Swiss Stock Exchanges. The Euro-Bond notes of the Company are listed on The Stock Exchange in London.

Independent Accountants
Price Waterhouse, West Los Angeles

Annual Meeting of Stockholders
Wednesday, February 6, 1985

Other Information
A copy of the Company's annual report to the Securities and Exchange Commission (Form 10-K) will be furnished without charge to any stockholder upon written request to Shareholder Services, Walt Disney Productions, P.O. Box 10099, Burbank, California 91510-0099.

Walt Disney Productions makes available to its stockholders a Dividend Reinvestment Plan. Those wishing a pamphlet about the plan should write to Shareholder Services, Walt Disney Productions, P.O. Box 10099, Burbank, California 91510-0099.

WALT DISNEY PRODUCTIONS AND SUBSIDIARIES

INDEX TO FINANCIAL STATEMENTS AND
SUPPLEMENTAL INFORMATION

The consolidated financial statements of Walt Disney
Productions and Subsidiaries have been included on the
following pages of this Annual Report:

Additional information, although not a required part of the
basic consolidated financial statements, may be read in
conjunction with the consolidated financial statements and
appears in the following supplemental section of this Annual
Report:

REPORT OF INDEPENDENT ACCOUNTANTS

To the Board of Directors and Stockholders
of Walt Disney Productions

In our opinion, the consolidated financial statements listed in
the index and appearing on pages 29, 31, 33 and 37 through 42,
present fairly the financial position of Walt Disney Productions
and its subsidiaries at September 30, 1984 and 1983, and the
results of their operations and the changes in their financial
position for each of the three years in the period ended
September 30, 1984, in conformity with generally accepted
accounting principles consistently applied after restatement
for the change, with which we concur, in the presentation of
the balance sheet as described in Note 1 and except for the
change, with which we concur, in the method of accounting for
investment tax credits as described in Note 4 to the
consolidated financial statements. Our examinations of these
statements were made in accordance with generally accepted
auditing standards and accordingly included such tests of the
accounting records and such other auditing procedures as we
considered necessary in the circumstances.

Price Waterhouse

West Los Angeles, California
November 27, 1984

NOTES TO CONSOLIDATED FINANCIAL STATEMENTS
(To be read in conjunction with the consolidated financial statements on pages 29, 31 and 33)

1. Description of the Business and Summary of Significant Accounting Policies

WALT DISNEY PRODUCTIONS and its subsidiaries (the Company) is a diversified international company engaged in family entertainment and community development with operations in four business segments; financial information regarding business segments appears on the Consolidated Statement of Income and in Note 11.

ENTERTAINMENT AND RECREATION
The Company operates the Disneyland amusement theme park in California and the Walt Disney World destination resort in Florida. In addition to an amusement theme park, the Magic Kingdom, and Epcot Center, the Walt Disney World complex includes three hotels, camping, golfing and other recreational facilities, a shopping village, a conference center and other lodging accommodations. The Company receives royalties on revenues generated by the Tokyo Disneyland amusement theme park in Tokyo, Japan, which is owned and operated by an unrelated Japanese corporation.

FILMED ENTERTAINMENT
The Company produces motion pictures for the theatrical, television and home video markets. The Company distributes its filmed product through its own distribution and marketing companies in the United States and through foreign subsidiaries in certain countries and other distribution companies throughout the rest of the world. The Company provides programming for, and operates, The Disney Channel, a pay television programming service.

COMMUNITY DEVELOPMENT
Through its new wholly owned subsidiary, Arvida Corporation (Note 2), the Company develops comprehensively planned, distinctive resort and primary home communities. The Company also develops commercial and industrial properties within or near many of its planned communities. Through various subsidiaries, the Company provides general real estate brokerage and resort and property management services.

CONSUMER PRODUCTS
The Company licenses the name Walt Disney, its characters, its literary properties and its songs and music to various manufacturers, retailers, printers and publishers. The Company also produces and distributes phonograph records, 16mm prints of product developed on educational subjects, computer software and a broad range of teaching aids. These activities are conducted through the character merchandising and publications, records and music publishing, and educational media divisions and subsidiaries of the Company.

The following summary of the Company's significant accounting policies is presented as an integral part of the consolidated financial statements.

Principles of Consolidation
The consolidated financial statements include the accounts of the Company and its domestic and foreign subsidiaries, all wholly owned.

The Consolidated Balance Sheet for fiscal 1983 has been restated to conform to a nonclassified presentation adopted in fiscal 1984, which does not distinguish between current and noncurrent assets and liabilities. The Company believes that a nonclassified balance sheet provides a more meaningful presentation for real estate inventories, film production costs and entertainment attractions consistent with the business cycles of the Company's operations. In addition, this conforms with the Company's presentation of changes in cash rather than working capital as shown in the Consolidated Statement of Changes in Financial Position.

Revenue Recognition
Generally, revenues are recorded when the earnings process is substantially complete and goods have been delivered or services performed. Revenues from participant/sponsors at the theme parks and Epcot Center are recorded over the period of the applicable agreements commencing with the opening of the attraction. Revenues from the theatrical distribution of motion pictures are recognized when motion pictures are exhibited domestically and when revenues are reported from foreign distributors; revenues from television licensing agreements are generally recorded when the film is available to the licensee and certain other conditions are met. Profit is recognized in full on sales of real estate when collectibility of the sales price is reasonably assured and the earnings process is virtually complete; if the sale does not meet requirements for recognition, profit is deferred until such requirements are met. Profit is recognized on residential unit sales at the time of closing.

Merchandise Inventories
Costs of merchandise, materials and supplies inventories are generally determined on the moving average basis and the retail method and are stated at the lower of cost or market.

Film Production Costs and Amortization
Costs of completed theatrical and commercial television film productions (negative costs), together with applicable capitalized exploitation costs, are amortized by charges to income in the proportion that gross revenues recognized by the Company during the year for each production bears to the estimated total gross revenues to be received. Estimates of total gross revenues are reviewed periodically and amortization is adjusted accordingly. If unamortized cost exceeds the estimated producers share of film rentals to be received, the carrying value of the film is adjusted to expected net realizable value. Programming costs for The Disney Channel are amortized on a straight-line basis over the estimated useful lives of the programs.

Real Estate Inventories
Real estate inventories are carried at cost not to exceed estimates of net realizable value determined on an individual project basis. Land and land development is apportioned among the projects on the basis of acreage. Marketing and other capitalized predevelopment costs relating to residential and commercial projects are charged to cost of real estate sales as related units are closed.

Entertainment Attractions and Other Property
The Company, at any one point in time, will have a number of projects in the concept, design, or construction phases related to entertainment and recreation attractions, buildings and equipment. All projects in progress are evaluated on a continuing basis and, upon completion, costs of major replacements and improvements are capitalized. If it is determined that a project in progress has no future use, the costs of such project are charged to income under the caption "Design Projects Abandoned."

Depreciation is provided principally on the straight line method using estimated service lives ranging from four to fifty years.

NOTES TO CONSOLIDATED FINANCIAL STATEMENTS, continued

Other Assets
Deferred preopening and start-up costs relating to Epcot Center and The Disney Channel are being amortized over five years.

Rights to the name, likeness and portrait of Walt Disney are being amortized over forty years.

Taxes on Income
Taxes are provided on all revenue and expense items included in the Consolidated Statement of Income, regardless of the period in which such items are recognized for income tax purposes, except for items representing a permanent difference between pretax accounting income and taxable income. In fiscal 1984, the method of accounting for investment tax credits was changed from the deferral method, which amortizes the credits over the estimated useful lives of the related assets, to the flow-through method, which reduces the provision for taxes on income in the year the related assets are placed into service (Note 4).

Stock Options
Proceeds from the sale of common stock issued under stock option plans are accounted for as capital transactions. If stock appreciation rights are granted in connection with options granted, income is charged or credited over the vesting period for the difference between the market price of the Company's stock and the option price of the appreciation rights outstanding.

Earnings per Share
Earnings per common and common equivalent share are computed on the basis of the average number of shares outstanding during each year, retroactively adjusted to give effect to all stock splits and stock dividends. It is assumed that all dilutive stock options are exercised at the beginning of each year and that the proceeds are used to purchase shares of the Company's common stock at the average market price during the year.

2. Acquisition

On June 6, 1984, the Company acquired all of the outstanding common stock of Arvida Corporation (Arvida) in exchange for 3.3 million shares of the Company's common stock. The acquisition was accounted for under the pooling of interests method. For reasons stated below, the Company's consolidated financial statements for periods ended prior to December 31, 1983 exclude the operating results of Arvida.

In December, 1983, all of the outstanding common stock of Arvida was acquired by Arvida Acquisition Company (AAC) from the Pennsylvania Company, a wholly owned subsidiary of The Penn Central Corporation. AAC was liquidated and merged into Arvida (the predecessor company) which became the surviving corporation. This acquisition of Arvida, effective December 31, 1983, was accounted for as a purchase and, accordingly, a new accounting basis was established. Because of these circumstances, the Company does not believe that Arvida's financial statements after December 31, 1983 are comparable to those of the predecessor company. Accordingly, Arvida's financial position and results of operations are included in the consolidated financial statements of the Company for the period commencing January 1, 1984.

Unaudited revenues and net income (before accounting change for investment tax credits) for the Company for the six months ended March 31, 1984 (the nearest interim period prior to the combination) were $648 and $31 million, respectively. Unaudited revenues and net income for Arvida for the three months ended March 31, 1984 were $61 and $9 million, respectively.

3. Unusual Charges

Management recently completed an analysis and evaluation of certain Company assets and of various options for growth in relation to newly defined corporate strategies and emerging business opportunities. Such strategies relate to a redirection of the Company's filmed entertainment business and a decision to limit to pre-Epcot Center levels further annual investments in the existing theme parks. As a result of this assessment, the Company recorded unusual charges of approximately $166 million in the fourth quarter of fiscal 1984. The charges include a provision for write-downs to estimated net realizable values of $112 million for motion picture and television properties in release, in production and under development (Filmed Entertainment segment), $40 million for the abandonment of certain projects in conceptual design and development for Walt Disney World or Disneyland (Corporate segment) and $14 million for the estimated cost of other restructuring measures (Corporate segment).

In addition to the above unusual charges, the Company incurred $20 million of certain nonrecurring corporate general and administrative expenses mostly in the fourth quarter of fiscal 1984. The expenses consisted principally of fees related to a terminated acquisition, costs of the Arvida merger and costs associated with changes in executive management.

4. Accounting Change

To conform with accounting practices predominantly used in industries in which the Company operates, the Company elected to change its method of accounting for investment tax credits (ITC) from the deferral method to the flow-through method in the fourth quarter of fiscal 1984. The Company was required to record the change effective October 1, 1983; it resulted in the recognition of $76 million of cumulative deferred ITC as part of net income in the first quarter of fiscal 1984 ($2.20 per share for the quarter and $2.12 per share for the year due to the greater number of average shares outstanding). If the flow-through method had been used for the first three quarters of fiscal year 1984, net income would not have been materially different from that reported. If the flow-through method had been used in fiscal years 1983 and 1982, net income would have increased to $111 million ($3.22 per share) and $139 million ($4.20 per share), respectively, due principally to the high level of credits earned on Epcot Center investments.

5. *Borrowings* (In thousands)

Borrowings consist of the following:

	1984	1983
Borrowings under unsecured revolving line of credit	$250,000	
Commercial paper	200,175	$118,200
Borrowings of subsidiary under unsecured real estate term loan and revolving line of credit	158,000	
15.75% Eurodollar notes, due September 1, 1986 and redeemable at option of Company after September 1, 1984, interest payable annually	100,000	100,000
12.50% Eurodollar notes, due March 15, 1989 and redeemable at option of Company after September 15, 1986, interest payable annually	75,000	75,000
8.60% yen term loan, due February 1, 1993, principal payable in semi-annual installments of $3,125	53,125	59,375
6.00% to 13.50% notes payable due in varying amounts through 1991, secured by real estate inventories and certain property	25,609	
	$861,909	$352,575

Revolving Line of Credit and Commercial Paper

The Company has available through May, 1987 an unsecured revolving line of bank credit of up to $1.3 billion for general corporate purposes. The Company has the option to borrow at various interest rates not to exceed the bank's prime rate. In May, 1987, any amounts outstanding may be converted into a four-year term loan at ¼ of 1% above the prime rate. The Company is required to pay a commitment fee on the unused portion of the line and to meet certain financial covenants, including net worth and capitalization ratio requirements. The line is available to support commercial paper borrowings and intermediate notes. As of September 30, 1984, the Company had outstanding $250 million under the line with interest at 12.36% and had issued $200 million of commercial paper used for current operations with interest at 11.38%.

Term Loans

Under a real estate term loan and revolving line of credit agreement, the Company's subsidiary, Arvida Corporation, has a $132 million term loan outstanding due in varying amounts through December, 1991. Arvida also has available through that date an unsecured revolving line of credit of up to $50 million for general real estate operating purposes, of which $26 million was outstanding at September 30, 1984. Arvida has the option to borrow at ¾ of 1% above the certificate of deposit or LIBOR rates. At September 30, 1984, interest averaged 12.44% on these borrowings. Arvida is required to meet, among other things, certain minimum net worth, capitalization and cash flow requirements. In addition, payment provisions of the term loan and line of credit agreement require scheduled payments and prepayments based on Arvida's cash flow levels and proceeds from certain asset sales, as defined.

The Company previously entered into an 8.60% Japanese yen term loan and a forward exchange contract which effectively converted $50 million of the $75 million 12.50% Eurodollar notes into yen equivalents. This 7.40% yen borrowing is due March 14, 1989 with interest payable annually. The Company has hedged these yen borrowings by designating its cumulative royalty receipts from Tokyo Disneyland to service principal and interest yen payments, thus offsetting the impact of exchange rate fluctuations.

Term loans and notes payable mature as follows: $10,800–1985; $28,500–1986; $36,800–1987; $41,800–1988; $52,800–1989; and $40,000 thereafter.

Eurodollar Offerings

In September, 1984, the Company authorized the issuance of 12.50% Eurodollar notes for $150 million; the proceeds were received in fiscal 1985. The notes will mature on October 1, 1987 and are not redeemable prior to maturity, except in the event of certain changes affecting United States tax law. The net proceeds from the sale of the notes (approximately $148 million) were used by the Company to reduce outstanding borrowings under the revolving line of credit.

On October 17, 1984, the Company called for the redemption of the $100 million 15.75% Eurodollar notes as of November 30, 1984.

Capitalization of Interest

The Company capitalizes interest costs on assets constructed for its theme parks, Epcot Center and real estate developments and on theatrical and television productions in process. In 1984, the Company capitalized $32.1 million of $75.8 million total interest costs incurred. In 1983, $25.4 million of a total $43.3 million in interest costs were capitalized. In 1982, the total interest costs incurred of $24.4 million were capitalized.

6. *Taxes on Income* (In thousands)

The income before provision and the provision (benefit) for taxes on income consist of the following:

	1984	1983	1982
Income (loss) before provision for taxes on income			
Domestic (including U.S. exports)	$ (7,445)	$140,725	$167,083
Foreign subsidiaries	24,178	22,735	11,710
Total income before provision (benefit) for taxes on income	$ 16,733	$163,460	$178,793
Provision (benefit) for taxes on income currently payable (refundable)			
Federal	$(54,007)	$(67,906)	$(29,109)
State	(105)	2,369	3,485
Foreign			
Foreign subsidiaries	8,821	8,737	5,275
Other	7,019	6,751	5,407
Total currently refundable	(38,272)	(50,049)	(14,942)
Deferred			
Federal	31,967	123,818	96,627
State	1,305	6,531	5,215
Investment credits amortized		(10,000)	(8,200)
Total deferred	33,272	120,349	93,642
Total provision (benefit) for taxes on income	$ (5,000)	$ 70,300	$ 78,700

WALT DISNEY PRODUCTIONS AND SUBSIDIARIES

NOTES TO CONSOLIDATED FINANCIAL STATEMENTS, continued

The significant components of deferred taxes on income included in the provision (benefit) for taxes on income are as follows:

	1984	1983	1982
Excess of tax over book depreciation and amortization	$ 73,810	$ 89,193	$ 54,090
Difference between investment credits claimed for tax purposes and amortization under deferral method for financial reporting purposes (Note 4)		17,000	39,741
Interest capitalized for financial reporting purposes	13,230	12,700	11,840
Epcot Center expenses deferred for financial reporting purposes	(2,790)	990	9,400
Difference between Epcot Center participant fees included in income for tax purposes and deferred for financial reporting purposes	(2,820)	(5,584)	(16,280)
Difference between unusual charges included in expense for financial reporting purposes and deferred for income tax purposes (Note 3)	(45,170)		
Other	(2,988)	6,050	(5,149)
Total provision for deferred taxes on income	$ 33,272	$120,349	$ 93,642

Primarily as a result of excess of tax over book depreciation relating to Epcot Center, the Company recorded estimated claims for refundable income taxes of $60,000 at September 30, 1984 ($70,000–1983). As a result of these losses for tax purposes, the Company has tax basis foreign tax credit carryforwards of approximately $11 million expiring in 1989.

The difference between the U.S. federal income tax rate and the Company's effective income tax (benefit) rate is explained below:

	1984	1983	1982
Federal income tax rate	46.0%	46.0%	46.0%
State income taxes, net of federal income tax benefit	3.9	2.9	2.6
Reduction in taxes resulting from investment tax credits (Note 4)	(53.8)	(6.1)	(4.6)
Difference in carrying values of certain Arvida assets and liabilities for tax and financial reporting purposes (Note 2)	(44.0)		
Nondeductible acquisition and other costs	11.2		
Amortization of Walt Disney name rights	2.6	0.3	
Other	4.1	(0.1)	
Effective income tax (benefit) rate	(30.0%)	43.0%	44.0%

7. Pension Programs (In thousands)

The Company contributes to various tax-qualified pension plans under union and industry-wide agreements. Contributions are based upon the hours worked or by gross wages paid to covered employees. The Company's share of the unfunded liability, if any, related to these multi-employer plans is not determinable.

In addition, the Company has tax-qualified pension plans covering most of its domestic salaried and hourly employees not covered by union or industry-wide pension plans, and a non-qualified, unfunded key employee retirement plan.

In May, 1984, the Company restructured its pension program with respect to its salaried employees. The restructured

pension program for salaried employees provides for the replacement and enhancement of certain benefits previously provided under the existing tax-qualified and non-qualified pension plans.

All of the pension plans maintained by the Company, except for the amended and restated non-qualified plan for key management employees, are funded by Company contributions, and, where applicable, by employee contributions to trusts administered by banks. A comparison of the accumulated plan benefits for these pension plans with net assets available for benefits as of the dates of the latest actuarial valuations is as follows:

	1984	1983
Vested	$60,700	$43,000
Nonvested	11,000	8,800
Actuarial present value of accumulated plan benefits	$71,700	$51,800
Net assets available for benefits	$73,100	$58,600

The 1984 actuarial present value of accumulated plan benefits was calculated based upon the plans' actuarial interest rate assumptions ranging from 9½% to 12%. The 1983 actuarial present value of accumulated plan benefits was calculated based on the Pension Benefit Guaranty Corporation weighted average interest rate assumption of 8¼%.

The Company's non-qualified and unfunded pension plan for key management employees as amended in May, 1984, provides certain benefits that have not been replaced by the restructured pension program for salaried employees. After adjusting for the restructuring of the pension program and funding of $24,338, the amount accrued as a liability under this plan was reduced to $4,273 at September 30, 1984 from $21,520 at September 30, 1983.

The aggregate amounts expensed for all of these plans were $11,100, $9,600 and $9,300 for fiscal years 1984, 1983 and 1982, respectively, including amortization of actuarially computed prior service costs, where applicable, over periods ranging up to thirty years. The May, 1984 program changes are estimated to increase annual pension expense $6 million, commencing in fiscal 1985.

8. Stock Option and Ownership Plans
(In thousands, except share data)

Stock Option Plans
The Company grants stock options under its 1973 and 1980 Stock Option Plans and under its 1981 Incentive Plan to key executive, management and creative personnel at prices equal to market price at date of grant. The options and prices set forth below have been adjusted, where applicable, for all subsequent stock splits and stock dividends.

Transactions under the various Plans during fiscal year 1984 were as follows:

	Number of Shares	
	Options Granted	Available For Grant
Outstanding September 30, 1983 ($20.77 to $80.63 per share)	996,200	639,958
Options terminated	(85,262)	73,882
Options granted	158,900	(158,900)
Options exercised	(85,043)	
SAR's exercised	(30,308)	
Outstanding September 30, 1984 ($20.77 to $64.31 per share)	954,487	554,940

WALT DISNEY PRODUCTIONS AND SUBSIDIARIES

Options are exercisable beginning not less than one year after date of grant. All options expire ten years after date of grant. At September 30, 1984, options on 176,343 shares granted under the 1973 Plan were exercisable at $20.77 to $55.25 per share; options on 317,869 shares granted under the 1980 Plan were exercisable at $51.75 to $64.31 per share; and options on 79,650 shares granted under the 1981 Stock Option Plan, a component of the 1981 Incentive Plan, were exercisable at $55.25 per share.

The 1980 Stock Option Plan and 1981 Incentive Plan permit the granting of stock appreciation rights (SAR's) in connection with any option granted under these plans or under the 1973 Stock Option Plan. In lieu of exercising a stock option, SAR holders are entitled, upon exercise of an SAR, to receive cash or common shares or a combination thereof in an amount equal to the excess of the fair market value of such shares on the date of exercise over the option price.

As of September 30, 1984, SAR's were outstanding with respect to 285,754 shares subject to options under the 1973 and 1980 Stock Option and 1981 Incentive Plans. These SAR's were granted to a limited number of key employees. Income and overhead accounts were credited with $905 during fiscal year 1984 (charged with $3,460 — 1983 and $1,869 — 1982) with respect to SAR's.

Effective September 22, 1984, the Company entered into employment agreements with certain executives, pursuant to which the Company has agreed, among other things, to provide for bonus compensation computed on the Company's net income in excess of a certain level, as defined.

In addition, stock options were subsequently granted such executives for the acquisition of an aggregate 970,000 common shares at $57.44 per share, becoming exercisable in annual installments from 1985 through 1989. The new stock option plan pursuant to which these options were granted is subject to approval at the annual meeting of stockholders in February, 1985.

Stock Ownership Plans

The Company has a Payroll Based Employee Stock Ownership Plan (PAYSOP) effective January 1, 1983 for all regular employees, as defined, with three years of service. Under the Plan's provisions, the Company claims an additional ½ of 1% of compensation of covered participants as an income tax credit and pays such an amount to a trust which then purchases shares of the Company's stock in the open market for the employees' benefit. Relating to fiscal 1983, $1,144 was used to purchase 21,409 shares of common stock.

The Company also had an Employee Stock Ownership Plan (ESOP) for salaried employees. This Plan was amended to comply with the Economic Recovery Tax Act of 1981 and as a result, contributions were terminated as of December 31, 1982. As of that date, under the Plan's provisions, the Company claimed an additional 1% of the Company's qualified capital investments as an investment tax credit and paid such an amount to a trust which then purchased shares of the Company's stock in the open market for the employees' benefit. Relating to fiscal 1983 and 1982, respectively, $1,131 and $4,711 have been used to purchase 21,484 and 74,612

shares of common stock. The Company also claimed a further tax credit equal to an additional ½% of the Company's qualified capital investments which was used to match employee contributions. Relating to fiscal years 1983 and 1982, respectively, the matching employer contributions of $360 and $2,115 have been used to purchase 13,790 and 67,106 shares of common stock.

9. Stockholders Equity
(In thousands, except per share data)

	Common Shares Issued and Outstanding		Retained Earnings
	Number	Amount	
Balance at September 30, 1981	32,433	$ 540,935	$626,183
Exercise of stock options	30	917	
Income tax benefit from exercise of stock options		198	
Common stock issued for Retlaw acquisition	888	46,200	
Dividends ($1.20 per share)			(39,742)
Net income			100,093
Balance at September 30, 1982	33,351	588,250	686,534
Exercise of stock options	128	4,784	
Income tax benefit from exercise of stock options		1,657	
Stock offering in February, 1983	1,100	70,883	
Common stock returned (i)	(70)	(3,640)	
Dividends ($1.20 per share)			(41,100)
Net income			93,160
Balance at September 30, 1983	34,509	661,934	738,594
Exercise of stock options	85	3,062	
Income tax benefit from exercise of stock options		856	
Common stock repurchased (ii)	(4,198)	(327,679)	
Common stock issued (Note 2)	3,333	21,815	
Dividends ($1.20 per share)			(40,941)
Net income			97,844
Balance at September 30, 1984	33,729	$ 359,988	$795,497

(i) The acquisition for common stock in January, 1982 of certain assets from Retlaw Enterprises, Inc. (a company owned by the family of the late Walter E. Disney) was adjusted in fiscal 1983 by the return of 70,000 common shares resulting from the settlement of a stockholders' suit.

(ii) On June 11, 1984, the Company repurchased 4.2 million shares of the Company's common stock from Reliance Insurance Company at an aggregate cost, including related expenses, of $327.7 million. This repurchase was financed by borrowings under the Company's revolving line of credit. On a pro forma basis, if the 4.2 million shares had been repurchased at the beginning of fiscal 1984, the effect would have been to reduce net income $14 million ($.43 per share) for fiscal 1984 on lower average number of shares outstanding of 33 million. In addition, dividends would have been reduced by $2.5 million. The pro forma information assumes interest on borrowed funds at 10% through June, 1984.

The repurchase agreement also provides that, if within one year of the repurchase date, a per share price in excess of $80.00 per share of the Company's common stock is paid pursuant to any merger or consolidation of the Company with or into any other entity or any sale of all or substantially all of the assets of the Company or any tender offer for all the Company's common shares which is recommended by the Company's Board of Directors, the Company is to pay Reliance the difference between such higher price and $80.00 per share multiplied by the 4.2 million shares repurchased.

On November 27, 1984, the Board of Directors authorized a stock repurchase program under which the Company may purchase, from time to time, up to 3.5 million shares of the Company's outstanding common stock.

WALT DISNEY PRODUCTIONS AND SUBSIDIARIES

NOTES TO CONSOLIDATED FINANCIAL STATEMENTS, continued

10. Detail of Certain Balance Sheet Accounts (In thousands)

Film Production Costs*	1984	1983
Released, less amortization	$ 66,746	$ 60,399
Completed, not yet released	4,511	26,599
In process	31,205	40,012
	$102,462	$127,010

*Includes theatrical and television film production and programming costs.

Real Estate Inventories	1984
Completed	$ 18,943
In progress	154,192
Land	56,289
	$229,424

Other Assets	1984	1983
Walt Disney name rights, net of amortization	$ 35,270	$ 35,995
Epcot Center and The Disney Channel preopening and start-up costs, net of amortization	24,948	32,545
Prepaid expenses	23,791	19,843
Other	34,627	23,247
	$118,636	$111,630

Accounts Payable, Payroll and Other Accrued Liabilities	1984	1983
Accounts payable	$128,325	$ 80,344
Payroll and employee benefits	79,573	56,662
Property, payroll and other taxes	17,703	13,830
Key employee retirement plan (Note 7)	4,273	21,520
Cash dividends payable	10,118	10,353
	$239,992	$182,709

Unearned Deposits and Advances	1984	1983
Epcot Center participation fees*	$ 93,372	$ 85,146
Other unearned deposits and advances	85,535	24,410
	$178,907	$109,556

*Pursuant to participation agreements with corporate sponsors, the Company expects to have received approximately $393 million in Epcot Center participant fees through 1995 of which $141 million has been received as of September 30, 1984.

11. Business Segments (In thousands)

The Company operates in four business segments: Entertainment and Recreation, Filmed Entertainment, Community Development and Consumer Products. These business segments are identified in the Description of the Business in Note 1.

The Consolidated Statement of Income presents revenues and operating income by business segment. Operating income excludes unusual charges of $166 million (Note 3). The Filmed Entertainment business segment includes operating losses incurred by The Disney Channel of $35 and $28 million for fiscal years 1984 and 1983, respectively. The Disney Channel commenced operations in April, 1983. Additional financial information relative to business segments follows.

Total consolidated revenues include foreign revenues (export sales) related to the following geographic areas:

	1984	1983	1982
Europe	$ 70,459	$ 68,464	$ 82,242
Far East and Australia	50,851	47,207	26,826
Western Hemisphere (excluding the United States)	23,691	22,082	24,706
Other	3,916	3,046	1,845
	$148,917	$140,799	$135,619

Capital expenditures for entertainment attractions and other property by business segment were:

	1984	1983	1982
Entertainment and recreation	$145,295	$287,940	$645,632
Filmed entertainment	23,959	1,845	2,794
Community development	6,509		
Consumer products	244	222	66
Corporate	6,044	1,195	273
	$182,051	$291,202	$648,765

Depreciation expense of entertainment attractions and other property by business segment was:

	1984	1983	1982
Entertainment and recreation	$100,497	$88,059	$40,078
Filmed entertainment	3,027	1,643	1,517
Community development	2,094		
Consumer products	147	135	118
Corporate	842	347	204
	$106,607	$90,184	$41,917

Amortization expense of film production and programming costs included in the Filmed Entertainment business segment, before unusual charges, was $54.1, $65.6 and $64.9 million for fiscal years 1984, 1983 and 1982, respectively.

Identifiable assets by business segment were:

	1984	1983	1982
Entertainment and recreation	$2,012,553	$2,018,787	$1,808,731
Filmed entertainment	185,750	180,201	146,337
Community development	351,952		
Consumer products	44,579	37,381	34,129
Corporate	144,609	144,826	113,619
	$2,739,443	$2,381,195	$2,102,816

12. Commitments and Contingencies

The Company's subsidiary, Buena Vista Distribution Co., Inc., is a defendant with other motion picture distributors in a number of private treble damage actions asserting claims under the federal anti-trust laws. These actions, which have been filed over several years and which seek damages aggregating hundreds of millions of dollars, are in various stages of pre-trial proceedings. The Company has denied the material allegations of the complaints in these actions, and in the opinion of management and counsel, the Company will not suffer any material liability by reason thereof.

During June and July, 1984, a number of lawsuits were filed alleging, among other things, breaches of fiduciary duties by members of the Company's Board of Directors in connection with the acquisition of Arvida (Note 2) and the Company's repurchase of its common stock from Reliance (Note 9). Plaintiffs seek, among other things, rescission of the two transactions. In the opinion of management and counsel, the Company does not expect to suffer any material monetary liability by reason thereof.

In addition, the Company is a defendant in various routine litigation incident to the conduct of its business. In the opinion of management, the Company will not suffer any material liability by reason thereof.

SUPPLEMENTARY INFORMATION REGARDING
INFLATION AND CHANGING PRICES

General Background

Inflation has become a subject of significance in the U.S. economy during the past decade. During periods of continuing inflation the purchasing power of the dollar is eroded, meaning that it requires more dollars to purchase the same goods and services.

The primary financial statements traditionally reflect the historic cost rather than the current cost of assets required to maintain an enterprise's productive capability. Transactions are recorded in terms of the number of dollars actually received or expended without regard to changes in the purchasing power of the currency or changes in the cost of goods and services consumed.

There is no universally accepted method for measuring the effect of inflation in financial statements. In recognition of the need, however, to provide readers of financial statements with information to assist them in assessing that impact, the Financial Accounting Standards Board issued Statement of Financial Accounting Standards No. 33, "Financial Reporting and Changing Prices" (SFAS 33). The general objectives of reporting the effects of changing prices as expressed in SFAS 33 are to help users assess (a) future cash flows, (b) the maintenance of operating capability, (c) financial performance, and (d) the maintenance of general purchasing power.

On November 20, 1984, the FASB issued Statement of Financial Accounting Standards No. 82, "Financial Reporting and Changing Prices: Elimination of Certain Disclosures" (SFAS 82), removing the need for the presentation of two supplementary income computations as required by SFAS 33. One computation, constant dollar, deals with the effect of general inflation; and the other, current cost, deals with the effects of changes in the specific prices of resources used in the operation of the enterprise. Although SFAS 82 will be effective for fiscal years ending on or after December 15, 1984, the Company adopted early the provisions of the Statement to its fiscal 1984 financial reporting.

In computing income from continuing operations adjusted for changing prices, the Company has not experienced a material difference in the amount disclosed under the two methods. As a result, consistent with SFAS 82, the Company has elected to present only constant dollar information beginning with fiscal year 1984. Under the constant dollar method, historical cost financial information is adjusted only for changes that have occurred in the general purchasing power of the dollar as measured by the Consumer Price Index for all Urban Consumers (CPI-U).

Constant dollar adjustments for the current fiscal year are as follows:

SUPPLEMENTARY STATEMENT OF CONSOLIDATED INCOME
ADJUSTED FOR CHANGING PRICES
Year ended September 30, 1984
(In thousands, except per share data)

	As Included In Primary Financial Statements (Historical Cost)	As Adjusted For General Inflation (Constant Dollar)
Revenues	$1,655,977	$1,655,977
Costs and expenses		
Cost of goods sold	311,630	315,150
Depreciation	106,607	159,100
Amortization	54,134	58,200
Other expenses and unusual charges	1,125,135	1,125,135
Interest expense — net	41,738	41,738
Taxes on income (benefit)	(5,000)	(5,000)
Total costs and expenses	1,634,244	1,694,323
Income (loss) from continuing operations	$ 21,733	$ (38,346)
Gain from decline in purchasing power of net amounts owed		$ 41,300

At September 30, 1984 the constant dollar/historical cost of inventories was $313,000, film production costs net of amortization was $114,000 and entertainment attractions and other property net of accumulated depreciation was $2,769,000.

Net assets at year end are increased by $836 million when the cost of inventories, film production costs and entertainment attractions and other property are adjusted to average 1984 dollars. This increase in the valuation of assets results in an increase in depreciation expense of $52 million. This adjustment of depreciation expense is the primary cause of the decrease in net income adjusted for the effects of inflation. In computing the above amounts, normal service lives and depreciation/amortization rates have been applied to the adjusted amounts. No adjustments are made to fully depreciated assets currently utilized in the Company's business. Revenues and all other expenses are considered to reflect the average price levels for the year and accordingly have not been adjusted.

In accordance with SFAS 33, no adjustment has been made to the provision (benefit) for income taxes included in the supplementary statement of income.

Net monetary assets represent cash or claims to cash less amounts owed. When prices are increasing, the holding of monetary assets results in a loss in general purchasing power. Similarly, amounts owed produce a gain in general purchasing power because the amount of money required to settle the liabilities represents dollars of diminishing purchasing power. At September 30, 1984, the excess of monetary liabilities over monetary assets resulted in a net gain in purchasing power. This gain is presented as supplementary information and has not been included in net income adjusted for changing prices.

As required by SFAS 33, certain selected financial data are restated based on the average CPI-U for the year for each of the five years shown. The amounts as expressed in average 1984 dollars are as follows:

WALT DISNEY PRODUCTIONS AND SUBSIDIARIES

SUPPLEMENTARY INFORMATION REGARDING
INFLATION AND CHANGING PRICES, continued

FIVE YEAR COMPARISON OF SELECTED SUPPLEMENTARY FINANCIAL DATA
ADJUSTED FOR EFFECTS OF CHANGING PRICES IN CONSTANT DOLLARS
In Average 1984 Dollars
(In thousands, except for per share data)

Year ended September 30	1984	1983	1982	1981	1980
Revenues	$1,655,977	$1,360,700	$1,109,900	$1,163,000	$1,175,300
Net income (loss) from continuing operations	(38,346)	50,500	65,200	95,200	121,900
Earnings (loss) per share from continuing operations	(1.07)	1.47	1.96	2.92	3.75
Net assets at year end	1,991,900	2,216,800	2,047,000	1,967,100	1,953,500
Cash provided by operations	414,036	351,000	295,900	244,100	262,700
Investment in entertainment attractions and other property	194,142	347,300	661,700	386,100	192,100
Investment in film production and programming costs	127,595	87,100	56,300	64,200	87,800
Cash dividends per common share	1.20	1.25	1.29	1.16	.93
Market price per common share at year end	59.13	63.29	61.01	54.10	60.73
Gain (loss) from decline in purchasing power of net amounts owed (monetary assets)	41,300	22,300	21,100	4,600	(25,700)
Average consumer price index	308	296	286	266	240

Management's Comments and Conclusions

Inflation accounting as required by SFAS 33 involves the use of numerous assumptions, approximations, and estimates, and should be viewed in that context and not as a precise indicator of the effects of inflation. The reader is cautioned not to attach too much significance to any one year's adjusted results. Even when several years are viewed consecutively, the information is considered to be of limited use until the reader completely understands the principles and concepts utilized in compiling the data.

Although not required information by SFAS 33, the Company has provided additional selected supplementary financial data relating to cash provided by operations, investment in entertainment attractions and other property and investment in film production and programming.

As noted previously, net income in this presentation has been significantly reduced from net income reported in the primary financial statements due to the additional theoretical depreciation which has been adjusted for inflation. However, the Company does not believe that this hypothetical calculation has much relevance to its operations. The Company believes that cash provided by operations provides a more meaningful insight into the impact of inflation, because it excludes non-cash charges such as depreciation. Cash provided by operations has increased at an annual average rate of 13% when expressed in average 1984 dollars (compared to an annual rate of 21% as reflected in the primary financial statements).

Elsewhere in this report the Company discusses its continuing program of investing in the future through its capital improvements program, intended to maintain and/or to increase its productive capability. However, the Company is not confronted with a problem of replacing very old and worn-out capital assets as a result of carefully planned and comprehensive refurbishing programs. As reflected in the selected data, the Company has invested almost $2.2 billion in productive assets over the last five years (compared to approximately $2.0 billion as reflected in the primary financial statements). To the extent that these expenditures are replacing existing assets, it is presumed that the costs in 1984 dollars are significantly higher than the costs of the original assets.

WALT DISNEY PRODUCTIONS AND SUBSIDIARIES

QUARTERLY FINANCIAL SUMMARY
(In thousands, except per share data)

	December 31**	March 31	June 30	September 30**
OPERATIONS BY QUARTER				
1984				
Revenues				
Entertainment and recreation	$224,895	$244,262	$314,610	$313,592
Filmed entertainment	46,585	73,612	67,841	56,514
Community development		61,185	74,609	68,590
Consumer products	30,679	28,242	26,259	24,502
	$302,159	$407,301	$483,319	$463,198
Income (Loss) Before Corporate Expenses and Unusual Charges				
Entertainment and recreation	$ 21,377	$ 38,348	$ 68,075	$ 64,895
Filmed entertainment	(6,120)	1,070	7,728	(429)
Community development		12,678	17,782	11,766
Consumer products	16,252	15,832	11,240	10,539
	$ 31,509	$ 67,928	$104,825	$ 86,771
Income Before Unusual Charges, Taxes on Income and Accounting Change	$ 16,091	$ 51,492	$ 81,557	$ 33,553
Net Income (Loss)	$ 85,102	$ 31,313	$ 45,436	$ (64,007)
*Earnings (Loss) per Share**	$2.46	$0.82	$1.23	($1.89)
1983				
Revenues				
Entertainment and recreation	$203,698	$239,741	$288,936	$298,827
Filmed entertainment	41,338	46,109	40,533	37,478
Consumer products	25,106	29,826	29,032	26,733
	$270,142	$315,676	$358,501	$363,038
Income (Loss) Before Corporate Expenses				
Entertainment and recreation	$ 24,898	$ 44,930	$ 67,438	$ 59,612
Filmed entertainment	5,780	6,512	(32,226)	(13,451)
Consumer products	11,841	17,812	15,793	11,436
	$ 42,519	$ 69,254	$ 51,005	$ 57,597
Income Before Taxes on Income	$ 30,414	$ 54,020	$ 38,230	$ 40,796
Net Income	$ 17,214	$ 30,020	$ 21,430	$ 24,496
*Earnings per Share**	$0.51	$0.87	$0.61	$0.70

*Quarterly earnings per share amounts do not necessarily total to the year end earnings per share amount due to the varying amounts of average shares outstanding during the periods.

**See Notes 3 and 4 of Notes to Consolidated Financial Statements for description of fourth quarter fiscal 1984 unusual charges, nonrecurring corporate general and administrative expenses and first quarter fiscal 1984 accounting change.

MARKET PRICE AND DIVIDEND DATA				
1984				
Price per share:				
High	$64	$68	$68½	$64½
Low	$47¼	$48⅜	$46¼	$45¼
Dividend per share	$0.30	$0.30	$0.30	$0.30
1983				
Price per share:				
High	$71½	$78¾	$84¾	$68¼
Low	$55	$60⅛	$65	$55⅞
Dividend per share	$0.30	$0.30	$0.30	$0.30

The principal market for trading Walt Disney Productions common stock is the New York Stock Exchange.

WALT DISNEY PRODUCTIONS AND SUBSIDIARIES

SELECTED FINANCIAL DATA
(In thousands, except Per Share and Other Data)

	1984	1983	1982	1981	1980
Statement of Income Data					
Revenues (Page 47)	$1,655,977	$1,307,357	$1,030,250	$1,005,040	$ 914,505
Income before corporate expenses	291,033	220,375	200,116	214,664	231,300
Corporate expenses	66,602	42,849	36,104	30,814	25,424
Interest expense (income) — net	41,738	14,066	(14,781)	(33,130)	(42,110)
Unusual charges*	165,960				
Taxes on income (benefit)	(5,000)	70,300	78,700	95,500	112,800
Change in accounting for investment tax credits*	(76,111)				
Net income	97,844	93,160	100,093	121,480	135,186
Balance Sheet Data					
Film production costs	102,462	127,010	108,067	120,640	120,408
Real estate inventories	229,424				
Entertainment attractions and other property, net of depreciation	1,937,346	1,871,809	1,673,238	1,069,369	762,546
Total assets	2,739,443	2,381,195	2,102,816	1,610,009	1,347,407
Borrowings	861,909	352,575	315,000	110,000	
Total liabilities and deferred credits	1,583,958	980,667	828,032	442,891	272,609
Total net assets (stockholders equity)	1,155,485	1,400,528	1,274,784	1,167,118	1,074,798
Statement of Changes in Financial Position Data					
Cash provided by operations	414,036	337,356	274,782	210,805	204,682
Cash dividends	40,941	41,100	39,742	32,406	23,280
Investment in entertainment attractions and other property	194,142	333,738	614,416	333,407	149,674
Investment in film production and programming costs	127,595	83,750	52,295	55,454	68,409
Per Share Data					
Net income (earnings)	$ 2.73	$ 2.70	$ 3.01	$ 3.72	$ 4.16
Cash dividends	1.20	1.20	1.20	1.00	.72
Stockholders equity	34.26	40.58	38.22	35.99	33.22
Average number of common and common equivalent shares outstanding during the year (in thousands)	35,849	34,481	33,225	32,629	32,513
Other Data					
Stockholders at close of year	62,000	60,000	61,000	60,000	62,000
Employees at close of year	28,000	30,000	28,000	25,000	24,000

*See Notes 3 and 4 of Notes to Consolidated Financial Statements for description of fourth quarter fiscal 1984 unusual charges, nonrecurring corporate general and administrative expenses and first quarter fiscal 1984 accounting change.

WALT DISNEY PRODUCTIONS AND SUBSIDIARIES

OTHER FINANCIAL DATA
(In thousands)

	1984	1983	1982	1981	1980
ENTERTAINMENT AND RECREATION					
Walt Disney World					
Admissions and rides	$ 295,921	$ 278,320	$153,504	$139,326	$130,144
Merchandise sales	182,804	172,324	121,410	121,465	116,187
Food sales	177,078	178,791	121,329	114,951	106,404
Lodging	104,779	98,105	81,427	70,110	61,731
Disneyland					
Admissions and rides	110,723	102,619	98,273	92,065	87,066
Merchandise sales	79,260	72,300	76,684	79,146	72,140
Food sales	46,770	45,699	44,481	44,920	41,703
Participant fees, Walt Disney Travel Co., Tokyo Disneyland royalties and other	100,024	83,044	28,502	29,828	28,005
	$1,097,359	$1,031,202	$725,610	$691,811	$643,380
Theme park total attendance					
Walt Disney World	21,121	22,712	12,560	13,221	13,783
Disneyland	9,869	9,980	10,421	11,343	11,522
	30,990	32,692	22,981	24,564	25,305
FILMED ENTERTAINMENT					
Theatrical					
Domestic	$ 70,679	$ 38,635	$ 55,408	$ 54,624	$ 63,350
Foreign	38,182	43,825	64,525	76,279	78,314
Television					
Worldwide	57,479	27,992	44,420	43,672	19,736
Home Video and Non-Theatrical					
Worldwide	78,212	55,006	37,749	22,231	10,565
	$ 244,552	$ 165,458	$202,102	$196,806	$171,965
COMMUNITY DEVELOPMENT					
Residential	$ 53,038				
Land and commercial property	90,166				
Resort operations and other	61,180				
	$ 204,384				
CONSUMER PRODUCTS					
Character merchandising	$ 42,750	$ 45,429	$ 35,912	$ 30,555	$ 29,631
Publications	18,184	20,006	20,821	24,658	22,284
Records and music publishing	33,734	30,666	26,884	27,358	23,432
Educational media	11,509	10,269	15,468	21,148	21,908
Other	3,505	4,327	3,453	12,704	1,905
	$ 109,682	$ 110,697	$102,538	$116,423	$ 99,160

Future and Present Values of Cash Flows

5

The Time Value of Money

Ignoring the effects of inflation, a dollar today is worth more than a dollar to be received a year from now. In other words, we would all prefer to receive a specific amount of money now rather than on some future date. This preference rests on the *time value of money*. The term *interest* is used to describe the price charged for using money over time.

When payments for the time value of money are made or accrued, *interest expense* is incurred; when payments for the time value of money are received or accrued, *interest revenue* is realized.

Business decisions often involve receiving cash or other assets *now* in exchange for a promise to make payments after one or more periods. A common example is a decision to borrow money. Another important group of business decisions involves investing cash now in order to receive cash, goods, or services in future periods.

Inflows of dollars on various future dates should not be added together as if they were of equal value. These future cash inflows must be restated at their *present values* before they are aggregated. The concept of the time value of money tells us that the more distant cash inflows have a smaller present value than cash inflows to be received within a shorter time span.

Similar reasoning applies to cash outflows. Before we add together cash outflows on various future dates, we must restate these outflows at their present values. The more distant the date of a cash outflow, the smaller is its present value.

As a simple example of this concept of present value, assume that you are trying to sell your car and you receive offers from three prospective buyers.

Buyer A offers you $8,000 to be paid immediately. Buyer B offers you $8,200 to be paid one year from now. Buyer C offers the highest price, $9,200, but this offer provides that payment will be made in five years. Assuming that the offers by B and C involve no credit risk and that money may be invested at 5% interest compounded annually, which offer would you accept? You should accept the offer of $8,000 to be received immediately, because the ***present value*** of the other two offers is less than $8,000. If you were to invest $8,000 today, even at the modest rate of interest of 5%, your investment would be worth more than $8,200 in one year and considerably more than $9,200 in five years.

This example suggests that the timing of cash receipts and payments has an important effect on the economic worth and the accounting values of both assets and liabilities. Consequently, investment and borrowing decisions should be made only after a careful analysis of the relative present values of the prospective cash inflows and outflows.

Uses of Present and Future Values in Financial Accounting

Accountants find many situations in which a reliable measurement of a transaction depends on the present value of future cash inflows and outflows. For example, the amount received for a bond issue by the issuer reflects the present value of the issuer's promise to make a series of future interest payments and to repay the principal when the bonds reach maturity. Some other examples of the need for measuring present or future values of cash flows are listed below:

1   ***Promissory Notes and Mortgages***   Measurement of the present value of such assets or liabilities when the interest rate is not specified or differs from the current fair rate of interest. (See Chapters 7 and 10.)

2   ***Bonds Payable***   Computation of interest expense and amortization of premium or discount by the effective interest method, and the determination of present value and interest revenue on investments in bonds. (See Chapters 14 and 15.)

3   ***Leases***   Measurement of amount to be recorded as an asset and liability under leases that are considered equivalent to acquisitions of assets, and the determination of periodic lease payments to obtain a desired rate of return on investment. (See Chapter 20.)

4   ***Pensions***   Measurement of pension costs (past and current) and funding programs for pension plans. (See Chapter 19.)

5   ***Plant Assets***   Measurement of plant assets acquired by issuance of debt securities (including installment contracts payable) when the interest rate is not specified or differs from the current fair rate of interest. (See Chapter 11.)

6   ***Sinking Funds***   Determination of periodic payments required to provide a fund for the retirement of long-term debt or preferred stock. (See Chapter 14.)

7   ***Depreciation***   Computation of periodic depreciation under the sinking fund and annuity methods of depreciation. (See the Appendix at the end of Chapter 12.)

Measurement of the present and future values implicit in the foregoing examples involves the use of compound interest principles (defined below). In this chapter we illustrate the basic principles of compound interest in a format that will be useful throughout this book. We also stress the use of compound interest tables (presented in the Appendix at the end of this chapter) as a basis for solving a wide range of financial accounting problems.

Simple Interest and Compound Interest

Interest is the growth in a *principal amount* representing the fee charged for the use of money for a specified time period. Because the concept of economic earnings is periodic, we typically think of return on investment in terms of *a rate of return per year.*

Simple interest is the return on a principal amount for one time period. We may also think of simple interest as a return for more than one time period if we assume that the interest itself does not earn a return, but this kind of situation occurs rarely in the business world. Simple interest usually is applicable only to short-term investment and borrowing transactions involving a time span of less than one year.

Interest generally is expressed in terms of an annual rate. The formula for simple interest is $I = prt$ (interest = principal $\times$ annual rate of interest $\times$ number of years or fraction of a year that interest accrues). For example, interest on $10,000 at 8% for one year is expressed as follows:

Formula for
simple interest

$$I = prt$$
$$I = \$10,000 \times 0.08 \times 1$$
$$I = \underline{\$800}$$

Compound interest is the return on a principal amount for two or more time periods, assuming that the interest for each time period is added to the principal amount at the end of each period and earns interest in all subsequent periods. Because most investment and borrowing transactions involve more than one time period, business executives evaluate proposed transactions in terms of periodic returns, each of which is assumed to be reinvested to yield additional returns.

For example, if interest at 8% is compounded quarterly for one year on a principal amount of $10,000, the total interest (compound interest) would be $824.32, as computed below:

Interest compounded
quarterly

Period	Principal $\times$ Rate $\times$ Time =	Compound interest	Accumulated amount
1st quarter	$10,000.00 $\times$ 0.08 $\times$ ¼	$200.00	$10,200.00
2d quarter	10,200.00 $\times$ 0.08 $\times$ ¼	204.00	10,404.00
3d quarter	10,404.00 $\times$ 0.08 $\times$ ¼	208.08	10,612.08
4th quarter	10,612.08 $\times$ 0.08 $\times$ ¼	212.24	10,824.32
Interest on $10,000 at 8% compounded quarterly for one year		$824.32	

In the computation of compound interest, the accumulated amount at the end of each period becomes the principal amount for purposes of computing interest for the following period.

FUTURE AND PRESENT VALUES OF A SINGLE AMOUNT

Amount of 1

The accumulated **amount** (small a) of a single amount invested at compound interest may be computed period by period by a series of multiplications, as illustrated on page 241 for $10,000 invested for one year at 8% compounded quarterly. If n is used to represent the number of periods that interest is to be compounded, i is used to represent the interest **per period,** and p is the principal amount invested, the **series of multiplications** to compute the accumulated amount a in the example above may be determined as follows:

Long-hand method for amount of 1

$$a = p(1 + i)^n$$
$$a = \$10,000 \ (1 + 0.02)^4$$
$$a = \$10,000 \ (1.02)(1.02)(1.02)(1.02)$$
$$a = \underline{\underline{\$10,824.32}}$$

It is important to observe that i is the **rate of interest for each time period** that interest is **compounded.** For example, the formulas for the compound amount a of 1 at 12%, assuming different compounding patterns, are:

12% interest at different compounding patterns

Interest at 12% per year compounded **annually** $= (1 + 0.12)^1 = 1.12$
Interest at 12% per year compounded **semiannually** $= (1 + 0.06)^2 = 1.1236$
Interest at 12% per year compounded **quarterly** $= (1 + 0.03)^4 = 1.125509$
Interest at 12% per year compounded **monthly** $= (1 + 0.01)^{12} = 1.126825$

The symbol $a_{\overline{n}|i}$ is the amount to which 1 will accumulate at i rate of interest per period for n periods. This symbol is read as "small a angle n at i." If annual interest of 8% is compounded quarterly for one year, the rate of interest per time period (one-fourth of a year) would be 2%, and the number of interest periods n would be 4. Thus, the amount of 1 formula at 8% compounded quarterly for one year is:

Amount of 1 formula

$$a_{\overline{n}|i} = (1 + i)^n \qquad \text{or} \qquad a_{\overline{4}|2\%} = (1 + 0.02)^4$$

Tables are available that give the value of $a_{\overline{n}|i}$. Use of these tables involves reference to a line showing the number of periods and a column showing the rate of interest per period. For example, Table 1 in the Appendix (page 263) shows that

$a_{\overline{4}|2\%}$ is equal to 1.082432, which means that $10,000 would accumulate to $10,824.32 in one year at 8% compounded quarterly. Compound interest tables generally are prepared for $1 and *the dollar sign is omitted*. This provides a convenient means of finding the accumulated amount of any number of dollars by multiplying the amount of 1 at i interest for n periods by the number of dollars involved in a problem or a business transaction.

Summary and Examples The amount of 1 formula, $a_{\overline{n}|i}$, is used to compute the future amount a of a principal amount p that earns compound interest at a specified interest rate i per period for n periods. A diagram for the amount of 1 is shown below:

Diagram for amount of 1

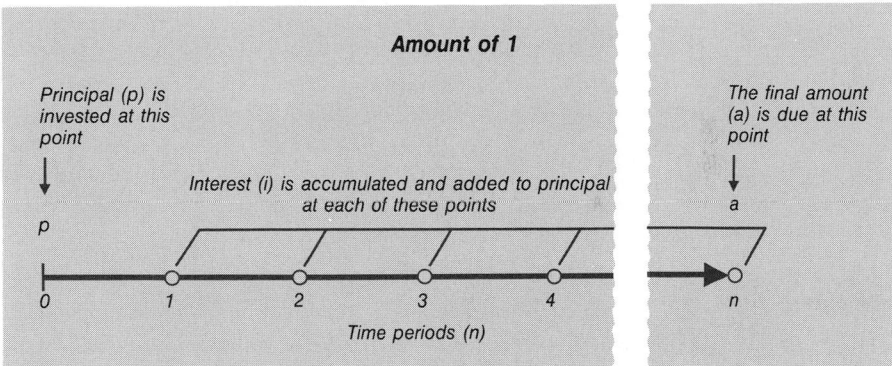

Example 1: Computation of the Amount of 1 for Longer Number of Periods Than Is Available in Table 1 of the Appendix If on the day her daughter was born, Candace Carlo deposited $10,000 in a savings account that guarantees to accumulate interest *quarterly* at 10% a year, what will be the amount in the savings account on her daughter's 18th birthday?

Solution The amount in the savings account on the daughter's 18th birthday will be $10,000 $(1 + 0.025)^{72}$. Because Table 1 in the Appendix at the end of this chapter does not go beyond 50 periods, the amount in the savings account on the daughter's 18th birthday may be computed as follows:

$$\$10,000\ (1 + 0.025)^{50} \times (1 + 0.025)^{22}$$
$$\$10,000\ (3.437109) \times (1.721571) = \underline{\$59,172}$$

Example 2: Determining the Interest Rate If $1,000 is deposited at compound interest on January 1, Year 1, and the amount on deposit on December 31, Year 10, is $1,806.11, what is the *semiannual interest rate* accruing on the deposit?

Solution The amount of 1 for 20 periods at the unstated rate of interest is 1.80611 ($1,806.11 ÷ $1,000 = 1.80611). Reference to Table 1 in the Appendix at the end of this chapter indicates that 1.806111 is the amount of 1 for 20 periods at 3%. Therefore, *the semiannual interest rate is 3%.*

Example 3: Amount Accumulated When Interest Rate Changes   Fanny deposited $10,000 in a fund that will earn 8% interest *compounded quarterly for the first four years,* and 10% interest *compounded semiannually for the next six years.* How much will Fanny have in the fund at the end of 10 years?

Solution   Using Table 1 in the Appendix at the end of this chapter, we have the following amount at the end of four years at 8% interest compounded quarterly:

$$\$10,000 \times a_{\overline{16}|2\%} = \$10,000 \ (1 + 0.02)^{16}$$
$$\$10,000 \times a_{\overline{16}|2\%} = \$10,000 \ (1.372786) \qquad \text{or} \qquad \underline{\$13,728}$$

And for the next six years at 10% compounded semiannually, we have:

$$\$13,728 \times a_{\overline{12}|5\%} = \$13,728 \ (1 + 0.05)^{12}$$
$$\$13,728 \times a_{\overline{12}|5\%} = \$13,728 \ (1.795856) \qquad \text{or} \qquad \underline{\$24,654}$$

In this case the interest rate *per period* changed at the end of four years from 2% to 5%. Therefore, it was first necessary to compute the amount on deposit at the end of four years ($13,728) and then to accumulate compound interest on this amount for six additional years at 10% compounded semiannually.

Present Value of 1

Many measurement and valuation problems in financial accounting require the computation of the discounted present value of a principal amount to be paid or received on a fixed future date. As the diagram below illustrates, the present value of 1 is closely related to the procedures used to compute the amount of 1:

Diagram for present value of 1

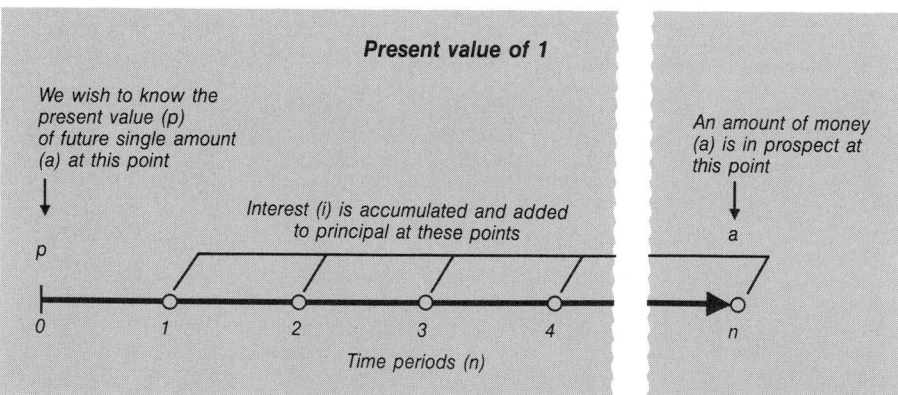

Present value of 1

We wish to know the present value (p) of future single amount (a) at this point

p

Interest (i) is accumulated and added to principal at these points

An amount of money (a) is in prospect at this point

a

0   1   2   3   4   n

Time periods (n)

From this diagram we see that the computation of the present value of a single future amount is a *reversal* of the process of finding the amount to which a present amount will accumulate. For example, we have seen (page 242) that $(1 + 0.02)^4 = 1.082432$ and that the principal amount p of $10,000 will accumulate to $10,824.32 in one year if interest is compounded quarterly. To find the principal p that must be invested now at 8% compounded quarterly to give us $10,824.32 in one year, we may proceed as follows: We know that $a = p(1 + i)^n$, and when we solve for p by dividing both sides of the equation by $(1 + i)^n$, we have the following:

$$p = \frac{a}{(1 + i)^n}$$

Now we substitute $(1 + 0.02)^4$ for $(1 + i)^n$ and $10,824.32 for a, and we have

$$p = \frac{\$10,824.32}{(1 + 0.02)^4} = \frac{\$10,824.32}{1.082432} = \underline{\underline{\$10,000}}$$

It should be clear that we may determine the present value p of any future amount a by dividing the future amount a by $(1 + i)^n$. Thus, the formula for the present value of 1 due in n periods at i rate of interest per period is:

Present value of 1 formula

$$p_{\overline{n}|i} = \frac{1}{(1 + i)^n}$$

The symbol $p_{\overline{n}|i}$ is read "small p angle n at i." The present value of 1 formula at 8% compounded quarterly for one year is:

$$p_{\overline{4}|2\%} = \frac{1}{(1 + 0.02)^4}$$

It is apparent that a table showing values for $1 \div (1 + i)^n$ at different interest rates i and different number of periods n would be useful. Table 2 in the Appendix at the end of this chapter provides such values. The value of $p_{\overline{4}|2\%}$ in that table is 0.923845; therefore, the present value of $10,824.32 discounted for one year at 8% compounded quarterly also may be computed as follows:

$$\$10,824.32 \times 0.923845 = \underline{\underline{\$10,000}}$$

Summary and Examples The present value of 1 formula, $p_{\overline{n}|i}$, is used to compute the discounted present value p of an amount a due or payable on some future date, discounted at a specified interest rate i per period for n periods.

Example 1: Proceeds from Issuance of "Zero Coupon Bonds" Growth Corporation issues bonds that pay no interest when the market rate of interest on this type of bond is 14% compounded semiannually. How much will Growth Corporation receive from the issuance of 25-year "zero coupon bonds" with a maturity value of $100 million?

Solution The proceeds from the issuance of the bonds is equal to the present value of $100 million discounted at 7% for 50 periods. Using Table 2 in the Appendix at the end of this chapter, the proceeds are computed as follows:

$$\$100,000,000 \times 0.033948 = \underline{\underline{\$3,394,800}}$$

Example 2: Present Value When Interest Rate Changes Paul Horsley wants to deposit cash in a savings account at the beginning of Year 1 so that he will have

$50,000 at the end of Year 6. How much must Horsley deposit at the beginning of Year 1 if the interest rate is 6% compounded semiannually for the first three years and 8% compounded quarterly for the next three years?

Solution   Using Table 2 in the Appendix at the end of this chapter, we have the following present value at the beginning of Year 4 of the $50,000 required at the end of Year 6:

$$\$50,000 \times p\,\overline{_{12}}_{|2\%} = \$50,000 \times 0.788493 = \$39,425$$

And at the beginning of Year 1, we have:

$$\$39,425 \times p\,\overline{_{6}}_{|3\%} = \$39,425 \times 0.837484 = \underline{\underline{\$33,018}}$$

Thus, Horsley must deposit $33,018 at the beginning of Year 1 to have $50,000 at the end of Year 6. Because the interest rate per period changed at the beginning of Year 4, it was necessary to prepare the solution in two steps.

Example 3: Determining the Approximate Interest Rate by Interpolation   If the present value of $100,000 discounted at an unstated rate of interest for 20 periods is $64,162.10, what was the approximate interest rate per period used in computing this present value?

Solution   From Table 2 in the Appendix at the end of this chapter, we obtain the following present values for different interest rates:

Estimating the rate of interest

$$p\,\overline{_{20}}_{|2\%} = 0.672971 \qquad p\,\overline{_{20}}_{|?\%} = 0.641621^* \qquad p\,\overline{_{20}}_{|2\frac{1}{2}\%} = 0.610271$$

difference = 0.03135

difference = 0.06270

*$64,162.10 ÷ $100,000 = 0.641621

The unknown interest rate is exactly at the midpoint between 2% and 2½%. Therefore, the approximate interest rate per period is 2¼%, computed as follows:

$$0.02 + 0.005 \left(\frac{0.03135}{0.06270} \right) \qquad \text{or} \qquad 0.02 + (0.005 \times \tfrac{1}{2}) = \underline{\underline{2\tfrac{1}{4}\%}}$$

Relationship of Amount of 1 and Present Value of 1 to *n* and *i*

In dealing with computations of accumulations and present values, it is useful to have some general idea of relationships as a basis for verifying the reasonableness of results. We may reason, for example, that $a\,\overline{_{n}}_{|i}$ should grow *larger* for increasing rates of interest *i* and for an increasing number of periods *n*, because the longer a principal amount accumulates interest the larger it grows, and **the higher the rate of interest the larger the future amount.** The reverse situation is true of present values. The longer the time period *n* or the higher the rate of interest *i*, **the smaller is the present value of any future amount.**

ANNUITIES

Many measurement situations in financial accounting involve periodic deposits, receipts, withdrawals, or payments (called *rents*), with interest at a stated rate compounded at the time that each rent is paid or received. These situations *are considered annuities if all the following conditions are present:*

1　The periodic rents are equal in amount.

2　The time period between rents is constant, such as a year, a quarter of a year, or a month.

3　The interest rate per time period remains constant.

4　The interest is compounded at the end of each time period.

When rents are paid or received at the end of each period and the total amount on deposit is determined at the time the final rent is made, the annuity is an ***ordinary annuity*** (or ***annuity in arrears***). Other types of annuities, that is, an ***annuity due*** (or ***annuity in advance***) and a ***deferred annuity,*** are discussed in subsequent sections of this chapter.

Amount of Ordinary Annuity of 1

The amount of an ***ordinary annuity*** (or ***annuity in arrears***) consists of the sum of the equal periodic rents and compound interest on the rents ***immediately after the final rent.*** The amount A to which an ordinary annuity of n rents of R dollars each will accumulate in n periods at i rate of interest per period is illustrated below:

Diagram for amount of ordinary annuity

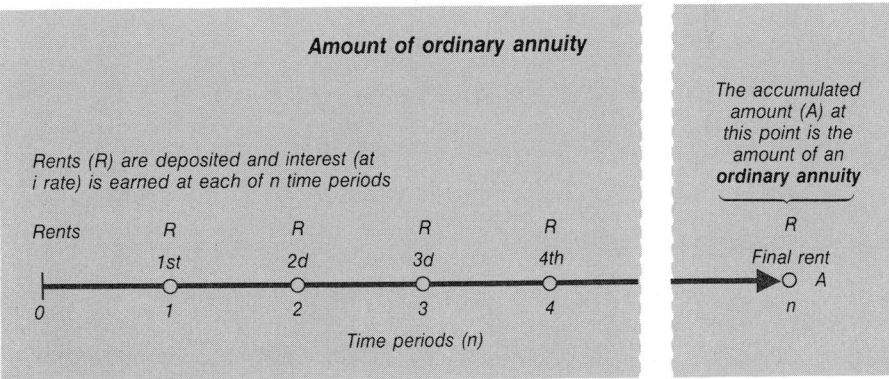

The amount A of an ordinary annuity of n rents of 1 at i interest rate per period is determined *by dividing by i the compound interest* that accumulates on a single deposit of 1 for n periods at i interest. This is expressed as follows:

Formula for amount of ordinary annuity of 1

$$A_{\overline{n}|i} = \frac{(1 + i)^n - 1}{i}$$

For example, the amount of an ordinary annuity of 16 rents of 1 at 2% is determined below:

Solving the formula

$$A_{\overline{16}|2\%} = \frac{(1 + 0.02)^{16} - 1}{0.02} = \frac{1.372786 - 1}{0.02} = \frac{0.372786}{0.02} = \underline{\underline{18.6393}}$$

The amount of 1 at 2% for 16 periods (1.372786) is taken from Table 1 in the Appendix at the end of this chapter. Dividing the compound interest of 0.372786 (1.372786 − 1 = 0.372786) by 0.02 gives the amount of an ordinary annuity of 16 rents of 1 at 2%. Tables such as Table 3 in the Appendix at the end of this chapter have been prepared to give the amount of ordinary annuities for different numbers of rents at varying interest rates. Note that in Table 3 the value for $A_{\overline{16}|2\%}$ is 18.64 (rounded to two decimal places). Table 3 in the Appendix is used to compute the amount of an ordinary annuity for rents of any dollar amount by the process of multiplication. For example, because the amount of an annuity of 16 rents of 1 at 2% is 18.64, the amount of an ordinary annuity of 16 rents of $500 is $9,320 ($500 × 18.64 = $9,320).

Other Applications of Amount of an Ordinary Annuity of 1 Formula

In the example above the amount of an ordinary annuity of 16 rents of 1 at 2% (18.64) and the periodic rent ($500) were known. From the information available we were able to compute the amount of the ordinary annuity of 16 rents of $500 at 2% as $9,320. Thus, four variables were involved:

1   The number of rents (16)

2   The interest rate per period (2%)

3   The amount of each periodic rent ($500)

4   The amount of the ordinary annuity immediately after the last rent ($9,320)

If any three of these variables are known, the fourth one may be determined by using Table 3 in the Appendix at the end of this chapter as illustrated below:

1   **Question**   How many quarterly rents of $500 are required to accumulate $9,320 if the amount on deposit earns interest at 8% compounded quarterly?

     Answer $9,320 ÷ $500 = 18.64, the amount of an ordinary annuity of 1 at 2% for an unknown number of rents. The 2% column in Table 3 in the Appendix at the end of this chapter shows that the *required number of rents is 16* because the amount of an ordinary annuity of 16 rents at 2% is 18.64 (rounded to two decimal places).

2   **Question**   If an amount of an ordinary annuity of 16 rents of $500 equals $9,320 immediately after the sixteenth rent, what is the interest rate?

Answer $9,320 ÷ $500 = 18.64, the amount of an ordinary annuity of 16 rents of 1 at an *unstated interest rate* per period. The line for 16 rents in Table 3 in the Appendix at the end of this chapter shows that the *interest rate per period is 2%*.

3 **Question** If the required amount of an ordinary annuity of 16 rents at 2% is $9,320, what periodic rents are required to accumulate this amount?

Answer Table 3 in the Appendix shows that the amount of an ordinary annuity of 16 rents at 2% is 18.64 (rounded). The *periodic rents are $500* ($9,320 ÷ 18.64 = $500).

Summary and Example The amount of an ordinary annuity of 1 formula, $A_{\overline{n}|i}$, is used to compute the future amount A of n equal periodic rents of R dollars that earn compound interest rate i per period. The periodic rent is computed by dividing the dollar amount to be accumulated by the amount of an ordinary annuity of 1 at the specified interest rate for the number of periods equal to the number of rents (deposits).

Example: Accumulation of a Fund to Retire Debt Bloom Company wants to accumulate $600,000 on December 31, Year 5, to retire a long-term note payable. Bloom intends to make five equal annual deposits in a fund that will earn interest at 6% compounded annually. The first deposit is made on December 31, Year 1. Compute the amount of the periodic deposits that Bloom must make and prepare a fund accumulation table to verify that $600,000 will be available on December 31, Year 5.

Solution The amount of the periodic deposits is $600,000 ÷ 5.637093 (the amount of an ordinary annuity of five rents of 1 at 6% from Table 3 in the Appendix at the end of this chapter), or $106,438 (rounded). The fund accumulation table appears below.

Example of fund buildup

Dec. 31, Year	Annual deposit	Interest earned at 6%	Increase in fund balance	Fund balance
1	$106,438		$106,438	$106,438
2	106,438	$ 6,386	112,824	219,262
3	106,438	13,156	119,594	338,856
4	106,438	20,331	126,769	465,625
5	106,438	27,937*	134,375	600,000

BLOOM COMPANY
Fund Accumulation Table

*Adjusted for slight rounding error.

Amount of an Annuity Due

The amount of an *annuity due* (or *annuity in advance*) is the total amount on deposit *one period after the final rent.* This is illustrated below for an annuity due of 16 rents:

Diagram for amount of annuity due

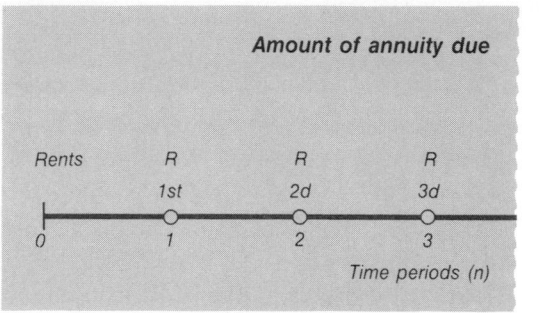 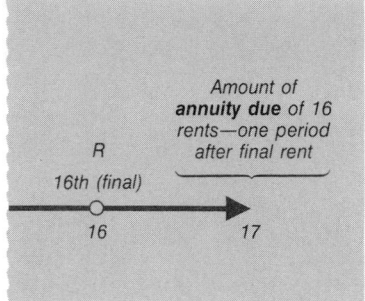

This diagram suggests that there are two ways of computing the amount of an annuity due of 16 rents of 1 at, say, 2% interest per period, as follows:

1 Take the amount of an ordinary annuity of 16 rents of 1 at 2% from Table 3 in the Appendix at the end of this chapter and accrue interest at 2% for one additional period:

$$18.639285 \times 1.02 = \underline{19.01207} \qquad [A_{\overline{n}|i} \times (1 + i)]$$

2 Take the amount of an ordinary annuity of 17 rents of 1 at 2% from Table 3 in the Appendix at the end of this chapter and subtract 1, the rent not made at the end of time period 17:

$$20.01207 - 1 = \underline{19.01207} \qquad (A_{\overline{n+1}|i} - 1)$$

The application of the amount of an annuity due is illustrated in the following example.

Example   Greco Corporation needs $200,000 on March 31, Year 5. This amount is to be accumulated by making 16 equal deposits in a fund at the end of each quarter, starting March 31, Year 1, and ending on December 31, Year 4. The fund will earn interest at 8% compounded quarterly. Compute the periodic rents (deposits) that Greco must make.

Solution   The balance in the fund on March 31, Year 5, represents the amount of an annuity due of 16 rents at 2% per period (19.01207 as determined above). Therefore, the periodic rents are: $200,000 ÷ 19.01207 = $10,519.63. This result may be verified as follows:

Ordinary annuity plus interest for 1 period = amount of annuity due

Amount of **ordinary annuity** of 16 rents of $10,519.63 at 2% on December 31, Year 4: $10,519.63 × 18.639285..............................	$196,078
Add: Interest for first quarter of Year 5: $196,078 × 0.02	3,922
Balance in fund on March 31, Year 5 (amount of an **annuity due** of 16 rents of $10,519.63 at 2%)	$200,000

Amount of Deferred Annuity

When the amount of an ordinary annuity remains on deposit for a number of periods beyond the final rent, the arrangement is known as a *deferred annuity*. The diagram on page 250 shows that the amount of an annuity due of 16 rents is also the amount of an ordinary annuity *deferred for only one period*. Thus, when the amount of an ordinary annuity continues to earn interest for one additional period, we have an annuity due situation; when the amount of an ordinary annuity continues to earn interest for more than one additional period, we have a deferred annuity situation.

The amount of a deferred annuity may be computed by multiplying the amount of the ordinary annuity by the amount of 1 for the period of deferral to accrue compound interest. Alternatively, we may take the amount of an ordinary annuity for all periods (including the period of deferral) and subtract from this the amount of the ordinary annuity for the deferral period when rents *were not made,* but interest continued to accumulate. The diagram below illustrates the relationship of an *ordinary annuity* of 16 rents, an *annuity due* of 16 rents, and an *ordinary annuity of 16 rents deferred for five periods:*

Diagram of three types of annuity amounts

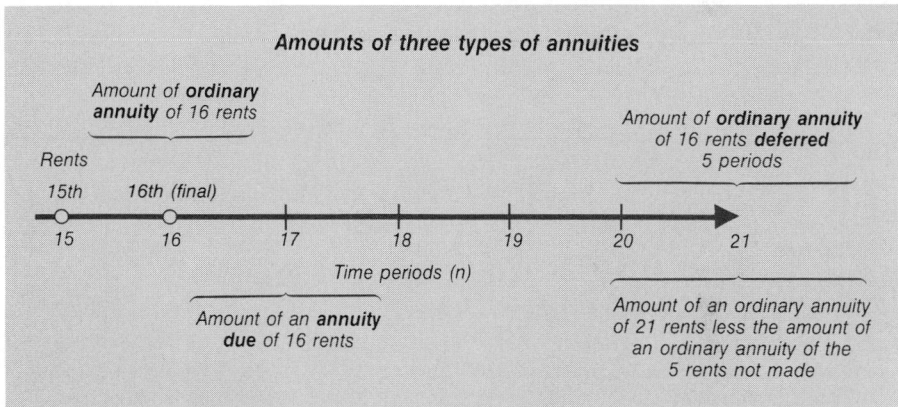

Using the Appendix at the end of this chapter, and assuming a 2% rate of interest per period, we may compute the amount of an ordinary annuity of 16 rents of 1 deferred for 5 periods (at time period 21) *two ways,* as follows:

Alternative computations for amount of deferred annuity

$$A_{\overline{16}|2\%} \times (1 + 0.02)^5 = 18.639285 \times 1.104081 = \underline{\underline{20.57928}}$$

or $\quad A_{\overline{21}|2\%} - A_{\overline{5}|2\%} = 25.783317 - 5.204040 = \underline{\underline{20.57928}}$

Present Value of Ordinary Annuity of 1

Present values of annuities are used more frequently in financial accounting than any of the compound interest concepts discussed to this point. For example, the computation of (1) the proceeds of bond issues, (2) the value of plant assets acquired in purchase-type business combinations or through capital leases, (3) the amount of past service pension costs, (4) the amount of debt or receivables under installment contracts, and (5) the amount of mortgage debt or investments in mortgage notes all require the application of the present-value-of-annuity concept.

A diagram depicting the present value (P) of an ***ordinary annuity (annuity in arrears)*** of five rents (R) is given below:

Diagram of present value of ordinary annuity

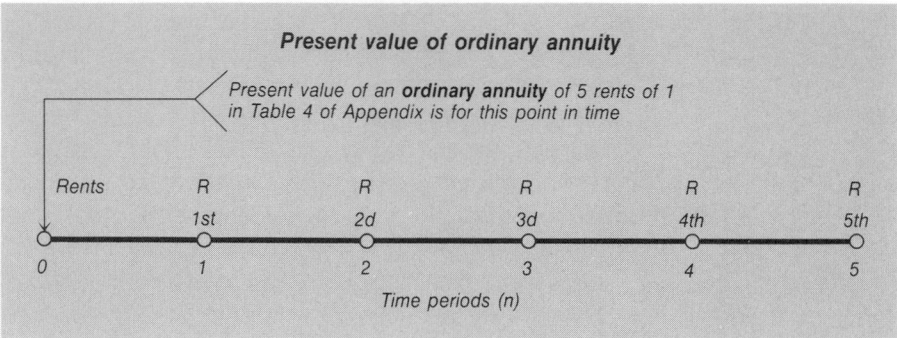

Present value of ordinary annuity

*Present value of an **ordinary annuity** of 5 rents of 1 in Table 4 of Appendix is for this point in time*

| Rents | R | R | R | R | R |
| | 1st | 2d | 3d | 4th | 5th |

| 0 | 1 | 2 | 3 | 4 | 5 |

Time periods (n)

The present value of an ordinary annuity of five rents depicted above is the value of the rents, discounted at compound interest, at a point in time ***one period before the first rent.*** The present value of an ordinary annuity is computed as the total of the present values of the individual rents, but the use of a table, such as Table 4 in the Appendix at the end of this chapter, is more efficient.

The present value (P) of an ordinary annuity of n rents at i rate of interest may be computed ***by dividing by i the compound discount*** on 1 for n periods at i rate of interest. This is illustrated below in the computation of the present value of an ordinary annuity of five rents at 8% per period:

Computation of present value of an ordinary annuity

$$P_{\overline{n}|i} = \frac{1 - \dfrac{1}{(1 + i)^n}}{i} = \frac{1 - \dfrac{1}{(1 + 0.08)^5}}{0.08} = \frac{1 - 0.680583}{0.08}$$

$$= \frac{0.319417}{0.08} = \underline{\underline{3.99271}}$$

The present value of 1 at 8% for five periods (0.680583) is taken from Table 2 in the Appendix at the end of this chapter. Dividing the compound discount of 0.319417 (1 − 0.680583 = 0.319417) by 0.08 gives the present value of an ordinary annuity of five rents of 1 at 8%. In Table 4 in the Appendix, the present value of an ordinary annuity of five rents of 1 at 8% is given as 3.992710, thus confirming the computation above.

To illustrate the application of the present value of an ordinary annuity of 1, assume the following: Evans Company has outstanding a $500,000 noninterest-bearing debt, payable $100,000 a year for five years starting on December 31, Year 1. What is the present value of this debt on January 1, Year 1, for financial accounting, if 8% compounded annually is considered a fair rate of interest? The present value of the debt on January 1, Year 1, is equal to the present value of an ordinary annuity of five rents of $100,000 at 8% per period. Therefore, the debt should be reported at $399,271 ($100,000 × 3.99271) in the accounting records on January 1, Year 1. The *repayment program* (*loan amortization table*) for this debt is summarized below:

Repayment program
for debt

| | EVANS COMPANY | | | |
| | Repayment Program for Debt of $399,271 at 8% Interest | | | |
Date	**Interest expense at 8% a year**	**Repayment at end of year**	**Net reduction in debt**	**Debt balance**
Jan. 1, Year 1				$399,271
Dec. 31, Year 1	$31,942	$100,000	$68,058	331,213
Dec. 31, Year 2	26,497	100,000	73,503	257,710
Dec. 31, Year 3	20,617	100,000	79,383	178,327
Dec. 31, Year 4	14,266	100,000	85,734	92,593
Dec. 31, Year 5	7,407	100,000	92,593	–0–

As illustrated in our earlier discussion of the amount of an ordinary annuity, Table 4 in the Appendix at the end of this chapter may be used to compute other variables in the formula for the present value of an ordinary annuity. For example, if we know that $P_{\overline{5}|8\%} = 3.99271$ and the present value of an ordinary annuity of five rents at 8% per period is $399,271, we may compute the periodic rent of $100,000 by dividing $399,271 by 3.99271.

Summary and Examples The present value of an ordinary annuity of 1 formula, $P_{\overline{n}|i}$, is used to compute the amount P that would settle a debt one period before the first rent of n equal rents of R dollars discounted at compound interest rate i per period. Stated differently, $P_{\overline{n}|i}$ is used to compute the value one period before the first rent of a series of equal cash inflows or outflows, discounted at a constant interest rate per period.

Example 1: Proceeds from Bonds Issued at a Discount Murphy Company issued $5 million face amount of 9%, five-year bonds on June 30, Year 5. The bonds pay interest on June 30 and December 31 and were issued to yield 10% compounded semiannually. Compute the proceeds of this bond issue.

Solution The proceeds of the bond issue may be computed as the total of (1) the present value of the $5 million to be paid at maturity, discounted at the 5% semiannual current rate of interest for 10 periods, plus (2) the present value of an ordinary annuity of 10 rents of $225,000 ($5,000,000 × 0.045 = $225,000) semiannual interest payments, also discounted at 5% per period. This approach is illustrated as follows:

Computation of proceeds of bonds payable

Present value of $5 million discounted at 5% for 10 six-month periods:

$5,000,000 × 0.613913 . . . . $3,069,565

Add: Present value of ordinary annuity of 10 rents of $225,000 dis-
counted at 5%: $225,000 × 7.721735   1,737,390

Proceeds of bond issue $4,806,955*

*$2 discrepancy between this amount and the amount computed below is caused by rounding in present value tables.

Alternative Solution   Because the 9% interest rate on the bonds is less than the 10% current fair rate of interest, the bonds were sold at a discount equal in amount to the present value of the semiannual interest *deficiency* (interest that will not be paid to bondholders) of $25,000 [$5,000,000 × (0.050 − 0.045) = $25,000] for 10 semiannual periods discounted at the 5% *current rate of interest per period.* Therefore, the proceeds from the bond issue also may be computed as follows:

Alternative computation of proceeds of bonds payable

Face amount of bonds $5,000,000

Less: Present value of ordinary annuity of 10 rents of $25,000 interest
deficiency discounted at 5% per period: $25,000 × 7.721735   193,043

Proceeds of bond issue $4,806,957

    Computation of the proceeds of ''zero coupon'' bonds is illustrated on page 245. In recent years some companies have issued bonds that bear a low nominal rate of interest. Such bonds have been issued at substantial discounts and are referred to as ''deep discount bonds.'' The proceeds of the issuance of bonds at a premium (when the interest rate paid on the bonds exceeds the current rate of interest) are computed similarly, as illustrated in Chapter 15.

Example 2: Note Receivable with Excessive Rate of Interest   On March 1, Year 1, Crane Company sold land that cost $80,000 for a $100,000, two-year, 15% promissory note. Interest of $15,000 is due on March 1, Year 2, and $115,000 (interest and face amount of the note) is due on March 1, Year 3. The fair rate of interest on this promissory note on March 1, Year 1, was 10% a year. Crane recorded the transaction *incorrectly* on March 1, Year 1, as follows:

Note Receivable 100,000

    Land 80,000

    Gain on Sale of Land 20,000

To record sale of land.

Compute the current fair value of the note receivable and prepare a correcting entry required as of March 1, Year 1, as well as journal entries to record the cash receipts on March 1, Year 2 and Year 3. Disregard accruals of interest revenue.

Solution   The current fair value of the note receivable is larger than its face amount because it bears an excessive rate of interest. The *current fair value* of the note receivable on March 1, Year 1, is computed below:

Computation of current fair value of note receivable on March 1, Year 1	*Present value of face amount of note (discounted at 10% for two years): $100,000 × 0.826446** $82,645
	Add: Present value of interest on note for two years (ordinary annuity of two rents of $15,000 at 10%): $15,000 × 1.735537† 26,033
	Current fair value of note receivable $108,678

*Table 2 in Appendix at the end of this chapter
†Table 4 in Appendix at the end of this chapter

The *correcting entry* as of March 1, Year 1, and the *journal entries to record the cash receipts* on March 1, Year 2 and Year 3, are shown below:

Correcting entry and journal entries to record cash receipts

March 1, Year 1

Premium on Note Receivable	8,678	
Gain on Sale of Land ($28,678 − $20,000)		8,678

To record premium on note receivable and increase the amount of the gain on the sale of the land from $20,000 to $28,678 ($108,678 − $80,000 = $28,678).

March 1, Year 2

Cash	15,000	
Interest Revenue ($108,678 × 0.10)		10,868
Premium on Note Receivable		4,132

To record receipt of interest and amortization of premium on note receivable.

March 1, Year 3

Cash	115,000	
Note Receivable		100,000
Interest Revenue [($108,678 − $4,132) × 0.10]		10,454‡
Premium on Note Receivable		4,546

To record receipt of principal and interest, and amortization of premium on note receivable.

‡Adjusted for $1 discrepancy because of rounding

Present Value of Annuity Due

The present value of an ordinary annuity falls one period before the first rent. In contrast, the **present value of an annuity due falls on the date the first rent is deposited or withdrawn.** For this reason, an annuity due often is referred to as an **annuity in advance.** The difference between the present value of an ordinary annuity and the present value of an annuity due is illustrated below:

Diagram of present values for ordinary annuity and annuity due

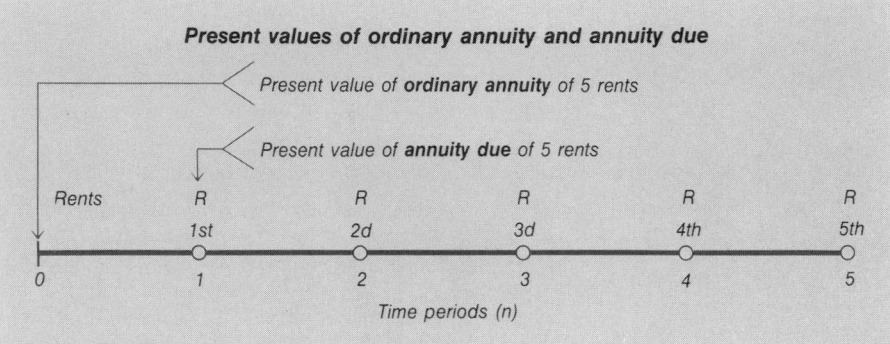

Present values of ordinary annuity and annuity due

*Present value of **ordinary annuity** of 5 rents*

*Present value of **annuity due** of 5 rents*

For example, we need the present value of an annuity due of n rents of 1 to compute the periodic rent payments on an installment contract or a lease when the first payment is due at the beginning of each period. The diagram above indicates that the present value at time period 1 of an annuity due of five rents may be computed (1) by adding interest for one period to the present value of an ordinary annuity of five rents, or (2) by obtaining the present value of an ordinary annuity of four rents and then adding 1, representing the ''extra'' rent at time period 1. These two approaches are illustrated below, using Table 4 in the Appendix at the end of this chapter, to compute the present value of an annuity due of five rents of 1 at 8% per period.

Two ways of computing present value of annuity due

> *Present value of ordinary annuity of five rents of 1 at 8%, plus interest at 8% on this present value for one period: 3.99271 × 1.08 = present value of annuity due $[P_{\overline{n}|i} \times (1 + i)]$* **4.312127**
>
> **or** *Present value of ordinary annuity of four rents of 1 at 8%, plus 1, the fifth rent at time period 1: 3.312127 + 1 = present value of annuity due $(P_{\overline{n-1}|i} + 1)$* **4.312127**

To illustrate the application of the present value of an annuity due of 1, assume the following: On January 1, Year 1, Cinema Corporation acquired a plant asset for $64,682. Cinema agreed to make five equal annual payments starting on January 1, Year 1, and ending on January 1, Year 5, at 8% compounded annually. The annual payments on the debt are determined below:

$$\$64,682 \div 4.312127 = \underline{\underline{\$15,000}}$$

The repayment program for this debt is presented below:

		CINEMA CORPORATION			
		Repayment Program for Debt of $64,682 at 8% Interest			
Jan. 1, Year	Debt at beginning of year	Payment at beginning of year	Balance accruing interest	Interest at 8%	Debt at end of year
1	$64,682	$15,000	$49,682	$3,975	$53,657
2	53,657	15,000	38,657	3,093	41,750
3	41,750	15,000	26,750	2,140	28,890
4	28,890	15,000	13,890	1,110*	15,000
5	15,000	15,000	–0–	–0–	–0–

*Adjusted for $1 discrepancy due to rounding of computations.

Present Value of Deferred Annuity

When periodic rents are postponed for more than one period, the present value of such an annuity on some date prior to the first rent may be computed by using two different methods as follows: (1) Discount the present value of the ordinary annuity portion at compound interest for the periods the annuity is deferred, or (2) determine the present value of an ordinary annuity equal to the total number of periods involved and subtract from this the present value of the "missing" ordinary annuity for rents equal in number to the number of periods the annuity is deferred. To illustrate, assume that Jedi, Inc., wants to know the amount at time period 0 that would pay a debt of five payments of $100,000 each, payments starting at time period 4, and interest compounded at 8% per time period. A diagram of the periodic rents (payments) follows:

Diagram of present
value of deferred
annuity

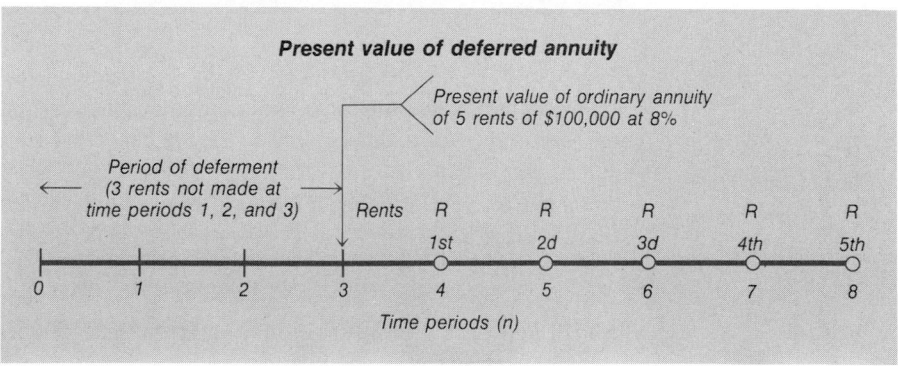

Using Tables 2 and 4 in the Appendix at the end of this chapter, we may compute the present value (at time period 0) of the ordinary annuity of five rents of 1 *deferred for three periods* as follows:

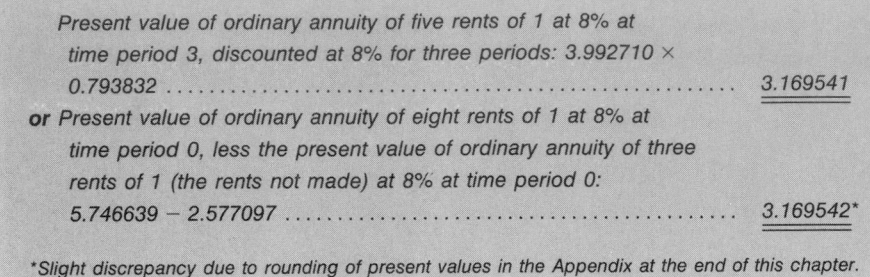

Two ways of computing present value of deferred annuity

Present value of ordinary annuity of five rents of 1 at 8% at time period 3, discounted at 8% for three periods: 3.992710 × 0.793832 .... **3.169541**

or *Present value of ordinary annuity of eight rents of 1 at 8% at time period 0, less the present value of ordinary annuity of three rents of 1 (the rents not made) at 8% at time period 0:*
5.746639 − 2.577097 .... **3.169542***

*Slight discrepancy due to rounding of present values in the Appendix at the end of this chapter.

Thus, cash in the amount of $316,954 ($100,000 × 3.169542 = $316,954) is needed at time period 0 to repay the debt diagrammed on page 257. The repayment of the debt is summarized below:

Proof that computation is correct

JEDI, INC.
Repayment Program for Debt of $316,954 at 8% Interest

Time period	Interest expense at 8% per period	Repayments	Net reduction in debt	Debt balance
0	Present value of debt			$316,954
1	$25,356			342,310
2	27,385			369,695
3	29,576			399,271
4	31,942	$100,000	$68,058	331,213
5	26,497	100,000	73,503	257,710
6	20,617	100,000	79,383	178,327
7	14,266	100,000	85,734	92,593
8	7,407	100,000	92,593	−0−

More Complex Situations

Many complex situations involving compound interest may be encountered in the business world. An understanding of the concepts discussed in the preceding pages enables accountants to analyze and solve problems requiring the application of compound interest principles. Because money may be invested readily to earn a return, there is a universal service charge (interest) for its use, and a specific amount of money available on a stated date has a different value at all other points in time. Compound interest procedures are a means of moving money inflows and outflows forward and backward in time on a basis that enables a comparison of values in equivalent terms.

For example, assume that you are given a choice of receiving $20,000 cash in two years or $30,000 in eight years. The choice is not obvious. Assuming a current fair interest rate of 10%, these amounts may be compared only by measuring their *present value or accumulated amount on a particular date.* If we choose *now* (time point zero), the following ***present-value*** analysis shows that the $20,000 in two years is preferable to receiving $30,000 in eight years:

Comparing present values of future cash flows at 10% interest

$$\$20,000(p_{\overline{2}|10\%}) = \$20,000 \times 0.826446^* = \underline{\$16,529}$$

$$\$30,000(p_{\overline{8}|10\%}) = \$30,000 \times 0.466507^* = \underline{\$13,995}$$

Table 2 in the Appendix at the end of this chapter.

We may reach the same conclusion by comparing ***the accumulated amounts*** of the two dollar amounts eight years from now as follows:

Comparing amounts on a fixed future date at 10% interest

$$\$20,000(a_{\overline{6}|10\%}) = \$20,000 \times 1.771561^* = \underline{\$35,431}$$

$30,000 at the end of eight years is equivalent to $\underline{\$30,000}$

Table 1 in the Appendix at the end of this chapter.

The receipt of $20,000 in two years again is shown to be preferable to the receipt of $30,000 in eight years, because if $20,000 is invested at 10% at the end of the second year, it would accumulate to $35,431 by the end of the eighth year. Any other point in time may be selected to make a similar comparison at 10% interest without changing the validity of the decision to receive $20,000 two years from today. However, if the interest rate were reduced materially, the option of receiving $30,000 in eight years would be more advantageous; for example, if we assume a 5% interest rate, the $20,000 received at the end of the second year would be worth only $26,802 ($20,000 × 1.340096 = $26,802) at the end of the eighth year. Thus, the option of receiving $30,000 in eight years would be preferable.

As another example, assume that at the beginning of Year 1 Kay Park deposited $50,000 in a fund that pays 8% interest compounded annually, and that she planned to withdraw from the fund as follows:

1 Equal amounts for three years starting at the end of Year 1

2 Equal amounts starting at the end of Year 4 and ending at the end of Year 6 ***that are three times as large as the first three withdrawals***

The diagram below indicates that the deposit of $50,000 is equal to (1) the present value of an ordinary annuity of three rents (*R*) at 8%, plus (2) the present value of an ordinary annuity of three rents three times as large as the first three rents (3*R*) deferred for three years:

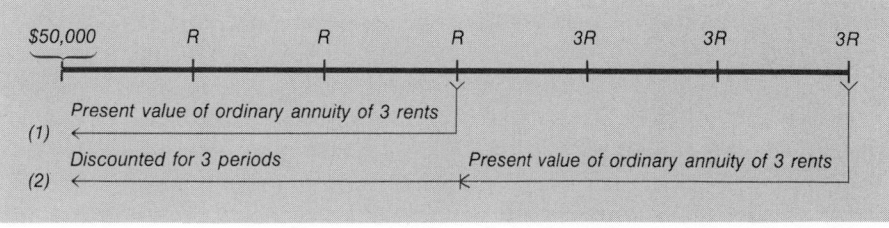

From the present value tables in the Appendix at the end of this chapter, the amount of R may be computed as follows:

$$R \ (2.577097) + 3R \ (2.577097 \times 0.793832) = \$50,000$$

$$8.714443R = \$50,000$$

$$R = \underline{\$5,738} \ \text{(amount of each of the first three withdrawals)}$$

$$3R = \underline{\$17,214} \ \text{(amount of each of the last three withdrawals)}$$

A table summarizing the compound interest accumulations and withdrawals by Kay Park follows:

KAY PARK
Interest Accumulations and Withdrawals—Fund of $50,000

End of year	Interest revenue at 8% a year	Withdrawals	Net reduction in fund	Fund balance
				$50,000
1	$4,000	$5,738	$1,738	48,262
2	3,861	5,738	1,877	46,385
3	3,711	5,738	2,027	44,358
4	3,549	17,214	13,665	30,693
5	2,455	17,214	14,759	15,934
6	1,280*	17,214	15,934	–0–

*Adjusted by $5 for rounding of amounts to nearest dollar.

Summary of Future Amounts and Present Values

The following list of future amounts and present values may be useful as a quick review of the essential concepts discussed in this chapter:

Essential concepts relating to future and present values of cash flows

1 FUTURE AMOUNT. Value on a future date of a *single amount* or a *series of rents* invested at compound interest.

  a *Amount of a single deposit.* Future value of a single deposit at the end of a specific number of periods at compound interest (Table 1 in the Appendix at the end of this chapter).

  b *Amount of an annuity.* Future value of a series of equal receipts or payments (rents) made at regular time intervals and at the same rate of interest compounded each time the receipts or payments are made.

    (1) *Amount of ordinary annuity (annuity in arrears)* is the amount accumulated at compound interest through a series of rents on the date the final rent is made (Table 3 in the Appendix at the end of this chapter).

(2) *Amount of annuity due* (*annuity in advance*)   is the amount accumulated at compound interest through a series of rents one period after the final rent is made. Thus, the amount of an annuity due of *R* rents is equal to the amount of an ordinary annuity of *R* rents plus interest for one additional period.

(3) *Amount of deferred annuity*   is the amount of an ordinary annuity that continues to earn compound interest for more than one period after the final rent is made.

2 PRESENT VALUE.   Value now of a *single amount* or a *series of rents* to be received in the future and discounted at compound interest to an earlier date (usually the date of a transaction, such as the acquisition of equipment on the installment plan).

a *Present value of 1.*   Value of a single amount due or payable on some future date discounted at compound interest (Table 2 in the Appendix at the end of this chapter).

b *Present value of an annuity.*   Value of a series of equal future receipts or payments (rents) made at regular time intervals and discounted at the same compound interest rate on each date rents are due.

(1) *Present value of ordinary annuity* (*annuity in arrears*)   is the discounted value of a series of future rents on a date one period before the first rent (Table 4 in the Appendix at the end of this chapter).

(2) *Present value of annuity due* (*annuity in advance*)   is the discounted value of a series of future rents on the date the first rent is received or paid.

(3) *Present value of deferred annuity*   is the discounted value of a series of future rents on a date that is more than one period before the date that the first rent is received or paid.

APPENDIX: COMPOUND INTEREST TABLES

Table 1 Future Amount of 1 at Compound Interest Due in n Periods: $a_{\overline{n}|i} = (1 + i)^n$

n \ i	½%	1%	1½%	2%	2½%	3%
1	1.005000	1.010000	1.015000	1.020000	1.025000	1.030000
2	1.010025	1.020100	1.030225	1.040400	1.050625	1.060900
3	1.015075	1.030301	1.045678	1.061208	1.076891	1.092727
4	1.020151	1.040604	1.061364	1.082432	1.103813	1.125509
5	1.025251	1.051010	1.077284	1.104081	1.131408	1.159274
6	1.030378	1.061520	1.093443	1.126162	1.159693	1.194052
7	1.035529	1.072135	1.109845	1.148686	1.188686	1.229874
8	1.040707	1.082857	1.126493	1.171659	1.218403	1.266770
9	1.045911	1.093685	1.143390	1.195093	1.248863	1.304773
10	1.051140	1.104622	1.160541	1.218994	1.280085	1.343916
11	1.056396	1.115668	1.177949	1.243374	1.312087	1.384234
12	1.061678	1.126825	1.195618	1.268242	1.344889	1.425761
13	1.066986	1.138093	1.213552	1.293607	1.378511	1.468534
14	1.072321	1.149474	1.231756	1.319479	1.412974	1.512590
15	1.077683	1.160969	1.250232	1.345868	1.448298	1.557967
16	1.083071	1.172579	1.268986	1.372786	1.484506	1.604706
17	1.088487	1.184304	1.288020	1.400241	1.521618	1.652848
18	1.093929	1.196147	1.307341	1.428246	1.559659	1.702433
19	1.099399	1.208109	1.326951	1.456811	1.598650	1.753506
20	1.104896	1.220190	1.346855	1.485947	1.638616	1.806111
21	1.110420	1.232392	1.367058	1.515666	1.679582	1.860295
22	1.115972	1.244716	1.387564	1.545980	1.721571	1.916103
23	1.121552	1.257163	1.408377	1.576899	1.764611	1.973587
24	1.127160	1.269735	1.429503	1.608437	1.808726	2.032794
25	1.132796	1.282432	1.450945	1.640606	1.853944	2.093778
26	1.138460	1.295256	1.472710	1.673418	1.900293	2.156591
27	1.144152	1.308209	1.494800	1.706886	1.947800	2.221289
28	1.149873	1.321291	1.517222	1.741024	1.996495	2.287928
29	1.155622	1.334504	1.539981	1.775845	2.046407	2.356566
30	1.161400	1.347849	1.563080	1.811362	2.097568	2.427262
31	1.167207	1.361327	1.586526	1.847589	2.150007	2.500080
32	1.173043	1.374941	1.610324	1.884541	2.203757	2.575083
33	1.178908	1.388690	1.634479	1.922231	2.258851	2.652335
34	1.184803	1.402577	1.658996	1.960676	2.315322	2.731905
35	1.190727	1.416603	1.683881	1.999890	2.373205	2.813862
36	1.196681	1.430769	1.709140	2.039887	2.432535	2.898278
37	1.202664	1.445076	1.734777	2.080685	2.493349	2.985227
38	1.208677	1.459527	1.760798	2.122299	2.555682	3.074783
39	1.214721	1.474123	1.787210	2.164745	2.619574	3.167027
40	1.220794	1.488864	1.814018	2.208040	2.685064	3.262038
41	1.226898	1.503752	1.841229	2.252200	2.752190	3.359899
42	1.233033	1.518790	1.868847	2.297244	2.820995	3.460696
43	1.239198	1.533978	1.896880	2.343189	2.891520	3.564517
44	1.245394	1.549318	1.925333	2.390053	2.963808	3.671452
45	1.251621	1.564811	1.954213	2.437854	3.037903	3.781596
46	1.257879	1.580459	1.983526	2.486611	3.113851	3.895044
47	1.264168	1.596263	2.013279	2.536344	3.191697	4.011895
48	1.270489	1.612226	2.043478	2.587070	3.271490	4.132252
49	1.276842	1.628348	2.074130	2.638812	3.353277	4.256219
50	1.283226	1.644632	2.105242	2.691588	3.437109	4.383906

Table 1 Future Amount of 1 (*continued*)

n \ i	3½%	4%	4½%	5%	5½%	6%
1	1.035000	1.040000	1.045000	1.050000	1.055000	1.060000
2	1.071225	1.081600	1.092025	1.102500	1.113025	1.123600
3	1.108718	1.124864	1.141166	1.157625	1.174241	1.191016
4	1.147523	1.169859	1.192519	1.215506	1.238825	1.262477
5	1.187686	1.216653	1.246182	1.276282	1.306960	1.338226
6	1.229255	1.265319	1.302260	1.340096	1.378843	1.418519
7	1.272279	1.315932	1.360862	1.407100	1.454679	1.503630
8	1.316809	1.368569	1.422101	1.477455	1.534687	1.593848
9	1.362897	1.423312	1.486095	1.551328	1.619094	1.689479
10	1.410599	1.480244	1.552969	1.628895	1.708144	1.790848
11	1.459970	1.539454	1.622853	1.710339	1.802092	1.898299
12	1.511069	1.601032	1.695881	1.795856	1.901207	2.012196
13	1.563956	1.665074	1.772196	1.885649	2.005774	2.132928
14	1.618695	1.731676	1.851945	1.979932	2.116091	2.260904
15	1.675349	1.800944	1.935282	2.078928	2.232476	2.396558
16	1.733986	1.872981	2.022370	2.182875	2.355263	2.540352
17	1.794676	1.947901	2.113377	2.292018	2.484802	2.692773
18	1.857489	2.025817	2.208479	2.406619	2.621466	2.854339
19	1.922501	2.106849	2.307860	2.526950	2.765647	3.025600
20	1.989789	2.191123	2.411714	2.653298	2.917757	3.207135
21	2.059431	2.278768	2.520241	2.785963	3.078234	3.399564
22	2.131512	2.369919	2.633652	2.925261	3.247537	3.603537
23	2.206114	2.464716	2.752166	3.071524	3.426152	3.819750
24	2.283328	2.563304	2.876014	3.225100	3.614590	4.048935
25	2.363245	2.665836	3.005434	3.386355	3.813392	4.291871
26	2.445959	2.772470	3.140679	3.555673	4.023129	4.549383
27	2.531567	2.883369	3.282010	3.733456	4.244401	4.822346
28	2.620172	2.998703	3.429700	3.920129	4.477843	5.111687
29	2.711878	3.118651	3.584036	4.116136	4.724124	5.418388
30	2.806794	3.243398	3.745318	4.321942	4.983951	5.743491
31	2.905031	3.373133	3.913857	4.538039	5.258069	6.088101
32	3.006708	3.508059	4.089981	4.764941	5.547262	6.453387
33	3.111942	3.648381	4.274030	5.003189	5.852362	6.840590
34	3.220860	3.794316	4.466362	5.253348	6.174242	7.251025
35	3.333590	3.946089	4.667348	5.516015	6.513825	7.686087
36	3.450266	4.103933	4.877378	5.791816	6.872085	8.147252
37	3.571025	4.268090	5.096860	6.081407	7.250050	8.636087
38	3.696011	4.438813	5.326219	6.385477	7.648803	9.154252
39	3.825372	4.616366	5.565899	6.704751	8.069487	9.703507
40	3.959260	4.801021	5.816365	7.039989	8.513309	10.285718
41	4.097834	4.993061	6.078101	7.391988	8.981541	10.902861
42	4.241258	5.192784	6.351615	7.761588	9.475526	11.557033
43	4.389702	5.400495	6.637438	8.149667	9.996679	12.250455
44	4.543342	5.616515	6.936123	8.557150	10.546497	12.985482
45	4.702359	5.841176	7.248248	8.985008	11.126554	13.764611
46	4.866941	6.074823	7.574420	9.434258	11.738515	14.590487
47	5.037284	6.317816	7.915268	9.905971	12.384133	15.465917
48	5.213589	6.570528	8.271456	10.401270	13.065260	16.393872
49	5.396065	6.833349	8.643671	10.921333	13.783849	17.377504
50	5.584927	7.106683	9.032636	11.467400	14.541961	18.420154

Table 1   Future Amount of 1 (*continued*)

n \ i	7%	8%	9%	10%	12%	15%
1	1.070000	1.080000	1.090000	1.100000	1.120000	1.150000
2	1.144900	1.166400	1.188100	1.210000	1.254400	1.322500
3	1.225043	1.259712	1.295029	1.331000	1.404928	1.520875
4	1.310796	1.360489	1.411582	1.464100	1.573519	1.749006
5	1.402552	1.469328	1.538624	1.610510	1.762342	2.011357
6	1.500730	1.586874	1.677100	1.771561	1.973823	2.313061
7	1.605781	1.713824	1.828039	1.948717	2.210681	2.660020
8	1.718186	1.850930	1.992563	2.143589	2.475963	3.059023
9	1.838459	1.999005	2.171893	2.357948	2.773079	3.517876
10	1.967151	2.158925	2.367364	2.593742	3.105848	4.045558
11	2.104852	2.331639	2.580426	2.853117	3.478550	4.652391
12	2.252192	2.518170	2.812665	3.138428	3.895976	5.350250
13	2.409845	2.719624	3.065805	3.452271	4.363493	6.152788
14	2.578534	2.937194	3.341727	3.797498	4.887112	7.075706
15	2.759032	3.172169	3.642482	4.177248	5.473566	8.137062
16	2.952164	3.425943	3.970306	4.594973	6.130394	9.357621
17	3.158815	3.700018	4.327633	5.054470	6.866041	10.761264
18	3.379932	3.996019	4.717120	5.559917	7.689966	12.375454
19	3.616528	4.315701	5.141661	6.115909	8.612762	14.231772
20	3.869684	4.660957	5.604411	6.727500	9.646293	16.366537
21	4.140562	5.033834	6.108808	7.400250	10.803848	18.821518
22	4.430402	5.436540	6.658600	8.140275	12.100310	21.644746
23	4.740530	5.871464	7.257874	8.954302	13.552347	24.891458
24	5.072367	6.341181	7.911083	9.849733	15.178629	28.625176
25	5.427433	6.848475	8.623081	10.834706	17.000064	32.918953
26	5.807353	7.396353	9.399158	11.918177	19.040072	37.856796
27	6.213868	7.988061	10.245082	13.109994	21.324881	43.535315
28	6.648838	8.627106	11.167140	14.420994	23.883866	50.065612
29	7.114257	9.317275	12.172182	15.863093	26.749930	57.575454
30	7.612255	10.062657	13.267678	17.449402	29.959922	66.211772
31	8.145113	10.867669	14.461770	19.194342	33.555113	76.143538
32	8.715271	11.737083	15.763329	21.113777	37.581726	87.565068
33	9.325340	12.676050	17.182028	23.225154	42.091533	100.699829
34	9.978114	13.690134	18.728411	25.547670	47.142517	115.804803
35	10.676581	14.785344	20.413968	28.102437	52.799620	133.175523
36	11.423942	15.968172	22.251225	30.912681	59.135574	153.151852
37	12.223618	17.245626	24.253835	34.003949	66.231843	176.124630
38	13.079271	18.625276	26.436680	37.404343	74.179664	202.543324
39	13.994820	20.115298	28.815982	41.144778	83.081224	232.924823
40	14.974458	21.724521	31.409420	45.259256	93.050970	267.863546
41	16.022670	23.462483	34.236268	49.785181	104.217087	308.043078
42	17.144257	25.339482	37.317532	54.763699	116.723137	354.249540
43	18.344355	27.366640	40.676110	60.240069	130.729914	407.386971
44	19.628460	29.555972	44.336960	66.264076	146.417503	468.495017
45	21.002452	31.920449	48.327286	72.890484	163.987604	538.769269
46	22.472623	34.474085	52.676742	80.179532	183.666116	619.584659
47	24.045707	37.232012	57.417649	88.197485	205.706050	712.522358
48	25.728907	40.210573	62.585237	97.017234	230.390776	819.400712
49	27.529930	43.427419	68.217908	106.718957	258.037669	942.310819
50	29.457025	46.901613	74.357520	117.390853	289.002190	1083.657442

Table 2   Present Value of 1 at Compound Interest Due in n Periods: $p_{\overline{n}|i} = \dfrac{1}{(1+i)^n}$

n \ i	½%	1%	1½%	2%	2½%	3%
1	0.995025	0.990099	0.985222	0.980392	0.975610	0.970874
2	0.990075	0.980296	0.970662	0.961169	0.951814	0.942596
3	0.985149	0.970590	0.956317	0.942322	0.928599	0.915142
4	0.980248	0.960980	0.942184	0.923845	0.905951	0.888487
5	0.975371	0.951466	0.928260	0.905731	0.883854	0.862609
6	0.970518	0.942045	0.914542	0.887971	0.862297	0.837484
7	0.965690	0.932718	0.901027	0.870560	0.841265	0.813092
8	0.960885	0.923483	0.887711	0.853490	0.820747	0.789409
9	0.956105	0.914340	0.874592	0.836755	0.800728	0.766417
10	0.951348	0.905287	0.861667	0.820348	0.781198	0.744094
11	0.946615	0.896324	0.848933	0.804263	0.762145	0.722421
12	0.941905	0.887449	0.836387	0.788493	0.743556	0.701380
13	0.937219	0.878663	0.824027	0.773033	0.725420	0.680951
14	0.932556	0.869963	0.811849	0.757875	0.707727	0.661118
15	0.927917	0.861349	0.799852	0.743015	0.690466	0.641862
16	0.923300	0.852821	0.788031	0.728446	0.673625	0.623167
17	0.918707	0.844377	0.776385	0.714163	0.657195	0.605016
18	0.914136	0.836017	0.764912	0.700159	0.641166	0.587395
19	0.909588	0.827740	0.753607	0.686431	0.625528	0.570286
20	0.905063	0.819544	0.742470	0.672971	0.610271	0.553676
21	0.900560	0.811430	0.731498	0.659776	0.595386	0.537549
22	0.896080	0.803396	0.720688	0.646839	0.580865	0.521893
23	0.891622	0.795442	0.710037	0.634156	0.566697	0.506692
24	0.887186	0.787566	0.699544	0.621721	0.552875	0.491934
25	0.882772	0.779768	0.689206	0.609531	0.539391	0.477606
26	0.878380	0.772048	0.679021	0.597579	0.526235	0.463695
27	0.874010	0.764404	0.668986	0.585862	0.513400	0.450189
28	0.869662	0.756836	0.659099	0.574375	0.500878	0.437077
29	0.865335	0.749342	0.649359	0.563112	0.488661	0.424346
30	0.861030	0.741923	0.639762	0.552071	0.476743	0.411987
31	0.856746	0.734577	0.630308	0.541246	0.465115	0.399987
32	0.852484	0.727304	0.620993	0.530633	0.453771	0.388337
33	0.848242	0.720103	0.611816	0.520229	0.442703	0.377026
34	0.844022	0.712973	0.602774	0.510028	0.431905	0.366045
35	0.839823	0.705914	0.593866	0.500028	0.421371	0.355383
36	0.835645	0.698925	0.585090	0.490223	0.411094	0.345032
37	0.831487	0.692005	0.576443	0.480611	0.401067	0.334983
38	0.827351	0.685153	0.567924	0.471187	0.391285	0.325226
39	0.823235	0.678370	0.559531	0.461948	0.381741	0.315754
40	0.819139	0.671653	0.551262	0.452890	0.372431	0.306557
41	0.815064	0.665003	0.543116	0.444010	0.363347	0.297628
42	0.811009	0.658419	0.535089	0.435304	0.354485	0.288959
43	0.806974	0.651900	0.527182	0.426769	0.345839	0.280543
44	0.802959	0.645445	0.519391	0.418401	0.337404	0.272372
45	0.798964	0.639055	0.511715	0.410197	0.329174	0.264439
46	0.794989	0.632728	0.504153	0.402154	0.321146	0.256737
47	0.791034	0.626463	0.496702	0.394268	0.313313	0.249259
48	0.787098	0.620260	0.489362	0.386538	0.305671	0.241999
49	0.783183	0.614119	0.482130	0.378958	0.298216	0.234950
50	0.779286	0.608039	0.475005	0.371528	0.290942	0.228107

Table 2 Present Value of 1 (*continued*)

n \ i	3½%	4%	4½%	5%	5½%	6%
1	0.966184	0.961538	0.956938	0.952381	0.947867	0.943396
2	0.933511	0.924556	0.915730	0.907029	0.898452	0.889996
3	0.901943	0.888996	0.876297	0.863838	0.851614	0.839619
4	0.871442	0.854804	0.838561	0.822702	0.807217	0.792094
5	0.841973	0.821927	0.802451	0.783526	0.765134	0.747258
6	0.813501	0.790315	0.767896	0.746215	0.725246	0.704961
7	0.785991	0.759918	0.734828	0.710681	0.687437	0.665057
8	0.759412	0.730690	0.703185	0.676839	0.651599	0.627412
9	0.733731	0.702587	0.672904	0.644609	0.617629	0.591898
10	0.708919	0.675564	0.643928	0.613913	0.585431	0.558395
11	0.684946	0.649581	0.616199	0.584679	0.554911	0.526788
12	0.661783	0.624597	0.589664	0.556837	0.525982	0.496969
13	0.639404	0.600574	0.564272	0.530321	0.498561	0.468839
14	0.617782	0.577475	0.539973	0.505068	0.472569	0.442301
15	0.596891	0.555265	0.516720	0.481017	0.447933	0.417265
16	0.576706	0.533908	0.494469	0.458112	0.424581	0.393646
17	0.557204	0.513373	0.473176	0.436297	0.402447	0.371364
18	0.538361	0.493628	0.452800	0.415521	0.381466	0.350344
19	0.520156	0.474642	0.433302	0.395734	0.361579	0.330513
20	0.502566	0.456387	0.414643	0.376889	0.342729	0.311805
21	0.485571	0.438834	0.396787	0.358942	0.324862	0.294155
22	0.469151	0.421955	0.379701	0.341850	0.307926	0.277505
23	0.453286	0.405726	0.363350	0.325571	0.291873	0.261797
24	0.437957	0.390121	0.347703	0.310068	0.276657	0.246979
25	0.423147	0.375117	0.332731	0.295303	0.262234	0.232999
26	0.408838	0.360689	0.318402	0.281241	0.248563	0.219810
27	0.395012	0.346817	0.304691	0.267848	0.235605	0.207368
28	0.381654	0.333477	0.291571	0.255094	0.223322	0.195630
29	0.368748	0.320651	0.279015	0.242946	0.211679	0.184557
30	0.356278	0.308319	0.267000	0.231377	0.200644	0.174110
31	0.344230	0.296460	0.255502	0.220359	0.190184	0.164255
32	0.332590	0.285058	0.244500	0.209866	0.180269	0.154957
33	0.321343	0.274094	0.233971	0.199873	0.170871	0.146186
34	0.310476	0.263552	0.223896	0.190355	0.161963	0.137912
35	0.299977	0.253415	0.214254	0.181290	0.153520	0.130105
36	0.289833	0.243669	0.205028	0.172657	0.145516	0.122741
37	0.280032	0.234297	0.196199	0.164436	0.137930	0.115793
38	0.270562	0.225285	0.187750	0.156605	0.130739	0.109239
39	0.261413	0.216621	0.179665	0.149148	0.123924	0.103056
40	0.252572	0.208289	0.171929	0.142046	0.117463	0.097222
41	0.244031	0.200278	0.164525	0.135282	0.111339	0.091719
42	0.235779	0.192575	0.157440	0.128840	0.105535	0.086527
43	0.227806	0.185168	0.150661	0.122704	0.100033	0.081630
44	0.220102	0.178046	0.144173	0.116861	0.094818	0.077009
45	0.212659	0.171198	0.137964	0.111297	0.089875	0.072650
46	0.205468	0.164614	0.132023	0.105997	0.085190	0.068538
47	0.198520	0.158283	0.126338	0.100949	0.080748	0.064658
48	0.191806	0.152195	0.120898	0.096142	0.076539	0.060998
49	0.185320	0.146341	0.115692	0.091564	0.072549	0.057546
50	0.179053	0.140713	0.110710	0.087204	0.068767	0.054288

Table 2   Present Value of 1 (*continued*)

n \ i	7%	8%	9%	10%	12%	15%
1	0.934580	0.925926	0.917431	0.909091	0.892857	0.869565
2	0.873439	0.857339	0.841680	0.826446	0.797194	0.756144
3	0.816298	0.793832	0.772183	0.751315	0.711780	0.657516
4	0.762895	0.735030	0.708425	0.683013	0.635518	0.571753
5	0.712986	0.680583	0.649931	0.620921	0.567427	0.497177
6	0.666342	0.630170	0.596267	0.564474	0.506631	0.432328
7	0.622750	0.583490	0.547034	0.513158	0.452349	0.375937
8	0.582009	0.540269	0.501866	0.466507	0.403883	0.326902
9	0.543934	0.500249	0.460428	0.424098	0.360610	0.284262
10	0.508349	0.463193	0.422411	0.385543	0.321973	0.247185
11	0.475093	0.428883	0.387533	0.350494	0.287476	0.214943
12	0.444012	0.397114	0.355535	0.318631	0.256675	0.186907
13	0.414964	0.367698	0.326179	0.289664	0.229174	0.162528
14	0.387817	0.340461	0.299246	0.263331	0.204620	0.141329
15	0.362446	0.315242	0.274538	0.239392	0.182696	0.122894
16	0.338735	0.291890	0.251870	0.217629	0.163122	0.106865
17	0.316574	0.270269	0.231073	0.197845	0.145644	0.092926
18	0.295864	0.250249	0.211994	0.179859	0.130040	0.080805
19	0.276508	0.231712	0.194490	0.163508	0.116107	0.070265
20	0.258419	0.214548	0.178431	0.148644	0.103667	0.061100
21	0.241513	0.198656	0.163698	0.135131	0.092560	0.053131
22	0.225713	0.183941	0.150182	0.122846	0.082643	0.046201
23	0.210947	0.170315	0.137781	0.111678	0.073788	0.040174
24	0.197147	0.157699	0.126405	0.101526	0.065882	0.034934
25	0.184249	0.146018	0.115968	0.092296	0.058823	0.030378
26	0.172195	0.135202	0.106393	0.083905	0.052521	0.026415
27	0.160930	0.125187	0.097608	0.076278	0.046894	0.022970
28	0.150402	0.115914	0.089548	0.069343	0.041869	0.019974
29	0.140563	0.107328	0.082155	0.063039	0.037383	0.017369
30	0.131367	0.099377	0.075371	0.057309	0.033378	0.015103
31	0.122773	0.092016	0.069148	0.052099	0.029802	0.013133
32	0.114741	0.085200	0.063438	0.047362	0.026609	0.011420
33	0.107235	0.078889	0.058200	0.043057	0.023758	0.009931
34	0.100219	0.073045	0.053395	0.039143	0.021212	0.008635
35	0.093663	0.067635	0.048986	0.035584	0.018940	0.007509
36	0.087535	0.062625	0.044941	0.032349	0.016910	0.006529
37	0.081809	0.057986	0.041231	0.029408	0.015098	0.005678
38	0.076457	0.053690	0.037826	0.026735	0.013481	0.004937
39	0.071455	0.049713	0.034703	0.024304	0.012036	0.004293
40	0.066780	0.046031	0.031838	0.022095	0.010747	0.003733
41	0.062412	0.042621	0.029209	0.020086	0.009595	0.003246
42	0.058329	0.039464	0.026797	0.018260	0.008567	0.002823
43	0.054513	0.036541	0.024584	0.016600	0.007649	0.002455
44	0.050946	0.033834	0.022555	0.015091	0.006830	0.002134
45	0.047613	0.031328	0.020692	0.013719	0.006098	0.001856
46	0.044499	0.029007	0.018984	0.012472	0.005445	0.001614
47	0.041587	0.026859	0.017416	0.011338	0.004861	0.001403
48	0.038867	0.024869	0.015978	0.010307	0.004340	0.001220
49	0.036324	0.023027	0.014659	0.009370	0.003875	0.001061
50	0.033948	0.021321	0.013449	0.008519	0.003460	0.000923

Table 3   Future Amount of Ordinary Annuity of 1 per Period: $A_{\overline{n}|i} = \dfrac{(1+i)^n - 1}{i}$

n \ i	½%	1%	1½%	2%	2½%	3%
1	1.000000	1.000000	1.000000	1.000000	1.000000	1.000000
2	2.005000	2.010000	2.015000	2.020000	2.025000	2.030000
3	3.015025	3.030100	3.045225	3.060400	3.075625	3.090900
4	4.030100	4.060401	4.090903	4.121608	4.152516	4.183627
5	5.050251	5.101005	5.152267	5.204040	5.256329	5.309136
6	6.075502	6.152015	6.229551	6.308121	6.387737	6.468410
7	7.105879	7.213535	7.322994	7.434283	7.547430	7.662462
8	8.141409	8.285671	8.432839	8.582969	8.736116	8.892336
9	9.182116	9.368527	9.559332	9.754628	9.954519	10.159106
10	10.228026	10.462213	10.702722	10.949721	11.203382	11.463879
11	11.279167	11.566835	11.863262	12.168715	12.483466	12.807796
12	12.335562	12.682503	13.041211	13.412090	13.795553	14.192030
13	13.397240	13.809328	14.236830	14.680332	15.140442	15.617790
14	14.464226	14.947421	15.450382	15.973938	16.518953	17.086324
15	15.536548	16.096896	16.682138	17.293417	17.931927	18.598914
16	16.614230	17.257864	17.932370	18.639285	19.380225	20.156881
17	17.697301	18.430443	19.201355	20.012071	20.864730	21.761588
18	18.785788	19.614748	20.489376	21.412312	22.386349	23.414435
19	19.879717	20.810895	21.796716	22.840559	23.946007	25.116868
20	20.979115	22.019004	23.123667	24.297370	25.544658	26.870374
21	22.084011	23.239194	24.470522	25.783317	27.183274	28.676486
22	23.194431	24.471586	25.837580	27.298984	28.862856	30.536780
23	24.310403	25.716302	27.225144	28.844963	30.584427	32.452884
24	25.431955	26.973465	28.633521	30.421862	32.349038	34.426470
25	26.559115	28.243200	30.063024	32.030300	34.157764	36.459264
26	27.691911	29.525632	31.513969	33.670906	36.011708	38.553042
27	28.830370	30.820888	32.986679	35.344324	37.912001	40.709634
28	29.974522	32.129097	34.481479	37.051210	39.859801	42.930923
29	31.124395	33.450388	35.998701	38.792235	41.856296	45.218850
30	32.280017	34.784892	37.538681	40.568079	43.902703	47.575416
31	33.441417	36.132740	39.101762	42.379441	46.000271	50.002678
32	34.608624	37.494068	40.688288	44.227030	48.150278	52.502759
33	35.781667	38.869009	42.298612	46.111570	50.354034	55.077841
34	36.960575	40.257699	43.933092	48.033802	52.612885	57.730177
35	38.145378	41.660276	45.592088	49.994478	54.928207	60.462082
36	39.336105	43.076878	47.275969	51.994367	57.301413	63.275944
37	40.532785	44.507647	48.985109	54.034255	59.733948	66.174223
38	41.735449	45.952724	50.719885	56.114940	62.227297	69.159449
39	42.944127	47.412251	52.480684	58.237238	64.782979	72.234233
40	44.158847	48.886373	54.267894	60.401983	67.402554	75.401260
41	45.379642	50.375237	56.081912	62.610023	70.087617	78.663298
42	46.606540	51.878989	57.923141	64.862223	72.839808	82.023196
43	47.839572	53.397779	59.791988	67.159468	75.660803	85.483892
44	49.078770	54.931757	61.688868	69.502657	78.552323	89.048409
45	50.324164	56.481075	63.614201	71.892710	81.516131	92.719861
46	51.575785	58.045885	65.568414	74.330564	84.554034	96.501457
47	52.833664	59.626344	67.551940	76.817176	87.667885	100.396501
48	54.097832	61.222608	69.565219	79.353519	90.859582	104.408396
49	55.368321	62.834834	71.608698	81.940590	94.131072	108.540648
50	56.645163	64.463182	73.682828	84.579401	97.484349	112.796867

Table 3 Future Amount of Ordinary Annuity of 1 (*continued*)

n \ i	3½%	4%	4½%	5%	5½%	6%
1	1.000000	1.000000	1.000000	1.000000	1.000000	1.000000
2	2.035000	2.040000	2.045000	2.050000	2.055000	2.060000
3	3.106225	3.121600	3.137025	3.152500	3.168025	3.183600
4	4.214943	4.246464	4.278191	4.310125	4.342266	4.374616
5	5.362466	5.416323	5.470710	5.525631	5.581091	5.637093
6	6.550152	6.632975	6.716892	6.801913	6.888051	6.975319
7	7.779408	7.898294	8.019152	8.142008	8.266894	8.393838
8	9.051687	9.214226	9.380014	9.549109	9.721573	9.897468
9	10.368496	10.582795	10.802114	11.026564	11.256260	11.491316
10	11.731393	12.006107	12.288209	12.577893	12.875354	13.180795
11	13.141992	13.486351	13.841179	14.206787	14.583498	14.971643
12	14.601962	15.025805	15.464032	15.917127	16.385591	16.869941
13	16.113030	16.626838	17.159913	17.712983	18.286798	18.882138
14	17.676986	18.291911	18.932109	19.598632	20.292572	21.015066
15	19.295681	20.023588	20.784054	21.578564	22.408664	23.275970
16	20.971030	21.824531	22.719337	23.657492	24.641140	25.672528
17	22.705016	23.697512	24.741707	25.840366	26.996403	28.212880
18	24.499691	25.645413	26.855084	28.132385	29.481205	30.905653
19	26.357181	27.671229	29.063562	30.539004	32.102671	33.759992
20	28.279682	29.778079	31.371423	33.065954	34.868318	36.785591
21	30.269471	31.969202	33.783137	35.719252	37.786076	39.992727
22	32.328902	34.247970	36.303378	38.505214	40.864310	43.392290
23	34.460414	36.617889	38.937030	41.430475	44.111847	46.995828
24	36.666528	39.082604	41.689196	44.501999	47.537998	50.815577
25	38.949857	41.645908	44.565210	47.727099	51.152588	54.864512
26	41.313102	44.311745	47.570645	51.113454	54.965981	59.156383
27	43.759060	47.084214	50.711324	54.669126	58.989109	63.705766
28	46.290627	49.967583	53.993333	58.402583	63.233510	68.528112
29	48.910799	52.966286	57.423033	62.322712	67.711354	73.629798
30	51.622677	56.084938	61.007070	66.438848	72.435478	79.058186
31	54.429471	59.328335	64.752388	70.760790	77.419429	84.801677
32	57.334502	62.701469	68.666245	75.298829	82.677498	90.889778
33	60.341210	66.209527	72.756226	80.063771	88.224760	97.343165
34	63.453152	69.857909	77.030256	85.066959	94.077122	104.183755
35	66.674013	73.652225	81.496618	90.320307	100.251364	111.434780
36	70.007603	77.598314	86.163966	95.836323	106.765189	119.120867
37	73.457869	81.702246	91.041344	101.628139	113.637274	127.268119
38	77.028895	85.970336	96.138205	107.709546	120.887324	135.904206
39	80.724906	90.409150	101.464424	114.095023	128.536127	145.058458
40	84.550278	95.025516	107.030323	120.799774	136.605614	154.761966
41	88.509537	99.826536	112.846688	127.839763	145.118923	165.047684
42	92.607371	104.819598	118.924789	135.231751	154.100464	175.950545
43	96.848629	110.012382	125.276404	142.993339	163.575989	187.507577
44	101.238331	115.412877	131.913842	151.143006	173.572669	199.758032
45	105.781673	121.029392	138.849965	159.700156	184.119165	212.743514
46	110.484031	126.870568	146.098214	168.685164	195.245719	226.508125
47	115.350973	132.945390	153.672633	178.119422	206.984234	241.098612
48	120.388257	139.263206	161.587902	188.025393	219.368367	256.564529
49	125.601846	145.833734	169.859357	198.426663	232.433627	272.958401
50	130.997910	152.667084	178.503028	209.347996	246.217476	290.335905

Table 3   Future Amount of Ordinary Annuity of 1 (*continued*)

n \ i	7%	8%	9%	10%	12%	15%
1	1.000000	1.000000	1.000000	1.000000	1.000000	1.000000
2	2.070000	2.080000	2.090000	2.100000	2.120000	2.150000
3	3.214900	3.246400	3.278100	3.310000	3.374400	3.472500
4	4.439943	4.506112	4.573129	4.641000	4.779328	4.993375
5	5.750740	5.866601	5.984711	6.105100	6.352847	6.742381
6	7.153291	7.335929	7.523335	7.715610	8.115189	8.753738
7	8.654021	8.922803	9.200435	9.487171	10.089012	11.066799
8	10.259803	10.636628	11.028474	11.435888	12.299693	13.726819
9	11.977989	12.487558	13.021036	13.579477	14.775656	16.785842
10	13.816448	14.486562	15.192930	15.937425	17.548735	20.303718
11	15.783599	16.645487	17.560293	18.531167	20.654583	24.349276
12	17.888451	18.977126	20.140720	21.384284	24.133133	29.001667
13	20.140643	21.495297	22.953385	24.522712	28.029109	34.351917
14	22.550488	24.214920	26.019189	27.974983	32.392602	40.504705
15	25.129022	27.152114	29.360916	31.772482	37.279715	47.580411
16	27.888054	30.324283	33.003399	35.949730	42.753280	55.717472
17	30.840217	33.750226	36.973705	40.544703	48.883674	65.075093
18	33.999033	37.450244	41.301338	45.599173	55.749715	75.836357
19	37.378965	41.446263	46.018458	51.159090	63.439681	88.211811
20	40.995492	45.761964	51.160120	57.274999	72.052442	102.443583
21	44.865177	50.422921	56.764530	64.002499	81.698736	118.810120
22	49.005739	55.456755	62.873338	71.402749	92.502584	137.631638
23	53.436141	60.893296	69.531939	79.543024	104.602894	159.276384
24	58.176671	66.764759	76.789813	88.497327	118.155241	184.167841
25	63.249038	73.105940	84.700896	98.347059	133.333870	212.793017
26	68.676470	79.954415	93.323977	109.181765	150.333934	245.711970
27	74.483823	87.350768	102.723135	121.099942	169.374007	283.568766
28	80.697691	95.338830	112.968217	134.209936	190.698887	327.104080
29	87.346529	103.965936	124.135356	148.630930	214.582754	377.169693
30	94.460786	113.283211	136.307539	164.494023	241.332684	434.745146
31	102.073041	123.345868	149.575217	181.943425	271.292606	500.956918
32	110.218154	134.213537	164.036987	201.137767	304.847719	577.100456
33	118.933425	145.950620	179.800315	222.251544	342.429446	644.665525
34	128.258765	158.626670	196.982344	245.476699	384.520979	765.365353
35	138.236878	172.316804	215.710755	271.024368	431.663496	881.170156
36	148.913460	187.102148	236.124723	299.126805	484.463116	1014.345680
37	160.337402	203.070320	258.375948	330.039486	543.598690	1167.497532
38	172.561020	220.315945	282.629783	364.043434	609.830533	1343.622161
39	185.640292	238.941221	309.066463	401.447778	684.010197	1546.165485
40	199.635112	259.056519	337.882445	442.592556	767.091420	1779.090308
41	214.609570	280.781040	369.291865	487.851811	860.142391	2046.953854
42	230.632240	304.243523	403.528133	537.636992	964.359478	2354.996933
43	247.776497	329.583005	440.845665	592.400692	1081.082615	2709.246473
44	266.120851	356.949646	481.521775	652.640761	1211.812529	3116.633443
45	285.749311	386.505617	525.858734	718.904837	1358.230032	3585.128460
46	306.751763	418.426067	574.186021	791.795321	1522.217636	4123.897729
47	329.224386	452.900152	626.862762	871.974853	1705.883752	4743.482388
48	353.270093	490.132164	684.280411	960.172338	1911.589803	5466.004746
49	378.999000	530.342737	746.865648	1057.189572	2141.980579	6275.405458
50	406.528929	573.770156	815.083556	1163.908529	2400.018249	7217.716277

Table 4 Present Value of Ordinary Annuity of 1 per Period: $P_{\overline{n}|i} = \dfrac{1 - \dfrac{1}{(1 + i)^n}}{i}$

n	½%	1%	1½%	2%	2½%	3%
1	0.995025	0.990099	0.985222	0.980392	0.975610	0.970874
2	1.985099	1.970395	1.955883	1.941561	1.927424	1.913470
3	2.970248	2.940985	2.912200	2.883883	2.856024	2.828611
4	3.950496	3.901966	3.854385	3.807729	3.761974	3.717098
5	4.925866	4.853431	4.782645	4.713460	4.645829	4.579707
6	5.896384	5.795476	5.697187	5.601431	5.508125	5.417191
7	6.862074	6.728195	6.598214	6.471991	6.349391	6.230283
8	7.822959	7.651678	7.485925	7.325481	7.170137	7.019692
9	8.779064	8.566018	8.360517	8.162237	7.970866	7.786109
10	9.730412	9.471305	9.222185	8.982585	8.752064	8.530203
11	10.677027	10.367628	10.071118	9.786848	9.514209	9.252624
12	11.618932	11.255077	10.907505	10.575341	10.257765	9.954004
13	12.556151	12.133740	11.731532	11.348374	10.983185	10.634955
14	13.488708	13.003703	12.543382	12.106249	11.690912	11.296073
15	14.416625	13.865053	13.343233	12.849264	12.381378	11.937935
16	15.339925	14.717874	14.131264	13.577709	13.055003	12.561102
17	16.258632	15.562251	14.907649	14.291872	13.712198	13.166118
18	17.172768	16.398269	15.672561	14.992031	14.353364	13.753513
19	18.082356	17.226009	16.426168	15.678462	14.978891	14.323799
20	18.987419	18.045553	17.168639	16.351433	15.589162	14.877475
21	19.887979	18.856983	17.900137	17.011209	16.184549	15.415024
22	20.784059	19.660379	18.620824	17.658048	16.765413	15.936917
23	21.675681	20.455821	19.330861	18.292204	17.332110	16.443608
24	22.562866	21.243387	20.030405	18.913926	17.884986	16.935542
25	23.445638	22.023156	20.719611	19.523456	18.424376	17.413148
26	24.324018	22.795204	21.398632	20.121036	18.950611	17.876842
27	25.198028	23.559608	22.067617	20.706898	19.464011	18.327031
28	26.067689	24.316443	22.726717	21.281272	19.964889	18.764108
29	26.933024	25.065785	23.376076	21.844385	20.453550	19.188455
30	27.794054	25.807708	24.015838	22.396456	20.930293	19.600441
31	28.650800	26.542285	24.646146	22.937702	21.395407	20.000428
32	29.503284	27.269589	25.267139	23.468335	21.849178	20.388766
33	30.351526	27.989693	25.878954	23.988564	22.291881	20.765792
34	31.195548	28.702666	26.481728	24.498592	22.723786	21.131837
35	32.035371	29.408580	27.075595	24.998619	23.145157	21.487220
36	32.871016	30.107505	27.660684	25.488842	23.556251	21.832253
37	33.702504	30.799510	28.237127	25.969453	23.957318	22.167235
38	34.529854	31.484663	28.805052	26.440641	24.348603	22.492462
39	35.353089	32.163033	29.364583	26.902589	24.730344	22.808215
40	36.172228	32.834686	29.915845	27.355479	25.102775	23.114772
41	36.987291	33.499689	30.458961	27.799489	25.466122	23.412400
42	37.798300	34.158108	30.994050	28.234794	25.820607	23.701359
43	38.605274	34.810008	31.521232	28.661562	26.166446	23.981902
44	39.408232	35.455454	32.040622	29.079963	26.503849	24.254274
45	40.207196	36.094508	32.552337	29.490160	26.833024	24.518713
46	41.002185	36.727236	33.056490	29.892314	27.154170	24.775449
47	41.793219	37.353699	33.553192	30.286582	27.467483	25.024708
48	42.580318	37.973959	34.042554	30.673120	27.773154	25.266707
49	43.363500	38.588079	34.524683	31.052078	28.071369	25.501657
50	44.142786	39.196118	34.999688	31.423606	28.362312	25.729764

Table 4   Present Value of Ordinary Annuity of 1 (*continued*)

n \ i	3½%	4%	4½%	5%	5½%	6%
1	0.966184	0.961538	0.956938	0.952381	0.947867	0.943396
2	1.899694	1.886095	1.872668	1.859410	1.846320	1.833393
3	2.801637	2.775091	2.748964	2.723248	2.697933	2.673012
4	3.673079	3.629895	3.587526	3.545951	3.505150	3.465106
5	4.515052	4.451822	4.389977	4.329477	4.270284	4.212364
6	5.328553	5.242137	5.157872	5.075692	4.995530	4.917324
7	6.114544	6.002055	5.892701	5.786373	5.682967	5.582381
8	6.873956	6.732745	6.595886	6.463213	6.334566	6.209794
9	7.607687	7.435332	7.268791	7.107822	6.952195	6.801692
10	8.316605	8.110896	7.912718	7.721735	7.537626	7.360087
11	9.001551	8.760477	8.528917	8.306414	8.092536	7.886875
12	9.663334	9.385074	9.118581	8.863252	8.618518	8.383844
13	10.302738	9.985648	9.682852	9.393573	9.117079	8.852683
14	10.920520	10.563123	10.222825	9.898641	9.589648	9.294984
15	11.517411	11.118387	10.739546	10.379658	10.037581	9.712249
16	12.094117	11.652296	11.234015	10.837770	10.462162	10.105895
17	12.651321	12.165669	11.707191	11.274066	10.864609	10.477260
18	13.189682	12.659297	12.159992	11.689587	11.246074	10.827603
19	13.709837	13.133939	12.593294	12.085321	11.607654	11.158116
20	14.212403	13.590326	13.007936	12.462210	11.950382	11.469921
21	14.697974	14.029160	13.404724	12.821153	12.275244	11.764077
22	15.167125	14.451115	13.784425	13.163003	12.583170	12.041582
23	15.620410	14.856842	14.147775	13.488574	12.875042	12.303379
24	16.058368	15.246963	14.495478	13.798642	13.151699	12.550358
25	16.481515	15.622080	14.828209	14.093945	13.413933	12.783356
26	16.890352	15.982769	15.146611	14.375185	13.662495	13.003166
27	17.285365	16.329586	15.451303	14.643034	13.898100	13.210534
28	17.667019	16.663063	15.742874	14.898127	14.121422	13.406164
29	18.035767	16.983715	16.021889	15.141074	14.333101	13.590721
30	18.392045	17.292033	16.288889	15.372451	14.533745	13.764831
31	18.736276	17.588494	16.544391	15.592811	14.723929	13.929086
32	19.068865	17.873552	16.788891	15.802677	14.904198	14.084043
33	19.390208	18.147646	17.022862	16.002549	15.075069	14.230230
34	19.700684	18.411198	17.246758	16.192904	15.237033	14.368141
35	20.000661	18.664613	17.461012	16.374194	15.390552	14.498246
36	20.290494	18.908282	17.666041	16.546852	15.536068	14.620987
37	20.570525	19.142579	17.862240	16.711287	15.673999	14.736780
38	20.841087	19.367864	18.049990	16.867893	15.804738	14.846019
39	21.102500	19.584485	18.229656	17.017041	15.928662	14.949075
40	21.355072	19.792774	18.401584	17.159086	16.046125	15.046297
41	21.599104	19.993052	18.566109	17.294368	16.157464	15.138016
42	21.834883	20.185627	18.723550	17.423208	16.262999	15.224543
43	22.062689	20.370795	18.874210	17.545912	16.363032	15.306173
44	22.282791	20.548841	19.018383	17.662773	16.457851	15.383182
45	22.495450	20.720040	19.156347	17.774070	16.547726	15.455832
46	22.700918	20.884654	19.288371	17.880067	16.632915	15.524370
47	22.899438	21.042936	19.414709	17.981016	16.713664	15.589028
48	23.091244	21.195131	19.535607	18.077158	16.790203	15.650027
49	23.276565	21.341472	19.651298	18.168722	16.862751	15.707572
50	23.455618	21.482185	19.762008	18.255925	16.931518	15.761861

Table 4   Present Value of Ordinary Annuity of 1 (*continued*)

n \ i	7%	8%	9%	10%	12%	15%
1	0.934579	0.925926	0.917431	0.909091	0.892857	0.869565
2	1.808018	1.783265	1.759111	1.735537	1.690051	1.625709
3	2.624316	2.577097	2.531295	2.486852	2.401831	2.283225
4	3.387211	3.312127	3.239720	3.169865	3.037349	2.854978
5	4.100197	3.992710	3.889651	3.790787	3.604776	3.352155
6	4.766540	4.622880	4.485919	4.355261	4.111407	3.784483
7	5.389289	5.206370	5.032953	4.868419	4.563757	4.160420
8	5.971299	5.746639	5.534819	5.334926	4.967640	4.487322
9	6.515232	6.246888	5.995247	5.759024	5.328250	4.771584
10	7.023582	6.710081	6.417658	6.144567	5.650223	5.018769
11	7.498674	7.138964	6.805191	6.495061	5.937699	5.233712
12	7.942686	7.536078	7.160725	6.813692	6.194374	5.420619
13	8.357651	7.903776	7.486904	7.103356	6.423548	5.583147
14	8.745468	8.244237	7.786150	7.366687	6.628168	5.724476
15	9.107914	8.559479	8.060688	7.606080	6.810864	5.847370
16	9.446649	8.851369	8.312558	7.823709	6.973986	5.954235
17	9.763223	9.121638	8.543631	8.021553	7.119630	6.047161
18	10.059087	9.371887	8.755625	8.201412	7.249670	6.127966
19	10.335595	9.603599	8.950115	8.364920	7.365777	6.198231
20	10.594014	9.818147	9.128546	8.513564	7.469444	6.259331
21	10.835527	10.016803	9.292244	8.648694	7.562003	6.312462
22	11.061241	10.200744	9.442425	8.771540	7.644646	6.358663
23	11.272187	10.371059	9.580207	8.883218	7.718434	6.398837
24	11.469334	10.528758	9.706612	8.984744	7.784316	6.433771
25	11.653583	10.674776	9.822580	9.077040	7.843139	6.464149
26	11.825779	10.809978	9.928972	9.160945	7.895660	6.490564
27	11.986709	10.935165	10.026580	9.237223	7.942554	6.513534
28	12.137111	11.051078	10.116128	9.306567	7.984423	6.533508
29	12.277674	11.158406	10.198283	9.369606	8.021806	6.550877
30	12.409041	11.257783	10.273654	9.426914	8.055184	6.565980
31	12.531814	11.349799	10.342802	9.479013	8.084986	6.579113
32	12.646555	11.434999	10.406240	9.526376	8.111594	6.590533
33	12.753790	11.513888	10.464441	9.569432	8.135352	6.600463
34	12.854009	11.586934	10.517835	9.608575	8.156564	6.609099
35	12.947672	11.654568	10.566821	9.644159	8.175504	6.616607
36	13.035208	11.717193	10.611763	9.676508	8.192414	6.623137
37	13.117017	11.775179	10.652993	9.705917	8.207513	6.628815
38	13.193473	11.828869	10.690820	9.732651	8.220993	6.633752
39	13.264928	11.878582	10.725523	9.756956	8.233030	6.638045
40	13.331709	11.924613	10.757360	9.779051	8.243777	6.641778
41	13.394120	11.967235	10.786569	9.799137	8.253372	6.645025
42	13.452449	12.006699	10.813366	9.817397	8.261939	6.647848
43	13.506962	12.043240	10.837950	9.833998	8.269589	6.650302
44	13.557908	12.077074	10.860505	9.849089	8.276418	6.652437
45	13.605522	12.108402	10.881197	9.862808	8.282516	6.654293
46	13.650020	12.137409	10.900181	9.875280	8.287961	6.655907
47	13.691608	12.164267	10.917597	9.886618	8.292822	6.657310
48	13.730474	12.189136	10.933575	9.896926	8.297163	6.658531
49	13.766799	12.212163	10.948234	9.906296	8.301038	6.659592
50	13.800746	12.233485	10.961683	9.914814	8.304498	6.660515

REVIEW QUESTIONS

1 Briefly explain the difference between simple interest and compound interest.

2 **a** Explain the meaning of $(1 + i)^n$ and define the symbols i and n.
  b Give the formula for each of the following:
   (1) Present value of 1
   (2) Amount of an ordinary annuity of 1
   (3) Present value of an ordinary annuity of 1

3 Define each of the following:
  a *Present value of an annuity due*
  b *Present value of a deferred annuity*
  c *Amount of an annuity due*
  d *Amount of a deferred annuity*

4 Write the formula, including the numerical value for i and n, for computing the compound amount of $500 invested for five years (do not compute the solution):
  a At 10% compounded semiannually
  b At 8% compounded quarterly
  c At 12% compounded monthly
  d At 6% compounded annually

5 The following values are taken from compound interest tables for the same number of periods n and at the same rate of interest i:
  a 13.180795
  b 1.790848
  c 0.558395
  d 7.360087
What does each of the four values represent? Explain.

6 Indicate the compound interest table that would be used in solving each of the following problems:
  a Sheila Jones wants to know how much she would have in her savings account at the end of five years if she deposits a single amount and leaves it to accumulate interest.
  b Eva Smith owes Olson $5,000 due in two years at no interest. Smith wants to know how much she should pay Olson now if they agree on a current fair rate of interest.
  c Charles Harrison owes a debt to Andersen that is payable in semiannual installments of $2,000 each. The first installment is due today. Harrison wants to know the amount he should pay to Andersen today to eliminate his debt.
  d Yo Takagaki wants to know what equal annual deposits he should make at the beginning of each of 10 years so that he will have $20,000 to acquire a cabin cruiser at the end of the tenth year. Interest at a fixed rate will be compounded annually on the cumulative amount in Takagaki's "cruiser fund."

7 Assume that you need the amount of 1 for 80 periods at 2% per period. You do not have access to a computer, and the compound interest table that you have available includes amounts through only 50 periods. Explain how you would compute $(1 + 0.02)^{80}$.

8   What are the four prerequisites of an annuity situation?

EXERCISES

Ex. 5-1   Select the best answer for each of the following multiple-choice questions:

1   Which of the following is the present value of an *ordinary annuity* of 10 rents of 1 at an interest rate of 6% per period?
a 1.790848   **b** 0.558395   **c** 13.180795   **d** 7.360087   **e** Some other amount

2   Which of the following is used to compute the present value of an *ordinary annuity* of 20 rents of 1 at 16% compounded quarterly?
a $p_{\overline{5}|16\%}$ **b** $P_{\overline{5}|16\%}$ **c** $p_{\overline{20}|4\%}$ **d** $P_{\overline{20}|4\%}$ **e** Some other formula

3   Present values of an *ordinary annuity* of 1 at 15% a year compounded annually are as follows: $n = 5$, 3.352155; $n = 6$, 3.784483; $n = 7$, 4.160420. The present value of an *annuity due* of 6 rents of 1 at 15% a year compounded annually is:
a 3.784483   **b** 4.352155   **c** 3.160420   **d** Some other amount

4   The present value of an *ordinary annuity* is used in the accounting valuations of all the following, except:
a Proceeds of a bond issue
b Present value of a noninterest-bearing promissory note due in five years
c Cost of a plant asset acquired through a 10-year capital lease; lease payments are due monthly starting at the inception of the lease
d Cost of a plant asset acquired on the installment plan with the first payment due one month after the date of acquisition

5   On January 10, Year 1, Irving Porton signed a contract to operate a fast-food restaurant for an initial franchise fee of $40,000. Of this amount, $15,000 was paid to Odom, Inc., when the contract was signed, and the balance is payable in five annual payments of $5,000 each beginning January 10, Year 2. The contract provides that the down payment is not refundable, and no future services are required of Odom, Inc. Porton's credit rating indicates that he is able to borrow money at 12% for a loan of this type. Information on present and future values (rounded) follows:

> *Present value of 1 at 12% for 5 periods* *0.567*
> *Future amount of 1 at 12% for 5 periods* *1.762*
> *Present value of an ordinary annuity of 5 rents of 1 at 12% a year* *3.605*

Porton should record the acquisition cost of the franchise on January 10, Year 1, at:
a $29,175   **b** $33,025   **c** $40,000   **d** $44,050   **e** Some other amount

6   For which of the following transactions would the use of the present value of an *annuity due* concept be appropriate in the computation of the present value of the asset obtained or liability incurred on the date of the transaction?
a A capital lease is entered into with the initial lease payment due one month subsequent to the signing of the lease contract
b A capital lease is entered into with the initial lease payment due on the date the lease contract was signed
c Ten-year, 8% bonds are issued on January 2 with interest payable semiannually on July 2 and January 2, yielding 7%

d Ten-year, 8% bonds are issued on January 2 with interest payable semiannually on July 2 and January 2, yielding 9%

Ex. 5-2 Presented below are the present values of 1 discounted at 8% for one through five periods. Each of the values is based on 8% interest compounded annually from day of deposit to day of withdrawal.

Periods	Present value of 1 discounted at 8% per period
1	0.926
2	0.857
3	0.794
4	0.735
5	0.681

Choose the best answer for each of the following four questions:

1 What amount should you deposit in a savings account today in order to have $5,000 three years from today?
a $5,000 ÷ 0.794
b $5,000 × 0.926 × 3
c ($5,000 × 0.926) + ($5,000 × 0.857) + ($5,000 × 0.794)
d $5,000 × 0.794

2 What amount should you have in your savings account today before withdrawal if you need $5,000 each year for four years, with the first withdrawal to be made today and each subsequent withdrawal at one-year intervals? (You will have a zero balance in your savings account after the fourth withdrawal.)
a $5,000 + ($5,000 × 0.926) + ($5,000 × 0.857) + ($5,000 × 0.794)
b ($5,000 ÷ 0.735) × 4
c ($5,000 × 0.926) + ($5,000 × 0.857) + ($5,000 × 0.794) + ($5,000 × 0.735)
d ($5,000 ÷ 0.926) × 4

3 If you deposit $8,000 in a savings account today, what amount will you have available two years from today?
a $8,000 × 0.857
b $8,000 × 0.857 × 2
c $8,000 ÷ 0.857
d ($8,000 ÷ 0.926) × 2

4 What is the present value today of $2,000 you will receive six years from today?
a $2,000 × 0.926 × 6
b $2,000 × 0.794 × 2
c $2,000 × 0.681 × 0.926
d Amount cannot be determined from the information given

Ex. 5-3 Heidi Mealy plans to take a vacation starting July 4, Year 5, shortly after she graduates from college. Mealy estimates that the cost of her vacation will be $6,000 and wants to accumulate that amount in a fund that pays quarterly interest of 2% by making eight quarterly deposits starting on October 1, Year 3, and ending on July 1, Year 5. The last four deposits will be twice as large as the first four deposits.

Compute the amount of each of the first four deposits and the amount of each of the last four deposits, and prepare a fund accumulation table similar to the one illustrated on page 249. Use the Appendix at the end of this chapter and round computations to the nearest dollar.

Ex. 5-4 On June 30, Year 1, Levine Corporation purchased merchandise at an auction for $40,000. The current fair value of the merchandise, according to Levine's personnel, was at least $48,000. Levine paid $10,000 cash and signed a 16% one-year promissory note for $30,000. Interest of $1,200 is payable on the note quarterly, starting on September 30, Year 1. You conclude that the current fair rate of interest on the note is 12% payable quarterly.

Record the purchase of the merchandise in the accounting records of Levine Corporation, assuming that the periodic inventory system is used. Use the Appendix at the end of this chapter and round computations to the nearest dollar.

Ex. 5-5 From the compound interest tables in the Appendix at the end of this chapter, compute the following values at 4%:
a Amount of 1 for 10 periods
b Present value of 1 for 20 periods
c Amount of ordinary annuity of 15 rents of 1
d Amount of annuity due of 15 rents of 1
e Amount of ordinary annuity of 15 rents of 1, deferred for 10 periods
f Present value of ordinary annuity of 25 rents of 1
g Present value of annuity due of 25 rents of 1
h Present value of ordinary annuity of 25 rents of 1, deferred for 5 periods

Ex. 5-6 Celestial Company acquired $10,000 face amount of noncallable 10% bonds that have a remaining term of 12 years. The bonds pay interest every six months. The present value of 1 at 4% for 24 periods is 0.390121, and the present value of 1 at 5% for 24 periods is 0.310068. The present value of an ordinary annuity of 1 at 4% for 24 periods is 15.246963, and the present value of an ordinary annuity of 1 at 5% for 24 periods is 13.798642.

Compute the amount paid for the bonds if the market rate of interest for bonds of comparable quality is 8% compounded semiannually. Round computations to the nearest dollar.

Ex. 5-7 On December 31, Year 1, Long Beach Development Company issued $10 million of 8% bonds payable. Interest is payable on December 31 of each year. The bonds mature on December 31, Year 11. The bonds were issued to yield an annual rate of 10%. The present value of an ordinary annuity of 10 rents of 1 at 10% is 6.144567; the present value of 1 for 10 periods at 10% is 0.385543.

Compute the amount received from issuance of the bonds. Round computations to the nearest dollar.

Ex. 5-8 Fred Dryer sold a parcel of land for $44,000. He received $12,000 cash on the date of sale and 16 promissory notes of equal amount due serially, one each six months starting six months from the date of sale. It was agreed that the notes will include interest in their face amount at 12% compounded semiannually.

Using the Appendix at the end of this chapter, compute (to the nearest dollar) the face amount of each note.

Ex. 5-9 Sonar Products, Inc., wants to accumulate a fund of $80,000 at the end of Year 10 to retire a debt. The fund will be accumulated by making 20 equal semiannual deposits starting on June 30, Year 1.

If the fund will earn interest at 6% compounded semiannually, compute the amount of each deposit. Use the Appendix at the end of this chapter and round computations to the nearest dollar.

Ex. 5-10 Ken Krueger has a 6% loan with an unpaid balance of $17,169. The principal and interest are payable quarterly at the rate of $1,000. Krueger has 20 more payments to make, having just made the payment due December 31, Year 5. The lender approaches Krueger and offers to reduce the principal of the debt from $17,169 to $16,500 if Krueger would take out a new loan for $16,500 at 10% (the current market rate), payable quarterly for the next five years.

Should Krueger refinance the loan? Use the Appendix at the end of this chapter and present computations (to the nearest dollar) in support of your answer. Disregard income tax considerations.

Ex. 5-11 Denise Stevens deposited $1,000 each quarter starting on June 30, Year 1, in a savings account that earned interest at 8% compounded quarterly. She has already made seven deposits, the last one on December 31, Year 2.

Using the tables in the Appendix at the end of this chapter, compute the amount (to the nearest dollar) Stevens has on deposit on each of the following dates (assuming that she made no withdrawals from the savings account):
a December 31, Year 2, including the deposit made on that date
b March 31, Year 3, including the deposit made on that date
c June 30, Year 5, assuming that Stevens made the last deposit on March 31, Year 5

Ex. 5-12 On January 1, Year 1, Alameda Company leased equipment from Pico Corporation. This lease was noncancelable and was in substance an installment purchase (a capital lease). The initial term of the lease was 12 years, with title passing to Alameda at the end of the twelfth year at no additional cost. Annual rent to be paid by Alameda was $10,000 at the beginning of each year. The first rent payment was made on January 1, Year 1. The equipment had an estimated economic life of 20 years, with no residual value. The interest rate generally paid by Alameda on similar financing arrangements was 8%. The present value of an *annuity due* of 12 rents of 1 at 8% is 8.138964.
a Compute the cost of the equipment to Alameda Company to the nearest dollar.
b Compute interest expense for Alameda Company for each of the first three years.

CASES

Case 5-1 The following letter was mailed by Hustler Finance Company to a resident of a large city:

Dear Ms. Creditworthy:

You are one of a select group of creditworthy individuals in your community who qualify for a unique opportunity. Without additional credit references or time-consuming technicalities, you are guaranteed a "Prestige Loan" of $10,000 now.

Because you are financially responsible, and you've always handled your financial obligations with efficiency, your loan *already has been approved.* The enclosed certificate entitles you to a loan of $10,000 any time you'd like to have it. So please call or come to our office at your earliest convenience.

Sincerely,

Homer Hustler

The certificate referred to in the letter indicated that the repayment of the loan was to be made in 24 equal monthly payments of $534 each.

Instructions

a What is the total amount a borrower would have to pay to Hustler Finance Company over the two-year period of this installment loan?

b Compute the approximate *annual rate* of interest (as a percentage) compounded monthly, using Table 4 in the Appendix at the end of this chapter.

c Is the rate of interest computed in *b* attractive for "creditworthy individuals" if the current bank prime interest rate is 15%? Why?

Case 5-2 While on an audit with a CPA firm at the end of Year 5, Michael Synn observed the following deferred compensation contract signed by his client:

"In lieu of any salary and bonus for Year 5, Mark Naughton will receive $25,000 at the end of Year 6 and each year thereafter through December 31, Year 11. Naughton will not be required to perform any services after December 31, Year 5. Six promissory notes in the amount of $25,000 each are hereby executed in evidence of this obligation."

The client of the CPA firm recorded this contract as follows:

Salaries Expense ($25,000 × 6)	150,000	
Notes Payable		150,000

To record salary and bonuses payable to Mark Naughton.

A staff assistant working under Synn's supervision stated: "This journal entry is proper; the expense is applicable to Year 5, and the notes meet all the traditional tests of a liability. The salary and bonus payments to Naughton had been over $130,000 a year for several years; therefore, the amount of $150,000 debited to Salaries Expense in Year 5 is reasonable."

Synn pointed out that there is no mention of interest in the contract with Naughton and that the client had to pay 8% interest on most of its bank loans in the last quarter of Year 5. He agreed that the notes were liabilities, but added that an auditor must ascertain not only that a liability exists but also that the amount of the liability on the balance sheet date is fairly stated.

Instructions

Use the appropriate table in the Appendix at the end of this chapter to reach your conclusions.

a Evaluate the positions taken by the staff assistant and by Michael Synn.

b What correcting entry, if any, would you recommend on December 31, Year 5, assuming that a Discount on Notes Payable ledger account is used?

c What journal entry should be made on December 31, Year 6, to record the first payment to Mark Naughton?

Case 5-3 Vincent Lee's godfather, Linton Chu, decided to make him a gift of $27,000. Chu gave Lee the option to receive the cash in any one of the following three patterns:

(1) One thousand dollars at the end of each of the first three years, starting one year from now; $3,000 at the end of each of the next three years; and $5,000 at the end of each of the last three years. Chu suggests that this arrangement might be preferable because Lee is young and will need more money as he grows older, not only because he will learn to spend more but also because inflation will increase his cost of living.

(2) Three thousand dollars at the end of each of the next nine years, starting one year from now. Chu pointed out that this option offers Lee the advantage of a steady cash flow.

(3) Five thousand dollars at the end of each of the first three years, starting one year from now; $3,000 at the end of each of the next three years; and $1,000 at the end of each of the last three years. Chu points out that he would not recommend this option to Lee because it would give him an excess of cash flow during the first three years that would be invested at a rate of interest lower than he (Chu) could earn. Lee had told Chu that he would invest all this money in San Francisco at 6% compounded annually; Chu had responded that he invests his money at 10% compounded annually in a Hong Kong bank.

After discussing these alternatives with several philosophy students at Golden Shark University, Lee said to Chu: "All three options are the same; obviously I shall receive an average of $3,000 at the end of each of the nine years, so it makes no difference. I'll take the first option." Chu responded, "I am happy to know that you are in school; there is much to learn."

Instructions

a Did Vincent Lee make the right decision? Why?

b What is the present value of each option at 6% interest compounded annually, given the following present value of 1 at 6%?

Periods	Present value of 1	Present value of ordinary annuity of 1
3	0.8396	2.6730
6	0.7050	4.9173
9	0.5919	6.8017

c Briefly evaluate the observations made by Linton Chu relative to each of the three options he presented to Vincent Lee.

Case 5-4   Caledonia Corporation borrowed $500,000, payable in 12 equal annual installments of $92,240. The effective interest rate is 15% a year and the total interest on the loan is $606,880 [($92,240 × 12) − $500,000 = $606,880]. The terms of the loan contract state that interest expense is to be computed in accordance with the "Rule of 78." Under the Rule of 78, the interest expense for each year is determined by multiplying the total interest payable on the loan by a fraction, the numerator of which is the number of periods remaining on the debt and the denominator of which is the sum of the periods' digits for the term of the loan. Thus, because the sum of the digits 1 through 12 is 78, Caledonia recorded interest expense of $93,366 ($606,880 × 12/78 = $93,366) in the first year of the loan.

Instructions

a Prepare a loan amortization table similar to the one on page 257 under the Rule of 78 approach of recording interest expense. Round computations to the nearest dollar.

b Prepare a loan amortization table under the effective interest method; that is, interest expense is computed at 15% a year on the balance of the loan outstanding. Round computations to the nearest dollar.

c Evaluate the appropriateness of the results obtained under the two approaches.

PROBLEMS

5-1   On July 1, Year 1, Sunset Company signed a three-year lease contract for a warehouse. The contract provided that Sunset has the option of either paying annual rent of $20,000 on July 1, beginning in Year 1, or paying total rent in advance at a 12% discount, compounded annually.

Instructions

(Use the Appendix at the end of this chapter and round computations to the nearest dollar.)

a What single amount would Sunset Company have to pay on July 1, Year 1, for the annual lease rent?

b Assume the same facts as above, except that the interest is compounded monthly. Compute the single amount Sunset Company would have to pay on July 1, Year 1.

c Explain the difference in the results obtained in **a** and **b.**

5-2   Fernando Slider has been a star baseball player for the Indianapolis Boomers for many years. Slider decided to become a free agent and offered his services to the highest bidder for four more years, before retiring to practice law in Miami. After many weeks of negotiations, Slider and his agent accepted the following offer from the Ohio White Shoes:

(1) An annual salary of $600,000 for four years, payable in monthly installments of $50,000, starting one month from today.

(2) A deferred compensation of $480,000, payable in monthly installments of $10,000 for four years, for services rendered during the four years of playing

baseball for the Ohio White Shoes. These payments will commence one month after the last payment of $50,000 is made to Slider.

(3) A "signing bonus" of $120,000 cash, payable immediately.

Headlines in sport pages around the nation stated that Slider had signed a "$3 million contract" with the Ohio White Shoes.

Instructions

Assuming that interest at the rate of 1½% a month is charged on personal loans to professional athletes, compute the present value today of the "$3 million contract" signed by Fernando Slider with the Ohio White Shoes. Use the Appendix at the end of this chapter and round computations to the nearest dollar.

5-3 The management of Sensormatic Company is evaluating a proposal to acquire a new drill press as a replacement for a less efficient old press that would be sold. The total cost of the new press is $180,000. If the new press is acquired, costs of $8,000 would be incurred in removing the old press. The old press has a carrying amount of $100,000 and a remaining economic life of ten years. Because of new technical improvements that have made the old press uneconomical, it has a current resale value of only $50,000.

Additional Information

(1) Management of Sensormatic provided you with the following comparison of annual production and operating costs:

	Old press	New press
Annual production (units)...............................	400,000	500,000
Annual operating costs:		
Labor	$ 30,000	$ 25,000
Depreciation (10% of asset carrying amount)............	10,000	18,000
Other costs	50,000	20,000
Total annual operating costs	$ 90,000	$ 63,000

(2) Management believes that if the old drill press is not replaced now, it would have to wait seven years before replacement would be economically justifiable.

(3) Both the old and the new drill press are expected to have a negligible residual value at the end of 10 years.

(4) If the new drill press is acquired, the management of Sensormatic will require a 15% return on the investment before income taxes.

(5) The present value of an ordinary annuity of 10 rents of 1 at 15% is 5.018769.

Instructions

a In order to assist the management of Sensormatic in reaching a decision on the proposal, prepare a working paper showing the computation of the following (disregard any effects of net incremental cash flow from increased sales of units produced by the new drill press):

(1) Net initial cash investment, before income taxes.

(2) Net present value of the net initial cash investment, before income taxes. Assume that the annual cash savings before income taxes are realized at the end of each year. Round computations to the nearest dollar.

b Would you recommend the acquisition of the new drill press? Explain.

5-4 This problem consists of four independent parts, each related to the business activities of Eleanor Corporation. Compute the answer (to the nearest dollar) for each part by using the tables in the Appendix at the end of this chapter.

(1) Eleanor plans to accumulate $500,000 on December 31, Year 10, to retire preferred stock. Eleanor deposited $125,000 in a fund on January 1, Year 1, that will earn interest at 10% compounded quarterly, and wants to know what additional amount it has to deposit in the fund at the end of each quarter for 10 years (starting on March 31, Year 1) to have $500,000 available at the end of Year 10. The periodic deposits also will earn interest at 10% compounded quarterly.

(2) Eleanor plans to make five equal annual deposits in a fund beginning June 1, Year 1, in order to be able to withdraw $50,000 at six annual intervals beginning June 1, Year 6. The amount on deposit will earn interest at 12% annually until the fund is exhausted. Compute the equal deposits that should be made to the fund.

(3) On June 30, Year 1, Eleanor acquired a machine for $80,000. The down payment was $10,000, and the balance is to be paid in 48 equal monthly payments, including interest at 18% compounded monthly. What is the amount of the monthly payment if the first payment is due one month from the date of acquisition?

(4) On April 1, Year 2, Eleanor made a deposit of $100,000 in a fund and left the fund undisturbed for four years to earn compound interest at a rate that did not change during the four-year period. At the end of four years, the fund had a balance of $132,088.60. If interest was compounded quarterly, what was the annual rate of interest earned on the deposit?

5-5 This problem consists of four separate parts, each relating to the business activities of Situs Company. Compute the answer (to the nearest dollar) for each part by using the tables in the Appendix at the end of this chapter.

(1) On July 1, Year 1, Situs issued $50 million of 20-year, 8% bonds, paying interest semiannually on January 1 and July 1. The bonds were issued to yield 9% compounded semiannually. What were the proceeds from this bond issue?

(2) On April 1, Year 1, Situs acquired a plant asset by paying $8,000 down and $8,000 at the beginning of each of the next 19 calendar quarters. What was the cost of the plant asset for financial accounting, assuming that the interest rate was 16% compounded quarterly?

(3) Situs has a promissory note receivable in the amount of $300,000 issued by Kore Corporation. The note calls for payment of $100,000 of principal at the end of each year starting in three years, plus interest at the rate of 12% a year on the unpaid balance of the note. Only interest is due at the end of the first two

years. Payments of $124,000 and $112,000 are due at the end of Year 4 and Year 5, respectively. Situs immediately discounted this note with a finance company at 10% interest compounded annually. How much did Situs receive from the finance company for the note?

(4) Situs wishes to accumulate a $10 million fund with Ida Trust Company for the retirement of bonds in 10 years. Situs plans to make 20 equal deposits of $243,929.25 starting in six months, to accumulate the $10 million fund. What semiannual interest rate will be earned by Situs on the balance of the fund?

5-6 As an accountant for Santa Rosa, Inc., you find the following memorandum on your desk from Howard Hinshaw, controller of Santa Rosa:

(1) On December 31, Year 1, we shall sign a noninterest-bearing note for $400,000 due in five years. The lender wants to earn 10% compounded annually on the amount advanced to us. Please compute the proceeds on this borrowing transaction and prepare a table showing our interest expense and net liability for each of the five years of the loan.

(2) Also on December 31, Year 1, the installment sale of the land in Eureka will be completed. The purchaser will pay us $100,000 a year for ten years starting a year from now. Our contract includes interest at 10% a year in the face amount of the notes. The land is carried in our accounting records at $550,000. I want you to prepare a journal entry to record the sale of the land and to prepare a table that will show interest revenue for each year and the carrying amount of the notes receivable at the end of each year. We shall record the note receivable at face amount.

Instructions

Prepare a memo to the controller of Santa Rosa, Inc., that includes the information he asked you to assemble. Use the Appendix at the end of this chapter and round all computations to the nearest dollar.

5-7 Midland Oil Company has a debt for $300,000 maturing on June 30, Year 10. Midland Oil plans to deposit $25,000 in a debt retirement fund on June 30 each year for eight years, starting on June 30, Year 3. In addition, Midland Oil plans to deposit a single amount on June 30, Year 2, that, together with the eight annual deposits in the debt retirement fund, will be sufficient to repay the debt on June 30, Year 10. The amount in the debt retirement fund earns interest at 7% compounded annually.

Midland Oil also has made annual deposits of $40,000 in a "contingency fund" at the end of each of the last four years. The balance in the "contingency fund" after the fourth deposit on December 31, Year 4, was $180,244. Interest on the "contingency fund" is compounded annually.

Instructions

(Use the Appendix at the end of this chapter and round computations to the nearest dollar.)

    a Compute the single amount that must be deposited on June 30, Year 2, if $300,000 is to be available on June 30, Year 10, in the debt retirement fund.

    b What was the annual rate of interest earned on the ''contingency fund'' through December 31, Year 4?

    c Compute the amount that may be withdrawn from the ''contingency fund'' at the end of each year for ten years, starting on December 31, Year 5, assuming that the amount on deposit in the ''contingency fund'' earns interest at 10% annually from January 1, Year 5, through December 31, Year 14.

5-8   Lynne Kawagoe was recently hired as an accountant by Oahu Corporation, and the first assignment was given to her as follows:

> ''To get your feet wet and to give you some practice with the calculator, I want you to prepare tables summarizing our interest expense or revenue and the liability or asset balance for these two transactions:
>
> (1) Today we acquired a machine for $54,173. We paid $10,000 down and agreed to make six equal semiannual payments, including interest at 12% compounded semiannually, starting six months from now.
>
> (2) We will need $200,000 five years from now to reline our furnaces. We want to deposit five equal amounts annually in a fund starting one year from now so that we will have the money we need in five years. We have arranged to invest the money with Punahoe Trust Company at 8% compounded annually.''

Instructions

a Compute (1) the amount of the semiannual payments on the contract for the acquisition of the machine, and (2) the amount of the annual deposits in the furnace relining fund. Use the Appendix at the end of this chapter and round computations to the nearest dollar.

b Prepare (1) a loan amortization table for the installment debt incurred in the acquisition of the machine, and (2) a fund accumulation table for the deposits to the furnace relining fund.

5-9   As a summer intern with Dugan and Ward, Certified Public Accountants, you are presented with the following situations:

(1) Client A inquired whether a proposed transaction made economic sense. The client sold a parcel of land for $51,000 and was given the choice of receiving $51,000 cash or $17,000 per year for four years starting one year from now. The client does not need cash but would like to earn 12% before income taxes annually on idle cash resources; consequently, the client wants to know what interest rate (to the nearest tenth) would be earned if the installment payment option is taken.

(2) Client B wants to know how much to pay for $100,000 face amount of 8% bonds that mature in five years if interest is payable semiannually and if 10% compounded semiannually is a fair return on this type of investment.

(3) Client C is negotiating to acquire a going concern and is uncertain whether the

asking price for goodwill (present value of future superior earnings) is reasonable. The seller wants $60,000 for goodwill, but the client does not want to pay more than the present value of projected superior earnings for the next three years discounted at 15% annually. Superior earnings (to be realized at the end of each year) were estimated as follows:

At end of first year	$40,000
At end of second year...	30,000
At end of third year	10,000

(4) On June 1, Year 1, Client D plans to make the first of four equal annual deposits in a fund that will earn 9% and will amount to $180,000 immediately after the last deposit on June 1, Year 4. The client wants to know the amount of each deposit and wants proof that $180,000 would be available on June 1, Year 4.

Instructions

Prepare appropriate computations and a working paper that will give each of the four clients the information requested. Use the Appendix at the end of this chapter and round all computations to the nearest dollar.

5-10   In the course of your December 31, Year 4, audit engagement for Dibble Company, the following situations required you to apply compound interest principles:

(1) A noninterest-bearing note receivable in the face amount of $150,000 and maturing in three years was received on December 31, Year 4, in partial payment of an account receivable. The accountant for Dibble credited the customer's account for $150,000, despite a written agreement that the customer was to receive credit for the "present value of the note discounted at 12% for three years, interest compounded semiannually."

(2) Dibble agreed to pay $20,000 a year for five years to a retiring executive, starting on December 31, Year 7. The liability *was not recorded* in the accounting records. The payments were in lieu of a year-end bonus that would have been taxed at a combined federal and state income tax rate of over 60%. Dibble regularly borrows money at a 9% annual rate of interest.

(3) Dibble wants to accumulate a fund of $125,000 in six years (December 31, Year 10) to retire a long-term note. On December 31, Year 1, the board of directors had passed a resolution instructing the treasurer to make ten equal annual deposits in a fund earning interest at 8% compounded annually. Because no one knew how to compute the equal deposits, the treasurer decided to deposit $10,000 at the end of each year. The fourth deposit was made on December 31, Year 4. What equal annual deposits should be made during the next six years, starting a year from now, if exactly $125,000 is to be accumulated on December 31, Year 10? Prepare a fund accumulation table to confirm that $125,000 will be available on December 31, Year 10.

(4) On December 31, Year 4, Dibble acquired a barge for $500,000. The contract calls for 20 payments of $32,629 every three months starting immediately. You have been asked by the president of Dibble to compute the approximate rate of interest charged on this contract every three months.

Instructions

Prepare journal entries for Dibble Company on December 31, Year 4, with supporting computations, to correct the accounting records for situations (1) and (2) above, and compute the answers for situations (3) and (4). Use the Appendix at the end of this chapter and round computations to the nearest dollar. Record notes receivable and notes payable at face amount.

5-11   This problem consists of three independent parts relating to the business activities of West Company.

(1) West invested $93,420 with Guardian Insurance Company on January 1, Year 1. The amount on deposit earned interest at 10% a year. West plans to withdraw the amount on deposit in three equal annual installments starting December 31, Year 4.

(2) West plans to accumulate a fund of $58,666 at Providence Bank at the end of five years by making five equal annual deposits starting one year from now. The fund will earn interest at 8% compounded annually.

(3) On January 1, Year 1, West invested $270,358 at 12% compounded annually with Executive Annuity Corporation. The amount invested and accrued interest are to be withdrawn in five equal installments starting on December 31, Year 1.

Instructions

(Use the Appendix at the end of this chapter and round computations to the nearest dollar.)

a Compute the three equal amounts that West Company will receive from Guardian Insurance Company, and prepare a table that shows that the entire amount on deposit will have been withdrawn by December 31, Year 6.

b Compute the annual deposits that West Company should make with Providence Bank and prepare a fund accumulation table for the five-year period.

c Compute the amounts West Company may withdraw each year from Executive Annuity Corporation, and prepare a table that shows that the amount invested will be exhausted by December 31, Year 5.

5-12   Late in Year 1, Vronsky Corporation was negotiating to acquire machinery. An analysis of the proposed use of the machinery indicates that it will result in the following cost savings over its economic life of 10 years and residual value at the end of Year 11:

Estimated annual cost savings after income taxes (assume that the savings will be realized at the end of each year):

Year 2 through Year 6	$60,000
Year 7 through Year 10	50,000
Year 11	25,000

Estimated residual value of machinery:

End of Year 11..	$10,000

Instructions

a Compute the amount that Vronsky Corporation should pay for the machinery, assuming that Vronsky requires a minimum of 12% annual rate of return on investments in plant assets. Use the Appendix at the end of this chapter and round computations to the nearest dollar.

b Assume that Vronsky Corporation acquired the machinery on December 31, Year 1, for the amount computed in **a,** and that it paid $100,000 cash as a down payment. The balance was payable in four equal annual installments (including interest at 10% a year) starting on December 31, Year 2. Prepare a journal entry for Vronsky to record the acquisition of the machinery.

c Compute the amount of each of the four annual payments on the loan. Use the Appendix at the end of this chapter and round computations to the nearest dollar.

d Prepare a loan amortization table similar to the one illustrated on page 257, and a journal entry to record the first payment on the loan on December 31, Year 2.

Working Capital

2

The motive power of a business enterprise is provided by its working capital components—cash, short-term investments, receivables, inventories, and current liabilities. Measurement of these components for balance sheet presentation also involves the recognition of revenue and expenses in the process of measuring periodic net income. Much of the criticism of financial statements in recent years has been directed at the accounting for doubtful accounts, inventories, profits and losses on construction-type contracts, and estimated liabilities such as product warranties.

Loss contingencies are recognized to present the financial position and results of operations of business enterprises in accordance with generally accepted accounting principles; gain contingencies generally are recorded in the accounting period in which realization takes place.

Cash and Short-Term Investments

6

CASH

Cash is a medium of exchange that a bank will accept for deposit and immediate credit to the depositor's account. Cash includes currency and coin, personal checks, bank drafts, money orders, credit card sales drafts, and cashiers' checks, as well as money on deposit with banks. Items sometimes confused with cash include postage stamps, postdated checks, and IOUs. Postage should be classified as a short-term prepayment; postdated checks and IOUs should be classified as receivables.

Deposits with a trustee, for example, a bond sinking fund that is not under the control of management of a business enterprise, should not be included in cash. As another example, many airline companies have millions of dollars in cash deposits with manufacturers for the acquisition of flight equipment. Such deposits do not qualify as current assets because they are not available for payment of current liabilities.

Certificates of deposit generally are classified as short-term investments rather than as cash because they are not available for immediate withdrawal. Strictly speaking, savings deposits also may not be withdrawn without prior notice to the bank, but banks seldom enforce this requirement. Consequently, savings deposits usually are viewed as cash. Petty cash funds and change funds are minor elements of cash under the control of management, even though these funds generally are intended to be used for specific purposes. The limitations placed on the use of these funds do not remove them from the category of cash but simply aid in the control of cash on hand.

In summary, the criteria generally used to define *cash* are that the item be a medium of exchange, be available immediately for the payment of current debts, and be free from any contractual restriction that would prevent management of the business enterprise from using the item to pay its creditors.

Management of Cash

The management of cash is of major importance in any business enterprise because cash is a means of acquiring goods and services. In addition, careful scrutiny of cash transactions is required because cash may be readily misappropriated.

The management of cash generally is centered around forecasting and internal controls. The responsibilities of management with respect to cash are: (1) to assure that there is sufficient cash to carry on the operations, (2) to invest any idle cash, and (3) to prevent loss of cash due to theft or misappropriation. Cash forecasting is necessary for the proper planning of future operations and to assure that cash is available when needed but that cash on hand is not excessive. Internal controls are necessary to assure that the cash is used for proper business purposes and not wasted, misused, or stolen. Management is responsible for controlling and protecting all assets of a business enterprise. However, special problems exist in controlling cash because of its highly liquid nature.

Internal Controls

The purpose of a *system of internal controls* is to assure that assets that belong to the business enterprise are received when tendered, are protected while in the custody of the enterprise, and are used only for authorized business purposes. Such a system consists of *administrative control* and *accounting control,* which are defined below.[1]

> *Administrative control* includes, but is not limited to, the plan of organization and the procedures and records that are concerned with the decision processes leading to management's authorization of transactions. Such authorization is a management function directly associated with the responsibility for achieving the objectives of the organization and is the starting point for establishing accounting control of transactions.
>
> *Accounting control* comprises the plan of organization and the procedures and records that are concerned with the safeguarding of assets and the reliability of financial records and consequently are designed to provide reasonable assurance that:
>
> **a** Transactions are executed in accordance with management's general or specific authorization.
>
> **b** Transactions are recorded as necessary (1) to permit preparation of financial statements in conformity with generally accepted accounting principles or any other criteria applicable to such statements, and (2) to maintain accountability for assets.
>
> **c** Access to assets is permitted only in accordance with management's authorization.
>
> **d** The recorded accountability for assets is compared with the existing assets at reasonable intervals and appropriate action is taken with respect to any differences.

---

[1]*Statement on Auditing Standards No. 1,* "Codification of Auditing Standards and Procedures," AICPA (New York: 1973), p. 20.

A system of internal controls is not designed primarily to detect errors but rather to reduce the opportunity for errors or dishonesty to occur. In an effective system of internal controls, no one person should carry out all phases of a business transaction from beginning to end. For example, if one person were permitted to order merchandise, receive it, write a check in payment, and record the transaction in the accounting records, there would be no protection against either fraud or errors. In large business enterprises, separate and independent departments are established for such functions as purchasing, receiving, selling, finance, and accounting, to assure that no one department handles all phases of a transaction.

The system of internal controls frequently may be improved by physical safeguards. Computers help to improve the efficiency and accuracy of the record-keeping function. Cash registers, safes, and prenumbered business forms are very helpful in safeguarding cash and establishing responsibility for it. Any system of internal controls must be supervised with care if it is to function effectively.

If an attempt is made to design a "foolproof" system of internal controls, it should be remembered that management's primary responsibility is profitable operation of the business enterprise. The cost of the system of internal controls must be balanced against the benefit to be derived in preventing errors and losses.

Controlling Cash Receipts and Payments

The objective sought in the control of cash receipts is to assure that all cash that is receivable by the business enterprise is collected and recorded without loss. The system of controlling cash payments should be designed to ensure that no unauthorized payments are made. Control is accomplished by division of responsibility to achieve independent verification of cash transactions without duplication of effort. Cash is safeguarded by keeping it in a safe, depositing it in banks, and through the use of special (imprest) cash funds.

Imprest Cash Fund (Petty Cash Fund)

The term *imprest cash fund* (or *petty cash fund*) refers to a fund of fixed amount used for small expenditures that are most conveniently paid in cash. The imprest fund is restored to its original amount at frequent intervals by the issuance of a check on the general bank account payable to the custodian of the fund. The replenishment check is equal in amount to the expenditures made from the fund. Imprest cash funds placed in the custody of responsible employees thus serve to maintain control over cash without involved procedures for small payments.

The size of a petty cash fund should be sufficient to meet the normal need for small cash payments for a period of two or three weeks. As each cash payment is made, a *voucher* or *receipt* is placed in the fund. The vouchers or receipts are reviewed and canceled when the petty cash fund is replenished. The petty cash fund is replenished when its cash is exhausted and at the end of the accounting period so that the expenses paid from the fund are recorded in the proper period and the year-end cash balance is stated correctly.

To illustrate the accounting for petty cash transactions, assume that on December 1, Year 6, Micro Systems Corporation established a petty cash fund of $250. On December 21, Year 6, the custodian requested replenishment for items paid to date.

The following itemized list of payments from petty cash was presented on December 21 for replenishment and on December 31 in connection with the Year 6 audit:

Summary of activity in
petty cash fund for
December, Year 6

MICRO SYSTEMS CORPORATION
Composition of Petty Cash Fund
December 21 and 31, Year 6

	Dec. 21	Dec. 31
Cash in fund	$ 9	$150
Office supplies expense	171	77
Miscellaneous selling expenses	65	25
Cash shortage (overage)	5	(2)
Totals	$250	$250

The journal entries required to record petty cash transactions for the month of December, Year 6, for Micro Systems Corporation are as follows:

Journal entries to
record petty cash
transactions

Year 6			
Dec. 1	Petty Cash Fund	250	
	Cash		250
	To record establishment of petty cash fund.		
21	Office Supplies Expense	171	
	Miscellaneous Selling Expenses	65	
	Cash Shortage (Overage)	5	
	Cash		241
	To record expenses incurred since Dec. 1, and		
	to record replenishment of petty cash fund.		
31	Office Supplies Expense	77	
	Miscellaneous Selling Expenses	25	
	Cash Shortage (Overage)		2
	Cash		100
	To record expenses incurred since Dec. 21, and		
	to record replenishment of petty cash fund.		

The Cash Shortage (Overage) ledger account in the foregoing journal entries is classified as revenue when it has a credit balance and as expense when it has a debit balance.

If for any reason the petty cash fund is not replenished at the end of an accounting period, it is still desirable that the expenses be recorded before the accounting records are closed. In this situation the December 31, Year 6, journal entry illustrated above would be changed in only one respect: the credit of $100 would be to Petty Cash Fund rather than to Cash. The effect on the financial statements is the same as if the fund actually had been replenished.

Change Fund

A *change fund* is used to facilitate the collection of cash from customers. The amount of the change fund is deducted from the total cash (including checks, money orders, etc.) on hand at the close of business each day to determine the daily cash collections. The cash should be counted and compared with the cash register tape daily. In general, change and petty cash funds are combined with cash on hand and in the bank and are presented as a single amount in the balance sheet.

Reconciliation of Bank Balances

The cash balance indicated in a bank statement seldom agrees with the cash balance indicated by the depositor's ledger account for cash. These two balances do not agree even though they purport to measure the same quantity, because there is a lag between the time that transactions are recorded by the bank and by the depositor. For example, the depositor credits the Cash ledger account when a check is prepared in payment of accounts payable. The bank does not reduce the depositor's account until the check is presented for payment by the payee. Another common difference between the two balances results when the deposit of cash receipts is made after the bank closes its records for the statement period. Both of these differences are self-correcting over time; the outstanding checks are presented for payment and the deposit is recorded by the bank within a few days.

There are also time lags in transactions initiated by the bank. For example, a depositor generally is not notified of the bank's charges for servicing the account or for collecting a promissory note receivable for the depositor until the bank statement is received.

In addition to items that involve merely a lag in the recording process, various errors may be made by the depositor or by the bank. The process of reconciling the balances forces a careful review of all transactions involving cash and provides a means of proving the accuracy of the depositor's accounting records. The value of this review stems from the fact that two independent parties have recorded the same transactions and that their records are being compared. When differences arise, they must be explained. Differences that are self-correcting require no further action. However, corrections must be made for omissions or other errors in recording transactions in the depositor's accounting records. Errors made by the bank should be called to its attention for correction.

Two forms of bank reconciliation are in common usage: (1) both the bank balance and the balance in the depositor's records are reconciled to a correct balance, and (2) the bank balance is reconciled to the balance in the depositor's records. The first form is illustrated on page 298, and the second form is illustrated on page 300.

Bank Balance and Depositor's Balance Reconciled to Correct Balance The Cash ledger account for Rossi Company shows a debit balance of $10,592.66 on December 31, Year 5. The bank statement indicates a balance on deposit of $12,269.02 on December 31. Receipts of December 31 in the amount of $1,144.60 were left in the bank's night depository on December 31 but were not included in the bank statement. The December bank statement included a debit memorandum for $13.50 for service charges for December. A credit memorandum included with the bank statement indicated that a note receivable in the amount of $2,000, left with the bank for collection, had been collected and credited to Rossi Company's account for $2,030, including interest revenue of $30. Comparison of the paid checks with the check stubs indicated that check no. 821 for $463.90 on December 15, for the acquisition of office equipment, had been entered erroneously in the cash payments journal as $436.90. In addition, the following checks issued in December, Year 5, had not been paid by the bank:

<table>
<tr><td style="text-align:left">Checks not paid by
the bank in December</td><td>No. 811 ....</td><td style="text-align:right">$421.96</td></tr>
<tr><td></td><td>No. 814 ....</td><td style="text-align:right">93.00</td></tr>
<tr><td></td><td>No. 822 ....</td><td style="text-align:right">250.00</td></tr>
<tr><td></td><td>No. 823 ....</td><td style="text-align:right">116.50</td></tr>
</table>

Also included with the bank statement was a check for $50 drawn by Robert Reeves, a customer of Rossi Company. This check was marked NSF (not sufficient

Reconciliation of bank balance and depositor's balance to correct cash balance

ROSSI COMPANY
Bank Reconciliation
December 31, Year 5

Balance in depositor's records		$10,592.66
Add: Note and interest of $30 collected by bank	$ 2,030.00	
Proceeds of U.S. Treasury bill that had been acquired for $9,652.00 (interest revenue = $348.00)	10,000.00	12,030.00
Subtotal		$22,622.66
Less: Bank service charges for December	$ 13.50	
NSF check drawn by Robert Reeves	50.00	
Error in recording check no. 821		
($463.90 − $436.90)	27.00	90.50
Correct cash balance		$22,532.16
Balance in bank statement		$12,269.02
Add: Deposit in transit	$ 1,144.60	
Proceeds of U.S. Treasury bill matured on		
December 31, Year 5	10,000.00	11,144.60
Subtotal		$23,413.62
Less: Outstanding checks:		
No. 811	$ 421.96	
814	93.00	
822	250.00	
823	116.50	881.46
Correct cash balance		$22,532.16

funds). Finally, an examination of the accounting records indicated that the bank had collected $10,000 for Rossi on December 31, Year 5, representing the maturity value of a U.S. Treasury bill, but the bank did not credit Rossi's account until January 2, Year 6. The U.S. Treasury bill had been acquired by the bank for Rossi at a discount for $9,652 and had been recorded at cost in the Short-Term Investments (U.S. Treasury bill) ledger account by Rossi.

A reconciliation of both the balance in the depositor's records and the balance in the bank statement to the correct cash balance on December 31, Year 5, is presented on page 298.

This form of bank reconciliation serves three functions: (1) to determine the correct cash balance to be reported in the balance sheet, (2) to disclose errors made in recording cash transactions, either by the bank or by the depositor, and (3) to provide information necessary to bring the accounting records up to date. The journal entry required to adjust the accounting records for errors and omissions is taken from the adjustments to the depositor's records in the bank reconciliation. All items appearing in the reconciliation as additions to or deductions from the "balance in depositor's records" must be included in the journal entry. The journal entry on December 31, Year 5, to adjust the accounting records of Rossi Company is shown below:

Journal entry to adjust accounting records for items in bank reconciliation

Cash	11,939.50	
Office Equipment	27.00	
Accounts Receivable: Robert Reeves	50.00	
Miscellaneous Expenses	13.50	
Interest Revenue ($30.00 + $348.00)		378.00
Notes Receivable		2,000.00
Short-Term Investments (U.S. Treasury bill)		9,652.00
To adjust Cash ledger account per December 31, Year 5, bank reconciliation.		

The balance in the depositor's records, $10,592.66, plus the debit of $11,939.50 in the journal entry, equal the correct cash balance of $22,532.16.[2] If there had been arithmetic errors in balancing the Cash account, these would be corrected, and the balance in the depositor's records in the bank reconciliation also would be changed. Errors of this type seldom are found in bank reconciliation procedures if a trial balance of the general ledger is prepared prior to the preparation of the bank reconciliation.

The deposit in transit and the outstanding checks will be processed by the bank in the regular course of business during January, Year 6.

Bank Balance Reconciled to Balance in Depositor's Records The second form of bank reconciliation reconciles the bank balance to the unadjusted balance of the

---

[2]As a general rule, the journal entry resulting from a bank reconciliation is the only example of an adjusting or correcting entry that involves the Cash ledger account.

depositor's Cash account in the general ledger. Then, the required adjustment to the Cash account is entered in the bank reconciliation, resulting in the correct cash balance. This type of bank reconciliation is illustrated below for Rossi Company:

Reconciliation of bank
balance to unadjusted
Cash ledger account
balance

ROSSI COMPANY
Bank Reconciliation
December 31, Year 5

Balance in bank statement		$12,269.02
Add: Deposit in transit	$1,144.60	
Bank service charges for December	13.50	
NSF check drawn by Robert Reeves	50.00	
Error in recording check No. 821 ($463.90 − $436.90)	27.00	1,235.10
Subtotal		$13,504.12
Less: Outstanding checks:		
No. 811	$ 421.96	
814	93.00	
822	250.00	
823	116.50	
Total outstanding checks	$ 881.46	
Note and interest of $30 collected by bank	2,030.00	2,911.46
Balance in depositor's records, unadjusted		$10,592.66
Add: Adjustment to Cash ledger account (see page 299)		11,939.50
Correct cash balance		$22,532.16

Comparison of Two Forms of Bank Reconciliation   Each of the two forms of bank reconciliation has advantages and disadvantages. The form that reconciles both the bank balance and the depositor's balance to the correct cash balance has the advantages of being ''self-balancing'' and clearly identifying items requiring adjustment in the depositor's accounting records. The disadvantage of this form is that it does not *directly* reconcile the bank balance to the unadjusted balance of the Cash ledger account.

The second form of bank reconciliation is preferred by many practicing accountants because it verifies the balance in the Cash ledger account (unadjusted). Any required adjusting journal entries for posting to the Cash account then are prepared. A disadvantage of the second form of bank reconciliation is that it does not present in one place all items requiring adjustment of the Cash ledger account. However, this disadvantage is mitigated by the fact that, generally, all reconciling items in a bank reconciliation require adjustment of the Cash account, *other than deposits in transit and outstanding checks.*

A difference in the two forms of bank reconciliation is found in the handling of the $10,000 collected by the bank on behalf of Rossi Company on December 31, Year 5, for the matured U.S. Treasury bill. This item appeared as a reconciling item in both sections of the first form of reconciliation, because neither the bank statement nor the depositor's Cash ledger account (unadjusted) reflected the $10,000 item on December 31, Year 5.

Reconciliation of Cash Receipts and Cash Payments (Proof of Cash)

Cash balances in the bank statement and the depositor's ledger are reconciled to establish the accuracy of the cash records on a specific date. A full reconciliation of cash receipts and payments (known as a *proof of cash*) also may be made to establish the accuracy of the cash balance and the effectiveness of internal controls over cash receipts and cash payments for a selected month or a longer period.

To illustrate a reconciliation of cash receipts and cash payments for Rossi Company, we need, in addition to the information already provided for the month of December, Year 5, the bank reconciliation for November and cash receipts and payments data for December from both the bank's and Rossi's records. This information is provided below and on page 302.

(1) The following bank reconciliation was prepared on November 30, Year 5:

Bank reconciliation on
November 30, Year 5

ROSSI COMPANY
Bank Reconciliation
November 30, Year 5

Balance in bank statement		$6,947.26
Add: Deposit in transit	$1,055.52	
Bank service charges for November	3.25	
NSF check drawn by James Price	75.00	1,133.77
Subtotal		$8,081.03
Less: Outstanding checks:		
No. 760	$ 244.18	
762	197.50	
763	88.49	
764	151.25	681.42
Balance in depositor's records, unadjusted		$7,399.61
Less: Adjustment to Cash ledger account (see journal entry below)		78.25
Correct cash balance		$7,321.36

(2) The adjusting journal entry on November 30, Year 5, based on the bank reconciliation above, was as follows:

Journal entry to adjust
accounting records
for items in bank
reconciliation

Miscellaneous Expenses	3.25	
Accounts Receivable: James Price	75.00	
Cash		78.25

To adjust Cash ledger account per November 30, Year 5, bank reconciliation.

(3) The cash receipts journal showed total cash received during December of $22,640.50, and the cash payments journal showed cash payments during De-

cember of $19,369.20. Thus, the unadjusted cash balance in Rossi's accounting records on December 31, Year 5, was $10,592.66, as follows:

Cash
ledger
account
for
December

	Cash			
Date	**Explanation**	**Debit**	**Credit**	**Balance**
Year 5				
Nov. 30	Unadjusted balance			7,399.61 dr
30	Adjustment for items in bank reconciliation		78.25	7,321.36 dr
Dec. 31	Cash receipts for December	22,640.50		29,961.86 dr
31	Cash payments for December		19,369.20	10,592.66 dr

(4) The bank statement for December indicated that the total deposits of cash during December were $24,581.42 and that the total checks paid, including bank charges of $13.50, amounted to $19,259.66. This resulted in an unadjusted bank balance amount on December 31, Year 5, of $12,269.02 ($6,947.26 + $24,581.42 − $19,259.66 = $12,269.02).

The cash receipts, cash payments, and the cash balances reflected in the bank statement and in the ledger of Rossi Company are reconciled to the correct balances for December, Year 5, as follows:

Proof
of cash

ROSSI COMPANY Proof of Cash December 31, Year 5				
	Balance, Nov. 30, Year 5	**Receipts**	**Payments**	**Balance, Dec. 31, Year 5**
Balances in bank statement	$6,947.26	$24,581.42	$19,259.66	$12,269.02
Deposits in transit:				
Nov. 30, Year 5	1,055.52	(1,055.52)		
Dec. 31, Year 5		1,144.60		1,144.60
Outstanding checks:				
Nov. 30, Year 5	(681.42)		(681.42)	
Dec. 31, Year 5			881.46	(881.46)
Other reconciling items:				
Bank service charges for December			(13.50)	13.50
NSF check drawn by Robert Reeves....			(50.00)	50.00
Error in recording check No. 821			(27.00)	27.00
Note and interest collected by bank.....		(2,030.00)		(2,030.00)
Balances in depositor's records	$7,321.36	$22,640.50	$19,369.20	$10,592.66
Add: Adjustment to Cash ledger account on Dec. 31, Year 5 (see page 299)				11,939.50
Correct cash balance...................				$22,532.16

The proof of cash for Rossi Company on December 31, Year 5, is explained below:

1   Reconciliation of cash receipts in bank statement and in depositor's records The $1,055.52 deposit in transit on November 30 is deducted from the deposits recorded by the bank in December because it was a receipt of cash in November. The $1,144.60 deposit in transit on December 31 is a receipt of cash in December and should be included in total cash receipts for December. The $2,030.00 proceeds of the note and interest collected by the bank must be deducted from the deposits recorded by the bank because the proceeds had not been entered in the accounting records (before adjustment) on December 31, Year 5.

2   Reconciliation of cash payments in bank statement and in depositor's records The outstanding checks of $681.42 on November 30 are included in the bank debits for December. These do not represent cash payments during December but rather were shown properly as cash payments in November. The outstanding checks of $881.46 on December 31 did not include any checks that were outstanding on November 30; therefore, this total is properly classified as a cash payment by Rossi during December. The bank service charges of $13.50 and the NSF check of $50.00 were included in the bank's debits for December but not in the accounting records (unadjusted). The bank recorded check no. 821 at its correct amount of $463.90; that amount is $27.00 larger than the $436.90 amount recorded in the depositor's records.

3   Reconciliation of bank and depositor cash balances The last column of the reconciliation is identical to the reconciliation of the bank and depositor balances to the correct cash balance illustrated on page 300. The journal entry required to adjust the accounting records of Rossi Company on December 31, Year 5, is the same as that illustrated on page 299.

Cash Overdraft

The issuance of checks in excess of the balance on deposit creates an *overdraft* in the bank account. Banks often (but not always) refuse to pay a check that exceeds the balance of the depositor's account. Such refusal prevents an overdraft from occurring. In the rare situation in which a business enterprise maintains only one bank account and that account is overdrawn on the balance sheet date, the overdraft amount is reported as a current liability. However, if an enterprise has other accounts in the same bank with larger positive balances, it is reasonable to present the net balance of cash as a current asset. This treatment is based on the reasoning that users of financial statements are interested in an enterprise's net cash position, rather than in the status of its individual bank accounts in a particular bank.

An overdraft in an account in one bank should not be offset against positive balances in other banks because no *right of offset* exists. The overdraft in the one bank account is a current liability, and the total of the positive balances is a current asset.

In rare instances, an accountant may discover a situation in which checks are written (and recorded) in excess of the amount on deposit, but the checks are not issued to creditors. In the preparation of financial statements, the credit balance in the Cash ledger account should be eliminated by a debit to the Cash account and a credit to the Accounts Payable account (or to other liability accounts) for the amount of the checks written but not issued.

Disclosure of Compensating Cash Balances

The Securities and Exchange Commission requires that companies filing financial statements with the SEC disclose compensating cash balances.[3] A *compensating balance* generally is defined as the portion of any demand deposit maintained by a depositor that constitutes support for existing borrowing arrangements with banks.

Disclosure of compensating-balance arrangements is required because such cash balances are not available for discretionary use by management on the balance sheet date. Because the maintenance of compensating cash balances affects liquidity and the effective cost of borrowing from banks, users of financial statements may find such information useful.

An example of disclosure of compensating cash balances, taken from the notes to the financial statements in an annual report of a publicly owned corporation, is presented below:

> *Compensating Balances*—Informal lines of credit agreements with several banks require the company to maintain average cash compensating balances equal to 20% of the average outstanding short-term bank loans or 10% of the amount of the credit line, whichever is higher. The agreements require interest on the loans at the prime rate and are subject to review from time to time and may be terminated at the option of either party.
>
> In 19—, the average compensating balance required to be maintained amounted to $4,354,000, and the amount required on December 31, 19—, was $4,008,000 after adjustment for estimated average float. The average amount of outstanding loans amounted to $9,461,000, and the maximum amount outstanding at the end of any month was $16,631,000. The unused available borrowings under the lines of credit agreements amounted to $58,150,000 on December 31, 19—. The weighted average interest rate on the short-term bank loans during the year amounted to 14.65%.

Credit Card Sales Drafts as Cash

Merchants making sales to customers who present bank credit cards prepare a *sales draft* to evidence the credit sale. One copy of the sales draft is given to the customer, another copy is retained by the merchant, and a third copy is deposited in the bank that issued the credit card. Usually the deposit of the sales draft must be made no later than three bank business days following the date of sale. Thus, the copy of the sales draft deposited in the bank by the merchant is the equivalent of *cash.* Accordingly, the journal entry to record a sale to a customer who presents a bank credit card is as follows:

---

[3]*Regulation S-X,* Rule 5-02 (1), SEC (Washington: 1984).

Journal entry to
record credit
card sale

Cash	345	
Sales		345
To record sale (sales draft no. 4672).		

Any undeposited sales drafts at the end of an accounting period are reported as undeposited cash (an addition to the bank balance) in the bank reconciliation on that date.

The bank that issued the credit card charges a *discount* on credit card sales drafts deposited by the merchant. The discount, which varies based on average amounts and monthly volume of sales drafts issued by the merchant, is either deducted from the gross amount of each sales draft deposited or subtracted monthly from the merchant's bank balance. In either case, the appropriate journal entry for the discount is a debit to an account such as Credit Card Discount Expense and a credit to Cash. The credit card discount expense is included with interest expense in the income statement for the merchant.

Electronic Banking

In recent years commercial banks have adopted various electronic systems for some of their services. *Electronic banking,* or *electronic funds transfer,* includes the following:[4]

Automated banking services such as automated teller machines

Point-of-sale services, which include the verification or guarantee of checks and direct charges to the bank account of a customer making a purchase from a retailer

Home banking services such as pay-by-telephone arrangements between a bank and its depositors

Automated clearinghouse services, which involve direct debits or credits to bank checking accounts without the preparation of formal checks or deposit slips

All four components of electronic banking have been designed to increase efficiency in the processing of banking transactions. However, because of limited documentary evidence provided by electronic banking, it is doubtful that checks and deposit slips will disappear completely from banking in the foreseeable future.

SHORT-TERM INVESTMENTS

Investment of Idle Cash

To achieve efficient use of all resources, management of a business enterprise frequently turns unproductive cash balances into productive resources through the

---

[4]Howard G. Johnson, "Understanding Electronic Banking," *Price Waterhouse Review* (1983, Number 1), pp. 8–12.

acquisition of short-term investments. In some cases an enterprise may follow a policy of owning investments that may be converted to cash as needed. Short-term investments acquired for the purpose of earning a return on excess cash resources are characterized by their salability at a readily determinable price. Stocks and bonds not widely owned or frequently traded usually do not meet the marketability test; consequently, securities of this type are not considered in this discussion.

Investments in securities of other companies acquired by a business enterprise as a means of exercising influence or control over the operations of such companies are of a quite different character and should not be considered as short-term investments. If the holding is for the purpose of exercising control, the effective operation of the enterprise may be hampered by the liquidation of the investment. Investments of this nature are discussed in Chapter 14.

In summary, short-term investments classified in the balance sheet as current assets must be readily salable and should not be held for purposes of bolstering business relations with the issuing company. There is no requirement that short-term investments be owned for a limited time only or that management express its intent as to the duration of the investment. The objectives of acquiring short-term investments are twofold: (1) to maximize the return on assets, and (2) to minimize the risk of loss from price fluctuations.

When excess cash is available for short periods, the investment media typically used are certificates of deposit, commercial paper, U.S. Treasury bills, and bonds (both government and corporate) with near-term maturities (in order to minimize price fluctuations). *Certificates of deposit* essentially are promissory notes issued by banks for varying periods of time. *Commercial paper* is the term used for short-term unsecured promissory notes issued by corporations and sold at a discount to investors, generally other companies. *U.S. Treasury bills* are issued at a discount by the United States Treasury with maturities of thirteen weeks, twenty-six weeks, and fifty-two weeks. Longer-term bonds and common stocks, although occasionally used as a medium for investing idle cash, do not meet the objective of limited price fluctuation. Long-term bond prices fluctuate with changes in the level of interest rates, as do prices of bonds with short-term maturities; the degree of fluctuation is greater for bonds with longer maturities. In contrast, common stocks are subject to wide price movements because of changes in investor sentiment, corporate earnings, and economic and political developments.

Recording Transactions in Short-Term Investments

At acquisition, short-term investments are recorded at cost, the price of the item in the market *plus any costs incident to the acquisition,* such as brokerage commission and transfer taxes. Bonds acquired between interest dates are traded on the basis of the market price plus the interest accrued since the most recent interest payment. The accrued interest is a separate asset acquired with the bonds. The cost of these two assets should be separated in the accounting records to achieve a clear picture of the results of the investment in bonds.

When short-term investments are sold, the difference between the carrying amount and the proceeds is recognized as a gain or a loss. A business enterprise that has numerous short-term investments may have a single Short-Term Investments (or

Marketable Securities) controlling account in the general ledger and a subsidiary ledger account for each individual investment, showing cost, maturity date, interest or dividends earned, and gain or loss on disposal.

Illustration On January 31, Year 5, Sawyer Company placed an order with a broker to acquire 100, $1,000, 9% Atlantic Railroad bonds that mature on November 30, Year 8, with interest dates May 31 and November 30. The bonds were acquired on the same day at 103 (103% of face amount), plus accrued interest of $1,500 for two months. The brokerage commission was $500. The total cost of the bonds and the total cash paid are computed below:

Computation of cost of short-term investment in bonds and total cash paid	Market price of bonds ($1,030 × 100)............................. $103,000
	Add: Brokerage commission 500
	Total cost of bonds... $103,500
	Add: Accrued interest for two months on $100,000, at 9% a year........ 1,500
	Total cash paid $105,000

The journal entry required to record the acquisition of the bonds is shown below:

Journal entry for acquisition of short-term investment in bonds	Short-Term Investments 103,500	
	Interest Receivable 1,500	
	Cash	105,000
	To record acquisition of 100 Atlantic Railroad bonds at 103 plus accrued interest of $1,500 and brokerage commission of $500.	

On April 30, Year 5, Sawyer Company sold the Atlantic Railroad bonds at 104¾ plus accrued interest for five months. The cash received from sale of the bonds, after brokerage commission of $500, is computed below:

Computation of cash received from sale of bonds	Market price of bonds ($1,047.50 × 100)............................. $104,750
	Less: Brokerage commission.. 500
	Net proceeds on sale of bonds..................................... $104,250
	Add: Accrued interest for five months on $100,000, at 9% a year........ 3,750
	Total cash received $108,000

The following journal entry is required for Sawyer Company on April 30, Year 5, to record the sale of the bonds:

Journal entry for sale
of short-term
investment
in bonds

Cash	108,000	
Short-Term Investments		103,500
Interest Receivable		1,500
Interest Revenue		2,250
Gain on Sale of Short-Term Investments		750

To record sale of Atlantic Railroad bonds at 104¾, less brokerage commission of $500, plus accrued interest of $3,750.

The gain of $750 realized on the sale of the Atlantic Railroad bonds is the result of a change in the market price of the bonds, which may have occurred for any number of reasons. The two most likely causes of such a gain are (1) a decline in the level of interest rates, or (2) a more favorable investor appraisal of this bond issue. If the level of interest rates had risen since January 31, Year 5, these bonds probably would have been sold at a loss.

The $1,500 of accrued interest on the bonds acquired on January 31, Year 5, might at that time have been recorded as a debit to the Interest Revenue ledger account. This procedure would require that the $3,750 of accrued interest received on April 30 be credited to the Interest Revenue ledger account. The net effect would be to show $2,250 ($3,750 − $1,500 = $2,250) as interest revenue for the three months the bonds were owned.

Discount or Premium on Short-Term Investments in Bonds   In accounting for short-term investments in bonds, it usually is unnecessary to amortize premiums or to accumulate discounts. Such temporary investments generally have near-term maturities; consequently, any premium or discount is likely to be negligible. The holding period by the investor also is likely to be short, which means that any change in market price usually is attributable to changes in interest rates and risk factors rather than to the approach of the maturity date. In theory, the amortization of premium or the accumulation of discount on short-term investments in bonds always is proper, but as a practical matter such amortization or accumulation would add little to the accuracy of financial statements.

Computation of Interest on Investment in Bonds   Accrued interest on notes and bonds issued by business enterprises generally is computed on the basis of a 360-day year. Any full month expired, whether it has 31 days, 30 days, or only 28 days, is viewed as one-twelfth of a year. Additional interest is determined on the basis of the number of days elapsed. For example, interest from April 25 to August 10 is computed for three months (May, June, and July) and 15 days (5 days in April and 10 days in August), or 105/360 of a year.

Interest on U.S. government securities is computed on the basis of a 365-day year; thus, the *exact number of days* for the interest computation period must be determined. Interest on a U.S. Treasury bond from April 25 to August 10, for example, would be 107/365 of a full year's interest.

Accounting for Commercial Paper and U.S. Treasury Bills

Unlike bonds, commercial paper and U.S. Treasury bills are noninterest-bearing. The interest revenue earned on these investments is measured by the *discount*—the difference between the face amount and the issuance price. The discount is *accumu-*

Journal entries for short-term investment in commercial paper

ROCHESTER COMPANY
Journal Entries

Year 1

Dec. 1	Short-Term Investments (Commercial Paper)	95,000	
	Cash		95,000
	To record acquisition of $100,000 face amount		
	of four-month commercial paper of Berg Company.		
31	Short-Term Investments (Commercial Paper)	1,226	
	Interest Revenue		1,226
	To record accrued interest for one month on		
	short-term investment in commercial paper of		
	Berg Company ($95,000 × 0.01291 = $1,226).		

Year 2

Jan. 31	Short-Term Investments (Commercial Paper)	1,242	
	Interest Revenue		1,242
	To record accrued interest for one month on		
	short-term investment in commercial paper of		
	Berg Company [($95,000 + $1,226) ×		
	0.01291 = $1,242].		
Feb. 28	Short-Term Investments (Commercial Paper)	1,258	
	Interest Revenue		1,258
	To record accrued interest for one month on		
	short-term investment in commercial paper of		
	Berg Company [($96,226 + $1,242) ×		
	0.01291 = $1,258].		
Mar. 31	Short-Term Investments (Commercial Paper)	1,274	
	Interest Revenue		1,274
	To record accrued interest for three months on		
	short-term commercial paper of Berg Company		
	[($97,468 + $1,258) × 0.01291 = $1,274].		
31	Cash	100,000	
	Short-Term Investments (Commercial Paper) .		100,000
	To record maturity of four-month commercial		
	paper of Berg Company.		

lated in the Short-Term Investments ledger account and recorded as interest revenue at the end of each account period during the stated term of the commercial paper or U.S. Treasury bills.

To illustrate, assume that Rochester Company on December 1, Year 1, invested $95,000 in Berg Company's four-month commercial paper with a face amount of $100,000. The discount is $5,000 ($100,000 − $95,000 = $5,000), the discount rate is 0.15 a year ($100,000 × 0.15 × $\frac{4}{12}$ = $5,000), and the effective rate of interest per month is 1.291%. Assuming that Rochester's fiscal year ends on December 31, the journal entries at the end of each month relating to the short-term investment in commercial paper are as illustrated on page 309.

In the journal entries on page 309 for Rochester Company, ***monthly interest revenue was computed by the interest method,*** in which the effective rate of interest, 1.291% a month, was applied to the ***carrying amount*** of the short-term investment in commercial paper at the beginning of each month. Alternatively, because of the insignificance of the differences in interest revenue in the two methods, the ***straight-line method*** of discount accumulation might have been used. Under this method, $1,250 of interest revenue, or one-fourth of the $5,000 discount, would be recorded each month. In both the interest method and the straight-line method, interest revenue for the four-month period that Rochester Company held the investment in commercial paper of Berg Company totals $5,000, and the carrying amount of the investment on the March 31, Year 2, maturity date is $100,000, the same as its face amount. The interest method and the straight-line method of discount accumulation are discussed further in Chapter 14.

Cost Selection The cost of short-term investments sold is not always as definite as in the preceding illustrations. If there are several acquisitions of the same bond or stock at different dates and prices, and a portion of the holdings is sold, some procedure of cost selection must be employed. Among the methods commonly used are specific identification, first-in, first-out, and average cost. For income tax purposes, only the specific identification and the first-in, first-out methods are acceptable.

Stock and bond certificates generally have serial numbers that facilitate determination of the cost of specific investments. By using the specific identification method, management may influence the amount of realized gain or loss by deliberately selecting the certificates to be sold from a high-cost lot or a low-cost lot. As an example, assume that Kane Company acquired 100 bonds of Lowe Corporation for $96,000 and a few months later acquired another 100 bonds for $99,000. A month later Kane sold 100 Lowe Corporation bonds for $98,000. The sale will show a gain of $2,000 or a loss of $1,000, depending on which bonds are sold.

Price Fluctuations and Valuation of Short-Term Investments

Normally, an asset is recorded at cost, and this cost is associated with the revenue generated from the use of the asset. If the asset loses its value without generating revenue, the cost is written off as a loss. The ***revenue realization principle*** usually allows recognition of increases in the value of an asset only when it is sold. Whether realization should be limited to the point of sale for short-term investments is a question worth considering. By definition, short-term investments are readily salable at a quoted market price. This same characteristic usually is not found in inventories or plant assets. This basic difference between these types of assets suggests that the traditional tests of revenue realization should not control the valuation of short-term investments.

The use of market prices to value short-term investments at the end of an accounting period has some advantages: (1) The income statement will show the results of decisions to hold or sell such investments period by period (for example, if the market price rises in one accounting period and falls in the next, the gain from holding short-term investments in the first period and the loss sustained by failure to sell at the higher price will be disclosed); (2) valuation at current market price eliminates the anomaly of carrying identical securities at different amounts because they were acquired at different prices; and (3) market value is more meaningful to creditors, who use the current section of a balance sheet to judge the debt-paying ability of the business enterprise.

The following example illustrates the issues that would arise if market value were used as the basis for valuation of short-term investments. On December 31, Year 1, Dixon Foundry has a portfolio of short-term investments that cost $148,000 and had a market value of $151,500. The question at issue is whether on December 31, Year 1, there has been a gain of $3,500 ($151,500 − $148,000 = $3,500). If we follow the traditional tests of revenue realization, *no gain would be recognized until the investments are sold.* If valuation at market price is accepted, the following journal entry would be recorded:

Journal entry to record short-term investments at market value

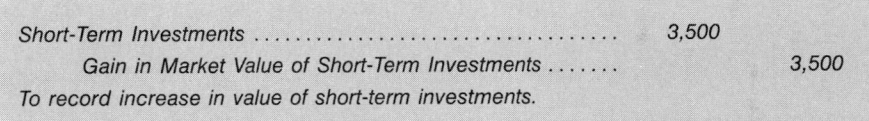

Short-Term Investments 3,500
  Gain in Market Value of Short-Term Investments 3,500
To record increase in value of short-term investments.

Thus, the gain would be recognized in the accounting period in which the price increased rather than in the period in which investments are sold.

On March 28, Year 2, the investments are sold for $149,800. Has there been a gain or a loss on the sale of investments? If the traditional revenue realization principle were followed, the increase in market price was not recognized earlier; because a sale has now taken place, a gain of $1,800 ($149,800 − $148,000 = $1,800) is recognized. If the investments were valued at market price on December 31, Year 1, the journal entry to record the sale on March 25, Year 2, would show a loss of $1,700 ($151,500 − $149,800 = $1,700) sustained since December 31, Year 1.

The question which must be answered is, "What event gives rise to the recognition of gains and losses from holding short-term investments?" The traditional answer has been "Sale of the investments," but the logic of this answer is questionable. In the opinion of the authors, the current market value of investments is the most relevant valuation because it is most likely to aid users in making decisions. It seems reasonable to anticipate that accountants eventually will find a satisfactory method of using current market prices to account for short-term investments.

Valuation at Cost or at Lower of Cost or Market

Despite the forcefulness of the arguments in favor of reporting short-term investments at market value, most business enterprises reported marketable securities at cost until the FASB issued *Statement No. 12*, "Accounting for Certain Marketable Securities," in 1975.[5] However, valuation at lower of cost or market was required when the decline in market value was substantial and was not "due to a mere temporary condition."[6] Recoveries in the market value of short-term investments that had been written down generally were not recognized.

Purpose and Applicability of *FASB Statement No. 12*   Because of the wide diversity of accounting practices applied to short-term and long-term investments in marketable securities, the FASB attempted to answer the following two questions in *Statement No. 12:*

1   Under what circumstances should marketable equity securities be written down below cost?

2   Should marketable equity securities that had been written down be written up at a later date?

FASB Statement No. 12 deals with **marketable equity securities** classified as current assets as well as marketable equity securities classified as noncurrent assets. In this section we are concerned primarily with the provisions of *FASB Statement No. 12* applicable to marketable equity securities carried as **short-term investments;** provisions of the *Statement* applicable to **noncurrent** marketable equity securities are discussed in Chapter 14. The *Statement* is applicable to most business enterprises as well as to personal financial statements. It does not apply to investments accounted for by the equity method (see Chapter 14), or to nonprofit organizations, mutual life insurance companies, and employee benefit plans. The *Statement* for the most part does not apply to business enterprises in industries having specialized accounting practices with respect to marketable equity securities. Such industries include investment companies, brokers and dealers in securities, stock life insurance companies, and fire and casualty insurance companies.

Definition of Terms   The FASB defined the following terms relating to marketable equity securities:[7]

1   *Equity securities* include instruments representing ownership shares or the right to acquire or dispose of ownership shares at fixed or determinable prices. Equity securities include common stocks, most preferred stocks (including convertible preferred stocks), stock warrants, and call or put options. The following *are not*

---

[5]*FASB Statement No. 12*, "Accounting for Certain Marketable Securities," FASB (Stamford: 1975).
[6]*Accounting Research and Terminology Bulletins, Final Edition*, AICPA (New York: 1961), Chap. 3A, p. 23.
[7]*FASB Statement No. 12*, pp. 3–5.

equity securities: preferred stock that by its terms either must be redeemed by the issuing enterprise or is redeemable at the option of the investor, treasury stock, and convertible bonds.

2 *Marketable* means that sales prices (or bid and ask prices) are currently available for an equity security on a national securities exchange or in the publicly reported over-the-counter market.

3 *Market price* refers to the price of a single share or unit of a marketable equity security.

4 *Market value* refers to the aggregate of the market price times the number of shares or units of each marketable equity security in a portfolio.

5 *Cost* refers to the original cost of a marketable equity security, unless a new cost basis has been assigned on recognition of an impairment of value that was deemed other than temporary. In such cases, the new cost basis is the cost.

6 *Valuation allowance* for a marketable equity securities portfolio represents the net unrealized loss in that portfolio.

7 *Carrying amount* of a marketable equity securities portfolio is the amount at which that portfolio of marketable equity securities is reported in the balance sheet, that is, cost reduced by the valuation allowance.

8 *Realized gain or loss* represents the difference between the net proceeds from the sale of a marketable equity security and its cost. (Such gain or loss results only on sale of a security.)

9 *Net unrealized gain or loss* on a marketable equity securities portfolio represents on any date the difference between the aggregate market value and aggregate cost. (Such gain or loss is recognized for financial accounting only at the end of an accounting period and is not a factor in the computation of taxable income.)

Accounting for Current Marketable Equity Securities   The FASB stated that the carrying amount of a marketable equity securities portfolio should be the lower of its aggregate cost or market value, as determined on each balance sheet date. The amount, if any, by which the aggregate cost of the portfolio exceeds market value is accounted for by use of a *valuation allowance.* The treatment of changes in the valuation allowance depends on whether the securities are current or noncurrent assets. In the case of a classified balance sheet, marketable equity securities are grouped into separate *current* and *noncurrent portfolios* for the purpose of comparing aggregate cost and market value. In the case of an unclassified balance sheet, marketable equity securities are treated as noncurrent assets.

   Realized gains and losses from sale of current or noncurrent marketable equity securities are included in the determination of net income of the accounting period in which they occur. Changes in the valuation allowance for a marketable equity securities portfolio *included in current assets* also are included in net income of the period in which they occur. Such changes in the valuation allowance result in *unrealized gains and losses.* A recovery in the aggregate market value of securities that had been written down to a market value below cost requires the recognition of an *unrealized gain* that is included in net income. However, increases in the aggregate market value of the current portfolio of marketable equity securities above aggregate cost are not recognized in the accounting records. (*Unrealized losses* on securities held in the *noncurrent portfolio* are not included in net income of the accounting period in which they occur; such losses are reported as direct reductions in stockholders' equity, and the adjusted valuation allowance is deducted from the cost of the noncurrent marketable equity securities.)

If there is a *change in the classification* of a marketable equity security between current and noncurrent, the security should be transferred between the corresponding portfolios at the lower of its cost or market value on the date of transfer. If market value is less than cost, *the market value becomes the new cost basis,* and the difference is recorded as a *realized loss.*

Unrealized gains and losses on marketable equity securities are not used to compute taxable income. Such gains and losses result in *temporary differences* between taxable income and pre-tax accounting income reported in the income statement. Interperiod tax allocation procedures, described in Chapter 3 and in Chapter 21, are applied to determine whether a net unrealized gain or loss should be affected by the applicable income tax effect.

WEBER COMPANY
Changes in Current Portfolio of Marketable Equity Securities
For Years Ended December 31, Year 1 through Year 3

	Cost	Market value	Unrealized gain (loss)
Dec. 31, Year 1			
Security A	$100,000	$ 80,000	$(20,000)
Security B	200,000	160,000	(40,000)
Security C	50,000	75,000	25,000
Totals	$350,000	$315,000	$(35,000)
Dec. 31, Year 2			
Security A	$100,000	$ 75,000	$(25,000)
Security B	100,000*	70,000	(30,000)
Security C	50,000	60,000	10,000
Totals	$250,000	$205,000	$(45,000)
Dec. 31, Year 3			
Security A	$100,000	$ 80,000	$(20,000)
Security B	100,000	90,000	(10,000)
Security C	50,000	65,000	15,000
Totals	$250,000	$235,000	$(15,000)

*On March 1, Year 2, one-half of the holdings of Security B (cost, $100,000) was sold for $75,000. There were no other sales of securities in Year 2 or Year 3.

Illustration To illustrate the application of *FASB Statement No. 12* to a current portfolio of marketable equity securities, assume that the changes in the portfolio of Weber Company from December 31, Year 1, through December 31, Year 3, are as set forth on page 314.

December 31, Year 1, the Date of Initial Application A valuation allowance of $35,000 is required for marketable equity securities included in the current portfolio to reflect the excess of total cost, $350,000, over total market value, $315,000. The unrealized loss of $35,000 is included in net income for Year 1. The journal entry to record the unrealized loss and the valuation allowance is:

Journal entry to establish valuation allowance for current portfolio of marketable equity securities

Unrealized Loss in Value of Marketable Equity Securities	35,000	
Allowance to Reduce Marketable Equity Securities		
to Market Value		35,000
To establish valuation allowance for decline in total market		
value of current portfolio of marketable equity securities.		

March 1, Year 2, Sale of Security at a Loss The sale of one-half of the holdings of Security B for $75,000 resulted in a *realized loss* of $25,000. The loss is included in net income for Year 2. The journal entry to record the sale is shown below:

Journal entry for sale of marketable equity security at a loss

Cash	75,000	
Realized Loss on Sale of Marketable Equity Securities	25,000	
Short-Term Investments		100,000
To record sale of Security B at a realized loss.		

December 31, Year 2, Increase in Valuation Allowance A valuation allowance of $45,000 is required for marketable equity securities in the current portfolio to reflect the excess of total cost, $250,000, over total market value, $205,000. Because the balance in the valuation allowance account is $35,000, an increase of $10,000 is required. The journal entry to record the increase in the valuation allowance is:

Journal entry to increase valuation allowance

Unrealized Loss in Value of Marketable Equity Securities	10,000	
Allowance to Reduce Marketable Equity Securities		
to Market Value		10,000
To record increase in valuation allowance as a result of		
further decline in total market value of current portfolio		
of marketable equity securities.		

December 31, Year 3, Recovery in Market Value of Portfolio There has been a market recovery during Year 3, as evidenced by the need to reduce the valuation allowance from $45,000 to $15,000. The difference of $30,000 is an ***unrealized gain*** and is included in net income for Year 3. The journal entry to record the reduction in the valuation allowance is:

Journal entry to reduce valuation allowance

Allowance to Reduce Marketable Equity Securities to Market Value	*30,000*	
Unrealized Gain in Value of Marketable Equity Securities		*30,000*
To reduce valuation allowance as a result of recovery in total market value of current portfolio of marketable equity securities.		

After the foregoing journal entries have been posted, the Short-Term Investments and Allowance to Reduce Marketable Equity Securities to Market Value ledger accounts appear as follows:

Ledger accounts for marketable equity securities

Short-Term Investments

Date	Explanation	Debit	Credit	Balance
12/31/1	Balance			350,000 dr
3/1/2	Sale of one-half of Security B holdings		100,000	250,000 dr

Allowance to Reduce Marketable Equity Securities to Market Value

Date	Explanation	Debit	Credit	Balance
12/31/1	($350,000 − $315,000)		35,000	35,000 cr
12/31/2	[($250,000 − $205,000) − $35,000]		10,000	45,000 cr
12/31/3	[($250,000 − $235,000) − $45,000]	30,000		15,000 cr

Note that on March 1, Year 2, the amount of the realized loss recognized was based on the actual cost of Security B ($100,000), not the market value at the end of the prior year ($80,000), and that the **valuation allowance is adjusted only on December 31, Year 2, at the end of the accounting period.** It also should be observed that the valuation of the entire current portfolio at lower of cost or market results in the recognition of the unrealized gain on Security C in Year 1, which defers recognition of part of the unrealized loss of $60,000 on Securities A and B. Also, the current versus noncurrent portfolio approaches adopted by the FASB may result in possible manipulative practices to avoid recognition of unrealized losses in the current portfolio. This may be achieved by the transfer of a security with a market value above cost from the noncurrent portfolio to the current portfolio.

■■■■■■■■■■■■■■■■ **Disclosure Requirements for Current Portfolio of Marketable Equity Securities**

The following information with respect to marketable equity securities included in the current portfolio is disclosed either in the financial statements or in a note to the financial statements:[8]

1   As of the date of each balance sheet presented, aggregate cost and aggregate market value, with identification as to which is the carrying amount.

2   As of the date of the latest balance sheet presented, the gross unrealized gains representing the excess of market value over cost for all marketable equity securities in the portfolio, and the gross unrealized losses representing the excess of cost over market value for all marketable equity securities in the portfolio.

3   For each accounting period for which an income statement is presented:
a Net realized gain or loss included in the determination of net income.
b The basis on which cost was determined in the computation of realized gain or loss (that is, average cost or other method used).

Financial statements are not adjusted for realized gains or losses or for changes in market prices when such events occur after the date of the financial statements but prior to their issuance. However, significant net realized and net unrealized gains and losses arising after the date of the financial statements, but prior to their issuance, applicable to securities owned on the date of the most recent balance sheet, are disclosed.

Balance Sheet Presentation of Cash and Short-Term Investments

Cash is the most liquid asset that a business enterprise owns, in the sense that it is most easily converted to other assets and services. This characteristic justifies its position as the first item in the current asset section of the balance sheet. There seldom is any reason to be concerned about the valuation of cash. There are few sources of possible loss except for theft, which cannot be anticipated. Loss due to bank failure has all but disappeared in recent years with the institution of the Federal Deposit Insurance Corporation. This agency of the United States government insures accounts up to $100,000 in banks covered under provisions of its charter. Therefore, cash is reported in the balance sheet at the amount that represents its current fair value. Terms of borrowing agreements, including requirements to maintain compensating balances, are disclosed in a note to the financial statements.

Short-term investments rank next to cash in liquidity and thus are listed below cash in the current assets section of the balance sheet. Whether short-term investments are reported at cost or at the lower of cost or market, disclosure of the current market value is required. The presentation of cash and short-term investments in a balance sheet, and the related notes to the financial statements on December 31, Year 4, are illustrated on page 318.

---

[8]Ibid., pp. 7–8.

Balance sheet
presentation
of cash and short-
term investments

Current assets:

Cash **(Note 1)**		$21,100,000
Short-term investments in corporate and U.S. government obligations, at cost, which approximates market value		9,000,000
Marketable equity securities, at cost **(Note 2)**	$12,000,000	
Less: Allowance to reduce marketable equity securities to market value	1,500,000	10,500,000

Note 1: *The company maintains lines of credit with a group of domestic banks for borrowing funds on a short-term and long-term basis. The company has agreed to maintain an average compensating balance of 10% of the unused lines of credit and 15% of the amounts borrowed. On December 31, Year 4, the aggregate compensating-balance requirement was approximately $11,250,000.*
Note 2: *The gross unrealized loss on December 31, Year 4, was $4,000,000, and the gross unrealized gain was $2,500,000. On February 15, Year 5, the gross unrealized loss was $3,200,000, and the gross unrealized gain was $2,950,000.*

REVIEW QUESTIONS

1   What are the usual components of *cash?*

2   How would you classify the following items in a balance sheet?
a Travel advances to employees
b Cash deposited with a trustee for the retirement of bonds payable
c Undeposited cash representing receipts of the prior day
d Customer's check returned by the bank marked NSF (not sufficient funds)
e A nonreturnable deposit with a real estate broker as an option on a tract of land
f Deposit in a foreign bank where there are restrictions on currency conversions
g U.S. Treasury bills temporarily held until cash is needed to make payments on building under construction
h A petty cash fund composed of the following:

Coin and currency	$110
Vouchers:	
Selling expenses	61
General and administrative expenses	29

3   What is *management's responsibility* with respect to cash? What techniques are used to aid in carrying out this responsibility?

4   **a** What is a system of *internal controls?*
     b Differentiate between *administrative control* and *accounting control.*
     c Why is internal control over cash and short-term investments particularly important?

5   Parr Company has a change fund of $100 in its cash register. The cash sales tickets for May 25 total $2,049.60, and cash in the cash register, verified by count, totals $2,154.25. Prepare the journal entry necessary to record sales for May 25.

6 Why are adjusting entries usually not made to record outstanding checks as liabilities or deposits in transit as cash on hand?

7 **a** What are three functions of a bank reconciliation?
b What function does the reconciliation of cash receipts and cash payments (proof of cash) serve?

8 **a** Describe two forms of bank reconciliation in common usage.
b Which form of bank reconciliation is preferred by many practicing accountants? Explain.

9 How is a material *cash overdraft* reported in the balance sheet?

10 Define *compensating cash balances* and state the reasons for disclosure of such balances in a note to the financial statements.

11 Explain the appropriate accounting for the *discount* charged by a bank on credit card sales drafts.

12 What is *electronic banking?*

13 Why is management concerned with investing cash that is temporarily in excess of current requirements in short-term investments? What may be done to eliminate or minimize the risk of loss from temporary fluctuations in the market price of securities held as short-term investments?

14 Do you support the use of current market value as the basis for valuing all short-term investments? Explain.

15 What two questions relative to marketable equity securities in a current portfolio did the Financial Accounting Standards Board attempt to answer in *Statement No. 12,* ''Accounting for Certain Marketable Securities''?

16 Define the following terms relating to the accounting for marketable equity securities:
a *Equity securities*
b *Valuation allowance*
c *Carrying amount*
d *Realized gain or loss*
e *Net unrealized gain or loss*

17 Briefly describe the accounting treatment of the valuation allowance to reduce marketable equity securities to market value. Include in your answer the treatment of realized gains and losses and changes in market value in subsequent accounting periods.

18 What information with respect to marketable equity securities is disclosed in the financial statements or in a note to the financial statements?

19 Should certificates of deposit be included in cash in the balance sheet for a business enterprise? Explain.

■■■■■■■ EXERCISES

Ex. 6-1   Select the best answer for each of the following multiple-choice questions:

1   When the aggregate market value of a business enterprise's current marketable equity securities portfolio is lower than its aggregate cost, the difference is:
a Accounted for as a current liability
b Disclosed in a note to the financial statements but not accounted for
c Accounted for as a valuation allowance deducted from the securities to which it relates
d Accounted for separately in the stockholders' equity section of the balance sheet

2   An analysis of Pickwick Corporation's short-term marketable equity securities portfolio acquired in Year 7 reveals the following totals on December 31, Year 7:

Aggregate cost of portfolio	$90,000
Aggregate market value of portfolio	80,000
Aggregate lower of cost or market value applied to each security	
in the portfolio	76,000

The amount of the valuation allowance that Pickwick should record on December 31, Year 7, is:
a $0   **b** $4,000   **c** $10,000   **d** $14,000   **e** Some other amount

3   Which of the following conditions generally exists before market value may be used as the basis for valuation of a business enterprise's current marketable equity securities?
a Management's intention must be to dispose of the securities within one year
b Market value must be less than cost for each security held in the enterprise's current marketable equity securities portfolio
c Market value must approximate historical cost
d The aggregate market value of the enterprise's current marketable equity securities portfolio must be less than the aggregate cost of the portfolio

4   Which of the following should not be included in cash in the balance sheet?
a Petty cash funds
b Certificates of deposit
c Dividends bank account
d Compensating balance for a 90-day note payable to bank
e None of the foregoing

5   In preparing its bank reconciliation for the month of March, Year 2, Derby Company has available the following information:

Balance in bank statement, Mar. 31, Year 2	$36,050
Deposit in transit, Mar. 31, Year 2	6,250
Outstanding checks, Mar. 31, Year 2.	5,750
Credit erroneously recorded by bank in Derby's account, Mar. 12, Year 2	250
Bank service charges for March, Year 2.	50

The correct balance of Derby Company's cash on March 31, Year 2, is:
a $35,250   **b** $36,250   **c** $36,300   **d** $36,550   **e** Some other amount

6 In the form of bank reconciliation preferred by many practicing accountants:

a The unadjusted cash account balance in the depositor's records is reconciled to the bank statement balance

b The bank statement balance is reconciled to the unadjusted cash account balance in the depositor's records

c Both the bank statement balance and the cash account balance in the depositor's records are reconciled to a correct balance

d The correct cash balance is reconciled to the balance in the bank statement

7 Interest revenue on short-term investments in commercial paper is measured by the:

a Discount

b Face amount times the nominal interest rate

c Face amount times the effective interest rate

d Present value times the effective interest rate

8 The unrealized loss in value of marketable equity securities included in current assets is presented in the:

a Income statement in the measurement of net income

b Balance sheet as a contra asset

c Balance sheet as a contra to stockholders' equity

d Statement of retained earnings as a prior period adjustment

Ex. 6-2 The December 31, Year 5, balance of Wynn Company's Cash ledger account was $4,000. Wynn had the following items in its safe on December 31, Year 5:

(1) *Check of customer, Canna Company, payable to Wynn, dated and recorded on Jan. 2, Year 6* *$1,000*

(2) *Check of customer, Lowe Company, payable to Wynn, deposited by Wynn on Dec. 26, Year 5, but returned by bank on Dec. 30, Year 5, marked NSF. No journal entry was made for the returned check. Wynn redeposited the check on Jan. 2, Year 6, and it cleared* *200*

(3) *Postage stamps received from mail-order customers* *75*

(4) *Check of Wynn Company payable to Keith Company, a supplier, dated and recorded on Dec. 31, Year 5. Wynn mailed the check on Jan. 2, Year 6* *500*

Compute the balance of cash to be included in Wynn Company's December 31, Year 5, balance sheet.

Ex. 6-3 On February 1, Year 2, Cree Company acquired for $84,000 commercial paper of Dorf Company with a face amount of $90,000, due June 1, Year 2. The discount rate was 20% a year, and the effective interest rate was 1.74% per month.

Prepare journal entries on February 1 and February 28, Year 2, for Cree Company, which has a February 28 fiscal year. Use the interest method to compute interest revenue and round all amounts to the nearest dollar.

Ex. 6-4 The reconciling items in the February 28, Year 5, bank reconciliation of Dundee Company were as follows:

Balance in bank statement, Feb. 28, Year 5	$16,600
Balance in Cash ledger account, Feb. 28, Year 5	11,060
Bank service charges for February, Year 5	50
Deposit in transit, Feb. 28, Year 5	1,200
Error in Dundee's recording of check no. 654 to vendor, Ace Company,	
($400 check recorded by Dundee as $40)............................	360
Interest on note receivable collected by bank for Dundee on Feb. 28,	
Year 5	300
NSF check of customer, Bell Company, charged back by bank on Feb. 28,	
Year 5	250
Outstanding checks (total) Feb. 28, Year 5	4,100
Principal of note receivable collected by bank for Dundee on Feb. 28,	
Year 5	3,000

Prepare a February 28, Year 5, bank reconciliation for Dundee Company in the form illustrated on page 300. Disregard the required adjustment to the Cash ledger account.

Ex. 6-5 The petty cash fund for Grant Company is $200. During March, Year 10, $30.00 was spent on entertainment expense, $36.20 was spent on office supplies expense, $53.00 was spent on postage expense, $40.00 was spent for merchandise, $32.90 was spent on miscellaneous items, and $7.90 remained on hand. Grant uses the periodic inventory system.

Prepare a journal entry to record the replenishment of the petty cash fund on March 31, Year 10.

Ex. 6-6 How are the following reconciling items included in a four-column reconciliation (proof of cash) for the month of November, Year 8? Explain.
a Outstanding checks on November 30, Year 8
b Bank service charge for month of October, Year 8, recorded in general journal in November, Year 8
c Deposit in transit on October 31, Year 8
d NSF check returned to depositor by the bank on November 17, Year 8; redeposited on November 18, Year 8, with no journal entry in the accounting records

Ex. 6-7 In auditing the financial statements of Rohr Company for Year 10, you review the following ledger account:

Short-Term Investment—Weiss Company Common Stock

Date	Explanation	Debit	Credit	Balance
Year 10				
Mar. 28	Acquired 200 shares at 26¼	5,250		5,250 dr
June 15	Dividend received		80	5,170 dr
Dec. 15	Dividend received		80	5,090 dr
23	Proceeds from sale of 100 shares		2,940	2,150 dr

You also find that a commission of $106 on the acquisition of the 200 shares of Weiss Company common stock was debited to the Miscellaneous Expenses ledger account.

Prepare a journal entry on December 31, Year 10, to correct Rohr Company's accounting records.

Ex. 6-8   Presented below is a condensed version of the bank reconciliation prepared by Lowell Company on March 31, Year 1.

LOWELL COMPANY
Condensed Bank Reconciliation
March 31, Year 1

Balance in bank statement		$11,120
Add: Deposit in transit	$1,390	
Service charge for March	8	1,398
Subtotal		$12,518
Less: Outstanding checks		2,008
Balance in Cash ledger account (before adjustment)		$10,510

Cash receipts and payments entered in the accounting records during the month of April, Year 1, are listed below:

Cash receipts..	$29,400
Cash payments (including adjusting entry for March bank service charge)	26,950

On April 30, Year 1, checks outstanding amounted to $2,950, and deposits in transit amounted to $1,911. There was no service charge for April, and no errors were made either by the bank or by Lowell.

Prepare a proof of cash for Lowell Company for the month of April, Year 1, similar to the illustration on page 302. Disregard the required adjustment to the Cash ledger account.

Ex. 6-9   Prepare journal entries to record the following transactions or events relating to short-term investments of Hadley Company during Year 4:

June 11 Acquired $50,000 face amount 15% bonds issued by Lamar Company. Total acquisition price was $52,800, which included accrued interest of $1,250 from April 11.

Oct. 11 Received semiannual interest on Lamar Company bonds, $3,750.

Dec. 11 Sold $20,000 face amount Lamar Company bonds for total consideration of $23,500, which included accrued interest of $500 from Oct. 11.

   31 Recorded accrued interest for 80 days on $30,000 face amount Lamar Company bonds.

Ex. 6-10   From the following data of Skiff Company for December, Year 7 (**a**) compute the cash balance in the accounting records before adjustments are recorded, and (**b**) prepare a journal entry to bring the accounting records up to date:

Balance in bank statement...	$15,500
Checks outstanding	6,400
Cash receipts recorded in the accounting records, not yet deposited	1,920
Bank service charges not recorded in the accounting records............	22
Promissory note collected by bank, not recorded in the accounting	
records (includes interest of $40)	4,040

Ex. 6-11 The following bank reconciliation was prepared for Howe Company on June 30, Year 6:

HOWE COMPANY
Bank Reconciliation
June 30, Year 6

Balance in bank statement, June 30, Year 6		$ 8,308
Add: Deposit in transit	$ 1,690	
Check incorrectly charged to Howe Company		
by bank	250	
Bank service charge for June	10	
NSF check from customer returned by bank	120	2,070
Subtotal		$10,378
Less: Proceeds of bank loan arranged on June 30,		
Year 6	$10,000	
Outstanding checks	2,940	
Error in recording check in payment of vendor's		
invoice...	18	12,958
Balance in accounting records, June 30, Year 6		$ (2,580)

(a) Compute Howe Company's correct cash balance on June 30, Year 6, and (b) prepare a journal entry to adjust Howe Company's Cash ledger account to the correct balance. Interest on the bank loan is payable at maturity, and all payments on vendors' invoices are debited to the Accounts Payable ledger account.

Ex. 6-12 Pearl Company began investing idle cash in marketable equity securities in Year 3. The cost and market value of the securities held in its current portfolio at the end of its December 31 fiscal years were as follows:

End of Year		Cost	Market value
3	....	$200,000	$210,000
4	....	310,000	260,000
5	....	280,000	210,000
6	....	400,000	425,000

Prepare journal entries for Pearl Company at the end of each year to adjust the valuation allowance to reduce current marketable equity securities to market value.

Ex. 6-13 The items required for the September 30, Year 9, bank reconciliation of Leward Company's demand (checking) account follow:

Balance in bank statement, Sept. 30, Year 9		$12,367.43
Balance in depositor's records, Sept. 30, Year 9		4,977.47
Bank service charges for month of September, Year 9 . .		6.50
Bank error in recording check no. 648:		
Drawn and recorded in depositor's records	$411.42	
Encoded incorrectly and paid by bank	41.42	
Net bank error		370.00
Outstanding checks:		
No. 643	$ 10.00	
651	50.00	
654	750.00	
655	750.00	
671	55.00	
673	750.00	
674	2,000.00	
675	14.00	
676	250.00	
678	5.00	
679	2,390.96	
680	1.50	
Total outstanding checks		7,026.46

Prepare a bank reconciliation for Leward Company on September 30, Year 9. Use the total for outstanding checks on September 30, Year 9; do not list individual checks. Reconcile both the bank balance and the depositor's balance to the correct cash balance.

CASES

Case 6-1 On December 31, Year 1, the end of its first year of operations, Key Company had a current marketable equity securities portfolio with a cost of $500,000 and a market value of $550,000. On December 31, Year 2, the end of its second year of operations, Key had a current marketable equity securities portfolio with a cost of $525,000 and a market value of $475,000. No securities were sold during Year 1. One security with a cost of $80,000 and a market value of $70,000 at the end of Year 1 was sold for $100,000 during Year 2.

Instructions

How should Key Company report the above facts in its balance sheets and income statements for Year 1 and Year 2? Discuss the rationale for your answer.

Case 6-2 Management of Kingsley Company foresees a period of three to five years of reduced operations. During this period, management does not expect to replace any plant assets. Management presents the board of directors with a plan (1) to maintain the ratio of dividends to net income at 60%, and (2) to invest all cash that accumulates in excess of normal operating needs in a diversified list of high-quality common stocks. Management also proposes that the common stocks be carried in the balance sheet at market value on the balance sheet date. Any change in market value from date of acquisition or the most recent valuation for financial statement purposes is to be included in the income statement.

Instructions

a What are the advantages of accounting for and reporting of investments in this manner?

b What objections might be made to this method of reporting the investments?

c Should the investments be reported as a current or a noncurrent asset? Why?

Case 6-3 Segura Company is projecting an increased level of operations for the coming year (Year 4), which will require an additional investment in inventories and accounts receivable. The minimum cash balance required is $50,000. After a detailed review of the prospects for Year 4, the controller prepared the following forecast of monthly cash balances (parentheses indicate projected cash deficiency):

January	$110,000	July	$395,000
February	50,000	August	450,000
March	(100,000)	September	80,000
April	(230,000)	October	(250,000)
May	(150,000)	November	(290,000)
June	150,000	December	(50,000)

Short-term investment decisions are made and loans are negotiated on the fifteenth day of each month in an amount equal to the projected cash surplus or deficiency for the month. Changes in the short-term investment or loan positions are made in multiples of $5,000.

Assume that surplus cash is to be invested in short-term U.S. Treasury notes bearing 10% interest and that borrowed funds cost 15%. The cash balance on January 1, Year 4, was $50,000.

Instructions

a Prepare a working paper to compute the net cost (interest expense less interest revenue on short-term investments) of short-term borrowing to finance the operations of Segura Company for the year ended December 31, Year 4. Round computations to nearest dollar.

b If Segura Company is to avoid short-term borrowing, how much long-term debt or equity capital must be raised? Would you recommend that Segura attempt to raise the capital or follow a policy of short-term borrowing? Why?

Case 6-4 Following are four unrelated situations involving marketable equity securities:

a A noncurrent portfolio with an aggregate market value in excess of cost includes one security whose market value has declined to less than one-half of the original cost. The decline in value is not considered to be temporary.

b The balance sheet does not classify assets and liabilities as current and noncurrent. The portfolio of marketable equity securities includes securities normally considered current that have an aggregate cost that exceeds market value by $2,000. The remainder of the portfolio has an aggregate market value that exceeds cost by $5,000.

c A marketable equity security, whose market value currently is less than cost, is classified as noncurrent but is to be reclassified as current.

d The noncurrent portfolio of marketable equity securities consists of the common stock of one company. At the end of the prior year the market value of the security was 50% of original cost, and this effect was reflected properly in a valuation allowance account. However, at the end of the current year the market value of the security had appreciated to twice the original cost. The security still is considered noncurrent at year-end.

Instructions

What is the effect on the balance sheet classification, carrying amount, and net income for each of the above situations? Complete your response to each situation before proceeding to the next situation.

Case 6-5   Since the issuance of *FASB Statement No. 12,* "Accounting for Certain Marketable Securities," Coldwater Company has intended to follow the practice of valuing its short-term investments in marketable equity securities at the lower of cost or market. On December 31, Year 10, the ledger account Marketable Equity Securities (Current Portfolio) had a balance of $260,000, and the ledger account Allowance to Reduce Marketable Equity Securities to Market Value had a balance of $40,000. The allowance account had been unchanged during Year 10; the balance of $40,000 was based on the following facts relating to the securities owned on December 31, Year 9:

Security	Cost	Market value	Allowance required
X Company common stock	$150,000	$120,000	$30,000
Y Company common stock	80,000	70,000	10,000
Z Company warrants to acquire			
common stock	30,000	75,000	
Totals	$260,000	$265,000	$40,000

During Year 10, the Y Company common stock was sold for $65,000, the difference between the $65,000 and the cost of $80,000 being debited to the Realized Loss on Sale of Marketable Equity Securities ledger account. The market values of the securities remaining on December 31, Year 10, were: X Company common stock, $90,000; Z Company warrants to acquire common stock, $40,000.

Instructions

a What argument supports the use of the lower-of-cost-or-market rule in the valuation of marketable equity securities?

b Did Coldwater Company apply the lower-of-cost-or-market rule correctly at the end of Year 9? Explain.

c What correcting entries are required for Coldwater Company on December 31,

Year 10, assuming that any error made in Year 9 is corrected as a prior period adjustment? Disregard income taxes.

d Assume that the president of Coldwater Company does not wish to recognize any unrealized loss in the value of marketable equity securities at the end of Year 10. Instead, the president wants to transfer a block of K Company common stock from the noncurrent portfolio to the current portfolio. The common stock of K Company is listed on the New York Stock Exchange with a market value of $200,000. K Company is a major customer of Coldwater, and its common stock was acquired many years ago at a cost of $100,000 to maintain good business relations between Coldwater Company and K Company. Would you approve the president's proposal? Explain.

PROBLEMS

6-1 On May 1, Year 5, Olman Company paid $942,184 for $1,000,000 face amount of Logan Company's four-month commercial paper maturing on August 31, Year 5, at a discount rate of 17.3448% a year. Olman prepares adjusting entries at the end of each month, and uses the interest method to compute interest revenue on commercial paper investments.

Instructions

a By reference to Table 2 in the Appendix at the end of Chapter 5, determine the effective interest rate per month on Olman Company's investment in Logan Company's commercial paper.

b Prepare journal entries for Olman Company's investment in commercial paper of Logan Company on May 1, May 31, June 30, July 31, and August 31, Year 5. Round all amounts to the nearest dollar.

6-2 On January 2, Year 8, Mission Company, which adjusts its accounting records and prepares financial statements at the end of each month, acquired for cash 1,000 shares of common stock of three companies as short-term investments, as follows:

	Cost*
1,000 shares of F Company common stock	$12,000
1,000 shares of G Company common stock	14,000
1,000 shares of H Company common stock	16,000
Total	$42,000

*Includes brokerage commissions

On February 14, Year 8, Mission sold 500 shares of G Company common stock for $6,200, nct of the brokerage commission. Market values per share of the three common stocks were as follows on January 31 and February 28, Year 8:

	Jan. 31, Year 8	Feb. 28, Year 8
F Company common stock	$13	$11
G Company common stock	12	11
H Company common stock	15	16

Instructions

Prepare journal entries for Mission Company on January 2, January 31, February 14, and February 28, Year 8.

6-3 The bank statement for Dingle Corporation showed a balance of $70,688.88 on December 31, Year 9. The balance of the Cash ledger account was $65,194.43. In comparing the bank balance with the cash balance in the accounting records, Dingle's accountant discovered the following:

(1) Checks amounting to $18,830.00 had not cleared the bank.
(2) A check in payment of an account payable was recorded in the accounting records for $857.20; the correct amount of the check was $875.20.
(3) A customer's check for $739.90 was returned marked NSF. No journal entry had been made in the accounting records to record this check.
(4) A deposit of $12,565.70 had not been recorded by the bank.
(5) The bank's charge for printing checks was $11.95.

Instructions

a Prepare a bank reconciliation for Dingle Corporation on December 31, Year 9, in the form illustrated on page 300.

b Prepare a journal entry for Dingle Corporation on December 31, Year 9, to bring the accounting records up to date. Record the journal entry's net effect on the Cash ledger account in the bank reconciliation prepared in **a.**

6-4 Seacoast Company was organized early in Year 1. During the next four years it completed the following transactions in the current portfolio of marketable equity securities:

Year 1: Acquired the following marketable equity securities:

Security A.. $100,000
Security B..   50,000
Security C..   75,000

Year 2: Sold Security A for $140,000, net of brokerage commission and other miscellaneous costs.

Year 3: Acquired Security D for $88,000.

Year 4: Sold Security B for $37,500, net of brokerage commission and other miscellaneous costs. Acquired Security E at a total cost of $180,000.

The market values of the current portfolio of marketable equity securities on December 31 of each year were as follows:

	Year 1	Year 2	Year 3	Year 4
Security A	$125,000			
Security B	30,000	$ 45,000	$ 35,000	
Security C	50,000	90,000	70,000	$ 55,000
Security D			85,000	80,000
Security E				175,000
Totals	$205,000	$135,000	$190,000	$310,000

Instructions

a Prepare journal entries for Seacoast Company to record the transactions in marketable equity securities listed above for the four-year period ended December 31, Year 4, including appropriate adjustments to the valuation allowance account at the end of each year. Disregard income taxes.

b Show how the current portfolio of marketable equity securities would be presented in Seacoast Company's balance sheet at the end of each of the four years ended December 31, Year 4. Supplementary disclosure pursuant to *FASB Statement No. 12,* "Accounting for Certain Marketable Securities," is not required.

6-5 Kain Company owned marketable equity securities on December 31, Year 5, that were appropriately reported as current assets in its balance sheet, as follows:

	Carrying amount, Dec. 31, Year 5
Bart Corporation, 1,500 shares of $100 par, 12% cumulative preferred stock, at cost (market value $140,000)	$110,000
Behrend Corp., 1,000 shares of $3 no-par convertible preferred stock, at cost (market value $230,000).....................................	225,000
Bella Company, 10,000 shares of common stock, at cost (market value $250,000)	200,000
Chockey, Inc., 3,000 shares of common stock, at cost (market value $92,000)...	90,000
Dempsey Company, 4,000 shares of common stock, at cost (market value $25,000)...	24,000
Total marketable equity securities	$649,000

During Year 6 the following transactions or events occurred:

(1) Bart Corporation could not pay dividends on preferred stock in Year 6 due to adverse business conditions. The market value of the stock was $120,000 on December 31, Year 6.

(2) Behrend Corp. pays cash dividends once a year to stockholders of record on May 31. The cash was received on June 10, Year 6. On June 15, Year 6, Kain converted 500 shares of Behrend Corp. $3 no-par convertible preferred stock to 1,000 shares of Behrend Corp. common stock, which had a market value of $114,000 on the date of the conversion and $116,000 on December 31, Year 6. The market value of the remaining $3 no-par convertible preferred stock was $117,000 on December 31, Year 6.

(3) Bella Company distributed a 10% stock dividend in Year 6. The market value of the common stock on December 31, Year 6, was $24 a share.

(4) Chockey, Inc., effected a 2 for 1 stock split in Year 6. The market value of the stock on December 31, Year 6, was $91,000.

(5) Dempsey Company declared cash dividends to stockholders of record on March 31, Year 6, and June 30, Year 6, of $0.40 a share on each date. The cash was received on April 15, Year 6, and July 15, Year 6, respectively. On July 24, Year 6, Kain sold all its shares of Dempsey for $7 a share.

Instructions

a Prepare a working paper to compute the aggregate cost and aggregate market value of Kain Company's current marketable equity securities on December 31, Year 6.

b Prepare a partial balance sheet and related note to the financial statements for Kain Company's marketable equity securities on December 31, Year 6.

c Compute and list the amounts of the Year 6 marketable equity securities transactions that should appear in Kain Company's income statement for Year 6.

6-6 On June 1, Year 2, Lew Corporation adopted a petty cash fund procedure for minor cash payments. Also on June 1, Year 2, Lew made an initial investment of idle cash in marketable equity securities. The fiscal year ends on June 30. The operations of the petty cash fund for the last month of the fiscal year ended June 30, Year 2, and the first month of the following fiscal year, and the acquisition of marketable equity securities, are summarized below:

June 1   The petty cash fund was established with a Lew check for $2,500 payable to the petty cash custodian.

1   Lew acquired 1,000 shares of Data Processing Associates, Inc., common stock at 40½, plus a commission of $825, as a short-term investment.

19   A request for replenishment of the petty cash fund was received by the accounts payable department, supported by appropriate signed vouchers summarized as follows:

Selling expenses	$ 468
Administrative expenses	678
Factory overhead costs	383
Special tools	192
Telephone, telegraph, and postage expenses	48
Miscellaneous expenses	308
Total	$2,077

20   A check for $2,077 was drawn payable to the petty cash custodian.

30   Lew's independent certified public accountant counted the petty cash fund in connection with year-end audit work and found the following:

Cash in petty cash fund		$1,010
Employees' checks with July dates (postdated checks)		180
Expense vouchers properly approved as follows:		
Selling expenses	$249	
Administrative expenses	387	
Factory overhead costs	89	
Office supplies expense	96	
Telephone, telegraph, and postage expenses	56	
Miscellaneous expenses	428	1,305
Total		$2,495

The petty cash fund was not replenished on June 30, Year 2.

June 30   The independent certified public accountant also noted that the closing market price of the Data Processing Associates, Inc., common stock on June 30 was $35 a share.

July 15   The employees' checks that were in the petty cash fund on June 30 were cashed, and the proceeds were placed in the petty cash fund.

31   A request for replenishment of the petty cash fund was received by the accounts payable department, and a check was drawn to restore the fund to its original balance of $2,500. The supporting vouchers for July expenditures are summarized below:

Selling expenses..	$ 160
Administrative expenses	164
Factory overhead costs.......................................	349
Telephone, telegraph, and postage expenses..................	35
Miscellaneous expenses	338
Total	$1,046

Instructions

a Prepare journal entries for the foregoing transactions of Lew Corporation, including any adjustment required on June 30, Year 2. Disregard income tax effects.

b Evaluate Lew Corporation's use of the petty cash fund.

6-7   Gilson, Inc., received the following bank statement for the month of September, Year 6:

GILSON, INC.
In Account with Valley Bank
Waco, Texas

Checks			Deposits	Date	Balance
				Sept. 1	3,658.75
310.00	35.48	130.00	820.00	Sept. 2	4,003.27
60.00	31.15	510.00	72.80	Sept. 5	3,474.92
70.00	515.00		361.00	Sept. 7	3,250.92
90.00			280.00	Sept. 8	3,440.92
13.30	62.50		510.00	Sept. 9	3,875.12
28.00			205.60	Sept. 12	4,052.72
650.00			180.14	Sept. 14	3,582.86
			345.00	Sept. 16	3,927.86
85.00			427.50	Sept. 19	4,270.36
24.10	125.06			Sept. 20	4,121.20
40.00	65.00		90.00	Sept. 21	4,106.20
162.40			360.00	Sept. 23	4,303.80
15.00			625.00	Sept. 26	4,913.80
355.00	270.00	225.00	130.25	Sept. 28	4,194.05
7.50s			280.50	Sept. 30	4,467.05

s = Service charge

The entries in Gilson's cash journals for the month of September are shown below:

	Cash Receipts Journal				Cash Payments Journal		
Date		**Explana-tion**	**Cash (debit)**	**Date**		**Explana-tion** **Check no.**	**Cash (credit)**
Sept	1		72.80	Sept	1	65	130.00
	3		361.00		1	66	90.00
	6		280.00		1	67	35.48
	8		510.00		2	68	31.15
	10		205.60		4–19	69–78	1,648.86
	13		180.14		20	79	24.10
	15		345.00		20	80	38.60
	17		427.50		20	81	65.00
	20		90.00		22	82	162.40
	22		360.00		23	83	150.00
	24		625.00		26	84	15.00
	27		130.25		28	85	270.00
	28		280.50		28	86	105.20
	29		1,710.10		28	87	225.00
	30		315.25		28	88	355.00
			5,893.14		30	89	25.00
					30	90	645.29
					30	91	155.00
							4,171.08

The Cash ledger account balance in Gilson's accounting records on August 31 agreed with the balance in the bank statement, although a deposit was in transit and two checks were outstanding. The balance of the Cash ledger account on September 30 was $5,380.81.

Instructions

a Prepare a bank reconciliation for Gilson, Inc., on September 30, Year 6. Use the form illustrated on page 300.

b Prepare the necessary journal entry to adjust Gilson, Inc.'s, Cash ledger account on September 30, Year 6. Record the journal entry's net effect on the Cash account in the bank reconciliation prepared in **a**.

6-8 On February 1, Year 1, Ryder Company had cash in excess of its immediate needs. Management decided to invest this cash, and any other cash that appeared to be temporarily in excess of current needs, in short-term U.S. government securities. The following transactions occurred during the fiscal year ended January 31, Year 2:

Year 1

Feb. 1   Acquired for $292,130, including accrued interest of $2,630, U.S. Treasury 10% bonds, due in two years, $300,000 face amount, with interest payable June 30 and December 31. (Debit Interest Receivable for $2,630.)

May 31	Sold for $152,455, including accrued interest of $6,205, one-half of the U.S. Treasury 10% bonds acquired February 1.
June 30	Received interest on U.S. Treasury 10% bonds, $7,500.
Aug. 1	Acquired 40 U.S. Treasury 12%, $1,000 bonds, interest payable April 1 and October 1, at 102 plus accrued interest of $1,604 and a commission of $125. These bonds mature three years after the next interest date.
Oct. 1	Received interest on U.S. Treasury 12% bonds, $2,400.
Dec. 15	Sold for $148,054, including accrued interest of $6,904, the remainder of the U.S. Treasury 10% bonds acquired February 1.

Year 2

Jan. 16	Acquired $100,000 face amount U.S. Treasury 14% notes for a price of $102,250. Interest is paid on these notes on January 16 and July 16.
31	Adjusted the accounting records to reflect interest accrued to the end of the fiscal year. Management decided that the premium on bonds and notes acquired will not be amortized. Interest on U.S. Treasury obligations is computed based on the exact number of days elapsed, using a 365-day year. Compute interest on each security to the nearest dollar.

Instructions

a Prepare journal entries to record the foregoing transactions of Ryder Company.

b The closing market quotes for the U.S. Treasury 12% bonds and the U.S. Treasury 14% notes on January 31, Year 2, were 102 and 105, respectively. Prepare a partial balance sheet for Ryder Company on January 31, Year 2, showing all data for short-term investments. Assume that short-term investments are reported at cost and that market value is shown parenthetically.

6-9 The following data pertaining to the cash transactions and bank account of Taurus Company for September, Year 4, are available to you:

(1)	Cash balance in accounting records, Sept. 30, Year 4	$28,104.50
(2)	Cash balance in bank statement, Sept. 30, Year 4	34,085.80
(3)	Bank service charge for September	14.00
(4)	Debit memo for printed checks delivered by the bank; the charge has not been recorded in the accounting records................	5.00
(5)	Deposit of Sept. 30 not recorded by bank until Oct. 1............	3,870.00
(6)	Outstanding checks, Sept. 30, Year 4.........................	8,128.30
(7)	Proceeds of a bank loan on Sept. 30 not recorded in the accounting records (interest payable at maturity).......................	2,970.00
(8)	Principal and interest on customer's promissory note, face amount $800, collected by the bank, net of collection fee of $3 charged by the bank	810.00
(9)	Check no. 1086 to a supplier entered in the accounting records as $1,879.10; deducted in the bank statement in the correct amount of	1,789.10
(10)	Stolen check lacking an authorized signature deducted from Taurus Company's account by the bank in error	867.50

(11) Customer's check returned by the bank marked NSF, indicating that the customer's balance was not adequate to cover the check; no journal entry has been made to record the returned check.....   *1,260.50*

Instructions

a Prepare a reconciliation of the cash balances of Taurus Company and the bank to the correct balance on September 30, Year 4.

b Prepare a journal entry to adjust Taurus Company's accounting records on September 30, Year 4.

6-10 You are the senior accountant in charge of the March 31, Year 2, audit of Lido Company. Lido's inexperienced accountant has prepared the bank reconciliation shown below for your consideration. You have reviewed the dollar amounts in the reconciliation, and have determined that they are accurate.

LIDO COMPANY
Bank Reconciliation
March 31, Year 2

Balance in general ledger, Mar. 31, Year 2.........................		*$69,316.66*
Add: Deposit in transit, mailed Mar. 31, Year 2		*8,197.66*
$9,200 note receivable and $47 interest collected by bank Mar. 31, Year 2, less $1.07 service charge........................		*9,245.93*
Bank service charge for March, Year 2		*10.88*
Check in payment of account payable, drawn and paid by bank as $91.73, recorded in cash payments journal as $917.30......		*825.57*
Subtotal		*$87,596.70*
Less: Outstanding checks:		
No. 413	*$ 185.22*	
419	*216.25*	
420	*96.44*	
421	*123.80*	
422	*314.55*	
423	*112.01*	
Total outstanding checks	*$1,048.27*	
Check of customer, J. K. Lane, deposited Mar. 26, Year 2, returned NSF by bank Mar. 31, Year 2 ..	*814.69*	*1,862.96*
Computed balance in bank statement, Mar. 31, Year 2..		*$ 85,733.74*
Unlocated difference................................		*(14,320.54)*
Balance in bank statement, Mar. 31, Year 2...........		*$ 71,413.20*

Instructions

a Prepare a corrected bank reconciliation for Lido Company on March 31, Year 2, in the form illustrated on page 300.

b Prepare a correcting journal entry for Lido Company's Cash ledger account on March 31, Year 2. Record the net effect of the journal entry in the reconciliation prepared in **a**.

6-11   The following information pertains to marketable equity securities in the current portfolio of Quaid Corporation on December 31, Year 3:

	Cost	Market value
1,000 shares of M Company common stock	$ 50,000	$ 55,000
2,000 shares of N Company common stock	125,000	120,000
500 shares of P Company convertible preferred stock .	60,000	62,000
Totals	$235,000	$237,000

Quaid was organized on March 4, Year 3, and did not establish a valuation allowance to reduce marketable equity securities to market value at the end of Year 3, because the aggregate market value of the current portfolio exceeded aggregate cost.

During Year 4, Quaid completed the following transactions in marketable equity securities in its current portfolio:

Feb. 10   Acquired 1,000 shares of H Company common stock for $33,000.

June 19   Sold 500 shares of P Company convertible preferred stock for $66,000.

Sept. 5   Acquired 800 shares of R Company common stock at a total cost of $47,500.

Market values of the securities in the current portfolio on December 31, Year 4, were as follows:

1,000 shares of M Company common stock	$ 60,000
2,000 shares of N Company common stock	110,000
1,000 shares of H Company common stock	25,000
800 shares of R Company common stock	50,000
Total market value..	$245,000

On May 1, Year 5, the 800 shares of R Company common stock were sold for $44,000. There were no other acquisitions or sales through December 31, Year 7. The market values of the equity securities held in the current portfolio on December 31 of each of the succeeding three years were as follows:

	Year 5	Year 6	Year 7
1,000 shares of M Company common stock .	$ 52,000	$ 48,000	$ 65,000
2,000 shares of N Company common stock ..	90,000	120,000	125,000
1,000 shares of H Company common stock ..	30,000	24,000	40,000
Totals	$172,000	$192,000	$230,000

Instructions

a Prepare journal entries to record Quaid Corporation's transactions relating to marketable equity securities for the four years (Year 4 through Year 7), including appropriate entries (if any) to the valuation allowance ledger account at the end of each year. Disregard income taxes.

b Prepare the balance sheet presentation of Quaid Corporation's current marketable equity securities at the end of each year (Years 4 through 7).

6-12 You have completed your examination of the cash on hand and in banks in your audit of Harvey Company's financial statements for the year ended December 31, Year 7, and noted the following:

(1) Harvey maintains a general bank account at National Bank and a payroll bank account at City Bank. All checks are signed by the company president, Douglas Harvey. Harvey uses a Vouchers Payable ledger account to accompany its voucher system for all cash payments.

(2) Data and reconciliations prepared by Harvey's accountant on November 30, Year 7, indicated that the payroll account had a $1,000 general ledger and bank balance with no in-transit or outstanding items, and the general bank account had a $12,405 general ledger balance with checks outstanding aggregating $918 (no. 1202 for $575 and no. 1205 for $343) and one deposit of $492 in transit to National Bank.

(3) Your surprise cash count on Tuesday, January 2, Year 8, revealed that customers' checks totaling $540 and a National Bank deposit slip for that amount dated December 29, Year 7, were in Harvey's safe and that no cash was in

**General Ledger
General Bank Account
(National Bank)**

Ref.	Debits	Credits	Balance
Bal.			$12,405
12-1	$ 496		12,901
1206		$ 1,675	11,226
1207		645	10,581
12-6	832		11,413
1208		1,706	9,707
12-8	975		10,682
1209		2,062	8,620
1210		3,945	4,675
1211		6,237	1,562*
12-12	8,045		6,483
12-15	9,549		16,032
1212		1,845	14,187
RT		241	13,946
1213		350	13,596
D		2,072	11,524
12-22	1,513		13,037
1214		2,597	10,440
1215		1,739	8,701
12-29	540		9,241
12-31	942		10,183
1216		1,120	9,063
	$22,892	$26,234	

*Credit balance

transit to National Bank at that time. Your examination of the general account prenumbered checks revealed check no. 1216 to be the first unused check; it ultimately was issued to a supplier.

(4) Harvey's general ledger accounts are prepared on a posting machine, and all transactions are posted in chronological sequence. The ledger account for the general bank account for December, Year 7, is shown on page 337.

(5) The December statements from both banks were delivered unopened to you. The City Bank statement contained deposits for $1,675; $1,706; $1,845; and $2,597 and 72 paid checks totaling $7,823. The National Bank statement is shown below:

NATIONAL BANK
Account: Harvey Company (General Account)

Date	Charges		Credits	Balance
Year 7				
Nov. 30				$12,831
Dec. 1			$ 492	13,323
5	$1,675	$ 267 RT	496	11,877
8	575		832	12,134
11	1,706	654	975	10,749
14	1,987 D	2,062	8,045	14,745
18	6,237	1,845	9,949	16,612
21	241 RT	546 RT	546 CM	16,371
22	2,072 D		1,513	15,812
26	2,597			13,215
28	362	4 DM	1,010 CM	13,859
29	12 DM		362	14,209
	Total charges—$22,842		Tot. Cr.—$24,220	

Legend: CM: Credit memo   D: Draft
RT: Returned check   DM: Debit memo

(6) You obtained cutoff bank statements from both banks on January 8, Year 8. The National Bank statement is presented below:

NATIONAL BANK
Account: Harvey Company (General Account)

Date	Charges		Credits	Balance
Dec. 29, Year 7				$14,209
Jan. 2, Year 8	$1,739	$3,945	$540	9,065
Jan. 5, Year 8	350		942	9,657

(7) You determine that the bank statements are correct except that National Bank incorrectly charged a returned check on December 21 but corrected the account with a credit the same day.

(8) The $362 check charged by National Bank on December 28 was check no. 2000 drawn payable to Harvey Company and endorsed "Harvey Company by Donald Hume." Your investigation showed that the amount credited by National Bank on December 29 was an unauthorized transfer from City Bank Payroll Account to National Bank General Account that had been made by Harvey's accountant, who made no related entry in Harvey's accounting records. The check was charged to Harvey's payroll bank account on January 2, Year 8, in the cutoff statement that you received from City Bank.

(9) Drafts charged against the National Bank account were for trade acceptances that were signed by Douglas Harvey and issued to a supplier.

(10) On December 28, a 60-day, 6%, $1,000 promissory note was collected by National Bank for Harvey for a $4 collection fee.

(11) The $12 debit memo from National Bank was a charge for printed checks.

(12) Check no. 1213 was issued to replace check no. 1205 when the latter was reported not received by a vendor. Because of the delay in paying this account, Harvey Company was no longer entitled to the 2% cash discount it had taken in preparing the original check. Harvey completed a stop payment order for check no. 1205.

Instructions

a Prepare a four-column reconciliation (proof of cash) for Harvey Company's general bank account for the month of December, Year 7. Use the form illustrated on page 302.

b Prepare an adjusting entry to correct the General Bank Account ledger account of Harvey Company on December 31, Year 7. Record the net effect on the account in the proof of cash prepared in **a.** Use separate accounts receivable ledger accounts for customers' returned checks, and the unauthorized cash payment by Donald Hume.

6-13 In connection with an audit of cash of Vail Company as of December 31, Year 15, you obtained the following information:

(1) Balances in bank statements:

Nov. 30	$ 195,700
Dec. 31	313,674

(2) Balances in accounting records:

Nov. 30	$ 164,826
Dec. 31	287,598

(3) Cash receipts for month of December:

In bank statement	$1,670,450
In accounting records	2,751,445

(4) Outstanding checks:

Nov. 30	$ 63,524
Dec. 31	75,046

(5) Dishonored checks are recorded as a reduction of cash receipts. Dishonored checks that are redeposited are recorded as a regular cash receipt. Dishonored checks returned by the bank and recorded by Vail amounted to $6,250 during the month of December; according to the accounting records, $5,000 of dishonored checks were redeposited. Dishonored checks recorded in the bank statement but not in the accounting records until the following months amounted to $250 on November 30 and $2,300 on December 31.

(6) On December 31, a $2,323 check on which a stop-payment order was in force was charged by the bank to Vail's account in error.

(7) Proceeds of a promissory note from Capp Company, collected by the bank on December 30, were not entered in the accounting records:

Principal amount of note	$2,000
Interest, $20, less collection charge of $5............................	15
Net proceeds	$2,015

(8) Vail has pledged its accounts receivable with the bank under a contract whereby the bank lends Vail 80% on the pledged accounts receivable. Accounting for and collection of the accounts are performed by Vail, and adjustments of the loan are made from daily sales reports and daily cash deposits.

The bank credits Vail's account and increases the amount of the loan for 80% of the reported sales. The loan contract states that the sales report must be accepted by the bank before Vail is credited. Sales reports are forwarded by Vail to the bank on the first day following the date of sales. The bank allocates 80% of each deposit to the payment of the loan and 20% to Vail's account. Thus, only 80% of each day's sales and 20% of each collection deposit are entered in the bank statement.

The accountant for Vail records the pledge of new accounts receivable (80% of sales) as a debit to Cash and a credit to Loans Payable to Bank on the date of sales. Of the collections on accounts receivable, 100% is recorded as a cash receipt; 80% of the collections is recorded in the cash payments journal as a payment on the loan. In a review of the loan contract, you learned the following facts:

(a) Included in the deposits in transit is cash from the pledged accounts receivable. Sales were $40,500 on November 30 and $42,250 on December 31. The balance of the deposit in transit on December 31 was made up from collections of $32,110, which were entered in the accounting records in the manner indicated above.

(b) Collections on accounts receivable deposited in December, other than deposits in transit, totaled $1,320,000.

(c) Sales for December totaled $1,600,000.

(9) Cash receipts from other sources that were deposited intact during December totaled $120,835.

(10) Interest on the bank loan for the month of December, charged by the bank but not recorded in the accounting records, amounted to $6,140.

Instructions

a Prepare for Vail Company a four-column reconciliation (proof of cash) of beginning and ending cash balances, cash receipts, and cash payments for December, Year 15.

b Prepare the adjusting journal entry required to bring Vail Company's accounting records up to date on December 31, Year 15. Record the net effect on the Cash account in the proof of cash prepared in **a.**

Receivables

7

The balance sheet of every business enterprise includes a variety of claims from other parties that generally provide a future inflow of cash. These *receivables* arise from transactions and events such as sale of goods or services, loans made, subscriptions obtained from investors for capital stock or bonds, claims for income tax refunds, claims resulting from litigation, and amounts due from leasing of assets.

Receivables from customers frequently represent a substantial part of a business enterprise's current assets. Poor screening of applicants for credit or an inefficient collection policy may result in large losses. Consequently, strong accounting controls and effective management of receivables are typical characteristics of most profitable enterprises.

Valuation of Receivables

For most receivables the amount of money to be received and the due date can be reasonably determined. Accountants thus are faced with a relatively certain future inflow of cash, and the problem is to determine the net amount of this inflow.

A number of factors must be considered in the valuation of a prospective cash inflow. One factor is the probability that a receivable actually will be collected. For any specific receivable, the probability of collection might be difficult to establish; however, for a large group of receivables a reliable estimate of collectibility generally can be made. The possible noncollectibility of receivables is an example of a *loss contingency* because a future event (inability to collect) confirming the loss is *probable* and the amount of the loss can be *reasonably estimated*.[1] If the estimate of possible uncollectible accounts can be made within a range, but no single amount appears to be a better estimate than any other amount within the range, the Financial Accounting Standards Board recommended that the minimum amount in the range be accrued.[2] In the measurement of the amount of possible uncollectible accounts, the FASB stated:[3]

> Whether the amount of loss can be reasonably estimated . . . will normally depend on, among other things, the experience of the enterprise, information about the ability of individual debtors to pay, and appraisal of the receivables in light of the current economic environment. In the case of an enterprise that

---

[1] *FASB Statement No. 5*, "Accounting for Contingencies," FASB (Stamford: 1975), p. 4.
[2] *FASB Interpretation No. 14*, "Reasonable Estimation of the Amount of a Loss (an interpretation of *FASB Statement No. 5*)," FASB (Stamford: 1976), p. 2.
[3] *FASB Statement No. 5*, pp. 11–12.

has no experience of its own, reference to the experience of other enterprises in the same business may be appropriate. Inability to make a reasonable estimate of the amount of loss from uncollectible receivables . . . precludes accrual and may, if there is significant uncertainty as to collection, suggest that the installment method, the cost recovery method, or some other method of revenue recognition be used. . . .

Another factor to be considered in the valuation of receivables is the length of time until collection. As stated in Chapter 5, an amount of money due at some future time is not worth as much as the same amount due immediately. The longer the time to maturity, the larger is the difference between the *maturity value* and the *present value* of a receivable. When the time to maturity is long, most contracts between debtors and creditors require the payment of a fair rate of interest, and the present value of such a contract is equal to its face amount. The present value of any noninterest-bearing receivable is less than the amount that will be received on the due date. If the time to maturity is short, this difference usually is ignored. For example, a 30-day unsecured trade account receivable almost always is recorded at its face amount. The difference between present value and face amount of longer-term receivables always should be considered, because this difference may be material.

Receivables from Sale of Goods and Services

The most common receivables result from revenue-producing activities, such as the sale of goods and services. The unsecured *trade account* is the most important of these. Contracts governing trade accounts receivable typically are informal and are supported by such documents as sales orders, invoices, and delivery contracts. Most trade accounts are noninterest-bearing. However, in the retail trade the addition of interest or a service charge to revolving charge accounts or installment receivables is a common practice. Manufacturers and wholesalers use disallowed cash discounts as a form of interest charge if payment is made after the discount period.

Some receivables from customers are represented by various commercial credit instruments such as promissory notes. Such instruments have a stronger legal status than ordinary trade accounts, and because the terms are specified in writing, the holder finds it easier to borrow against them.

A customer who requests an extension of time on a trade account often is asked to sign a promissory note so that the payee may discount the note and receive cash. Most notes and other commercial credit instruments bear interest, because they involve credit for long periods of time. Amounts due from employees and owners of a business enterprise may be included among trade receivables if they result from the sale of goods and services at the usual credit terms.

Receivables from Miscellaneous Sources

Some receivables result from transactions not directly related to the sale of goods and services. For example, short-term advances to affiliated companies, subcontractors, or customers are made in anticipation of future benefits. A claim against an insurance company and a claim based on a legal suit for damages are other examples of miscellaneous receivables. Prospective refunds of amounts previously paid, such as a claim for refund of prior years' income taxes, represent receivables whenever the collection of the claim is reasonably certain. Issuance of capital stock and bonds on a subscription basis and disposal of plant assets also represent sources of miscellaneous receivables. Any type of receivable that is material in amount should be listed separately in the balance sheet. Miscellaneous receivables that are expected to be collected in one year are classified as current assets; long-term receivables are classified under Investments.

Accruals of interest, dividends, rent, and royalties are current receivables that represent a prospective inflow of cash. Rent and interest receivable accrue as a function of time. Dividends usually are not recorded as receivables prior to the ex-dividend date. Royalties usually accrue as a result of the manufacture or sale of products or the extraction of natural resources.

Occasionally, a receivable arises out of a debit balance in trade accounts payable when, for one reason or another, overpayment has been made to a supplier. If the purchaser expects a cash refund, the amount involved clearly is a receivable. The rule against offsetting assets and liabilities requires that any sizable debit balance in trade accounts payable be treated as a receivable rather than as an offset against other trade accounts payable. Similarly, a large credit balance in customers' accounts is reported as a current liability. An advance payment on a purchase contract is reported as a prepayment for goods rather than as a receivable. Receivables arising from leasing transactions are discussed in Chapter 20.

TRADE ACCOUNTS RECEIVABLE

A large portion of retail trade in the United States involves credit in some form; at the wholesale and manufacturing level almost all sales transactions are on a credit basis. Terms on ordinary trade accounts receivable range from the 10 days typically allowed for taking cash discounts to as long as six months or a year in some cases.

Accounting System and Internal Controls   Business enterprises with a large volume of credit sales usually computerize their accounting records. A computerized system enables the operator to record the credit sale, post to the controlling account, and post to subsidiary ledger accounts in a single operation. Such a system also facilitates the preparation of financial statements and an aging of trade accounts receivable (as illustrated on page 352) at appropriate intervals.

A procedure known as *cycle billing* may be used by department stores and public utilities with a large number of customers. Accounts receivable subsidiary ledgers are divided into a number of groups on the basis of geographical location, type of customer, or alphabetically, with each group having its own subcontrol account. The customers in each subcontrol group are billed at different times during a month. This procedure has the advantage of spreading the work of preparing customer statements more evenly during the month and assuring a more uniform cash flow from collection of trade accounts receivable.

It is possible to reduce record keeping by the elimination of the formal subsidiary trade accounts receivable ledgers. Invoices for credit sales may be sorted by subcontrol groups, and the total amount is entered directly in the trade accounts receivable controlling account. The individual invoices then are filed according to customer. At the end of the month or cycle billing period, the amount receivable from each customer is summarized in a statement, the duplicate copy of which becomes the subsidiary ledger for that customer. Invoices are reproduced (to provide a file copy) and are mailed to each customer along with the statement of the customer's account.

Effective internal controls over the sale of goods and related cash collections are an integral part of the system for handling trade accounts receivable. The responsibility for recording sales and collections of trade accounts receivable should not be assigned to individuals who handle cash receipts or who prepare bank deposit slips and bank reconciliations. Without such segregation of duties, a dishonest employee could abstract cash collections from customers and conceal the theft by recording the collection as a debit to the Sales Returns and Allowances ledger account, or by writing off the receivable as uncollectible.

Recording Trade Accounts Receivable and Revenue

Two important questions faced by accountants in recording trade accounts receivable are:

1   At what point in the earning process should a trade account receivable be recorded?

2   How should the net amount of a trade account receivable be measured so that this asset and the related revenue and expenses will be recorded accurately?

Trade accounts receivable generally are recorded when sales are made and title to the goods passes. As stated in Chapter 3, receivables for services are recorded only as services are performed. Receivables are not recorded when a customer's order is received or when goods are produced; and shipments on *consignment* are not sales, because title to the goods does not pass until *consignees* sell the goods. However, receivables should be recorded for work completed on construction-type contracts.[4]

When it is determined that revenue has been realized and recording of the claim against a customer is warranted, the question of measuring the amount of the receivable (and the revenue) still remains. For example, assume that a parcel of land is sold by a land developer for $5,000. The customer may pay either $5,000 cash or $1,000 down and $1,100 at the end of each year for five years. If the sale is made on the deferred payment plan, should the receivable be recorded by the land developer at $4,000 ($5,000 cash price less the $1,000 down payment) or at $5,500, the face amount of the five remaining payments of $1,100 each? Is the revenue realized by the land developer in the current year $5,000, $6,500, or some other amount? The amount of revenue is dependent on the valuation of the consideration received

---

[4]Accounting for consignment shipments is covered in *Modern Advanced Accounting* of this series; procedures relating to construction-type contracts are covered in Chapter 9.

(including receivables) from revenue transactions. Thus, the land developer should record the receivable at $4,000 and recognize revenue of $5,000 at the time the land is sold. Accounting for trade accounts receivable centers on two issues: (1) the amount due, and (2) the estimate of the probability that the receivable will be collected. A number of problems relating to these issues are discussed in the following sections.

MEASURING TRADE ACCOUNTS RECEIVABLE

Trade Discounts In some industries it is customary to bill customers a gross price subject to one or more trade discounts. The gross price usually is the suggested price for resale, and the trade discount represents the difference between gross (list) price and the price to the purchaser before cash discounts. The use of fixed list prices and varying trade discounts enables the seller to change prices, or to grant special discounts to certain customers, without reprinting catalogs or price lists. For financial accounting, these discounts should be recognized for what they are—a convenient means of pricing. The amount that a customer will pay is the net price after the trade discount, and this is the amount at which the receivable and the related revenue are recorded.

Cash (Sales) Discounts Cash discounts are used to establish a *cash price* when payment is received shortly after delivery of goods, as distinct from a higher *deferred payment price*. For example, if an invoice for $10,000 provides for terms of 2/10, n/30, the customer has two alternatives: (1) pay $9,800 in 10 days, or (2) wait the full 30 days and pay $10,000. The differential of $200 represents an effective interest rate of 36.7% for the use of the $9,800 for the extra 20-day period, and thus offers a strong incentive for payment before the 10-day discount period expires.[5]

A theoretical valuation of receivables subject to cash discounts should allow for the probability that discounts will be taken. In the case cited above, for example, if the probability is high that the customer will take the discount, the receivable is worth only $9,800. If the customer is expected to pay the face amount, the receivable is worth $10,000.

In dealing with a large number of receivables, accountants find that past experience usually is a good guide in estimating customer reaction to discounts that are available to be taken. In view of the generous saving inherent in the cash price, the assumption that most customers will take the discounts probably is justified.

Several approaches may be used to account for sales discounts. For example, entries to the Trade Accounts Receivable and Sales ledger accounts may be recorded at the face amount of the receivables, and discounts taken by customers are recorded by debits to the Sales Discounts ledger account. No journal entry is made at the end of the accounting period to anticipate discounts that may be taken by customers on outstanding trade accounts receivable.

---

[5]There are eighteen 20-day periods in one year; therefore, the annualized rate earned may be computed as follows: ($200 × 18) ÷ $9,800 = 0.367.

Alternatively, the same procedure may be followed, except that an adjusting entry is made at the end of the accounting period to accrue discounts that may be taken by customers on outstanding receivables. The Sales Discounts ledger account is debited and the Allowance for Sales Discounts account is credited for the amount of potential discounts that may be taken on outstanding receivables. The balance in the Allowance for Sales Discounts ledger account is deducted from trade accounts receivable in the balance sheet. Actual discounts taken by customers at the beginning of the following accounting period may be debited to the Allowance for Sales Discounts ledger account. If a reversing entry is made to eliminate the allowance account, discounts taken then may be recorded in the usual manner by debits to the Sales Discounts ledger account.

Under the first approach, trade accounts receivable and pre-tax income are overstated by the amount of estimated sales discounts not accrued. These overstatements are eliminated under the alternative approach, which is consistent with the objective of reporting trade accounts receivable and revenue at *net realizable values* in the financial statements. However, we should point out that accrual of sales discounts is not allowed for income tax purposes.

Estimated Collection Costs   Valuation of trade accounts receivable on the balance sheet date should take into account any direct costs (that are material in amount) of collecting outstanding receivables. For example, the estimated legal costs that may be incurred in the collection of outstanding receivables may be recognized as an expense of the current accounting period, and the related allowance account is deducted from trade accounts receivable in the balance sheet. Observe the following title of the valuation account used by a publicly owned company:

Estimated collection costs deducted from face amount of receivables

Accounts receivable:	
Installment accounts receivable, substantially all of which are due within one year	$58,216,135
Other trade receivables	926,889
Total face amount of accounts receivable	$59,143,024
Less: **Allowance for returns, losses, and collection costs**	13,563,641
Total accounts receivable (net)	$45,579,383

Sales Returns and Allowances   The value assigned to trade accounts receivable also should recognize the probability that some customers will return goods that are unsatisfactory or will make other claims requiring reduction in the net amount receivable. Potential sales returns and allowances reduce the amount that ultimately will be collected from customers and thus reduce the net realizable value of trade accounts receivable. If the amounts are material, as in the recorded music and catalog sales industries, periodic income measurement is improved by an adjustment for estimated returns and allowances.

To illustrate, assume that experience shows that sales returns average 10% of accounts receivable, and that an average of 60% of the original selling price ultimately is realized from the returned goods. If trade accounts receivable at the end of the accounting period amount to $100,000 and the perpetual inventory system is in use, the appropriate end-of-period adjusting entry is illustrated below:

Accrual of sales returns

Inventory—Anticipated Sales Returns (at net realizable value)		
[($100,000 × 0.10) × 0.60]	*6,000*	
Sales Returns ($100,000 × 0.10)	*10,000*	
Cost of Goods Sold		*6,000*
Allowance for Sales Returns		*10,000*
To record anticipated sales returns.		

The effect of this journal entry is to reduce current assets and the gross profit on sales by $4,000—the difference between the original selling price and the estimated net realizable value of the goods returned. This adjusting entry may be reversed on the first day of the next accounting period; then, as sales returns are made by customers, the Sales Returns ledger account is debited and Trade Accounts Receivable is credited.

The accrual of sales returns at the end of an accounting period is widely used in industries experiencing material amounts of returns.[6] However, the accrual of sales returns (as in the case of accrual of sales discounts) is not allowed for income tax purposes.

Allowance for Freight-Out   Occasionally goods are sold with the understanding that a customer will pay the freight charges and then deduct that amount from the remittance. In such instances both trade accounts receivable and sales may be recorded net of the freight charges. Alternatively, both trade accounts receivable and sales may be recorded at the gross amount billed to the customer, along with a debit to Freight-Out and a credit to Allowance for Freight-Out. The balance in the allowance account is deducted from trade accounts receivable in the balance sheet.

Sales and Excise Taxes   Many government units impose sales and excise taxes on particular products or on sales transactions. Usually, the seller is responsible for the remittance of these taxes to the government. An excise tax imposed on the manufacture of a product is a part of the cost of production, but an excise tax on the sale of the product is imposed on the purchaser and is collected by the seller.

If sales and excise taxes are collected as separately disclosed additions to the selling price, they should not be confused with revenue but should be credited to a liability account. Whether this is done at the time of each sale or as an adjustment at the end of the accounting period is a matter of convenience.[7] Generally, it is prefer-

---

[6]See also discussion on page 108 in Chapter 3.
[7]Business enterprises account for sales and excise taxes in a variety of ways: Some do not report such taxes either in sales or in expenses; others include such taxes in gross sales, then deduct them in the computation of net sales; still other enterprises report sales and excise taxes either as part of cost of goods sold or as operating expenses. The amounts of excise taxes may be staggering: For example, some years ago one enterprise reported gross sales of $145 million less excise taxes of $110 million, with net sales of only $35 million.

able to record the tax liability at the time of sale. For example, if a day's sales amount to $20,000 and are subject to a 6% sales tax, the sales tax payable is $1,200, and the journal entry to record sales is:

Recording one day's sales and sales tax payable

Trade Accounts Receivable (or Cash) ($20,000 × 1.06)	21,200	
Sales Tax Payable ($20,000 × 0.06)		1,200
Sales		20,000
To record sales and sales tax liability.		

Container Deposits   Customers may be charged for deposits on containers, with the understanding that the deposits will be refunded when the containers are returned. The containers, such as drums, are depreciable plant assets of the business enterprise that owns them. If container deposits are collected in cash, the only problem is the correct accounting for the refund obligation. When containers are returned, the liability is canceled by the refund of the deposit; if containers are not returned, the liability no longer exists, and the difference between the amount of the deposit and the cost of the containers not returned represents a gain or loss which, as a matter of convenience, may be recorded in the ledger account for the depreciation of containers. At the end of an accounting period, an adjusting entry is required to record the estimate of the containers that will not be returned.

In some cases, container deposits are debited to the Trade Accounts Receivable ledger account. This creates an uncertainty with respect to the amount that will be collected. Until the uncertainty is resolved, trade accounts receivable show a separate item for the amount billed to customers for containers.

Estimating Probability of Collection

Thus far we have considered the problem of determining the amount due from customers under the terms of credit sales. The other major valuation problem is to evaluate the probability that customers will pay their accounts. Because a business enterprise does not make a credit sale unless ultimate collection is reasonably assured, the probability of noncollection with respect to a specific sale is presumably low. However, the best efforts of a capable credit department cannot eliminate all uncollectible accounts. Furthermore, the managerial objective is not to minimize doubtful accounts expense but to maximize net income. Too stringent a credit policy may cause loss of sales volume, which more than offsets the reduction in the doubtful accounts expense.

Receivables that will never be collected have a zero value, and the related revenue will not be realized. The objective in the estimation of doubtful accounts expense is to prevent an overstatement of assets and revenue in the accounting period in which sales are made.

In the ledger, the estimate of doubtful accounts is carried as a credit balance in a valuation account titled Allowance for Doubtful Accounts or Allowance for Uncollectible Accounts. This is known as the *allowance method* of accounting for doubtful accounts expense. A separate valuation account is used, because it is not known which specific receivables will prove uncollectible and because the Trade Accounts Receivable controlling account must agree with the subsidiary ledger detail. In the balance sheet, the allowance account is deducted from trade accounts receivable to measure their net realizable value.[8]

The doubtful accounts expense may be classified several ways in the income statement. Logically, doubtful accounts expense should be classified as an offset against gross sales, because it represents revenue that will not be collected. In practice, doubtful accounts expense usually appears among operating expenses, under the assumption that credit "losses" are a normal expense of operations. Finally, some consider doubtful accounts expense as a financial management item and report it as "other expense." Because each of these reporting practices produces the same net income, the issue is not a major one.

Two kinds of evidence are used in estimates of doubtful accounts expense: (1) the average relationship between sales and uncollectible accounts in past years, and (2) an analysis of the quality and age of outstanding receivables at the end of an accounting period.

Estimate of Doubtful Accounts Expense Based on Sales   The average percentage of credit sales not collected in past accounting periods is a logical basis for estimating the portion of current credit sales that will prove uncollectible. This approach, often referred to as the *income statement approach*, is simple to apply and makes possible an estimate of doubtful accounts expense as soon as credit sales are recorded. It results in a sound matching of costs and revenue, and is especially appropriate in the preparation of interim reports. For example, if credit sales for the first quarter of the current year are $250,000, and doubtful accounts expense is estimated at 2% of credit sales, the following adjusting entry is required:

Adjusting entry to record doubtful accounts expense

Doubtful Accounts Expense ($250,000 × 0.02)   5,000
Allowance for Doubtful Accounts   5,000
To record estimated doubtful accounts expense at 2% of
credit sales for first quarter of year.

If the ratio of cash sales to credit sales is relatively constant, estimates of doubtful accounts expense as a percentage of *total sales* may produce reasonably accurate results. Strictly speaking, however, the estimate of doubtful accounts expense should be based on *credit sales* only. The estimate may be further refined by analyses of the experience for different classes of customers.

Application of the appropriate percentage to the credit sales for an accounting period provides an estimate of the sales of the period that will not be collected. The degree of error in the estimate cannot be determined until the record of collection experience is in. Because this approach initially ignores the balance in the Allowance for Doubtful Accounts ledger account, a periodic test should be made to make certain that the allowance account is neither overstated nor understated.

[8]*APB Opinion No. 12*, "Omnibus Opinion—1967," AICPA (New York: 1967), p. 188.

Estimate of Doubtful Accounts Expense Based on Receivables   An effective way to test the adequacy of the allowance for doubtful accounts and to estimate doubtful accounts expense is to make an analysis of accounts receivable by age group and probability of collection. This procedure is known as the **balance sheet approach** of estimating doubtful accounts expense. Generally, a significant correlation exists between the length of time an account receivable is past due and the collectibility of the receivable. A summary that classifies the balances of all accounts receivable according to whether the amounts are not yet due, or are past due by varying lengths of time, is known as an **aging of accounts receivable.**

The number of different age classes to be used depends on actual experience and the terms of sale. An estimate of the average collection experience for each age class provides a basis for estimating the portion of outstanding trade accounts receivable that may prove to be uncollectible.

An aging summary of trade accounts receivable for Midwest Company on December 31, Year 5, is illustrated below:

Analysis of trade accounts receivable by age

MIDWEST COMPANY
Aging of Trade Accounts Receivable
December 31, Year 5

Credit terms: Net 30 days

Classification by due dates	Balances in each category (summarized from analysis of individual accounts)	Estimated uncollectibles, %	Estimated doubtful accounts
Not yet due	$2,400,000 (75.0%)	1	$24,000
Under 30 days past due .	416,000 (13.0%)	3	12,480
30–60 days past due	208,000 (6.5%)	5	10,400
61–120 days past due . . .	96,000 (3.0%)	10	9,600
121–180 days past due . .	48,000 (1.5%)	30	14,400
Over 180 days past due .	32,000 (1.0%)	Individual analysis	25,000
Totals	$3,200,000 (100.0%)		$95,880

The percentages shown next to each category are useful in detecting an imbalance between current and past-due accounts. When an aging of receivables is used as a basis for the estimate of doubtful accounts expense, the current provision is an amount sufficient to bring the balance in the Allowance for Doubtful Accounts ledger account **to the amount indicated by the aging analysis.** For example, if the balance of the Allowance for Doubtful Accounts for Midwest Company on December 31, Year 5, is $55,000 after interim provisions of $60,000 and write-offs of $70,000 during Year 5 (debit Allowance for Doubtful Accounts and credit Trade Accounts Receivable), the analysis above requires the following adjusting entry to bring the allowance account balance to the required $95,880:

Adjustment based on aging	Doubtful Accounts Expense ($95,880 − $55,000) 40,880

Doubtful Accounts Expense ($95,880 − $55,000) *40,880*
   Allowance for Doubtful Accounts *40,880*
To adjust allowance to required balance of $95,880.

A summary of the allowance account for the year ended December 31, Year 5, for Midwest Company follows:

Allowance for Doubtful Accounts

Date	Explanation	Debit	Credit	Balance
Year 5				
Jan. 1	Balance			65,000 cr
Jan.–Dec.	Interim provisions during Year 5		60,000	125,000 cr
Jan.–Dec.	Write-offs during Year 5	70,000		55,000 cr
Dec. 31	Adjustment at year-end		40,880	95,880 cr

A simpler method sometimes followed is to increase the allowance *to a specified percentage* of receivables or to increase the allowance *by a specified percentage* of receivables. These procedures are not recommended because the results they produce are less accurate than those obtained through a comprehensive aging analysis.

In the process of aging trade accounts receivable, management should evaluate current financial statements of major customers to make a better assessment of the probability of collection. The credit department of a business enterprise is assigned responsibility for a continuing analysis of the financial statements of existing and prospective customers so that sales are not made to those who represent excessive risk of nonpayment.

Doubtful Accounts Expense and Income Measurement

It is unlikely that estimated uncollectible accounts receivable will agree with actual write-offs applicable to each year's revenue. As long as there is a reasonably close correlation between the annual estimate and actual experience, minor discrepancies from year to year may be ignored.

When an *unusual* and *infrequent* event takes place, such as the destruction of a customer's business by a major and infrequent earthquake that results in a material write-off of accounts receivable, special analysis of the write-off is required. If such a write-off was a direct result of the earthquake, the effect of the write-off is an *extraordinary loss*. However, any portion of the write-off that would have resulted from a valuation of accounts receivable in the normal course of business is not included in the determination of the extraordinary loss.[9] Extraordinary items are discussed in Chapter 3.

---

[9]*APB Opinion No. 30,* "Reporting the Results of Operations- . . . ," AICPA (New York: 1973), p. 566.

A major adjustment to the allowance for doubtful accounts or a revision of the method used to compute doubtful accounts expense is viewed by the Accounting Principles Board as a *change in accounting estimate:*

> Future events and their effects cannot be perceived with certainty; estimating, therefore, requires the exercise of judgment. Thus accounting estimates change as new events occur, as more experience is acquired, or as additional information is obtained.[10]

> The Board concludes that the effect of a change in accounting estimate should be accounted for in (a) the period of change if the change affects that period only, or (b) the period of change and future periods if the change affects both. A change in an estimate should not be accounted for by restating amounts reported in financial statements of prior periods or by reporting pro forma amounts for prior periods.[11]

The effect of a change in an accounting estimate on income before extraordinary items, net income, and earnings per share of the current accounting period *is disclosed if material in amount* Estimates made each period in the ordinary course of accounting for doubtful accounts expense need not be disclosed.

In income tax returns, a change in estimate may be treated differently from the method used for financial accounting. Income tax regulations provide that an excessive or inadequate balance in the allowance for doubtful accounts may be corrected by adjusting the rate used in estimating doubtful accounts expense in future years.

Write-Off and Subsequent Collection of Receivables

When the decision is made to write off receivables, the debit to the Allowance for Doubtful Accounts and the credit to the Trade Accounts Receivable ledger accounts have no effect on either the carrying amount of accounts receivable or the net income of the accounting period in which the write-off occurs. If a receivable that has been written off is collected later, Trade Accounts Receivable is debited and the Allowance for Doubtful Accounts is credited. This reverses the write-off, and the collection then is recorded in the usual manner. This method has the advantage of providing in the customer's subsidiary ledger account a complete record of credit experience with that customer.

Direct Write-Off Method for Doubtful Accounts Expense

Some business enterprises may elect to record doubtful accounts expense only as specific receivables are considered to be uncollectible. This *direct write-off method* of accounting for doubtful accounts expense overstates the carrying amount of receivables and does not match doubtful accounts expense with revenue, because receivables representing sales in Year 1, for example, may be recorded as an expense in Year 2, and receivables originating in Year 2, may be recorded as an expense in Year 3 or Year 4.

---

[10]*APB Opinion No. 20,* "Accounting Changes," AICPA (New York: 1971), p. 338.
[11]Ibid., p. 397. (A complete discussion of changes in accounting estimate is included in Chapter 22.)

Under the direct write-off method, uncollectible receivables are written off by a debit to Doubtful Accounts Expense and a credit to Trade Accounts Receivable. Collection of receivables written off in a previous accounting period is recorded by a credit to Doubtful Accounts Recovered (a miscellaneous revenue item), and the recovery of receivables written off earlier in the current period is recorded by a credit to Doubtful Accounts Expense to eliminate an expense recorded prematurely.

Either the allowance method or the direct write-off method may be used for income tax purposes, but the method adopted must be followed consistently. The allowance method generally is more advantageous for income tax purposes, because deductible expenses are anticipated, and income taxes are not paid on revenue that may never be collected.

Installment Accounts Receivable

Many individuals and business enterprises find it convenient to buy certain items on the installment plan. The installment contract, in essence a promissory note providing for payment over an extended period of time, is widely used at the retail level. Most enterprises that sell goods on the installment plan have adequate financial resources to carry their own installment accounts receivable. Some enterprises, however, sell or assign their installment accounts receivable to finance companies.

Installment accounts receivable from the sale of goods or services in the ordinary course of business, including those due more than one year from the balance sheet date, are included in current assets (net of any unearned interest and finance charges). This classification is appropriate because installment receivables arise in the operating cycle from revenue-generating activities. For example, a recent balance sheet of a publicly owned corporation included the following:

Unearned interest and finance charges are deducted from gross installment accounts receivable

Current assets:	
Installment accounts receivable (easy payment and revolving charge accounts)	*$9,854,000*
Less: Unearned interest and finance charges of $410,000, and allowance for doubtful accounts of $130,000	*(540,000)*
Net installment accounts receivable	*$9,314,000*

The unearned interest and finance charges are recognized as revenue only when realized and are disclosed separately in the income statement.

Analysis of Trade Accounts Receivable

Trade accounts receivable are an important factor in an analysis of financial liquidity and a projection of cash flows. Changes in the length of the average collection period or the number of days' sales in trade receivables, for example, should be analyzed carefully, and action should be initiated to correct unfavorable trends. A discussion of several analytical techniques for trade accounts receivable appears in Chapter 24.

USE OF RECEIVABLES AS A SOURCE OF CASH

Business enterprises generally raise the cash needed for current operations through the collection of trade accounts receivable. It is possible to accelerate this process by (1) *pledging* receivables as collateral for loans, (2) *selling* receivables, or (3) *assigning* receivables. In some industries, such procedures are quite common; in other industries, this may be done only in times of absolute necessity.

Enterprises engaged in the buying of receivables are known as *factors,* and the process of selling receivables is called *factoring.* Factors generally buy receivables outright, that is, *without recourse.* Alternatively, factors or other lending institutions may buy receivables *with recourse,* or may lend money to the owner of the receivables under a legal arrangement known as an *assignment.* In such cases customers generally are instructed to make payments directly to the factors or other lenders. Factoring is an important source of ready cash in industries such as textiles, apparel, furniture, and consumer electronics.

A pledge of accounts receivable as collateral for a loan involves no special accounting problems. Accounting for the sale and the assignment of accounts receivable is described in the following sections.

Sale of Receivables without Recourse

The purpose of selling receivables *without recourse* is to shift to the purchaser of the receivables the risk of credit losses, the effort of collection, and the waiting period that result from the granting of credit. The "without recourse" applies only to the inability of customers to pay, not to disputes as to quality or price of the merchandise.

The acceptance of credit cards by retail merchants is a familiar form of sale (factoring) of receivables without recourse. For example, when merchants accept American Express, MasterCard, or Visa credit cards, they avoid accounting costs and doubtful accounts expense, and obtain cash almost immediately, in return for a 4 to 7% fee (discount). The amount of the fee depends on the volume of business a merchant generates for the credit card company. The fee or discount may be recorded by the merchant as a loss on sale of receivables, or as an interest and factoring expense because the sale of receivables is essentially a financing transaction.

Sale of Receivables with Recourse

When receivables are sold *with recourse,* the seller (transferor) in effect guarantees the receivables, and the purchaser (transferee) is reimbursed for failure of debtors to pay the full amounts anticipated at the time of sale.

Generally, the sale of ordinary trade receivables with recourse results in receipt of proceeds that are less than the face amount of the receivables sold. Similarly, the sale of installment accounts receivable that bear a lower interest rate than the discount rate used in the sale of the receivables results in proceeds that are less than the carrying amount of the receivables. For example, a sale for $18,500 of trade accounts receivable with a face amount of $20,000 and a carrying amount of $19,400 is recorded as follows:

Sale of accounts receivable at a loss

Cash	18,500	
Allowance for Doubtful Accounts...........................	600	
Loss on Transfer (Sale) of Trade Accounts Receivable	900	
Trade Accounts Receivable		20,000

To record sale of trade accounts receivable on a recourse basis.

However, the sale of installment accounts receivable that bear a higher interest rate than the discount rate used to compute the proceeds on the sale would result in a gain. To illustrate, assume the following ledger account balances for installment accounts receivable that are *considered fully collectible:*

Carrying amount of installment accounts receivable to be sold

Installment accounts receivable, including interest at 1½% a month, payable at the rate of $723 a month for 36 months starting in one month... $26,028

Less: Deferred interest revenue... 6,028

Carrying amount of installment accounts receivable [equal to the present value of ordinary annuity of 36 payments of $723 a month at 1½% a month: $723 × 27.660684 (Table 4 in the Appendix at the end of Chapter 5) = $20,000]... $20,000

If these receivables are sold with recourse at a price to yield 1% a month to the transferee, the proceeds on the sale are computed below:

Proceeds on sale of installment accounts receivable

Present value of ordinary annuity of 36 payments of $723 a month, with interest at 1% a month: $723 × 30.107505 (Table 4 in the Appendix at the end of Chapter 5) $21,768

The *sale* of the receivables is recorded by the transferor as follows:

Transferor's journal entry to record sale of installment accounts receivable on recourse basis at a gain

Cash	21,768	
Deferred Interest Revenue	6,028	
Installment Accounts Receivable		26,028
Gain on Transfer (Sale) of Installment Accounts Receivable		1,768

To record sale of installment accounts receivable on a recourse basis. Receivables bear interest at 1½% a month but were sold to yield 1% a month to transferee.

The *acquisition* of the receivables and the receipt of the first monthly installment of $723 is recorded by the transferee as follows:

Transferee's journal
entries to record
acquisition of
installment accounts
receivable and receipt
of first monthly
installment

Installment Accounts Receivable	*26,028*	
Deferred Interest Revenue		*4,260*
Cash		*21,768*

To record acquisition of installment accounts receivable on a recourse basis at a price to yield 1% a month.

Cash	*723*	
Deferred Interest Revenue	*218*	
Installment Accounts Receivable		*723*
Interest Revenue ($21,768 × 0.01)		*218*

To record receipt of first monthly installment.

A sale of receivables with recourse frequently has the characteristics of a borrowing contract collateralized by the receivables. *FASB Statement No. 77,* ''Reporting by Transferors for Transfers of Receivables with Recourse,'' requires a transfer of receivables *with recourse* to be recognized as a *sale* if all the following conditions are met:[12]

1   The transferor surrenders control of the future economic benefits embodied in the receivables.

2   The transferor's obligation under the recourse provisions can be reasonably estimated.

3   The transferee cannot require the transferor to repurchase the receivables except pursuant to the recourse provisions.

If any of these conditions is not met, the amount of the proceeds from the transfer of receivables is reported as a liability resulting from a borrowing transaction.[13] When a transfer of receivables qualifies as a sale, all *probable adjustments*[14] in connection with the recourse obligations are accrued by the transferor in the measurement of the gain or loss on the transfer (sale) of the receivables. The proceeds received from the sale of receivables and the amount of transferred receivables that remain uncollected at the end of the accounting period are disclosed in a note to the transferor's financial statements.

Assignment of Receivables

Instead of selling receivables, a business enterprise may borrow money using the receivables as collateral. This may involve a pledge of the receivables under a contract providing that the proceeds from the collection of the receivables must be

---

[12]*FASB Statement No. 77,* ''Reporting by Transferors for Transfers of Receivables with Recourse,'' FASB (Stamford, 1983), p. 2.
[13]Ibid., p. 3.
[14]Including, for example, adjustments for *(a)* failure to collect for any reason, *(b)* estimated effects of prepayments, and *(c)* defects in the legal title of the transferred receivables.

used to retire the loan. Alternatively, receivables may be *assigned* under a more formal arrangement whereby a borrower (*assignor*) pledges the receivables to a lender (*assignee*) and signs a promissory note payable. Assignment gives the assignee the same right to bring action to collect the receivables that the assignor possesses. The assignor retains the credit risks and continues collection efforts, and promises to make good any receivables that cannot be collected. In most cases, customers are not notified of the assignment and make payments directly to the assignor; however, they may be instructed to make payments to the assignee. The assignor generally has some equity in the assigned receivables because the financing company advances less than 100% of the face amount of the receivables assigned.

The primary accounting problem raised by assignment of receivables is to measure the assignor's equity in the assigned receivables and the liability to the assignee. Assigned receivables are transferred to a separate ledger account, As-

Journal entries for assignment of accounts receivable

Transaction	Journal entries in assignor's accounting records	
Jan. 2: Assigned accounts receivable of $50,000. Finco, Inc., remitted 90% of receivables, less 2% fee ($45,000 × 0.02 = $900).	Assigned Accounts Receivable ... 50,000	
	Accounts Receivable	50,000
	Cash 44,100	
	Interest Expense 900	
	Notes Payable to Finco, Inc.	45,000
Jan. 31: Collected $30,150 and paid this amount to Finco, Inc., including interest at 1% a month on $45,000 unpaid balance of loan. Balances on Jan. 31 are as follows:	Cash 30,150	
	Assigned Accounts Receivable	30,150
Assigned accounts receivable ($50,000 − $30,150) $19,850	Notes Payable to Finco, Inc....... 29,700	
Note payable to Finco, Inc. ($45,000 − $29,700) 15,300	Interest Expense ($45,000 × 0.01)................ 450	
	Cash	30,150
Feb. 28: Collected $17,000 and paid balance owed to Finco, Inc., plus interest at 1% a month on $15,300 unpaid balance of loan.	Cash 17,000	
	Assigned Accounts Receivable	17,000
	Notes Payable to Finco, Inc....... 15,300	
	Interest Expense ($15,300 × 0.01)................ 153	
	Cash	15,453
Feb. 28: Transferred balance of assigned receivables to the Accounts Receivable ledger account.	Accounts Receivable 2,850	
	Assigned Accounts Receivable ($19,850 − $17,000)	2,850

signed Accounts Receivable, and a liability to the assignee is recorded. As collections are received by the assignor, assigned receivables are reduced, and the liability to the assignee is correspondingly reduced when cash is remitted by the assignor to the assignee. Fees and interest charges are included in the remittance and are recorded as expenses.

To illustrate, assume that on January 2, Year 1, Adams Company assigned receivables of $50,000 to Finco, Inc., and received $45,000, less a fee of 2% on the amount advanced. Interest at 1% of the unpaid balance of the loan was to be paid monthly. The journal entries for Adams to record the assignment and subsequent transactions are shown on page 359.

The assignor's equity in assigned receivables generally is reported in the assignor's balance sheet by deducting the balance of notes payable to the assignee from the amount of the assigned receivables. Offsetting the liability against the asset may be justified in this situation because collections of assigned receivables must be used to liquidate the loan. The presentation of assigned receivables by Adams Company on January 31, Year 1, is illustrated below:

Balance sheet presentation of assignor's equity in assigned receivables

Current assets:		
Accounts receivable		$200,000
Assigned accounts receivable	$19,850	
Less: Notes payable to Finco, Inc. (assignee)	15,300	
Equity in assigned accounts receivable		4,550
Total accounts receivable		$204,550

Disclosure of accounts receivable pledged, assigned, or sold, including any possible loss contingency, is made in the balance sheet or in a note to the financial statements.

NOTES RECEIVABLE

The term *notes receivable* (or *promissory notes*) is used in accounting to designate several types of credit instruments. A promissory note is a written contract containing an unconditional promise by the *maker* to pay a certain sum of money to the *payee* under terms clearly specified in the contract. Most promissory notes used as a basis for business transactions are *negotiable,* which means that a *holder in due course* may sell the notes, discount them, or borrow against them.

Notes receivable often are used when the goods sold have a high unit or aggregate value and the purchaser of the goods wants to extend payment beyond the normal 30- to 90-day period of trade credit. In the banking and commercial credit fields, notes are the typical form of credit instrument used to support lending transactions. Notes receivable also may result from sale of plant assets, or from a variety of other business transactions.

Valuation of Notes Receivable

As in the case of accounts receivable, the proper valuation of notes receivable and similar credit instruments is their current fair value (or present value) at the time of acquisition. Accountants can value notes receivable because their terms generally provide reliable evidence of the rights inherent in them. Except for questions of collectibility, there is little uncertainty with respect to the amounts that will be received and the dates on which the amounts will be received.

Notes receivable, just as trade accounts receivable, may prove to be uncollectible. If a business enterprise uses notes as a regular credit medium and has a large volume outstanding, the amounts of probable uncollectible notes may be estimated, and an allowance for such notes established by procedures similar to those for accounts receivable.

Strictly speaking, there is no such thing as a noninterest-bearing note; there are only *notes that contain a stated provision for interest and notes that do not.* The time value of money is present in any case, because the present value of a promise to pay a stated amount of cash on a fixed or determinable date is not as large as the amount to be paid at maturity. The so-called noninterest-bearing note has a lower present value than its face amount by an amount equivalent to an interest charge. In contrast, if a note bears a fair rate of interest, its *face amount* and *present value* are the same on the date of issuance.

This point may be illustrated by an example. Suppose that two promissory notes are received in connection with the sale of goods. In settlement of the first sale, Customer W gives a one-year, 12% note, with a face amount of $25,000. In settlement of the second sale, Customer X gives a one-year note with a face amount of $28,000, but with no interest provision specified in the note. If accountants considered only the face amount of the notes, they might be tempted to record the two notes as follows:

Note from Customer X is not recorded correctly	**Customer W**			**Customer X**		
	Notes Receivable ...	25,000		Notes Receivable ...	28,000	
	Sales		25,000	Sales		28,000
	To record sale exchange for 12% promissory note.			To record sale in exchange for noninterest-bearing promissory note.		

A careful examination of the evidence indicates that the two promissory notes are identical, assuming that 12% is a reasonable annual rate of interest. Both customers have promised to pay $28,000 at the end of one year, and both notes have a present value of $25,000 ($28,000 ÷ 1.12 = $25,000). A logical method of accounting is to record both notes at $25,000, and to record interest of $3,000 as it is realized. Thus, the note receivable from Customer X may be recorded at $25,000 (the same as the note from Customer W), or preferably by use of a Discount on Notes Receivable ledger account (resulting in a *carrying amount* of $25,000) as illustrated at the top of page 362.

The correct way to record note from Customer X

Notes Receivable	28,000	
Discount on Notes Receivable		3,000
Sales		25,000

To record sale to Customer X in exchange for noninterest-bearing promissory note.

The discount on notes receivable is amortized periodically as interest revenue, and any unamortized balance at the end of an accounting period is deducted from Notes Receivable in the balance sheet.

In practice, noninterest-bearing, short-term notes received from customers often are recorded at the outset at face amount (maturity value). The foregoing analysis shows that this procedure overstates assets and fails to recognize interest revenue. Although generally accepted accounting principles require that notes be recorded at present value, trade notes and accounts receivable with customary trade terms not exceeding one year may be recorded at face amount. When the amount of the unearned implicit interest is substantial, this procedure may result in a significant overstatement of assets, stockholders' equity, and net income in the accounting period that the notes and accounts receivable are recorded.

Discounting Notes Receivable

Negotiable notes receivable may be sold or discounted. The term *sale* is appropriate when a note is indorsed to a bank or finance company on a *without recourse* basis; that is, in the event the maker of the note defaults, the bank or finance company has no recourse against the seller of the note. The term *discounted* applies when an enterprise borrows against notes receivable and indorses them on a *with recourse* basis, which means that the borrower must pay the note if the maker does not.

The *proceeds* received when a note is discounted are computed by deducting from the *maturity value* of the note the amount of interest (discount) charged by the bank or finance company. Banks usually compute the discount on the maturity value of the note rather than on the proceeds (amount actually borrowed), which gives the bank a higher *effective rate of interest* than the rate of interest used to discount the note.

To illustrate these points and the accounting involved, assume that Scott Company discounts at a bank two notes receivable arising from the sale of merchandise. Both notes have a face amount of $100,000 and are due in one year. Note Y is noninterest-bearing; note Z bears interest at a 15% annual rate. The bank also charges a 15% discount rate. If we assume that the notes are discounted with recourse immediately upon receipt, the proceeds and the difference between the proceeds and the present value are determined as illustrated at the top of page 363.

The difference between the proceeds and the present value of each note represents additional interest charged by the bank because the 15% discount is computed on maturity value rather than on the amount actually borrowed (proceeds). The additional interest is recognized as an expense over the remaining term of the note.

Proceeds and present value of notes discounted

	Note Y (no interest)	Note Z (15% interest)
Face amount of notes	$100,000	$100,000
Add: Interest to maturity	–0–	15,000
Maturity value of notes..........................	$100,000	$115,000
Less: Bank discount (15% of maturity value for		
one year)	15,000	17,250
Proceeds on notes	$ 85,000	$ 97,750
Present value @ 15% (maturity value ÷ 1.15)	86,957	100,000
Difference between proceeds and present value ..	$ 1,957	$ 2,250

The journal entries to record the receipt and the discounting of the two notes are shown below:[15]

Journal entries for discounted notes receivable

Note Y (no interest)	Note Z (15% interest)
At time of sale:	
Notes Receivable 100,000	Notes Receivable 100,000
Discount on Notes	Sales 100,000
Receivable 13,043	
Sales 86,957	
At time notes are discounted:	
Cash 85,000	Cash 97,750
Discount on Notes	Deferred Interest
Receivable 13,043	Expense 2,250
Deferred Interest	Notes Receivable .. 100,000
Expense................ 1,957	
Notes Receivable .. 100,000	

An alternative procedure for recording discounted notes is to credit Notes Receivable Discounted (a contra-asset account) rather than Notes Receivable. In the balance sheet, the balance in the Notes Receivable Discounted ledger account is deducted from Notes Receivable. When the note is paid at maturity, Notes Receivable Discounted is debited and Notes Receivable is credited. Because most discounted notes are paid at maturity, this journal entry may be avoided by crediting Notes Receivable at the time notes are discounted.

---

[15]An alternative approach is to view the proceeds received from the bank as the "true" present value of the notes. This interpretation calls for the recording of the two notes and related sales at $85,000 and $97,750, respectively; thus, the need to record deferred interest expense when the notes are discounted is eliminated.

If Scott Company had held the notes for some time before discounting them with recourse, interest revenue realized prior to the time the notes are discounted must be recognized. Assuming that Scott held the two notes for six months before discounting them at 12%, the following journal entries would be appropriate:

Note Y (no interest)		Note Z (15% interest)	
To accrue interest revenue			
for six months:			
Discount on Notes Receivable	6,522	Interest Receivable	7,500
Interest Revenue	6,522	Interest Revenue	7,500
Interest revenue: $86,957 \times		Interest revenue: $100,000 \times	
$0.15 \times 6/12 = \$6,522$		$0.15 \times 6/12 = \$7,500$	
To record discounting of			
notes at 12% for six months:			
Cash	94,000	Cash	108,100
Discount on Notes Receivable	6,521	Interest Receivable	7,500
Notes Receivable	100,000	Notes Receivable	100,000
Deferred Interest Revenue	521	Deferred Interest Revenue	600
Proceeds: $100,000 -		Proceeds: $115,000 -	
($100,000 \times 0.12 \times 6/12)		($115,000 \times 0.12 \times 6/12)	
= \$94,000		= \$108,100	

The $521 excess of the proceeds of $94,000 over the carrying amount of $93,479 ($100,000 - $6,521 = $93,479) from the discounting of Note Y represents additional interest revenue to be recognized over the remaining six-month term of the note. Similarly, the $600 excess of the proceeds of $108,100 over the carrying amount of $107,500 ($100,000 + $7,500 = $107,500) from the discounting of Note Z is recorded as deferred interest revenue. In both cases, the additional interest revenue results from the fact that the notes were discounted by Scott Company at 12%, a rate *less than the annual yield rate of 15%* to Scott.

If a discounted note is *dishonored,* Scott Company would be required to pay the bank the maturity value of the note plus any protest fees charged by the bank. Notice of the dishonor of a discounted note must be given promptly; therefore, the indorser may assume that payment has been made if no notice is received within a few days after maturity date. When a note is dishonored, the amount paid to the bank is debited to Accounts Receivable (or Dishonored Notes Receivable). Subsequent collection from the maker of the note is recorded as a credit to this receivable; failure to collect requires that this receivable be written off against the allowance for doubtful accounts.

The party discounting notes receivable is contingently liable on the notes until the maker pays them in full at maturity. The *loss contingency* may be disclosed (1) in a note to the financial statements, (2) parenthetically in the balance sheet, or (3) by use of a Notes Receivable Discounted ledger account deducted from Notes Receivable. Disclosure by means of a note to the financial statements is by far the most common practice. A detailed discussion of loss contingencies is presented in Chapter 10.

Accounting for Notes Receivable under *APB Opinion No. 21*

APB Opinion No. 21, "Interest on Receivables and Payables," is applicable if the face amount of a receivable (especially a promissory note) does not reasonably measure the present value of the consideration given in exchange. Such situations arise when no interest is explicitly stated or if the stated rate of interest is not appropriate. For example, assume that Caine Company exchanges land with a carrying amount of $6,000 for a five-year noninterest-bearing promissory note with a face amount of $10,000. It would be improper for Caine to record a gain of $4,000 on this exchange because the present value of the five-year note is far less than its $10,000 face amount. Assuming that 10% is the current fair rate of interest, the present value (rounded) of the note is $6,209 ($10,000 × 0.6209 = $6,209), thus indicating a gain on the exchange of only $209 ($6,209 − $6,000 = $209).

APB Opinion No. 21 applies to secured and unsecured promissory notes, debentures, bonds, mortgage notes, equipment obligations, and some accounts receivable and payable; however, it does not apply to "receivables and payables arising from transactions with customers or suppliers in the normal course of business which are due in customary trade terms not exceeding approximately one year."[16] A summary of *APB Opinion No. 21* as it relates to receivables is presented in the following paragraphs.

Notes Received Solely for Cash Interest on a cash loan generally is the difference between the actual amount of cash received by the borrower and the total amount agreed to be repaid to the lender. The amount of cash loaned to the borrower may differ from the face amount of the promissory note receivable because the stated interest rate may differ from the prevailing rate for similar notes. This difference indicates that the present value of the note receivable differs from its face amount at the time of issuance. The difference between the face amount of the note and its present value is recorded as a premium or discount and is amortized over the term of the note.

When a promissory note is received solely for cash equal to its face amount and no other right or privilege is exchanged, the note receivable is presumed to have a present value on the issuance date *equal to the amount of cash exchanged.* Thus, if a noninterest-bearing promissory note with a face amount of $10,000 is received in exchange for cash of $10,000, the transaction is recorded as follows:

Journal entry to record loan evidenced by noninterest-bearing note

Note Receivable	10,000	
Cash		10,000
To record cash loan evidenced by noninterest-bearing		
promissory note.		

---

[16]*APB Opinion No. 21,* "Interest on Receivables and Payables," AICPA (New York: 1971), p. 418.

No interest revenue is recorded on this loan; the note is deemed to have a present value equal to the cash transferred because no other right or privilege is exchanged between the lender and borrower. When cash and other rights or privileges are exchanged for a note receivable, the current fair value of the rights or privileges must be measured and recorded by the lender.

Notes Received in Exchange for Cash and Other Rights or Privileges Instead of issuing a note solely for cash, the parties may agree to exchange other rights or privileges (stated or unstated). These rights and privileges are given accounting recognition by taking into account any implicit discount or premium on the note. For example, assume that on November 30, Year 1, Lori Company lends $112,000 to a supplier for one year, without interest, although the going rate of interest for this type of loan is 12%. In return, the supplier agrees to sell a stated quantity of scarce merchandise to Lori during the month of December at a favorable price. Neither of these transactions was made in the normal course of business at the usual trade terms. The merchandise was purchased for $300,000 on December 5 and sold prior to December 25. Lori's fiscal year ends on December 31. The note has a present value of $100,000 ($112,000 ÷ 1.12 = $100,000); hence, the logical conclusion is that Lori obtained a property right (lower cost of merchandise) with a value of $12,000. Consequently, the loan to the supplier, the purchase of merchandise, the accrual of interest on December 31, Year 1, and the loan repayment on November 30, Year 2, are recorded by Lori as illustrated below and at the top of page 367.

LORI COMPANY
Journal Entries

November 30, Year 1:

Note Receivable	112,000	
Property Right with Supplier	12,000	
Cash		112,000
Discount on Note Receivable		12,000

To record noninterest-bearing one-year loan to supplier.

December 5, Year 1:

Purchases (or Inventories)	312,000	
Accounts Payable (or Cash)		300,000
Property Right with Supplier		12,000

To record purchase of merchandise.

December 31, Year 1:

Discount on Note Receivable	1,000	
Interest Revenue		1,000

To record interest revenue ($100,000 × 0.12 × 1/12 = $1,000).

November 30, Year 2:

Cash	112,000	
Discount on Note Receivable	11,000	
Note Receivable		112,000
Interest Revenue		11,000

To record receipt of loan repayment and interest revenue
($100,000 × 0.12 × $^{11}/_{12}$ = $11,000).

If the loan to the supplier had been recorded by Lori Company as a debit to Note Receivable and a credit to Cash for $112,000, the following errors would have resulted in its financial statements for the year ended December 31, Year 1:

1 Purchases and cost of goods sold would have been understated by $12,000 in the income statement.

2 Interest revenue would have been understated by $1,000 in the income statement.

3 Income before income taxes would have been overstated by $11,000 ($12,000 − $1,000 = $11,000) in the income statement.

4 The carrying amount of notes receivable would have been overstated by $11,000 in the balance sheet.

In the supplier's accounting records, the loan from Lori Company is recorded as follows:

Parallel journal entry in supplier's accounting records

Cash	112,000	
Discount on Note Payable...............................	12,000	
Note Payable		112,000
Obligation to Customer		12,000

To record noninterest-bearing one-year loan from customer.

When the merchandise is sold to Lori Company, the supplier debits the Obligation to Customer ledger account and credits the Sales account for $12,000. The Discount on Note Payable account is amortized on a straight-line basis to Interest Expense over the one-year term of the loan.

When notes are received in exchange for assets or services, and interest either is not stated or is unreasonably low, the notes are recorded at the current fair value of the assets or services or at the market value of the notes, whichever is more clearly evident. In the absence of exchange prices for the assets or services, or evidence of the market value of the notes, the ***present value*** of the notes must be computed. This computation is made at the time the note is acquired, and any subsequent changes in interest rates are disregarded.[17]

---

[17]Ibid., pp. 421–422.

Computation of Present Value of a Note Receivable　The *current fair rate of interest* used to compute the present value of a note receivable depends on factors such as the credit standing of the issuer, terms of the note, the quality of collateral offered by the issuer, and the general level of interest rates. The interest rate selected for this purpose should approximate the rate at which the debtor could obtain similar financing from other sources.

To illustrate the computation of the present value of notes receivable, assume that on December 31, Year 1, Software, Inc., presents a $39,930 invoice for services to a client. The client protested the amount of the invoice and as a compromise was allowed to pay the invoice in three annual installments of $13,310, starting on December 31, Year 2. Software, Inc., received three noninterest-bearing promissory notes for $13,310 each, dated December 31, Year 1. How should these notes be entered in the accounting records of Software, Inc., if the current fair rate of interest is 10% a year? First, the present value of the three notes is computed from Table 4 in the Appendix at the end of Chapter 5, as follows:

Computation of present value of notes	*Amount of annual receipts (notes)* $13,310
	Multiply by present value of ordinary annuity of three rents
	of 1 at 10% interest 2.486852
	Present value of three annual receipts of $13,310 at 10% interest $33,100

The journal entries to record the original billing for services, the receipt of the notes by Software, Inc., on December 31, Year 1, and three annual receipts from the client are illustrated below and on page 369 (we have assumed that the promissory notes are recorded at the face amount of $39,930 and that a Discount on Notes Receivable ledger account is used to record the $6,830 implicit interest to be realized over the term of the notes):

Journal entries for notes	***December 31, Year 1:***	
	Accounts Receivable 39,930	
	*　　Fees Revenue*	39,930
	To record billing for services.	
	December 31, Year 1:	
	Notes Receivable 39,930	
	Fees Revenue 6,830	
	*　　Discount on Notes Receivable ($39,930 − $33,100)*	6,830
	*　　Accounts Receivable*	39,930
	To record receipt of noninterest-bearing notes with a face	
	amount of $39,930, payable in three annual installments of	
	*$13,310 each. The notes are recorded at their **present value***	
	based on an interest rate of 10% a year.	

December 31, Year 2:

Cash	13,310	
Discount on Notes Receivable	3,310	
Notes Receivable		13,310
Interest Revenue		3,310

To record collection of first note. Interest for first year:
($39,930 − $6,830) × 0.10 = $3,310.

December 31, Year 3:

Cash	13,310	
Discount on Notes Receivable	2,310	
Notes Receivable		13,310
Interest Revenue		2,310

To record collection of second note. Interest for second year:
($26,620 − $3,520) × 0.10 = $2,310.

December 31, Year 4:

Cash	13,310	
Discount on Notes Receivable	1,210	
Notes Receivable		13,310
Interest Revenue		1,210

To record collection of third note. Interest for third year:
($13,310 − $1,210) × 0.10 = $1,210.

In the second journal entry on December 31, Year 1, the discount of $6,830 is recorded as a reduction in the previously recorded Fees Revenue ledger account. The discount then is amortized as interest revenue over the three-year term of the notes at 10% a year, applied to the carrying amount of the notes receivable *at the beginning of each year.* The Discount on Notes Receivable ledger account and the balance sheet presentation of notes receivable by Software, Inc., are illustrated below and at the top of page 370.

Discount on Notes Receivable ledger account and balance sheet presentation of notes receivable

	Discount on Notes Receivable				
Date	**Explanation**	**Debit**	**Credit**	**Balance**	
Year 1					
Dec. 31	Original amount of discount		6,830	6,830 cr	
Year 2					
Dec. 31	Amortization	3,310		3,520 cr	
Year 3					
Dec. 31	Amortization	2,310		1,210 cr	
Year 4					
Dec. 31	Amortization	1,210		–0–	

	December 31,		
Current assets:	Year 1	Year 2	Year 3
Notes receivable	$39,930	$26,620	$13,310
Less: Discount on notes receivable	6,830	3,520	1,210
Carrying amount of notes receivable	$33,100	$23,100	$12,100

Notes receivable that bear a nominal (low) rate of interest would be accounted for in a similar manner. For an example of accounting procedures for a note that bears an unreasonably high rate of interest, see pages 254–255 of Chapter 5.

Presentation of Receivables in the Balance Sheet

In the current asset section of the balance sheet, material amounts of the following classes of receivables are reported separately: (1) notes and other receivables arising from written negotiable contracts, (2) ordinary trade receivables, (3) installment accounts receivable, (4) receivables from the U.S. government, and (5) other current claims. Negotiable notes and contracts have a special status because of the ease with which they may be converted to cash through discounting.

Any discount or premium relating to notes receivable is reported in the balance sheet as a deduction from or as an addition to the face amount of the notes. The description of notes receivable should include the effective interest rate. Receivables that have been pledged are identified, and any receivables that will not be collected within a year or the operating cycle are excluded from the current assets category. A credit balance in an individual account receivable, if material in amount, is reported as a current liability. Receivables from officers, employees, and stockholders generally are classified as noncurrent unless current collection is assured.

The presentation of various types of receivables and related accounts in the balance sheet is illustrated below and at the top of page 371.

Presentation of receivables and related accounts in the balance sheet

Receivables (current assets):	
Trade notes receivable (net of unearned discounts of $5,000)	$ 105,000
Trade accounts receivable (net of allowances for doubtful accounts, returns, and discounts of $47,000)	220,000
Installment receivables (net of unearned interest and finance charges of $2,700,000 and allowance for doubtful accounts of $52,000) (Note 1)	1,900,000
Current amount receivable from affiliated company, interest at 11% . .	45,000
Miscellaneous (including $4,000 debit balance in accounts payable) .	10,000
Total current receivables	$2,280,000

(continued)

Investments (noncurrent assets):

Receivable from sale of equipment (due with interest at 13% in
  three years).. $ 150,000
Notes due from officers and employees 85,000
Dishonored notes receivable (net of $6,000 allowance for doubtful
  notes) 12,000

Current liabilities:

Container deposits by customers .... $ 17,500
Accounts receivable with credit balances......................... 4,250

Note 1 *The installment receivables arise from sales of partially finished homes for time payments over periods of 12 to 20 years and are secured by first deeds of trust. Of the gross amount of $4,652,000, an amount of $4,410,000 is due after one year. These installment receivables are included in current assets because they arise and are collected during the company's operating cycle.*

REVIEW QUESTIONS

1   Briefly discuss the significance of accounts receivable in an analysis of the financial position of a business enterprise.

2   What is meant by *valuation of receivables?* If accountants generally require that assets be recorded at *cost,* why are trade accounts receivable not recorded at the cost of the merchandise sold?

3   What is the distinction between *trade receivables* and *miscellaneous receivables?* Give two examples of each type of receivable.

4   At what point are trade receivables recorded? Are shipments to consignees recorded as receivables?

5   Describe a *cycle billing system* and state its advantages.

6   Describe how the following items affect the valuation of trade accounts receivable: *trade discounts, sales discounts, sales returns and allowances, allowance for freight-out,* and *sales and excise taxes.*

7   Describe two methods of accounting for cash (sales) discounts.

8   Some accountants classify doubtful accounts expense as an operating expense, while others classify it as a contra-revenue account. Discuss the reasoning behind these alternative positions. What objection, if any, do you have to the ledger account title ''Loss from Bad Debts''?

9   What is an *aging of accounts receivable?* Describe how such an analysis may be used to estimate doubtful accounts expense and to analyze the quality of trade accounts receivable.

10   According to *APB Opinion No. 20,* ''Accounting Changes,'' how is a change in the method for estimating doubtful accounts expense and a material increase or decrease in the allowance for doubtful accounts reported in financial statements or in a note to the financial statements?

11 Briefly discuss the logic of basing the estimate of doubtful accounts expense on (**a**) total sales, (**b**) credit sales, and (**c**) a fixed percentage of trade accounts receivable at the end of an accounting period.

12 Discuss the accounting procedures necessary to record recoveries of accounts receivable previously written off (**a**) if an allowance for doubtful accounts is used, or (**b**) if the direct write-off method is used.

13 Explain the distinction between *factoring* and *assigning* trade accounts receivable.

14 When receivables are transferred *with recourse,* what three conditions must be met in order to record the transfer as a sale?

15 Equicorp sold merchandise with a selling price of $10,500 on an installment contract covering 24 months. Payments of $500 were to be made by the customer each month. Interest charges of $1,500 were added to the sales price to compute gross installment accounts receivable. Equicorp recorded the sale by a debit to Installment Accounts Receivable and a credit to Sales for $12,000. Evaluate this procedure.

16 What errors result when a noninterest-bearing note receivable due in one year is recorded at its face amount? Explain.

17 Describe various ways that a potential loss contingency relating to notes receivable discounted may be presented in financial statements or in a note to the financial statements.

18 According to *APB Opinion No. 21,* ''Interest on Receivables and Payables,'' how should a low-interest, one-year loan for $250,000 by Luke Company to a supplier who agreed to sell material to Luke at a favorable fixed price be recorded? Explain the approach used in recording this transaction and prepare a journal entry for Luke to record the loan, assuming that the present value of the note receivable is $220,000.

EXERCISES

Ex. 7-1 Select the best answer for each of the following multiple-choice questions:

1 A method of estimating doubtful accounts expense that focuses on the income statement rather than the balance sheet is the allowance method based on:
a Direct write-off of uncollectible trade accounts receivable
b Aging of trade accounts receivable
c Credit sales
d The balance of trade accounts receivable

2 On March 28, Year 1, Swiss Company received a $120,000, 12%, 90-day note from a customer. Immediately, Swiss discounted the note at a bank; the discount rate was 16%. In its journal entry to record the discounting of the note, Swiss debits the Cash ledger account for:

a $118,800   **b** $115,200   **c** $118,656   **d** $120,000   **e** Some other amount

3   Balog Company received a $30,000, six-month, 10% promissory note from a customer. After holding the note for two months, Balog was in need of cash and discounted the note at Olympic Bank at a 12% discount rate. The amount of cash received by Balog from the bank was:

a $31,260   **b** $30,870   **c** $30,300   **d** $30,240   **e** Some other amount

4   On January 1, Year 1, Sting Company lent $20,000 cash to Ross, Inc. The promissory note signed by Ross did not bear interest and was due on December 31, Year 2. No other rights or privileges were exchanged. The prevailing interest for a loan of this type was 12%. The present value of 1 for two periods at 12% is 0.797. Sting recognizes interest revenue in Year 1 of:

a $0   **b** $1,913   **c** $2,030   **d** $2,400   **e** Some other amount

5   Hunt Company prepared an aging of its accounts receivable on December 31, Year 2, and determined that the net realizable value of the receivables on that date was $50,000. Additional information follows:

Accounts receivable, Dec. 31, Year 1	$48,000
Accounts receivable, Dec. 31, Year 2	54,000
Allowance for doubtful accounts, Dec. 31, Year 1 (credit balance)	6,000
Accounts receivable written off as uncollectible during Year 2	5,000

Hunt's doubtful accounts expense for the year ended December 31, Year 2, was:

a $3,000   **b** $4,000   **c** $5,000   **d** $7,000   **e** Some other amount

6   The following ledger account balances were taken from the December 31, Year 1, trial balance of Singer Company:

Credit sales	$750,000
Sales discounts	15,000
Allowance for doubtful accounts (credit balance)	18,000

During Year 1, $30,000 of uncollectible accounts receivable were written off. Past experience indicates that 3% of gross credit sales proves to be uncollectible. What is the balance of the Allowance for Doubtful Accounts ledger account on December 31, Year 1, after provision for doubtful accounts expense is made for Year 1?

a $10,050   **b** $10,500   **c** $22,050   **d** $34,500   **e** Some other amount

7   On January 1, Year 1, Gray Company sold a building that cost $190,000 and had accumulated depreciation of $80,000 on the date of sale. Gray received a $200,000 noninterest-bearing promissory note due on January 1, Year 4. There was no established exchange price for the building, and the note had no ready market. The prevailing rate of interest for a note of this type on January 1, Year 1, was 10%. The present value of 1 at 10% for three periods is 0.75. What amount of interest revenue should be included in Gray's Year 1 income statement?

a $6,750   **b** $15,000   **c** $16,667   **d** $20,000   **e** Some other amount

8   Kong Corporation provides an allowance for its doubtful accounts receivable. On December 31, Year 1, the allowance for doubtful accounts had a credit balance of $8,000. Each month Kong records doubtful accounts expense in an amount equal to 2% of credit sales. Total credit sales during Year 2 amounted to $2,000,000. During Year 2, uncollectible accounts receivable totaling $22,000 were written off against the allowance account. An aging of accounts receivable on December 31, Year 2, indicated that an allowance of $42,000 was required for doubtful accounts as of that date. Accordingly, doubtful accounts expense previously accrued during Year 2 should be increased by:

a $62,000   **b** $42,000   **c** $26,000   **d** $16,000   **e** Some other amount

Ex. 7-2   In auditing the financial statements of Status Corporation for the current fiscal year, you find that the following items are included in trade accounts receivable (both controlling account and subsidiary ledger):

Customers' accounts with credit balances . . . . $ 2,950
Receivables from officers 12,500
Advances to employees 2,200
Customers' accounts known to be uncollectible 2,880

Prepare a correcting journal entry for Status Corporation to reclassify items that are not trade accounts receivable and to write off the uncollectible accounts receivable.

Ex. 7-3   On September 30, Year 1, the following notes receivable from customers are discounted at the bank. The bank charges a 10% discount rate on the maturity value of the notes. Compute the proceeds of each note, using 360 as the number of days in a year.

a 90-day, $24,000, 10% note dated September 30, Year 1
b 90-day, $18,000, noninterest-bearing note dated August 15, Year 1
c 60-day, $6,000, 8% note dated September 15, Year 1
d 6-month, $12,000, 15% note dated August 1, Year 1

Ex. 7-4   Wool Corporation began operations in Year 1 and had accounts receivable of $300,000 on December 31, Year 1. In determining the valuation of receivables on December 31, Year 1, management wished to recognize the following:

Estimated doubtful accounts $6,240
Estimated collection costs 1,800
Estimated price adjustments and other allowances on outstanding
   receivables (no returns of merchandise are anticipated) 3,000
Estimated cash (sales) discounts 3,600

a Prepare an adjusting entry for Wool Corporation on December 31, Year 1, to recognize management's estimate of the net realizable value of accounts receivable. No accounts were written off in Year 1.

b Show how accounts receivable are reported in Wool Corporation's balance sheet on December 31, Year 1.

Ex. 7-5 Albert Company acquired merchandise at a cost of $4,000. The merchandise was offered for sale by Albert at a list price of $6,500, before a trade discount of 20% and a cash discount of 2% if the invoice was paid within 10 days. Albert bills customers net of the trade discount, records accounts receivable and sales at the invoice price, and uses the perpetual inventory system.

Prepare journal entries for Albert Company to record (**a**) the sale and the cost of the goods sold, and (**b**) the collection of the account receivable within 10 days.

Ex. 7-6 From the following information, compute the doubtful accounts expense for Year 1: Beginning balance in Trade Accounts Receivable was $80,000; beginning credit balance in Allowance for Doubtful Accounts was $6,000; ending balance in Trade Accounts Receivable was $110,000, of which 4% was estimated to be uncollectible. During Year 1, $7,490 of accounts receivable were written off as uncollectible.

Ex. 7-7 Certain information relative to the operations of Murphy Company for Year 10 follows:

Trade accounts receivable, Jan. 1	$16,000
Trade accounts receivable collected during year	52,000
Cash sales	10,000
Inventories, Jan. 1	24,000
Inventories, Dec. 31	22,000
Purchases	40,000
Gross profit on sales	18,000

Compute the amount of Murphy Company's trade accounts receivable on December 31, Year 10.

Ex. 7-8 Your accounts receivable clerk, who earns a salary of $950 a month, has just acquired a new luxury car. You decide to test the accuracy of the accounts receivable balance of $30,400 as shown in the general ledger at the end of the year. All sales are on credit.

The following information is available for your first year of operation: Collections from customers, $125,000; payments for merchandise purchases, $130,000; ending inventories, $40,000; and ending accounts payable to merchandise suppliers, $30,000. All goods purchased were marked to sell at 40% above cost (selling price equals 140% of cost).

Compute the amount of any apparent shortage in trade accounts receivable at the end of the year.

Ex. 7-9 Watt Company prepared the following journal entry on April 30, Year 4:

Notes Receivable	20,000	
Discount on Notes Receivable		3,471
Sales		16,529

To record sale of merchandise and receipt of noninterest-bearing note due April 30, Year 6. Present value of note at 10% annual rate of interest is $16,529.

Prepare journal entries for Watt Company on April 30, Year 5, and April 30, Year 6, the end of the fiscal years.

Ex. 7-10   Cristy Company, which adjusts its accounting records and prepares financial statements at the end of each month, uses the income statement approach for estimating doubtful accounts expense. In past years, uncollectible accounts have averaged 3% of net credit sales. Relevant data for Cristy's doubtful accounts for the month of February, Year 3, follow:

Cash sales	$ 62,800
Credit sales	352,200
Cash discounts on credit sales......................................	14,300
Sales returns and allowances on credit sales	3,900
Balance of Allowance for Doubtful Accounts, Jan. 31, Year 3 (credit)	69,900
Uncollectible trade accounts receivable written off, Feb. 28, Year 3	70,200

Prepare journal entries for Cristy Company on February 28, Year 3, to record the write-off of uncollectible trade accounts receivable and the provision for doubtful accounts for the month of February.

Ex. 7-11   The following accounts appear in the general ledger of Delphine Company on December 31, Year 7:

Sales	$1,200,000
Accounts receivable	500,000
Allowance for doubtful accounts (debit balance)	2,000

Prepare a journal entry for Delphine Company on December 31, Year 7, to record doubtful accounts expense for each independent assumption below:
a The allowance for doubtful accounts is increased to a balance of $15,000.
b Delphine recognizes 2% of sales as doubtful accounts expense.
c Through an aging of the accounts, $24,750 of accounts receivable is estimated to be uncollectible.

Ex. 7-12   On March 1, Beckman Company assigned accounts receivable of $60,000 to Rec-Fin, Inc., and received $54,000, less a 2% fee on $54,000. Interest is charged at the rate of 1% a month of the unpaid balance. Beckman made collections on the assigned accounts and remitted the proceeds at the end of each month to Rec-Fin, Inc. Collections in March were $30,000.

Prepare journal entries for Beckman Company to record the March transactions relating to the assignment of accounts receivable.

Ex. 7-13   Excelsior Corporation sold a machine with a cost of $20,000 and a carrying amount of $2,000 for $9,000, payable $1,014 down and promissory notes of $2,662 at the end of each of the next three years. No interest was mentioned in the contract, although 10% a year would have been a fair rate of interest for this type of transaction.

Compute (without using compound interest tables) the present value of the $7,986 to be received over the next three years and prepare a journal entry for

Excelsior Corporation to record the sale of the machine as recommended in *APB Opinion No. 21*, "Interest on Receivables and Payables." Verify your answer by using Table 4 in the Appendix at the end of Chapter 5.

Ex. 7-14 The information below is available for Terry Lanni Company:

	Amounts in thousands		
	Year 1	Year 2	Year 3
Credit sales....................................	$ 900	$1,100	$1,000
Cash sales	600	800	700
Total sales	$1,500	$1,900	$1,700
Accounts receivable (end of year)	$ 170	$ 230	$ 220
Allowance for doubtful accounts (end-of-year credit balance)................................	47	30	46
Accounts receivable written off during the year...	2	50	14

Assuming there was no change in the method used to estimate doubtful accounts during the three-year period, compute the balance of the Allowance for Doubtful Accounts ledger account of Terry Lanni Company at the beginning of Year 1.

Ex. 7-15 On December 31, Year 5, Friedman Corporation had the following installment receivables:

Installment accounts receivable, including deferred interest revenue at 2% a month; due at the rate of $3,200 a month for 28 months, starting Jan. 31, Year 6..	$89,600
Less: Deferred interest revenue..	21,500
Carrying amount of installment accounts receivable, Dec. 31, Year 5......	$68,100

Friedman transferred the receivables to a private investor on a recourse basis for an amount to yield 1½% a month to the investor. The transfer qualified as a sale under the provisions of *FASB Statement 77*, "Reporting by Transferors for Transfers of Receivables with Recourse."

a Using the Appendix at the end of Chapter 5, compute the proceeds from Friedman Corporation's transfer (sale) of the installment accounts receivable.

b Prepare a journal entry for Friedman Corporation on December 31, Year 5, to record the transfer (sale) of the installment accounts receivable to the private investor.

Ex. 7-16 Olmstead Corporation operates in an industry that has a high rate of uncollectible accounts. On June 30, Year 6, before any year-end adjustments, the balance of the trade accounts receivable was $600,000, and the allowance for doubtful accounts had a credit balance of $48,000. The adjusted year-end balance for the allowance for doubtful accounts will be based on the following aging analysis:

Days outstanding	Amount	Probability of collection
Less than 15 days....................................	$350,000	0.95
Between 16 and 30 days	110,000	0.90
Between 31 and 45 days	50,000	0.80
Between 46 and 60 days	40,000	0.70
Between 61 and 75 days	20,000	0.60
Between 76 and 90 days	10,000	0.40
Over 90 days	20,000	0.00
Total	$600,000	

a Compute the required balance of Olmstead Corporation's allowance for doubtful accounts on June 30, Year 6.

b Prepare any journal entries required for Olmstead Corporation on June 30, Year 6.

CASES

Case 7-1   On July 1, Year 10, Rover Company, a calendar-year company, sold merchandise on credit and received in return an interest-bearing promissory note from the customer. Rover will receive interest at the prevailing rate for a note of this type. Both the principal and interest are due on June 30, Year 11.

On December 31, Year 10, Rover had significant amounts of trade accounts receivable as a result of credit sales to its customers. Rover uses the allowance method based on credit sales to estimate doubtful accounts expense. Based on past experience, 1% of credit sales normally will not be collected. This pattern is expected to continue.

Instructions

a When should Rover Company recognize interest revenue from the note receivable? Discuss the rationale for your answer.

b Assume that the note receivable was discounted without recourse at a bank on December 31, Year 10. How does Rover Company determine the amount of the discount and what is the appropriate accounting for the discounting transaction?

c Discuss the rationale for using the allowance method based on credit sales to estimate doubtful accounts expense. Contrast this method with the allowance method based on the balance of trade accounts receivable.

d How should Rover Company report the allowance for doubtful accounts in its balance sheet on December 31, Year 10? Also, describe the alternatives, if any, for presentation of doubtful accounts expense in Rover's income statement.

Case 7-2   Business transactions often involve the exchange of plant assets, merchandise, or services for promissory notes or similar instruments that may stipulate no interest rate or an interest rate that varies from prevailing rates.

Instructions

a When a promissory note is exchanged for plant assets, merchandise, or services, what value should be placed on the promissory note,
  (1) if it bears interest at a reasonable rate and is issued in a bargained transaction entered into at arm's length? Explain.
  (2) if it bears no interest and/or is not issued in a bargained transaction entered into at arm's length? Explain.

b If the carrying amount of a promissory note differs from the face amount,
  (1) how is the difference accounted for? Explain.
  (2) how is the difference presented in the balance sheet? Explain.

Case 7-3 During the audit of accounts receivable of Daley Company, the president, Roberta Daley, asked why the current year's expense for doubtful accounts is debited because some accounts may become uncollectible next year. She then said that she had read that financial statements should be based on reliable evidence, and that it seemed to her to be much more reliable and objective to wait until specific accounts receivable actually were determined to be uncollectible before an expense is recognized.

Instructions

a Discuss the theoretical justification of the allowance method as contrasted with the direct write-off method of accounting for doubtful accounts.

b Describe the following two methods of estimating doubtful accounts. Include a discussion of how well each accomplishes the objectives of the allowance method of accounting for doubtful accounts.
  (1) The percentage-of-sales method
  (2) The aging method

c Of what merit is the president's contention that the allowance method lacks the reliability of the direct write-off method? Discuss in terms of accounting's measurement function.

Case 7-4 As a result of earthquake losses, Sally Company, one of the oldest and largest customers of Barge Transport, Inc., suddenly and unexpectedly became insolvent. Approximately 30% of the total sales of Barge have been made to Sally during each of the past several years.

The account receivable from Sally is uncollectible and is equal to 25% of total accounts receivable, an amount that is considerably in excess of what was determined to be an adequate allowance for doubtful accounts at the end of the preceding year.

Instructions

How should Barge Transport, Inc., record the write-off of the Sally Company account receivable, if it uses the allowance method of accounting for doubtful accounts? Justify your suggested treatment.

Case 7-5   The annual report for Year 10 of Allied Corporation, which operates a group of correspondence and resident schools, included the following relating to contracts receivable and sales:

Current assets:

Contracts receivable, less allowance for doubtful contracts of
$3,228,180 **(Note 2)** . . . . $ 6,599,399

Current liabilities:

Estimated costs to service contracts . . . . $ 264,281

Unearned tuition revenue **(Note 2)**   1,074,226

Income statement:

Sales, net of discounts and allowances of $2,076,911 . . . . $14,350,698

Provision for doubtful contracts receivable   3,863,800

Note 2—Contracts receivable:

Students in home-study courses enter into contracts that contain various payment plans, generally for a term of one to three years. Similarly, home-study courses generally are completed over a term of one to three years. Revenue from home-study courses and estimated costs to service the contracts are recorded when the contract is received.

Many of the contracts receivable are due from resident students and represent advance registrations for classes that will begin subsequent to December 31, Year 10. Tuition revenue on these contracts and a portion of tuition applicable to the classes in progress on December 31, Year 10, net of an allowance for cancellations, have been deferred and will be credited to revenue as earned over the period of attendance.

It is estimated that gross contracts receivable of approximately $1,900,000 on December 31, Year 10, are not expected to be realized within one year. However, it is not practicable to state separately the long-term portion of contracts receivable in the balance sheet because of the difficulty of determining the allowance for doubtful contracts relating to the long-term contracts receivable.

Instructions

Briefly evaluate the accounting practices of Allied Corporation. Your answer should refer to such accounting concepts or principles as revenue realization, matching of costs and revenue, conservatism, reliability, and classification of contracts receivable as current assets based on the length of Allied's operating cycle.

PROBLEMS

7-1   In the second half of Year 3, Jakarta Imports Company required additional cash for its operations and used trade accounts receivable to raise cash as follows:

(1) On July 1, Jakarta Imports assigned $300,000 of trade accounts receivable to Finance Company. Jakarta Imports received an advance from Finance of 85% of the assigned receivables, less a fee of 3% on the advance. Prior to December 31, Year 3, Jakarta Imports collected $190,000 on the assigned receivables, and remitted $185,000 to Finance, $13,500 of which represented interest on the advance (loan payable).

(2) On November 10, Jakarta Imports sold $310,000 of trade accounts receivable for $280,000. The receivables had a carrying amount of $290,000 and were sold on a nonrecourse basis.

(3) On December 31, Jakarta Imports obtained a loan of $125,000 from Rosen Bank by pledging $180,000 of trade accounts receivable.

Instructions

Prepare journal entries to record the foregoing transactions of Jakarta Imports Company.

7-2 The accountant for Kai Trading Company was hired at the beginning of Year 6. On December 31, Year 6, before making any adjusting entries, the accountant prepared a trial balance that included the following ledger account balances:

	Debit	*Credit*
Notes receivable (received in exchange for trade		
accounts receivable)	*$ 50,000*	
Trade accounts receivable	*300,000*	
Allowance for doubtful accounts	*7,500*	
Sales		*$2,000,000*
Sales returns and allowances	*18,850*	
Sales discounts	*25,540*	

Instructions

Prepare an adjusting entry for Kai Trading Company on December 31, Year 6, to provide for estimated doubtful accounts under each of the following independent assumptions. Explain the basis for each journal entry.

a Kai Trading's experience indicates that 70% of all sales are credit sales, and that on the average 3% of gross credit sales prove uncollectible.

b An analysis of the aging of trade accounts receivable indicates that potential uncollectible accounts and notes receivable on December 31, Year 6, amount to $30,000.

c Kai Trading's policy is to maintain an allowance for doubtful accounts equal to 5% of outstanding trade accounts receivable, including notes received from customers.

d The allowance for doubtful accounts is increased by 2% of gross sales, and an allowance for sales discounts of $9,000 on outstanding trade accounts receivable is established.

7-3 On January 1, Year 1, Long Beach Corporation sold to Tab Tillman a parcel of land with a carrying amount of $450,000. Tillman gave Long Beach $80,000 cash and $600,000 noninterest-bearing promissory notes payable in six equal annual installments of $100,000, with a first payment on the notes due on January 1, Year 2. Neither the land nor the notes had readily ascertainable current fair value. The market rate of interest for notes of this type is 15% a year. The fiscal year for Long Beach ends on December 31.

Instructions

a Prepare journal entries for Long Beach Corporation to record the sale of the land in Year 1, the collection on the notes receivable in Year 2, and adjusting entries on December 31, Year 1 and Year 2. Use the Discount on Installment Notes Receivable ledger account. Include supporting computations as part of the explanation for each journal entry. Round all computations to the nearest dollar and use the Appendix at the end of Chapter 5.

b Show how the notes receivable are presented in the balance sheet of Long Beach Corporation on December 31, Year 2.

7-4 The following information is taken from the trial balance Westwood Restaurant Supplies on September 30, Year 10, the end of its fiscal year:

	Debit	Credit
Notes receivable from customers (due within one year		
at 12% interest)	$100,000	
Trade accounts receivable	310,000	
Allowance for doubtful accounts and notes	7,300	
Allowance for sales discounts		$ 2,200
Allowance for sales returns		–0–
Sales—cash		250,000
Sales—credit		730,000
Sales returns	12,500	
Sales discounts	14,250	

Accounts receivable written off during the year were debited to the Allowance for Doubtful Accounts and Notes ledger account; merchandise returns by customers were recorded in the Sales Returns account; and sales discounts allowed to customers were recorded in the Sales Discounts account. Westwood Restaurant Supplies uses the perpetual inventory system.

Instructions

a Prepare journal entries for Westwood Restaurant Supplies on September 30, Year 10, to adjust the Allowance for Doubtful Accounts and Notes, the Allowance for Sales Discounts, and the Allowance for Sales Returns ledger accounts based on the following information:

(1) Aging of trade accounts receivable and notes receivable indicates that the following balances are required on September 30, Year 10:

Allowance for doubtful accounts and notes	$20,800
Allowance for sales discounts	8,200

(2) Based on many years of experience, management of Westwood Restaurant Supplies estimated that of the $310,000 of accounts receivable on September 30, Year 10, $20,000 selling price of merchandise will be returned. The net realizable value of the returned merchandise was estimated at $11,200. Westwood Restaurant Supplies follows the practice of establishing an inventory account for the merchandise expected to be returned by customers (see pages 348–349).

b Assuming that the allowance accounts are adjusted correctly on September 30, Year 10, show how sales, doubtful accounts expense, and receivables appear in the financial statements of Westwood Restaurant Supplies for the fiscal year ended September 30, Year 10. Doubtful accounts expense is reported as an operating expense in the income statement.

7-5 In auditing the financial statements of Malta James Corporation for Year 5, you discover the following information:

(1) On April 30, Year 5, Malta James received a noninterest-bearing promissory note for $30,000 maturing in one year, as payment for a consulting fee. The fee originally was established at $27,000, but, because the client was short of cash, Malta James agreed to accept the note. The note was recorded at $30,000 by a debit to Notes Receivable and a credit to Fees Revenue. A discount account representing unearned interest revenue generally is used by Malta James.

(2) Malta James sold a parcel of land on June 30, Year 5, for $10,000 cash and a noninterest-bearing promissory note of $50,000 due in three years. The land had a cost of $39,600, and Gain on Disposal of Land was credited for $20,400. You ascertain that the present value of the note on June 30, Year 5, discounted at 12%, was $35,589.

(3) A promissory note receivable of $9,000, on which interest receivable of $550 had been recorded in the Interest Receivable ledger account, was discounted at a bank at a rate of interest higher than the rate on the note. Proceeds of $9,440 were credited to Notes Receivable. Malta James does not use a Notes Receivable Discounted ledger account. The note matures early in Year 6.

(4) Interest accrued on investment in bonds on December 31, Year 5, amounts to $7,115.

(5) Malta James has recorded doubtful accounts expense only as specific accounts receivable were deemed to be worthless. You ascertain that an allowance for doubtful accounts of $11,200 is required on December 31, Year 5, after worthless accounts receivable of $4,100 are written off.

Instructions

Prepare an adjusting or correcting journal entry for Malta James Corporation on December 31, Year 5, for each item (1) through (5) above. The accounting records are still open for Year 5. Disregard income tax considerations and round all computations to the nearest dollar.

7-6 From inception of its operations in Year 1, Ray-Randall Company had no allowance for doubtful accounts. Uncollectible accounts receivable were expensed as written off, and recoveries were credited to revenue as collected. On March 1, Year 5 (after the Year 4 financial statements were issued), management recognized that Ray-Randall's accounting policy with respect to doubtful accounts **was not correct**, and determined that an allowance for doubtful accounts was necessary. A policy was established to maintain an allowance for doubtful accounts based on Ray-Randall's historical uncollectible accounts percentage applied to year-end accounts receivable. The historical uncollectible accounts percentage is to be recomputed each year based on all available past years up to a maximum of five years.

Information from Ray-Randall's accounting records is presented at the top of page 384.

Year	Credit sales	Accounts receivable written off	Recoveries of written-off accounts receivable
1	$1,500,000	$15,000	$-0-
2	2,250,000	58,000	2,700
3	2,950,000	52,000	2,500
4	3,300,000	65,000	4,800
5	4,000,000	63,000	5,000

Accounts receivable balances were $1,450,000 and $1,660,000 on December 31, Year 4, and December 31, Year 5, respectively.

Instructions

a Prepare a journal entry for Ray-Randall Company to establish the allowance for doubtful accounts as of January 1, Year 5. Show supporting computations in the explanation for the journal entry.

b Prepare a working paper to analyze the changes in Ray-Randall Company's Allowance for Doubtful Accounts ledger account for the year ended December 31, Year 5. Show supporting computations.

7-7 From inception of operations to December 31, Year 1, Ausman Corporation provided for uncollectible trade accounts receivable under the allowance method: provisions were made monthly at 2% of credit sales; accounts receivable written off were debited to the allowance account; recoveries of accounts receivable previously written off were credited to the allowance account; and no year-end adjustments to the allowance account were made. Ausman's usual credit terms are net 30 days.

The balance in the allowance for doubtful accounts was $130,000 on January 1, Year 2. During Year 2 credit sales totaled $9,000,000, interim provisions for doubtful accounts were made at 2% of credit sales, $90,000 of accounts were written off, and recoveries of accounts previously written off amounted to $15,000. Ausman installed a computer facility in November, Year 2, and an aging of trade accounts receivable was prepared for the first time on December 31, Year 2. A summary of the aging follows:

Classification by month of sale	Balance in each category	Estimated percent uncollectible
Nov.–Dec., Year 2	$1,140,000	2
July–Oct., Year 2	600,000	10
Jan.–June, Year 2	400,000	25
Prior to Jan. 1, Year 2	130,000	75
Total	$2,270,000	

Based on the review of collectibility of the trade accounts receivable in the "prior to Jan. 1, Year 2," category, additional receivables totaling $60,000 were written off on December 31, Year 2. Effective with the year ended December 31, Year 2, Ausman adopted a new accounting method for estimating the allowance for doubtful accounts at the amount indicated by the year-end aging analysis of trade accounts receivable.

Instructions

a Prepare a working paper for Ausman Corporation to analyze the changes in the allowance for doubtful accounts for the year ended December 31, Year 2. Show supporting computations.

b Prepare Ausman Corporation's journal entry for the year-end adjustment to the allowance for doubtful accounts balance on December 31, Year 2.

7-8 The following information appeared in the balance sheet for Wolfgang Company on December 31, Year 4:

Note receivable			$ 24,000
Interest receivable			1,000
Trade accounts receivable		$280,000	
Less: Allowance for doubtful accounts.........	$11,200		
Allowance for sales returns	4,000	15,200	264,800
Total notes and trade accounts receivable ...			$289,800

The note receivable is a six-month, 10% promissory note for $24,000 from Ace Company dated July 31, Year 4. (A 60-day, 12% promissory note for $36,000 from Burr Company dated November 15, Year 4, had been discounted at Arizona Bank on November 30, Year 4.)

A summary of transactions and other information relating to notes and trade accounts receivable for January, Year 5, follows:

Jan. 11 Received a 90-day, 12% promissory note from a customer, Karen Young, in exchange for a trade account receivable of $18,000. The fair rate of interest for the note is 12%.

13 Collected $732 from John Ruiz on a trade account receivable written off in Year 4.

15 Notice was received from Arizona Bank that Burr Company paid the $36,000 note due January 14, together with the interest of $720. Wolfgang does not use a Notes Receivable Discounted ledger account.

20 Uncollectible accounts totaling $6,100 were written off.

30 Received payment on Ace Company note, including interest of $1,200.

31 Credit sales for the month totaled $712,400.

31 Collections on trade accounts receivable, not including the account of John Ruiz, were as follows:
  (1) From accounts outstanding on December 31, Year 4, after $5,000 in sales discounts, $244,000.
  (2) From current month's sales, after $8,410 in sales discounts, $370,000.

31 Recorded accrued interest for 20 days on note from Karen Young.

31 Aging of trade accounts receivable showed that $20,000 was required in the allowance for doubtful accounts, and $9,120 was required in the allowance for sales returns.

Instructions

a Prepare journal entries for Wolfgang Company for the transactions and other information given for the month of January. Wolfgang does not reverse any adjusting entries.

b Show how the information relating to notes and trade accounts receivable appears in Wolfgang Company's balance sheet on January 31, Year 5.

7-9 The Allowance for Doubtful Accounts ledger account of Arapaho Corporation for Year 5 is summarized below:

Allowance for Doubtful Accounts

Date	Explanation	Debit	Credit	Balance
Year 5				
Jan. 1	Balance			29,800 cr
Mar. 31	Provision		10,530	40,330 cr
31	Write-off, Year 3 accounts	9,870		30,460 cr
June 30	Provision		9,720	40,180 cr
30	Write-off, Year 4 accounts	9,100		31,080 cr
Sept. 30	Provision		14,200	45,280 cr
30	Write-off, Year 4 accounts	6,840		38,440 cr
Dec. 31	Provision		12,550	50,990 cr
31	Write-off, Year 5 accounts	14,190		36,800 cr

Arapaho sells on 30-day credit terms and has followed a practice of debiting Doubtful Accounts Expense in an amount equal to 4% of sales. Arapaho's accountant prepares quarterly income statements and makes adjusting entries at the end of each quarter in order to measure the interim net income. At the end of Year 5, the accountant suggested that an aging be made of trade accounts receivable to test the adequacy of the Allowance for Doubtful Accounts ledger account balance. The aging of accounts receivable on December 31, Year 5, follows:

Current accounts, outstanding 30 days or less.........................	$290,000
31 to 60 days old...	85,200
61 to 120 days old...	50,000
121 days to 6 months old...	31,000
Over 6 months old	26,800
Balance of controlling account, Dec. 31, Year 5.....................	$483,000

After discussion with the credit manager of Arapaho, the accountant determined that the following percentages represented a reasonable estimate of the doubtful accounts in each category: current, 3%; 31 to 60 days old, 5%; 61 to 120 days old, 10%; 121 days to 6 months old, 20%; over 6 months old, 30%.

Instructions

a On the basis of the foregoing information, test the adequacy of the balance in Arapaho Corporation's Allowance for Doubtful Accounts ledger account on December 31, Year 5.

b Prepare an adjusting journal entry for Arapaho Corporation on December 31, Year 5, based on your analysis. The accounting records have not been closed for Year 5.

7-10 Paris Fashions Company began operations on January 2, Year 3, and reported net income of $25,000 in Year 3, $33,000 in Year 4, and $50,000 in Year 5. The accounting records for the year ended December 31, Year 5, are closed.

Paris Fashions did not use the accrual basis of accounting for some items. It was agreed that adjustments should be made in the accounting records to report the assets, liabilities, and owners' equity on the accrual basis of accounting.

Trade accounts receivable at the end of each year consisted of the following:

	December 31,		
	Year 3	Year 4	Year 5
Relating to sales made in:			
Year 3..................................	$20,000	$ 6,000	$ 3,000
Year 4..................................		24,000	7,500
Year 5..................................			35,000

Doubtful accounts expense was recorded when trade accounts receivable were deemed uncollectible. Based on an aging of the receivables, an allowance for doubtful accounts should be established as of December 31, Year 5, and should be estimated as follows: Current-year receivables, 5%; receivables relating to sales of Year 4, 20%; receivables relating to sales of Year 3, 60%. Doubtful accounts expense previously recorded and years of sale are summarized below:

Doubtful accounts expense recorded		Doubtful accounts expense recorded for sales made in		
Year	Amount	Year 3	Year 4	Year 5
3	$1,500	$1,500		
4	2,000	1,400	$ 600	
5	5,500	500	2,000	$3,000
Totals	$9,000	$3,400	$2,600	$3,000

Salaries and insurance were recorded as expense when paid. The amounts of accrued salaries and unexpired insurance at the end of each year were as follows:

	December 31,		
	Year 3	Year 4	Year 5
Salaries payable	$ 800	$ 1,050	$ 1,420
Salaries paid..............................	20,000	25,000	26,500
Unexpired insurance......................	600	800	150
Insurance premiums paid	2,500	2,000	2,200

Instructions

a Compute the required balance in the Allowance for Doubtful Accounts ledger account on December 31, Year 5, for Paris Fashions Company.

b Compute Paris Fashions Company's net income for Year 5, under the accrual basis of accounting. First, prepare a working paper to compute each of the following expenses for Year 5, under the accrual basis of accounting. (Disregard income taxes.)

(1) Doubtful accounts expense

(2) Salaries expense

(3) Insurance expense

c Prepare a correcting entry to restate the accounting records of Paris Fashions to the accrual basis of accounting on December 31, Year 5. Close the net adjustment to net income for the three-year period to the Retained Earnings ledger account. (Disregard income taxes.)

7-11 Laser Research Company was organized in Year 1, and it adopted a policy of providing for doubtful accounts expense at the rate of 3% of credit sales. A record of Laser Research's experience for the past three years appears below:

	Year 3	Year 2	Year 1
Credit sales	$535,000	$380,000	$320,000
Cash collected on credit sales of:			
Year 1			$211,580
Year 2		$318,420	85,000
Year 3	$370,000	47,000	10,000
Accounts of respective years written off as uncollectible:			
Year 1			500
Year 2		8,180	8,800
Year 3	2,200	6,400	4,120
Balance of trade accounts receivable, Dec. 31, Year 3	162,800		
Totals	$535,000	$380,000	$320,000

Laser Research's accountant made no journal entries affecting trade accounts receivable other than entries to record sales, cash collections from customers, the annual provision for doubtful accounts, and the write-offs of uncollectible accounts against the allowance account.

Laser Research engaged you at the end of Year 3 to make an examination of its financial statements for the purpose of supporting a loan application. You have the foregoing data available as a basis for determining the adequacy of the allowance for doubtful accounts. You propose to adjust the allowance to conform to the actual experience relating to doubtful accounts expense during Years 1 and 2.

Instructions

a Set up ledger accounts in three-column form for Trade Accounts Receivable (controlling account), Allowance for Doubtful Accounts, and Doubtful Accounts

Expense, and post all journal entries as Laser Research Company's accountant made them in Years 1 through 3. Also post closing entries for Year 1 and Year 2 to Doubtful Accounts Expense.

b Prepare and post to the accounts set up in **a,** any adjusting entries you deem necessary for Laser Research Company on December 31, Year 3, assuming that the accounting records have not been closed. Explain briefly the reasons for your adjustments and the basis for your determination of the proper allowance for doubtful accounts on December 31, Year 3. Laser Research Company records corrections of prior years' doubtful accounts expense in the current year's doubtful accounts expense.

7-12   Kay Furniture Company operates a furniture manufacturing business in New York. Although sales have been increasing rapidly, Kay Furniture has not been able to earn a consistently satisfactory net income because of price competition, losses as a result of excessive inventories, inability to collect on several large trade accounts receivable, and ineffective controls over manufacturing costs. Kay Furniture pays bills promptly, but its customers do not. As a result, Kay Furniture is short of cash and is unable to obtain material and equipment to start production of a new line of dining room furniture.

In an effort to obtain a loan, Mary Kay, the president of Kay Furniture, requested a working capital statement from her accountant with instructions to "make it look good." The accountant prepared the following statement of working capital:

KAY FURNITURE COMPANY
Statement of Working Capital
April 1, Year 5

Current assets:		
Cash		$ 8,925
Trade accounts receivable (net of $12,000 received from		
customers as deposits on special orders; allowances		
for doubtful accounts, sales discounts, and sales		
returns have not been used)		73,000
Inventories, at cost		49,150
Receivable from U.S. Treasury for claim for tax refund		
filed (net of income taxes payable of $4,000, which		
were due on Mar. 15, Year 5)		2,800
Receivable from subsidiary company (no due date)		34,000
Miscellaneous current assets		8,250
Total current assets		$176,125
Less: Current liabilities:		
Accounts payable	$50,450	
Wages payable	5,000	
Notes payable and miscellaneous current liabilities,		
including property taxes of $1,800 due on Apr. 10,		
Year 5	15,000	70,450
Working capital (current ratio 2.5 to 1)		$105,675

Kay presented the foregoing statement to three bankers, hoping to obtain a loan of $50,000 for one year. Each turned her down, giving reasons as follows:

Banker A: "We do not extend credit on the basis of partial balance sheets and without an income statement. We also like to see a cash forecast for the coming year. Incidentally, you should hire a certified public accountant who understands generally accepted accounting principles to audit your financial statements."

Banker B: "You have a satisfactory working capital position and do not need a loan. Besides, we are fully loaned up at the present time."

Banker C: "Because you do not need the money immediately, I would suggest that you take the following actions before we make a final decision on your loan request:

(1) Make a stronger effort to collect trade accounts receivable, write off the worthless accounts receivable, and provide an allowance for additional uncollectible accounts;
(2) Curtail production until inventories are reduced, auction some slow-moving items to raise cash, and postpone payments on payables as long as possible;
(3) Obtain the services of an accountant who can help to implement a cost reduction program, improve inventory controls, and reduce credit losses."

Instructions

a Evaluate the position taken by each of the three bankers.
b Assuming that $8,000 of the trade accounts receivable is uncollectible, that an allowance of 6% of the remaining accounts receivable is considered adequate, and that the market value (replacement cost) of inventories is approximately $41,200, prepare a revised statement of working capital for Kay Furniture Company as of April 1, Year 5.
c Prepare a reconciliation of the difference between the $105,675 working capital determined by Kay Furniture Company's accountant and your computation of working capital in part **b** above.

7-13 Lydia Corporation finances some of its current operations by assigning accounts receivable to High Finance Company. On May 1, Year 8, it assigned accounts receivable amounting to $300,000. High Finance advanced 80% of the accounts receivable assigned, less a fee of 2% of the total accounts receivable assigned. Customers were instructed to make payment directly to High Finance. Collections in excess of the loan and the fee were to be remitted to Lydia. At the time of remittance, the accountant for Lydia transferred any balance in Assigned Accounts Receivable to the Accounts Receivable ledger account.

The status of assigned accounts receivable at the end of May and June follows:

May 31 Lydia received a statement that showed that High Finance had collected $180,000 of the assigned accounts receivable and had made an additional charge for interest of 1½% of assigned accounts receivable outstanding on May 31. This charge was to be deducted from the first remittance of cash by High Finance to Lydia.

June 30 Lydia received a second statement from High Finance, together with a check for the amount due. The statement indicated that High Finance had collected an additional $66,000 and had made an additional charge for interest of 1½% of assigned accounts receivable outstanding on June 30, Year 8.

Instructions

a Prepare journal entries to record the foregoing transactions of Lydia Corporation. Debit all financing and interest charges to Interest Expense.

b Show how the information regarding assigned receivables is presented in the balance sheet of Lydia Corporation (1) on May 31, and (2) on June 30, Year 8.

7-14 Garment Factoring Company was incorporated in December, Year 1, for the purpose of factoring (purchasing) accounts receivable. Garment Factoring was authorized to issue 100,000 shares of $5 par common stock, all of which were issued at par.

Garment Factoring charges its clients a fee of 5% of all accounts receivable factored and assumes all credit risks. In addition to the 5% fee, 10% of gross accounts receivable is withheld on all purchases of accounts receivable and is credited to the Payable to Clients ledger account. This account is used for merchandise returns made by customers of the clients for which a credit memorandum would be due. Payments are made to its clients by Garment Factoring at the end of each month to adjust the Payable to Clients ledger account so that it equals 10% of the uncollected accounts receivable as of the end of the month.

Based on the collection experience of other factoring enterprises, the management of Garment Factoring decided to make monthly provisions to the Allowance for Doubtful Accounts ledger account based on 1% of all accounts receivable purchased during the month.

Garment Factoring also decided to recognize fees revenue only on the factored accounts receivable that have been collected; however, for accounting simplicity all fees originally are credited to Fees Revenue, and an adjusting entry is made to Unearned Fees Revenue at the end of each quarter, based on 5% of accounts receivable then outstanding.

Operations of Garment Factoring during the first quarter of Year 2 resulted in the following:

Accounts receivable factored:

January	*$400,000*
February	*500,000*
March	*800,000*

Collections on accounts receivable for the first quarter of Year 2 totaled $950,000. Operating expenses paid during the first quarter of Year 2 were as follows:

Salaries expense	*$19,500*
Office rent expense	*9,500*
Advertising expense	*800*
Equipment rent expense	*1,600*
Miscellaneous expenses	*1,450*

On January 31, Year 2, a six-month, 12% bank loan was obtained for $200,000, with interest payable at maturity.

For the first three months of the year, Garment Factoring rented all its office furniture and equipment; however, on March 31, Year 2, it acquired office furniture and equipment for $20,200, payable within 10 days. This acquisition was not entered in the accounting records.

Instructions

a Prepare a six-column (two columns each for Transactions for Quarter, Income Statement, and Balance Sheet) working paper to summarize the activities of Garment Factoring Company for the quarter ended March 31, Year 2. (Disregard all withholding taxes and the employer's liability for FICA and income taxes.)

b Prepare a balance sheet for Garment Factoring Company on March 31, Year 2.

7-15 Marten Company has not prepared financial statements for three years, since December 31, Year 1. Marten has used the accrual basis of accounting and had reported income on a calendar-year basis prior to Year 2. During the past three years (Years 2, 3, and 4), Marten has maintained cash records and has entered credit sales in an accounts receivable ledger; however, no general ledger postings have been made, and an allowance for doubtful accounts has not been used.

The balances at the beginning and end of the three-year period accumulated as a result of your examination are presented below:

	December 31,	
	Year 4	Year 1
Aging of accounts receivable:		
Less than one year old	$14,562	$7,700
1 to 2 years old	1,900	600
2 to 3 years old	2,138	
Over 3 years old (known to be uncollectible)	1,100	
Totals	$19,700	$8,300
Inventories..	$ 9,400	$5,800
Accounts payable (merchandise purchases)	6,500	4,305

Other information compiled from Marten Company's accounting records follows:

	Year 4	Year 3	Year 2	Total
Cash received on account, relating to:				
Current year's accounts receivable......	$103,938	$80,900	$74,400	$259,238
Accounts receivable of the prior year....	8,400	7,500	6,700	22,600
Accounts receivable of two years prior ..	262	200	300	762
Total cash received in Years 2 to 4....	$112,600	$88,600	$81,400	$282,600
Accounts to be written off in addition to				
the $1,100 that are over 3 years old......	$ 1,062	$ 820	$ 1,988	$ 3,870
Cash sales	15,600	13,200	13,500	42,300
Payments for merchandise purchases	86,900	70,600	62,500	220,000
Of receivables remaining Dec. 31, Year 4,				
estimated uncollectible percentage.......	10%	50%	80%	

No accounts receivable have been written off as uncollectible during the three-year period. The rate of gross profit for Marten Company has remained relatively constant for many years.

Instructions

a Prepare a working paper for Marten Company showing the gross profit on sales for Years 2, 3, and 4. (Hint: First, compute cost of goods sold as a percentage of sales for the three-year period.)

b Prepare adjusting entries for Marten Company on December 31, Year 4, to (1) establish an adequate allowance for doubtful accounts, and (2) write off accounts receivable that are uncollectible. Debit Retained Earnings for the amount required to establish the allowance for doubtful accounts. (Disregard income taxes.)

c Marten Company wishes to know what percentage of credit sales would be reasonable as an estimate of yearly doubtful accounts expense in the future, based on Marten's experience of the past three years. Support your recommendation with appropriate computations.

7-16 You are examining Marina Corporation's financial statement for the year ended December 31, Year 5. Your analysis of the journal entries for Year 5 in the Notes Receivable ledger account is summarized below:

MARINA CORPORATION
Analysis of Notes Receivable Ledger Account
For Year Ended December 31, Year 5

Date Year 5	Analysis of transactions	Notes Receivable Debit (Credit)
Jan. 1	Balance	$118,000
Feb. 28	Received 12%, $25,000 promissory note due Oct. 28, Year 5, from Daley Company, whose account receivable was past due. Memorandum entry only.	
28	Discounted Daley Company's note at 15% for 8 months..	(24,300)
Aug. 31	Received principal of $10,000 and interest of $8,400 due from Allen Company and, in accordance with agreement, two principal payments of $10,000 each in advance..................................	(38,400)
Sept. 4	Paid protest fee on promissory note dishonored by Chark Company	25
Oct. 29	Paid protest fee of $30 and maturity value of Daley Company's promissory note to bank. Note discounted Feb. 28, Year 5, was dishonored	27,030
30	Accepted fixtures with a current fair value of $26,500 in full settlement from Daley Company	(26,500)
Nov. 1	Received check in settlement of Bailey Company's promissory note	(8,960)

(continued)

Dec. 31	Received noninterest-bearing demand promissory note from James Edge, Marina's treasurer		6,200
31	Received payment on Chark Company's promissory note, including interest for one year and late-payment penalty of $75		(43,700)
31	Accrued interest on Allen Company's note for 6 months at 12%		2,400
	Balance of Notes Receivable ledger account		$ 11,795

Additional Information

(1) Notes receivable on January 1, Year 5, consisted of the following:

Note from Allen Company dated Aug. 31, Year 1, payable in annual installments of $10,000 plus interest at 12% each Aug. 31	$ 70,000
Note from Bailey Company dated Nov. 1, Year 4, due Nov. 1, Year 5, bearing interest at 12%.	8,000
Note from Chark Company dated Dec. 31, Year 4, due Sept. 1, Year 5, bearing interest at 9%.	40,000
Total notes receivable, Jan. 1, Year 5	$118,000

(2) Balance in the Interest Receivable ledger account on January 1, Year 5, consisted of the following:

Allen Company's note ($70,000 × 0.12 × 4/12)	$2,800
Bailey Company's note ($8,000 × 0.12 × 2/12)	160
Total interest receivable	$2,960

(3) No journal entries were made during Year 5 to the Interest Receivable ledger account, and only one credit entry for $2,400 on December 31 appeared in the Interest Revenue ledger account.

(4) All promissory notes were from trade customers unless otherwise indicated, and were fully collectible (even if later dishonored).

(5) Debits and credits offsetting related credit and debit entries to the Notes Receivable ledger account were correctly recorded unless the facts indicate otherwise.

Instructions

a Prepare a working paper to adjust or correct each journal entry of Marina Corporation for Year 5 and to reclassify it, if necessary. Enter your adjustments in the proper columns to correspond with the date of each entry and use a Notes Receivable Discounted ledger account for notes that are discounted. Do not combine related entries for different dates. Your completed working paper will provide the basis for a single journal entry to correct all entries to the Notes Receivable ledger account and the related ledger accounts for Year 5. Use the following headings for the working paper:

Date Year 5	Analysis of transactions	Notes Receivable (as recorded) Debit (Credit)	Adjustments or reclassifications required				
			Notes Receivable Debit (Credit)	Accounts Receivable Debit (Credit)	Interest Revenue Debit (Credit)	Other ledger accounts Account title	Debit (Credit)
Jan. 1	Balance	118,000					

b From the "Adjustments or reclassifications required" section of the working paper in **a,** prepare a single journal entry to correct Marina Corporation's accounting records on December 31, Year 5.

Inventories: Cost and Cost Flow Assumptions

8

Nature of Inventories

Inventories consist of goods held for sale to customers, partially completed goods, and material and supplies to be used in production. Inventory items are acquired and sold continuously by a merchandising enterprise; or acquired, placed in production, converted to a finished product, and sold by a manufacturing enterprise. The sale of merchandise or finished products is the primary source of revenue for most nonservice business enterprises.

In a retail or merchandising operation, inventories consist principally of products purchased for resale in their existing form. A retail enterprise also may have an inventory of supplies such as wrapping paper, cartons, and stationery. A manufacturing enterprise has several types of inventories: material, parts, and factory supplies; goods in process; and finished goods.

Material and parts are basic commodities or other products obtained directly from natural resources or acquired from others, which will be incorporated physically into the finished product. *Factory supplies* are similar to material, but their relation to the end product is indirect. For example, in the manufacture of shirts, cloth is inventoried as material, whereas the cleaning supplies and the oil to lubricate the machinery are classified as factory supplies. *Goods in process* consists of partially completed products and includes the cost of direct material, direct labor, and factory overhead. *Finished goods* are items that are complete and ready for sale and include the same cost elements as those in goods in process.

Inventory Procedures

Two methods may be employed to ascertain the inventory quantities on hand—the periodic system and the perpetual system. Both systems may be employed simultaneously for various inventories, such as material, finished goods, and goods in process.

The *periodic inventory system* relies on a physical count of the goods on hand as the basis for control, management decisions, and financial accounting. Although this procedure may give accurate results on a specific date, there is no continuing record of the inventory. The *perpetual inventory system* requires a continuous record of all receipts and withdrawals of each item of inventory. The perpetual record sometimes is kept in terms of quantities only. This procedure provides a better basis for control than is obtained under the periodic system. When the perpetual system is used, a physical count of the goods owned by the business enterprise *must be made periodically* to verify the accuracy of the inventories reported in the accounting records. Any discrepancies discovered must be corrected so that the perpetual inventory records are in agreement with the physical count.

COST AND QUANTITY ACCUMULATION

Timing Errors in the Recording of Purchases and Sales

When the cost of goods available for sale during a specific accounting period is being accumulated, decisions frequently must be made as to whether certain goods become the property of the purchaser in the current period or in the succeeding period. If acquisitions of goods are not recorded in the period in which they become the property of the purchaser, errors in the financial statements will result.

Three common types of timing errors in recording inventory purchases may occur. The errors and their effects on financial statements are:

1   A purchase is recorded properly, but goods are not included in the ending inventories. The result is to understate current assets and net income.

2   A purchase is not recorded, but goods are included in the ending inventories. The result is to state the assets properly but to understate current liabilities and to overstate net income.

3   A purchase is not recorded, and goods are not included in the ending inventories. Net income in this case is unaffected because both purchases and ending inventories are understated by the same amount, but both current assets and current liabilities also are understated.

The first two errors are most likely to occur when the periodic inventory system is used; the third type may occur under either the periodic or the perpetual system, but it is more likely when the perpetual system is used. In most cases, timing errors are counterbalanced in the following accounting period; however, the fact that the errors may be self-correcting does not remove the need for correct presentation of financial position and results of operations for each period.

The valuation of inventories has important effects on both the balance sheet and the income statement. The investment in inventories frequently is a major part of a business enterprise's total assets, and the valuation of inventories has a direct effect on the determination of the cost of goods sold. The effect of inventory valuation on the financial statements for a merchandising enterprise that has a single class of inventory is illustrated at the top of page 399.

In this illustration the cost of goods available for sale is $900,000, composed of the beginning inventory and the cost of goods purchased during Year 10. The cost of goods available for sale is allocated between the inventory on hand on December 31, Year 10, $150,000, and the cost of goods that have been sold during Year 10, $750,000. The cost of goods sold for Year 10 is the difference between the cost of

Valuation of inventory determines the cost of goods sold

Beginning inventory (current asset in balance sheet on Dec. 31, Year 9)	$200,000
Add: Purchases during Year 10	700,000
Cost of goods available for sale during Year 10	$900,000
Less: Ending inventory (current asset in balance sheet on Dec. 31, Year 10)	150,000
Cost of goods sold during Year 10	$750,000

goods available for sale and the cost of the ending inventory. Any failure to determine accurately either the cost of goods available for sale or the ending inventory may have a material effect on financial statements.

Goods in Transit

Orders for goods that *have not* been filled by the seller present little difficulty for accountants. The orders that *have* been filled by the seller but not received by the purchaser are the crucial ones. The problem that must be resolved in these cases is to determine whether the goods in transit are the property of the purchaser or of the seller. The passage of title from the seller to the purchaser marks the time when the legal responsibility for the goods changes from one party to the other.

Contracts for purchases usually specify which party is responsible for the goods and the exact location where the responsibility changes. This point usually is indicated by the letters *"FOB,"* meaning *"free on board,"* followed by the designation of a particular location, for example, "FOB Denver." This means that title is held by the seller until the goods are delivered to a common carrier in Denver that will act as an agent for the purchaser.[1] The following example illustrates this concept.

KC Shirt Shop orders 200 shirts from Denver Fashions to be shipped "FOB Denver," the invoice to be paid within 10 days after shipment. When Denver Fashions delivers the goods to the common carrier that acts as an agent of KC Shirt Shop, title to the goods passes to KC Shirt Shop. At this time, KC Shirt Shop would record the purchase if it knew that the goods were shipped. The freight charges in this case must be paid by KC Shirt Shop; however, the liability for freight charges does not arise until the carrier delivers the goods to KC Shirt Shop.

If KC Shirt Shop (located in Kansas City) also orders 1,000 shirts from Chicago Fabrics to be delivered "FOB Kansas City," the shirts are the property of Chicago Fabrics until they are delivered, and KC Shirt Shop does not record an asset or a liability until the shirts are received.

Goods on Consignment and Installment Sales

Goods may be transferred by one party to another without the typical sale and purchase contract. The party receiving the goods, the *consignee,* agrees to accept the goods without any liability beyond that of providing reasonable protection from

---

[1]Other important FOB designations are "FOB point of destination," which means that title passes at the purchaser's plant, and "FOB point of shipment," meaning that title passes at the seller's plant.

loss or damage, until the goods are sold by the consignee to a third party. At this time the consignee must remit to the shipper, the *consignor,* the sales price less a commission and costs incurred in connection with the sale. The consignor retains title to the goods until the time of sale to the third party, and the consignee, acting only as an agent, never has title to the goods. Therefore, until the goods are sold by the consignee, they remain the property of the consignor and must be included in the consignor's inventories at cost, including the handling and shipping costs involved in the transfer to the consignee. The consignee does not own the consigned goods and, therefore, does not include them in its inventories.

When goods are sold on the installment plan, the seller usually retains legal title to the goods until full payment has been received; however, such goods are excluded from the inventories of the seller. The expectation is that customers will make payment in the ordinary course of business; therefore, strict adherence to the "passing-of-title" rule is not considered a realistic approach to the recording of installment sales transactions.

Inventoriable Costs

The two most important functions of accounting for inventories are to determine (1) the quantity of goods to be included in inventories, and (2) the cost of the inventories on hand. The first function involves the *taking of inventory,* the second the *valuation of inventory.*

Taking of Inventory   As we have already indicated, a complete physical inventory of goods owned by a business enterprise must be taken periodically under both the periodic inventory system and the perpetual inventory system. The physical inventory generally is taken on or near the end of the enterprise's fiscal year, typically at a time when the enterprise has suspended operations. The taking of a physical inventory is a complex and time-consuming activity that requires extensive planning and control to assure accuracy. Inventory teams consisting of the enterprise's employees or outside experts count, weigh, or measure the goods owned by the enterprise, using tags or sheets to record the counts. Care must be taken to assure that all goods owned by the enterprise, regardless of their location, are included in the physical inventory, and that customer-owned goods or consigned goods in possession of the enterprise are excluded.

Valuation of Inventory   After the quantity of goods owned has been determined, the starting point in the valuation process is to ascertain the inventoriable cost elements of goods purchased or products manufactured. For inventory items purchased from outsiders, the net invoice cost generally is considered to be the inventoriable cost. *Net invoice cost* is the invoice price of the item less any cash (purchases) discounts *available* to the purchaser. As stated in Chapter 3, cash discounts should not be included in inventory cost, regardless of whether the purchaser takes advantage of the discounts or fails to do so.

In theory, if a specific cost is expected to contribute to the production of revenue, that cost should be associated with the goods acquired. Thus, a theoretical justification exists for adding the indirect costs of ordering, freight-in, handling, and storing to the net invoice cost to determine the total cost of goods acquired. However, the work involved in the allocation of these costs to inventories often exceeds the benefits derived from the increased accuracy in the valuation of inventories. Furthermore, the allocation of some indirect costs to goods acquired may be highly subjective.

Although the assignment to inventories of all costs incurred in the preparation of goods for sale is desirable, unrealistic allocations of indirect costs should be avoided to prevent a false impression of precision in the measurement of inventory costs. When costs are incurred that are necessary for the acquisition or production of goods but are not expected to produce future benefits or are not material in amount, the costs usually are not included in inventories. Instead, such costs are considered **period costs** to be deducted from current revenue. The foregoing discussion is summarized in the diagram below:

Flow of inventory costs to the financial statements

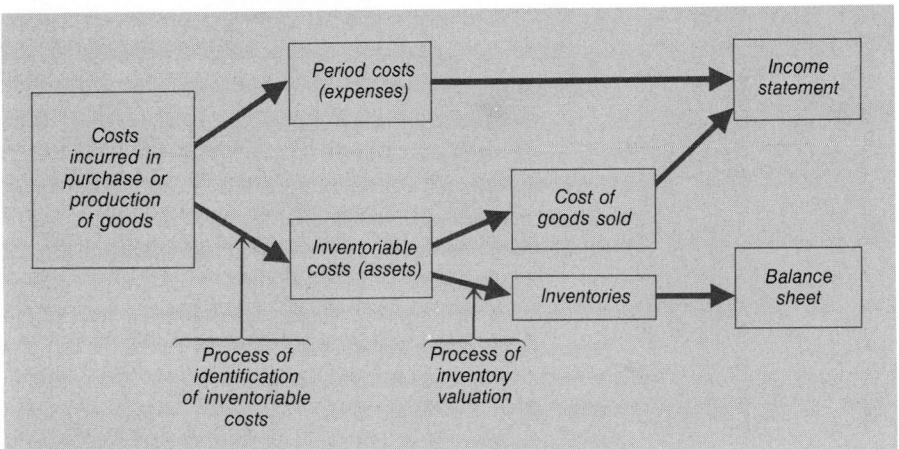

Purchased Inventories All costs incurred in the ordering, securing, handling, and storing of goods theoretically are as much a part of the total cost of the goods as the net invoice cost itself. The following example involving the purchase of shirts by KC Shirt Shop described on page 399 illustrates the determination of the cost of goods acquired.

Assume that the invoice from Denver Fashions indicates the price of the 200 shirts to be $10 each, with terms 2/10, n/30. This means that KC Shirt Shop must pay Denver Fashions either $1,960 [(200 × $10) × 0.98 = $1,960] within 10 days of the date of the invoice or $2,000 (200 × $10 = $2,000) within 30 days after the date of the invoice. The net invoice cost is $1,960. If payment is not made within 10 days, the $40 ($2,000 − $1,960 = $40) cash discount lost is recorded in a Purchases Discounts Lost ledger account (a financing expense) and is not included in the cost of inventories.

The cost of deciding to order these particular shirts, the actual cost of ordering them, the transportation cost, and the handling and storage cost incurred after receipt of the shirts, are costs that logically might be added to the net invoice cost of $1,960. However, for the reasons discussed in the preceding section, these costs typically are expensed.

Manufactured Inventories   In many ways the problems of measuring inventory costs are the same for a manufacturing enterprise as they are for a retailing enterprise. This is particularly true of material and other purchased inventoriable items. The major difference is found in the measurement of the cost of finished goods and goods in process. Tracing the movement of goods and costs through the production process often is difficult, but if it is done with reasonable care, the resulting information is useful to management and outsiders.

As stated earlier, four classes of inventory usually are found in a manufacturing enterprise: (1) material and parts, (2) goods in process, (3) finished goods, and (4) factory supplies. The costs of these inventories emerge as a part of the general process of the measurement of the costs of the three elements (direct material, direct labor, and factory overhead) that flow through the manufacturing process, and of the tracing of these costs to specific quantities of partially finished and finished products as illustrated below:

Flow of production costs

> *Direct material*
> *Direct labor*   } → *goods in process* → *finished goods*
> *Factory overhead**
>
> **Heat, light, and power; indirect material; indirect labor; rent; depreciation; insurance; supplies; maintenance; property taxes; etc.*

For a manufacturing enterprise, a sound *cost accounting system* is an essential component of *financial accounting.* Two types of *cost systems* may be used to accumulate product costs for a manufacturing enterprise: the job order cost system and the process cost system.

The *job order cost system* is used when an enterprise manufactures several distinct products. For example, the job order system is used for a construction or specialty product enterprise. Each product or group of products is distinct in some way, and the production costs are identified with a specific job. *Job order cost sheets* are used to accumulate the cost of direct material, direct labor, and factory overhead incurred on each job. Costs entered in job order cost sheets make up the goods in process inventory until the jobs are completed. The cost of completed jobs is a part of the finished goods inventory until the goods are sold.

The *process cost system* is used when large numbers of similar units are produced on an assembly-line operation. The production process typically is divided into *cost centers* or departments, based on logical divisions for the assignment of responsibility. Direct material, direct labor, and factory overhead costs then are accumulated by cost center, and the goods in process inventory is the sum of all costs incurred on the partially finished units in the various cost centers. The finished goods inventory is composed of all costs incurred to produce the completed goods on hand.

When the process cost system is used, the cost to produce a complete unit of product usually is determined from departmental *cost of production reports.* Such reports show how the total costs incurred were assigned to any *by-products* (or scrap) and to the *main products.* By-products usually are priced at net realizable value; if such value is immaterial, no cost is assigned to by-products.

Accountants frequently encounter situations in which production costs in a specific manufacturing process relate to two or more products. The allocation of these *joint costs* is necessary to determine the unit cost of each product and frequently is made on the basis of the *relative sales value* of the *joint products.* Dividing the total costs by the total sales value of the joint product determines the *cost percentage,* which then is applied to the unit selling price of each product to determine the estimated unit cost of each product.

Many enterprises engaged in manufacturing activities use standard costs as an integral part of their cost systems. *Standard costs* are estimates of what costs *should be* under relatively ideal conditions. The basic purpose of standard costs is to aid in measuring the efficiency of an operation, but standard costs also may be used for inventory valuation. The factors that make standard costs a useful control tool serve to reduce their usefulness for inventory valuation purposes. To be a good control tool a standard cost of a product should represent what cost *ought to be,* not what it *is* or *has been.* When standard costs are used for inventory valuation, accountants should ascertain that the standard costs are reasonable estimates of costs actually incurred.

COST FLOW ASSUMPTIONS

The term *cost flow* refers to the inflow of costs when goods are purchased or manufactured and to the outflow of costs when goods are sold. The cost remaining in inventories is the difference between the inflow and outflow of costs. During a specific accounting period, such as a year or a month, identical goods may be purchased or manufactured at different costs. Accountants then face the problem of determining which costs apply to items in inventories and which apply to items that have been sold. The critical issue in accounting for inventories is summarized below:[2]

A major objective of accounting for inventories is the proper determination of income through the process of matching appropriate costs against revenues.

Cost for inventory purposes may be determined under any one of several assumptions as to the flow of cost factors (such as, first-in, first-out, average, and last-in, first-out); the major objective in selecting a method should be to choose the one which, under the circumstances, most clearly reflects periodic income.

The *assumed flow of costs* to be used in the assignment of costs to inventories and to goods sold need not conform to the physical flow of goods. *Cost flow assumptions relate to the flow of costs, rather than to the physical flow of goods.* The question of which physical units of identical goods were sold and which remain in inventories is not relevant to income measurement and inventory valuation.

All methods of inventory valuation are based on the *cost principle;* no matter which method is selected, the inventory is stated *at cost.* In selecting an inventory

---

[2]*Accounting Research and Terminology Bulletins—Final Edition,* AICPA (New York: 1961), chap. 4, pp. 28–29.

valuation method (or cost flow assumption), accountants are *matching costs with revenue,* and the ideal choice is the method that *"most clearly reflects periodic income."* The most widely used methods of inventory valuation are:

1. First-in, first-out method (fifo)

2. Last-in, first-out method (lifo)

3. Weighted-average method

4. Specific identification method

A recent survey of 600 corporate annual reports indicated that fifo was used by 366 companies; lifo was used by 408 companies; average cost was used by 235 companies; and 52 companies applied a variety of other methods to the valuation of inventories. Obviously, many of the companies included in the survey used more than one method.[3]

First-In, First-Out Method

The first-in, first-out method assumes a flow of costs based on the assumption that the oldest goods on hand are sold first. This assumption about cost flow generally conforms to reality; management usually finds it desirable to keep the oldest goods moving out to customers in order to keep fresh or new goods on hand. The method is systematic and is easy to apply; it adheres to the cost principle; and the cost assigned to inventories is likely to be in close harmony with the current prices being paid for inventory replacements.

To understand the application of the fifo method, assume the following data for the month of January relating to item X in the inventories of West Company:

A total of 2,000 units was available for sale . . . and 1,300 units were sold

WEST COMPANY Record of Purchases of Item X during January		
Jan. 1 Inventory on hand	200 units @ $7	$ 1,400
Jan. 8 Purchase	1,100 units @ $8	8,800
Jan. 25 Purchase	300 units @ $9	2,700
Jan. 30 Purchase	400 units @ $10	4,000
Totals	2,000	$16,900

A physical inventory taken on January 31 shows 700 units on hand. The inventory could be composed of any combination of 700 units on hand at the beginning of January or purchased during January. If we follow the fifo procedure, however, we assume that the inventory on January 31 is composed of the items that were acquired *most recently.* The computation of the inventory cost on January 31, based on the fifo assumption, is illustrated at the top of page 405.

---

[3]*Accounting Trends & Techniques, 38th ed.,* AICPA (New York: 1984), p. 123.

Fifo inventory of 700 units is on hand

WEST COMPANY
Inventory of Item X: First-In, First-Out Method

Jan. 30 (last purchase)	400 units @ $10	$4,000
Jan. 25 (next-to-last purchase)......................	300 units @ $9	2,700
Totals	700	$6,700

The cost of goods sold consists of the earliest costs incurred and amounts to $10,200 (total goods available, $16,900, less ending inventory, $6,700, equals $10,200). *The fifo method gives the same result whether the periodic or perpetual inventory system is used* because each withdrawal of goods is from the oldest stock on hand.

Last-In, First-Out Method

The last-in first-out method assumes a flow of inventory costs based on the assumption that the most recently purchased goods are sold first, because current costs are incurred to make current sales and to maintain adequate inventories on hand. Under this view, the latest costs are most closely associated with current revenue; thus, the matching principle of income measurement is carried out. In the balance sheet, inventories under the lifo method are valued at the *earliest costs incurred.*

The following data for the month of January relating to item X in the inventory of West Company are the same as those used for the fifo illustration on page 404, except for the addition of the number of units sold and the dates when the sales were made:

Summary of purchases and sales

WEST COMPANY
Record of Purchases and Sales of Item X during January

	Purchases				Sales	
Date		Units	Price	Total	Date	Units sold
Jan. 1	Inventory on hand	200	$ 7	$ 1,400	Jan. 6	100
Jan. 8	Purchase	1,100	8	8,800	Jan. 9	200
Jan. 25	Purchase	300	9	2,700	Jan. 15	400
Jan. 30	Purchase	400	10	4,000	Jan. 27	600
	Totals	2,000		$16,900		1,300

The cost assigned to the ending inventory under lifo depends on whether the periodic or the perpetual inventory system is used.

Periodic Inventory System Based on the information given above, the cost of the 700 units on hand on January 31 is computed under lifo periodic inventory procedures as shown at the top of page 406.

WEST COMPANY
Inventory of Item X; Last-In, First-Out Method
(Periodic Inventory System)

Jan. 1 (beginning inventory)	200 units @ $7	$1,400
Jan. 8 (first purchase)	500 units @ $8	4,000
Totals	700	$5,400

The lifo inventory on January 31 is composed of two layers: the 200 units on hand on January 1, plus the layer of 500 units added during January. Should sales exceed purchases in any subsequent period, the costs of units comprising the most recently added layer or layers would be removed from inventory and transferred to cost of goods sold. The cost of the original layer would not be reduced until all subsequently added layers had been assigned to cost of goods sold. The cost of goods sold for January is $11,500 ($16,900 cost of goods available for sale, less $5,400 cost of inventory on January 31, equals $11,500), and consists of the most recent purchases.

Perpetual Inventory System Unlike the first-in, first-out method, the last-in, first-out method does not produce the same result when the perpetual inventory system is used. When the perpetual system is used, each withdrawal must come from the most recent purchase; however, this may mean that items may be withdrawn from the beginning inventory or the earliest purchase when purchases lag behind sales. If we assume the same record of purchases and sales as on page 405, the costs assigned to the goods sold under lifo perpetual inventory procedures is $10,600, as computed below:

WEST COMPANY
Cost of Goods Sold (Item X): Last-In, First-Out Method
(Perpetual Inventory System)

Jan. 6	100 units @ $7	$ 700
Jan. 9	200 units @ $8	1,600
Jan. 15	400 units @ $8	3,200
Jan. 27	600 units { 300 @ $9	2,700
	{ 300 @ $8	2,400
Totals	1,300	$10,600

The ending inventory under the lifo perpetual inventory system amounts to $6,300 ($16,900 − $10,600 = $6,300), and consists of the following:

... and ending inventory under perpetual inventory system

WEST COMPANY
Inventory of Item X: Last-In, First-Out Method
(Perpetual Inventory System)

Jan. 1 (Balance of beginning layer not sold)	100 units @ $7	$ 700
Jan. 8	200 units @ $8	1,600
Jan. 30	400 units @ $10	4,000
Totals	700	$6,300

Thus, it is apparent that the results of the lifo method of valuing the inventory under the perpetual inventory system may vary somewhat, depending on the timing of sales and purchases.

Unit-Lifo Method The practical problems of determining the cost of inventory under the lifo procedure may be overwhelming, especially without the aid of a computer. When there are large numbers of similar items and numerous transactions, the weighted-average unit cost of the items purchased during an accounting period is considered the cost for purposes of pricing additions to inventory for the period. Such a procedure eliminates the need for identifying the cost of particular units. This adaptation is used in conjunction with the periodic inventory system and is called the ***unit-lifo method.*** Given the data presented on page 405 for West Company, the unit-lifo inventory on January 31 is computed below:

Illustration of unit-lifo method

WEST COMPANY
Inventory of Item X: Unit-Lifo Method

Beginning inventory	200 units @ $7.00	$1,400
Layer added in January	500 units @ $8.61*	4,305
Totals	700	$5,705

*Computation of weighted-average unit cost for units acquired in January:	
Cost of purchases	$15,500
Total units purchased in January	1,800
Weighted-average unit cost of purchases ($15,500 ÷ 1,800)	$ 8.61

The unit-lifo method is applied only when there is an increase in the inventory during an accounting period. The layer added in January retains its identity in subsequent months as long as the inventory consists of 700 units or more. However, if the inventory decreased to 400 units in February, the inventory on February 28 would consist of 200 units at $7 and only 200 units at $8.61.

Dollar-Value Lifo Method

The determination of lifo cost for a single inventory item, as illustrated in the preceding sections, is not difficult. However, a business enterprise that has several product lines consisting of numerous items in its inventories would have difficulty in applying lifo cost to each of the individual items, especially if the earliest costs dated back many years. Such an enterprise might use the dollar-value lifo inventory method to simplify the application of lifo procedures. Under *dollar-value lifo,* inventory items constituting a single product line or otherwise having similar characteristics are accumulated in *pools.* Individual items in each pool are assigned lifo costs in accordance with the procedures described on pages 405–406. The total lifo cost of each pool becomes base-year cost for that pool, with a *cost index* of 100. Total base-year costs for all pools constitutes the lifo inventories on the date of adoption of the dollar-value lifo method.

Subsequent ending inventories in each pool are valued first at *current cost;* total current cost then is converted to equivalent base-year cost by use of the appropriate cost index. Any increase in the ending inventory for each pool, in terms of base-year costs, is valued at costs prevailing during the current year. In practice, the cost index as of the *end of the current year* is used to value the added layer; practical limitations of computing several indexes during a year have led to this procedure. A decrease in the ending inventory for each pool in terms of base-year cost is deducted from the most recent layer added to the inventory, at the costs prevailing in the year when the layer was added. Thus, dollar-value lifo measures changes in inventories in terms of *dollar amounts* rather than in terms of *units.*

There are four techniques for applying the dollar-value lifo method: *double-extension, link-chain, index,* and *retail.* These techniques differ primarily in the computation of the cost indexes. The dollar-value retail lifo method is illustrated in Chapter 9, together with other retail methods; the other three techniques are described and illustrated in the following sections.

Double-Extension Dollar-Value Lifo   Under the double-extension dollar-value lifo technique, the ending inventories subsequent to the base year for each pool are computed with two values—*current cost* and *base-year cost.* The ratio of total current cost to total base-year cost is the pool's *cost index* for the year, and is used to value any increase (*lifo layer*) in the pool for that year. The term "double-extension" refers to the two computations of quantities times unit costs.

To illustrate, assume that on December 31, Year 1, Lastin Company adopted the dollar-value lifo method, with the double-extension technique, for costing its two inventory items, Alpha and Beta, which constitute a single pool. Details of quantities and unit costs for the two items on December 31, Years 1 through 4, follow:

Data for double-extension dollar-value lifo illustration

	LASTIN COMPANY Quantities and Unit Costs of Inventory Items December 31, Year 1 through Year 4							
Item	**Quantities on December 31,**				**Unit costs on December 31,***			
	Year 1	**Year 2**	**Year 3**	**Year 4**	**Year 1**	**Year 2**	**Year 3**	**Year 4**
Alpha	4,000	5,000	6,000	5,600	$3.00	$3.60	$3.90	$4.20
Beta	6,000	8,000	9,000	8,400	4.00	4.80	5.20	5.60

*December 31, Year 1, unit cost is lifo cost; unit costs on December 31, Years 2 through 4, are current costs.

Lastin's December 31, Year 1, inventory at lifo cost is $36,000 [(4,000 × $3.00) + (6,000 × $4.00) = $36,000], which amount constitutes *base-year inventory*. The cost indexes for Years 2, 3, and 4 are computed by the double-extension technique as follows:

Computation of cost indexes for dollar-value lifo method by double-extension technique

LASTIN COMPANY
Computation of Cost Indexes for Dollar-Value Lifo—Double-Extension Technique
For Years Ended December 31, Year 2 through Year 4

Item	Quantity	Unit cost		Total cost	
		Current year	Base year	Current year	Base year
Dec. 31, Year 2:					
Alpha	5,000	$3.60	$3.00	$18,000	$15,000
Beta	8,000	4.80	4.00	38,400	32,000
Totals	13,000			$56,400	$47,000

Cost index: $56,400 ÷ $47,000 = 1.20, or 120

Dec. 31, Year 3:					
Alpha	6,000	$3.90	$3.00	$23,400	$18,000
Beta	9,000	5.20	4.00	46,800	36,000
Totals	15,000			$70,200	$54,000

Cost index: $70,200 ÷ $54,000 = 1.30, or 130

Dec. 31, Year 4:					
Alpha	5,600	$4.20	$3.00	$23,520	$16,800
Beta	8,400	5.60	4.00	47,040	33,600
Totals	14,000			$70,560	$50,400

Cost index: $70,560 ÷ $50,400 = 1.40, or 140

By use of total inventory for the base year, December 31, Year 1 ($36,000), and the cost indexes computed by the double-extension technique, Lastin computes its ending inventories by the dollar-value lifo method as follows (the inventories at base-year costs and the indexes are taken from the preceding table):

Dollar-value lifo method illustrated (double-extension technique)

LASTIN COMPANY
Computation of Dollar-Value Lifo Inventories—Double-Extension Technique
December 31, Year 1 through Year 4

December 31,	Inventories at base-year costs	Determination of inventory layers	Dollar-value lifo inventories at year-end
Year 1	$36,000	$36,000 × 1.00	$36,000
Year 2	$47,000	$36,000 × 1.00	$36,000
		11,000 × 1.20	13,200
		$47,000	$49,200

(continued)

Year 3	$54,000	$36,000 × 1.00	$36,000
		11,000 × 1.20	13,200
		7,000 × 1.30	9,100
		$54,000	$58,300
Year 4	$50,400	$36,000 × 1.00	$36,000
		11,000 × 1.20	13,200
		3,400 × 1.30	4,420
		$50,400	$53,620

Explanation of Computations

Year 2: The increase in the ending inventories, in terms of base-year costs, is $11,000 ($47,000 − $36,000 = $11,000). This increase is converted to year-end costs by multiplying it by 1.20, the end-of-Year 2 cost index. The $13,200 product is the Year 2 **lifo layer;** this amount is added to the base-year ending inventories of $36,000 to obtain the $49,200 dollar-value lifo inventories on December 31, Year 2.

Year 3: The increase in the ending inventories, in terms of base-year costs, is $7,000 ($54,000 − $47,000 = $7,000). This increase is converted to year-end costs by multiplying it by 1.30, the end-of-Year 3 cost index. The $9,100 product is the Year 3 **lifo layer;** this amount is added to the Year 2 ending inventories of $49,200 (at dollar-value lifo) to obtain the $58,300 dollar-value lifo inventories on December 31, Year 3.

Year 4: The decrease in the ending inventories, in terms of base-year costs, is $3,600 ($54,000 − $50,400 = $3,600). This decrease, termed a **lifo liquidation,** is attributed to the Year 3 lifo layer, in accordance with the last-in, first-out cost flow assumption. Thus, the residual Year 3 lifo layer, in terms of base-year costs, is $3,400 ($7,000 − $3,600 = $3,400). The Year 4 cost index of 140 is not used in the computation of the dollar-value lifo inventories on December 31, Year 4, or at any subsequent year-end, because no lifo layer was added in Year 4. The $4,680 decrease ($58,300 − $53,620 = $4,680) in the December 31, Year 4, dollar-value lifo inventories may be verified by multiplying the $3,600 Year 4 lifo liquidation, at base-year costs, by 1.30, the cost index for Year 3 ($3,600 × 1.30 = $4,680).

Link-Chain Dollar-Value Lifo The link-chain dollar-value lifo technique is a variation of the double-extension technique in which *beginning-of-year costs,* rather than *base-year costs,* are used to compute the denominator for the computation of the cost index for each year subsequent to the base year. Each successive year's cost index is multiplied by the preceding year's cost index to obtain a *cumulative cost index* through a *chaining* technique. The cumulative cost indexes are used to compute the dollar-value amounts of the lifo layers for the years to which they relate. If there are no changes in the items comprising a specific inventory pool during a year, the cost index computed by the double-extension technique would be identical to the cumulative cost index computed by the link-chain technique.

To illustrate the link-chain technique for dollar-value lifo, we return to the data for the Lastin Company illustration on page 408. Computations of the cumulative cost indexes for Lastin by the link-chain technique are shown on page 411.

Computation of cost indexes for dollar-value lifo method by link-chain technique

LASTIN COMPANY
Computation of Cost Indexes for Dollar-Value Lifo—Link-Chain Technique
For Years Ended December 31, Year 2 through Year 4

Item	Quantity	Unit cost		Total cost	
		End-of-year	Beginning-of-year	End-of-year	Beginning-of-year
December 31, Year 2:					
Alpha	5,000	$3.60	$3.00	$18,000	$15,000
Beta	8,000	4.80	4.00	38,400	32,000
Totals	13,000			$56,400	$47,000

Cost index for year: $56,400 ÷ $47,000 = 1.20, or 120
Cumulative (link-chain) cost index: 1.20 × 1.00 = 1.20, or 120

Item	Quantity	Unit cost		Total cost	
December 31, Year 3:					
Alpha	6,000	$3.90	$3.60	$23,400	$21,600
Beta	9,000	5.20	4.80	46,800	43,200
Totals	15,000			$70,200	$64,800

Cost index for year: $70,200 ÷ $64,800 = 1.083, or 108
Cumulative (link-chain) cost index: 1.08 × 1.20 = 1.30, or 130

Item	Quantity	Unit cost		Total cost	
December 31, Year 4:					
Alpha	5,600	$4.20	$3.90	$23,520	$21,840
Beta	8,400	5.60	5.20	47,040	43,680
Totals	14,000			$70,560	$65,520

Cost index for year: $70,560 ÷ $65,520 = 1.077, or 108
Cumulative (link-chain) cost index: 1.08 × 1.30 = 1.40, or 140

Because there were no changes in the items comprising Lastin Company's inventory pool during the three years ended December 31, Year 4, the cumulative cost indexes computed above are identical to those computed by the double-extension technique (page 409). Thus, the dollar-value lifo inventory amounts would be identical to those shown on pages 409–410 under the double-extension dollar-value lifo approach.

If a new product had been included in Lastin's December 31, Year 4, inventory pool, for example, a base-year cost for the new product would be obtained or simulated for use in the double-extension technique, but the January 1, Year 4, cost would be used for the new product in the link-chain technique. The December 31, Year 4, cumulative cost index under the link-chain technique thus would differ from the December 31, Year 4, cost index under the double-extension technique because the December 31, Year 3, cumulative cost index did not include the effect of the new product.

Index Dollar-Value Lifo   For a business enterprise having numerous inventory pools, both the double-extension and the link-chain techniques may involve numerous computations to derive appropriate cost indexes. Such enterprise may choose to use specific cost indexes published by the U.S. Department of Labor that are appropriate for the enterprise's inventory pools. In the absence of an appropriate specific price index, an accountant may take samples of the inventory pools and value the samples at both current-period and base-period prices. The total cost in terms of the current period's prices then is divided by the total cost in terms of the base period's prices. The cost index thus determined is used to value the entire inventory pool. In the computation of this index, discontinued and new products deserve special consideration. The best approach is to eliminate these items from the computation. They in turn must be valued separately, and in many cases the only feasible way is to refer to particular invoice costs. The cost index for a sample of inventory items may be computed as illustrated below. This computation indicates that current-period prices have risen on the average by 10% from base-period prices ($7,700 ÷ $7,000 = 1.10).

Computation of cost index by sampling from inventory pool

Items	Inventory quantity	Unit costs		Total costs	
		End of current period	Base period	End of current period	Base period
A	150	$40.00	$36.00	$6,000	$5,400
B	60	15.00	13.00	900	780
C	200	4.00	4.10	800	820
				$7,700	$7,000

The key feature of the dollar-value lifo method, regardless of the technique used to determine cost indexes, is the conversion of the beginning and ending inventories of each pool to base-year costs. The difference between the two converted inventory amounts indicates the increase or decrease in the inventory expressed in terms of base-year costs. The lifo layers then must be valued at costs prevailing when the layers were added to the inventory.

Base Stock Method

The *base stock method* is similar to lifo, but, because it is not acceptable for income tax purposes and has little theoretical support, it seldom is used in practice. This method assumes a continuous existence of a minimum stock of goods, the cost of which is considered to be a permanent asset. Any excess over the base stock is considered a temporary increase and is priced at *current replacement costs;* any decrease in the base stock is considered to be temporary and is assigned to cost of goods sold at current replacement costs.

The base stock method differs from lifo in that it uses current replacement costs as an element in the pricing of inventory; in contrast, lifo relies exclusively on actual costs.

Weighted-Average Method

The weighted-average method of inventory valuation is based on the assumptions that all goods are commingled and that no particular batch of goods is retained in the inventories. Thus, the inventories are valued on the basis of average prices paid for the goods, weighted according to the quantity purchased at each price. Given the information for West Company on page 404, the ending inventory and cost of goods sold are determined under the weighted-average method (periodic inventory system) as follows:

Weighted-average method under periodic inventory system

WEST COMPANY Inventory and Cost of Goods Sold (Item X): Weighted-Average Method (Periodic Inventory System)	
Cost of goods available for sale	$16,900
Total units available for sale	2,000
Unit cost = total cost ÷ number of units ($16,900 ÷ 2,000)	$ 8.45
Inventory valuation (700 × $8.45)	$ 5,915
Cost of goods sold ($16,900 − $5,915)...............................	$10,985

This method produces a result, for both inventory valuation and income measurement, that lies between the results achieved under fifo and those achieved under lifo. The weighted-average method does not produce an inventory value consistent with the current cost of the items in inventory; by its nature it lags behind market prices. During a period of rising prices the inventory cost tends to be below replacement cost; during a period of falling prices it tends to be above replacement cost.

When the perpetual inventory system is used, the weighted-average method gives the result of a ***moving weighted average.*** Under the perpetual system, a new weighted-average unit cost is computed after each purchase, and for this reason is known as the moving-weighted-average method. Units sold are priced at the latest weighted-average unit cost. Given the information for West Company on page 405, the moving-weighted-average method is illustrated at the top of page 414.

Specific Identification Method

At first thought one might argue that each item of inventory should be identified with its ***actual*** cost and that the total of these amounts should constitute the inventory value. Although such a technique might be possible for a business enterprise handling a small number of items, for example, an automobile dealer, it becomes completely inoperable in a complex manufacturing enterprise when the identity of the individual item is lost. Practical considerations thus make specific identification inappropriate in most cases.

Even when specific identification is a feasible means of valuation, it may be undesirable from a theoretical point of view. The method permits income manipulation when there are identical items acquired at varying prices. By choosing to sell the item that was acquired at a specific cost, management may cause material distortions in income. For example, assume that Grain Company acquires 1 million

Weighted-average
method under
perpetual inventory
system

WEST COMPANY
Inventory of Item X: Moving-Weighted-Average Method
(Perpetual Inventory System)

	Units	Amount
Jan. 1 inventory	200 @ $ 7.00	$1,400
Less: Jan. 6 sale	(100) @ $ 7.00	(700)
Balance, Jan. 6	100 @ $ 7.00	$ 700
Add: Jan. 8 purchase	1,100 @ $ 8.00	8,800
Balance, Jan. 8 (new unit cost computed)	1,200 @ $ 7.92	$9,500*
Less: Jan. 9 sale	(200) @ $ 7.92	(1,584)
Balance, Jan. 9	1,000 @ $ 7.92	$7,916*
Less: Jan. 15 sale	(400) @ $ 7.92	(3,168)
Balance, Jan. 15	600 @ $ 7.92	$4,748*
Add: Jan. 25 purchase	300 @ $ 9.00	2,700
Balance, Jan. 25 (new unit cost computed)	900 @ $ 8.28	$7,448*
Less: Jan. 27 sale	(600) @ $ 8.28	(4,968)
Balance, Jan. 27	300 @ $ 8.28	$2,480*
Add: Jan. 30 purchase	400 @ $10.00	4,000
Balance, Jan. 31 (inventory at new unit cost)	700 @ $ 9.26	$6,480*

*Slight discrepancy due to rounding of average cost to nearest cent.

bushels of wheat in four equal lots of 250,000 bushels each, at costs of $3.50, $4, $4.50, and $5 a bushel. Grain Company receives an order to sell 250,000 bushels at $4.75 a bushel. If management is accounting for inventory in accordance with specific identification, it can determine the income reported for the period by selecting the batch of wheat that will produce the desired objective. The results of the transaction could range from a profit of $312,500 if the $3.50 wheat were sold, to a loss of $62,500 if the $5 wheat were sold. If an assumption regarding the flow of costs were adopted (fifo or lifo, for example), the effect of such arbitrary decisions on reported income would be removed.

Summary of Inventory Valuation Methods

The inventory valuation and cost of goods sold for West Company as determined in the preceding illustrations are summarized at the top of page 415. Results from use of the specific identification method are not shown, because we did not identify the composition of the units in inventory by date of purchase.

In the West Company example in which prices were rising, the costs assigned to inventory range from a high of $6,700 under the fifo method to a low of $5,400 when the lifo method is used in conjunction with the periodic inventory system. The disparity in inventory valuation under the various cost flow assumptions depends on the trend and volatility of prices paid for new purchases and, of course, on the length of time the lifo method has been in use.

Summary of cost flow
assumptions

Cost flow assumption	Goods available for sale	Inventory	Cost of goods sold
WEST COMPANY			
Inventory and Cost of Goods Sold (Item X): Various Cost Flow Assumptions			
First-in, first-out method	$16,900	$6,700	$10,200
Last-in, first-out method:			
Periodic system	16,900	5,400	11,500
Perpetual system	16,900	6,300	10,600
Unit lifo	16,900	5,705	11,195
Weighted-average method			
(periodic system)	16,900	5,915	10,985
Moving-weighted-average			
method (perpetual system)	16,900	6,480	10,420

INVENTORY VALUATION AND INFLATION

Although both lifo and fifo are accepted inventory valuation methods, they may lead to significant differences in the financial statements during a period of inflation. Neither method achieves an entirely satisfactory reporting of both inventories and cost of goods sold when prices are going up. Therefore, it is not surprising that a controversy has evolved around the relative importance of working capital and net income. In an inflationary period, this controversy is somewhat overshadowed by the managerial and income tax implications of inventory valuation procedures.

Effect on Working Capital and Net Income

As illustrated earlier, the fifo method has the effect of assigning the most recently incurred costs to inventories, whereas the lifo assumption assigns the first costs incurred to inventories. During periods of rising price levels, inventories valued on the fifo basis approximate more closely the current cost of the inventories; the cost of items valued on the lifo basis are less than the current cost. The difference between the inventories valued at lifo and at current cost depends on the magnitude of the price level increases. The lifo method produces a seriously distorted inventory valuation when it is used over a long period during which the price level increases steadily or when the price level increases rapidly.

The understatement of inventories resulting from the use of the lifo method is objectionable because of the effect on working capital, current ratio, and inventories turnover rate. The problem is rather serious if no indication is included in the financial statements of the degree of understatement. The advocates of lifo minimize the importance of this understatement by arguing that the income statement is more important than the balance sheet. They argue that *a more accurate measure of net income* may justify a less meaningful balance sheet. Despite these views by proponents of lifo, the Securities and Exchange Commission requires companies subject to its jurisdiction that use lifo to disclose in a note to the financial statements the excess of replacement or current cost over the lifo value of inventories.[4]

Proponents of the lifo method argue that realized revenue should be matched with the cost of acquiring goods at or near the time the revenue is realized. They contend that during periods of rising prices, for example, two types of profits, inventory profits and operating profits, may be included in net income, unless diligence is exercised to avoid the inclusion of inventory profits. **Inventory profits** arise as a result of holding inventories during periods of rising inventory costs, and are measured by the **difference between the original cost of the goods sold and their current cost at the time of sale. Operating profits** result from sales of a product at a price above current cost. Because the lifo method matches the most recently incurred costs with realized revenue, it tends to exclude inventory profits from net income. Supporters of lifo favor the exclusion of inventory profits from net income, on the premise that inventories that are sold must be replaced and that inventory profits are **fictitious** and **illusory**.

Those supporting the fifo method of inventory valuation agree that there may be two types of profits, but they consider both to be an element of income realized at the time of sale. They argue that if the proponents of lifo are interested in measuring **real** rather than **monetary** income, they should extend their proposal to use current costs to value all assets. The cost of goods sold should not be the most recently incurred costs but rather the costs that **will be incurred** to replace the items that have been sold. This method has been referred to as the **next-in, first-out (nifo)** method of inventory valuation. At the present time, the nifo method is not acceptable, because it violates the cost principle.

The measurement of **real income** poses another problem during a period of inflation. To illustrate, assume that an inventory item was purchased for $100 when the general price-level index was 120, and was sold for $150 when the general price-level index was 132 and the current cost of the item was $124. The apparent gross profit of $50 ($150 − $100 = $50) on the sale of the item may be allocated between the (1) general price-level adjustment, (2) holding gain, and (3) operating profit as follows:

Analysis of gross profit

General price-level adjustment: ($100 × 132/120) − $100 (original cost)	*$10*
Holding gain: $124 (current cost) − $100 (original cost) − $10 (general price-level adjustment computed above)	*14*
Operating profit: $150 (selling price) − $124 (current cost)	*26*
Total difference between selling price and original cost ($150 − $100)	*$50*

The **holding gain** of $14 is the increase accruing as a result of owning the item while the specific price (current cost) of the item was rising. The holding gain does not include the $10 increase in price of the item caused by general inflation. The total of the price-level adjustment and the holding gain, $24, is the **inventory profit**

---

[4]*Regulation S-X,* Rule 5-02-6(c), Securities and Exchange Commission (Washington: 1984).

(difference between the current cost of $124 and the original cost of $100). Finally the *operating profit* of $26 is the real economic reward to the enterprise for handling and selling the item.

Managerial and Income Tax Implications

The proponents of lifo argue that this method is an invaluable aid to management because it excludes inventory profits from net income. External factors that are beyond the control of management often create inventory profits. Moreover, inventory profits are reinvested in inventories, which means that disposable (spendable) income is measured more accurately by the use of lifo.

Fifo advocates agree that management may need information about the current cost of the inventory and its effect on net income; however, they maintain that this information may be compiled without distorting working capital and net income. Moreover, they argue that if the inventory profits are excluded from net income, similar profits derived from other investments also should be excluded. If management decisions regarding dividend declarations, wage negotiations, and prices are based on the concept of disposable income, a more extensive modification of the determination of net income is needed than that achieved by lifo. Adherents of fifo also criticize the distortions of net income caused by lifo liquidations. When these occur, cost of goods sold includes costs that may differ significantly from current costs. For example, in the Year 4 example for Lastin Company (page 410), cost of goods sold includes $4,680 ($3,600 $\times$ 1.30 = $4,680) attributable to the lifo liquidation, compared with current cost of approximately $5,040 ($3,600 $\times$ 1.40 = $5,040). In recognition of this deficiency of the lifo method, the Securities and Exchange Commission requires companies that it supervises to disclose the effect of material lifo liquidations on their net income.[5]

Despite the theoretical arguments in support of lifo, the dominant reason for its popularity is the income tax benefits that result from the use of this method. During periods of rising prices, taxable income and income taxes are reduced through the use of lifo. If prices later fall to the level at the time lifo was adopted, this reduction is simply a deferral of taxes. If prices continue to rise, the reduction will be permanent. In either case, the lifo user gains, because a postponement of taxes has economic value. The federal income tax law requires that lifo must be used for the financial accounting income statement if it is used for income tax purposes, although different lifo techniques may be applied.[6]

The income tax benefits of lifo are not guaranteed. If prices fall below levels at the time lifo was adopted, or if the quantity of inventories is reduced below the amount on hand at the inception of lifo, it is conceivable that the lifo method could produce a tax disadvantage. Before adopting lifo solely for income tax reasons, management should consider such factors as the expected course of prices, future income tax rates, inventory fluctuations, the enterprise's net income pattern, and the existence of provisions in the income tax law (such as operating loss carrybacks and carryforwards) that even out the tax burden over periods of income and loss.

---

[5]*Staff Accounting Bulletin 40,* Topic 11F, Securities and Exchange Commission (Washington: 1981).
[6]*U.S. Treasury Regulations,* Section 1.472-2(e)(8).

The Securities and Exchange Commission has expressed concern about the application of the lifo inventory method by some business enterprises. In alleging that financial accounting practices for lifo have been unduly influenced by income tax regulations, the SEC identified abuses of the lifo method such as the following:[7]

1   Incorrect designation of preexisting inventory items as new products and including them in a pool at current cost, rather than at base-year cost, under the double-extension technique for dollar-value lifo.

2   Manipulation of net income by creation of lifo liquidations.

3   Inference in presidents' letters or other sections of corporate annual reports that a fifo-based net income, rather than lifo-based net income of the income statement, constitutes "real" earnings.

In recognition of the foregoing and other problems, the AICPA's Accounting Standards Executive Committee (AcSEC) submitted an *Issues Paper* to the Financial Accounting Standards Board dealing with the lifo method of inventory valuation, which the SEC endorsed in *Staff Accounting Bulletin 58*.

VALUATION OF INVENTORIES AT LOWER OF COST OR MARKET

We have indicated that valuation of inventories includes ascertaining the number of units, determining an appropriate unit cost, and computing the total cost. We now consider another possibility: that of a decrease in the economic value of inventories below their cost. If some items of inventories are used for display or demonstration, a part of the cost of these units should be expensed prior to their sale. Whenever an asset contributes to the realization of revenue and a part of the usefulness of the asset is consumed, a part of the cost of the asset should be deducted from such revenue.

Assume, for example, that the owner of Delphine's Dress Shop wants her store to have a reputation as *the* fashion shop in her area. To accomplish her objective she knows that she must stock the extreme styles in sufficient volume to satisfy a substantial part of her clientele. In many cases she will buy more dresses than she expects to sell in order to maintain her reputation. To obtain a proper measure of net income and to value her inventories properly, a part of the cost of the excess supply of dresses will have to be charged against revenue prior to the sale of these dresses. The problem is one of ascertaining the amount of the cost that should be charged off. The loss of economic value is believed to have contributed to the realization of revenue, and the selling price of dresses on hand will have to be reduced. The expired cost of dresses still on hand may be added to the cost of goods sold.

---

[7]*Codification of Financial Reporting Policies,* Securities and Exchange Commission (Washington: 1982), Sec. 205.02.

Obsolescence of Inventories

In other situations part of the cost of inventories must be deducted from revenue even though no benefit has accrued to the business enterprise. Inventory items frequently become unsalable at regular prices because of obsolescence, damage, or deterioration. If items that are to become a part of a manufactured article are damaged or spoiled during the production process, the loss need not be segregated, but may become a part of the cost of the completed product. This procedure is acceptable, provided the damage or loss is expected as a part of the normal operation of the plant. However, unusual loss or damage should not be included in the cost of manufactured goods.

Damaged or obsolete goods frequently are valued at *net realizable value*— estimated selling price less direct costs of completion and disposal. A more severe standard is to write the goods down to replacement cost—the price that would be paid for the goods in their present condition. In some cases an arbitrary percentage of the cost is written off; this is difficult to defend, but it may be necessary if a more objective basis is not available. Finally, when there is doubt about the existence of any net realizable value, the cost of the goods should be reduced to scrap value, or to zero in the absence of scrap value.

Price Fluctuations and Valuation of Inventories

Price changes that result in loss of economic usefulness of inventories should be deducted from revenue in the accounting period in which the loss takes place. Because the cost of the inventories is determined by negotiation between the purchaser and supplier based on the purchaser's expectation of realizing a desired gross profit margin on resale, a significant decline in the selling price of inventories requires a reduction in the carrying amount of inventories. The inventory value that is most appropriate in such situations is *replacement cost* (or a "derived market" price), that is, a price that will allow recovery of the adjusted cost of the inventories and yield a desired gross profit margin.

At present, generally accepted accounting principles hold that gains attributable to price increases should not be recognized until inventories are sold. However, losses resulting from decreases in the replacement cost of inventories are recognized in the accounting period in which the losses occur. The basis for this *lower-of-cost-or-market rule* is found in the concept of conservatism.

Lower-of-Cost-or-Market Procedures

The lower-of-cost-or-market (LCM) rule requires that inventories be priced at the lower of these two values (cost price or market price). The benefits attributed to this method of inventory valuation are (1) the loss, if any, is identified with the accounting period in which it occurred, and (2) goods are valued at an amount that measures the expected contribution to revenue of future periods. The following principle supports the lower-of-cost-or-market rule:[8]

---

[8]*Accounting Research and Terminology Bulletins—Final Edition*, chap. 4, p. 30.

A departure from the cost basis of pricing the inventory is required when the utility of the goods is no longer as great as its cost. Where there is evidence that the utility of goods, in their disposal in the ordinary course of business, will be less than cost, whether due to physical deterioration, obsolescence, changes in price levels, or other causes, the difference should be recognized as a loss of the current period. This is generally accomplished by stating such goods at a lower level commonly designated as *market.*

A precise measurement of *utility* is almost impossible, and the adoption of the LCM price is a practical means of approximating the decline in utility of goods in inventories.

What is meant by ''market'' in the expression ''lower of cost or market''? Is it the price at which the item will be sold, or is it the price that would be paid to purchase the item? Current practice requires the use of the current price, that is, *replacement cost,* with certain limitations. Replacement cost is a broader term than purchase price because it includes incidental acquisition costs. Replacement cost also may be applied to manufactured inventories by reference to the prevailing prices for direct material, direct labor, and factory overhead. If replacement cost is not reasonably determinable or exceeds the amount expected to be realized by the sale of the items, *net realizable value* is used instead of replacement cost. The net realizable value is determined by subtracting from the expected selling price all prospective *direct costs* of completing and selling the item. The following limits (*ceiling* and *floor*) have been placed on ''market'' (''replacement cost'').[9]

> As used in the phrase *lower of cost or market* the term *market* means current replacement cost (by purchase or by reproduction, as the case may be) except that:
>
> **1** Market should not exceed the net realizable value (i.e., estimated selling price in the ordinary course of business less reasonably predictable costs of completion and disposal); and
>
> **2** Market should not be less than net realizable value reduced by an allowance for an approximately normal profit margin.

Thus, the *ceiling* is equal to the selling price reduced by the estimated costs of completion and sale; and the *floor* is equal to the ceiling reduced by the normal gross profit. *Replacement cost is used as ''market'' price if it falls between the ceiling and the floor; the ceiling amount is used as ''market'' price when replacement cost is above the ceiling; and the floor amount is used as ''market'' price when replacement cost is below the floor.* This general rule is diagramed on page 421 for a unit costing $40, with three different assumptions as to replacement cost ($38, $34, and $28), a ceiling limit on market price of $36, and a floor limit on market price of $30.

When the ceiling, replacement cost, and floor amounts are ranked from highest to lowest, the amount in the middle is used as the ''market'' price. Once the ad-

---

[9]Ibid., chap. 4, p. 31.

Applying the "ceiling" and "floor" tests

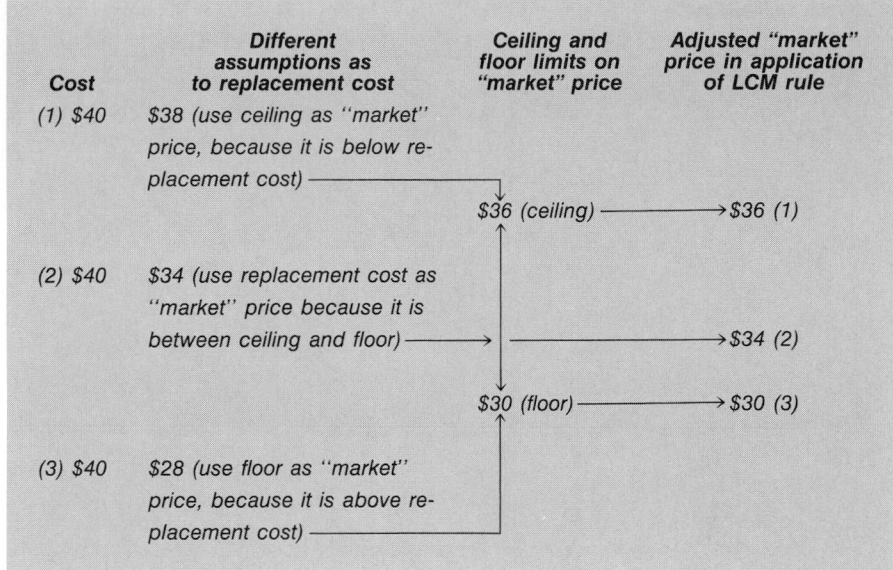

Cost	Different assumptions as to replacement cost	Ceiling and floor limits on "market" price	Adjusted "market" price in application of LCM rule
(1) $40	$38 (use ceiling as "market" price, because it is below replacement cost)	$36 (ceiling)	$36 (1)
(2) $40	$34 (use replacement cost as "market" price because it is between ceiling and floor)		$34 (2)
(3) $40	$28 (use floor as "market" price, because it is above replacement cost)	$30 (floor)	$30 (3)

justed amount for market price is determined, ***the final step is to compare the cost of the inventory item with the adjusted market price*** to determine the LCM valuation. In each of the three assumptions in the diagram, the adjusted market price is less than cost, and is the value assigned to inventory under the LCM rule. This adjusted market price is used as the "cost" for future comparisons with market prices.

Although replacement cost is the basic concept of market, it should not be used blindly. When the replacement cost of an item is higher than its net realizable value, conservatism requires that the item be written down to its net realizable value. Otherwise, a loss that is already apparent would be deferred. For this reason, net realizable value must be the ***ceiling.*** In contrast, if a business enterprise is required to write down its inventories, it might be tempted to "take a big bath" and write off an excessive amount. In the following year, the gross profit on sales would be overstated; thus, investors would have an impression of a strong "turnaround." To prevent this type of manipulation, the write-down of inventories must not be below the ***floor.***

Taxpayers using the LCM rule may not write down excessive inventories below replacement costs, unless such inventories actually have been scrapped, sold, or offered for sale at prices lower than replacement costs. The Internal Revenue Service has defined "excessive inventories" as goods that are (1) held for sale, (2) in excess of any reasonably foreseeable future demand, and (3) not scrapped or sold at reduced prices.

Illustrations of Selection of "Market" and "Lower of Cost or Market"   The additional examples on page 422 illustrate the application of the LCM rule. The inventory value for each item is in bold face type. Completion and selling costs are $6 for each item, and the normal gross profit margin is 25% of the selling price.

Application of LCM
rule to five examples

	Inventory items				
	A	**B**	**C**	**D**	**E**
Selling price	$20	$20	$28	$36	$36
Cost (determined by specific identification, fifo, weighted-average, etc.)	16	15	20	25	**20**
Selling price less $6 completion and selling costs **(ceiling)**	**14**	**14**	22	30	30
Selling price less completion and selling costs and normal gross profit margin of 25% of selling price **(floor)**	9	9	15	**21**	21
Replacement cost on inventory date	15	16	**17**	20	19

Explanations

Item A   Replacement cost of $15 exceeds the ceiling of $14, which is the adjusted market price; because cost is $16, the inventory value is $14, the lower of cost or adjusted market price.

Item B   Replacement cost of $16 exceeds the ceiling of $14, which is the adjusted market price; inventory value is $14, although replacement cost of $16 exceeds cost of $15.

Item C   Replacement cost of $17 is between the ceiling-floor limit ($22 to $15); replacement cost is the adjusted market price; inventory value is $17, because it is less than cost of $20.

Item D   Replacement cost of $20 is below the floor of $21, which is the adjusted market price; the inventory value is $21, because it is less than cost of $25.

Item E   Replacement cost of $19 is below the floor of $21, which is the adjusted market price; the inventory value is $20, or cost, because cost is lower than adjusted market price of $21. In this case, the normal gross profit margin will be realized when the unit is sold; therefore, no loss in value is recognized.

Application of LCM   The LCM rule may be applied to (1) each individual item in inventories, (2) major categories of inventories, or (3) inventories as a whole. Regardless of which of the three methods is adopted, each inventory item should be priced at cost and at market as a first step in the valuation process. The item-by-item method produces the lowest inventory value, and the application of the LCM rule to inventories as a whole produces the highest value. For income tax purposes, the item-by-item method must be used. For financial accounting, the authors favor the application of the LCM rule to inventories as a whole because this approach is consistent with the rule established for marketable equity securities in *FASB Statement No. 12,* ''Accounting for Certain Marketable Securities'' (see page 313). The illustration at the top of page 423 for Ann Company demonstrates the variation in LCM amounts that result from the application of these three methods.

Applying
LCM to
each item
results in
lowest
inventory
value

ANN COMPANY
Determination of Value of Inventories by Use of the LCM Rule—End of Year 1

Inventory categories	Cost	Market	(1) Item by item	(2) Category of inventories	(3) Inventories as a whole
No. 1: Item A	$ 6,000	$ 9,000	$ 6,000		
Item B	10,000	9,500	9,500		
Subtotals	$16,000	$18,500		$16,000	
No. 2: Item C	$15,000	$17,000	15,000		
Item D	20,000	14,000	14,000		
Subtotals	$35,000	$31,000		31,000	
Totals	$51,000	$49,500			$49,500
Valuation of inventories ...			$44,500	$47,000	$49,500

In the valuation of inventories for a manufacturing enterprise, goods in process and finished goods inventories must be adjusted for any decline in the price of material, direct labor, and factory overhead costs.

Subsequent Valuation Problems Suppose that at the end of Year 2, item D in the illustration above is still on hand and that the market value has risen from $14,000 to $19,000. What valuation should be assigned to item D at the end of Year 2? Generally, accountants have held that, once an inventory item has been written down, this lower value *is considered cost* for future comparisons with "market." Therefore, in the application of the item-by-item method, the value of item D is $14,000 at the end of Year 2 because the item was written down to this amount at the end of Year 1.

For *interim reporting purposes,* this rule was modified by the Accounting Principles Board as follows:[10]

> Inventory losses from market declines should not be deferred beyond the interim period in which the decline occurs. Recoveries of such losses on the same inventory in later interim periods of the same fiscal year through market price recoveries should be recognized as gains in the later interim period. Such gains should not exceed previously recognized losses. Some market declines at interim dates, however, can reasonably be expected to be restored in the fiscal year. Such *temporary* market declines need not be recognized at the interim date since no loss is expected to be incurred in the fiscal year.

Valuation Allowance for Write-Down of Inventories

When inventories are written down below cost, the reduction may be credited to an inventory valuation account. This procedure accomplishes the objective of a write-down, and at the same time permits the cost of the inventory to be reported in the

---

[10]*APB Opinion No. 28,* "Interim Financial Reporting," AICPA (New York: 1973), pp. 524–525.

balance sheet. Use of a valuation account is especially appropriate with the perpetual inventory system, because it eliminates the necessity of adjusting the detailed inventory records (maintained at actual costs) to lower market prices.

The journal entry to record the reduction of inventories at the end of Year 1 from a cost of $100,000 to a market valuation of $92,000 is illustrated below for Karen Company:

Recording inventory valuation account

> Cost of Goods Sold (or Loss from Price Decline in
>   Inventories) ($100,000 − $92,000)   8,000
>   Allowance for Price Decline in Inventories   8,000
>   To record the reduction in value of inventories caused by
>   declining prices.

In the balance sheet at the end of Year 1, inventories are listed at cost and are reduced to a lower market by deduction of the allowance for price decline from cost. This procedure is illustrated for Karen Company below:

Balance sheet presentation of inventories after write-down

> Current assets:
>   Inventories (at first-in, first-out cost) $100,000
>   Less: Allowance for price decline in inventories 8,000 $92,000

If the write-down of inventories is material, it may be shown separately from cost of goods sold in the income statement or disclosed in a note to the financial statements.

The inventory valuation allowance is not needed after the goods in question are sold. Therefore, at the time the cost of beginning inventories is transferred to Income Summary (or to the Cost of Goods Sold ledger account), the allowance account also is closed, to reduce the cost of beginning inventories to market value. For example, the following journal entry is made at the end of Year 2 by Karen Company to close beginning inventories, assuming that the periodic inventory system is used:

Closing journal entry when inventory valuation account is used

> Income Summary   92,000
> Allowance for Price Decline in Inventories   8,000
>   Inventories (beginning)   100,000
>   To close beginning inventories to Income Summary.

If the market value of inventories at the end of Year 2 is below cost, an allowance for price decline in inventories again should be established.

An inventory allowance account similar to the one illustrated above is used by some business enterprises to reduce inventories from fifo or average cost to a lifo basis. Such an account is established by a debit to Cost of Goods Sold or Income

Summary and a credit to Allowance to Reduce Inventory to Lifo Basis. The valuation allowance, sometimes referred to as a *lifo reserve account,* is used to preserve inventory cost on the fifo or average cost basis for internal accounting purposes while obtaining the advantages of using lifo for income tax purposes.

Valuation of Purchase Commitments at Lower of Cost or Market

If at the end of an accounting period a business enterprise has a contract to purchase goods at a fixed price that is higher than the current price of the goods, a loss should be recognized. In other words, the outstanding purchase commitment should be valued on a lower-of-cost-or-market basis by recognition of a current loss and the accrual of a current liability. These accounting procedures are described in Chapter 10.

Appraisal of the Lower-of-Cost-or-Market Rule

The lower-of-cost-or-market rule originated in an era of emphasis on balance sheet conservatism. It exemplifies an old accounting axiom: "Anticipate no profit and provide for all possible losses." By reducing inventories to market, accountants also reduce net income for the current accounting period. However, if the price of the goods rises, generally accepted accounting principles do not permit the value of inventories to be increased. Such action would result in the recognition of income before revenue is realized.

The treatment of damaged and obsolete goods was discussed earlier, in accordance with the principle of valuing inventory at cost less an amount that measures any decline in utility. Also, the argument has been presented that a decline in prices casts a shadow over a part of the inventory cost because the revenue in future accounting periods may not be adequate to provide a normal margin of profit. Thus, accountants have been led to the conclusion that the goods have lost a part of their economic utility, and that the unrecoverable portion of inventory cost should be deducted from current revenue.

One should not dismiss such an argument lightly; unrecoverable costs are not assets. However, every price decline does not necessarily mean that the cost of goods in inventories will not be recovered. The price system is not so sensitive that it transmits related price movements quickly and uniformly throughout the economy. The indiscriminate application of the lower-of-cost-or-market rule should not be allowed to replace sound professional judgment in the valuation of inventories. There are instances when recognition of losses prior to sale is justified. However, a careful evaluation of the particular circumstances is necessary before the amount of the loss may be determined. The ceiling and floor limits on "market" serve a useful function in making such an evaluation.

Anticipation of Price Declines

The lower-of-cost-or-market rule is applicable to price declines that actually have occurred, *not to possible future price declines.* The AICPA has made the following distinction between inventory losses that may be measured objectively and those that are conjectural in nature:[11]

> It has been argued with respect to inventories that losses which will have to be taken in periods of receding price levels have their origins in periods of rising prices, and that therefore reserves to provide for future price declines should be created in periods of rising prices by charges against the operations of those periods. Reserves of this kind involve assumptions as to what future price levels will be, what inventory quantities will be on hand if and when a major price decline takes place, and finally whether loss to the business will be measured by the amount of the decline in prices. The bases for such assumptions are so uncertain that any conclusions drawn from them would generally seem to be speculative guesses rather than informed judgments.

Only *actual* losses on goods included in inventories that arise from price declines should be included in net income; *possible* future losses should not be entered in the accounting records.

Inventories and Financial Reporting Standards

The objectives of reporting inventories in the balance sheet are to reveal the type, the relative liquidity, and the basis of valuation of the inventories. In reporting the investment in inventories, as in reporting other assets, accountants are concerned with disclosing all significant information; they are particularly concerned that the investment in inventories has been determined on a basis consistent with that of preceding years. If a change is made in the method of determining inventory cost, the change should be explained fully as to its effect on the current and prior year's financial statements. The accounting problems of reporting changes in inventory valuation methods are discussed in Chapter 22.

When a valuation account is used as a means of valuing the inventory at the lower of cost or market or on the last-in, first-out basis, this account is subtracted from inventory cost in the balance sheet, as illustrated on page 424.

Financial accounting standards require that the various categories of inventories be indicated under the general caption "Inventories," and that the basis of valuation and the method of determining costs be disclosed. The Financial Accounting Standards Board requires disclosure of current cost of inventories by large publicly owned corporations in a supplementary section of the annual report. In addition, the SEC requires companies using the lifo method of inventory valuation to disclose the excess of replacement or current cost over the stated lifo values of inventories and the effect of material lifo liquidations on net income.

Inventories that have been pledged as collateral for loans are included in the Inventories section rather than being offset against the loans secured by the inventories. Such financing agreements are described in a note to the financial statements. Firm purchase commitments also are disclosed in a note to the financial statements. Most business enterprises report inventories in a single amount, accompanied by an

---

[11]*Accounting Research and Terminology Bulletins—Final Edition,* chap. 6, p. 42.

explanatory note. An example for two years from an annual report of a publicly owned company follows:

Inventories in the balance sheet

	Year 10	Year 9
Inventories **(Note 3)**	$75,863,808	$79,407,280

Note 3—Inventories are valued on the balance sheet dates as follows:

	Year 10	Year 9
Logs, pulpwood, clips, and sawdust	$14,808,908	$10,337,848
Lumber and other manufactured wood products	9,092,589	9,759,782
Pulp, paper, and converted paper products	33,522,887	41,204,047
Material and supplies	18,439,424	18,105,603
Totals	$75,863,808	$79,407,280
Valued at lower of cost or market:		
First-in, first-out basis	$ 9,525,121	$ 9,423,818
Last-in, first-out basis	17,128,752	16,049,015
Average-cost basis	49,209,935	53,934,447
Totals	$75,863,808	$79,407,280

If the last-in, first-out inventory had been priced at current cost, the values would have been $11,404,000 higher on December 31, Year 10, and $12,637,000 higher on December 31, Year 9. There was no significant liquidation of prior years' lifo layers during Year 10 or Year 9.

The above inventories were used to compute cost of goods sold. The beginning inventories for Year 9 were $52,484,190.

REVIEW QUESTIONS

1   What features distinguish inventory costs from other costs that are allocated between deferred and expired portions?

2   There are two systems of maintaining inventory records: (**a**) *periodic inventory system,* and (**b**) *perpetual inventory system.* What are the basic differences between the two systems, and under what circumstances should each be used?

3   Why is the valuation of inventories critical to financial reporting? What criteria should accountants use in deciding between alternative methods of valuation?

4   At the end of the accounting period, the following purchase invoices dated December 27 are on hand, but the goods have not been received. How would you treat each invoice in the determination of the ending inventories?
a Invoice amount, $12,670; terms, 2/10, n/30; "FOB shipping point."
b Invoice amount, $14,860; terms, 1/5, n/30; "FOB destination."

5   Indicate the effects on the financial statements for the current year and succeeding years of each of the following types of errors in accounting for inventories. Indicate the direction of error, that is, overstatement, understatement, or no effect.
a An invoice for goods shipped "FOB shipping point" has been received, but no

journal entry has been made to record the purchase. The goods have not been received and are not included in the ending inventories.

b An invoice for goods shipped, but not received, has been recorded correctly to indicate that the goods belong to the purchaser, but the items have not been included in the ending inventories.

c Goods that have been received, but the purchase of which has not been entered in the accounting records, are included in the ending inventories.

d The ending inventories do not include goods shipped on consignment. The transfer of these goods to the consignee has been recorded as a sale, even though they remain in the consignee's possession at the end of both the current year and the succeeding year.

6   Describe the process of *taking of inventory*.

7   Lieber Company had goods costing $38,500 on consignment from Maxwell Company on June 30, Year 8, the end of Lieber's fiscal year. How should the consigned goods be treated in Lieber's June 30, Year 8, physical inventory under the periodic inventory system?

8   What costs should be included in the cost of inventories? What objectives are considered in deciding what costs are to be included in inventories?

9   Midtown Company is licensed to manufacture and sell a certain product under a patent owned by Alan Bella. A royalty of 10 cents is payable to Bella for each unit sold. For financial accounting Midtown treats royalty payments as a selling expense and does not accrue a royalty liability on the unsold units in inventories. The property tax assessor claims that 10 cents should be treated as a production cost and included in the valuation of inventories. Do you agree with the tax assessor? Explain.

10   If two or more *joint products* are produced in a single department of a manufacturing enterprise, how are the total production costs incurred in the department allocated to the joint products?

11   The *specific identification* method of inventory valuation has been supported by some accountants as the ideal method of achieving a matching of costs and revenue. What objections may be raised to the use of this method for the valuation of inventories?

12   Differentiate between the *weighted-average method* and the *moving-weighted-average method* of determining cost of inventories.

13   Frank Caliri tells you that he is considering changing from the fifo to the lifo method of inventory valuation for his single proprietorship, and that he would like your advice on the matter. He admits that his primary objective is to reduce his income tax liability, and his friends tell him this is a good way to do it. What factors would you consider in advising Caliri?

14   Identify the four techniques for applying the dollar-value lifo method of inventory valuation.

15 In the application of the double-extension technique for the dollar-value lifo method of valuing inventories, it is necessary to value ending quantities of an inventory pool at both current costs and base-year costs. Why? Would a valuation of end-of-year quantities at beginning-of-year costs be acceptable?

16 Under what conditions may a portion of the cost of inventories be written off prior to the sale of the items comprising the inventories?

17 Define the term *market* as used in the inventory valuation procedure referred to as the lower-of-cost-or-market rule.

18 What are the arguments against the use of the lower-of-cost-or-market rule in the valuation of inventories?

19 Is there any difference, insofar as inventory valuation is concerned, between an item with a cost of $50 that regularly sells for $75 but has been so physically damaged that it may be sold for no more than $55, and a like item that has no physical damage, but the cost of replacing the item has declined to $30?

20 Under what conditions, if any, is it appropriate to enter anticipated inventory price declines in the accounting records?

21 Under what conditions, if any, should losses from price declines involving future purchase commitments be entered in the accounting records?

22 The balance sheet for Emery Corporation included the following:

Inventories.	$80,000,000
Less: Allowance to reduce inventories to last-in, first-out basis.	15,200,000
Net inventories	$64,800,000

What is the probable reason for the use of the inventories valuation ledger account by Emery Corporation?

23 What objectives do accountants seek to achieve in reporting inventories in the balance sheets of business enterprises?

EXERCISES

Ex. 8-1 Select the best answer for each of the following multiple-choice questions:

1 Which of the following inventory cost flow methods could use dollar-value pools?
a Specific identification
b Weighted-average
c First-in, first-out
d Last-in, first-out
e None of the foregoing

2 Is the moving-weighted-average inventory cost flow method applicable to the following inventory systems?

	Periodic	Perpetual
a	Yes	Yes
b	Yes	No
c	No	No
d	No	Yes

3   The following pertains to an inventory item:

Cost	$60
Estimated selling price	68
Estimated cost of disposal	1
Normal gross profit margin	11
Replacement cost	51

Under the lower-of-cost-or-market rule, this inventory item is valued at:
a $51   **b** $56   **c** $60   **d** $67   **e** Some other amount

4   During Year 4, Olsen Company discovered that the ending inventories reported in its financial statements were understated as follows:

Year	Understatement
1	$50,000
2	60,000
3	0

Olsen uses the periodic inventory system. Ending inventory quantities are converted to dollar amounts by the fifo cost flow method. Assuming no other accounting errors, Olsen's retained earnings balance on December 31, Year 3, is:
a Correct
b $ 60,000 understated
c $ 60,000 overstated
d $110,000 understated

5   Wye Company, which uses the periodic inventory system, failed to record a $6,000 purchase of merchandise that was received on March 31, Year 7, but included the cost of the merchandise in the March 31, Year 7, physical inventory (fifo basis). The effect of this error on Wye's financial statements for the fiscal year ended March 31, Year 7, was to:
a Overstate current assets and understate current liabilities
b Overstate net income and understate current liabilities
c Understate net income and understate current assets
d Understate current assets and understate current liabilities

6   Cash discounts on purchases should not be included in inventory cost:
a Only if the purchaser takes advantage of the discounts
b Only if the purchaser fails to take advantage of the discounts
c Regardless of whether the purchaser takes advantage of the discounts or pays the full invoice price
d If management of the purchasing enterprise decides to exclude the discount from inventory cost

7 Ending inventories differ depending on whether the perpetual inventory system or the periodic inventory system is used, under the following cost-flow assumptions:

a First-in, first-out and last-in, first-out
b Specific identification and weighted-average
c Last-in, first-out and weighted-average
d First-in, first-out and weighted-average

Ex. 8-2 Janis Manufacturing Company, which uses the perpetual inventory system, recorded the following data pertaining to material X:

		Units		
Date	*Received*	*Cost*	*Issued*	*On hand*
Jan. 1		$1.00		400
8	600	1.10		1,000
12			800	200
15	400	1.21		600

Compute the moving-weighted-average cost per unit of material X for Janis Manufacturing Company on January 15.

Ex. 8-3 Stationers Company had 200 calculators on hand on January 1, Year 9, costing $18 each. Purchases and sales of calculators during the month of January, Year 9, were as follows:

Date	*Purchases*	*Sales*
Jan. 12		150 @ $28
14	100 @ $20	
29	100 @ $22	
30		100 @ $32

Stationers does not maintain perpetual inventory records. According to a physical count, 150 calculators were on hand on January 31, Year 9.

Compute the cost of Stationers Company's January 31, Year 9, inventory of calculators under **(a)** the fifo method, and **(b)** the lifo method of inventory valuation.

Ex. 8-4 Dexter Company sells water beds. The perpetual inventory balance was $19,600 in the accounting records on December 31, Year 4. Some events that occurred near the end of Year 4 are listed below:

(1) Beds shipped to a customer on January 2, Year 5, costing $2,000, were included in inventory on December 31, Year 4. The sale was recorded in Year 5.
(2) Beds costing $9,000 received on December 30, Year 4, were recorded as having been received on January 2, Year 5.
(3) Beds received costing $1,900 were entered twice in the perpetual inventory record.
(4) Beds shipped "FOB shipping point" on December 28, Year 4, which cost

$8,000, were not recorded as a sale by Dexter until January 3, Year 5. The beds were included in the ending inventory.

(5) Beds on hand that cost $2,300 were not entered in the accounting records in Year 4.

Prepare a working paper showing the correct amount of Dexter Company's inventory on December 31, Year 4.

Ex. 8-5 Longo Company was established April 1, Year 1, and adopted the dollar-value lifo method, double-extension technique, for valuing inventories, which consisted of a single pool having two products, ergo and farad. Quantities and unit costs of the two products on March 31, Year 2, Year 3, and Year 4, were as follows:

| | Quantities, Mar. 31, | | | Unit costs, Mar. 31,* | | |
Item	Year 2	Year 3	Year 4	Year 2	Year 3	Year 4
Ergo	10,000	12,000	16,000	$6.00	$6.20	$6.38¼
Farad	20,000	24,000	30,000	2.00	2.40	2.42

*March 31, Year 2, unit cost is lifo cost; unit costs on March 31, Year 3 and Year 4 are current costs.

Compute the cost indexes for Longo Company on March 31, Year 3 and Year 4, by the double-extension technique under the dollar-value lifo method. (The year ended March 31, Year 2, is the base year.)

Ex. 8-6 The following information relates to a commodity of Willis Company for the month of January:

Inventory, Jan. 1	100 units @ $5
Purchases....................................	400 units @ $6; 100 units @ $7
Inventory, Jan. 31	200 units

a Compute the balance of Willis Company's January 31 inventory under the first-in, first-out cost flow assumption.

b Compute Willis Company's cost of goods sold for January under the last-in, first-out cost flow assumption.

Ex. 8-7 The following information was available from the inventory records of Rue Company for January:

	Units	Unit cost	Total cost
Balance, Jan. 1	2,000	$9.775	$19,550
Purchases:			
Jan. 6	1,500	10.300	15,450
Jan. 26	3,400	10.750	36,550
Sales:			
Jan. 7	(1,800)		
Jan. 31	(3,500)		
Balance, Jan. 31	1,600		

a Assuming that Rue Company maintains perpetual inventory records, compute the inventory on January 31 under the moving-weighted-average method, rounded to the nearest dollar.

b Assuming that Rue Company maintains periodic inventory records, compute the inventory on January 31 under the weighted-average method, rounded to the nearest dollar.

Ex. 8-8 Lansing Corporation uses the periodic inventory system and the first-in, first-out method to determine the cost of its inventories. The physical inventory on October 31, Year 6, is summarized below:

Item no.	Unit cost*	Inventory (units)	Freight-in applicable to inventory
101	$ 3	6,000	$ 915
102	5	9,000	675
103	6	4,500	1,110
104	10	2,400	960

*Before cash (purchases) discounts

Lansing regularly takes a 2% discount on all purchases (excluding freight-in) and allocates an appropriate portion of freight-in to the ending inventories. Additional information available on October 31, Year 6, is presented below:

Beginning inventories (Nov. 1, Year 5)	$100,500
Purchases (net of returns and discounts)...........................	535,500
Freight-in...	19,500
Sales (net of returns)	721,500
Sales discounts..	9,300

a Compute the cost of Lansing Corporation's inventories on October 31, Year 6.

b Compute the amount of Lansing Corporation's gross profit on sales for the year ended October 31, Year 6.

Ex. 8-9 Presented below is the inventory activity for a product for the month of April:

Date	Transaction	Units	Cost	Total	Units sold
Apr. 1	Inventory	1,200	$8.00	$ 9,600	
4	Purchase	800	8.25	6,600	
7	Sale				600
10	Purchase	500	8.10	4,050	
13	Sale				1,000
16	Purchase	600	7.90	4,740	
19	Sale				900
22	Purchase	300	7.90	2,370	
25	Purchase	600	8.00	4,800	
28	Sale				500
	Totals	4,000		$32,160	3,000

Assuming that the periodic inventory system is used, compute the April 30 inventory cost under each of the following cost flow assumptions:

a First-in, first-out
b Last-in, first-out
c Weighted-average (round the average to the nearest cent)

Ex. 8-10 Shown below are three different sets of assumptions (cases) relating to an item in inventories:

	Case 1	Case 2	Case 3
Cost	$22,400	$20,000	$28,000
Selling price	$30,000	$30,000	$30,000
Cost to complete and ship to customers	$ 4,000	$ 4,000	$ 4,000
Normal gross profit on selling price	25%	25%	10%
Replacement cost	$20,000	$18,000	$26,500

Compute the inventory valuation at lower of cost or market for each case.

Ex. 8-11 Kort Company manufactures a single product. On December 31, Year 1, Kort adopted the dollar-value lifo method, using a specific cost index. The inventory on that date under the lifo method was $310,000. Inventory data for succeeding years are as follows:

Year ended Dec. 31,	Inventories at year-end costs	Specific cost indexes (Year 1 = 100)
Year 2	$363,000	110
Year 3	420,000	120
Year 4	430,000	125

Compute the inventory amounts for Kort Company on December 31, Year 2, Year 3, and Year 4, under the dollar-value lifo method.

Ex. 8-12 The controller of Grody Corporation, a retail enterprise that uses the periodic inventory system, made three different computations of gross profit for the first quarter ended March 31, Year 10. These computations appear below:

	Sales ($10 a unit)	Cost of goods sold	Gross profit
Computation 1	$280,000	$118,550	$161,450
Computation 2	280,000	116,900	163,100
Computation 3	280,000	115,750	164,250

The cost of goods sold in each computation is based on the data presented at the top of page 435.

	Units	Unit cost	Total cost
Beginning inventory, Jan. 1	10,000	$4.00	$ 40,000
Purchase, Jan. 20	8,000	4.20	33,600
Purchase, Feb. 12	5,000	4.13	20,650
Purchase, Mar. 14	7,000	4.30	30,100
Purchase, Mar. 27	12,000	4.25	51,000
Totals	42,000		$175,350

Nancy Rogers, the president of Grody, cannot understand how three different gross profit amounts were computed from the same data. As controller, you have explained to her that the three computations are based on three different assumptions concerning the flow of inventory costs; that is, first-in, first-out; last-in, first-out; and weighted average. Computations 1, 2, and 3 were not necessarily prepared in this sequence of cost flow assumptions.

Prepare a working paper to compute the cost of goods sold and the composition of the ending inventory for Grody Corporation under each of the three cost flow assumptions.

Ex. 8-13 Wigg Corporation uses the dollar-value lifo method of pricing inventories, computing cost indexes by sampling items from its single pool. The inventories valued at end-of-year current costs and the cost indexes are given below:

Year	Inventories at year-end cost	Cost indexes at end of year
1 (base year)	$ 80,000	100
2	102,000	125
3	127,400	130
4	140,000	140
5	101,250	135

Prepare a working paper to show the computation of Wigg Corporation's ending inventories under the dollar-value lifo method for Years 1 through 5.

Ex. 8-14 You are given the following data about four items included in the inventories of Wold Corporation:

	Item			
	W	X	Y	Z
Cost	$50	$62	$29	$46
Replacement cost	52	48	25	44
Sales price less selling and completion costs	53	59	23	42
Sales price less selling and completion costs and less normal gross profit	47	51	20	38

Indicate which amount is to be used in valuing Wold Corporation's ending inventories in accordance with the lower-of-cost-or-market rule.

Ex. 8-15 The inventories for Carlton Company consist of two major categories listed below:

	Quantities	Unit cost	Market
Category A:			
Item XP	80	$ 7	$ 6
Item XQ	40	8	9
Item XR	30	10	8
Category B:			
Item YS	100	$ 4	$ 3
Item YT........................	150	9	8
Item YU	300	12	14

Prepare a summary similar to the one illustrated on page 423 to compute inventory values for Carlton Company under the lower-of-cost-or-market rule applied to (1) each item, (2) separate categories, and (3) inventories as a whole.

CASES

Case 8-1 Langley Company sells goods from its store and on consignment through Consignee Company.

Instructions

Answer the following questions:

a Should Langley Company include in its inventories goods purchased from its suppliers but not yet received if the shipping terms are FOB shipping point? Explain.

b Should Langley Company include freight-in costs as part of the cost of inventories? Explain.

c Langley Company purchased an item for inventories three times during the current year, each time at a higher cost than the previous purchase. What would have been the effects on ending inventories and cost of goods sold if Langley had used the weighted-average cost method instead of the first-in, first-out cost method in accounting for the purchases under the perpetual inventory system?

d What are goods on consignment and how should they be presented in the balance sheet of Langley Company? Explain.

Case 8-2 In Year 8, Crossling Company, which values its inventories by the dollar-value lifo method with the double-extension technique, treated an item as a new product in one of its inventory pools because production of the item had been moved during Year 8 from Crossling's Chicago factory to its Houston factory. Substantial cost savings were a result of the production change. Because of the new product designation, Crossling used a base-year cost for the item of $650 a unit, which was equal to the cost of producing the item in Houston during Year 8. The base-year cost of the item in the Chicago plant was $340, which was the cost of production in Year 1.

Instructions

Do you consider Crossling Company's use of $650, rather than $340, as the base-year cost of the Houston-manufactured product to be consistent with dollar-value lifo valuation of inventories? Explain.

(Adapted from *Codification of Financial Reporting Policies* of the Securities and Exchange Commission)

Case 8-3   Taylor Company purchases goods from various suppliers. Taylor's policy is to take all cash discounts offered by suppliers. Taylor uses the periodic inventory system and values its inventories at the lower of first-in, first-out cost or market.

Instructions

a Discuss the propriety of each of the following alternative methods for accounting for cash discounts on purchases:

(1) Credit discounts taken to the Other Revenue ledger account when payments are made to suppliers.

(2) Reduce cost of goods sold for the accounting period in which payments are made to suppliers.

(3) Reduce cost of goods purchased from suppliers on the date of purchase.

b Identify the effects on both the balance sheet and the income statement of Taylor Company's use of the last-in, first-out method instead of the first-in, first-out method of inventory valuation for a substantial time period when purchase prices of goods are rising. State why these effects take place.

c Why is the lower-of-cost-or-market rule used in the valuation of inventories? Explain.

Case 8-4   In order to effect an approximate matching of current costs with related sales revenue, the last-in, first-out (lifo) method of pricing inventories may be used.

Instructions

a Describe the establishment of and subsequent pricing procedures for each of the following lifo inventory methods:

(1) Lifo applied to units of product when the periodic inventory system is used.

(2) Application of the dollar-value lifo method by the double-extension technique.

b Discuss the specific advantages and disadvantages of the dollar-value lifo method. Disregard income tax considerations.

c Discuss the general advantages and disadvantages claimed for lifo methods. Disregard income tax considerations.

Case 8-5   Lamb Corporation has valued its year-end inventories at the lower of first-in, first-out cost or market for many years. During this period purchases costs had tended to move in a rather general upward trend. For the past three years the general trend of purchases costs has been erratic, and management of Lamb has become concerned with the effect on net income of the lower-of-cost-or-market rule for inventory valuation. You have been requested to analyze the situation and make a recommendation to management supported by computations and accounting theory. The inventories on January 1, Year 1, were valued (both cost and market) at $60,000; additional data are given below:

	Year 3	Year 2	Year 1
Sales	$425,000	$325,000	$375,000
Net purchases	300,000	225,000	260,000
Year-end inventories:			
At fifo cost.............................	75,000	70,000	60,000
At market	55,000	82,000	45,000

Instructions

a Prepare partial income statements for Lamb Corporation for each of the three years using (1) first-in, first-out cost, and (2) lower of cost or market to determine cost of goods sold.

b Draft a report to management of Lamb Corporation explaining the effect of their present procedure on net income. Assuming that this pattern of fluctuating net income is expected to continue, which method of valuation would you recommend? Why?

PROBLEMS

8-1 Layne Corporation, a manufacturer of small tools that uses the periodic inventory system, provided the following information from its accounting records for the year ended December 31, Year 6:

Inventories, Dec. 31, Year 6 (based on physical count of goods in
  Layne's plant at cost on Dec. 31, Year 6)........................... $1,750,000
Accounts payable, Dec. 31, Year 6 1,200,000
Net sales (sales less sales returns) for Year 6....................... 8,500,000

Additional Information

(1) Included in the physical count of finished goods were tools billed to a customer FOB shipping point on December 31, Year 6. These tools had a cost of $28,000 and were billed at $35,000. The shipment was on Layne's loading dock, to be picked up by the common carrier.

(2) Material was in transit from a vendor to Layne on December 31, Year 6. The invoice cost was $50,000, and the material was shipped FOB shipping point on December 29, Year 6.

(3) Work-in-process inventory costing $20,000 was sent to an outside processor for plating on December 30, Year 6.

(4) Tools returned by customers and held pending inspection in the returned goods area on December 31, Year 6, were not included in the physical count. On January 8, Year 7, the tools (cost $26,000) were inspected and returned to finished goods inventory. Credit memos totaling $40,000 were issued to the customers on the same date.

(5) Tools shipped to a customer FOB destination on December 26, Year 6, were in

transit on December 31, Year 6, and had a cost of $25,000. On notification of receipt by the customer on January 2, Year 7, Layne issued a sales invoice for $42,000.

(6) Material with an invoice cost of $30,000, received from a vendor at 5:00 p.m. on December 31, Year 6, was recorded in a receiving report dated January 2, Year 7. The material was not included in the physical count, but the invoice was included in accounts payable on December 31, Year 6.

(7) Material received from a vendor on December 26, Year 6, was included in the physical count. However, the related $60,000 invoice was not included in accounts payable on December 31, Year 6, because the accounts payable copy of the receiving report was lost.

(8) On January 3, Year 7, a monthly freight bill in the amount of $4,000 was received. The bill specifically related to material purchased in December, Year 6, one-half of which was still in the material inventory on December 31, Year 6. The freight charges were not included in either inventories or accounts payable on December 31, Year 6.

Instructions

Using the working paper format shown below, prepare adjustments as of December 31, Year 6, to the amounts in Layne Corporation's accounting records. Show separately the effect, if any, of each of the eight transactions on the December 31, Year 6, amounts. If the transactions have no effect on the initial amount shown, leave the column blank.

	Inventories	Accounts payable	Net sales
Unadjusted amounts	$1,750,000	$1,200,000	$8,500,000
Adjustments—increase (decrease):			
(1)			
(2)			
(8)			
Adjusted amounts	$	$	$

8-2 Roman Company began operations on January 2, Year 1, with 200 units of item X at a cost of $1,800. The following data pertaining to purchases of item X were taken from the accounting records at the end of Year 1:

Purchase no.	Number of units	Total cost
1	24	$ 240
2	84	924
3	126	1,244
4	96	864
5	170	2,125
Totals	500	$5,397

A physical inventory on December 31, Year 1, revealed that 220 units of item X remained in stock. Roman Company uses the periodic inventory system.

Instructions

Based on the data provided, compute for Roman Company (a) the cost of inventory on December 31, Year 1, and (b) the cost of goods sold during Year 1, under each of the following cost flow assumptions:

(1) Last-in, first-out
(2) First-in, first-out
(3) Weighted-average (Round unit cost to nearest cent and total cost to nearest dollar.)

8-3   Geary Company adopted the dollar-value lifo inventory method on July 1, Year 1, when it began operations. Data for inventories (which constitute a single lifo pool) for Geary's first four fiscal years were as follows:

Item	Quantities, June 30,				Unit costs, June 30,*			
	Year 2	Year 3	Year 4	Year 5	Year 2	Year 3	Year 4	Year 5
Largo	100	120	180	200	$1.00	$1.20	$1.40	$1.50
Macho	400	500	600	700	7.00	7.40	7.50	7.80
Norad	300	350	320	400	5.00	5.30	5.40	5.50

*June 30, Year 2 (base year) unit cost is lifo cost; unit costs on June 30, Years 3–5, are current costs.

Instructions

Compute cost indexes (rounded to two decimal places) for Geary Company's use in the dollar-value lifo method under the following techniques:
a Double-extension
b Link-chain

8-4   The following information relating to product Q was taken from the accounting records of Dempsey Corporation for the three-month period ending March 31, Year 2:

	Units	Unit cost
Jan. 1, Year 2 (beginning inventory)	800	$ 9.50
Purchases:		
Jan. 5	1,500	10.00
Jan. 25	1,200	10.50
Feb. 16 .!...	600	11.00
Mar. 26	900	11.50

The inventory on March 31, Year 2, consisted of 1,600 units. Dempsey uses the periodic inventory system.

Instructions

Compute the cost of Dempsey Corporation's inventory on March 31, Year 2, under each of the following inventory methods (show supporting computations):

a First-in, first out

b Last-in, first-out

c Weighted-average

8-5 Quebec Company manufactures and sells four products, the inventories of which are priced at the lower of fifo cost or market. Quebec considers a gross profit margin of 30% of selling price to be normal for all four products.

The following information was compiled on December 31, Year 4:

Product	Units	Fifo unit cost	Cost to replace	Estimated cost to dispose	Expected selling price
W	500	$35.00	$42.00	$15.00	$ 80.00
X	200	47.50	45.00	20.50	95.00
Y	480	17.50	18.00	5.00	21.00
Z	240	45.00	46.00	26.00	100.00

Instructions

Prepare a working paper for Quebec Company on December 31, Year 4, containing unit values (including "floor" and "ceiling") for determining the lower of cost or market on an individual product basis. Underscore for each product the unit value for the purpose of inventory valuation resulting from the application of the lower-of-cost-or-market rule. The last column of the working paper should contain the value assigned to each product and the total valuation of inventories.

8-6 On December 31, Year 1, Seymour Company adopted the dollar-value lifo inventory method for its single pool, using an appropriate specific cost index. The inventory on that date under the lifo inventory method was $200,000. Inventory data for the five succeeding years are as follows:

Dec. 31, Year	Inventories at respective year-end prices	Specific cost indexes (base year = 100)
2	$231,000	105
3	299,000	115
4	300,000	120
5	273,000	130
6	330,000	150

Instructions

Compute Seymour Company's inventories on December 31, Years 2 through 6, under the dollar-value lifo method.

8-7 On January 2, Year 1, Grover Company changed its inventory cost flow method to the lifo cost method from the fifo cost method for its material inventory. The change was made for both financial accounting and income tax purposes. Grover uses the unit-lifo method under which substantially identical material is grouped into lifo inventory pools; weighted-average costs are used in valuing annual incremental layers. The composition of the December 31, Year 3, inventory for the Class F material inventory pool was as follows:

	Units	Weighted-average unit cost	Total cost
Base year inventory, Dec. 31, Year 1	9,000	$10.00	$ 90,000
Incremental layer, Year 2	3,000	11.00	33,000
Incremental layer, Year 3	2,000	12.50	25,000
Inventory, December 31, Year 3...............	14,000		$148,000

Inventory transactions for the Class F material inventory pool during Year 4 were as follows:

(1) On March 1, Year 4, a total of 4,800 units were purchased at a unit cost of $13.50 for $64,800.
(2) On September 1, Year 4, a total of 7,200 units were purchased at a unit cost of $14.00 for $100,800.
(3) A total of 15,000 units were used in production during Year 4.

The following transactions for the Class F material inventory pool took place during Year 5:

(1) On January 10, Year 5, a total of 7,500 units were purchased at a unit cost of $14.50 for $108,750.
(2) On May 15, Year 5, a total of 5,500 units were purchased at a unit cost of $15.50 for $85,250.
(3) On December 29, Year 5, a total of 7,000 units were purchased at a unit cost of $16.00 for $112,000.
(4) A total of 16,000 units were used in production during Year 5.

Instructions

a Prepare a working paper to compute the inventory (units and dollar amounts) of Grover Company's Class F material inventory pool on December 31, Year 4. Show supporting computations.

b Prepare a working paper to compute the cost of Class F material used in production by Grover Company for the year ended December 31, Year 4.

c Prepare a working paper to compute the inventory (units and dollar amounts) of Grover Company's Class F material inventory pool on December 31, Year 5. Show supporting computations.

8-8   Digby Company sells a single product that has been steadily increasing in selling price in recent months. The inventory on January 1, Year 9, and the purchases and sales for Year 9 are presented at the top of page 443.

	Number of units	Unit cost	Average selling price
Jan. 1, Inventory	8,000	$3.50	
Jan. 10, Purchase	3,000	4.00	
Jan. 21, Purchase	5,000	5.00	
Jan. 1–31, Sales for month..........	10,000		$ 9.00
Feb. 5, Purchase..................	4,000	6.00	
Feb. 18, Purchase.................	6,000	7.00	
Feb. 1–28, Sales for month	9,000		11.00
Mar. 5, Purchase..................	5,000	7.80	
Mar. 22, Purchase.................	10,000	8.25	
Mar. 1–31, Sales for month	13,000		13.00

Digby uses the periodic inventory system. Physical inventories are taken at the end of each month.

Instructions

a Compute the cost of Digby Company's inventories on hand at the end of each of the first three months of Year 9 under (1) the first-in, first-out cost flow assumption, and (2) the last-in, first-out cost flow assumption.

b Prepare a comparative statement summarizing the gross profit on sales for each month, assuming that inventories are valued under (1) the first-in, first-out cost flow assumption, and (2) the last-in, first-out cost flow assumption. Use the following form:

	(1) First-in, first-out			**(2) Last-in, first-out**		
	January	February	March	January	February	March
Sales ..						

8-9 The following data were taken from the inventory records of Carney Tool Company on December 31, Year 2:

Department	Item number	Quantity (units)	Fifo unit cost	Market (per unit)
Garden tools	10	140	$24.00	$25.00
	11	350	12.10	11.70
	12	10	8.00	9.60
Electric tools	20	60	4.00	3.00
	21	14	14.00	13.00
	22	8	36.00	37.00
Miscellaneous.................	30	70	2.40	2.00
	31	80	4.90	4.50
	32	100	1.20	1.30

Instructions

a Value Carney Tool Company's inventories under the lower-of-cost-or-market rule applied to: (1) each individual item, (2) major categories, and (3) inventories as a whole.

b Which value in **a** would you recommend for inclusion in Carney Tool Company's financial statements for the year ended December 31, Year 2? Why is the value you recommended preferable to the other two?

8-10 On January 1, Year 1, Lucas Company, Inc., adopted the dollar-value lifo inventory method for both financial accounting and income taxes. However, Lucas continued to use the fifo inventory method for internal accounting and management purposes. In applying the dollar-value lifo method Lucas used the double-extension technique and the multiple-pools approach under which substantially identical inventory items are grouped into inventory pools. The following data were available for Inventory Pool No. 1, which is comprised of products A and B, for the two years following the adoption of dollar-value lifo:

	Units	Unit cost	Total cost
Inventory, Jan. 1, Year 1:			
Product A	12,000	$30 (1)	$360,000
Product B	8,000	25 (1)	200,000
Totals	20,000		$560,000
Inventory, Dec. 31, Year 1:			
Product A	17,000	35 (2)	$595,000
Product B	9,000	28 (2)	252,000
Totals	26,000		$847,000
Inventory, Dec. 31, Year 2:			
Product A	13,000	40 (2)	$520,000
Product B	10,000	32 (2)	320,000
Totals	23,000		$840,000

(1) Lifo cost
(2) Current cost

Instructions

a Prepare a working paper for Lucas Company, Inc., to compute the cost indexes for December 31, Year 1 and Year 2, under the double extension technique. (January 1, Year 1, is the base year.) Round the indexes to two decimal places.

b Prepare a working paper to compute the dollar-value lifo inventory totals for Lucas Company, Inc., on December 31, Year 1 and Year 2, under the double extension technique. Round all amounts to the nearest dollar.

8-11   Malone Furniture Company reported income before income taxes as follows:

Year 2	$132,600
Year 3	115,000
Year 4	125,000
Total	$372,600

Malone uses the periodic inventory system. An analysis of inventory on December 31, Year 4, indicates the following:

(1) The inventory on December 31, Year 1, was correct.

(2) Furniture costing $340 was received in Year 2 and included in the inventory on December 31, Year 2; however, the journal entry to record the purchase was made on January 6, Year 3, when the invoice was received.

(3) The December 31, Year 2, inventory included 1,000 units of item Z, which cost $73.00 a unit, erroneously priced at $37.00 a unit.

(4) Furniture that cost $500 and sold at $700 was shipped to a customer FOB shipping point on December 31, Year 3, and was not included in the December 31, Year 3, inventory; however, the sale was not recorded until January 5, Year 4.

(5) Furniture costing $6,000 shipped FOB shipping point was recorded as a purchase in Year 3 when the invoice was received; however, it was not included in the December 31, Year 3, inventory because it was not received until January 6, Year 4.

(6) Furniture costing $5,750 was sold on December 31, Year 3 for $8,000 and billed on that date. This sale was recorded on December 31, Year 3, but the furniture was included in the ending inventory because it had not been separated from other stock and was not shipped until January 3, Year 4. (Assume that the sale should have been recorded in Year 4.)

(7) The inventory on December 31, Year 4, was correct.

Instructions

a Compute Malone Furniture Company's corrected income before income taxes for each of the three years and the total for the three years (Years 2 through 4).

b Prepare a journal entry to correct Malone Furniture Company's accounting records on December 31, Year 4, assuming that the accounting records have not been closed. Any corrections to income of Year 3 (or earlier) should be made to the Retained Earnings ledger account. Disregard income taxes.

8-12   During the first two years of operations, Ritt Corporation, which uses the periodic inventory system, purchased units of a product as shown at the top of page 446.

	Year ended April 30, Year 3				Year ended April 30, Year 4		
Purch. no.	Number of units	Unit cost	Total cost	Purch. no.	Number of units	Unit cost	Total cost
1	13,000	$4.00	$ 52,000	6	12,000	$3.25	$ 39,000
2	4,000	3.75	15,000	7	6,000	3.50	21,000
3	12,000	3.50	42,000	8	4,000	3.50	14,000
4	5,000	3.50	17,500	9	5,000	3.75	18,750
5	8,000	3.00	24,000	10	16,000	4.00	64,000
	42,000		$150,500		43,000		$156,750

The replacement cost of the units on April 30, Year 3, was $4.00 a unit, and on April 30, Year 4, was $4.20 a unit. There were 16,000 units on hand on April 30, Year 3, and 21,000 on hand on April 30, Year 4.

Instructions

a Compute the inventory and the cost of goods sold of Ritt Corporation for each year under (1) the first-out method, and (2) the last-in, first-out method.

b If 800 units had been stolen during the year ended April 30, Year 4, and Ritt Corporation wanted to separate the theft loss from the cost of goods sold, how would Ritt determine the amount of the loss?

8-13   The perpetual inventory records of Keylime Company indicate that the purchases, sales, and inventory quantities for product KB-80 for the month of March, Year 7, were as follows:

		Purchases		
Date		Units	Unit cost	Sales (units)
Mar. 1 Inventory		800	$ 8	
6				500
10		700	9	
18				800
22		900	10	
30				600

Instructions

a Compute the cost of the ending inventory and the cost of goods sold for Keylime Company for March, Year 7, assuming that the perpetual inventory system is used, under each of the following methods. The following columnar headings are suggested: Date, Transaction, Units, Unit Cost, Balance.

(1) First-in, first-out
(2) Last-in, first-out
(3) Moving-weighted-average (Round unit cost to nearest tenth of a cent.)

b Assuming that the periodic inventory system is used, compute the cost of the ending inventory and the cost of goods sold for Keylime Company for March, Year 7, under each of the following methods:

(1) First-in, first-out

(2) Last-in, first-out

(3) Weighted-average (Round unit cost to nearest tenth of a cent.)

   c Where differences occur between the results in **a** and **b**, explain why they exist. Under what conditions would you recommend use of the perpetual inventory system? The periodic inventory system?

8-14   Uptown Department Store decided in December, Year 1, to adopt the dollar-value lifo method for computation of the ending inventories on a pool basis for Year 2 and each year thereafter. Management believed that published cost indexes were too general for its use; therefore, it decided to compute an index of cost changes by sampling its stock of goods. The inventory on December 31, Year 1, was $75,000, and Year 1 was considered the base year for purposes of the dollar-value lifo method.

   The following sample data for pool 2 were accumulated as the basis for inventory valuation:

	Number of units, Dec. 31,			Unit cost, Dec. 31			
Item	**Year 2**	**Year 3**	**Year 4**	**Year 1***	**Year 2†**	**Year 3†**	**Year 4†**
G	40	80	40	$ 10.00	$ 12.00	$ 13.00	$ 13.00
L	80	100	102	12.00	13.75	14.40	15.00
R	30	40	43	8.00	9.00	10.00	10.00
V	100	120	100	14.00	14.50	16.00	17.30
Total cost at end-of-year costs				$75,000	$99,000	$117,000	$108,750

*Lifo cost
†Current cost

Instructions

   a Compute the cost indexes for pool 2 of Uptown Department Store for Year 2, Year 3, and Year 4.

   b Compute the dollar-value lifo inventories of Uptown Department Store for pool 2 on December 31, Year 2, Year 3, and Year 4.

8-15   The trial balance for Marcia Company shown on page 448 has been adjusted for all items except ending inventories and income taxes.

MARCIA COMPANY
Trial Balance
December 31, Year 2

	Debit	Credit
Cash	$ 21,000	
Accounts receivable (net)	40,000	
Inventories, Dec. 31, Year 1 (at cost)	52,000	
Short-term prepayments.............................	4,000	
Land	125,000	
Buildings	200,000	
Accumulated depreciation of buildings		$ 60,500
Equipment.......................................	225,000	
Accumulated depreciation of equipment		105,000
Accounts payable		55,000
Mortgage note payable ($12,000 due in Year 3)		50,000
Common stock, no par, 10,000 shares issued and		
outstanding		90,000
Retained earnings, Dec. 31, Year 1		266,500
Dividends	50,000	
Sales		505,000
Sales returns and allowances	10,000	
Sales discounts	5,000	
Purchases (including freight-in)	280,000	
Purchases discounts...............................		3,500
Selling expenses	73,000	
General and administrative expenses.................	50,500	
Totals	$1,135,500	$1,135,500

Additional Information

(1) Inventories on December 31, Year 2, consisted of the following:

	Cost	Replacement cost (net of freight-in and purchases discounts)
Inventories (cost includes freight-in but has not been reduced for 2% purchases discounts)	$87,000	$75,000

The controller of Marcia wants to recognize the decline in the market value of the December 31, Year 2, inventories by setting up an Allowance for Price Decline in Inventories; the write-down would be included in the cost of goods sold in the income statement. The cost of the December 31, Year 2, inventories should be reduced for purchases discounts that normally are taken. You also ascertain that the cost of ending inventories includes $4,700 of worthless goods and $2,300 of freight-in. Freight-in applicable to the worthless goods amounts to $65. Purchases discounts of 2% are offered on the invoice price of all purchases.

(2) Assume that Marcia pays income taxes at the rate of 45%, and that it had 10,000 shares of common stock outstanding throughout Year 2.

Instructions

a Determine the adjusted cost of Marcia Company's inventories on December 31, Year 2, and prepare a journal entry to record the estimated loss in value of the inventories caused by declining prices. Assume that the amount of the ending inventories had been entered in the accounting records by an appropriate closing entry.

b Prepare an income statement for Marcia Company for the year ended December 31, Year 2. Include the write-down of inventories to market in cost of goods sold.

c Prepare a balance sheet for Marcia Company on December 31, Year 2.

d Prepare a statement of retained earnings for Marcia Company for the year ended December 31, Year 2.

Inventories:
Special Valuation Methods

9

Inventory valuation methods based on cost flow assumptions and the application of the lower-of-cost-or-market rule are described in Chapter 8. Special inventory valuation methods, such as the *retail* and *gross profit* methods, are discussed in this chapter. In addition, the accounting for construction-type contracts (which involves the valuation of construction work in process inventories) is included in this chapter.

RETAIL METHOD

The retail method of estimating the cost of inventories is used primarily by retailing enterprises. Under the periodic inventory system, the cost of the ending inventories is subtracted from the total cost of goods available for sale to compute the cost of goods sold. Under the retail method, a record of goods available for sale at selling prices is kept separate from the accounting records, and sales for the accounting period are deducted from this total to determine the ending inventories at selling prices. The ending inventories valued at selling prices then are reduced to estimated cost by multiplying the inventories at selling prices by the cost percentage computed for the accounting period.

Some uses of the retail method of estimating the cost of inventories are:

1   To verify the reasonableness of the cost of inventories at the end of the accounting period. By using a different set of data from that used in pricing inventories, accountants may establish that the valuation of inventories is reasonable.

2   To estimate the cost of inventories for interim accounting periods and for income tax purposes.

3   To permit the valuation of inventories when selling prices are the only available data. The use of this method allows management to mark only the selling prices on the merchandise and eliminates the need for reference to specific purchase invoices.

Illustration of Retail Method

The retail method of estimating inventories (at average cost) is illustrated by the following simplified example for Robb Company:

Key step in the retail method is the computation of a cost percentage

ROBB COMPANY
Estimate of Inventories by Retail Method
End of Current Year

	Cost	Retail
Beginning inventories	$ 40,000	$ 50,000
Net purchases	150,000	200,000
Goods available for sale	$190,000	$250,000
Cost percentage ($190,000 ÷ $250,000) 76%		
Less: Sales and normal shrinkage		220,000
Ending inventories, at retail		$ 30,000
Estimated ending inventories, at cost ($30,000 × 0.76)	$ 22,800	

Although the retail method enables estimation of the value of inventories without a physical count of the items on hand, the accountant should insist that a physical inventory be taken periodically. Otherwise, *shrinkage* due to shoplifting, breakage, and other causes might go undetected and might result in an increasingly overstated inventories valuation.

Normal shrinkage in the inventories may be estimated on the basis of the goods that were available for sale. The method frequently used is to develop a percentage from the experience of past years, such as 2% of the retail value of goods available for sale. This percentage is used to determine the estimated shrinkage, which is deducted, together with sales, from goods available for sale at retail prices to compute the estimated inventories at retail prices.[1] The cost of normal shrinkage is included in the cost of goods sold; the cost of abnormal shrinkage (theft, unusual spoilage, etc.) that is material in amount is reported separately in the income statement.

The estimated cost of the inventories is computed by use of a *cost percentage,* that is, the relationship between the cost of goods available for sale during an accounting period and their retail value. The reliability of this procedure rests on the conditions that (1) a uniform relationship exists between selling price and cost for all goods available for sale during the period, or (2) if the markup on individual inventory items differs, the distribution of items in the ending inventories is roughly the same as the ''mix'' in the total goods available for sale during the period. When one of these conditions is not present, the accuracy of the retail method is improved by applying it to the individual departments of the business enterprise, and adding the resulting departmental inventories to compute the estimated cost of the total inventories.

---

[1]When sales are made to employees or selected customers at a special discount price, such discounts are added to sales to compute the estimated inventories at retail prices.

Retailing Terminology

The following terms are used in the application of the retail method of estimating the cost of inventories:

Original selling price The price at which goods originally are offered for sale.

Markup The initial margin between the selling price and cost. It also is referred to as *gross margin* or *mark-on*.

Additional markup An increase above the original selling price.

Markup cancellation A reduction in the selling price after there has been an additional markup. The reduction does not reduce the selling price below the original selling price. Additional markups less markup cancellations are referred to as *net markups.*

Markdown A reduction in selling price below the original selling price.

Markdown cancellation An increase in the selling price, following a markdown, that does not increase the new selling price above the original selling price. Markdowns less markdown cancellations are referred to as *net markdowns.*

To illustrate these terms, assume that an item that cost $20 is priced to sell for $30 a unit. The *markup* is $10 (50% of cost or 33⅓% of selling price). In response to strong demand for the item an *additional markup* of $3 is added, so that the selling price is increased to $33. As the demand slackens, the price is reduced to $31 by a *markup cancellation* of $2. Subsequently, in order to dispose of the remaining units, the selling price is reduced to $25 by a markup cancellation of $1 and a *markdown* of $5. Finally, if management concludes that the remaining units will be sold at a price of $28, a *markdown cancellation* of $3 is required to increase the selling price from $25 to $28.

Retail Method—Valuation at Average Cost

An understanding of the meaning of each term defined above is important in the application of the retail method, because the treatment of net markups and net markdowns affects the estimate of the cost of ending inventories. The data below

	Cost	Retail*
Beginning inventories	$15,810	$ 27,000
Net purchases	75,190	110,000
Additional markups		5,000
Markup cancellations		(2,000)
Markdowns		(10,875)
Markdown cancellations		875
Net sales		(90,000)
Ending inventories, at retail		$ 40,000

*All amounts other than net sales are taken from separate records.

Data for illustration of retail method

for Elmo Company are used to illustrate the treatment of net markups and net markdowns in the application of the retail method on December 31, Year 1.

The inventories at *average cost* for Elmo Company on December 31, Year 1, are estimated by the retail method as follows:

Net markdowns are used to compute cost percentage for estimation of ending inventories at average cost

ELMO COMPANY
Estimate of Inventories by Retail Method—Valuation at Average Cost
December 31, Year 1

	Cost	Retail
Beginning inventories	$15,810	$ 27,000
Net purchases	75,190	110,000
Net markups ($5,000 − $2,000)		3,000
Less: Net markdowns ($10,875 − $875)		(10,000)
Goods available for sale	$91,000	$130,000
Cost percentage ($91,000 ÷ $130,000) 70%		
Less: Net sales		(90,000)
Ending inventories, at retail		$ 40,000
Estimated ending inventories, at average cost ($40,000 × 0.70)	$28,000	

The cost percentage of 70% is determined after net markups are added to, and net markdowns are deducted from, the goods available for sale at retail prices. This procedure results in estimating the ending inventories at *average cost.* The estimated cost of $28,000 for the ending inventories is accurate only if the goods on hand consist of a representative sample of all goods available for sale during Year 1. For example, if the ending inventories do not include any goods that were on hand on January 1, Year 1, the cost percentage should be computed without use of the beginning inventories amounts. Similarly, if all goods on which the net markups and net markdowns were made have been sold, both the net markups and the net markdowns should be excluded from the computation of the cost percentage. Under such circumstances, however, the net markups and net markdowns still are used to compute the ending inventories at retail prices.

Retail Method—Valuation at Lower of Average Cost or Market

The retail method may be adapted to produce inventory valuations approximating the lower of average cost or market when there have been changes in the costs and selling prices of goods during the accounting period. The crucial factor in the estimate of cost of the ending inventory by the retail method is the treatment of net markups and net markdowns in the computation of the cost percentage. The *inclusion of net markups* and the *exclusion of net markdowns* in the computation of the cost percentage produce an inventory valued at the *lower of average cost or market.* This is sometimes called the *conventional retail method* and is illustrated for Elmo Company at the top of page 455.

Net markdowns are not used to compute cost percentage for estimation of ending inventories at lower of average cost or market

ELMO COMPANY
Estimate of Inventories by Retail Method—Valuation at Lower of Average Cost or Market
December 31, Year 1

	Cost	Retail
Beginning inventories	$15,810	$ 27,000
Net purchases	75,190	110,000
Net markups ($5,000 − $2,000)		3,000
Goods available for sale	$91,000	$140,000
Cost percentage ($91,000 ÷ $140,000) 65%		
Less: Net sales		(90,000)
Net markdowns ($10,875 − $875)		(10,000)
Ending inventories, at retail		$ 40,000
Estimated ending inventories, at lower of average cost		
or market ($40,000 × 0.65)	$26,000	

Net markups and net markdowns change the relationship between the retail price and the cost for goods available for sale, and thus affect the estimate of the ending inventories and the cost of goods sold computed by the retail method.

In the illustration above, the cost percentage is 65%, and the estimate of the ending inventories at *lower of average cost or market* is $26,000. When both the net markups and the net markdowns were used in the computation of the cost percentage, the percentage was 70%, and the estimate of the ending inventories at *average cost* was $28,000. The inclusion of net markups in the computation of the cost percentage assumes that the net markups apply proportionately to items sold and to items on hand at the end of the accounting period; however, net markdowns are assumed to apply only to the goods sold. Because the retail price of goods to which the markdowns apply is less than the original retail price, the net markdowns as well as sales must be deducted from goods available for sale at retail price to determine the inventories at retail price. If these assumptions are correct, the exclusion of net markdowns in the computation of the cost percentage values the ending inventories at actual average cost. However, if the net markdowns apply both to goods sold and to goods on hand, the exclusion of net markdowns from the computation of the cost percentage results in an inventory valuation at the *lower of average cost or market.*

As stated previously, the retail method is based on an assumption that the ending inventories are composed of the same mix of items as the total pool of goods from which sales were made. If there are markdowns for special sale promotions, this assumption implicit in the retail method may not be valid. Some markdowns may apply to goods available for sale and to goods in ending inventories in equal proportions, but others may apply only to goods that have been sold. In essence, we are saying that there are really two lines of merchandise, "special sale" items and regular items, on which the markups are different. The two lines may not be held in equal proportions in the goods available and in the ending inventories. Attempts to handle the two lines in one computation are likely to prove inadequate as a means of estimating meaningful inventory cost amounts.

Retail Method—Valuation at Last-In, First-Out

The preceding discussion illustrated two variations of the retail method that produce inventory estimates at *average cost* and at the *lower of average cost or market.* If the last-in, first-out method is used to estimate the cost of inventories, the conventional retail method must be modified. The retail method may be adapted to approximate lifo cost of the ending inventories by the computation of a cost percentage for purchases of the current accounting period only. The objective is to estimate the cost of *any increase* (lifo layer) in inventories during the accounting period.

Because lifo is a cost (not lower-of-cost-or-market) method of inventory valuation, both net markups and net markdowns are included in the computation of the cost percentage for purchases of the current period, in accordance with the discussion of the average-cost procedure on pages 453–454.

The modification of the retail method necessary to value inventory at lifo cost is shown below for Elmo Company (using the same data as in previous illustrations). For purposes of this illustration, assume that selling prices have remained unchanged and that net markups and net markdowns *apply only to the goods purchased during Year 1.*

Exclude beginning inventories from computation of the cost percentage when retail lifo method is used

ELMO COMPANY
Estimate of Inventories by Retail Method—Valuation at Lifo Cost
December 31, Year 1

	Cost	Retail
Beginning inventories	$15,810	$ 27,000
Net purchases	75,190	110,000
Net markups ($5,000 − $2,000)		3,000
Less: Net markdowns ($10,875 − $875)		(10,000)
Goods available for sale, at retail		$130,000
Less: Net sales		90,000
Ending inventories, at retail		$ 40,000
Cost percentage for net purchases, including net markups and net markdowns ($75,190 ÷ $103,000*) 73%		
Ending inventories, at lifo cost:		
Beginning inventories layer	$15,810	$ 27,000
Add: Layer added in Year 1 ($13,000 × 0.73)	9,490	13,000
Ending inventories, at retail		$ 40,000
Estimated ending inventories, at lifo cost	$25,300	

*$110,000 + $3,000 − $10,000 = $103,000.

The inventories on December 31, Year 1, are composed of the cost of the beginning inventories plus the estimated cost of the layer added during Year 1. If in Year 2 the inventories decreased, the decrease would be taken from the layer added in Year 1, $9,490, and then from the layer on hand at the beginning of Year 1,

$15,810. For example, if the ending inventories for Elmo Company totaled $30,000 at retail prices (a decrease of $10,000 during Year 2) on December 31, Year 2, the inventories at lifo cost would be computed as illustrated below:

	Cost	Retail
Inventories, Dec. 31, Year 2, at lifo cost:		
Inventory layer, Jan. 1, Year 1	*$15,810*	*$27,000*
Layer added in Year 1 ($3,000 × 0.73)	*2,190*	*3,000*
Ending inventories, at retail		*$30,000*
Estimated ending inventories, Dec. 31, Year 2, at lifo cost	*$18,000*	

Note the cost of layer added in previous year

Under retail lifo procedures, computation of a cost percentage for current year's purchases is required *only when an increase in inventories (at retail) occurs during the current year.* The cost percentage is computed for the sole purpose of pricing the incremental layer in inventories. In contrast, if a decrease (lifo liquidation) in inventories takes place, the ending inventories consist of a fraction of the beginning inventories cost. For example, if the ending inventories at retail for Elmo Company on December 31, Year 2, amounted to only $13,500, or one-half of the layer on January 1, Year 1, the estimated inventories at lifo cost would be determined on December 31, Year 2, as follows:

Inventories consist of one-half of prior year's beginning inventories

$$\$15,810 \times \frac{\$13,500}{\$27,000} = \underline{\underline{\$7,905}}$$

Retail Method—Valuation at First-In, First-Out

The cost of the inventories on a first-in, first-out basis may be estimated from the data used to determine the lifo cost. For example, the estimated cost of the inventories on December 31, Year 1, for Elmo Company on the first-in, first-out basis would be $29,200 ($40,000 × 0.73, the cost percentage applicable to Year 1 purchases). If the cost percentage for the following year (Year 2) was 68% and the inventories at retail amounted to $30,000, the estimated inventories fifo cost would be $20,400 ($30,000 × 0.68 = $20,400).

Changes in Price Levels and the Retail Lifo Method

Let us now remove the simplifying assumption of the stability of selling prices. In reality, retail prices do change from one accounting period to another, and this is particularly significant for pricing inventories at retail lifo. Because the procedure employed under these circumstances is similar to that used in conjunction with dollar-value lifo described in Chapter 8, it is known as the *dollar-value retail lifo method.* The ending inventories at retail prices must be converted to beginning-of-year prices to ascertain the increase in the inventories at beginning-of-year prices. An appropriate cost index must be used to convert from end-of-year prices to beginning-of-year prices. There are several indexes published regularly by various governmental agencies and trade associations that may be used. For example, the Bureau of Labor Statistics regularly publishes national indexes for 20 major groups of retail departments, as well as for soft goods and durable goods.

The procedure for estimating the cost of the ending inventories under the dollar-value retail lifo method and assuming increasing selling prices, is shown below for Todd Company. The sales price index at the beginning of Year 5, *when lifo was adopted,* is assumed to be 100, and the index at the end of Year 5 is assumed to be 110, an increase of 10%.[2] In order not to complicate the example, we assume that there were no net markups or net markdowns in Year 5.

Dollar-value retail lifo method when prices are rising

TODD COMPANY
Dollar-Value Retail Lifo Method
December 31, Year 5

	Cost	Retail
Inventories, Jan. 1, Year 5 (date lifo was adopted)	$18,000	$ 30,000
Purchases during Year 5 (cost percentage is 65%)	65,000	100,000
Goods available for sale during Year 5, at retail prices		$130,000
Less: Net sales during the period		75,000
Inventories, Dec. 31, Year 5, at retail prices		$ 55,000
Computation of increase in inventories, at end-of-year retail prices:		
Inventories, Dec. 31, Year 5, at beginning-of-year retail prices ($55,000 ÷ 1.10)		$ 50,000
Less: Inventories, Jan. 1, Year 5, at retail prices		30,000
Increase in inventories, at beginning-of-year retail prices . .		$ 20,000
Increase in inventories, at end-of-year retail prices ($20,000 × 1.10)		$ 22,000
Ending inventories, at dollar-value retail lifo cost:		
Beginning inventories layer	$18,000	
Add: Layer added in Year 5 ($22,000 × 0.65)	14,300	
Estimated ending inventories, at dollar-value retail lifo cost . .	$32,300[3]	

GROSS PROFIT METHOD

The gross profit method is useful for several purposes: (1) to control and verify the validity of inventory cost; (2) to estimate interim inventory valuations between physical counts; and (3) to estimate the inventory cost when necessary information

---

[2]When the base-period index is other than 100, the percentage increase is determined by dividing the index at the end of the current period by the base-period index and subtracting 100. For example, if the base-period index is 125 and the index at the end of the current period is 150, the increase would be 20% [(150 ÷ 125) − 100 = 0.20].

[3]Failure to recognize the increase in the price level would result in an erroneous ending inventory cost of $34,250, as illustrated below:

	Lifo cost	Selling price
Beginning inventories layer	$18,000	$30,000
Incremental layer [lifo cost = ($55,000 − $30,000) × 0.65]	16,250	25,000
Estimated ending inventories	$34,250	$55,000

normally used is lost or unavailable. The procedure involved is one of reducing sales to a cost basis; that is, cost of goods sold is estimated. The estimated cost of goods sold then is subtracted from the cost of goods available for sale to compute the estimated cost of the ending inventories.

In the event that both merchandise and inventory records are destroyed by fire, the inventory cost may be estimated by use of the gross profit method. The gross profit and cost of goods sold percentages are obtained from prior years' financial statements, which presumably are available. The beginning inventories amount for the current year is the ending inventories amount of the preceding year. Net purchases are estimated from copies of the paid checks returned by the bank and through correspondence with suppliers. Sales are computed by reference to cash deposits and by an estimate of the outstanding accounts receivable through correspondence with customers.

Gross Profit Method Is Really a "Cost Percentage" Method

The key step in the application of the gross profit method is the development of an accurate *cost percentage,* obtained by deduction of the gross profit rate from 100%. Frequently the best available measure is an average of the cost percentages for recent years, adjusted for any changes in costs and selling prices that have taken place in the current year.

To illustrate the computation of the cost of inventories by the gross profit method, assume the following data for Dubin Corporation for Year 4:

Cost percentage of 80% means that gross profit is 20%

Beginning inventories, at cost	$ 40,000
Net purchases	200,000
Net sales	225,000
Average cost percentage for past three years	80%

Assuming that the cost percentage for Year 4 remained at 80%, the cost of the inventories on December 31, Year 4, is estimated as follows:

The key step in the gross profit method is the estimate of cost of goods sold

DUBIN CORPORATION
Estimate of Cost of Inventories by Gross Profit Method
December 31, Year 4

Beginning inventories, at cost		$ 40,000
Add: Net purchases		200,000
Cost of goods available for sale		$240,000
Less: Estimated cost of goods sold:		
Net sales	$225,000	
Cost percentage	0.80	180,000
Estimated ending inventories, at cost		$ 60,000

The cost of the ending inventories estimated by the gross profit method is reasonably consistent with the usual method of valuing inventories. This follows from the fact that the gross profit percentage is based on historical records that reflect the particular method of valuing the inventories. If the inventories are valued at lifo, the estimated inventories will approximate lifo cost; therefore, if the gross profit method is used as a basis for recovering an insured fire loss, the inventories should be restated for insurance purposes to current fair value at the time of the fire.

Sometimes the gross profit percentage is stated as a percentage of cost. In such situations the gross profit percentage must be restated to a percentage of net sales to compute the cost percentage (based on net sales) for the period. For example, if the gross profit is stated as 25% of cost, the gross profit percentage may be restated to 20% of net sales as follows:

Restatement of gross profit percentage based on cost to percentage based on net sales

(1) 25% = ¼ gross profit based on cost
(2) Add numerator of fraction to denominator to make ⅕
(3) ⅕ = 20% gross profit based on net sales

When 20% is subtracted from 100%, we have the cost percentage of 80% of net sales. Alternatively, the cost percentage based on net sales may be determined directly as follows:

Direct computation of cost percentage

Let X = cost as percentage of net sales

$0.25X$ = gross profit percentage (based on cost)

then $X + 0.25X = 100\%$ of net sales

$1.25X = 100\%$

$$X = \frac{100\%}{1.25}$$

$X = 80\%$ (cost percentage based on net sales)

Applying the Gross Profit Method to Departments

If there are several classes of merchandise that have different markup percentages, the gross profit method yields accurate results only if the inventory for each class of merchandise is computed individually. The use of a combined cost percentage would require the unlikely assumption that the various classes of merchandise are sold in the same relative proportions each year. To illustrate this point, assume that the gross profit percentages for Dawson Company have averaged 50% for Department A and 30% for Department B in recent years. Thus, the cost percentage is 50% for Department A and 70% for Department B; the combined cost percentage has averaged 65% in recent years. The cost of the combined ending inventories for Year 8 may be estimated as shown at the top of page 461.

Use of the combined cost percentage (based on prior years' experience) produces an inventories estimate of $50,000, although the sum of the two departmental ending inventories is estimated at $65,000 ($35,000 + $30,000 = $65,000). The source of the error is clear when we note that the cost percentage for Year 8, determined by combining the departmental results, is not 65% but 60%, because a

DAWSON COMPANY
Estimate of Cost of Departmental and Combined Inventories by Gross Profit Method
For Year 8

	Dept. A	Dept. B	Combined
Beginning inventories, at cost	$ 20,000	$ 40,000	$ 60,000
Net purchases	90,000	95,000	185,000
Cost of goods available for sale	$110,000	$135,000	$245,000
Less: Estimated cost of goods sold:			
Net sales	$150,000	$150,000	$300,000
Average cost percentage, **prior years**	0.50	0.70	0.65
Estimated cost of goods sold	$ 75,000	$105,000	$195,000
Estimated ending inventories, at cost	$ 35,000	$ 30,000	$ 50,000

higher-than-usual proportion of total sales in Year 8 was made by Department A, which has a lower cost percentage. The **actual** combined cost percentage (60%) for Year 8 is determined below:

Total sales ($150,000 + $150,000) $300,000
Total estimated cost of goods sold ($75,000 + $105,000) $180,000
Combined cost percentage for Year 8 ($180,000 ÷ $300,000) 60%

If the combined Year 8 cost percentage of 60% is used, the aggregate ending inventories would be computed correctly at $65,000 ($245,000 − $180,000 = $65,000). Stated simply, separate departmental cost percentages should be used to estimate the cost of inventories by the gross profit method when the cost percentages differ materially among departments.

Gross Profit Method for Interim Reports

The gross profit method frequently is used in the preparation of interim reports. It should be clear that the use of the gross profit method results in an **estimated cost** of inventories. If the reporting enterprise normally values inventories at lower of cost or market for annual reporting purposes, it must follow the same procedure for interim reporting purposes. Thus, the estimated cost obtained by use of the gross profit method must be compared with current replacement costs to determine whether a write-down to a lower "market" is required. The gross profit method may be used for interim reports even though annual inventories are determined by use of one of the cost flow assumptions described in Chapter 8. Enterprises that use the gross profit method for interim reports "should disclose the method used . . . and any significant adjustments that result from reconciliations with the annual physical inventory."[4]

----

[4]*APB Opinion No. 28*, "Interim Financial Reporting," AICPA (New York: 1973), p. 524.

OTHER VALUATION METHODS

Valuation of Inventories at Replacement Costs

The valuation of inventories at replacement costs has been advocated by accountants who believe that the current asset section of the balance sheet should reflect current fair values. The cost methods of inventory valuation frequently understate the value of inventories, particularly during periods of rising prices. The significance of replacement costs as a measure of inventory value varies considerably depending on the type of inventories involved. In the retail market, the selling prices of staple commodities, such as sugar, copper, cotton, etc., tend to follow cost prices closely. In such situations, replacement costs of inventories are important to management and outsiders.

Replacement-cost valuation of inventories in the preparation of financial statements is not generally accepted. Perhaps the closest practical approach is the first-in, first-out method. Unless prices are rising rapidly, the fifo method of pricing presents inventories in the balance sheet at or near current replacement costs without a departure from the cost principle. The need for disclosure of replacement or current costs of inventories arises when the last-in, first-out method is used for pricing inventories.

The theoretical objection to the use of replacement costs as a method of inventory is implicit in the arguments previously presented. Some of the advantages of inventory valuation at replacement costs may be achieved by disclosure of current replacement costs of inventories in a note to the financial statements. Some accountants have argued for the adoption of replacement costs as a means of pricing inventories whether replacement costs are more or less than actual costs. They base their argument on the fact that the economic utility of inventories is indicated by the current costs of replacement. A valid point made by proponents of replacement costs is that if replacement costs are objective and more useful when they are lower than actual costs, they also possess those attributes when they are higher than actual costs.

The consistent use of replacement costs for the valuation of inventories would require some broadening of the revenue realization principle as presently applied. Under generally accepted accounting principles, revenue emerges at the time inventories are sold and converted to accounts receivable (or cash), as indicated in the following diagram:

Revenue is realized
when inventories
are sold

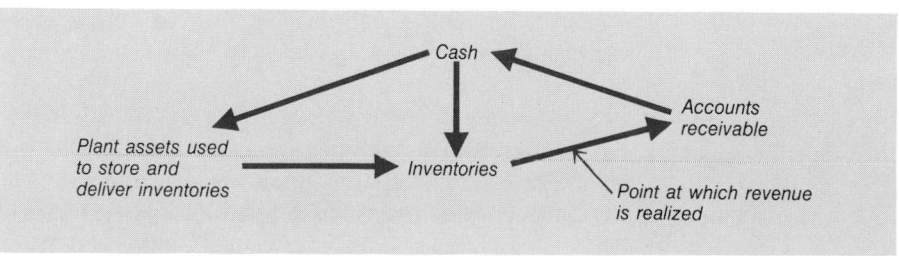

If replacement costs were adopted for inventory valuation, ***holding gains and losses*** represented by the difference between actual costs and replacement costs would be recognized and included in income prior to the sale of finished products. The information resulting from such a procedure would be useful in accounting periods when prices were changing significantly. The real issue is whether replacement costs can be determined with sufficient objectivity to provide a reliable basis for financial accounting. At present, valuation of inventories at replacement costs that are *higher* than actual costs is not acceptable.

Restatement of inventory costs to constant purchasing power is another approach to the problem of changing prices. This subject is found in Chapter 25.

Valuation of Inventories at Net Selling Prices

The valuation of inventories at *net selling prices* (sales prices less direct costs of completion and disposal) has some appeal, especially when one considers that economic value is added as the goods are brought to market. For example, in a retail store, goods are more valuable than they were at the wholesaler's warehouse; value is added by the process of bringing the goods nearer the ultimate market. In a manufacturing enterprise, costs are blended together, and a product emerges that is more valuable than the sum of the production costs. However, this method of inventory valuation has not been widely adopted for two reasons: (1) the lack of objectivity in determining the net selling price, and (2) the fact that the selling price has not been realized in cash or cash equivalents. Accountants generally consider revenue to be realized at the time of sale of goods, not at the time of production.

The valuation of inventories at net selling prices is appropriate for some types of business enterprises producing commodities that have readily determinable market prices. When the production of such commodities is complete, revenue may be considered realized. In some enterprises having selling prices established by contract, the sale is reasonably assured, and completed inventories may be valued at net selling prices.

The use of net selling prices to value inventories moves the point of revenue realization back one step in the earning process. As costs are incurred during the process of bringing an item to market, income is earned in the most fundamental sense. Each activity necessary to advance the goods closer to the customer and ultimately to close the sale transaction adds an element of income—the increase in selling price over the added cost. Therefore, if there are costs still to be incurred, there is still an element of income to be earned. The valuation of inventories at net selling prices means that a portion of income may be prematurely recognized before it is realized through sale.

Supplies and Short-Term Prepayments

In addition to inventories of merchandise, finished goods, material, parts, and goods in process, a business enterprise may have several types of supplies on hand. For example, inventories of supplies may include office supplies, promotional materials, shipping supplies, and factory supplies. The problems of determining cost and valuation of supplies are similar to those for inventories discussed in Chapter 8. Supplies are acquired for use in operations, and any quantities remaining on hand at the end of an accounting period are included in the current assets section of the balance sheet.

The term *prepaid expenses* is widely used to describe unexpired costs that are expected to be consumed within a relatively short period of time. However, this term is somewhat of a misnomer and should be replaced by a more descriptive title such as *short-term prepayments.* Prepaid expenses are costs of goods and services that have not been consumed in the revenue-earning process. Strictly speaking, both depreciable plant assets and inventories fall within this definition. Plant assets are classified separately because they provide services over long time periods; inventories require separate disclosure because of their materiality and importance. There is a presumption that short-term prepayments will be consumed within one year or within the business enterprise's next operating cycle, and for this reason they are included in the current assets section of the balance sheet.

ACCOUNTING FOR CONSTRUCTION-TYPE CONTRACTS

Contracts for construction of buildings, roads, bridges, dams, and similar projects often require more than one year to complete. Because of their unique features, such contracts present special problems of asset valuation and revenue recognition. Among these features are the following:[5]

1   A unique property is produced at the jobsite owned by the customer.

2   The contract typically is obtained by bidding or negotiation, which requires the contractor to estimate the cost to complete the construction project and the desired profit margin.

3   Although the contractor acquires material for a construction project, the work in progress is owned by the customer.

4   Most contractors use *progress billings* or advances from customers as a source of financing their construction work, in addition to final billings for the completed projects.

5   The original contract may be modified by *change orders* during the process of construction.

The four basic types of construction contracts are:[6]

1   *Fixed-price* (or *lump-sum*) *contracts,* which provide for a single price for all work performed by the contractor

2   *Unit-price contracts,* which include a fixed price for each unit of output under the contract

3   *Cost-type contracts,* which provide for reimbursement of specified costs incurred by the contractor plus a fee for the contractor's services

---

[5]*Audit and Accounting Guide,* "Construction Contractors," AICPA (New York: 1981), pp. 3, 6–7, 9.
[6]Ibid., p. 4.

4 *Time-and-material contracts,* which provide for a fixed hourly rate for the contractor's direct labor hours, plus payment for cost of material and other specified items

Methods of Accounting for Construction-Type Contracts

As stated in Chapter 3, the two methods of accounting for construction-type contracts are the percentage-of-completion method and the completed-contract method. The two methods are not free-choice alternatives for the same circumstances.[7]

Most contractors employ the *percentage-of-completion method* of accounting for financial accounting. This method requires the accrual of gross profit and revenue over the term of the contract based on the progress achieved each year. If the work performed in a year is estimated to represent 40% of the total work required on the contract, 40% of the total estimated gross profit and revenue is considered realized. The recognition of gross profit and revenue is accomplished by increasing the carrying amount of the Cost of Contracts in Progress ledger account, which is comparable with the Goods in Process inventory account of a manufacturing enterprise. Estimates of work performed on a contract during a year may be based on one of the following input or output measures:[8]

1 *Input measures*

a Costs incurred to date as a percentage of the total estimated cost (*cost-to-cost method*)

b Labor hours, labor dollars, machine hours, or material quantities incurred to date as a percentage of the related estimated totals (*efforts-expended methods*)

2 *Output measures*

a Units produced, units delivered, or contract milestones (such as completion of the foundation of a building) completed to date as a percentage of the related estimated totals (*units-of work-performed methods*)

b Value added to the project to date as a percentage of estimated total value of the completed project (*value-added method*)

Physical inspection of the project may be required to substantiate the percentage of completion estimated by one of the foregoing methods.

Under the *completed-contract method* of accounting, no gross profit is recognized for a construction project until it is *substantially completed;* that is, when remaining costs and potential risks are insignificant in amount.[9] The completed-contract method is appropriate for financial accounting only if a contractor has primarily short-term contracts that are completed in a year or less or if estimates of input or output measures of completion are not reasonably dependable or are subject to inherent hazards such as those described on page 472.[10]

---

[7]*FASB Statement No. 56,* "Designation of AICPA Guide . . . on Contractor Accounting . . . As Preferable . . ." (Stamford: 1982), p. 2.

[8]*Audit and Accounting Guide,* "Construction Contractors," pp. 129–130.

[9]Ibid., p. 132.

[10]Ibid., p. 21.

Under both the percentage-of-completion and the completed-contract methods of accounting, an estimated loss under a construction-type contract is *recognized in full in the accounting period it becomes apparent,* with a debit to Provision for Loss on Uncompleted Contract and a credit to Estimated Loss on Uncompleted Contracts. The provision (debit-balance account) is included in the income statement as an element of cost of realized contract revenue, and the estimated loss (credit-balance account) is presented in the balance sheet as a liability or as a deduction from the cost of contracts in progress.[11]

Accounting for Construction-Type Contract: Profit Anticipated

To illustrate the accounting for a construction-type contract, assume that a small bridge is to be constructed by Cabot Construction Company beginning in Year 1 at a fixed price of $900,000, with estimated construction costs totaling $750,000. The bridge is expected to be completed in Year 3. The construction costs incurred, cost estimates, and other data are presented below in summary form for each year of the three-year period:

Data for illustration

	Year 1	Year 2	Year 3
Construction costs incurred	$125,000	$495,000	$145,000
Estimated cost to complete the bridge	625,000	155,000	–0–
Progress billings to customer	110,000	565,000	225,000
Collections from customer on billings	90,000	520,000	265,000
Operating expenses incurred (selling, general, and administrative)	15,000	30,000	22,500

We illustrate the *cost-to-cost method* of estimating the percentage of completion of the bridge construction; other techniques for estimating work performed are similar in their application.

Percentage-of-Completion Method   If Cabot Construction Company determines the estimated percentage of completion of the bridge by the cost-to-cost method, the percentages and the related contract revenue, cost of contract revenue, and gross profit are computed as shown on page 467.

Note in the exhibit on page 467 that the computation of the cost of contract revenue for each year produces an amount equal to the actual construction costs incurred for that year (see data for illustration above). This equality always results from the use of the cost-to-cost method of estimating the percentage of completion, but not from one of the other methods described on page 465.

The journal entries for Cabot Construction Company for each year of the construction project under the *percentage-of-completion method* are shown on page 468.

---

[11]Ibid., pp. 25–26, 173–174.

Computations under
percentage-of-
completion method

CABOT CONSTRUCTION COMPANY
Computation of Contract Revenue, Cost of Contract Revenue, and Gross Profit—
Percentage-of-Completion Method
For Years 1, 2, and 3

	Year 1	Year 2	Year 3
Total estimated revenue (fixed price)	$900,000	$900,000	$900,000
Total construction costs incurred to date **(a)** .	$125,000	$620,000	$765,000
Estimated cost to complete.................	625,000	155,000	
Total estimated or actual cost **(b)**	$750,000	$775,000	$765,000
Total estimated or actual gross profit	$150,000	$125,000	$135,000
Percentage of completion (cost-to-cost method) [**(a)** ÷ **(b)**]	16⅔%	80%	100%
Contract revenue:			
Year 1 ($900,000 × 0.16⅔)	$150,000		
Year 2 [($900,000 × 0.80) − $150,000]		$570,000	
Year 3 [$900,000 − ($150,000 + $570,000)]			$180,000
Cost of contract revenue:			
Year 1 ($750,000 × 0.16⅔)	125,000		
Year 2 [($775,000 × 0.80) − $125,000]		495,000	
Year 3 [$765,000 − ($125,000 + $495,000)]			145,000
Gross profit for year	$ 25,000	$ 75,000	$ 35,000

Comments on the journal entries on page 468 (identified by numbers) follow:

(1) As indicated on page 465, the Cost of Contracts in Progress ledger account is similar to the Goods in Process inventory account of a manufacturing enterprise. In the Cost of Contracts in Progress account are recorded the material, direct labor, and overhead costs incurred by the contractor, as well as costs associated with work performed by *subcontractors.*

(2) The Progress Billings ledger account *is not a revenue account,* despite its being associated with entries to the Accounts Receivable account. As stated on page 464, progress billings to the customer are a means of financing (together with bank loans) for a contractor; the timing of progress billings is provided in the construction contract and may or may not bear a direct relationship to the percentage of completion of the project. Note, for example, that the $110,000 of Cabot Construction Company's progress billings in Year 1 represent approximately 12% of the total contract price ($110,000 ÷ $900,000 = 12.22%), compared with the 16⅔% computation of the percentage of completion for Year 1 (see exhibit above).

Thus, the Progress Billings ledger account is a contra to the Cost of Contracts in Progress and the Estimated Earnings on Contracts in Progress ledger accounts. In essence, the balance of the Progress Billings ledger account on any date prior to completion of the construction project represents the *customer's equity interest* in the project.

(3) The collections from customer, recorded by a credit to Accounts Receivable, require no additional comments.

Illustrative
journal
entries
under
per-
centage-
of-
comple-
tion
method

CABOT CONSTRUCTION COMPANY
Journal Entries—Percentage-of-Completion Method

Accounts and explanations of transactions	Year 1		Year 2		Year 3	
	Debit	Credit	Debit	Credit	Debit	Credit
(1) Operating Expenses............	15,000		30,000		22,500	
Cost of Contracts in Progress	125,000		495,000		145,000	
Material Inventory, Cash, etc. .		140,000		525,000		167,500
To record operating expenses and construction costs.						
(2) Accounts Receivable	110,000		565,000		225,000	
Progress Billings		110,000		565,000		225,000
To record billings on contract.						
(3) Cash	90,000		520,000		265,000	
Accounts Receivable		90,000		520,000		265,000
To record collections from customer.						
(4) Cost of Contract Revenue	125,000		495,000		145,000	
Estimated Earnings on Contracts in Progress	25,000		75,000		35,000	
Contract Revenue............		150,000		570,000		180,000
To record contract revenue estimated on the basis of cost incurred to total estimated cost. (See computations on p. 467)						
(5) Progress Billings..............					900,000	
Cost of Contracts in Progress .						765,000
Estimated Earnings on Contracts in Progress						135,000
To record approval of project by customer.						

(4) As indicated on page 466, when the cost-to-cost method is used to estimate the percentage of completion of a construction-type contract, the cost of contract revenue for an accounting period is identical to the total construction costs incurred in that period. Thus, the debits to the Cost of Contract Revenue account are the same as the debits to the Cost of Contracts in Progress account in journal entries in (1). However, the Cost of Contract Revenue account, being similar to cost of goods sold of a manufacturing enterprise, appears in the income statement of the contractor and is closed at the end of each accounting period.

The Estimated Earnings on Contracts in Progress ledger account is a *positive valuation account* for the Cost of Contracts in Progress account. The use of a separate account for the accrual of earnings on a contract under the percentage-of-completion method preserves the record of actual costs incurred on the contract in the Cost of Contracts in Progress account and still achieves the goal of increasing the carrying amount of the contracts in progress asset.

The Contract Revenue ledger account is similar to the Sales account of a manufacturing enterprise. The total of the credits to this account during the term of the construction contract is equal to the total contract price.

(5) When the construction project has been completed and approved by the customer, the asset and contra-asset amounts related to the project are removed from the related ledger accounts. No revenue or expenses are recognized by this journal entry because the total revenue and costs applicable to the contract were included in the journal entries in (4).

The presentation of contract revenue and cost of contract revenue in the income statement is illustrated below for Cabot Construction Company under the *percentage-of-completion* method:

Presentation in income statements: Percentage-of-completion method

	Year 1	Year 2	Year 3
Contract revenue	$150,000	$570,000	$180,000
Less: Cost of contract revenue	125,000	495,000	145,000
Gross profit	$ 25,000	$ 75,000	$ 35,000

The balance sheets for Cabot Construction Company include the amounts shown below when the *percentage-of-completion method* is used:

Presentation in balance sheets: Percentage-of-completion method

	End of Year 1	End of Year 2	End of Year 3
Current assets:			
Contract receivables	$ 20,000	$ 65,000	$ 25,000
Costs and estimated earnings in excess of billings on uncompleted contract **(Note)**	40,000	45,000	

Note: Costs, estimated earnings, and billings on uncompleted contracts:

	End of Year 1	End of Year 2
Costs incurred on uncompleted contract..........	$125,000	$620,000
Estimated earnings	25,000	100,000
Subtotal	$150,000	$720,000
Less: Billings to date	110,000	675,000
Costs and estimated earnings in excess of billings on uncompleted contract	$ 40,000	$ 45,000

If on the date of a balance sheet the balance of the Progress Billings contra-asset ledger account exceeds the total of the balances of the Cost of Contracts in Progress and Estimated Earnings on Contracts in Progress accounts, the excess is included in current liabilities in the contractor's balance sheet. For example, suppose that the balance of Cabot Construction Company's Progress Billings ledger account had been $180,000, rather than $110,000, at the end of Year 1. The $30,000 excess ($180,000 − $150,000 = $30,000) of the contra-asset account over the total of the two asset accounts would be presented as follows in the current liabilities section of Cabot's end-of-Year 1 balance sheet:

<table>
<tr><td>Credit excess in
balance sheet</td><td>Current liabilities:
Billings in excess of costs and estimated earnings
on uncompleted contract ....</td><td>$30,000</td></tr>
</table>

The billings in excess of costs and estimated earnings current liability of a contractor resembles the deferred revenue liability of a manufacturing enterprise that receives payments in advance for finished goods to be shipped subsequently to customers. Costs and estimated earnings in excess of billings and billings in excess of costs and estimated earnings are *current* assets and liabilities, respectively, because the operating cycle of a contractor encompasses the total time required to complete construction contracts, even though that time exceeds one year.

Completed-Contract Method   Assuming that Cabot Construction Company used the completed-contract method of accounting, rather than the percentage-of-completion method, for the small bridge construction project described on page 466, Cabot would record no gross profit on the project until Year 3, when the project was completed. The journal entries for Cabot Construction Company to record the transactions related to the construction of the bridge under the *completed-contract method* are shown on page 471.

Assuming that the bridge construction contract was the only construction contract of Cabot Construction Company, its income statements for Year 1 and Year 2 would show pre-tax losses of $15,000 and $30,000, respectively, the amounts of operating expenses for those years. Cabot's income statement for Year 3 includes the following items under the *completed-contract method:*

<table>
<tr><td>Presentation in the
income statement for
Year 3: Completed-
contract method</td><td>Contract revenue...</td><td>$900,000</td></tr>
<tr><td></td><td>Less: Cost of contract completed.....................................</td><td>765,000</td></tr>
<tr><td></td><td>Gross profit...</td><td>$135,000</td></tr>
<tr><td></td><td>Operating expenses..</td><td>22,500</td></tr>
<tr><td></td><td>Income before income taxes.......................................</td><td>$112,500</td></tr>
</table>

The $135,000 gross profit recognized by Cabot in Year 3 under the completed-contract method is equal to the total gross profit for Years 1, 2, and 3 under the percentage-of-completion income statements on page 469 ($25,000 + $75,000 + $35,000 = $135,000).

Illustrative journal entries under completed contract method

CABOT CONSTRUCTION COMPANY
Journal Entries—Completed-Contract Method

Accounts and explanations of transactions	Year 1 Debit	Year 1 Credit	Year 2 Debit	Year 2 Credit	Year 3 Debit	Year 3 Credit
(1) Operating Expenses..........	15,000		30,000		22,500	
Cost of Contracts in Progress .	125,000		495,000		145,000	
Material Inventory, Cash, etc.		140,000		525,000		167,500
To record operating expenses and construction costs.						
(2) Accounts Receivable	110,000		565,000		225,000	
Progress Billings		110,000		565,000		225,000
To record billings on contract.						
(3) Cash	90,000		520,000		265,000	
Accounts Receivable		90,000		520,000		265,000
To record collections from customer.						
(4) Progress Billings					900,000	
Cost of Contract Revenue					765,000	
Contract Revenue..........						900,000
Cost of Contracts in Progress						765,000
To record contract revenue and applicable construction costs on substantial completion of project.						

The balance sheets for Cabot Construction Company include the following amounts when the ***completed-contract*** method is used:

Presentation in balance sheets: Completed contract method

	End of Year 1	End of Year 2	End of Year 3
Current assets:			
Contract receivables......................................	$20,000	$65,000	$25,000
Costs in excess of billings on uncompleted contract (**Note**)...	15,000		
Current liabilities:			
Billings in excess of costs on uncompleted contract (**Note**)...		$55,000	

(continued)

Note: *Costs and billings on uncompleted contract:*

	End of Year 1	End of Year 2
Costs incurred on uncompleted contract.....................	$125,000	$620,000
Less: Billings to date	110,000	675,000
Costs in excess of billings (billings in excess of costs) on uncompleted contract	$ 15,000	$ (55,000)

It is important to emphasize that, as pointed out on page 465, Cabot Construction Company does not have the *option* of using either the percentage-of-completion method or the completed-contract method of accounting for the bridge construction contract. Because the construction project extends over three years, Cabot may use the completed-contract method only if estimates of measures of completion *are not reasonably dependable or are subject to inherent hazards.* Estimates of costs are a critical part of the bidding and negotiating process for construction contracts; thus, situations in which estimates of completion under, for example, the cost-to-cost method would not be dependable are rare. With respect to inherent hazards, the AICPA stated:[12]

> . . . inherent hazards that make otherwise reasonably dependable contract estimates doubtful involve events and conditions that would not be considered in the ordinary preparation of contract estimates and that would not be expected to recur frequently, given the contractor's normal business environment. . . . Such hazards may relate, for example, to contracts whose validity is seriously in question (that is, which are less than fully enforceable), to contracts whose completion may be subject to the outcome of pending legislation or pending litigation, or to contracts exposed to the possibility of the condemnation or expropriation of the resulting properties.

Thus, the situations in which the completed-contract method of accounting is appropriate for construction-type contracts may be rare. Income tax laws permit the use of the completed-contract method of accounting in specified circumstances. If the percentage-of-completion method is used for financial accounting and the completed-contract method for income tax purposes, income tax allocation is required. This topic is discussed in Chapter 21.

Accounting for Construction-Type Contract: Loss Anticipated

We have indicated on page 466 that an anticipated loss on a construction-type contract is recognized when it is identified, under both the percentage-of-completion and the completed-contract methods.

To illustrate, assume that City Contractors on January 2, Year 1, entered into a contract to construct a building on the customer's land at a fixed price of

---

[12]Ibid., p. 122.

$1,000,000, with construction expected to be completed late in Year 2. In its bid on the project, City estimated total construction costs of $850,000, with an anticipated gross profit of $150,000. Construction costs incurred during Year 1 totaled $400,000; estimated costs to complete on December 31, Year 1, totaled $640,000; and construction costs incurred during Year 2 totaled $650,000. Progress billings totaled $300,000 in Year 1 and $700,000 in Year 2. The building was completed on November 29, Year 2.

Under both the percentage-of-completion method and the completed-contract method of accounting, City Contractors would prepare the following journal entry on December 31, Year 1, to record the $40,000 estimated loss [($400,000 + $640,000) − $1,000,000 = $40,000] on the contract:

Journal entry to record estimated loss on contract

Provision for Loss on Uncompleted Contract	40,000	
Estimated Loss on Uncompleted Contracts		40,000
To provide for estimated loss on building contract.		

The income statement for Year 1 under the percentage-of-completion method would show contract revenue, $400,000 (the amount of the construction costs incurred in Year 1); cost of contract revenue, $440,000 ($400,000 construction costs incurred plus $40,000 provision for loss = $440,000); and a gross loss of $40,000 ($400,000 − $440,000 = $40,000). Only the $40,000 gross loss would appear in the income statement for Year 1 under the completed-contract method. An additional gross loss of $10,000 ($650,000 − $640,000 = $10,000) would appear in the income statement for Year 2 under both the percentage-of-completion method and the completed-contract method.

For the balance sheet for City Contractors on December 31, Year 1, the $400,000 balance of the Cost of Contracts in Progress ledger account would be reduced by the $40,000 balance of the Estimated Loss on Uncompleted Contracts account and the $300,000 balance of the Progress Billings account; the net amount of $60,000 ($400,000 − $40,000 − $300,000 = $60,000) would appear as "costs in excess of billings on uncompleted contracts," under both the percentage-of-completion method and the completed-contract method of accounting.

Evaluation of Accounting for Construction-Type Contracts

Generally accepted accounting principles appropriately limit severely the situations in which the completed-contract method of accounting may be used for construction-type contracts. The percentage-of-completion method is consistent with the accrual basis of accounting because it apportions total revenue under a construction-type contract to the accounting periods in which the construction activity took place. Although the percentage-of-completion method theoretically abandons the revenue realization principle, the abandonment is more conceptual than real. The customer under the construction contract realizes benefits throughout the course of construction; thus, for the contractor, the earning process may be considered to occur throughout the construction period, rather than solely when the project is substantially completed. In contrast, the purchaser of goods realizes no benefits from the goods before they are received; thus, recognition of revenue for sales of merchandise is appropriate when the goods are delivered. The only merit for the completed-contract method of accounting for a construction-type contract that extends over several accounting periods is the postponement of revenue recognition under conditions of substantial uncertainty, as described on page 472.

Disclosures Regarding Construction-Type Contracts

Contractors should disclose the method of recognizing gross profit on construction-type contracts in the "Summary of Significant Accounting Policies" note to the financial statements.[13] In addition, the Securities and Exchange Commission requires extensive disclosures regarding construction-type contracts extending over a period longer than 12 months. The SEC stated that such disclosure is necessary because long-term contracts involve inventories and receivables with *unique risk and liquidity characteristics.* The disclosures required include the amount of inventoried costs, the nature of cost elements included in inventories, the amount of progress billings netted against inventories, and the principal assumptions used to determine total contract costs.[14]

REVIEW QUESTIONS

1   For what purposes may the *retail method* of inventory estimation be used?

2   Differentiate among (**a**) *markup* and *additional markup,* (**b**) *markup cancellation* and *markdown,* and (**c**) *markdown cancellation* and *additional markup.*

3   Describe the computation of the cost percentage when inventories are valued at estimated average cost by the retail method.

4   Describe the computation of the cost percentage when inventories are valued at the estimated lower of average cost or market by the retail method.

5   What is the basic assumption as to the composition of the ending inventories when the retail method is applied on the basis of average cost or on the basis of the lower of average cost or market?

6   Describe the application of the retail method when cost is estimated on a last-in, first-out basis.

7   Describe the procedure required to estimate inventories on the *retail lifo* basis after retail prices have increased.

8   List three uses that may be made of the *gross profit method* of estimating inventories.

9   (**a**) Differentiate between gross profit as a percentage of net sales and as a percentage of cost. (**b**) Convert the following gross profit percentages based on net sales to gross profit percentages based on cost: 16⅔%, 25%, and 50%. (**c**) Convert

---

[13]*APB Opinion No. 22,* "Disclosure of Accounting Policies," AICPA (New York: 1972), p. 436.
[14]*Regulation S-X,* Rule 5-02-6(d), Securities and Exchange Commission (Washington: 1984).

the following gross profit percentages based on cost to gross profit percentages based on net sales: 25%, 50%, and 150%.

10   Explain the possible limitations of the use of an average-cost percentage for prior years to estimate the cost of inventories by the gross profit method.

11   Under what conditions may inventories be valued at net selling prices? Explain.

12   Why are short-term prepayments included in the current assets section of the balance sheet?

13   What are three features of construction-type contracts?

14   Differentiate between *fixed-price* and *unit-price* construction-type contracts.

15   There are two methods of accounting for operations involving construction-type contracts. What are the two methods? What criteria are used in choosing between the methods? How do you justify a departure from the accepted practice of recognizing revenue only at the time of sale?

16   When a business enterprise adopts the percentage-of-completion method of accounting for construction-type contracts, there are several generally used methods of estimating the portion completed. What are three of these methods?

17   Under the percentage-of-completion method of accounting for construction-type contracts, anticipated profits are recorded only as the construction progresses, but anticipated losses are recorded in full as soon as they are ascertained. Why does this inconsistency exist?

EXERCISES

Ex. 9-1   Select the best answer for each of the following multiple-choice questions:

1   Under the retail method of estimating the cost of inventories, which of the following is included in the computation of goods available for sale at both cost and retail?
a Freight-in
b Purchases returns
c Net markups
d Net markdowns
e None of the foregoing

2   When a construction-type contract is expected to result in a loss, the loss is recorded as soon as it is determinable under:
a The completed-contract method only
b The percentage-of-completion method only
c Both the completed-contract method and the percentage-of-completion method
d Neither the completed-contract method nor the percentage-of-completion method

3   The completed-contract method of accounting for construction-type contracts is preferable when:

a A contractor is involved in numerous construction projects

b The contracts are of a relatively long duration

c Estimates of costs to complete and extent of progress toward completion are reasonably dependable

d Lack of dependable estimates or inherent hazards cause forecasts to be doubtful

4   Included in the computation of the cost percentage for the conventional retail method of estimating cost of inventories are:

a Markups but not freight-in

b Net markdowns but not net markups

c Shrinkage but not purchases returns and allowances

d Net markups but not net markdowns

5   The gross profit method for estimating the cost of ending inventories is used for all the following except:

a Determination of end-of-year inventories under the periodic inventory system

b Control and verification of inventory cost

c Estimation of interim inventory valuations between physical counts

d Estimation of inventory valuation when necessary information normally used is lost or unavailable

6   The Progress Billings ledger account used in accounting for construction-type contracts is a/an:

a Asset account

b Liability account

c Revenue account

d Contra-asset account

e Contra-liability account

7   The gross profit percentage for Rice Company has been 20% of cost for the past several years. Rice had net sales of $600,000 for the year ended February 28, Year 12. The estimated cost of goods sold of Rice for the year ended February 28, Year 12, is:

a $100,000   b $120,000   c $480,000   d $500,000   e Some other amount

8   Contractors, Inc., uses the percentage-of-completion, cost-to-cost method of accounting for its construction-type contracts. On January 2, Year 1, Contractors began work on a $6,000,000 contract, which was completed in Year 2. The accounting records included the following data for the contract:

	Year 1	Year 2
Construction costs incurred	$1,800,000	$3,600,000
Estimated cost to complete...........................	3,600,000	
Progress and other billings to customer	2,200,000	3,800,000
Collections from customer on billings	1,400,000	4,600,000

The gross profit on the contract for Year 1 is:

a $200,000   b $220,000   c $300,000   d $400,000   e Some other amount

Ex. 9-2   Colby Company estimates its ending inventories by the lower-of-average-cost-or-market retail method. For the month ended August 31, Year 6, the following amounts were available:

Beginning inventories, at cost	$ 15,000
Beginning inventories, at retail	20,000
Net markdowns	3,000
Net markups	24,000
Net purchases, at cost	75,000
Net purchases, at retail	100,000
Net sales	85,000

Compute Colby Company's estimated inventories (under the lower-of-average-cost-or-market retail method) on August 31, Year 6.

Ex. 9-3 The following data were taken from the records of Dolby Department Store for the year ended January 31, Year 8:

	Cost	Retail
Inventories, Feb. 1, Year 7	$180,000	$260,000
Net markdowns		80,000
Net markups		20,000
Net purchases	660,000	920,000
Net sales		960,000

Dolby estimates normal shrinkage at 2% of the retail value of goods available for sale.

Compute the estimated inventories of Dolby Department Store on January 31, Year 8, under the lower-of-average-cost-or-market retail method.

Ex. 9-4 The following information was taken from the accounting and other records of Willoughby Company for the year ended May 31, Year 5:

	Cost	Retail
Beginning inventories	$25,000	$ 46,200
Purchases (net)	120,000	191,800
Net markups		12,000
Sales (net)		178,000
Net markdowns		3,800

You are to assume that all net markups and net markdowns apply to purchases of the year ended May 31, Year 5, and that it is appropriate to treat the entire inventories as a single department, with no markdowns having occurred during the year ended May 31, Year 4.

Compute the estimated ending inventories at last-in, first-out cost by the retail method.

Ex. 9-5 During the year ended December 31, Year 7, the index of selling prices for merchandise sold by Berg Company increased from 90 to 108.

From the information that follows, compute Berg Company's estimated ending inventories at last-in, first-out cost, taking into account the increase in selling prices.

	Cost	Selling price	Cost percentage
Beginning inventories (date lifo was adopted)	$ 40,000	$ 50,000	80%
Purchases	150,000	200,000	75%
Goods available for sale	$190,000	$250,000	
Less: Net sales		180,000	
Ending inventories		$ 70,000	

Ex. 9-6 The following data are available for the month of May, Year 3, for Sharon's Store:

	Cost	Retail
Inventories, May 1, Year 3	$107,600	$160,000
Purchases	346,400	447,200
Purchases returns	6,000	7,200
Sales (net of returns and allowances)		489,000
Markdowns		42,000
Additional markups		58,000
Markdown cancellations		26,000
Markup cancellations		18,000

Compute the estimated inventories of Sharon's Store on May 31, Year 3, at the lower of average cost or market by the retail method.

Ex. 9-7 The following information is available for Chester Company for the three months ended March 31, Year 6:

Inventories, Jan. 1, Year 6	$ 900,000
Net purchases	3,000,000
Freight-in	200,000
Net sales	4,800,000

Chester's gross profit margin has averaged 33⅓% of cost of goods sold for the past several years.

Compute Chester Company's estimated inventories on March 31, Year 6, under the gross profit method.

Ex. 9-8 Higbie Company's gross profit margin on sales has averaged 30% for many years. Higbie suspects that employees may have been stealing goods from its inventories during Year 4. Physical inventories under the periodic inventory system were $550,000 on January 1, Year 4, and $600,000 on December 31, Year 4. Net sales and net purchases for Year 4 were $3,000,000 and $2,250,000, respectively.

Compute the estimated cost of goods stolen by Higbie Company's employees during Year 4.

Ex. 9-9 Seeley Company uses the gross profit method to estimate monthly inventories. In recent months gross profit has averaged 35% of net sales. The following data are available for the month of January, Year 9:

Inventories, Jan. 1, Year 9	$ 26,580
Purchases	120,000
Purchases returns	5,000
Freight-in	6,000
Gross sales	169,000
Sales returns and allowances	10,000

Compute the estimated cost of Seeley Company's inventories on January 31, Year 9, by the gross profit method.

Ex. 9-10   You took a physical inventory for your single proprietorship at the close of business on July 20, Year 2. The inventory totaled $20,500. Your fiscal year ends on June 30; therefore, you must estimate an inventory amount on June 30, Year 2. You find that during the period July 1 through July 20 sales were $70,500; sales returns, $1,800; gross purchases, $65,000; purchases returns, $1,200; freight-in, $600.

Compute the estimated cost of the inventory on June 30, Year 2, assuming that goods are sold at prices 20% above cost.

Ex. 9-11   On July 10, Year 10, a fire destroyed the goods in process inventory of Tallman Company. Inventories of material and finished goods were not damaged. Physical inventories taken after the fire were as follows:

Material	$ 65,000
Finished goods	120,000
Total	$185,000

Inventories on January 1, Year 10, were as shown below:

Material	$ 45,000
Goods in process	80,000
Finished goods	150,000
Total	$275,000

The accounting records disclosed the following for January 1 through July 10, Year 10:

Sales (net)	$380,000
Purchases of material (net)	117,500
Direct labor costs	92,000
Factory overhead costs	58,200

The gross profit in recent years has averaged 25% of cost of finished goods sold.

Compute the estimated cost of the goods in process inventory of Tallman Company destroyed by the fire.

Ex. 9-12   Haywood Construction Company records gross profit under the percentage-of-completion method for its construction-type contracts. During Year 8, Haywood entered into a fixed-price contract to construct a bridge for $15,000,000. Construction costs incurred and estimated cost to complete the bridge were as follows:

	Cumulative construction costs incurred to date	Estimated cost to complete
Dec. 31, Year 8	$ 1,000,000	$8,000,000
Dec. 31, Year 9	5,500,000	5,500,000
Dec. 31, Year 10	10,000,000	2,000,000

Compute the amount of gross profit that Haywood Construction Company should recognize on the bridge contract under the percentage-of-completion, cost-to-cost method of accounting for the year ended December 31, Year 10.

Ex. 9-13   On April 1, Year 10, Lary Construction Company entered into a fixed-price contract to construct an apartment building for $6,000,000. Lary accounted for this contract under the percentage-of-completion, cost-to-cost method. Information relating to the contract is as follows:

	Dec. 31, Year 10	Dec. 31, Year 11
Percentage of completion	20%	60%
Estimated total cost when completed	$4,500,000	$4,800,000
Cumulative gross profit recognized	$ 300,000	$ 720,000

Compute the amount of construction costs incurred by Lary Construction Company during the year ended December 31, Year 11.

Ex. 9-14   In Year 1, Dodd Construction Company contracted to construct a building for $800,000. The building was completed in Year 2. Dodd uses the percentage-of-completion, cost-to-cost method of accounting for construction-type contracts. Data relating to this contract are summarized below:

	Year 1	Year 2
Construction costs incurred	$180,000	$442,800
Estimated cost to complete the building	420,000	–0–
Progress and other billings to customer	200,000	600,000
Collections from customer on billings	160,000	590,000

Prepare journal entries for Dodd Construction Company for Year 1 and Year 2 relating to this contract. Journal entries to close nominal accounts are not required.

Ex. 9-15   In Year 1, Garcia Corporation began work under a construction-type contract. The fixed price was $800,000, and the construction was expected to be completed in three years. Garcia uses the percentage-of-completion, cost-to-cost method of accounting. The revenue to be recognized each year is based on the proportion of construction costs incurred to total estimated costs to complete the contract. The information relating to this contract in the financial statements for the year ended December 31, Year 1, follows:

Balance sheet:

Contract receivables		$20,000
Costs incurred and estimated earnings on uncompleted contract	$200,000	
Less: Billings to date	188,000	

(continued)

Costs and estimated earnings in excess of billings on uncompleted contract	*12,000*
Income statement:	
Gross profit	*$20,000*

a Compute the amount of cash collected by Garcia Corporation on this contract in Year 1.

b Compute the total estimated gross profit of Garcia Corporation on this contract.

Ex. 9-16 Rey Construction Company began operations in Year 3. By December 31, Year 3, the first construction project was finished and a second project was partially completed. Information as of December 31, Year 3, follows:

	Project No. 1	*Project No. 2*
Construction costs incurred	*$ 80,000*	*$105,000*
Percentage of completion	*100%*	*70%*
Fixed price	*$100,000*	*$200,000*
Progress and other billings to customers	*$100,000*	*$115,000*
Collections from customers on billings	*$ 92,000*	*$ 75,000*

a Prepare journal entries for Rey Construction Company for Year 3 (excluding closing entries) to record the transactions relating to the two projects, assuming that the percentage-of-completion, cost-to-cost method of accounting for construction-type contracts is used.

b Prepare a partial balance sheet for Rey Construction Company on December 31, Year 3, under the percentage-of-completion method of accounting.

Ex. 9-17 Carson Contractors, Inc., entered into a $600,000 fixed-price construction-type contract on January 2, Year 6. Because Carson's estimates of measures of completion were subject to inherent hazards, Carson adopted the completed-contract method of accounting. Data regarding the contract for Year 6 are shown below:

Construction costs incurred	*$280,000*
Estimated cost to complete construction.............................	*410,000*
Progress billings to customer..	*250,000*
Collections from customer on billings	*220,000*

Prepare journal entries for Carson Contractors, Inc., for Year 6 for the contract. Journal entries to close nominal ledger accounts are not required.

Ex. 9-18 Krone Construction Company adopted the percentage-of-completion, cost-to-cost method of accounting for its $2,800,000 fixed-price construction-type contract with Biggers, Inc., dated April 1, Year 3. The following data relate to the contract for the year ended December 31, Year 3:

Construction costs incurred	*$1,152,000*
Estimated cost to complete construction.............................	*1,728,000*
Progress billings to customer.......................................	*1,080,000*
Collections from customer on billings...............................	*900,000*

Prepare all journal entries for Krone Construction Company, except entries to close nominal ledger accounts, for the contract for Year 3.

CASES

Case 9-1   Dru Department Store uses the conventional retail method as a means of controlling the investment in inventories at its branch stores. Dru's main accounting office summarizes the recorded activity at each branch and estimates the ending inventories monthly. The estimate is then compared with a normal inventory investment based on expected volume. Normal shrinkage is estimated at 1% of the retail value of goods available for sale. Store managers are required to explain deviations of 5% or more from the expected normal inventory. The following data have been accumulated for the South Branch on April 30, Year 5:

	Cost	*Retail*
Net sales		$630,000
Beginning inventories	$150,000	222,000
Net purchases	560,000	823,000
Net markups		20,000
Net markdowns		9,000

Instructions

a The normal inventories of the South Branch total $220,000 at lower of cost or market. Compute the estimated amount of the ending inventories at retail and at lower of average cost or market and indicate the nature of the explanation to be made by the South Branch store manager.

b What effect, if any, would the following factors have on the effectiveness of the retail method as a control device?

(1) A widely fluctuating shrinkage factor

(2) A shift in the volume of goods handled at various markups

(3) Additional markups related to goods sold by the end of the accounting period

(4) Markdowns incorrectly treated as markup cancellations

(5) Additional markups included with markdown cancellations

Case 9-2   Broadmoor Company has used the gross profit method for estimating the investment in inventories and as a test of the physical inventory at the end of each year. Broadmoor has two lines of merchandise that have produced gross profit margins of 25% and 35%, respectively, on selling price over the past several years. The gross profit margin for Broadmoor's total sales has averaged 30% of sales.

The operation data for the year ended January 31, Year 7, were as follows:

	Economy line	*Quality line*	*Total*
Sales	$100,000	$200,000	$300,000
Beginning inventories	10,000	25,000	35,000
Purchases	90,000	130,000	220,000
Gross profit margins on selling price	25%	35%	30%

A physical inventory of the merchandise on January 31, Year 7, totaled $50,000, but the manager's estimate by the gross profit method indicated ending inventories should be $45,000. The manager of Broadmoor is of the opinion that the discrepancy is too large to accept without explanation. A test sample selected revealed that the gross profit margins on the two lines were unchanged at 25 and 35%.

Instructions

a Show how the manager of Broadmoor Company computed the January 31, Year 7, inventories by the gross profit method.

b Compute the January 31, Year 7, inventories of Broadmoor Company by the gross profit method in the manner in which it should be used in this situation.

c Explain to the manager of Broadmoor Company why the difference exists between the physical inventory and the estimate of the value of inventories on January 31, Year 7, under the gross profit method.

Case 9-3 Lalo Construction Company had three construction-type contracts in progress on December 31, Year 1, the data for which are presented below:

Contract	Fixed price	Estimated total costs	Construction costs incurred to date (all in Year 1)	Progress billings to date	Collections from customers to date
X	$ 750,000	$ 600,000	$400,000	$450,000	$415,000
Y	1,000,000	1,050,000	525,000	400,000	380,000
Z	900,000	675,000	202,500	225,000	202,500

Instructions

a Prepare partial income statements and balance sheets for Lalo Construction Company for Year 1 reporting the details of the foregoing contracts under (1) the completed-contract method, and (2) the percentage-of-completion, cost-to-cost method. Use adjacent columns for (1) and (2). Show total revenue and applicable costs in the partial income statements, and show supporting computations.

b What are the differences between the two sets of financial statements?

c Which set of financial statements do you think presents the more meaningful data about the construction-type contracts of Lalo Construction Company? Explain.

Case 9-4 The two methods of accounting for construction-type contracts are the percentage-of-completion method and the completed-contract method.

Instructions

a Discuss how realized contract revenue and gross profits on construction-type contracts are computed and recorded under these two methods.

b Under what circumstances is it preferable to use one method instead of the other?

c Why is realized contract revenue as measured by progress billings not generally accepted for construction-type contracts?

d How are construction costs and progress billings reported in the balance sheet under the percentage-of-completion method and under the completed-contract method?

PROBLEMS

9-1   Con-Tract Company has a construction-type contract with Customer Company with a fixed price of $1,200,000, which it entered into on April 1, Year 4, the beginning of a fiscal year. Data with respect to the contract for the three years ended March 31, Year 7, were as follows:

| | Year ended March 31, | | |
	Year 5	Year 6	Year 7
Construction costs incurred	$200,000	$250,000	$400,000
Estimated cost to complete construction			
at end of year............................	600,000	350,000	–0–
Progress and other billings to Customer			
Company	300,000	400,000	500,000
Collections from Customer Company on			
billings	270,000	360,000	450,000
Operating expenses incurred	50,000	60,000	70,000

Instructions

Prepare journal entries for Con-Tract Company's operations during the three years ended March 31, Year 7, under the percentage-of-completion, cost-to-cost method of accounting for the construction-type contract. Round all amounts to the nearest dollar. Use the following format for your working paper:

| | Year ended March 31, | | | | | |
| | Year 5 | | Year 6 | | Year 7 | |
Accounts and Explanation	Debit	Credit	Debit	Credit	Debit	Credit

9-2   The controller of Retail Sellers, Inc., estimated that normal inventory shrinkage of Retail ranged between 1% and 1.5% of the retail value of goods available for sale. To test that estimate, the controller authorized the taking of a physical inventory on July 31, Year 7, midway through the fiscal year ending January 31, Year 8. The July 31, Year 7, physical inventory totaled $301,800 at retail prices. Data for the conventional retail inventory method for the six months ended July 31, Year 7, follow:

	Cost	Retail
Beginning inventories	$ 247,400	$ 288,400
Net markdowns		40,600
Net markups		120,400
Net purchases	2,674,200	2,911,200
Net sales		2,931,100

Instructions

a Compute the estimated inventories of Retail Sellers, Inc., on July 31, Year 7, and compare it with the physical inventory at retail on that date to determine whether normal inventory shrinkage falls within the range estimated by the controller.

b Compute the estimated lower of average cost or market of the physical inventory of Retail Sellers, Inc., on July 31, Year 7.

9-3 Ward Construction Company began operations on March 1, Year 2. During Year 2, Ward entered into a contract with Stevens Corporation to construct a building. At that time, Ward estimated that it would take four years to complete the building at a total cost of $4,800,000. The fixed price for the construction of the building was $6,200,000. During Year 2, Ward incurred $1,250,000 of construction costs related to this project, and Stevens was billed and paid 30% of the contract price. The remaining costs to complete the contract were estimated at $3,750,000 on December 31, Year 2.

Instructions

Prepare working papers for Ward Construction Company to compute (1) the amount of gross profit realized on the construction-type contract for the year ended December 31, Year 2, and (2) the amount to be shown as "costs and estimated earnings in excess of billings on uncompleted contract" or "billings in excess of costs and estimated earnings on uncompleted contract" on December 31, Year 2, under each of the following accounting methods:
a Percentage-of-completion, cost-to-cost method
b Completed-contract method

9-4 This problem consists of two unrelated parts.
a Logan Company uses the retail method to estimate its inventories. Information relating to the computation of inventories on December 31, Year 1, is as follows:

	Cost	Retail
Inventories, Jan. 1, Year 1	$ 55,000	$ 90,000
Net sales		620,000
Net purchases	355,000	580,000
Freight-in	7,600	
Additional markups		60,000
Markup cancellations		10,000
Markdowns		25,000
Markdown cancellations		5,000

Estimated normal shrinkage is 3% of the retail value of goods available for sale.

Instructions

Compute the estimated cost of Logan Company's inventories on December 31, Year 1, at the lower of average cost or market. Use the retail method and show supporting computations.

b On June 28, Year 1, a fire at Watt Company's warehouse caused severe damage to its inventories. Watt estimated that the cost of the undamaged inventories after the fire was $30,000, and that its gross profit rate was 30% of net sales. The following information was available from the accounting records:

Inventories, June 1, Year 1	*$250,000*
Net purchases from June 1 to June 28, Year 1	*350,000*
Net sales from June 1 to June 28, Year 1	*550,000*

Instructions

Compute the estimated cost of Watt Company's inventories lost in the fire. Use the gross profit method and show supporting computations.

9-5 Information relating to the operations of the sportswear department of Amy's Fashion Shop for the year ended December 31, Year 10, is presented below:

	Cost	*Retail*
Beginning inventories	*$ 49,600*	*$ 83,600*
Purchases	*257,800*	*406,900*
Freight-in	*10,400*	
Purchases returns	*4,200*	*7,000*
Additional markups		*15,000*
Markup cancellations		*8,500*
Markdowns		*8,000*
Markdown cancellations		*1,600*
Sales		*396,500*
Sales returns		*6,700*

Normal shrinkage is estimated at 1% of the retail value of goods available for sale.

Instructions

a Compute the December 31, Year 10, inventories of Amy's Fashion Shop at the lower of average cost or market by the retail method.

b Compute the December 31, Year 10, inventories of Amy's Fashion Shop by the retail lifo method.

9-6 San Remo Company uses the retail method to estimate ending inventories for its monthly financial statements. The following data pertain to a single department for the month of May, Year 8:

Inventories, May 1:	
At cost	*$ 19,000*
At retail	*30,000*
Purchases (exclusive of freight-in and returns):	
At cost	*83,558*
At retail	*146,495*
Freight-in	*5,100*
Purchases returns:	
At cost	*2,100*
At retail	*2,800*
Additional markups	*2,500*
Markup cancellations	*265*
Net markdowns	*800*
Sales (net of sales returns)	*138,200*

Normal shrinkage is 1½% of the retail value of goods available for sale.

Instructions

a Using the conventional retail method, prepare a working paper to compute San Remo Company's estimated inventories at lower of average cost or market on May 31, Year 8. Round all amounts to nearest dollar.

b Assume that San Remo Company used the conventional retail inventory method to estimate the cost of its May 31, Year 8, inventories at $30,600, and that a physical inventory revealed only $26,000 of inventories at lower of cost or market. Identify factors that may have caused the difference between the computed inventories and the physical inventory.

9-7 This problem consists of two unrelated parts, one for Archer Company and one for Bowman Company.

Archer Company uses the retail lifo method. Information relating to the computation of Archer's inventories on December 31, Year 5, follows:

	Cost	Retail
Inventories, Jan. 1, Year 5	$ 30,200	$ 45,000
Purchases	120,000	171,000
Freight-in	22,000	
Net sales		190,000
Net markups		40,000
Net markdowns		11,000

Bowman Company prepares quarterly financial statements and estimates inventories at the end of each quarter by the gross profit method, because the relationship of selling prices and costs remains relatively stable during each year. The inventories on December 31 are determined by a physical count. The data below for the first three quarters of the year ending December 31, Year 5, were taken from Bowman's accounting records:

	Mar. 31	June 30	Sept. 30
Sales	$993,600	$963,000	$808,500
Sales returns	13,000	20,000	8,000
Sales discounts	600	3,000	500
Purchases	745,000	735,000	665,000
Freight-in	9,500	9,100	8,210
Purchases returns and allowances	500	2,400	4,630
Operating expenses	102,000	103,000	94,400

The physical inventories for Bowman Company on December 31, Year 4, totaled $105,000.

Instructions

a Assuming that there was no change in the price index during the year, compute the estimated cost of the inventories on December 31, Year 5, for Archer Company by the retail lifo method.

b Assuming that the gross profit rate for the prior fiscal year was 20% of net sales and that this rate is expected to prevail throughout Year 5, prepare quarterly income statements for Bowman Company for the first three quarters of Year 5. Income taxes expense is estimated at 45% of pre-tax income.

9-8   This problem consists of two parts.

a The June 30, Year 3, physical inventories of Dalbert Company, which uses the periodic inventory system, totaled $623,300 at first-in, first-out cost, which was lower than market. The controller of Dalbert, believing that the physical inventories might be understated, decided to use the gross profit method, because Dalbert's gross profit percentage had been constant at 33⅓% of cost of goods sold for several years. Data for the gross profit method for June 30, Year 3, follow:

Beginning inventories, at fifo cost	$ 482,400
Net purchases	6,822,000
Net sales	8,794,400

Instructions

Using the gross profit method, estimate the June 30, Year 3, inventories of Dalbert Company at fifo cost, and compute the difference between the estimate and the physical inventories amount of $623,300.

b In reviewing the records of purchases, sales, and consignments for the year ended June 30, Year 3, Dalbert Company's controller found the following items:
   (1) Goods costing $23,800, shipped FOB shipping point by the supplier on June 28, Year 3, had been recorded in the Purchases ledger account on June 30, Year 3, but had not been included in the physical inventories on that date because the goods were not received until July 2, Year 3.
   (2) Goods billed to a customer at $20,000 on June 30, Year 3, and physically segregated in the shipping department for the customer's later pickup had been included erroneously in the June 30, Year 3, physical inventories at cost.
   (3) Goods with a selling price of $102,000, on consignment from Dalbert to Consignee Company, had not been included in Dalbert's June 30, Year 3, physical inventories.

Instructions

Correct Dalbert Company's June 30, Year 3, physical inventories total of $623,300 for any effects of the foregoing items, and compute any remaining difference between Dalbert's corrected June 30, Year 3, physical inventories and the estimated inventories computed in **a**.

9-9   This problem consists of two unrelated parts.

a On July 1, Year 7, Crewe Construction Company entered into a $4,000,000 fixed-price contract with Farley Company, which was expected to be profitable, to construct an office building over a two-to-three-year period. Because of inherent hazards in estimates of input or output measures, Crewe adopted the completed-contract method of accounting for the project. Information with respect to the contract for Years 7 through 9, follows:

	Year ended Dec. 31,		
	Year 7	Year 8	Year 9
Construction costs incurred	$ 350,000	$2,150,000	$1,750,000
Estimated costs to complete...........	3,150,000	1,700,000	
Progress and other billings to customer	720,000	1,440,000	1,840,000

Instructions

Compute the amounts to be shown in Crewe Construction Company's balance sheets on December 31, Years 7 through 9, as "costs in excess of billings on uncompleted contract" or "billings in excess of costs on uncompleted contract." Show supporting computations of gross profit or loss to be recognized on the contract by Crewe Construction Company for the years ended December 31, Years 7 through 9.

b On April 1, Year 9, Builder Company entered into a $2,400,000 fixed-fee contract to construct a building for Dalton Company. Builder estimated a two-year construction period at an estimated total cost of $2,000,000. For the year ended December 31, Year 9, Builder incurred construction costs of $700,000 under the contract, and billed Dalton a total of $500,000. Estimated costs on December 31, Year 9, to complete the building totaled $1,400,000. Builder adopted the percentage-of-completion, cost-to-cost method of accounting for the contract.

Instructions

Prepare a journal entry on December 31, Year 9, for Builder Company to recognize contract revenue and cost of contract revenue for the construction-type contract.

9-10 Adam Corporation is a small manufacturing company. On March 31, Year 6, a fire completely destroyed the inventory of goods in process. The material and finished goods inventories were not damaged. After the fire a physical inventory was taken. The material was valued at $37,500 and the finished goods at $62,000, at first-in, first-out cost.

The inventories on January 1, Year 6, consisted of:

Material	$ 15,500
Goods in process	60,500
Finished goods	85,000
Total	$161,000

A review of the accounting records disclosed that the sales and gross profit on sales for the last three years were:

	Sales	Gross profit on sales
Year 3	$400,000	$120,000
Year 4	380,000	110,500
Year 5	250,000	88,800

The sales for the first three months of Year 6 were $150,000. Material purchases were $62,500, freight-in on purchases was $5,000, and direct labor cost for the three months was $50,000. For the past two years factory overhead cost has been applied at 75% of direct labor cost.

Instructions

Compute the estimated cost of Adam Corporation's inventory of goods in process destroyed by the fire on March 31, Year 6, using the weighted-average gross profit for the last three years.

9-11   This problem consists of three unrelated parts.

a Arn Company lost all its inventories by fire on January 1, Year 10. A physical inventory had not been taken on December 31, Year 9. The following data are available for the three preceding years:

	Year 7	Year 8	Year 9
Inventories, Jan. 1	$161,600	$168,000	$170,160
Sales	724,000	788,000	812,000
Sales returns...........................	12,000	8,000	12,000
Purchases	644,000	656,000	720,000
Purchases returns	36,000	32,000	40,000
Operating expenses	198,000	221,000	240,000
Accounts receivable, Dec. 31	55,000	50,000	60,000
Accounts payable, Dec. 31...............	28,000	35,000	40,000

Instructions

Assuming that the gross profit percentage for Year 9 was estimated to be the same as the weighted-average gross profit percentage for the two previous years, compute the estimated cost of Arn Company's inventories destroyed by fire on January 1, Year 10.

b Burr Company uses the retail method to estimate its inventories. The following information was available for Burr Company for Year 10:

	Cost	Retail
Beginning inventories	$ 40,500	$ 65,000
Purchases (net of returns)	290,000	405,000
Freight-in	2,000	
Net markups		5,000
Net markdowns		9,000
Employee discounts		2,000
Net sales		410,000

Instructions

Compute Burr Company's estimated inventories by the retail method on December 31, Year 10, on the basis of lower of average cost or market.

c Corb Company entered into a construction-type contract early in Year 10. The fixed price was $800,000, and Corb expected to earn a gross profit of $180,000 on the contract. The following information was available through the end of Year 12:

Year ended Dec. 31,	Cumulative construction costs incurred to date	Estimated costs to complete construction
Year 10	$ 49,600	$570,400
Year 11	172,800	467,200
Year 12	504,000	126,000

Instructions

Compute the gross profit to be recognized by Corb Company in each year (Years 10 through 12) under the percentage-of-completion, cost-to-cost method for the construction-type contract.

9-12 On January 1, Year 2, Moy Company adopted the retail method of accounting for its inventories. When you undertook the preparation of Moy's interim report of earnings for the six months ended June 30, Year 2, the data below were available:

	Cost	Retail
Inventories, Jan. 1, Year 2	$ 76,200	$120,000
Markdowns		31,500
Additional markups		58,500
Markdown cancellations		19,500
Markup cancellations		13,500
Purchases	265,860	335,400
Sales		366,000
Purchases returns and allowances	4,500	5,400
Sales returns and allowances		20,000

Instructions

a Prepare a working paper to compute Moy Company's estimated June 30, Year 2, inventories under the retail method of accounting. The inventories are to be valued at last-in, first-out cost. Assume that net markups and markdowns apply only to purchases.

b Without prejudice to your solution to part **a,** assume that you computed the June 30, Year 2, inventories to be $132,300 at retail and the cost percentage to be 80%. The general price level had increased from 100 on January 1 to 105 on June 30, Year 2. Prepare a working paper to compute Moy Company's estimated June 30, Year 2, inventories at the June 30 price level, using the dollar-value retail lifo method. Round amounts to nearest dollar and percentage.

9-13 On April 15, Year 5, a fire damaged the office and warehouse of Weeden Company. The only accounting record saved was the general ledger, from which the following trial balance was prepared:

WEEDEN COMPANY
Trial Balance
March 31, Year 5

	Debit	Credit
Cash	$ 23,800	
Accounts receivable	27,000	
Inventories, Dec. 31, Year 4	36,000	
Land	24,000	
Building and equipment................................	120,000	
Accumulated depreciation of building and equipment		$ 46,000
Other assets	3,600	
Accounts payable		23,700
Accrued liabilities		7,200
Common stock, $2.50 par		100,000
Retained earnings		47,700
Sales		135,400
Purchases	103,000	
Operating expenses	22,600	
Totals	$360,000	$360,000

Additional Information

(1) Weeden's fiscal year ends on December 31.

(2) An examination of the April, Year 5, bank statement and paid checks disclosed that checks written during the period April 1 to 15 totaled $11,600: $5,700 paid on accounts payable as of March 31, $2,000 for April purchases, and $3,900 for operating expenses. Deposits during the same period amounted to $10,650, all of which consisted of receipts on account from customers, with the exception of a $450 refund from a vendor for goods returned in April.

(3) Correspondence with suppliers disclosed unrecorded purchases on April 15, Year 5, of $3,500, including $1,300 for shipments in transit on April 15.

(4) Customers acknowledged indebtedness of $26,400 as of April 15, Year 5. It also was estimated that customers owed another $5,000 that will never be acknowledged or recovered. Of the acknowledged indebtedness, $700 probably will be uncollectible. All sales were on credit.

(5) Assume that the weighted-average gross profit percentage for the past two years was in effect during Year 5. Weeden's financial statements included the following:

	Year ended Dec. 31,	
	Year 3	Year 4
Net sales	$300,000	$400,000
Net purchases	174,000	226,000
Beginning inventories	35,000	45,000
Ending inventories	45,000	36,000

(6) Goods with an estimated cost of $8,250 were salvaged and sold for $4,800. The remainder of the inventories was lost in the fire.

Instructions

Prepare a working paper to compute the amount of Weeden Company's inventory fire loss on April 15, Year 5, including a supporting computation of the cost of goods sold percentage.

9-14 Provo Construction Company constructs water treatment plants for small communities. All its construction-type contracts are accounted for by the percentage-of-completion method, except for two contracts that are accounted for by the completed-contract method because of inherent hazards in estimates of input or output measures.

The following information on construction-type contracts is available for the year ended December 31, Year 5:

Construction-Type Contracts: Percentage-of-Completion Method

Fixed prices of construction-type contracts accounted for by the percentage-of-completion method totaled $6,050,000. Costs incurred on these contracts were $1,500,000 in Year 4 and $3,000,000 in Year 5. On December 31, Year 5, it was estimated that additional costs of $1,000,000 were required to complete these contracts. Revenue of $1,750,000 was recognized in Year 4, and progress billings totaled $4,900,000, of which $4,600,000 had been collected. No construction-type contracts accounted for by the percentage-of-completion method were completed in Year 5.

Construction-Type Contracts: Completed-Contract Method

The two construction-type contracts accounted for by the completed-contract method were started in Year 4. One had a fixed price of $5,000,000. Costs incurred were $1,400,000 in Year 4 and $1,600,000 in Year 5. Progress billings totaled $3,100,000, of which $2,900,000 had been collected. Although it was difficult to estimate the additional costs required to complete this contract, Provo expected the contract to be profitable.

The second contract had a fixed price of $4,000,000. Costs incurred were $1,200,000 in Year 4 and $2,600,000 in Year 5. Progress billings totaled $3,200,000, of which $2,900,000 had been collected. Although it was difficult to estimate the additional costs required to complete this contract, Provo expected a loss of approximately $100,000.

Additional Information

(1) Operating expenses totaled $200,000 for Year 5.
(2) Other revenue amounted to $45,500 for Year 5.

Instructions

Prepare an income statement for Provo Construction Company for the year ended December 31, Year 5, stopping at income (or loss) before income taxes. Show supporting computations. Disregard income tax and deferred tax considerations. Notes to the income statement are not required.

9-15 Dykes Construction began operations on January 5, Year 10. Construction activities for Year 10 are summarized below:

Contract	Fixed price	Construction costs incurred	Estimated cost to complete	Progress and other billings to customers	Collections from customers on billings
P	$ 310,000	$187,500	$ 12,500	$160,000	$155,000
Q	415,000	195,000	248,000	249,000	210,000
R	350,000	320,000	–0–	350,000	300,000
S	300,000	16,500	183,500	20,000	
Totals	$1,375,000	$719,000	$444,000	$779,000	$665,000

The controller of Dykes Construction has asked you to compute the amounts of contract revenue for the year ended December 31, Year 10, to be recognized under the percentage-of-completion method of accounting for construction-type contracts.

Additional Information

(1) All contracts are with different customers.
(2) Any work remaining to be done on the contracts is expected to be completed in Year 11.
(3) Dykes Construction's accounting records have been maintained by the percentage-of-completion, cost-to-cost method.

Instructions

a Prepare a working paper for Dykes Construction to compute the amount of contract revenue, cost of contract revenue, and gross profit or loss realized on each contract for the year ended December 31, Year 10, under the percentage-of-completion, cost-to-cost method. Show supporting computations.

b Prepare a working paper under the percentage-of-completion method to compute the amounts that would appear in Dykes Construction's balance sheet on December 31, Year 10, for:
  (1) Costs and estimated earnings in excess of billings on uncompleted contracts
  (2) Billings in excess of costs and estimated earnings on uncompleted contracts

9-16 Pacific Corporation began operations on October 15, Year 1, with contract X as its only construction-type contract during Year 1. A trial balance on December 31, Year 2, follows:

PACIFIC CORPORATION
Trial Balance
December 31, Year 2

	Debit	Credit
Cash	$ 23,300	
Accounts receivable	136,480	
Cost of contracts in progress	461,120	
Estimated earnings on contracts in progress	8,000	

(continued)

Progress billings		$459,400
Plant assets	135,500	
Accumulated depreciation of plant assets................		13,880
Accounts payable		70,820
Deferred income tax credits		2,400
Common stock, $5 par....................................		235,000
Retained earnings		3,500
Operating expenses	20,600	
Totals	$785,000	$785,000

Additional Information

(1) Pacific determines gross profit on construction-type contracts under the percentage-of-completion, cost-to-cost method for both financial accounting and income taxes.

(2) During Year 2, there were three contracts in progress, the fixed prices of which had been estimated as follows:

	Contract X	Contract Y	Contract Z
Material and labor costs	$169,000	$34,500	$265,700
Indirect costs	30,000	5,500	48,000
Total costs	$199,000	$40,000	$313,700
Add: Gross profit	40,000	3,000	30,300
Total fixed price	$239,000	$43,000	$344,000

(3) Progress billings to customers are credited to the Progress Billings ledger account. Contract revenue is recognized at year-end by offsetting debits to the Cost of Contract Revenue and Estimated Earnings on Contracts in Progress ledger accounts.

(4) All contract costs are debited to the Cost of Contracts in Progress ledger account. Original cost estimates compiled by engineers are considered reliable. Data on costs to December 31, Year 2, are shown below:

		Costs incurred to date		
Contract	Original cost estimates	Total	Material and labor costs	Indirect costs
X	$199,000	$115,420	$ 92,620	$22,800
Y	40,000	32,000	26,950	5,050
Z	313,700	313,700	265,700	48,000
Totals	$552,700	$461,120	$385,270	$75,850

(5) On December 31, Year 1, accumulated costs on contract X were $39,800, or 20% of the total; no costs had been accumulated on contracts Y and Z. All work on contract Z was completed prior to December 31, Year 2, and the full contract price had been billed to the customer.

(6) Pacific is subject to an income tax rate of 45%.

Instructions

a Prepare a working paper for Pacific Corporation to compute the percentage of completion of contracts on December 31, Year 2.

b Prepare a working paper for Pacific Corporation to compute contract revenue, cost of contract revenue, and gross profit to be recognized in Year 2.

c Prepare a working paper for Pacific Corporation to compute estimated income taxes expense for the year ended December 31, Year 2.

d Prepare journal entries for Pacific Corporation on December 31, Year 2, to record (1) contract revenue, cost of contract revenue, and gross profit for Year 2; (2) income taxes for Year 2; and (3) approval of completed contract Z by the customer.

Current Liabilities and Contingencies

10

In Chapter 1, *liabilities* are defined as "probable future sacrifices of economic benefits arising from present obligations of a particular entity to transfer assets or provide services to other entities in the future as a result of past transactions or events."[1] Liabilities are recorded when obligations are incurred, and are measured at the amounts to be paid or at the present value of these amounts. The distinction between current liabilities and long-term liabilities is important in an evaluation of the financial position of a business enterprise and its ability to meet maturing obligations. Some liabilities are definitely determinable, both as to existence and as to amount; other liabilities exist, but their amount is estimated; and certain loss contingencies require the accrual of liabilities. Current liabilities and contingencies are discussed in this chapter.

Distinction between Current Liabilities and Long-Term Liabilities

Traditionally, one year marked the accounting boundary between current and long-term liabilities. When strictly applied this one-year rule may result in a misleading financial picture, particularly when the *operating cycle* of a business enterprise exceeds one year.

The modern viewpoint is that current liabilities are obligations for which payment will require the use of current assets or the creation of other current liabilities in one year or during the next operating cycle, if longer. The definition of current liabilities is closely related to the definition of current assets. Thus, current liabilities include obligations for items that have entered into the operating cycle, such as payables to suppliers and employees, cash advances from customers and accruals for rents, taxes, product warranties, etc. Obligations incurred outside of the operat-

---

[1]See page 19.

ing cycle and not payable in one year are not current liabilities; obligations that will be liquidated by the issuance of shares of capital stock are included in stockholders' equity in the balance sheet.

Current liabilities also include obligations that are or will be payable on demand within one year (or the enterprise's operating cycle, if longer) from the balance sheet date, even though liquidation may not be expected within that period. Similarly, long-term obligations that are or will be callable by creditors because of the debtor's violations of provisions of the debt agreement also are included among current liabilities. However, the reclassification of such obligations from long-term to current is not appropriate if creditors have waived or lost their right to demand payment, or if it is probable that the violations will be cured within a specified grace period.[2]

The amount of current liabilities reported in the balance sheet is of great interest to users of financial statements. Short-term credit is an important source of financing for most business enterprises. Certain current obligations such as trade accounts payable and accrued liabilities regularly arise from business operations; however, other obligations result from decisions by management to obtain cash during periods of expanding or peak business activity. Financial analysts keep a close watch on the amount of current liabilities, the relationship of current assets to current liabilities, and the relationship between cash balances and current liabilities. These relationships are important indicators of financial stability and *solvency*—the ability to pay debts as they mature.

Recognition and Valuation of Current Liabilities

Every business enterprise faces the prospect of a wide variety of future cash outlays in order to continue in operation. For example, an enterprise must purchase material, pay wages, pay for services, replace plant assets, and pay taxes. We might take an extreme view and consider the ***present value*** of all these future cash outflows as the total debt of the enterprise at a specific time. This would correspond to the concept of assets as the present value of all future cash inflows. However, these theoretical extremes are beyond the accountants' power of measurement. As a practical matter, we need a basis for establishing some limits on the liability concept.

A logical starting point is to say that the amounts of all legally enforceable debts should appear as liabilities in the balance sheet. But what about legal obligations that are highly uncertain in amount? Because liabilities must be quantified, the ability to measure them with reasonable accuracy is essential. Then we must consider whether a strict legal test excludes any obligations to convey assets that are significant in an economic sense. The process of measuring net income may require that a valuation be placed on highly uncertain future cash outflows that result from past transactions and events, because the costs incurred must be matched with current revenue.

These two elements, ***measurability*** and ***relation to past transactions and events,*** lead us to conclude that liabilities should be defined to include all future cash outflows that result from past transactions and events and that may be meas-

---

[2]*FASB Statement No. 78,* ''Classification of Obligations That Are Callable by the Creditor,'' FASB (Stamford: 1983), pp. 2–3.

ured with reasonable accuracy. Because we are dealing with *future payments,* the element of uncertainty plays an important role in accounting for current liabilities.

In theory, the measure of any liability at the time it is incurred is the present value of the required future cash outflow.[3] In practice, however, most current liabilities are recorded at face amount. The difference between the present value of a current liability and the amount that will be paid at maturity usually is not material because of the short time period involved.

To emphasize the importance of the degree of uncertainty, the measurement of current liabilities is discussed under the following headings: (1) definitely measurable liabilities, (2) liabilities dependent on operating results, and (3) contingencies.

DEFINITELY MEASURABLE LIABILITIES

Liabilities in this category are the results of contracts or the operation of federal and state statutes such that the amount of an obligation and its due date are known with reasonable certainty. The accounting problems are to ascertain that an obligation exists, to measure it as accurately as possible, and to enter it in the accounting records.

Trade Accounts Payable

The accounting procedures for recording and controlling the payments for the purchase of goods and services generally are designed so that the existence, amount, and due date of such liabilities are readily determinable. Accountants give particular attention to transactions occurring near the end of one accounting period and at the beginning of the next period to see that the recording of purchases of goods and services is consistent with that of the related liability. For example, if goods are purchased and received near the end of a period but an invoice has not arrived, the goods may have been included in inventories, but the recording of the liability may have been overlooked.

Trade accounts payable may be recorded at *face amount* or *net of purchases discounts offered* by suppliers. When trade accounts payable are recorded at face amount, the Purchases Discounts ledger account is credited for discounts taken, and a material amount of discounts available to be taken at the end of an accounting period is accrued by a debit to Allowance for Purchases Discounts (a contra-liability ledger account). The balance of the Purchases Discounts account is deducted from the amount of purchases in the income statement. When trade accounts payable are recorded net of purchases discounts, the Purchases Discounts Lost account is debited for discounts *not taken* and for any estimated discounts that *will not be taken.* In the income statement, the amount of purchases discounts lost is reported under Other Expenses.

---

[3]The present value of a liability is the sum of expected future payments discounted to the present date at an appropriate rate of interest. *APB Opinion No. 21,* "Interest on Receivables and Payables," states that presentation of liabilities at their discounted present value is not required for "payables arising from transactions with customers or suppliers in the normal course of business which are due in customary trade terms not exceeding approximately one year." *APB Opinion No. 21* also does not apply to estimates of warranty obligations assumed in connection with sales of property, goods, or services.

To illustrate, assume the following activity relating to trade accounts payable for Year 10:

1 Purchased $900,000 of merchandise on terms of 2/10, n/30.

2 Paid invoices for purchases of $600,000 within the discount period and for purchases of $100,000 after the discount period lapsed.

3 Estimated at the end of Year 10 that 25% of the $200,000 outstanding trade accounts payable would not be paid within the discount period.

The journal entries (explanations omitted) for Year 10 and the presentation of trade accounts payable in the balance sheet at the end of Year 10 under the two alternative approaches are presented below:

Trade accounts payable recorded at face amount or net of purchases discounts

Trade accounts payable recorded at face amount		**Trade accounts payable recorded net of purchases discounts**	
(1) Purchases	900,000	Purchases	
Trade Accounts		($900,000 × 0.98).	882,000
Payable	900,000	Trade Accounts	
		Payable	882,000
(2) Trade Accounts		Trade Accounts	
Payable	700,000	Payable	
Cash	688,000	($700,000 × 0.98).	686,000
Purchases Dis-		Purchases Discounts	
counts		Lost ($100,000 ×	
($600,000 ×		0.02)	2,000
0.02)	12,000	Cash	688,000
(3) Allowance for Pur-		Purchases Discounts	
chases Dis-		Lost [($200,000 ×	
counts	3,000	0.25) × 0.02]	1,000
Purchases Dis-		Trade Accounts	
counts		Payable	1,000
[($200,000 × 0.75) ×			
0.02]	3,000		
Presentation in balance sheet at end of Year 10:			
Trade accounts payable	$200,000	Trade accounts payable .	$197,000
Less: Allowance for			
purchases discounts..........	3,000		
Carrying amount of trade			
accounts payable	$197,000		

Most business enterprises plan to take advantage of all cash discounts available and thus prefer to record trade accounts payable at the net amount. The added cost of departures from this policy is indicated in the Purchases Discounts Lost ledger account.

Loan Obligations and Refinancing of Short-Term Debt

In this category are included short-term promissory notes (including *commercial paper*[4]) issued as evidence of borrowing, and any portion of long-term debt due within one year. If long-term debt currently maturing is expected to be retired from sinking funds, from the proceeds of new long-term debt or equity securities, or through conversion to common stock, current funds will not be required. Therefore, such debt is reported as long-term, and the reason for this classification is described in a note to the financial statements. Similarly, short-term debt that is expected to be refinanced on a long-term basis may be excluded from current liabilities.

Promissory Notes   The accounting for promissory notes payable is similar to the accounting for promissory notes receivable described in Chapter 7. When a promissory note bears a current fair rate of interest, its face amount is equal to its present value at the time of issuance; however, when a promissory note bears no interest or an unreasonably low rate of interest, the present value of the note payable is less than its face amount. The discount on such a note represents an adjustment (increase) to interest expense over the term of the note.

To illustrate the accounting for a promissory note issued at a discount, assume that on July 1, Year 1, Karlinsky Company issues a one-year noninterest-bearing note as consideration for the acquisition of office equipment. The face amount of the note is $150,000 and the current fair rate of interest on the note is 12% compounded quarterly. From Table 2 in the Appendix at the end of Chapter 5, we find that the present value of this note is $133,273 ($150,000 × 0.888487 = $133,273). The journal entries for the last six months of Year 1 and the presentation of the note in Karlinsky's balance sheet on December 31, Year 1, are on page 502.

On March 31, Year 2, interest expense of $4,242 ($141,389 × 0.12 × 3/12 = $4,242) would be recorded, and on June 30, Year 2, interest expense of $4,369 [($141,389 + $4,242) × 0.12 × 3/12 = $4,369] would be recorded. These journal entries increase the carrying amount of the note to its maturity value of $150,000.

Promissory notes payable that bear an unreasonably high rate of interest require the recording of a premium. The accounting for such notes is illustrated on pages 254–255 of Chapter 5. The accounting for notes payable that include other rights or privileges, together with the accounting for the related notes receivable, is illustrated on page 367 in Chapter 7.

As stated in Chapter 7, the cash received from a transfer (sale) of receivables *with recourse* is reported in the balance sheet as a liability when one of the following conditions exists:[5]

---

[4]*Commercial paper* (as defined in Chapter 6, page 306) is the term used in the money market for short-term unsecured promissory notes issued by corporations at a discount to investors, generally other corporations.

[5]*FASB Statement No. 77,* "Reporting by Transferors for Transfers of Receivables with Recourse," FASB (Stamford: 1983), pp. 2–3.

Journal entries:

Year 1

July 1   Office Equipment   133,273

         Discount on Note Payable   16,727

            Note Payable   150,000

         *To record issuance of a one-year noninterest-
bearing promissory note. The current fair rate of interest on the note is 12% compounded quarterly.*

Sept. 30   Interest Expense   3,998

            Discount on Note Payable   3,998

         *To record interest expense for three
months ($133,273 × 0.12 × 3/12 = $3,998).*

Dec. 31   Interest Expense   4,118

            Discount on Note Payable   4,118

         *To record interest expense for three months
[($133,273 + $3,998) × 0.12 × 3/12 = $4,118].*

Presentation in balance sheet on
  December 31, Year 1:

Note payable $150,000

Less: Discount on note payable ($16,727 − $3,998 − $4,118)   8,611

Carrying amount of note payable $141,389

1   The transferor does not surrender control of the future economic benefits embodied in the receivables.

2   The transferor's obligations under the recourse provisions cannot be reasonably estimated.

3   The transferee can require the transferor to repurchase the receivables.

Refinancing of Short-Term Debt   When a business enterprise expects to refinance short-term debt on a long-term basis, a question arises as to the proper classification of such debt. *FASB Statement No. 6,* "Classification of Short-Term Obligations Expected to Be Refinanced. . . ," requires that a short-term debt be classified as a current liability unless the enterprise *intends to refinance the debt on a long-term basis* and can demonstrate its *ability to carry out the refinancing.*[6]

    Refinancing means replacing short-term debt with either long-term debt or equity securities, or renewing, extending, or replacing the short-term debt with

---

[6]*FASB Statement No. 6,* "Classification of Short-Term Obligations Expected to Be Refinanced. . . ," FASB (Stamford: 1975), p. 4.

other short-term debt for more than one year (or beyond the operating cycle of the business enterprise, if applicable) from the date of the balance sheet. *Ability to refinance* on a long-term basis must be demonstrated either by (1) actually having issued long-term debt or equity securities to replace short-term debt after the date of the balance sheet but before the balance sheet is issued, or by (2) having entered into a firm financing contract that will enable the debtor enterprise to refinance short-term debt at maturity.

When a short-term debt is classified as other than a current liability, the reasons for such classification are disclosed in a note to the financial statements. Specific disclosures required include a general description of the refinancing contract, the terms of any new debt incurred or to be incurred, and the terms of any equity securities issued or to be issued pursuant to the refinancing. An example of such disclosure from a balance sheet dated December 31, Year 10, follows:

Disclosure of
refinancing contract
in balance sheet

Current liabilities:	
Trade accounts payable	$1,800,000
Income taxes payable	1,150,000
Other current liabilities	370,000
Total current liabilities	$3,320,000
Long-term debt:	
12% notes payable (**Note 1**)	3,200,000
Total liabilities	$6,520,000

Note 1 *The company has entered into a refinancing contract with Boise Bank to borrow up to $5,000,000 at any time through Year 12. Amounts borrowed under the contract mature three years from the date of the loan and bear interest at 2% above Boise Bank's prime interest rate. The contract requires the company to maintain working capital of at least $6,000,000 and prohibits the payment of cash dividends and acquisition of treasury stock without prior approval by Boise Bank. Because the company intends to borrow at least $3,200,000 under the refinancing contract to retire the 12% notes payable that mature on March 31, Year 11, the notes have been classified as long-term debt.*

A related issue is whether a short-term debt should be excluded from current liabilities if it is repaid after the balance sheet date and then is replaced by a long-term debt before the balance sheet is issued. Because repayment of the short-term debt before funds are obtained through a long-term refinancing requires the use of current assets, the Financial Accounting Standards Board concluded that the short-term obligation *shall not be excluded from current liabilities* on the balance sheet date.[7]

Liabilities Relating to Payrolls

Employers act as tax collectors for the federal and state governments with respect to taxes withheld from employees. Employers also may withhold from salaries and wages amounts for such items as union dues, state disability insurance, group life insurance, and contributory pension plans. Accountants must be familiar with the general provisions of payroll tax legislation.

---

[7]*FASB Interpretation No. 8,* "Classification of a Short-Term Obligation Repaid Prior to Being Replaced by a Long-Term Security (an interpretation of *FASB Statement No. 6*)," FASB (Stamford: 1976), p. 2.

Social Security Taxes (FICA) The Federal Insurance Contributions Act provides for old age and survivors' benefits for employees and members of their families, and hospitalization insurance (Medicare) provides for medical costs. These payroll taxes are referred to as *social security taxes* and are levied against both the employer and its employees at the same rate, based on the employees' gross earnings. Both the rates and base earnings have been increased many times in recent years and are scheduled to change in the future. For purposes of discussion and problems in this chapter, we assume that a rate of 7% applies for both the employer and its employees on earnings up to $40,000.

Federal Unemployment Tax The Federal Unemployment Tax Act (FUTA) provides for a system of unemployment insurance established in cooperation with state governments. Generally, employers of one or more persons are subject to the federal unemployment tax. In 1984, the tax applied to the first $7,000 of earnings paid to each employee during the calendar year. The federal tax was levied only on employers at a rate of 3.5%, with a credit against the federal tax up to 2.7% of taxable earnings allowed for contributions that an employer made to a state plan. Thus, the effective federal unemployment tax was 0.8% (3.5% − 2.7% = 0.8%) of earnings up to $7,000 per employee. The amount of annual earnings subject to the tax and the tax rate are changed periodically. For example, the rate was increased to 6.2% in 1985, and a credit of up to 5.4% was allowed for contributions to a state plan.

State Unemployment Tax The provisions of the various state laws governing unemployment compensation differ from the federal law, and differ among various states. Most state laws tax only employers, but a few apply taxes on employees as well. An important feature of all state unemployment tax laws is the *merit rating provision,* under which a reduction in the tax rate levied by the state is granted to employers whose unemployment experience is better than a specified standard. Thus, employers whose employee turnover rate is low may be entitled to a lower state tax rate. To make this type of incentive toward stable employment effective, the federal law provides that an employer who pays a lower *merit rate* to the state is entitled to a maximum credit against the federal tax.

Income Taxes Withheld Employers of one or more persons are required to withhold from employees' earnings an amount approximating the federal income tax due on those earnings. A number of cities and states also levy income taxes and require that income taxes be withheld. An employer is required to withhold income taxes only if the legal relationship of employer and employee exists; this excludes payments to persons who perform services as *independent contractors* rather than as employees. Certain other limited classes of wage payments are exempt from income tax withholding.

    The amount of income taxes withheld is determined by formula or may be obtained from tables prepared by the government; it varies according to the length of the pay period, the amount of each employee's taxable earnings, and the marital status and the number of dependents of each employee. The employer remits income taxes withheld and FICA taxes to the taxing authorities at regular intervals.

Compensated Absences and Special Termination Benefits Vacation, holiday, and illness pay (collectively referred to as *compensated absences*) are a standard element of most employment contracts. The right to such pay usually depends on the length of employment, and may increase after an employee completes a specified term of service.

When does a liability for compensated absences come into existence for financial accounting? Does it arise only when an employee has met all the conditions, or does it accrue through the employment period? For example, it seems clear that an employee who earns $500 a week and is entitled to a two-week vacation is paid $26,000 for 50 weeks of work, or $520 a week ($26,000 ÷ 50 = $520). This reasoning suggests that the vacation pay accrued at the rate of $20 a week during the 50 weeks prior to the vacation. Whether a legal liability exists for the vacation pay depends on the terms of the employment contract. If the paid vacation is contingent on the employee's remaining in service until the vacation period, the legal obligation does not arise until this condition has been met. However, an obligation exists that meets the tests of a liability, because the employer estimates the liability for vacation pay on the basis of employee turnover experience. Generally, the probability is high that a future cash outflow for vacation pay will take place, and the recording of a liability is appropriate.

Liabilities for employees' compensation for future absences are accrued if *all* of the following conditions are met:[8]

1   The employer's obligation to compensate employees for future absences is attributable to services already rendered by employees.

2   The obligation relates to rights that *vest* (are not contingent on an employee's future service) or *accumulate* (may be carried forward to one or more accounting periods subsequent to that in which it is earned).

3   Payment of the compensation is probable.

4   The amount can be reasonably estimated.

Inability to estimate a liability for compensated absences that meet the first three tests above is disclosed in a note to the financial statements.

Special termination benefits may be offered by employers to their employees as consideration for early retirement. Such termination benefits may consist of a lump-sum payment, periodic future payments, or a combination of these. The Financial Accounting Standards Board requires that employers record an expense and a liability when their employees accept the offer and the amount may be reasonably estimated. The amount thus recorded consists of the lump-sum payment to employees plus the present value of any expected future payments.[9]

Recording Payroll Liabilities The liability aspect of the problem of accounting for payroll centers on the amounts due employees, the liabilities associated with

---

[8]*FASB Statement No. 43*, "Accounting for Compensated Absences," FASB (Stamford: 1980), pp. 2–3.
[9]*FASB Statement No. 88*, "Employers' Accounting for . . . Termination Benefits," FASB (Stamford: 1985), p. 5.

withholdings from employees' earnings, and the employer's share of payroll taxes and fringe benefits. There is also a cost side to the problem. The total costs incurred for employee services, including gross earnings, payroll taxes, and other fringe benefits, must be allocated to cost centers or profit centers to provide useful cost information for management.

To illustrate the recording of a payroll in the accounting records, we assume the following payroll data for Corbin Company for the month of May. Because May is the fifth month of the year, some employees have received salaries in excess of the limits subject to payroll taxes, so that the amount subject to payroll taxes is less than the total amount earned. We also assume that Corbin is entitled to a merit rate of 2% on the state unemployment tax. A summary of total salaries and the amounts of salaries subject to vacation pay and payroll taxes for the month of May are presented below for Corbin Company:

CORBIN COMPANY
Payroll Data for Month of May

	Total salaries	Salaries subject to vacation pay, 4%	Salaries subject to payroll taxes		
			FICA taxes, 7%	Federal unemployment tax, 0.8%	State unemployment tax, 2%
Salaries	$100,000	$100,000	$100,000	$60,000	$70,000
Vacation pay		$ 4,000			
Payroll taxes expense ...			$ 7,000	$ 480	$ 1,400

The employer's total payroll taxes expense is $8,880 ($7,000 + $480 + $1,400 = $8,880). The amounts withheld from employees' salaries and the computation of employees' *net take-home pay* are summarized below:

<table>
<tr><td>Total salaries ....</td><td></td><td>$100,000</td></tr>
<tr><td>Withholdings:</td><td></td><td></td></tr>
<tr><td> FICA taxes..</td><td>$ 7,000</td><td></td></tr>
<tr><td> Income taxes withheld ....</td><td>13,200</td><td></td></tr>
<tr><td>   Hospital insurance premiums (private plans) ....</td><td>1,500</td><td>21,700</td></tr>
<tr><td> Employees' net take-home pay ....</td><td></td><td>$ 78,300</td></tr>
</table>

Amounts withheld and employees' net take-home pay

The payroll for the month of May is recorded in the journal entry on page 507.

Payroll taxes on employers become a legal liability when salaries and wages actually are paid, rather than at a time services are rendered by employees. For example, if salaries and wages accrued at year-end amount to $4,500, payroll taxes would not be levied on these earnings until the following year. However, the matching principle requires that payroll taxes be accrued for financial accounting when payroll taxes are material in amount.

<table>
<tr><td>Journal entry to record payroll</td><td></td><td></td></tr>
</table>

Journal entry to record payroll		
Salaries Expense	100,000	
Vacation Pay Expense	4,000	
Payroll Taxes Expense	8,880	
FICA Taxes Payable ($7,000 + $7,000)		14,000
Liability for Income Taxes Withheld		13,200
Hospital Insurance Premiums Payable		1,500
Federal Unemployment Tax Payable		480
State Unemployment Tax Payable		1,400
Vacation Pay Payable		4,000
Accrued Payroll		78,300
To record payroll for month of May.		

Other Current Liabilities

Cash Dividends When a cash dividend is declared by a corporation's board of directors, the corporation incurs a legal obligation to pay the dividend on a specified date. Because the time between declaration and payment is short, a dividend payable in cash is a current liability. *Dividends in arrears* on cumulative preferred stock are disclosed in a note to the financial statements because no liability exists until such dividends are declared by the board of directors. Undistributed *stock dividends* are not included among current liabilities, because no cash outlay will be required; the balance in the Stock Dividends to Be Distributed ledger account is included in the stockholders' equity section of the balance sheet. Dividends are discussed in more detail in Chapter 16.

Advances from Customers When a business enterprise receives payments in advance from its customers, a liability is created. This liability is sometimes referred to as a *deferred revenue* or *deferred credit.* The enterprise is obligated to perform by delivery of goods or services, or to refund the advance if it fails to perform. Generally, the cost of performance will not be as large as the advance, because there is an element of unrealized profit in the price charged. The profit element emerges as goods are delivered or services are performed; prior to this time the enterprise essentially is a trustee of the funds received from its customers. As performance takes place, the amount of the liability diminishes and is transferred to revenue. The costs of performance are recognized as expenses, and income (or loss) emerges.

    Advances from customers that are expected to be realized as revenue within a year or during the next operating cycle (if longer than a year) are classified as current liabilities. Examples include deposits on sales orders received, magazine subscriptions received in advance, and billings in excess of costs incurred on construction-type contracts. Advances from customers that are not expected to be realized as revenue within one year or the next operating cycle are classified as noncurrent liabilities. It may be argued that certain short-term deferred revenue, such as rents and interest received in advance, should be classified as noncurrent liabilities because the realization of such revenue is not expected to require current expenditures. Although this position has some merit, it has not been widely accepted, because the amounts involved generally are immaterial and because it may be difficult to estimate the expenditures to be incurred in the process of realizing such deferred revenue items.

Amounts received from customers as *container deposits* generally are refunded when the containers are returned (usually within a short period); therefore, such deposits are classified among current liabilities in the balance sheet.

Accrued Liabilities   The term *accrued liabilities* (or *accrued expenses*) is used to designate obligations that come into existence as the result of past contractual commitments or laws that levy taxes on income, real and personal properties, payrolls, and sales. Because of their materiality, income tax liabilities are listed separately among the current liabilities. Most other accrued liabilities may be combined under one heading, or, as is the case of accrued interest on short-term loans, combined with the liability to which they relate. The problems involved in accounting for property taxes and accrued losses on firm purchase commitments require special attention.

Property taxes are based on the assessed value of real and personal property and usually represent the primary source of revenue for local governmental units. Legally, property taxes arise as of a particular date, usually on the *lien date,* the date the taxes become a lien against the property.

The two accounting issues relating to property taxes are: (1) When should the liability for property taxes be recorded? (2) To which accounting period does the tax expense relate? Because the legal liability for property taxes arises on the lien date, the liability may be recorded on that date. However, the AICPA took the position that accrual of property taxes during the fiscal year of the taxing units generally is the most acceptable method.[10] Because property taxes are expenses associated with the use of property during the fiscal year of the taxing units, it seems reasonable to expense the property taxes during that period.

To illustrate, assume that Morris Company's plant assets are subject to property taxes by local taxing units. The fiscal years of the local taxing units cover the period from July 1 to June 30. Property taxes of $36,000 are assessed on March 15, Year 1, covering the fiscal year starting on July 1, Year 1. The lien date is July 1, Year 1, and taxes are payable in two installments of $18,000 each on December 10, Year 1, and on April 10, Year 2.

The accounting for property taxes for the period from July 1, Year 1, to June 30, Year 2, assuming that Morris accrues property taxes monthly, is illustrated on page 509.

Under this method of accounting for property taxes, neither prepaid property taxes nor property taxes payable would appear in the December 31, Year 1, balance sheet of Morris Company.

An *accrued loss on a firm purchase commitment* at the end of an accounting period requires the recording of a current liability. To assure a steady supply of merchandise or material, a business enterprise may enter into a contract for the future delivery of such goods at a fixed price for the ordered goods. It is assumed in

[10]*Accounting Research and Terminology Bulletins—Final Edition,* AICPA (New York: 1961), pp. 83–84.

Property taxes accrued over fiscal year of taxing units

Explanation	Journal entries
July 1, Year 1. Liability of $36,000 comes into existence on July 1, Year 1, the lien date.	No journal entry required.
At the end of July, August, September, October, and November, Year 1, to record **monthly** property taxes expense.	Property Taxes Expense ($36,000 ÷ 12) 3,000 Property Taxes Payable 3,000
Dec. 10, Year 1. To record payment of first installment of property tax bill.	Property Taxes Payable ($3,000 × 5) . . . 15,000 Prepaid Property Taxes . . . . 3,000 Cash 18,000
Dec. 31, Year 1. To record **monthly** property taxes expense.	Property Taxes Expense . . . . 3,000 Prepaid Property Taxes 3,000
At the end of January, February, and March, Year 2, to record **monthly** property taxes expense.	Property Taxes Expense . . . . 3,000 Property Taxes Payable 3,000
Apr. 10, Year 2. To record payment of second installment of property tax bill.	Property Taxes Payable ($3,000 × 3) . . 9,000 Prepaid Property Taxes . . . . 9,000 Cash 18,000
At end of April, May, and June, Year 2, to record **monthly** property taxes expense.	Property Taxes Expense . . . . 3,000 Prepaid Property Taxes 3,000

this discussion that the contract is ***not subject to cancellation,*** regardless of changes in market price. As stated in Chapter 8, if the price of the goods at the end of an accounting period is less than the contract price, the lower-of-cost-or-market rule is applied to the purchase contract and the loss is recognized in the accounting records. However, if a loss will not ***in fact*** be incurred because of the price decline, no loss or liability is recorded. According to the AICPA, ''The utility of such commitments is not impaired, and hence there is no loss, when the amounts to be realized from the disposition of the future inventory items are adequately protected by firm sales contracts or when there are other circumstances which reasonably assure continuing sales without price decline.''[11]

A sustained loss is recognized in the accounting period in which the price decline occurs, and the value of the goods under contract is reduced as though these goods were on hand. The journal entries to record an assumed loss of $15,000 and the subsequent purchase of the goods at a fixed price of $100,000 are illustrated below:

Journal entries for loss on firm purchase commitment

Year of price decline:

Loss on Firm Purchase Commitment	15,000	
Liability Arising from Firm Purchase Commitment		15,000
To record loss due to decline in price of goods ordered.		

Year of purchase:

Inventories (or Purchases).................................	85,000	
Liability Arising from Firm Purchase Commitment	15,000	
Trade Accounts Payable		100,000
To record purchase of goods under contract on which a loss		
due to price decline was recorded in the previous year.		

The loss on firm purchase commitment is listed separately in the income statement if it is material in amount. The liability recorded in the year of price decline is the estimated amount the purchaser would be required to pay if the contract were canceled. When the goods are purchased, this estimated liability is transferred to Trade Accounts Payable. If the expectation is that the purchase will be made during the operating cycle of the business enterprise, the liability arising from the firm purchase commitment is presented as a current liability in the balance sheet.

If contracts to purchase goods at fixed prices may be canceled by the prospective purchaser without penalty, no liability is recognized for declines in market prices because such unfavorable contracts generally would be canceled.

LIABILITIES DEPENDENT ON OPERATING RESULTS

The amount of certain obligations cannot be measured until operating results are known. These include income taxes, bonuses, profit-sharing distributions, and royalties. There is no particular accounting problem in determining such liabilities at the end of a fiscal year, when the operating results are known. However, difficulties may arise in estimating such obligations for *interim reports*.

---

[11]Ibid., p. 35.

Income Taxes

The most familiar example of a liability whose amount is dependent on operating results is income taxes. Individual proprietors and members of a partnership are subject to personal income taxes on their share of the net income of the business enterprise. Thus, single proprietorships and partnerships are not taxable entities and therefore do not report income tax liabilities in their balance sheets.

Corporations, estates, and trusts are taxable entities and are subject to income taxes. Income tax liabilities, therefore, appear in the balance sheets of such entities. In most cases a corporation is required to make payments of its estimated income tax liability in advance. The remaining tax not covered by the estimated payments is payable by the due date of the income tax return. The estimated tax payments may be debited to the Prepaid Income Taxes ledger account, to the Income Taxes Expense account, or to the Income Taxes Payable account if the accrued tax liability previously was recorded. A credit balance in the Income Taxes Payable ledger account is reported as a current liability at the end of the accounting period.

As stated in Chapter 3, a problem arises in accounting for income tax obligations because of temporary differences between **taxable income** and **pre-tax accounting income.** As a result of these differences, interperiod allocation of income taxes is required, and the amount of current income taxes payable at the end of a fiscal year may differ materially from the amount of income taxes expense reported in the income statement. Consequently, Deferred Tax Benefit and Deferred Income Tax ledger account balances appear in the balance sheet. These balances may be current or noncurrent, depending on the reasons for the differences between taxable income and pre-tax accounting income. A complete coverage of this topic appears in Chapter 21.

The accounting for income taxes in interim reports appears in Chapter 21 and in **Modern Advanced Accounting** of this series.

Bonus and Profit-Sharing Plans

Contracts covering rents, royalties, or employee compensation sometimes call for conditional payments in an amount dependent on revenue or income for an accounting period. We use the term **bonus** to describe conditional payments of this type.

Expenses based on revenue cause little difficulty. For example, if an operating lease specifies rent of $500 a month plus 1% of all sales in excess of $100,000 a year, rent expense accrues at the rate of $500 a month, and when sales reach $100,000 each additional dollar of sales creates an additional rent obligation.

Some bonus plans provide for a bonus based on income. The plans generally are drawn so that the income amount used to compute the bonus is clearly defined. For example, the bonus may be based on (1) income before income taxes and bonus, (2) income after bonus but before income taxes, or (3) net income.

To illustrate the computations involved, assume that Larson Company has a bonus plan under which a branch manager receives 20% of the income over $20,000 earned by the branch. Income for the branch amounted to $80,000 before the bonus and income taxes. Assume for purposes of illustration that income taxes are 40% of pre-tax income. The bonus under each of the three plans listed above is computed as follows:

Plan 1   The bonus is based on income in excess of $20,000 before deduction of income taxes and the bonus:

$$\text{Bonus} = 0.2(\$80,000 - \$20,000) = \underline{\underline{\$12,000}}$$

Plan 2   The bonus is based on income in excess of $20,000 after deduction of the bonus but before deduction of taxes:

$$
\begin{aligned}
B &= \text{Bonus} \\
B &= 0.2(\$80,000 - \$20,000 - B) \\
B &= \$16,000 - \$4,000 - 0.2B \\
1.2B &= \$12,000 \\
B &= \underline{\underline{\$10,000}}
\end{aligned}
$$

The computation of the bonus may be proved by taking 20% of the amount by which the income after the bonus exceeds $20,000. Thus, 20% of $50,000 ($80,000 − $10,000 − $20,000 = $50,000) equals the bonus of $10,000.

Plan 3   The bonus is based on net income in excess of $20,000 after deduction of both the bonus and income taxes:

$$
\begin{aligned}
B &= \text{Bonus} \\
T &= \text{Income taxes} \\
B &= 0.2(\$80,000 - \$20,000 - T - B) \\
T &= 0.4(\$80,000 - B)
\end{aligned}
$$

Substituting for T in the first equation, the bonus is computed as follows:

$$
\begin{aligned}
B &= 0.2[\$60,000 - 0.4(\$80,000 - B) - B] \\
B &= \$12,000 - \$6,400 + 0.08B - 0.2B \\
1.12B &= \$5,600 \\
B &= \underline{\underline{\$5,000}}
\end{aligned}
$$

The computation of the bonus may be proved by taking 20% of the amount by which the net income after the bonus of $5,000 and income taxes of $30,000 ($75,000 × 0.40 = $30,000) exceeds $20,000. Therefore, 20% of $25,000 ($80,000 − $5,000 − $30,000 − $20,000 = $25,000) equals the bonus of $5,000.

The journal entry to record the bonus under **Plan 3** follows:

Journal entry to record bonus	*Bonus Expense*	*5,000*	
	Bonus Payable		*5,000*
	To record liability for bonus to branch manager.		

Bonus Expense is presented as an operating expense in the income statement and Bonus Payable as a current liability in the balance sheet.

Some current liabilities may be based on operating results other than income. These include, for example, royalties for use of patents, royalties based on extraction of natural resources, and rentals for the use of films or other artistic works.

CONTINGENCIES

A loss contingency is defined in Chapter 4 as a potential loss, the existence of which is conditional on the happening of some future event. Until the issuance of *FASB Statement No. 5,* "Accounting for Contingencies," the distinction between potential liabilities from loss contingencies and estimated liabilities was not clear.[12] Similarly, some confusion existed as to which contingencies required accrual in the accounting records, which contingencies required disclosure in a note to the financial statements, and which general risk contingencies required neither accrual nor disclosure. *FASB Statement No. 5* established definitive accounting principles for various types of contingencies.

Accounting Principles for Contingencies

A *contingency* is an existing condition, a situation, or a set of circumstances involving uncertainty as to possible gain (*gain contingency*) or loss (*loss contingency*) to a business enterprise that ultimately will be resolved when a future event or events occurs or fails to occur. (The term *loss* is used here to include some items that commonly are referred to as *expenses*.) Resolution of the uncertainty surrounding a gain contingency generally results in an acquisition of an asset or the reduction of a liability; resolution of the uncertainty surrounding a loss contingency generally results in reduction of an asset or the incurrence of a liability. The likelihood that the future event or events will confirm the loss may be *probable* (likely to occur), *reasonably possible* (more than remote but less than likely), or *remote* (slight chance of occurring).

The FASB stated that "not all uncertainties inherent in the accounting process give rise to contingencies." The preparation of financial statements requires estimates for many business activities, and the use of estimates does not necessarily mean that a contingency exists. For example, the measurement of depreciation and income taxes expense involves estimates, but neither item is a contingency. The expiration of the cost of depreciable assets and the incurrence of the obligation to

---

[12]*FASB Statement No. 5,* "Accounting for Contingencies," FASB (Stamford: 1975).

pay income taxes are certain; however, the periodic amounts entered in the accounting records require the use of estimates.

Among the examples of loss contingencies identified by the FASB are: (1) Collectibility of receivables; (2) obligations related to product warranties and product defects; (3) risk of loss or damage to property by fire, explosion, or other hazards; (4) threat of expropriation of assets; (5) pending or threatened litigation and actual or possible claims and assessments; (6) guarantees of indebtedness of others; and (7) agreements to reacquire receivables or other assets that have been sold.[13]

Accrual of Loss Contingencies   An estimated loss or expense from a loss contingency shall be accrued by a charge to income if **both** of the following conditions are met:[14]

   a Information available prior to issuance of the financial statements indicates that it is **probable that an asset had been impaired or a liability had been incurred** at the date of the financial statements. It is implicit in this condition that it **must be probable** that one or more future events will occur confirming the fact of the loss.
   b The amount of loss can be **reasonably estimated.**
   (Emphasis added)

When the range of loss can be reasonably estimated but no single amount within the range appears to be a better estimate than any other amount within the range, **the minimum amount in the range should be accrued,** and the amount of any additional possible loss is disclosed in a note to the financial statements.[15] For example, assume that on the balance sheet date Ellen Company had lost a lawsuit, but the amount of damages remains unresolved. A reasonable estimate is that the judgment will be for not less than $2 million or more than $6 million. No amount between $2 million and $6 million appears to be a better estimate than any other amount. Ellen records this loss contingency as follows:

Journal entry to record contingency loss

Litigation Loss	2,000,000	
Liability from Litigation		2,000,000
To record minimum amount of contingency loss.		

Ellen Company also discloses the possibility of an additional loss of $4 million in a note to its financial statements. Both accrued and actual loss contingencies are included in the measurement of income before extraordinary items, unless such losses meet the criteria for classification as extraordinary items described in Chapter 3 (pages 134–135).

---

[13]Ibid., p. 2.
[14]Ibid., p. 4.
[15]*FASB Interpretation No. 14,* "Reasonable Estimation of the Amount of a Loss. . . ." FASB (Stamford: 1976), p. 2.

The important points to keep in mind are: (1) a loss contingency is accrued only when it is probable that an asset has been impaired or a liability incurred, (2) it must be probable that a future event or events will confirm the existence of the loss, and (3) the amount of the loss can be reasonably estimated. The absence of insurance (sometimes improperly referred to as *self-insurance*) covering property losses, or the possibility that injury claims will be made against a business enterprise, for example, does not indicate that an asset has been impaired or that a liability has been incurred. *Mere exposure to risk does not require accrual of a loss.*

A summary of the provisions of *FASB Statement No. 5* follows:

Summary of *FASB Statement No. 5,* "Accounting for Contingencies"

Probability that contingency exists	Contingency can be reasonably estimated	Contingency cannot be reasonably estimated
1 Loss contingencies:		
a Probable	Accrued and included in financial statements	Not accrued, but reported in a note to the financial statements
b Reasonably possible	Not accrued, but reported in a note to the financial statements	Not accrued, but reported in a note to the financial statements
c Remote	Not accrued; a note to the financial statements is permitted but not required	Not accrued; a note to the financial statements is permitted but not required
2 Gain contingencies:		
a Probable	Not accrued, except in unusual situations; disclosure in a note to the financial statements is required	Not accrued, but disclosed in a note to the financial statements in a manner that **does not give an impression gain is likely**
b Reasonably possible	Not accrued, but disclosed in a note to the financial statements in a manner that **does not give an impression realization of gain is likely**	Not accrued, but disclosed in a note to the financial statements in a manner that **does not give an impression realization of gain is likely**
c Remote	No disclosure required	No disclosure required

Included in the category of accruable loss contingencies are estimates of doubtful accounts expense and sales returns when the customers have a right to return merchandise. Both these contingencies are discussed in Chapter 7. The accounting for other accruable contingencies such as product warranty expense, gift certificates outstanding, service contracts outstanding, and coupons and trading stamps outstanding are described in the section beginning at the bottom of this page.

Loss Contingencies That Are Not Accrued　Certain loss contingencies that do not meet the two criteria for accrual, but which are at least *reasonably possible,* are disclosed in a note to the financial statements. The disclosure should indicate the nature of the contingency and provide an estimate of the possible loss, or state that such an estimate cannot be made. An example of such a loss contingency is a legal action against a business enterprise in which an unfavorable outcome is reasonably possible, but a reasonable estimate of loss cannot be made.

If the probability of loss from a nonaccruable contingency is *remote,* the contingency still may be disclosed. Such contingencies include guarantees of indebtedness of others and agreements to reacquire receivables that had been sold. Disclosure is not required for a loss contingency involving claims or lawsuits not yet filed, unless it appears *probable* that a claim or lawsuit will be filed and that an unfavorable outcome is *reasonably possible.* General or unspecified business risks do not meet the conditions for accrual and need not be disclosed in a note to the financial statements.

Gain Contingencies　Contingencies that might result in gains are not recorded until the gains are realized or realizable. This is consistent with the general principles of revenue realization. Although disclosure is made of contingencies that *might* result in gains, care should be exercised not to give an impression that realization of such gains is *likely.* Examples of gain contingencies include probable favorable outcome of plaintiff litigation and potential future income tax benefits of operating loss carryforwards.

Accounting for Loss Contingencies When Liability Has Been Incurred

The accrual of loss contingencies requires a debit to a loss or expense ledger account and a credit to either an asset (or asset valuation) account or an estimated liability account. The term *estimated liability* is used to describe an obligation that definitely exists but is uncertain as to amount and due date. The primary accounting problem relating to an estimated liability is to obtain a reasonable estimate of the amount of the liability. An estimated liability may be current or long-term. The accounting for certain contingencies that require the recognition of estimated current liabilities is described in the following sections.

Product Warranties　Estimating the liability that arises in connection with various kinds of product warranties often poses a difficult problem. Warranties to replace or repair a product if it proves unsatisfactory during some specified time period are made by most business enterprises. Such liabilities arise at the time of sale and may be recorded at the time of sale or at the end of the accounting period. The following journal entries are made if the liability is recorded at the time of sale:

Journal entries for product warranty liability recorded at the time of sale

Product Warranty Expense .... *XXX*	
Liability under Product Warranty	*XXX*
To record estimated liability under product warranty.	
Liability under Product Warranty .... *XXX*	
Cash (or Accounts Payable, Inventories of Parts, etc.) .	*XXX*
To record costs of servicing customer claims.	

The balance in the liability ledger account at the end of an accounting period should be reviewed and adjusted if necessary to make certain that it is a reasonable measure of potential customer claims on outstanding product warranties.

An acceptable alternative is to make no journal entry in the liability account at the time of sale; Product Warranty Expense is debited as actual costs are incurred in servicing customer claims and outstanding potential claims are recorded at the end of the accounting period.

Income tax regulations allow a deduction for product warranty expense only when the cost has been incurred. In the past, many business enterprises followed the income tax regulations in their accounting records, thus overstating net income and understating current liabilities. When the outstanding liability under a product warranty is significant, neither the income tax law nor the uncertainty of the amount of expense to be incurred is a valid reason for failure to recognize the expense and the related current liability in the financial statements.

Gift Certificates   Some business enterprises issue tickets, tokens, or gift certificates that are promises to perform services or to furnish merchandise on some later date. The amount of the liability is equal to the amount advanced by customers. As redemptions are made, the liability ledger account is debited and a revenue account is credited. Examples of this type of transaction are coupons issued by garages and gasoline stations, tickets and tokens issued by transportation enterprises, and gift certificates sold by retail stores. Because such advances are in small individual amounts and numerous, it is almost certain that some never will be presented for redemption. Estimating the amount of forfeited claims is simplified when there is an agreement that the obligation expires after a stated time. When the offer is of indefinite duration, it is necessary to estimate the amounts of potential claims that will not be redeemed and to transfer this amount from the liability ledger account to a revenue account.

Service Contracts   Business enterprises selling or servicing household appliances often sell service contracts to customers under which the enterprises agree to service the appliance for a specified period of time. The amounts received for such service contracts constitute unearned revenue that will be earned (realized) by performance over the term of the contract. To illustrate, assume that an enterprise sells television service contracts for $150 each, agreeing to service customers' sets for one year. If 1,000 such service contracts are sold, the journal entry is:

Journal entry for sale of service contracts

Cash (or Trade Accounts Receivable)	*150,000*	
Unearned Service Contract Revenue		*150,000*
To record sale of 1,000 service contracts at $150 each.		

During the ensuing 12-month period, the unearned service contract revenue will be realized, and actual costs of servicing the television sets will be recognized as expenses. On the basis of experience, it often is possible to establish a pattern of probable service calls as a guide for recognizing revenue. For example, if the bulk of the service calls tend to be made in the first part of the year covered by the service contract, a policy of recognizing revenue for, say, 30% of the contract price in the first month, 20% in the second month, and 5% in each of the 10 subsequent months might be reasonable. The journal entries below are illustrative of this procedure for the first month of the service contract period, if we assume that costs of $30,735 were incurred in servicing the contracts during the first month:

Journal entries for revenue realized and costs incurred under service contracts

Unearned Service Contract Revenue	*45,000*	
Service Contract Revenue		*45,000*
To recognize 30% of unearned service contract revenue as		
realized revenue for the first month of the contract period		
($150,000 × 0.30 = $45,000).		
Service Contract Expense	*30,735*	
Inventory of Parts		*14,250*
Cash, Accrued Payroll, etc.		*16,485*
To recognize expense incurred under service contracts.		

At the end of the first month, the balance of $105,000 ($150,000 − $45,000 = $105,000) in the Unearned Service Contract Revenue ledger account is reported among current liabilities in the balance sheet.

Coupons and Trading Stamps In an effort to promote the sale of certain products, a business enterprise may issue coupons exchangeable for prizes such as cash or merchandise. In such cases, the enterprise incurs a liability equal to the cost of the prizes that are expected to be claimed by customers.

The liability for prizes to be distributed is based on the enterprise's past and anticipated experience with redemptions of coupons. For example, assume that in Year 1 Lena Company issued coupons that may be redeemed for prizes costing $2,500 if all the coupons are presented for redemption. If past experience indicates that only 80% of the coupons issued will be presented for redemption, the liability is $2,000 ($2,500 × 0.8 = $2,000), the maximum cost of prizes that are expected to be claimed by Lena's customers.

The purchase of prize merchandise to be given to customers is recorded in an inventory ledger account. For example, the journal entry to record the purchase of $2,800 of prize merchandise by Lena Company in Year 1 is illustrated below:

Journal entry for purchase of prizes

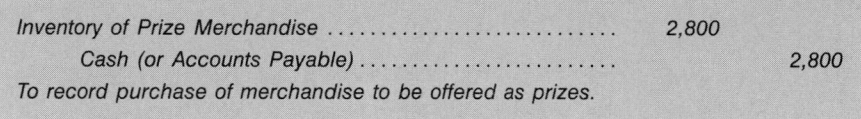

Inventory of Prize Merchandise	*2,800*	
Cash (or Accounts Payable)		*2,800*
To record purchase of merchandise to be offered as prizes.		

Generally, the cost of the coupons is immaterial in amount and is not accounted for separately; if the cost of coupons is material, the cost also may be recorded in an inventory ledger account. Assuming that Lena Company's customers present coupons during Year 1 in exchange for prize merchandise costing $1,500, the following journal entry would be required:

Journal entry for redemption of coupons for prizes

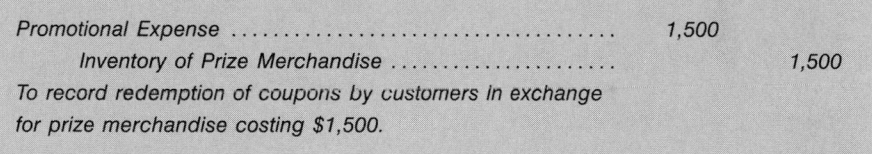

Promotional Expense	*1,500*	
Inventory of Prize Merchandise		*1,500*
To record redemption of coupons by customers in exchange for prize merchandise costing $1,500.		

An adjusting journal entry is required at the end of each accounting period to recognize the estimated expense and liability relating to the coupons outstanding. In our example, the total cost of prizes expected to be claimed by Lena Company's customers was estimated at $2,000, of which $1,500 was redeemed during Year 1. Thus, an additional expense and a liability of $500 ($2,000 − $1,500 = $500) are recorded at the end of Year 1 as follows:

Adjusting entry to record liability for unredeemed coupons

Promotional Expense	*500*	
Liability for Coupons Outstanding		*500*
To record estimated liability for coupons outstanding at the end of Year 1.		

At the end of Year 1, the inventory of prize merchandise is $1,300 ($2,800 − $1,500 = $1,300). This inventory is listed among the current assets in Lena Company's balance sheet; the liability for coupons outstanding, $500, is included among current liabilities; and the promotional expense for the year, $2,000 ($1,500 + $500 = $2,000), is classified as a selling expense in the income statement.

A slightly different situation exists when a retailer gives its customers *trading stamps* to be redeemed by another enterprise engaged in the sale and redemption of trading stamps. The retailer pays a fixed price for the trading stamps, which are recorded in an Inventory of Trading Stamps ledger account. When stamps are issued to customers, an operating expense ledger account is debited, and the Inventory of Trading Stamps ledger account is credited. The obligation to redeem the stamps is assumed by the enterprise that sells and redeems trading stamps. The trading stamp enterprise usually records the proceeds from the sale of stamps in a revenue ledger account and also records a liability for the cost of merchandise and related service costs to be incurred when stamps are redeemed. When merchandise is issued for redeemed stamps, the liability is debited and the inventory of merchandise is credited.

Operating Reserves   Some business enterprises debit an expense ledger account and credit an *operating reserve* account for costs such as repairs or maintenance that have not yet been incurred. Also, estimated future payments for deferred compensation, restoration of leased properties, plant closing and relocation costs, and disposal of an industry segment sometimes are reported as current liabilities.

The recording of these estimated costs presumably is an effort to implement accrual accounting by recognition of an expense or loss when an obligation to incur costs in the future may be identified with reasonable certainty. The operating reserve ledger account is debited when such costs are incurred. However, there is some evidence that operating reserves at times have been used by management as "income-smoothing" devices. Accountants should analyze the nature of these "reserves" to determine whether a liability has been incurred or an asset impaired, or whether the reserves improperly relieve future accounting periods of expenses and losses.

When costs that are expensed for annual accounting periods clearly benefit interim periods, each interim period is charged for an appropriate portion of such costs by the use of accruals and deferrals.[16] Costs expected to be incurred in carrying out the disposal of a business segment are accrued and included in the measurement of the gain or loss on the disposal of the segment.[17] Such accrued costs are included among the current liabilities in the balance sheet.

Disclosure of Contingencies Not Accrued

If a loss contingency does not meet the two conditions for accrual described on page 514, and the likelihood of loss is *reasonably possible* or even, in some cases, remote, the loss contingency is disclosed in a note to the financial statements. The disclosure includes the nature of the contingency and, if possible, an indication of the amount involved. Some examples of contingencies that are not accrued are discussed and illustrated in the following sections.

Guarantees of Indebtedness of Others   A loss contingency may arise from the discounting of notes receivable *with recourse,* from the assignment of accounts receivable with recourse, and from accommodation indorsements of the obligations of other parties such as customers, employees, or affiliated companies. In such cases little question exists as to the amount of the obligation or its due date. The central issue is whether the debtor will pay the liability. If the probability is strong that the debtor will make payment, the chance of the indorser's being required to pay is remote. An example of disclosure of this type of loss contingency is illustrated at the top of page 521.

---

[16]*APB Opinion No. 28,* p. 526.
[17]*APB Opinion No. 30,* "Reporting the Results of Operations—. . . ," AICPA (New York: 1973), p. 563.

In connection with providing for its future bituminous coal supply, the company . . . has guaranteed obligations of certain coal suppliers (including five owned and two controlled coal companies) aggregating $131.6 million.

Pending or Threatened Litigation If a business enterprise is the defendant in a lawsuit calling for the payment of damages, a loss contingency exists. The outcome of such litigation seldom may be predicted with any assurance. The decision of the court either may release the enterprise of any obligation, or may establish an enforceable claim against it. However, the possibility of an appeal to a higher court still may exist. Another possible outcome is an out-of-court settlement between the parties, thus ending the litigation.

Even though the evidence available on the balance sheet date does not favor the defendant, it is hardly reasonable to expect the defendant to disclose in its financial statements a dollar estimate of possible damages. Such disclosure could influence unfavorably the chances of an out-of-court settlement or encourage the plaintiff to intensify its efforts. As a generalization, then, we may say that a loss contingency from pending litigation should be disclosed in a note to the financial statements, but this disclosure will seldom, if ever, reach the point of estimating the dollar amount of damages. To do so would weaken the defendant's position in the dispute. An example of disclosure of an asserted claim follows:

In January, 1985, a purported class action was filed in the U.S. District Court for the Southern District of New York against the corporation, certain of its present and former directors and its independent accountants. Plaintiffs allege that the corporation's Annual Reports for 1982 and 1983 and other statements and reports failed to make proper disclosures with respect to the corporation's financial condition and earnings, resulting in violation of Section 10(b) of the Securities Exchange Act of 1934 and Rule 10b-5 thereunder and constituting common law fraud. Plaintiffs seek damages in an unspecified amount on behalf of the alleged class consisting of all persons who acquired the corporation's common stock during the period of the alleged wrongful conduct. Management denies the claims asserted.

In the area of threatened litigation or unasserted claims against a client, a letter of audit inquiry to the client's lawyers is the auditors' primary means of obtaining confirmation of the information provided by management concerning litigation, claims, and assessments. This audit procedure has been a source of considerable controversy between auditors and lawyers. The issue boils down to a struggle between the principle of *disclosure* and the *confidentiality of lawyer-client communications.*[18]

Actual or Possible Claims and Assessments The Internal Revenue Service may disagree with the treatment of items in the computation of taxable income and (during the period of the statute of limitations) may assess additional taxes. Because this loss contingency is well-recognized and understood, no specific disclosure is

---

[18]*Statement on Auditing Standards No. 12,* ''Inquiry of a Client's Lawyer Concerning Litigation, Claims, and Assessments,'' AICPA (New York: 1976).

required prior to the time that an actual assessment has been made. Except in cases of fraud or failure to file a tax return, the statute of limitations on federal income tax deficiencies is three years; thus, on any date only income taxes of the last three years may be in doubt as to matters involving an interpretation of the law. A note to the financial statements may indicate that income tax returns have been examined and final determination of income taxes has been made for certain years. The following disclosure of a proposed income tax deficiency is given as an example:

> The Internal Revenue Service issued a notice of deficiency of $823,000, plus interest, relating primarily to the allocation of the purchase price to acquired assets and the subsequent valuations of inventories. The company has petitioned the United States Tax Court; however, no trial date has been set. In the event any portion of the deficiency is sustained, the adjustments would represent timing differences that should result in tax deductions in future years; consequently, there would be no material adverse effect on the financial statements.

Future Liabilities and Commitments

Most business enterprises are continuously planning future operations. In many instances, commitments may be made that will result in substantial liabilities in the near future. On any balance sheet date, an enterprise ordinarily will have made certain commitments that are of a recurring nature and normal in amount; these do not require special disclosure. However, when unusual and material commitments have been made, their nature and amount are disclosed. Examples are commitments for an unusually large purchase of material, major acquisitions of natural resources or plant assets, payments to be made contingent on earnings of acquired enterprises, or unusually large commitments for advertising and product development costs. An example of disclosure of commitments appears below:

> The company has commitments under contracts for the acquisition of land and for the construction of buildings. Portions of such contracts not completed at year-end are not included in the financial statements. Such unrecorded commitments amounted to approximately $58,575,000 at the end of 1985 as compared with $83,757,000 at the end of 1984.

Presentation of Current Liabilities in the Balance Sheet

The two issues that arise in connection with the presentation of current liabilities in the balance sheet are: (1) the order of presentation, and (2) the extent of disclosure necessary for different types of current liabilities. Current liabilities may be reported in the *order of maturity* or according to *amount* (largest to smallest). It is difficult to satisfy both objectives, and the usual compromise is to rank current liabilities in order of amount, unless differences in maturity dates are significant. However, cash overdrafts and promissory notes payable maturing shortly after the balance sheet date usually are listed first.

In the balance sheet, the discount or premium on notes payable is deducted from or added to the face amount of the notes. The description of the notes payable includes the effective interest rate, and the face amount of the notes is disclosed in the financial statements or in a note to the financial statements.[19]

The matter of detail will depend to some extent on the purpose for which the balance sheet is prepared. In a balance sheet prepared in support of an application for a short-term loan, current liabilities may be listed in more detail; for presentation in annual reports, the classification illustrated below is recommended:

Balance sheet presentation of current liabilities

Current liabilities:	
Notes payable to banks (interest rate, 13%)	$ 600,000
Notes payable to trade creditors (interest rate, 15%; face amount, $475,000, less discount of $30,000)	445,000
Trade accounts payable	325,200
Current maturities of long-term debt (including bonds payable, mortgage notes payable, and equipment contracts payable)	150,500
Income taxes payable	112,500
Dividends payable	25,000
Advances from customers and deferred revenue	16,000
Other accrued liabilities (payroll, interest, royalties, etc.)	12,900
Total current liabilities	$1,687,100

If the due date of any liability can be extended, or if a liability has been refinanced prior to the issuance of financial statements, the details are disclosed parenthetically or in a note to the financial statements. Any short-term liability that is expected to be liquidated by the issuance of capital stock is reported in the stockholders' equity section of the balance sheet, accompanied by an appropriate note explaining the reason for such classification.

REVIEW QUESTIONS

1 Liabilities sometimes are described as ''equities of outsiders in the assets of a business enterprise.'' Do you agree with this description of liabilities? Explain.

2 Distinguish between a *liability* and a *commitment*. Should the currently maturing installment of a deferred compensation contract that is to be liquidated by the issuance of common stock be reported as a liability in the balance sheet? Explain.

3 What is the basis for distinguishing between a *current liability* and a *long-term liability?*

4 Distinguish among the following: *definitely measurable liability, liability dependent on operating results, estimated liability, loss contingency.* Give one or more example of each.

5 Under what circumstances is it proper to report a currently maturing debt as a noncurrent liability in the balance sheet?

---

[19]*APB Opinion No. 21,* ''Interest on Receivables and Payables,'' AICPA (New York: 1971), p. 423.

6   **a** What are the liabilities that generally arise in connection with a payroll?
b When are *special termination benefits* recorded by an employer?

7   When should deferred revenue (or unearned revenue) be reported as a current liability? When should deferred revenue be reported as a noncurrent liability?

8   When is the liability for property taxes entered in the accounting records? Over what period are property taxes recognized as expenses? Explain.

9   Describe the generally accepted accounting principles for an accrued loss on a *firm purchase commitment.*

10   Where should the liability for current year's income taxes appear in the balance sheet of a partnership? Explain.

11   Motowne, Inc., acquired certain patent rights in return for royalties equal to ''10% of income.'' What difficulties may arise in the interpretation of this contract?

12   **a** Define a *contingency* and differentiate between a *gain contingency* and a *loss contingency.*
b Give some examples of gain contingencies and loss contingencies.
c What two conditions must be met before a loss contingency is entered in the accounting records?

13   On December 31, Year 6, Georgia Granite Company had an investment of $2 million in the bonds of Coe Company, which has filed for bankruptcy. A reasonable estimate of the probable loss ranges from $600,000 to $900,000. No amount of the estimated loss in this range appears to be a better estimate than any other amount. How should Georgia Granite account for this loss contingency in its financial statements for the year ended December 31, Year 6?

14   Briefly describe the accounting for promotional plans involving coupons and prizes, product guarantees, and the sale of service contracts.

15   **a** Michigan Cement Corporation does not carry workers' compensation insurance, but it does have its own plan for payments to disabled employees. Should estimated obligations to employees under this plan be reported as a liability by Michigan Cement Corporation in its balance sheet?
b Are potential losses on ''self-insurance'' plans properly reported as liabilities in the balance sheet? Why?

16   Included among the current liabilities of Amaro Corporation is an item described as ''Excess of Checks Outstanding over Balance on Deposit, $59,300.'' The current liabilities of Zinc Corporation include ''Estimated Costs of Closing Lomita Plant, $1,980,000.'' Explain the nature of these two current liabilities.

17   Indicate how each of the following items is reported in the balance sheet:
a Bank overdraft
b Customers' accounts with credit balances
c Service guarantee on products sold
d Bonds maturing in three months, to be paid from a sinking fund
e Stock dividend to be distributed in the form of common stock of the issuing corporation

f Dividends in arrears on cumulative preferred stock

g Interest (discount) on a note payable, deducted from the face amount of the note to determine the net proceeds received

h Estimated payments to be made to employees under a three-year union contract

i Potential payments to stockholders of an acquired company based on future earnings of the acquired company.

18 Under what circumstances are commitments for future expenditures disclosed in financial statements? How should this disclosure be made?

19 List some general guidelines for reporting current liabilities in the balance sheet of a business enterprise.

EXERCISES

Ex. 10-1   Select the best answer for each of the following multiple-choice questions:

1   According to *FASB Statement No. 5,* "Accounting for Contingencies," an estimated loss or expense from a loss contingency is accrued if the amount of the loss or expense can be reasonably estimated and information available prior to issuance of the financial statements indicates that, on the date of the financial statements, the impairment of an asset or the incurrence of a liability is:
a Probable   **b** Reasonably possible   **c** Certain   **d** Remote

2   In July, Year 7, Nyquist, Inc., filed suit in federal court against Dean Corporation seeking to recover $750,000 for patent infringement. A court verdict was rendered in August, Year 9, awarding Nyquist $500,000 in damages. Dean has appealed the verdict, but a final decision is not expected before Year 12. Nyquist's counsel believes it is probable that Nyquist will be successful against Dean for an estimated amount of $400,000. What amount does Nyquist recognize as a gain in the year ended December 31, Year 11?
a $0   **b** $400,000   **c** $500,000   **d** $750,000   **e** Some other amount

3   Cone Company, a manufacturer of paint, is preparing annual financial statements on December 31, Year 3. Because of a recently proven health hazard in one of its paints, the United States government has indicated clearly its intention of having Cone recall all cans of this paint sold in the last six months. The management of Cone estimates that this recall would cost $800,000. What accounting recognition, if any, should be accorded this situation?
a No recognition
b Disclosure in a note to the financial statements
c Operating expense of $800,000
d Extraordinary loss of $800,000

4   Lucero, Inc., provides an incentive compensation plan under which its president is to receive a bonus equal to 10% of Lucero's income in excess of $100,000 before deduction of income taxes but after deduction of the bonus. If income before income taxes and the bonus is $320,000, the amount of the bonus is:
a $20,000   **b** $22,000   **c** $32,000   **d** $44,000   **e** Some other amount

5   Swanny's is a retail store operating in a state with a 5% retail sales tax. The state law provides that the retail sales tax collected during the month must be remitted to the state during the following month. If the amount collected is remitted to the state on or before the twentieth day of the following month, the retailer may keep 2% of the sales tax collected. On April 10, Swanny's remitted $16,905 sales tax to the state tax division for March retail sales. What was the amount of the March retail sales subject to sales tax?

a $331,340   **b** $331,480   **c** $338,100   **d** $345,000   **e** Some other amount

6   Monica Company was sued for negligence in permitting local residents to be exposed to toxic chemicals from its plant. Monica lost the suit, and its lawyers have concluded that it is probable that Monica will be liable for a judgment costing anywhere from $250,000 to $1,250,000. However, the lawyers state that the most probable cost is $500,000. As a result of the above facts, Monica should accrue:

a A loss contingency of $250,000, and disclose an additional contingency of up to $1,000,000

b A loss contingency of $500,000, and disclose an additional contingency of up to $750,000

c A loss contingency of $500,000, but not disclose any additional contingency

d No loss contingency, but disclose a contingency of $250,000 to $1,250,000

7   On January 2, Year 5, Lee Company borrowed $200,000 from its major customer, Sun Corporation, evidenced by a promissory note payable in three years. The note did not bear interest. Lee agreed to supply Sun's merchandise needs for the loan period at favorable prices. The market rate of interest for this type of loan is 14%. Assume that the present value (at the market rate of interest) of the $200,000 note is $135,000 on January 1, Year 5. What amount of interest expense is included in Lee's Year 5 income statement?

a $0   **b** $18,900   **c** $21,667   **d** $28,000   **e** Some other amount

8   Ability to refinance a short-term debt on a long-term basis is evidenced by:

a Actually having issued other short-term debt to replace the short-term debt after the date of the balance sheet but before it is issued

b Planning to issue equity securities to replace the short-term debt after the date of the balance sheet

c Having entered into a firm financing contract that will enable the debtor to refinance the short-term debt when it becomes due

d None of the foregoing

9   Reyes Company estimates its annual warranty expense at 2% of annual net sales. The following data are available:

Net sales for Year 5	$4,000,000
Warranty liability ledger account:	
December 31, Year 4 balance	$60,000 credit
Warranty payments during Year 5	50,000 debit

After estimated warranty expense for Year 5 is recorded, the warranty liability ledger account will show a December 31, Year 5, balance of:

a $10,000   **b** $70,000   **c** $80,000   **d** $90,000   **e** Some other amount

10 During Year 1, Charles Company introduced a new line of machines that carry a three-year warranty against manufacturer's defects. Based on industry experience, warranty expense is estimated at 2% of net sales in the year of sale, 4% in the year after sale, and 6% in the second year after sale. Net sales and actual warranty payments for the first three years were as follows:

	Net sales	Actual warranty payments
Year 1	$ 200,000	$ 3,000
Year 2	500,000	15,000
Year 3	700,000	45,000
Totals	$1,400,000	$63,000

What amount does Charles report as a liability under product warranty on December 31, Year 3?
a $0   **b** $5,000   **c** $68,000   **d** $105,000   **e** Some other amount

11 Laura Company sells its products in reusable, expensive containers. The customer is charged a deposit for each container delivered and receives a refund for each container returned within two years after the year of delivery. Laura accounts for the containers not returned within the time limit as being sold for the amount of the deposit. Information for Year 3 is as follows:

Containers held by customers on December 31, Year 2, from deliveries in:		
Year 1	$ 50,000	
Year 2	145,000	$195,000
Containers delivered in Year 3		260,000
Containers returned in Year 3 from deliveries in:		
Year 1	$ 30,000	
Year 2	85,000	
Year 3	95,000	210,000

What amount does Laura report as a liability for returnable containers on December 31, Year 3?
a $165,000   **b** $215,000   **c** $225,000   **d** $245,000   **e** Some other amount

12 The balance in Ashe Company's Trade Accounts Payable ledger account on December 31, Year 2, was $700,000 before any necessary year-end adjustments relating to the following:

(1) Goods were in transit from a vendor to Ashe on December 31, Year 2. The invoice cost was $50,000, and the goods were shipped FOB shipping point on December 29, Year 2. The goods were received on January 4, Year 3.

(2) Goods shipped FOB shipping point on December 20, Year 2, from a vendor to Ashe were lost in transit. The invoice cost was $25,000. On January 5, Year 3, Ashe filed a $25,000 claim against the common carrier.

(3) Goods shipped FOB destination on December 21, Year 2, from a vendor to Ashe were received on January 6, Year 3. The invoice cost was $15,000.

What amount does Ashe report as trade accounts payable on its December 31, Year 2, balance sheet?

a $725,000   **b** $740,000   **c** $750,000   **d** $775,000   **e** Some other amount

Ex. 10-2 On December 31, Year 3, Muriel Company issued a two-year noninterest-bearing promissory note with a face amount of $58,320 for the purchase of scrap metal. The transaction was recorded as follows:

| Purchases .... 58,320 | |
| Note Payable .... | 58,320 |

a Prepare a correcting journal entry for Muriel Company on December 31, Year 3, assuming that a fair rate of interest is 8% a year and that the accounting records are still open for Year 3. Use the Appendix at the end of Chapter 5 to determine the present value of the note.
b Prepare an adjusting entry for Muriel Company on December 31, Year 4, to record interest expense on the note.
c Show how the note is presented in Muriel Company's balance sheet on December 31, Year 4.

Ex. 10-3 Rio Company had $6 million of short-term commercial paper outstanding on June 30, Year 6, the end of its fiscal year. On that date, Rio had a firm contract to refinance the commercial paper by issuance of long-term debt. However, because Rio had excess cash in July, it retired $2 million of the commercial paper. On August 10, Year 6, Rio issued $12 million long-term bonds, and on August 15, it issued financial statements for the year ended June 30. The proceeds of the $12 million long-term bond issue were to be used as follows:

(1) To increase working capital, $2 million
(2) To pay balance of commercial paper, $4 million
(3) To finance construction of new warehouse, $6 million

Indicate how the foregoing information is to be presented in Rio Company's balance sheet on June 30, Year 6.

Ex. 10-4 The following information was taken from the accounting records of Grau Company for the first three months of its operations:

Month	Total salaries earned	Income taxes withheld	FICA taxes withheld (7%)	Remitted to Internal Revenue Service
January	$ 2,600	$ 290	$182	
February	3,400	360	238	$ 654 (1)
March	4,000	410	280	836 (2)
Totals	$10,000	$1,060	$700	$1,490

(1) Income taxes withheld ($290), FICA taxes withheld ($182), and employer's FICA taxes for January ($182).
(2) Income taxes withheld ($360), FICA taxes withheld ($238), and employer's FICA taxes for February ($238).

Journal entries to record the payroll for January and February, including taxes on the employer (FICA, 7%; state unemployment tax, 2.7%; and federal unemployment tax, 0.8%) were recorded properly. Remittances to the Internal Revenue Service were debited to the respective liability ledger accounts. All salaries earned through March 31 were subject to payroll taxes.

a Prepare a journal entry to record Grau Company's payroll for the month of March. Record all payroll taxes on the employer in the Payroll Taxes Expense ledger account.

b Prepare a journal entry for Grau Company on April 30 to record payment of the balance of the amount due for income taxes withheld, FICA taxes, and the full amount of state unemployment tax for the first quarter of the year. Federal unemployment tax is not due until the amount payable exceeds $100.

Ex. 10-5   On October 29, Year 5, Ernst Company contracted to purchase 7,500 tons of material in Year 6 at a fixed price of $100 a ton. The contract was not subject to cancellation. On December 31, Year 5, the replacement cost of the material was $88 a ton.

Prepare a journal entry for Ernst Company on December 31, Year 5, to recognize the loss on the firm purchase commitment.

Ex. 10-6   Raymond ZeBrack has an employment contract under which he is to receive a bonus of 20% of Kyle Company's net income in excess of $100,000. Kyle's income before the bonus and income taxes for the year is $385,000. Income taxes are 45% of taxable income.

Compute the amount of Raymond ZeBrack's bonus, rounded to the nearest dollar, assuming that it is based on Kyle Company's net income in excess of $100,000 after deduction of both the bonus and income taxes.

Ex. 10-7   At the end of a fiscal year, the auditors for Moran Company found the following contingencies that had not been entered in the accounting records:

a Stella Davis, a former officer of Moran, has threatened to sue Moran for $1 million "to recover the contributions she made to the success of the company's marketing program for which she was not compensated adequately." In the opinion of Moran's management and outside attorneys, the suit has absolutely no merit and probably will never be filed by Davis.

b Moran has guaranteed a debt of $500,000 issued by certain affiliated companies. The affiliated companies are in a strong financial position, and Moran's management does not consider that any of the companies will default on their debt.

c Moran's management is of the opinion that $100,000 should be set aside for general business risks that cannot be identified at the present time.

d Moran has been sued for industrial espionage, and the damages sought by the plaintiff amount to $200,000. Moran's outside counsel and management are of the opinion that the suit has merit and that the amount of the damages may range from a minimum of $25,000 to a maximum of $75,000. No amount in this range is a better estimate than any other amount.

For each situation described above, prepare a journal entry for Moran Company to record the contingency or briefly explain why a journal entry is not required.

Ex. 10-8   Adams Company sold a machine (that it had manufactured) on credit early in Year 5 for $1,200, along with a one-year warranty. Maintenance on each machine during the warranty period averages $100.

Prepare journal entries for Adams Company to record the sale of the machine and the cash expenditure of $85 to service the machine during Year 5, assuming that the Product Warranty Expense ledger account is debited at the time of sale and that Adams uses the periodic inventory system.

Ex. 10-9   In Year 1, Palmer Corporation began selling a new line of products that carry a two-year warranty against defects. Based on past experience with other products, the estimated warranty costs related to dollar sales are as follows:

First year of warranty 2%
Second year of warranty 5%

Sales and actual warranty payments for Year 1 and Year 2 are presented below:

	Year 1	Year 2
Sales	$500,000	$700,000
Actual warranty payments	10,000	30,000

Compute Palmer Corporation's estimated warranty liability at the end of Year 2.

Ex. 10-10   In an effort to increase sales, Remo Company launched a sales promotional campaign on June 30, Year 5, whereby Remo placed a coupon in each package of product sold, the coupons being redeemable for a premium. Each premium costs Remo $2, and five coupons must be presented by a customer to receive a premium. Remo estimated that only 60% of the coupons issued will be redeemed. For the six months ended December 31, Year 5, the following information is available:

Packages of product sold	Premiums purchased	Coupons redeemed
800,000	60,000	200,000

Compute Remo Company's estimated liability for premium claims outstanding on December 31, Year 5.

Ex. 10-11   Cord Company distributes to consumers coupons that may be presented (on or before a stated expiration date) to grocers for discounts on certain products of Cord. The grocers are reimbursed when they send the coupons to Cord. In Cord's experience, 40% of the coupons are redeemed, and generally one month elapses between the date a grocer receives a coupon from a consumer and the date Cord receives it. During Year 8, Cord issued two separate series of coupons as follows:

Date issued	Total value	Consumer expiration date	Amount disbursed as of Dec. 31, Year 8
Jan. 1, Year 8	$100,000	June 30, Year 8	$34,000
July 1, Year 8	120,000	Dec. 31, Year 8	42,000

Compute Cord Company's liability for unredeemed coupons on December 31, Year 8.

Ex. 10-12   Sinbad Company offers a coupon with each unit of product sold. A customer who submits 100 coupons is given a choice of prizes consisting of a football, a basketball, or a baseball glove. These prizes cost $5 each. The Promotional Expense ledger account is debited as redemptions are made during the year and also at the end of the year when an estimate is made of outstanding coupons that will be redeemed. The following summary transactions occurred in Year 1:

    a Acquired for cash 800 coupon books, each containing 1,000 coupons, for a total cost of $800. (Debit Inventory of Coupons.)

    b Issued 500,000 coupons to customers.

    c Acquired for cash 2,200 items of prize merchandise (footballs, basketballs, and baseball gloves).

    d Issued 1,500 prizes to customers.

    e Of the coupons issued, it is estimated that an additional 120,000 will be redeemed.

        Prepare journal entries to record each of the transactions of Sinbad Company.

Ex. 10-13   On January 6, Year 1, Plaga, Inc., acquired prize merchandise costing $5,000 for distribution in a promotional campaign, and related coupons costing $100 (an immaterial amount). During Year 1, prize merchandise costing $3,100 was distributed to customers in exchange for coupons. Coupons redeemable for $8,000 of prize merchandise were issued to customers. The controller of Plaga estimated that 90% of the coupons would be presented by customers who obtained the coupons from cartons of Plaga's product. No expiration date appeared on the coupons.

        Prepare journal entries for Plaga, Inc., in connection with the promotional campaign.

CASES

Case 10-1   Salcedo Company has been sued for $2,000,000 for an injury caused to a child as a result of alleged negligence while the child was visiting Salcedo's plant on March 10, Year 5. The lawsuit was filed on July 6, Year 5. Salcedo's lawyer states that it is probable that Salcedo will lose the lawsuit and be found liable for anywhere from $200,000 to $900,000. However, the lawyer states that the most probable estimated loss is $400,000.

Instructions

How should Salcedo Company report the probable effect of the lawsuit in its Year 5 financial statements? Discuss the rationale for your answer. Include in your answer disclosures, if any, that should be made in Salcedo's financial statements or in a note to the financial statements.

Case 10-2   Bennington Company sells two products, product X and product Y. Each product carries a one-year warranty. For product X, the warranty costs are based on past experience and normally amount to 1% of sales. For product Y, the warranty costs cannot be reasonably estimated because it is a new product; however, the chief engineer believes that warranty costs will be incurred.

Instructions

How should Bennington Company report the estimated warranty costs for each of the two products? Discuss the rationale for your answer. Do not discuss deferred income tax implications or disclosures that should be made in the financial statements or in a note to the financial statements.

Case 10-3   On June 30, Year 3, Horsley Company has a bank loan due on September 30, Year 3. The loan has been in existence for five years, but both Horsley and the bank intend to renew it indefinitely. The loan is collateralized by the cash surrender value of life insurance policies.

For several years, Horsley has been offering to officers and employees the right to acquire its 15% bonds that are redeemable at face amount at the holder's request at any time after two years from the date of issuance. In the past, executive incentive bonuses have been paid by the issuance of these bonds. During the past 10 years, bonds redeemed were less than 10% of bonds outstanding, and evidence indicates that no bondholders intended to redeem their bonds in the year ending June 30, Year 4.

Instructions

State how you would classify the cash surrender value of the life insurance policies, the bank loan, and the 15% bonds payable in the balance sheet of Horsley Company on June 30, Year 3. Give reasons for your answer.

Case 10-4   The balance sheet of Denny Company on December 31, Year 5, *did not* include among the current liabilities the following items (all of which are material in amount):

(1) Promissory notes payable to a group of twelve stockholders, the notes to become due and payable on demand of at least eight of the stockholders
(2) A promissory note payable due March 31, Year 6, in settlement of which the holder accepted 1,000 shares of preferred stock on January 15, Year 6.
(3) Rent collected one year in advance
(4) Bonds payable maturing on March 31, Year 6

Instructions

Assuming that in each case the exclusion from current liabilities was based on sound reasoning, give the arguments in support of the financial statement presentation used by Denny Company. If your answer involves assumptions as to facts not given in the case, state your assumptions.

Case 10-5   Promotek Company was organized on January 2, Year 1, to sell trading stamps to retailers who distribute the stamps gratuitously to their customers. Books for accumulating the stamps and catalogs illustrating the merchandise for which the stamps may be exchanged are given free to retailers for distribution to stamp recipients. Centers with inventories of merchandise have been established for redemption of the stamps. Retailers may not return unused stamps

The analysis on page 533 shows Promotek's expectations as to percentages of a normal month's activity that will be attained. For this purpose, a "normal month's activity" is defined as the level of operations expected when expansion of activities ceases or tapers off to a stable rate. Promotek expects that this level will be attained in the third year and that sales of stamps will average $2,000,000 a month throughout the third year.

Month	Actual stamp sales, %	Merchandise purchases, %	Stamp redemptions, %
6th	30	40	10
12th	60	60	45
18th	80	80	70
24th	90	90	80
30th	100	100	95

Promotek adopted a fiscal year ending on December 31, Year 1.

Instructions

a Discuss the accounting alternatives that should be considered by Promotek Company for the recognition of revenue and related expenses.

b For each accounting alternative discussed in **a** above, identify the ledger accounts that are used and indicate how each is classified in Promotek Company's balance sheet.

Case 10-6   A condensed balance sheet of Candide Corporation on December 31, Year 5, is presented below:

CANDIDE CORPORATION
Condensed Balance Sheet
December 31, Year 5

Assets

Current assets	$15,000,000
Other assets	25,000,000
Total assets	$40,000,000

Liabilities & Stockholders' Equity

15% Note payable to bank, due Feb. 1, Year 6	$ 2,500,000
18% Note payable to insurance company, due July 10, Year 6	1,500,000
Accounts payable and accrued liabilities	5,000,000
16% Bonds payable, due Dec. 31, Year 25	12,500,000
Stockholders' equity	18,500,000
Total liabilities & stockholders' equity	$40,000,000

Before Candide issued a classified balance sheet on March 1, Year 6, as of December 31, Year 5, you ascertained that Candide intended to refinance the two notes payable on a long-term basis. During December, Year 5, Candide negotiated a financing contract with Equitable Bank for a maximum amount of $4 million at any time through December 31, Year 6. The terms of the contract are as follows:

(1) Funds will be made available at the request of Candide, and any amount borrowed will mature three years from the date of borrowing. Interest at the prevailing bank prime interest rate will be due quarterly.

(2) An annual commitment fee of 1% will be charged by the bank on the difference between the amount borrowed by Candide and $4 million.

(3) The contract is cancelable by the bank only if:

(i) Candide's working capital, excluding borrowings under the contract, falls below $6 million.

(ii) Candide becomes obligated under a lease contract to pay annual rent in excess of $1 million.

(iii) Candide acquires treasury stock without prior approval of the bank.

(iv) Candide guarantees indebtedness of other business enterprises in excess of $200,000.

Instructions

a Is Candide Corporation's intention to refinance sufficiently finalized to permit the classification of the two notes payable as noncurrent liabilities in a classified balance sheet dated December 31, Year 5?

b Assuming that the two notes payable are properly excluded from Candide Corporation's current liabilities in the balance sheet dated December 31, Year 5, prepare a note to the financial statements to describe the refinancing contract.

PROBLEMS

10-1   Account balances and other data relating to liabilities, contingencies, and commitments of Computer Memories, Inc., on December 31, Year 5, are as follows:

Notes payable, due Feb. 1, Year 6	$ 80,000
Notes payable, due Oct. 31, Year 8	100,000
Discount on notes payable, due Oct. 31, Year 8	4,100
Notes payable to officers (renewed annually)	60,000
Trade accounts receivable (excluding $40,000 sold to a factor on a recourse basis)	171,200
Trade accounts payable	101,750
Bonds payable ($100,000 due on June 30 of each year)	800,000
Accrued payroll	4,280
FICA and income taxes withheld and accrued	1,770
Miscellaneous accrued liabilities	2,600
Stock dividend to be distributed (at stated value of common stock)	20,000
Income taxes payable	32,100
Deferred income tax credits (resulting from use of Accelerated Cost Recovery System for income tax purposes)	145,000
Liability for coupons outstanding	7,500
Unearned service contract revenue (contracts are for one year)	6,000

On October 10, Year 5, Computer Memories signed a noncancelable contract to purchase merchandise in Year 6 at a fixed price of $60,000; this merchandise had a market value of $52,000 on December 31, Year 5. On January 3, Year 6, $50,000 of the $80,000 principal amount of notes payable due February 1, Year 6, was refinanced on a long-term basis due February 1, Year 9.

Instructions

Prepare the current liabilities section of Computer Memories, Inc.'s balance sheet on December 31, Year 5, and list any contingencies and commitments that should be disclosed in a note to the financial statements.

10-2 The general manager of Incentive Systems, Inc., wants a bonus based on income of the current accounting period, which the general manager estimates will be approximately $660,000 before the bonus and income taxes.

Instructions

If the bonus rate is established at 10% and income taxes amount to 45% of taxable income, compute the estimated amount of the bonus to the general manager under each of the following assumptions. (Round all amounts to nearest dollar.)
a Bonus is based on income before income taxes and bonus.
b Bonus is based on income after bonus but before income taxes.
c Bonus is based on net income (after income taxes and bonus).

10-3 Listed below are selected transactions and events for Innovative Design Company relating to current liabilities during the year ended December 31, Year 8:

Jan. 10   Purchased merchandise for $30,000. A 2% discount is offered by suppliers. Innovative Design records purchases and accounts payable net of discounts and uses the periodic inventory system.

19   Paid $21,560 on invoice of January 10. The invoice amount was for $22,000 and was paid within the discount period.

31   Paid balance of January 10 invoice, $8,000, after the discount period.

Apr. 1   Issued one-year promissory note to a supplier in settlement of an invoice for $12,500 dated March 31. The invoice had been recorded net of 2% purchases discount; that is, $12,250. The face amount of the note was $14,210, including interest at 16% on $12,250 for one year. The note was recorded at face amount.

30   Wages for April were $16,000 before the following withholdings:

Income taxes	*$2,380*
FICA, 7%..	*1,120*

Innovative Design records payroll taxes at the end of each month in a Payroll Taxes Expense ledger account. All wages for April are subject to 2.7% state unemployment tax and 0.8% federal unemployment tax.

May 20   Declared dividends on common stock as follows:

Cash..	*$18,000*
Stock...	*3%*

The dividends were to be paid or distributed to stockholders on June 25. There are 300,000 shares of $5 par common stock outstanding;

the current market price of the common stock is $30 a share. (Debit Retained Earnings for total amount of dividends.)

June 25   Paid the cash dividend and distributed the stock dividend declared on May 20.

Dec. 31   Innovative Design sells service contracts on its products and credits Deferred Service Contract Revenue when payments are received from customers. For Year 8, $7,400 of the service contract revenue was considered realized.

    31   Recorded interest expense for Year 8 on the promissory note issued to the supplier on April 1.

Instructions

Prepare journal entries to record the foregoing transactions and events of Innovative Design Company.

10-4   Southern Milling Company acquired a machine on July 1, Year 1, for $10,000 and an 18-month, $45,000 face amount promissory note on which interest was payable at the annual rate of 10% on December 31 and June 30. The current fair rate of interest on a note of comparable quality was 16% compounded semiannually.

Instructions

(Round all computations to the nearest dollar.)

a Compute the cost of Southern Milling Company's machine and record the acquisition of the machine on July 1, Year 1. Use the Appendix at the end of Chapter 5 to determine the present value of the note payable.

b Prepare journal entries for Southern Milling Company to record the following:

(1) Payment of interest on the note and adjustment of the Discount on Note Payable ledger account on December 31, Year 1.

(2) Payment of interest on the note and adjustment of the Discount on Note Payable ledger account on June 30, Year 2.

(3) Payment of the note (principal and interest) and adjustment of the Discount on Note Payable ledger account on December 31, Year 2.

c Show how the note payable is presented in Southern Milling Company's balance sheet on December 31, Year 1.

10-5   Greenly Company, a publisher of trade magazines, is preparing its December 31, Year 5, financial statements and must determine the proper accounting treatment for each of the following situations:

(1) Greenly sells subscriptions to several magazines for a one-year, two-year, or three-year period. Cash receipts from subscribers are credited to Unearned Magazine Subscriptions Revenue, and this account had a balance of $2,400,000 on December 31, Year 5. Outstanding subscriptions on December 31, Year 5, expire as follows:

During Year 6	*$650,000*
During Year 7	*900,000*
During Year 8	*400,000*

(2) On January 2, Year 5, Greenly discontinued collision, fire, and theft coverage on its delivery vehicles and became "self-insured" for these risks. Actual losses of $45,000 during Year 5 were debited to Delivery Expense. The Year 4 premium for the discontinued coverage amounted to $100,000, and the controller wants to set up a reserve for self-insurance by a debit to Delivery Expense of $55,000 and a credit to Reserve for Self-Insurance of $55,000.

(3) A suit for breach of contract seeking damages of $1,000,000 was filed by an author against Greenly on July 1, Year 5. Greenly's legal counsel believes that an unfavorable outcome is probable. A reasonable estimate of the court's award to the author is in the range between $200,000 and $550,000. No amount in this range is a better estimate of potential damages than any other amount.

(4) During December, Year 5, a competitor filed suit against Greenly for industrial espionage claiming $2,000,000 in damages. In the opinion of management and Greenly's legal counsel, it is reasonably possible that damages will be awarded to the plaintiff. However, the amount of potential damages awarded to the plaintiff cannot be reasonably estimated.

(5) An investment of Greenly's in a foreign country has been expropriated. The carrying amount of the investment is $800,000, but Greenly expects to recover at least $1,000,000 on insurance policies covering this investment.

Instructions

For each situation above, prepare a journal entry for Greenly Company on December 31, Year 5, or explain why an entry is not required. Show any supporting computations.

10-6 While auditing the financial statements of Tao & Company for the year ended December 31, Year 3, you found that the following contingencies had not been entered in the accounting records:

(1) Doubtful accounts are estimated at $16,200 as a result of aging of the accounts receivable. The unadjusted balance of Allowance for Doubtful Accounts on December 31, Year 3, was a *debit balance* of $5,100.

(2) In prior years, Tao had not accrued estimated claims for injuries to customers as a result of their using Tao's products because such claims were covered by insurance. In Year 3, Tao discontinued the insurance. A reasonable estimate of outstanding claims on December 31, Year 3, was $31,000.

(3) A former employee has sued Tao for $500,000, alleging age discrimination. Tao's attorney does not think the suit has any merit but has suggested that Tao pay the former employee an out-of-court settlement of $8,000, because the cost of defending the suit was estimated at $50,000. Tao agreed, and the former employee signed appropriate settlement papers.

(4) Tao has lost a breach of contract suit, but the amount of damages has not been determined. The plaintiff is seeking damages of $100,000. Management and legal counsel are of the opinion that the damages the court would find for the plaintiff would be a minimum of $12,500 and a maximum of $50,000. No amount within this range is a better estimate of potential damages than any other amount.

(5) Tao is an indorser on notes receivable discounted at a bank in the amount of $150,000, including interest. All but one of the makers of the notes are financially sound companies. The one maker had issued a one-year 10% unsecured promissory note of $20,000 to Tao. The note matures on January 30, Year 4, but the maker's bankruptcy trustee has estimated that only 50% of the maturity value of unsecured notes will be paid.

(6) A lower court has awarded $200,000 in damages to Tao in litigation in which Tao was the plaintiff. The defendants have appealed the decision to a higher court, which is not expected to issue a decision for a year or more.

(7) During Year 3, Tao discontinued collision coverage on its motor vehicles and assumed the risk for this loss contingency. Actual losses of $15,000 during Year 3 were debited to Delivery Expense. Because the premiums for collision insurance in past years averaged $45,000, the controller wants to record a "reserve for self-insurance" by increasing the balance of the Delivery Expense ledger account by $30,000.

(8) Management has requested your consent to record a provision for unspecified general business risks for $120,000 by a debit to an expense ledger account.

Instructions

For each contingency described above, prepare a journal entry for Tao & Company to record the contingency, or briefly explain why an entry would not be in accordance with generally accepted accounting principles.

10-7 Sandra Corporation sells tomato juice in six-packs, cases, and through vending machines. In order to promote the drink, Sandra launched in Year 10 a promotional plan called "Toma." For every 10 bottle caps and 10 cents turned in, customers receive a ball-point pen and become eligible for a grand prize of $100 cash, one of which is awarded for every 12,500 bottle caps turned in. Sandra estimates that only 30% of the bottle caps will be presented for redemption. A summary of transactions for Year 10 follows:

(1) Sold 4,000,000 bottles of juice for $2,261,600 cash.
(2) Acquired 80,000 ball-point pens for $32,000 cash. (Debit Inventory of Prize Merchandise.)
(3) Expenses paid in cash and attributable to the promotional plan were $8,750.
(4) A total of 60,000 ball-point pens were distributed as prizes to customers, and an appropriate number of grand prizes were awarded on December 31, Year 10.

At the end of each year, Sandra recognizes a liability equal to the estimated cost of potential prizes outstanding. The 10 cents received for each pen is considered sufficient to cover the direct expenses of handling each request; therefore, neither the estimated direct expenses nor the potential remittances from customers are accrued at the end of the year.

Instructions

a Prepare journal entries for Sandra Corporation to record the transactions relating to the promotional plan for the year ended December 31, Year 10. Expenses of the promotional plan are recorded in a Promotional Expense ledger account.

b Compute the balances of all ledger accounts relating to the promotional plan of Sandra Corporation and explain how each account would appear in the financial statements for the year ended December 31, Year 10.

10-8 Bronson Company operates a retail store and must determine the proper December 31, Year 7, accrual for the following expenses:

(1) Bronson's store lease calls for fixed rent of $1,500 a month, payable at the beginning of each month, and additional rent equal to 5% of net sales in excess of $250,000 each calendar year, payable on January 31 of the following year. Net sales of the retail store for the year ended December 31, Year 7, were $2,200,000.

(2) Bronson has personal property subject to a city property tax. The city's fiscal year is from July 1 to June 30, and the tax, assessed at 3% of personal property owned on April 30, is payable on June 30 of the same year. Bronson has estimated that its personal property tax will amount to $8,400 for the city's fiscal year ending June 30, Year 8.

(3) All of Bronson's employees are entitled to two weeks of paid vacation for each full year in Bronson's employ. Unused vacation time may be accumulated and carried forward to succeeding years and will be compensated at the salary rate in effect at the time the vacation is taken. Mary Beal started her employment with Bronson on January 2, Year 1. As of December 31, Year 7, when Beal's salary was $522 a week, Beal had used nine weeks of her accumulated vacation time. In December, Year 7, Beal notified Bronson that she intended to use her accumulated vacation time in June, Year 8. Bronson regularly scheduled salary increases in July of each year. Bronson properly did not deduct compensation for unused vacation time in its income tax return for Year 7.

(4) Bronson operates in a state that levies a 10% tax on corporate income after federal income taxes. The state income tax for any year is an allowable deduction for the federal income tax for that year, but is not deductible for the state income tax for any year. The federal income tax is 40% of all taxable income. During the year ended December 31, Year 7, Bronson had $100,000 of income subject to both state and federal income taxes, before deduction of either state or federal income taxes.

Instructions

Compute to the nearest dollar the amount to be included in Bronson Company's current liabilities on December 31, Year 7, for each of the following:
a Lease rental
b Personal property taxes
c Accumulated vacation pay
d Federal and state income taxes

10-9 Described below are selected transactions and events of Plainview Company for the year ended December 31, Year 6:

(1) Plainview is obligated under an operating lease for the payment of minimum monthly rent of $1,000 in advance, plus additional rent (payable by the tenth

day of the following month) equal to 8% of the net income earned by its branch store, after both total rent and a 40% provision for income taxes have been deducted. Operating income of the branch store during January, Year 6, (before rent and income taxes) was $20,000. Income taxes expense is recorded monthly. (Compute rent expense to the nearest dollar and debit Rent Expense for both the rent advance on January 2 and the accrual of rent on January 31.)

(2) Plainview issues gift certificates in denominations of $5, $10, and $25. The certificates are redeemable in merchandise having an average gross profit of 25% of selling price. During March, Plainview sold $31,000 of gift certificates and redeemed certificates having a sales value of $27,400. It is estimated that 8% of the certificates issued will not be redeemed. Plainview uses the periodic inventory system, and thus does not compute the cost of goods sold until the end of the year. The sales of gift certificates are recorded in a Liability for Gift Certificates Outstanding ledger account.

(3) Sales during June totaled $777,000, of which $487,500 were on credit. Plainview operates in a state that has a 6% sales tax. Included in the sales amount are sales taxes to be collected from customers on all items except food, which is exempt from sales tax. Food sales amounted to 40% of total sales before the sales tax was added.

(4) Salaries for November, Year 6, were $250,000, of which $80,000 represented amounts paid over $40,000 and $150,000 represented amounts paid over $7,000 to certain employees. Income taxes withheld totaled $32,000, and FICA tax withholdings were at the rate of 7% (on wages up to $40,000 a year). Plainview is subject to a state unemployment tax rate of 2.7% and a federal unemployment tax rate of 0.8% (on wages up to $7,000 a year). Payroll taxes on the employer are recorded in separate expense ledger accounts. Record the accrued payroll and related payroll tax liabilities in the same journal entry.

Instructions

a Prepare journal entries for Plainview Company to record the transactions and events described above. An entry to record the accrual of income taxes for January should be made in part (1).

b Prepare a list of all current liability ledger accounts of Plainview Company involved in the journal entries in a. (Do not include account balances.)

10-10   Monte Rico Corporation started mining in Year 5 on certain land leased from Highlands Company. Monte Rico previously had paid minimum royalties of $56,000 to Highlands, none of which was earned, during a 3½-year period prior to Year 5. The royalty provisions in the lease contract are as follows:

(1) Minimum annual royalty is $16,000, with a minimum of $4,000 payable quarterly. Unearned minimum royalties may be recovered in any subsequent quarter from earned royalties in excess of minimum royalties.

(2) Earned royalty shall be 10 cents per ton shipped from the mine plus a per-ton amount equal to 3% of the amount that the market value of the ore at the mine exceeds $4 a ton.

Operations of Monte Rico for Year 5 are summarized at the top of page 541.

Quarter	Tons shipped	Market value at destination, per ton	Freight from mine to destination, per ton
1st	None		
2d	150,000	$11.50	$3.50
3d	300,000	12.50	3.50
4th	None		

Instructions

a Compute the amount of royalty to be paid to Highlands Company by Monte Rico Corporation for Year 5, and the amount of unearned minimum royalty on December 31, Year 5.

b How is the unearned minimum royalty paid reported in the balance sheet of Monte Rico Corporation on December 31, Year 5? Explain.

10-11 Four transactions completed by Bavaria Company during the year ended December 31, Year 7, are described below:

(1) On February 20, Year 7, Bavaria was offered a stock of merchandise being closed out by a manufacturer. Bavaria purchased the merchandise on February 26 for $72,000, and paid for it on March 1 by issuing a noninterest-bearing promissory note for $81,000, due on March 1, Year 8. Bavaria uses the periodic inventory system and records notes payable at face amount. The discount of $9,000 on the note payable is amortized by the straight-line method and represents a fair rate of interest.

(2) On July 1, property taxes on Bavaria's retail stores for the ensuing 12-month period became a lien against the property. Bavaria's controller estimated that property taxes for the year in the amount of $13,200 would be paid on November 1. Taxes in the amount of $13,300 were paid on November 1.

   Bavaria does not record the liability for property taxes on the lien date; however, it records the current year's portion of taxes as an expense at the time of payment.

(3) On November 2, Bavaria purchased $30,000 of merchandise from Y Company, terms 2/10, n/30; and $10,000 of merchandise from Z Company, terms 2/10, n/e.o.m. Bavaria records accounts payable net of cash discounts offered. The invoice from Y Company was paid on November 10, but the invoice from Z Company was not paid until November 25, and the cash discount was lost.

(4) On December 1, Bavaria launched a special one-month promotion of one of its products. Included in each product package sold during December was a coupon that, if returned to Bavaria with $1 enclosed, entitled the customer to receive a toy. Bavaria's sales manager estimated that 50% of the customers would accept the offer, which would cost Bavaria $1.20 for each toy claimed plus 30 cents in packaging and shipping costs. Bavaria acquired 50,000 toys for cash. During December, Year 7, 100,000 of the products were sold for $4 cash each, and 30,000 coupons were presented for redemption. (Credit the Packaging and Shipping Expense ledger account for 30 cents for each coupon redeemed because actual costs incurred in packaging and shipping were recorded

in that account.) On December 31, Year 7, on the basis of experience to date, it was estimated that only 12,000 additional coupons will be presented by customers before the offer expires. Toys that will not be distributed as prizes may be sold for 40 cents each. The inventory of prize merchandise expected to be sold should be written down to net realizable value by a debit to the Promotional Expense ledger account.

Instructions

a Prepare journal entries for Bavaria Company to record the transactions described above.

b Assume that no journal entries have been made other than the entries to record the foregoing transactions as they occurred. Prepare adjusting entries for Bavaria Company on December 31, Year 7, relating to each of the four transactions.

c Prepare a list of ledger accounts used in **a** and **b** and indicate the financial statement classification, that is, current asset, current liability, cost of goods sold, operating expense, etc., for each account. (Do not include ledger account balances.)

10-12 A summary of the financial position of Sorrento Company on December 31, Year 8, is presented below and on page 543.

Cash—includes an overdraft of $1,250 with Suburban Bank, receivables from employees of $300, and checks from customers of $3,500 dated January 10, Year 9, that have been recorded as cash receipts	$ 44,300
Customers—includes promissory notes of $20,000 (accrued interest of $800 has not been recorded), trade accounts of $77,500 (including an uncollectible account of $1,200 that should be written off), and an allowance for doubtful accounts of $1,300. Aging of accounts indicates that an allowance of $4,200 is required on December 31, Year 8. Customer's promissory note of $12,000 maturing on March 31, Year 9, has been discounted at a bank	96,200
Inventories—include $2,000 of prize merchandise, $6,800 of worthless goods, and $5,000 of goods on consignment from Capri Company	60,000
Prepayments—include tools of $2,000, cash surrender value of life insurance policies of $3,100, long-term utility deposits of $1,000	12,500
Fixtures—net of $34,500 accumulated depreciation	197,000
Total assets	$410,000

Current liabilities, recorded in a single ledger account that includes the following:

Promissory note payable due in three annual installments; interest at 15% since Sept. 1, Year 8, has not been accrued	$45,000	
Trade accounts payable	46,000	
Payable to Capri Company for consigned goods	5,000	
Liability for coupons outstanding	1,500	$ 97,500

(Sorrento has been sued for damages of $25,000 but does not anticipate that any liability will result.)

(continued)

Stockholders' equity—100,000 shares of no-par value common stock issued for $120,000 (less 1,000 shares of treasury stock reacquired for $2,800) and retained earnings of $195,300 ....   *312,500*

      Total liabilities & stockholders' equity............................   *$410,000*

Instructions

Prepare a revised balance sheet for Sorrento Company, including appropriate notes to the financial statements. Disregard the income tax effect of any corrections to previously reported net income. A working paper to determine correct ledger account balances is recommended in the following form:

Ledger accounts	Unadjusted ledger account balances		Adjustments and corrections		Corrected ledger account balances	
	Debit	Credit	Debit	Credit	Debit	Credit

10-13   Systems Dynamics Corporation requests that you make an estimate of its product warranty liability on June 30, Year 9.

Systems Dynamics manufactures television tubes and sells them under a six-month warranty to replace defective tubes without charge. On December 31, Year 8, Systems Dynamics reported a Liability for Product Warranty of $374,800. By June 30, Year 9, this account had been reduced to $55,920 by debits for the net cost of defective tubes returned that had been sold in Year 8. The net cost of replacing defective tubes sold in Year 9 (January to May) was recorded in the Product Warranty Expense ledger account.

System Dynamics began Year 9 expecting tube returns to equal 8% of the dollar volume of sales for the year. However, as a result of the introduction of new models during Year 9, this estimated percentage of returns was increased to 10% on May 1. It is assumed that no tubes sold during a specific month are returned in that month. Each tube is stamped with a date at the time of sale so that the warranty may be administered properly. The following table indicates the likely pattern of sales returns during the six-month period of the warranty, starting with the month following the sale of the tubes:

Month following sale	Percentage of total returns expected
First..	20
Second	30
Third..	20
Fourth, fifth, and sixth (10% each month)	30

Gross sales of tubes for the first six months of Year 9 were:

January	$3,600,000	April	$2,850,000
February	3,300,000	May	2,000,000
March....................	4,100,000	June	1,960,000

The warranty offered by Systems Dynamics also covers payment of the shipping cost on defective tubes returned and on new tubes shipped as replacements.

This shipping cost averages approximately 10% of the selling price of the tubes returned. The manufacturing cost of the tubes is roughly 80% of the selling price, and the residual value of returned tubes averages 20% of their selling price. Returned tubes on hand on December 31, Year 8, were carried in inventories at 20% of their original selling price.

Instructions

a Prepare a working paper to estimate Systems Dynamics Corporation's liability under its product warranty on June 30, Year 9.

b Prepare an adjusting journal entry for Systems Dynamics Corporation on June 30, Year 9. (Income tax considerations may be disregarded.)

10-14 The following list of Synchronicity Corporation's liabilities on December 31, Year 1, was prepared by an inexperienced accounting intern:

Trade notes payable (rates of interest, 12 to 15%)	$ 480,000
13% equipment contract payable (due $25,000 plus interest at the end of each month)	500,000
14% note payable (due June 1, Year 2)	350,000
12% note payable (due in annual installments of $100,000 on Jan. 31 of each year)	600,000
Trade accounts payable	1,050,000
Income taxes payable (net of $200,000 previously paid on the estimated amount due for Year 1, and including $135,000 of deferred income tax credits as a result of use of the Accelerated Cost Recovery System for income tax purposes)	174,000
Allowance for sales returns	25,000
Deposits on returnable containers	14,500
Interest payable	74,167
Miscellaneous current liabilities	32,100
Total liabilities	$3,299,767

Additional Information

(1) The financial statements for the year ended December 31, Year 1, were to be issued on February 1, Year 2. On January 23, Year 2, the principal amount of the 12% note payable was refinanced on a long-term basis by the issuance of an $800,000, 13½% mortgage note to Knapp Mortgage Company. The mortgage note matures on January 23, Year 7.

(2) On January 25, Year 2, a noncancelable agreement was reached with Troy Bank to refinance the principal amount of the 14% note payable on a long-term basis. The terms of the agreement are readily determinable but will not be finalized until February 4, Year 2. Both Synchronicity and Troy Bank are financially capable of honoring the agreement, and there have been no violations of any provisions of the agreement as of January 31, Year 2.

(3) Trade accounts payable were recorded at gross invoice amounts. A 2% cash discount is offered by suppliers on 80% of the trade accounts payable outstand-

ing on December 31, Year 1. Synchronicity wishes to establish an allowance for purchases discounts on December 31, Year 1.

(4) On November 28, Year 1, Synchronicity signed a noncancelable contract to purchase merchandise at a fixed price of $2,000,000 during the second quarter of Year 2. The market value of the merchandise under contract was $1,910,000 on December 31, Year 1. Neither the contract nor the price decline of the merchandise has been entered in the accounting records.

(5) During Year 1, Synchronicity issued coupons with a face amount of $280,000 to its customers. The expiration date of the coupons was December 31, Year 1, but redemptions are honored up to three months after the expiration date. Approximately 80% of the coupons issued are expected to be redeemed, and handling costs of 15% of the face amount of redeemed coupons generally are incurred by Synchronicity. Through December 31, Year 1, the face amount of the coupons redeemed amounted to $155,000, and handling costs of $23,100 were incurred and recorded in the Promotional Expense ledger account. The estimated amount of outstanding coupons on December 31, Year 1, and the related handling costs have not been recorded.

(6) The allowance for sales returns, the deposits on returnable containers, the interest payable, and the miscellaneous current liabilities were measured and recorded in conformity with generally accepted accounting principles.

Instructions

a Assuming that the accounting records have not been closed for Year 1, prepare a single journal entry as of December 31, Year 1, to correct Synchronicity Corporation's accounting records. Disregard income tax considerations.

b Prepare the liabilities section of Synchronicity Corporation's December 31, Year 1, balance sheet, including notes to the financial statements required by generally accepted accounting principles. (Reminder: The financial statements for the year ended December 31, Year 1, are to be issued on February 1, Year 2.)

Long-Term Assets and Liabilities

3

Accounting for long-term assets and liabilities provides accountants with some of their most challenging problems. The cost of plant assets, intangible assets, and long-term investments are measured and recorded; the cost of plant assets (other than land) and intangible assets is allocated to revenue over their economic lives; disposals of long-term assets require the recognition of gains and losses; exchanges of plant assets may result in deferral of an indicated gain if no monetary assets are received; accounting for long-term investments in equity securities may require the application of the equity method of accounting or the lower of cost or market rule, depending on the amount and nature of such investments; and the issuance and retirement of long-term liabilities involve some unusual accounting issues.

The use of long-term assets and proceeds from long-term borrowing requires periodic depreciation, depletion, and amortization. The differentiation between capital expenditures and revenue expenditures, selection of appropriate methods of depreciation, depletion and amortization for long-term assets, and the method of amortization for discount and premium on long-term debt have a significant impact on the measurement of income.

Other accounting problems arise in connection with long-term assets and liabilities, such as the capitalization of interest during construction, research and development costs, the estimate of goodwill for a business enterprise, the restructuring of debt, and in-substance defeasance of debt. These and additional topics are discussed and illustrated in this part.

Plant Assets: Acquisition and Disposal

11

Nature of Plant Assets

The terms *plant assets; plant and equipment; property, plant, and equipment;* or *fixed assets* often are used to describe the tangible assets used by a business enterprise in its operations. *Use in operations* distinguishes these assets from other tangible assets that are reported in the balance sheet as Investments. Land held as a prospective building site, for example, is an investment. When a building is constructed on the land and is placed in service, the land is reported in the balance sheet under plant assets. A characteristic common to all plant assets is that they yield services over many years. Plant assets other than land have a limited economic life; consequently, the cost of such assets must be allocated as depreciation expense to the accounting periods receiving benefit from their use.

Classification of Assets Used in Operations

Assets used in operations may be divided into tangible and intangible categories as follows:

Tangible Assets Tangibility is the characteristic of bodily substance, as exemplified by a tract of timber, a bridge, or a machine.

1 *Plant assets* Included in this category are properties acquired for use in operations. Examples are land, buildings and structures of all types, machinery, equipment, furniture, tools, orchards, returnable containers, and leasehold improvements. Plant assets generally are acquired for use rather than for sale. In yielding services over many accounting periods, a plant asset does not change in physical characteristic; that is, it does not become physically incorporated in the finished goods of a business enterprise. For example, a building or machine wears out and eventually loses its ability to perform efficiently, but its physical components remain relatively unchanged. In contrast, material is incorporated in finished goods.
a *Land* Unlike the other kinds of tangible property, land has an indefinite economic life. In general, land does not deteriorate with the passage of time and is

549

not physically exhausted through use. There may be exceptional cases. Agricultural land may suffer a loss of usefulness through erosion or failure to maintain fertility. Building sites may be damaged or destroyed by slides, floods, or earthquakes. Generally, land is accounted for as a nondepreciable asset.

b *Property having a limited economic life* With the exception of land, all other plant assets have limited economic lives. The cost of such assets is allocated through the process of *depreciation* to the cost of the goods and services produced. Depreciation is discussed in Chapter 12.

2   *Natural resources* This term includes *wasting assets* that are subject to exhaustion through extraction. The principal types of wasting assets are mineral deposits, oil and gas deposits, and standing timber. In essence, natural resources are long-term inventories acquired for sale or use in production over a number of years. The cost of acquiring and developing wasting assets is allocated to expense in the form of *depletion* charges. Depletion also is discussed in Chapter 12.

Intangible Assets Intangibility denotes a lack of physical substance. Examples of intangible assets (as this term is used in financial accounting) include patents, copyrights, trademarks, franchises, organization costs, and goodwill. The cost of acquired intangible assets is *amortized* over their estimated economic lives, but not in excess of 40 years.[1] Research and development costs incurred in the creation of internally developed intangible assets are recognized currently as expenses.

Accounting for Plant Assets

A plant asset is a *bundle of future services*. The cost of acquiring such an asset is a measure of the amount invested in future services that will be provided by the asset. At the time of acquisition, cost is also an objective measure of the exchange value of an asset. The market price represents the simultaneous resolution of two independent opinions (the acquirer's and the seller's) as to the current fair value of the asset changing ownership. There are cases where the acquirer pays too high a price because of errors in judgment or excessive construction costs, and it is sometimes possible to acquire plant assets at bargain prices. These, however, are exceptional cases; accountants seldom have reliable evidence to support either "unfortunate" or "bargain" acquisitions. Accountants use cost as the basis of recording and reporting plant assets because it is reliable and because it is a measure of the investment in future services.

The problem of determining *carrying amount* (often referred to as *carrying value* or *book value*) subsequent to acquisition is also important. As a plant asset is used in operations, a portion of the original bundle of services (cost) is used up. This is illustrated in the diagram on page 551. The carrying amount of a plant asset thus is reduced by depreciation, because a smaller bundle of potential services remains at the end of each accounting period.

Because plant assets generally have long economic lives, it is possible that their current fair value may rise above or fall below carrying amount between the time of acquisition and the time the services are used. When such price movements

---

[1] A more complete discussion of intangible assets appears in Chapter 13.

Bundle of asset services is used up and is called depreciation

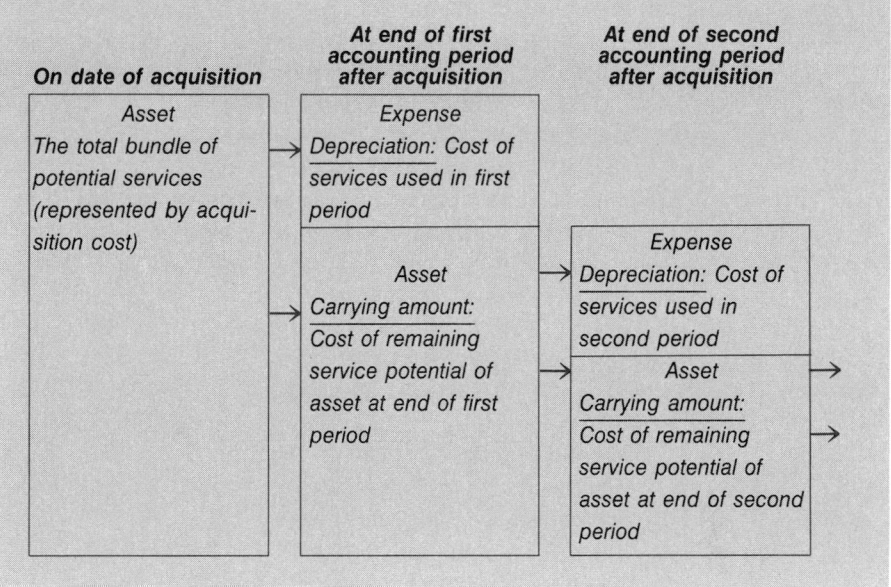

On date of acquisition	At end of first accounting period after acquisition	At end of second accounting period after acquisition
Asset *The total bundle of potential services (represented by acquisition cost)*	*Expense* *Depreciation: Cost of services used in first period*	
	Asset *Carrying amount:* *Cost of remaining service potential of asset at end of first period*	*Expense* *Depreciation: Cost of services used in second period*
		Asset *Carrying amount:* *Cost of remaining service potential of asset at end of second period*

are material, a question arises about the continuing significance of historical cost. This issue is discussed in Chapter 25.

COST OF PLANT ASSETS

The total cost of a plant asset is the cash outlay, or its equivalent, made to acquire the asset and place it in operating condition. This is a clear and simple statement of the principle involved; however, problems arise in the application of this principle to practical situations. In essence, these problems raise three questions: (1) What is included in the cost of plant assets? (2) How is the cost of plant assets measured? and (3) How are costs incurred subsequent to the acquisition date recorded? Each of these questions is examined in the following sections.

What Is Included in the Cost of Plant Assets?

Until a plant asset is ready to perform the services for which it was acquired, it is not complete. Some plant assets, such as a truck or a computer, are complete and ready to function at acquisition. The cost of such assets may be measured by the total of the invoice price (including sales tax) and transportation costs. Other assets, for example an automobile assembly line or the machinery for a paper mill, must be assembled, installed, and tested. *All expenditures* connected with the assembling, installing, and testing logically are viewed as a part of cost of the asset.

Capital Expenditures and Revenue Expenditures   Initial expenditures that are included in the cost of assets are called *capital expenditures,* and such expenditures are said to be *capitalized;* expenditures treated as current expenses are called *revenue expenditures.* The distinction between capital expenditures and revenue expenditures is important in the periodic measurement of net income. If the cost of acquiring plant assets is recognized as a current expense, income of the current accounting period is understated, and income of future periods, when the asset services are used, will be overstated.

The theoretical test to distinguish a capital expenditure from a revenue expenditure is simple: Have the services acquired been consumed entirely within the current accounting period, or will there be a carryover of services to future periods? As we shall see, this test is not always easy to apply. Many business enterprises follow an arbitrary procedure of debiting all asset expenditures of relatively small amounts (for example, those under $250) to expense accounts, to minimize accounting effort. Unless these small expenditures are significantly large in the aggregate, such practices, if consistently followed, are reasonable and efficient. They are condoned as a matter of expedience, because they do not materially distort periodic measurement of net income.

Specific types of capital expenditures and revenue expenditures after acquisition, such as additions, betterments, replacements, and repairs, are covered in a subsequent section of this chapter.

Land Special problems arise in the determination of the initial cost of land. Generally, the acquisition cost of land includes: (1) the acquisition price; (2) all costs of closing the transaction and obtaining title, such as real estate commission, legal fees, escrow fees, title investigations, and title insurance; (3) all costs of surveying, clearing, draining, or filling to make the land suitable for the desired use, including the cost of demolishing existing unneeded structures; and (4) costs of landscaping.

It sometimes is necessary to examine the terms of the acquisition contract to determine the price paid for land. Suppose, for example, that an acquirer agrees to pay $80,000 for a parcel of land in addition to delinquent property taxes of $5,000 and past-due mortgage note payments of $1,500. The acquisition cost of the land in this case includes all the additional consideration and is $86,500 ($80,000 + $5,000 + $1,500 = $86,500), not $80,000.

When newly acquired land is not in the condition necessary for the intended use, the acquirer will incur certain costs that should be recorded as part of the cost of the land. For example, costs of clearing trees, or of leveling hills or filling low spots, are included in the cost of the land. Any salvage material recovered in the process of clearing land represents a *cost offset.*

Land held as a potential building site or for investment purposes is not currently used in operations and should be reported under Investments in the balance sheet rather than as a part of the plant assets category. The *carrying costs,* such as property taxes and weed control incurred prior to the time that the land is placed in use, are capitalized (added to the cost of the land). When the site is placed in use, the land is reclassified from the investment category to the plant assets category, and future carrying costs are recognized as expenses.

Land Improvements Land improvement costs are capital expenditures and are either recorded as a part of land cost or recorded in a separate Land Improvements ledger account. Improvements such as landscaping and drainage, which have indefinite economic lives, are added to land cost. The cost of land improvements such as sidewalks, streets, and sewers may or may not have indefinite economic lives. In many localities, the cost of streets, sewers, and similar improvements are paid by the owners of the benefited property, but the local governmental unit agrees to maintain and replace them if they are built to standard specifications. In such cases the special assessment expenditure is a part of land cost, because it is permanent in nature. If the property owner is responsible for eventual replacement of land improvements, however, they have limited economic lives and are recorded in a separate Land Improvements ledger account to facilitate depreciation accounting.

Buildings The distinction between land and building costs may be of considerable importance because of the potential effect on net income. For example, suppose that a parcel of land is acquired as the site for a new building. On the land is an old building that must be razed before the new building can be constructed. Is the cost of tearing down the old building (net of any salvage recovery) a current expense, a part of the cost of the new building, or a part of land cost? If it is a current expense, it is deducted from revenue immediately; if it is a part of the cost of the new building, it will be depreciated over the economic life of the building; if it is a part of land cost, it will not be depreciated. What are the standards to be used in the application of these guidelines?

The primary issue is the nature of the relationship between the expenditure and a particular plant asset. Accountants must ask: What is the asset that has been acquired, and is the cost at issue reasonably related to the acquisition of this particular asset? If land is acquired for a building site, the entire cost of bringing the land into suitable condition as a building site, including cost of razing existing structures, is allocated to the land; in contrast, excavation costs incurred to construct the foundation for a new building are a part of the cost of the building.

The line of reasoning outlined above may be used to determine the appropriate accounting for various costs incurred during the construction of a new building. The examples below are illustrative:

Cost Incurred	*Accounting treatment*
1 Cost of temporary structures used for offices or for storing tools and material during construction of a new building.	***Record as cost of new building.*** This is a necessary cost of constructing the new building.
2 Cost of tearing down an old building previously used in operations in order to construct a new building.	***Record as a loss on retirement of old building.*** This cost is related to the services of the old building.
3 Cost of liability insurance coverage during construction of a new building.	***Record as cost of new building.*** This is an ordinary and necessary cost of constructing the new building.

When a building is constructed, all costs necessary to complete the construction should be included in the cost of the building. These may include architects' fees, building permit, and a variety of overhead costs. When a completed building is acquired, all costs relating to the acquisition (termite inspection fee, for example) that are applicable to future revenue should be capitalized. Separate ledger accounts may be used for the building shell (foundation, walls, and floors), partitions, air-conditioning units, roof, wiring, and siding.

Cost that will not benefit future accounting periods should not be capitalized. For example, suppose that immediately after the acquisition of a building it is found that extensive repairs are necessary. The proper treatment of such costs must rest on evidence as to the circumstances of the acquisition. If the acquirer recognized the need for these repairs at the time of acquisition, the repair costs are a part of the cost of placing the building in serviceable condition and should be capitalized. The reasoning is that paying $100,000 for a rundown building and $50,000 for renovation is equivalent to paying $150,000 for a renovated building. However, if a building is acquired for $150,000 under the assumption that it is in condition for occupancy and it is later discovered that there are serious defects requiring an expenditure of $50,000 to correct, any portion of the $50,000 expenditure that does not result in an improved structure or add to the originally anticipated economic life of the building should be deducted from revenue as incurred.

A similar line of reasoning may be used to reject proposals to treat the carrying amounts of obsolete plant assets replaced as part of the cost of the new plant assets acquired. The cost, and thus the service potential, of the new assets is not increased by the obsolescence of assets no longer in service. Future periods will benefit from the ownership and use of new assets, not from the retirement of the obsolete plant assets or from the failure to depreciate such assets fast enough.

Leaseholds and Leasehold Improvements   A *leasehold* is a personal property right granting to the *lessee* the use of real property for a specified length of time. The contract under which this right is granted is called a *lease,* and the owner of the property is known as the *lessor.* A lease contract generally requires monthly rent payments. On rare occasions, leases provide for a lump-sum payment of the entire rent in advance.[2] A lease contract gives the lessee the right to use the property in exchange for a contractual obligation to make future rent payments. Thus, it may be appropriate to record both the leased asset and the corresponding obligation to pay rent in the accounting records of the lessee. This topic is discussed in Chapter 20.

Leasehold improvements in the form of buildings or structural alterations sometimes are made on leased property. Accounting for leasehold improvements by the lessee is comparable with accounting for similar owned property, except that economic life should be related to the term of the lease. If the economic life of the leasehold improvements is less than the lease term, the cost of the improvements is amortized over their economic life. However, a building expected to last 20 years that is built on land leased for 15 years with no renewal option has a 15-year economic life to the lessee, and a residual value equal to any amount that the lessor agrees to pay to the lessee at the end of the lease term. When the lease contract contains a provision to renew at the option of the lessee, the length of economic life becomes uncertain, except in terms of the present intentions of the lessee. In the

---

[2]The lump-sum leasehold is almost extinct, largely because of the income tax law, which requires the lessor to include the entire amount received in taxable income in the year of receipt, without regard to the lease term.

foregoing example, if the lease contract contained a renewal option for an additional five-year period, the economic life for the building would be either 15 or 20 years, depending on the intent of the lessee with respect to renewal.

The lessor generally does not record leasehold improvements made by the lessee. However, if the lessor pays for any of the improvements, the cost should be recorded in a plant asset ledger account by the lessor and depreciated over the estimated economic life of the improvements.

Machinery and Equipment   This category may encompass a wide variety of items, including all types of machinery, furniture, fixtures, ships, vehicles of all types, tools, containers, patterns and dies, computers, and other office equipment. Cost of machinery and equipment items is determined and allocated to revenue through the process of depreciation. Several topics relating to the acquisition of machinery, equipment, and buildings are discussed in the following pages.

Self-Constructed Plant Assets   Occasionally, a building, machine, or equipment may be constructed by a business enterprise for its own use, either because this is an economical method of acquisition or because the quality and specifications of the asset may be controlled better if the asset is self-constructed. Determining the cost of the completed asset in this situation raises a number of issues.

Accountants generally agree that all direct costs incurred in construction activities should be capitalized. *Direct costs* are defined as costs that are identified specifically with the construction project in the sense that they would not have been incurred otherwise. Direct costs include the cost of material, labor, design, engineering, etc. Whether any overhead should be included in the cost of the self-constructed asset is a controversial issue.

The basic issue is whether overhead costs that will not change as the result of a self-construction project should be included in the cost of the new asset. Some enterprises have engineering and construction departments that regularly engage in new construction. The overhead costs incurred in these departments benefit current revenue-producing activities as well as the new construction. But what of the overhead costs of a regular producing department that undertakes the construction of a plant asset? It is difficult to imagine a situation in which any significant self-construction project could be undertaken without some increase in overhead. However, there are several fixed overhead costs that will not increase as a result of construction activities. If these fixed costs are allocated between regular production and self-construction projects, the result may be that the average manufacturing cost for units produced will be reduced during accounting periods in which self-construction activities are undertaken. Pre-tax income during the construction period thus would be increased by the amount of the fixed overhead costs allocated to the self-constructed asset. The three possible approaches to this issue are the following:

1   *Allocate no overhead costs to the self-constructed asset*   This approach has little to recommend it. At least some overhead costs are the direct result of new construction, and charging such incremental overhead costs to current operations is a clear case of distortion of income by the failure to recognize a capital expenditure.

2 *Allocate only incremental overhead costs to the self-constructed asset* This approach may be defended on the grounds that incremental overhead costs represent the relevant cost that management considered in making the decision to construct the asset. Fixed overhead costs, it is argued, are period costs. Because they would have been incurred in any case, there is no relationship between the fixed overhead costs and the self-constructed project. This approach has been widely used in practice because it does not distort the cost of normal operations.

3 *Allocate a portion of all overhead costs to the self-constructed asset* The argument for this approach is that the proper function of cost allocation is to relate all costs incurred in an accounting period to the output of that period. If an enterprise is able to construct an asset and still carry on its regular activities, it has benefited by putting to use some of its *idle capacity,* and this fact should be reflected in larger income. To charge the entire overhead to only a portion of the productive activity is to disregard facts and to understate the cost of the self-constructed asset. This line of reasoning has considerable merit.

If a plant asset is constructed for less than the lowest bid received from an outside contractor, the asset is recorded at actual cost; no "profit" is recognized. Profits are generated from asset *use and disposal,* not from asset *acquisition;* the *cost saving* will be realized through lower depreciation expense over the economic life of the asset.

Interest during Construction Period During the time it takes to complete a self-construction project, cash is tied up in material, labor, and other construction costs. Is the interest cost incurred in borrowing funds for this purpose a part of the cost of the constructed asset? This has been a controversial question in financial accounting.

Generally, accountants regard interest as a cost of financing, not as a cost of obtaining asset services. If X pays cash for an asset and Y borrows cash to acquire an identical asset, there is no logical basis for claiming that Y has an asset with a higher cost because it has paid interest on borrowed funds. This reasoning, applied to self-constructed assets, suggests that interest on funds borrowed and used in construction should not be capitalized.

The opposing view is that interest during construction is a cost of acquiring future asset services. Funds are immobilized during the construction period. In deciding to construct an asset, management of the business enterprise must have determined that the value created would be sufficient to cover all costs, including interest. Furthermore, interest on investment is included in the price of the asset if it is acquired in finished form. Therefore, it may be argued, the interest on funds employed in construction of an asset should be added to the cost of the asset rather than expensed.

In 1979, the FASB issued *Statement No. 34,* "Capitalization of Interest Cost," which established the current standards of accounting and reporting for capitalized interest cost.[3] The FASB pointed out that the cost of any asset includes

[3]*FASB Statement No. 34,* "Capitalization of Interest Cost," FASB (Stamford: 1979). The remaining discussion in this section is based on pages 2–8 of this *Statement.*

all costs "incurred to bring it to the condition and location necessary for its intended uses." When a period of time is needed to bring the asset to that condition and location, the interest cost incurred in these efforts should be included in the cost of the asset. Such a period of time is called the *acquisition period.* The objectives of this accounting treatment of interest cost are (1) to measure more accurately the total investment in the asset, and (2) to charge this investment, including interest cost, to future revenue that will benefit from the use of the asset.

Capitalization of interest cost *is required* for assets that are constructed for a business enterprise's own use, and for assets intended for sale or lease that are constructed as clearly identifiable projects, such as ships and parcels of real estate; interest cost *is not capitalized* for inventories that are routinely produced in large quantities on a repetitive basis, assets that are either in use or ready for use, and assets that are not intended for use in the activities of the enterprise. For example, the interest cost relating to idle land is not capitalized; however, if the land is being developed for a particular purpose, the interest paid on any debt incurred in the acquisition and development of the land is capitalized. Thus, if land is to be used as a parking lot or sold as developed land, interest is included in the cost of the land. However, if land is to be used to construct buildings for the enterprise's own use or for resale, interest is added to the cost of the buildings.

The amount of interest property capitalized is that portion of interest cost during the acquisition period that *could have been avoided if the asset had not been acquired.* Needless to say, the application of this concept is not easy. *If a project is financed by a specific loan, the interest actually paid on the loan is capitalized.* However, if a project is financed from internally generated funds or from general borrowings, the average effective interest rate on all outstanding debt is used to compute the amount of interest capitalized. The total amount of interest capitalized in an accounting period must not exceed the total amount of interest cost actually incurred by the business enterprise in that period. The acquisition period begins when the following three conditions are present:

1   Expenditures for a specific asset have been incurred.

2   Activities to prepare the asset for use are in progress.

3   Interest cost is being incurred.

Interest capitalization continues as long as all three of these conditions are present and ends when the asset is completed and is ready for use. The total interest cost incurred and the total interest cost capitalized in an accounting period must be disclosed in a note to the financial statements (see page 230).

To illustrate the computation of interest cost capitalized as part of the cost of an asset, assume that Clark Steel Company constructed a blast furnace in the current year. The construction activity started on March 1, and the furnace was ready for use on December 1. Thus, the acquisition period was nine months. On March 1, Clark borrowed $400,000 at 15% for five years to pay for the parts and material acquired on that date, and financed additional costs of $360,000 from its general borrowing of approximately $4,000,000, which carried an average interest rate of 12%. The additional costs of $360,000 were incurred at a rate of $40,000 a month from March 1 through December 1. Thus, the average amount of the accumulated additional costs was $180,000 ($360,000 ÷ 2 = $180,000) during the acquisition period. The total interest cost included in the cost of the blast furnace is computed below:

Computation of interest
capitalized as part of
cost of plant asset

	Interest capitalized
Specific borrowing on Mar. 1 ($400,000 × 0.15 × 9/12)	$45,000
Average accumulated additional costs from Mar. 1 to Dec. 1	
($180,000 × 0.12 × 9/12)	16,200
Total interest cost included in cost of blast furnace	$61,200

Assuming that Clark Steel Company debits interest cost to the Interest Expense ledger account when it is incurred, the journal entry to capitalize the interest cost included in the cost of the blast furnace is as follows:

Journal entry to
record capitalized
interest cost

Machinery and Equipment	61,200	
Interest Expense		61,200
To capitalize interest cost included in cost of blast furnace.		

The total cost of the blast furnace for financial accounting is $821,200 ($400,000 + $360,000 + $61,200 = $821,200). Note that no interest cost is capitalized after the furnace is placed in use on December 1, even though interest continues to accrue on the $400,000 loan for the acquisition of parts and material needed for the construction of the blast furnace.

Ledger Account for Self-Constructed Plant Assets   A Construction in Progress ledger account generally is used to record the costs incurred in the self-construction of plant assets. This account is debited with the material, labor, overhead costs, and interest cost incurred in the construction of the assets. During the period of construction, depreciation is not recorded for the self-constructed assets because they are not producing revenue. If several plant assets are being constructed in an accounting period, a subsidiary ledger may be established for the **work orders** used to record costs accumulated for each asset, similar to job order cost accounting for manufactured goods. When construction is completed, the appropriate plant asset ledger account is debited and the Construction in Progress ledger account is credited for the total cost incurred in the construction of the asset.

How Is Cost of Plant Assets Measured?

We have reviewed some of the problems that arise in the determination of what is included in the cost of plant assets. Now, let us examine the problems that arise in the measurement of the cost of plant assets when the method of acquisition obscures the acquisition price. The objective of cost measurement is to determine the cash outlay or its equivalent necessary to obtain the asset.

Cash Discounts   When assets are acquired under terms that allow the deduction of a discount for the payment of cash in a specified period of time, the term "cash equivalent" may be interpreted to mean the invoice price, net of the discount. For example, if M Company acquires a plant asset for $10,000, terms 2/10, n/30, it has the choice of either paying cash (in a 10-day period) of $9,800, or deferring payment for an additional 20 days, at an added cost of $200. If payment is made in the 10-day period, the cost of the asset is only $9,800; if payment is deferred for 20 days, the additional $200 paid is a penalty for late payment and is not included in the cost of the asset.

Deferred Payment Contracts   In many cases, payment for a plant asset is delayed for long time periods. For example, suppose that equipment is acquired under a contract calling for payments of $1,490 at the end of each year for 10 years. To assume that the present value of the liability, and thus the cost of the equipment, is $14,900 ($1,490 × 10), is to ignore the fact that there is an interest charge included in the contract. To arrive at a basis for recording this acquisition, accountants must look for evidence of the cash-equivalent price of the equipment. If the equipment may be acquired for $10,000 cash, this amount becomes the measure of cost. If no conclusive evidence of a cash price is available, the rate of interest implicit in the contract price should be determined. The present value of an ordinary annuity of 10

Journal entries for acquisition of plant asset on installment plan

On acquisition date:

Equipment	10,000	
Discount on Equipment Contract Payable	4,900	
Equipment Contract Payable		14,900

To record acquisition of equipment under contract requiring payment of $1,490 at the end of each of 10 years. Present value of equipment contract payable at 8% is $10,000.

Payment on contract at end of first year:

Interest Expense	800	
Equipment Contract Payable	1,490	
Cash		1,490
Discount on Equipment Contract Payable		800

To record interest expense on equipment contract for first year ($10,000 × 0.08 = $800) and payment of first installment.

Payment on contract at end of second year:

Interest Expense	745	
Equipment Contract Payable	1,490	
Cash		1,490
Discount on Equipment Contract Payable		745

To record interest expense on equipment contract for second year [($13,410 − $4,100) × 0.08 = $745] and payment of second installment.

rents of 1 at an unstated interest rate is 6.71 ($10,000 ÷ $1,490 = 6.71), and Table 4 of the Appendix at the end of Chapter 5 shows that 6.71 is the present value of 10 equal payments of 1 *at 8% interest.* Thus, the present value of 10 equal payments of $1,490 at 8% interest is approximately $10,000.[4] Assuming that an 8% rate of interest is reasonable, the acquisition of the equipment and the first two payments are recorded under the interest method as illustrated on page 559.

When payment is deferred for relatively short time periods, the amount of interest implicit in the acquisition price may not be material in amount and may be ignored. However, if the length of time and the amount of interest involved are material, a reasonable estimate of the cash-equivalent acquisition price is required.[5]

Property often is acquired by assuming a purchase-money obligation. A *purchase-money mortgage,* for example, is a loan created at the time property is acquired, collateralized by the property, and having priority over any subsequently created lien on the property.

Lump-Sum Acquisitions   A single negotiated price may be paid for two or more assets. If the assets have different economic lives, it is necessary to allocate the total lump-sum cost among them to provide a proper basis for the computation of depreciation. The most common example of this situation is the acquisition of real property—land and building—for a single price. Because the economic life of land is indefinite and the economic life of a building is limited, an allocation of the total cost is necessary. Assume, for example, that a building and the land on which it is located are acquired for $250,000 (see escrow statement on page 561). How is an accountant to determine how much of the $250,000 applies to the land and how much to the building? An examination of the negotiations that preceded the transaction may show that the price was settled on under the assumption that $200,000 applied to the building and $50,000 to the land. If such evidence is not available or is considered to be unrealistic, the accountant must look elsewhere for more objective evidence of *relative values* as a basis for cost allocation. If, for example, the assessed valuation for property tax purposes is $161,000 for the building and $69,000 for land, the allocation of the total cost of $250,000 is made as follows:

Allocation of joint costs by relative value method

	Assessed valuation	Relative value	×	Total cost	=	Allocation of cost
Building	$161,000	70%				$175,000
				$250,000		
Land	69,000	30%				75,000
Totals	$230,000	100%				$250,000

The Escrow Statement   Parties to a real estate transaction generally engage an agent (bank or escrow company) to handle the details of the transaction. When the

---

[4]$1,490 × 6.71 = approximately $10,000.
[5]See *APB Opinion No. 21,* "Interest on Receivables and Payables," AICPA (New York: 1971).

transaction is closed, each party receives an *escrow statement,* which shows the complete details of the transaction. The escrow statement shows (as charges and credits) items such as selling price of the property, mortgage note assumed by the acquirer, transfer taxes, commission charged to the seller, escrow fees, cash received from the acquirer, any amount paid to either party to complete the transaction, etc. The allocation of property taxes, interest on the mortgage note, insurance, rents, and other items also is summarized in the escrow statement. A condensed escrow statement for the acquirer of the property discussed in the preceding section is shown below:

Escrow statement
for building and land

WESTERN ESCROW COMPANY
Escrow Statement for Acquirer

Escrow No. 1-879   *Date: November 1, Year 1*

Items	Charges	Credits
Acquisition price of property.............................	$246,700	
Balance of mortgage note assumed......................		$104,000
Interest at 12% from Oct. 16, Year 1, to Nov. 1, Year 1		520
Property taxes prorated, $6,600 a year from July 1, Year 1, to Nov. 1, Year 1		2,200
Fire insurance prorated, $480 a year from Nov. 1, Year 1, to May 1, Year 2	240	
Deposited in escrow by acquirer.........................		143,570
Title policy (acquirer agreed to pay full amount)	1,490	
Revenue stamps (tax on transaction)	290	
Recording fee..	20	
Escrow fee (acquirer agreed to pay full amount)	1,500	
Check to balance (made payable to acquirer).............	50	
Totals	$250,290	$250,290

The escrow statement for the acquirer shows that the acquisition price of the property was $246,700, a debit in the escrow statement. The acquirer was charged $240 for unexpired insurance, and additional costs of $3,300 ($1,490 + $290 + $20 + $1,500 = $3,300) allocable to the property. Thus, the total cost of the property is $250,000 ($246,700 + $3,300 = $250,000). The acquirer was credited for $104,000, representing the unpaid balance of the mortgage note assumed, $520 of accrued interest on the mortgage note and $2,200 of accrued property taxes that the acquirer must pay on a later date, and $143,570 that previously was deposited in escrow to apply on the acquisition price. (The cash deposit had been recorded in the Escrow Deposit ledger account.) The "check to balance" of $50 is the amount of cash returned to the acquirer to close the escrow on November 1, Year 1.

The escrow statement for the acquirer provides the information needed to record the acquisition of the property as illustrated at the top of page 562.

A similar escrow statement prepared for the seller provides the required information to record the sale of the property by the seller.

Cash	50	
Building	175,000	
Land	75,000	
Unexpired Insurance	240	
Interest Payable		520
Property Taxes Payable		2,200
Mortgage Note Payable		104,000
Escrow Deposit		143,570

*To record acquisition of building and land per Escrow No.
1-879. The total cost of $250,000 is allocated on the basis
of property tax valuation of building and land (see allocation
on page 560).*

Securities Issued in Exchange for Plant Assets

When a corporation issues shares of its common stock for a plant asset, the appropriate basis for recording such a transaction is not always clear. The current fair value of the plant asset acquired is the cash equivalent received by the corporation for its shares of common stock.[6] Conversely, the current fair (or market) value of the common stock given in exchange is a measure of the consideration for the asset. Thus, accountants are faced with the problem of obtaining independent evidence of (1) the current fair value of the plant asset, and (2) the current fair value of the common stock given in exchange. We should expect these two values to be roughly equivalent; if they are not, a choice between them must be made based on the factors considered by management in completing the transaction and on the validity of each valuation.

Shares of common stock represent an interest in the net assets of a corporation, including the plant asset being acquired. The market price of the common stock issued thus is not an entirely independent variable, because it depends to some extent on the value of the asset received in exchange. This reasoning indicates that our first choice should be independent evidence of the current fair value of the asset acquired, determined by appraisal, from previous bid prices, or from other objective sources. For example, if a machine that was appraised at $180,000 is acquired in exchange for 2,000 shares of $50 par common stock, the exchange is recorded as follows:

Machinery	180,000	
Common Stock, $50 par (2,000 × $50)		100,000
Paid-in Capital in Excess of Par		80,000

*To record exchange of 2,000 shares of $50 par common
stock for machine appraised at $180,000.*

---

[6]Procedures for recording assets acquired pursuant to business combinations accounted for as *purchases* and as *pooling of interests* are discussed briefly in Chapter 16.

In some cases, evidence of the market value of shares of common stock is easier to obtain and more reliable than evidence as to the current fair value of an asset. This is particularly true if the common stock is listed on a stock exchange and daily quotations of market price are available.

Plant Assets Acquired by Gift Normally, there is a presumption against the idea that anyone makes a gift to a business enterprise. However, a corporation may receive property under conditions that may be interpreted as the receipt of a gift. For example, assume that the City of Stillwater is trying to attract industry to its area. In order to induce Tanner Company to locate a manufacturing plant in its city, the City Council of Stillwater agrees to donate a building site and to construct a building for Tanner, in return for which Tanner promises to operate a plant employing 200 persons for a period of 10 years. The land has a current fair value of $400,000, and the building has a current fair value of $2,000,000.

How should this transaction be recorded? If we adopt the view that the sole responsibility of accountants is to keep track of costs incurred, we might argue that no cost is involved in the acquisition of the land and building in this instance, and therefore no journal entry is required. This is, however, too narrow a view of the scope of accounting. A primary justification for recording asset acquisitions at cost is that cost at that time represents more satisfactory evidence of current fair value than any other basis. When cash outlay no longer is a reasonable basis for asset accountability or income measurement, accountants should be prepared to deal with the problem on its merits, rather than adhering solely to the cost principle. If a business enterprise receives an asset at no cost, *the asset should be recorded at its current fair value,* determined on the basis of the best evidence available. Referring to the Tanner Company example, the donation of the land and building results in an increase in the net assets of Tanner and is recorded as follows:

Recording a
donated asset

Land	400,000	
Building	2,000,000	
Donated Capital		2,400,000
To record at current fair value property donated by City		
of Stillwater.		

Conditions sometimes are attached to a gift of property so that title is not transferred until the conditions are met (for example, continuing operations for a specified number of years). As long as indications are that the enterprise receiving the gift of property intends to comply, and is capable of complying, with the conditions, depreciation expense should be recorded in the regular manner, both before and after title is acquired, in order that the services obtained from the use of the asset are recognized as expenses.

Investment Tax Credit Federal income tax statutes provide for a reduction of income taxes paid by individuals and corporations by an amount known as the *investment tax credit.* The investment tax credit is subject to a number of limitations and has been amended frequently and even suspended. The credit generally ranges from 6% to 10% of the cost of depreciable property other than buildings and their structural components. To illustrate, if a corporate enterprise acquired for $100,000 a plant asset that qualified for a 10% investment tax credit, it would be entitled to a reduction of $10,000 ($100,000 × 0.10 = $10,000) in its federal income taxes payable.

Two methods have been used to recognize the effect of the investment tax credit in the accounting records.

1   The *flow-through method,* which reduces income taxes expense by the amount of the investment tax credit in the year the plant asset is acquired. This method is favored by most business executives on grounds that immediate tax reduction is the intent of the federal income tax law. Because income taxes expense is reduced in the year depreciable plant assets are acquired, this method allows business enterprises to increase net income by acquiring depreciable plant assets that qualify for the investment tax credit.

2   The *deferral method,* which requires the amortization of the benefit arising from the investment tax credit over the economic life of the depreciable plant asset acquired. Under this method the investment tax credit is viewed as a reduction in the effective cost of the asset, although it generally is reported as a deferred credit in the balance sheet and is amortized by periodic credits to the Income Taxes Expense ledger account.

The deferral method is favored by most accountants because it avoids an immediate increase in net income as a result of acquisition of plant assets, and thus provides a more meaningful measurement of net income. However, most individuals and corporations use the flow-through method.[7] Accounting for the investment tax credit is discussed further in Chapter 21.

Costs Subsequent to Acquisition

Expenditures relating to plant assets normally are made throughout the economic life of the assets. Whether these expenditures should be charged against current revenue *(revenue expenditures)* or whether they should be capitalized *(capital expenditures)* often is a difficult question. The general approach for dealing with these expenditures may be stated as follows: Expenditures that result in additional asset services, more valuable asset services, or extension of economic life are capitalized and allocated to future revenue; expenditures to maintain plant assets in good operating condition are recognized as expenses. This approach is consistent with the principle of matching expired costs and revenue and should be applied to any expenditure of significant amount. *Future benefit is a characteristic of all capitalized costs relating to plant assets; costs that are applicable to current or past revenue are recognized as expenses or losses.*

Although the general approach outlined in the preceding paragraph enables accountants to distinguish between capital expenditures and revenue expenditures

---

[7]*Accounting Trends & Techniques,* 38th ed., AICPA (New York: 1984), p. 289.

incurred subsequent to acquisition of plant assets, a brief discussion relating to different types of such expenditures is appropriate.

Additions   An *addition* is a capital expenditure for a new and separate plant asset or an extension of an existing asset. The construction of a new wing on an existing building is an example of an addition to buildings. The installation of two-way communication radios in a fleet of delivery trucks is an example of an addition to equipment. The addition of entirely new units is identical in nature to the acquisition of new plant assets and raises no accounting problems not discussed previously. When the addition involves an enlargement or extension of an existing plant asset, the only problem is to determine whether any portion of the service potential of the existing asset has been removed or lost in the process. For example, if in connection with the construction of a building addition, it is necessary to remove the old heating unit and install one with a larger capacity, the old heating unit should be retired. The journal entry to record the addition is accompanied by another entry to remove the cost of the old heating unit and its related accumulated depreciation from the accounting records and to recognize any resulting loss.

Improvements, Renewals, and Replacements   Improvements (or betterments), renewals, and replacements are nonrecurring capital expenditures that add to the service potential of plant assets. The additional value may be the result of extending the economic life, increasing the rate of output, or lowering the cost of operation per unit of output. Therefore, such capital expenditures are related to future services and should be matched with revenue in the accounting periods in which the services are used. Improvements and renewals may be accomplished through the substitution of better component parts and thus may be labeled "replacements." The distinction between these different expenditures is obscure and is not relevant to the basic accounting issues involved. Costs of this type often are referred to as *plant renovation* (or *plant modernization*) *costs*.

To the extent that renovation involves the substitution of a new part for an old one, the proper accounting is to remove the cost of the old part from the asset ledger account (and the appropriate amount from the related accumulated depreciation account) and to substitute the cost of the new part. If the renovation does not involve a substitution but results only in some modification of the plant asset, the costs incurred are added to the carrying amount of the asset by a debit to either the asset ledger account or the accumulated depreciation account. These three procedures are explained below:

1   A considerable improvement in accounting for plant assets is possible if property units are defined in terms of major components and separate economic lives are used to depreciate these components. To illustrate, suppose that a glass-lined food storage tank is constructed at a cost of $200,000, of which $40,000 is estimated to be the cost of the glass lining. The estimated economic life of the tank is 20 years; the lining must be replaced approximately every five years. If a single ledger account, Storage Tanks, is used, there will be a problem of dealing with the periodic replacement of the lining. A better procedure is to use two ledger accounts, Storage Tanks and Tank Lining, and to depreciate the former over 20 years and the latter over five years. Now, assume that at the beginning of the fifth year the glass lining had to be replaced at a cost of $54,000, but a new material was used that is expected to last ten years, with no net residual value. The journal entries to record the lining replacement are shown below:

Journal entries for replacement of a component of a plant asset

Accumulated Depreciation of Tank Lining ($40,000 × ⅘)	32,000	
Loss on Retirement of Tank Lining	8,000	
Tank Lining		40,000
To record removal of old tank lining. Carrying amount of old tank lining is recognized as a loss.		
Tank Lining	54,000	
Cash		54,000
To record replacement of old lining with new material.		

Depreciation of the new lining is recorded at $5,400 ($54,000 ÷ 10 = $5,400) in each of the next ten years, and the Storage Tanks ledger account is undisturbed by these events.

2   A capital expenditure that does not replace an existing part may enlarge the capacity or improve the efficiency of a plant asset without prolonging its economic life. Such an expenditure is recorded in the asset ledger account and depreciated over the remaining economic life of the asset. This procedure is similar to the one previously suggested for additions.

3   The cost of plant asset renovation often is debited directly to Accumulated Depreciation. The rationale for this procedure is that such an expenditure extends the economic life of the asset and thus restores some of the service potential (cost) previously written off. This procedure is sound in theory and may be used for income tax purposes, but it should not be followed indiscriminately, particularly when capital expenditures for additions and replacements are involved.

Rearrangements and Moving Costs   Costs of rearranging machinery and equipment to provide a more efficient plant layout may be recorded in a separate ledger account and amortized over the period of time expected to benefit from the rearrangement (usually a short period because of the possibility of further rearrangements). Costs of moving the entire plant or office may be recorded similarly, unless the moving results from some unusual and infrequent event, in which case the costs of moving are included as part of the related extraordinary loss. In practice, most business enterprises record moving costs as expenses.

Ordinary Repairs and Maintenance   Minor repair and maintenance revenue expenditures usually are required throughout the economic life of a plant asset to keep it in efficient operating condition. The distinguishing characteristic of such expenditures is that they neither add to the value of the asset nor materially prolong its economic life. The preferable procedure is to recognize these costs as expenses, because maintenance activities are recurring and the costs are related to current revenue. However, any unusual or extraordinary repairs arising from fire or other casualties are recognized as losses if not covered by insurance.

A questionable approach to the problem of dealing with repair costs that vary widely from one accounting period to another and are significant in amount is to **anticipate** such costs and allocate them to expense over the economic life of the appropriate plant asset. Under this procedure, the total expected repair costs are estimated at the time each asset is acquired, and Repairs Expense is debited each accounting period for a portion of the estimated lifetime repair costs. The offsetting credit is to an account titled Allowance for Estimated Repairs. Actual repair expenditures are debited to the allowance account. For income tax purposes, only the actual expenditures are deductible in the year incurred.

To illustrate, assume that repair costs for an item of equipment are expected to average $250 a year, that no repair costs are incurred in Year 1, and that repair costs of $400 are incurred in Year 2. The journal entries required during the first two years are shown below:

Journal entries for accrual of repair costs

End of Year 1:
Repairs Expense	250	
Allowance for Estimated Repairs		250
To record estimated repairs expense.		

During Year 2:
Allowance for Estimated Repairs	400	
Cash, Parts, Accrued Payroll, etc.		400
To record actual costs of repairs.		

End of Year 2:
Repairs Expense	250	
Allowance for Estimated Repairs		250
To record estimated repairs expense.		

At the end of the second year, the allowance ledger account has a credit balance of $100 ($500 − $400 = $100). Conceivably, a debit balance might appear in the allowance account if major repairs occurred early or if the estimate of repair costs were too low.

A number of criticisms of this method may be raised. Some accountants have argued that it is an **operating reserve** (income-smoothing device) and that it tends to obscure the fact that repair costs may increase as an asset becomes older. Others question whether reliable estimates of repair costs can be made. Finally, the classification of the Allowance for Estimated Repairs ledger account poses difficulties. A credit balance in the allowance account is not considered a part of stockholders' equity because it is illogical to debit an expense and increase stockholders' equity. Classification as a liability may be questioned, because no legal obligation for an expenditure exists. Treating the allowance as an asset valuation ledger account (to be deducted from or added to the cost of the related plant asset in the balance sheet) assumes that the "accrued repairs" represent additional depreciation and thus reduce the carrying amount of the asset. This is probably the least objectionable alternative, because it is consistent with the reporting of a debit balance in the allowance account as an asset—in the nature of a prepayment of repair costs.

Anticipation of repair costs does not fit neatly in the conceptual model of financial accounting. Year-to-year accrual of estimated repair costs lacks sufficient objectivity and might encourage managements of business enterprises to adopt other income-smoothing practices.

RETIREMENTS, DISPOSALS, AND EXCHANGES

When a plant asset is retired, sold, or exchanged, the accumulated depreciation on the asset first is brought up to date. The second requirement is to remove from the accounting records all ledger account balances relating to the asset and to recognize any gain or loss from the disposal of the asset. Some of the more common situations involving the retirement, disposal, or exchange of plant assets include the following:

1   A fully depreciated plant asset with no residual value is *retired* without receipt of any proceeds; no gain or loss is recognized on such retirement.

2   A partially depreciated plant asset is *retired* without receipt of any proceeds; a loss is recognized on such retirement.

3   A fully or partially depreciated plant asset is *retired* or *sold* with some recovery of net residual value; a gain or loss is recognized on such retirement or sale.

4   A fully or partially depreciated asset is *exchanged* for other assets without any cash being received or paid; the guidelines for the recognition of a gain or loss on such a *nonmonetary exchange transaction* are:

a If a loss is indicated by the terms of the transaction, the *loss always is recognized.*

b If a gain is indicated in an *exchange of dissimilar assets that results in the completion of the earning process* (such as the exchange of an inventory item that cost $1,000 for a plant asset with a current fair value of $1,500), the *gain is recognized.*

c If a gain is indicated in an *exchange of similar assets that does not complete the earning process* (such as an exchange of an inventory item for another inventory item or an exchange of a plant asset with a similar plant asset), the *gain is not recognized.*

5   A fully or partially depreciated plant asset may be exchanged for a *similar asset,* with cash being paid or received by the parties to the transaction. In such exchanges, *an indicated loss is recognized in full, but only a portion of any indicated gain is recognized by the party receiving cash.*

The accounting procedures for the foregoing situations are described in the following sections.

████████████████ ### Retirements and Disposals of Plant Assets

When a fully depreciated plant asset with no net residual value is retired, and no proceeds are received, the retirement is recorded by a debit to the accumulated depreciation ledger account and a credit to the plant asset account; when a partially depreciated plant asset is retired and no proceeds are received, a loss is recognized equal to the difference between cost and accumulated depreciation; when a fully or partially depreciated plant asset is retired or sold with some recovery of net residual value, a gain or loss is recognized equal to the difference between the carrying amount of the asset and the proceeds received. For example, assume that equipment with a cost of $6,000 with no net residual value has been depreciated at an annual rate of 10% for eight years. In the middle of the ninth year the equipment is sold for $1,750 cash (net of any direct costs incurred on the sale). The journal entries to record this sale are shown below:

Depreciation Expense ($6,000 × 0.10 × ½)	300	
Accumulated Depreciation of Equipment		300
To record depreciation at 10% for six months on equipment		
costing $6,000 with no net residual value.		
Cash	1,750	
Accumulated Depreciation of Equipment ($6,000 × 0.10 × 8½)	5,100	
Gain on Disposal of Equipment		850
Equipment		6,000
To record sale of equipment.		

Depreciation first is brought up to date when a plant asset is sold

The proper interpretation of any gain or loss that may result from the retirement or sale of a plant asset often is uncertain. To the extent that it stems from errors in estimates of economic life or net residual value, the "gain" or "loss" is an adjustment of previously reported net income. To the extent that it is caused by changes in the current fair value of the asset, the gain or loss is also an element of net income for the current year. In most cases a combination of these factors is present. Material gains and losses (or provisions for losses) from the sale or abandonment of plant assets are included in the determination of income before extraordinary items.

Standby Plant Assets

Plant assets sometimes are retired from active service and are neither sold nor abandoned but are kept on a *standby status* for use in emergency or to meet peak-load requirements. When this occurs, the plant assets are written down to their standby or residual values. Depreciation of such assets is discontinued while they remain idle. When the amount of standby plant assets is significant, it should be reported under the Other Noncurrent Assets caption in the balance sheet.

Exchanges of Plant Assets

Prior to the issuance of *APB Opinion No. 29,* "Accounting for Nonmonetary Transactions," exchanges of plant assets for similar plant assets were recorded in a variety of ways for financial accounting. Such transactions frequently were recorded according to income tax requirements; that is, the plant asset acquired was recorded at the carrying amount of the plant asset given in exchange plus any cash paid or less any cash received, and no gain or loss was recognized. Alternatively, a gain or loss was recognized when the current fair value of the plant asset given in exchange was used to record the transaction, and the plant asset acquired generally was recorded at the current fair value of the asset exchanged, plus any cash paid or less any cash received.

APB Opinion No. 29 differentiated *monetary exchanges* involving cash and receivables or payables from *nonmonetary exchanges* involving, for example, inventories, investments in common stocks, and plant assets. An *exchange* was defined as a transfer between business enterprises that results in one enterprise receiving assets or services or satisfying obligations by surrendering other assets or services or incurring other obligations.[8] The portion of the *basic principle* in *APB Opinion No. 29* that relates to exchanges of plant assets appears below:[9]

> The Board concludes that in general accounting for nonmonetary transactions should be based on the fair values of the assets (or services) involved which is the same basis as that used in monetary transactions. Thus, the cost of a nonmonetary asset acquired in exchange for another nonmonetary asset is the fair value of the asset surrendered to obtain it, and a gain or loss should be recognized on the exchange. The fair value of the asset received should be used to measure the cost if it is more clearly evident than the fair value of the asset surrendered.

The Accounting Principles Board modified this basic principle in several important respects. First, the accounting for exchanges is based on the current fair values of assets unless such values are not reasonably determinable. If current fair values are not reasonably determinable, the asset acquired is recorded at the carrying amount of the asset given in exchange plus any cash paid, and no gain or loss is recognized. Second, if an exchange transaction does not result in the completion of the earning process (realization), the asset acquired also is recorded at the carrying amount of the asset surrendered. An example of such a transaction is an exchange of a plant asset for a similar plant asset. However, if the terms of the transaction indicate that the asset surrendered has a current fair value that is less than its carrying amount, a loss is recognized. Finally, if cash (or other monetary consideration) is received in an exchange of assets, the recipient of the cash is deemed to have realized a gain on the exchange equal in amount to the excess of the cash received over the proportionate share of the carrying amount of the asset given in exchange. A transaction in which a plant asset and cash are received in exchange for another plant asset *is viewed as a sale to the extent of cash received, and as an exchange to the extent of the current fair value of the plant asset received.*

---

[8]*APB Opinion No. 29,* "Accounting for Nonmonetary Transactions," AICPA (New York: 1973), p. 541.
[9]Ibid., p. 547.

The procedures to be followed in recording exchanges of plant assets pursuant to *APB Opinion No. 29* are summarized below:

1   Compute the indicated gain or loss on the exchange. The gain or loss is equal to the difference between the current fair value of the asset surrendered and its carrying amount.

2   If the computation in **1** results in a loss, the entire indicated loss is recognized for financial accounting, and the asset acquired is recorded at the current fair value of the asset surrendered plus any cash paid (or less any cash received). *An indicated loss always is recognized.*

3   If the computation in **1** results in a gain, and the earning process is completed, the full indicated gain is recognized; if the earning process is not completed and cash is paid (or no cash is involved in the exchange), no gain is recognized; if cash is received in the exchange, only a portion of the gain is recognized as follows:

Gain is recognized on the cash part of the "sale" when the earning process is not completed

$$\text{Gain} \times \frac{\text{cash received}}{\text{cash received} + \text{current fair value of asset received}} = \text{gain recognized}$$

The procedures for recording exchanges of similar plant assets are illustrated in the examples on page 572. The plant asset exchanged has a carrying amount of $6,000 (cost of $20,000 less accumulated depreciation of $14,000). Each example involves similar plant assets with comparable current fair values, adjusted for any cash paid or received. For each example, the indicated gain or loss is the difference between the current fair value of the old asset and its carrying amount.

The indicated losses in each of the first three examples are recognized for financial accounting. In the next two examples, no gain is recognized because no cash was received in Example **4** and because cash was paid in Example **5**. However, in Example **6**, 10% of the indicated gain of $4,000 is recognized because 10% of the total consideration received consisted of cash, and to that extent *the earning process was completed.*

If the exchanges in the last three examples involved dissimilar assets, the entire indicated gain would be recognized for financial accounting *because the earning process would be considered completed.* Exchanges of plant assets that are material in amount, either individually or in the aggregate, are disclosed in a note to the financial statements. Such disclosure includes the nature of the exchanges, the basis of accounting for the assets transferred, and the amount of gain or loss recognized.

Involuntary Conversions

The services of plant assets occasionally are lost through condemnation, fire, or other involuntary means. In the accounting for such events, the amount of any loss or gain is recognized, and all amounts relating to such assets are removed from the accounting records. For example, assume that certain land and buildings owned by a business enterprise are condemned by the state for the construction of a highway,

Examples
of ex-
change
transac-
tions in-
volving
similar
plant
assets
(earning
process
not com-
pleted)

Exchange transaction	*Journal entry (explanation omitted)*

1 Loss of $2,000 is indicated; no cash is involved. *Current fair value of old asset is $4,000. (Cost of new asset is $4,000 current fair value of old asset.)*

Plant asset (new)................... 4,000
Accumulated Depreciation 14,000
Loss on Exchange of Plant Asset 2,000
    Plant Asset (old)   20,000

2 Loss of $2,500 is indicated; cash of $1,000 is paid. *Current fair value of old asset is $3,500. (Cost of new asset is $3,500 current fair value of old asset plus $1,000 cash paid, or $4,500).*

Plant Asset (new) 4,500
Accumulated Depreciation 14,000
Loss on Exchange of Plant Asset 2,500
    Cash   1,000
    Plant Asset (old)   20,000

3 Loss of $1,000 is indicated; cash of $200 is received. *Current fair value of old asset is $5,000. (Cost of new asset is $5,000 current fair value of old asset less $200 cash received, or $4,800).*

Cash 200
Plant Asset (new) 4,800
Accumulated Depreciation 14,000
Loss on Exchange of Plant Asset 1,000
    Plant Asset (old)   20,000

4 Gain of $6,500 is indicated; no cash is involved. *Current fair value of old asset is $12,500. (Cost of new asset is $6,000 carrying amount of old asset.)*

Plant Asset (new) 6,000
Accumulated Depreciation 14,000
    Plant Asset (old)   20,000

5 Gain of $6,500 is indicated; cash of $1,000 is paid. *Current fair value of old asset is $12,500. (Cost of new asset is $6,000 carrying amount of old asset plus $1,000 cash paid, or $7,000.)*

Plant Asset (new) 7,000
Accumulated Depreciation 14,000
    Cash   1,000
    Plant Asset (old)   20,000

6 Gain of $4,000 is indicated; cash of $1,000 is received. *Current fair value of old asset is $10,000, indicating a current fair value of new asset of $9,000. The portion of indicated gain recognized is:*

$$\$4,000 \times \left(\frac{\$1,000}{\$1,000 + \$9,000}\right) = \$400$$

(Cost of new asset is $6,000 carrying amount of old asset, less $1,000 cash received, plus $400 gain recognized, or $5,400; alternatively, the cost of new asset may be computed by deducting the gain not recognized from the current fair value of the new asset: $9,000 − $3,600 = $5,400.)

Cash 1,000
Plant Asset (new) 5,400
Accumulated Depreciation 14,000
    Plant Asset (old)   20,000
    Gain on Exchange of Plant
      Asset   400

and that the state sets a price of $140,000 as the condemnation award. Accumulated depreciation of the building is $120,000, and its cost was $160,000; the cost of the land was $40,000. The journal entry to record this involuntary conversion follows:

Recording involuntary conversion

Cash	140,000	
Accumulated Depreciation of Building	120,000	
Building		160,000
Land		40,000
Gain on Condemnation of Property		60,000
To record disposal of property condemned by state.		

The position of the Financial Accounting Standards Board on involuntary conversions is summarized below.[10]

> Involuntary conversions of nonmonetary assets to monetary assets are monetary transactions for which gain or loss shall be recognized even though an enterprise reinvests or is obligated to reinvest the monetary assets in replacement of nonmonetary assets.

The FASB addressed this topic because many business enterprises applied the income tax rule for an involuntary conversion of plant assets. In most cases no gain is recognized for income tax purposes at the time of an involuntary conversion if the owner of the property uses the funds received to replace the involuntarily converted asset.

When depreciable plant assets or merchandise are destroyed by fire or other casualties, accountants often assist in measuring and recording the losses sustained. For example, inventories on hand at the time of fire may have to be estimated by the gross profit method described in Chapter 9.

Insurance on Plant Assets   Most business enterprises insure assets for possible losses resulting from fire, theft, explosion, and other insurable events. A *deductible clause* usually limits recovery to a loss in excess of a specified amount, such as $100.

Insurance policies provide for recovery of loss based on the replacement cost (current fair value) of the asset destroyed. The carrying amount of an asset, although irrelevant in determining the amount of recovery from insurance companies, is used to measure the loss or gain as a result of the casualty. For example, if $10,000 is collected from an insurance company on complete destruction of an asset with a carrying amount of $7,500, a gain of $2,500 results.

The amount of insurance carried on an asset should never exceed the current fair value of the asset, because the amount recovered never exceeds the current fair value of the asset. When inadequate insurance is carried on an asset, the insured in effect becomes a ''coinsurer'' with the insurance company. For example, if an asset

---

[10]*FASB Interpretation No. 30*, ''Accounting for Involuntary Conversions of Nonmonetary Assets to Monetary Assets''—an interpretation of *APB Opinion No. 29*, FASB (Stamford: 1979), p. 1.

worth $5,000 that is insured for only $4,000 is totally destroyed, the insurance company would bear $4,000 of the loss and the owner would absorb the remaining $1,000 of the loss.

Coinsurance Clause in an Insurance Policy If it were possible to obtain insurance coverage for only a fraction of the current fair value of an asset, the owner would benefit by receiving full reimbursement of most losses with a minimum insurance coverage and cost. However, insurance companies usually include a ***coinsurance clause*** in the insurance policy to prevent this approach to low-cost insurance protection. A coinsurance clause requires that an asset be insured for a specified minimum amount, usually 80% of current fair value, if a loss is to be absorbed fully (up to the face amount of the policy) by the insurance company. If the insurance coverage is below the specified percentage, the owner absorbs a portion of the loss, even though the loss does not exceed the face amount of the policy.

To illustrate the application of a coinsurance clause in a fire insurance policy, assume the following:

Data for illustration

Carrying amount of machinery damaged by fire (cost, $140,000)	$ 55,000
Insurance carried (face amount of policy)	60,000
Current fair value of machinery on date of fire	100,000
Coinsurance required by policy (80% of current fair value)	80,000
Amount of fire loss (based on current fair value of machinery)	40,000

The recovery from the insurance company is determined under the coinsurance formula as follows:

$$\frac{\$60,000 \text{ (amount of insurance)}}{\$80,000 \text{ (coinsurance requirement)}} \times \$40,000 \text{ (loss)} = \underline{\underline{\$30,000}}$$

It is important to note the following points regarding property insurance:

1   The amount of insurance coverage is not dependent on the cost or the carrying amount of the asset. (Cost and carrying amount are irrelevant for purposes of measuring either the amount of insurance that may be carried or the amount of recoverable loss).

2   Recovery on the loss is dependent on the current fair value of the asset, the amount of insurance carried, and the minimum amount of insurance required by the coinsurance clause.

3   If insurance is carried equal to or in excess of the amount required by the coinsurance clause, any loss up to the face amount of the policy is fully recoverable; if less than the required amount of insurance is carried, the loss is absorbed in part by the ***insured.***

4 If the amount of insurance carried exceeds the coinsurance requirement, there is no need to apply the coinsurance formula.

A careful study of the coinsurance formula indicates that *the recoverable portion of the loss always is the lower of (1) the amount of the loss adjusted by the coinsurance formula, or (2) the face amount of the policy.*

Two or More Insurance Policies If an asset is insured under two or more policies that do not have coinsurance clauses, any loss is shared by the insurance companies in proportion to the amount of insurance written by each company; the same procedure applies when the insurance policies contain identical coinsurance requirements. If two or more insurance policies cover the same asset, and the policies have *different* coinsurance clauses, *the coinsurance formula is applied to each policy separately.* However, the loss absorbed by any insurance company will not exceed its proportion of the total insurance carried with all insurance companies. For example, assume that a building with a current fair value of $400,000 is insured under two policies as follows:

Policy A: $150,000, with an 80% coinsurance clause

Policy B: $150,000, with a 70% coinsurance clause

Assuming that a fire causes damage of $240,000 to the building, how much of the loss will be recovered under each policy? If neither policy had a coinsurance clause, each insurance company absorbs 50% of the loss ($120,000) because each policy represents 50% of the total insurance ($300,000). If both policies had a 70% coinsurance requirement, each insurance company absorbs $120,000 of the loss because the total insurance carried ($300,000) exceeds the minimum insurance required by the coinsurance clause ($400,000 × 0.70 = $280,000). However, because policy A has an 80% coinsurance clause in this case, the recovery under each policy is determined as follows:

Allocation of loss between two insurance companies

Policy A:

$$\frac{\$150,000 \text{ (insurance under policy A)}}{\$320,000 \text{ (coinsurance req. for policy A)}} \times \$240,000 \text{ (loss)} = \underline{\$112,500}$$

Policy B:

$$\frac{\$150,000 \text{ (insurance under policy B)}}{\$300,000 \text{ (total insurance on building)}} \times \$240,000 \text{ (loss)} = \underline{\$120,000}$$

The recovery under policy A is $15/32$ of the loss, which is less than the pro rata coverage of $15/30$, because the coinsurance requirement under this policy *was not met.* In contrast, the recovery under policy B is $15/30$ of the loss, because the total insurance on the building ($300,000) exceeds the minimum required under policy B ($280,000). Thus, the coinsurance formula is not applicable to policy B.

Insurance contracts vary in form and complexity. The discussion here is brief and simplified. Although accountants need not be experts in insurance contracts, they should have a basic understanding of insurance to be able to account properly for premiums paid and proceeds received, and to help clients formulate a sound property insurance program.

REVIEW QUESTIONS

1   Define the following terms: *tangible asset, natural resource, intangible asset,* and list a few examples of each.

2   What are the arguments in favor of using historical cost as the basis of accounting for plant assets? Might this be referred to as an asset *valuation procedure?*

3   How is the cost of a plant asset determined for financial accounting? What three issues are involved in accounting for the cost of plant assets?

4   What is meant by the terms *capital expenditure* and *revenue expenditure?* How are these terms related to the accounting principles of revenue realization and matching of costs and revenue?

5   Which of the following are capital expenditures? Indicate the appropriate accounting treatment of any item that is not a capital expenditure.
a Cost of grading land prior to construction
b Cost of installing equipment, including cost of spoiled material during test runs
c Tax assessment for street paving
d Delinquent property taxes on land acquired
e Cost of maintaining equipment in good operating condition
f Cost of moving and reinstalling equipment in another part of factory
g Cost of repairs to used equipment; need for repair was discovered immediately after acquisition of the equipment
h Cost of demolishing an old building in preparation for new construction (old building was used for 24 years and was fully depreciated)
i Cost of insurance policy covering possible damages that may arise during construction of a new building
j Excess of operating expenses over revenue during first year of operations
k Cost of removing soil to build foundation for new building

6   Duke Company has constructed a special-purpose machine for its own use. Direct labor and material costs were $10,000. Variable overhead costs were 10% of direct costs, and fixed overhead costs allocable to the constructed machine were $2,400. Duke's engineers estimate that an equivalent machine would cost $15,000 if acquired for cash. At what amount should the machine be recorded? Why? Is there a profit on the self-construction? Assuming that the machine could have been acquired for $8,000, at what amount should the machine be recorded for financial accounting?

7   Capitalizing interest cost during construction is an accepted accounting procedure; adding interest on an installment contract to the cost of the asset acquired is not. Explain the distinction between these two situations.

8   What position did the FASB take in *Statement No. 34,* "Capitalization of Interest Cost," on the capitalization of interest cost?

9   Discuss the accounting problem that arises in each of the following situations involving plant assets, and explain the proper accounting procedure:
a Assets are acquired under a deferred payment plan
b A group of assets is acquired for a lump-sum price
c Assets are acquired in exchange for common stock or bonds of the acquiring corporation
d Assets are acquired by gift

10   What is the *investment tax credit* and how, in your opinion, should it be treated for financial accounting?

11   Briefly describe the accounting procedures appropriate for the following:
a Additions
b Improvements, renewals, and replacements
c Ordinary repair and maintenance costs
d Extraordinary repairs as a result of fire damage not covered by insurance
e Gain or loss on involuntary conversion of land to cash

12   The accountant for Waddell Company estimates annual repair costs on equipment and prepares a journal entry each year debiting Repairs Expense and crediting Allowance for Repairs, which sometimes shows a credit balance and sometimes a debit balance. What is the appropriate classification of the latter ledger account in the balance sheet? Why?

13   Evans Company debits the cost of major repairs of plant assets to the Accumulated Depreciation ledger account. Evaluate this procedure.

14   How are gains and losses on retirements, disposals, or exchanges of plant assets reported in the income statement?

15   **a** Describe the *basic principle* stated in *APB Opinion No. 29,* "Accounting for Nonmonetary Transactions," relating to accounting for exchanges of plant assets.
b List three modifications of the basic principle stated in *APB Opinion No. 29.*

16   Describe the conditions in which exchange transactions involving plant assets require the recognition of gains and losses for financial accounting.

17   What is meant by *coinsurance?* Describe the coinsurance formula. May the destruction of insured property result in a gain for financial accounting? Explain.

EXERCISES

Ex. 11-1   Select the best answer for each of the following multiple-choice questions:

1 On June 25, Year 7, Lino Printers, Inc., incurred the following costs for one of its printing presses:

Acquisition of collating and stapling attachment.......................	$42,000
Installation of attachment..	18,000
Replacement parts for overhaul of press	13,000
Labor and plant overhead costs applicable to overhaul of press.........	7,000
Total costs	$80,000

The overhaul resulted in a substantial increase in the output of the printing press. Neither the attachment nor the overhaul increased the estimated economic life of the press. The amount of the foregoing costs that Lino Printers debits to the Printing Presses ledger account is:

a $42,000   **b** $55,000   **c** $60,000   **d** $80,000   **e** Some other amount

2   Mansfield Company acquired equipment under a deferred payment contract on December 31, Year 3. The contract required the payment of $20,000 on December 31, Year 3, and $20,000 on December 31 of each of the following five years. The amount that Mansfield debits to the Equipment ledger account is:
a The present value of an ordinary annuity of six rents of $20,000
b $120,000
c $120,000 less imputed interest
d $120,000 plus imputed interest
e Some other amount

3   In an arm's length transaction, Lewis Company and Clark Company exchanged similar plant assets, with no cash involved in the exchange. Current fair values of both plant assets were available. Clark's accounting for the exchange is based on the:
a Current fair value of the asset surrendered by Clark
b Current fair value of the asset received by Lewis
c Carrying amount of the asset surrendered by Clark
d Carrying amount of the asset received from Lewis

4   Which of the following costs is debited to the Land ledger account?
a Landscaping of the land
b Sidewalks constructed and maintained by owner of the land
c Parking lot constructed and maintained by owner of the land
d Parking structure constructed and maintained by owner of the land

5   The *acquisition period* for the capitalization of interest cost incurred for a plant asset begins when all the following conditions are present, except:
a The plant asset has been placed in use
b Interest cost is being incurred
c Expenditures for the plant asset have been incurred
d Activities to prepare the plant asset for use are in progress

6   Plant assets retired from active service but kept on a standby status for use in emergency are:
a Depreciated over their remaining estimated economic lives
b Written down to residual values
c Written off in total as an extraordinary loss
d Included in the current assets section of the balance sheet

7   The method of accounting for the investment tax credit that reduces income taxes expense by the amount of the credit in the year the qualifying plant asset is acquired is the:
a Flow-through method   **b** Reduction method   **c** Deferral method
d Credit method

8   Corsair Company paid $7,000 cash and exchanged an old machine that had a cost of $10,000, a carrying amount of $4,000, and a current fair value of $5,000, for a similar new machine with a current fair value of $12,000. In the journal entry to record the transaction in accordance with generally accepted accounting principles, Corsair:
a Credits Gain on Exchange of Plant Assets, $1,000
b Credits Machinery (old), $4,000
c Debits Machinery (new), $11,000
d Credits Machinery (old), $5,000

Ex. 11-2   Among the Year 8 transactions involved in Grange Company's acquisition of land for the construction of a new building, so that Grange could give up leased premises, were the following:

Mar. 16   Paid billing from subcontractor for clearing trees and brush from land, $15,000
     18   Received $2,000 from firewood dealer for timber salvaged from land-clearing operation
     30   Paid billing from subcontractor for cost of razing old building acquired with land, $140,000
Apr. 18   Paid billing from subcontractor for construction of parking lot to be maintained by Grange, $80,000

Prepare journal entries for the foregoing transactions of Grange Company.

Ex. 11-3   On July 11, Year 8, Lupo Corporation acquired land with a current fair value of $590,000 in exchange for $200,000 face amount of bonds payable and 20,000 shares of its $2 par common stock. The stock was trading at $20 on the New York Stock Exchange on July 11, Year 8.
     Prepare a journal entry to record Lupo Corporation's acquisition of land.

Ex. 11-4   On April 15, Year 4, Fonville Company exchanged 10,000 shares of its no-par common stock, with a stated value of $25 a share and a current fair value of $60 a share, for land for a future plant site. Fonville received $75,000 for scrap from the demolition of an existing building on the land that was razed at a cost of $120,000.
     Compute the amount that Fonville Company should debit to the Land ledger account as the cost of the acquired land.

Ex. 11-5   The costs incurred by Armine Baeza to acquire land and construct a building were as follows:

Land (including miscellaneous acquisition costs)	*$150,000*
Construction insurance	*3,500*

Building construction contract (excluding excavation)...................	220,000
Architect fees...	2,000
Street and sidewalk installation (maintenance by the city)..............	4,000
Costs of excavation for foundation	3,100
Property taxes on land (prior to construction)	1,600
Advertising costs to attract tenants	1,250
Interest cost during acquisition period on loan to pay contractor.........	2,600

Determine the cost of Armine Baeza's (**a**) land, and (**b**) building for financial accounting.

Ex. 11-6   Lupina, Inc., replaced a used machine with a new one having a list price of $10,000, subject to a 2% cash discount if paid promptly. Net cost of removing the used machine to make room for the new one amounted to $800. Installation of the new machine cost $400. Costs of testing the new machine were $250 for operator's time and $325 in spoiled material. The cash discount was lost because of late payment of the invoice.

Compute the cost of Lupina, Inc.'s, new machine for financial accounting.

Ex. 11-7   On January 2, Year 6, Ramirez Company contracted with Construction Specialists, Inc., for a new building at a fixed price of $4,000,000. Construction Specialists estimated a three-year construction period for the building. Also on January 2, Year 6, Ramirez borrowed $4,000,000, payable in 10 annual installments of $400,000, plus interest at 11% a year, beginning January 2, Year 7. During Year 6, Ramirez made progress payments totaling $1,500,000 to Construction Specialists; the average amount of accumulated payments was $650,000 for Year 6. Ramirez invested unused borrowed cash in short-term commercial paper, from which Ramirez realized interest revenue of $250,000 during Year 6.

Compute the amount of Ramirez Company's capitalized interest cost for the year ended December 31, Year 6.

Ex. 11-8   On June 30, Year 10, Silvy Company acquired equipment at a bankruptcy auction. The acquisition price consisted of the following:

Cash down payment	$ 72,150
Four noninterest-bearing promissory notes in the face amount of	
$50,000 each, payable annually on June 30, commencing in Year 11 ...	200,000
Total acquisition price	$272,150

Record the acquisition of the equipment in the accounting records of Silvy Company, assuming that a fair rate of interest is 10% compounded annually. Use the appropriate table in the Appendix at the end of Chapter 5 and round computations to the nearest dollar.

Ex. 11-9   On December 31, Year 1, Woodrow Company acquired equipment under a deferred payment contract requiring the payment of $100 a month for 12 months, beginning on January 31, Year 2. The interest rate implicit in the contract was 1½% a month. Compound interest tables provide the following values:

$a\,\overline{12}_{1\frac{1}{2}\%} = 1.20$ $\qquad$ $p\,\overline{12}_{1\frac{1}{2}\%} = 0.84$ $\qquad$ $A\,\overline{12}_{1\frac{1}{2}\%} = 13.04$ $\qquad$ $P\,\overline{12}_{1\frac{1}{2}\%} = 10.91$

Prepare journal entries for Woodrow Company for the deferred payment contract on December 31, Year 1; January 31, Year 2; and February 28, Year 2. Round all amounts to the nearest dollar.

Ex. 11-10 Dilworth, Inc., acquired three machines at an auction for a lump-sum cost of $14,500, and also paid $500 to have the machines delivered to its place of business. The current fair values of the three machines were as follows:

Machine X..	$10,000
Machine Y..	6,000
Machine Z..	4,000
Total current fair value	$20,000

Determine the cost allocated to each machine acquired by Dilworth, Inc., using the relative current fair values of the machines as a basis of allocating the total cost of the machines.

Ex. 11-11 Selleck Company sold land and a building to Ackwire Company. The property had cost Selleck $39,000, including $10,000 allocated to land. Depreciation of $3,500 had been recorded on the building by Selleck. At the close of escrow, the following escrow statements were submitted to Selleck and Ackwire:

	Escrow statement to Selleck Company		Escrow statement to Ackwire Company	
	Charges	Credits	Charges	Credits
Selling price		$40,300	$40,300	
Cash deposited in escrow				$10,400
Prorated property taxes	$ 120			120
Prorated interest	70			70
Prorated insurance		200	200	
Mortgage note assumed by acquirer	30,160			30,160
Commission to broker............	2,370			
Title search fee	150		150	
Escrow fee	210			
Cash to seller	7,420			
Cash to acquirer			100	
Totals	$40,500	$40,500	$40,750	$40,750

a Prepare a journal entry to record the sale of the property in Selleck Company's accounting records.

b Prepare a journal entry to record the acquisition of the property in Ackwire Company's accounting records. The value assigned to land is $15,500. Ackwire had recorded the cash deposited in escrow, $10,400, in an Escrow Deposit ledger account. Record any accrued or deferred expenses in nominal ledger accounts.

Ex. 11-12   Alice Arnold, a single proprietor, has been maintaining her own accounting records. At the end of Year 3, after the accounting records were adjusted but before they were closed, you were engaged to review the records. The items that require correction are listed below:

(1) Installation costs for fixtures, $1,200, were debited to Maintenance Expense. The fixtures have a five-year economic life, with no net residual value, and were installed at the beginning of Year 3. Assume use of the straight-line method of depreciation.

(2) A machine acquired on January 2, Year 1, at a cost of $5,500 has been depreciated on a straight-line basis over a five-year period, with no net residual value. The machine was sold on June 30, Year 3. Arnold debited Cash and credited Machinery for $2,100, the proceeds on the sale. No depreciation was recorded on this machine in Year 3, but you conclude that one-half year's depreciation should have been recorded.

Prepare a correcting journal entry for Alice Arnold on December 31, Year 3, for each of the two items described above.

Ex. 11-13   Prepare journal entries to record the exchange of machine A for machine B in each of the following situations:

a Carlton Corporation acquired machine B by trading in machine A and paying $5,000 cash. Machine A cost $95,000 and had accumulated depreciation of $25,000 on the date of exchange. Machine B could have been acquired for $80,000 cash. The machines are similar.

b Assume the same facts as in **a,** except that instead of paying $5,000 cash, Carlton received $20,000 cash.

c Assume the same facts as in **a,** except that instead of paying $5,000 cash, Carlton received $5,000 cash. Machine B could have been acquired for $50,000 cash.

Ex. 11-14   On June 1, Year 7, Zane Company replaced its obsolete air conditioning system having a carrying amount of $30,000 and a current fair value of $10,000 with a new system having a current fair value of $190,000. Zane paid the air conditioning contractor $180,000 and permitted the contractor to keep the obsolete air conditioner. Accumulated depreciation on the obsolete system was $50,000.

Prepare a journal entry to record Zane Company's acquisition of the new air conditioning system.

Ex. 11-15   On February 28, Year 2, Hix Company traded a machine with a cost of $60,000, a carrying amount of $20,000, and a current fair value of $25,000, to Cox Company for a similar new machine with a cost and current fair value of $23,000. In addition, Hix received $2,000 from Cox.

Prepare journal entries to record the foregoing transaction in the accounting records of **a** Hix Company, and **b** Cox Company.

Ex. 11-16   In Year 2, Leah Gold sold for $55,000 a parcel of land that had cost $25,000. The contract required a down payment of $15,000 and a noninterest-bearing promissory note for $40,000 due in four years.

Record the sale of land in Gold's accounting records, assuming that the present value of the note (discounted at compound interest of 12% for four years) was $25,421, and that 12% was a fair rate of interest on this type of note. Assume that the note receivable is recorded at face amount.

Ex. 11-17 On October 15, Year 9, a fire caused $100,000 in damage to Banning Company's building that had a current fair value of $300,000 and a carrying amount of $175,000. Banning had a fire insurance policy in the amount of $120,000 with an 80% coinsurance clause for the building.

Compute the maximum amount that the insurance carrier will pay to Banning Company as a result of the fire loss.

Ex. 11-18 A machine has a carrying amount of $13,000 and a current fair value of $20,000. Determine the amount recoverable from the insurance company in each case below, assuming that each insurance policy contains an 80% coinsurance clause:

Case	Insurance coverage	Loss incurred
A	$10,000	$12,000
B	12,000	11,000
C	14,000	8,000
D	16,000	18,000
E	18,000	17,000

CASES

Case 11-1 Among the principal topics related to the accounting for the plant assets of a business enterprise are acquisition and retirement.

Instructions

a What expenditures are capitalized when equipment is acquired for cash?

b Assume that the current fair value of equipment acquired is not determinable by reference to a similar acquisition for cash. Describe how the acquiring enterprise determines the capitalizable cost of equipment acquired by exchanging for it each of the following:

(1) Bonds having an established market price

(2) Common stock not having an established market price

(3) Similar equipment having a determinable current fair value

c Describe the factors that determine whether expenditures relating to plant assets already in use should be capitalized.

d Describe how to account for the gain or loss on the sale of plant assets for cash.

Case 11-2 Plant assets generally represent a significant portion of the total assets of most business enterprises. Accounting for the acquisition and use of such assets is, therefore, an important part of financial accounting.

Instructions

a Distinguish between revenue expenditures and capital expenditures and explain why this distinction is important.

b Identify six costs that should be capitalized as the cost of land. For your answer, assume that land with an existing building is acquired for cash and that the existing building is to be removed in order that a new building may be constructed on the site.

c At what amount should a business enterprise record a plant asset acquired under a deferred payment plan?

d In general, at what amount should plant assets received in exchange for other nonmonetary assets be recorded? Specifically, at what amount should a business enterprise record a new machine acquired in exchange for a similar used machine and a cash payment?

Case 11-3   Olmo Company found three suitable sites, each having certain unique advantages, for a new plant facility. In order to investigate thoroughly the advantages and disadvantages of each site, one-year options were acquired for an amount equal to 5% of the contract price of each site. The costs of the options could not be applied against the contract prices. Before the options expired, one of the sites was acquired at a price of $60,000. The option on this site had cost $3,000; the two options not exercised had cost $3,500 each.

Instructions

Present arguments in support of recording the cost of the land acquired by Olmo Company at each of the following amounts: **a** $60,000; **b** $63,000; and **c** $70,000.

Case 11-4   Rondo Company has completed payment for a new building constructed at a cost of $2 million. After reviewing the contracts and cost data, Rondo's controller suggests using the following classifications in future accounting for this building: (1) foundation, framing, and sheathing, (2) outside finish, (3) interior finish, (4) roof, (5) electric wiring and fixtures, (6) partitions, (7) acoustical ceiling, (8) furnace and boiler, and (9) plumbing system.

Instructions

Discuss the advantages and the disadvantages of following such a system of accounting for Rondo Company's building, particularly its effect on accounting for maintenance, depreciation, and retirements.

Case 11-5   Hi-Tech Company manufactures electrical appliances, most of which are used in homes. Hi-Tech's engineers have designed a new type of blender which, through the use of a few attachments, will perform more functions than any blender currently on the market. Demand for the new blender can be projected with reasonable accuracy. In order to manufacture the blenders, Hi-Tech needs a specialized machine that is not available from outside sources. Therefore, Hi-Tech decided to construct the specialized machine in its own plant.

Instructions

a Hi-Tech Company's plant may be operating at capacity or below capacity. Compare the problems in determining the cost to be assigned to the specialized machine at these different levels of operations.

b Discuss the effect of projected demand in units for the new blenders (which may be steady, decreasing, or increasing) on the determination of a depreciation method to be used for the specialized machine.

Case 11-6 Kalish Company has two manufacturing departments, A and B. During Year 5 the manager of Department A obtained a bid of $75,000 from an outside vendor for a machine needed in the department. The manager of Department B, however, convinced management of Kalish that the machine could be manufactured in Department B more economically, and the decision was made to allow Department B to undertake the project. The machine was finished near the end of Year 5, at a cost of $16,000 for material, $24,000 for direct labor, $10,000 for variable factory overhead, and $12,000 for fixed overhead allocated on the basis of direct labor cost.

The controller of Kalish entered the equipment in the accounting records at a cost of $50,000 (excluding fixed factory overhead). The manager of Department B requested that the equipment be recorded at $75,000, stating, "If my employees had not been working on this machine, they could have been engaged in profitable production. If you record the machine at $50,000 my department is going to look bad in the reports at the end of the year. When will I ever get credit for the $25,000 ($75,000 − $50,000) I have earned for Kalish by manufacturing the machine?"

Instructions

a What are the basic issues involved in this controversy?

b If the Department B manager's position were accepted, would the net income of Kalish Company during the current and subsequent accounting periods be changed? Explain.

c Evaluate the two positions and state which one you favor and why.

PROBLEMS

11-1 On January 2, Year 4, Brock Corporation acquired land (Land Site No. 101) with a building for $600,000. Additionally, Brock paid a real estate broker's commission of $36,000, legal fees of $6,000, and title guarantee insurance of $18,000. The closing escrow statement indicated that the land appraised value was $500,000 and the building appraised value was $100,000. Shortly after acquisition, the building was razed at a cost of $75,000.

Brock entered into a $3,000,000 fixed-price construction-type contract with Barnett Builders, Inc., on March 1, Year 4, for the construction of an office building on Land Site No. 101. The building was completed and occupied on September 30, Year 5. Additional construction costs were incurred as follows:

Plans, specifications, and blueprints	*$12,000*
Architects' fees for design and supervision	*95,000*

To finance the construction cost, Brock borrowed $3,000,000 on March 1, Year 4. The loan was payable in 10 annual installments of $300,000 plus interest at the rate of 14%. Brock's average amounts of accumulated building construction costs were as follows:

For the period March 1 to December 31, Year 4 .... $ 900,000
For the period January 1 to September 30, Year 5.................... 2,300,000

Instructions

a Prepare a working paper for Brock Corporation to determine the composition of the total cost of Land Site No. 101 on September 30, Year 5.

b Prepare a working paper for Brock Corporation to determine the composition of the total cost of the office building completed on September 30, Year 5. Show supporting computations.

11-2 On December 31, Year 1, the assets included in the plant assets section of Oliver Company's balance sheet had the following balances:

Land.. $100,000
Buildings.. 800,000
Leasehold improvements 500,000
Machinery and equipment 700,000

During Year 2 the following transactions occurred:

(1) Land Site No. 20 was acquired for $1,000,000. To acquire the land, Oliver paid a $60,000 commission to a real estate agent. Costs of $16,000 were incurred to clear the land. During the course of clearing the land, timber and gravel were recovered and sold for $5,000.

(2) A second tract of land (Land Site No. 21) with a building was acquired for $300,000. The closing escrow statement indicated that the appraised value of the land was $200,000 and the appraised value of the building was $100,000. Shortly after acquisition, the building was demolished at a cost of $30,000. A new building was constructed for $150,000, plus the following costs:

Excavation fees $11,000
Architectural design fees.. 8,000
Building permit fee 1,000
Imputed interest cost (not incurred) on funds used during construction ... 10,500

The building was completed and occupied on September 30, Year 2.

(3) A third tract of land (Land Site No. 22) was acquired for $600,000 and was listed with a real estate broker for sale.

(4) Extensive work was done to a building occupied by Oliver under a lease that expires on December 31, Year 11. The total cost of the work was $125,000, which consisted of the following:

Painting of ceilings (estimated economic life is 1 year) .... $ 10,000
Electrical work (estimated economic life is 10 years) 35,000

(continued)

Construction of extension to the working area (estimated economic
life is 20 years) 80,000

Total cost $125,000

The lessor paid one-half the costs incurred in connection with the extension to the working area. The lease is classified as an operating lease for financial accounting.

(5) During December, Year 2, costs of $65,000 were incurred to improve leased office space. The operating lease will terminate on December 31, Year 4, and is not expected to be renewed.

(6) A group of new machines was acquired under a royalty contract requiring payment of royalties based on units of production for the machines. The invoice price (after a 2% cash discount) of the machines was $78,600, freight costs were $2,100, unloading costs were $1,500, and royalty payments for Year 2 were $13,000.

Instructions

a Prepare an analysis of the changes in each of the following ledger accounts of Oliver Company for the year ended December 31, Year 2 (disregard the related accumulated depreciation accounts):

Land

Buildings

Leasehold Improvements

Machinery and Equipment

b List the items that were not used to determine the answer to **a** above, and indicate where, or if, these items should be included in Oliver Company's financial statements.

11-3 Four independent situations relating to plant assets are described below for Lasswell Corporation. Separate instructions are given for each situation.

a A machine was acquired for $52,000 on May 1, Year 1. At the time of acquisition, the machine was estimated to have an economic life of 10 years and a net residual value of $4,000. Monthly depreciation was recorded under the straight-line method. On March 1, Year 10, the machine was sold for $4,200.

Instructions

Compute Lasswell Corporation's gain or loss on the disposal of the machine.

b A used delivery truck was traded in for a new delivery truck. Information relating to the trucks follows:

Used delivery truck:

Cost .... $ 8,000

Accumulated depreciation 6,000

Estimate of current fair value made by Lasswell's accountant 1,600

New delivery truck:

List price $10,000

(continued)

Cash price without trade-in.	9,500
Cash paid with trade-in	7,800

Instructions

Prepare a journal entry for Lasswell Corporation to record the foregoing exchange transaction in conformity with generally accepted accounting principles.

c Land, building, and equipment were acquired for $90,000 from an insolvent enterprise. At the time of acquisition, $6,000 was paid to have the assets appraised. The appraisal indicated the following current fair values of the assets:

Land.	$60,000
Building	40,000
Equipment.	20,000

Instructions

Determine the cost allocated to Lasswell Corporation's land, building, and equipment for financial accounting.

d A building was appraised at $100,000. A fire occurred, causing $48,600 damage to the building. The building was insured for $60,000 under a policy that included an 80% coinsurance clause.

Instructions

Compute the amount of the loss that Lasswell Corporation will recover under the insurance policy.

11-4 This problem consists of five independent situations relating to plant assets of Larch Corporation. Each situation contains specific instructions.

a Larch Corporation has two fire insurance policies. Policy A with Ace Fidelity covers the furniture at a face amount of $108,000 and the office building at a face amount of $360,000. Policy B with Bravo Indemnity covers only the office building at a face amount of $140,000. A fire caused losses to the furniture and the office building. The relevant data are summarized below:

	Furniture	Office building	
Insurance policies	A	A	B
Current fair values before fire	$150,000	$700,000	$700,000
Current fair values after fire	$ 25,000	$406,000	$406,000
Face amounts of insurance policies	$108,000	$360,000	$140,000
Coinsurance requirements	80%	80%	75%

Instructions

Compute the amount to be recovered by Larch Corporation from each insurance company for the loss on each asset category. Show computations, rounded to the nearest dollar.

b A truck was inspected thoroughly when it was noticed that the diesel engine, which normally lasts four years, was in need of an overhaul and that the trailer needed replacement. The engine cost $2,000 new and was two and a half years old. However, with a $900 overhaul, it was expected to last two more years. The old trailer cost $5,000, had a carrying amount of $750, and was scrapped by Larch Corporation. The price of new trailers had increased by $3,000 since the old one was acquired. Larch accounts for each truck component separately and computes depreciation under the straight-line method.

Instructions

Prepare journal entries for Larch Corporation to record the overhaul of the engine and the replacement of the trailer.

c Larch Corporation exchanged a used automobile for a new automobile. The used automobile had a cost of $6,500, a carrying amount of $1,500, and a current fair value of $2,000 when exchanged. In addition, Larch paid $7,200 cash for the new automobile. The list price of the new automobile was $9,300, and the cash price was $9,200.

Instructions

Prepare a journal entry for Larch Corporation to record the exchange of the used automobile for the new automobile.

d Larch Corporation exchanged 1,000 shares of treasury stock (its $50 par common stock) for land. The treasury stock had cost $60 a share, and had a market price of $82 a share on the exchange date. Larch received $1,200 for scrap when an existing building was removed from the land at a cost of $20,000.

Instructions

Compute the cost of Larch Corporation's land for financial accounting.

e Larch Corporation received $20,000 cash and a used computer with a current fair value of $180,000 for an old computer with a current fair value of $200,000 and a carrying amount of $150,000.

Instructions

Compute the gain (if any) that Larch Corporation should recognize on this exchange transaction and the cost of the used computer for financial accounting.

11-5 Josten Company acquired a new machine and retired an old machine that cost $16,000 and had a carrying amount of $4,000 at the time of retirement. Josten had received offers from two vendors to sell the new machines as follows:

(1) Maye Company offered its machine for $18,000 and agreed to allow $1,000 on the old machine as a trade-in.
(2) Noye Company offered its machine for $17,500, terms 2/10, n/30, but would not accept a trade-in.

Josten accepted Noye's offer and sold its old machine for $700 after incurring $220 in labor costs to remove it from the building. Additional costs incurred in placing the new machine in use were as follows:

Freight (paid in cash)...	$1,190
Installation:	
Material	350
Labor	440
Travel expenses paid to Noye Company's engineer, who supervised the	
installation (There was no charge for the engineer's time.)	210
Costs incurred in testing new machine:	
Operator's wages	160
Spoiled material...	200

During the removal of the used machine, a section of the factory floor was damaged and had to be repaired at a cost of $400 paid to an independent contractor. The damage was caused by extreme carelessness of Josten's employees.

As a result of an error in the treasurer's department, the Noye Company invoice was not paid until 30 days after invoice date; therefore, the cash discount could not be taken.

Instructions

Prepare journal entries for Josten Company, together with supporting computations, to record the retirement of the used machine and the acquisition of the new machine. Credit Material Inventory for the cost of material used and Accrued Payroll for labor costs incurred.

11-6   In auditing the financial statements of Lambeth Company for the fiscal year ended December 31, Year 5, you discover the following:

(1) Machine W with a cash selling price of $18,800 was acquired on April 1, Year 5, in exchange for $20,000 face amount of bonds payable trading at 94 and maturing on April 1, Year 15. The accountant recorded the acquisition by a debit to Machinery and a credit to Bonds Payable for $20,000. Straight-line depreciation was recorded based on a five-year economic life and amounted to $2,400 for nine months. In the computation of depreciation, a net residual value of $4,000 was used.

(2) Machine X listed at a cash price of $6,400 was acquired on January 2, Year 5. Lambeth paid $1,000 down and $500 a month for 12 months. The last payment was made on December 30, Year 5. All cash payments were debited to Machinery. Straight-line depreciation, based on a five-year economic life and no net residual value, was recorded at $1,400 for the year. Freight of $400 on Machine X was debited to the Freight-in ledger account.

(3) On December 28, Year 5, Machine Y was recorded at $5,100, which included the carrying amount of $1,100 for an old machine accepted as a trade-in and cash of $4,000. The cash price of Machine Y was $4,500, and the trade-in allowance was $500.

(4) Machine Z was acquired on January 10, Year 5, in exchange for past-due accounts receivable of $14,000 on which an allowance of 20% had been established on December 31, Year 4. The current fair value of the machine on January 10 was $11,000. The machine was recorded by a debit to Machinery and a credit to Accounts Receivable for $14,000. No depreciation was recorded

on Machine Z, because it was not used in operations. In March, Machine Z was exchanged for 100 shares of Lambeth's outstanding common stock with a market price of $105 a share. The Treasury Stock ledger account was debited for $14,000, the carrying amount of Machine Z.

Instructions

Record any correcting journal entries required for Lambeth Company on December 31, Year 5, for each transaction (1) through (4) above. Assume that revenue and expense ledger accounts have not been closed for Year 5. Amortize bond discount by the straight-line method.

11-7 On July 10, Year 5, Sayle Company sold a building to Beyer Company. The escrow statements for the seller and the acquirer are presented below:

	Sayle Company (Seller)		Beyer Company (Acquirer)	
	Charges	Credits	Charges	Credits
Sale Price		$310,000	$310,000	
First mortgage note assumed by acquirer	$120,000			$120,000
Purchase-money mortgage note, 12%	80,000			80,000
Prorations:				
Property taxes from July 1 to July 10, Year 5	250			250
Insurance		200	200	
Interest accrued	350			350
Fees:				
Escrow	100		100	
Title insurance			790	
Recording and legal	40		60	
Revenue stamps (taxes)			550	
Cash deposited in escrow account on July 10, Year 5				111,100
Items paid from escrow account:				
Commission	18,600			
Remittance to seller	90,860			
Totals	$310,200	$310,200	$311,700	$311,700

Additional Information

(1) A Suspense ledger account was used by Sayle to record cash received in connection with the sale, including monthly receipts on the purchase-money mortgage. The Suspense ledger account had a credit balance of $94,450 on September 30, Year 5.

(2) The purchase-money mortgage note payments are $1,000 a month, plus accrued interest on the unpaid balance. The first payment was received on August 10

and amounted to $1,800; the second payment was received on September 9 and amounted to $1,790. Both amounts were credited by Sayle to the Suspense ledger account.

(3) The building and land had been acquired by Sayle on July 1, Year 1, for $270,000. The building was depreciated over a 40-year economic life under the straight-line method. Accumulated depreciation on December 31, Year 4, was $17,500. A half-year's depreciation has been consistently recorded for assets acquired or sold during the year. No depreciation had been recorded by Sayle for Year 5.

Instructions

a Determine the net proceeds to Sayle Company for the land and for the building. The sales price and expenses of sale were allocated by Sayle as follows: land, 30%; building, 70%.

b Prepare journal entries to record the sale and related transactions in Sayle Company's accounting records. Prepare a supporting analysis showing the gain or loss on the sale of land and the gain or loss on the sale of building. Disregard income taxes, and do not record cash received from Beyer Company on the purchase-money mortgage note because the receipts already had been recorded.

c Prepare a journal entry to record the acquisition of land and building in Beyer Company's accounting records. The acquisition price, including all fees, is allocated 30% to land and 70% to building.

11-8 Lang Company offered More Company $200,000 cash for used machinery. More responded that the price offered was acceptable but for income tax reasons it did not want an all-cash transaction. More then offered to sell the machinery to Lang for a $50,000 cash down payment, the balance payable in five equal annual installments of $30,000 each with interest payable annually at 6% on the unpaid balance. In addition, Lang agreed to sign a contract to purchase merchandise from More.

Lang decided that, although More's merchandise prices were in excess of current market prices, the 6% interest rate on the promissory note was sufficiently below the 10% that Lang would have to pay to borrow elsewhere to make the contract acceptable. Accordingly, on July 1, Year 7, Lang accepted More's proposal, made the down payment, signed the 6% promissory note and the contract for the purchase of the merchandise, and accepted delivery of the used machinery.

Instructions

a Record the acquisition of the used machinery in the accounting records of Lang Company on July 1, Year 7. On that date, the discounted value of the five-year, 6% promissory note, based on an interest rate of 10%, was $135,490.

b Prepare journal entries for Lang Company on December 31, Year 7, to record the following:

(1) Interest expense for six months. Use the interest method of amortization for the discount on the note payable and round to the nearest dollar.

(2) Depreciation for six months. Assume a four-year economic life for the used machinery, no net residual value, and the straight-line method of depreciation.

(3) Any required adjustment to cost of goods sold. Assume that one-half of the merchandise contracted for with More had been purchased and that the merchandise purchased had been sold by December 31, Year 7.

11-9   Bosnia Company was incorporated on January 4, Year 10, but was unable to begin manufacturing activities until July 1, Year 10, because its plant was not finished until that date.

On December 31, Year 10, Bosnia's record of the construction and accounting for the plant appeared in a Plant ledger account as follows:

Plant

Date	Explanation	Debit	Credit	Balance
Year 10				
Jan. 31	Cost of land and old building	325,000		325,000 dr
Feb. 28	Cost of removing old building	7,400		332,400 dr
Mar. 1	Proceeds from sale of salvaged			
	material from old building		3,000	329,400 dr
May 1	Partial payment for new building	175,000		504,400 dr
1	Legal fees	4,000		508,400 dr
June 1	Second payment for new building	175,000		683,400 dr
1	Insurance premium (May 1, Year 10			
	to Apr. 30, Year 13)	3,600		687,000 dr
1	Special tax assessment	5,000		692,000 dr
30	Expenses	24,000		716,000 dr
July 1	Final payment for new building	175,000		891,000 dr
Dec. 31	Write-up of new building per			
	appraisal	50,000		941,000 dr
31	Depreciation expense for 6 months			
	($941,000 × 0.02)		18,820	922,180 dr

Additional Information

(1) On January 31, Bosnia paid $25,000 cash and issued 3,000 shares of 8% cumulative preferred stock, $100 par, for land and an old building. On January 30, a large block of preferred stock had been traded in the market for $105 a share. The preferred stock issued was recorded at par.

(2) The demolition company charged $7,400 for removal of the old building. The salvaged material from the old building was sold for $3,000.

(3) Legal fees covered the organization of Bosnia, $1,500; acquisition of land, $2,000; and construction contract for the new building, $500.

(4) Insurance on the new building was acquired on May 1. The three-year premium was paid on June 1, on receipt of the invoice.

(5) The special tax assessment covered street improvements.

(6) The expenses were for the period from January 2 to June 30 and include president's salary, $12,000; salary of plant superintendent who supervised construction of the new building, $10,000; and office salaries, $2,000. The president's salary and office salaries are considered organization costs.

(7) During the six months' construction period, a new union contract for construction workers was negotiated calling for an increase of 15% in wages, and there were increases in construction material costs. On the basis of these facts, the plant superintendent suggested that the building be written up by $50,000 to recognize the increase in the current cost of the building. The credit was recorded in the Retained Earnings ledger account.

(8) The new building was to be depreciated at the rate of 4% a year, with no net residual value. Depreciation of $18,820 for six months was debited to the Depreciation Expense ledger account.

Instructions

a Prepare a working paper to classify the transactions of Bosnia Company in appropriate ledger accounts. Provide separate columns for Land and for Building; other accounts should be analyzed in a Miscellaneous column.

b Prepare a single journal entry on December 31, Year 10, to correct the accounting records of Bosnia Company. The accounting records have not been closed for the year ended December 31, Year 10.

11-10   Coal Company completed certain transactions in the current year to simplify its operations, to improve its competitive position, and to resolve several business disputes. Three transactions involved transfers of mining claims to stockholders of Coal Company, and three transactions were with Olson Corporation, a competitor. The transactions are listed below:

(1) Mining claim No. 1, carried in the accounting records at a cost of $5,000, was sold to a stockholder of Coal Company for $12,000 cash.

(2) Mining claim No. 2, carried in the accounting records at a cost of $3,000, was exchanged for 200 shares of Coal's outstanding common stock. The common stock was trading for $125 a share at the time of the exchange. (Record the common stock acquired in the Treasury Stock ledger account.)

(3) Mining claim No. 3, carried in the accounting records at a cost of $20,000, was transferred to Betty Strong, a stockholder, in consideration of her withdrawal of a patent infringement suit against Coal. When asked for an estimate of the current fair value of the mining claims, the president of Coal answered that it was ''anyone's guess.'' Further questioning elicited the reluctant response, ''Claim No. 1 probably was worth about $12,000 and each of the other two claims was worth about twice that.'' You have concluded that no more precise estimates of current fair values were obtainable.

(4) Coal exchanged its 5% common stock investment in Belmont Company, carried at cost of $90,000, for a plant site owned by Olson Corporation appraised at $200,000.

(5) Coal traded certain inventory items located in Chicago for similar items held by Olson Corporation in Tulsa. To equalize trading values, Olson also paid $2,000 cash to Coal. The cost of the inventory items given up by Coal was $8,200, and the current fair value was $10,000. Coal uses the perpetual inventory system.

(6) Coal obtained production jigs and dies from Olson Corporation, giving in exchange a used milling machine and cash of $1,700. The milling machine, car-

ried in Coal's accounting records at a cost of $20,000, was considered similar to jigs and dies; accumulated depreciation was $12,000. Olson was willing to pay the $10,500 appraised value of the milling machine in cash, but Coal insisted on an exchange for the jigs and dies.

Instructions

Prepare journal entries for Coal Company to record each of the six transactions described above.

11-11   Margo Beatty maintains her accounting records on a cash basis. On February 28, Year 10, she sold property, acquired 17 years earlier for $110,000, to Lana Conley for $161,200. The cost allocated to the building was $70,000, and the accumulated depreciation to the date of the sale was $42,500.

     The escrow statements on February 28 for the acquirer and the seller are shown below:

Acquirer's Escrow Statement (City Escrow Co., Escrow No. 911)

Acquisition price of property	$161,200	
Deposit of cash by acquirer on Jan. 30 (recorded in		
Escrow Deposit ledger account)		$ 83,100
Title fee (one-half)	430	
Drawing and recording deed	15	
Fire insurance, prorated	1,430	
Mortgage note assumed by acquirer		78,460
Property taxes for period Jan. 1 to Feb. 28, Year 10,		
accrued and unpaid		200
Lease deposits		850
Rent, prorated		340
Interest accrued on mortgage note		185
Cash to acquirer	60	
Totals	$163,135	$163,135

Seller's Escrow Statement (City Escrow Co., Escrow No. 911)

Selling price of property		$161,200
Title fee (one-half)	$ 430	
Drawing and recording deed	15	
Property taxes for period Jan. 1 to Feb. 28, Year 10		
accrued and unpaid	200	
Interest accrued on mortgage note	185	
Lease deposits	850	
Rent, prorated	340	
Mortgage note assumed by acquirer	78,460	
Fire insurance, prorated		1,430
Revenue stamps (tax on real estate transfers)	150	
Real estate broker's commission	10,300	
Cash to seller	71,700	
Totals	$162,630	$162,630

Instructions

a Prepare a working paper to show how Margo Beatty should determine the gain or loss on the foregoing transaction. Disregard income taxes.

b Prepare a journal entry to record the foregoing transaction in the accounting records of Margo Beatty.

c Prepare a journal entry to record the foregoing transaction in the accounting records of Lana Conley, assuming that $100,000 of total cost is allocated to land and that items representing future expenses or revenue are recorded in nominal (expense and revenue) ledger accounts.

11-12 Nakota Corporation manufactures auto parts. On August 31, Year 2, a fire completely destroyed Nakota's building, goods in process inventory, and machinery.

Additional Information

(1) The cost of plant assets destroyed and the related accumulated depreciation ledger accounts on August 31, Year 2, were as follows:

	Cost	Accumulated depreciation
Building	$40,000	$17,500
Machinery	15,000	4,500

At present prices, the cost to replace the destroyed property are: building, $80,000; machinery, $37,500. At the time of the fire it was estimated that the building was 50% depreciated, and the destroyed machinery was one-third depreciated. Insurance companies agreed that the insurable value (current fair value) of the building and machinery was $65,000 on the date of fire.

(2) After the fire, a physical inventory was taken. The inventories of material and finished goods had a cost (and current fair value) of $26,000 and $52,000, respectively.

(3) The inventories on December 31, Year 1, were: material, $20,000; goods in process, $48,000; and finished goods, $54,000.

(4) The sales of the first eight months of Year 2 were $150,000, and purchases of material were $55,000. Direct labor for the eight months was $40,000; for the past five years factory overhead has been applied at the rate of 80% of direct labor cost. The gross profit for the last five years has averaged 30% of net sales.

(5) Insurance is carried with two companies, each policy with an 80% coinsurance clause. The amounts of insurance carried with each company are listed below:

	Building and machinery	Inventories
Acme Insurance Company	$42,000	$64,800
Zenith Indemnity Company	20,000	21,600

Instructions

a Compute the estimated cost of Nakota Corporation's inventory of goods in process lost in the fire on August 31, Year 2.

b Compute Nakota Corporation's expected recovery from each insurance company, assuming that the estimated cost of inventories lost is accepted as a measure of current fair value on the date of the fire.

c Assuming that Nakota Corporation recovers the loss determined in part **b,** what is the loss or gain from fire reported in its income statement for the year ended December 31, Year 2? Disregard the income tax effect of the loss or gain.

11-13 On September 20, Year 8, a fire damaged the office and warehouse of Wholesalers, Inc., whose fiscal year ends on December 31. The only accounting record salvaged was the general ledger, from which the following information was obtained as of August 31, Year 8:

	Debit	Credit
Accounts receivable	$25,000	
Inventory, Dec. 31, Year 7	60,920	
Accounts payable		$ 27,500
Sales, Jan. 1 to Aug. 31, Year 8		100,000
Purchases, Jan. 1 to Aug. 31, Year 8	80,000	

Additional Information

(1) The September bank statement and paid checks disclosed that checks written during the period September 1 to 20 totaled $15,000: $8,000 for accounts payable as of August 31, $2,000 for September purchases, and $5,000 for operating expenses. Deposits during the same period amounted to $11,500, which consisted of receipts from customers, with the exception of a $1,300 refund from a supplier for goods returned in September.

(2) Correspondence with suppliers disclosed unrecorded obligations of $7,200 on September 20, for merchandise purchased during September.

(3) Customers confirmed payables of $29,500 to Wholesalers, Inc., as of the close of business on September 20, Year 8.

(4) The following insurance on inventory was in effect on the date of the fire:

	Amount of coverage	Coinsurance requirement
Allied Mutual	$30,000	80%
Blue Regional	20,000	70%
Claim Free	10,000	None

(5) The insurance companies agreed that the fire loss claim should be based on the assumption that the overall gross profit rate of 40% of sales for the past two years was in effect during Year 8 and that the cost of inventory so determined is a reasonable estimate of the current fair value of the inventory.

(6) Inventory with a cost of $22,400 was recovered in good condition. The remainder of the inventory was a total loss. The office and the warehouse building were not insured. Wholesalers, Inc., paid $4,150 to repair the damage to the office, but the warehouse was a total loss. The warehouse (excluding land) cost $50,000 to construct, was fully depreciated, and had a current fair value of $10,000 on the date of the fire.

Instructions

a Prepare a working paper for Wholesalers, Inc., to compute the approximate cost of inventory lost in the fire on September 20, Year 8.

b Prepare a working paper for Wholesalers, Inc., to compute the pro rata claim to be filed with each insurance company.

c Assuming that Wholesalers, Inc., is indemnified as determined in part **b,** what is the loss or gain from fire included in its income statement for Year 8? Disregard income tax effect of the loss or gain.

11-14 The inexperienced accountant for Wintergreen Company, a service enterprise that began operations on February 1, Year 2, made a number of errors in accounting for Wintergreen's plant assets. Wintergreen's plant asset ledger accounts on December 31, Year 2, were as follows:

Land and Building

Date	Explanation	Debit	Credit	Balance
Year 2				
Feb. 1	Check to close escrow	24,600		24,600 dr
Apr. 5	Routine painting of building	5,210		29,810 dr
June 1	Grading and paving of new parking lot	22,400		52,210 dr
Sept. 30	Cost of completed new wing of building	78,700		130,910 dr

Automobiles

Date	Explanation	Debit	Credit	Balance
Year 2				
Feb. 1–				
Oct. 1	$420 × 9 monthly rent on leased automobile	3,780		3,780 dr
Oct. 31	Down payment on new automobile	5,000		8,780 dr
Nov. 30	Monthly payment on new automobile	392		9,172 dr
Dec. 31	Monthly payment on new automobile	392		9,564 dr

Furniture and Equipment

Date	Explanation	Debit	Credit	Balance
Year 2				
Feb. 1	Furniture and equipment acquired for cash	15,000		15,000 dr
Sept. 26	Routine repairs to microcomputer	720		15,720 dr
Dec. 1	Furniture and equipment acquired for common stock	4,000		19,720 dr

Additional Information

(1) On January 2, Year 2, after issuing common stock for cash, Wintergreen made a $100,000 deposit in escrow for the acquisition of land and a building. The accountant debited an Escrow Expense ledger account for the deposit. The statement issued to Wintergreen by the escrow company at the close of the escrow on February 1, Year 2, was as follows:

FIDELITY ESCROW COMPANY
Escrow Statement for Acquirer

Escrow No. 2758   **Date: Feb. 1, Year 2**

Items	*Charges*	*Credits*
Acquisition price of property............................	$369,200	
Balance of mortgage note assumed by acquirer		$240,000
Interest at 10% from Jan. 16, Year 2, to Feb. 1, Year 2 ...		1,000
Property taxes prorated, $14,400 a year from July 1, Year 1, to Feb. 1, Year 2		8,400
Fire insurance prorated (coverage for period from Feb. 1, Year 2, to June 1, Year 2)	120	
Deposited in escrow by acquirer........................		100,000
Title policy (acquirer agreed to pay full amount)	1,850	
Revenue stamps (tax on transaction)	360	
Recording fee..	70	
Escrow fee (acquirer agreed to pay full amount)	2,400	
Check to balance		24,600
Totals	$374,000	$374,000

(2) An appraisal of the building obtained by Wintergreen on February 1, Year 2, established the current fair value of the building at $204,500.

(3) On February 1, Year 2, Wintergreen leased an automobile under a one-year cancelable operating lease at $420 a month rent.

(4) Wintergreen acquired furniture and equipment costing $15,000 on February 1, Year 2. When the invoice for the equipment was paid on February 10, Year 2, the $300 cash discount was credited to the Purchases Discounts ledger account.

(5) On October 31, Year 2, Wintergreen terminated the automobile lease dated February 1, Year 2, and acquired an automobile with a cash price of $15,000. Terms of the sale were as follows:

Cash price of automobile	$15,000
Less: Down payment	5,000
Balance payable over 36 months	$10,000
Add: Interest at 13¾% for three years on $10,000.....................	4,125
Total contract payable (36 payments of $392 beginning Nov. 30, Year 2)..	$14,125

The effective interest rate on the deferred payment contract for the automobile was 2% a month.

(6) On December 1, Year 2, Wintergreen acquired furniture and equipment with a cash price of $4,400 in exchange for 400 shares of Wintergreen's no-par common stock with a stated value of $10 a share.

Instructions

Prepare correcting journal entries for Wintergreen Company on December 31, Year 2, the end of its first fiscal year. Disregard depreciation and income taxes. Round all amounts to the nearest dollar and record expense prorations (from the escrow statement) in asset and liability accounts.

Plant Assets:
Depreciation
and Depletion

12

In Chapter 11 we describe plant assets as a "bundle of future services," and consider the problem of determining the acquisition cost of the future services embodied in such assets. In this chapter we are concerned with the problem of measuring the portion of the services of plant assets and natural resources "withdrawn from the bundle" and consumed in business operations.

Depreciation is the portion of the cost of plant assets that is deducted from revenue for asset services used in the operations of a business enterprise. In practice, depreciation describes the cost of the expired services of tangible plant assets. For financial accounting, *depletion* refers to the estimated cost of natural resources such as oil, gas, timber, and iron ore that have been removed from their source. Recording the expired service cost of intangible assets, such as patents and goodwill, is called *amortization,* and is discussed in Chapter 13.

DEPRECIATION

The concept of depreciation is linked closely to the measurement of net income. Because part of the service potential of depreciable plant assets is exhausted in the revenue-generating process each accounting period, the cost of these services must be deducted from revenue in the measurement of net income; the expired cost must be recovered before a business enterprise is considered "as well off" as at the beginning of the period. Depreciation is the measurement of this expired cost.

Depreciation has been one of the most misunderstood concepts of accounting. In the early history of accounting, it was necessary to convince users of accounting information that depreciation was a cost (expense) of doing business. Business executives tended to view depreciation as a matter of "setting aside something" during profitable years for the replacement of depreciable assets. When earnings were high, large amounts of depreciation might be recorded; when earnings were low or losses were incurred, depreciation was not recorded. Today, it is universally agreed that depreciation is an expense that must be recognized regardless of the level of earnings, and that depreciation accounting does not involve "setting aside" cash or other assets in a fund to replace depreciable assets.

Accounting for depreciation is a process of *cost allocation,* not asset valuation. The acquisition of plant assets means that asset services have been acquired in advance of their use. Between the time of acquisition and the time of use, the value of these services may change materially because of supply and demand factors or changes in price levels. Therefore, the measurement of the historical cost of plant asset services that are used may differ from the current cost of similar services. This difference is germane to a variety of managerial decisions; however, the question of revaluing depreciable assets (in effect, revaluing the remaining unused services) at some time subsequent to acquisition should not be confused with the cost allocation problem. In this chapter we deal only with the allocation of the cost of plant assets and natural resources. The revaluation of plant assets and depreciation expense in response to increases in current costs and the general price level is considered in Chapter 25.

Factors in the Estimation of Periodic Depreciation

The estimate of periodic depreciation is dependent on the following three variables:

1   *Economic life* This involves choosing the unit in which economic life of plant assets is to be measured and estimating how many units of service are embodied in each asset. The units may be measured in years, hours of operation, or number of items produced.

2   *Depreciation base* The depreciation base is the cost of asset services that will be used; it usually is less than the total cost of the asset because net residual (salvage) value is subtracted from cost to compute the depreciation base.

3   *Method of cost allocation* The problem here is to determine the amount of services that has been used in each accounting period. A corollary issue is to decide whether all units of service have an equal cost, or whether some units of service have a larger or smaller cost than others.

Estimate of Economic Life

The economic life of a plant asset is the total units of service expected to be derived from the asset. Accountants commonly measure economic life of a plant asset in terms of time units, for example, months or years. Economic life of a plant asset also may be measured in terms of output or activity, expressed in such physical units as miles or machine-hours. For example, the estimated economic life of a truck may be described as *four years* or *200,000 miles.* Forces that tend to limit the economic life of a plant asset should be considered in the determination of the type of *unit of service* to use for a specific asset or group of assets. The causes of a decrease in economic life may be divided into *physical deterioration* (including casualties), and *functional* or *economic* factors.

Physical deterioration results largely from wear and tear from use and the forces of nature. These physical forces terminate the usefulness of plant assets by rendering them incapable of performing the services for which they were intended and thus set the maximum limit on economic life. Unusual events such as accidents, floods, and earthquakes also serve to terminate or reduce the economic life of plant assets.

Functional or *economic factors* may render a plant asset that is in good physical condition no longer useful because it is not economical to keep the asset in service, or because of legal or income tax considerations related to the use of the asset. Two primary causes of functional depreciation are obsolescence and inadequacy. *Obsolescence* refers to the effect of innovations and technological improvements on the economic life of plant assets. An inevitable result of research and development activities is the obsolescence of existing plant assets. Jet airliners, for example, made piston-driven aircraft uneconomical for major airlines to operate. Thus, obsolescence terminated the economic life of many piston-driven aircraft and sent them to the used-plane market even though they had a physical potential of many more years of service.

Inadequacy refers to the effect of growth and changes in the scale of a business operation in terminating the economic life of plant assets. A warehouse may be in sound condition, but if more space is required than may be provided economically by the addition of a separate building, the old warehouse has become inadequate, and its economic life, from the standpoint of the business enterprise, is terminated. In a general sense, any plant asset whose capacity is such that it cannot be operated efficiently or does not fit the requirements of the enterprise is *inadequate*.

In a highly developed industrial society, functional factors of depreciation probably have a greater influence on economic lives of plant assets than physical deterioration, particularly with respect to special-purpose equipment. Estimates of economic life, therefore, are influenced by these factors.

The choice of an appropriate *unit* of economic life for a plant asset also requires a determination of the causes of depreciation. The objective is to choose the unit most closely related to the cause of service exhaustion. When the economic life of a plant asset is limited largely by the effect of physical deterioration, a unit that reflects physical use of the asset is appropriate. For example, hours of service might be chosen as the unit of economic life for an electric motor, or miles of service for a truck. In contrast, the physical deterioration that limits the economic life of buildings probably is related more closely to the passage of time than to usage. Thus, an estimated economic life in terms of years is more appropriate for buildings.

No estimate of economic life can be made with high precision. The best procedure is to start with an estimate of physical economic life as a maximum, modify this for the probable effects of obsolescence and inadequacy, and then be prepared to adjust these estimates in the light of actual experience. If the estimated economic life of a plant asset is revised, the undepreciated cost of the asset is allocated to the remaining units of service.

The Depreciation Base

The depreciation base (or depreciable cost) of a plant asset is the portion of its cost that is allocated to depreciation expense during its economic life. Because the owner of an asset may sell it before its serviceability is ended, the initial cost of a plant asset, as determined by the guidelines described in Chapter 11, is not necessarily its depreciation base. For example, a car rental company may pay $12,000 for a new car and sell it at the end of three years for $5,000, even though its economic life is much longer. The depreciation base is $7,000, the difference between cost and *residual value*.

The scrapping or removal of plant assets such as buildings, structures, and heavy equipment may involve substantial costs in the year of retirement. Theoretically, removal costs should be estimated and included in the depreciation base. The inclusion of removal costs in the depreciation base means that the entire cost involved in obtaining services from plant assets will be allocated to the revenue generated by the assets, without regard to the timing of the expenditure. In practice, however, removal costs may be either disregarded or netted against the estimated residual value of the assets. The depreciation base for a plant asset thus becomes:

Depreciation base
of plant asset

Depreciation base = cost − estimated residual value (net)

In some instances, net residual value (gross residual value minus estimated removal costs) is likely to be so small or uncertain that it may be disregarded in the computation of the depreciation base.

Depreciation Methods—Cost Allocation

When the economic life of a plant asset has been estimated, and its depreciation base established, there remains the problem of determining the portion of cost that will expire with each unit of economic life. There are two major variables to be considered in reaching a solution to this problem:

1   The *quantity* of services used may be equal or may differ during each accounting period of economic life.

2   The *cost* of various units of service may be equal or may differ during each accounting period of economic life.

Because of the relatively high degree of uncertainty that underlies estimates of economic life and service use, the distinction between these two variables may become blurred. We may illustrate by reference to a situation that is familiar—the depreciation of an automobile used for business purposes. Assume that the automobile cost $10,000, has an expected net residual value of $1,000, and is estimated to have an economic life of 100,000 miles. The average depreciation expense per unit of service (1 mile) is 9 cents [($10,000 − $1,000) ÷ 100,000 = $0.09]. However, the miles of service used in each accounting period may vary. If 20,000 miles are driven during the first year and 30,000 miles during the second year, there has been a variation in the *quantity* of service used, and depreciation expense of $1,800 for the first year and $2,700 for the second recognizes this fact.

However, even if the automobile is driven 20,000 miles each year for five years, there may be a difference in the *cost* of the miles of service in each of these five accounting periods. The miles of service when the automobile is new and operating efficiently may be more valuable (and thus presumably more costly) than the miles of service during later years. Therefore, the assumption that each mile bears the same depreciation expense may not be reasonable, and we might compute depreciation on the assumption that early miles cost more than later miles. For example, depreciation might be computed at 12 cents a mile for the first 20,000 miles, 10 cents for the next 20,000 miles, and so forth.

There are several depreciation methods that attempt to recognize these factors in varying degrees. They may be classified as follows:

1   Straight-line method (based on expiration of time)

2   Accelerated methods (based on expiration of time)
   a Fixed-percentage-of-declining-balance
   b Double-declining-balance and other arbitrary fixed-percentage methods
   c Sum-of-the-years'-digits

3   Output (or units-of-production) method (based on physical service or production)

4   Retirement-replacement-betterment method

5   Interest methods

Depreciation under the straight-line and accelerated methods is a function of time rather than use. In contrast, depreciation under the output method is a function of actual usage rather than the passage of time.

Depreciation that is a function of time generally is computed to the nearest month, although other procedures consistently applied may be acceptable. For example, one-half of a full year's depreciation may be recognized in both the year of acquisition and the year of disposal of a plant asset. Descriptions of the most widely used depreciation methods follow:

Straight-Line Method   The distinguishing characteristic of the straight-line method of depreciation is that each full year of service absorbs an equal portion of cost. Depreciation per year is computed as follows:

Straight-line method means equal periodic expense

$$\text{Depreciation per year} = \frac{\text{cost} - \text{estimated net residual value}}{\text{years of economic life}}$$

To illustrate the straight-line method of depreciation, assume that a machine is acquired on January 2, Year 1, for $7,000 and that the net residual value of the

Carrying amount of machine decreases by $1,500 each year of its economic life

Date	Depreciation expense for year	Accumulated depreciation	Carrying amount
Jan. 2, Year 1			$7,000
Dec. 31, Year 1	$1,500	$1,500	5,500
Dec. 31, Year 2	1,500	3,000	4,000
Dec. 31, Year 3	1,500	4,500	2,500
Dec. 31, Year 4	1,500	6,000	1,000*

*Net residual value

machine at the end of four years of economic life is estimated at $1,000. The depreciation expense, accumulated depreciation, and *carrying amount* (cost less accumulated depreciation) of the machine over its economic life are presented at the bottom of page 605. At the end of each year, depreciation expense on this machine is recorded as follows:

Journal entry to record depreciation

Depreciation Expense......................................	1,500	
Accumulated Depreciation of Machinery		1,500
To record depreciation for year.		

Accelerated Methods   The assumption that plant assets yield either a greater quantity of service or more valuable service in early years of their economic life has led accountants to devise methods of depreciation that result in larger amounts of depreciation in early years of economic life, and smaller amounts in later years. These methods, known as *accelerated methods* of depreciation, were not widely used until they were incorporated in the federal income tax laws. The three most widely used accelerated methods of depreciation are described in the following sections.

1 Fixed-Percentage-of-Declining-Balance Method   Under this method (frequently called the *declining-balance method*), a percentage depreciation rate is computed that, when applied to the carrying amount of the asset at the beginning of each accounting period, results in reducing the carrying amount of the asset to estimated net residual value at the end of its economic life. Because the rate computed is applied on a constantly declining carrying amount, the depreciation expense decreases each year. The formula for the computation of the required rate per year (when n = years of economic life) is:

Formula to compute fixed percentage

$$\text{Depreciation rate} = 1 - \sqrt[n]{\frac{\text{net residual value}}{\text{cost}}}$$

In the application of this formula a net residual value of at least $1 must be used, because it is impossible to reduce any amount to zero by applying a constant percentage to the successively declining carrying amount. The depreciation rate for a plant asset that cost $10,000, has a net residual value of $1,296, and has an economic life of four years, is computed below:

Formula solved

$$\text{Depreciation rate} = 1 - \sqrt[4]{\frac{\$1,296}{\$10,000}} = 1 - \frac{6}{10} = \underline{\underline{40\%}}$$

If this formula yields a rate of, say, 39.69%, rounding the rate to 40% would not be objectionable, because measurement of depreciation at best is only a rough estimate. This formula yields a *precise rate* that depreciates a plant asset to a carrying amount equal to its net residual value. Other *arbitrary rates* (discussed below) have been introduced by income tax laws. The tabulation below shows depreciation expense for the four-year economic life for a fixed percentage of 40% on the declining carrying amount of the plant asset:

Amount of depreciation decreases each year under declining-balance method

| Year of economic life | Carrying amount at beginning of year | Depreciation expense | | Accumulated depreciation |
		Amount (40% of carrying amount at beginning of year)	Percentage of total	
1	$10,000	$4,000	46.0	$4,000
2	6,000	2,400	27.6	6,400
3	3,600	1,440	16.5	7,840
4	2,160	864	9.9	8,704
Balance	1,296*			
		$8,704	100.0	

*Net residual value

It should be noted that the carrying amount at the end of the fourth year is equal to the estimated net residual value, $1,296, and that annual depreciation expense decreases rapidly. (In this example, because the depreciation rate is 40%, the depreciation expense in the second year and each of the succeeding years of economic life is only 60% of the expense reported a year earlier.)

2 Double-Declining-Balance and Other Arbitrary Fixed-Percentage Methods
Modifications of the fixed-percentage-of-declining-balance method of depreciation introduced by federal income tax laws are termed the *double-declining-balance* (or *200%-declining-balance*) *method,* the *150%-declining-balance method,* and the *125%-declining-balance method.* Under these methods, depreciation is computed by applying arbitrary percentages to the carrying amount of the plant asset at the beginning of each year of its economic life. *The asset is not depreciated below net residual value under these methods;* thus, net residual value is taken into account only as a limiting factor in the application of the double-declining-balance and the other arbitrary fixed-percentage methods.

To illustrate the double-declining-balance method of depreciation, we shall use the example of a plant asset costing $22,000, having a net residual value of $2,000, and an economic life of four years. The depreciation percentage is 50% (¼ = 25%; 25% × 2 = 50%).

In the tabulation at the top of page 608, depreciation for Year 2 and Year 3 is 50% of the prior-year depreciation. However, depreciation for Year 4 has no such relationship to the Year 3 depreciation; it is merely the amount required to reduce the carrying amount of the plant asset to its net residual value at the end of its economic life of four years.

Double-declining-
balance method
of depreciation

Year of economic life	Carrying amount at beginning of year	Depreciation expense		Accumulated depreciation
		Amount (50% of carrying amount at beginning of year)	Percentage of total	
1	$22,000	$11,000	55.0	$11,000
2	11,000	5,500	27.5	16,500
3	5,500	2,750	13.8	19,250
4	2,750	750†	3.7	20,000
Balance	2,000*			
		$20,000	100.0	

*Net residual value
†Amount required to reduce carrying amount to net residual value

Fractional-Period Depreciation under Double-Declining-Balance Method   The acquisition during the year of a plant asset that is to be depreciated under the double-declining-balance method does not require the allocation of each full year's depreciation between two fiscal years because the fixed percentage is applied to the carrying amount (undepreciated cost) of the plant asset at the beginning of each year. However, in the last full year of asset life, depreciation is computed for a

Double-declining-
balance depreciation
involving fractional
periods, **with no
allocation** of each
full year's depreciation
between two fiscal
years

Period ended	Carrying amount at beginning of period	Depreciation expense		Accumulated depreciation
		Amount (40% of carrying amount at beginning of period times fraction of period)	Percentage of total	
12/31/4	$8,000	$2,400*	32.0	$2,400
12/31/5	5,600	2,240	29.9	4,640
12/31/6	3,360	1,344	17.9	5,984
12/31/7	2,016	806	10.7	6,790
12/31/8	1,210	484	6.5	7,274
12/31/9	726	226‡	3.0	7,500
Balance	500†			
		$7,500	100.0	

*($8,000 × 0.40) × $9/12$ = $2,400
†Net residual value
‡Amount required to reduce carrying amount to net residual value

fraction of a year (or an amount that reduces the beginning-of-year carrying amount of the asset to net residual value).

For example, depreciation expense under the double-declining-balance method of depreciation for a plant asset having an economic life of five years, residual value of $500, and a cost of $8,000 on April 1, Year 4, is computed for the six years ended December 31, Year 9, as illustrated at the bottom of page 608.

If, instead of the foregoing method, double-declining-balance depreciation had been computed by the allocation of each full year's depreciation between two fiscal years, only the depreciation for the last two years would be different, as demonstrated below:

Double-declining-balance depreciation involving fractional periods **with** **allocation** of each full year's depreciation between two fiscal years

Period ended	Computation of depreciation	Depreciation expense	Accumulated depreciation	Carrying amount
12/31/4	[($8,000 × 0.40) × 9/12] (4/1/4 to 12/31/4)	$2,400	$2,400	$5,600
12/31/5	[($8,000 × 0.40) × 3/12] + [($4,800 × 0.40) × 9/12]	2,240	4,640	3,360
12/31/6	[($4,800 × 0.40) × 3/12] + [($2,880 × 0.40) × 9/12]	1,344	5,984	2,016
12/31/7	[($2,880 × 0.40) × 3/12] + [($1,728 × 0.40) × 9/12]	806	6,790	1,210
12/31/8	[($1,728 × 0.40) × 3/12] + ($537* × 9/12)	576	7,366	634
12/31/9	($537* × 3/12)(1/1/9 to 3/31/9)	134	7,500	500†
		$7,500		

*Amount required to reduce carrying amount to net residual value
†Net residual value

Depreciation for Year 8 in the foregoing computation is $92 larger ($576 − $484 = $92) than in the computation on page 608; conversely, depreciation for Year 9 above is $92 less ($226 − $134 = $92) than in the computation on page 608. This is because the depreciation of $710 ($1,210 − $500 = $710) for the final year of asset life is allocated to two fiscal years under the *allocation method*.

3 Sum-of-the-Years'-Digits Method   Under this method, a decreasing depreciation expense is computed by a simple mathematical procedure relating to arithmetic progressions. The sum of a series of digits representing the years of economic life of a plant asset becomes the denominator of the depreciation fraction in any year.[1] The

---

[1]The formula for determining the sum of any arithmetic progression of n consecutive digits is $n\left(\dfrac{n+1}{2}\right)$. Thus, the sum of all digits from 1 to 15 is $15\left(\dfrac{16}{2}\right)$, or 120. Tables are available that provide the decimal equivalent of the depreciation rate for each year of economic life.

numerator of the depreciation fraction for each year is the remaining years of economic life *at the beginning of the year.* Because the denominator remains constant and the numerator declines each year, the result is a decreasing depreciation expense. Furthermore, because the total of the numerators of the depreciation fractions is equal to the denominator, the sum of all the fractions is 1, and 100% of the depreciation base ultimately is allocated to depreciation expense.

The tabulation below illustrates the application of the sum-of-the-years'-digits method to a plant asset costing $22,000, having a net residual value of $2,000, and an economic life of four years:

Sum-of-years'-
digits method
of depreciation

Year of economic life	Depreciation fraction	Depreciation base ($22,000 − $2,000)	Depreciation expense	Accumulated depreciation	Carrying amount
					$22,000
1	4/10	$20,000	$8,000	$ 8,000	14,000
2	3/10	20,000	6,000	14,000	8,000
3	2/10	20,000	4,000	18,000	4,000
4	1/10	20,000	2,000	20,000	2,000*
Sum 10					

*Net residual value

Fractional-Period Depreciation under the Sum-of-the-Years'-Digits Method
Under accelerated methods, depreciation is determined for each full unit of economic life. A question of mechanics arises when plant assets are acquired during the year and less than a full year's depreciation is to be recorded during the first and last fiscal years of economic life. A logical solution to this problem for the sum-of-the-years'-digits method of depreciation is to compute the depreciation for each full year of economic life, and then allocate each full year's depreciation between two different fiscal years.

To illustrate, assume the following data for a plant asset for which the sum-of-the-years' digits method of depreciation is used:

Data for illustration
of fractional-period
depreciation

Cost of plant asset, acquired Apr. 1, Year 4............................ $8,000
Estimated economic life.. 5 years
Sum of the years' digits $\left[5\left(\frac{5+1}{2}\right)\right]$.................................. 15
Estimated net residual value... $500

The computation of depreciation for the first partial year (Year 4) and the remaining years under the sum-of-the-years'-digits method is demonstrated in the tabulation at the top of page 611.

Computation of
depreciation under
sum-of-the-years' digits
method for fractional
periods

Period ended	Computation of depreciation	Depreciation expense	Accumulated depreciation	Carrying amount
12/31/4	[($7,500 × 5/15) × 9/12] (4/1/4 to 12/31/4)	$1,875	$1,875	$6,125
12/31/5	[($7,500 × 5/15) × 3/12] + [($7,500 × 4/15) × 9/12]	2,125	4,000	4,000
12/31/6	[($7,500 × 4/15) × 3/12] + [($7,500 × 3/15) × 9/12]	1,625	5,625	2,375
12/31/7	[($7,500 × 3/15) × 3/12] + [($7,500 × 2/15) × 9/12]	1,125	6,750	1,250
12/31/8	[($7,500 × 2/15) × 3/12] + [($7,500 × 1/15) × 9/12]	625	7,375	625
12/31/9	[($7,500 × 1/15) × 3/12] (1/1/9 to 3/31/9)	125	7,500	500*

*Net residual value

Output Method   A more realistic allocation of the cost of some plant assets may be obtained by dividing the depreciation base by the estimated units of use or production (machine-hours, units of product produced, or miles driven) rather than by the years of economic life. For example, a bus company might compute depreciation on its vehicles under a mileage basis. If a bus cost $30,000 and is estimated to have an economic life of 200,000 miles and no residual value, the depreciation rate per mile of operation is 15 cents ($30,000 ÷ 200,000 = $0.15). At the end of each year, the amount of depreciation is determined by multiplying the number of miles the bus was driven during the year by the 15-cent rate.

The estimated economic life of a plant asset under the output method is measured in terms of potential physical services or units of output, and periodic depreciation is based on the actual use of the asset. As a result, *total depreciation expense* for each fiscal year varies if use varies, but the *depreciation per unit of output is constant.* The output method of depreciation is particularly appropriate when plant asset use fluctuates widely from year to year, and depreciation is more closely related to actual use than to functional obsolescence.

Some accountants have suggested that certain plant assets should be depreciated on the basis of periodic appraisals. This method may result in periodic depreciation expense of certain plant assets that closely parallels the output method, because the current fair value of a plant asset depends to a considerable extent on the amount of its usage. The *appraisal method* requires a determination of the value of services that *remain in the asset* at the end of each accounting period. Depreciation is estimated by appraising each plant asset at the end of an accounting period, and expensing an amount sufficient to reduce the carrying amount of the asset to its appraised value. The appraisal method of depreciation is appropriate for short-lived plant assets such as small tools, dies, dishes, and kitchen utensils.

Retirement-Replacement-Betterment Method   The methods of depreciation discussed thus far represent an attempt to measure the expiration of a plant asset's cost as it occurs. An alternative approach, advocated in the past by some regulated industries, is to recognize depreciation only at the time assets reach the end of their economic lives. Under the ***retirement-replacement-betterment*** method, plant asset ledger accounts include the full cost of all plant assets currently in use. Costs of replacing plant assets are recognized as expense unless the replacement represents a betterment. For a betterment, the current fair value of the plant asset replaced is recognized as expense, and the amount by which the cost of the betterment exceeds such current fair value is debited to the plant asset ledger account. When a plant asset is retired, its cost is recognized as expense and removed from the plant asset ledger account.

There are two objections to the retirement-replacement-betterment method. The first is that no depreciation is recorded until retirement of plant assets occurs. Not only is net income overstated in the early years of economic life, but also the original plant asset cost appears in the balance sheet, despite the fact that a portion of this cost has expired. The second objection is that depreciation expense is determined by the number of plant assets replaced and the cost of the new assets. The probability that the cost of replacements or retirements in a fiscal year will coincide with the cost of asset services used during that year is rather slim. The force of this objection is increased when it is noted that the plant asset replacement policy of a business enterprise is likely to vary in response to the availability of funds for capital expenditures, the stage of the business cycle, the earnings prospects of the enterprise, and the income tax incentives available.

The retirement-replacement-betterment method is seldom used today, because the Interstate Commerce Commission now requires railroads subject to its jurisdiction to use conventional depreciation accounting for railroad track structures in their reports to the Commission. Previously, the Commission had required the use of retirement-replacement-betterment accounting, and railroads used that method in their financial accounting as well as in their reports to the Commission.

Interest Methods   The ***annuity*** and ***sinking-fund*** methods of depreciation involve the application of compound interest concepts in the measurement of periodic depreciation. These methods are illustrated in the Appendix starting on page 626.

Composite Depreciation Method   Many business enterprises find it expedient to account for depreciation of certain kinds of plant assets on a ***composite*** or ***group basis,*** to minimize the record keeping for individual assets. Composite or group depreciation is a process of averaging the economic lives of a number of plant assets and computing depreciation on the entire class of assets as if it were an operating unit. The term ***composite*** generally refers to a collection of somewhat dissimilar plant assets; the term ***group*** usually refers to a collection of similar assets. The procedures for the computation of periodic depreciation are essentially the same in either case.

Several methods may be used to develop a composite or group depreciation rate to be applied to the total cost of a group of plant assets. The computation of a ***straight-line composite depreciation rate*** for a group of machines owned by Wilbur Company is illustrated at the top of page 613.

Straight-line composite
depreciation rate

WILBUR COMPANY
Computation of Straight-Line Composite Depreciation Rate for Machinery

Machine	Cost	Net residual value	Depreciation base	Economic life (years)	Annual depreciation expense
W	$ 6,000	$–0–	$ 6,000	5	$1,200
X	10,000	1,200	8,800	8	1,100
Y	15,000	1,000	14,000	10	1,400
Z	19,000	1,000	18,000	12	1,500
Totals	$50,000	$3,200	$46,800		$5,200

Composite depreciation rate based on cost: $5,200 ÷ $50,000 = 10.4%

Composite economic life of machines: $46,800 ÷ $5,200 = 9 years

The composite depreciation rate is 10.4%, and the composite economic life of the machines is 9 years. Thus, the application of the 10.4% composite rate to the cost of $50,000 will reduce the composite net residual value of the machines to $3,200 in exactly 9 years [$50,000 − ($5,200 × 9) = $3,200].

Once the composite depreciation rate is computed, *it is continued in use until a material change occurs in the composition of plant assets or in the estimate of their economic lives.* The assumptions underlying the use of composite depreciation methods are that (1) plant assets are regularly retired near the end of their economic lives, (2) retired plant assets are regularly replaced with similar assets, and (3) proceeds on retirement are approximately equal to the net residual value used for the computation of the composite depreciation rate. If assets are not replaced, for example, the use of the 10.4% rate computed above eventually would result in the recording of excessive depreciation.

In the determination of yearly depreciation, the 10.4% rate is applied to the balance of the Machinery ledger account at the beginning of the year, which balance excludes the original cost of all machines retired prior to the beginning of the year. Thus, for each of the first five years, annual depreciation is $5,200; and in the sixth year (assuming machine W was replaced at the end of the fifth year with a similar machine costing $9,000), depreciation would be $5,512 [($50,000 − $6,000 + $9,000) × 10.4% = $5,512]. The composite depreciation rate is not revised when plant assets are replaced with comparable assets, and the asset group should not be depreciated below net residual value at any time.

When composite depreciation procedures are employed, a record is not maintained for accumulated depreciation or individual plant assets. When an asset is retired from use or sold, a journal entry is required to remove the original cost from the plant asset account, and any difference between original cost and the proceeds received is debited to Accumulated Depreciation; a gain or loss is not recognized because gains and losses are assumed to offset over time. To illustrate, if machine W were sold at the end of the fourth year for $1,500, the journal entry to record the sale would be as follows:

Cash	*1,500*	
Accumulated Depreciation of Machinery	*4,500*	
Machinery		*6,000*

*To record sale of machine W. Composite depreciation method
is used; therefore, no gain or loss is recognized.*

The primary disadvantage of the composite depreciation method is that the averaging procedure may obscure significant variations from average. The accuracy of the straight-line composite depreciation rate may be verified by recomputing depreciation on the straight-line basis for individual plant assets. Any significant discrepancies between the two results require a change in the composite depreciation rate.

The advantages claimed for the composite method are simplicity, convenience, and a reduction in the amount of detail involved in plant asset records and depreciation computations. The availability of computers has reduced the force of this argument. In many cases unit plant asset records are now feasible, although composite methods previously were considered a necessity.

The requisites for the successful operation of composite depreciation procedures are that there be a large number of homogeneous plant assets, of relatively small individual value, with similar economic lives. Telephone and electric transmission poles, underground cables, railroad tracks, and hotel furniture are examples of plant assets for which composite depreciation methods may give satisfactory results.

DEPRECIATION FOR INCOME TAX PURPOSES

The depreciation methods described in the foregoing pages apply to financial accounting. Federal income tax law provides for rapid writeoffs of depreciable plant assets under the Accelerated Cost Recovery System (ACRS).[2] Under ACRS, the plant assets of a business enterprise are allocated to one of four possible *recovery periods* as follows:

  3 years: automobiles and light trucks
  5 years: most machinery and equipment
10 years: theme parks, mobile homes, railroad tank cars
19 years: depreciable real property

The recovery periods must be used regardless of the estimated economic lives of the plant assets involved, and *net residual values are disregarded for ACRS.* A specified percentage of the cost of the plant assets is expensed as the *cost recovery* for the

---

[2]The ACRS cost recovery percentages incorporate one-half year's depreciation in the year of acquisition, use of 150%-declining-balance method, and a switch to the straight-line method at an optimal time for maximizing cost recoveries.

year, depending on the applicable recovery period. For example, the cost of a plant asset in the three-year recovery period category is depreciated at the rate of 25% in the first year, 38% in the second year, and 37% in the third year. These percentages apply regardless of the date of acquisition of the plant asset, its estimated economic life, and its estimated net residual value.

Illustration of ACRS

To illustrate the application of ACRS for federal income tax purposes, assume that on January 2, Year 1, Webley Company acquired for $10,000 a machine with an estimated economic life of eight years and an estimated net residual value of $2,800. Webley adopted the sum-of-the-years'-digits method of depreciation for financial accounting and ACRS for income tax purposes. The machine qualified for a *five-year recovery period* under ACRS, the cost recovery percentages for which are 15% in the first year, 22% in the second year, and 21% for each of the third, fourth, and fifth years. Disregarding the effect of the investment tax credit and the annual expensing provision (see page 616), Webley's depreciation expense for financial accounting and for income tax purposes is set forth below:

Comparison of depreciation expense for financial accounting and for income tax purposes

Year	Depreciation expense			
	Financial accounting		**Income tax purposes**	
	Computation	*Amount*	*Computation*	*Amount*
1	$7,200 × 8/36*	$1,600	$10,000 × 0.15	$ 1,500
2	$7,200 × 7/36	1,400	$10,000 × 0.22	2,200
3	$7,200 × 6/36	1,200	$10,000 × 0.21	2,100
4	$7,200 × 5/36	1,000	$10,000 × 0.21	2,100
5	$7,200 × 4/36	800	$10,000 × 0.21	2,100
6	$7,200 × 3/36	600		
7	$7,200 × 2/36	400		
8	$7,200 × 1/36	200		
	Total	$7,200	Total	$10,000

$$* \frac{8(8 + 1)}{2} = 36$$

Thus, except in Year 1, ACRS provides a much faster depreciation writeoff, for a larger total amount, than does the sum-of-the-years'-digits method used for financial accounting.

Special Features of ACRS

Among the many features of ACRS other than those described in the preceding section are an annual expensing provision for plant assets, an election to use straight-line depreciation, and the effects of the investment tax credit.

Annual Expensing Provision   Federal income tax law permits the expensing of a specified maximum amount of the cost of depreciable plant assets instead of deducting depreciation expense over the appropriate recovery period. Thus, assuming that the annual expensing limitation was $10,000 in the example on page 615, Webley Company may have elected to deduct the entire cost of the machine in Year 1. In so doing, Webley would lose any investment tax credit applicable to the machine.

Election to Use Straight-Line Depreciation   Instead of using the cost recovery percentages provided by ACRS, a business enterprise may elect to deduct depreciation for income tax purposes computed under the straight-line method over the specified cost recovery period for the applicable plant asset, or over permissable longer periods. Under this election, the enterprise must incorporate estimated net residual value in the computation of depreciation and must generally limit the depreciation expense deduction for the year of acquisition of the plant asset to one-half of a year's depreciation.

Effects of Investment Tax Credit   If a business enterprise takes the maximum allowable investment tax credit as a reduction of income taxes payable in the year of acquisition of a plant asset, the depreciation base of the asset for ACRS must be *decreased by one-half of the allowable investment tax credit.* Alternatively, the enterprise may reduce the allowable investment tax credit percentage by 2% to avoid the required reduction of the depreciation base.

   The foregoing discussion of depreciation for income tax purposes indicates that such depreciation and financial accounting depreciation often may differ for a business enterprise. In such circumstances, interperiod income tax allocation generally is required. This issue is discussed in Chapter 21.

DEPRECIATION METHODS AND MANAGEMENT DECISIONS

In highly industrialized nations, plant assets play a large part in the productive process. It is easy to see that the cost of direct material and direct labor becomes a part of finished product. It is not always so clearly recognized, however, that a business enterprise also sells to its customers the services of the plant assets used to manufacture and market its products.

   The importance of depreciation stems from the various management decisions that are affected by it. To the extent that depreciation is a significant part of operating costs, and that operating costs are relevant in business decisions, the relative merits of various depreciation methods are significant in decisions relating to the following areas:

1   Measurement of net income and the impact of inflation

2   Computation of income taxes payable

3   Investment of capital

   The effect of different depreciation methods in relation to each of these decision areas is discussed in the following sections.

Depreciation, Net Income Measurement, and Inflation

The purpose of depreciation accounting is to measure the amount that must be recovered from revenue to compensate for the portion of plant asset cost that has been used up. This idea is embodied in the phrase *maintenance of capital,* which often is used in relation to income measurement.

The widespread use of the straight-line method of depreciation results from its simplicity and convenience. Two objections may be leveled against the straight-line method, each of which becomes a supporting argument for some other method of depreciation.

1   It does not allow for the fact that productivity of plant assets may decline with age.

2   It does not take into account variations in the rate of plant asset use.

Some business executives suggest that the decline in productivity of many plant assets is so pronounced that the value (and thus the cost) of asset services in the early stages of economic life is materially greater than in later years. If this is true, accelerated methods of depreciation may achieve a better matching of costs and revenue than the straight-line method. Originally, the declining productivity argument centered on a rising curve of repair and maintenance costs as assets aged. In recent years, greater weight has been given to the effects of obsolescence. Often, the period of high earnings on new plant assets is short because of the inroads of innovation and competition.

The use of the straight-line depreciation method makes depreciation a fixed period cost by assumption, and thereby fails to allow for the loss of service potential related to wear and tear through usage. If a plant asset is used twice as much in one year as another, it would be unrealistic to assume that the amount and cost of asset services consumed is the same in both years. This objection to straight-line depreciation becomes an argument for the use of a measure of output as the unit of economic life, which would tend to make depreciation a variable cost rather than a fixed cost.

During an inflationary period, any depreciation method based on historical cost tends to understate the amount of capital consumed (depreciation). Thus, a part of reported net income essentially represents *return of capital.* Users of financial statements should consider this shortcoming in the traditional income measurement model and should make appropriate adjustments to restate depreciation and net income in terms of current cost of plant assets. A more detailed discussion of the impact of inflation on depreciation accounting appears in Chapter 25.

Depreciation Policy and Income Taxes

Probably the strongest influence on depreciation policy is the federal income tax law. The direction of the influence is toward rapid depreciation deductions. Depreciation expense reduces taxable income and income taxes expense. Taxpayers may not deduct more than the actual cost of a depreciable asset over its economic life, but income taxes may be postponed by maximizing depreciation deductions, and deferred taxes represent an interest-free loan for the period of the postponement. The only possible tax disadvantage of large initial depreciation deductions is that income tax rates might increase sufficiently during the economic life of a plant asset to more than offset the interest savings.

Federal income tax provisions such as ACRS do not require estimates of economic lives or net residual value of plant assets, without regard to issues of accounting theory or economic reality. If such practices applied only to the computation of taxable income, no damage would be done to the validity of financial statements. For many business enterprises, however, the convenience of keeping only one set of depreciation records is such that the accounting records often are made to conform to federal income tax requirements.

If income tax depreciation and financial accounting depreciation substantially are equivalent, there are practical advantages to maintaining the accounting records on a tax basis. Tax deductions, however, are shaped by matters of public policy and the need for revenue by the federal and state governments, and are in no way related to the objectives of financial accounting. Material divergence between income tax and financial accounting data is possible. For example, many business enterprises use ACRS depreciation methods for federal income tax purposes but use the straight-line method for financial accounting.

Allowing relatively large depreciation deductions for income tax purposes is a means of subsidizing business investment. As a result, proposals for speeding up depreciation allowances as a means of stimulating investment or encouraging certain kinds of investment frequently are made in the U.S. Congress. Therefore, the continued usefulness of accounting data for managerial and investment purposes may depend on maintaining a state of independence between financial accounting and income tax rules.

Depreciation and Capital Investment Decisions

The two most important questions relating to the role of depreciation in a capital investment decision are: (1) Is depreciation a relevant cost in the decision? (2) How does depreciation affect the cash flows from the investment?

Depreciation Expense May Be Either an Incremental Cost or a Sunk Cost   In essence, two kinds of costs are relevant to the decision to invest capital in productive assets: (1) *future costs,* that is, costs that will be incurred as the result of the decision; and (2) *incremental costs,* that is, costs that will change as the result of the decision. The expense represented by depreciation on existing plant assets is attributable to an investment made at some time in the past. Except to the extent that an existing plant asset may be sold and some portion of the past investment recovered, no present decision can change the amount of cost that has been sunk into that asset. Thus, depreciation often has been referred to as a *sunk cost.*

A decision to invest in productive facilities should be based on an analysis of incremental costs and revenue. The carrying amount of existing plant assets (a sunk cost that cannot be changed in the short run) is an irrelevant factor and may be disregarded (except for income tax considerations). Most managerial decisions as to alternative actions such as acquiring or leasing, acquiring or making, or accepting or not accepting a special order, depend on an analysis of incremental costs and revenue. Depreciation may or may not represent a relevant cost in comparing such alternative courses of action. Depreciation on special equipment acquired for a specific activity is always an incremental cost to that activity, but depreciation on existing plant assets is an incremental cost only if the use of the assets for the specific activity reduces their economic life or residual value.

We have oversimplified the problem in this discussion, but a valid generalization may be drawn. Whether or not depreciation should be regarded as an incremental cost depends on whether the limiting factor in plant asset life is obsolescence or use, and whether the asset in question is being used to capacity. For this reason, depreciation expense computed for purposes of income determination generally has a low level of relevance for decision making.

Effect of Depreciation on Cash Flows   Investment decisions frequently are made on the basis of the expected rate of return on the investment. In the computation of the rate of return, *net cash flow* from the investment generally is a more useful concept than *net income* from the investment. Depreciation expense does not generate cash directly; it is an expense that does not reduce cash, but is deducted to compute taxable income. Thus, depreciation expense indirectly generates larger cash flows from operations by reducing income taxes. For this reason, depreciation is viewed as a powerful instrument for increasing cash flows and reducing the *payback period* (the number of years required to recover an investment in a plant asset) on new investments in plant assets.

To illustrate the relationships between depreciation and cash flows, assume the following annual results for an asset that is rented to others:

Depreciation does not require a cash outflow in the current accounting period	

Amount of cash received as rental revenue	$5,000
Less: All expenses (except income taxes and depreciation of $2,000)	1,200
Net cash received	$3,800
Income taxes, 45% of income after depreciation [($3,800 − $2,000) × 0.45]	810
Net cash flow each year	$2,990

The annual net cash flow of $2,990 also may be determined by adding the depreciation expense of $2,000 to the net income of $990 ($3,800 − $2,000 − $810 = $990). Determination of the present value of net cash flows from an investment is a critical procedure in the evaluation of investment alternatives under *capital budgeting* techniques.

Depreciation Procedures and Records

Property Records   The typical business enterprise employs many different kinds of plant assets having varying characteristics and economic lives. Precision in accounting for the use of such assets is facilitated by detailed and complete property records. Property records may be maintained on ledger cards, punched cards, magnetic tapes, or in a computer storage.

An ideal system is to maintain a record for each plant asset. The record should show, for each asset, its cost, additions, economic life, net residual value, date of installation, location, basis and amount of periodic depreciation, and other information such as the serial number. In addition to providing thorough support for depreciation and retirement journal entries, such property records are useful for maintaining internal control for plant assets.

Accumulated Depreciation Ledger Account In theory, depreciation could be recorded as a credit to the plant asset ledger accounts because depreciable plant assets basically are long-term deferred charges. The direct write-off procedure often is used for large numbers of small-value plant assets when periodic inventories are taken to determine the portion of asset cost remaining on hand. For larger assets, the usual practice is to credit a contra-asset ledger account titled Accumulated Depreciation, Allowance for Depreciation, or Reserve for Depreciation.[3] The primary argument for the use of a separate ledger account is to preserve information about the cost of plant assets and the proportion of cost that has expired. Also, in an analysis of account balances, it is convenient to be able to distinguish plant additions and retirements from adjustments in accumulated depreciation.

The Accumulated Depreciation ledger account is frequently, but improperly, referred to as a *valuation account.* The Accumulated Depreciation account represents the portion of the acquisition cost of a plant asset that has been allocated to expense through the process of depreciation. Its purpose is not to value a plant asset in terms of current prices, but rather to determine the unallocated cost (or carrying amount) of a plant asset on a specific date.

Depreciation (Lapsing) Schedules When the number of individual items within each class of plant assets is not large, a *depreciation schedule* (sometimes known as a *lapsing schedule*) may be used. Lapsing schedules may take many forms and often are prepared by the use of computer spreadsheets if the number of assets is large. A depreciation schedule is a means of maintaining unit property records with a minimum of effort. Its purposes are to facilitate the computation of periodic depreciation, and to provide a continuing record of asset costs and the related accumulated depreciation.

A typical lapsing schedule includes columns for cost, estimated net residual value, accumulated depreciation, and *prospective depreciation charges* throughout the economic life for each plant asset. If a plant asset is retired at the end of its economic life, its cost is deducted from the cost column, and its accumulated depreciation to date is deducted from the accumulated depreciation column. The retirement is recorded in the general journal or the cash receipts journal, together with any gain or loss. If a plant asset is retired prematurely, it is not necessary to erase or change the originally scheduled depreciation amounts. It is more convenient to cancel the future depreciation charges by recording appropriate *deductions* on the line used to record the retirement.

Disclosure of Depreciation in Financial Statements

Because of the significant effects on financial position and results of operations that stem from depreciation expense and the depreciation methods used, the following

---

[3]The 1984 edition of *Accounting Trends & Techniques,* published by the AICPA, reported that of the 600 companies surveyed, 508 companies used the terms *accumulated depreciation* and *accumulated depreciation and amortization* (or *depletion*); 67 companies used the terms *allowance for depreciation* and *allowance for depreciation and amortization* (or *depletion*); and only 25 companies used other captions.

disclosures are made in the financial statements or in notes to the financial statements:[4]

1   Depreciation expense for the accounting period

2   Balances of major classes of depreciable plant assets, by nature or function

3   Accumulated depreciation, either by major classes of depreciable plant assets or in total

4   A general description of the method or methods used in the computation of depreciation with respect to major classes of depreciable plant assets

The 1984 edition of *Accounting Trends & Techniques,* published by the AICPA, showed that 564 of the 600 companies surveyed used the straight-line method of depreciation, and 148 companies used one or more of the accelerated depreciation methods; only 65 companies used the output method. If a change in the method of computing depreciation is made, the effect of the change on the current year's net income is disclosed in a note to the financial statements. Similarly, the effect of any unusual depreciation charges is disclosed. Accounting for changes in depreciation methods, changes in economic lives of depreciable plant assets, and corrections of errors in the recording of depreciation in prior accounting periods are discussed in Chapter 22.

DEPLETION OF NATURAL RESOURCES

Depreciable plant assets usually retain their physical characteristics as they are used in operations. In contrast, *natural resources* in essence are long-term inventories of material that will be removed physically from their source. In either case—whether accountants are dealing with a ''bundle of services'' or a ''store of material''—the basic problem is to determine the cost of the units of services or material that are consumed during each accounting period. The portion of the cost (or other valuation) assigned to property containing natural resources that is applicable to the units removed from the property is known as *depletion.*

The Depletion Base

The *depletion base* of property containing natural resources is the acquisition cost less the estimated net residual value of the property after the resources have been removed. The estimated cost of dismantling, abandoning, or restoring the property is taken into account in the determination of the net residual value of the property.

Acquisition cost of a natural resource includes the price paid for the property and legal fees, broker's fees, and other fees incurred to acquire the property.

In the lumber industry, substantial costs are incurred for fire protection, insect and disease control, property taxes, and other maintainance costs applicable to standing timber that will not be harvested for a considerable length of time. These

---

[4]*APB Opinion No. 12,* ''Omnibus Opinion—1967,'' AICPA (New York: 1967), p. 188.

costs, known as *carrying costs,* are capitalized (added to the cost of the property) while the property is being developed. For example, if carrying costs of $400,000 are applicable to a tract of timber, and during an accounting period 20% of the timber is cut, 80%, or $320,000, is applicable to uncut timber and is capitalized.

Exploration and Development Costs

In the production of natural resources such as petroleum, considerable exploration costs, and development costs such as preparation of sites, drilling and equipping wells, and construction of production facilities, are incurred. These costs are capitalized as part of the petroleum enterprise's wells and related equipment and facilities.[5]

The Problem of "Dry Holes"   What if the expenditures made to acquire, explore, and develop natural resources prove unproductive? Under one view, termed the *successful efforts method,* if each specific property is considered a separate venture, the logical interpretation is that no asset exists, and a loss therefore has occurred. A contrasting theory, termed the *full cost method,* holds that from the viewpoint of the enterprise as a whole, particularly if it is seeking constantly to maintain its natural resource base by exploration and acquisition of new deposits, a certain amount of unproductive effort may be treated as a normal cost of discovering new natural resource deposits. If, for example, 10 dry wells are drilled for each producing oil well brought in, the argument that 11 drillings are necessary to bring in a producing well and that the cost of a producing well includes the cost of 10 unsuccessful efforts has some merit. The problem is analogous to that of accounting for spoilage in manufacturing. If a certain amount of spoilage is considered normal, it is treated as a part of the cost of the good units produced; if the amount of spoilage is abnormal, it is recognized as a loss.

   In *FASB Statement No. 19,* "Financial Accounting and Reporting for Oil and Gas Producing Companies," the Financial Accounting Standards Board expressed a preference for the successful efforts method of accounting.[6] However, the Securities and Exchange Commission permits use of the full cost method by companies that report to it.[7]

Estimate of Recoverable Units

The estimate of economic lives for plant assets is a relatively simple undertaking compared with the estimate of recoverable units of natural resources. The quantity of ore in a vein and the recoverable deposit in petroleum-producing property often are difficult to determine, and revisions may be necessary as production takes place and new evidence becomes available. Adding to the problem is the fact that changes in the method of extraction may make it possible to work deposits of natural resources that originally were deemed uneconomical.

---

[5]*FASB Statement No. 19,* "Financial Accounting and Reporting by Oil and Gas Producing Companies," FASB (Stamford: 1977) pp. 6–7.

[6]Ibid., p. 5.

[7]*Codification of Financial Reporting Policies,* Securities and Exchange Commission (Washington: 1982), Sec. 406.

Ideally, the recoverable deposit of a natural resource should be measured in units of *desired* product, such as an ounce of silver or a pound of copper, rather than in units of *mined* product, such as a ton of raw ore. If depletion is based on tons of mined ore, the same charge will be applied to a ton of high-grade ore as to a ton of low-grade ore. This treatment is hardly logical in terms of the way mining property is valued and in terms of efforts by accountants to match costs and revenue.

Cost Depletion

Conceptually, any of the methods of depreciation previously discussed might be applied in a comparable manner to the computation of depletion. However, the straight-line method is of doubtful applicability because the exhaustion of natural resources is a matter of physical output rather than the passage of time. Accelerated methods have not been widely used to measure depletion, despite the fact that the productivity of natural resources may decline rapidly when the unit cost of recovery increases as production moves from richer to poorer deposits.

By far the most widely used method of depletion for financial accounting is the output (units-of-production) method, which produces a constant depletion charge per unit of the natural resource removed. To illustrate, assume that early in Year 7 Lowell Company acquired mining property for $720,000. It is estimated that there are 1.2 million recoverable units of the natural resource, and that the land will have a net residual value (after restoration costs) of $60,000 when the resource is exhausted. The depletion per unit of output is computed as follows:

Formula to compute depletion per unit

$$\text{Depletion} = \frac{\text{cost} - \text{net residual value}}{\text{estimated total recoverable units}}$$

$$= \frac{\$720,000 - \$60,000}{1,200,000 \text{ units}} = \$0.55 \text{ per unit}$$

If Lowell Company removed 300,000 units of the natural resource from the ground in Year 7, the journal entry to record depletion is as follows:

Journal entry to record depletion

Depletion (300,000 × $0.55) 165,000
    Accumulated Depletion of Mining Property 165,000
To record depletion for Year 7.

The amount of cost depletion is included in the cost of the inventory of the natural resource and is recognized as an expense (cost of goods sold) only when the inventory is sold. For example, if in Year 7 Lowell Company sold 200,000 of 300,000 units extracted, the cost of goods sold for Lowell for Year 7 is determined as follows (costs other than depletion are assumed):

	Total	Unit cost
Cost of goods sold:		
Depletion	$165,000	$0.55
Material, labor, and overhead (other than depletion		
and depreciation)	237,000	0.79
Depreciation of equipment	15,000	0.05
Total cost of production (300,000 units)	$417,000	$1.39
Less: Ending inventory (100,000 units × $1.39)	139,000	
Cost of goods sold (200,000 units × $1.39)	$278,000	

When additional costs are incurred in the development of mining properties or estimates of recoverable units are revised, the depletion rate should be recomputed. Depletion previously recorded should not be revised. The new depletion rate is computed by dividing the carrying amount (cost less accumulated depletion, less net residual value) of the mining property (including any additional development costs) by the new estimate of recoverable units.

Depreciation of Plant Assets Associated with Natural Resources

Buildings and equipment used to remove natural resources may have an economic life shorter than the time required to complete the removal, in which case the depreciation of these assets should be recorded over their economic lives. Otherwise, depreciation is computed by the output method, similar to the computation of depletion.

Percentage Depletion for Income Tax Purposes

For income tax purposes, a special depletion method known as *percentage* or *statutory depletion* may be used by taxpayers engaged in most mining activities. Under this procedure the depletion deduction may be computed as a percentage of the gross income received, without regard to the cost of the property or the number of units produced. Some examples of percentage depletion (subject to change by Congress at any time) follow:

Oil and gas (small independent producers)	15%
Gold, silver, oil shale, copper, and iron ore	15%
China clay, rock asphalt, borax, and granite	14%
Coal and sodium chloride..	10%
Gravel, peat, sand, and magnesium chloride.............................	5%

Taxpayers have the option of using either cost depletion or percentage depletion, whichever is more advantageous. The only limitation on percentage depletion is that it may not exceed 50% of the taxable income from the property before depletion. To illustrate, assume the following for Arizona Copper Company for Year 5:

Information for
percentage depletion
illustration

Sale of copper ore (200,000 tons)	$15,000,000
Expenses (excluding depletion)......................................	$ 6,500,000
Depletion base (cost) of ore-bearing property......................	$ 4,000,000
Estimated tons of ore recoverable from property....................	1,000,000
Cost depletion per ton of ore ($4,000,000 ÷ 1,000,000)	$ 4
Income tax rate	45%

The taxable income and net income for financial accounting of Arizona Copper Company for Year 5 are computed below:

Percentage depletion
is $2,250,000 and
cost depletion is
$800,000

	Taxable income	Financial accounting income
Sale of copper ore	$15,000,000	$15,000,000
Expenses (excluding depletion)	(6,500,000)	(6,500,000)
Income before depletion	$ 8,500,000	
Depletion:		
Percentage basis for income tax purposes		
($15,000,000 × 0.15)	(2,250,000)	
Cost basis for financial accounting		
(200,000 tons of ore × $4 a ton)		(800,000)
Taxable income	$6,250,000	
Income taxes expense ($6,250,000 × 0.45)		(2,812,500)
Net income		$ 4,887,500

In the computation of taxable income for Year 5, percentage depletion is $2,250,000 ($15,000,000 × 0.15 = $2,250,000), because this amount exceeds cost depletion of $800,000 and is less than 50% of the $8,500,000 income before depletion ($8,500,000 × 0.50 = $4,250,000). However, if expenses excluding depletion amounted to $12,000,000, percentage depletion would be limited to $1,500,000 ($3,000,000, the income before depletion, × 0.50 = $1,500,000). For property to which the percentage method applies, depletion should be computed under both the cost method and the percentage method, and the larger deduction taken for income tax purposes.

The primary advantage of percentage depletion arises not because it may be larger than cost depletion in a certain year, but because the cumulative amount of depletion deductions is not limited by the depletion base. There is no cost base for percentage depletion, and taxpayers may deduct depletion on their income tax returns many times in excess of the cost of the property. *Percentage depletion is not recorded in the accounting records;* it represents a special income tax benefit granted by the United States Congress to specified natural resource industries as a matter of public policy.

APPENDIX: INTEREST METHODS OF DEPRECIATION

For many years the *annuity* and *sinking-fund* methods of depreciation have received attention from accounting theorists because of their focus on cost recovery and rate of return on the investment in depreciable plant assets. A depreciable plant asset represents a bundle of future services to be received periodically over the economic life of the asset. The cost of such an asset may be viewed as the present value of the equal periodic rents (services) discounted at a rate of interest consistent with the risk factors identified with the investment in the plant asset.

Annuity Method   The annuity method of depreciation is appropriate when the periodic cost (depreciation) of using a long-lived plant asset is considered to be equal to the total of the expired cost of the asset and the implicit interest on the unrecovered investment in the asset. Depreciation Expense is debited and Accumulated Depreciation and Interest Revenue are credited periodically, as explained in the example below.

Assume that a computer with an economic life of five years and a net residual value of $67,388 is acquired by Dorsey, Inc., for $800,000. If the fair rate of interest for this type of investment is 10% compounded annually, the yearly depreciation expense is computed as illustrated below:

Computation of annual depreciation expense under annuity method

$$\text{Depreciation} = \frac{\text{cost of asset less present value of net residual value}}{\text{present value of ordinary annuity of 5 rents of 1 at 10\%}}$$

$$= \frac{\$800,000 - (\$67,388 \times 0.620921^*)}{3.790787\dagger}$$

$$= \frac{\$800,000 - \$41,843}{3.790787}$$

$$= \underline{\underline{\$200,000}}$$

*Present value of 1 for five periods at 10% (Table 2 in the Appendix at the end of Chapter 5).
†See Table 4 in the Appendix at the end of Chapter 5.

A summary of the results of the annuity method of depreciation, and the journal entries to record depreciation for the first two years, are shown on page 627.

The summary on page 627 shows that: (1) Depreciation expense computed by the annuity method is debited for $200,000 each year; (2) interest revenue is credited each year with 10% of the unrecovered investment (carrying amount of the computer); (3) the difference between annual depreciation expense and interest revenue is credited to Accumulated Depreciation; and (4) the carrying amount of the computer at the end of Year 5 is $67,388, the net residual value at the end of its economic life. The total depreciation expense over the economic life of the computer exceeds its depreciable cost by $267,388 ($1,000,000 − $732,612 = $267,388), an amount equal to the implicit interest revenue recognized during the

DORSEY, INC.
Summary of Annuity Method of Depreciation

Year	Depre-ciation expense	Implicit interest revenue (10% of carrying amount)	Credit to Accu-mulated Depre-ciation ledger account	Balance of Accu-mulated Depre-ciation ledger account	Carrying amount of com-puter
0					$800,000
1	$ 200,000	$ 80,000	$120,000	$120,000	680,000
2	200,000	68,000	132,000	252,000	548,000
3	200,000	54,800	145,200	397,200	402,800
4	200,000	40,280	159,720	556,920	243,080
5	200,000	24,308	175,692	732,612	67,388
	$1,000,000	$267,388	$732,612		

Journal entries:

	Year 1	Year 2
Depreciation Expense...............	200,000	200,000
Interest Revenue	80,000	68,000
Accumulated Depreciation	120,000	132,000

To record depreciation by annuity method.

economic life of the computer. The net charge to income over the five-year period is equal to the depreciation base of the computer and ***increases*** each year. The annuity method of depreciation thus tends to produce a more constant rate of return on investment than, say, the straight-line method of depreciation. Consequently, the use of the annuity method of depreciation for assets acquired under capital leases has been advocated by some accountants in recent years.

Sinking-Fund Method   The sinking-fund method of depreciation might be used when a fund is to be accumulated to replace a plant asset at the end of its economic life. Under the sinking-fund method, the amount of annual depreciation expense is equal to the increase in the asset replacement fund. The increase in the fund consists

Computation of annual sinking-fund deposits under sinking-fund method of depreciation

$$\text{Sinking-fund deposits} = \frac{\text{cost of asset less net residual value}}{\text{amount of ordinary annuity of 5 rents of 1 at 10\%}}$$

$$= \frac{\$800,000 - \$67,388}{6.1051^*}$$

$$= \underline{\$120,000}$$

*See Table 3 in the Appendix at the end of Chapter 5.

of the equal periodic deposits (rents) plus the interest revenue realized at the assumed rate on the sinking-fund balance.

We shall illustrate the sinking-fund method of depreciation with the same example as we used to illustrate the annuity method, that is, a computer acquired by Dorsey, Inc., for $800,000 with an economic life of five years and a net residual value of $67,388 at the end of five years. If we again assume a 10% annual compound rate of interest, the annual deposits to the sinking fund are determined as shown at the bottom of page 627.

A summary of the results of the sinking-fund method of depreciation, and the journal entries to record depreciation for the first two years, are as follows:

DORSEY, INC.
Summary of Sinking-Fund Method of Depreciation

Year		Sinking fund				Depreciation and carrying amount	
	Annual deposit	Realized interest revenue (10% of fund balance)	Total fund increase	Fund balance	Depreciation expense	Balance of Accumulated Depreciation ledger account	Carrying amount of computer
0							$800,000
1	$120,000		$120,000	$120,000	$120,000	$120,000	680,000
2	120,000	$ 12,000	132,000	252,000	132,000	252,000	548,000
3	120,000	25,200	145,200	397,200	145,200	397,200	402,800
4	120,000	39,720	159,720	556,920	159,720	556,920	243,080
5	120,000	55,692	175,692	732,612	175,692	732,612	67,388
	$600,000	$132,612	$732,612		$732,612		

Journal entries:	Year 1		Year 2	
Sinking Fund	120,000		132,000	
Depreciation Expense..............	120,000		132,000	
Cash		120,000		120,000
Interest Revenue				12,000
Accumulated Depreciation		120,000		132,000
To record depreciation by sinking-fund method.				

The foregoing summary and journal entries show that: (1) Depreciation expense computed by the sinking-fund method is debited each year for *increasing* amounts equal to the total increase in the sinking fund; (2) interest revenue is credited each year with earnings at 10% on the fund balance; (3) the net charge to income (depreciation expense less interest revenue) each year remain constant at $120,000; and (4) the carrying amount of the computer at the end of Year 5 is $67,388, the net residual value at the end of its economic life.

The sinking-fund method of depreciation may be used without the accumulation of a sinking fund. However, depreciation expense still would be recorded equal to the hypothetical fund increases, as illustrated on page 628. The sinking-fund method of depreciation is used by only a few utility companies.

REVIEW QUESTIONS

1 Some business enterprises, particularly those owning improved real estate, may report an intermediate amount in their income statement labeled as ''income before depreciation.'' Comment on this practice.

2 Distinguish among the terms *depreciation, amortization,* and *depletion.* How is depreciation accounting related to the replacement of a plant asset at the end of its economic life?

3 What are the three variables used in the computation of periodic depreciation expense? Is depreciation a valuation procedure or a cost allocation procedure?

4 The manager of an electric utility stated, ''Our transmission lines are kept in good operating condition by regular repairs and maintenance, and their efficiency is relatively constant—they just don't depreciate!'' Do you agree with this statement? Explain.

5 What is meant by the term *estimated economic life* of a plant asset, and how is it measured?

6 What are the major causes of a decrease in the economic life of a plant asset? How accurately may the causes be identified for a specific asset?

7 Jordan Company acquires delivery trucks for $18,000. These trucks have an economic life of six years based on physical deterioration and a net residual value of $3,000. Jordan typically sells a truck for $7,000 after operating it 100,000 miles. What is the depreciation base for a delivery truck? What is its estimated economic life to Jordan?

8 Both the quantity of plant asset services used each accounting period and the relative value of the asset services are factors in the choice of a method of depreciation. Explain.

9 **a** List the methods that may be used to compute depreciation.
  b State two objections to the straight-line method of depreciation.
  c List some advantages of the straight-line method of depreciation.

10 Many depreciable plant assets exhibit a declining productivity with advancing age. Explain how this fact may be used both as an argument for and as an argument against use of the straight-line method of depreciation.

11 During Year 5, a strike halted manufacturing operations of Arcadia, Inc., for four months. Depreciation of its spinning and weaving machines for the full year under the straight-line method is $216,000. Arcadia's operations for Year 5 resulted in a net loss of $132,000 (after deduction of depreciation expense). The president of

Arcadia suggests that the depreciation expense for Year 5 should be reduced because of the low volume of operations. Do you agree?

12   Describe a situation in which the use of the *output method* of depreciation is appropriate.

13   What is meant by a *composite* or *group basis method of depreciation?* What are the advantages and limitations of this method?

14   Explain why the use of Accelerated Cost Recovery System (ACRS) methods is advantageous for federal income tax purposes.

15   What principle should be applied to determine whether depreciation is a fixed or a variable expense? Why is depreciation called a ''noncash expense''?

16   What disclosures relating to depreciation and depreciation methods are made in the financial statements or in notes to the financial statements?

17   Bronze Corporation acquired for $800,000 land from which it expects to extract 1 million tons of Grade A ore and 2 million tons of Grade B ore. Grade A ore is three times as valuable as Grade B ore. Compute depletion per ton of each grade of ore extracted. Explain the term *percentage depletion.*

18   Plant assets or natural resources donated to a business enterprise generally are recorded by the enterprise, and depreciation or depletion on such assets is allocated to expense. Justify this practice.

EXERCISES

Ex. 12-1   Select the best answer for each of the following multiple-choice questions:

1   If a plant asset with a five-year economic life is sold during the second year, how would use of the sum-of-the-years'-digits method of depreciation instead of the straight-line method of depreciation affect the gain or loss on disposal of the asset?

Gain	*Loss*
a Decrease	Increase
b Increase	Decrease
c No effect	No effect
d No effect	Decrease

2   Which of the following depreciation methods involves the same computational techniques as those used for depletion?

a Straight-line   **d** Output
b Sum-of-the-years'-digits   **e** None of the foregoing
c Double-declining-balance

3   The composite depreciation method:

a Is applied to a group of homogeneous plant assets

b Is an accelerated method of depreciation

c Does not involve the recognition of a gain or loss on the retirement of an individual plant asset of the group

d Disregards net residual value in the computation of the depreciation base

4　On November 1, Year 1, Platte Company acquired for $50,000 equipment having an economic life of 10 years and a net residual value of $2,000. Platte adopted the double-declining-balance method of depreciation for the equipment. If Platte computes depreciation to the nearest month, depreciation expense for the equipment for the year ended April 30, Year 3, is:

a $7,680　　**b** $9,000　　**c** $9,600　　**d** $10,000　　**e** Some other amount

5　The effect of growth and changes in the scale of a business enterprise's operations in terminating the economic life of plant assets is termed:

a Depreciation　　**b** Obsolescence　　**c** Inadequacy　　**d** Economies of scale

6　The formula for determining the sum of an arithmetic progression, used in the sum-of-the-years'-digits method of depreciation, is:

a $2n(n + 1)$　　**b** $\dfrac{n + 1}{2n}$　　**c** $n(n + 1)$　　**d** $n\left(\dfrac{n + 1}{2}\right)$　　**e** None of the foregoing

7　On January 2, Year 6, Dragoon Company acquired for $120,000 equipment with an economic life of eight years and a net residual value of $12,000. Dragoon adopted the sum-of-the-years'-digits method of depreciation for the equipment. On December 31, Year 7, accumulated depreciation on the equipment totals:

a $15,000 less than under the straight-line method of depreciation
b $15,000 less than under the double-declining-balance method of depreciation
c $18,000 more than under the straight-line method of depreciation
d $18,000 more than under the double-declining-balance method of depreciation

Ex. 12-2　Yazoo Company leased a building under an operating lease and immediately acquired equipment for $430,000 and spent $45,000 to have special platforms and supporting encasements built. The lease contract provides that when the lease expires Yazoo must remove the equipment, demolish the platforms and encasements, and restore the building to its original condition, an operation that is expected to cost $20,000.

　　Compute the depreciation base of Yazoo Company's equipment, including platforms and encasements.

Ex. 12-3　Determine the fractions to be used in the computation of depreciation expense under the sum-of-the-years'-digits method for each of the following:

a The third year of a six-year economic life
b The sixth year of a 10-year economic life
c The seventh year of an eight-year economic life

Ex. 12-4　A plant asset cost $56,000, had an economic life of eight years, and an estimated net residual value of $2,000.

a Compute depreciation expense for the first year of economic life under the sum-of-the-years'-digits method of depreciation.
b Assume that this asset was acquired on April 1, Year 1. Compute depreciation expense for the full year ended December 31, Year 2, under the sum-of-the-years'-digits method of depreciation.

Ex. 12-5   On October 1, Year 1, Lessing Company, whose fiscal year is the calendar year, acquired for $4,000 a machine with an economic life of four years and a net residual value of $250. Lessing adopted the double-declining-balance method of depreciation for the machine.

Compute depreciation expense for Lessing Company for Year 1 through Year 5, using two methods to determine depreciation expense for fractional years. Round all amounts to the nearest dollar. (*Note:* Depreciation expense should be the same for both methods of computation.)

Ex. 12-6   On January 2, Year 3, Lucas Company acquired for $1,000,000 a machine with an economic life of eight years and a net residual value of $100,000. Lucas adopted the sum-of-the-years'-digits method of depreciation for the machine.

Compute the carrying amount of the machine on December 31, Year 4.

Ex. 12-7   Deluxe Corporation has three machines, each with an economic life of five years. Deluxe records a full-year's depreciation expense in the year in which plant assets are acquired, and no depreciation expense in the year of disposal of plant assets. Details of Deluxe's three machines on December 31, Year 3, follow:

Machine	Year acquired	Cost	Net residual value	Accumulated depreciation
No. 1	Year 2	$100,000	$20,000	$64,000
No. 2	Year 1	55,000	10,000	36,000
No. 3	Year 1	70,000	14,000	33,600

a Compute Deluxe Corporation's depreciation expense for machine No. 1 for Year 4, under the double-declining-balance method used by Deluxe Corporation for the machine.

b Compute Deluxe Corporation's depreciation expense for machine No. 2 for Year 4, under the same method used by Deluxe Corporation for the machine for Year 1 through Year 3.

c Compute the gain or loss realized by Deluxe Corporation on June 30, Year 4, when it sold machine No. 3, which it had been depreciating under the straight-line method, for $28,000.

Ex. 12-8   A machine with an estimated economic life of five years, or 100,000 units of output, was acquired by Webb Company on October 4, Year 1. The cash price of the machine was $9,000, which was to be paid for as follows:

Cash...	$ 1,500
Old machine accepted as trade-in (carrying amount is equal to current fair value)	500
Four installments payable at the rate of $2,000 every six months (includes $1,000 interest and financing charges)	8,000
Total	$10,000

Compute Webb Company's depreciation expense for the three months ended December 31, Year 1 and for Year 2, assuming that the net residual value of the machine is $1,500, under each of the following methods:

a Straight-line

b Sum-of-the-years'-digits

c Double-declining-balance

d Output (8,000 units were produced in Year 1 and 33,000 units in Year 2)

Ex. 12-9 Romero Company acquired a plant asset at the beginning of Year 1 for $16,000. The asset has an economic life of four years and a net residual value of $1,000.

Compute the depreciation on Romero Company's asset for Year 1, under each of the following methods;

a Straight-line

b Sum-of-the-years'-digits

c Fixed-percentage-of-declining-balance (Compute the theoretically correct rate and prove that it yields a net residual value of $1,000 at the end of four years.)

Ex. 12-10 On January 3, Year 1, Lund Company acquired equipment that had an estimated economic life of 10 years and a net residual value of $20,000. The depreciation expense for Year 5 was $12,000 under the sum-of-the-years'-digits method.

Compute the cost of the equipment acquired by Lund Company.

Ex. 12-11 The controller of Producto Company maintains records of plant assets under the composite method. A list of plant assets acquired on January 2, Year 1, follows:

Plant assets	Cost	Net residual value	Economic life (years)
A-101	$4,000	$400	3
A-102	1,500	300	4
A-103	7,000	750	5

a Compute Producto Company's straight-line composite depreciation rate based on cost.

b Assuming that on December 31, Year 3, asset A-101 was sold for $1,200, prepare a journal entry for Producto Company to record the sale.

Ex. 12-12 At the beginning of Year 1, Tangiers Company acquired 20 similar machines for $4,000 each and developed a straight-line group depreciation rate of 30% based on the following expectations:

	Year 2	Year 3	Year 4
Number of machines to be retired at end of year	5	10	5
Net residual value of machines to be retired	$6,000	$4,000	none

The retirements and proceeds realized were exactly as expected. The 30% depreciation rate is correct.

Record all transactions of Tangiers Company for the four-year period in T accounts and explain the balance in the Accumulated Depreciation of Machinery ledger account at the end of Year 4.

Ex. 12-13 An analysis of the Machinery ledger account of Locado Corporation for Year 8 appears below:

Jan. 2 Acquisition of four machines with an economic life of five years	$24,000
6 Installation cost for the four machines..........................	800
Total debits...	$24,800
Dec. 28 Less: Credit representing proceeds on disposal of one machine	
(debit was recorded in the Cash ledger account).............	4,200
31 Balance of Machinery ledger account........................	$20,600

a Prepare a journal entry for Locado Corporation to record depreciation expense for Year 8 for the four machines. The estimated net residual value of each machine is $700. Use the straight-line method of depreciation.

b Prepare a journal entry for Locado Corporation to correct the accounting records on December 31, Year 8, including the gain or loss (which was not recognized on December 28) on the disposal of the one machine. The accounting records have not been closed for Year 8.

Ex. 12-14 On January 2, Year 5, Oscar Company acquired for $14,000 an automobile with an economic life of five years and a net residual value of $1,000. For financial accounting, Oscar adopted the double-declining-balance method of depreciation; for federal income tax purposes, Oscar elected the Accelerated Cost Recovery System, with no expensing of the maximum permitted by federal income tax laws.

Compute depreciation expense for Oscar Company's automobile for (**a**) financial accounting, and (**b**) income tax purposes for each of the five years ending December 31, Year 9. Disregard the investment tax credit. Round all amounts to the nearest dollar.

Ex. 12-15 Elezar Company acquired land containing a natural resource. Elezar is required by its acquisition contract to restore the land to a condition suitable for recreational use after it extracts the natural resource. Geological surveys indicate that the recoverable amount of the natural resource is estimated at 3 million tons, and that the land will have a value of $600,000 after restoration. Relevant cost information follows:

Land..	$6,000,000
Restoration of land..	920,000
Geological surveys..	400,000

Assuming that Elezar Company maintains no inventories of the extracted natural resource, compute the depletion per ton of the natural resource extracted.

Ex. 12-16 Data regarding Copper Company for the year ended April 30, Year 2, follow:

Sales of copper ore (100,000 tons)................................	$8,000,000
Expenses (excluding depletion)...................................	$3,100,000

Depletion base, May 1, Year 1.....................................	$6,000,000
Estimated tons of copper ore recoverable, May 1, Year 1	1,200,000
Income tax rate	45%
Percentage depletion rate for copper...............................	15%

Compute the following for Copper Company for the year ended April 30, Year 2:

a Cost depletion (there was no beginning or ending inventory of copper ore)

b Percentage depletion

Ex. 12-17 Colorado Ore Company acquired mining property for $1.2 million. The property was expected to yield 800,000 tons of ore, after which the property would have a net residual value of $200,000. During the first year of operations, 60,000 tons of ore were mined and sold for $800,000. Operating expenses other than cost depletion amounted to $350,000. The ore mined is eligible for a 15% percentage depletion for income tax purposes. Income taxes are 45% of taxable income.

Compute for Colorado Ore Company's first year of operations the amount of (**a**) cost depletion on the mining property, (**b**) income taxes expense, and (**c**) net income for financial accounting.

CASES

Case 12-1 Proponents of the *successful efforts method* and the *full cost method* of accounting for natural resources acquisition, exploration, and development costs have argued the relative merits of the two methods for many years. Presently, the Financial Accounting Standards Board prefers the successful efforts method, but the Securities and Exchange Commission permits use of the full cost method in reports filed by companies subject to the jurisdiction of the SEC.

Instructions

a Present arguments in support of the successful efforts method of accounting.

b Present arguments in support of the full cost method of accounting.

c Is the successful efforts method or the full cost method more consistent with the conceptual framework of financial accounting theory? Explain.

Case 12-2 Werdling Company began operations on leased premises under an operating lease on January 2, Year 1. On that date, Werdling invested $100,000 in machinery and equipment having an economic life of 10 years and a net residual value of $20,000. Werdling prefers a depreciation method based on expiration of time for financial accounting, but does not wish to use a composite or group depreciation method. The controller asks your advice on what method or methods of depreciation to adopt for the purpose of (1) maximizing financial accounting net income, and (2) minimizing taxable income for Year 1. The income tax rate is 45%.

Instructions

Present a report addressed to the controller of Werdling Company setting forth your recommendations on how Werdling may best achieve its stated objectives. Support your proposal with underlying computations, assuming that there will be no more acquisitions of plant assets during Year 1. Disregard issues of interperiod income tax allocation and the investment tax credit, and assume a $10,000 maximum expensing limitation for income tax purposes.

Case 12-3
The controller of Dublin Corporation is preparing accounting policies for Dublin in its first month of operations. Dublin has a variety of plant assets, including a significant investment in highly specialized equipment. You have been asked to assist the controller with this project.

Instructions

a Define *depreciation* as the term is used in financial accounting.
b Identify the factors that are relevant in the measurement of annual depreciation expense on plant assets and explain whether these factors are determined objectively or whether they are based on judgment.
c Explain why depreciation is shown in the ''Financial Resources Provided from Operations'' section of the statement of changes in financial position.

Case 12-4
Arlo Steel Corporation computes depreciation based on the level of its production activity. In the third quarter of Year 7, Arlo Steel, according to a financial news story, ''returned to profit a sum equal to $0.25 a share that had been recognized as depreciation in the previous six months but that it determined had not been needed.''

Instructions

a Evaluate Arlo Steel Corporation's depreciation policy.
b Do you believe that Arlo Steel Corporation is smoothing its net income by means of its depreciation policy or trying to match the service potential (cost) of its assets with the economic benefits derived (tons of steel produced)?

Case 12-5
Luna Company owned an old factory building that had a carrying amount of $200,000. Machinery and equipment in the building had a carrying amount of $300,000. In Year 5, Luna built a new building at a cost of $1.2 million and installed new equipment costing $650,000. Some of the equipment in the old building was replaced, and both plants were operated at near capacity from Year 5 to Year 10. Depreciation was recorded under the straight-line method.

In Year 10, Luna shut down the old plant because of a decline in sales. The controller of Luna proposes to stop recording depreciation on the old building and machinery, stating that while the old plant is useful, it is not wearing out; furthermore, depreciating the old plant increases costs, overstates inventories, and places Luna in a poor position to bid for new orders because its production costs are high.

Instructions

Discuss and evaluate the controller's position. What recommendation would you make to Luna Company?

Case 12-6
An article in a financial journal stated that the net income for Cann Oil Company has decreased from $5 million in Year 3 to only $2 million in Year 4, largely

because of increases in depletion and depreciation. These increases were necessary because an independent consultant prepared revised estimates of oil and gas reserves that were substantially less than Cann's previous estimates. The article further stated that the revised estimates do not affect Cann's revenue or cash flow, and that revisions in estimates of oil and gas reserves are not unusual in the oil and gas industry. The president of Cann was quoted, "Because we are a relatively small oil and gas company, these revisions affect us more seriously than they do large companies."

Instructions

a How do you suppose the revised depletion and depreciation amount was determined? Should understatements of depletion and depreciation in prior years result in understatements of net income in subsequent years?

b How can independent auditors verify the estimates of deposits of natural resources?

c Explain why an increase in depletion and depreciation does not affect Cann Oil Company's revenue or cash flow.

d Why do revisions in estimates of oil and gas reserves affect a small company "more seriously" than they do large companies? Do such revisions affect the percentage depletion allowed for income tax purposes?

PROBLEMS

12-1 Kase Corporation made a study of its five-year experience with a group of trucks. The appraised values of the trucks at the end of each year and average miles driven each year for each truck during a typical five-year period are shown in the table below:

Year	Miles driven	Appraised value (% of cost)
1	40,000	80%
2	60,000	55
3	40,000	40
4	30,000	30
5	30,000	25

Instructions

Using the foregoing information, compute Kase Corporation's depreciation expense each year during the five-year economic life of a truck that cost $36,000 and is expected to have a net residual value of $9,000, under each of the following depreciation methods (round all computations to the nearest dollar):

a Appraisal
b Straight-line
c Output
d Sum-of-the-years'-digits
e Double-declining-balance

12-2   On January 2, Year 2, Lokey Company, a machine-tool manufacturer, acquired new equipment for $1,000,000. The equipment was eligible for a 10% investment tax credit, which Lokey accounted for by the flow-through method. The equipment had an estimated economic life of five years, and the net residual value was estimated to be $100,000. Lokey estimated that the equipment would produce 10,000 units in its first year. Production was expected to decline by 1,000 units a year over the remaining four years of economic life of the equipment.

The following depreciation methods may be used for financial accounting:

(1) Double-declining-balance
(2) Straight-line
(3) Sum-of-the-years'-digits
(4) Output

Lokey plans to use the Accelerated Cost Recovery (ACRS), with a five-year recovery period, for federal income tax purposes. In so doing, Lokey must reduce the depreciation base by one-half of the investment tax credit. Lokey elects not to use the annual expensing option.

Instructions

a Compute Lokey Company's ACRS depreciation deductions for federal income tax purposes for the three-year period ended December 31, Year 4. Disregard investment tax credit limitations.
b Which depreciation method would result in the maximization of Lokey Company's net income for financial accounting for the three-year period ended December 31, Year 4? Prepare a working paper to show the amount of accumulated depreciation on December 31, Year 4, under the method selected. Show supporting computations. Disregard present values and income taxes.

12-3   The cash price of a machine acquired by Mosby Manufacturing Corporation on September 30, Year 1, was $62,400, including sales taxes; it was paid for as follows:

Cash down payment	$ 7,800
Common stock, 600 shares with a current fair value of $42 a share	25,200
Promissory note payable in 24 monthly installments of $1,500 each, including interest, beginning Oct. 31, Year 1	36,000
Total (paid or payable)	$69,000

The following additional costs were incurred before the machine was ready to be used in operations:

Installation costs	$2,400
Direct costs of trial runs	1,200

The machine was expected to produce 100,000 units during its economic life. It was placed in service on October 4, Year 1.

Instructions

a Determine the cost of Mosby Manufacturing Company's machine for financial accounting. Assume that the discount on the promissory note is equal to the difference between the total payments to be made and the cash price of the machine.

b Assuming that the net residual value of the machine is $6,000 and that the economic life is five years, compute Mosby Manufacturing Corporation's depreciation expense for Year 1 (three months) and Year 2 under each of the following methods:

(1) Straight-line method
(2) Sum-of-the-years'-digits method
(3) Double-declining-balance method
(4) Output method (the machine produced 5,000 units in Year 1 and 21,000 units in Year 2)

12-4 In auditing the financial statements of Vista Corporation, you note the following journal entries in the Machinery ledger account:

Debits:

Jan. 2, Year 3 Acquisition of machine A (invoice cost)	$22,000	
2, Year 3 Installation of machine A	2,000	
Sept. 30, Year 3 Acquisition of machine B (invoice cost)	30,000	
Mar. 31, Year 4 Acquisition of machine C (invoice cost)	16,000	
July 1, Year 5 Repairs as a result of flooding	4,500	$74,500

Credits:

Dec. 31, Year 3 Depreciation for Year 3	$10,800	
Dec. 31, Year 4 Depreciation for Year 4	11,840	
April 1, Year 5 Proceeds on sale of machine A	8,560	
Dec. 31, Year 5 Depreciation for Year 5	7,460	38,660
31, Year 5 Balance		$35,840

Depreciation expense was recorded at the end of each year at 20% of the balance of the Machinery ledger account. The economic life of the machines was five years, and the net residual value of each machine was 10% of invoice cost.

Instructions

a Prepare a working paper to compute the correct balances of the Machinery and Accumulated Depreciation of Machinery ledger accounts of Vista Corporation on December 31, Year 5. Use the straight-line method of depreciation.

b Using the information in **a**, prepare a single correcting journal entry to restate the accounting records of Vista Corporation to conform with generally accepted accounting principles on December 31, Year 5. The revenue and expense ledger accounts for Year 5 are still open. Record the correction of any errors in depreciation expense for Years 3 and 4 in the Retained Earnings ledger account as a prior period adjustment. Disregard income taxes.

12-5 The following entries were in an improperly established Property ledger account in the accounting records of Scoville Company at the end of Year 1:

Debit entries:

Feb.	1 Amount paid to acquire building site......................	$ 45,000
	12 Cost of removing old building from site	10,000
	15 Contract price for new building, which was completed on Apr. 1	159,000
Apr.	1 Insurance and other costs directly connected with construction of new building	9,000
	Total debits	$223,000

Credit entries:

Feb.	12 Proceeds from sale of material obtained from dismantling of old building	$ 6,000
Dec.	31 Depreciation expense for Year 1—5% of balance of Property ledger account, $217,000 (Debit was recorded in the Depreciation Expense ledger account)	10,850
	Total credits	16,850
	31 Balance	$206,150

Instructions

a Prepare a correcting journal entry for Scoville Company on December 31, Year 1, assuming that the economic life of the new building is 20 years, that no net residual value is anticipated, and that depreciation expense under the straight-line method is to be recognized for nine months in Year 1. The accounting records have not been closed for Year 1.

b Compute depreciation expense for Scoville Company's building for Year 1, Year 2, and Year 3 under the following methods: (1) straight-line, (2) double-declining-balance, and (3) sum-of-the-years'-digits.

12-6 Cable Products Company acquired 15 used machines on January 2, Year 1, for $60,000. The machines are not identical but perform similar functions. The machines have an average economic life of four years, and the residual value for each machine will approximately equal the removal costs. A composite depreciation method (straight-line) is used to allocate the cost of the machines to expense. Depreciation expense on assets retired or sold is computed for a full year.

Machines retired or sold and the proceeds on sale are summarized below:

End of	Machines retired or sold	Proceeds on sale
Year 3	3	$ 700
Year 4	10	1,200
Year 5	2	100

New machines of this type were not acquired as replacements.

Instructions

a Prepare a cost allocation working paper for Cable Products Company under the composite depreciation method for the five-year period ended December 31, Year 5, during which the assets were used. Use the working paper headings below:

End of year	Depreciation expense	Machinery ledger account		Accum. Dep. ledger account		Carrying amount
		Debit (Credit)	Balance	Debit (Credit)	Balance	

b Prepare a similar working paper for Cable Products Company, but assume (1) that nothing was received on the sale of the machines, and (2) that two machines were retired at the end of Year 3, eleven machines were retired at the end of Year 4, and two machines were retired at the end of Year 5.

c Comment on differences between the results obtained in **a** and **b**.

12-7 Selected ledger accounts included in the plant assets section of Lopez Corporation's balance sheet on December 31, Year 8, had the following balances:

Land...	$175,000
Land improvements	90,000
Buildings..	900,000
Machinery and equipment	850,000

During Year 9, the following transactions were completed:

(1) Land was acquired for $125,000 as a potential future building site.

(2) A facility consisting of land and buildings was acquired from Chu Company in exchange for 10,000 shares of Lopez's common stock. On the exchange date, Lopez's common stock had a current fair value of $48 a share. The facility was carried in Chu's accounting records on the exchange date at $89,000 for land and $130,000 for buildings. Appraised value on the exchange date for property tax purposes was $120,000 for land and $240,000 for buildings.

(3) Machinery and equipment were acquired at a cost of $300,000. Additional costs were incurred as follows:

Freight and unloading	$15,000
Sales and use taxes..	12,000
Installation...	25,000

(4) Expenditures totaling $80,000 were made for new parking lots, streets, and sidewalks at Lopez's various plant locations. These expenditures had an economic life of 15 years.

(5) Machine Q, which had been acquired for $50,000 on January 2, Year 1, was scrapped on June 30, Year 9. Double-declining-balance depreciation based on a 10-year economic life had been recorded.

(6) Machine R was sold for $20,000 on July 1, Year 9. The cost of the machine was $36,000 on January 2, Year 6, and it was depreciated under the straight-line method over an economic life of seven years and a net residual value of $1,000.

Instructions

a Prepare an analysis of the changes in each of the following ledger accounts of Lopez Corporation for Year 9:

Land

Land improvements

Buildings

Machinery and equipment

(Disregard the related accumulated depreciation ledger accounts.)

b List and compute the items in the fact situations that were not used to determine the answer to **a** above, showing the pertinent amounts and supporting computations for each item. In addition, indicate where, or if, these items should be included in the financial statements.

12-8 On January 2, Year 1, Diggers, Inc., acquired for cash the following:

(1) Land costing $1,800,000 with a net residual value of $200,000 and an estimated total mineral ore content of 400,000 tons

(2) A building on the land costing $600,000 with a net residual value of $100,000 and an economic life of 10 years (disregarding the mineral content of the land)

(3) Mining machinery and equipment costing $200,000 with a net residual value of $50,000 and an economic life of five years

   Diggers estimated that eight years of mining would exhaust the mineral content of the land. Diggers uses the straight-line method of depreciation, where appropriate, for plant assets.

   During Year 1, Diggers mined 22,000 tons of ore. On January 2, Year 2, the remaining ore content was estimated at 360,000 tons. During Year 2, Diggers mined 42,000 tons of ore.

Instructions

Compute the depletion and the depreciation amounts to be included in the cost of ore inventory for Diggers, Inc., for both Year 1 and Year 2. Show supporting computations. Round all amounts to the nearest dollar.

12-9 A two-year record of the Equipment ledger account in the accounting records of Stowe Company, which began operations January 2, Year 1, is shown below. Stowe has a policy of taking a full year's depreciation in the year of acquisition and no depreciation in the year of disposal of plant assets.

Year	Cost of equipment	Economic life (years)	Net residual value	Disposals	
				Year acquired	Cost
1	$110,000	10	20% of cost		
2	84,000	6	20% of cost	1	$20,000

Instructions

Prepare a working paper for Stowe Company showing for the two-year period the additions, disposals, and ending balances for the Equipment ledger account, and for the related Accumulated Depreciation of Equipment account, using the following depreciation methods:

a Straight-line

b Sum-of-the-years'-digits

c Double-declining-balance

12-10 On July 1, Year 5, Bayless Company, which has a December 31 fiscal year, established a new manufacturing department that requires several different types of machinery. Bayless uses the sum-of-the-years'-digits method of depreciation and takes a full year's depreciation in the year of acquisition, but no depreciation in the year of disposal, of plant assets. The transactions involving the machines in the new department for a period of three years are described below:

July 1, Year 5 Acquired the following machines:

Machine No.	Cost	Net residual value	Economic life (years)
100	$40,000	$8,500	6
101	15,300	1,300	7
102	47,500	2,500	5

Jan. 2, Year 6   Acquired machine No. 103 for $60,000. Economic life 10 years; net residual value $5,000.

May 1, Year 7   Sold machine No. 100 for $20,000 and replaced it with machine No. 104, which was acquired for $54,000 and has a net residual value of $10,800 at the end of eight years of economic life.

Oct. 1, Year 8   Exchanged machine No. 102 for a similar new machine (No. 105), paying $43,500 in cash and receiving a trade-in allowance (equal to current fair value) of $15,000. Machine No. 105 has an economic life of 10 years and no net residual value.

Instructions

a Prepare a working paper for Bayless Company showing the computation of depreciation expense for each of the years ended December 31, Years 5, 6, 7, and 8, and the balances in the Machinery ledger account and Accumulated Depreciation of Machinery account on December 31, Year 8.

b Prepare journal entries for Bayless Company to record the sale of machine No. 100 and the trade-in of machine No. 102. Show computation of the carrying amount of these machines at the time of sale or exchange. Any gain or loss is to be recognized consistent with the provisions of *APB Opinion No. 29,* "Accounting for Nonmonetary Transactions," as summarized in Chapter 11 (pages 569–571).

12-11   Dakota Mining Company paid $1,850,000 for land containing valuable ore and spent $450,000 in developing the property during Year 1, preparatory to beginning mining activities on January 2, Year 2. Dakota's geologists estimated that the mineral deposit would produce 8 million tons of ore over a 15-year period, and it was estimated that the land will have a net residual value of $300,000 after the ore deposit is exhausted.

A record of plant asset expenditures during the last half of Year 1, exclusive of the development costs previously mentioned, follows:

Asset	Economic life (years)	Cost
Mine buildings	30	$200,000
Railroad and hoisting equipment.....................	20	600,000
Miscellaneous mining equipment.....................	10	250,000

The buildings, railroad, and hoisting equipment could not be removed economically from the mine location, but the miscellaneous mining equipment was movable and had alternative uses.

Operations during Year 2 are summarized below:

Tons of ore mined	1,000,000
Tons of ore sold at $5.10 a ton (FOB at the mine)..................	950,000
Mining labor and other operating costs (exclusive of depreciation and depletion)	$2,400,000
Selling and administrative expenses...............................	$ 625,750

Income taxes expense for the year (based on percentage depletion) was $492,000.

Instructions

a Prepare an income statement for Dakota Mining Company for Year 2, showing the computation of depletion and depreciation per ton of ore mined in a supporting exhibit. Use the straight-line method of depreciation, with no net residual value for the miscellaneous mine equipment. Dakota had 200,000 shares of common stock outstanding during Year 2.

b Early in Year 3, Dakota Mining Company received an offer from an Indonesian company to purchase 500,000 tons of ore at a price of $3.90 a ton delivered in Indonesia. Dakota estimated that it would cost $1.40 a ton to ship the ore to Indonesia, and believed that accepting this offer would not affect the domestic price. It was estimated that the cost of acquiring and developing additional ore property had not increased. One-fourth of Dakota's "mining labor and other operating costs" are fixed as long as at least 600,000 tons of ore are produced annually. Would you recommend that Dakota Mining Company accept the offer from the Indonesian company? Present computations to support your conclusion.

12-12   City Trucking Company acquired 100 trucks on January 2, Year 1, for $600,000. The controller of City decided to use the group depreciation method for these trucks, and estimated the composite rate at 21% ($126,000 ÷ $600,000 = 0.21) as follows:

Year	Number of trucks to be retired	Cost	Net residual value	Depreciation base	Economic life, years	Annual depreciation expense
1	5	$ 30,000	$ 21,000	$ 9,000	1	$ 9,000
2	20	120,000	72,000	48,000	2	24,000
3	30	180,000	59,400	120,600	3	40,200
4	30	180,000	36,000	144,000	4	36,000
5	15	90,000	6,000	84,000	5	16,800
	100	$600,000	$194,400	$405,600		$126,000

At the end of Year 7, when the last truck had been retired, the controller prepared the following summary of City's actual experience:

Year	Number of trucks retired	Proceeds received on retirement
1	4	$ 17,200
2	11	32,800
3	28	74,700
4	42	49,600
5	8	5,000
6	5	1,800
7	2	800
	100	$181,900

City had followed group depreciation procedures and recognized no gain or loss when the trucks were retired.

Instructions

a Reconstruct City Trucking Company's Trucks and Accumulated Depreciation of Trucks ledger accounts as they would have appeared had the controller's estimates been realized, and the computed rate of 21% had been used as a basis for recording depreciation. Would the controller's rate have produced accurate results if the assumptions had been correct? Why?

b On the basis of hindsight, that is, the actual record of experience with the 100 trucks, compute the group depreciation rate that should have been used by City Trucking Company. Also determine the group economic life of the trucks.

c Using the rate computed in b, reconstruct City Trucking Company's Trucks and Accumulated Depreciation of Trucks ledger accounts. Explain any balance of the Accumulated Depreciation of Trucks account at the end of Year 7 and state why this balance, if any, differs from the balance of the Accumulated Depreciation of Trucks account obtained in a.

12-13   Lido Corporation, a manufacturer of steel products, began operations on October 1, Year 2. Lido's accounting department has begun the depreciation analysis shown below:

LIDO CORPORATION
Depreciation Analysis
For Years Ended September 30, Years 3 and 4

Assets	Acquisition date	Cost	Net residual value	Depre- ciation method	Esti- mated life (years)	Depreciation for year ended Sept. 30, Year 3	Year 4
Land L	Oct. 1, Year 2	$ (a)	*	*	*	*	*
Building B . .	Oct. 1, Year 2	(b)	$64,060	Straight- line	(c)	$14,000	$ (d)
Land LL	Oct. 2, Year 2	(e)	*	*	*	*	*
Building BB	(Under con- struction)	210,000 to date	none	Straight- line	30	none	(f)
Donated equipment .	Oct. 2, Year 2	(g)	2,000	150%-de- clining- balance	10	(h)	(i)
Machine M .	Oct. 2, Year 2	(j)	5,500	Sum-of-the- years'- digits	10	(k)	(l)
Machine MM	Oct. 1, Year 3	(m)	none	Straight- line	12	none	(n)

*Not applicable

You have been asked to assist in completing the foregoing analysis. In addition to ascertaining that the data already in the analysis were correct, you have obtained the following information from Lido's accounting records:

(1) Depreciation is computed from the first of the month of acquisition to the first of the month of disposal.
(2) Land L and building B were acquired from a predecessor corporation. Lido paid a total of $830,500 for the land and building. At the time of acquisition, the land had an appraised value of $72,000 and the building had an appraised value of $828,000.
(3) Land LL was acquired on October 2, Year 2, in exchange for 3,000 shares of Lido's common stock. On the date of acquisition, the common stock had a par value of $5 a share and a current fair value of $25 a share. During October, Year 2, Lido paid $10,400 to demolish an existing building on this land to construct a new building (building BB).
(4) Construction of building BB began on October 1, Year 3. By September 30, Year 4, Lido had paid $210,000 of the estimated total construction costs of $300,000. Estimated completion and occupancy date was July, Year 5.

(5) Equipment was donated to Lido by the city of Pineridge. An independent appraisal of the equipment on the date of donation placed the current fair value at $16,000.

(6) The total cost of $110,000 for machine M included installation costs of $550 and normal repairs and maintenance of $11,000 incurred through January 31, Year 4. Machine M was sold on February 1, Year 4.

(7) On October 1, Year 3, machine MM was acquired under a deferred payment contract requiring a down payment of $3,760 and 10 annual installments of $4,000 each beginning October 1, Year 4. The current fair rate of interest was 8%. The following data are available from present value tables:

Present value of 1 at 8%

10 periods	*0.463*
11 periods	*0.429*
15 periods	*0.315*

Present value of ordinary annuity of 1 at 8%

10 rents	*6.710*
11 rents	*7.139*
15 rents	*8.559*

Instructions

For each lettered item in the foregoing analysis for Lido Corporation, supply the correct amount. Round each amount to the nearest dollar. Do not recopy the analysis, but show supporting computations.

Intangible Assets

13

Nature of Intangible Assets

The basic characteristic that distinguishes intangible assets from tangible assets is that the former are not physical in nature. In legal terminology this distinction is maintained consistently, the term *intangibles* being applied to all non-physical properties, including cash, accounts and notes receivable, and investments in corporate securities. Intangible assets for financial accounting include patents, copyrights, trademarks, trade names, secret formulas, organization costs, franchises, licenses, and goodwill (the excess of cost of an acquired business enterprise over the current fair value of identifiable net assets acquired).

One reason for distinguishing between tangible and intangible assets is that it often is difficult to identify intangible assets. Because one can ''stub a toe'' on a tangible asset, it is relatively easy to know when a tangible asset exists. Evidence of the existence of intangible assets may be vague, and the relationship between costs incurred and the emergence of an asset may be difficult to establish objectively. The economic value of both tangible and intangible assets is dependent on their ability to generate future revenue and earnings, and this often is as difficult to measure for tangible assets as it is for intangibles. However, physical existence is not a guarantee of economic value (obsolete machinery, for example), nor does the absence of physical existence preclude economic value (the Listerine formula, for example). For some business enterprises, the value of intangible assets may exceed the value of their tangible assets.

Cost of Intangible Assets

A business enterprise may acquire intangible assets from others, or it may develop internally certain types of intangible assets. The general objectives in accounting for intangible assets are comparable with those for tangible assets; the initial cost is determined and deducted from the revenue that the assets help to generate. A significant and permanent decline in the value of an intangible asset is expensed in the year the decline occurs. Generally, such write-offs are not considered extraordinary items.

When an intangible asset is acquired from others, its cost may be measured with little difficulty. It may be necessary to estimate the value of nonmonetary assets given in exchange for intangible assets, or to allocate the total cost among various assets acquired as a group. The principles used in dealing with these problems, described in Chapter 11 for plant assets, also are applicable to intangible assets. Accounting for intangible assets *developed* by business enterprises is no longer a problem for accountants, because all costs incurred in the ''in house'' development of most intangible assets are recognized as expenses.

In 1970, the Accounting Principles Board took the following position in *APB Opinion No. 17,* ''Intangible Assets,'' relative to recording intangible assets:[1]

> The Board concludes that a company should record as assets the costs of intangible assets acquired from other enterprises or individuals. Costs of developing, maintaining, or restoring intangible assets which are not specifically identifiable, have indeterminate lives, or are inherent in a continuing business and related to an enterprise as a whole—such as goodwill—should be deducted from income when incurred.

> Intangible assets acquired singly should be recorded at cost at date of acquisition. Cost is measured by the amount of cash disbursed, the fair value of other assets distributed, the present value of amounts to be paid for liabilities incurred, or the fair value of consideration received for stock issued. . . .

> Intangible assets acquired as part of a group of assets or as part of an acquired company should also be recorded at cost at date of acquisition. Cost is measured differently for specifically identifiable intangible assets and those lacking specific identification. The cost of identifiable intangible assets is an assigned part of the total cost of the group of assets or enterprise acquired, normally based on the fair values of the individual assets. The cost of unidentifiable intangible assets is measured by the difference between the cost of the group of assets or enterprise acquired and the sum of the assigned costs of individual tangible and identifiable intangible assets acquired less liabilities assumed. Cost should be assigned to all specifically identifiable intangible assets; cost of identifiable assets should not be included in goodwill.

The Accounting Principles Board classified all intangible assets into two categories: (1) those that are specifically *identifiable,* and (2) those that are *unidentifiable.* As indicated in the foregoing quotation, the APB required the costs of developing, maintaining, or restoring intangible assets that are not specifically identifiable (such as goodwill) to be expensed when incurred. Four years later, the Financial Accounting Standards Board wrestled with one of the most difficult problems related to intangible assets, namely, the accounting for research and development costs, and reached the conclusion that ''all research and development costs . . . shall be charged to expense when incurred.''[2]

Amortization of Intangible Assets

The process of systematically writing off the cost of intangible assets is called *amortization.* For many years, accountants approached the question of amortization

---

[1]*APB Opinion No. 17,* ''Intangible Assets,'' AICPA (New York: 1970), p. 339.
[2]*FASB Statement No. 2* ''Accounting for Research and Development Costs,'' FASB (Stamford: 1974), p. 6.

by classifying intangible assets into two categories: (1) those having a *limited* term of existence, such as patents, and (2) those with an *indefinite* or *unlimited* term of existence, such as goodwill. Those with a limited economic life were amortized; those with an indefinite or unlimited economic life were maintained intact until they became worthless, at which time they were written off. This gave management of business enterprises considerable leeway in accounting for intangible assets. However, the Accounting Principles Board established the following amortization policy for intangible assets acquired after October 31, 1970:[3]

> The Board believes that the value of intangible assets at any one date eventually disappears and that the recorded costs of intangible assets should be amortized by systematic charges to income over the periods estimated to be benefited.

According to the APB, then, all intangible assets acquired after October 31, 1970, and those with a limited term of existence acquired on or before October 31, 1970, must be amortized. Factors that should be considered in estimating the economic life of an intangible asset include:[4]

1   Legal, regulatory, or contractual provisions when they place a limit on the maximum economic life.

2   Provisions for renewal or extension of rights or privileges covered by specific intangible assets.

3   Effects of obsolescence, customer demand, competition, rate of technological change, and other economic factors.

4   Possibility that economic life of intangible assets may be related to life expectancies of certain groups of employees.

5   Expected actions of competitors, regulatory bodies, and others.

6   An apparently unlimited economic life of an intangible asset may in fact be only indefinite, and future benefits cannot be reasonably projected.

7   An intangible asset may be a composite of many individual factors with diverse economic lives.

The period of amortization for intangible assets is determined after a careful review of all relevant factors. This review enables management of a business enterprise to make a reasonable estimate of the economic life of most intangible assets. According to *APB Opinion No. 17,* the period of amortization for any intangible asset *should not exceed 40 years,* and if a longer economic life is expected, the amortization period should be 40 years. No minimum period for amortization was specified in *APB Opinion No. 17.*

In the opinion of the authors, the maximum period of amortization of 40 years is much too long for most intangible assets. During the current era of rapid techno-

---

[3]*APB Opinion No. 17,* pp. 339–340.
[4]Ibid., p. 340.

logical innovations and changes in consumer tastes, few intangible assets retain their usefulness for 40 years. Consequently, many business enterprises probably overstate their net income by amortizing unidentifiable intangible assets over the maximum period allowed. Conversely, mandatory amortization of some types of intangible assets that tend to increase in value over time (such as licenses to operate radio or television stations) may be unrealistic. Amortization of these intangible assets (even over a 40-year period) may result in an understatement of total assets, stockholders' equity, and net income.

The accounting procedures for the amortization of intangible assets are comparable with those employed for depreciable plant assets. The cost of intangible assets should be amortized in a systematic manner over their estimated economic lives. *APB Opinion No. 17* requires use of the *straight-line* method of amortization, unless management of the business enterprise presents a convincing case that some other systematic method is more appropriate. For example, if there is evidence that the value of services provided by an intangible asset in early accounting periods of its economic life is significantly higher than the value in later years, an appropriate accelerated method of amortization may be used.

The amortization of intangible assets may be credited directly to the asset ledger account, leaving a balance representing the unamortized cost. This is a matter of custom rather than accounting logic. For example, the journal entry to record the amortization of patents in the amount of $4,200 is illustrated below:

Recording periodic amortization	*Patent Amortization Expense* 4,200	
	Patents (or Accumulated Amortization of Patents)	4,200
	To record amortization of patents.	

The amortization of intangible assets may be either a factory overhead cost or an operating expense, depending on the nature and use of the assets. For example, the amortization of a patent on a manufacturing process is included in factory overhead costs, and the amortization of a trademark used to promote products is a selling expense.

Disclosure of the method and the period of amortization for intangible assets, as well as the amount of amortization for the accounting period, is required in a note to the financial statements. The period used to amortize intangible assets is reviewed continually to determine whether changing circumstances require a change in the estimate of economic life. When a change is made in the estimated economic life of an intangible asset, the unamortized cost is allocated over the *remaining economic life* of the asset. The remaining economic life may be longer or shorter than the original estimate. The revised economic life, however, must not exceed 40 years from the date the intangible asset was acquired. A review of the amortization policy also may indicate that a material amount of unamortized cost of intangible assets should be written off. However, a single loss year or even several loss years does not necessarily justify a write-off of all or a large part of the unamortized cost of an intangible asset.

IDENTIFIABLE INTANGIBLE ASSETS

Certain intangible assets, such as patents, copyrights, and franchises, are identifiable as distinct and separable property rights; others, such as goodwill, are difficult to identify. The more common identifiable intangible assets are discussed in the following sections.

Patents

A patent is a grant by the federal government giving the owner the exclusive right to manufacture and sell a particular invention for a period of 17 years. Patent rights may be assigned in part or in their entirety. Frequently, licensing contracts require payments of royalties to the owner of a patent for the right to use a patented innovation or to manufacture a patented product. Legally, patents may not be renewed, but in practice their economic lives often are extended by obtaining patents on slight variations and improvements near the end of the legal life of the original patent.

A patent has economic value only if the protection it affords against competition results in increased earnings through an ability to operate at a lower cost, to manufacture and sell a product, or to obtain a higher price for goods and services. The economic life of a patent generally is much shorter than its legal life; therefore, amortization should be recognized over the period of usefulness.

If a patent is acquired from others, its cost is measured by the acquisition price plus any incidental costs. The acquisition of a patent from another party is recorded as follows:

<table>
<tr><td>Journal entry to record acquisition of an intangible asset</td><td>Patents . . . .</td><td>60,000</td><td></td></tr>
<tr><td></td><td>Cash . . . .</td><td></td><td>60,000</td></tr>
<tr><td></td><td>To record acquisition of patent.</td><td></td><td></td></tr>
</table>

A patent does not include automatic protection against infringement; patent owners must prosecute those who attempt to infringe their patents and defend against infringement suits brought by owners of similar patents. The cost of successfully establishing the legal validity of a patent should be capitalized (added to the carrying amount of the patent), because such cost will benefit revenue over the remaining economic life of the patent. However, a patent infringement suit may take years to resolve, and the accounting treatment of legal costs during this period must recognize the uncertainties involved by expensing such costs. If the legal decision is favorable, legal costs may be paid by the losing party; if the legal decision is adverse, both the amount of damages paid and the unamortized cost of the patent should be written off, because no further economic benefits are expected to result from the patent.

The right to use a patent owned by others under a licensing contract is not recorded as an intangible asset, unless a lump-sum payment is made at the outset of such a contract. The periodic royalty payments are recorded as factory overhead costs or as operating expense, depending on the use made of the patent.

If a patent is developed as a result of a business enterprise's research and development efforts, the cost assigned to the patent *includes only the direct legal costs and fees incurred in obtaining the patent*. No research and development costs incurred internally are assigned to the patent, because all such costs must be expensed as incurred. Accounting for research and development costs is covered in another section of this chapter.

Copyrights

A copyright is a grant by the federal government giving an author, creator, or artist the exclusive right to publish, sell, or otherwise control literary or artistic products for the life of the author plus 50 years. A business enterprise may obtain the rights granted under copyrights by paying royalties, by acquisition of the copyright from the author, or by obtaining a copyright on a literary or artistic product developed by the enterprise. The problems that arise in measuring the cost of copyrights are comparable with those discussed in connection with patents.

Although a copyright has a long legal life, its economic life is limited to the period for which a commercial market exists for the publication. In order to achieve a proper matching of costs and revenue, copyright costs are amortized against the total revenue that is anticipated from the copyright. Because of the difficulty encountered in estimating copyright revenue and because experience indicates that such revenue generally results over only a few years, copyrights typically are amortized over a relatively short period of time. On occasion, copyrights thought to be worthless may bounce back to life with renewed vigor. An outstanding example is old movies: Their production and copyright costs previously had been fully amortized, but these films became extremely valuable with the development of television. However, this increase in the value of copyrights was not reflected in the balance sheets of motion picture producers.

Licenses and Contracts

Many business enterprises expend considerable amounts to obtain licenses to engage in certain types of business activities or to acquire rights to use copyrighted materials owned by others. For example, Federal Communications Commission (FCC) licenses, network-affiliation contracts, and film rights probably are the most valuable assets of an enterprise engaged in the broadcasting industry. Without an FCC license, it would be impossible for a broadcaster to earn revenue; a network-affiliated station is more valuable than an independent station because of network-supplied programming. The rights to show old movies are an important source of revenue for television broadcasters.

The cost of a license or a contract is amortized over the accounting periods expected to benefit. An FCC license generally is amortized over a period of 40 years; a network-affiliation contract is amortized over the period specified in the contract; and film rights acquired by a television station generally are amortized on an accelerated basis, because first showings generate more advertising revenue than reruns.[5] If a license or a contract is canceled or for any reason becomes worthless, any unamortized cost is recognized as an expense.

---

[5] *FASB Statement No. 63*, "Financial Reporting by Broadcasters," FASB (Stamford: 1982), pp. 2–3.

Trademarks, Trade Names, and Secret Formulas

Trademarks, trade names, secret formulas, and various distinctive labels are important means of building and maintaining customer acceptance for many products. The value of such product identification and differentiation stems from the ability of the business enterprise to sell products in large volume and at prices higher than those for unbranded products.

Trademarks, trade names, secret formulas, and labels are property rights that may be licensed, assigned, or sold. Their economic lives continue as long as they are used, and their cost is amortized over their economic lives or 40 years, whichever is shorter.

The value of trademarks, trade names, or secret formulas often is enhanced as the enterprise succeeds in building consumer confidence in the quality of products distributed under a particular brand name. Presumably this growth in value is not without cost, because enterprises spend large sums for advertising and otherwise promoting trade names. The relationship between promotional expenditures and the increase in the value of a trade name is nebulous; therefore, accountants do not assign a cost to this intangible asset, except when it is acquired from another party.

Organization Costs

The organization of a corporate business enterprise usually requires a considerable amount of time, effort, and cost. Compensation must be paid to those who conceive, investigate, and promote the idea; legal fees relating to drafting of the corporate charter and bylaws, accounting fees, and incorporation fees are incurred; and costs may be incurred in conducting initial meetings of stockholders and directors. All these expenditures are made with the expectation that they will contribute to future revenue. Therefore, the cost of organizing a corporate enterprise logically should be treated as an asset and not as an expense. However, items such as operating losses incurred by a corporation in the early years, bond discount and issuance costs, large initial advertising expenditures, or discount and issuance costs on common stock, are not included in organization costs. Expenditures incurred in connection with the issuance of shares of common stock, such as professional fees and printing costs, generally are deducted from the proceeds received for the stock. Similar expenditures relating to the issuance of bonds or other debt instruments are deferred and amortized over the term of the debt.

Theoretically, the costs of organization have an economic life as long as the corporate enterprise remains a going concern. Because the life of most corporations is unlimited, organization costs may be viewed as a permanent asset that will continue in existence until the corporation goes out of business. Despite the logic of this position, organization costs generally are amortized over a five-year period, because the federal income tax law permits amortization over a period of "not less than five years." However, amortization over a maximum period of 40 years is permitted by generally accepted accounting principles.

Franchises

A *franchise* is a right or privilege received by a business enterprise for the exclusive right to engage in business in a specified geographic area. The franchise may be acquired from a governmental unit or from another enterprise. For example, public utilities generally receive a franchise from state or federal agencies and are subject to specific regulations; a retailer may obtain an exclusive right from a manufacturer to sell certain products in a specified territory; an operator of a restaurant may obtain the right to utilize trade names and recipes developed by another enterprise; and a cable television company may obtain exclusive rights for television programming in one or more communities.

Some franchises granted by manufacturers or retail chains (*franchisors*) may cost substantial amounts. The amount paid for such a franchise is recorded by the *franchisee* as an intangible asset and amortized over its expected economic life. The proceeds received by franchisors are recognized as revenue when the contractual commitments to franchisees are fulfilled.[6] If the right to operate under a franchise is limited to 10 years, for example, the amortization period should not exceed 10 years. Although some franchises prove to be worthless in a short period of time, others may increase substantially in value if the location and product (or service) prove successful.

An *operating right* issued by the Interstate Commerce Commission or a similar state agency to a motor carrier (trucker) to transport goods with limited competition over specified routes is a form of a franchise. Many trucking enterprises acquired such rights to transport goods interstate at substantial costs. The Motor Carrier Act of 1980 deregulated the interstate trucking industry, thus reducing or eliminating the value of these intangible assets. Consequently, the FASB required that ''Unamortized costs of interstate operating rights subject to the provisions of the Act shall be charged to income and, if material, reported as an extraordinary item . . . in the income statement.''[7]

Leasehold Costs

An existing lease right and a lump-sum payment to acquire rights to explore for oil and minerals on land are valuable property rights that may be included with intangible assets in the balance sheet. However, because such assets represent rights to use tangible assets, they generally are included under plant assets in the balance sheet.

UNIDENTIFIABLE INTANGIBLE ASSETS: GOODWILL

Thus far we have discussed the major types of identifiable intangible assets. However, the earning power of most prosperous business enterprises is attributable to a variety of factors that cannot be specifically identified, either as tangible assets or as intangible assets. Accountants, business executives, and lawyers often refer to these factors collectively as goodwill.

In ordinary usage the term *goodwill* is associated with a kindly feeling or benevolence. However, in business and law goodwill has a different meaning. The most acceptable evidence of goodwill is the ability of a business enterprise to earn a

---

[6]For a complete discussion on this topic, see *FASB Statement No. 45,* ''Accounting for Franchise Fee Revenue,'' FASB (Stamford: 1981).

[7]*FASB Statement No. 44,* ''Accounting for Intangible Assets of Motor Carriers,'' FASB (Stamford: 1980), p. 2.

rate of return on net assets (owners' investment) in excess of a normal rate for the industry in which the enterprise operates. *Goodwill is the difference between the value of a business enterprise as a whole and the sum of the current fair values of its identifiable tangible and intangible net assets.* Goodwill is in essence a ''master valuation account''—the missing link that reconciles the current fair value of an enterprise as a going concern with the current fair value of the sum of its identifiable parts.

Nature of Goodwill

The first procedure toward an understanding of goodwill is to estimate the current fair value of a business enterprise as a going concern. The current fair value of the enterprise may be greater than the amount of identifiable tangible and intangible net assets, because of the presence of unidentifiable intangible assets. A simple example may help to clarify this point. Assume that Parke Company is offered for sale and that the balance sheet below is used as a basis for negotiating a fair price:

Net assets
(stockholders' equity)
is $400,000

PARKE COMPANY			
Balance Sheet			
December 31, Year 10			
Cash and receivables	$130,000	Liabilities..................	$100,000
Inventories	90,000	Common stock, $1 par	250,000
Plant assets (net)	280,000	Retained earnings	150,000
		Total liabilities & stock-	
Total assets	$500,000	holders' equity.........	$500,000

We shall assume that Parke Company is expected to earn an average net income of $60,000 a year indefinitely in the future. Because the current fair value of net assets depends directly on the earning power of the assets, we may value Parke as a going concern, without reference to its balance sheet, by determining the present value of future earnings of $60,000 a year. A logical way of appraising this is in terms of the rate of return on alternative investment opportunities of comparable risk. We shall assume this rate to be 10%. If it is possible to earn a 10% return on similar investments, the current value of the prospect of receiving $60,000 a year *in perpetuity* may be computed by determining the amount which must be invested at 10% to earn an annual return of $60,000. This procedure is called *capitalization of income,* and the result in this case is a value for the net assets of Parke of $600,000 ($60,000 ÷ 0.10 = $600,000), compared with a carrying amount of only $400,000 ($500,000 − $100,000 = $400,000).

If the net assets of Parke Company are worth $600,000, why are they reported in the balance sheet at only $400,000? One reason is that Parke's accounting records do not reflect the current fair value of identifiable net assets. Inventories and plant assets, for example, might be worth considerably more than carrying amount, and liabilities might be overstated. If these discrepancies are identified during the negotiations, appropriate adjustments should be made.

It is possible, however, that the carrying amount of each asset and liability included in the balance sheet closely approximates its current fair value, but still Parke Company's net assets are worth $200,000 more than carrying amount. Is this an accounting exception to the principle that the whole must equal the sum of its parts, or is it possible that some of the parts are not included in the balance sheet? The latter is the more likely explanation, and it is apparent that the missing parts are those characteristics of Parke Company that enable it to earn $60,000 a year (10% of $600,000) rather than $40,000 a year (10% of $400,000). Parke apparently has intangible assets that are not included in its balance sheet. Any of the identifiable intangible assets previously discussed in this chapter is a possible source of the unexplained $200,000 in the current fair value of Parke as a going concern.

For purposes of this illustration, we assume that Parke Company has a patent worth $50,000 that is not included in the balance sheet, because it was developed internally or because it had been fully amortized. After all identifiable assets, both tangible and intangible, have been appraised, only $150,000 ($200,000 − $50,000) remains unexplained, and we have isolated the *imputed value* of all unidentifiable intangible assets, that is, *goodwill.* Goodwill exists as an asset only because it is impossible to identify separately all sources of the prospective earning power of a business enterprise. This analysis may be summarized as follows for Parke Company:

Imputed value
of goodwill

Current fair value of total assets		*$700,000**
Less: Current fair value of tangible net assets	*$400,000*	
Current fair value of patent not included in the		
accounting records	*50,000*	
Liabilities	*100,000*	*550,000*
Unidentifiable intangible asset (goodwill)		*$150,000*

*$600,000 net assets + $100,000 liabilities = $700,000

If patents of $50,000 and goodwill of $150,000 were added to the assets of Parke Company, the carrying amount of its *net assets* would be $600,000 (assets of $700,000, less liabilities of $100,000). Therefore, if Parke earned $60,000, its earnings no longer would be large in relation to the carrying amount of its net assets. Thus, the ability to earn a *superior rate of return* on net assets that *do not include* goodwill is evidence that goodwill exists; the ability to earn a normal rate of return on assets that *include* the goodwill and all identifiable intangible assets is evidence of the existence of goodwill in the amount computed.

Negative Goodwill

Goodwill, as we have defined it, may be either positive or negative in amount. Suppose, for example, that the prospective earnings of Parke Company had been estimated at only $36,000 a year indefinitely into the future and that its identifiable net assets are fairly stated at $400,000. On a 10% yield basis, the capitalized value of these earnings is $360,000 ($36,000 ÷ 0.10 = $360,000), and it is evident that the carrying amount of the net assets exceeds the current fair value of Parke as a whole by $40,000 ($400,000 − $360,000 = $40,000). This $40,000 is termed *negative goodwill.*

When the earning potential of a business enterprise is such that the enterprise as a whole is worth less than its net assets, the owners would be better off to dispose of the assets piecemeal, pay the liabilities, and terminate the enterprise. In reality this may not be done because of concern for the welfare of employees, willingness of the owners to continue operating an unprofitable enterprise, optimism about future prospects, or other considerations. Because the presence of negative goodwill suggests that liquidation is the best course of action, positive goodwill is more likely to be found in going concerns than negative goodwill. Although negative goodwill exists in many unprofitable enterprises, it is not isolated and reported in the balance sheet; the only evidence of its existence is a *low rate of earnings* on the net assets of the enterprises.

If an enterprise with negative goodwill is sold as a going concern, the value assigned to the net assets acquired by the acquirer should not exceed the *cost actually paid.* The total current fair value of identifiable assets acquired less the liabilities assumed occasionally may exceed the price paid for the acquired enterprise. According to *APB Opinion No. 16,* ''Business Combinations,'' such an excess over cost should be allocated to reduce the carrying amounts assigned to noncurrent assets (other than long-term investments in marketable securities). If this allocation reduces noncurrent assets to zero, any remaining excess is classified as a deferred credit and amortized over a period not exceeding 40 years.[8]

Recording of Goodwill (Excess of Cost over Net Assets Acquired)

The high degree of certainty about the future assumed in the measurement of goodwill of Parke Company in the foregoing example does not exist in the real world. Assessing the earnings potential of a business enterprise is an uncertain process, and any resulting estimate of goodwill is a matter of judgment and opinion.

In the face of this uncertainty, accountants have adopted a conservative stance with respect to goodwill. It is generally accepted that goodwill should be recorded in the accounting records only when its amount is substantiated by an arm's-length transaction. Because goodwill cannot be either sold or acquired separately, accounting recognition of goodwill is restricted to those occasions in which the entire net assets of a business enterprise, or a substantial interest in the net assets representing a clearly defined segment of a business enterprise, are acquired and goodwill may be established with reasonable objectivity.[9] In such cases goodwill frequently is labeled as *Excess of Cost over Net Assets Acquired.*

---

[8]*APB Opinion No. 16,* ''Business Combinations,'' AICPA (New York: 1970), p. 321.
[9]Cases in which goodwill is recorded in connection with changes in owners of partnerships and in the preparation of consolidated financial statements are presented in *Modern Advanced Accounting* of this series. Our discussion at this point is limited to goodwill arising out of the *purchase* of the entire business enterprise for cash. When a going business enterprise is acquired in exchange for shares of common stock, the transaction may be accounted for as a *pooling of interests.* Goodwill may be recorded in a purchase-type transaction, but not in a pooling of interests.

Limiting the recording of goodwill to *purchased goodwill* is admittedly not an ideal solution to the problem. Internally developed goodwill actually may exist in a business enterprise and not be recorded; conversely, goodwill acquired in the past may appear in the accounting records when there is no current evidence (in terms of earning power) that it actually exists. The financial statements of business enterprises that have changed ownership will appear to be inconsistent with those of enterprises that have had a continuing existence. For example, assume that Parke Company, which is discussed on pages 657–658, has identifiable net assets of $450,000 and that a new company is formed to acquire its net assets for $600,000 cash. The beginning balance sheet of the new company would include goodwill of $150,000. Is there any justification for a rule that prohibits the recording of $150,000 goodwill in the accounting records of Parke but permits the inclusion of this amount in the balance sheet of the new company?

On balance, an affirmative answer is warranted. Specific assets represent resources in which the capital of a business enterprise is invested, to the extent that it has been possible to determine them. The periodic adjustment of these asset valuations by a variable amount labeled ''goodwill'' to a level consistent with the present value of future earnings not only would be highly subjective but also would obscure the significant relationship between actual investment and earning power. If $150,000 of goodwill had been recorded by Parke, not only would there be a serious question as to the validity of this amount, but also the high level of earnings on investment that Parke had been able to attain would be concealed. The investment of the new owners, however, was not $450,000, but $600,000. The new owners paid $150,000 for future superior earnings, and if only $150,000 of superior earnings should materialize, this amount will not represent income to the new owners but a *recovery of their investment.* The position that goodwill should be recorded only when it is evidenced by an acquisition appears to be consistent with the accounting concept of reliability and the valuation principle.

Estimate of Goodwill

The price to be paid for a business enterprise is established as the result of bargaining between independent parties. The bargaining process includes the possible existence of goodwill. The amount of goodwill *to be recorded,* however, is determined after the terms of the contract are set by deducting the current fair value of all identifiable net assets from the total acquisition price. Accountants are interested in the process of estimating goodwill because they often are called upon to aid in establishing the current fair value of an enterprise at the time of negotiations for the acquisition or sale of an enterprise and in court cases.

Procedures generally required to estimate the current fair value of a business enterprise, and thus the amount of goodwill, are listed below:

1   Estimate the current fair value of all identifiable tangible and intangible assets of the enterprise, and deduct from this total the amount of all liabilities. The difference is the current fair value of the *identifiable net assets* of the enterprise.

2   Forecast the average annual earnings that the enterprise *expects to earn* in future years with the use of its present resources.

3   Choose an appropriate rate of return to estimate the normal annual earnings the enterprise *should earn* on its identifiable net assets.

4   Compute the amount of expected annual *superior earnings,* if any.

5   Capitalize the expected annual superior earnings, if any, at an appropriate rate (or rates) of return to estimate the present value of such earnings. *The present capitalized value of any expected annual superior earnings is the estimated value of goodwill for the enterprise.*

In the following sections, an estimate of goodwill is developed for Reed Company (which is for sale) to serve as a basis for a discussion of the problems that arise in connection with each of the foregoing procedures.

Estimate of the Current Fair Value of Identifiable Net Assets Because carrying amounts and current fair values of assets seldom correspond, an appraisal of identifiable assets is necessary to establish the current fair value of the business enterprise (excluding goodwill) and to identify the assets that generate the earnings of the enterprise.

The fair values of current assets, such as cash and accounts receivable, usually approximate their carrying amounts. Inventories, if verified by a physical inventory and priced on a first-in, first-out or average-cost basis, also may be reasonably stated. Last-in, first-out inventories, however, probably are stated in terms of costs incurred many years earlier and should be adjusted to current fair value. The carrying amounts of plant assets are not likely to approximate current fair values. Various methods of indirect valuation may be employed to appraise such assets on a going-concern basis. The current fair value of all identifiable intangible assets should be estimated, even if these assets do not appear in the accounting records. The liabilities of the business enterprise should be reviewed and measured at present value, and any unrecorded liabilities should be estimated and recorded. Liabilities that will

Data for estimates
of goodwill

Items	Carrying amount	Adjust-ments	Estimated current fair value
REED COMPANY Carrying Amount and Current Fair Value of Identifiable Net Assets December 31, Year 10			
Cash, accounts receivable, and short-term prepayments	$142,000	$ (2,000)	$140,000
Inventories (last-in, first-out)	178,000	42,000	220,000
Plant assets (net)......................	480,000	120,000	600,000
Patents and secret formulas		30,000	30,000
Total identifiable assets	$800,000	$190,000	$990,000
Less: Liabilities........................	160,000	10,000	170,000
Identifiable net assets................	$640,000	$180,000	$820,000

not be assumed by the new owners are disregarded unless payment from present assets is contemplated before the enterprise changes ownership. Identifiable assets at current fair values, less the present or current fair value of liabilities to be assumed by the new owners, is the adjusted amount (estimated current fair value) of identifiable net assets for purposes of estimating the value of goodwill.

The assumed data for Reed Company on page 661 illustrate the process of estimating the current fair value of identifiable net assets of a business enterprise.

Forecast of Expected Average Annual Earnings   The aggregate value of a business enterprise depends on its future earnings, not on its past earnings. Thus, the key procedure in an estimate of the current fair value of an enterprise is a forecast of its future earnings, a process which, unfortunately, is never more than an intelligent guess. Because the immediate past history of an enterprise ordinarily provides the best available evidence and is most relevant, the usual procedure is to compute the average annual earnings of an enterprise during the past three to six years and to project them into the future, adjusting for any changing conditions that may be foreseen. The estimate of future conditions and earnings generally is made by the parties to the transaction and not by accountants. A single year's performance clearly is not a sufficient basis for judgment; however, little may be gained by reaching too far into the past, because both the internal and the external conditions influencing business operations may have changed significantly.

In the compilation of the past earnings record suitable for estimating future earnings, two points should be considered:

1   We are not interested in establishing what past earnings were, but in learning what past experience tells us about probable future earnings.

2   Our objective is to obtain an estimate of future earnings that is consistent with the adjusted current fair values of specific identifiable tangible and intangible assets and liabilities.

It seldom is possible to obtain satisfactory data by computing an average of past reported earnings. A more reasonable approach is to work from actual revenue and expense amounts, because changes in revenue and expenses are likely to be related to projected economic and operating conditions. The effect on earnings of a 10% increase in revenue and a 15% increase in operating expenses, for example, may have to be determined. Past data should be adjusted for changes in the value of assets. For example, if inventories and equipment are understated in terms of current fair values, adjustments of past cost of goods sold and depreciation expense must be made. Extraordinary items generally are omitted from past earnings. In view of the subjectivity of estimates and income measurement, immaterial adjustments may be disregarded.

In the evaluation of an average of past data, particular attention must be given to *significant trends.* For example, two business enterprises may have the same five-year average sales, but if the sales of one enterprise have increased in each of the past five years, while the sales of the other have declined steadily, the average sales amounts of the two enterprises should be interpreted differently.

An important point, often overlooked in the adjustment of past earnings in the light of future expectations, is that improvements in earnings expected as a result of the efforts of new owners and management should be distinguished carefully from prospective improvements that are related to existing conditions. If the acquirer of a business enterprise expects to make changes in management, production methods, products, and marketing techniques to increase earnings in the future, these changes should not be considered in the valuation of the enterprise because they will flow from the efforts of the new owners. However, the final price paid for goodwill in any transaction is a matter of bargaining between the acquirer and the seller.

The working paper below is a continuation of the Reed Company example. It represents an assumed computation on December 31, Year 10, of estimated future earnings, based upon an average of the results experienced over the past five years. This estimate might be interpreted by the prospective acquirer to indicate a probable range of future annual earnings for Reed of, say, between $90,000 and $120,000 a year. However, for illustrative purposes, we use the amount of $116,000.

Computation of estimated average future earnings

REED COMPANY
Estimate of Average Future Earnings
December 31, Year 10

Revenue:		
Average annual revenue for past five years, which is expected to be typical of future years (extraordinary items have been excluded)		$920,000
Expenses:		
Average cost of goods sold and operating expenses for past five years, excluding depreciation expense and income taxes expense	$635,600	
Add: Anticipated annual increase in wages and fringe benefits expense as a result of a new union contract ..	45,800	
Less: Average of the five-year increase in inventory valuation not included in the last-in, first-out basis of pricing inventories ($42,000 ÷ 5)	(8,400)	
Depreciation and amortization:		
Average depreciation expense on carrying amounts of assets	24,000	
Add: Increase in depreciation expense on the basis of current fair value (25% increase in value)	6,000	
Amortization expense of patents and secret formulas, not previously carried in the accounting records ($30,000 divided by the economic life of 6 years). ...	5,000	708,000
Expected average future earnings before income taxes ...		$212,000
Less: Estimated income taxes expense (45%)		95,400
Estimated average future earnings		$116,600

Normal Rate of Return   The rate of return used to capitalize future earnings and to separate superior earnings from ordinary earnings is determined by the risks and investment alternatives involved. The objective is to approximate the rate necessary to attract capital to the business enterprise under review, given the existing risk conditions. The cost of capital, as other costs, varies in relation to a variety of factors. The primary cause of differences in the rate of return necessary to attract capital to a specific investment is the amount of risk involved.

Data on average earnings rates for enterprises in particular industries are available in financial services, trade association studies, and government publications. Care should be exercised in the use of such data to be sure that they are applied to comparable situations; for example, that the earnings rate consistently is assumed to be either before or after income taxes. We assume for purposes of illustration that a reasonable normal rate of return for Reed Company is 10% *after income taxes*.

Estimate of Future Superior Earnings   The amount of estimated future superior earnings may be defined as the amount of earnings expected in excess of normal earnings on the current fair value of identifiable tangible and intangible net assets.

All variables necessary to compute the estimated future superior earnings of Reed Company have been discussed and now may be illustrated. The current fair value of Reed's identifiable net assets is $820,000 (see data on page 661), and its average future earnings are estimated at $116,000. Because a 10% after-tax rate of return is sufficient to attract an investment in Reed, its estimated future superior earnings may be computed as follows:

Estimated average future earnings	$116,000
Less: 10% return on current fair value of identifiable net assets	
($820,000 × 0.10)	82,000
Estimated future superior earnings	$ 34,000

Superior earnings: the ultimate source of goodwill

This computation shows that $82,000 ($820,000 × 0.10 = $82,000) a year is necessary to support a valuation of $820,000 for the identifiable net assets of Reed Company. Because Reed's prospects are for earnings in excess of $82,000, the source of this excess earning power must be the unidentifiable intangible assets (goodwill) that enable Reed to earn a higher-than-normal rate of return.

Estimate of Present Value of Superior Earnings—The Final Procedure   A number of different methods may be used to value the estimated future superior earnings, and thus determine an estimate of goodwill. Four methods are illustrated below and on the following pages:

Method 1

Estimated future superior earnings are capitalized at the normal rate of return. One assumption is that the superior earnings of $34,000 a year, as determined above, will continue unimpaired into the future and that this prospect is attributable entirely to the existing resources of Reed Company. The annual superior earnings are *capi-*

talized to answer the following question: How much capital should be invested if the annual return on the investment is $34,000 in perpetuity, and the desired rate of return is 10% a year? Under this approach, goodwill is estimated at $340,000 as follows:

<table>
<tr><td></td><td></td></tr>
<tr><td>*Value of estimated annual average earnings of $116,000 capitalized at*</td><td></td></tr>
<tr><td>*10% in perpetuity ($116,000 ÷ 0.10)* ....</td><td>*$1,160,000*</td></tr>
<tr><td>*Less: Estimated current fair value of identifiable net assets* ....</td><td>*820,000*</td></tr>
<tr><td>*Estimated amount of goodwill* ....</td><td>*$ 340,000*</td></tr>
<tr><td>**Alternative computation:**</td><td></td></tr>
<tr><td>*Value of estimated future superior earnings capitalized at 10% in*</td><td></td></tr>
<tr><td>*perpetuity (goodwill) ($34,000 ÷ 0.10)* ....</td><td>*$ 340,000*</td></tr>
</table>

What objection do you see in this approach?

There are serious flaws in the assumptions on which this method rests. It may be reasonable to forecast that a business enterprise will earn a 10% return on its net assets over a long period of time, but the assumption that superior earning power will persist in perpetuity in the face of competitive pressures and the hazards of free enterprise is optimistic, to say the least. Furthermore, even if superior earnings do continue for a business enterprise, it seldom is possible to trace their origin to conditions that existed at the time of acquisition of the enterprise. The forces that erode superior earnings are such that a persistent ability to earn a higher-than-normal rate of return ultimately will be due to some additional propellant in the form of research, innovations, efficiency, and strategy on the part of the new owners and management.

Method 2

Estimated future superior earnings are discounted for a limited number of years to determine the present value of such earnings. The estimate of goodwill may be modified in several ways to allow for the uncertain nature of superior earnings. One approach is to assume that any estimated future superior earnings will continue for a **limited period**, for example, three or five years. The **present value** of a series of superior earnings at a specified rate of return may be computed by the use of present value concepts described in Chapter 5. In the Reed Company example, if estimated future superior earnings of $34,000 a year will continue for a five-year period, the present value of this prospect discounted at 10% is approximately $129,000, computed as follows:

A conceptually sound approach for estimating goodwill

<table>
<tr><td>*Estimated future superior earnings (assume receipt at end of each year)* .</td><td>*$ 34,000*</td></tr>
<tr><td>*Present value of ordinary annuity of five rents of 1 each,*</td><td></td></tr>
<tr><td>*discounted at 10%* ....</td><td>*3.790787*</td></tr>
<tr><td>*Present value of estimated future superior earnings (goodwill)*</td><td></td></tr>
<tr><td>*($34,000 × 3.790787)* ....</td><td>*$128,887*</td></tr>
</table>

Method 3

Estimated future superior earnings are capitalized at a higher-than-normal rate of return. A variation of **Method 1** is to capitalize estimated future superior earnings at a higher discount rate than is used to capitalize normal earnings. For example, if the normal rate of return is considered to be 10%, a rate of 20% or 30% may be used to capitalize superior earnings. The higher assumed rates of return allow for higher risk, because the prospect that superior earnings will continue unimpaired into the future is *much more uncertain* than the prospect of continued normal earnings. Referring once more to the Reed Company illustration, if superior earnings of $34,000 a year are capitalized at 30%, for example, goodwill is estimated at approximately $113,000 as follows:

Estimated future superior earnings	$ 34,000
Capitalization rate	0.30
Capitalized value of estimated future superior earnings discounted at 30% in perpetuity (goodwill) ($34,000 ÷ 0.30)	$113,333

Higher capitalization rate recognizes that superior earnings are subject to erosion

Under this approach, the earnings prospects of Reed Company have been divided into two layers—$82,000 of normal earnings, and $34,000 ($116,000 − $82,000 = $34,000) of superior earnings—and a different discount rate has been used to value each layer. Any number of different layers and any number of different discount rates might be used to estimate goodwill.

Method 4

Estimated future superior earnings for a stated number of years are acquired. Another approach to the estimate of goodwill is to multiply estimated future superior earnings by a number of years and to refer to the result as a "number of years of estimated future superior earnings acquired." For example, a goodwill estimate of $170,000 may be described as "the acquisition of five years of estimated future superior earnings of $34,000 a year." Such loose statements may obscure the real issues involved. As noted previously, the present value of five years of estimated future superior earnings of $34,000 discounted at 10% is approximately $129,000, not $170,000. Therefore, no reason exists for paying $170,000 for superior earnings of $170,000 to be received over a five-year period if money is worth 10% compounded annually.

Summary of Methods

Uncertainty and subjectivity surround each of the variables involved in an estimate of goodwill. The probable amount of future earnings, the portion that represents superior earnings, the length of time, and the appropriate rate of return to be used in the valuation of superior earnings—all are variables not subject to objective verification. They may be estimated only within a *reasonable* range. The illustrated methods indicate the following possible range (from highest to lowest) in the estimated value of goodwill for Reed Company:

Results of preceding
four approaches
compared

Estimated future superior earnings of $34,000 are capitalized at 10%	
in perpetuity	*$340,000*
Estimated future superior earnings of $34,000 for five years are	
acquired	*170,000*
Estimated future superior earnings of $34,000 for five years are	
discounted at 10% (rounded).	*129,000*
Estimated future superior earnings of $34,000 are capitalized at	
30% (to recognize a higher risk factor) in perpetuity (rounded)	*113,000*

In a transaction involving the acquisition of Reed Company, the value established for goodwill probably would be somewhere between $340,000 and $113,000, depending on the relative bargaining power of the acquirer and the seller. Inability to agree on a specific value for goodwill frequently results in an agreement to pay a minimum amount for goodwill, to be supplemented by additional payments *contingent* on future superior earnings of the acquired enterprise. Such agreements may raise numerous accounting questions. For example, (1) How should the future payments be recorded? (2) How should the earnings on which the contingent payments are based be measured? (3) How should future contingent payments be disclosed by the acquirer?

It sometimes is suggested that the market value of a corporation's common stock provides a basis for estimating the current fair value of the corporation. Thus, if Reed Company, whose net assets have a current fair value of $820,000, has 200,000 shares of common stock outstanding, quoted on the market at $6 a share, this suggests that Reed is worth $1,200,000 (200,000 × $6 = $1,200,000), and that goodwill is $380,000 ($1,200,000 − $820,000 = $380,000). This conclusion would have some merit if the market price of $6 a share applied to the entire issue of 200,000 shares, or to a block representing a substantial and controlling interest in Reed Company. However, only a small fraction of the total shares outstanding normally is offered for sale on the market at any one time. The market prices of this small *floating supply* of common stock may fluctuate widely, and are influenced by short-run factors that may be unrelated to Reed Company's long-run prospects. Furthermore, there is no quoted market price for the common stock of most small corporations. Stock prices may be useful as evidence of *relative* values in the negotiation of a business combination involving an exchange of common stock, and they also may substantiate or invalidate the estimates of goodwill reached independently. However, common stock prices seldom are useful in the direct valuation of goodwill.

Non-Compete Agreements

When a business enterprise is acquired, the acquirer may pay an amount in excess of the current fair value of the identifiable net assets acquired. Typically, the excess is recorded as goodwill. However, there are situations in which a part of the acquisition price may be attributable to an agreement by the seller not to engage in a competing enterprise for a specified period of time. The acquirer of a retail store or a restaurant, for example, would not want the former owner to establish a competing enterprise in the same geographic area.

A *non-compete agreement* is incorporated in the contract for the sale of a business enterprise, in words such as "the seller agrees not to engage in the restaurant business in the City of Ames for a period of five years." Such an agreement obviously has value to the acquirer, and a reasonable portion of the acquisition price should be assigned to it in the contract. Although the value of a non-compete agreement is difficult to determine, the acquirer and seller should be able to agree on a fair price. The value assigned to goodwill does not include the value assigned to the non-compete agreement, because the latter represents an *identifiable* intangible asset. For example, if Bates Company, with identifiable net assets of $100,000 at current fair value, is acquired for $150,000, it appears that the acquirer paid $50,000 for goodwill. However, if the parties assign a value of $30,000 to a non-compete agreement for five years, the acquisition of Bates is recorded as follows:

A non-compete agreement may be amortized for income tax purposes

Net Assets	100,000	
Non-Compete Agreement	30,000	
Goodwill	20,000	
Cash		150,000

To record the acquisition of Bates Company, with non-compete agreement and goodwill valued separately.

The advantage of reducing the recorded amount of goodwill is that the non-compete agreement is amortized at the rate of $6,000 a year over its economic life of five years, and this amortization is a deductible expense for income tax purposes; amortization of goodwill is not a deductible expense in the computation of taxable income.

Controversy over Amortization of Goodwill

Whether goodwill arising out of the acquisition of a business enterprise should be amortized has been a controversial issue for many years. After the issuance of *APB Opinion No. 17,* "Intangible Assets," many business executives and accountants disagreed with the mandatory amortization of acquired goodwill.

It has been argued that goodwill has an indefinite economic life and, therefore, should not be amortized until there is evidence that it no longer exists. Supporters of this view maintain that as long as earnings are sufficient to indicate that goodwill is unimpaired, it is a permanent asset. To amortize goodwill in the absence of a decline in earnings, it is argued, would obliterate the superior earnings that supported the recording of the goodwill in the first place.

The argument against the amortization of acquired goodwill is particularly strong when earnings are at a level that indicates that goodwill continues to exist. It is doubtful that continuing goodwill stems solely from conditions existing at the time of acquisition. A more likely situation is that goodwill is maintained through the successful efforts of the new owners and management of the business enterprise to stay ahead of competition. It is unlikely that the exact amount of original goodwill that has dissipated will be replaced by internally developed goodwill. Retaining acquired goodwill intact in the accounting records would be an attempt to compensate for the accounting inconsistency of recording acquired goodwill and not recording internally developed goodwill. Expenditures for research and development and advertising necessary to maintain superior earning power are recorded as expenses. If acquired goodwill is amortized, there would be a duplication of expenses—the current expenditures incurred to build and maintain goodwill, and the periodic amortization of previously acquired goodwill.

The opposing view is that the amount paid for goodwill represents the acquisition of an unidentifiable intangible asset and superior earnings for a limited number of years. It is argued that goodwill does not last forever and that the realization of superior earnings is not income to the new owners but rather a recovery of capital. Amortization of acquired goodwill is supported on practical grounds, because the value of the goodwill is likely to become zero at some future date. Thus, the investment in goodwill should be accounted for in the same manner as other productive assets having a limited economic life. If expectations were realized, that is, if earnings continued unchanged for the period of years used to estimate and amortize acquired goodwill, the amortization will result in less-than-normal earnings on the investment of the new owners during the amortization period. This squares with reality, because the payment for superior earnings makes their ultimate emergence a *return of investment,* not income.

Both sides in this controversy agree that goodwill should be written down in the face of clear evidence that is overstated. If superior earnings are eroded by competition and other economic conditions, the disappearance of goodwill is recognized as a loss.

ACCOUNTING FOR RESEARCH AND DEVELOPMENT (R&D) COSTS

Many business enterprises spend large amounts of money on research aimed at the discovery and development of improved processes and products. Some research expenditures result in patentable discoveries and some produce nonpatentable benefits in the form of better production methods and techniques. However, significant amounts of research and development (R&D) costs produce no measurable benefits to future revenue.

Enterprise managements had almost complete discretion to defer or to expense R&D costs until 1970, when the Accounting Principles Board stated that "a company should record as expenses the costs to develop intangible assets which are not specifically identifiable."[10] However, this accounting principle was vague and did not prevent the accumulation of vast sums of R&D costs in the balance sheets of many enterprises. In some instances such costs could not be related to specific future revenue and were often written off in a "year of the big bath," because of deterioration in demand for the enterprises' products or for other economic reasons.

[10]*APB Opinion No. 17*, p. 334.

The AICPA recognized the need to develop sharper accounting standards for R&D costs, and in 1973 published *Accounting Research Study No. 14,* "Accounting for Research and Development Expenditures." *ARS No. 14* recommended, among other things, that costs incurred in continuing research programs should be recorded as expenses immediately, and that costs of any substantial development projects should be deferred and amortized over the future accounting periods that they are intended to benefit.[11] This study provided background material for the Financial Accounting Standards Board in the development of *FASB Statement No. 2,* "Accounting for Research and Development Costs," the current source of accounting standards for R&D costs.

Accounting for Research and Development Costs

FASB Statement No. 2 was issued in an effort to reduce the diversity of accounting practices and to establish standards of disclosure for R&D costs. The *Statement* specified the activities and costs that should be identified as R&D for financial accounting. The main conclusion of the *Statement* was that all R&D costs, other than fully reimbursable costs incurred for others under contract, *shall be recorded as expenses when incurred.*[12] R&D costs previously deferred were required to be written off as a *prior period adjustment.* When financial statements were presented for accounting periods preceding the write-off of R&D costs, the financial statements and summaries based on such statements were *restated retroactively to reflect the prior period adjustment.* The nature of the restatement and its effect on net income and earnings per share for each accounting period presented were disclosed in the period of change. The FASB also required disclosure of total R&D costs expensed in each accounting period for which an income statement is presented.

The Financial Accounting Standards Board defined *research* and *development* as follows: *Research* is aimed at discovery of new knowledge with the hope that such knowledge will be useful in developing new products (including services) or processes, or in bringing about improvements in existing products or processes. *Development* is the translation of research findings into a plan or design for new or improved products or processes; it includes the conceptual formulation, design, and testing of product alternatives, construction of prototypes, and operation of pilot plants; it does not include routine or periodic alterations to existing products and processes or market research and market testing activities. *Activities typically included* in R&D are listed below:[13]

1   Laboratory research aimed at discovery of new knowledge

2   Searching for applications of new research findings

3   Conceptual formulation and design of possible new products or processes

4   Testing in search for or evaluation of new products or processes

---

[11]Oscar S. Gellein and Maurice S. Newman, *Accounting Research Study No. 14,* "Accounting for Research and Development Expenditures," AICPA (New York: 1973), pp. 6–8.

[12]*FASB Statement No. 2,* "Accounting for Research and Development Costs," FASB (Stamford: 1974), p. 6.

[13]Ibid., p. 4.

5 Modification of the formulation or design of products or processes

6 Design, construction, and testing of preproduction prototypes and models

7 Design of tools, jigs, molds, and dies involving new technology

8 Design, construction, and operation of a pilot plant that is not of a scale economically feasible to the enterprise for commercial production

9 Engineering activity required to advance the design of a product to the point that it meets predetermined specifications and is ready for manufacture

Activities typically excluded from R&D are: (1) engineering follow-through, quality control, and troubleshooting during production; (2) routine efforts to improve products and adapt to changing customer needs; (3) routine design (or changes in design) of tools, jigs, molds, and dies; and (4) legal services in connection with patent applications or litigation to protect existing patents, and the sale or licensing of patents. Costs incurred in these activities generally are expensed, except legal costs incurred in connection with patent applications or litigation that are expected to benefit future revenue.

Costs that are classified as *R&D costs* for financial accounting are:[14]

1 Material consumed in R&D activities and depreciation and amortization of assets used in R&D activities. Material and assets acquired for an R&D project that have no alternative uses should be recognized as expenses as acquired.

2 Salaries, wages, and other related costs of personnel engaged in R&D activities.

3 Contract services performed by others in connection with R&D activities. Intangible assets acquired from others that have alternative future uses should be capitalized and amortized over a period of 40 years or less.

4 A reasonable allocation of indirect costs (general and administrative costs that are not clearly related to R&D activities should not be included with R&D costs).

The main provision of *FASB Statement No. 2,* that is, ''all research and development costs . . . shall be charged to expense when incurred,'' was a compromise solution to a difficult financial accounting problem. Those who opposed the deferral of R&D naturally were pleased with the position of the FASB. However, some accountants and corporate executives questioned the logic of immediate write-offs of R&D costs that have a high probability of contributing to future revenue.

Admittedly, there is a considerable degree of uncertainty as to the future benefits of individual R&D projects. ''Estimates of the rate of success of R&D projects vary markedly—depending in part on how narrowly one defines a 'project' and how one defines 'success'—but all such estimates indicate a high failure rate.''[15] Because a direct relationship between R&D costs and specific future revenue generally

---

[14]Ibid., pp. 5–6.
[15]Ibid., p. 15.

is difficult to establish, the recognition of such costs as expenses is a conservative application of the matching principle. For income tax purposes, all R&D costs may be expensed as incurred, and most business enterprises regularly expense such costs in their income tax returns. Thus, *FASB Statement No. 2* eliminated a major difference between financial accounting and income tax rules.

Deferred Charges

The term *deferred charges* frequently is used to describe long-term prepayments subject to amortization. For example, the costs of issuing bonds produce benefits by providing funds for use by a business enterprise; however, the funds provided contribute to revenue over the entire term of the bonds. Similarly, the cost of machinery rearrangements presumably results in a more efficient and valuable plant and, therefore, should be allocated to revenue over an appropriate number of years. Other examples of deferred charges include noncurrent prepaid income taxes, preoperating (or start-up) costs, and certain pension costs.

The use of the term *deferred charges* may be criticized, because all assets other than cash, receivables, investments, and land are forms of deferred charges to revenue. Most deferred charges may be classified either as plant assets (machinery rearrangement) or as intangible assets (oil exploration costs). If a deferrable cost is not classified under plant assets or intangible assets, it should be included under Other Noncurrent Assets in the balance sheet to avoid a separate category for deferred charges.

The deferral of an expenditure may be justified only if an asset with future service potential has resulted. If the future service potential of any cost incurred is obscure, it should be recognized as an expense.

Accounting for Development-Stage Enterprises

In the 1970s, a special category of deferred charges received considerable attention. Costs incurred by business enterprises in the development stage were designated as *preoperating* or *start-up costs*. Such costs generally were deferred and amortized over a relatively short period after the enterprise emerged from the development stage and started generating revenue. Preoperating costs that were applicable to abandoned projects and other costs that were not expected to contribute to revenue in future accounting periods were written off in the accounting period in which the loss of service potential became apparent.

Accounting practices for enterprises in the development stage varied considerably. Consequently, the FASB issued *Statement No. 7,* ''Accounting and Reporting by Development Stage Enterprises,'' which specified guidelines for identifying enterprises in the development stage and the standards of accounting and reporting applicable to such enterprises. An enterprise is considered to be in a development stage if it is devoting most of its efforts to establishing a new business and planned principal operations have not begun, or, if they have begun, no significant revenue has been realized. A development-stage enterprise typically devotes most of its efforts to financial planning, raising capital, exploring for and developing natural resources, research and development, establishing sources of supply, acquiring plant assets, and gearing up for production.[16] A summary of the accounting and disclosure requirements of *FASB Statement No. 7* follows:[17]

1   Financial statements issued by development-stage enterprises should present financial position, changes in financial position, and results of operations *in conformity with generally accepted accounting principles that apply to established operating enterprises.*

2   In issuing the same basic financial statements as an established operating enterprise, development-stage enterprises also should disclose the following information:

a   A balance sheet, including any cumulative net losses reported with a descriptive caption, such as ''deficit accumulated during the development stage,'' in the owners' equity section.

b   An income statement, showing amounts of revenue and expenses for each accounting period covered by the income statement and, in addition, cumulative amounts from the enterprise's inception.

c   A statement of cash flows, showing the sources and uses of financial resources for each accounting period for which an income statement is presented and, in addition, cumulative amounts from the enterprise's inception.

3   A statement of owners' equity, showing for a corporation, for example, for each issuance of securities from the enterprise's inception: (*a*) the date and number of shares of capital stock, stock warrants, or other securities issued for cash and for other consideration; (*b*) the dollar amounts assigned to the consideration received; and (*c*) the nature of the noncash consideration and the basis for assigning current fair values to the noncash consideration.

In addition, the financial statements must be identified as those of a development-stage enterprise and must include a description of the nature of the development-stage activities. The financial statements for the first fiscal year in which an enterprise no longer is considered to be in the development stage should disclose that in prior years *it had been in the development stage.*

Plant and Intangible Assets in the Balance Sheet

There is a noticeable trend in financial reporting toward including all noncurrent assets (other than investments) under a single major heading labeled ''plant assets,'' ''plant and equipment,'' or ''property, plant, and equipment.'' Tangible and intangible assets are reported separately, and plant assets held for sale are included under Other Noncurrent Assets. The methods of depreciation and amortization used, as well as the amounts of depreciation and amortization expense for the latest accounting period, should be disclosed.

In a recent survey of 600 public companies, 399 reported intangible assets being amortized and 123 reported intangible assets (presumably acquired before

[16]*FASB Statement No. 7*, ''Accounting and Reporting by Development Stage Enterprises,'' FASB (Stamford: 1975), pp. 3–4.
[17]Ibid., pp. 5–6.

October 31, 1970) not being amortized.[18] The most common types of intangible assets reported were goodwill (excess of cost over net assets acquired in business combinations), patents, trademarks, brand names, copyrights, licenses and contracts, and franchises. The following example illustrates the presentation of plant assets and intangible assets in the balance sheet:

Presentation of plant assets and intangible assets in the balance sheet

Plant assets:		
Land, at cost	$ 350,000	
Buildings (cost $1,640,000, less accumulated depreciation of $185,000)	1,455,000	
Equipment (cost $870,000, less accumulated depreciation of $150,000)	720,000	
Tools and patterns (at unamortized cost)	25,000	
Total plant assets (net)		$2,550,000
Intangible assets:		
Patents (amortized over 12 years)..................	$ 85,000	
Trademarks and trade names (amortized over 20 years)	100,000	
Organization costs (amortized over 40 years)	15,000	
Goodwill (amortized over 40 years)	180,000	
Total intangible assets (net)		380,000

Note: Depreciation and amortization expense amounted to $310,000 for the latest accounting period. The straight-line method is used to compute depreciation and amortization for both financial accounting and income tax purposes.

REVIEW QUESTIONS

1   Accountants use the term *intangible assets* in a more limited sense than the legal meaning of this term. Explain why this is so. What are two categories of intangible assets?

2   Why is the identification and measurement of the cost of intangible assets more difficult than it is for tangible assets? What are some similarities between tangible assets and intangible assets?

3   Lennox Corporation has just been organized. The costs of forming Lennox and issuing its common stock amounted to $85,000. One officer of Lennox suggests that this amount be charged immediately against the amount invested by stockholders in excess of the par value of common stock. Another officer suggests that the amount be amortized over a period of five years by direct charges to retained earnings. Evaluate these two proposals.

4   In the computation of the equity (book value) per share of common stock, security analysts generally disregard intangible assets. Evaluate this practice.

[18]*Accounting Trends & Techniques,* 38th ed., AICPA (New York: 1984), p. 158.

5 Roe Company applied for and received a patent on a manufacturing process. The legal fees and patent application fees totaled $10,000. Research costs leading to the patent were estimated at $60,000. Shortly after the patent was issued, Roe spent $25,000 in legal fees in a successful defense against a suit in which it was claimed that Roe's patent infringed a patent owned by a competitor.

a At what amount should the patent be recorded?

b What is the legal life of the patent?

c What factors should be considered in the determination of the patent's economic life?

6 What amortization policy should be followed for *copyrights, trademarks, secret formulas,* and *licenses and contracts?*

7 It has been argued, on the grounds of conservatism, that all intangible assets should be written off immediately on acquisition. Present arguments against this position.

8 What expenditures generally are included in *organization costs?*

9 What is meant by the term *goodwill?* What are the tests of the existence of goodwill? What is meant by the term *negative goodwill?* Is negative goodwill reported in the balance sheet?

10 In negotiations for the sale of a going business enterprise, an intangible factor called *goodwill* sometimes is estimated by capitalizing average superior earnings, that is, by dividing average superior earnings by an assumed earnings-rate factor. Explain how the average superior earnings are determined, and justify the capitalization of superior earnings in the estimation of the amount of goodwill.

11 What is the distinction between *capitalizing* estimated future earnings and *computing the present value* of estimated future earnings?

12 "If all individual assets and liabilities of a business enterprise are identified and valued properly, goodwill will not exist." Do you agree with this quotation?

13 Acquired goodwill usually is recorded and included in the balance sheet; internally developed goodwill is not. Explain the reason for this accounting practice.

14 List five procedures that may be followed to estimate the amount of goodwill of a business enterprise. May the market value of its outstanding common stock be used to estimate the amount of goodwill of a publicly owned corporation?

15 Lento Company has identifiable net assets with an estimated current fair value of $1 million. Lento has an indicated ability to earn $160,000 a year, and the normal earnings rate in its industry is 10%. Describe three methods that might be used to estimate the amount of goodwill of Lento Company.

16 What are two major provisions of *FASB Statement No. 2,* "Accounting for Research and Development Costs"?

17 Harlow Company conducts research on the development of new products, improvement of existing products, and improvement of its manufacturing process.

How should the costs incurred by Harlow in its research and development activities be recorded for financial accounting?

18 **a** Define *development-stage enterprises*.

   b Briefly summarize the accounting and disclosure requirements for development-stage enterprises, as required by *FASB Statement No. 7*, ''Accounting and Reporting by Development Stage Enterprises.''

EXERCISES

Ex. 13-1 Select the best answer for each of the following multiple-choice questions:

1 During the year ended April 30, Year 3, Keene Company incurred $176,000 in research and development costs for an invention that was patented on May 1, Year 3. Legal costs incurred for the patent were immaterial and were expensed during the year ended April 30, Year 4. The patent had a legal life of 17 years and an economic life of eight years on May 1, Year 3. On May 1, Year 7, Keene incurred legal fees of $16,000 in a successful defense of the patent. Keene's patent amortization expense for the year ended April 30, Year 8, is:

a $0   **b** $1,231   **c** $4,000   **d** $26,000   **e** Some other amount

2 Which of the following is not a consideration in the determination of economic life of an intangible asset?

a Legal, regulatory, or contractual provisions
b Provisions for renewal or extension
c Expected actions of competitors
d Cost of the intangible asset
e None of the foregoing

3 Goodwill represents the excess of the cost of an acquired business enterprise over the:

a Total of the current fair values of the enterprise's identifiable assets less its liabilities
b Total of the current fair values of the enterprise's tangible assets less its liabilities
c Total of the current fair values of the enterprise's intangible assets less its liabilities
d Carrying amount of the net assets of the enterprise

4 On May 1, Year 6, newly organized Nolan Corporation incurred organization costs of $240,000. Nolan decided to amortize the organization costs over the minimum period permitted by federal income tax laws. The unamortized balance of Nolan's Organization Costs ledger account on April 30, Year 7, is:

a $0   **b** $48,000   **c** $192,000   **d** $240,000   **e** Some other amount

5 Which of the following activities is excluded from the definition of research and development costs?

a Design of tools involving new technology
b Routine design of tools
c Construction of preproduction models
d Construction of a pilot plant not of a scale economically feasible for commercial production

6 Henkel Company acquired a franchise from Marx Corporation on January 2, Year 1, for $100,000. The franchise had a carrying amount of $15,000 in Marx's accounting records on January 2, Year 1. The economic life of the franchise was 50 years on the date of acquisition; it had no legal limitation on its life. Henkel decided to amortize the cost of the franchise over the maximum term possible. Henkel's franchise amortization expense for Year 1 is:

a $375   **b** $2,000   **c** $2,500   **d** $15,000   **e** Some other amount

7 In the negotiations for the acquisition of Fargo Company's net assets by Dover Company, it was agreed that the amount to be paid by Dover for Fargo's goodwill would be determined by capitalizing the $60,000 estimated future superior earnings of Fargo's identifiable net assets at a 10% normal rate of return. The carrying amount and current fair value of Fargo's identifiable net assets were $1,800,000 and $2,500,000, respectively. The amount that Dover will pay for Fargo's goodwill is:

a $180,000   **b** $240,000   **c** $600,000   **d** $700,000   **e** Some other amount

8 On July 1, Year 4, Todd Company acquired for $89,250 a patent with a remaining economic and legal life of 15 years, expiring on June 30, Year 19. During the year ended June 30, Year 8, Todd determined that the remaining economic life on July 1, Year 4, should have been 10 years rather than 15 years. Todd's patent amortization expense for the year ended June 30, Year 8, is:

a $5,250   **b** $8,925   **c** $10,200   **d** $17,850   **e** Some other amount

Ex. 13-2 On January 2, Year 5, Keko Company acquired for $192,000 a patent with a remaining legal life of 12 years and an estimated economic life of eight years. On January 2, Year 9, Keko paid legal fees of $12,000 in a successful defense of the patent.

Compute Keko Company's patent amortization expense for Year 9.

Ex. 13-3 On January 2, Year 2, Adam Corporation acquired a patent with a remaining legal life of 15 years and an estimated economic life of eight years. The cost of the patent was $124,000. On January 2, Year 6, Adam paid $48,000 to Ted Dale, who had claimed in a Year 5 lawsuit that the patent acquired in Year 2 infringed on one of his inventions.

Prepare journal entries for Adam Corporation to record the acquisition of the patent, the payment on the patent infringement judgment, and the amortization for Year 6. Amortization is recorded as a credit in the Patents ledger account.

Ex. 13-4 On January 2, Year 1, Loy Company acquired for $85,000 a patent for a new consumer product. At the time of acquisition, the legal life of the patent was 17 years. Because of the competitive nature of the product, the patent was estimated to have an economic life of five years. On January 5, Year 4, the product was removed from the market under governmental order because of a potential health hazard present in the product.

Compute the amount that Loy Company should recognize as a loss in Year 4, assuming amortization is recorded at the end of each year.

Ex. 13-5   On January 2, Year 1, Carlo Company sold to Dow Company a patent that had a carrying amount of $23,000 in Carlo's accounting records. Dow gave Carlo an $80,000 noninterest-bearing note payable in five equal annual installments of $16,000, with the first payment due and paid on January 2, Year 2. There was no established market price for the patent, and the note payable had no ready market. The prevailing rate of interest for a note of this type on January 2, Year 1, was 12%. Information on present value and future amount factors is shown below:

	Periods				
	1	2	3	4	5
Present value of 1 at 12%.........	0.893	0.797	0.712	0.636	0.567
Present value of an ordinary annuity of 1 at 12%....................	0.893	1.690	2.402	3.037	3.605
Future amount of 1 at 12%........	1.120	1.254	1.405	1.574	1.762
Future amount of an ordinary annuity of 1 at 12%....................	1.000	2.120	3.374	4.779	6.353

Compute the income or loss before income taxes (rounded to the nearest dollar) of Carlo Company for the years ended December 31, Year 1, and Year 2, as a result of the foregoing information.

Ex. 13-6   On May 1, Year 7, Willard Music Company acquired from a composer for $80,000 the copyright for a popular song written by the composer. For the year ended April 30, Year 8, Willard amortized the copyright over the maximum economic life permitted by generally accepted accounting principles. On May 1, Year 8, Willard concluded that the economic life of the copyright would not exceed five more years because of an unexpected decline in popularity of the composer's works.

Prepare journal entries for Willard Music Company for the acquisition of the copyright on May 1, Year 7, and for amortization of the copyright for the years ended April 30, Year 8 and Year 9.

Ex. 13-7   The Organization Costs ledger account for Vista Company appeared as follows on April 30, Year 4, the date Vista began operations:

Organization Costs

Date	Explanation	Debit	Credit	Balance
Year 4				
Mar. 1	Fees paid to promoters	10,000		10,000 dr
4	Fees paid to attorneys for drafting corporate charter and bylaws	5,000		15,000 dr
5	Incorporation fee paid to State of California	500		15,500 dr
31	Discount on $100,000 bond issued at 99	1,000		16,500 dr
31	Bond issue costs paid	1,500		18,000 dr
Apr. 15	Payment of costs incurred in issuing 10,000 shares of $1 par common stock at $15 a share	2,500		20,500 dr

Prepare a single correcting journal entry for Vista Company's Organization Costs ledger account on April 30, Year 4. Disregard amortization.

Ex. 13-8 The income before income taxes of Leslie Company for Year 1 was $330,000, and included the following:

Extraordinary gains	$80,000
Extraordinary losses	35,000
Profit-sharing payments to employees	25,000
Amortization of goodwill	15,000
Amortization of identifiable intangible assets	17,500
Depreciation of building (straight-line method)	44,000

The building is worth three times as much as carrying amount, and the remaining economic life will be increased by 100% by the new owner of Leslie. The new owner will continue the profit-sharing payments to employees. These payments are based on income before depreciation and amortization.

Compute the normal earnings of Leslie Company for Year 1 for purposes of measuring the possible existence of superior earnings and goodwill.

Ex. 13-9 On April 1, Year 10, Oliver Corporation acquired the assets and assumed the liabilities of Wong Company, a single proprietorship, for $400,000 cash. The condensed balance sheet of Wong Company on the date of acquisition is shown below:

WONG COMPANY
Condensed Balance Sheet
April 1, Year 10

Assets	$480,000	Liabilities		$150,000
		James Wong, capital		330,000
Total assets	$480,000	Total liabilities & capital		$480,000

Oliver valued the tangible and identifiable assets of Wong Company at $515,000, and restated the liabilities at $162,500. Included in the acquisition contract was a provision that James Wong could not operate a competing business enterprise for three years; the acquisition price of $400,000 included $25,000 for the non-compete agreement.

Prepare a journal entry to record the acquisition of Wong Company on April 1, Year 10, in the accounting records of Oliver Corporation.

Ex. 13-10 Net income and stockholders' equity of Nell's Restaurant for a three-year period are shown below:

Year	Net income	Stockholders' equity at end of year
1	$62,000	$180,000
2	75,000	230,000
3	91,000	220,000

At the end of Year 3, James Lu acquired Nell's Restaurant on the following basis:

(1) 20% is considered a normal return on restaurant investments.
(2) Payment for goodwill is to be determined by capitalizing at 40% the average annual net income that is in excess of 20% of average stockholders' equity for the past three years.
(3) Net assets, which do not include any goodwill, will be recorded by Lu at the carrying amounts reported by Nell's Restaurant.

Prepare a journal entry in the accounting records of James Lu to record the acquisitions of Nell's Restaurant at the end of Year 3.

Ex. 13-11 Western Company is planning to acquire Eastern Company. The past earnings of Eastern have averaged $40,000 a year. It is estimated that Eastern's earnings will be 20% larger in the future. Normal earnings for Eastern are $19,000 a year.

Compute the amount that Western Company should pay for Eastern Company's goodwill, assuming that:
a Goodwill is equal to the total of superior earnings for five years.
b Goodwill is estimated by capitalization of superior earnings at 25%.

Ex. 13-12 San Company acquired the net assets of Paulo Company for $100,000. In acquiring the net assets, the owners of San determined that Paulo had unrecorded goodwill. They decided to capitalize the estimated annual superior earnings of Paulo at 20% to determine the amount of goodwill. This computation resulted in an estimate of goodwill at $20,000. A rate of 10% on net assets before recognition of goodwill was used to determine normal annual earnings of Paulo because it was the rate that is earned on net assets in the industry in which Paulo operates. All other assets of Paulo were recorded properly.

Compute the estimated annual earnings of Paulo Company.

Ex. 13-13 Nimoy Corporation incurred research and development (R&D) costs in Year 10 as follows:

Material used in R&D projects...	$160,000
Equipment acquired that will be used in future R&D projects............	800,000
Depreciation for Year 10 on foregoing equipment	200,000
Labor costs of employees involved in R&D projects	400,000
Consulting fees paid to outsiders for R&D projects	50,000
Indirect costs reasonably allocable to R&D projects	80,000
Fully reimbursable R&D costs	77,200

Compute the amount of R&D costs that should be reported as research and development expense in the income statement of Nimoy Corporation for Year 10.

Ex. 13-14 From the following amounts, prepare the intangible assets section of Earley Company's balance sheet:

Deposits with advertising agency that will be used to promote sales	$ 4,500
Organization costs	25,000

Discount on bonds payable	$15,500
Excess of cost over net assets of acquired enterprise	40,000
Patents.	24,400
Franchise to operate in state of Illinois	10,000
Marketing costs of introducing new products	15,000
Research and development costs expected to benefit future accounting periods.	42,000

CASES

Case 13-1 On June 30, Year 1, your client, Hight Corporation, was granted two patents covering plastic cartons that it had been producing and marketing profitably for the past three years. One patent covered the manufacturing process, and the other covered the related products.

Executives of Hight informed you that the patents represent the most significant breakthrough in the industry in the past 30 years. The products had been marketed under the following registered trademarks: Safetainer, Duratainer, and Sealrite. Licenses under the patents already had been granted by Hight to other manufacturers in the United States and abroad and were producing substantial royalties.

On July 1, Year 2, Hight commenced patent infringement suits against several companies whose names you recognize as those of substantial and prominent competitors. Management of Hight is optimistic that these suits will result in a permanent injunction against the manufacture and sale of the infringing products, and in the collection of damages for lost profits caused by the alleged infringements.

The financial vice president of Hight has suggested that the patents be recorded at the discounted value of expected net royalty receipts.

Instructions

a Explain the meaning of *intangible assets* and *discounted value of expected net royalty receipts.* How is discounted value of royalty receipts computed?

b What basis of valuation for Hight Corporation's patents is in accordance with generally accepted accounting principles? Give supporting reasons for this basis.

c Assuming no problems of implementation and disregarding generally accepted accounting principles, what is the preferable basis of valuation and amortization for patents?

d What disclosure, if any, should be made regarding the infringement suits in a note to the financial statements of Hight for the year ended September 30, Year 2?

Case 13-2 Litchy Corporation, a retail fuel distributor, has increased its annual sales volume to a level three times the annual sales of the dealership that it acquired in Year 1 to begin operations.

In Year 6, the board of directors of Litchy received an offer to negotiate the sale of Litchy. The majority of the board want to increase the carrying amount of goodwill in the balance sheet to reflect the larger sales volume developed through intensive promotion and the favorable market price of fuel. However, some board members prefer to eliminate goodwill from the balance sheet "to prevent possible misinterpretations.'' Goodwill had been recorded in Year 1 in conformity with generally accepted accounting principles.

Instructions

a Define *goodwill* and list the techniques used to estimate its value in negotiations to acquire a business enterprise. To what extent does the value of goodwill depend on sales volume?

b Why are the carrying amount and current fair value for goodwill of Litchy Corporation different?

c Discuss the propriety of increasing or eliminating the carrying amount of goodwill prior to negotiations for the sale of a business enterprise.

Case 13-3 Some years ago the annual report of Canfield Communications Corporation (CCC) included the following message to stockholders:

> Because amortization of intangible assets as required by *APB Opinion No. 17,* ''Intangible Assets,'' is significant to CCC's earnings and because management of CCC does not agree with the amortization requirement of *APB Opinion No. 17,* we hereby make our views known in the hopes you will then be in a better position to analyze our financial statements and the performance of CCC.
>
> Intangible assets represent the difference between the total amount paid in a purchase-type business combination and the fair market value of the tangible assets acquired (also commonly referred to as goodwill). In the broadcasting industry, the amount paid for intangible assets includes the station's Federal Communications Commission broadcast license, its network affiliation contract, an established audience, established program format, and established advertising clients. In the newspaper industry, the amount paid for intangible assets includes the paper's established circulation lists, editorial reference library, established news development resources, community loyalty developed through editorial policies and support of local activities, and established advertising clients. The Accounting Principles Board, in issuing *APB Opinion No. 17* requiring the amortization of intangible assets acquired after October 31, 1970, apparently made the assumption that goodwill gradually loses its value over a period of years and established an arbitrary maximum economic life of 40 years.
>
> Management is in absolute disagreement with the required amortization of the intangible assets related to broadcast stations and newspapers where the intangibles are clearly marketable assets that retain their value and, in many instances, increase in value over the years. We believe there is a sufficient number of business combinations each year in the broadcast and newspaper fields to demonstrate this fact. We simply do not accept a conclusion that one rule for the amortization of intangible assets fits all business enterprises.
>
> It is management's opinion that intangible assets should not be expensed (in whole or in part) until it becomes apparent that there has been or will be a measurable diminution in their value. Should it become apparent in years subsequent to the acquisition that a downward adjustment is necessary, it should

be the responsibility of management to determine the amount of the adjustment and the accounting period or periods to which such adjustment should be applied. Such a determination should, of course, be subject to the approval of the independent public accountants.

Instructions

Do you agree with the management of Canfield Communications Corporation? Explain your position.

Case 13-4 Niles Company was in the process of developing Novo, a revolutionary new product. A new division of Niles was formed to develop, manufacture, and market Novo. As of December 31, Year 7, Novo had not been manufactured for resale; however, a prototype unit of Novo had been built and was in operation.

Throughout Year 7 the new division incurred certain costs. These costs included design and engineering studies, prototype manufacturing costs, administrative costs (including salaries of administrative personnel), and market research costs. In addition, approximately $500,000 in equipment (estimated economic life of 10 years) was acquired for use in developing and manufacturing Novo. Approximately $200,000 of this equipment was built specifically for the design development of Novo. The remaining $300,000 of equipment was used to manufacture the preproduction prototype, and will be used to manufacture Novo once it is in commercial production.

Instructions

a What are the definitions of *research* and of *development* according to *FASB Statement No. 2,* ''Accounting for Research and Development Costs''?

b Briefly indicate the practical and conceptual reasons for the conclusion reached by the Financial Accounting Standards Board on accounting and reporting practices for research and development costs.

c In accordance with *FASB Statement No. 2,* how are the various costs of Niles Company described above reported in the financial statements for the year ended December 31, Year 7?

PROBLEMS

13-1 Lambert Company began operations on January 2, Year 1. On December 31, Year 1, its accounting records included the asset ledger account reproduced on page 684. (Lambert posts journal entries at month-end only.)

Instructions

a Prepare a working paper to allocate the items in Lambert Company's Research and Development ledger account on December 31, Year 1, to the correct ledger accounts. Use the following columnar headings:

Date
Description
Amount

Research and Development

Date	Explanation	Debit	Credit	Balance
Year 1				
Jan. 31	Material, salaries, and indirect costs related to general R&D activities	14,000		14,000 dr
Feb. 28	Engineering salaries and indirect costs related to production troubleshooting	3,500		17,500 dr
Mar. 31	Material, salaries, and indirect costs incurred for customer Raymond Company	6,300		23,800 dr
Apr. 30	Fee of Leslie Engineering Company regarding general R&D activities	1,700		25,500 dr
June 30	Fee from Raymond Company		8,400	17,100 dr
July 31	Engineering salaries and indirect costs related to routine tool design	2,400		19,500 dr
Aug. 31	Legal fee for patent acquired on product developed through general R&D activities	3,600		23,100 dr
Dec. 31	Allocation of Year 1 salaries of officers, none of whom was engaged in R&D (credit was to Officers' Salaries Expense ledger account)	14,400		37,500 dr

Research and Development Expense
Engineering Expense
Research and Development Fee Revenue (net)
Tooling Expense
Patents
Officers' Salaries Expense

b Prepare a single journal entry to correct Lambert Company's accounting records on December 31, Year 1. The patent acquired on August 31, Year 1, had an estimated economic life of six years.

13-2 Stratton Company has provided information on intangible assets as follows:

(1) A patent was acquired from Cobb Company for $1,500,000 on January 2, Year 7. Stratton estimated the remaining economic life of the patent to be 10 years. The patent was carried in the accounting records of Cobb at $1,250,000 when it was sold to Stratton. On January 3, Year 8, Stratton management, based on developments in the industry, estimated that the remaining economic life of the patent acquired on January 2, Year 7, was only six years from January 1, Year 8.

(2) In Year 8, a franchise was acquired from Wok Company for $600,000. In addition, 3% of revenue from the franchise must be paid to Wok as a royalty. Revenue from the franchise for Year 8 was $2,000,000. Stratton's management estimated the economic life of the franchise to be eight years, and decided to take a full year's amortization in the year of acquisition.

(3) Stratton incurred research and development costs in Year 8 as follows:

Material	$ 80,000
Salaries and wages	140,000
Indirect costs	160,000
Total research and development costs	$380,000

Stratton's management estimated that these costs would be recouped by December 31, Year 11.

Instructions

Prepare a working paper for the computation of the amount of (1) intangible assets to be included in Stratton Company's balance sheet on December 31, Year 8, and (2) all expenses related to research and development and intangible assets to be included in Stratton's income statement for the year ended December 31, Year 8. Assume that amortization is recorded as a credit to each intangible asset ledger account.

13-3 The following information was obtained from the accounting records of Logan Company and Cabot, Inc., on January 2, Year 6, in connection with the proposed merger of the two companies:

	Logan Company	Cabot, Inc.
Assets other than goodwill	$2,625,000	$1,593,000
Liabilities	975,000	720,000
Average income before income taxes for Year 1 through Year 5	408,000	281,400

The current fair values of assets, including goodwill, are to be determined as follows: 20% is considered a reasonable pre-tax return on net assets, excluding goodwill; average pre-tax income for Years 1 through 5 in excess of 20% on such net assets on January 2, Year 6, is to be capitalized at 25% to determine goodwill. The following adjustments to average pre-tax income are required before determination of the going-concern value of each company:

(1) Equipment of Logan has a current fair value that is $150,000 in excess of its carrying amount; the equipment has a remaining economic life of 10 years.

(2) At the beginning of Year 1, Cabot debited the cost of a franchise to expense. The franchise cost $54,000 and had an estimated economic life of 10 years. The current fair value of the franchise on January 2, Year 6, was $27,000.

(3) Included in the net income of Cabot for Years 1 through 5 are extraordinary gains of $46,500 and extraordinary losses of $99,000.

Instructions

Prepare a working paper showing for both Logan Company and Cabot, Inc., the valuation of:

a Net assets other than goodwill

b Goodwill

c The company as a whole

13-4 Clovis Corporation performs subcontracting work for several major aircraft manufacturers. On January 2, Year 3, Clovis acquired from Researchers, Inc., a patent for a new type of navigational instrument. The economic life of the patent was equal to its legal life, which expires on January 2, Year 18. Clovis planned to incorporate the technology covered by the patent in one of its major projects after addition of several new features to the patent.

In January, Year 4, while auditing the financial statements of Clovis Corporation for Year 3, you reviewed the ledger account below that summarizes costs incurred in the development of the new and improved patent for the navigational instrument.

Navigational Instrument Project

Date	Explanation	Debit	Credit	Balance
Year 3				
Jan. 2	Cost of patent acquired from Researchers, Inc.	60,000		60,000 dr
30	Legal costs incurred in connection with acquisition of patent from Researchers, Inc.	4,000		64,000 dr
June 30	Costs of improving patent:			
	Blueprints for improvements	300		64,300 dr
	Assembly and testing of proto- types and models	25,400		89,700 dr
	Other R&D costs incurred	19,300		109,000 dr
July 5	Cost of settlement of a threatened infringement suit on patent ac- quired from Researchers, Inc.	5,000		114,000 dr
Dec. 31	Proceeds on sale of R&D data de- veloped in Year 3 (at related cost)		7,500	106,500 dr
31	Royalty received on license granted to competitor to use a design for a navigational instrument		13,100	93,400 dr

The improved patent was ready for use on July 1, Year 3, but the new navigational instrument was not sold to aircraft manufacturers until Year 4.

Instructions

a Prepare a working paper to summarize the costs that should be included in Clovis Corporation's Patents ledger account in accordance with generally accepted accounting principles.

b Prepare a single journal entry to eliminate Clovis Corporation's Navigational Instrument Project ledger account and to record the items in this account in conformity with generally accepted accounting principles. Assume that the nominal (revenue and expense) ledger accounts have not been closed for Year 3.

c Prepare a journal entry for Clovis Corporation, if required, to record the amortization of the patent for Year 3. If no entry is required, explain why.

13-5 Telecom Company operates two television stations. On August 31, Year 10, Telecom contracted with a film distributor for a series of films. The contract gave Telecom an option to telecast the films as follows:

40 initial weekly telecasts starting on September 1, Year 10
12 reruns of the best films during the summer of Year 11
50 more reruns from September of Year 11 to August of Year 12

Telecom plans to telecast the original series during prime viewing hours, the summer reruns as a late show, and second-year reruns as a late-late show. The expected revenue from advertisers on both stations is estimated by Telecast management as follows:

Revenue from original 40 weeks	$420,000
Revenue from 12 summer reruns	108,000
Revenue from 50 second-year reruns (late-late shows)	72,000

The cost of the film rental rights is $240,000, which Telecom will pay in installments over a two-year period at the rate of $18,000 a month during the first year (starting on September 30, Year 10) and $3,745 a month during the second year. These payments include interest at 1% a month on the carrying amount of the outstanding liability.

Instructions

a Prepare a journal entry for Telecom Company to record the film rental contract on August 31, Year 10, assuming that Telecom elects to make payments on the installment basis. Use a Discount on Contract Payable ledger account.

b Prepare a working paper for Telecom Company showing amortization of cost of the film rental rights for each telecast over the two-year period.

c Prepare journal entries for Telecom Company to record:
  (1) The first payment on the contract on September 30, Year 10
  (2) Amortization of the cost of the film rental rights for the year ended December 31, Year 10 (after 17 telecasts have been run)

d If Telecom Company decided in August, Year 11, not to rerun the films during the second year, what journal entry should be made at that time to write off the unamortized film rental rights?

13-6 Linager Company is being audited at the end of Year 1, its first year of operations. The accountant for Linager recorded numerous transactions in the Intangible Assets ledger account. You have been assigned to audit this account, which included the following entries for Year 1:

Debit entries in Intangible Assets ledger account:

Jan.	2 Incorporation fees	$ 6,500
	2 Cost of common stock certificates (engraving, etc.)..........	2,100
	10 Legal fees in connection with organization of company	15,000
Mar.	1 Costs of advertising campaign during Year 1	20,000
July	1 Operating loss for first six months of Year 1................	22,200
	7 R&D costs on abandoned projects........................	45,000
Aug.	1 Goodwill recorded by credit to Retained Earnings ledger account based on estimate of future earnings..............	50,000
Sept.	25 R&D costs of computer program for payroll system..........	8,000
Oct.	10 General R&D costs.......................................	40,400
Nov.	1 Acquisition of patent (remaining economic life of five years from Nov. 1, Year 1)	25,200
Dec.	30 Bonus to design supervisor for "creative contribution to the product lines for Year 1"...........................	4,800
	Total debits...	$239,200

Credit entries in Intangible Assets ledger account:

Jan.	15 Proceeds on issuance of common stock in excess of par	$80,500	
Oct.	1 Proceeds from sale of potentially patentable design of new product. The costs of developing this design were debited to R&D expense in Year 1 and exceeded $15,000	6,000	86,500
Dec.	31 Balance		$152,700

Instructions

a Prepare journal entries to correct Linager Company's ledger accounts, assuming that the nominal (revenue and expense) accounts have not been closed for Year 1. Any amount allocated to organization costs is amortized over five years.

b Prepare the intangible assets section of Linager Company's balance sheet on December 31, Year 1.

13-7 Petrol Corporation is considering the acquisition of Texas Drillers, Inc., on March 31, Year 4. Relevant data for Texas Drillers, Inc., follow:

Net assets (stockholders' equity)....................................	$ 749,000
Total assets...	1,200,000
Pre-tax earnings for three most recent fiscal years ($141,000 + $140,000 + $115,000)...............................	396,000
Cash dividends paid during three most recent years.................	135,000

Texas Drillers has a valuable patent that is fully amortized and will be transferred to Petrol at a valuation of $126,000. Other assets of Texas Drillers have a current fair value equal to carrying amount. The estimated remaining economic life of the patent is five years. The earnings of Texas Drillers during the next four fiscal years are expected to average 20% more than the average earnings of the past three fiscal years (before patent amortization).

Instructions

Estimate the amount of goodwill of Texas Drillers, Inc., under each of the following independent assumptions:

a Average estimated future pre-tax earnings are capitalized at 15% to compute the total value of net assets of Texas Drillers, Inc.

b Pre-tax earnings at the rate of 14%, based on identifiable net assets at current fair value, are considered normal for Texas Drillers, Inc.'s type of business. Goodwill is estimated to be equal to average superior earnings capitalized at 20%.

c Normal pre-tax earnings rate on identifiable net assets at current fair value is considered to be 12½%, and goodwill is estimated at an amount equal to esti⁎ mated superior earnings for three years.

d Pre-tax earnings of $120,700 are considered normal. Goodwill is estimated to be equal to the present value of average superior earnings (before income taxes) for four years, discounted at 20%. The present value of an ordinary annuity of four rents of 1 at 20% is 2.5887.

13-8 Ludwig Company, a closely owned business enterprise, has not issued financial statements since it was incorporated in Year 1. You have been engaged to audit the financial statements of Ludwig for the year ended December 31, Year 15. Management of Ludwig plans to present financial statements to an investment banker in conjunction with a preliminary discussion of the possibility of issuing common stock to the public. Management desires to report the maximum net income for Year 15 under generally accepted accounting principles.

This problem relates solely to your audit of the Intangible Assets ledger account summarized below:

Debit entries in Intangible Assets ledger account:

2/1/1	Organization costs	$ 18,000
12/31/1	Goodwill acquired in business combination	40,000
12/31/1	Net loss incurred in development stage	55,500
7/1/5	Patent (estimated remaining economic life 15 years)	25,200
12/31/9	Goodwill acquired in business combination	66,000
12/31/10	Non-compete agreement covering six-year period	12,000
12/31/11	Research and development costs resulting in new and improved products and processes	32,500
12/31/12	Financing costs related to five-year loan of $2 million from Local Insurance Company, arranged on 12/31/12	33,000
12/31/14	Research and development costs—new products	45,000
12/31/15	Research and development costs—new processes	85,000
12/31/15	Balance	$412,200

No credit entries have been made in the Intangible Assets ledger account since Ludwig was organized, and no amortization has been recorded for any of the items included in the account. You ascertain that the dollar amounts for all debits to the Intangible Assets ledger account were determined correctly. Management agreed with your suggestion that the organization costs should have been amortized over a five-year period, and that there has been no decline in the economic value of any goodwill acquired.

Instructions

(Disregard income tax considerations.)

a Observing management's desire to report the maximum net income for Year 15 in conformity with generally accepted accounting principles, prepare a working paper analysis of Ludwig Company's Intangible Assets ledger account. Any unamortized balance of an intangible asset as of December 31, Year 15, should be recorded in a separate ledger account. Use the following format (disposition of organization costs is given as an example):

Description of item	Amount recorded in Intangible Assets ledger account	Prior period adjustment (debit)	Expense (or factory overhead) for Year 15	Other ledger accounts debited	
				Amounts	Accounts
Organization costs— should have been fully amortized prior to Year 15	$ 18,000	$ 18,000			

b Prepare a single journal entry for Ludwig Company to eliminate the Intangible Assets ledger account and to correct the accounting records on December 31, Year 15. The accounting records have not been closed for Year 15.

13-9 Lon Webb is investigating the possibility of acquiring Peg's Place, a single proprietorship owned by Peggy Price. The condensed balance sheet of Peg's Place on December 31, Year 5, follows:

PEG'S PLACE
Condensed Balance Sheet
December 31, Year 5

Assets		Liabilities & Proprietor's Capital	
Current assets	$191,500	Current liabilities	$160,000
Land	115,000	12% mortgage note	
Buildings	540,000	payable	400,000
Less: Accumulated depre-		Total liabilities	$560,000
ciation	(50,000)		
Equipment	186,000		
Less: Accumulated depre-			
ciation	(42,500)	Peggy Price, capital	380,000
		Total liabilities & proprie-	
Total assets	$940,000	tor's capital	$940,000

Webb examined the foregoing balance sheet and determined that all assets were fairly stated, except that land was worth at least $195,000. An independent public accountant had examined the income statements of Peg's Place for each of the five years ended December 31, Year 5, and reported that income, before interest on the mortgage note payable and income taxes, amounted to $100,000 for Year 5. The average unpaid balance of the mortgage note payable during the next four years will be $370,000. Because of an expected increase in sales volume, the income before interest and income taxes for each of the next four years is expected to increase at a compound rate of 10% a year. The present facilities of Peg's Place are sufficient to handle the expected increase in volume. Price is asking $525,000 cash for Peg's Place. Webb considers 15% a normal rate of return (before income taxes) for a business enterprise of this type.

Instructions

a Prepare an estimate of the goodwill of Peg's Place on December 31, Year 5, under each of the following methods. Round estimates of expected average income before income taxes and goodwill to the ***nearest hundred dollars.***

    (1) Capitalization of the average expected superior income before income taxes over the next four years at 15%.

    (2) Acquisition of expected superior income before income taxes for the next four years.

    (3) Present value of average superior income before income taxes expected to be realized at the end of each of the next four years, discounted at 15%. (The present value of an ordinary annuity of four rents of 1 at 15% a year is 2.855.)

    (4) Capitalization of the first $5,000 of expected average superior income before income taxes at $12\frac{1}{2}$%, the next $5,000 at 20%, and the remainder at 25%.

b Should Lon Webb pay the amount Peggy Price is asking? Explain.

c Assume that Lon Webb's investigation indicates that Peg's Place will earn an average income before income taxes of $72,000 a year for an indefinite period. What maximum amount should Webb be willing to pay for Peg's Place? Prepare a journal entry to record the acquisition in Lon Webb's accounting records (assume a single proprietorship), under the assumption that Webb acquired Peg's Place for the maximum price you computed.

Long-Term Investments

14

In Chapter 6 we discuss short-term investments, such as investments in shares of International Business Machines Corporation common stock or in Exxon Corporation bonds. Such investments may be converted quickly to cash and are classified as current assets. Many business enterprises (termed *investors*) also make long-term investments in corporate securities (stocks, bonds, mortgage notes, long-term receivables, etc.) to create close business ties with other companies (termed *investees*). These long-term investments are not current assets because they do not represent resources available to meet working capital needs.

The basis of distinction between short-term investments and long-term investments lies in the nature and purpose of the investment. Investments that are readily marketable and that may be sold without disrupting business relationships or impairing the operations of the business enterprise are classified as current assets. Investments made to foster business relationships with other enterprises are classified as long-term investments. Also, investments that do not meet the test of ready marketability are considered long-term, even if these investments do not promote business relationships. Long-term investments are listed immediately below the current assets section of the balance sheet.

Objectives of Long-Term Investments

A business enterprise may make long-term investments in the securities of other corporations for many reasons. For example, these investments may be used to create close ties to major suppliers or to retail outlets. The rights of ownership inherent in common stock investments give an investor in such securities a degree of influence or control over the management of the investee. Thus, many enterprises use investments in common stock as a means of gaining control of a competitor, acquiring ownership of a company with a strong cash position, or diversifying by acquiring an ownership interest in investees in order to obtain dividend revenue and capital appreciation.

Consolidated Financial Statements

A company that acquires a controlling interest in the common stock of another company is termed the *parent company,* and the controlled company is the

693

subsidiary. The investment in the common stock of the subsidiary is a long-term investment for the parent company. In addition to the separate financial statements prepared for the parent company and for the subsidiary, *consolidated financial statements* also are prepared. Consolidated financial statements disregard the legal fact that each enterprise is a separate legal entity and treat the parent company and its subsidiaries as a single economic entity.

Viewing both parent company and subsidiary as a single economic entity is an alternative to treating the subsidiary as an investment owned by the parent company. The circumstances in which consolidated financial statements are appropriate and the manner in which they are prepared are discussed fully in *Modern Advanced Accounting* of this series.

Acquisition Cost

The cost of an investment in securities includes the acquisition price plus brokerage fees and any other expenditures incurred in the transaction. If assets other than cash are given in payment for the securities and the current fair value of such noncash assets is unknown, the current market price of the securities may be used to establish the cost of the securities acquired and the value of the noncash assets given in exchange. When neither a market price for the securities nor the current fair value of the assets given in exchange is known, accountants must rely on independent appraisals to establish values for recording the transaction.

If two or more securities are acquired for a lump sum, the total cost should be allocated among the various securities. If the various securities acquired are publicly traded, the existing market prices serve as the basis for apportionment of the total cost. This type of cost apportionment is termed *relative market value allocation.*

For example, assume that X Company acquires from Y Company 100 units of five shares of common stock and one share of preferred stock each, at a price of $240 a unit, when the common stock is trading at $30 and the preferred stock at $100 a share. The portion of the cost allocated to the common stock is $24,000 × 150/250, or $14,400, and the portion allocated to the preferred stock is $24,000 × 100/250, or $9,600. If only one class of the stock is publicly traded, that class usually is recorded at its market value, and the remaining portion of the cost is considered the cost of the other class. When neither class of stock trades in the open market, the apportionment of the cost may have to be delayed until current fair values or market values of the securities are established.

ACCOUNTING FOR LONG-TERM INVESTMENTS IN COMMON STOCK

Measuring Return on Investment

What is the "return" on an investment in common stock? One point of view is that the investor's return consists of the stream of dividends received from the investment. A second point of view is that the investor's return consists of a proportionate share of the net income (minus preferred dividends, if any) of the investee, without regard to whether this income is distributed in the form of dividends during the accounting period. Supporting the latter point of view is the fact that the earnings of the investee that are not distributed as dividends are retained by the investee, with a resultant increase in the investee's stockholders' equity. A third interpretation of the investor's return consists of the dividends received plus (or minus) the change in the market value of the investment.

Three different accounting methods exist, depending on which return an investor wishes to measure. These methods are:

1   *Cost method.* Investment income consists only of dividends received.

2   *Equity method.* Investment income consists of the investor's proportionate share of the investee's net income.

3   *Market value method.* Investment income includes dividends received and changes in the market value of the investment.

The market value method (as an alternative to the cost method) is illustrated for short-term investments in Chapter 6. However, the market value method is much less appropriate for long-term investments. By definition, long-term investments are not held to take advantage of short-term fluctuations in market prices. When an investor intends to hold investments in securities for long periods of time, the daily changes in market price lose significance. Therefore, either the cost method or the equity method generally is used to account for long-term investments in common stock.

Accounting for Dividends Received

The payment of dividends on capital stock (both preferred and common) is a discretionary act, requiring that the board of directors first declares the dividend. For this reason, investors should not accrue dividend revenue over a period of time as they do interest revenue on a bond. There are three acceptable alternatives for the recognition of dividend revenue under the cost method of accounting: (1) when the dividend is declared (***declaration date***), (2) when the dividend "accrues" to the current stockholder even if the stock is subsequently sold (***ex-dividend date***), or (3) when the dividend is received (***payment date***). Most investors record dividend revenue on the date of receipt. For purpose of consistency, all illustrations in this chapter recognize dividend revenue on the date the dividend is received.

Not all dividends received represent revenue to the investor. Sometimes corporations may pay dividends in excess of net income. In such cases the amount by which the cash distribution ***exceeds total earnings to date*** is considered a ***return of capital,*** termed a ***liquidating dividend,*** rather than dividend revenue.

Some accountants have suggested that, from the viewpoint of any stockholder, a liquidating dividend may be deemed to have occurred if dividends received exceed total net income of the investee after the date the investment was acquired. Practical application of such a concept may be difficult, because corporations do not measure net income on a daily basis, whereas the acquisition of shares of common stock by individual investors occurs throughout the year. Moreover, some large investors make a series of acquisitions of an investee's common stock without disrupting the market price of the stock. Only in special circumstances would an investor be able to determine that a dividend received represented net income earned prior to the date of a specific acquisition of common stock.

For income tax purposes, liquidating dividends are defined with respect to the investee paying the dividend, rather than with respect to individual investors. Tax laws recognize liquidating dividends only to the extent that total dividends paid exceed total net income *over the life of the investee.*

The Cost Method of Accounting for Long-Term Investments in Common Stocks

When an investor owns only a small portion (for example, less than 20%) of the total outstanding common stock of an investee, the investor has little or no influence over the investee. In this case, the investor cannot influence the investee's dividend policy, and the only portion of the investee's income that reaches the investor is the dividends paid by the investee. Thus, when the investor has little or no influence over the investee, the dividends received represent the only return realized by the investor. Under these circumstances, the *cost method* of accounting for the investment in common stock is appropriate.

When the cost method of accounting is used, the investment ledger account is maintained in terms of the cost of the common stock acquired. Revenue is recognized by the investor only to the extent of dividends received. However, if a material portion of the dividends received represents a distribution of investee's earnings realized prior to the time the stock was acquired, that portion of the dividends is a *return of capital* (a *liquidating dividend*), not revenue. Changes in the net assets of the investee are disregarded unless a *significant* and *permanent* impairment of value of the investment occurs. Finally, long-term investments in marketable equity securities may be written down to a lower of cost or market. The three events that may cause a departure from the cost basis are discussed below.

Liquidating Dividends   Because liquidating dividends represent a return of capital, receipt of such dividends by the investor is recorded by a credit to the investment ledger account. To illustrate the accounting for a liquidating dividend, assume that Toko Company acquired 15% of the outstanding common stock of Duran Company early in Year 1. During Year 1, Duran reported net income of $100,000 and paid a cash dividend of $150,000. Because the dividend exceeded by a material amount the net income of Duran for the period Toko owned Duran common stock, Toko records the dividend as follows:

Journal entry for liquidating dividend

Cash ($150,000 × 0.15)	22,500	
Dividend Revenue ($100,000 × 0.15)		15,000
Investment in Duran Company Common Stock		7,500
To record receipt of dividend, including distribution of $7,500		
in excess of net income since the investment was acquired.		

Permanent Decline in Value of Investment Operating losses of the investee that reduce the investee's net assets substantially and seriously impair its future prospects are recorded as losses by the investor. A portion of the long-term investment has been lost, and this fact is recorded by reducing the carrying amount of the investment. The following excerpt from *FASB Statement No. 12,* "Accounting for Certain Marketable Securities," supports this approach:[1]

> If the decline is judged to be other than temporary, the cost basis of the individual security shall be written down to a new cost basis and the amount of the write-down shall be accounted for as a realized loss. The new cost basis shall not be changed for subsequent recoveries in market value.

For example, the journal entry to record a permanent decline of $210,000 in the value of long-term investments in Gray Company common stock is as follows:

Journal entry for permanent decline in value of long-term investments

Realized Loss in Value of Long-Term Investments	*210,000*	
Investments in Gray Company Common Stock		*210,000*
To record a permanent decline in value of long-term investments in common stock.		

The realized loss is included in the computation of income before extraordinary items in the income statement.

Although *FASB Statement No. 12* gave little guidance for the determination of the existence of a permanent decline in the value of long-term investments, consideration should be given to the following:

1 The length of time the security has been owned

2 The length of time the market value of the security has been below the investor's cost and the extent of the decline

3 The financial condition and prospects of the investee

4 The financial condition of the investor

5 The materiality of the decline in value of the investment in relation to the net income and stockholders' equity of the investor

Valuation at Lower of Cost or Market Special accounting procedures are required by *FASB Statement No. 12* when the aggregate market value of a noncurrent portfolio of marketable equity securities, accounted for by the *cost method,* is below aggregate cost. Such a portfolio is valued at the lower of cost or market. However, in contrast to the valuation of the current portfolio of marketable equity

---

[1]*FASB Statement No. 12,* "Accounting for Certain Marketable Securities," FASB (Stamford: 1975), p. 11.

securities discussed in Chapter 6, the unrealized loss in value of a noncurrent portfolio of marketable equity securities *is not included in net income*. Instead, the
unrealized loss is reported as a *reduction of stockholders' equity*.[2]

To illustrate the accounting for long-term investments in marketable equity
securities at lower of cost or market, assume the following: On January 2, Year 1,
Investor Company made long-term investments of $200,000 in the common stock
of several publicly owned corporations, setting up a subsidiary ledger to account for
the separate investments. The aggregate market value of the investments was
$160,000 at the end of Year 1 and $184,000 at the end of Year 2. The journal entries
to record the acquisition and to value the long-term investments in marketable
equity securities at lower of cost or market at the end of Year 1 and at the end of
Year 2 are:

Journal entries to record acquisition and to value long-term investments in marketable equity securities

Jan. 2, Year 1

Long-Term Investments in Marketable Equity Securities 200,000
    Cash   200,000
To record acquisition of long-term investments.

Dec. 31, Year 1

Unrealized Loss in Value of Long-Term Investments in Marketable Equity Securities..................................... 40,000
    Allowance to Reduce Long-Term Investments in Market-
      able Equity Securities to Market Value...............   40,000
*To establish allowance for decline in market value of long-
term investments in marketable equity securities
($200,000 − $160,000 = $40,000).*

Dec. 31, Year 2

Allowance to Reduce Long-Term Investments in Marketable
  Equity Securities to Market Value ($40,000 − $16,000) 24,000
    Unrealized Loss in Value of Long-Term Investments
      in Marketable Equity Securities   24,000
*To reduce the allowance to a balance of $16,000
($200,000 − $184,000 = $16,000) required at end of Year 2.*

When a long-term investment in marketable equity securities is sold at a price
below original cost, a *realized loss* is recorded; however, *no journal entry is made
in the unrealized loss and allowance accounts until the end of the accounting
period*. For example, assume that on July 10, Year 3, Investor Company sold
long-term investments that cost $100,000 for $75,000, and that on December 31,
Year 3, the aggregate market value of the remaining investments (cost, $100,000)
was $90,000. The journal entry for the sale and the adjusting entry at the end of
Year 3 are illustrated at the top of page 699.

---

[2]Ibid., p. 7.

Journal entries
to record sale
of investments
and to adjust
allowance at end
of Year 3

July 10, Year 3

Cash 75,000
Realized Loss on Sale of Long-Term Investments in Marketable Equity Securities 25,000
        Long-Term Investments in Marketable Equity Securities   100,000
To record sale of long-term investments in marketable equity
securities.

Dec. 31, Year 3

Allowance to Reduce Long-Term Investments in Marketable
   Equity Securities to Market Value ($16,000 − $10,000) 6,000
       Unrealized Loss in Value of Long-Term Investments in
          Marketable Equity Securities 6,000
To reduce the allowance to a balance of $10,000 ($100,000 −
$90,000 = $10,000) required at end of Year 3.

The ledger accounts that are associated with Investor Company's long-term investments in marketable equity securities on December 31, Year 3, appear as follows:

Investor Company's
ledger accounts

Long-Term Investments in Marketable Equity Securities

Date	Explanation	Debit	Credit	Balance
Year 1				
Jan. 2	Acquisition of common stock of several publicly owned corporations	200,000		200,000 dr
Year 3				
July 10	Sale of common stock		100,000	100,000 dr

Allowance to Reduce Long-Term Investments in Marketable Equity Securities to Market Value

Date	Explanation	Debit	Credit	Balance
Year 1				
Dec. 31	($200,000 − $160,000)		40,000	40,000 cr
Year 2				
Dec. 31	($200,000 − $184,000)	24,000		16,000 cr
Year 3				
Dec. 31	($100,000 − $90,000)	6,000		10,000 cr

Unrealized Loss in Value of Long-Term Investments in Marketable Equity Securities

Date	Explanation	Debit	Credit	Balance
Year 1				
Dec. 31	($200,000 – $160,000)	40,000		40,000 dr
Year 2				
Dec. 31	($200,000 – $184,000)		24,000	16,000 dr
Year 3				
Dec. 31	($100,000 – $90,000)		6,000	10,000 dr

The balance sheets of Investor Company at the end of each year include the following information:

Balance sheet presentation of long-term investments in marketable equity securities

	Dec. 31, Year 1	Dec. 31, Year 2	Dec. 31, Year 3
Investments:			
Long-term investments in marketable equity securities, at cost	$ 200,000	$ 200,000	$ 100,000
Less: Allowance to reduce long-term investments in marketable equity securities to market value	40,000	16,000	10,000
Long-term investments in marketable equity securities, at lower of cost or market	$ 160,000	$ 184,000	$ 90,000
Stockholders' equity:			
Total paid-in capital and retained earnings..........................	$XXX,XXX	$XXX,XXX	$XXX,XXX
Less: Unrealized loss in value of long-term investments in marketable equity securities	(40,000)	(16,000)	(10,000)
Total stockholders' equity	$XXX,XXX	$XXX,XXX	$XXX,XXX

Nature of Unrealized Loss Ledger Account   In requiring the unrealized loss in value of long-term investments in marketable equity securities to be deducted from the total paid-in capital and retained earnings of a corporation, the Financial Accounting Standards Board authorized the creation of an unusual ledger account. The accounting standards established for the unrealized loss on long-term investments appear to be a compromise between the supporters of lower-of-aggregate-cost-or-market accounting for long-term investments in marketable equity securities and the opponents of including in the income statement unrealized gains and losses resulting from fluctuations in the market value of long-term investments. The provisions of *FASB Statement No. 12* did not apply to certain industries such as life insurance and casualty insurance.

The Equity Method of Accounting for Long-Term Investments in Common Stocks

When an investor owns enough common stock of an investee to exercise significant influence over the investee's management, the dividends paid by the investee no longer may be an appropriate measure of the return on the investment. This is because the investor may influence the investee's dividend policy. In such a case, dividends paid by the investee may reflect the *investor's* income tax considerations and cash needs, rather than the profitability of the investment in common stock.

For example, assume that an investor owns 100% of the common stock of an investee. For two years the investee had significant net income but paid no dividends, because the investor had no need for additional cash. In the third year, the investee has a net loss but pays a large cash dividend. It would be misleading for the investor to report no investment income while the investee was operating profitably, and then to show large investment income in a year when the investee operated at a loss.

The investee need not be 100% owned for the investor to have significant influence over its operating and financial policies. When the common stock of the investee is widely held, an investor owning much less than 50% of the common stock may have effective influence over the investee, because it is doubtful that the remaining outstanding shares will vote as an organized block.

When the investor has a significant degree of influence over the operating and financial policies of the investee, the equity method of accounting more fairly presents the benefits accruing to the investor than does the cost method. When the investor has little or no influence over the operating and financial policies of the investee, the benefits received by the investor may be limited to the dividends received, indicating the cost method of accounting to be more appropriate. The key criterion in selecting between the methods is the *degree of influence* the investor is able to exercise over the investee.

To achieve uniformity in accounting practice, the Accounting Principles Board took the position in *APB Opinion No. 18,* "The Equity Method of Accounting for Investments in Common Stock," that "an investment (direct or indirect) of *20% or more* of the voting stock of an investee should lead to a presumption that in absence of evidence to the contrary an investor has the ability to exercise significant influence over an investee."[3] Thus, investments representing 20% or more of the voting stock of an investee usually are accounted for by the equity method of accounting. However, if the investor owns 20% or more of the voting stock but is unable to exercise significant influence over the investee, use of the cost method is required. Investments of less than 20% usually are accounted for by the cost method of accounting, unless clear-cut ability to influence the operating and financial policies of the investee may be demonstrated. Investments in preferred stock are accounted for by the cost method, because preferred stockholders usually do not have either voting rights or a residual equity in net income.

When the equity method of accounting is used, an investment in common stock initially is recorded at the cost of the stock acquired, but is adjusted for changes in

---

[3]*APB Opinion No. 18,* "The Equity Method of Accounting for Investments in Common Stock," AICPA (New York: 1971), p. 355. See also *FASB Interpretation No. 35,* "Criteria for Applying the Equity Method . . . ," FASB (Stamford: 1981). (Emphasis added.)

the net assets of the investee subsequent to acquisition. The investor's proportionate share of the investee's net income is recorded as *investment income,* causing an increase in the investment ledger account. If the investee's net income includes extraordinary items, the investor records its share of such items as extraordinary (if material in amount to the investor), rather than as ordinary investment income. Dividends paid by the investee are recorded by the investor as a conversion of the investment to cash, causing the investment ledger account to decrease.

Illustration of Equity Method of Accounting   To illustrate the equity method of accounting, assume that on January 2, Year 1, Investor Company acquired 40% of the common stock of Lee Company for $300,000, which corresponded with the carrying amount of Lee's net assets. On December 31, Year 1, Lee reported net income of $70,000 (including a $10,000 extraordinary gain) and declared and paid dividends of $30,000. Investor Company accounts for its investment in Lee Company as follows (disregarding income tax effects):

Journal entries for equity method of accounting—first year of affiliation

Year 1				
Jan. 2	Investment in Lee Company Common Stock	300,000		
	Cash		300,000	
	To record acquisition of 40% of common stock of Lee Company at carrying amount of Lee's net assets.			
Dec. 31	Investment in Lee Company Common Stock	28,000		
	Investment Income (ordinary)..............		24,000	
	Investment Income (extraordinary)		4,000	
	To record 40% of net income of Lee Company for Year 1 ($60,000 × 0.40 = $24,000; $10,000 × 0.40 = $4,000).			
31	Cash	12,000		
	Investment in Lee Company Common Stock		12,000	
	To record dividends received from Lee Company ($30,000 × 0.40 = $12,000).			

After the foregoing journal entries have been posted, the investment and investment income ledger accounts appear as follows (before closing entries for the investment income accounts):

Investor's ledger accounts under equity method of accounting

	Investment in Lee Company Common Stock			
Date	**Explanation**	**Debit**	**Credit**	**Balance**
Year 1				
Jan. 2	Cost of investment	300,000		300,000 dr
Dec. 31	Share of net income			
	($70,000 × 0.40)	28,000		328,000 dr
31	Dividends received			
	($30,000 × 0.40)		12,000	316,000 dr

Investment Income (Ordinary)				
Date	Explanation	Debit	Credit	Balance
Year 1 Dec. 31	Share of net income ($60,000 × 0.40)		24,000	24,000 cr

Investment Income (Extraordinary)				
Date	Explanation	Debit	Credit	Balance
Year 1 Dec. 31	Share of net income ($10,000 × 0.40)		4,000	4,000 cr

Note that the net effect of Investor's accounting for Lee's net income and dividends was to increase the balance of the investment ledger account by $16,000. This corresponds with 40% of the increase in Lee's net assets as a result of undistributed earnings during Year 1 [($70,000 − $30,000) × 0.40 = $16,000].

Problems in the Application of Equity Method Four problems may arise in the application of the equity method of accounting. First, intercompany profits (gains) and losses resulting from transactions between the investor and the investee must be eliminated until realized by a transaction with an unaffiliated entity. Second, when the acquisition cost of an investment differs from the carrying amount of the investee's identifiable net assets, adjustments may have to be made to the investment income recorded by the investor. Third, use of the equity method of accounting requires the investor to establish a Retained Earnings of Investee ledger account to be used in end-of-period closing entries. Fourth, the equity method of accounting may have to be applied *retroactively* if the investor acquires its influencing investment in a series of transactions instead of a single one. (A change from the equity method of accounting to the cost method for a long-term investment in common stock creates no special problems.)

Intercompany Profits (Gains) or Losses An investor or an investee may sell merchandise or, less frequently, plant or intangible assets to its affiliate. If so, any unrealized profit (gain) or loss must be excluded from the net income of the investor.

To illustrate, assume that on November 30, Year 2, Investor sold merchandise costing $50,000 to Lee Company for $80,000, or a gross profit rate of 37½% ($30,000 ÷ $80,000 = 0.375). On December 31, Year 2, the inventories of Lee included $60,000 (at billed price) of this merchandise. In addition, on December 31, Year 2, Lee sold merchandise that cost $30,000 to Investor for $50,000; none of this merchandise was sold by Investor to its customers on that date. If Lee reported net income of $95,000 (none of which was an extraordinary item) for Year 2, but did not declare or pay dividends for that year, Investor prepares the following journal entries on December 31, Year 2, under the equity method of accounting (disregarding income tax effects):

Investment in Lee Company Common Stock
   [($95,000 − $20,000) × 0.40]   30,000
         Investment Income (ordinary)   30,000
To record 40% of net income of Lee Company for Year 2
after elimination of $20,000 unrealized gross profit ($50,000 −
$30,000 = $20,000) remaining in Investor's inventories on
Dec. 31, Year 2.

Income Summary ($60,000 × 0.375)   22,500
         Deferred Gross Profit on Sales   22,500
To defer unrealized gross profit attributable to merchandise
in Lee Company's inventories on Dec. 31, Year 2.

The net effect of the two foregoing journal entries is to reduce Investor's net income (disregarding income tax effects) by $30,500, computed as follows:

Investor's share of unrealized gross profit of Lee Company
   ($20,000 × 0.40) .... $ 8,000
Investor's unrealized gross profit on sales to Lee Company
   ($60,000 × 0.375)   22,500
Total reduction of Investor's net income $30,500

A review of the foregoing illustration of intercompany profits emphasizes the necessity of excluding unrealized intercompany profits (gains) and losses from an investor's net income. The investor's ability to influence the operating and financial policies of an investee enables the investor to determine to a large degree the quantity and unit price of merchandise sold by investor to investee, and vice versa. Obviously, if unrealized intercompany profits were not eliminated from the investor's net income, the investor might reach a desired earnings per share amount merely by selling merchandise to, or purchasing merchandise from, an investee.

Cost in Excess of Equity Acquired   Often an investor will pay more than the *underlying equity* of an investment because current fair values of the investee's identifiable assets may be larger than their carrying amounts, or because the investee has unrecorded goodwill. In either case, this excess of cost over the underlying equity will benefit the investor only over the economic lives of the undervalued (or unrecorded) assets.

To the extent that the excess of cost over the underlying equity was paid to acquire an interest in specific undervalued assets, this amount should be amortized over the economic lives of those assets. The journal entry to reflect the amortization is as follows:

<table>
<tr><td>Journal entry for amortization of excess of cost over underlying equity acquired</td><td>Investment Income (ordinary) XXX
    Investment in Investee Company Common Stock XXX
To adjust investment income for amortization of excess of
cost over underlying equity of Investee's net assets.</td></tr>
</table>

To the extent that the excess cost was incurred because of implied goodwill, the excess is amortized over the estimated economic life of the goodwill. The Accounting Principles Board took the position that amounts paid for goodwill should be amortized over a period of not more than 40 years.[4] If the excess of the cost over the underlying equity is small, it usually is amortized as goodwill, rather than allocated to identifiable assets. Accounting for goodwill is discussed in Chapter 13.

Cost Less than Equity Acquired   When an investor acquires an investment in common stock at a cost less than the underlying equity, it is assumed that specific identifiable assets of the investee are overvalued. If these assets have limited economic lives, the investor allocates the excess of the underlying equity over cost to investment income over the economic lives of the assets. The journal entry to record this amortization is shown below:

<table>
<tr><td>Journal entry for amortization of excess of underlying equity acquired over cost</td><td>Investment in Investee Company Common Stock XXX
    Investment Income (ordinary) XXX
To adjust investment income for amortization of excess of
underlying equity of Investee's net assets over cost.</td></tr>
</table>

Note that this adjustment *increases* investment income. The rationale for this action is that the investee's reported net income is understated because the investee has recorded depreciation or amortization based on overstated carrying amounts of assets.

Investor's Closing Entries under Equity Method   The corporation laws of most states provide that only dividends received from an investment in common stock may be included in the retained earnings of the investor as a source of dividends to the investor's shareholders. Thus, an investor that uses the cost method of accounting for an investment in common stock closes the Dividend Revenue ledger account to the Retained Earnings account.

In contrast, an investor that uses the equity method of accounting for an investment in common stock closes the balances of the Investment Income ledger accounts to Retained Earnings only if the investee declared dividends in the amount of its net income accrued by the investor under the equity method of accounting. Any amount of investment income not paid as dividends by the investee is closed to the investor's Retained Earnings of Investee ledger account rather than to Retained

---

[4]*APB Opinion No. 17*, ''Intangible Assets,'' AICPA (New York: 1970), p. 340.

Earnings, because those **undistributed earnings** of the investee are not available (in most states) for the declaration of dividends by the investor.

To illustrate, return to the Investor Company-Lee Company illustration on pages 702–704 and assume that, after Year 1 closing entries for all revenue (including investment income) and expense ledger accounts of Investor had been posted, the Income Summary ledger account had a credit balance of $432,000 on December 31, Year 1. During Year 1, investee Lee had reported net income of $70,000 and declared and paid dividends of $30,000. Therefore, Investor's 40% share of Lee's undistributed earnings for Year 1 is $16,000 [($70,000 − $30,000) × 0.40 = $16,000]. Investor's journal entry to close the Income Summary ledger account on December 31, Year 1, is as follows:

Investor's closing entry under equity method of accounting

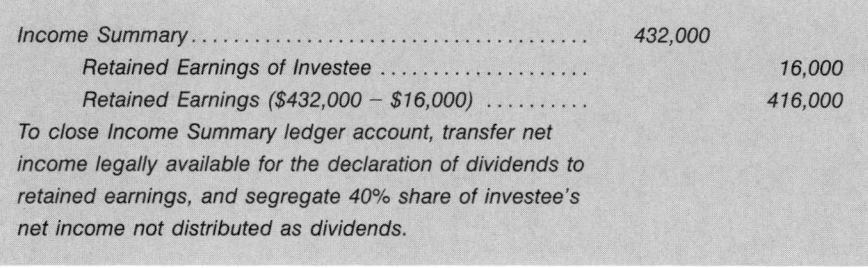

Income Summary	432,000	
Retained Earnings of Investee		16,000
Retained Earnings ($432,000 − $16,000)		416,000

To close Income Summary ledger account, transfer net income legally available for the declaration of dividends to retained earnings, and segregate 40% share of investee's net income not distributed as dividends.

Because Lee Company did not declare or pay dividends in Year 2 (see page 703), Investor's December 31, Year 2, journal entry to close the Income Summary ledger account would credit Retained Earnings of Investee for $30,000, the amount of Lee's Year 2 net income recorded by Investor under the equity method of accounting.

Retroactive Application of Equity Method If an investor acquires sufficient voting stock to influence an investee in a **series of acquisitions** rather than a **single one,** the equity method of accounting is applied **retroactively** when the investor has acquired 20% of the investee's common stock, as stated on page 703. Prior to acquiring the ability to influence the investee, the investor accounts for the investment under the cost method of accounting.

To illustrate, assume that on January 2, Year 1, Ingo Company acquired for $50,000 a 10% interest in the outstanding common stock of Leslie, Inc., which had total stockholders' equity of $500,000 on that date. Leslie had net income of $60,000 for Year 1 and declared and paid dividends of $25,000 on December 31, Year 1. Thus, Leslie's undistributed earnings in Year 1 amounted to $35,000 ($60,000 − $25,000 = $35,000). On January 2, Year 2, Ingo acquired an additional 20% interest in Leslie's outstanding common stock for $107,000. After the acquisition of the additional 20% interest, Ingo was able to exercise significant influence over the operating and financial policies of Leslie; consequently, Ingo now recognizes its $3,500 share of Leslie's Year 1 undistributed earnings of $35,000 ($35,000 × 0.10 = $3,500).

The following journal entries illustrate Ingo's application of the cost method of accounting for its investment in Leslie during Year 1, and the retroactive application of the equity method of accounting for the investment on January 2, Year 2. (The closing entry for Ingo's Dividend Revenue ledger account on December 31, Year 1, is not illustrated.)

Investor's journal entries for retroactive application of equity method

Year 1

Jan. 2 Investment in Leslie, Inc., Common Stock 50,000
            Cash   50,000
        To record acquisition of 10% of the common stock of
        Leslie, Inc., at carrying amount ($500,000 × 0.10
        = $50,000).

Dec. 31 Cash ($25,000 × 0.10) 2,500
            Dividend Revenue   2,500
        To record receipt of dividend from Leslie, Inc.

Year 2

Jan. 2 Investment in Leslie, Inc., Common Stock 107,000
            Cash   107,000
        To record acquisition of 20% of the common stock of
        Leslie, Inc., at carrying amount [($500,000 +
        $60,000 − $25,000) × 0.20 = $107,000].

    2   Investment in Leslie, Inc., Common Stock 3,500
            Retained Earnings of Investee   3,500
        To change retroactively accounting for investment
        in Leslie, Inc., to equity method from cost method,
        and to record retroactively 10% share of Leslie's net
        income for year ended Dec. 31, Year 1, as follows:
          Share of Leslie's net income, Year 1
            ($60,000 × 0.10) $6,000
          Less: Dividend revenue recorded in Year 1   2,500
          Prior period adjustment to Retained
            Earnings of Investee ledger account $3,500

        (Income tax effects are disregarded.)

After the foregoing journal entries have been posted, Ingo Company's investment ledger account appears as follows:

Investor's ledger account

Investment in Leslie, Inc., Common Stock

Date	Explanation	Debit	Credit	Balance
Year 1				
Jan. 2	Cost of investment—10% interest	50,000		50,000 dr
Year 2				
Jan. 2	Cost of investment—20% interest	107,000		157,000 dr
2	Retroactive application of equity			
	method of accounting	3,500		160,500 dr

Ingo Company's retroactive application of the equity method of accounting on January 2, Year 2, has adjusted the balance of its investment ledger account to equal its 30% interest in the net assets (stockholders' equity) of Leslie, Inc., on that date [($500,000 + $60,000 − $25,000) × 0.30 = $160,500]. Further, the $3,500 balance of Ingo's Retained Earnings of Investee account is equal to Ingo's 10% share of the undistributed earnings of Leslie for Year 1 [($60,000 − $25,000) × 0.10 = $3,500]. For Year 2 and future years, as long as Ingo's interest in Leslie's outstanding common stock remains at 30%, Ingo debits its investment account for 30% of Leslie's net income and credits the account for 30% of Leslie's net losses and dividends.

When the investor's ownership is reduced below 20% or when the investor loses the ability to exercise significant influence over the investee, the investor discontinues use of the equity method and adopts the cost method, but the investment ledger account *is not adjusted retroactively.*[5] Any previously accrued undistributed earnings of the investee remain in the investment account.

Summary of Procedures under the Equity Method of Accounting   Accounting procedures under the equity method may be summarized as follows:

1   The investment initially is recorded at cost.

2   The investor subsequently recognizes its proportionate share of the investee's net income (after elimination of intercompany profits) by a debit to the investment ledger account and a credit to Investment Income. In event of a loss, Investment Loss is debited and the investment account is credited.

3   The investor views its share of dividends declared and paid by the investee as a conversion of the investment to cash. Thus, the investor debits Cash and credits the investment ledger account.

4   The investor adjusts the recorded amount of investment income or loss by the amortization of any excess of cost of its investment over the underlying equity associated with the investee's depreciable assets or goodwill. This adjustment consists of a debit to Investment Income (or Loss) and a credit to the investment ledger account.

5   The investor adjusts the recorded amount of investment income or loss by the amortization of any excess of the underlying equity over cost by a debit to the investment ledger account and a credit to Investment Income (or Loss).

6   At the end of an accounting period, the investor closes the undistributed adjusted earnings of the investee to the Retained Earnings of Investee ledger account.

Comparative Illustration of the Cost and Equity Methods of Accounting for Long-Term Investments in Common Stocks

To illustrate the differences in the cost and equity methods, assume that on January 2, Year 1, Investor Company acquired 4,000 shares (20%) of the outstanding com-

[5]*APB Opinion No. 18,* p. 359.

mon stock of Investee Company for $1,000,000. On the date of acquisition, the carrying amount of Investee's identifiable net assets was $4,550,000. Investor was willing to pay more than the underlying equity for the investment because it was estimated that Investee owned land worth $100,000 more than its carrying amount, depreciable plant assets worth $150,000 more than their carrying amounts, and enough goodwill to make a 20% interest in Investee worth the $1,000,000 cost.

The excess of the cost of the investment over the underlying equity is analyzed below:

Analysis of excess of cost of investment over underlying equity

Cost of investment..	$1,000,000
Less: Underlying equity ($4,550,000 × 0.20)	910,000
Excess of cost over underlying equity acquired	$ 90,000
Composition of excess:	
20% interest in undervalued land ($100,000 × 0.20)	$ 20,000
20% interest in undervalued depreciable plant assets ($150,000 × 0.20)...	30,000
Implied goodwill ($90,000 − $20,000 − $30,000)	40,000
Excess of cost over underlying equity acquired	$ 90,000

The undervalued depreciable plant assets have an average remaining economic life of 10 years, and Investor's policy with respect to goodwill is to amortize it over 40 years.

During Year 1, Investee reported net income of $430,000, after an extraordinary loss of $50,000, and declared and paid dividends of $200,000 at year-end. Investor's accounting for its investment in Investee during Year 1 is illustrated on page 710 under the cost and equity methods of accounting.

Note that no adjustment is made under either the cost or the equity method for the $20,000 excess of cost over the underlying equity representing Investor's 20% interest in Investee's undervalued land. This is because land is not depreciated. The results for Year 1 are illustrated below for the two methods of accounting:

Comparison of results of equity method and cost method

	Cost method of accounting	Equity method of accounting
Investment in common stock of Investee Company (ending balance)....................	$1,000,000	$1,042,000
Investment income (loss) recognized by Investor Company:		
Ordinary income	$ 40,000	$ 92,000
Extraordinary loss		(10,000)

INVESTOR COMPANY
Comparison of Cost and Equity Methods of Accounting
For Year 1

Date	Explanation	Cost Method (Investor assumed to have no influence over Investee)	Equity Method (Investor assumed to have influence over Investee)

Year 1
Jan. 2
	To record acquisition of 4,000 shares of Investee Company's common stock.	Investment in Investee Company Common Stock 1,000,000
		    Cash 1,000,000
			Investment in Investee Company Common Stock 1,000,000
			    Cash 1,000,000

Dec. 31	To record receipt of dividend of $40,000 from Investee Company ($200,000 × 0.20 = $40,000).	Cash 40,000
		    Dividend Revenue .. 40,000
			Cash 40,000
			    Investment in Investee Company Common Stock... 40,000

31	To record $86,000 share of Investee Company's net income ($430,000 × 0.20 = $86,000) including $10,000 share of extraordinary loss ($50,000 × 0.20 = $10,000).	(No journal entry)	Investment Loss (extraordinary) .... 10,000 Investment in Investee Company Common Stock .... 86,000 Investment Income (ordinary) 96,000
31	To amortize a portion of the excess of investment cost over the underlying equity, as follows: Depreciable plant assets ($30,000 ÷ 10 years) ..... $3,000 Goodwill ($40,000 ÷ 40 years) .... 1,000 Total amortization........ $4,000	(No journal entry)	Investment Income (ordinary) .... 4,000 Investment in Investee Company Common Stock ... 4,000

ACCOUNTING FOR LONG-TERM INVESTMENTS IN BONDS

A bond contract represents a promise to pay an amount of money at maturity and a series of interest payments (usually every six months) during the term of the contract. Investors acquire corporate bonds to earn a *return on investment.* The effective rate of return (*yield*) on bonds to investors is determined by the price investors pay for the bonds (because the terms of the contract are fixed). The yield on the bonds to investors generally will differ from the effective interest cost to the borrower when the bonds are acquired by investors subsequent to the issuance date.

Computation of Acquisition Price of Long-Term Investment in Bonds

The cost of an investment in bonds is the present value of the future cash receipts pursuant to the bond contract, measured in terms of the *market rate of interest* at the time of investment. The *stated (nominal) rate of interest* in the bond contract measures the cash to be received periodically by the investor. If the rate of return demanded by investors is exactly equal to the nominal rate, the bonds may be acquired at the face amount. If the market rate of interest exceeds the nominal rate, the bonds may be acquired at a *discount,* because the investor is demanding a higher return than the bond contract offers; therefore, to equate the yield on the bond with the market rate of interest, the bond is acquired at a price below face amount. If the market rate of interest is *below* the nominal rate, the investor will be willing to pay a *premium* for the bond, that is, a price above face amount.

To illustrate the computation of the acquisition price of bonds (using the present value concepts described in Chapter 5), assume that $200,000 of 7% bonds of Villa Company maturing in 15 years are acquired by Kane Company to yield 8% compounded semiannually. The bonds pay interest semiannually starting six months from date of acquisition. Because the market rate of interest exceeds the nominal rate, the bonds are acquired at a discount, as shown below (using the Appendix at the end of Chapter 5):

Computation of acquisition price of bonds issued at a *discount*

Present value of $200,000 discounted at 4% for 30 six-month periods ($200,000 × 0.308319)...	$ 61,664
Add: Present value of ordinary annuity of 30 rents of $7,000 (semiannual interest payments) discounted at 4% ($7,000 × 17.292033)...	121,044
Acquisition price of bonds (discount of $17,292)	$182,708*

*Alternative computation [$200,000 − ($1,000 semiannual interest "deficiency" × 17.292033) = $182,708]

If the market rate of interest was only 6% compounded semiannually, the bonds paying semiannual interest at 7% a year would be acquired at a premium, as shown at the top of page 712.

Computation of
acquisition price
of bonds issued
at a *premium*

Present value of $200,000 discounted at 3% for 30 six-month periods	
($200,000 × 0.411987)	*$ 82,397*
Add: Present value of ordinary annuity of 30 rents of $7,000	
discounted at 3% ($7,000 × 19.600441)	*137,203*
Acquisition price of bonds (premium of $19,600)	*$219,600**

*Alternative computation [$200,000 + ($1,000 semiannual "extra" interest × 19.600441) = $219,600]

Acquisition of Bonds between Interest Dates

Interest on a bond contract accrues with the passage of time in accordance with the provisions of the contract. The issuer pays the contractual rate of interest on the stated date to the investor owning the bond on that date. The investor who acquires a bond between interest dates must pay the previous owner the market price of the bond plus the interest accrued since the last interest payment. The investor is paying the previous owner of the bond the interest applicable to the first portion of the interest period and will in turn collect that portion plus the additional interest earned by holding the bond until the next interest payment date.

Illustration   On July 1, an investor acquired 10 bonds ($1,000 face amount each) of Ray Company, which had been issued several years ago. The bond contract provides for interest at 8% a year, payable semiannually on April 1 and October 1. The market rate of interest is higher than 8% at the present time, and the bonds are currently quoted at 97¾ plus accrued interest for three months. The journal entry for the investor to record the acquisition of the 10 bonds is:

Investor's journal
entry to record
acquisition of bonds
between interest dates

Investment in Ray Company Bonds ($10,000 × 0.9775)	*9,775*	
Interest Receivable ($10,000 × 0.08 × 3/12)	*200*	
Cash		*9,975*
To record acquisition of 10 bonds plus accrued interest of		
$200 for three months.		

The $200 paid by the investor for accrued interest may be debited to Interest Revenue; if so, when the first $400 interest payment ($10,000 × 0.08 × 6/12 = $400) is received on October 1, the entire amount is credited to Interest Revenue.

Discount and Premium on Long-Term Investments in Bonds

On the date of acquisition of bonds, the investment ledger account is debited for the cost of acquiring the bonds, including brokerage and other fees, but excluding any accrued interest. A separate discount or premium ledger account as a valuation account seldom is used. The subsequent treatment of the investment might be handled in one of three ways: (1) The investment might be carried at cost, ignoring the *accumulation* of discount or *amortization* of premium; (2) the investment ledger account balance might be revalued periodically to reflect market value changes; or

(3) the discount or premium might be accumulated· or amortized to reflect the change in the carrying amount of the bonds based on the effective rate of interest prevailing at the time of acquisition.

The first alternative (the cost basis) is used primarily in accounting for short-term bond investments, as discussed in Chapter 6, for convertible bonds (see page 720), and for other bonds for which the discount or premium is insignificant. The discount or premium on convertible bonds seldom is related to the level of interest rates, but rather reflects the effect of the price of the common stock to which the bond is convertible. These securities are subject to wide price movements related to changes in the market price of common stocks; therefore, the amortization of premium or accumulation of discount by investors does not seem appropriate for convertible bonds.

The second alternative (valuation at market) is not in accord with the present interpretation of the realization principle or the concept of conservatism, especially during periods of rising bond prices. Changes in market prices of bonds held as long-term investments may be of less significance to the investor than changes in prices of short-term investments, because the long-term investments frequently are held to maturity, at which time market price and face amount of the bonds are equal. When the investment in bonds is in jeopardy because of serious cash shortages of the issuer, it generally is acceptable to write the investment down to its expected net realizable value and to recognize a loss.

The third alternative (the systematic accumulation and amortization) is the preferred treatment for long-term investments in bonds. This approach recognizes that the interest revenue represented by the discount, or the reduction in interest revenue represented by the premium, accrues over the term of the bonds. This method is consistent with the principle that requires assets other than cash and receivables to be recorded at cost.

Interest Revenue

The periodic interest payments provided for in a bond contract represent the total interest revenue to an investor holding a bond to maturity only if the investor acquired the bond at its face amount. If an investor acquires a bond at a premium, the amount received on maturity of the bond will be less than the amount of the initial investment, thus reducing the cumulative interest revenue by the amount of the premium. Similarly, if the bond is acquired at a discount, the amount received at maturity will be larger than the initial investment, thereby increasing the cumulative interest revenue by the amount of the discount.

When an investor intends to hold bonds to maturity, there is little logic in treating the discount or premium as a gain or loss occurring on the maturity date. Rather, the increase in the carrying amount of the bonds as a discount disappears should be viewed as part of the revenue accruing to the investor over the entire period the bonds are owned. Similarly, the decrease in value when a premium disappears is a cost the investor is willing to incur during the holding period to receive periodic interest payments higher than the market rate at the time the bonds were acquired. Thus, the amount of the discount or premium is viewed as an integral part of the periodic interest revenue earned by the investor. The accumulation of a discount increases periodic interest revenue, and the amortization of a premium decreases periodic interest revenue.

An extreme illustration of this concept has occurred for certain corporate and governmental *zero coupon* bonds, which provided no periodic interest payments at all. Instead, these bonds were issued at a *deep discount,* and the gradual growth in the redemption value of the bonds toward their maturity value (accumulation of the discount) was the investor's only return. Although the investor received no cash proceeds until the bonds matured, interest revenue was being earned. To measure the periodic interest revenue, the accumulation of the discount had to be recognized as interest revenue over the term of the bonds.

Methods of Discount Accumulation or Premium Amortization

The methods of amortization for bond discount and bond premium by the issuer are discussed in Chapter 15. These methods present precisely the same problem for the investor as for the issuer. The purpose of *accumulating the discount* or *amortizing the premium* is to measure accurately the periodic interest revenue derived from the investment in bonds.

Interest Method   The *interest method* produces a constant rate of return on the investment in bonds. That is, the periodic interest revenue always represents the *same percentage return* on the carrying amount of the investment. Thus, when a discount on a long-term investment in bonds is being accumulated and the balance in the investment ledger account is increasing, the interest revenue recorded each interest period also *increases;* this is accomplished by accumulating an ever-increasing portion of the discount each period. When the premium on a long-term investment in bonds is being amortized and the balance in the investment account is decreasing, the interest revenue recorded each interest period also *decreases.* Under the interest method, the interest revenue is computed for each interest period by multiplying the balance of the investment account by the effective interest rate at the time the investment was made. The accumulation of the discount (or amortization of the premium) thus is the difference between the periodic cash receipt and the interest revenue for the period computed by the effective rate of interest.

Straight-Line Method   Under the *straight-line method,* the discount or premium is spread uniformly over the term of the bonds. Although the bonds may be sold by the investor or redeemed by the issuer prior to maturity, the accumulation or amortization always *is based on the years remaining to maturity.* The straight-line method is simple to apply and avoids the necessity for determining the yield rate. *The primary objection to the straight-line method is that it produces a constant amount of interest revenue each accounting period, which results in an uneven rate of return on the investment.* For this reason, the interest method is conceptually superior to the straight-line method, especially with respect to *deep discount* bonds.

Use of the interest method for discount accumulation and premium amortization is required by generally accepted accounting principles; however, the straight-line method may be used if it does not result in a materially different amount of interest revenue.

Journal entries and investment ledger accounts for acquisition of bonds and accumulation of discount

KANE COMPANY
Journal Entries

	Interest method		Straight-line method	
(1) Bonds acquired to yield 8% compounded semiannually:				
Investment in Villa Company Bonds	182,708		182,708	
Cash		182,708		182,708
To record acquisition of 7% bonds at a discount of $17,292 to be accumulated over 30 six-month periods.				
Cash	7,000		7,000	
Investment in Villa Company Bonds	308		576	
Interest Revenue		7,308		7,576
To record receipt of interest at the end of the first six-month period ($200,000 × 0.07 × ½ = $7,000).				
Accumulation of discount:				
Interest method: ($182,708 × 0.04) − $7,000 = $308.				
Straight-line method: $17,292 ÷ 30 = $576.				
Cash	7,000		7,000	
Investment in Villa Company Bonds	321		576	
Interest Revenue		7,321		7,576
To record receipt of interest at the end of the second six-month period ($200,000 × 0.07 × ½ = $7,000).				
Accumulation of discount:				
Interest method: [($182,708 + $308) × 0.04] − $7,000 = $321.				
Straight-line method: $17,292 ÷ 30 = $576.				

Investment		Investment	
182,708		182,708	
308		576	
321		576	
(183,337)		(183,860)	

Illustration   The computation of periodic discount to be accumulated or premium to be amortized and the related journal entries and ledger accounts are illustrated with the examples for Kane Company on pages 711–712. The Kane Company examples involved (1) the acquisition of $200,000 face amount of 7% bonds maturing in 15 years (or 30 semiannual periods) to yield 8% compounded semiannually, and (2) the acquisition of the same bonds to yield 6% compounded semiannually. The journal entries to record the investment, receipt of interest for the first year, and the related accumulation or amortization under the interest method and the straight-line method are presented on pages 715–717 (all computations are rounded to the nearest dollar). The investment ledger account under each method appears below the journal entries.

When the bonds are acquired at a discount and the interest method of accumulation is used, the investment ledger account balance is increased to $183,016 ($182,708 + $308 = $183,016) at the end of the first six-month period; therefore, interest revenue for the second six-month period is $7,321 ($183,016 × 0.04 = $7,321), which required $321 of the discount to be accumulated.

When the bonds are acquired at a premium and the interest method of amortization is used, the investment ledger account balance is reduced to $219,188 ($219,600 − $412 = $219,188) at the end of the first six-month period; therefore, interest revenue for the second six-month period is $6,576 ($219,188 × 0.03 = $6,576), which required $424 of the premium to be amortized.

Interest revenue on long-term bond investments, just as interest revenue on any other investment, is accrued only on significant dates. The significant dates are: (1) interest payment dates, (2) the end of the investor's accounting period, and (3) the time of any transaction (such as the sale of any portion of the investment) involving the particular investment that does not coincide with a regular interest payment date. The discount also is accumulated or the premium amortized in accordance with whatever method of accumulation or amortization is used.

SPECIAL PROBLEMS IN ACCOUNTING FOR LONG-TERM INVESTMENTS IN SECURITIES

Cost Identification

Investments in securities may pose a problem as to which costs should be offset against revenue in the period of sale. For example, assume that an investor acquires 1,000 shares of Z Company common stock at a price of $80 a share, and 1,000 shares at $90 a share. Several years later, the investor sells 1,000 shares of Z Company common stock for $84 a share. Should the investor recognize a $4,000 gain or a $6,000 loss?

The answer to this question requires making a *cost flow assumption,* as with inventories. Because securities usually are identified by a certificate number, it would be possible to use specific identification of stock certificates to establish the cost of the 1,000 shares sold. However, an alternative cost flow assumption might be adopted. The alternative methods of cost flow include: (1) fifo—the first shares acquired are assumed to be the first ones sold; (2) lifo—the last shares acquired are assumed to be the first ones sold; and (3) weighted-average cost—each share is assigned the same cost basis.

Journal entries and investment ledger accounts for acquisition of bonds and amortization of premium

KANE COMPANY
Journal Entries

	Interest method		Straight-line method	
(2) Bonds acquired to yield 6% compounded semiannually:				
Investment in Villa Company Bonds........................	219,600		219,600	
Cash		219,600		219,600
To record acquisition of 7% bonds at a premium of $19,600 to be amortized over 30 six-month periods.				
Cash	7,000		7,000	
Investment in Villa Company Bonds		412		653
Interest Revenue		6,588		6,347
To record receipt of interest at the end of the first six-month period ($200,000 × 0.07 × ½ = $7,000).				
Amortization of premium: Interest method: $7,000 − ($219,600 × 0.03) = $412. Straight-line method: $19,600 ÷ 30 = $653.				
Cash	7,000		7,000	
Investment in Villa Company Bonds		424		653
Interest Revenue		6,576		6,347
To record receipt of interest at the end of the second six-month period ($200,000 × 0.07 × ½ = $7,000).				
Amortization of premium: Interest method: $7,000 − [($219,600 − $412) × 0.03] = $424. Straight-line method: $19,600 ÷ 30 = $653.				

Investment		Investment	
219,600	412	219,600	653
	424		653
	(836)		(1,306)

Income tax rules require the use of either the specific identification method or the fifo method to measure the *gain or loss.* Neither lifo nor weighted-average cost is an acceptable method for income tax purposes. The specific identification method usually is more advantageous for income tax purposes, because it allows the investor to select for sale the securities that will have the most desirable tax consequences. For financial accounting, most investors use the same method of cost selection used for income tax purposes to simplify record keeping. However, weighted average is the only cost flow assumption that recognizes the economic equivalence of identical securities. In our illustration of successive acquisitions of the common stock of Z Company at different prices, it is undeniable that each share of Z Company common stock owned has exactly the same current fair value regardless of the price paid to acquire it. The weighted-average cost flow assumption recognizes the economic reality that, except for income tax purposes, it makes no difference which 1,000-share certificate is sold and which is retained.

Accounting for Stock Dividends and Stock Splits

Stock dividends and stock splits do not result in revenue to investors. The income tax regulations are in agreement with financial accounting on this point.[6]

> Since a shareholder's interest in the corporation remains unchanged by a stock dividend or split-up except as to the number of share units constituting such interest, the cost of the shares previously held should be allocated equitably to the total shares held after receipt of the stock dividend or split-up. When any shares are later disposed of, a gain or loss should be determined on the basis of the adjusted cost per share.

The investor's accounting procedure to record receipt of additional shares from a stock dividend or stock split usually is a memorandum entry that indicates the number of shares of stock received and the new cost per share.

Property Dividends

When a corporation distributes a dividend in the form of merchandise, securities of other corporations, or other noncash assets, the investor records the property received at its current fair value. Income tax regulations also require the use of current fair value to measure dividend revenue from property dividends received.

Stock Warrants and Stock Rights

A *stock warrant* is a certificate issued by a corporation conveying to the owner *rights* to acquire shares of its common stock at a specified price in a specified time period. A single right attaches to each share of outstanding stock, and two or more rights usually are required to acquire one new share at the specified price. For example, when rights are issued, the owner of 100 shares of common stock will receive a warrant representing 100 rights and specifying the number of rights re-

---

[6]*Accounting Research and Terminology Bulletins—Final Edition,* AICPA (New York: 1961), chap. 7b, p. 51.

quired to acquire one new share of common stock. The term of these rights usually is limited to a few weeks. The rights must be exercised or sold before the expiration date or they become worthless.

Accounting for Stock Warrants Acquired for Cash The accounting problems involved when an investor acquires warrants in the open market are similar to those relating to the acquisition of any security. The acquisition price, plus brokerage fees and other acquisition costs, is debited to Investment in Stock Warrants, and Cash is credited. When warrants are acquired in conjunction with the acquisition of other securities, the total cost must be allocated to the various securities included in the package, based on relative market values.

When the warrants are used to acquire common stock, the initial cost of the warrants used plus the cash paid is the cost of the stock. The Investment in Common Stock ledger account is debited; Cash and Investment in Stock Warrants are credited. If the market price of the common stock differs from this combined cost, this fact is disregarded until the stock is sold, at which time a gain or loss is recognized.

Accounting for Stock Warrants Acquired from Issuer Stock warrants for rights are distributed to the stockholders of a corporation in proportion to their holdings of common stock. The receipt of stock warrants for rights may be compared with the receipt of a stock dividend. The issuer distributes no assets; instead, a method has been provided for an additional investment by the present stockholders. Until the stockholders elect to exercise or sell their warrants, their investment in the corporation is represented by (1) shares of common stock that have been acquired, and (2) stock warrants for rights to acquire additional shares of common stock at a price below the current market price. The cost of the original common stock investment consists now of the cost of the common stock and the warrants; therefore, the cost of the original investment is apportioned between these two parts of the investment on the basis of relative market values. The common stock will trade in the market on a "rights-on" basis until the ex-rights date, at which time the stock sells "ex-rights," and the stock warrants have a market of their own. Relative market value allocation may be used to apportion the cost between the common stock and the stock warrants as follows:

Allocation of cost of common stock investment to stock warrants

$$
\left.\begin{array}{c}\text{Cost assigned}\\\text{to stock warrants}\end{array}\right\} = \left(\begin{array}{c}\text{Cost of original}\\\text{investment in common stock}\end{array}\right)
$$

$$
\times \left(\frac{\text{market value of one right}}{\begin{array}{c}\text{market value}\\\text{of one share of}\\\text{stock ex-rights}\end{array} + \begin{array}{c}\text{market}\\\text{value of}\\\text{one right}\end{array}}\right)
$$

To illustrate, assume that on June 1, Year 7, Lott Company received warrants from Anne Corporation for 10,000 rights to acquire one additional share of Anne's common stock for four rights plus $80. On that date, Lott's Investment in Anne Company Common Stock ledger account (10,000 shares) had a balance of

$432,000. On the "ex rights" date, market values of Anne's securities were as follows: common stock, $95 a share; stock warrants, $5 a right.

Lott Company prepares the following journal entry to record the receipt of the stock warrants:

Journal entry for allocation of cost to stock warrants

Investment in Anne Corporation Stock Warrants		
($432,000 × $5/$100)	21,600	
Investment in Anne Corporation Common Stock		21,600
To allocate cost of Anne Corporation investment to stock		
warrants received June 1, Year 7, based on relative market		
values of Anne's common stock and stock warrants.		

If Lott subsequently exercised all the rights to acquire 2,500 shares of Anne's common stock, the following journal entry would be appropriate:

Journal entry for exercise of stock rights

Investment in Anne Corporation Common Stock		
[(2,500 × $80) + $21,600]	221,600	
Cash (2,500 × $80)		200,000
Investment in Anne Corporation Stock Warrants		21,600
To record acquisition of 2,500 shares of Anne Corporation		
common stock at $80 a share plus rights.		

If Lott allowed the warrants to lapse without exercising the rights, it would debit a realized loss ledger account and credit Investment in Anne Corporation Stock Warrants in the amount of $21,600.

Convertible Securities

An investor may invest in bonds or preferred stocks that are convertible to the common stock of the investee at the option of the investor. The characteristics of convertible securities are discussed in Chapters 15 and 17. At this point, we consider the action to be taken by investors who exercise the **conversion option** (**feature**) and receive common stock in exchange for convertible bonds or convertible preferred stock.

The market value of the common stock received may differ materially from the carrying amount of the converted securities. However, it is virtually universal practice to assign the carrying amount of the convertible security to the common stock acquired in exchange. Thus, **no gain or loss is recorded at the time of conversion,** for either financial accounting or income tax purposes. This treatment is supported by the theoretical argument that investors contemplate conversion when they acquire a convertible security. Thus, no gain or loss is recognized until the common stock acquired by conversion is sold.

The following journal entry illustrates the **carrying amount** (or **book value**) **method** for the conversion of an investment in Quincy Company bonds with a carrying amount of $96,720 to Quincy's common stock with a current market value of $120,000:

Journal entry for
conversion of bonds to
common stock—
carrying amount
(or *book value*)
method

Investment in Quincy Company Common Stock	96,720	
Investment in Quincy Company Convertible Bonds		96,720
To record conversion of bonds to common stock.		

Some accountants have proposed recording the common stock acquired by conversion of bonds at the market value of the stock. Under this *market value method,* the journal entry to record the conversion would be as follows:

Journal entry to
record conversion of
bonds to common
stock—
*market value
method*

Investment in Quincy Company Common Stock	120,000	
Investment in Quincy Company Convertible Bonds		96,720
Unrealized Gain on Conversion of Bonds		
($120,000 − $96,720)		23,280
To record conversion of bonds to common stock.		

The difficulty with the market value method is the financial statement presentation of the unrealized gain ledger account. The realization principle precludes inclusion of the unrealized gain in the income statement; and the gain does not fit the definition of a liability or stockholders' equity.

OTHER LONG-TERM INVESTMENTS

Long-Term Receivables

As indicated in Chapter 4 (page 173) and Chapter 7 (page 345), receivables not collectible during the next year or operating cycle, whichever is longer, are excluded from current assets and may be reported with other long-term investments in the balance sheet. Among such receivables are long-term notes and installment contracts receivable and notes receivable from officers, employees, or affiliated companies not collectible in the next year or operating cycle. The current portion of installment contracts receivable and other notes receivable collectible in installments is reported with other current assets in the balance sheet. Adequate allowances for doubtful amounts are required for long-term receivables as they are for current accounts and notes receivable. If a long-term receivable acquired in exchange for goods or services is noninterest-bearing or pays an interest rate that is materially different from the current market rate, the receivable is valued in accordance with the standards described in Chapter 7 (pages 366–370).

Investments in Special-Purpose Funds

Occasionally, a business enterprise accumulates a fund of cash, usually invested temporarily in securities, for a special purpose. Funds generally are created to pay a liability or to acquire specific assets. In general, funds are treated as long-term investments only when they are established by contract, and the resources of the funds are not available to management for general operating needs. A fund is classified as a current asset if it is created voluntarily and may be used for operating purposes.

The transactions that must be accounted for in connection with fund accumulation and administration are: (1) the transfer of assets to the fund, (2) the investment of the assets in internally managed funds, (3) the collection of revenue and payment of expenses if the fund is managed internally, and (4) the use of fund assets for the intended purpose.

There are two methods of handling funds: (1) The fund may be established and operated internally; or (2) the assets may be deposited with a ***trustee*** (a bank, for example) who receives deposits, invests cash, collects revenue, pays expenses, and renders an appropriate accounting to the responsible officials.

Typically, funds that are created voluntarily are operated internally, whereas those created by contract are handled by a trustee. The periodic deposit in the fund generally is set in advance. It may be related to the level of operations, or it may be set either as a stated amount each period or as a stated amount less earnings on fund assets for the period. The method of determining the amount and time for the deposit generally may be found by referring to the document authorizing the establishment of the fund. In cases when the fund is committed irrevocably for the purpose designated, and cash actually is deposited with a trustee, the fund itself may not appear among the assets of the business enterprise, and the liability that is to be paid from fund assets may be excluded from the liabilities. This procedure is used most often when the liability does not exceed the fund balance, which means that the enterprise has no liability other than that for the periodic deposits stipulated in the contract. Most employee pension and benefit plans discussed in Chapter 19 are of this type.

Bond sinking funds usually are included under long-term investments, and bonds outstanding are shown as a long-term liability. The sinking fund should not be offset against the bond liability. A sinking fund and other similar funds usually are included in the balance sheet as an asset even though they are held by trustees.

One of the most common methods of accumulating a sinking fund is to deposit fixed amounts at periodic intervals. The periodic deposit is computed by use of an amount of annuity formula described in Chapter 5.

The transactions relating to the acquisition and sale of securities, and the accrual and collection of revenue for the sinking fund, are accounted for in the same manner in which transactions relating to regular investments are recorded.

Cash Surrender Value of Life Insurance Policies

When a business enterprise is dependent on certain officers for direction and management, life insurance policies may be acquired on the lives of these officers, with the enterprise named as the beneficiary. Certain types of insurance policies combine a savings program and an insurance plan. When these are acquired, the accumulated amount of the savings portion of the insurance premium is reported in the balance sheet as a long-term investment.

The savings part of a life insurance policy is referred to as the ***cash surrender value*** of the policy. This is the amount the enterprise would receive in the event that the policy were canceled; this same amount also may be used as collateral for a loan.

The following data represent the first four years' experience of White Company, which has a $100,000 life insurance policy on one of its officers:

Breakdown of gross
life insurance premium

Year	Gross premium	Cash value increase	Insurance expense
1	$3,040	$ 30	$3,010
2	3,040	250	2,790
3	3,040	260	2,780
4	3,040	280	2,760

From these limited data, we can readily see the increase in the asset and the decreasing annual cost of life insurance. The journal entries for the first two years are as follows:

Journal entries for
payment of life
insurance premiums
for first two years

Year 1	Insurance Expense	3,010	
	Cash Surrender Value of Life Insurance Policy	30	
	Cash		3,040
	To record the payment of life insurance premium.		

Year 2	Insurance Expense	2,790	
	Cash Surrender Value of Life Insurance Policy	250	
	Cash		3,040
	To record the payment of life insurance premium.		

In the event of death of the insured officer, White Company would collect the face amount of the insurance policy. The journal entry to record this event, assuming death occurred early in Year 3, would be as follows:

Journal entry for
receipt of proceeds of
life insurance policy

Year 3	Cash	100,000	
	Gain on Settlement of Life Insurance Policy ..		99,720
	Cash Surrender Value of Life Insurance Policy		280
	To record collection of life insurance proceeds.		

For financial accounting, the gain is included in income before extraordinary items in the income statement. For income tax purposes, the premiums paid on life insurance policies in which the business enterprise is the beneficiary are *not deductible*. Similarly, the gain on the settlement on the death of the insured party is not taxable income for the beneficiary.

Presentation in Financial Statements

Long-term investments that cannot be sold without impairing business relationships are classified immediately following current assets in the balance sheet.

The following illustration is indicative of the features of the investments section of a balance sheet, including the required disclosures for significant investments accounted for under the equity method of accounting:

Investments:

Common stock of Arletz Company, at cost.............................	$ 60,450
Common stock of Fenby, Inc., at underlying equity (**Note 1**).........	286,200
12% bonds of Jardine Company due December 31, Year 9, at cost	
less unamortized discount of $5,971	94,029
Sinking fund for 10% bonds due June 30, Year 14	348,721
Receivable from affiliated company	50,000
Cash surrender value of life insurance policies	283,400
Total investments	$1,122,800

Note 1 The 35% investment in the outstanding common stock of Fenby, Inc., is accounted for by the equity method of accounting. The difference of $60,000 between the cost of the investment and the underlying equity on the date of acquisition is attributable to goodwill and is being amortized over a 20-year economic life. Aggregate market value of the investment was $320,000 on December 31, Year 5.

Dividends and interest revenue normally are listed under the caption Other Revenue and are included in the determination of income before extraordinary items. When the equity method of accounting is used, ordinary investment income (or loss) also is included in Other Revenue (or Other Expenses), but the investor's share of any material extraordinary item of the investee retains its extraordinary nature and is classified as an extraordinary item of the investor. Because of the nature of long-term investments, gains and losses from sales occur relatively infrequently. A business enterprise with numerous long-term investments may expect occasional gains and losses from sales of these investments and generally should include such gains and losses in income before extraordinary items, under the caption of Other Revenue or Other Expenses.

REVIEW QUESTIONS

1   Distinguish between the asset categories of short-term investments and long-term investments. Might the same securities constitute short-term investments for one business enterprise and long-term investments for another? Explain.

2   What is the *cost* of a security acquired for cash? Acquired in exchange for assets for which current fair value is not readily determinable? Acquired as part of a group acquisition?

3   Explain three concepts of the "return on investment" to an investor in common stock and identify the appropriate accounting method for each concept.

4   Why should dividend revenue not be accrued over time by an investor as is interest revenue? What are the alternatives for the recognition of dividend revenue?

5   An investor acquired 1,000 shares of Anne Company common stock on May 15 for $75 a share when the carrying amount of Anne's common stock was composed of the following:

Common stock, $10 par	$1,000,000
Additional paid-in capital	2,000,000
Retained earnings	4,500,000
Total stockholders' equity	$7,500,000

On May 16, Anne declared a dividend of $3 a share. What was the nature of this distribution from the point of view of the investor? Of Anne? What was the legal interpretation of this distribution to the investor?

6   Distinguish between the *cost* and *equity* methods of accounting for a long-term investment in common stock. When is each appropriate?

7   Identify three events that necessitate a write-down of a long-term investment under the cost method of accounting.

8   Compare the accounting for dividends from an investee under the cost and equity methods of accounting for a long-term investment in common stock. How is the difference in accounting for dividends justified?

9   Is the elimination of unrealized intercompany profits on merchandise shipments by an investor to an investee different from the reverse situation? Explain.

10   How may the acquisition price of a long-term investment in common stock affect the subsequent measurement of investment income or loss under the equity method of accounting?

11   Explain the use of the Retained Earnings of Investee ledger account under the equity method of accounting for a long-term investment in common stock.

12   Why does the effective yield of a long-term investment in bonds often differ from the interest rate stated in the bond contract? Explain the effect of interest rate fluctuations on bond prices.

13   Why is the discount or premium on long-term bond investments treated as an adjustment of interest revenue rather than as a gain or loss on sale, redemption, or maturity of the bonds?

14   Distinguish between the *interest method* and the *straight-line method* of accumulating a discount and amortizing a premium on a long-term investment in bonds.

15   What is the theoretical support for the use of a weighted average as a basis for determining cost when units of the same equity security are acquired on different dates and at different prices?

16   From an investor's point of view, is there any significant difference between a stock dividend and a stock split? Does either represent revenue to an investor?

17   What are *stock warrants for rights?* How are they accounted for by an investor?

18   When a convertible bond is converted to common stock, what journal entry does the investor make? Would your answer be different if the market price of the common stock were known? If the market price were not known? Explain.

19   Why is the *cash surrender value* of an insurance policy on the life of an officer of a business enterprise included as a long-term investment in the balance sheet of the enterprise?

EXERCISES

Ex. 14-1   Select the best answer for each of the following multiple-choice questions:

1   On January 2, Year 6, Lido Company acquired (as a long-term investment) 5,000 shares of DeKalb Company's common stock at $60 a share. The 5,000 shares were less than 10% of DeKalb's outstanding common stock. On December 15, Year 6, when the market value of DeKalb common stock was $47 a share, Lido determined that the market value decline was permanent. The market value of DeKalb common stock was $46 a share on December 31, Year 6.

The Realized Loss on Value of Long-Term Investments ledger account balance for Lido Company on December 31, Year 2, is:

a $0   **b** $5,000   **c** $65,000   **d** $70,000   **e** Some other amount

2   An investor that uses the equity method of accounting for a 40%-owned investee, which had net income of $20,000 and declared and paid dividends of $5,000 during Year 6, prepared the following journal entries (explanations omitted) on December 31, Year 6:

Investment in Investee Common Stock	8,000	
Investment Income		8,000
Cash...	2,000	
Dividend Revenue		2,000

The effect of the foregoing journal entries on the balance sheet of the investor on December 31, Year 6, is to:

a Understate the investment ledger account and retained earnings
b Overstate the investment ledger account and retained earnings
c Overstate the investment ledger account and understate retained earnings
d State financial position correctly

3   For a noncurrent marketable equity securities portfolio, which of the following is included in net income of the investor for a specific accounting period?
a Realized gains during the period
b Unrealized losses during the period
c Accumulated changes in the valuation allowance ledger account balance
d Increases in the valuation allowance ledger account balance during the period

4   Investor Company received stock warrants for 10,000 rights to acquire one additional share of Investee Company common stock for one right plus $100 cash. The cost of Investor's 10,000 shares of Investee common stock on which the rights were received was $240,000. On the "ex-rights" date, the market value of one right was $8 and the market value of one share of Investee common stock was $112. In the journal entry to record receipt of the stock warrants, Investor debits the Investment in Investee Company Stock Warrants ledger account for:
a $12,000   **b** $16,000   **c** $80,000   **d** $92,000   **e** Some other amount

5   On January 2, Year 5, Margold Company established a sinking fund for a bond issue due on January 2, Year 15. On December 31, Year 7, the bank serving as independent trustee for the sinking fund reported a fund balance of $364,000, representing $300,000 of Margold's annual deposits to the fund and earnings of $64,000. How is the sinking fund reported in Margold's December 31, Year 7, balance sheet?
a No part of the sinking fund is included in the balance sheet
b $64,000 is included with current assets
c $364,000 is included with current assets
d $364,000 is included with long-term investments

6   The following journal entry (explanation omitted) appeared in the accounting records of Jax Company on April 30, Year 7, the end of its fiscal year:

Realized Loss in Value of Long-Term Investments *60,000*
  Investments in Common Stocks *60,000*

A possible explanation for the foregoing journal entry is:
a To record decline in market value of long-term investments in marketable equity securities
b To record loss on sale of common stocks
c To record a permanent decline in value of long-term investments in common stocks
d None of the foregoing

7   Liquidating dividends received from an investee are credited to the Investment in Investee Company Common Stock ledger account under:
a The equity method of accounting only
b The cost method of accounting only
c Both the equity method and the cost method of accounting
d Neither the equity method nor the cost method of accounting

8   The method of premium amortization or discount accumulation on long-term investments in bonds that produces a constant rate of return on the investment is the:
a Equity method
b Interest method
c Constant-rate method
d Straight-line method

9   The accumulated balance of the valuation allowance for a long-term marketable equity securities portfolio is a component of:
a Current assets
b Noncurrent assets
c Noncurrent liabilities
d Net income
e None of the foregoing

Ex. 14-2   The following transactions or events relate to Bowen Company's long-term investment in Weber Company common stock (1,500,000 shares outstanding):

| | Apr. 10 | Acquired 500 shares of common stock at $22 a share, plus brokerage commission of $400. |

Apr. 10   Acquired 500 shares of common stock at $22 a share, plus brokerage commission of $400.

June 15   Acquired 1,000 shares of common stock at $29 a share, plus brokerage commission of $712.

Aug. 31   Weber distributed a 20% stock dividend.

a Prepare journal entries for Bowen Company to record the foregoing transactions

b Compute the cost per share of Bowen Company's investment in Weber Company common stock, assuming (1) the two acquisitions are treated as separate lots (to permit the use of fifo), and (2) a weighted average is computed for the investment as a whole.

c Prepare a journal entry for Bowen Company to record the sale of 800 shares of Weber Company common stock at $25 a share, assuming the cost of the shares sold is determined by (1) fifo, and (2) weighted average.

Ex. 14-3   On January 2, Year 9, Clarence Company acquired for $500,000 as a long-term investment a 30% interest in the outstanding common stock of Foley, Inc. On that date, Foley had identifiable net assets with a carrying amount and current fair value of $1,600,000. During Year 9, Foley declared and paid dividends of $40,000 and reported net income of $180,000.

     Compute the maximum amount of investment income that Clarence Company may recognize under the equity method of accounting for its investment in Foley, Inc., common stock for Year 9, disregarding income taxes.

Ex. 14-4   On January 2, Year 5, Luna Corporation acquired for $800,000 a 20% interest in the outstanding common stock of Jewel Company. Luna's long-term investment enabled it to exercise significant influence over Jewel's operating and financial policies. Jewel's stockholders' equity attributable to the common stock acquired by Luna was $600,000; the $200,000 excess paid by Luna was attributable to Jewel's patent, which had a remaining economic life of 10 years on January 2, Year 5. Jewel reported net income of $220,000 and declared and paid dividends of $80,000 during Year 5.

     Compute the balance of Luna Corporation's Investment in Jewel Company Common Stock ledger account on December 31, Year 5. Disregard income taxes.

Ex. 14-5   On January 2, Year 7, Dobb Company acquired 40% of the 300,000 outstanding shares of common stock of Lidden Company for $1,800,000, when 40% of the underlying equity of Lidden was $1,400,000. The excess of cost over the underlying equity was assigned to goodwill. Dobb amortizes goodwill over a 20-year period, with a full year's amortization taken in the year of acquisition. As a result of this transaction, Dobb had the ability to exercise significant influence over Lidden's operating and financial policies. Lidden's net income for the year ended December 31, Year 7, was $500,000. During Year 7, Lidden declared and paid $325,000 in dividends.

     Compute the investment income to be recognized by Dobb Company for its long-term investment in Lidden Company common stock for the year ended December 31, Year 7. Disregard income taxes.

Ex. 14-6   On May 1, Year 2, the beginning of a fiscal year, Lindell Corporation acquired 40% of the outstanding shares of common stock of Madison Company for $440,000, including implicit goodwill of $40,000 that had a 10-year economic life. For the year ended April 30, Year 3, Madison had net income of $100,000, and on April 1, Year 3, Madison declared common stock dividends totaling $30,000, payable April 30, Year 3, to stockholders of record on April 15, Year 3.

   Prepare Lindell Corporation's journal entries for its investment in Madison Company common stock on May 1, Year 2, April 1, Year 3, and April 30, Year 3, under the equity method of accounting. Disregard income taxes.

Ex. 14-7   Norman Company owns 40% of the outstanding common stock of Saxon Company; this long-term investment enables Norman to exercise significant influence over the operating and financial policies of Saxon. Norman acquired its investment at a price equal to 40% of Saxon's stockholders' equity on the date of acquisition. For the year ended December 31, Year 6, Saxon reported net income of $180,000, but did not declare or pay dividends. Included in Norman's December 31, Year 6, inventories is merchandise billed at $160,000 by Saxon, at a 30% gross profit rate. Included in Saxon's December 31, Year 6, inventories is merchandise billed at $550,000 by Norman, at a gross profit rate of 20%.

   Prepare journal entries for Norman Company on December 31, Year 6, to account for its investment in Saxon Company common stock under the equity method of accounting and to eliminate unrealized intercompany profits in inventories. Disregard income taxes.

Ex. 14-8   On January 2, Year 5, Investor Company acquired 20% of the 100,000 outstanding shares of Investee Company common stock. During Year 5, Investee reported net income of $140,000.

   Compute the equity per share of Investee Company stock and the carrying amount per share of Investor Company's long-term investment in Investee's common stock under each of the following independent assumptions (disregarding income taxes):

   a Investor acquired Investee's common at the underlying equity of $12 a share, and correctly accounted for the investment by the cost method of accounting. Investee declared and paid dividends of $80,000 during Year 5.

   b Same facts as case **a,** except that Investee declared and paid dividends of $160,000 during Year 5.

   c Same facts as case **a,** except that Investor correctly used the equity method of accounting to account for the investment.

   d Same facts as case **c,** except that Investor acquired the Investee common stock at a price of $15 a share, although the underlying equity was only $12 a share. The excess of cost over underlying equity was paid because a patent with a remaining economic life of six years was undervalued in Investee's accounting records.

Ex. 14-9   On January 2, Year 3, Olive Company acquired as a long-term investment at a 10% yield rate 100 of the $1,000 face amount, 8% bonds of Edgar Company maturing on January 2, Year 13. Interest on the bonds is paid annually on each January 2, beginning Year 4. Information on present value factors is as follows:

$P\,\overline{10}|8\% = 0.4632$ $P\,\overline{10}|10\% = 0.3855$ $P\,\overline{10}|8\% = 6.7101$ $P\,\overline{10}|10\% = 6.1446$

Prepare journal entries for Olive Company on January 2, Year 3, to record the acquisition of the Edgar Company bonds and on December 31, Year 3, to accrue interest on the bonds for a full year. Use the interest method to accumulate bond discount and round computations to the nearest dollar.

Ex. 14-10   On July 1, Year 8, Ford Company acquired 500 of the $1,000 face amount, 14% bonds of Nixon Company for $460,481, at a yield rate of 16% a year. The bonds, which mature on January 1, Year 15, pay interest semiannually on January 1 and July 1. Ford recorded the bonds as a long-term investment and adopted the interest method for accumulating the discount on the bonds.

Compute the carrying amount, rounded to the nearest dollar, of the Nixon Company 14% bonds in Ford Company's balance sheet on December 31, Year 8.

Ex. 14-11   The following data (rounded to the nearest dollar) are the beginning of an amortization table prepared by Hogan Company to account for its long-term investment in $80,000 face amount bonds of Popp Company, maturing in 17 years, which pay interest annually:

Year	Payment received	Interest revenue	Accumulation of discount	Carrying amount of investment
				$61,132
1	$4,000	$4,585	$585	61,717
2	4,000	4,629	629	62,346
3				

a Is the discount being accumulated by the straight-line method or the interest method? Explain.

b What is the nominal rate of interest on the bonds?

c What is the effective yield on the long-term investment in bonds?

d Prepare a journal entry to record Hogan Company's interest revenue in Year 2.

e Compute the amounts to be entered in each column of the table for Year 3.

f What would be the interest revenue recognized each year if the discount were accumulated by the straight-line method?

g Compute the percentage return (to the nearest tenth of one percent) on the carrying amount of the investment in Years 1 and 3, assuming that the discount was accumulated by the straight-line method.

Ex. 14-12   Lew Company owns 300 shares of the outstanding common stock of Parke Corporation, which has several hundred thousand shares of common stock publicly traded. The 300 shares were acquired as a long-term investment by Lew in Year 3 for $105 a share. On June 20, Year 5, Parke distributed stock warrants for rights to its stockholders to acquire one new share of Parke common stock for $120 cash and three rights. On June 20, Year 5, each share of Parke common stock had a market value of $134 ex-rights, and each right had a market value of $6.

Compute the cost of each new share of Parke Company common stock that Lew Company acquired by exercising the rights on July 18, Year 5.

Ex. 14-13 Prepare journal entries for Nebbitt Company to record the following transactions for long-term investments:

Feb. 10 Nebbitt acquired 1,000 shares of Nobe Company common stock at $88 a share.

Mar. 31 Nobe issued a 10% stock dividend to common stockholders.

June 30 Nobe issued stock warrants for rights to common stockholders, enabling the acquisition of one additional share of Nobe common stock at $90 for every five shares held. Nobe common stock was trading ex-rights at $114 a share, and the rights had a market value of $6 each.

July 18 Nebbitt exercised 1,000 rights to acquire new shares of Nobe common stock.

20 Nebbitt sold the remaining stock warrants for 100 rights for $6.50 each.

Oct. 12 Nebbitt sold 400 shares of Nobe common stock for $48,000. The shares sold were specifically identified as being from those acquired on February 10.

Ex. 14-14 Prepare a single journal entry for Roxy Company on December 31, Year 4, to correct the following ledger account. Include supporting computations in the explanation for the journal entry. The accounting records have not been closed for Year 4. (*Note:* Credits to the account represent *net cash* received.)

Investment in Tupp Company Common Stock (Long-Term)

Date	Explanation	Debit	Credit	Balance
Year 4				
Jan. 18	Acquired 200 shares (½% interest)	24,000		24,000 dr
Mar. 6	Sold 40 shares received as a 20% stock dividend on this date		3,800	20,200 dr
July 26	Received cash dividend of $1.50 a share		300	19,900 dr
Aug. 21	Sold stock warrants for 200 rights received on this date (3% of adjusted cost is allocable to rights)		700	19,200 dr
Dec. 20	Sold 100 shares after a 2 for 1 stock split effective Oct. 10, Year 4		5,350	13,850 dr

CASES

Case 14-1 On July 1, Year 5, Drosser Company acquired for cash 40% of the outstanding common stock of Furman, Inc. Both Drosser and Furman have a December 31 fiscal year. Furman reported its net income for Year 5 to Drosser, and also declared and paid cash dividends in Year 5 to its stockholders.

Instructions

How should Drosser Company report the foregoing facts in its balance sheet on December 31, Year 5, and its income statement for the year then ended? Explain. (Disregard income taxes.)

Case 14-2 During your examination of the financial statements of Lure Company, which has never before been audited, you discover that the cash surrender value of a $250,000 life insurance policy on the president, for which Lure was the beneficiary, had not been entered in the accounting records. The president stated that the total premium on the policy was debited to the Insurance Expense ledger account each year because Lure had no intention to "cash in" the policy or to use the cash surrender value as collateral for a loan from the insurance company or a bank. Therefore, asserted the president, it would be misleading for Lure to record as an asset an amount never expected to be realized or used by Lure.

Instructions

Evaluate the position of the president of Lure Company.

Case 14-3 For the past five years Root Company has maintained a long-term investment (accounted for and reported correctly) in Koler Company amounting to a 10% interest in the common stock of Koler. The cost of the investment was $700,000, and the underlying net equity in Koler on the date of acquisition was $620,000. On January 2, Year 7, Root acquired an additional 15% of the common stock of Koler for $1,200,000; the underlying equity of the additional investment on January 2 was $1,000,000. Koler has been profitable and has paid dividends annually since Root's initial acquisition.

Instructions

Discuss how the increase in Root Company's ownership of Koler Company common stock affects the accounting for and reporting of the investment in Koler. Include in your discussion adjustments, if any, to the amount shown prior to the increase in investment to bring the amount into conformity with generally accepted accounting principles. Also indicate how the investment in Koler Company common stock is reported in Root's financial statements for Year 7 and subsequent accounting periods.

Case 14-4 Null Company has been operating profitably for many years. On March 1, Year 4, Null acquired 50,000 shares of Tulak Company common stock for $2,000,000. The 50,000 shares represented 25% of Tulak's outstanding common stock. Both Null and Tulak have a fiscal year ending August 31.

For the year ended August 31, Year 4, Tulak reported net income of $800,000, earned ratably throughout the year. During November, Year 3, and February, May, and August, Year 4, Tulak declared and paid regular quarterly cash dividends of $125,000.

Instructions

a What criteria should Null Company consider in determining whether its investment in Tulak Company should be classified as a current asset or a noncurrent asset in Null's August 31, Year 4, balance sheet? Confine your discussion to the decision criteria for determining the balance sheet classification of the investment.

b Assume that the investment is classified as a long-term investment in Null Company's balance sheet. The cost of the investment equaled Null's equity in Tulak Company's net assets; carrying amounts were not materially different from current fair values (individually or collectively). How much investment income does Null recognize as a result of its investment in Tulak common stock for the year ended August 31, Year 4? Explain.

Case 14-5 Nickleby Company acquired 45,000 of 150,000 outstanding shares of common stock of Zane Company on January 2, Year 6, at $30 a share. The carrying amount of Zane's common stock on December 31, Year 5, was $22.75 a share. During the year following the acquisition of the stock by Nickleby, Zane earned $325,000 and declared and paid dividends of $1.10 a share. The management of Nickleby is concerned about the appropriate method of presenting the investment in Zane in the financial statements. The controller argues that Nickleby had earned 30% of Zane's net income, because it owns 30% of Zane's common stock. The financial vice president argues that the investment must be carried at cost as are all other nonmonetary assets, and that the net income of Nickleby should include only the dividends received from Zane.

Instructions

a Attempt to resolve this debate by pointing out the relevant issues on both sides of the argument.

b The vice president counters your points in favor of the controller's position with the statement that, ''What you say makes sense until you try to explain what the dollar amount of the investment represents. It is not market value of the common stock, because the current market price is $29 a share, and it most certainly is not cost.'' Present your answer to the vice president.

PROBLEMS

14-1 On June 1, Year 9, Liston Company acquired as a long-term investment 800 of the $1,000 face amount, 8% bonds of Welsh Corporation for $738,300. The bonds were acquired to yield 10% interest. The bonds pay interest on June 1 and December 1 and mature on June 1, Year 14. Liston uses the interest method to accumulate bond discount. On November 1, Year 10, Liston sold the bonds for $785,000, including accrued interest of $26,667.

Instructions

Prepare a working paper to compute the pre-tax income or loss from the bond investment recorded by Liston Company for the years ended December 31, Year 9 and Year 10. Show supporting computations and round all amounts to the nearest dollar.

14-2   On April 1, Year 9, Chatt Company acquired 6% convertible bonds of Curtin, Inc., with face amount of $1,500,000 for $1,818,000 plus accrued interest for two months. The bonds pay interest semiannually on February 1 and August 1 and mature in 8 years and 10 months from date of acquisition. Each $1,000 bond is convertible on any interest date to 40 shares of common stock.

On August 1, Year 9, 500 bonds were converted to Curtin common stock. On the date of conversion the Curtin common stock was selling for $40 a share. On September 1, Year 9, a 10% stock dividend was declared on the common stock, to be distributed on October 10 to stockholders of record on September 20. On December 1, Year 9, 5,500 shares of Curtin common stock were sold for $35 a share.

Instructions

a Prepare journal entries for Chatt Company for the foregoing transactions or events, including receipt of interest on August 1, Year 9, and the accrual of interest on December 31, Year 9, assuming that the conversion of the bonds is recorded by the carrying amount (book value) method.

b Justify your reason for amortizing or not amortizing the premium on Chatt Company's investment in convertible bonds.

14-3   On January 2, Year 3, Kirby Company paid $700,000 for 10,000 shares (a 10% interest) of Lude Company outstanding common stock. On that date the carrying amount of Lude's identifiable net assets was equal to the current fair value of $6,000,000. Kirby did not have the ability to exercise significant influence over the operating and financial policies of Lude. Kirby received dividends of $0.90 a share from Lude on October 1, Year 3, and Lude reported net income of $400,000 for the year ended December 31, Year 3.

On July 1, Year 4, Kirby paid $2,300,000 for 30,000 additional shares of Lude's outstanding common stock, for an additional 30% interest. The current fair value of Lude's identifiable net assets equaled the carrying amount of $6,500,000 on July 1, Year 4. As a result of this transaction, Kirby had the ability to exercise significant influence over the operating and financial policies of Lude. Kirby received dividends from Lude during Year 4 as follows: $1.10 a share on April 1, and $1.35 a share on October 1. Lude reported net income of $300,000 for the six months ended June 30, Year 4, and $200,000 for the six months ended December 31, Year 4. Kirby amortizes goodwill over an economic life of 40 years.

Instructions

a Prepare a working paper to show the pre-tax income or loss reported by Kirby company from its investment in Lude Company for the year ended December 31, Year 3.

b Prepare a working paper to compute the balance of Kirby Company's investment in Lude Company common stock on December 31, Year 3 and Year 4, for inclusion in comparative balance sheets to be issued by Lude in its annual report for Year 4.

14-4   On October 1, Year 7, Lansing Company acquired for cash 200,000 shares, representing 45%, of the outstanding common stock of Berst Company. As a result of the acquisition, Lansing had the ability to exercise significant influence over the operating and financial policies of Berst. Goodwill of $500,000 was appropriately computed by Lansing on the date of the acquisition.

On January 2, Year 8, Lansing also acquired 300,000 shares, representing 30% of the outstanding common stock of Ansel Company. The amount of cash paid for the Ansel common stock was $2,500,000. The stockholders' equity section of Ansel's balance sheet on January 2, Year 8, was as follows:

Common stock, $2 par...	$2,000,000
Additional paid-in capital...	1,000,000
Retained earnings	3,500,000
Total stockholders' equity	$6,500,000

Furthermore, on January 2, Year 8, the current fair value of Ansel's plant assets was $4,000,000, and the carrying amount was $3,600,000. For all other assets and liabilities of Ansel the current fair values and carrying amounts were equal. As a result of the acquisition, Lansing had the ability to exercise significant influence over the operating and financial policies of Ansel.

Assume that Lansing amortizes goodwill to the nearest month over the maximum period allowed by generally accepted accounting principles.

Instructions

Prepare a working paper for computation of the amount of goodwill and accumulated amortization for Lansing Company on December 31, Year 8, and the goodwill amortization for the year ended December 31, Year 8. Show supporting computations.

14-5   Coco Company has supplied you with the following information regarding two long-term investments that were made during Year 4. Coco uses a single Investments ledger account.

(1) On January 2, Year 4, Coco acquired 40% of the 500,000 shares of outstanding common stock of Filbert Company for $2,400,000, equal to 40% of the carrying amount of the net assets of Filbert. Net income of Filbert for Year 4 was $750,000, including $80,000 unrealized intercompany profit on sales of merchandise to Coco. Filbert declared and paid dividends of $0.50 a share in Year 4. The market price of Filbert's common stock was $14 a share on December 31, Year 4. Coco exercised significant influence over the operating and financial policies of Filbert.

(2) On July 1, Year 4, Coco acquired 15,000 shares, representing 5% of the outstanding common stock of Leach Company, for $450,000. Leach's net income for the six months ended December 31, Year 4, was $350,000; for the year ended December 31, Year 4, net income was $600,000. Leach declared and paid dividends of $0.30 a share each quarter during Year 4 to stockholders of record on the last day of each quarter. The market price of Leach's common stock was $34 a share on December 31, Year 4.

Instructions

a Prepare a working paper to compute the balance in Coco Company's Investments ledger account on December 31, Year 4. Show supporting computations. Disregard income taxes.

b Compute the investment income, under the accrual basis of accounting for dividends, reported by Coco Company for the year ended December 31, Year 4. Show supporting computations. Disregard income taxes.

14-6   In Year 5, Liggett Corporation acquired 1% of the outstanding common stock of Yorba Company as a long-term investment. The accountant for Liggett was inexperienced and made the following errors in recording the transactions relating to the investment in the common stock of Yorba: (1) Shares received as a 10% stock dividend were valued at the current market price and recorded by a debit to the investment ledger account and a credit to Dividend Revenue; (2) the net cash proceeds on the sales of shares of Yorba common stock and stock warrants for rights were credited to the investment ledger account; and (3) a cash dividend was credited to the investment ledger account.

On June 9, Year 5, the common stock of Yorba was trading ex-rights at $98, and the rights were trading at $2. The activity in the investment ledger account during Year 5 is presented below:

Investment in Yorba Company Common Stock (Long-Term)

Date	Explanation	Debit	Credit	Balance
Year 5				
Jan. 18	Acquired 4,000 shares (1% interest)	374,000		374,000 dr
Feb. 28	Received 400 shares as 10% stock			
	dividend (400 × $100)	40,000		414,000 dr
Mar. 6	Sold 400 shares received Feb. 28		38,000	376,000 dr
May 25	Received cash dividend			
	(4,000 × $1.10)		4,400	371,600 dr
June 27	Sold stock warrants for 4,000			
	rights received June 9		7,850	363,750 dr
Dec. 20	Sold 3,200 shares (20%) after a 4			
	for 1 split effective Oct. 10		98,800	264,950 dr

Instructions

a Prepare a working paper to summarize the transactions in Liggett Company's investment in Yorba Company Common Stock ledger account as the transactions should have been recorded. Use the following column headings:

Date	Transac-tions	Number of shares	Cost	Proceeds on sale	Gain of (loss)
Year 5					
Jan. 18					

b Prepare a single journal entry to correct the accounting records of Liggett Company as of December 31, Year 5. Assume that the accounting records have not been closed for Year 5.

14-7 At the beginning of Year 1, Le Moyne Company acquired 10,000 shares, representing 6% of the outstanding shares of Merk Company common stock, for $300,000 as a long-term investment. At the end of Year 1, the market value of the investment was $258,000. Late in Year 2, Le Moyne sold 2,000 shares of Merk common stock for $55,000. At the end of Year 2, the market value of the remaining 8,000 shares of Merk common stock was $215,000.

Instructions

a Prepare journal entries for Le Moyne Company to record realized and unrealized gains or losses relating to the investment in Merk Company common stock.

b Show how the investment in Merk Company common stock and the unrealized loss are presented in the balance sheets of Le Moyne Company at the end of Year 1 and Year 2. Disregard disclosures in notes to the financial statements.

14-8 The following transactions and adjustments relate to long-term investments of Logan Company during Year 6:

Apr. 30 Acquired $60,000 face amount 16% bonds of March Company at a cost of $63,760 plus accrued interest. The bonds pay interest semiannually on March 1 and September 1, and mature 94 months from the date of acquisition.

July 10 Acquired for a total of $155,000 a package of 500 shares of 12%, $100 par, preferred stock and 1,000 shares of common stock of Niles Company. The preferred and common stock were trading at $80 a share and $120 a share, respectively.

Sept. 1 Received semiannual interest payment on the March Company bonds. Premium is amortized by the straight-line method when interest is received and at the end of the fiscal year.

Oct. 15 Received the quarterly dividend on the Niles Company preferred stock.

25 Received new shares from a 2 for 1 stock split of the Niles Company common stock.

Dec. 31 Prepared appropriate adjusting entry (or entries), including amortization of premium, for the end of the fiscal year.

Instructions

Prepare journal entries for Logan Company to record the foregoing transactions and adjustments.

14-9 On July 1, Year 5, Lubell Company acquired 25% of the outstanding shares of common stock of Slocum Company at a total cost of $720,000. The underlying equity of the stock acquired by Lubell was only $600,000. Lubell was willing to pay more than the underlying equity for the Slocum common stock for the following reasons:

(1) Slocum owned depreciable plant assets (10-year remaining economic life) with a current fair value $60,000 more than their carrying amount.

(2) Slocum owned land with a current fair value $300,000 more than its carrying amount.

(3) Lubell believed that Slocum possessed enough goodwill to justify the remainder of the cost. Lubell's accounting policy with respect to goodwill is to amortize it over 10 years.

Slocum earned net income of $540,000 uniformly over the year ended December 31, Year 5. On December 31, Year 5, Slocum declared and paid a cash dividend of $360,000. Both Lubell and Slocum close their accounting records on December 31.

Instructions

a Compute the total imputed amount of goodwill of Slocum Company, based on the price paid by Lubell Company for Slocum's common stock.

b Assuming that Lubell Company's investment does not enable it to exercise significant influence over Slocum Company, prepare all journal entries for Lubell relating to the investment for the year ended December 31, under the cost method of accounting.

c Assuming that Lubell Company's investment enables it to exercise significant influence over Slocum Company, prepare all journal entries for Lubell Company relating to the investment for the year ended December 31, under the equity method of accounting.

14-10 Noria Company acquired as a long-term investment $500,000 face amount of Tork Company bonds on September 30, Year 2. The bonds have a 14% nominal rate with interest payable semiannually on March 31 and September 30. The remaining term of the bonds is 10 years, and the bonds have an effective yield to maturity of 16% compounded semiannually.

Instructions

(Round all computations to the nearest dollar.)

a Using the tables in the Appendix at the end of Chapter 5, compute the amount that Noria Company paid for the Tork Company bonds.

b Prepare tables for Noria Company for the first two years to show the accumulation of the discount and the computation of interest revenue on the Tork Company bonds, under both the interest method and the straight-line method.

c Prepare journal entries for Noria Company to record the first year's transactions, excluding the acquisition of the bonds and closing entries, under both the interest method and the straight-line method. Noria's fiscal year ends on September 30.

14-11 On June 30, Year 2, Alber Company acquired as a long-term investment 20% of the 100,000 outstanding shares of common stock of Nemo Company. The stockholders' equity of Nemo on June 30, Year 2, was as follows:

Common stock, $10 par	$1,000,000
Additional paid-in capital	1,750,000
Retained earnings	2,350,000
Total stockholders' equity	$5,100,000

Alber paid $1,410,000 cash for the common stock of Nemo. The excess of the cost over the underlying equity was paid because (1) the land owned by Nemo had a current fair value $550,000 more than its carrying amount; (2) the depreciable plant assets of Nemo were worth $450,000 more than their carrying amount; (3) Nemo had at least the amount of goodwill imputed by the cost of Alber's 20% interest. The accounting policy of Alber with respect to goodwill is to amortize over 40 years. The depreciable plant assets of Nemo had a remaining economic life of 12 years on June 30, Year 2.

During the last six months of Year 2, Nemo earned net income of $270,000, after an extraordinary loss of $45,000, and declared and paid dividends of $1 a share. In Year 3, Nemo reported a net loss of $90,000 and declared and paid dividends of $2 a share. Both Alber and Nemo end their fiscal year on December 31.

Instructions

a Compute the total imputed amount of Nemo Company's goodwill based on the cost of Alber Company's 20% interest in Nemo.

b Prepare Alber Company's journal entries for Year 2 and Year 3 relating to the investment in Nemo under the cost method of accounting. Assume that all end-of-period adjustments are made and that dividends are received at the end of each year.

c Prepare Alber Company's journal entries for Year 2 and Year 3 relating to the investment in Nemo under the equity method of accounting.

d On January 2, Year 4, Alber Company decided that Nemo Company's goodwill no longer had any value and that the investment ledger account balance should be reduced by Alber's portion of unamortized goodwill. Prepare a journal entry to record Alber Company's write-off of goodwill, assuming that the equity method of accounting had been in use.

14-12 Quarry Company acquired three lots of Moto Company common stock as follows:

Lot No.	Number of shares	Cost of each share	Brokerage and other costs
1	2,000	$28	$600
2	800	36	300
3	1,200	30	400

Moto issued a 10% stock dividend on May 10 and stock warrants for rights on August 15 entitling common stockholders to acquire for $40 one new share for every 10 shares held. Shortly after the stock warrants for rights were issued, the common stock was trading ex-rights at $49 a share, and the rights at $1 a right. Quarry sold 1,000 rights at $1.125 a right, less brokerage commission of $45. The remaining rights were exercised. Moto has 5,000,000 shares of common stock outstanding.

Instructions

a Compute Quarry Company's gain or loss on the sale of rights under (1) fifo, (2) lifo, and (3) average cost of the common stock to determine the cost of the rights sold. Round cost of each right to the nearest tenth of a cent.

b Prepare a working paper for Quarry Company to show the number of shares of Moto Company common stock in each lot, the total cost of each lot, and the unit cost of each lot (to the nearest cent), assuming the use of fifo in part **a** and considering the shares acquired through the exercise of rights as lot no. 4.

14-13   At the beginning of Year 1, Galber Company issued at face amount $500,000 of 15%, 10-year bonds, interest to be payable annually. A sinking fund was established at the same time to accumulate the $500,000 at the end of 10 years. Galber was to make payments of $28,492 to the fund at the end of each year. The fund balance was to be invested to earn 12% a year.

In addition to the sinking fund, Galber acquired at the beginning of Year 1 a $100,000 life insurance policy on Lois Hatch, Galber's president. The terms of the insurance policy were as follows:

Year	Gross premium	Cash surrender value at end of year
1	$7,770	$ 1,340
2	7,770	7,460
3	7,770	13,780
4	7,770	20,290
5	7,770	27,030
6	7,770	34,020
7	7,770	41,290
8	7,770	48,880
9	7,770	56,830
10	7,770	65,210

Instructions

a Prepare for Galber Company a fund accumulation table for the sinking fund for the first three years. Round all computations to the nearest dollar.

b Prepare for Galber Company a table to determine the effect on net income of the life insurance policy for each of the first three years.

c Prepare journal entries for Galber Company for all transactions involving the bonds, the sinking fund, and the life insurance policy for each of the first three years.

14-14   The following transactions and events relate to the long-term investments of Marquez Company for the year ended December 31, Year 2:

Jan. 2   Acquired 30,000 of 100,000 outstanding shares of Garth Company common stock for $15 a share. Underlying equity was $12 a share; Marquez attributed the excess of cost over equity acquired to goodwill, to be amortized over 30 years. The acquisition gave Marquez a significant degree of influence over Garth.

Jan. 6   Acquired $100,000 of Haggis Company first mortgage 18% bonds at face amount plus accrued interest for 36 days. Interest was payable semiannually on December 1 and June 1, with maturity on December 1, Year 11. The bonds were callable at 106 (106% of face amount).

Feb. 15   Acquired 1,000 shares of Ingle Company $10 par common stock for $65,280. Ingle had 200,000 shares of common stock outstanding.

May 5   Received cash dividend of 65 cents a share on Ingle Company common stock.

June 1   Received semiannual interest on Haggis Company bonds.

Aug. 5   Received cash dividend of 65 cents a share and a 2% stock dividend on Ingle Company common stock.

Sept. 30   Sold the shares of Ingle Company common received as a stock dividend for $70 a share and acquired 50, $1,000 16% subordinated debenture bonds of James Company at 94 (94% of face amount), with interest payable semiannually on March 31 and September 30, and with maturity 10 years from date of acquisition. The bonds were callable at 102 (102% of face amount).

Oct. 1   Received cash dividend of 75 cents a share from Garth Company. (The dividend was paid from earnings.)

Nov. 5   Received cash dividend of 70 cents a share on Ingle Company common stock.

Dec. 1   Received semiannual interest on Haggis Company bonds and surrendered to Haggis 60 of the $1,000 bonds at the call price of 106, in accordance with the provisions of the bond indenture.

31   Garth Company reported net income of $164,000 for Year 2, including an extraordinary gain of $44,000.

Instructions

a Prepare journal entries for Marquez Company for the foregoing transactions and events and record any adjustments required on December 31, Year 2. Accumulate the discount on the bonds of James Company to the nearest month, under the straight-line method. The market value of Ingle Company common stock on December 31, Year 2, was $75,000.

b Prepare a listing of long-term investments to appear in the balance sheet of Marquez Company on December 31, Year 2.

14-15   Rampe, Inc., had the following long-term receivables on December 31, Year 3:

Note receivable from sale of electronics division...................... $1,500,000

Note receivable from officer   400,000

Additional information

(1) The $1,500,000 note receivable is dated May 1, Year 3, bears interest at 9%, and represents the balance of the consideration received from the sale of Rampe's electronics division to Carlin Company. Principal payments of

$500,000 plus appropriate interest are due on May 1, Year 4, Year 5, and Year 6. The first principal and interest payment was made on May 1, Year 4. Collection of the note installments from Carlin is reasonably assured.

(2) The $400,000 note receivable is dated December 31, Year 1, bears interest at 8%, and is due on December 31, Year 6. The note is due from Robert Finley, president of Rampe, and is collateralized by 10,000 shares of Rampe common stock. Interest is payable annually on December 31, and all interest payments were paid on their due dates through December 31, Year 4. The market price of Rampe common stock was $45 a share on December 31, Year 4.

(3) On April 1, Year 4, Rampe sold a patent to Bell Company for a $100,000 noninterest-bearing note due on April 1, Year 6. There was no market price for the patent, and the note had no ready market. The prevailing rate of interest for a note of this type on April 1, Year 4, was 15%. The present value of 1 discounted for two periods at 15% is 0.756. The patent had a carrying amount of $40,000 on January 1, Year 4, and the amortization for the year ended December 31, Year 4, would have been $8,000. Collection of the note receivable from Bell is reasonably assured.

(4) On July 1, Year 4, Rampe sold a parcel of land to Carr Company for $200,000 under an installment sale contract. Carr made a $60,000 cash down payment on July 1, Year 4, and signed a four-year promissory note with an effective interest rate of 16% for the $140,000 balance. The equal annual payments of principal and interest on the note are $50,000, payable on July 1, Year 5, through July 1, Year 8. The land could have been sold for $200,000 cash. The cost of the land to Rampe was $150,000. Collection of the note installments from Carr is reasonably assured.

Instructions

a Prepare the long-term receivables section of the investments section of Rampe, Inc.'s, balance sheet on December 31, Year 4.

b Prepare a working paper to compute the current portion of the long-term receivables and interest receivable for presentation in Rampe, Inc.'s, balance sheet on December 31, Year 4.

c Prepare a working paper to compute interest revenue from the long-term receivables and gains on sales of assets for presentation in Rampe, Inc.'s, income statement for the year ended December 31, Year 4.

Long-Term Debt

15

Liabilities that do not require the payment of cash, the shipment of goods, or the rendering of services in one year (or the next operating cycle, whichever is longer) for their liquidation are designated *long-term liabilities,* or *long-term debt.* Examples of long-term debt are: bonds, mortgage notes, promissory notes, deposits received for utilities service, some obligations under pension and deferred compensation plans, certain types of lease obligations, deferred income tax credits, and some deferred revenue items.

Long-term debt may be *collateralized* (secured) by liens on business property of various kinds, for example, equipment (equipment notes), real property (mortgages), or securities (collateral trust bonds). Many companies issue *debenture bonds* that are backed only by the general credit standing of the issuer, and some companies have issued *commodity backed bonds* that are redeemable at prices linked to the prices of specified products such as gold and silver. The title of a long-term debt obligation, such as First Mortgage Bonds Payable, may indicate the nature of collateral for the debt. Bonds may be issued that pay no interest *(zero-coupon bonds)* or that pay an exceptionally low rate of interest *(deep-discount bonds).*

As noted in Chapter 10, some current liabilities involve no specific mention of interest payments. Because money has a time value, some amount of interest probably is included in the face amount of such liabilities, but often it is disregarded because of the relatively small amounts involved. However, the interest factor in long-term debt is significant and must be given accounting consideration. Accounting for bonds is covered in this chapter; pensions and leases are discussed in Chapters 19 and 20, respectively; and deferred income tax credits are covered in Chapter 21.

Types of Bonds

Bonds are a means of dividing long-term debt into a number of small units. Usually, bonds are issued in $1,000 denominations, or in multiples of $1,000. Occasionally, additional denominations of $100 or $500 are used. In this way, amounts of money larger than that which could be borrowed from a single source may be obtained from a large number of investors. The specific conditions of the borrowing and any restrictions on the issuer (such as limitations on dividend payments and additional borrowing) are contained in a contract between the issuer of the bonds and the bondholders, which is known as the *bond indenture*. This contract usually is held by a *trustee,* such as a bank or a trust company, who acts as an independent third party to protect the interests of both the issuer and the bondholders.

Bonds may be issued by corporations, by nations, by state and local governments, and by governmental agencies. They may be *registered bonds* or *coupon bonds*. Interest on registered bonds is paid only to the owner of record, but interest on coupon bonds is paid to persons presenting the periodic interest coupons.[1] *Serial bonds* mature in predetermined installments; *term bonds* mature on a single fixed maturity date.

A bond issue may rank behind previously issued *senior bonds* and thus may be described as *subordinated debentures* or *second mortgage bonds*. Most bonds are *callable*[2] at the option of the issuer. Some bond issues are *convertible* to common stock of the issuer at the option of the bondholder. *Revenue bonds* (issued by municipalities, turnpikes, bridge authorities, etc.) pay interest and principal only from specific revenue sources. Occasionally, bonds are *guaranteed* by a business enterprise or governmental unit other than the issuer. High-risk bonds issued by companies with a weak financial position are termed *junk bonds*.

Bonds may be privately placed with a single institution or issued to investment bankers, who in turn reissue the bonds in smaller lots to individual investors. Investment bankers may *underwrite* the bond issue, thus guaranteeing a fixed price to the issuer and assuming the risk in selling the issue to the public. If a bond issue is underwritten, the entire issue is recorded in the accounting records of the issuer at the time of sale to underwriters. Unissued bonds represent potential indebtedness that may be incurred without further authorization from the board of directors or additional pledge of properties. Authorized and unissued bonds are reported in the balance sheet parenthetically or in a note to the financial statements.

Financial Management Considerations

When financial managers decide to borrow money by issuing bonds, they must resolve a number of questions before they issue the bonds. First, they must relate the need for funds to the amount of long-term debt that may be undertaken safely by studying the financial position and earning prospects of the company. They must forecast the ability of the company to meet bond sinking fund requirements or periodic maturities of serial bonds. A decision must be made regarding the features of the bonds, such as collateral to be offered, call provisions, convertibility, etc. It is apparent that a great deal of advance preparation precedes the issuance of bonds payable.

---

[1]The Tax Equity and Fiscal Responsibility Act of 1982 placed severe restrictions on the deductibility of bond interest expense for coupon bonds, thus making such bonds less popular.

[2]The call provision protects the issuer, which may wish to retire the debt in advance, particularly when interest rates have fallen and it may secure more favorable financing. Bondholders who are repaid at this time must reinvest their funds at a lower rate of interest, and therefore insist on a call premium as compensation for the reduced interest rate. Call premiums generally are established on a decreasing scale as the bonds approach maturity.

ACCOUNTING FOR ISSUANCE OF BONDS AND INTEREST EXPENSE

Issuance of Term Bonds

In a typical term bond contract, the issuer promises two essentially different kinds of future payments: (1) the payment of a fixed amount (*face amount* or *principal*) on a specified date; and (2) the periodic payment of interest, usually at six-month intervals, in an amount expressed as a percentage of the face amount of the bonds. In the light of expectations as to what interest rate is necessary to attract the required funds, a rate of interest is set. The interest expense actually incurred on the bonds is determined by the price at which the bonds are sold; thus, the *effective interest rate* (sometimes called the *yield rate*) is set by the money market.

Interest on bonds expressed as a percentage of the face amount is referred to as the *nominal* or *contract rate.* If the effective interest rate is identical to the nominal rate, the bonds will sell at face amount. If the effective interest rate is higher than the nominal rate, the bonds will sell at a *discount.* (*Zero-coupon bonds* pay no interest and thus are issued at a *deep discount.*) Conversely, if the effective interest rate is less than the nominal rate, the bonds will sell at a *premium.* Differences between the nominal rate and the yield rate thus are adjusted by changes in the price at which the bonds are issued.

To illustrate, assume that $100,000 of five-year, 7% term bonds are authorized by a corporation's board of directors.[3] The bonds, which promise $100,000 at the end of five years and $7,000 annual interest, then are offered to a group of investment bankers comprising an *underwriting syndicate.* The prices bid by the underwriters will depend on their expectations as to the effective rate of interest for this type of bonds. Under two different assumptions as to the effective annual interest rate, the proceeds are determined as follows, using the present value tables in the Appendix at the end of Chapter 5:

Computation of proceeds of 7% bonds issued at a *discount* (8% effective rate) and at a *premium* (6% effective rate)

Amount bid for 7% term bonds, assuming an effective rate of 8%		*Amount bid for 7% term bonds, assuming an effective rate of 6%*	
Present value of $100,000 due in 5 years at 8%, with interest paid annually ($100,000 × 0.680583)	*$68,058*	*Present value of $100,000 due in 5 years at 6%, with interest paid annually ($100,000 × 0.747258)*	*$ 74,726*
Present value of $7,000 every year for 5 years at 8% ($7,000 × 3.992710)	*27,949*	*Present value of $7,000 every year for 5 years at 6% ($7,000 × 4.212364)*	*29,487*
Proceeds of bond issue	*$96,007*	*Proceeds of bond issue*	*$104,213*

---

[3]Although bonds issued in amounts as small as $100,000, paying interest annually and maturing in five years, are not found in the business world, these amounts are used to facilitate the illustration.

The underwriters would expect to resell these bonds to investors at a higher price and thus a lower effective interest rate, to give them a margin to cover their costs and earn a profit. However, the yield rate to the issuer is determined by the price it receives from the underwriters. The journal entries to record the issuance of 7% term bonds at a discount and at a premium on December 31, Year 1, are shown below:

Issued at effective rate of 8%			*Issued at effective rate of 6%*		
Cash	96,007		Cash	104,213	
Discount on Bonds			Premium on		
Payable	3,993		Bonds Payable		4,213
Bonds Payable . .		100,000	Bonds Payable .		100,000
To record issuance of			To record issuance of		
bonds at a discount.			bonds at a premium.		

Journal entries to record the issuance of 7% term bonds at a **discount** *(8% effective rate) and at a* **premium** *(6% effective rate)*

Bond Discount and Premium in the Balance Sheet

At the time of issue, the carrying amount of bonds payable is equal to the proceeds received, because these proceeds are computed as the present value of all future payments at the yield rate set by the money market. Bond discount and bond premium are valuation amounts relating to bonds payable. This is stated in *APB Opinion No. 21,* "Interest on Receivables and Payables," in relation to notes (but is equally applicable to bonds) as follows:[4]

> . . . the discount or premium should be reported in the balance sheet as a direct addition to or deduction from the face amount of the note. It should not be classified as a deferred charge or deferred credit. The description of the note should disclose the effective interest rate; . . . Issue costs should be reported in the balance sheet as deferred charges.

Using the amounts from the foregoing illustration, bonds payable on the date of issuance are presented in the balance sheet as follows:

Balance sheet presentation of bonds payable and related discount or premium on date of issuance

Bonds issued at a discount			*Bonds issued at a premium*	
Long-term debt:			*Long-term debt:*	
7% bonds payable, due in			7% bonds payable, due in	
5 years (face amount) . . .	$100,000		5 years (face amount) . . .	$100,000
Less: Discount	3,993		Add: Premium	4,213
Carrying amount	$ 96,007		Carrying amount	$104,213

---

[4]*APB Opinion No. 21,* "Interest on Receivables and Payables," AICPA (New York: 1971), p. 423.

Term Bond Interest Expense

Because differences between the effective rate and the nominal rate of interest are reflected in bond prices, the amount of premium or discount affects the periodic interest expense of the issuer. This is illustrated by a comparison of the five-year interest expense under each of the two assumptions in the foregoing sections as to effective interest rates:

Comparison of five-year interest expense on bonds issued at a *discount* (8% effective rate) and at a *premium* (6% effective rate)

Assuming an effective rate of 8%		Assuming an effective rate of 6%	
Nominal interest ($7,000 × 5 annual payments)	$35,000	Nominal interest ($7,000 × 5 annual payments)	$35,000
Add: Discount ($100,000 − $96,007)	3,993	Less: Premium ($104,213 − $100,000)	4,213
Five-year interest expense . . .	$38,993	Five-year interest expense . . .	$30,787

If the bonds are issued to yield 8%, the discount of $3,993 represents an additional amount of interest that will be paid by the issuer at maturity. Similarly, if the bonds are issued to yield 6%, the premium of $4,213 represents an advance paid by bondholders for the right to receive larger annual interest checks and is viewed as a reduction in the effective interest expense. The premium in effect is returned to bondholders in the form of larger periodic interest payments.

The present value of the bonds on the date of issuance differs from their face amount because the market rate of interest differs from the periodic interest payments provided for in the bond contract. Therefore, the process of *amortizing* the bond discount or premium in conjunction with the computation of periodic interest expense is a means of recording the *change in the carrying amount of the bonds as they approach maturity.* In the bond discount case, the increase in the carrying amount of the bonds is caused by the decrease in bond discount through amortization. Similarly, in the bond premium case, the decrease in the carrying amount of the bonds is caused by the decrease in bond premium through amortization. In either case, the carrying amount of the bonds payable will be $100,000 on the maturity date.

Interest Method of Amortization for Term Bonds

In theory, the bond interest expense in each accounting period should equal the effective interest expense, that is, the effective rate of interest applied to the *carrying amount* of the bonds at the beginning of that period. This approach to the computation of interest expense is known as the *interest method of amortization.* The interest method generally should be used to amortize the discount or premium on bonds payable. However, the straight-line method may be used as a matter of expediency if the difference in results between the two methods is not material. The Accounting Principles Board stated that ''the interest method of amortization is

Discount amortization
for term bonds under
interest method

Term Bonds Issued at a Discount
Annual Interest Expense Determined by Interest Method of Amortization
($100,000, 5-year bonds, interest at 7% payable annually,
issued for $96,007, to yield 8% compounded annually)

Date	(A) Interest paid (7% of face amount)	(B) Interest expense (8% of bonds' carrying amount)	(C) Discount amorti- zation (B − A)	(D) Bond discount balance (D − C)	(E) Carrying amount, end of year ($100,000 − D)
12/31/1				$3,993	$ 96,007
12/31/2	$7,000	$7,681	$681	3,312	96,688
12/31/3	7,000	7,735	735	2,577	97,423
12/31/4	7,000	7,794	794	1,783	98,217
12/31/5	7,000	7,857	857	926	99,074
12/31/6	7,000	7,926	926		100,000

Journal entries: Dec. 31, Year 2   Dec. 31, Year 3

	Dec. 31, Year 2	Dec. 31, Year 3
Bond Interest Expense	7,681	7,735
Cash	7,000	7,000
Discount on Bonds Payable	681	735

To record interest expense, including amortization of discount.

Ledger accounts:

Bond Interest Expense

Date	Explanation	Debit	Credit	Balance
12/31/2	($96,007 × 0.08)	7,681		7,681 dr
12/31/2	Closing entry		7,681	−0−
12/31/3	($96,688 × 0.08)	7,735		7,735 dr
12/31/3	Closing entry		7,735	−0−

Discount on Bonds Payable

Date	Explanation	Debit	Credit	Balance
12/31/1	Date of issuance	3,993		3,993 dr
12/31/2	Amortization ($7,681 − $7,000)		681	3,312 dr
12/31/3	Amortization ($7,735 − $7,000)		735	2,577 dr

theoretically sound and an acceptable method.''[5] Subsequently, the APB took a
more explicit stand in relation to the amortization of discount or premium on notes
receivable and payable (but equally applicable to bonds payable) as follows:[6]

[5]*APB Opinion No. 12*, ''Omnibus Opinion—1967,'' AICPA (New York: 1967), p. 194.
[6]*APB Opinion No. 21*, p. 423.

. . . the difference between the present value and the face amount should be treated as discount or premium and amortized as interest expense or income over the life of the note in such a way as to result in a constant rate of interest when applied to the amount outstanding at the beginning of any given period. This is the "interest" method. . . . However, other methods of amortization

Premium amortization for term bonds under interest method

Term Bonds Issued at a Premium
Annual Interest Expense Determined by Interest Method of Amortization
($100,000, 5-year bonds, interest at 7% payable annually,
issued for $104,213, to yield 6% compounded annually)

Date	(A) Interest paid (7% of face amount)	(B) Interest expense (6% of bonds' carrying amount)	(C) Premium amor-tization (A − B)	(D) Bond premium balance (D − C)	(E) Carrying amount, end of year ($100,000 + D)
12/31/1				$4,213	$104,213
12/31/2	$7,000	$6,253	$747	3,466	103,466
12/31/3	7,000	6,208	792	2,674	102,674
12/31/4	7,000	6,160	840	1,834	101,834
12/31/5	7,000	6,110	890	944	100,944
12/31/6	7,000	6,056*	944		100,000

*Adjusted $1 for rounding.

Journal entries:

	Dec. 31, Year 2	Dec. 31, Year 3
Bond Interest Expense	6,253	6,208
Premium on Bonds Payable	747	792
Cash	7,000	7,000

To record interest expense, including amorti-zation of premium.

Ledger accounts:

Bond Interest Expense

Date	Explanation	Debit	Credit	Balance
12/31/2	($104,213 × 0.06)	6,253		6,253 dr
12/31/2	Closing entry		6,253	−0−
12/31/3	($103,466 × 0.06)	6,208		6,208 dr
12/31/3	Closing entry		6,208	−0−

Premium on Bonds Payable

Date	Explanation	Debit	Credit	Balance
12/31/1	Date of Issuance		4,213	4,213 cr
12/31/2	Amortization ($7,000 − $6,253)	747		3,466 cr
12/31/3	Amortization ($7,000 − $6,208)	792		2,674 cr

may be used if the results obtained are not materially different from those which would result from the "interest" method.

Term Bonds Issued at a Discount   When term bonds are issued at a discount, the carrying amount of the bonds increases as they approach maturity; thus, interest expense *increases* in each period. Annual interest expense over the term of the bonds, journal entries to record interest expense for the first two years, and ledger accounts for Bond Interest Expense and Discount on Bonds Payable are shown on page 748.

Term Bonds Issued at a Premium   When term bonds are issued at a premium, the carrying amount of the bonds decreases as they approach maturity, and the amount of periodic interest expense *decreases* over the term of the bonds. Annual interest expense, journal entries to record interest expense for the first two years, and ledger accounts for Bond Interest Expense and Premium on Bonds Payable are illustrated on page 749.

Straight-Line Method of Amortization for Term Bonds

The additional interest expense (discount) or reduction of interest expense (premium) may be allocated evenly over the term of the bonds. This method, known as

Discount amortization for term bonds under straight-line method

Term Bonds Issued at a Discount
Annual Interest Expense Determined by Straight-Line Method of Amortization
($100,000, 5-year bonds, interest at 7% payable annually,
issued for $96,007 to yield 8% compounded annually)

Date	(A) Interest paid (7% of face amount)	(B) Discount amortization (⅕ of $3,993)	(C) Interest expense (A + B)	(D) Bond discount balance (D − B)	(E) Carry amount, end of year ($100,000 − D)
12/31/1				$3,993	$ 96,007
12/31/2	$7,000	$799	$7,799	3,194	96,806
12/31/3	7,000	799	7,799	2,395	97,605
12/31/4	7,000	799	7,799	1,596	98,404
12/31/5	7,000	799	7,799	797	99,203
12/31/6	7,000	797*	7,797*		100,000

*$2 adjustment to compensate for rounding average interest expense to the nearest dollar.

Journal entries:	Dec. 31, Year 2	Dec. 31, Year 3
Bond Interest Expense......................	7,799	7,799
Cash	7,000	7,000
Discount on Bonds Payable	799	799

To record interest expense, including amortization of discount.

the *straight-line method of amortization,* results in a uniform periodic interest expense. Although this method does not give the accurate results obtained by use of the interest method of amortization, it frequently is encountered in practice. As previously stated, the use of the straight-line method is acceptable if it is applied to immaterial amounts of discount or premium.

Term Bonds Issued at a Discount   When term bonds are issued at a discount, the carrying amount of the bonds increases as they approach maturity, and periodic interest expense remains constant over the term of the bonds. Annual interest expense over the term of the bonds and journal entries to record interest expense for the first two years are shown on page 750.

Term Bonds Issued at a Premium   When term bonds are issued at a premium, the carrying amount of the bonds decreases as they approach maturity, and periodic interest expense remains constant over the term of the bonds. Annual interest expense and journal entries to record interest expense for the first two years are shown below:

Premium amortization for term bonds under straight-line method

	Term Bonds Issued at a Premium				
	Annual Interest Expense Determined by Straight-Line Method of Amortization				
	($100,000, 5-year bonds, interest at 7% payable annually,				
	issued for $104,213, to yield 6% compounded annually)				
Date	(A) Interest paid (7% of face amount)	(B) Premium amortization (⅕ of $4,213)	(C) Interest expense (A − B)	(D) Bond premium balance (D − B)	(E) Carrying amount, end of year ($100,000 + D)
12/31/1				$4,213	$104,213
12/31/2	$7,000	$843	$6,157	3,370	103,370
12/31/3	7,000	843	6,157	2,527	102,527
12/31/4	7,000	843	6,157	1,684	101,684
12/31/5	7,000	843	6,157	841	100,841
12/31/6	7,000	841*	6,159*		100,000

*$2 adjustment to compensate for rounding average interest expense to the nearest dollar.

	Dec. 31, Year 2	Dec. 31, Year 3
Journal entries:		
Bond Interest Expense.....................	6,157	6,157
Premium on Bonds Payable	843	843
Cash	7,000	7,000
To record interest expense, including amortization of premium.		

A comparison of periodic interest expense under the interest method shown on pages 748 and 749 with the straight-line method shown on pages 750 and above reveals the extent of the error involved in the use of a simple average in the straight-line method. For example, if the bonds payable were issued at a discount, the interest expense for each year ranges from $7,681 to $7,926; the use of the straight-line method results in a constant annual interest expense of $7,799. In the first year, for example, interest expense on a $100 million bond issue would be approximately $118,000 more under the straight-line method. In choosing the method to use, accountants should balance the simplicity of the straight-line method against the materiality of the difference involved. The longer the term of the bond issue and the larger the discount or premium relative to the face amount of the bonds, the larger will be the difference between straight-line interest expense and the interest expense determined by the interest method of amortization.

Another advantage of the interest method of amortization of bond discount or premium is that the carrying amount of the bonds at the end of each accounting period equals the present value of the bonds at the yield rate. For example, the table on page 748 shows the carrying amount of the bonds on December 31, Year 3, three years prior to maturity, to be $97,423. This amount equals the present value of the bonds at the original 8% yield rate, computed by reference to the tables in the Appendix at the end of Chapter 5, as follows:

Carrying amount of bonds issued at a discount amortized by interest method is equal to present value of bonds at yield rate

Present value of $100,000 due in 3 years at 8%, with interest payable annually ($100,000 × 0.793832)	*$79,383*
Add: Present value of $7,000 every year for 3 years at 8% ($7,000 × 2.577097)	*18,040*
Present value of bonds (equal to carrying amount)	*$97,423*

When interest is paid semiannually or when interest payment dates do not coincide with the end of the fiscal year, a policy of amortizing the discount or the premium only at the end of the fiscal year may be adopted to minimize the routine work involved when the straight-line method of amortization is used.

Bond Issue Costs

A number of costs are incurred in connection with a bond issue: fees paid to accountants, attorneys, and other experts in connection with the preparation of the bond contract and prospectus; printing and engraving costs; fees of the Securities and Exchange Commission; and costs incurred in advertising the issue. These are costs for the use of the funds borrowed and are allocated to the years that the bonds are outstanding. Amortization of bond issue costs is recorded by a debit to Bond Issue Expense, as illustrated in the Electronics Company example on page 754.

As noted on page 746, bond issue costs are classified as an asset (deferred charges) and are amortized on a straight-line basis over the term of the bonds because revenue benefits from the use of the bond proceeds over this period. An alternative procedure advocated by some accountants (but which is not in accordance with generally accepted accounting principles) is to add bond issue costs to bond discount or deduct them from bond premium. This procedure implies that the amount of funds made available to the borrower is equal to the net proceeds of the bond issue after deduction of all costs of borrowing. Under this procedure, bond issue costs increase the interest expense during the term of the bonds.

Bonds Issued between Interest Dates

Bond interest payments usually are made semiannually on dates specified in the bond contract. When term bonds are issued on a date other than an interest payment date, an adjustment for this factor may be made by reducing the amount of the interest payment for the first ''short'' interest period. However, it is more convenient to add to the price of bonds the amount of interest that has accrued since the last interest payment date. Investors, in effect, prepay the issuer of the bonds for the portion of the full six-month interest payment to which they are not entitled. Thus, investors will receive the full six-month interest payment on the next semiannual interest payment date.

Assume that Electronics Company issued $100,000 of 10-year, 12% term bonds, with interest payable semiannually on April 1 and October 1 of each year. The bonds were issued on June 1, Year 1, for $107,080 plus accrued interest of $2,000 ($100,000 × 0.12 × $\frac{2}{12}$ = $2,000) for two months. The bonds were dated April 1, Year 1, and bond issue costs amounted to $2,360. Note that this borrowing actually runs for 9 years and 10 months, or 118 months, and the accounting for the bonds and the related bond issue costs should reflect this fact. Assuming that the straight-line method of amortization is used for the bond premium, the monthly interest expense is determined below:

<table>
<tr><td rowspan="5">Computation of interest expense for each month for term bonds issued at a premium</td><td>Actual interest paid to investors over 10-year period ($12,000 × 10).....</td><td>$120,000</td></tr>
<tr><td>Less: Premium received on issuance of bonds.......................</td><td>(7,080)</td></tr>
<tr><td>Accrued interest received from investors (Apr. 1–June 1, Year 1)</td><td>(2,000)</td></tr>
<tr><td>Total interest expense (9 years and 10 months) ....</td><td>$110,920</td></tr>
<tr><td>Monthly interest expense ($110,920 ÷ 118 months)...................</td><td>$ 940</td></tr>
</table>

Because the monthly interest accrual is $1,000 ($12,000 ÷ 12 months = $1,000) and the monthly interest expense is $940, the monthly premium amortization is the difference, or $60 ($7,080 ÷ 118 = $60). Monthly amortization of bond issue costs is $20 ($2,360 ÷ 118 = $20). Assuming that amortization of the bond issue costs and the premium is recorded only at the end of the year, the journal entries for Electronics Company relating to the bond issue during Year 1 are shown on page 754.

It would be possible to *credit* Bond Interest Expense (rather than Bond Interest Payable) on June 1 for $2,000, the amount of the accrued interest for two months acquired by bondholders. On October 1, Bond Interest Expense would be debited for $6,000, thus leaving a balance of $4,000 in Bond Interest Expense representing interest incurred from June 1 to October 1. It also would be possible to amortize the premium and bond issue costs at the time interest is paid, as well as at the end of the fiscal year, but there is little point in following such an inefficient procedure when the straight-line method of amortization is used.

Serial Bonds

Thus far we have considered term bonds having a single fixed maturity date. Another type of bond contract, known as a *serial bond*, provides for payment of the

ELECTRONICS COMPANY
Journal Entries for Term Bonds Issued between Interest Dates

Year 1

June 1	Bond Issue Costs	2,360	
	Cash		2,360
	To record costs of issuing bonds.		
1	Cash	109,080	
	Bonds Payable............................		100,000
	Bond Interest Payable		2,000
	Premium on Bonds Payable		7,080
	To record issuance of bonds and accrued interest for 2 months ($100,000 × 0.12 × $2/12$ = $2,000).		
Oct. 1	Bond Interest Payable	2,000	
	Bond Interest Expense	4,000	
	Cash ($100,000 × 0.12 × $6/12$)..............		6,000
	To record interest payment for first 6 months.		
Dec. 31	Bond Interest Expense	2,580	
	Premium on Bonds Payable	420	
	Bond Issue Expense...........................	140	
	Bond Issue Costs		140
	Bond Interest Payable		3,000

To accrue interest expense for 3 months and record amortization of bond issue costs and premium for 7 months. Amounts determined as follows:

Bond interest payable ($100,000 × 0.12 × $3/12$)...........................	$3,000
Less: Amortization of premium ($7,080 × $7/118$)	420
Bond interest expense (net)	$2,580
Amortization of bond issue costs ($2,360 × $7/118$)	$ 140

principal in periodic installments. Serial bonds have the advantage of gearing the issuer's debt repayment to its periodic cash inflow from operations.

As in the case of term bonds, serial bonds may be issued at a premium or a discount in response to the difference between the nominal and the effective interest rate. The proceeds of a serial bond issue are somewhat more difficult to compute because of the varying maturities, but the approach is the same: The present value of the series of principal payments plus the present value of the interest payments, all at the effective interest rate, equals the proceeds received for the bonds.

At this point the question arises: Is there any single interest rate applicable to a serial bond issue? We often refer loosely to *the rate* of interest, when in fact in the market at any one time there are several interest rates, depending on the terms, nature, and length of the bond contract offered. In a specific serial bond issue, the terms of all bonds in the issue are the same except for the differences in maturity. However, because short-term interest rates often differ from long-term rates, it is likely that each maturity will sell at a different yield rate, so that there will be a different discount or premium relating to each maturity.

In accounting for an issue of serial bonds under these conditions, each maturity may be treated as a separate bond issue. Thus, if $500,000 of five-year, 10% serial bonds are issued, to be repaid in the amount of $100,000 each year, and each maturity sells at a price reflecting a different yield rate, the problem would be treated as a summarized accounting for five separate bond issues of $100,000 each, maturing in one, two, three, four, and five years, respectively. Each maturity would have a related discount or premium, and interest expense on each maturity would be computed as previously illustrated for term bonds.

In many cases, however, this degree of precision in accounting for serial bond issues is not possible because the yield rate for each maturity is not known. Underwriters may bid on an entire serial bond issue on the basis of an average yield rate and may not disclose the particular yield rate for each maturity that was used to determine the bid price. In this situation we may have to assume that the same yield rate applies to all maturities in the issue, and proceed accordingly.

If the interest method is to be used in accounting for serial bond interest expense, the procedure is similar to that illustrated in connection with term bonds. The interest expense for each accounting period is an amount equal to the effective interest rate applied to the carrying amount of the serial bonds outstanding during that period, and the difference between this amount of interest expense and the actual interest payments represents the amortization of the bond discount or premium. The result is a constant rate of interest expense in relation to the carrying amount of the serial bonds outstanding.

A variation of the straight-line method, known as the **bonds outstanding method,** results in a decreasing amount of premium or discount amortization each accounting period proportionate to the decrease in the amount of outstanding serial bonds.

Accounting for Serial Bonds Illustrated

To illustrate the variation in the pattern of interest expense under each of these methods, assume that at the beginning of Year 1 James Company issued $100,000 of five-year, 5% serial bonds, to be repaid in the amount of $20,000 each year. To simplify the illustration, assume that interest payments are made annually and that no bond issue costs were incurred. If the bonds are issued to yield 6% a year, the proceeds total $97,375, as determined at the top of page 756 from the 6% column in Table 2 in the Appendix at the end of Chapter 5.

Computation of
proceeds
(present value) of
serial bonds issued
at a single effective
interest rate

JAMES COMPANY
Computation of Proceeds of Serial Bond Issue
Beginning of Year 1

Principal and interest due at end of Year 1:
($20,000 + $5,000) × 0.943396 .... $23,585
Principal and interest due at end of Year 2:
($20,000 + $4,000) × 0.889996 21,360
Principal and interest due at end of Year 3:
($20,000 + $3,000) × 0.839619 19,311
Principal and interest due at end of Year 4:
($20,000 + $2,000) × 0.792094 17,426
Principal and interest due at end of Year 5:
($20,000 + $1,000) × 0.747258 15,693
Proceeds of serial bond issue at 6% yield basis $97,375

The accounting problem is to determine how the discount of $2,625 ($100,000 − $97,375 = $2,625) should be amortized over the term of the serial bond issue. Tables to determine periodic discount amortization and interest expense under the *interest* and *bonds outstanding* methods are illustrated below and on page 757.

Discount amortization
table for serial
bonds—interest
method

JAMES COMPANY
Amortization of Discount on Serial Bonds by Interest Method

Year	(A) Carrying amount of bonds ($100,000 −E − F)	(B) Interest expense (6% of A)	(C) Interest payment	(D) Discount amortization (B − C)	(E) Bond discount balance (E − D)	(F) Cumulative principal payment
Issue	$97,375				$2,625	
1	78,217	$ 5,842	$ 5,000	$ 842	1,783	$ 20,000
2	58,910	4,693	4,000	693	1,090	40,000
3	39,444	3,534	3,000	534	556	60,000
4	19,811	2,367	2,000	367	189	80,000
5		1,189	1,000	189		100,000
Totals		$17,625	$15,000	$2,625		

The bonds outstanding method in this case produces results that are a close approximation of the interest method because of the short term of the issue and the relatively small discount. The longer the term of the bonds and the larger the discount or premium, the larger would be the discrepancy between the two methods.

Under the straight-line method, discount amortization is $525 a year ($2,625 ÷ 5 = $525). The bonds outstanding method is essentially a straight-line method because it results in a constant periodic amortization of discount or premium

Discount amortization
table for serial
bonds—bonds out-
standing method

			(A)	(B)	
Year	Bonds out-standing (face amount)	Fraction of total of bonds out-standing	Amortization of discount ($2,625 × fraction)	Interest payments (5% of bonds out-standing)	Interest expense (A + B)
		JAMES COMPANY			
	Amortization of Discount on Serial Bonds by Bonds Outstanding Method				
1	$100,000	10/30	$ 875	$ 5,000	$ 5,875
2	80,000	8/30	700	4,000	4,700
3	60,000	6/30	525	3,000	3,525
4	40,000	4/30	350	2,000	2,350
5	20,000	2/30	175	1,000	1,175
Totals	$300,000	30/30	$2,625	$15,000	$17,625

per $1,000 face amount of bonds outstanding. In this example, the amount of annual discount amortization for each $1,000 bond outstanding is computed by dividing the total discount by the sum of the bonds outstanding over the term of the serial bond issue: ($2,625 ÷ $300,000 = $8.75 per $1,000 bond). If the discount amortization for each $1,000 bond is determined at the time of issuance, it is a simple process to compute the appropriate amount of discount applicable to any amount of bonds in a specific year throughout the term of a serial bond issue. Thus, in the fourth year, when $40,000 of bonds were outstanding, the discount to be amortized is computed as follows: $40,000 of bonds times $8.75 per $1,000 face amount of bonds equals $350 ($8.75 × 40 = $350).

Bond Sinking Funds

Some bond indentures require that a sinking fund be established for the retirement of the bonds. Ordinarily, a sinking fund would not be created in connection with the issuance of serial bonds; such bonds are retired periodically in lieu of making sinking fund deposits. A disadvantage inherent in bond sinking funds is that a portion of the money borrowed for planned business purposes is not being used in this manner if cash must be deposited periodically in a sinking fund. Accounting for sinking funds and their balance sheet presentation are discussed in Chapter 14 (pages 721–722).

EXTINGUISHMENT OF LONG-TERM DEBT

If the principal of term bonds or serial bonds is paid on the maturity date, no gain or loss results because the carrying amount and face amount of the bonds, and the cash paid, are the same amount. The journal entry to record the payment of the bonds at maturity is a debit to Bonds Payable and a credit to Cash.

Occasionally, because of favorable interest rates or other considerations, the issuer of bonds may retire them before maturity by exercising the call provision, by acquiring the bonds in the open market, in a ***debt-equity swap,*** in a ***refunding,*** or by means of an ***in-substance defeasance.*** These ***extinguishments*** of long-term debt are discussed in the following sections. Typically, a gain or loss (before income tax effect) on the extinguishment of term or serial bonds prior to maturity is recorded equal to the difference between the amount paid to retire the bonds and their carrying amount, including any unamortized bond issue costs. In all examples in this chapter, the income tax effect on the gains or losses from extinguishment of bonds payable is disregarded. The amortization of any bond discount or premium and bond issue costs should be adjusted to the date of extinguishment ***before*** the journal entry to record the extinguishment is prepared.

Extinguishment by Calling Bonds

To illustrate the accounting for extinguishment of long-term debt by exercise of the call provision of term bonds, assume that $20,000 (20%) of the Electronics Company term bonds described on page 753 were called on December 1, Year 2, or 18 months after the bonds were issued. If the bonds were redeemed at the call price of 103 (103% of face amount), plus accrued interest of $400 ($20,000 × 0.12 × $\frac{2}{12}$ = $400) for two months, the journal entries on page 759 would be required.

Gains and losses on extinguishment of bonds reflect the changes in interest rates since the bonds were issued. ***Material gains and losses*** on the extinguishment of bonds (net of related income tax effect) ***are reported as extraordinary items*** in the income statement. On this point, ***FASB Statement No. 64,*** "Extinguishments of Debt . . .," stated:[7]

> Gains and losses from extinguishment of debt that are included in the determination of net income shall be aggregated and, if material, classified as an extraordinary item, net of related income tax effect. . . . The conclusion does not apply, however, to gains and losses from extinguishments of debt made to satisfy sinking-fund requirements that an enterprise must meet within one year of the date of the extinguishment. Those gains and losses shall be aggregated and the amount shall be identified as a separate item.

The reason for the ***extraordinary items*** treatment of gains and losses from extinguishments of bonds, which do not meet the ***unusual in nature*** and ***infrequent in occurrence*** criteria for extraordinary items described in Chapter 3 (pages 134–136) is that management of the issuer of the bonds controls the amount and timing of the gains and losses on extinguishment of bonds. Management would thus be able to manipulate ordinary earnings, absent the extraordinary items treatment for gains and losses on extinguishment of bonds.

When an entire bond issue is ***called for redemption,*** the entire unamortized premium or discount and bond issue costs are written off. Losses generally result on such redemptions because the sliding call prices ordinarily are in excess of bond carrying amounts on corresponding call dates.

---

[7]*FASB Statement No. 64,* "Extinguishments of Debt Made to Satisfy Sinking-Fund Requirements," FASB (Stamford: 1982), p. 2.

ELECTRONICS COMPANY
Journal Entries to Record Extinguishment of Term Bonds through Call

Year 2

Dec. 1   Premium on Bonds Payable   132

       Bond Issue Expense............................   44

          Bond Interest Expense.....................   132

          Bond Issue Costs   44

To record amortization on $20,000 (or 20%) of bonds
for period Jan. 1 to Dec. 1, Year 2 (the date of extin-
guishment) as follows:

    Amortization of bond premium:

       $7,080 \times 0.20 \times {}^{11}/_{118} = \$132.$

    Amortization of bond issue costs:

       $2,360 \times 0.20 \times {}^{11}/_{118} = \$44.$

1   Bonds Payable..................................   20,000

      Premium on Bonds Payable ($1,416 − $216)   1,200

      Bond Interest Expense ($20,000 \times 0.12 \times {}^{2}/_{12}$)   400

          Cash ($20,600 + $400)   21,000

          Bond Issue Costs ($472 − $72).............   400

          Gain on Extinguishment of Bonds   200

To record extinguishment of bonds at 103, plus
accrued interest of $400 for 2 months. The gain is
determined as follows:

    Original issuance proceeds ($107,080 \times

    0.20) $21,416

    Less: Original bond issue costs

    ($2,360 \times 0.20)   472

      Subtotal $20,944

    Amortization for 18 months:

      Premium ($60 \times 0.20 \times 18).................   (216)

      Bond issue costs ($20 \times 0.20 \times 18)...........   72

    Carrying amount less unamortized bond

    issue costs on extinguishment $20,800

    Amount paid to extinguish bonds

    ($20,000 \times 1.03)   20,600

    Gain on extinguishment of bonds .... $ 200

If bonds are called but not formally retired, a Treasury Bonds ledger account may be debited for the face amount of the *treasury bonds* held, but a gain or loss still should be recognized as illustrated above. The Treasury Bonds account is not an asset; it is deducted from bonds payable in the balance sheet. Interest is not paid on treasury bonds unless they are held as an investment by a company-sponsored fund, such as an employee pension fund.

Extinguishment by Open-Market Acquisition

If interest rates are rising and bond prices are falling, it may be appropriate for the issuer to realize a substantial gain by acquiring its bonds in the open market from present bondholders at a substantial discount.

To illustrate the extinguishment of serial bonds by open-market acquisition, assume that $10,000 of James Company bonds (see pages 755–757) are acquired at 85 (85% of face amount) at the end of Year 2, two years prior to the scheduled retirement date. The bond interest had been paid for Year 2. The discount applicable to the bonds acquired is determined by the bonds outstanding method as follows:

Computation of discount applicable to serial bonds acquired in open market

Discount applicable to Year 3: $525* $\times \dfrac{10,000}{60,000}$ . . . . $ 87.50

Discount applicable to Year 4: $350* $\times \dfrac{10,000}{40,000}$ 87.50

Total discount applicable to acquired bonds . . . . $175.00†

*From Column A in table on page 757.
†Because the discount amortization amounts to $8.75 per $1,000 per year, this amount may be determined as follows: $8.75 × 10 × 2 = $175. Similar procedures may be used to compute amortization of discount on serial bonds when the "bond year" and the fiscal year of the issuer do not coincide.

The journal entry to record the extinguishment follows:

Journal entry for extinguishment of serial bonds

Bonds Payable	10,000	
Discount on Bonds Payable		175
Cash ($10,000 × 0.85)		8,500
Gain on Extinguishment of Bonds		1,325

To record extinguishment of serial bonds, two years prior to scheduled maturity date.

Extinguishment through Debt-Equity Swap

Instead of using cash to acquire its outstanding bonds in the open market, the issuer may enter into a **debt-equity swap** arrangement with an investment banking house to serve as a broker. The broker acquires the issuer's bonds over a period of time in the open market and exchanges the bonds for shares of the issuer's common stock, which may be unissued or in the treasury. The issuer thus retires the bonds acquired in the *swap* with the broker. By this means, the issuer extinguishes long-term debt without using cash, and improves its **debt-to-equity ratio** (the ratio of total liabilities to total stockholders' equity).

To illustrate, assume that a broker acquired in the open market $500,000 face amount of Casper Corporation's 10% bonds for a total cost of $450,000. The bonds had a carrying amount of $505,000 in Casper's accounting records ($500,000 face amount, plus $12,000 premium, and less $7,000 bond issue costs) on December 31,

Year 4. On that date, Casper issued to the broker 10,000 shares of its $1 par common stock with a current fair value of $48 a share in exchange for the bonds.

The journal entry to record Casper Corporation's debt-equity swap is as follows:

<table>
<tr><td>Journal entry for
debt-equity swap</td><td>

Bonds Payable...	500,000	
Premium on Bonds Payable	12,000	
Bond Issue Costs		7,000
Common Stock, $1 par (10,000 × $1)		10,000
Paid-in Capital in Excess of Par (10,000 × $47)		470,000
Gain on Extinguishment of Bonds		
[($512,000 − $7,000) − $480,000].................		25,000
To record extinguishment of bonds in a debt-equity		
swap with broker.		

</td></tr>
</table>

Extinguishment through Refunding

Refunding is the process of retiring a bond issue with the proceeds of a new bond issue. When refunding occurs at the time the old bonds mature, the carrying amount of such bonds is equal to face amount; no gain or loss arises from the retirement of the old bonds, and the issuance of the new bonds is recorded in the usual manner.

A problem arises when refunding occurs prior to the maturity of the old bonds. This usually happens when interest rates have declined and the issuer decides to reduce its interest expense by calling the old bonds (paying the required penalty in the form of a call premium) and issuing new bonds at a lower yield rate. If the two transactions (calling the old bonds and issuing new ones) are viewed as separate and unrelated transactions, no issues are raised that have not already been discussed. Calling and retiring the old bonds results in a gain or loss equal to the difference between carrying amount and call price; the new bonds are recorded in the usual manner. However, some accountants have argued that the loss on the refunding prior to maturity should be deferred and amortized over part of, or the entire, term of the new bond issue.

For example, assume that Cleve Corporation has outstanding $1,000,000 of 12% bonds having 10 years to maturity and a carrying amount of $960,000 (face amount of $1,000,000, less unamortized discount of $40,000). Cleve calls the bonds at 105, using the proceeds of a new 20-year issue of 10% bonds (which we assume were issued at face amount). Bonds having a carrying amount of $960,000 thus are refunded at a cost of $1,050,000, and a question arises as to the treatment of the $90,000 difference ($1,050,000 − $960,000 = $90,000). Three solutions have been proposed:

1   Recognize $90,000 (net of income tax effect) as a loss at the time of refunding.

2   Record the $90,000 (net of income tax effect) as a deferred charge and amortize it over the remaining term of the retired bonds (in this case 10 years).

3   Record the $90,000 (net of income tax effect) as a deferred charge and amortize it over the term of the new bonds (in this case 20 years).

The first alternative has the weight of logic in its favor. The amount of unamortized bond discount at any time measures the liability for additional interest that will accrue during the remaining term of bonds to compensate for the fact that the nominal rate of interest is less than the effective rate of interest. In order to eliminate the old bond contract, the issuer is required to pay this $40,000 of interest now, and, in addition, a $50,000 call premium. These costs are *related* to past periods but are *caused* by the current decline in the interest rate and management's decision to refund. Deferral of these costs would penalize future accounting periods, because the new 10% bonds could have been issued even if the 12% bonds had not been outstanding.

The Accounting Principles Board did not make a distinction between refunding and other types of extinguishment; it required that gains and losses on refunding, net of income tax effect, "should be recognized currently in income of the period of extinguishment. . . ."[8]

Arguments for the amortization over the remaining term of old bonds are based on the principle that when a cost is incurred, the benefits of which are expected to be realized over a period of years, the cost should be recognized as an expense over those years. It may be argued that the unamortized bond discount and the call premium paid to refund the old bonds are costs incurred to obtain the benefit of lower interest expense during the remaining term of the old bonds. The payment of a call premium necessary to cancel an unfavorable bond contract and the write-off of unamortized discount on the contract may be viewed as events relating to the old bond contract and not as benefits to be derived from the new bond contract. For example, if a higher nominal rate of interest had been set on the old bonds, they would have been issued at face amount, and there would be no unamortized discount to write off on the refunding date.

The third method rests on the premise that because the new bonds are a continuation of the old, the costs of both the old and new borrowings should be expensed over the term of the new bonds. The term of the new bonds generally is longer than the unexpired term of the old bonds. It was suggested that deferral of the "loss" was appropriate when the refunding takes place because of currently lower interest rates or anticipated higher rates in the future. This position assumes that the key reason for the refunding is to obtain a lower interest cost over the term of the new bonds.

Although students should be familiar with the alternatives discussed above, we must emphasize that *only the first method (immediate recognition of gains and losses) is sanctioned by generally accepted accounting principles.*

Deciding When to Refund a Bond Issue

A decline in interest rates is not in itself a sufficient basis for a decision to refund a bond issue. The out-of-pocket costs of refunding must be compared with the present value of future interest savings. In addition, the income tax impact of refunding and bond indenture features on both the old and new bonds must be considered. Unamortized discount and bond issue costs applicable to the old bonds may be deducted

---

[8]*APB Opinion No. 26,* "Early Extinguishment of Debt," AICPA (New York: 1972), pp. 501–502.

for income tax purposes in the year of refunding. The call premium also is deductible for income tax purposes, but the issue costs of the new bonds must be amortized over their term. Future interest rates also should be considered, because a further decline in rates may mean that refunding may be made under even more favorable conditions on a later date.

Extinguishment by In-Substance Defeasance

The conventional method of extinguishing long-term debt such as bonds payable is payment of cash or the issuance of common stock pursuant to the conversion of convertible bonds. Common stock also is issued to extinguish bonds payable in a debt-equity swap.

In FASB Statement No. 76, ''Extinguishment of Debt,'' the Financial Accounting Standards Board addressed another method of debt extinguishment—*in-substance defeasance.* The term *defeasance* indicates that the debtor is released from legal liability for bonds payable or other debt. *In-substance* means that the *legal form* of defeasance is not present, but that *substantively* the debt has been extinguished by action of the debtor.

The Financial Accounting Standards Board provided the following criteria for in-substance defeasance of debt:[9]

> A debtor shall consider debt to be extinguished for financial reporting purposes in the following circumstances:
>
> . . . .
>
> The debtor irrevocably places cash or other assets in a trust to be used solely for satisfying scheduled payments of both interest and principal of a specific obligation and the possibility that the debtor will be required to make future payments with respect to the debt is remote. In this circumstance, debt is extinguished even though the debtor is not legally released from being the primary obligor under the debt obligation.
>
> The following requirements regarding the nature of the assets held by the trust shall be met to effect an extinguishment of debt . . .:
>
> **a** The trust shall be restricted to owning only monetary assets (money or a claim to receive a sum of money that is fixed or determinable without reference to future prices of specific goods and services) that are *essentially risk free* as to the amount, timing, and collection of interest and principal. . . . For debt denominated in U.S. dollars, essentially risk-free monetary assets shall be limited to:
>
> (1) Direct obligations of the U.S. government
>
> (2) Obligations guaranteed by the U.S. government
>
> (3) Securities that are backed by U.S. government obligations as collateral . . .
>
> **b** The monetary assets held by the trust shall provide cash flows (from interest and maturity of those assets) that approximately coincide, as to timing and

---

[9]*FASB Statement No. 76,* ''Extinguishment of Debt,'' FASB (Stamford: 1983), pp. 1–3.

amount, with the scheduled interest and principal payments on the debt that is being extinguished.

Illustration of In-Substance Defeasance of Bonds Payable   To illustrate the in-substance defeasance of debt, assume that Magno, Inc., had the following ledger account balances related to bonds payable on May 31, Year 4, the end of a fiscal year:

Data for illustration

8% bonds payable, due May 31, Year 13, interest payable May 31 and Nov. 30, callable at 102	$8,000,000
Discount on bonds payable (based on 10% yield rate)	935,167
Bond issue costs	72,000

Because 9% U.S. Treasury bonds due May 31, Year 13, were trading at a yield rate of 16% on May 31, Year 4, Magno was able to acquire $8,000,000 face amount of the bonds for $5,375,872, computed as follows:

Computation of cost of 9% U.S. Treasury bonds

$8,000,000 × 0.250249*	$2,001,992
$360,000 × 9.371887**	3,373,880
Total cost of U.S. Treasury bonds	$5,375,872

*From Table 2 of the Appendix at the end of Chapter 5.
**From Table 4 of the Appendix at the end of Chapter 5.

Magno then transferred the 9% U.S. Treasury bonds to an irrevocable trust for servicing Magno's 8% bonds payable, which had the same interest payment dates (May 31 and November 30) and same maturity date (May 31, Year 13) as the U.S. Treasury bonds. The trustee would use the $360,000 ($8,000,000 × 0.045 = $360,000) semiannual interest received on the 9% U.S. Treasury bonds to pay the semiannual interest of $320,000 ($8,000,000 × 0.04 = $320,000) on Magno's bonds and the trustee's fee of $40,000 semiannually. Further, the trustee would use the $8,000,000 proceeds received for the 9% U.S. Treasury bonds on May 31, Year 13, to extinguish the $8,000,000 principal of the 8% Magno bonds that mature on the same date. (If the $40,000 interest differential were insufficient to cover the trustee's fee for servicing the bonds, Magno would have to accrue the *present value* of the deficiency in full on May 31, Year 4; the trustee would refund to Magno any excess of the $40,000 over the semiannual trustee's fee.)[10]

Because the acquisition of the 9% U.S. Treasury bonds and transfer of the bonds to the irrevocable trust comply with the provisions of ***FASB Statement No. 76*** outlined on page 763, the following journal entries are appropriate for Magno, Inc., on May 31, Year 4:

---

[10]Ibid., p. 3.

Journal entries for in-
substance defeasance
of bonds payable

MAGNO, INC.
Journal Entries for In-Substance Defeasance of Bonds Payable

Investment in 9% U.S. Treasury Bonds	5,375,872	
Cash		5,375,872

*To record acquisition of $8,000,000 face amount of 9% U.S.
Treasury bonds due May 31, Year 13, at a 16% yield rate.*

Bonds Payable.......................................	8,000,000	
Discount on Bonds Payable		935,167
Bond Issue Costs		72,000
Investment in 9% U.S. Treasury Bonds		5,375,872
Gain on Extinguishment of Bonds		1,616,961

*To record transfer of 9% U.S. Treasury bonds to irrevoca-
ble trust for servicing of 8% bonds payable. The transaction constitutes an in-substance defeasance of bonds,
with a resultant gain on extinguishment.*

As a result of the foregoing transactions, Magno, Inc., has realized a pre-tax extraordinary gain (assuming the amount is material) of $1,616,961 for the year ended May 31, Year 4. In contrast, Magno would have incurred an extraordinary loss (if material) of $1,167,167 if it had called the bonds at 102 on May 31, Year 4. The $1,167,167 loss would have been computed as follows:

Computation of loss if
bonds had been called

Call price of bonds ($8,000,000 × 1.02)	$8,160,000
Less: Carrying amount of bonds, May 31, Year 4	
($8,000,000 − $935,167 − $72,000)........................	6,992,833
Loss if bonds had been called	$1,167,167

Thus, by using the in-substance defeasance technique to extinguish bonds payable, a business enterprise may realize a gain, rather than the loss that typically results from calling the bonds. Further, an in-substance defeasance may be accomplished more quickly and efficiently than a debt-equity swap, in which the broker must acquire bonds in the open market over a substantial period of time to avoid undue upward pressure on prices of the bonds (and accompanying downward pressure on the yield rate for the bonds).

Evaluation of Accounting Principles for In-Substance Defeasance of Debt The accounting principles for in-substance defeasance of debt enacted by the Financial Accounting Standards Board are highly controversial. Critics claim that the setting aside of assets in trust does not constitute a disposal of the assets or the extinguishment of a liability, with resultant gain or loss. The assets continue to exist in the possession of a trustee, and the liability is still outstanding. In the opinion of the authors, although financial accounting emphasizes economic substance over legal form in most business transactions, the accounting for in-substance defeasance of debt borders on being "cute accounting," a term given by the Securities and Exchange Commission to accounting techniques that stretch financial accounting concepts to the limits of credibility. Nonetheless, the SEC has sanctioned the accounting principles for in-substance defeasance of debt established in *FASB Statement No. 76.*

OTHER TOPICS RELATING TO LONG-TERM DEBT

Convertible Bonds

Current Practice   A *convertible bond* may be exchanged at the holder's option for a stipulated number of shares of common stock. The conversion feature of a convertible bond enables the holders of such a security to enjoy the status of a creditor and at the same time participate in the price appreciation of the common stock. According to *APB Opinion No. 14,* "Accounting for Convertible Debt . . . ," "no portion of the proceeds from the issuance of . . . convertible debt securities . . . should be accounted for as attributable to the conversion feature."[11] Based on this principle, the accounting for the issuance and conversion of bonds is illustrated in the example below.

Assume that Lucien Company issued at face amount $10 million of 10-year, 12% convertible bonds. Interest on the bonds is payable semiannually. Each $1,000 bond is convertible to 30 shares of Lucien's $20 par common stock. The journal entries to record the issuance and subsequent conversion of the bonds (immediately after the periodic interest had been paid) are illustrated below:

Journal entries for issuance and conversion of bonds

Cash	*10,000,000*	
Convertible Bonds Payable		*10,000,000*
To record issuance of 10-year, 12% convertible bonds at face amount.		
Convertible Bonds Payable	*10,000,000*	
Common Stock, $20 par		*6,000,000*
Paid-in Capital in Excess of Par		*4,000,000*
To record conversion of 10-year, 12% convertible bonds to 300,000 shares of $20 par common stock.		

When common stock is issued in exchange for convertible bonds, the carrying amount of the bonds is assigned to the common stock. Thus, no gain or loss is recognized on a conversion of bonds to common stock under this *carrying amount* (or *book value*) *method.* Additional discussion of convertible bonds appears in Chapter 17.

---

[11]*APB Opinion No. 14.* "Accounting for Convertible Debt and Debt Issued with Stock Purchase Warrants," AICPA (New York: 1969), p. 207.

Evaluation of Current Practice   Current practice for recording the issuance of convertible bonds *does not,* in the opinion of the authors, recognize the economic substance of such transactions. When convertible bonds are issued, a portion of the proceeds logically is attributable to the conversion feature, a factor that is reflected in a lower nominal rate of interest. Because the bondholder receives a "call" on the issuer's common stock, a portion of the proceeds attributable to the conversion feature should be recorded as paid-in capital, and a bond discount (or a reduced bond premium) should be recorded. The discount (or reduced premium) is equal to the difference between the amount at which the bonds were issued and the estimated amount for which they would have been issued *in the absence of the conversion feature.*

To illustrate, assume that the $10 million of 10-year, 12% convertible bonds were issued at face amount by Lucien Company (see page 766) when similar non-convertible bonds were yielding 14% compounded semiannually. Present value tables indicate that 12% nonconvertible bonds would be issued for $8,940,599 to yield 14% compounded semiannually. The journal entry to record the issuance of the bonds by Lucien Company, *if a value is assigned to the conversion feature,* follows:

Journal entry for issuance of convertible bonds, *assuming a value is assigned to the conversion feature*

Cash	10,000,000	
Discount on Convertible Bonds Payable	1,059,401	
Convertible Bonds Payable		10,000,000
Paid-in Capital—Conversion Feature of Bonds		
Payable		1,059,401

To record issuance of 10-year, 12% convertible bonds valued at $8,940,599 (excluding value of conversion feature).

The discount would be amortized over the term of the bonds, thus increasing the amount of interest expense. If the bonds were converted prior to maturity, the carrying amount of the bonds would be transferred to the Common Stock and Paid-in Capital in Excess of Par ledger accounts.

In *APB Opinion No. 10,* "Omnibus Opinion—1966," the Accounting Principles Board required the assignment of a value to the conversion feature of convertible bonds as illustrated above, but a few years later, in *APB Opinion No. 14,* "Accounting for Convertible Debt . . . ," it reversed its position. Opposition by corporate managements and investment bankers to the separate accounting for the conversion feature, and the resultant increase in interest expense recognized by the issuer, probably was responsible for the reversal of position by the Accounting Principles Board. In the opinion of the authors, the final position of the APB is difficult to support conceptually. However, *the student is reminded that the earlier illustration on page 766 is in accord with generally accepted accounting principles.*

Extinguishment of Convertible Bonds   Should a gain or loss be recorded on the extinguishment of convertible bonds before maturity or conversion? A convertible bond is a hybrid security; thus, a simple answer to this question is difficult. When convertible bonds are trading at a large premium because of their conversion feature, and management of the issuer decides to retire the entire issue of bonds, it may call the bonds to force bondholders to convert. However, if management plans to retire only a portion of the bond issue, it could not exercise the call privilege and would have to pay the going market price for the bonds or initiate a debt-equity swap.

Because convertible bonds that are trading at a large premium are, in effect, an equity security, accounting theory suggests that the difference between the carrying amount of the bonds and the amount paid to retire them should be debited to paid-in capital, and not recognized as a loss. Under these circumstances the extinguishment of the convertible bonds may be viewed as equivalent to an acquisition of common stock for retirement. When convertible bonds are trading at a substantial discount, not because of high market rates of interest but because the issuer's common stock is trading at a low market price, extinguishment of such bonds may be viewed as giving rise to paid-in capital. This line of reasoning is based on the fact that the intent of issuing convertible bonds is to raise equity capital, and the low market price of the bonds is caused by the fact that the value of the bonds as an equity security has decreased. Despite arguments along these lines, the Accounting Principles Board in *Opinion No. 26,* "Early Extinguishment of Debt," stated:[12]

> The extinguishment of convertible debt before maturity does not change the character of the security as between debt and equity at that time. Therefore, a difference between the cash acquisition price of the debt and its net carrying amount should be recognized currently in income in the period of extinguishment as losses or gains.

In the opinion of the authors, this principle in some cases may result in material gains or losses being reported in the income statement that are in substance increases or decreases in paid-in capital.

Bonds Issued with Stock Warrants Attached

When bonds are issued that are not convertible to common stock but, instead, include *detachable stock warrants* giving the bondholder the right to acquire a certain number of shares of the issuer's common stock at a fixed price, a separate value is assigned to the warrants, based on the relative market values of the two

Journal entry for issuance of bonds with stock warrants attached

Cash	*10,000,000*	
Discount on Bonds Payable	*500,000*	
Bonds Payable		*10,000,000*
Paid-in Capital—Stock Warrants		*500,000*
To record issuance of bonds with common stock		
warrants attached.		

---

[12]*APB Opinion No. 26,* p. 502.

securities, because the two securities usually are traded separately in the market. If only one security has a market value, such value is assigned to the one security, and the remainder of the proceeds is assigned to the other security. Thus, if $10 million of bonds, with stock warrants attached that have a market value of $500,000, are issued for $10 million, the issuance would be recorded as shown on page 768.

Because the warrants are valued at $500,000, the bonds in effect were issued at 95. The Accounting Principles Board supported this approach in *APB Opinion No. 14,* "Accounting for . . . Debt Issued with Stock Purchase Warrants," as follows:[13]

> The Board is of the opinion that the portion of the proceeds of debt securities issued with detachable stock purchase warrants which is allocable to the warrants should be accounted for as paid-in capital. The allocation should be based on the relative fair values of the two securities at the time of issuance. Any resulting discount or premium on the debt securities should be accounted for as such. . . . However, when stock purchase warrants are not detachable from the debt and the debt security must be surrendered in order to exercise the warrant, the two securities taken together are substantially equivalent to convertible debt. . . .

When the stock warrants are exercised, the carrying amount of the warrants is treated as part of the proceeds from the issuance of common stock. This topic is discussed in more detail in Chapter 17.

Zero-Coupon (Deep-Discount) Bonds

Zero-coupon bonds do not pay interest; thus, they are in substance a long-term version of *commercial paper* issued by corporations (see Chapter 6, page 306 and Chapter 10, page 501 for a discussion of commercial paper). Because of their long term to maturity, zero-coupon bonds are issued at a *deep discount.* Because zero-coupon bonds do not bear interest, the only journal entries subsequent to issuance and prior to extinguishment of the bonds are entries for amortization of the deep discount.

To illustrate, assume that on January 2, Year 5, Tillson Company issued $5,000,000 of 20-year, zero-coupon bonds to yield 16% compounded semiannually to finance a plant expansion program. The cash received by Tillson was $230,155 ($5,000,000 × 0.046031* = $230,155). Journal entries of Tillson for the Year ended December 31, Year 5, are shown on page 770 (disregarding bond issue costs).

Why would Tillson Company incur long-term debt with a face amount of $5,000,000 for the receipt of only $230,155 cash? The answer is threefold: (1) Tillson avoids the payment of interest throughout the term of the bonds; (2) Tillson obtains an income tax deduction for interest each year without actually paying any interest; and (3) interest expense (exclusive of capitalized interest cost of the plant expansion) during the early years of the bonds' term is significantly lower than in

---

[13]*APB Opinion No. 14,* p. 209.
*From the 8% column of Table 2 in the Appendix at the end of Chapter 5.

Journal entries for zero-coupon bonds

Year 5

Jan. 2 Cash 230,155

Discount on Bonds Payable 4,769,845

      Bonds Payable 5,000,000

To record issuance of 20-year, zero-coupon

bonds to yield 16% compounded semiannually.

June 30 Bond Interest Expense ($230,155 × 0.08) 18,412

      Discount on Bonds Payable 18,412

To record interest expense on zero-coupon

bonds.

Dec. 31 Bond Interest Expense [($230,155 + $18,412)

    × 0.08] 19,885

      Discount on Bonds Payable 19,885

To record interest expense on zero-coupon bonds.

the later years, when the revenue provided by the expanded plant facilities is significant.

Miscellaneous Long-Term Debt

Other long-term debt such as notes payable to banks, equipment contracts payable, purchase-money obligations, and mortgage notes payable frequently is found in the balance sheets of business enterprises. The essential accounting problems related to these liabilities are similar to those applicable to bonds payable. The important point is that all long-term debt initially should be recorded at the present value of the amounts to be paid. This is particularly important when debts are incurred in connection with acquisition of noncash assets or are assumed by the combinor (acquiring company) in a business combination. In the acquisition of a business enterprise, if liabilities are not fairly valued, the amount of unidentifiable intangibles (goodwill) and the periodic amortization of such intangibles will be misstated.

As pointed out in Chapter 4, a variety of other "deferred credit" or "quasi-liability" items sometimes are included under long-term debt in balance sheets of business enterprises. These may range from unearned revenue items to items such as "excess of equity in net assets of subsidiary over cost," deferred investment tax credits, and deferred income tax credits.

Accounting for Restructured Debt

Business enterprises that encounter financial difficulties sometimes are able to negotiate more favorable terms with creditors for existing current or long-term debt. The result of such an arrangement is referred to as a *restructuring of debt* and may include the following provisions:

1   Extension of the due date of principal and interest payments

2   Reduction in the rate of interest on existing debt

3   Forgiveness by creditors of a portion of principal or accrued interest

In *FASB Statement No. 15,* "Accounting by Debtors and Creditors for Troubled Debt Restructurings," the Financial Accounting Standards Board defined ***troubled debt restructurings*** as those in which the creditor, for reasons related to the debtor's financial difficulties, grants a concession to the debtor that it would not otherwise consider.[14] If the concession involves the creditor's acceptance of noncash assets, preferred stock, or common stock with a current fair value less than the carrying amount of the troubled debt, the debtor recognizes a gain on restructuring of payables that, if material in amount, is reported as an extraordinary item.[15] However, the Financial Accounting Standards Board concluded that no gain be recognized by debtors when ***only a modification of terms is involved,*** unless the carrying amount of the restructured debt exceeds the total future cash payments specified by the new terms.[16] If the carrying amount of the restructured debt exceeds future cash payments, the debtor reduces the carrying amount of the debt, and all cash payments are recorded as reductions in the debt. Thus, the debtor recognizes a gain equal to the reduction in the carrying amount of the restructured debt, and no interest expense is recognized between the date of restructuring and the revised maturity date of the restructured debt.

To illustrate the accounting for a debt restructuring as a result of a ***modification of terms,*** assume that Paul Corporation has the following troubled debt on December 31, Year 10:

Composition of troubled debt on Dec. 31, Year 10, prior to restructuring

Note payable, 12%, due Dec. 31, Year 11	*$5,000,000*
Interest payable	*600,000*

On December 31, Year 10, the troubled debt was restructured as follows: (1) $500,000 of the note principal and the $600,000 of interest payable were forgiven by the creditor, (2) the maturity date was extended to December 31, Year 15, and (3) the interest rate was reduced from 12% to 8% a year on the $4,500,000 reduced principal amount of the note and was payable on December 31, Year 15. Because the total future cash payments under the new terms amount to $6,300,000 (principal of $4,500,000 and interest of $1,800,000 for five years at 8%), which exceeds the $5,600,000 total carrying amount of the debt prior to the restructuring, no gain is recognized by Paul on the restructuring. The excess of the total payments over the carrying amount of the debt, $700,000 ($6,300,000 − $5,600,000 = $700,000), is recognized as interest expense at a computed effective interest rate of 2.38363%* on the carrying amount of the debt ($5,600,000 for Year 11) as follows:

---

[14]*FASB Statement No. 15,* "Accounting by Debtors and Creditors for Troubled Debt Restructurings," FASB (Stamford, 1977), p. 1.
[15]Ibid., pp. 6, 7, 10.
[16]Ibid., p. 7.
*Computed by use of a computer program or by iteration from Table 2 in the Appendix at the end of Chapter 5.

Computation of annual
interest expense on
restructured troubled
debt

Year 11 $5,600,000 × 0.0238363	$133,483
Year 12 $5,733,483 × 0.0238363	136,665
Year 13 $5,870,148 × 0.0238363	139,923
Year 14 $6,010,071 × 0.0238363	143,258
Year 15 $6,153,329 × 0.0238363	146,671*
Total interest expense on restructured troubled debt........	$700,000

*Difference of $2 due to rounding

Paul Corporation records the troubled debt restructuring, interest expense, and the payment on December 31, Year 15, as follows:

Journal entries for restructured troubled debt not involving a **gain** on restructuring

Note Payable	5,000,000	
Interest Payable	600,000	
Discount on Restructured Note Payable	700,000	
Restructured Note Payable ($4,500,000 +		
$1,800,000)		6,300,000
To record restructuring of troubled debt on Dec. 31, Year 10, including reduction in interest rate from 12% to 8%.		
Interest Expense	133,483	
Discount on Restructured Note Payable		133,483
To recognize interest expense for year ended Dec. 31, Year 11.		
Interest Expense ($700,000 − $133,483)	566,517	
Discount on Restructured Note Payable		566,517
To recognize interest expense (in summary form) for the 4 years ended Dec. 31, Year 15.		
Restructured Note Payable	6,300,000	
Cash		6,300,000
To record payment of principal and interest on Dec. 31, Year 15.		

Over the five-year period ended December 31, Year 15, Paul Corporation recognizes interest expense in the amount of $700,000 ($133,483 + $566,517 = $700,000), and the restructured note payable is eliminated on December 31, Year 15, by payment of $4,500,000 and $1,800,000 interest, or a total of $6,300,000.

However, if the interest rate had been reduced from 12% to 4%, **payable annually,** the total future cash payments under the new terms would be $5,400,000 (principal of $4,500,000 and interest of $900,000 for five years at 4%), which is $200,000 less than the $5,600,000 pre-restructuring carrying amount of the troubled debt. In this case, the debtor would record the troubled debt restructuring (including a gain of $200,000) and the subsequent payments as follows:

<table>
<tr><td>Journal entries for restructured troubled debt involving a *gain* on restructuring</td><td>

Note Payable 5,000,000

Interest Payable 600,000

  Restructured Note Payable (including interest of

    $900,000 for five years) 5,400,000

    Gain on Restructuring of Troubled Debt 200,000

To record restructuring of troubled debt on Dec. 31, Year 10, including reduction in interest rate from 12% to 4%.

Restructured Note Payable 900,000

  Cash 900,000

To record payments of interest at the rate of $180,000 each year for five years (Dec. 31, Years 11 through 15).

Restructured Note Payable 4,500,000

  Cash 4,500,000

To record payment of principal on Dec. 31, Year 15.

</td></tr>
</table>

Troubled debt restructurings may take many forms and involve complex accounting issues. The foregoing examples were designed to illustrate relatively simple modifications of terms without any cash or other consideration being issued to the creditor in the debt restructurings.

Distinguishing between Long-Term Debt and Equity

Because interest is deductible in the computation of taxable income, and a payment designated as a dividend is not, it is inevitable that creative financial managers will devise liability contracts that bestow on the securities as many of the characteristics of ownership as possible without destroying their income tax status as debt. As a result, the dividing line between long-term debt and equity (stockholders' equity) often is blurred. An example on the liability side is *subordinated income bonds*. Such bonds are secured only by the general credit standing of the issuer, and the bond contract provides that interest will be paid only when and if earnings are sufficient. Interest payments on such a bond usually are cumulative, but failure to pay interest does not give bondholders the right to interfere in corporate affairs. It is clear that a substantial amount of risk, comparable with that borne by stockholders, attaches to such bonds. The basic characteristic distinguishing subordinated income bonds from preferred stock is that the bonds have a maturity date. The absence of a maturity date would give the Internal Revenue Service grounds for holding that subordinated income bonds are equivalent to preferred stock.

On the stockholders' equity side of the dividing line, some forms of preferred stock are similar to debt. A preferred stock issue that has no voting rights, provides a stated cumulative dividend, and requires redemption on specified dates represents only a limited form of ownership equity. Such preferred stock, in effect, represents "a liability masquerading as stockholders' equity," and requires special reporting in the balance sheet. This type of redeemable preferred stock is discussed in Chapter 16.

The question arises, in dealing with such cases, whether a distinction may be drawn with sufficient clarity to make a clear-cut division in accounting between long-term liabilities and stockholders' equity. Some accountants have argued that the entire right side of the balance sheet should be labeled "equities," and that the distinction between liabilities and stockholders' equity may not be important. This is an extreme position, however, and is not consistent with the definitions of *liabilities* and *equities* on page 19 of Chapter 1.

Long-Term Debt in the Balance Sheet

All long-term debt should be described in the balance sheet or in a note to the financial statements. Business enterprises having large amounts of long-term debt in the form of numerous issues often show only one amount in the balance sheet and support this with a note to the financial statements that presents the details of maturity dates, interest rates, call provisions, conversion features, assets pledged as collateral, and limitations on dividends or other restrictions imposed on the issuer. (For example, see *Note 5* on page 230.)

The Financial Accounting Standards Board requires disclosure of the combined aggregate amount of maturities and any sinking fund requirements of all long-term borrowings for each of the five years following the balance sheet date.[17] Also, the FASB requires substantial disclosures regarding troubled debt restructurings[18] and in-substance defeasance of debt.[19]

Any portion of long-term debt that matures in one year is listed as a current liability, unless the retirement of the debt will not require the use of current assets. If, during the ensuing year, long-term debt is expected to be converted to common stock, refunded, or repaid from a sinking fund, there is no reason to change its classification to a current liability. However, the expected method of retirement should be disclosed.

REVIEW QUESTIONS

1   Define the following: *debenture bonds, term bonds, serial bonds, convertible bonds, bond indenture, nominal (contract) rate, effective (yield) rate,* and *call premium.*

2   Bonds with a nomimal rate of interest of 10% are issued to yield 12%. Will the bond sell at a premium or a discount? Explain.

3   A $1 million bond issue is issued for $990,000 and is callable at 105. A few months later the bonds are trading at 106. List possible reasons for the increase in the market price of the bonds and explain the significance of the increase to the issuer.

4   Viking Company plans to issue $1 millicı 12%, 10-year bonds. What will be the average annual interest expense if the bonds are issued at 104? At 97?

[17]*FASB Statement No. 47*, "Disclosure of Long-Term Obligations," FASB (Stamford: 1981), pp. 4–5.
[18]*FASB Statement No. 15*, pp. 11–12.
[19]*FASB Statement No. 76*, p. 3.

5   If bonds are issued at a premium and the **_interest method_** is used to amortize the premium, will the annual interest expense increase or decline over the term of the bonds? Explain.

6   Canton Company has just issued $100 million of 15-year debenture bonds at a discount. At an annual stockholders' meeting, a stockholder asks the controller to explain the nature of bond discount and issue costs, which are included among Canton's assets at $4,829,000. The controller answers, ''This represents prepaid interest of $4.7 million and bond issue costs of $129,000 on our bonds, which are being amortized over the term of the debt.'' Evaluate the controller's answer.

7   Explain the appropriate balance sheet classification of:
a Premium on bonds payable
b Discount on bonds payable
c Bond issue costs

8   Why is the **_interest method_** of amortization of premium or discount on bonds payable considered conceptually superior to the **_straight-line method?_** Explain.

9   Explain how the interest accrued on bonds may be accounted for when bonds are issued between interest dates.

10   Describe the accounting for the difference between the carrying amount of bonds payable and the amount paid to extinguish the bonds. How is the difference entered in the accounting records and reported in the financial statements when bonds are refunded?

11   List some factors that management of a business enterprise should consider in deciding when to refund a bond issue.

12   Explain the following techniques for extinguishment of long-term bonds:
a **_Debt-equity swap_**
b **_In-substance defeasance_**

13   What are the advantages to a growing corporation of issuing convertible bonds?

14   What is the generally accepted practice in regard to the assignment of a value to the conversion feature of convertible bonds? Present an argument in favor of assigning to the conversion feature a part of the proceeds received on the issuance of convertible bonds.

15   Briefly describe the accounting for bonds that include detachable stock warrants to acquire the issuer's common stock.

16   An executive of a railroad was quoted as saying, ''Debt management is a continuous process that is essential to good operations. I shall never take on debt without a sinking fund.'' Comment on the executive's position.

17   Pardee Company has outstanding an issue of **_10% subordinated debentures_** and an issue of **_10% cumulative preferred stock,_** both callable at face amount or par. What is the basic distinction between these two securities that determines their balance sheet classification?

18 Explain the debtor's accounting for a troubled debt restructuring involving only a modification of terms:

a When the carrying amount of the debt *exceeds* the total future cash payments specified by the new terms

b When the carrying amount of the debt *is less than* the total future cash payments specified by the new terms

19 What disclosures regarding long-term debt are typically included in a note to the financial statements?

EXERCISES

Ex. 15-1 Select the best answer for each of the following multiple-choice questions:

1 Lemon Company borrowed $200,000 from Colonial Bank under a 16%, three-year promissory note dated December 31, Year 1, with interest payable annually on December 31, Year 2, through Year 4. The December 31, Year 2, interest payment was made on time by Lemon. During Year 3, Lemon experienced financial difficulties that made default on the note payable likely unless Colonial made concessions. On December 31, Year 3, Colonial agreed to accept $10,000 cash and land with a current fair value of $140,000 and a carrying amount of $100,000 from Lemon in full settlement of the note and accrued interest payable. Disregarding income taxes, the amount of Lemon Company's extraordinary gain (because of materiality) on the troubled debt restructuring is:

a $0 **b** $50,000 **c** $82,000 **d** $122,000 **e** Some other amount

2 One July 1, Year 2, Ramon Corporation issued $1,000,000 face amount, 10%, 20-year bonds with detachable stock warrants attached for $1,060,000. Each $1,000 bond had a detachable stock warrant enabling the acquisition of one share of Ramon's $50 par common stock for $60. Immediately after issuance of the bonds, market values of Ramon's securities were as follows:

10% bonds (ex-warrants)	$1,040
Stock warrants	20
$50 par common stock	56

In the journal entry to record issuance of the bonds, Ramon Corporation credits Premium on Bonds Payable for:

a $0 **b** $20,000 **c** $40,000 **d** $60,000 **e** Some other amount

3 If the cash received for bonds issued with detachable stock warrants attached exceeds the total of the face amount of the bonds and the current fair value of the stock warrants, the excess is credited to:

a Paid-in Capital in Excess of Par or Stated Value

b Retained Earnings

c Premium on Bonds Payable

d Paid-in Capital—Stock Warrants

4 For a troubled debt restructuring involving only a modification of terms, the debtor recognizes a gain if the carrying amount of the restructured debt:

a Exceeds the total future cash payments specified by the new terms

b Is less than the total future cash payments specified by the new terms

c Exceeds the present value of the future cash payments specified by the new terms

d Is less than the present value of the future cash payments specified by the new terms

5 How is the current fair value of detachable warrants attached to issued bonds accounted for?

a No value is accounted for

b The value is credited to a paid-in capital ledger account

c The value is credited to a retained earnings reserve ledger account

d The value is credited to a liability ledger account

6 On January 2, Year 2, Ludwig Company issued $500,000 face amount of 9%, 10-year bonds at 95. Interest on the bonds is payable on January 1 and July 1. Bond issue costs paid by Ludwig on January 2, Year 2, totaled $20,000. If Ludwig uses the straight-line method of amortization for bond discount and issue costs, the carrying amount of the bonds payable in Ludwig Company's December 31, Year 2, balance sheet is:

a $459,500   b $477,500   c $495,500   d $522,500   e Some other amount

7 The yield rate of interest for bonds that are issued for more than face amount is:

a Less than the nominal rate

b Equal to the nominal rate

c Larger than the nominal rate

d Independent of the nominal rate

8 On May 1, Year 7, Quando Company issued $1,000,000 face amount of 10% debenture bonds dated March 1, Year 7, with interest payable March 1 and September 1. The debenture bonds were issued at face amount plus accrued interest. Quando Company's debit to the Cash ledger account on May 1, Year 7, is:

a $966,667   b $983,333   c $1,016,667   d $1,033,333   e Some other amount

9 On April 1, Year 4, when the market rate of interest for comparable bonds was 14%, Wiley Corporation issued $500,000 face amount of 12%, 10-year bonds with interest payable semiannually. The discount of $52,970 on the bonds was amortized under the interest method. Discount amortization on October 1, Year 4, is:

a $1,277   b $2,659   c $3,191   d $3,723   e Some other amount

Ex. 15-2   Leach Company plans to issue $5 million, 12% bonds, due 20 years from date of issue. Interest is payable semiannually.

Compute the proceeds of Leach Company's bond issue if the effective rate of interest compounded semiannual is (a) 10%, and (b) 14%. Use the present value tables in the Appendix at the end of Chapter 5.

Ex. 15-3   On September 30, Year 2, the end of a fiscal year, Loman Company issued $1,000,000 face amount of 20-year, 24% "junk bonds" for $1,195,581, a 20% yield. Interest on the bonds was payable each March 31 and September 30. Loman uses the interest method of amortizing bond discount and bond premium.

Prepare journal entries for Loman Company to record the issuance of the bonds on September 30, Year 2, and the payment of interest on March 31 and September 30, Year 3. Disregard bond issue costs.

Ex. 15-4   On January 2, Year 5, Gayle Company issued 12% bonds with a face amount of $1,000,000. The bonds mature in 10 years, and interest is paid semiannually on June 30 and December 31. The bonds were issued for $894,060 to yield 14% compounded semiannually.

Using the interest method, compute the amount that should be debited by Gayle Company to Bond Interest Expense in Year 5. Round all amounts to the nearest dollar.

Ex. 15-5   Lazar Company plans to finance the acquisition of plant assets by issuing 10% bonds. Management projects earnings, *before* deduction of bond interest expense and income taxes expense, at $4,664,000 a year. Lazar's income tax rate is 40%. Management wants its net earnings *after* deduction of bond interest and income taxes to be 10 times the bond interest expense.

Assuming that the bonds may be issued to yield 10%, compute the face amount of bonds that should be issued by Lazar Company.

Ex. 15-6   Landau Corporation uses the interest method to amortize at a 10% yield rate the premium on its 11%, 20-year bonds with a face amount of $1,000,000 and a carrying amount of $1,017,729 on June 30, Year 23, two years prior to maturity of the bonds. Interest on the bonds is payble on June 30 and December 31.

Prepare a three-column Premium on Bonds Payable ledger account for Landau Corporation and post thereto journal entries for December 31, Year 23, June 30 and December 31, Year 24, and June 30, Year 25. Round all amounts to the nearest dollar.

Ex. 15-7   On October 1, Year 8, Likert Company issued $6 million serial bonds requiring the payment of $1.2 million principal each year, beginning October 1, Year 9.
a Explain how a $270,000 discount on Likert Company's bond issue would be amortized if the bonds outstanding method were used.
b How much of the discount would be amortized for the year ended December 31, Year 10, under the bonds outstanding method?
c Assuming, as a separate case, that Likert Company's bonds required the payment of $1.2 million at the end of each of five years, starting at the end of the third year after issue date, prepare a schedule of discount amortization computed under the bonds outstanding method.

Ex. 15-8   On September 30, Year 13, the accounting records of Losswell Company had the following ledger account balances related to $500,000 face amount of 16%, 10-year bonds payable that had been issued October 1, Year 5, to yield 18%. Interest on the bonds was payable April 1 and October 1. All end-of-period adjustment had been made as of September 30, Year 13.

Bond interest payable	*$ 40,000*
Bond issue costs	*10,000*
Discount on bonds payable	*16,199*
16% bonds payable	*500,000*

On September 30, Year 13, Losswell called the entire bond issue at the call price of 102.

Prepare a journal entry for Losswell Company to record the call (and extinguishment) of the bonds on September 30, Year 13. Disregard income taxes.

Ex. 15-9   On December 31, Year 12, Beale Company had outstanding 10 million of 12%, 20-year bonds due in seven years and nine months. The premium on the bonds on October 1, Year 12, was $840,000.

Prepare journal entries for Beale Company (**a**) to record the accrual of interest and amortization of the premium for the three months ended December 31, Year 12, and (**b**) to record the call of $1 million of the bonds on January 2, Year 13, at 102 plus accrued interest for three months, assuming that premium is amortized on a straight-line basis and that reversing entries are not used. Disregard bond issue costs and income taxes.

Ex. 15-10   On December 1, Year 6, Kier Company issued 13%, $2,000,000 face amount bonds for $2,200,000, plus accrued interest. Interest is payable on February 1 and August 1. Bond issue costs may be disregarded. On December 31, Year 8, the carrying amount of the bonds, inclusive of the unamortized premium, was $2,100,000. On July 1, Year 9, Kier acquired the bonds in the open market at 98, plus accrued interest. Kier appropriately uses the straight-line method for the amortization of bond premium because the results do not differ materially from the interest method.

Compute the gain or loss on the extinguishment of Kier Company's bonds. Show supporting computations and disregard income taxes.

Ex. 15-11   On November 30, Year 4, Ginger Company issued 10,000 shares of its no-par common stock (stated value $10 a share, current fair value $38 a share) to an investment banker in a debt-equity swap for $500,000 face amount of Ginger's 10% bonds maturing November 30, Year 8, which had been issued to yield 14%. The bonds paid interest on May 31 and November 30. Bond issue costs amounted to $20,000 on November 30, Year 4. Ginger amortized bond discount under the interest method.

Prepare a journal entry to record Ginger Company's debt-equity swap on November 30, Year 4. Disregard income taxes.

Ex. 15-12   On March 31, Year 7, Newland Corporation completed an in-substance defeasance of its $600,000 face amount, 10% bonds due March 31, Year 15, which had been issued on March 31, Year 5, to yield 12%. The bonds, which paid interest March 31 and September 30, had a call price of 103 on March 31, Year 7. Newland amortizes bond discount under the interest method. Newland accomplished the in-substance defeasance by acquiring and placing in an irrevocable trust $600,000 face amount of

U.S. Treasury bonds due March 31, Year 15, which had a nominal interest rate of 12% and a yield rate of 16% on March 31, Year 7. Interest payment dates for the 12% U.S. Treasury bonds were the same as those for Newland's 10% bonds. The trustee agreed to accept the semiannual interest differential of $6,000 as a fee for servicing Newland's 10% bonds. Bond issue costs may be disregarded.

a Compute Newland Company's gain on the in-substance defeasance of its 10% bonds on March 31, Year 7. Disregard income taxes.

b Compute the loss that Newland Company would have incurred had it called the 10% bonds at 103 on March 31, Year 7.

Ex. 15-13　On April 1, Year 8, Ardell Company issued $1,000,000 face amount of 10%, 10-year convertible bonds to yield 12% compounded semiannually. Ardell's investment bankers estimated that a 14% yield rate, compounded semiannually, would have applied had Ardell's bonds been nonconvertible. Bond issue costs may be disregarded.

a Prepare a journal entry to record Ardell Company's issuance of 10% convertible bonds on April 1, Year 8, in accordance with generally accepted accounting principles, that is, with no value assigned to the conversion feature.

b Prepare a journal entry to record Ardell Company's issuance of 10% convertible bonds on April 1, Year 8, assuming a value had been assigned to the conversion feature.

Ex. 15-14　On September 1, Year 1, Exx Company issued for $198,000, $200,000 face amount of 12%, 20-year bonds, with interest payable March 1 and September 1. Each $1,000 bond had 10 detachable stock warrants attached entitling the owner to acquire one share of Exx's $10 par common stock for each warrant plus $20 cash. Shortly after issuance of the bonds, they were trading at 100 ex-warrants, and the warrants were trading at $10 each. Bond issue costs may be disregarded.

　　　Prepare a journal entry to record Exx Company's issuance of 12% bonds with detachable stock warrants attached on September 1, Year 1.

Ex. 15-15　Ellidge Corporation, which uses the interest method to amortize bond discount, issued $10,000,000 face amount, 20-year, zero-coupon bonds on March 31, Year 5, to yield 14% compounded semiannually.

　　　Show how the amounts related to Ellidge Corporation's zero-coupon bonds appear in its balance sheet on March 31, Year 6, assuming Ellidge paid $80,000 bond issue costs on March 31, Year 5.

Ex. 15-16　Cagle Company issued $1 million face amount, 9% bonds with detachable stock warrants attached. The bonds were issued for $1,015,000. Immediately after issuance, the bonds were quoted ex-warrants at 96, and the warrants had a total market value of $90,000.

　　　Prepare a journal entry to record Cagle Company's issuance of the bonds, assuming that no accrued interest was charged to acquirers of the bonds and that total proceeds were allocated on the basis of the relative market values of the bonds and stock warrants. Disregard bond issue costs.

Ex. 15-17   Mogo Company had a $10,000,000 note payable outstanding on June 30, Year 8, which was due in one year. Interest at 10% a year had been paid through June 30, Year 8. Mogo's fiscal year ends on June 30. Because of Mogo's poor financial condition, the creditor agreed to restructure the troubled loan on June 30, Year 8, as follows: The maturity date of the note was extended to June 30, Year 10; $1,500,000 of the principal was forgiven; and the interest rate was reduced to 5% a year on the reduced amount of principal.

Compute the gain on the restructuring of the troubled debt and prepare journal entries for Mogo Company to record the restructuring of the troubled debt and all payments on the note through June 30, Year 10.

Ex. 15-18   On August 31, Year 2, Ryder Company acquired machinery from Carroll, Inc., on a five-year, 8% promissory note in the amount of $493,604. Interest on the note was payable annually. On August 31, Year 3, Ryder informed Carroll that it was unable to pay interest of $39,488 on the note for the year ending that date because of a weak financial position. Thereupon, Carroll agreed to restructure the troubled debt by (1) forgiving $33,092 of the unpaid interest; (2) extending the due date for *total* interest to August 31, Year 7, the due date of the note; and (3) reducing the interest rate to 5% on the unpaid principal and interest on August 31, Year 3.

a Compute the effective interest rate on the unpaid balance of Ryder Company's restructured troubled debt on August 31, Year 3.

b Prepare journal entries for Ryder Company on August 31, Year 3, to record the restructuring of the troubled debt, and on August 31, Year 4, to record interest expense for one year on the restructured troubled debt.

CASES

Case 15-1   One method for a corporation to accomplish long-term debt financing is through the issuance of bonds.

Instructions

a Describe the accounting for the proceeds from bonds issued with detachable stock warrants attached.

b Explain the differences between a serial bond and a term bond.

c For a five-year term bond issued at a premium, why does amortization of the premium for the first year under the interest method differ from amortization under the straight-line method? Include in your discussion a statement as to whether premium amortization under the interest method is greater or less than amortization under the straight-line method for the first year.

d When bonds are issued at a discount between interest dates, what journal entry is prepared and how is the subsequent amortization of the discount affected? Include in your discussion an explanation of how the amount of each debit and credit item in the journal entry for issuance of the bonds is computed.

e Describe the financial statement presentation of a gain or loss from extinguishment of bonds payable.

Case 15-2   **a** The appropriate method of amortizing a premium or discount on bonds payable is the interest method.

Instructions

(1) What is the interest method of amortization, and how is it different from and similar to the straight-line method of amortization?

(2) How is amortization computed under the interest method, and why and how do amounts computed under the interest method differ from amounts computed under the straight-line method?

b Gains or losses from the extinguishment of bonds that are refunded may be accounted for in three ways:

Amortized over the remaining term of the old bonds

Amortized over the term of the new bonds

Recognized in full in the accounting period of the refunding

Instructions

(1) Discuss the supporting arguments for each of the three methods of accounting for gains and losses from the extinguishment of debt that is refunded.

(2) Which of the above methods is generally accepted, and how should the appropriate amount of gain or loss be reported in the income statement?

Case 15-3   The balance sheet of Noland Company on December 31, Year 5 follows:

NOLAND COMPANY
Balance Sheet
December 31, Year 5
(in thousands of dollars)

Assets

Current assets:	
Cash	$ 5,000
Short-term investments (at cost, market value $15.2 million)	15,000
Accounts receivable (net)	10,000
Inventories	24,000
Short-term prepayments	1,000
Total current assets	$ 55,000
Plant assets (net)	40,000
Other noncurrent assets	5,000
Total assets	$100,000

Liabilities & Stockholders' Equity

Current liabilities	$ 35,000
12% bonds payable, callable at 105, each $1,000 bond	
convertible to 25 shares of common stock	40,000
Total liabilities	$ 75,000

(continued)

Stockholders' equity:

Common stock, no par or stated value, 2,000,000 shares
authorized, 1,000,000 shares issued and outstanding ..... $ 5,000
Retained earnings 20,000
Total stockholders' equity 25,000
Total liabilities & stockholders' equity $100,000

The president of Noland believes that Noland is facing a serious financing problem, which she outlines for you as follows:

"We must raise approximately $50 million dollars over the next two years in order to finance the expansion of our product lines and sales territories. My banker friends tell me that our balance sheet is not in good shape. They have pointed out repeatedly that our current ratio (current assets divided by current liabilities) is significantly below the industry standard of 2 to 1 and that approximately 75% of our assets are financed by borrowed capital. They feel this is much too high, considering the type of industry we are in. We don't want to issue more common stock to the public, and apparently we can't issue additional bonds unless our balance sheet can be cleaned up. I wish we had paid more attention to the management of our assets: We have $15 million invested in low-yielding securities, our accounts receivable and inventories are twice as large as they ought to be, and we have been paying out too much in dividends. Our profits have been growing steadily, and we pay a dividend of $3 a share on our stock. As a result, our stock is trading at $55 a share and our bonds at 140 on the open market. I would appreciate your advice on this matter."

Instructions

Briefly outline a course of action the president should follow in "cleaning up" the balance sheet of Noland Company and raising the $50 million needed for expansion. Disregard the effects of income taxes in your answer.

Case 15-4 Olmo Company was organized two years ago by two experienced business executives and several members of the faculty at a local university. The main product line of Olmo consists of medium-size computers and software for all types of data-processing and information systems. Olmo's assets total $15 million and the liabilities amount to $10.5 million, consisting of $3 million of short-term debt and $7.5 million of long-term notes payable to an insurance company. There are 100,000 shares of common stock issued and outstanding. In order to expand its activities, Olmo needs $5 million in long-term capital. Members of the board of directors have discussed various proposals for raising the capital and have asked for your advice regarding the following alternatives:

(1) Issue bonds bearing interest at 13% with a sinking-fund provision.
(2) Issue 10% bonds at face amount. The bonds would be convertible to 40,000 shares of Olmo's common stock at $125 a share. The current market price of the common stock is $96 a share.

(3) Issue 9% preferred stock at a par of $100. The preferred stock would be callable at $105 a share and convertible to three-fourths of one share of common stock for one share of preferred.

(4) Issue 60,000 shares of common stock at $85 a share through a rights offering. Stockholders would be given stock warrants for rights to acquire one additional share of common stock for every 10 shares held.

Instructions

Evaluate the advantages and disadvantages of each of the four alternatives proposed by Olmo Company's board of directors.

Case 15-5   The directors of Miller Company are considering the issuance of $15 million of bonds. Miller does not need the money immediately, but Director Alan, a former banker, has convinced the board that the bonds should be issued "while interest rates are low and money is readily available."

Director Krueger, partner of a leading investment banking firm, also recommended that bonds should be issued because interest rates are beginning to rise and a nominal rate of 12% probably would command a modest premium. However, Krueger believes that the directors are making a mistake in not considering the issuance of convertible debentures for the following reasons:

(1) It would be cheaper for Miller (a rate of about 9% probably would be sufficient).

(2) Miller's stockholders' equity will need "beefing up" as Miller continues to expand its operations.

(3) It is essentially a means of issuing common stock at about 20% above the current market price.

Director Barney, vice president of finance, suggested that a 13% rate be assigned to nonconvertible bonds, stating, "A large premium is a sign of financial strength of our company; if interest rates continue to advance, 12% bonds will sell at a discount, and I don't want people thinking that our credit is so poor that we have to give a discount in order to sell our bonds."

Director Carla, a public relations executive, disagreed with Director Barney. She stated that investors are "bargain hunters" who would be more willing to invest in bonds at a discount than at a premium. She would assign an 11% interest rate to the bonds, stating "discount on bonds payable is prepaid interest, and it will not hurt us to get a jump on our interest payments to bondholders."

Instructions

Evaluate the view expressed by each of the four directors of Miller Company.

Case 15-6   Crowe Company recently issued $1 million face amount, 14%, 30-year subordinated debentures at 97. The debentures are callable at 103 on any date on 30 days notice, beginning 10 years after issuance. The debentures are convertible to $10 par common stock of Crowe at the conversion price of $12.50 a share for each $500 (or multiple thereof) of the face amount of the debentures. Debenture issue costs may be disregarded.

Instructions

a Explain how the conversion feature of convertible debentures has a value (1) to the issuer, and (2) to the investor.

b Management of Crowe Company has suggested that in recording the issuance of the debentures a portion of the proceeds should be assigned to the conversion feature.

(1) What are the financial accounting arguments for assigning a value to the conversion feature of the debentures?

(2) What are the financial accounting arguments supporting accounting for the convertible debentures as a single element?

PROBLEMS

15-1 On September 1, Year 1, Lingo Company issued $1,000,000 face amount of 18%, 20-year bonds for $1,119,246, a 16% yield rate. Interest on the bonds was payable each March 1 and September 1. Bond issue costs of $50,000 were paid on September 1, Year 1. Lingo uses the interest method of amortization for bond premium.

Instructions

Prepare journal entries for Lingo Company to record the issuance of the bonds and the payment of bond issue costs on September 1, Year 1, the payment of interest on March 1, Year 2, and the accrual of interest on August 31, Year 2, the end of the fiscal year. Lingo prepares adjusting entries only at the end of the fiscal year.

15-2 The balance sheet of Wolfram Corporation on September 30, Year 11, included the following items:

14% bonds payable, due Sept. 30, Year 26, interest payable Mar. 31 and Sept. 30...	$2,500,000
Discount on bonds payable, at 16% yield rate	281,445
Bond issue costs...	36,000

Instructions

a Prepare journal entries to record the payment of bond interest by Wolfram Corporation on March 31, Year 12, and September 30, Year 12, assuming bond discount is amortized by the interest method. Amortization of bond issue costs is recorded on each interest payment date by the straight-line method.

b Prepare a working paper to compute the gain or loss on Wolfram Corporation's call (and extinguishment) of the 14% bonds at 102 on September 30, Year 12, the end of a fiscal year.

15-3 On January 2, Year 4, Ruiz Company issued $1,000,000 of five-year, 9% serial bonds to be repaid in the amount of $200,000 on January 2, Year 5 through Year 9. Interest is payable at the end of each year. The bonds were issued to yield an annual rate of 10%. Bond issue costs may be disregarded.

Instructions

a Prepare a working paper to compute the proceeds received by Ruiz Company from the issuance of the serial bonds. Show supporting computations (rounded to the nearest dollar) and use the Appendix at the end of Chapter 5.

b Prepare a working paper for Ruiz Company for the amortization of the bond discount by the interest method for the full term of the bond issue. Show supporting computations, rounded to the nearest dollar.

15-4 On December 1, Year 5, Windsor, Inc., issued 10-year bonds of $2 million at 102. Interest is payable on June 1 and December 1 at the rate of 12%. On April 1, Year 7, Windsor acquired in the open market 600 of these bonds at 96, plus accrued interest. The accounting period for Windsor ends on December 31. Bond issue costs may be disregarded.

Instructions

Prepare journal entries for Windsor, Inc., to record the following. (Round all amounts to the nearest dollar and disregard the effects of income taxes.)

a The issuance of the bonds on December 1, Year 5.

b Interest payments and amortization in Year 6. Amortization is recorded by the straight-line method at the time of interest payments and at the end of the calendar year. Windsor, Inc., does not prepare reversing entries for the accrual of bond interest at the end of the calendar year.

c The extinguishment of $600,000 face amount of bonds on April 1, Year 7. (Hint: First amortize premium for three months on the bonds retired, with a credit to Bond Interest Expense.)

15-5 On July 1, Year 1, Crimson Company issued bonds with a face amount of $1,000,000 maturing in 10 years. The nominal interest rate was 10%, payable semiannually on June 30 and December 31. The bonds were issued to yield 12% compounded semiannually. Disregard bond issue costs.

On June 30, Year 2, Crimson issued $500,000 face amount of bonds with stock warrants attached. These bonds had a nominal interest rate of 8%, payable semiannually, and were issued at 105. One detachable warrant to acquire common stock was attached to each $1,000 bond. The current fair value of each bond without the warrant was $966. Disregard bond issue costs.

Instructions

a Using the Appendix at the end of Chapter 5, compute the amount of cash received by Crimson Company for the 10% bonds issued on July 1, Year 1.

b Prepare journal entries for Crimson Company to record the following:

(1) Issuance of 10% bonds on July 1, Year 1

(2) Payment of interest and amortization (under the interest method) on December 31, Year 1

(3) Payment of interest and amortization (under the interest method) on June 30, Year 2

c Prepare a journal entry for Crimson Company to record the issuance of the 8% bonds on June 30, Year 2.

15-6 The balance sheet of Ergo Corporation on June 30, Year 5, included the following:

12% first mortgage bonds payable, maturing on June 30, Year 20 .... $20,000,000

Discount on bonds payable 600,000

Bond issue costs... 132,000

Instructions

a Compute the annual interest expense for Ergo Corporation's first mortgage bonds payable, including amortization of bond issue costs. Straight-line amortization is used.

b Prepare a journal entry for Ergo Corporation to record the open market acquisition of $4 million of bonds at 105 on July 1, Year 10. Ergo's fiscal year ends on June 30. Disregard income taxes.

c Show how the amounts relating to bonds payable are presented in the balance sheet of Ergo Corporation on June 30, Year 15.

15-7 On July 1, Year 5, Pons Company issued $5 million of 9%, 20-year bonds with interest payable on March 1 and September 1. Pons received proceeds of $5,120,500, including accrued interest from March 1, Year 5. Bond issue costs may be disregarded. The bonds mature on March 1, Year 25. On December 31, Year 5, Pons completed a debt-equity swap with an investment banking firm by issuing 110,000 shares of $10 par common stock with a current fair value of $45 a share in exchange for the entire bond issue. The accrued interest was paid in cash.

Instructions

Prepare journal entries for Pons Company on the following dates (disregard income taxes):

a July 1, Year 5 (issuance of bonds)

b September 1, Year 5 (payment of interest and amortization of discount for two months under the straight-line method)

c December 31, Year 5 (accrual of interest and amortization of discount from September 1 to December 31 and issuance of common stock in debt-equity swap)

15-8 In July, Year 1, the board of directors of Noble Arms, Inc., authorized the issuance of $50 million of 10%, 20-year bonds payable. The bonds were dated September 1, Year 1, and interest was payable semiannually on March 1 and September 1. The bonds were issued to underwriters on September 1, Year 1. Noble Arms amortizes discount and premium under the interest method on each interest payment date and at the end of the accounting period. Bond issue costs may be disregarded.

Instructions

Prepare journal entries for Noble Arms, Inc., to record the issuance of the bonds, the adjusting entry on December 31, Year 1 (the close of the fiscal year), the journal entries to record the first two semiannual interest payments in Year 2, and the adjusting entry on December 31, Year 2, assuming that:

a The bonds were issued to the underwriters to yield 9%. (Use the Appendix at the end of Chapter 5 and round all computations to the nearest dollar.)

b The bonds were issued to the underwriters to yield 11%.

15-9   Loredo Company was authorized to issue $10 million of 10-year, 12% convertible bonds due December 31, Year 15. Each $1,000 bond is convertible to 40 shares of Loredo's $10 par common stock, and the bond indenture contained an antidilution provision. The bonds were issued to underwriters on March 1, Year 6, for net proceeds of $10,129,200, including accrued interest. Interest is payable semiannually on June 30 and December 31. Discount is amortized by the straight-line method. Bond issue costs may be disregarded.

Late in Year 6, Loredo declared a 10% stock dividend on the common stock, and in Year 7 the common stock was split 2 for 1. The interest payments and the amortization of discount by the straight-line method were correctly recorded through December 31, Year 7. On May 1, Year 8, bonds with a face amount of $1,000,000 were converted, and the accrued interest on these bonds was paid.

Instructions

a Prepare a journal entry for Loredo Company to record the issuance of bonds on March 1, Year 6. No value was assigned to the conversion feature of the bonds.

b Prepare a journal entry for Loredo Company to record, for the first four months of Year 8, the payment of interest and the amortization of discount on the bonds converted on May 1, Year 8.

c Prepare a journal entry for Loredo Company to record the conversion of $1,000,000 face amount of bonds on May 1, Year 8. (An antidilution provision in the bond indenture provides for a proportionate adjustment in the number of shares to which each bond may be converted if the common stock is split or if stock dividends are distributed.)

15-10   John Corporation issued $2 million of 11% serial bonds for $2,072,000 on January 2, Year 1. The bonds mature at the rate of $400,000 a year starting on December 31, Year 1. Interest is payable on June 30 and December 31. Bond issue costs may be disregarded.

Instructions

a Prepare a working paper for John Corporation showing the amortization of the premium and total interest expense for each year through Year 5. Amortization is computed by the bonds outstanding method.

b On July 1, Year 2, $200,000 face amount of the bonds, which were *scheduled to be retired on December 31, Year 4,* were acquired by John Corporation in the open market at 101. Prepare a journal entry for John to record the extinguishment of the bonds, assuming that the amortization of the premium was recorded through June 30, Year 2, when the semiannual interest was paid.

15-11   Rickert Company issued $4 million face amount of three-year, 9% bonds. Interest is payable semiannually on June 30 and December 31. The bonds were issued on January 1, Year 1, at a price that gave Rickert an effective interest cost of 5% semiannually. Bond issue costs may be disregarded.

Instructions

a Compute the proceeds of Rickert Company's bond issue and prepare an amortization table, similar to that illustrated on page 748, showing the interest expense for each six-month period by the interest method. (Use the Appendix at the end of Chapter 5 and round all computations to the nearest dollar.)

b Using the data in the amortization table prepared in **a**, prepare journal entries for Rickert Company to record the issuance of the bonds, the interest payments at the end of the first six months and at the end of the last six months of the bond issue, and the extinguishment of the bonds at maturity on December 31, Year 3.

15-12 Norbert Corporation issued $10 million of 10-year, 12% convertible bonds on September 30, Year 1, for $9,064,000, plus interest for three months. Bond issue costs of $23,400 were incurred and recorded in a separate ledger account. No value was assigned to the conversion feature. Interest is payable semiannually on June 30 and December 31. The bonds were callable after June 30, Year 6, and until June 30, Year 8, at 104, thereafter until maturity, at 102; and were convertible to $2.50 par common stock as follows:

(1) Until June 30, Year 6, at the rate of six shares for each $1,000 bond
(2) From July 1, Year 6, to June 30, Year 9, at the rate of five shares for each $1,000 bond
(3) After June 30, Year 9, at the rate of four shares for each $1,000 bond

The bonds mature on June 30, Year 11. Norbert prepares adjusting entries monthly and closes its accounting records yearly on December 31. Bond discount and bond issue costs are amortized on a straight-line basis.

The following transactions occurred in connection with the bonds:

July 1, Year 7: $2 million of bonds were converted to common stock.

Jan. 1, Year 9: $1 million of bonds were acquired in the open market at 98 and were extinguished.

June 30, Year 9:   The remaining $7 million of bonds were called for redemption. In order to obtain the necessary funds for redemption and business expansion, Norbert issued $12 million of 10% bonds at face amount. These bonds were dated May 31, Year 9, and were due on May 31, Year 29. Bond issue costs of $40,600 were paid.

Instructions

Prepare journal entries for Norbert Company to record the foregoing transactions, including monthly adjustments where appropriate, on each of the following dates. (Do not prepare closing entries, and include supporting computations as part of journal entry explanations.)

a September 30, Year 1. (Record bond issue costs in a separate journal entry.)

b December 31, Year 1. (Record one month's interest and amortization in a separate journal entry before recording the payment of interest.)

c July 1, Year 7.

d January 1, Year 9.

e June 30, Year 9. (Record the accrual of interest and related amortization of discount and issue costs, the payment of interest, the redemption of $7 million of 12%, convertible bonds, and the issuance of $12 million of 10% bonds and payment of bond issue costs in separate journal entries.)

15-13   The balance sheet of Matsudo Company on June 30, Year 7, included the following long-term debt:

> Bonds payable due June 30, Year 12, interest at 12% payable June 30
> and December 31, less discount at 14% yield rate on issue date,
> $70,236 . . . . $ 929,764
> Bonds payable due December 31, Year 15, interest at 14% payable
> June 30 and December 31   2,000,000

On June 30, Year 7, bond issue costs amounted to $48,000 for the 12% bonds payable and $51,000 for the 14% bonds payable.

In a desire to "clean up" the long-term debt section of its balance sheet, Matsudo completed the following transactions on June 30, Year 7:

(1) Issuance of 15,000 shares of $10 par common stock with a current fair value of $60 a share to an investment banker in a debt-equity swap. The investment banker had acquired the 12% bonds from several institutional investors for a total cost of $782,000.

(2) Acquisition of $2,000,000 face amount of 14% U.S. Treasury bonds due December 31, Year 15, interest payable June 30 and December 31, at a yield rate of 16%, and transfer of the bonds to an irrevocable trust for servicing of Matsudo's 14% bonds payable. The present value of the trustee's fees during the remaining term of Matsudo's 14% bonds payable was estimated at $105,000.

(3) Issuance of $30,000,000 zero-coupon, 20-year bonds to yield 18% compounded semiannually. Bond issue costs were paid in the amount of $290,000.

Instructions

a Prepare journal entries for Matsudo Company on June 30, Year 7, to record the foregoing transactions. (Use the Appendix at the end of Chapter 5 and round all amounts to the nearest dollar.)

b Prepare the long-term debt section of Matsudo Company's balance sheet on June 30, Year 7. Disregard disclosures required in notes to the financial statements.

Stockholders' Equity

Stockholders' Equity

4

The accounting for assets and liabilities has a direct impact on the measurement of net income. In contrast, the accounting for stockholders' equity generally does not affect revenue and expense measurements.

Invested capital for a corporation is differentiated from earned capital, legal capital is differentiated from other sources of paid-in capital, and the portion of capital legally available for the declaration of dividends must be clearly identified. Specific accounting procedures apply to different types of dividends. The amount of retained earnings transferred to paid-in capital as a result of stock dividends varies with the size of such dividends. Legal requirements have a strong influence on generally accepted accounting principles for stockholders' equity.

Numerous forms of stock warrants, convertible securities, and employee capital accumulation plans currently are used by business corporations. Contraction of stockholders' equity through treasury stock acquisitions has become an important financial strategy in recent years. The accounting for treasury stock transactions and the computation of earnings per share also are included in this part.

Paid-In Capital, Retained Earnings, and Dividends

16

One of the striking features of the United States economy is the dominant role played by corporations. Corporations are responsible for the bulk of the national output of goods and services; they also are the principal source of employment, a major medium for the investment of capital, and a leading factor in the research and development activities that are so vital in keeping the economy growing and competitive in the world markets.

Efficiency of production and distribution in many industries requires more capital than can be obtained by a single proprietor or a partnership. The large amounts of capital needed for successful entry into many fields of business are most easily acquired by issuing shares of common stock to the public. Corporations have reached their dominant role largely because of their efficiency for the concentration of capital. Because most corporations have numerous stockholders who do not participate directly in management, complete accounting and internal control systems are of critical importance as a means of protecting the interests of absentee owners of corporate securities.

Several specific advantages of the corporate form of organization help explain why corporations are so successful in attracting capital. Among these advantages are the following:

1 *Limited liability* A stockholder has no personal liability for debts of the corporation. Creditors must look for payment only to the corporation itself and not to the personal resources of the owners. Freedom from personal liability is an important factor in encouraging investors to acquire common stock of corporations.

2 *Liquidity of investments in corporate securities* The owners of corporate securities (especially securities listed on stock exchanges) may sell all or part of their investment for cash at any time. The liquidity of corporate securities is a major reason for their popularity.

3 *Continuity of existence* A corporation is a separate legal entity with unlimited life, whereas a partnership may be terminated by the death or retirement of any partner.

4 *Separation of the functions of management and ownership* By attracting capital from a large number of investors and selecting management on a basis of executive ability, a corporation achieves expert direction of large amounts of economic and human resources.

Structure of the Corporation

To form a corporation, one or more incorporators submit an application to the corporation commissioner or other designated official of a state government. The application identifies the incorporators, states the nature of the business, and describes the capital stock to be issued. After payment of an incorporation fee and approval of the application, *articles of incorporation* are approved by the state as evidence of the legal existence of the corporation. The incorporators, who must be *subscribers* to shares of the corporation's common stock, elect a *board of directors* and approve *bylaws* to serve as general guides for the operation of the corporation. The board of directors appoints *officers* to serve as active managers of the corporation. Corporate officers usually include a president, one or more vice-presidents, a treasurer, a controller, and a secretary. The organization process is completed by the issuance of shares of common stock to the subscribers as evidence of their ownership of the corporation.

The corporate form of organization is not limited to companies organized for profit. The term *public corporation* is applied to government-owned units (such as the Federal Deposit Insurance Corporation), whereas the terms *private corporation* and *business corporation* include all companies that are owned by investors. Within the meaning of *private corporation* are both the *nonstock* corporations (churches, universities, and hospitals that are not organized for profit) and *stock* corporations, which operate to earn net income and which issue shares of capital stock to investors. Our attention is focused on the stock corporation. Within this group, one may also recognize subgroups such as *close corporations* with common stock held by a small number of owners (perhaps a family), and *publicly owned corporations* with capital stock available for acquisition by the public. The capital stock of publicly owned corporations may be *listed* (traded on organized stock exchanges) or *over-the-counter* (an unlisted market in which dealers buy from and sell to the public).

Although the laws governing the formation and operation of a stock corporation vary among the states, these state laws all emphasize certain basic concepts. Every state recognizes the corporation as a separate entity and provides for the issuance of shares of capital stock as units of ownership.

Ownership Equity of the Corporation

In the balance sheet of a single proprietorship, the owner's equity is shown as a single amount. For a partnership, the owner's equity of each partner is presented, without any distinction between paid-in capital and retained earnings. However, in the balance sheet of a corporation, a basic objective in reporting the stockholders' equity is to distinguish clearly between paid-in capital and retained earnings.

Why should the stockholders' equity be subdivided? One reason is that stockholders and creditors need to know whether a corporation that pays dividends is distributing earnings or is returning invested capital. The owners of single proprietorships and partnerships may withdraw capital in any amounts they choose, even though such withdrawals may exceed earnings. In a corporation, however, only the retained earnings ordinarily are available for dividends. This reflects corporate policy and desire for continuity of existence as well as legal considerations. Consequently, accountants maintain a clear distinction between paid-in capital and retained earnings. Any further classification of stockholders' equity usually rests on legal requirements rather than on accounting principles.

The framers of corporation laws have attempted to protect creditors by creating the concept of *legal capital*—an amount of stockholders' equity not subject to withdrawal. In recognition of these legal requirements, accountants generally classify stockholders' equity by subdividing paid-in capital between legal capital (the aggregate par or stated value of capital stock) and additional paid-in capital. Legal capital generally is not subject to withdrawal; in some states, however, additional paid-in capital legally is available for dividends, provided that stockholders are notified of the source of the dividends.

Components of Stockholders' Equity

The following components of stockholders' equity generally are used in a balance sheet:

1 Capital stock (legal capital)

2 Additional paid-in capital (paid-in capital in excess of par or stated value, donated capital, etc.)

3 Retained earnings (or deficit)

4 Unrealized loss in value of long-term investments in marketable equity securities (discussed in Chapter 14)

5 Cumulative translation adjustments (discussed in *Modern Advanced Accounting* of this series)

A subtotal entitled "total paid-in capital" may be inserted in the stockholders' equity section of the balance sheet to show the aggregate of the capital stock and additional paid-in capital.

The question of "appraisal capital" has little practical importance, because corporations generally have adhered to the cost principle of asset valuation. If any appreciation in the value of assets is included in the stockholders' equity, it should be shown separately and given a title such as *unrealized appreciation from revaluation of assets* or simply *appraisal capital.*

Additional Paid-in Capital   Additional paid-in capital arises principally from the following sources:

1   Excess of issuance proceeds over the par or stated value of capital stock

2   Conversion of convertible bonds or preferred stock to common stock

3   Excess of proceeds from reissuance of treasury stock over the cost of the treasury stock

4   Reduction of par or stated value of capital stock

5   Donations of assets to the corporation by stockholders or governmental units

6   Excess of market price of capital stock over par or stated value of stock issued as a stock dividend

7   Amount assigned to detachable stock warrants attached to bonds or preferred stock

Although capital from all these sources may be combined into the single balance sheet item of Additional Paid-in Capital, a separate ledger account is needed for each source. If any part of additional paid-in capital is distributed as a dividend, management generally must inform the stockholders that the dividend is a *return of capital* and not a distribution of earnings.

Neither operating losses nor extraordinary losses should be debited to additional paid-in capital ledger accounts. Other examples of improper debits to paid-in capital accounts include the write-off of acquired goodwill and the write-down of plant assets to net realizable value. These items are included in the income statement of the period in which they are recognized. Although debits to additional paid-in capital ledger accounts are infrequent, they are appropriate in situations such as the following:

1   Declaration of a liquidating dividend.

2   Redemption of preferred stock, originally issued for more than par, at a price in excess of par. For example, X Corporation redeemed at a call price of $104 a portion of its $100 par preferred stock originally issued at a price of $105. The $4 a share *redemption premium* may be debited to additional paid-in capital.

3   Absorption of a deficit as part of a quasi-reorganization.

4   Out-of-pocket costs of issuing capital stock, such as accountants' fees, legal fees, underwriting discounts and commissions, and printing costs.

Retained Earnings   Retained earnings represents the accumulated net income of a corporation, minus amounts distributed to stockholders and amounts transferred to paid-in capital accounts as a result of stock dividends. Revenue and expenses from continuing and discontinued operations, gain or loss from disposal of a business segment, extraordinary items, and cumulative effect of a change in accounting principle are included in the measurement of net income, which is transferred to the Retained Earnings ledger account. A negative amount (debit balance) in the Retained Earnings account is termed a *deficit.*

PAID-IN CAPITAL

Rights Associated with Ownership of Capital Stock

If a corporation has only one class of capital stock, stockholders usually have certain basic rights to be exercised in proportion to the number of shares of capital stock they own. These rights include: (1) right to vote for directors and thus to be represented by management, (2) right to receive dividends declared by the board of directors, (3) preemptive right to acquire additional shares of capital stock in proportion to present holdings in the event that the corporation increases the amount of capital stock outstanding, and (4) right to share in the distribution of cash or other assets if the corporation is liquidated. Variations in these rights may be encountered. For example, the preemptive right attached to existing shares of capital stock may prove inconvenient to a corporation interested in acquiring other companies by issuance of additional shares of capital stock. Consequently, this preemptive right has been eliminated (with the approval of stockholders) by many corporations.

Common Stock and Preferred Stock

When only one type of capital stock is issued, it has the basic rights described above and is called *common stock.* However, many corporations, in an effort to appeal to all types of investors, offer two or more classes of capital stock with different rights or priorities attached to each class. Stock that carries certain preferences over the common stock, such as a prior claim on dividends, is called *preferred stock.* Often a preferred stock has no voting rights, or only limited voting rights. The characteristics of preferred stocks vary widely among corporations; it is unwise, therefore, to assume that a preferred stock has any particular rights or priorities without positive determination of its status. The special rights of a particular preferred stock are set forth in the articles of incorporation and in the preferred stock certificates issued by the corporation.

When only one class of stock, that is, common stock, is issued by a corporation, it may be labeled as ''Capital Stock'' in the ledger and in the balance sheet.

Class A and Class B Stock

Corporations that issue more than one class of capital stock may designate the various issues by letter, such as Class A stock and Class B stock. In such cases one of the issues is common stock and the other issue has some preference or restriction of basic rights. To determine the significant characteristics of such capital stock, it is necessary to examine the articles of incorporation and stock certificates.

Characteristics of Preferred Stock

The following features are associated with most preferred stock issues:

1　Preference as to dividends at a stated rate or amount

2　Preference as to assets in event of liquidation of the corporation

3　Callable at the option of the corporation

4　Absence of voting rights

A preference as to dividends does not give assurance that dividends will be paid; it signifies only that the stated dividend rate applicable to the preferred stock must be paid before any dividends are paid on the common stock. Unlike interest on bonds and notes payable, dividends do not accrue. A liability to pay a dividend arises only when the board of directors declares a dividend. Any dividend action by the board must take into consideration (1) whether the corporation legally may pay a dividend, and (2) whether the present cash position and future cash needs make it advisable to pay a dividend.

Many preferred stocks have a par value, and this feature permits the dividend rate to be stated either as a percentage of par value or as a fixed dollar amount. For example, some years ago Georgia-Pacific Corporation issued a 5½%, $100 par, preferred stock, and Sperry Corporation issued a $4.50 preferred stock with a par value of $25 but with a prior claim of $100 in the event of redemption or liquidation. The annual dividend on no-par preferred stock is stated at a fixed dollar amount, such as "$4.50 Cumulative Preferred Stock."

Cumulative and Noncumulative Preferred Stock　Most preferred stocks have a cumulative provision as to dividends. If all or any part of the stated dividend on a cumulative preferred stock is not paid in a year, the unpaid portion *accumulates* and must be paid in a subsequent year *before any dividend is paid on the common stock*.

A dividend is said to have been *passed* if the directors fail to declare a dividend on the established date for dividend action. Any omitted dividends on cumulative preferred stock constitute *dividends in arrears*. The amount of preferred dividends in arrears is not a liability of the corporation, because no liability exists until the board of directors declares a dividend. However, no dividends may be declared on common stock until any dividends in arrears on preferred stock, as well as the current period's preferred dividend, have been paid. Thus, the amount of any dividends in arrears on preferred stock is important to investors and always is disclosed, usually in a note to the financial statements.

In the case of noncumulative preferred stocks, a dividend omitted or passed in one year is lost forever to shareholders. Because most investors refuse to acquire noncumulative preferred stocks, they seldom are issued.

As an illustration of the significance of dividends in arrears and the inherent weakness of a noncumulative preferred stock, assume that Garwood Corporation has three classes of capital stock as follows:

Three classes of
capital stock issued
by a corporation

6% cumulative preferred stock, $10 par, issued and outstanding 200,000 shares...	$2,000,000
7% noncumulative second preferred stock, $25 par, issued and out- standing 80,000 shares	2,000,000
Common stock, $10 par, issued and outstanding 200,000 shares	2,000,000

Assume also that operations of Garwood Corporation were unprofitable in Years 1, 2, and 3 and no dividends were declared during those three years. In Year 4, however, a large net income was earned, and Garwood's directors decided on December 31, Year 4, that $900,000 should be distributed as dividends. Despite the equal amounts of capital represented by the three capital stock issues, the dividend payments favor the cumulative preferred stock and the common stock. The holders of the noncumulative second preferred stock receive relatively little, as illustrated below:

Distribution of
dividends totaling
$900,000 to three
classes of capital
stock

	6% cumulative preferred stock	7% noncumulative second preferred stock	Common stock
Dividends in arrears ...	$360,000 (1)		
Preferred dividends, current year..........	120,000 (2)	$140,000 (3)	
Remainder, to common stock			$280,000 (4)
Total dividends paid .	$480,000	$140,000	$280,000

(1) ($2,000,0000 × 0.06) × 3 = $360,000
(2) $2,000,000 × 0.06 = $120,000
(3) $2,000,000 × 0.07 = $140,000
(4) $900,000 − ($480,000 + $140,000) = $280,000

Participating and Nonparticipating Preferred Stock A preferred stock is *nonparticipating* unless the stock certificate specifically provides for participation. Participating preferred stocks are rare. A *fully participating* preferred stock shares equally with the common stock in any dividends paid after the common stock has received a dividend at a rate equal to the preference rate on the preferred stock. For example, assume that in the current year Lude Corporation declared the usual 10% dividend on its fully participating $100 par preferred stock and also declared a dividend of $10 a share on the $100 par common stock. If any additional dividend is declared on the common stock, a corresponding additional amount must be declared on the preferred stock. A *partially participating* preferred stock is one with a ceiling established limiting the extent to which it participates in dividends with the common stock.

Convertible Preferred Stock Many corporations make their preferred stock attractive to investors by including a *conversion option* that entitles the stockholders to exchange their preferred stock for common stock in a stated ratio. The holders of convertible preferred stock have the advantage of a preferred claim on dividends and also the option of switching to common stock, which enjoys unlimited participation in dividends.

Preferred stock usually will be converted to common if the dividend rate on the common stock is increased. As long as the conversion option is open, the preferred stockholder gains the benefit of any increase in market price of the common stock without actual conversion, because market price of the preferred increases in proportion to any increase in the price of the common stock. It is sometimes said that the market prices of a common stock and the related convertible preferred stock are "in gear." The primary determinant of when to convert is the relative yields of the common and preferred stock at the prevailing market prices. In addition, consideration may be given to the greater assurance of continued dividend payments on the preferred stock. For some preferred stocks the conversion option expires after a specified number of years; for others the conversion period is unlimited; and in some cases the conversion terms are subject to change on specified future dates.

Callable Preferred Stock Most preferred stocks may be called *at the option of the issuer*. The call feature is advantageous to the issuer because the capital obtained through issuance of callable preferred stock is available as long as needed and may be repaid whenever the issuer desires. The *call price* is specified in the preferred stock contract and usually is set a few points above the issuance price. The existence of the call price tends to set a ceiling on the market price of nonconvertible preferred stock. Any dividends in arrears must be paid when a cumulative preferred stock is *called*.

If a convertible preferred stock is called, the holders of the stock have the option of converting to common stock rather than surrendering their investment in the corporation. As a result, the market price of outstanding convertible preferred stocks tends to move with the price of the common stock, even though it may be significantly above the call price.

Redeemable Preferred Stock Some preferred stocks are subject to mandatory redemption by the issuer on a specific date and at a specific price. Other preferred stocks may be redeemable at the option of the stockholders. Another category of preferred stocks is redeemable from future earnings of the issuer or in some other manner not controlled by the issuer. Preferred stocks having these characteristics are referred to collectively as *redeemable preferred stocks*. The issuer does not control the timing of the redemption of redeemable preferred stocks. In contrast, callable preferred stocks are subject to retirement *at the option of the issuer*.

Both the Financial Accounting Standards Board and the Securities and Exchange Commission require corporations having outstanding redeemable preferred stock to disclose the following in a note to the financial statements:[1]

---

[1]*FASB Statement No. 47,* "Disclosure of Long-Term Obligations," FASB (Stamford: 1981), pp. 4–5; *Codification of Financial Reporting Policies,* Securities and Exchange Commission (Washington: 1982), Sec. 211.04.

1   Redemption terms of the preferred stock

2   Amounts of the preferred stock that must be redeemed during each of the five years subsequent to the balance sheet date

3   Changes in the amounts of redeemable preferred stock outstanding during the accounting period

In addition, the SEC prohibits both the use of the conventional ''Stockholders' Equity'' caption by corporations having redeemable preferred stock and the presentation of a combined total for redeemable preferred stock, other preferred stock, and common stock.[2]

Liquidation Preference   Most preferred stocks have preference over common stock as to assets in the event of liquidation of the corporation. The claims of creditors take preference over both preferred and common stock. The preference of a cumulative preferred stock as to assets usually includes any dividends in arrears in addition to the stated liquidation value. Not every preferred stock has a prior claim on assets; the status of the stock in the event of liquidation depends on the specific provisions of the preferred stock contract.

The preference that a preferred stock has in the event of liquidation is disclosed in the balance sheet or in a note to the financial statements. In *APB Opinion No. 10,* the Accounting Principles Board stated:[3]

> Companies at times issue preferred (or other senior) stock which has a preference in involuntary liquidation considerably in excess of the par or stated value of the shares. The relationship between this preference in liquidation and the par or stated value of the shares may be of major significance to the users of the financial statements. . . . Accordingly, the Board recommends that, in these cases, the liquidation preference of the stock be disclosed in the equity section of the balance sheet in the aggregate, . . . rather than on a per share basis. . . .

Is Preferred Stock Debt or Equity?   The preferred stockholder is in some respects more a creditor than an owner. Typically, the preferred shareholder provides capital to the corporation for an agreed rate of return and has no voice in management. If the corporation prospers, it probably will increase the dividend rate on its common stock, but it will not consider increasing the dividend on preferred stock. Unless it is redeemable, preferred stock generally has no maturity date, but the preferred stockholder's relationship with the corporation may be terminated if the corporation chooses to call the preferred stock.

The uncertain status of preferred stock is emphasized by the SEC's prohibition against the inclusion of redeemable preferred stock in the stockholders' equity section of the balance sheet. However, the SEC did not require the inclusion of redeemable preferred stock among the liabilities of the corporation. Thus, the balance

---

[2]*Codification of Financial Reporting Policies,* Sec. 211.01.
[3]*APB Opinion No. 10,* ''Omnibus Opinion—1966,'' AICPA (New York: 1966), p. 148.

sheet status of redeemable preferred stock—as well as preferred stock in general—is not clear.

Par Value and No-Par-Value Stock

In the early history of United States corporations, all capital stock was required to have a par value, but now most state laws permit corporations to choose between par and no-par-value stock. A corporation that chooses to issue par value capital stock may set the par at any amount desired, such as $1, $5, or $100 a share. If a corporation subsequently splits its stock, the par value of each share is reduced accordingly. For example, General Motors common stock, which originally had a par value of $100, has been split many times and now has a par value of $1.66⅔ a share.

The par value of capital stock is the amount per share to be entered in the Capital Stock ledger account. This portion of the value of assets originally invested in the corporation must be kept permanently in the enterprise. The par value of the capital stock issued thus signifies a ''cushion'' of ownership equity for the protection of creditors.

The par value device originally was introduced for the protection of creditors but proved less effective than anticipated, because the intent of the law could be circumvented by the issuance of capital stock in exchange for nonmonetary assets. In the era before rigorous federal and state security laws, large amounts of capital stock sometimes were issued for mining claims, patents, goodwill, and other assets of unproved value. These assets usually were recorded at the par value of the capital stock issued in exchange, with the result of gross overstatement of assets and stockholders' equity.

To avoid this abuse of the par value concept, most states enacted legislation permitting corporations to issue capital stock without par value. It was argued that many investors had incorrectly assumed that any capital stock was worth as much as its par value, and that the use of no-par stock would force investors to consider more fundamental factors such as earnings, dividends, and current fair values of assets owned by the corporation.

No-par capital stock may have a *stated value* assigned by the board of directors, or it may have no stated value. The stated value assigned to no-par capital stock by the directors is the amount credited to the Capital Stock ledger account when the stock is issued, and represents legal capital. Any excess of the issuance proceeds over the stated value is credited to the Paid-in Capital in Excess of Stated Value ledger account. The entire issuance proceeds for no-par capital stock without a stated value is the legal capital and is credited to the Capital Stock ledger account in full.

The trend for corporations to set par values of capital stock at quite low amounts, such as $0.10 or $1 a share, has lessened the effectiveness of the arguments for no-par stock and has reduced some of the significance attached to the term *par value*.

Accounting for Capital Stock Transactions

A clear understanding of the following terms is necessary in accounting for capital stock transactions:

1 *Authorized capital stock* is the number of shares of capital stock that the state has authorized a corporation to issue. Typically, a corporation obtains authorization for a much larger number of shares than it plans to issue in the foreseeable future. The securing of authority to issue shares of stock does not bring an asset into existence, nor does it give the corporation any capital. Authorization merely affords a legal opportunity to obtain assets through the issuance of stock. Consequently, authorization of capital stock does not constitute a transaction or event to be entered in the accounting records. A notation of the authorization in the general journal and in the ledger account for capital stock is appropriate.

2 *Issued capital stock* is the number of shares of authorized capital stock that have been issued to date. Issued capital stock includes treasury stock, as defined below.

3 *Unissued capital stock* describes the authorized shares of capital stock that have not been issued to investors.

4 *Outstanding capital stock* is the number of shares of authorized capital stock that have been issued and presently are held by stockholders.

5 *Treasury stock* is the corporation's own capital stock that had been issued, fully paid, and has been acquired by the corporation but not canceled. Treasury stock is included in issued capital stock as defined above, but is not part of outstanding capital stock.

6 *Subscriptions receivable for capital stock* represent an asset—a receivable from investors who have promised to pay the subscription price at a future date.

7 *Subscribed capital stock* refers to authorized but unissued shares of capital stock that are earmarked for issuance under existing contracts with subscribers. The subscribed capital stock is issued when a subscription contract is collected in full. If financial statements are prepared between the date of obtaining capital stock subscriptions and the date of issuing the stock, the subscribed stock is included in the stockholders' equity section of the balance sheet.

Ledger Accounts for Paid-in Capital

Investments of capital by stockholders usually require the use of two types of stockholders' equity ledger accounts: (1) capital stock accounts, and (2) accounts for paid-in capital in excess of par or stated value.

Capital Stock Ledger Accounts A separate ledger account is used for each class of capital stock. The number of shares authorized may be recorded by a memorandum entry in the general journal and also may be indicated in the ledger accounts as shown at the top of page 806.

Ledger Accounts for Paid-in Capital in Excess of Par or Stated Value Capital stock often is issued at a price in excess of the par or stated value. This additional paid-in capital is credited to a ledger account with a descriptive title indicating its source, such as Paid-in Capital in Excess of Par: Preferred Stock or Paid-in Capital

Capital stock ledger
accounts illustrated

8% Cumulative Preferred Stock, $100 par

Date	Explanation	Debit	Credit	Balance
Year 7 Oct. 1	(Authorized 10,000 shares, callable at $105 a share)			

Common Stock, no-par, stated value $5

Date	Explanation	Debit	Credit	Balance
Year 7 Oct. 1	(Authorized 1,000,000 shares)			

in Excess of Stated Value: Common Stock. The following journal entries illustrate issuance of capital stock:

Journal entries for
issuance of preferred
and common stock

Cash (9,000 × $102)	918,000	
8% Cumulative Preferred Stock (9,000 × $100)		900,000
Paid-in Capital in Excess of Par: Preferred Stock		18,000
To record issuance of 9,000 shares of $100 par cumulative preferred stock for $102 a share.		
Cash (600,000 × $15)	9,000,000	
Common Stock (600,000 × $5)		3,000,000
Paid-in Capital in Excess of Stated Value: Common		
Stock		6,000,000
To record issuance of 600,000 shares of no-par common stock, stated value $5 a share, for $15 a share.		

In the preparation of financial statements, it is not necessary to use the exact titles of the ledger accounts as long as the sources of capital are disclosed. For example, the paid-in capital indicated by the preceding account titles and transactions might appear as shown in the balance sheet illustrated on page 807.

Some accountants prefer to list the paid-in capital applicable to the preferred stock with the listing of preferred stock, and to place the paid-in capital applicable to the common stock with the listing of common stock. Other accountants combine the various sources of paid-in capital under a single caption such as Additional Paid-in Capital. Other sources of additional paid-in capital (such as from treasury stock transactions) are discussed elsewhere in this chapter and in Chapters 17 and 18.

Paid-in capital in
the balance sheet

Stockholders' equity:

8% cumulative preferred stock, $100 par (callable at $105 a share), authorized 10,000 shares, issued and outstanding 9,000 shares		$ 900,000
Common stock, no-par, stated value $5, authorized 1 million shares, issued and outstanding 600,000 shares		3,000,000
Paid-in capital in excess of par or stated value:		
On preferred stock	$ 18,000	
On common stock	6,000,000	6,018,000
Total paid-in capital............................		$9,918,000

Discount and Assessments on Capital Stock

Many states now prohibit the issuance of capital stock at less than par value. In planning a capital stock issue, a corporation may set the par value as low as it pleases. Because par value usually is set at an amount considerably below the issuance price, the question of discount on capital stock is no longer of much practical importance. However, if capital stock is issued at a price below par, the amount of the discount is debited to the Discount on Capital Stock ledger account, which appears as a deduction (or negative element of paid-in capital) in the stockholders' equity section of the balance sheet.

Although most states require that capital stock issued to the public be nonassessable, occasionally a corporation may make an assessment against its stockholders. If the capital stock originally was issued at a discount, the amount received by assessment is credited to the Discount on Capital Stock ledger account. If the debit balance in the discount account thus is eliminated, any remaining portion of the assessment is credited to a separate stockholders' equity ledger account such as Paid-in Capital from Assessment of Stockholders.

Issuance Price and Subsequent Market Price of Capital Stock

The preceding discussion of the issuance of capital stock at prices above and below par raises a question as to how a corporation decides on the issuance price. For a new issue of capital stock, the issuer usually sets an issuance price based on factors such as the (1) expected future earnings and dividends, (2) financial condition and reputation of the issuer, and (3) current conditions in the security markets. After capital stock has been issued, the subsequent market price at which it is traded among investors tends to reflect the progress and prospects of the issuer and factors such as the state of investor confidence and the general trend of the economy. The current market prices of capital stock generally bear no discernible relationship to par value or to original issuance price.

Subscriptions for Capital Stock

The preceding sections have illustrated the issuance of capital stock for cash. Often, capital stock is issued under a subscription contract requiring payment by subscribers on a later date. Generally, the stock certificates are not issued until the subscription price is collected in full.

The increase in assets caused by obtaining a stock subscription receivable is offset by an increase in stockholders' equity. The ledger accounts to be credited (in the case of par value common stock) are Common Stock Subscribed and Paid-in Capital in Excess of Par: Common Stock. On a later date when the stock is issued, the Common Stock Subscribed ledger account is debited and the Common Stock account is credited. If financial statements are prepared between the obtaining of subscriptions and the issuance of the common stock, the Common Stock Subscribed account appears in the stockholders' equity section of the balance sheet.

Journal Entries   Assume that subscriptions are received for 10,000 shares of $10 par common stock at a price of $50 a share. The journal entry to record the subscriptions follows:

Journal entry to record subscriptions for common stock	*Subscriptions Receivable: Common Stock (10,000 × $50) ....* 500,000	
	Common Stock Subscribed (10,000 × $10)	100,000
	Paid-in Capital in Excess of Par: Common Stock	400,000
	To record subscriptions for 10,000 shares of $10 par common stock at $50 a share.	

All subscribers paid one-half of the amounts due on their subscriptions. The journal entry to record the collection of the subscriptions is:

Collection of subscriptions	*Cash ($500,000 × ½) ....* 250,000	
	Subscriptions Receivable: Common Stock	250,000
	To record collection of one-half of subscriptions receivable.	

Subscribers paid the balance due on their subscriptions with the exception of one subscriber who had subscribed for 100 shares. The journal entries to record the collection of the subscriptions and the issuance of common stock are illustrated below:

Collection of subscriptions and issuance of common stock	*Cash (9,900 × $25) ....* 247,500	
	Subscriptions Receivable: Common Stock	247,500
	To record collection of balance due on subscriptions for 9,900 shares	
	Common Stock Subscribed (9,900 × $10) 99,000	
	Common Stock, $10 par	99,000
	To record issuance of 9,900 shares after collection of subscriptions in full.	

Defaults by Subscribers If subscribers fail to pay all or part of their subscriptions, the disposition of the subscription contracts and of any amounts paid by the subscribers depends on the laws of the state and the policies of the corporation. If no payment has been made by the subscribers and nothing can be collected from them, the corporation should reverse the journal entries that recorded the subscriptions. If the subscribers have made one or more partial payments prior to default, the entire amount paid in prior to default may be refunded. As an alternative, the amount refunded may be the amount paid in minus any costs and ''loss'' incurred by the corporation in reissuing the subscribed stock. Another possible alternative calls for amending the subscription contracts to permit the issuance of a reduced number of shares corresponding to the cash collected. Still another alternative under some state laws calls for forfeiture by the subscribers of the amount paid prior to the default.

Default by a subscriber requires the writing off of the outstanding subscription receivable; the journal entry also includes a debit to the Common Stock Subscribed ledger account and usually a debit to the Paid-in Capital in Excess of Par: Common Stock account. If the corporation retains any amounts paid in on defaulted subscriptions without issuing common stock, this increase in paid-in capital may be credited to a separate ledger account with a title such as Paid-in Capital from Defaults on Stock Subscriptions. For example, if the $2,500 (100 × $50 × ½ = $2,500) paid by the defaulting subscriber for 100 shares in the foregoing example is forfeited, the journal entry to record the forfeiture is as follows:

Journal entry to record forfeiture by defaulting subscriber

Common Stock Subscribed (100 × $10)	1,000	
Paid-in Capital in Excess of Par: Common Stock (100 × $40) .	4,000	
Subscriptions Receivable: Common Stock		2,500
Paid-in Capital from Defaults on Stock Subscriptions . .		2,500
To record forfeiture of $2,500 paid by subscriber for 100 shares of common stock.		

Nature of Stock Subscriptions Receivable From the corporation's viewpoint, an amount receivable under a stock subscription contract generally is regarded as an asset (a special type of receivable). When there are many subscribers, the subscriptions receivable ledger account is a controlling account supported by a subsidiary ledger containing an account with each subscriber. In the balance sheet, the subscriptions receivable ledger account balance is included with the current assets, provided that early collection is anticipated.

Some accountants argue that stock subscriptions do not represent assets, and that they should be shown as contra items in the stockholders' equity section of the balance sheet. Under this view, stock subscriptions receivable are contrasted with ordinary trade receivables; and it is argued that the stock subscriptions are a dubious claim against the subscribers because the corporation has not delivered merchandise or rendered services to them. As a practical matter, stock subscriptions constitute valid legal claims and usually are collected in full.

Stockholders' Ledger, Stock Transfer Journal, and Stock Certificate Book

In addition to maintaining a ledger account for each class of capital stock, a corporation must maintain detailed subsidiary records showing the identity of stockholders. A *stockholders' ledger* contains a separate account for each stockholder showing the number of shares owned. The stockholders' ledger is maintained in number of shares of stock rather than in dollars. When a stockholder sells capital stock to another investor, an entry must be made in the *stock transfer journal* and posted to the stockholders' ledger to decrease the number of shares of capital stock held by the first stockholder and to set up an account for the new stockholder. No entry would be necessary in the general journal, because the amount of capital stock outstanding remains unchanged.

A *stock certificate book* also is needed to control the amount of capital stock outstanding. When a stock certificate is issued, the name of the owner and number of shares are listed on the certificate stub. When a stockholder sells capital stock, the original certificate is canceled and attached to the stub, and a new certificate is issued to the new stockholder. The open stubs in the stock certificate book indicate the number of shares of capital stock outstanding. Most large corporations retain an independent *stock registrar* and *transfer agent* to control stock certificates and to maintain stock transfer journals and stockholders' ledgers. Such records are maintained by computers when the volume of transactions is large.

Issuance of Two Types of Securities as a Unit

Corporations sometimes offer preferred and common stock as a unit, with no indication of the issuance price of either security considered separately. Such unit offerings raise a question as to how the proceeds should be allocated between the two securities. The same question arises when a corporation issues two or more kinds of securities to acquire another business enterprise. The aggregate par value of preferred and common stock issued as a unit usually is less than the proceeds received. How should the proceeds received be allocated to the two securities? If either security is issued concurrently for cash, the market price of that security may be used as evidence of its value; the remainder of the proceeds is applicable to the other security. If both securities have market values, the proceeds received are allocated to the two securities based on the *relative market values* of the securities.

Capital Stock Issued in Exchange for Assets or Services

When capital stock is issued for assets other than cash, the current fair value of the assets or the current fair value of the stock, *whichever is more clearly evident,* is used to record the assets received and the related amount of paid-in capital. In the absence of an arm's-length sale of assets for cash, opinions may differ as to the current fair value of the assets received. Consequently, it is appropriate to consider how much the capital stock would have been issued for if offered for cash. The underlying reasoning is that the exchange of capital stock for assets essentially is the equivalent of issuing the stock for cash and using the cash to acquire the assets.

If the corporation's capital stock is actively traded, the price of the stock on the date of the exchange constitutes reliable evidence as to the values exchanged. However, if stock sales are infrequent and small in amount, there is no assurance that the corporation could have issued a large block of stock for cash without forcing the price down.

Either treasury stock or previously unissued capital stock may be exchanged for assets. However, the cost of treasury stock used for this purpose does not constitute a proper basis of valuation for the exchange unless by chance the cost is equal to the current fair value of the stock.

The establishing of valuations for assets acquired in exchange for capital stock is the responsibility of the corporation's board of directors. The decisions of the board and the use of appraisals or other valuation techniques should be set forth in the corporate minutes. Under no circumstances should the par or stated value of the capital stock issued in exchange for assets be regarded as the decisive factor in establishing the current fair value of the assets acquired by a corporation.

The valuation problem when a corporation issues capital stock for personal services parallels that described in Chapter 11 for the issuance of capital stock for plant assets. The current fair value of the services received is a proper basis of valuation, but the current fair value of the stock often is more clearly evident and also is acceptable for establishing the accounting basis for the transaction.

Watered Stock and Secret Reserves

A corporation's common stock is said to be *watered* if the stockholders' equity is *overstated* because of an overstatement of assets or an understatement of liabilities. *Watered stock* usually relates to inflated asset values, and the most direct approach to eliminating ''water'' from a corporation's balance sheet is through writing down the overstated assets. The reduction in carrying amount of the assets may be accompanied by a reduction of retained earnings, or of the par or stated value of the common stock outstanding. Because such a write-down affects each stockholder proportionally, no real loss is involved; the proportionate equity of each stockholder in the net assets of the corporation is unchanged.

The existence of *secret reserves* in a corporation's balance sheet means that stockholders' equity is *understated* because assets are understated or liabilities are overstated. An understatement of stockholders' equity may be achieved by using inappropriate depreciation rates, by excessive provision for doubtful accounts, by using the last-in, first-out inventory method in periods of rising price levels, by recognizing capital expenditures as expenses, or by any similar action that understates assets or overstates liabilities. The deliberate creation of secret reserves is inconsistent with the maintenance of integrity in financial accounting.

Stock Splits

When the market price of a corporation's common stock reaches a high trading range such as $100 a share or more, the corporation may decide to split the stock. A stock split of, say, 3 for 1 of a stock trading at $150 a share causes the number of shares held by each stockholder to triple and should cause the market price to drop to approximately $50 a share.

A stock split causes no change in the total stockholders' equity and no change in paid-in capital or retained earnings. The par or stated value per share of common stock is reduced in proportion to the increase in number of shares. For example, in a 4 for 1 split of $10 par common stock, the new stock has a par value of $2.50.

When common stock is split, the old stock certificates usually are not exchanged for new certificates. The corporation issues to stockholders certificates for a sufficient number of additional shares to bring their total holdings up to the number indicated by the split. A stockholder who owned 100 shares of common stock prior to the previously mentioned 4 for 1 split of $10 par common stock would receive 300 additional shares of $2.50 par common stock. The stockholder would continue to hold the original certificate for 100 shares of $10 par common stock, even though the par value of all the shares is now $2.50. Eventually, the old $10 par certificates will disappear from circulation.

Because the only ledger account affected by a stock split is the Common Stock account, the stock split may be recorded in a memorandum entry. Alternatively, a journal entry such as the following may be made to record the reduction in par value per share and the increase in the number of outstanding shares:

Journal entry for a stock split

Common Stock, $10 par	10,000,000	
Common Stock, $2.50 par		10,000,000
To record a 4 for 1 stock split carried out by reducing		
par value from $10 to $2.50 a share and issuing 3 million		
additional shares of common stock, thus increasing total		
outstanding shares from 1 million to 4 million.		

A *reverse stock split,* as the name suggests, is the opposite of a stock split. The number of outstanding shares of common stock is reduced proportionately for all stockholders. For example, the outstanding common stock might be reduced from 3 million shares to 300,000 shares in a 1 for 10 reverse stock split. All stockholders would surrender their stock certificates in exchange for one-tenth as many new shares. A reverse stock split does not affect the assets or liabilities of the corporation and, therefore, does not change the stockholders' equity. Reverse stock splits are rare and usually are effected only by corporations with common stock that has dropped in market price to an extremely low level. A reverse stock split tends to increase the market price per share in inverse proportion to the reduction in number of shares outstanding.

RETAINED EARNINGS

The illustration below indicates the debits and credits entered in the Retained Earnings ledger account:

Composition of typical Retained Earnings ledger account

Retained Earnings	
Net loss	Net income
Dividends declared	Prior period adjustments (to correct
Prior period adjustments (to correct	material errors made in prior periods)
material errors made in prior periods)	

As explained in Chapter 3, (pages 134–136), generally accepted accounting principles require that extraordinary items be included in the determination of net income rather than being entered directly in retained earnings. ***Prior period adjustments*** are entered directly in the Retained Earnings ledger account and are not included in the determination of net income. The following items are prior period adjustments and are excluded from net income.[4]

1   Correction of an error in the financial statements of a prior period

2   Adjustments that result from realization of income tax benefits of preacquisition operating loss carryforwards of purchased subsidiaries

Prior period adjustments do not include normal recurring corrections and adjustments arising from the use of estimates in the accounting process. Thus, changes in depreciation rates because of revised estimates of economic lives of plant assets are not prior period adjustments; they are reflected in operations of the current and future accounting periods.

After listing the principal components of retained earnings, it may be useful to mention a few items that ***do not*** belong in retained earnings. These are:

1   Treasury stock transactions that result in a ''gain'' or a ''loss''

2   Donations of assets (such as the gift of a plant site to a corporation by a city seeking to attract new industries)

3   Increases in stockholders' equity resulting from write-ups of plant assets to current fair values in excess of carrying amounts

Let us consider briefly why each of these items does not belong in retained earnings. The reissuance of treasury stock at an amount in excess of cost increases additional paid-in capital, and the reissuance of treasury stock at an amount below cost decreases additional paid-in capital. The receipt of donated assets is not a source of earnings and is recorded in a separate paid-in capital ledger account such as Donated Capital. Increases in the carrying amounts of plant assets, if recorded at all, produce unrealized increases in stockholders' equity and require separate classification; to include such increases in retained earnings would suggest that they are realized and available for dividends.

Restrictions on Retained Earnings

The board of directors of a corporation may restrict or appropriate a portion of the retained earnings by transfer to a separate ledger account. For example, appropriations of retained earnings (sometimes called ***reserves***) may be made for expansion of plant, retirements of bonds, redemption of preferred stock, and general business contingencies. Although the practice of appropriating retained earnings is not widely followed, the Financial Accounting Standards Board sanctioned such practice as follows:[5]

---

[4]*FASB Statement No. 16,* ''Prior Period Adjustments,'' FASB (Stamford: 1977), p. 5.
[5]*FASB Statement No. 5,* ''Accounting for Contingencies,'' FASB (Stamford: 1975), p. 7.

Some enterprises have classified a portion of retained earnings as "appropriated" for loss contingencies. In some cases, the appropriation has been shown outside the stockholders' equity section of the balance sheet. Appropriation of retained earnings is not prohibited . . . provided that it is shown within the stockholders' equity section of the balance sheet and is clearly identified as an appropriation of retained earnings. Costs or losses shall not be charged to an appropriation of retained earnings, and no part of the appropriation shall be transferred to income.

An appropriation of retained earnings is recorded as follows (amount is assumed):

Retained Earnings	100,000	
Retained Earnings Appropriated for Plant Expansion . . .		100,000
To record appropriation of retained earnings under resolution of board of directors.		

A portion of retained earnings may be restricted and thus not available as a basis for dividend declaration for a variety of legal, contractual, or discretionary reasons. The almost universal practice is to disclose such a restriction in a note to the financial statements, rather than to establish an appropriation of retained earnings. An example of such disclosure follows:

The company's articles of incorporation and credit agreements with commercial banks contain restrictions limiting the payment of cash dividends. Retained earnings of $30 million dollars on December 31, 19—, are free of such restrictions.

DIVIDENDS

Cash Dividends

The usual meaning of *dividend* is a distribution of assets to stockholders in proportion to the number of shares of capital stock owned. The term *dividend,* when used by itself, generally means a cash dividend; this usage is followed throughout this book. The ratio of cash dividends declared to current net income is termed the *dividend payout ratio.* Corporations frequently distribute additional shares of their common stock to stockholders as *stock dividends.* Strictly speaking, a stock dividend is not a dividend at all because no assets are distributed to stockholders. However, stock dividends are of considerable practical importance and pose some challenging accounting questions that are discussed in a subsequent section of this chapter.

No obligation to pay a dividend exists until the board of directors formally declares a dividend. Dividend action by the board consists of a resolution specifying the following information:

1 Date of declaration

2 Date of record

3 Date of payment

4 Amount per share

On the *date of declaration* of a cash dividend, the appropriate journal entry is a debit to Dividends (or directly to the Retained Earnings ledger account) and a credit to Dividends Payable, a current liability. When the Dividends ledger account is used, it is closed to Retained Earnings at the end of the accounting period. If the corporation has both common and preferred stock, a separate Dividends ledger account may be used for each (for example, Dividends: Common Stock, and Dividends: Preferred Stock).

The *date of record* is specified in the dividend declaration and usually follows the date of declaration by a few weeks. To qualify for the dividend, a person must be listed as a stockholder in the corporation's stockholders' ledger on the date of record. Capital stocks of corporations listed on the stock exchanges trade *ex-dividend* five business days before the date of record, thus facilitating compilation of the list of owners on the record date. An investor who acquires capital stock before the ex-dividend date is entitled to receive the dividend; conversely, a stockholder who sells capital stock before the ex-dividend date is selling the right to receive the dividend that has been declared as well as the shares of stock.

The *date of payment* of a dividend usually is set for a few weeks after the date of record. Payment is recorded by a debit to Dividends Payable and a credit to Cash.

The *amount per share* may be stated, for example, as "regular quarterly dividend of $0.25 a share," or as an "extra year-end dividend of $1 a share."

As indicated in the preceding discussion, general requirements for declaration and payment of a cash dividend include (1) existence of retained earnings, (2) an adequate cash position, and (3) action by the board of directors. As protection for creditors, state laws place various other restrictions on the declaration of dividends.

Dividends Paid in the Form of Nonmonetary Assets

Most dividends are in cash, but occasionally a corporation may declare a dividend in the form of merchandise or other nonmonetary assets, such as securities of another corporation held as a short-term or long-term investment. When such *nonmonetary* dividends are declared, the *current fair value* (not the *carrying amount*) of the nonmonetary asset distributed is the appropriate amount to be recorded as a dividend. Similarly, stockholders record the receipt of the nonmonetary dividend at the current fair value of the asset received.

APB Opinion No. 29, "Accounting for Nonmonetary Transactions," established the following principle of accounting for nonmonetary dividends:[6]

---

[6]*APB Opinion No. 29,* "Accounting for Nonmonetary Transactions," AICPA (New York: 1973), pp. 547–548.

A transfer of a nonmonetary asset to a stockholder or to another entity in a nonreciprocal transfer should be recorded at the fair value of the asset transferred, and a gain or loss should be recognized on the disposition of the asset.

If the current fair value of the nonmonetary asset distributed is not objectively measurable at the time of the distribution, the only feasible alternative may be to record the dividend at the carrying amount of the nonmonetary asset.

To illustrate the accounting for a dividend paid in the form of a nonmonetary asset, assume that Dover Corporation owns 10% of the common stock of Lange Company with a carrying amount of $400,000 in the accounting records of Dover. On December 31, Year 10, when the current fair value of this long-term investment is $750,000, the board of directors of Dover authorizes the distribution of the Lange common stock as a dividend to the shareholders of Dover. The journal entries for Dover to record the declaration and distribution of this nonmonetary dividend are as follows:

Journal entries for nonmonetary dividend

Dividends (or Retained Earnings)	750,000	
Dividend Payable in Common Stock of Lange Company		750,000
To record declaration of nonmonetary dividend.		
Dividend Payable in Common Stock of Lange Company	750,000	
Investment in Lange Company Common Stock		400,000
Realized Gain on Disposal of Investments		350,000
To record payment of nonmonetary dividend.		

It would be possible for Dover to record the unrealized gain on the investment in common stock of Lange before the declaration of the nonmonetary dividend is recorded. This procedure might be followed to avoid recording a liability in excess of the carrying amount of the asset that will be used to liquidate the dividend liability. If a balance sheet is prepared for Dover after the declaration but before the distribution of the nonmonetary dividend, the asset to be distributed is classified as a current asset because the dividend payable is a current liability.

Liquidating Dividends

The term *liquidating dividend* may be used in the following situations:

1   A pro rata distribution of assets to stockholders that reduces paid-in capital rather than retained earnings

2   A pro rata distribution to stockholders by a corporation having wasting assets such as mineral deposits or timberlands, representing a return of invested capital

3   A pro rata distribution to stockholders when a corporation is liquidated

A liquidating dividend may be recorded as a debit to a specific paid-in capital ledger account or to a separate account such as Liquidating Dividend Distributed.

Any balance in this account is deducted from total paid-in capital in the balance sheet.

Corporations generally must inform their stockholders when a dividend, or a portion of a dividend, represents a return of invested capital. Liquidation dividends are recorded by stockholders as reductions in the cost of their investment rather than as revenue, as illustrated on page 696 of Chapter 14. This procedure generally is applicable for both financial accounting and income tax purposes.

A spin-off is closely related to a liquidating dividend, except that a spin-off may involve a reduction in retained earnings. A *spin-off* is a transfer by a corporation of selected assets to a new corporation in exchange for its capital stock, which then is distributed pro rata to stockholders of the first corporation.

Generally, *a gain is not recognized on a distribution of a liquidating dividend or on a transfer of assets to a new corporation in a spin-off, but a loss is recognized.* This point is covered in *APB Opinion No. 29* as follows:[7]

> Accounting for the distribution of nonmonetary assets to owners of an enterprise in a spin-off or other form of reorganization or liquidation or in a plan that is in substance the rescission of a prior business combination should be *based on the recorded amount (after reduction, if appropriate, for an indicated impairment of value)* of the nonmonetary assets distributed. (Emphasis added.)

A distribution to shareholders of common stock of an investee that has been accounted for under the equity method is considered a spin-off. Thus, no gain is recognized pursuant to such a distribution.

Stock Dividends

Many corporations distribute stock dividends to their stockholders. A *stock dividend* is a distribution of additional shares of capital stock, called *dividend shares,* to stockholders in proportion to their existing holdings. ''Common on common'' is the usual type of stock dividend; such a distribution is known as an *ordinary stock dividend,* and is assumed in the discussion that follows. When a stock dividend is declared, Retained Earnings (or Stock Dividends) is debited and one or more paid-in capital ledger accounts are credited.

Distribution of a stock dividend causes no change in the assets or liabilities of a corporation; the only effect is a transfer between stockholders' equity ledger accounts. Because there is no decrease in the net assets of the corporation, a stock dividend does not give stockholders anything they did not have before. The number of shares of common stock held by each stockholder is increased, but each share represents a smaller equity in the corporation.

The principal argument for stock dividends is that they enable a ''growth company'' to retain accumulated earnings, yet provide the stockholders with additional shares of common stock as evidence of the growth in the net assets of the corporation. Most stockholders view stock dividends as distributions of corporate

---

[7]Ibid., p. 549.

earnings in an amount equal to the market value of the dividend shares received. Such a view is strengthened by the fact that small stock dividends often do not cause a decline in the market price of the common stock, and the *total* market value of the original common stock often remains unchanged.

Securities that are convertible to common stock (such as convertible bonds and convertible preferred stock) contain an *antidilution clause* that requires *adjustment of the conversion ratio* to compensate for the "reduced size" of a share of common stock after a stock dividend or a stock split. If, for example, a preferred stock is convertible to three shares of common stock, the conversion ratio is increased to 3.3 shares after a 10% stock dividend on the common stock, and to 6.6 shares after a 10% stock dividend that is followed by a 2 for 1 split.

Accounting for Stock Dividends

What amount of retained earnings should be transferred to paid-in capital ledger accounts for each share of common stock issued as a stock dividend? Although the legal requirement in most states is the par or stated value of the dividend shares, generally accepted accounting principles for small stock dividends require the transfer of an amount equal to the *market price per share* prior to the dividend. Both the SEC and the AICPA support the use of market price as a measure of the amount of retained earnings transferred to paid-in capital for all stock dividends that increase the number of outstanding shares of common stock by less than 20 or 25%. For larger stock dividends, only the par or stated value per share is transferred from retained earnings to paid-in capital. The reasons underlying this difference in treatment of small and large stock dividends are explained in the following sections.

Small Stock Dividends   The AICPA has suggested 20 or 25% as a dividing line between *large* and *small* stock dividends. Above this amount it may be assumed that the purpose of the common stock distribution is to reduce the market price of the common stock, as in the case of a stock split. Below this level it may be assumed that the dividend shares will be regarded by most stockholders as a distribution of earnings.

Large Stock Dividends   A large stock dividend, such as one increasing the number of outstanding shares of common stock by 25% or more, may cause a material decrease in the market price per share of common stock. Such dividends are in the nature of stock splits. In other words, the amount of retained earnings transferred to paid-in capital pursuant to a large stock dividend is an amount equal to the aggregate par or stated value of the dividend shares. The following somewhat extreme example illustrates the probable reaction to a large stock dividend by a shareholder. Assume that Stockholder A owns 10 shares of $10 par common stock of Bragg Company, with a current market price of $150 a share. Bragg distributed a 100% stock dividend, and the market price of its common stock promptly dropped to approximately $75 a share. Stockholder A no doubt will recognize that the so-called "stock dividend" is not a distribution of earnings but is similar to a 2 for 1 split.

Corporations should avoid the use of the word "dividend" in notices relating to large stock dividends that reduce materially the market price per share of outstanding common stock. If legal considerations require use of the word "dividend,'' the transaction might be described as a *stock split effected in the form of a stock dividend.* For example, a few years ago Liz Claiborne, Inc., effected a 2 for 1 stock split through a 100% stock dividend by transferring $5,255,698 from retained earnings to its $1 par Common Stock ledger account.

Illustrative Journal Entries for Stock Dividends   Assume that Rosen Company has 1 million authorized shares of $5 par common stock, of which 500,000 shares are outstanding. The market price is $80 a share, and a quarterly cash dividend of 50 cents has been paid for several years. Current earnings are large and increasing annually, but Rosen plans to conserve cash for expansion of plant assets. Thus, the board of directors decides to issue a 2% stock dividend rather than to increase the current annual cash dividend of $2 a share. A journal entry *summarizing both the declaration and the distribution* of the 2% stock dividend is presented below to emphasize the end results of the stock dividend:

Condensed journal entry for declaration and distribution of small stock dividend

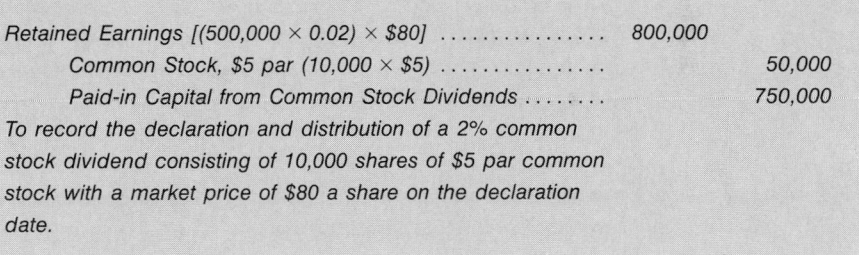

Retained Earnings [(500,000 × 0.02) × $80] 800,000
   Common Stock, $5 par (10,000 × $5)   50,000
   Paid-in Capital from Common Stock Dividends   750,000
To record the declaration and distribution of a 2% common stock dividend consisting of 10,000 shares of $5 par common stock with a market price of $80 a share on the declaration date.

The foregoing illustration of a journal entry for a small stock dividend could appear as *three separate journal entries.* The first entry would record declaration of the stock dividend by a debit to Common Stock Dividends for the market value of the shares to be issued, a credit to Common Stock Dividends to Be Distributed for the par value of the dividend shares, and a credit to Paid-in Capital from Common Stock Dividends for the excess of the market value over the par value of the shares to be issued. The second journal entry would record issuance of the shares by a debit to Common Stock Dividends to Be Distributed and a credit to Common Stock. At the end of the year, the Common Stock Dividends ledger account is closed to Retained Earnings. If a balance sheet is prepared between the date of declaration of the stock dividend and the date of distribution, the account Common Stock Dividends to Be Distributed is included in stockholders' equity below common stock.

If Rosen Company had declared and distributed a large stock dividend, say 50%, the following journal entry would be required:

Condensed journal entry for declaration and distribution of large stock dividend

Retained Earnings [(500,000 × 0.50) × $5] 1,250,000
   Common Stock, $5 par   1,250,000
To record the declaration and distribution of a 50% common stock dividend consisting of 250,000 shares of $5 par common stock.

Fractional Shares   When a small stock dividend is declared, stockholders owning only a few shares of common stock are entitled to receive only a fraction of a share. For example, in the foregoing illustration of a 2% stock dividend declared by Rosen Company, the holder of less than 50 shares of common stock is entitled to only a fraction of a share. To avoid the inconvenience of issuing fractional shares, most corporations offer stockholders the alternative of receiving in cash the market value of the fraction of a share due, or of paying sufficient cash to the corporation to qualify for a full share of common stock.

Business Combinations— Purchase versus Pooling of Interests

In recent years many corporations have been combined to obtain the economies of large-scale operation and the financial strength arising from diversification in various industries. Business combinations are discussed at length in *Modern Advanced Accounting* of this series. Our purpose at this point is to call attention to the difference in impact on retained earnings of the *purchase method* and the *pooling-of-interests method* of accounting for business combinations. In a *purchase,* the outstanding common stock of the acquired corporation usually is paid for in cash or through issuance of debt securities; in a *pooling,* the outstanding common stock of another corporation is acquired by issuance of common stock.

When a business combination is accounted for as a *purchase,* the acquiring corporation records its investment at the cost established by cash paid or current fair value of securities issued in exchange for outstanding common stock of the acquired corporation. *The retained earnings of the corporation acquired do not become part of combined retained earnings.* Revenue and expenses of the two corporations are combined only from the date of the business combination.

In contrast, when a business combination is accounted for as a *pooling of interests,* the net assets of the two corporations are combined at their carrying amounts. The current fair values of the common stock issued and of net assets acquired are disregarded. The pooling-of-interests method of accounting rests on an assumption of continuity of ownership, and the *retained earnings of the two corporations generally are added together to measure the amount of retained earnings of the combined enterprise.* The net income of the combined enterprise includes revenue and expenses of both corporations for the entire year in which the business combination occurred.

Quasi-Reorganizations

A *quasi-reorganization* occurs when a corporation in financial difficulties modifies its capital structure without being forced to do so by creditors and without coming under the supervision of a bankruptcy court.[8]

Typically, a quasi-reorganization involves writing off a deficit against additional paid-in capital; sometimes there is a reduction in the par or stated value of

---

[8]The word *quasi* means resembling or seemingly, but not actually. Thus, a quasi-reorganization resembles, but is not, a formal corporate reorganization under the Bankruptcy Code, which is described in *Modern Advanced Accounting* of this series.

common stock and a write-down of overvalued assets. Following a quasi-reorganization, the corporation is considered from an accounting standpoint to have a *fresh start,* and the way is cleared for reporting net income and declaring dividends in future years. Although the write-down of assets and the elimination of a deficit obscure historically significant data, the procedure is generally accepted because it results in more relevant asset values. Furthermore, a quasi-reorganization may help a corporation to regain its place as a profitable business enterprise without the stigma that attaches to a large deficit, continuous operating losses, and inability to declare cash dividends.

Sequence of Procedures in a Quasi-Reorganization   A quasi-reorganization typically involves the following procedures:

1   After stockholders approve the quasi-reorganization, assets that are considered to be overstated are written down to current fair value by a debit to Retained Earnings. If the current fair value of any asset exceeds carrying amount, increasing the carrying amount of such an asset generally is discouraged.

2   The deficit in retained earnings following the asset write-downs is eliminated against additional paid-in capital. Gains or losses realized subsequent to the quasi-reorganization that are attributable to the period prior to the quasi-reorganization are recorded as increases or decreases in additional paid-in capital.

3   If additional paid-in capital at the time of the quasi-reorganization is insufficient to absorb the deficit, the par or stated value of common stock is reduced to establish a paid-in capital ledger account that may be used to absorb the deficit.

4   Retained earnings following a quasi-reorganization must be identified (dated), generally for a period not exceeding 10 years, as accruing since the effective date of the quasi-reorganization. In subsequent balance sheets, this disclosure, called *dating the retained earnings,* may appear as follows:

"Dating retained earnings" subsequent to a quasi-reorganization

> *Retained earnings accumulated since June 30, Year 8, when a deficit of $4,202,000 was written off against additional paid-in capital as part of quasi-reorganization* *$1,917,400*

Illustration of a Quasi-Reorganization   To illustrate the accounting for a quasi-reorganization, assume that Lumen Corporation acquired another enterprise's identifiable net assets and goodwill at substantial costs, and that several years of unprofitable operations resulted in the balance sheet at the top of page 822.

The existence of the $1,600,000 deficit and the substantial carrying amount of plant assets and goodwill make it impossible for Lumen to report earnings or to pay dividends. To overcome these obstacles, let us assume that management proposes to effect a quasi-reorganization on December 31, Year 15, as follows:

1   The carrying amount of plant assets is to be reduced by $2,100,000, consisting of a $4,000,000 reduction in cost and a $1,900,000 reduction in accumulated depre-

LUMEN CORPORATION
Balance Sheet
December 31, Year 15

Assets

Current assets		$ 6,200,000
Plant assets	$12,500,000	
Less: Accumulated depreciation	5,700,000	6,800,000
Goodwill (net)		1,000,000
Total assets		$14,000,000

Liabilities & Stockholders' Equity

Liabilities:		
Current liabilities		$ 3,900,000
Long-term debt		500,000
Total liabilities		$ 4,400,000
Stockholders' equity:		
Common stock, no-par, $10 stated value	$10,000,000	
Paid-in capital in excess of stated value	1,200,000	
Total paid-in capital	$11,200,000	
Retained earnings (deficit)	(1,600,000)	9,600,000
Total liabilities & stockholders' equity		$14,000,000

Journal entries for quasi-reorganization		
Retained Earnings	3,100,000	
Accumulated Depreciation	1,900,000	
Plant Assets		4,000,000
Goodwill (net)		1,000,000
To write down carrying amount of plant assets and goodwill as part of quasi-reorganization.		
Common Stock, $10 stated value	10,000,000	
Common Stock, $5 stated value		5,000,000
Paid-in Capital in Excess of Stated Value		5,000,000
To reduce the stated value of common stock from $10 to $5 a share as part of quasi-reorganization.		
Paid-in Capital in Excess of Stated Value	4,700,000	
Retained Earnings		4,700,000
To eliminate deficit as part of quasi-reorganization.		

ciation; in addition, the entire goodwill of $1,000,000 is to be written off, thus increasing the amount of the deficit from $1,600,000 to $4,700,000 ($1,600,000 + $2,100,000 + $1,000,000 = $4,700,000).

2   The stated value of common stock is to be reduced from $10 a share to $5 a share, thus increasing the paid-in capital in excess of stated value from $1,200,000 to $6,200,000 [$1,200,000 + (1,000,000 × $5) = $6,200,000].

3   The deficit of $4,700,000 is to be written off against paid-in capital in excess of stated value, resulting in a zero balance in the Retained Earnings ledger account and a $1,500,000 ($6,200,000 − $4,700,000 = $1,500,000) balance in the Paid-in Capital in Excess of Stated Value account.

The journal entries to record the quasi-reorganization of Lumen Corporation on December 31, Year 15, are shown at the bottom of page 822.

Any retained earnings accumulated after December 31, Year 15, are available as a basis for dividend declaration and are dated in balance sheets following the quasi-reorganization. For example, assume that Lumen Corporation reported net income of $375,000 and declared cash dividends of $125,000 in Year 16; the stockholders' equity section of Lumen's balance sheet on December 31, Year 16, would be as follows:

Stockholders' equity one year after quasi-reorganization

Stockholders' equity:	
Common stock, no-par, $5 stated value a share....................	$5,000,000
Paid-in capital in excess of stated value...........................	1,500,000
Total paid-in capital...	$6,500,000
Retained earnings, accumulated since Dec. 31, Year 15, at which time a deficit of $4,700,000 was written off against paid-in capital in excess of stated value as part of quasi-reorganization............	250,000
Total stockholders' equity..	$6,750,000

Because replacement costs of plant assets have been increasing steadily in recent years, quasi-reorganizations seldom are encountered in practice. Corporations experiencing severe financial difficulties are more likely to undergo a restructuring of debt or a formal reorganization under the supervision of a bankruptcy court.

REVIEW QUESTIONS

1   Why do corporations often issue two or more types of capital stock?

2   What are the basic rights inherent in the ownership of capital stock? What modification of these basic rights usually is found in preferred stock?

3   If a corporation with cumulative preferred stock outstanding fails to declare any dividend during a year, what disclosure is made in a note to the financial statements?

4   What is *redeemable preferred stock?*

5   Distinguish between a *conversion provision* in a preferred stock and a *call provision.* May a preferred stock be both convertible and callable? If so, may both provisions be exercised?

6   In what respects does the status of preferred stockholders resemble that of bondholders rather than common stockholders? How does preferred stock differ from bonds payable?

7   For what purpose was the par value concept originally required for capital stock?

8   State briefly the accounting principle to be followed in recording the issuance of capital stock in exchange for nonmonetary assets or services.

9   Are most preferred stocks:
a Voting or nonvoting?
b Cumulative or noncumulative?
c Participating or nonparticipating?
d Callable or redeemable?

10   May a corporation have both *watered stock* and *secret reserves?* Explain.

11   How is a *nonmonetary dividend* recorded by the issuer?

12   Distinguish between a *stock split* and a *stock dividend.*

13   Weeks Corporation distributes a 3% common stock dividend each year, in addition to paying an annual cash dividend of $2 a share to common shareholders. How is the amount of the debit to the Retained Earnings ledger account for the stock dividend determined?

14   Stock splits and stock dividends may be used by a corporation to increase the number of shares of its common stock outstanding.
a What is meant by a *stock split effected in the form of a stock dividend?*
b How is a common stock dividend that has been declared but not distributed classified in a balance sheet? Why?

15   In what ways might a corporation offer creditors protection against excessive cash dividend payments to stockholders?

16   To eliminate a deficit of $700,000, Coker Corporation obtained approval from its stockholders for a "quasi-reorganization and a reverse split." One new share of $5 par common stock was issued for each two old shares of $10 par common stock. The entire issue of 100,000 old shares was retired. Prepare the journal entries to record the exchange of shares of common stock and the elimination of the deficit.

17   Under what circumstances is a corporation's retained earnings "dated"? Does dating of retained earnings refer to an item in the balance sheet or to a ledger account?

EXERCISES

Ex. 16-1 Select the best answer for each of the following multiple-choice questions:

1 DeFoe Corporation has 1,000,000 authorized shares of $3 par common stock of which 600,000 shares are issued and outstanding. When the market value of its common stock was $8 a share, DeFoe declared a 16⅔% common stock dividend. The journal entry (explanation omitted) summarizing *both the declaration and the distribution* of the common stock dividend is:

a *Retained Earnings* *300,000*
     Common Stock *300,000*

b *Paid-in Capital in Excess of Par: Common Stock* *300,000*
     Common Stock *300,000*

c *Retained Earnings* *800,000*
     Common Stock *300,000*
     Paid-in Capital from Common Stock Dividends *500,000*

d *Paid-in Capital in Excess of Par: Common Stock* *800,000*
     Common Stock *300,000*
     Retained Earnings *500,000*

2 The following increases in aggregate or individual ledger account balances of Lindsay Company during Year 9 were as follows:

Total assets	*$356,000*
Total liabilities	*108,000*
Common stock	*240,000*
Paid-in capital in excess of par	*24,000*

If the only debit to the Retained Earnings ledger account for Year 9 was for cash dividends of $52,000, Lindsay Company's net income for Year 9 was:
a $16,000   **b** $36,000   **c** $52,000   **d** $68,000   **e** Some other amount

3 Authorized common stock is issued on a subscription basis at a price in excess of par. Additional paid-in capital is recorded when the subscribed common stock is:
a Contracted for   **b** Paid for   **c** Issued   **d** Authorized

4 The Subscriptions Receivable: Common Stock and Common Stock Subscribed ledger accounts used in connection with common stock subscriptions are, respectively:
a Asset and liability accounts
b Asset and stockholders' equity accounts
c Asset and contra-asset accounts
d Contra-stockholders' equity and stockholders' equity accounts

5 Which of the following is not an acceptable debit to an additional paid-in capital ledger account?
a Write-off of bond discount at the time of issuance of the bonds
b Out-of-pocket costs of issuing capital stock

c Declaration of a liquidating dividend

d Redemption premium on preferred stock

e All of the foregoing

6   Outstanding common stock is always equal to:

a Authorized common stock less unissued common stock

b Issued common stock plus subscribed common stock

c Unissued common stock less issued common stock

d Issued common stock less treasury stock: common

7   With respect to subscriptions for capital stock, an additional paid-in capital ledger account is credited when:

a Capital stock is subscribed at a price in excess of par or stated value

b Subscribed capital stock is issued after subscribers pay the subscription price, which exceeded par or stated value

c A subscriber defaults and the corporation retains the amount paid on the defaulted subscription

d Either **a, b,** or **c** occurs

e Either **a** or **c** occurs

8   On July 14, Year 4, Lucerne Company exchanged 1,000 shares of its $8 par common stock for land with an appraised value of $23,000. The closing market price of Lucerne's common stock on the New York Stock Exchange was $21 a share on July 14, Year 4. As a result of the exchange, Lucerne's additional paid-in capital was increased by:

a $0   **b** $8,000   **c** $13,000   **d** $15,000   **e** Some other amount

Ex. 16-2   Wisely Corporation was incorporated on January 2, Year 8, with the following authorized capitalization:

(1) 5,000 shares of 8% cumulative preferred stock, $10 par

(2) 20,000 shares of no-par common stock, stated value $40 a share

During Year 8, Wisely issued 12,000 shares of common stock for a total of $600,000 and 3,000 shares of preferred stock at $16 a share. In addition, on December 20, Year 8, subscriptions for 1,000 shares of preferred stock were received at a price of $18 a share. The subscribed shares were paid for on January 2, Year 9.

Compute the amount that Wisely Corporation reports as total paid-in capital in its December 31, Year 8, balance sheet.

Ex. 16-3   Polar Corporation received authorization to issue an additional 100,000 shares of no-par common stock with a stated value of $10 a share. The stock was offered to subscribers at a subscription price of $50 a share. Subscriptions were recorded by a debit to Subscriptions Receivable: Common Stock and a credit to Common Stock Subscribed and an additional paid-in capital ledger account. A short time later, subscribers who had contracted to acquire 100 shares defaulted on their contracts after paying 40% of the subscription price. Costs of reissuing the 100 shares totaled $200. The method used by Polar to record the default depends on the contractual and legal rights of the defaulting subscribers and especially on the statutes of the state of incorporation.

Identify four methods of accounting at the time of the default for the amount paid in by subscribers prior to the default. Prepare a journal entry for Polar Corporation for each method to show how the default would be recorded. Omit explanations for the journal entries.

Ex. 16-4 The condensed balance sheet of Ollie's, a single proprietorship, on December 31, Year 2, was as follows:

OLLIE'S
Balance Sheet
December 31, Year 2

Assets

Current assets	$100,000
Plant assets (net of $120,000 accumulated depreciation)	80,000
Total assets	$180,000

Liabilities & Proprietor's Capital

Liabilities	$ 40,000
Oliver Miller, capital	140,000
Total liabilities & proprietor's capital.	$180,000

Current fair values of Ollie's current assets and plant assets (net) were $110,000 and $290,000, respectively, on December 31, Year 2; current fair values of liabilities on that date equaled their carrying amounts. On January 2, Year 3, Ollie's was incorporated as Ollie's, Inc., with 2,000 shares of $20 par common stock issued to Oliver Miller.

Compute the credit to the Paid-in Capital in Excess of Par ledger account of Ollie's, Inc., on January 2, Year 3.

Ex. 16-5 Loco Company had net income for Year 4 of $10,600,000 and earnings per share of common stock of $5.00. Included in the measurement of net income was $1,000,000 of bond interest expense on Loco's long-term debt. The income tax rate for Year 4 was 45%. Dividends declared on preferred stock were $600,000. Forty percent of the net income available for common stock was declared as dividends.

Compute the dividends declared on common stock by Loco Company for Year 4.

Ex. 16-6 Kendall Company was organized on January 2, Year 5, and issued the following capital stock:

(1) 50,000 shares of $10 par, fully participating, 9% cumulative preferred stock, at $25 a share (authorized 150,000 shares)
(2) 200,000 shares of $5 par common stock at $12 a share (authorized 500,000 shares)

The net income for Year 5 was $420,000, and cash dividends of $234,000 were declared in Year 5.

Compute the dividends declared by Kendall Company on the preferred stock and common stock during Year 5.

Ex. 16-7   On September 15, Year 8, Nillo Corporation declared a nonmonetary dividend of 1,000 shares of Wimble, Inc., appropriately carried at cost of $9,000 as a long-term investment. The market price of Wimble's outstanding common stock on September 15, Year 8, was $14 a share.

Compute the debit to Retained Earnings and the credit to Realized Gain on Disposal of Investments ledger accounts resulting from Nillo Corporation's dividend declaration on September 15, Year 8.

Ex. 16-8   Suffolk Company declared and distributed dividends as follows:

(1) The entire long-term investment in the common stock of Ney Company, a wholly owned subsidiary accounted for by the equity method of accounting, was distributed to Suffolk's stockholders. The carrying amount of this investment on the date of distribution was $725,000; Suffolk made the distribution instead of accepting a cash offer of $2,000,000 for the common stock of Ney from an independent investor. This distribution is considered a spin-off for financial accounting.

(2) Suffolk's 5% common stock interest in Haig Company was distributed to stockholders. The long-term investment in Haig was carried at cost of $62,000; the current fair value of this investment was $92,000.

Prepare single journal entries for Suffolk Company for the declaration and distribution of each of the two dividends described above.

Ex. 16-9   The stockholders' equity of Nako Company on July 31, Year 6, is presented below:

Stockholders' equity:

Common stock. $20 par, authorized 400,000 shares, issued and out-	
standing 150,000 shares	*$3,000,000*
Paid-in capital in excess of par	*140,000*
Retained earnings	*390,000*
Total stockholders' equity	*$3,530,000*

On August 1, Year 6, the board of directors of Nako declared a 5% stock dividend on common stock, to be distributed on September 15. The market price of Nako's common stock was $35 a share on August 1, Year 6, and $40 a share on September 15, Year 6.

Compute the amount of Nako Company's debit to the Retained Earnings ledger account as a result of the declaration and distribution of the stock dividend.

Ex. 16-10   Golan Company had substantial retained earnings but was short of cash. Accordingly, on September 20, Year 3, the board of directors of Golan declared the following dividends, distributable October 19, Year 3, to stockholders of record October 5, Year 3:

(1) 2,000 shares of Harold Company $1 par common stock, with a cost and carrying amount of $20,000. Golan's investment in Harold did not enable it to influence Harold's operating or financial policies.

(2) A 15% stock dividend on the 100,000 outstanding shares of Golan's $10 par common stock.

Per-share market values of the common stock of Golan and Harold on September 20, Year 3, were $14 and $23, respectively.

Prepare journal entries for Golan Company to record the declaration of the dividends on September 20, Year 3.

Ex. 16-11 The stockholders' equity section of the balance sheet of Norwalk Company at the beginning of Year 5 contained the following items:

Stockholders' equity:

12% convertible preferred stock, $100 par, authorized, issued,	
and outstanding 10,000 shares (Note 1)..........................	*$1,000,000*
Common stock, $5 par, authorized 1,000,000 shares, issued and out-	
standing 400,000 shares	*2,000,000*
Retained earnings	*6,000,000*
Total stockholders' equity	*$9,000,000*

Note 1: *The preferred stock is convertible at any time to common stock at a conversion ratio of four common shares for each preferred share, with the conversion ratio subject to adjustment for any dilution of the common stock.*

On January 10, Year 5, a 5% common stock dividend was declared, to be distributed January 30 to stockholders of record January 15. On March 1, Year 5, all the preferred stock was converted to common stock. Market price a share for the common stock was as follows: January 10, $41; January 15, $42; January 30, $43; March 1, $45.

Post the transactions and events of Norwalk Company described above in appropriate ledger accounts and determine the balances of the following accounts after giving consideration to all the listed transactions: (**a**) Common Stock, (**b**) Paid-in Capital in Excess of Par: Common Stock, and (**c**) Retained Earnings. Also compute Norwalk's total stockholders' equity after giving effect to these transactions.

Ex. 16-12 The stockholders' equity of Farber Company on December 31, Year 9, prior to a quasi-reorganization completed on that date was as follows:

Stockholders' equity:

Common stock, $10 par, authorized, issued, and outstanding	
700,000 shares	*$7,000,000*
Paid-in capital in excess of par	*1,600,000*
Retained earnings (deficit)	*(900,000)*
Total stockholders' equity	*$7,700,000*

Inventories were carried in Farber's accounting records on December 31, Year 9, at market value of $6,000,000, which was $500,000 less than cost. Farber's plant assets, carried at $12,000,000 net of accumulated depreciation, had a current fair value of $8,000,000 on December 31, Year 9. Under the provisions of the quasi-reorganization, the par value of Farber's common stock was reduced to $5 a share.

Prepare the stockholders' equity section of Farber Company's balance sheet on December 31, Year 9, following completion of the quasi-reorganization. Show supporting computations.

Ex. 16-13   The condensed balance sheet of Nolo Corporation on June 30, Year 6, prior to a quasi-reorganization, was as follows:

NOLO CORPORATION
Balance Sheet
June 30, Year 6

Assets

Current assets..	$ 550,000
Plant assets (net of $650,000 accumulated depreciation)............	1,350,000
Other assets	200,000
Total assets	$2,100,000

Liabilities & Stockholders' Equity

Liabilities..	$ 600,000
Common stock, $50 par, 32,000 shares issued and outstanding.......	1,600,000
Paid-in capital in excess of par	300,000
Retained earnings (deficit)...	(400,000)
Total liabilities & stockholders' equity	$2,100,000

The quasi-reorganization was to be implemented by an increase of $350,000 in accumulated depreciation, a $150,000 write-down of other assets, and an appropriate reduction in the par value of the common stock.

Compute the revised par value, per share and total, of Nolo Corporation's common stock on June 30, Year 6, following the quasi-reorganization.

Ex. 16-14   From the following information, prepare the stockholders' equity section of the balance sheet of Goth Corporation on October 31, Year 6:

Subscriptions receivable: common stock	$ 55,000
Paid-in capital in excess of par: preferred stock	50,000
Common stock, $5 par, authorized 40,000 shares, issued and outstanding 20,000 shares..	100,000
Paid-in capital in excess of par: common stock	150,000
Retained earnings, unappropriated	327,000
Retained earnings appropriated for general contingencies	125,000
Common stock subscribed...	25,000
12% cumulative preferred stock, $50 par, authorized 20,000 shares, issued and outstanding 10,000 shares................................	500,000
Paid-in capital from donation of plant site by city of Prado	140,000

CASES

Case 16-1   Problems may be encountered in accounting for transactions involving the stockholders' equity section of the balance sheet.

Instructions

[Assume that only one class of capital stock (common stock) is authorized.]

a Describe the accounting for the subscription of common stock at a price in excess of the par value of the common stock.

b Describe the accounting for the issuance of no-par common stock for cash at a price in excess of the stated value of the common stock.

c Explain the significance of the three dates that are important in accounting for cash dividends to stockholders. Describe the journal entry, if any, prepared on each date.

d Assume retained earnings are available for the declaration of stock dividends. What is the effect of a 10% common stock dividend on retained earnings and total stockholders' equity?

Case 16-2 Obsolescence has become a major problem in the inventories of Robin Company. Lack of attention to inventory turnover rates, combined with a change in product design to permit use of lighter-weight materials, has caused much of the existing inventories to become obsolete. An analysis of the inventories on December 31, Year 5, indicated that the carrying amount of inventories should be reduced by $1,100,000 because of obsolescence.

The income of Year 5 before the obsolescence loss and income taxes was estimated at $210,000. The stockholders' equity before year-end adjusting entries for Year 5 was as follows:

Stockholders' equity:

Common stock, $1 par...	$1,000,000
Additional paid-in capital.......................................	600,000
Retained earnings...	400,000
Total stockholders' equity	$2,000,000

The board of directors informs you that it regards obsolescence as an extraordinary item and that a decision has been made to write down inventories by the full amount of the obsolescence loss; to debit $400,000 to retained earnings and $600,000 to additional paid-in capital; and to recognize a loss of only $100,000 in Year 5.

Instructions

Evaluate the proposed treatment of the obsolescence loss in the light of generally accepted accounting principles. Disregard income tax considerations. Compute the amount of Robin Company's income or loss before income taxes for Year 5 and explain how the obsolescence loss should be reported. Disregard other adjustments that may be required in the computation of income or loss before income taxes.

Case 16-3 You are engaged in an audit of the financial statements of Mickelson Company on March 31, Year 1, the end of its first year of operations. During your examination of the stockholders' equity accounts, you discover that Mickelson issued common stock to three customers at a price substantially below the market prices of the stock on the dates of issuance.

Mickelson's controller proposes to present the difference between market value of the common stock and the proceeds received from the customers as an extraordinary loss in Mickelson's income statement for the year ended March 31,

Year 1. The controller points out that all other common stock issuances were for proceeds equal to current market value, and that the "discount" allowed to the customers who acquired Mickelson's common stock was for the purpose of encouraging future purchases of merchandise by those customers. The controller acknowledged, however, that the customers acquiring Mickelson's common stock at a discount from market value had no long-term contractual commitment to purchase merchandise from Mickelson.

Instructions

Do you concur with the controller's proposal for the accounting for Mickelson Company's discount from market value on common stock? Explain.

Case 16-4 The independent auditor of Neeham Company explained to its president that the use of the last-in, first-out inventory method during an extended period of rising prices and the expensing of research and development costs are among the accepted accounting practices that may create *secret reserves*. The auditor also pointed out that *watered stock* is the opposite of secret reserves.

Instructions

a What are *secret reserves?* How may secret reserves be created or enlarged?
b What is the basis for the statement that the two specific practices cited above tend to create secret reserves?
c Is it possible to create secret reserves in connection with accounting for liabilities? If so, explain or give an example.
d What are the objections to the creation of secret reserves?
e What is *watered stock?*
f Describe the general circumstances in which watered stock may arise.
g What actions may be taken to eliminate "water" from a balance sheet?

Case 16-5 After the cancellation of some of its government contracts, Ludwig Company began production under a new long-term government contract. During the period of operating losses resulting from the contract cancellations, Ludwig had suspended dividend payments on all four capital stock issues. These four issues consisted of a $7 cumulative, $100 par, first preferred stock; a $2.50 noncumulative, convertible, $50 par, preferred stock; an 8%, $100 par, noncumulative preferred stock; and common stock. Ten thousand shares of each issue of capital stock were outstanding. All dividends had been paid through Year 3, but Ludwig had been unable to pay any dividends in Year 4 or Year 5. During Year 6, Ludwig's financial position improved, and at a director's meeting near the end of Year 6, a proposal was made to pay a dividend of $2.25 a share on the common stock to stockholders of record December 31, Year 6.

Edward Cobb, who owned 100 shares of the $2.50 noncumulative, convertible, $50 par, preferred stock, had been considering converting those 100 shares to common stock at the existing conversion ratio of four shares of common stock for each share of the convertible preferred stock. The conversion ratio was scheduled to drop to 3½ to one at the end of Year 6. Observing that the market price of the common stock was rising rapidly, Cobb explained that he was "torn between a desire to retain his preferred stock until the dividend of $2.25 a share was received and a desire to convert promptly before the price of the common stock went higher and the conversion ratio was reduced."

Instructions

a Determine the amount of cash needed by Ludwig Company for dividend payments if the proposal to pay a $2.25 dividend on the common stock is adopted. (Assume that there is no conversion of preferred stock.)

b Advise Edward Cobb on the merits of converting the Ludwig Company preferred stock at this time as opposed to converting after the dividends have been paid and the conversion ratio decreased. Explain the issues involved.

Case 16-6 A few months after the organization of Lund Corporation, one of the principal stockholders, Norman Chow, offered to transfer land and a factory to Lund in exchange for 11,000 shares of Lund's $10 par common stock. Under the terms of the offer, an existing mortgage note payable of $28,000 on the factory was to be assumed by Lund.

The board of directors of Lund determined that the factory was well-suited to Lund's needs. The board was informed by the secretary of Lund that 15,000 authorized but unissued shares of common stock were available.

One member of the board, Rita Worth, opposed the idea of assuming the mortgage note payable, on the grounds that long-term debt could prove burdensome for a new company without established earning power, and suggested making a counteroffer of 13,800 shares with the understanding that Chow pay the mortgage note in full on the date title to the land and factory was received.

A second director, Carl Lope, argued against further issuance of common stock, pointing out that Lund had just obtained $325,000 cash from issuance of 26,000 shares of common stock and that this cash should be used to acquire plant assets. Lope proposed that Lund offer Chow $110,000 cash, assume the mortgage note, and pay it in full immediately.

A third director, Mary Fine, urged prompt acceptance of Chow's offer without modification. Fine produced documents showing that the land and factory had been acquired by Chow 10 years previously for $206,000 and that Chow's accounting records indicated depreciation to date of $36,000. In conclusion, Fine stated that these facts showed that Lund would be saving $32,000 by accepting Chow's offer.

Instructions

a Comment on the logic and reasonableness of the views expressed by each of the three directors. Explain how each computed the amounts mentioned.

b Indicate which deal you believe would be most advantageous to Lund Corporation, assuming that it was acceptable to Norman Chow.

c Assuming that Lund Corporation accepted the original offer by Norman Chow, prepare the journal entry to record the transaction, and explain the reasoning underlying the entry. Assume that land is worth 25% as much as the factory building.

Case 16-7   After receiving a common stock certificate for three shares, Ruth Ross, a stock-holder of Tillman Corporation, expressed this reaction:

"Tillman Corporation has just declared another stock dividend despite that letter of protest I wrote to the president last year. I wrote that I hate to see a company declare a stock dividend because it causes a transfer of retained earnings to paid-in capital. Such a transfer obviously reduces the amount available for cash dividends."

"You are absolutely right," said Wilma Wade. "When I acquired Tillman common stock I was hoping for an increase in cash dividends over a period of time, but the declaration of stock dividends certainly reduces my expectations for cash dividends. Let's write the president another letter."

Instructions

Evaluate the opinions expressed by Ruth Ross and Wilma Wade from the standpoint of accounting principles, and also in the light of customary dividend practices. Identify any elements of truth in the statements by Ross and Wade and any lack of logic in the conclusions they reached.

Case 16-8   Lee Corb, CPA, was asked by the president of a client for an explanation of a "quasi-reorganization." The president was unfamiliar with the procedure and was concerned that a competitor might have an advantage because it had carried out a quasi-reorganization.

Instructions

Prepare the report that Lee Corb should provide to the president explaining a quasi-reorganization. The report should include the following points:

a Definition and accounting features of a quasi-reorganization.

b Purpose of a quasi-reorganization. Under what conditions should a quasi-reorganization be considered?

c Authorization necessary to implement a quasi-reorganization.

d Disclosure required in the financial statements following a quasi-reorganization.

e Possible competitive advantage to a corporation that effected a quasi-reorganization.

PROBLEMS

16-1   Mendel Corporation's post-closing trial balance on December 31, Year 10, was as follows:

MENDEL CORPORATION
Post-Closing Trial Balance
December 31, Year 10

	Debit	Credit
Accounts payable		$ 290,000
Accounts receivable	$ 550,000	
Accumulated depreciation of building and equipment ...		200,000

(continued)

Additional paid-in capital: common stock:		
In excess of par		$1,560,000
From stock dividends		250,000
Allowance for doubtful accounts		30,000
Allowance to reduce long-term investments in		
marketable equity securities to market value		25,000
Bonds payable		400,000
Building and equipment	$1,100,000	
Cash	220,000	
Common stock, $1 par		150,000
Dividends payable on preferred stock		4,000
Inventories	620,000	
Land	560,000	
Long-term investments, at cost	310,000	
Preferred stock, $50 par		500,000
Short-term investments, at cost	215,000	
Short-term prepayments	40,000	
Retained earnings		231,000
Unrealized loss in value of long-term marketable equity		
securities	25,000	
Totals	$3,640,000	$3,640,000

Additional Information

(1) On December 31, Year 10, Mendel had the following numbers of shares of preferred stock and common stock:

	Preferred stock	Common stock
Authorized	50,000	500,000
Issued	10,000	150,000
Outstanding	10,000	150,000

(2) The $4 cumulative preferred stock has a liquidation preference of $50 a share.

Instructions

Prepare the stockholders' equity section of Mendel Corporation's balance sheet on December 31, Year 10.

16-2 Tinsel Company began operations in January, Year 1, and had the following net income or (loss) for each of its first five years of operations:

Year 1	$ (150,000)
Year 2	(130,000)
Year 3	(120,000)
Year 4	260,000
Year 5	1,022,000

On December 31, Year 5, Tinsel's capital stock ledger accounts were as follows:

(1) *10% nonparticipating, noncumulative preferred stock, $100 par,*
authorized, issued, and outstanding 1,000 shares .... $ 100,000
(2) *8% fully participating, cumulative preferred stock, $100 par,*
authorized, issued, and outstanding 10,000 shares 1,000,000
(3) *Common stock, $10 par, authorized 100,000 shares, issued*
and outstanding 50,000 shares 500,000

Tinsel has never paid a cash dividend or distributed a stock dividend. There has been no change in the capital stock ledger accounts since Tinsel began operations. The appropriate state law permits dividends only from retained earnings.

Instructions

Prepare a working paper to show the maximum amount available for cash dividends to Tinsel Company's shareholders on December 31, Year 5, and how it would be distributed to the holders of the common stock and each of the preferred stock issues. Show supporting computations.

16-3 On January 4, Year 1, Kelly Company was organized and received authority from the state to issue capital stock as follows:

(1) $5 preferred stock, $100 par, 250,000 shares
(2) Common stock, no-par, stated value $5 a share, 1,000,000 shares

After this authorization to issue capital stock, the following transactions affecting stockholders' equity occurred during the first quarter of Year 1:

Jan. 15 Received subscriptions for 25,000 shares of preferred stock at $105 a share. A payment of 40% of the subscription price accompanied each subscription; the balance was to be paid on March 15. (Record the full amount subscribed and then, in a separate journal entry, record the cash collections for 40% of this amount.)

17 Received subscriptions for 125,000 shares of common stock at $20 a share, payable March 1.

30 Issued 1,500 shares of common stock in payment for legal and accounting services reasonably valued at $30,000 relating to the organization of Kelly Company.

Mar. 1 Received payment in full of the amount due on common stock subscriptions and issued the stock certificates.

15 Received payment in full of the balance due on preferred stock subscriptions and issued the stock certificates.

30 Issued 5,000 shares of preferred stock for $520,000.

30 Issued 6,000 shares of common stock and 2,500 shares of preferred stock in exchange for assets for which the board of directors established the following current fair values:

Land	*$154,000*
Building	*190,000*
Delivery equipment	*20,000*
Inventories	*15,000*

Mar. 31 Net income earned to March 31 amounted to $176,000. No dividends had been declared.

Instructions

a Prepare journal entries to record the foregoing transactions of Kelly Company.

b Prepare the stockholders' equity section of Kelly Company's balance sheet on March 31, Year 1.

16-4 The board of directors of Hobb Corporation declared a 6% common stock dividend on October 1, Year 8, to be distributed on October 25 to stockholders of record October 15. The market price of Hobb's common stock was as follows on those dates: October 1, $63; October 15, $66; and October 25, $70. The accounting records of Hobb are maintained on the basis of a fiscal year ended September 30.

On October 28, Year 8, the board of directors declared a cash dividend of $0.90 a share on the common stock. The dividend was payable December 1 to stockholders of record November 18.

The stockholders' equity section of Hobb's balance sheet on September 30, Year 8, is shown below. For October, Year 8, Hobb's net income was $41,750.

> Stockholders' equity:
>
> Common stock, $15 par, authorized 200,000 shares, issued and out-
> standing 60,000 shares .... $ 900,000
> Paid-in capital in excess of par................................. 1,250,000
> Total paid-in capital... $2,150,000
> Retained earnings... 2,380,000
> Total stockholders' equity $4,530,000

Instructions

a Prepare journal entries for Hobb Corporation for the declaration and the distribution of the dividends during the month of October, Year 8. Debit Retained Earnings for dividend declarations. Also prepare a journal entry to record the net income for October (debit Income Summary).

b Prepare the stockholders' equity section of Hobb Corporation's balance sheet on October 31, Year 8.

16-5 Mose Corporation was organized on September 5, Year 2, with authorization to issue 600,000 shares of $5 par common stock and 22,500 shares of $50 par, 8% cumulative preferred stock. On September 15, Year 2, the assets of a single proprietorship were acquired in exchange for 12,000 shares of preferred stock, plus the assumption of a mortgage note payable of $276,000. The assets acquired were valued by a firm of independent appraisers at $900,000. On September 20, subscriptions were obtained for 30,000 shares of common at a price of $15 a share.

All subscriptions were collected and recorded on October 5, except for a subscription by Laura Caines for 300 shares. Caines paid $1,500 but defaulted on the balance of the contract. On October 10, the 300 shares were issued for cash by Mose at a price of $13 a share. In accordance with statutes of the state, Mose refunded the amount paid by Caines after deducting the "loss" realized on the issuance of the 300 shares.

No dividends were declared on the common stock. A quarterly dividend of $1 a share on the preferred stock was declared on November 9, payable on December 15, to stockholders of record on December 1. Operations for the period ended December 31, Year 2, resulted in net income of $72,500.

Instructions

a Prepare journal entries for the capital stock transactions of Mose Corporation and the dividend declaration and payment.

b Prepare the stockholders' equity section of Mose Corporation's balance sheet on December 31, Year 2.

16-6 Oliver Corporation maintains its accounting records on the basis of a fiscal year ending March 31. The stockholders' equity section of the balance sheet on March 31, Year 6, appears below:

Stockholders' equity:

Common stock, $10 par, authorized 250,000 shares, issued and out-standing 100,000 shares	$1,000,000
Paid-in capital in excess of par	2,675,000
Total paid-in capital	$3,675,000
Retained earnings	2,420,000
Total stockholders' equity	$6,095,000

On April 1, Year 6, the board of directors of Oliver declared a cash dividend of $1 a share payable on April 29 to common stockholders of record April 15.

On April 10, Year 6, the board of directors of Oliver also declared a 3% stock dividend distributable on May 31 to common stockholders of record May 15. The market price of the common stock on April 10 was $50 a share. The net income for April amounted to $78,500.

Instructions

a Prepare journal entries for Oliver Corporation for the declaration and the distribution of the dividends and to record net income for April. Debit Income Summary to record the net income.

b Prepare the stockholders' equity section of Oliver Corporation's balance sheet on April 30, Year 6, and a statement of retained earnings for the month ended April 30, Year 6, similar in format to the one on page 167.

16-7 The market price of Luci Corporation's common stock on June 30, Year 1, was $52 a share. The stockholders' equity on that date included substantial retained earnings, in addition to 250,000 shares of $2 par common stock that had been issued at a price of $12 a share. A total of 500,000 shares was authorized to be issued.

A nonmonetary dividend (short-term investments) of $1.10 a share was declared on March 10, Year 2, payable April 25, Year 2, to stockholders of record March 31, Year 2. The carrying amount of the short-term investments distributed as the nonmonetary dividend was $180,000.

A cash dividend of $1.50 a share was declared on June 1, Year 2, payable July 20, Year 2, to stockholders of record July 1, Year 2; a 5% stock dividend was declared at the same time and with the same dates of record and distribution. The cash dividend was not applicable to the shares of common stock issued as a stock dividend. The market price per share of the common stock was $55 on June 1, Year 2, and $56 on June 30, Year 2.

For the year ended June 30, Year 2, net income amounted to $1,643,700 (including the effect, if any, of the nonmonetary dividend), which represented an earnings rate of 10% on total stockholders' equity as of June 30, Year 1.

Instructions

a Record Luci Corporation's transactions and events affecting stockholders' equity during Year 2 in the general journal. Debit Income Summary to record the net income for the year ended June 30, Year 2.

b Prepare a statement of retained earnings for Luci Corporation for the year ended June 30, Year 2, similar in format to the one on page 167.

c Prepare the stockholders' equity section of Luci Corporation's balance sheet on June 30, Year 2.

16-8 Current conditions require that Vance Company carry out a quasi-reorganization on December 31, Year 6. Selected balance sheet items prior to the quasi-reorganization were as follows:

(1) Inventories were carried in the accounting records on December 31, Year 6, at market value of $3,000,000. The cost of the inventories was $3,250,000.

(2) Plant assets were carried in the accounting records on December 31, Year 6, at $6,000,000, net of accumulated depreciation. Plant assets had a current fair value of $5,000,000, and were to be written down to that amount by a credit to Accumulated Depreciation.

(3) Stockholders' equity on December 31, Year 6, consisted of the following:

Stockholders' equity:	
Common stock, $10 par, authorized, issued, and outstanding	
350,000 shares	$3,500,000
Additional paid-in capital	800,000
Retained earnings (deficit)	(450,000)
Total stockholders' equity	$3,850,000

The par value of the common stock was to be reduced from $10 a share to $5 a share.

Instructions

a Prepare journal entries to record the quasi-reorganization of Vance Company on December 31, Year 6.

b Prepare the stockholders' equity section of Vance Company's balance sheet on December 31, Year 6, after the quasi-reorganization had been effected. Show supporting computations. Disregard income tax and deferred tax considerations.

16-9 Farley Corporation was authorized to issue 500,000 shares of $25 par, 8% cumulative preferred stock, and 1,500,000 shares of no-par common stock with a stated value of $2.50 a share.

Early operations of Farley were profitable, but a prolonged strike caused a net loss of $910,000 for the fiscal year ended June 30, Year 6. Because of the loss, Farley declared no dividends on its common stock during the year ended June 30, Year 6. Dividends on preferred stock were declared and paid earlier in Year 6 in the amount of $120,000, but dividends were in arrears on the preferred stock on June 30, Year 6, in the amount of $360,000.

A trial balance of the ledger on May 31, Year 6, included the following:

8% cumulative preferred stock, $25 par	$6,000,000
Common stock, no-par, $2.50 stated value	1,000,000
Subscriptions receivable: preferred stock	618,000
Retained earnings (June 30, Year 5)	1,476,000
Paid-in capital in excess of par: preferred stock	198,000
Preferred stock subscribed	600,000
Paid-in capital in excess of stated value: common stock	1,375,000
Subscriptions receivable: common stock	525,000
Common stock subscribed	250,000
Dividends: preferred stock	120,000

Transactions during June, Year 6, relating to capital stock included the issuance on June 5 of 4,200 shares of common stock in exchange for a patent. An additional 30,000 shares of common stock were issued for cash on June 5 at a price of $6.50 a share. Cash was collected on June 21 representing payment in full for common stock subscriptions covering 20,000 shares. These subscriptions had been received and recorded prior to May 31. All common stock offerings by Farley prior to May 31, Year 6, had been at the same price.

Instructions

a Compute the average price at which the preferred stock was issued by Farley Corporation.

b Compute the price at which the common stock was issued by Farley Corporation prior to June, Year 6.

c Prepare journal entries to record Farley Corporation's transactions and events (including closing entries for the net loss and dividends) during June that affected the stockholders' equity ledger accounts.

d Prepare the stockholders' equity section of Farley Corporation's balance sheet on June 30, Year 6, including any applicable notes to the financial statements.

16-10   The stockholders of Putney Corporation have voted approval for Putney to carry out a quasi-reorganization effective October 1, Year 3. Putney's balance sheet on September 30, Year 3, follows:

PUTNEY CORPORATION
Balance Sheet
September 30, Year 3

Assets

Current assets		$1,080,000
Plant assets	$800,000	
Less: Accumulated depreciation	395,000	405,000

(continued)

Goodwill (net)	$1,520,000
Total assets	$3,005,000

Liabilities & Stockholders' Equity

Liabilities:

Current liabilities		$ 305,000
12% bonds payable		250,000
Total liabilities		$ 555,000

Stockholders' equity:

10.5% preferred stock, $100 par (dividends in arrears,		
$42,000)...	$ 200,000	
Common stock, $10 par	2,200,000	
Retained earnings	50,000	2,450,000
Total liabilities & stockholders' equity		$3,005,000

Putney is engaged in the manufacture of space exploration equipment and has acquired several small business enterprises at prices in excess of the current fair value of their identifiable net assets. The acquisition prices included, among other things, payment for research work and for the services of technically trained personnel. The value assigned to the acquired assets was based on the par value of common stock issued in the purchase-type business combinations. The market value of Putney's common stock was approximately equal to its par value.

In recent months, several major research projects were abandoned, and some key employees left Putney. As a result, many contracts were lost, and the goodwill was deemed to be worthless. In order to get a "fresh start" for financial accounting, the following actions were taken to carry out a quasi-reorganization effective October 1, Year 3, approved by stockholders:

(1) Inventories were written down by $140,000 and the allowance for doubtful accounts was increased by $10,000.
(2) The carrying amount of plant assets was reduced to $250,000 by an increase in accumulated depreciation.
(3) The goodwill was written off.
(4) The par value of common stock was reduced to $1 a share.
(5) The dividends in arrears on the preferred stock were paid in cash, and 80,000 shares of $1 par common stock were issued to the preferred stockholders in exchange for their stock.
(6) Following the asset write-offs, the deficit was eliminated against paid-in capital in excess of par: common stock.
(7) During the last quarter of Year 3, Putney earned net income of $85,000, and as a result, current assets increased by $120,000, current liabilities increased by $10,000, and accumulated depreciation increased by $25,000. Current liabilities also increased by $7,000 as a result of additional income taxes assessed for Year 1 because of an error in the computation of income taxes payable.

Instructions

a Prepare journal entries for Putney Corporation to record the quasi-reorganization on October 1, Year 3, and to summarize the transactions and events for the last quarter of Year 3.

b Compute the balance of Putney Corporation's retained earnings on December 31, Year 3.

16-11 On January 1, Year 9, the stockholders' equity of Albert Company was as follows:

Stockholders' equity:

12% convertible preferred stock, $100 par, authorized 10,000 shares, issued and outstanding 5,000 shares *(Note 1)*	$ 500,000
Common stock, $2 par, authorized 1,000,000 shares, issued and outstanding 350,000 shares	700,000
Common stock subscribed, 8,000 shares	16,000
Paid-in capital in excess of par: common stock	3,500,000
Total paid-in capital.	$4,716,000
Retained earnings	5,262,600
Total stockholders' equity	$9,978,600

Note 1: Preferred stock was issued at par, is callable at $105, and is convertible to common stock at a rate of 3 for 1, subject to an antidilution provision.

During the quarter ended March 31, Year 9, the following transactions were completed:

Jan. 7   Collected $310,000 representing payment in full for all outstanding common stock subscriptions; issued the common stock.

31   Declared the regular quarterly dividend on the preferred stock to be paid March 3 to stockholders of record February 19.

Feb. 1   Declared a 10% common stock dividend to be distributed March 4 to stockholders of record February 20.

Mar. 3   Paid quarterly dividend on the preferred stock.

4   Distributed the 10% common stock dividend.

15   Issued 11,000 shares of common stock for cash at $44 a share.

30   All preferred stock was converted to common stock.

31   Issued 100,000 shares of common stock in exchange for the net assets of Raye Corporation (appraised at $4.5 million) in a purchase-type business combination.

31   Net income for the quarter ended March 31, Year 9, was $877,700. (Debit the Income Summary ledger account.)

Market prices of Albert Company's common stock during Year 9 were as follows: January 7, $40; February 1, $38; February 20, $40; March 4, $42; March 15, $44; March 31, $45.

Instructions

a Prepare journal entries for the transactions and events of Albert Company described above.

b Prepare a statement of stockholders' equity (including retained earnings) for Albert Company for the quarter ended March 31, Year 9, similar in format to the one on page 181.

16-12 On December 31, Year 1, the end of its first year of operations, Watson Company prepared a balance sheet containing the following items, among others:

Subscriptions receivable: preferred stock		$ 208,000
Subscriptions receivable: common stock		720,000
8% cumulative preferred stock, $100 par, authorized		
200,000 shares, issued and outstanding 44,000 shares . . $4,400,000		
8% cumulative preferred stock subscribed 4,000 shares . . 400,000		4,800,000
Common stock, $10 par, authorized 400,000 shares,		
issued and outstanding 47,000 shares . . . . $ 470,000		
Common stock subscribed 48,000 shares 480,000		950,000
Paid-in capital in excess of par:		
On preferred stock		32,000
On common stock		1,930,000

Watson had been organized on January 2, Year 1, and had immediately received subscriptions for 40,000 shares of 8% cumulative preferred stock. Subscriptions for common stock were received on the same date. (The number of common shares subscribed and the subscription price can be determined from information given in the problem.) On May 5 subscriptions were received for an additional 8,000 shares of 8% cumulative preferred stock at a price of $104 a share.

Cash payments were received from subscribers at frequent intervals for several months after subscription. Watson issued stock certificates only when subscribers had paid in full. On December 22, Year 1, Watson issued 15,000 shares of its common stock in exchange for a tract of land with a current fair value of $480,000. (Subscriptions were not used in this transaction.)

Instructions

a Prepare journal entries for all the transactions completed during Year 1 by Watson Company as indicated by the December 31, Year 1, account balances. Assume that collections on the preferred stock subscriptions were made on a first-in, first-out basis.

b Compute the amount of paid-in capital for each class of Watson Company's capital stock on December 31, Year 1. Also determine the amount of stated (legal) capital applicable to the common stock.

Warrants, Convertible Securities, and Employee Capital Accumulation Plans

17

In this chapter we consider stock warrants, convertible securities, and employee capital accumulation plans such as stock option and stock purchase plans. A common characteristic of these securities or plans is that they provide for **contingent** issuances of common stock, and less frequently preferred stock and convertible bonds payable, at the election of the holder prior to the expiration of a specified time period.

STOCK WARRANTS AND WARRANTS TO ACQUIRE BONDS

As explained in Chapter 14, a *stock warrant* is a certificate issued by a corporation conveying to the owner rights to acquire shares of the issuer's common stock at a specified price in a specified time period. The term *right* means the privilege attaching to each outstanding stock warrant to acquire a specified number of shares of common stock. For example, the owner of 100 shares of common stock might receive a stock warrant for 100 rights, which would permit the owner to acquire 10 shares of common stock (because 10 rights are needed to acquire one additional share of common stock) at a price (the *exercise price*) below the current market price.

The use of rights is not limited to the acquisition of additional shares of common stock. Some corporations have issued warrants for rights to their common stockholders entitling them to acquire convertible bonds at a specified price. The use of rights in the acquisition of bonds is considered later in this chapter. At this point we are concerned only with rights that entitle the owner to acquire common stock at a specified price and in a specified time period.

When stock warrants are outstanding, the issuer should disclose the number of shares of common stock held in reserve to meet the contractual commitments to issue additional shares of common stock. This disclosure may be made in the stockholders' equity section of the balance sheet or in a note to the financial statements.

Stock Warrants to Existing Stockholders

When stock warrants are issued to existing stockholders as a preliminary step to raise capital through the issuance of additional shares of common stock, the issuer receives nothing in exchange for the warrants when they are *issued*. Only when the warrants are *exercised* does the issuer receive cash.

Stock warrants granted to existing stockholders as a preliminary step to raising capital through the issuance of additional common stock usually expire in a few weeks. The issuer thus may complete rapidly its program of raising capital through the issuance of additional common stock to present stockholders before offering stock to other investors. Stock warrants of this type are transferable, and some investors obtain warrants by acquisition from other investors. When investors who have acquired warrants from other investors exercise the warrants, the cost of the warrants is combined with the amount paid to the issuer to measure the cost of the shares of common stock acquired, as explained on page 719.

The acquisition price specified in stock warrants granted to existing stockholders always is set below the current market price of the common stock, thus giving a market value to the stock warrants. In the illustration on page 847 of a stock warrant for common stock issued by Pacific Gas and Electric Company, 15 rights were needed for each share of common stock to be acquired at the acquisition price (not shown) of $25.65. The market price of the common stock at the time the warrants were issued was $27.62. The term of the warrants was short—they were issued March 6 and expired on March 27. Through use of these warrants Pacific Gas and Electric issued over 4 million shares of common stock and raised capital in excess of $102 million during the three-week term of the warrants. The warrants were traded

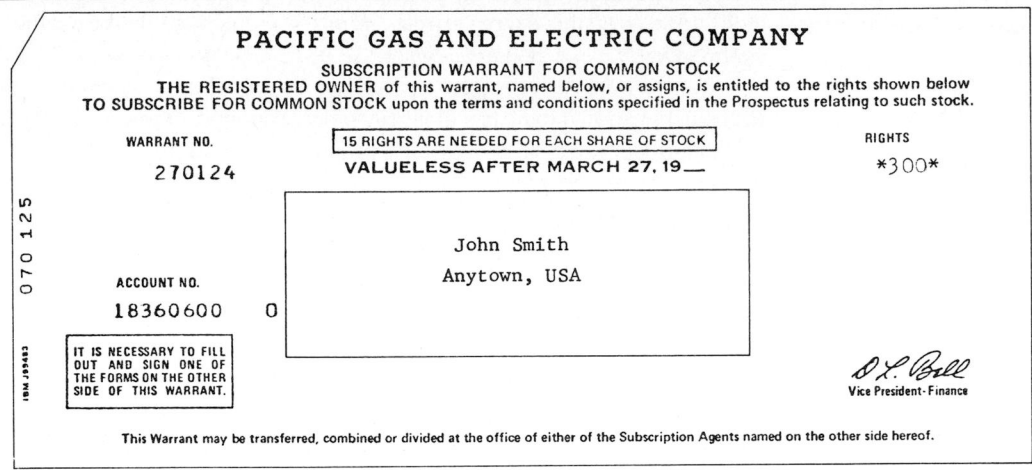

on the New York Stock Exchange throughout their brief term, with the market price per warrant varying between $0.125 and $0.50.

The issuance of stock warrants to stockholders does not require debits or credits to any ledger accounts of the issuer, although a memorandum entry stating the number of warrants issued and the terms involved may be used. When the warrants are exercised by the owners, they receive shares of common stock at the specified price. This transaction requires the usual journal entry for issuances of common stock.

Contingent Stock Warrants to Customers

To encourage volume purchases of its products, a corporation may issue *contingent stock warrants* to its customers giving them rights to acquire a specified number of shares of the corporation's common stock at prices *in excess* of the market price of the stock on the issuance date of the warrants. The contingent warrants would become exercisable at the end of a specified period only if the customers purchased stated quantities of the issuer's products. The underlying assumption is that the market price of the issuer's common stock would increase over the specified exercise price during the term of the warrants.

In *Staff Accounting Bulletin No. 57,* the Securities and Exchange Commission mandated accounting for contingent stock warrants to customers in a manner consistent with *FASB Statement No. 5,* "Accounting for Contingencies."[1] Prior to the date the contingent warrants become exercisable, the issuer must determine whether it is *probable* that (1) the customers holding the warrants will make the requisite purchases, and (2) the market price of the common stock on the date the warrants become exercisable will exceed the exercise price. (If the market price of the common stock is expected to be *less* than the exercise price, the customers would not exercise the warrants.) *If the two outcomes are probable,* the issuer must include a pro rata portion of the anticipated excess of the market price of the com-

---

[1] *Staff Accounting Bulletin No. 57,* Securities and Exchange Commission (Washington: 1984).

mon stock over the exercise price in cost of goods sold during the term of the contingency.

To illustrate, assume that on April 1, Year 5, Weir Corporation issued contingent stock warrants to its principal customer, Harvey Company. The warrants specified that if Harvey purchased Weir's products at a total price of $500,000 during the two years ended March 31, Year 7, Harvey could acquire 10,000 shares of Weir's no-par common stock (stated value $10 a share) at a price of $25 a share during a two-month period ending May 31, Year 7. The market price of Weir's common stock on April 1, Year 5, was $22 a share. On March 31, Year 6, because Harvey's purchases during the year ended that date had totaled $320,000 and the market price of Weir's common stock on March 31, Year 6, was $25 a share (and was expected to be $27 a share on March 31, Year 7), Weir considered that it was probable that Harvey would make purchases sufficient to earn the warrants. Accordingly, Weir prepared the following journal entry on March 31, Year 6:

Journal entry for contingent stock warrants that are probable of exercise

Cost of Goods Sold {[10,000 × ($27 − $25)] × ½}	10,000	
Paid-in Capital: Stock Warrants		10,000
To increase cost of goods sold for one-half (attributable to first year of two-year period) of expected difference between market price of common stock and exercise price of contingent stock warrants on March 31, Year 7.		

Assuming that Harvey's purchases from Weir totaled $240,000 during the year ended March 31, Year 7, and that the market price of Weir's common stock on March 31, Year 7, was $28 a share, Weir would prepare the following journal entry on that date:

Journal entry for contingent stock warrants that have become exercisable

Cost of Goods Sold {[10,000 × ($28 − $25)] − $10,000}	20,000	
Paid-in Capital: Stock Warrants		20,000
To increase cost of goods sold for difference between market price of common stock and exercise price of contingent stock warrants, less $10,000 debited to cost of goods sold for year ended March 31, Year 6.		

The net result of the foregoing two journal entries is that cost of goods sold and additional paid-in capital of Weir Corporation have been increased by $30,000 ($10,000 + $20,000 = $30,000) over a two-year period because contingent stock warrants have become exercisable. Assuming that Harvey Company exercises the stock warrants on April 16, Year 7, Weir prepares the following journal entry:

Cash (10,000 × $25)	*250,000*	
Paid-in Capital: Stock Warrants ($10,000 + $20,000)	*30,000*	
Common Stock, $10 stated value (10,000 × $10)		*100,000*
Paid-in Capital in Excess of Stated Value		*180,000*
To record issuance of 10,000 shares of common stock to		
Harvey Company on exercise of stock warrants.		

If Harvey Company had allowed the stock warrants to lapse by failing to exercise them by May 31, Year 7, Weir would leave the $30,000 amount permanently in the Paid-in Capital: Stock Warrants ledger account.

Warrants to Acquire Convertible Bonds

The preemptive right of common stockholders to acquire additional shares of common stock in proportion to their present holdings in the event that a corporation increases the amount of stock outstanding is discussed in Chapter 16. This preemptive right logically applies also to any new issues of convertible bonds or convertible preferred stock because these securities eventually may be converted to common stock.

During periods of high stock prices, convertible bonds are a popular form of financing. Warrants may be issued to common stockholders entitling them to acquire convertible bonds at a specified price, and usually with the provision that the warrants will expire if not exercised within a month or two. For example, National Cash Register issued to its common stockholders warrants for rights to acquire convertible bonds maturing in 20 years. Ten rights and $100 cash were required to acquire $100 face amount of bonds. The warrants traded for several weeks on the New York Stock Exchange at prices varying between $1 and $2 a right; concurrently, the convertible bonds were trading on a *when-issued* basis at prices ranging from $108 to $116 for each $100 face amount. (Securities distributed on a ''when-issued'' basis do not require delivery until after the scheduled date of issuance.)

The accounting procedures for warrants to acquire convertible bonds are similar to the procedures described for warrants to acquire common stock. The issuer prepares no journal entry when the warrants are issued but must maintain memorandum records of the number of warrants issued, exercised, and outstanding. When the warrants are exercised, the appropriate journal entry is a debit to Cash and a credit to the liability account for the convertible bonds. Usually, the exercise price for the bonds is face amount; thus, no discount or premium is involved when the convertible bonds are issued.

Stock Warrants Issued in Combination with Bonds or Preferred Stock

A corporation may add to the attractiveness of its bonds or preferred stock by including a detachable stock warrant to acquire its common stock at a specified price. The longer the term of the warrant, the greater its speculative appeal; detachable stock warrants issued with bonds or preferred stock often run for several years, and some have no expiration date.

When bonds are issued with detachable stock warrants, the interest rate on the bonds usually is less than if the bonds were offered alone. Similarly, preferred stock accompanied by detachable stock warrants for the acquisition of common stock may attract investors even though the dividend rate on the preferred stock is less than would otherwise be necessary. In other words, a part of the proceeds to the corporation from issuing bonds or preferred stock with detachable stock warrants attached represents payment by investors for the warrants. Therefore, the accounting for these "combination packages" of securities *requires that part of the proceeds be recorded as attributable to the warrants.*

Accounting for bonds payable issued with detachable stock warrants is illustrated in Chapter 15. Therefore, our discussion here is focused on the issuance of detachable stock warrants in combination with preferred stock.

Warrants giving the owner the right to acquire common stock at a specified price at any time during a span of years have an economic value regardless of whether the specified exercise price is higher than, lower than, or equal to the market price of the common stock when the warrants are issued. Because the detachable stock warrants often are traded separately from the preferred stock or bond with which they were originally issued, objective evidence is available for the allocation of the proceeds between the two types of securities.

In *APB Opinion No. 14,* "Accounting for Convertible Debt and Debt Issued with Stock Purchase Warrants," the Accounting Principles Board stated that "the portion of the proceeds of debt securities issued with detachable stock warrants which is allocable to the warrants should be accounted for as paid-in capital. The allocation should be based on the *relative fair values of the two securities at time of issuance.*"[2] Although this discussion related specifically to bonds issued with detachable stock warrants, the reasoning also appears applicable to detachable stock warrants issued with preferred stock.

Assume, for example, that Meeker, Inc., issued 1 million shares of $25 par preferred stock at $26½ and included with each share a detachable stock warrant to acquire one share of $5 par common stock at $30 at any time during the next 10 years. The common stock had a current market price of $26. The warrants had a

Journal entry to record issuance of preferred stock and detachable stock warrants

Cash (1,000,000 × $26.50)	26,500,000	
Preferred Stock (1,000,000 × $25)		25,000,000
Paid-in Capital in Excess of Par: Preferred Stock		
(1,000,000 × $0.50)		500,000
Paid-in Capital: Stock Warrants (1,000,000 × $1) .		1,000,000
To record issuance of 1 million shares of $25 par		
preferred stock at $25½ and 1 million detachable		
stock warrants with market price of $1 each.		

---

[2]*APB Opinion No. 14,* "Accounting for Convertible Debt and Debt Issued with Stock Purchase Warrants," AICPA (New York: 1969), p. 209.

value because of the likelihood that the market price of the common stock would increase above $30 a share during the next 10 years. Assume also that immediately after issuance the warrants had a market price of $1 each and the preferred stock had a market price of $25.50 a share. The journal entry to record the proceeds of the preferred stock offering is shown on page 850.

The Paid-in Capital: Stock Warrants ledger account is included in the stockholders' equity section of the balance sheet with other types of additional paid-in capital. If the warrants are exercised and the common stock issued at $30 a share, the journal entry is as follows:

Journal entry for exercise of warrants for common stock

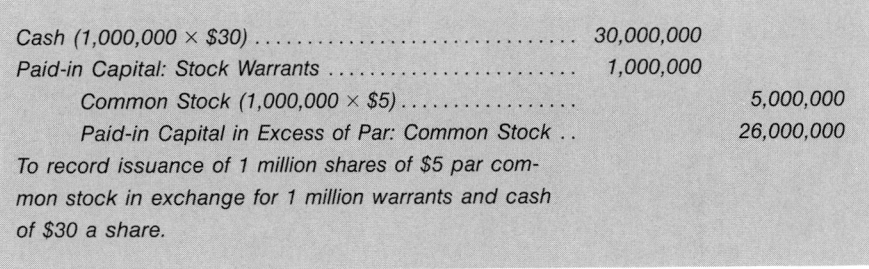

Cash (1,000,000 × $30)	30,000,000	
Paid-in Capital: Stock Warrants	1,000,000	
Common Stock (1,000,000 × $5)		5,000,000
Paid-in Capital in Excess of Par: Common Stock . .		26,000,000

To record issuance of 1 million shares of $5 par common stock in exchange for 1 million warrants and cash of $30 a share.

If a part of the detachable stock warrants is not exercised and expires, the balance of the Paid-in Capital: Stock Warrants ledger account remains a part of Meeker's paid-in capital.

CONVERTIBLE SECURITIES

Conversion of Bonds to Common Stock

As explained in Chapter 15, bonds that allow investors to exchange their bonds for common stock are known as *convertible bonds,* and this feature is called a *conversion option.* Inclusion of the conversion option makes bonds more attractive to investors and enables the issuer to obtain funds at an interest rate below the rate that would be paid on nonconvertible bonds. The conversion feature also may have the effect of providing for a gradual retirement of debt as the bondholders elect to exchange their bonds for common stock. Thus, by issuing convertible bonds, a corporation in effect issues common stock at a price substantially in excess of the market price of the common stock at the time the bonds are issued.

When convertible bonds are converted, the retirement of the debt and the issuance of common stock are recorded. To illustrate, assume that Skagg Corporation had outstanding $10,000,000 of 12% convertible bonds, carried in its accounting records at $10,400,000, including $400,000 unamortized bond premium. The bonds were convertible to $25 par common stock with a market price of $125 a share, at a *conversion ratio* of 10 shares of common stock for each $1,000 bond. Assume that Skagg called the bonds and that all bondholders presented their bonds for conversion.

In effect, Skagg has exchanged common stock with a total market value of $12,500,000 (10,000 × 10 × $125 = $12,500,000) for bonds payable with a carrying amount of $10,400,000. Two alternative methods have been suggested for accounting for the conversion—the *carrying amount method* (or *book value method*) and the *market value method.*

Carrying Amount (Book Value) Method   The carrying amount (book value) method of accounting for the conversion of convertible bonds is based on the view that on the issuance date of the convertible bonds, the proceeds received reflected the prospect that the bonds might be exchanged for common stock at some later time. Thus, the proceeds represented the market value of the bonds *and* the conversion option. When conversion takes place, *the carrying amount of the bonds measures the increase in paid-in capital from the issuance of common stock,* as illustrated in the following journal entry for Skagg Corporation:

Journal entry to record conversion of bonds—*carrying amount (book value) method*

12% Convertible Bonds Payable	10,000,000	
Premium on Bonds Payable	400,000	
Common Stock, $25 par (100,000 × $25)		2,500,000
Paid-in Capital in Excess of Par		7,900,000
To record conversion of bonds to 100,000 shares of common stock.		

Market Value Method   Adherents of the market value method of accounting for convertible bonds maintain that the issuance of common stock in the conversion of bonds should reflect the market value of the stock, just as issuances of common stock for cash or in nonmonetary transactions do. In their view, the issuance of common stock with a market value of $12,500,000 to liquidate long-term debt with a carrying amount of $10,400,000 results in a $2,100,000 loss ($12,500,000 − $10,400,000 = $2,100,000) to Skagg Corporation, in the same manner as though Skagg had issued the common stock for $12,500,000 cash and paid the cash to the holders of the convertible bonds to extinguish the debt. Under the market value method, Skagg would prepare the following journal entry:

Journal entry to record conversion of bonds—*market value method*

12% Convertible Bonds Payable	10,000,000	
Premium on Bonds Payable	400,000	
Loss on Conversion of Bonds Payable	2,100,000	
Common Stock, $25 par (100,000 × $25)		2,500,000
Paid-in Capital in Excess of Par (100,000 × $100) . .		10,000,000
To record conversion of bonds to 100,000 shares of common stock with a market price of $125 a share.		

Evaluation of the Two Methods   The carrying amount (book value) method of accounting for the conversion of convertible bonds appears to be more in accordance with generally accepted accounting principles than does the market value method. The latter method presumes that the current market price for the issuer's common stock is an appropriate measure of the value of the common stock issued in the conversion of bonds. However, this presumption disregards the fact that large blocks of stock often may not be traded at the market price for smaller lots. Further, the issuer has not entered the stock market when it issues common stock to bondholders; the entry into the market took place *when the bonds were issued.* To assign current market value of the common stock to the stock issued to bondholders implies that a *bargained exchange transaction* has taken place when none did.

When preferred stock or common stock is issued to extinguish convertible bonds in an *exchange offer* designed to improve the issuer's debt-to-equity ratio, a gain or loss always is recognized. Such exchanges are not made pursuant to the conversion option; thus, the current fair value of the securities issued measures the consideration paid to extinguish the bonds, and a gain or loss is recognized.

Induced Conversion of Convertible Bonds In order to reduce the cash outflow from interest payments or to improve its *debt ratio* (total liabilities divided by total assets), a corporation having outstanding convertible bonds may attempt to induce conversion of the bonds. One method would be to call the bonds at a time when the conversion ratio was favorable (that is, the market price of the corporation's common stock exceeded the conversion price). However, there is no assurance that *all* bondholders would respond to a call by converting their bonds to common stock; thus, the corporation might have to pay substantial amounts of cash for called bonds that were not converted. Thus, another method to induce conversion of convertible bonds is to "sweeten" the conversion feature by either reducing the conversion price or paying cash or other consideration to bondholders who convert.

In *FASB Statement No. 84,* the Financial Accounting Standards Board required recognition of an expense equal to the current fair value of consideration issued or paid by a corporation to induce conversion of convertible bonds.[3] (Alternative treatments of such consideration might have been as a loss on extinguishment of the bonds or as a reduction of paid-in capital attributable to the common stock issued for the bonds converted.) For example, assume that Lacey Company had 9% convertible bonds outstanding on May 31, Year 6, at face amount and carrying amount of $10 million, which were convertible to 200,000 shares of Lacey's $1 par common stock with a market price of $45 a share on May 31. Because the conversion price of $50 a share ($10,000,000 ÷ 200,000 = $50) exceeded the $45 market price of the common stock, Lacey "sweetened" the conversion feature by reducing the conversion price to $40 a share. Assuming all bondholders converted their bonds on May 31, Year 6, and disregarding bond issue costs, Lacey recognized bond conversion expense of $2,250,000, computed as follows:

Computation of bond conversion expense	*Market value of common stock issued in induced conversion* *{($10,000,000 ÷ $40) × $45}*..$11,250,000 *Less: Market value of common stock that would have been issued* *under original conversion price (200,000 × $45)*......................9,000,000 *Bond conversion expense*..$ 2,250,000

[3] *FASB Statement No. 84,* "Induced Conversions of Convertible Debt," FASB (Stamford: 1985), p. 2.

Lacey Company's journal entry on May 31, Year 6, for the induced conversion of the bonds is as follows:

9% Convertible Bonds Payable	10,000,000	
Bond Conversion Expense	2,250,000	
Common Stock (250,000 × $1)		250,000
Paid-in Capital in Excess of Par		12,000,000
To record induced conversion of 9% convertible bonds.		

The result of the foregoing journal entry (disregarding any income tax effect) is a *net* increase in Lacey Company stockholders' equity of $10,000,000 ($12,250,000 total paid-in capital less $2,250,000 bond conversion expense equals $10,000,000), which is equal to the carrying amount of the bonds converted.

Characteristics of Convertible Preferred Stock

Many preferred stocks are convertible to common stock at the option of the preferred stockholders. The appeal of convertible preferred stock lies in the fact that it combines certain attributes of both common stock and preferred stock in a single security. Because convertible preferred stock may be exchanged for common stock in a fixed ratio (the *conversion ratio*), it has the same appreciation potential as the related common stock. The status of convertible preferred stock as a *senior security* with a stated annual dividend rate gives it the same reduced risk inherent in nonconvertible preferred stock.

The conversion ratio is set when the convertible preferred stock is issued, but the ratio is subject to adjustment in the event a stock split or a stock dividend is distributed on the common stock. For example, assume that each share of Lansberry Corporation's $2 cumulative convertible preferred stock was convertible to 1½ shares of its common stock. When the common stock was split 3 for 1, the conversion ratio increased to 4½ (1½ × 3 = 4½) shares of common stock for each share of the convertible preferred stock.

Conversion of Preferred Stock to Common Stock

Investors who acquire convertible preferred stock are influenced by the possibility that conversion would be advantageous on some future date. Therefore, the proceeds received by the issuer for convertible preferred stock may be regarded as the appropriate amount of paid-in capital applicable to the common stock that investors receive on exercise of their conversion option, in accordance with the carrying amount (book value) method of accounting. Accordingly, when preferred stock conversions are recorded, any additional paid-in capital applicable to the preferred stock is eliminated by transfer to the paid-in capital ledger accounts representing the common stock being issued. Assume, for example, that Wilkie, Inc., had a $100 par preferred stock convertible at the option of the preferred stockholders to four shares of $10 par common stock. The preferred stock had been issued at a price of $105 a share, resulting in the following ledger account balances:

Ledger account balances related to convertible preferred stock

Convertible preferred stock, $100 par	$1,000,000
Paid-in capital in excess of par: preferred stock	50,000

If 100 shares of preferred stock are presented for conversion, the journal entry is as follows under the carrying amount (book value) method:

Journal entry to record conversion of preferred stock—*carrying amount (book value) method*

Convertible Preferred Stock (100 × $100)	10,000	
Paid-in Capital in Excess of Par: Preferred Stock (100 × $5)	500	
Common Stock (100 × 4 × $10)		4,000
Paid-in Capital in Excess of Par: Common Stock		6,500

To record issuance of 400 shares of $10 par common stock in exchange for 100 shares of $100 par convertible preferred stock.

In the rare situation in which the par or stated value of the common stock in a conversion transaction exceeds the par or stated value of the preferred stock being converted, a debit to the Retained Earnings ledger account would be necessary. Note, however, that the amount of retained earnings *is not increased* by a conversion of preferred stock to common stock.

EMPLOYEE CAPITAL ACCUMULATION PLANS

Stock option and stock purchase plans represent an important element of executive compensation. Collectively, plans such as employee stock ownership plans, stock appreciation rights plans, and comparable plans often are referred to as *employee capital accumulation plans* because they enable employees to obtain compensation in the form of common stock or cash, in addition to salaries and wages. The popularity of employee capital accumulation plans is evidenced by the fact that 527 companies of 600 surveyed by the American Institute of Certified Public Accountants had stock option plans.[4]

Stock Option and Stock Purchase Plans

A *stock option plan* gives officers and key employees of a corporation who are granted stock options the opportunity to acquire the corporation's common stock at the *exercise price* (or *option price*) in a specified time period. Thus, a stock option is in essence a *call* on the issuer's common stock at a fixed price over a period of years with no risk to the owner. The opportunity for gain is unlimited, and the chance of loss is zero. For example, assume that an executive of Wylie Corporation received an option on January 2, Year 3, to acquire 1,000 shares of Wylie's com-

[4]*Accounting Trends & Techniques,* 38th ed., AICPA (New York: 1984), p. 228.

mon stock at $20 a share (the current market price) at any time from January 2, Year 5 (the *vesting date*) until December 31, Year 12 (the *expiration date*). If, during the period the stock option is exercisable, the market price of Wylie's common stock increased to, for example, $70 a share, the executive could exercise the stock option and acquire for $20,000 (1,000 × $20 = $20,000) common stock with a market value of $70,000 (1,000 × $70 = $70,000). If Wylie split its common stock or issued a stock dividend during the term of the stock option, the exercise price and the number of shares under option would be adjusted accordingly, under an *antidilution* provision of the stock option plan. Thus, recipients of stock options are rewarded by increases in the market price of the issuer's common stock—a fact that is intended to motivate the recipients to remain in the issuer's employ and to be more productive.

A *stock purchase plan* is similar to a stock option plan, except that employees typically may elect to participate in such a plan by authorizing the corporation to deduct specified amounts from the employees' salaries or wages for use in acquiring the corporation's common stock (which may be treasury stock) at a price less than the market price of the stock. Thus, an employee may choose to participate or not to participate in a stock purchase plan; in contrast, the employer selects recipients of stock options under a stock option plan.

Income Tax Treatment of Stock Option and Purchase Plans

The Internal Revenue Code has long provided for favorable income tax treatment for stock option and stock purchase plans meeting specified requirements. Typically, recipients of *incentive stock options* (as defined in the Internal Revenue Code) do not have taxable income when they receive or exercise the options, and they may be taxed at the more favorable capital gain rate when they sell the stock acquired under the options. Similarly, an employee who sells common stock acquired under a stock purchase plan that meets requirements of the Internal Revenue Code may be taxed at the capital gain rate.

Theoretical Issues Involved in Stock Option Plans

From a theoretical viewpoint, the valuation of the compensation expense inherent in stock options is a difficult and challenging problem. In current practice, however, the problem of valuation of stock options generally is ignored, and the accounting procedures for the options are designed to comply with income tax rules. Because present income tax rules state that the receipt of stock options under an incentive stock option plan does not constitute income to the recipient, and that no compensation expense may be deducted by the issuer when the exercise price is equal to or in excess of the market price of the common stock, the difficult problem of determining the current fair value of stock options generally is avoided *by assuming that the options have no value.*

Although this treatment of stock options may be convenient for administration of the income tax laws, the current practice clearly has little theoretical support. Because stock options generally represent an important part of the total compensation cost of a corporation, it has been suggested that the options be valued at the amount for which options could be issued to the public at the time similar options are granted to employees. However, the framers of accounting standards have not found this line of reasoning persuasive because stock options are designed to give employees additional compensation and are not available for public issuance.

In the opinion of the authors, the current practice of not recording compensation expense for many stock option plans results in an understatement of compensation expense and paid-in capital, and a corresponding overstatement of net income and retained earnings. The basic accounting principle of matching costs with revenue suggests that the compensation expense implicit in stock option plans should be accrued throughout the term of the option. Such accruals would require the use of estimates (perhaps based on market prices of common stock from year to year). Thus, the two major accounting problems relating to stock option plans may be identified as (1) the measurement of any compensation cost implicit in stock options, and (2) the allocation of such compensation cost among accounting periods. The current generally accepted accounting principles addressing these two problems are found in *APB Opinion No. 25*, ''Accounting for Stock Issued to Employees.''[5]

APB Opinion No. 25, "Accounting for Stock Issued to Employees"

APB Opinion No. 25 provided a historical summary of the problems encountered in accounting for stock options and set forth the current accounting and disclosure requirements for stock option plans. Generally, such accounting and disclosure requirements depend essentially on whether the stock options are viewed as ***noncompensatory*** or ***compensatory***.

Noncompensatory Stock Option Plan   A stock option plan that is designed to raise capital or induce widespread ownership of the issuer's common stock among officers and employees is classified for financial accounting as a ***noncompensatory plan***. Essential characteristics of a noncompensatory plan listed in *APB Opinion No. 25* are (1) participation of all full-time employees; (2) offering of common stock on an equal basis or as a uniform percentage of salary to all employees; (3) a limited time for exercise of the option; and (4) a discount from market price no greater than would be reasonable in an offering of common stock to existing stockholders. In such noncompensatory plans, no compensation is presumed to be involved. Consequently, the issuer recognizes no compensation expense in its accounting records and claims no deduction for income tax purposes.

The exercise of noncompensatory stock options is recorded as is any issuance of common stock, as illustrated below for the issuance of 1,000 shares of $5 par common stock to employees at $40 a share:

Journal entry for exercise of noncompensatory stock options

Cash (1,000 × $40)	*40,000*	
Common Stock, $5 par (1,000 × $5)		*5,000*
Paid-in Capital in Excess of Par		*35,000*
To record issuance of 1,000 shares of common stock at $40		
a share pursuant to exercise of noncompensatory stock		
options by employees.		

[5]*APB Opinion No. 25*, ''Accounting for Stock Issued to Employees,'' AICPA (New York: 1972).

The noncompensatory type of stock option plan was summarized in *APB Opinion No. 25* to clear the way for consideration of the more controversial issues of accounting for compensatory stock option plans.

Compensatory Stock Option Plan   Any stock option plan not possessing the four specified characteristics of a noncompensatory plan is classified as a *compensatory plan* even though compensation cost may not be recognized. The features of a compensatory plan may vary in an almost endless number of respects. For example, the *grantee* (employee granted the stock option) may be obligated to continue in the employment of the issuer or of its subsidiaries. The number of shares of common stock specified in the stock option plan may be acquired at one time or in installments during each year of the plan's term. The consideration received by the issuer for common stock issued under a compensatory stock option plan may include cash, notes receivable, or other assets, as well as services from the employee. In compensatory plans, services from the grantee always represent part of the consideration for the common stock issued.

A key provision of *APB Opinion No. 25* is that compensation for services received as consideration for the stock options granted is measured by the difference (''*spread*'') between *the market price of the stock on the measurement date* (defined below) *and the amount that the employee is required to pay* (exercise price). In the application of this principle, determination of the measurement date for ascertaining compensation cost touches the theoretical core of the problem. The *measurement date* is the *first date on which are known both the number of shares of common stock to be received by each grantee and the exercise price.* On the measurement date the issuer of the stock options and the grantees presumably reach agreement as to the amount of total compensation to be paid, and the issuer forgoes any alternative uses of the common stock reserved for the exercise of the options. For most stock option plans, the measurement date is the date that the options are granted.

APB Opinion No. 25 required that an issuer should recognize compensation cost under compensatory stock option plans when the exercise price is less than the market price of the common stock on the measurement date. Because the exercise price in many stock option plans is set at or above the market price of the common stock on the date of grant, no compensation cost is recognized for such plans. When compensation cost is recognized, it should be allocated to the accounting periods subsequent to the adoption of a stock option plan that benefit from the services provided by the grantees. The following guidelines for accruing compensation cost under compensatory stock option plans are presented in *APB Opinion No. 25:*[6]

> Compensation cost in stock option, purchase, and award plans should be recognized as an expense of one or more periods in which an employee performs services and also as part or all of the consideration received for stock issued to the employee through a plan. The grant or award may specify the period or periods during which the employee performs services, or the period or periods

---

[6]Ibid., pp. 474–475.

may be inferred from the terms or from the past pattern of grants or awards. . . .

An employee may perform services in several periods before an employer corporation issues stock . . . for those services. The employer corporation should accrue compensation expense in each period in which the services are performed. If the measurement date is later than the date of grant or award, an employer corporation should record the compensation expense each period from date of grant or award to date of measurement based on the quoted market price of the stock at the end of each period.

If stock is issued in a plan before some or all of the services are performed, part of the consideration recorded for the stock issued is unearned compensation and should be shown as a separate reduction of stockholders' equity. The unearned compensation should be accounted for as expense of the period or periods in which the employee performs service.

Accruing compensation expense may require estimates, and adjustment of those estimates in later periods may be necessary. . . . For example, if a stock option is not exercised (or awarded stock is returned to the corporation) because an employee fails to fulfill an obligation, the estimate of compensation expense recorded in previous periods should be adjusted by decreasing compensation expense in the period of forfeiture.

The reporting of unearned (deferred) compensation cost as a reduction of stockholders' equity is appropriate because the entire recorded consideration relating to issuance of common stock has not been received. When the services are performed, the debit balance in the Deferred Compensation Cost ledger account is recognized as compensation expense.

Illustration of Compensatory Stock Option Plan: Measurement Date Is Grant Date; Exercise Price Equals Market Price   To illustrate the accounting for a compensatory stock option plan when the measurement date is the grant date, assume the following facts: On January 2, Year 1, Clark Corporation granted to key employees options to acquire 10,000 shares of its $10 par common stock at $20 a share in exchange for services to be performed over the next three years. The market price of the common stock on that date was $20 a share. The options were exercised on December 31, Year 3, when the market price of the common stock was $31 a share.

Although Clark Corporation's stock option plan is a compensatory one, no compensation cost is recognized because the exercise price is equal to the market

Journal entry for compensatory stock options: measurement date is grant date; exercise price equals market price	*Cash (10,000 × $20)* *200,000*	
	Common Stock (10,000 × $10)	*100,000*
	Paid-in Capital in Excess of Par	*100,000*
	To record issuance of 10,000 shares of common stock at $20 a share pursuant to compensatory stock option plan.	

price on the measurement date, which is January 2, Year 1, the grant date. Accordingly, the **only** journal entry prepared by Clark for its stock options is on December 31, Year 3, the **exercise date,** as shown at the bottom of page 859.

Thus, although Clark's employees received common stock with a market value of $310,000 (10,000 × $31 = $310,000) for cash of only $200,000, no compensation expense is recognized by Clark under the provisions of **APB Opinion No. 25.**

Illustration of Compensatory Stock Option Plan: Measurement Date Is Grant Date; Exercise Price Is Less Than Market Price Let us change the assumptions in the foregoing illustration to provide that the market price of Clark Corporation's common stock on January 2, Year 1, the measurement (and grant) date, was $23, rather than $20, a share. In such circumstances, the following journal entries are prepared by Clark (income tax effects are disregarded):

Journal entries for compensatory stock options: measurement date is grant date; exercise price less than market price

Year 1			
Jan. 2	Deferred Compensation Cost [10,000 × ($23 − $20)]	30,000	
	Common Stock Options		30,000
	To record compensatory stock options on grant date		
	to acquire 10,000 shares of common stock at $20 a		
	share. Market price of common stock is $23 a share.		
Dec. 31	Compensation Expense ($30,000 ÷ 3)	10,000	
	Deferred Compensation Cost		10,000
	To record compensation expense for Year 1.		
Year 2			
Dec. 31	Same journal entry as on Dec. 31, Year 1.		
Year 3			
Dec. 31	Same journal entry as on Dec. 31, Year 1.		
31	Cash (10,000 × $20)	200,000	
	Common Stock Options	30,000	
	Common Stock (10,000 × $10)		100,000
	Paid-in Capital in Excess of Par		130,000
	To record issuance of 10,000 shares of common		
	stock at $20 a share pursuant to compensatory		
	stock option plan.		

In the foregoing situation compensation expense of only $30,000 is recognized, despite the employees having received common stock with a market value of $110,000 ($310,000 − $200,000 = $110,000) in excess of the amount of cash they paid for the common stock.

The common stock options and deferred compensation cost are included in the additional paid-in capital section of the balance sheet on December 31, Year 1, as follows:

Balance sheet presentation of stock options and related deferred compensation

Common stock options.....................................	$30,000	
Less: Deferred compensation cost	20,000	$10,000

Illustration of Variable Compensatory Stock Option Plan: Measurement Date Is Two Years after Grant Date; Market Price Ultimately Exceeds Exercise Price

To illustrate the accounting for a *variable* compensatory stock option plan when the measurement date is *subsequent* to the grant date (because the exercise price and the number of shares of common stock that may be acquired by employees have not been determined), assume the following facts: On January 2, Year 1, Dome Corporation adopted a compensatory stock option plan for key employees to acquire an *estimated* 20,000 shares of $1 par common stock at an exercise price estimated at $20 a share. The market price of the common stock on January 2, Year 1, is $19 a share. Both the number of shares to be issued and the exercise price are to be determined on December 31, Year 2, the measurement date. The options were granted on January 2, Year 1, in consideration for services to be performed during Years 1 and 2, and may be exercised at any time starting on January 2, Year 3. The number of shares of common stock covered by the compensatory stock option plan, the exercise price, and the market price of the common stock on the relevant dates are as follows:

Data regarding compensatory stock option plan

	January 2, Year 1 (grant date)	December 31, Year 1	December 31, Year 2 (measurement date)
Number of shares optioned..................	20,000 (est.)	20,000 (est.)	21,000 (actual)
Exercise price..............	$20 (est.)	$20 (est.)	$22 (actual)
Market price of common stock	$19	$25	$33

No journal entry is required on January 2, Year 1, because the estimated exercise price exceeded the market price of the common stock and because the measurement date is December 31, Year 2. On December 31, Year 1, *estimated compensation expense and deferred compensation cost* are recorded as follows:

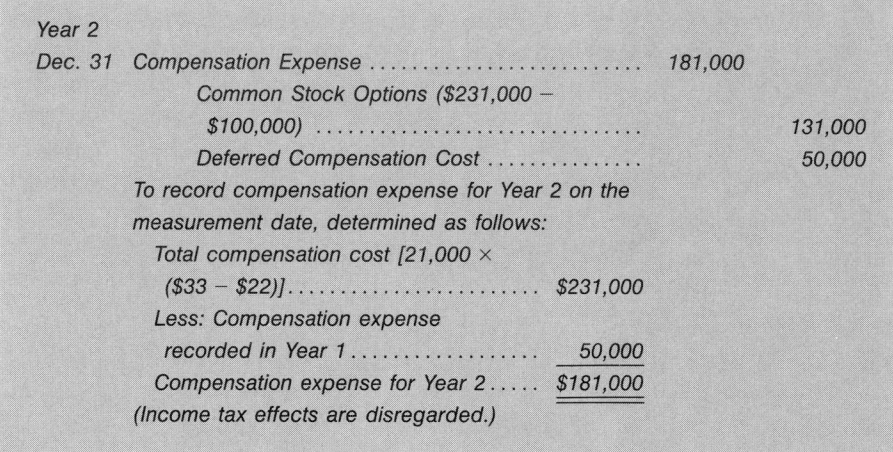

Journal entry for compensatory stock option plan prior to measurement date (which is later than grant date)

```
Year 1
Dec. 31  Compensation Expense ($100,000 ÷ 2) ...........      50,000
         Deferred Compensation Cost .....................      50,000
             Common Stock Options [20,000 ×
             ($25 − $20)] .............................                    100,000
         To record estimated compensation expense for Year
         1 based on market price of common stock, estimated
         number of shares optioned, and estimated exercise
         price. (Income tax effects are disregarded.)
```

On the measurement date, December 31, Year 2, the journal entry below is prepared:

Journal entry for compensatory stock option plan on measurement date (which is later than grant date)

```
Year 2
Dec. 31  Compensation Expense ........................     181,000
             Common Stock Options ($231,000 −
             $100,000) .............................                    131,000
             Deferred Compensation Cost ..............                   50,000
         To record compensation expense for Year 2 on the
         measurement date, determined as follows:
             Total compensation cost [21,000 ×
             ($33 − $22)].......................   $231,000
             Less: Compensation expense
             recorded in Year 1.................      50,000
             Compensation expense for Year 2 .....  $181,000
         (Income tax effects are disregarded.)
```

In the foregoing situation, total compensation cost of $231,000 is measured by the difference between the market price of the common stock under option, $693,000 (21,000 × $33 = $693,000) and the total exercise price to be paid by employees, $462,000 (21,000 × $22 = $462,000), or $231,000 ($693,000 − $462,000 = $231,000). Thus, accounting standards for stock option plans provide for differing measurements of compensation cost, depending on whether the measurement is *on,* or *subsequent to,* the grant date.

At the time the stock options are exercised by Dome Corporation's employees, a journal entry similar to the last entry illustrated on page 860 is prepared by Dome.

When compensation expense under stock option plans is reported by the issuer in an accounting period other than that in which the expense is deductible for income tax purposes, a *timing difference* results that requires the application of interperiod income tax allocation procedures. This topic is covered in Chapter 21.

If grantees should terminate before performing the services required for exercise of the stock options, the appropriate portions of common stock options and deferred compensation cost must be written off. For example, if on January 2, Year

2, grantees of 1,000 of Dome Corporation's common stock options terminated their employment and thus did not perform required services during Year 2, Dome would prepare the following journal entry on January 2, Year 2:

Journal entry for
write-off of stock options
of terminated grantees

Common Stock Options ($100,000 × $\frac{1}{20}$)   5,000
    Deferred Compensation Cost ($50,000 × $\frac{1}{20}$)   2,500
    Compensation Expense ($50,000 × $\frac{1}{20}$)   2,500
*To write off common stock options, deferred compensation
cost, and Year 1 compensation expense applicable to grantees of 1,000 stock options who terminated their employment
before completing the service period required for the options.
(Income tax effects are disregarded.)*

The foregoing journal entry reduces compensation expense for Year 2 by the amount of compensation expense of Year 1 attributable to the terminated grantees.

Also, a decline in the market price of the issuer's common stock may require a credit to Compensation Expense. For example, *if the market value of Dome Corporation's common stock had been $24 a share instead of $33 a share on December 31, Year 2,* Dome would prepare the following journal entry on December 31, Year 2:

Journal entry for
reduction of
compensation
expense related
to stock options

Common Stock Options {$100,000 − [21,000 × ($24 − $22)]} . . .   58,000
    Deferred Compensation Cost   50,000
    Compensation Expense   8,000
*To record reduction of compensation expense for Year 2
on the measurement date, determined as follows:*
  Total compensation cost 21,000 × ($24 − $22) $42,000
  Less: Compensation expense recorded in Year 1 . . .   <u>50,000</u>
  Reduction of compensation expense for Year 2 . . . .   <u>($ 8,000)</u>
(Income tax effects are disregarded.)

Journal Entries for Stock Purchase Plans   The accounting for compensation cost associated with stock purchase plans is similar to that for stock option plans. However, many stock purchase plans provide for withholding from employees' salaries or wages to accumulate the total purchase price. A liability ledger account is credited for such withholdings in the journal entries for payroll; when common stock is issued under the stock purchase plan, the liability account (rather than Cash) is debited.

Accounting for Stock Appreciation Rights

In recent years, a modification of stock options known as stock appreciation rights has become popular. *Stock appreciation rights* are awards entitling employees to receive cash, common stock, or a combination of cash and common stock in an amount equivalent to any excess of the market value of a stated number of shares of the issuer's common stock over a stated price.[7] Although stock appreciation rights may be granted separately, they typically are granted in conjunction with stock options, in a *tandem* (or *variable*) *plan.* Stock option plans that include stock appreciation rights typically provide that the stock options are forfeited if the stock appreciation rights are exercised, and vice versa. The following discussion of such plans is adapted from *FASB Interpretation No. 28,* ''Accounting for Stock Appreciation Rights . . .''

Compensation expense for a stock option plan that includes stock appreciation rights usually is measured under the presumption that grantees will exercise the stock appreciation rights, which require no cash payment, rather than the stock option, which requires a cash payment. The compensation element of stock appreciation rights is measured by the excess of the market price of the common stock over the exercise price. Changes in the market price of the common stock during the period from the grant date to the measurement date (which always is the exercise date) require changes in the measurement of compensation expense. The measurement date for stock appreciation rights is the date the rights are exercised because the number of shares of common stock to be issued is indeterminable until the exercise date. The compensation expense is accrued proportionately for each accounting period during which the grantees perform services required by the stock option plan. If no service period is specified, the vesting period is used to recognize compensation expense. Typically, the *vesting period* runs from the grant date to the date the stock options or stock appreciation rights become exercisable.

Compensation expense accrued in one accounting period is increased or decreased in subsequent periods for changes in the market price of the common stock, but it is never reduced below zero. If grantees elect to exercise the stock option rather than the stock appreciation rights, the compensation expense previously recognized for the stock appreciation rights becomes part of the paid-in capital for the common stock issued.

Illustration of Accounting for Stock Appreciation Rights   Under a tandem stock option plan that had been approved by its stockholders, Winfield Corporation granted stock options with stock appreciation rights to its employees on January 2, Year 1. The options were to expire on December 31, Year 10, cover 10,000 shares of Winfield's $1 par common stock, and were exercisable beginning January 2, Year 4. No service period was specified for the grantees; therefore, *the vesting period is three years and the measurement date is not known until grantees exercise the options.* The exercise price was $15 a share, which was equal to the market price of Winfield's common stock on January 2, Year 1. The per-share market prices of Winfield's common stock were as shown at the top of page 865.

On January 2, Year 4, grantees exercised *stock appreciation rights* for 7,000 of the 10,000 shares of common stock covered by the stock option plan, as follows:

(1) Grantees of options for 4,000 shares elected to receive cash.

---

[7]*FASB Interpretation No. 28,* ''Accounting for Stock Appreciation Rights and Other Variable Stock Option or Award Plans,'' FASB (Stamford: 1978), p. 7.

Jan. 2, Year 1	$15
Dec. 31, Year 1	18
Dec. 31, Year 2	21
Dec. 31, Year 3, and Jan. 2, Year 4	25

(2) Grantees of options for 3,000 shares elected to receive 1,200 shares of Winfield's common stock in lieu of cash.

Thus, the measurement date for 7,000 (4,000 + 3,000 = 7,000) shares covered by the stock option plan was January 2, Year 4. The measurement date for the remaining 3,000 shares under option (10,000 − 7,000 = 3,000) remains unknown until grantees of those options exercise either the stock appreciation rights or the stock options of Winfield's *tandem plan.* Because of the existence of the two alternatives, the measurement date for tandem plans must be the exercise date.

The following journal entries are prepared for Winfield Corporation's stock option plan, under the assumptions that grantees will elect the stock appreciation rights alternative, that the vesting period is three years (January 2, Year 1, to January 2, Year 4), and that income tax effects are disregarded:

Journal entries for stock appreciation rights

Year 1			
Dec. 31	Compensation Expense	10,000	
	Compensation Payable		10,000
	To record compensation expense under stock option		
	plan for Year 1, determined as follows:		
	Total compensation cost [10,000 ×		
	($18 − $15)] $30,000		
	Portion vested on Dec. 31, Year 1 .... ⅓		
	Compensation expense for Year 1 .... $10,000		

Year 2			
Dec. 31	Compensation Expense	30,000	
	Compensation Payable		30,000
	To record compensation expense under stock option		
	plan for Year 2, determined as follows:		
	Total compensation cost [10,000 ×		
	($21 − $15) $60,000		
	Portion vested on Dec. 31, Year 2 ...... ⅔		
	Accrued compensation cost, Dec. 31,		
	Year 2 .... $40,000		
	Less: Compensation expense for Year 1 . 10,000		
	Compensation expense for Year 2 .... $30,000		

Year 3

Dec. 31 Compensation Expense 60,000
    Compensation Payable   60,000
  To record compensation expense under stock option
  plan for Year 3, determined as follows:
   Total compensation cost [10,000 ×
    ($25 − $15)] $100,000
   Portion vested on Dec. 31, Year 3 .....   ³⁄₃

   Accrued compensation cost, Dec. 31,
    Year 3 .... $100,000
   Less: Compensation expense for Year
    1 and Year 2 ($10,000 + $30,000)   40,000
   Compensation expense for Year 3 ..... $ 60,000

Year 4

Jan. 2 Compensation Payable ($100,000 × 0.70) 70,000
   Cash   40,000
   Common Stock (1,200 × $1)   1,200
   Paid-in Capital in Excess of Par (1,200 × $24)   28,800
  To record exercise of stock appreciation rights as
  follows:
   Cash [4,000 × ($25 − $15)] $40,000
   Common stock $\left[\dfrac{3,000 \times (\$25 - \$15)}{\$25}\right]$ .. *1,200 sh*

Note that a Compensation Payable liability ledger account is credited in the foregoing journal entries that debit Compensation Expense because until employees exercise the stock appreciation rights, there is uncertainty as to how much cash will be paid and how many shares, if any, of common stock will be issued.

For Year 4 through Year 10, or until all the stock appreciation rights are exercised, Winfield Corporation must debit or credit the Compensation Payable ledger account for the effects of annual changes in the market price of Winfield's common stock, because the stock appreciation rights were fully vested on January 2, Year 4. The offsetting credit or debit is to the Compensation Expense ledger account. However, total compensation expense is not reduced below zero. Accrued compensation applicable to any options that expire on December 31, Year 10, would be written off by a debit to Compensation Payable and a credit to Compensation Expense.

The accounting for stock appreciation rights of Winfield Corporation resulted in total compensation expense of $100,000 for Year 1 through Year 3. Note that, had Winfield accounted for the tandem stock option plan under the assumption that this was a stock option plan *only,* Winfield would have recorded *no compensation expense* for Year 1 through Year 3. This outcome results because the measurement date for the stock options is January 2, Year 1 (the number of shares under option and the exercise price being known on that date), and there is no difference between the exercise price and the market price of Winfield's common stock on January 2, Year 1. This significant difference in the computation of compensation cost for a tandem stock option plan is troublesome for accountants because benefits to grantees are essentially the same under a straight stock option plan as under a tandem plan that includes stock appreciation rights.

Accounting for Stock Options Involving Junior Stock

Recently, some stock option and stock purchase plans have involved *junior stock,* which is a specific type of capital stock issued to employees that is subordinate to the issuer's common stock in terms of voting, liquidation, and dividend rights and is convertible to common stock of the issuer if certain performance goals are achieved or if certain transactions occur.[8] Thus, the measurement date for stock option and purchase plans involving junior stock generally is later than the grant date because the attainment of the performance goals or the occurrence of the specified transactions is after the grant date. The following discussion of stock option plans involving junior stock is adapted from *FASB Interpretation No. 38,* "Determining the Measurement Date for . . . Plans Involving Junior Stock."

The *measurement date for plans involving junior stock is the same as for stock option plans with variable terms,* that is, the first date on which are known both the number of shares of the issuer's common stock to be issued in exchange for the junior stock and the exercise price, if any. Compensation cost for junior stock is accrued by the issuer only if it becomes *probable* that the required performance goals will be achieved or the specified transactions will occur. The compensation cost, which is the difference between the market price of the issuer's common stock on the measurement date and the amount the employee paid or will pay for the junior stock, *is accrued between the date that attainment of the requirements for conversion of the junior stock to common stock becomes probable and the measurement date.* If junior stock may not be converted to common stock until *after* the measurement date, the period for accrual of compensation cost ends on the date the junior stock first becomes convertible or the end of the employee's required service period, whichever occurs first. The procedure for measuring compensation expense for each accounting period during the term of accrual of compensation cost is the same as for stock appreciation rights, as discussed in the preceding section.

Illustration of Accounting for Junior Stock   On January 2, Year 1, under a plan approved by stockholders, Rebo Corporation issued to key employees stock options involving 10,000 shares of junior stock that was convertible in a 1 to 1 ratio to 10,000 shares of Rebo's $1 par common stock, starting on January 2, Year 5, if the employees remained with Rebo through that date and if the amount of Rebo's earnings per share for Year 4 was at least $2 a share more than Year 1 earnings per share. The employees paid Rebo $5 a share for the junior stock. Not until December 31, Year 2, did Rebo management judge that it was *probable* that Year 4 earnings

---

[8]*FASB Interpretation No. 38,* "Determining the Measurement Date for Stock Option, Purchase, and Award Plans Involving Junior Stock," FASB (Stamford: 1984), p. 1.

per share would be at least $2 a share more than the $3.18 earnings per share for Year 1. Market prices per share of Rebo's common stock were as follows:

Jan. 2, Year 1	$ 8
Dec. 31, Year 1	11
Dec. 31, Year 2	14
Dec. 31, Year 3	17
Dec. 31, Year 4	20
Dec. 31, Year 5	21

On December 31, Year 4, it was *certain* that Year 4 earnings per share would exceed $5.18; thus, December 31, Year 4, was the measurement date.

Following are journal entries (disregarding income tax effects) for Rebo Corporation for the junior stock:

Journal entries for stock options involving junior stock

Year 1

Jan. 2   Cash (10,000 × $5) 50,000

  Junior Stock Issued 50,000

To record issuance of 10,000 shares of junior stock to employees.

Year 2

Dec. 31   Compensation Expense 30,000

  Compensation Payable 30,000

To record compensation expense under stock option plan involving junior stock as follows:

Total compensation cost [10,000 × ($14 − $5)]	$90,000
Portion vested on Dec. 31, Year 2	⅓
Compensation expense for Year 2	$30,000

Year 3

Dec. 31   Compensation Expense 50,000

  Compensation Payable 50,000

To record compensation expense under stock option plan involving junior stock as follows:

Total compensation cost [10,000 × ($17 − $5)]	$120,000
Portion vested on Dec. 31, Year 3	⅔
Accrued compensation cost, Dec. 31, Year 3	$ 80,000
Less: Compensation expense for Year 2	30,000
Compensation expense for Year 3	$ 50,000

Year 4

Dec. 31	Compensation Expense	70,000	
	Compensation Payable		70,000

To record compensation expense under stock option plan
involving junior stock as follows:

Total compensation cost [10,000 ×		
($20 − $5)]	$150,000	
Portion vested on Dec. 31, Year 4..........	³/₃	
Accrued compensation cost, Dec. 31,		
Year 4..................................	$150,000	
Less: Compensation expense for Year 2		
and Year 3.............................	80,000	
Compensation expense for Year 4..........	$ 70,000	

Year 5

Jan. 2	Compensation Payable	150,000	
	Junior Stock Issued	50,000	
	Common Stock (10,000 × $1)		10,000
	Paid-in Capital in Excess of Par		190,000

To record conversion of 10,000 shares of junior stock
to 10,000 shares of common stock.

The following aspects of the foregoing journal entries should be noted:

1   The Junior Stock Issued ledger account is credited for the $50,000 paid by employees for the junior stock because such stock is not the conventional common stock of a corporation. Until the junior stock is converted to common stock, the paid-in capital ledger accounts applicable to common stock are not affected.

2   There is no journal entry for compensation expense on December 31, Year 1, because Rebo Corporation's management had not determined on that date that attainment of the required Year 4 earnings per share in the amount of $5.18 ($3.18 + $2.00 = $5.18) was *probable.*

3   Once attainment of the required Year 4 earnings per share of $5.18 had been determined to be probable, on December 31, Year 2, Rebo begins accruing compensation cost over the remaining three-year period of employee service.

4   Total consideration for the common stock issued on January 2, Year 5, is $200,000, the $50,000 paid by employees for the junior stock plus the $150,000 compensation measured and recognized in Year 2 through Year 4.

If junior stock does not become convertible to common stock, and the issuer pays cash to employees to reacquire the junior stock from them, total compensation cost is measured by the difference between the cash paid to employees and the amount employees paid for the junior stock.

Accounting for Employee Stock Ownership Plans (ESOP)

Closely related to stock option plans described in the preceding pages are employee stock ownership plans (ESOP). Such plans may be established under the provisions of the Employee Retirement Income Security Act (ERISA) of 1974. An employee stock ownership plan is a *qualified* stock bonus plan designed to invest primarily in the common stock of the corporation sponsoring such a plan for its employees.[9] An ESOP acquires common stock of the employer, either directly from the employer (as periodic contributions) or by using borrowed funds. Subsequently, the ESOP distributes the employer's common stock to employees in accordance with a predetermined formula that may be based on years of service, attainment of a stated age, retirement, etc. The debt of an ESOP usually is collateralized by a pledge of the employer's common stock owned by the ESOP and by either a guarantee by the employer or a commitment by the employer to make periodic contributions to the ESOP. The periodic contributions are deductible expenses in the computation of the employer's taxable income.

In the accounting records of the employer, the periodic contributions to the ESOP are recognized as *compensation expense,* and any debt of the ESOP guaranteed by the employer is reported as a liability in the balance sheet of the employer. However, assets of the ESOP are not included in the balance sheet of the employer because such assets are owned by employees, not by the employer. When the liability for the guarantee of the debt of the ESOP is recorded by the employer, the offsetting debit is recorded in the Deferred Compensation Cost ledger account. This account is reported as a deduction from stockholders' equity (similar to the treatment of deferred compensation cost recognized under stock option plans). When the ESOP reduces the debt guaranteed by the employer (presumably using cash contributions from the employer), both the liability and the deferred compensation cost are reduced. The American Institute of Certified Public Accountants summarized these accounting requirements as follows:[10]

> . . . the offsetting debit to the liability recorded by the employer should be accounted for as a reduction of shareholders' equity. Therefore, when new shares are issued to the ESOP by the employer, an increase in shareholders' equity should be reported only as the debt that financed that increase is reduced. . . . When outstanding shares, as opposed to unissued shares, are acquired by the ESOP, shareholders' equity should similarly be reduced by the offsetting debit until the debt is repaid. . . . The liability is initially recorded because the guarantee or commitment is in substance the employer's debt. Therefore, it should not be reduced until payments are actually made. Similarly, the amount reported as a reduction of shareholders' equity should be reduced only when the ESOP makes payment on the debt. These two accounts should move symmetrically.

The amount recognized as expense by the employer is the amount (cash or current fair value of common stock) contributed to the ESOP. In the computation of

---

[9]*Employee Retirement Income Security Act of 1974,* Title II, Subtitle B, Sec. 2003.
[10]*Statement of Position No. 76-3,* "Accounting Practices for Certain Employee Stock Ownership Plans," AICPA (New York: 1976), pp. 3–4.

earnings per share, the employer treats all shares of its common stock owned by the ESOP as issued and outstanding.[11]

Illustration of Accounting for ESOP   On January 2, Year 4, Tilbury Corporation established an employee stock ownership plan, contributing $50,000 cash and 100,000 shares of no-par common stock (stated value $5 a share) with a current fair value of $12 a share. On March 31, Year 4, the ESOP borrowed $250,000 from a bank on a 12%, two-year promissory note indorsed by Tilbury. On April 3, Year 4, the ESOP acquired 10,000 shares of Tilbury's common stock from Tilbury at $13 a share. On December 31, Year 4, Tilbury contributed $122,500 to the ESOP, which immediately paid $100,000 principal and $22,500 interest ($250,000 × 0.12 × $^9/_{12}$ = $22,500) on the promissory note.

Tilbury Corporation's journal entries for the foregoing transactions are as follows:

Journal entries for ESOP

Year 4

Jan. 2   Compensation Expense ($50,000 + $1,200,000) ...   1,250,000
  Cash   50,000
  Common Stock, no par (100,000 × $5)   500,000
  Paid-in Capital in Excess of Stated Value
  [100,000 × ($12 − $5)]   700,000
  To record contribution of cash and common stock to ESOP.

Mar. 31   Deferred Compensation Cost   250,000
  Indorsed Note Payable of ESOP   250,000
  To record liability for indorsed promissory note payable of ESOP.

Apr. 3   Cash (10,000 × $13)   130,000
  Common Stock, no par (10,000 × $5)   50,000
  Paid-in Capital in Excess of Stated Value ...   80,000
  To record issuance of common stock to ESOP.

Dec. 31   Compensation Expense   122,500
  Cash   122,500
  To record contribution of cash to ESOP.

31   Indorsed Note Payable of ESOP   100,000
  Deferred Compensation Cost   100,000
  To record reduction of liability and deferred compensation cost resulting from ESOP's payment on indorsed promissory note.

---

[11]Ibid., p. 5.

In Tilbury Corporation's December 31, Year 4, balance sheet, the $150,000 balance ($250,000 − $100,000 = $150,000) of the Deferred Compensation Cost ledger account is deducted from total paid-in capital to compute total stockholders' equity.

Disclosure of Employee Capital Accumulation Plans

Because of their significance to a business enterprise, employee capital accumulation plans are disclosed in a note to the financial statements. The disclosure may be extensive, especially if there are several such plans in effect. An important feature of the disclosure is the number of shares of authorized but unissued common stock that are reserved for exercise of stock options and for employee stock purchase plans.

An example of disclosure of employee capital accumulation plans is on pages 231–232 of Chapter 4.

Stockholders' Equity in the Balance Sheet

The balance sheet presentation of stockholders' equity is illustrated below for Database Company:

Stockholders' equity section of balance sheet

DATABASE COMPANY
Stockholders' Equity Section of Balance Sheet
December 31, Year 8

$4 convertible, cumulative preferred stock, $100 par, callable at		
$106 a share, authorized, issued, and outstanding 100,000 shares .		$10,000,000
Common stock, $2.50 par, authorized 2,000,000 shares, issued and		
outstanding 1,000,000 shares.....................................		2,500,000
Additional paid-in capital:		
On common stock..		5,000,000
Common stock options...............................	$420,000	
Less: Deferred compensation cost	250,000	170,000
Stock warrants		500,000
Total paid-in capital...		$18,170,000
Retained earnings		4,100,000
Total stockholders' equity		$22,270,000

Note that this illustration discloses the following information:

1   Par or stated value of each class of capital stock issued and outstanding

2   Dividend preference and call price of the convertible cumulative preferred stock (conversion terms of preferred stock would be described in a note to the financial statements)

3   Number of shares authorized, issued, and outstanding for each class of capital stock

4   Additional paid-in capital from various sources

5   Total amount of paid-in capital, retained earnings, deferred compensation cost as a deduction from the value assigned to common stock options, and the total amount of stockholders' equity

In balance sheets of large business enterprises, the need for concise presentation may require some of the information concerning paid-in capital to be disclosed in a note to the financial statements rather than in the balance sheet. For example, the information concerning preferred stock preferences, conversion ratios, and sources of additional paid-in capital, may be disclosed thus. In addition, the number of shares of authorized but unissued common stock reserved for conversion of convertible bonds and preferred stock and for employee capital accumulation plans is disclosed in a note to the financial statements.

Pro Forma Financial Statements

When significant new financial changes are in prospect for a business enterprise, accountants may be asked to prepare financial statements that give effect to the planned transactions. Such statements are called *pro forma financial statements.* For example, when two or more companies are planning a business combination, the stockholders and management of each company will want pro forma financial statements for the combined enterprise to facilitate analysis of the financial position and earnings of the combined enterprise.

Another use for pro forma financial statements arises when a purchase-type business combination of two companies occurs *during* the current year. A pro forma income statement for a full year may be prepared to show the operating results that *would have* resulted for the entire year *if* the combination had taken place at the beginning of the current year.

Pro forma financial statements also are useful in situations other than business combinations. For example, a business enterprise might be considering the issuance of preferred stock to obtain cash with which to call bonds outstanding. In weighing the merits of this action, management will need a pro forma balance sheet to show the financial position of the enterprise as it would have appeared if these transactions had been carried out. Because the substitution of preferred stock for bonds would eliminate interest expense and have a bearing on taxable income, it also is desirable to prepare a pro forma income statement showing how the net income and earnings per share of the past year would have been modified if the changes in the capital structure had been in effect.

Other potential uses of pro forma financial statements are in connection with the contemplated disposal of a business segment and the change in a business enterprise from a partnership to a corporation.

In Rule 11-01 of *Regulation S-X,* the Securities and Exchange Commission prescribed the form and content of pro forma financial information to be filed with the Commission by companies subject to its jurisdiction in circumstances such as those described in the preceding paragraphs. Among the SEC's requirements are the following:

1   An introductory paragraph that describes the proposed transactions, the entities involved, the periods covered by the pro forma information, and what the pro forma information shows.

2   A pro forma condensed balance sheet, pro forma condensed income statements, and accompanying explanatory notes. The pro forma financial statements are in columnar form showing condensed historical amounts, pro forma adjustments, and the pro forma amounts.

3   Pro forma adjustments that are directly attributable to the proposed transaction, expected to have a continuing impact, and factually supportable.

REVIEW QUESTIONS

1   How are outstanding common stock warrants presented in the financial statements of a business enterprise?

2   What are *contingent stock warrants* issued to customers of a business enterprise?

3   Dane Corporation issued warrants to the holders of its 600,000 shares of common stock on November 30, Year 4, entitling them to acquire one convertible $1,000 bond at face amount for each 100 shares of common stock owned. The warrants expired on January 28, Year 5. On December 31, Year 4, bonds in the face amount of $2,500,000 had been issued through the exercise of warrants. What disclosure is made of these events in Dane Corporation's balance sheet on December 31, Year 4, or in a note to the financial statements?

4   Is the *preemptive right* that is inherent in common stock ownership logically applicable only to additional issuances of common stock, or should it also apply to additional issuances of convertible bonds and convertible preferred stock? Explain.

5   If common stock warrants are assigned a value at the time of issuance, what accounting is necessary if the warrants are not exercised and expire?

6   How are owners of convertible preferred stock or convertible bonds protected from the dilutive effects of stock dividends and stock splits on the issuer's common stock?

7   What treatment is given to the current fair value of common stock issued in exchange for convertible bonds? Explain.

8   What are the two major accounting problems relating to stock option plans?

9   Moore Corporation issued five-year stock options to its key executives on May 21, Year 6, at 100% of the market price of the common stock on that date. State arguments for and against recognizing compensation expense corresponding to the estimated current fair value of these options.

10   What are the major differences between a *compensatory stock option plan* and a *noncompensatory plan?* Does the issuer recognize compensation expense applicable to either?

11 What date does *APB Opinion No. 25,* ''Accounting for Stock Issued to Employees,'' stipulate for use in the measurement of compensation for employee services relating to stock option plans? How is the amount of compensation cost measured?

12 What are *stock appreciation rights?* How are they related to stock option plans?

13 What is the *vesting period* for stock appreciation rights?

14 Is a journal entry required when *junior stock* is issued to employees in connection with a stock option plan? Explain.

15 Define an *employee stock ownership plan* (ESOP) and briefly describe the accounting requirements for the employer relating to such a plan.

16 Define *pro forma financial statements* and state some examples of circumstances in which pro forma financial statements may be prepared.

EXERCISES

Ex. 17-1 Select the best answer for each of the following multiple-choice questions:

1 Compensation cost under a compensatory stock option plan for which the measurement date is the grant date is recognized in the issuer's income statement:
a On the date grantees of the stock options retire
b Of each accounting period subsequent to the adoption of the plan in which grantees of the stock options are required to render services
c On the exercise date
d On the date the stock option plan is adopted

2 Under a compensatory stock option plan for which the measurement date is the grant date, what ledger account is credited on the measurement date?
a Retained Earnings
b Common Stock Options
c Deferred Compensation Cost
d Compensation Expense
e None of the foregoing

3 A company's granting to its shareholders of the opportunity to acquire additional shares of common stock at a specified price during a specified time period is an example of a:
a Dividend reinvestment plan
b Stock right
c Stock dividend
d Stock option
e Contingent stock warrant

4 If the common stock for a compensatory stock option plan is issued before some or all of the services are performed by the grantee employees, a part of the consideration recorded for the stock issued is unearned compensation and is shown in the balance sheet as a line item in:

a Noncurrent liabilities

b Stockholders' equity

c Current assets

d Noncurrent assets

e Some other classification

5   A company issued to its shareholders warrants for rights to acquire for $25 a share 50,000 unissued shares of $10 par common stock. The Paid-in Capital in Excess of Par ledger account is credited when the warrants:

a Are issued

b Expire

c Become exercisable

d Are exercised

6   Stock appreciation rights are a modification of stock option plans that permit employees to receive:

a Cash only

b Common stock only

c A combination of cash and common stock

d Any of the foregoing

7   If the par or stated value of common stock issued in a conversion transaction exceeds the par or stated value of the converted preferred stock, the excess is debited to:

a Loss on Conversion of Preferred Stock

b Paid-in Capital in Excess of Par: Common Stock

c Retained Earnings

d Conversion Expense

8   When convertible bonds are converted to common stock, the journal entry to record the conversion under the market value method includes the effect of:

a The market value of the bonds but not of the common stock

b The market value of the common stock but not of the bonds

c The market values of both the bonds and the common stock

d The market value of either the bonds or the common stock

9   On September 1, Year 3, Oak Company issued 100,000 shares of 12%, $100 par preferred stock together with 100,000 warrants to acquire one share of Oak's $10 par common stock for one warrant plus $20 cash. The warrants had an aggregate market value of $400,000 on September 1, Year 3. Oak records the exercise of 20,000 warrants on September 29, Year 3, with the following journal entry (explanation omitted):

a Cash...	400,000	
Paid-in Capital: Stock Warrants	80,000	
Common Stock		200,000
Paid-in Capital in Excess of Par: Common Stock		280,000

b *Cash*	*400,000*		
Common Stock		*200,000*	
Paid-in Capital in Excess of Par: Common Stock		*200,000*	
c *Cash*	*400,000*		
Paid-in Capital: Stock Warrants		*80,000*	
Common Stock		*200,000*	
Paid-in Capital in Excess of Par: Common Stock		*120,000*	
d *Cash*	*400,000*		
Common Stock Warrants	*400,000*		
Common Stock		*200,000*	
Paid-in Capital in Excess of Par: Common Stock		*600,000*	

Ex. 17-2 The $10 par common stock of Hull Corporation presently is trading at $30 a share. Hull has 10 million authorized shares of common stock, of which 4 million are issued and outstanding. Because of a need for additional capital, Hull issued to its common stockholders stock warrants for rights permitting the acquisition of one new share of common stock in exchange for five warrants and $28 cash. The warrants expire 30 days after the date of issuance.

a Prepare a journal entry, if any, for Hull Corporation to record the issuance of the stock warrants.

b Assuming that all the stock warrants were exercised, prepare a journal entry for Hull Corporation to record the exercise of the stock warrants.

c Assuming that only 80% of the stock warrants were exercised before the expiration date, prepare the required journal entry or entries for Hull Corporation.

Ex. 17-3 On January 2, Year 6, Tandy Company issued contingent stock warrants to a major customer, Hurley Company. The warrants were to be excercisable at $18 a share for 5,000 shares of Tandy's $5 par common stock during the month of January, Year 8, if Hurley's purchases of Tandy's products totaled $250,000 for Year 6 and Year 7 combined. On December 31, Year 6, Tandy considered it probable that Hurley would make purchases sufficient to earn the warrants. Hurley's purchases from Tandy totaled $285,000 for the two years ended December 31, Year 7; market prices per share of Tandy's common stock were as follows:

Jan. 2, Year 6 (actual)	*$16*
Dec. 31, Year 7 (estimated on Dec. 31, Year 6)	*19*
Dec. 31, Year 7 (actual)	*21*

Compute Tandy Company's increase in cost of goods sold for Year 6 and Year 7, with respect to the contingent stock warrants.

Ex. 17-4 Burk Corporation issued for $8,250,000, 150,000 shares of $50 par preferred stock, together with detachable stock warrants entitling the holders to acquire one share of common stock for each share of preferred stock on presentation of a warrant and $25 cash. At the time of issuance, the common stock was trading on the stock exchange at $23 a share. The warrants began trading on the stock exchange at a price of $4 each, and the preferred stock began trading at $51 a share. The warrants expire in six months.

Prepare a journal entry for Burk Corporation to record the issuance of the preferred stock with warrants attached.

Ex. 17-5   On July 1, Year 7, Wing Corporation issued for $525,000 a total of 5,000 shares of $100 par, 10% noncumulative preferred stock, together with one detachable stock warrant for each share of preferred stock issued. Each warrant contained a right to acquire one share of Wing's $10 par common stock for $15 a share. The market price of the warrants on July 1, Year 7, was $2.50 a warrant. On October 31, Year 7, when the market price of the common stock was $19 a share and the market price of the warrants was $3 a warrant, 4,000 rights were exercised.

Prepare a journal entry for Wing Corporation to record the exercise of the rights and the issuance of the common stock.

Ex. 17-6   Newton Corporation had two issues of securities outstanding: common stock and a 9% convertible bond issue with a face amount of $10,000,000. Interest payment dates of the bond issue were June 30 and December 31. The conversion option in the bond indenture entitled the bondholders to receive 40 shares of $10 par common stock in exchange for each $1,000 bond. On June 30, Year 9, the holders of $900,000 face amount of bonds exercised the conversion option. The market price of the bonds on that date was $1,425 a bond, and the market price of the common stock was $35 a share. The amount of the unamortized bond discount on the date of conversion was $500,000.

Compute the amount that Newton Corporation credits to the Paid-in Capital in Excess of Par ledger account on June 30, Year 9, as a result of the conversion, under the carrying amount (book value) method.

Ex. 17-7   On December 31, Year 11, Lyle Company had outstanding $2,000,000 face amount of 8% convertible bonds that were to mature on December 31, Year 15, with interest payable semiannually on June 30 and December 31. The Premium on Bonds Payable ledger account had a balance of $45,000 on December 31, Year 11, which was being amortized by the straight-line method. Each $1,000 bond was convertible to 60 shares of Lyle's $10 par common stock. On December 31, Year 12, when the market price of Lyle's common stock was $18 a share, a bondholder converted 200 of the bonds.

Compute the amount that Lyle Company credits, as a result of the conversion of the bonds, to the Paid-in Capital in Excess of Par ledger account on December 31, Year 12, under the market value method.

Ex. 17-8   Kopp Corporation has outstanding two issues of securities: convertible preferred stock and common stock. Both securities are traded on the New York Stock Exchange. Assume that you acquired 100 shares of the 8%, $100 par convertible preferred stock at $103 a share when it was originally issued by Kopp. The preferred stock is convertible to four shares of $1 par common stock at any time. When you invested in the convertible preferred stock, the common stock had a market price of $22 a share. Now, several years later, the common stock has a market price of $90 a share, and you decide to convert your preferred stock to common stock.

Prepare a journal entry for Kopp Corporation to record the conversion, under the carrying amount (book value) method.

Ex. 17-9 In Year 3, Alba Corporation issued for $105 a share, 8,000 shares of $100 par, 12% convertible preferred stock. One share of preferred stock could be exchanged for three shares of Alba's $5 par common stock at the option of the preferred shareholder. In August, Year 4, all the preferred stock was converted to common stock. The market price of the common stock on the date of the conversion was $30 a share.

Compute the total amount that Alba Corporation credits to paid-in capital in excess of par for common stock as a result of the issuance of the preferred stock and its subsequent conversion to common stock, under the carrying amount (book value) method.

Ex. 17-10 On September 29, Year 4, grantees of options to acquire 10,000 shares of Nako Company's $5 par common stock at an exercise price of $40 a share exercised their options. On the September 1, Year 1, grant date (which was the measurement date), the market price of Nako's common stock was $50 a share. On September 29, Year 4, the market price of Nako's common stock was $60 a share. Nako had correctly recognized compensation expense related to the compensatory stock options.

Prepare a journal entry for Nako Company to record the exercise of the stock options on September 29, Year 4. Disregard income taxes.

Ex. 17-11 On July 18, Year 4, Cortez Corporation granted stock options to certain of its key employees as additional compensation. The options permitted the acquisition of 10,000 shares of Cortez common stock at $32 a share. On the grant date, the market price of the common stock was $38 a share. The options were exercisable beginning January 2, Year 5, and expire on December 31, Year 6. On February 3, Year 5, when the common stock was trading at $45 a share, all the options were exercised.

Compute the total amount of compensation cost that Cortez Corporation should recognize for the issuance of the stock options. Disregard income taxes.

Ex. 17-12 On January 2, Year 5, Liebold, Inc., granted its president an option to acquire 1,000 shares of Liebold's no-par, no stated value common stock at $40 a share beginning January 2, Year 7, after the president had completed two years of service. The market price of Liebold's common stock on December 31, Year 5, was $55 a share.

Compute the amount of Liebold, Inc.'s total compensation cost with respect to the stock option if the market price of Liebold's common stock on January 2, Year 5, was (**a**) $40 a share, and (**b**) $45 a share. Disregard income taxes.

Ex. 17-13 On July 1, Year 7, the beginning of a fiscal year, Yew Corporation granted stock options with stock appreciation rights to officers and key managers. The options covered 25,000 shares of Yew's $5 par common stock, and were exercisable beginning on July 1, Year 9, if the grantees remain employed by Yew for the entire two-year period ending on that date. The exercise price was $20 a share. Market prices of a share of Yew's common stock were as follows:

July 1, Year 7..	$20
June 30, Year 8...	24
June 30, Year 9...	31

Prepare journal entries for Yew Corporation's stock options on June 30, Year 8, and on June 30, Year 9. Disregard income taxes.

Ex. 17-14   On September 30, Year 5, the first date on which Roman Company's 50,000 outstanding stock options with stock appreciation rights became exercisable, Roman's Compensation Payable ledger account had a credit balance of $500,000, representing the excess of the $30 a share market price of Roman's $1 par common stock on September 30, Year 5, over the $20 a share exercise price on the grant date (September 30, Year 1) times the 50,000 shares under option [50,000 × ($30 − $20) = $500,000]. On September 30, Year 5, grantees of options for 20,000 shares of Roman's common stock elected to receive cash, and grantees of options for 30,000 shares of common stock elected to receive 10,000 shares of common stock in lieu of cash.

Prepare a journal entry on September 30, Year 5, to record Roman Company's distribution of cash and common stock for the exercise of stock appreciation rights by grantees.

Ex. 17-15   On January 2, Year 6, Norell Company issued 5,000 shares of junior stock to selected employees for cash of $12 a share. The junior stock was convertible to Norell's $10 par common stock on a share-for-share basis beginning January 2, Year 8, if the employees served Norell continuously during the two-year period ended on that date and if Norell's earnings per share for Year 7 was 50% larger than the earnings per share for Year 5, an outcome that Norell considered probable on December 31, Year 6. The market price of Norell's common stock was $16 a share on January 2, Year 6. As of December 31, Year 6, the anticipated market price on December 31, Year 7 was $22 a share, and the actual market price was $25 a share on December 31, Year 7.

Prepare journal entries for Norell Company on January 2 and December 31, Year 6, and December 31, Year 7. Disregard income taxes.

Ex. 17-16   Brel Corporation established an employee stock ownership plan (ESOP) in Year 1. Selected transactions relating to the ESOP during Year 1 were as follows:

(1) Brel contributed $20,000 cash and 2,000 shares of its $1 par common stock to the ESOP. The market price of the common stock at this time was $22 a share.

(2) The ESOP borrowed $500,000 from First National Bank and acquired an additional 20,000 shares of Brel's common stock at $23 a share. One-half of these shares were acquired in the open market and the other half directly from Brel, which guaranteed the loan from First National Bank.

(3) The ESOP repaid $40,000 of the loan from First National Bank and also paid $50,000 interest on the loan.

Prepare journal entries for Brel Corporation to record the transactions described above.

████████████████ **CASES**

Case 17-1   On February 1, Year 7, DeSoto Corporation issued $10,000,000 face amount of 10-year, 12% convertible bonds at a discount. Interest on the bonds was payable February 1 and August 1. Each $1,000 bond was convertible to 10 shares of DeSoto's no-par, $5 stated value common stock. On February 1, Year 10, a bond-holder converted 1,000 bonds to 10,000 shares of DeSoto's common stock, which had a market price of $110 a share on that date.

Instructions

Describe how DeSoto Corporation accounts for the conversion of the bonds to common stock under both the carrying amount (book value) and the market value methods. Discuss the rationale for each method.

Case 17-2   Witt Corporation issued to preferred stockholders warrants for two rights for each share of preferred stock outstanding, and to common stockholders warrants for one right for each share of common stock outstanding. The preferred stock is cumulative, but is neither convertible nor participating. The warrants provided that 10 rights and $1,000 cash would be required to acquire $1,000 face amount of 9% convertible bonds, and that the warrants would expire in 60 days. A total of 2 million rights was issued.

Some stockholders sold their warrants immediately, and trading in the warrants began at $30 a right. The convertible bonds, although not yet issued, traded on a "when-issued" basis, meaning that delivery would not be required until after the scheduled issuance date. All rights issued were exercised before the expiration date, and the convertible bonds were issued.

Instructions

a Was the issuance of warrants for rights by Witt Corporation typical of current practice? Explain.

b What was the approximate trading price of the convertible bonds on a "when-issued" basis?

c Would a common stockholder who sold the warrants instead of exercising them own a smaller share of the net assets of Witt Corporation than before the warrants were issued? Explain.

d Prepare a journal entry for Witt Corporation to record the exercise of warrants for 2 million rights and the issuance of the convertible bonds.

Case 17-3   A corporation has a noncompensatory stock purchase plan for all of its employees and a compensatory stock option plan for its officers.

Instructions

a Compare and contrast the accounting on the date the common stock is issued for the noncompensatory stock purchase plan and the compensatory stock option plan.

b What journal entry is prepared for the compensatory stock option plan on the grant date?

Case 17-4   Lenora Corporation granted 10-year stock options to five executives. The options for 50,000 shares of $1 par common stock had an exercise price of $25 a share. The market price of common stock on the grant date was $28. Each of the five executives who were granted 10,000-share options under the plan was given the right to exercise the options at any time within a 10-year period and could sell the common stock acquired at any time. Lenora's common stock is listed on the New York Stock Exchange and is actively traded.

In a discussion of the plan after its adoption by the stockholders, one executive suggested that the difference between the market price and the exercise price be debited to the Retained Earnings ledger account because the cost to Lenora was attributable to the past services of the five executives. Another executive expressed the view that there was no cost to Lenora because no payment of cash or other assets would be required for Lenora.

Instructions

a In the light of *APB Opinion No. 25*, ''Accounting for Stock Issued to Employees,'' is there a cost to Lenora Corporation that should be recognized? If so, should it be recognized at the time the options are granted, when they are exercised, or at some other time?

b Prepare the journal entry, if any, for Lenora Corporation to record issuance of the stock options, and the journal entry to record the exercise of the options for 50,000 shares of common stock. The market price on the date the options were exercised was $40. Observe the concepts set forth in *APB Opinion No. 25* in your solution. Disregard income taxes.

Case 17-5   On January 2, Year 10, Riesbord Corporation adopted a stock option plan to grant selected executives options for 500,000 shares of its $1 par common stock. The options were granted on May 1, Year 10, at an exercise price of $25 a share, the market price of the common stock on that date. All options were exercisable one year later and for four years thereafter, providing that the grantee was employed by Riesbord on the exercise date.

The market price of Riesbord's common stock was $40 a share on May 1, Year 11. All options were exercised before December 31, Year 11, on dates when the market price of the common stock was between $40 and $50 a share.

Instructions

It has been said that the exercise of a stock option would dilute the equity of existing stockholders.

a How could this happen? Discuss.

b What condition could prevent a dilution of existing equities from taking place with regard to Riesbord Corporation's stock option plan? Explain.

Case 17-6   Ward Carle, president of Olav Corporation, commented during the course of a directors' meeting that Olav had achieved increases in both sales and net income during each of the past seven years. Also, the market price of both the common stock and the convertible preferred stock had been in an uptrend. Carle also stated:

"We have 50,000 shares of 12%, $100 par, convertible preferred stock outstanding, which was originally issued for $5,100,000. This stock is callable at $106 and convertible at any time to our $5 par common stock in the ratio of three shares of common for each share of preferred. We have been paying $1 a year dividends on our common stock and do not plan any increase in the near future. Although our earnings have been increasing, we need to reinvest these earnings to take advantage of opportunities for growth. Our common stock is now trading for $70 a share, so apparently our stockholders are more interested in earnings than in dividends."

After these comments, Carle invited questions or suggestions from the directors. Director Anne Asche offered the following suggestion:

"Our convertible preferred stock is too small an issue for a corporation of our size. I propose that we call it at once and get rid of it. If everyone is forced to convert to common stock, the additional common dividend will increase by only $150,000 a year, and we shall save $600,000 a year in preferred dividends. Also, we may transfer the $100,000 of paid-in capital in excess of par on preferred stock now in our balance sheet to our retained earnings or include it as an extraordinary gain in this year's income statement. If some preferred stockholders fail to convert, we shall have a larger gain on those shares equal to the excess of the market price over the call price. And if we want convertible preferred stock in the future we shall be able to issue it at less than the 12% rate we're now paying. Consequently, calling the preferred stock will give us several benefits and cost us nothing."

Instructions

a Evaluate point by point the proposal by Director Anne Asche. For each point indicate (and explain) your agreement or disagreement.

b What is the probable market price of Olav Corporation's convertible preferred stock? Explain.

c Prepare the journal entry (or entries) for Olav Corporation that would be necessary if Asche's plan to call the preferred stock is carried out.

PROBLEMS

17-1 On January 2, Year 8, Yolo Corporation granted to officers and key employees options to acquire 20,000 shares of Yolo's $10 par common stock at an exercise price of $25 a share. The options were exercisable during a four-year period beginning January 2, Year 10, by officers and employees still employed by Yolo. The market price of Yolo's common stock was $33 a share on January 2, Year 8.

On March 31, Year 10, options for 12,000 shares of common stock were exercised when the market price of the common stock was $40 a share.

Instructions

a Prepare journal entries for Yolo Corporation to record the issuance of the stock options, debits to Compensation Expense on December 31, Year 8 and Year 9, and the exercise of the stock options. Disregard income taxes.

b Show how the balance sheet ledger accounts affected by the journal entries in **a** are presented in Yolo Corporation's balance sheets on December 31, Year 8 and Year 9.

17-2   The stockholders' equity section of Kapper Company's December 31, Year 4, balance sheet was as follows:

KAPPER COMPANY
Stockholders' Equity Section of Balance Sheet
December 31, Year 4

Common stock, no par or stated value, authorized 500,000 shares,
issued and outstanding 200,000 shares .... $ 842,000
Retained earnings 348,200
    Total stockholders' equity $1,190,200

On December 31, Year 4, the market price of Kapper's common stock was $12 a share.

On January 2, Year 5, Kapper issued 200,000, 60-day stock warrants to common stockholders for rights to acquire one additional share of common stock for one warrant and $10 cash.

Also on January 2, Year 5, Kapper issued contingent stock warrants to Nolo Company, a principal customer, specifying that Nolo could acquire 5,000 shares of Kapper's common stock at $15 a share during a 60-day period beginning January 2, Year 7, if Nolo purchased Kapper's products at a total price of $280,000 during the two years ending December 31, Year 6.

Additional Information
(1) On January 18, Year 5, stock warrants to acquire 140,000 shares of Kapper's common stock were exercised by common stockholders.
(2) On March 3, Year 5, the remaining 60,000 stock warrants issued to common stockholders expired.
(3) On December 31, Year 5, when the market price of Kapper's common stock on December 31, Year 6, was expected to be $17 a share, Kapper's management deemed it probable that Nolo would purchase more than $280,000 of Kapper's products.
(4) On December 31, Year 6, when the market price of Kapper's common stock was $19 a share, Kapper's management determined that Nolo's purchases of Kapper's products during the preceding two years totaled $302,000.
(5) On January 28, Year 7, Nolo exercised the contingent stock warrants to acquire 5,000 shares of Kapper's common stock.

Instructions
a Prepare journal entries for Kapper Company's stock warrants, as required, on January 2, January 18, March 3, and December 31, Year 5; December 31, Year 6; and January 28, Year 7. If no journal entry is required, so state and explain why.
b Prepare the stockholders' equity section of Kapper Company's balance sheet on December 31, Year 6. Kapper had retained earnings of $562,700 on that date.

17-3   The stockholders' equity section of Marcello Corporation's balance sheet on December 31, Year 7, was as follows:

MARCELLO CORPORATION
Stockholders' Equity Section of Balance Sheet
December 31, Year 7

12% cumulative preferred stock, $100 par, authorized, issued, and outstanding 20,000 shares	$2,000,000
Common stock, $1 par, authorized 1,000,000 shares, issued and outstanding 400,000 shares	400,000
Additional paid-in capital:	
On preferred stock	200,000
On common stock	640,000
Total paid-in capital	$3,240,000
Retained earnings	1,260,000
Total stockholders' equity	$4,500,000

On January 2, Year 8, Marcello established an employee stock ownership plan (ESOP), contributing $100,000 cash and 50,000 shares of unissued common stock with a current fair value of $8 a share to the ESOP.

Additional Information

(1) On March 1, Year 8, the ESOP borrowed $300,000 from a bank on a 12%, two-year promissory note indorsed by Marcello. The ESOP then acquired from Marcello 20,000 shares of unissued common stock at $7 a share.

(2) On June 6, Year 8, the ESOP acquired in the open market 10,000 shares of Marcello's outstanding common stock at $11 a share.

(3) On October 17, Year 8, two retiring employees were granted a total of 250 shares of Marcello's common stock owned by the ESOP.

(4) On December 31, Year 8, Marcello contributed $180,000 to the ESOP, which immediately paid it to the bank for interest to date and part of the principal.

Instructions

a Prepare journal entries for Marcello Corporation, as required, for the foregoing transactions. If no journal entry is required, so state and explain why.

b Prepare the stockholders' equity section of Marcello Corporation's balance sheet on December 31, Year 8. Marcello had retained earnings of $1,582,000 on that date.

17-4   On January 2, Year 3, under a stock option plan that had been approved by shareholders, Joyce Company issued to key employees 20,000 shares of junior stock at $25 cash a share. The junior stock was convertible to Joyce's no-par, $15 stated value common stock beginning on January 2, Year 6, on a 1 to 1 basis if the employees were still serving on that date and if Joyce's earnings per share for Year 5 had reached a specified level. Joyce's December 31, Year 2, balance sheet had the following stockholders' equity:

JOYCE COMPANY
Stockholders' Equity Section of Balance Sheet
December 31, Year 2

$9 convertible, cumulative preferred stock, $100 par, callable at $105 a share, authorized, issued and outstanding 50,000 shares ...	$ 5,000,000
Common stock, no-par, stated value $15, authorized 10,000,000 shares, issued and outstanding 6,000,000 shares	90,000,000
Additional paid-in capital:	
On preferred stock	250,000
On common stock...	22,800,000
Total paid-in capital	$118,050,000
Retained earnings..	32,700,000
Total stockholders' equity	$150,750,000

Additional Information

(1) On December 31, Year 3, Joyce's management determined that it was probable that the employees who had acquired junior stock would remain employed during the service period and that the specified level for earnings per share for Year 5 would be attained.

(2) On December 31, Year 5, Joyce called the $9 convertible, cumulative preferred stock. Holders of 30,000 shares of preferred stock exercised the conversion option to obtain 60,000 shares of Joyce's common stock. Holders of the remaining shares of preferred stock accepted the cash payment from Joyce. Joyce uses the carrying amount (book value) method for conversions.

(3) Market prices of Joyce's common stock were as follows:

Jan. 2, Year 3	$40
Dec. 31, Year 3	46
Dec. 31, Year 4	44½
Dec. 31, Year 5	52

(4) Earnings per share for Year 5 exceeded the specified level for conversion of the junior stock.

Instructions

a Prepare journal entries for Joyce Company in connection with the stock option plan involving junior stock and for the call and conversion of the preferred stock. Disregard income taxes.

b Prepare the stockholders' equity section of Joyce Company's balance sheet on December 31, Year 5. Joyce's retained earnings balance on that date was $46,900,000.

17-5 On January 2, Year 6, Lindstrom Corporation issued $100,000,000 face amount of 8%, 10-year convertible bonds at 101. The bonds, which paid interest semiannually on January 2 and July 2, were convertible on the basis of 10 shares of Lindstrom's $10 par common stock for each $1,000 bond. Because of the immateriality of the premium, Lindstrom adopted the straight-line method of amortization.

Additional Information

(1) On January 2, Year 8, holders of $40,000,000 face amount of the bonds exercised the conversion option.

(2) On January 2, Year 16 (the maturity date of the bonds), because of severe liquidity problems Lindstrom made an offer to the remaining bondholders to issue 10 shares of $50 par, 12% convertible preferred stock with a current fair value of $55 a share in exchange for each $1,000 bond. Because Lindstrom's bonds were trading at 45 (45% of face amount) and its common stock was trading at only $40 a share on January 2, Year 16, all bondholders accepted the exchange offer rather than converting to Lindstrom's common stock. The preferred stock was convertible to Lindstrom's common stock on a share-for-share basis.

(3) On January 2, Year 20, when Lindstrom's common stock was trading at $60 a share, Lindstrom called the 12% convertible preferred stock at the call price of $52 a share. All preferred stockholders converted to common stock.

Instructions

Prepare journal entries for Lindstrom Corporation on January 2, Year 6; January 2, Year 8; January 2, Year 16; and January 2, Year 20. Use the carrying amount (book value) method to record the conversions of both the bonds and the preferred stock. Disregard income tax effects.

17-6   On August 31, Year 10, the stockholders' equity section of Mercer Corporation's balance sheet was as follows:

MERCER CORPORATION
Stockholders' Equity Section of Balance Sheet
August 31, Year 10

Common stock, $2.50 par, authorized 5,000,000 shares, issued and outstanding 3,000,000 shares	$ 7,500,000
Paid-in capital in excess of par	38,400,000
Total paid-in capital	$45,900,000
Retained earnings	16,600,000
Total stockholders' equity	$62,500,000

During August, Year 10, Mercer completed plans for a September public offering of 200,000 shares of $6 preferred stock, par value $50 a share. Accompanying each preferred share was a detachable stock warrant entitling the holder to acquire one share of $2.50 par common stock at $40 a share at any time within the next 10 years. The common stock was trading at $36 a share. As soon as the terms of the preferred stock and warrants offering were announced, the warrants began trading separately on the stock exchange at $3.50 each on a "when-issued" basis.

The entire issue of 200,000 shares of preferred stock with warrants attached was issued on September 1, Year 10, at $55 a share. During the next few months the market price of the common stock increased, and on December 1, Year 10, it traded at $66 a share. On December 1, Year 10, 40,000 warrants were exercised, and Mercer issued 40,000 shares of common stock.

Instructions

a Prepare journal entries for Mercer Corporation to record the issuance of the preferred stock and detachable stock warrants on September 1, Year 10, and the issuance of common stock on December 1, Year 10. (Journal entries are not required for dividends.)

b Prepare the stockholders' equity section of Mercer Corporation's balance sheet on December 31, Year 10, assuming that net income since August 31, Year 10, was $4,500,000 and that on November 1, Year 10, a quarterly dividend of $1.50 a share was declared on the preferred stock, payable December 2, Year 10, to stockholders of record on November 20, Year 10. Dividends of $1,500,000 were declared on the common stock subsequent to August 31, Year 10.

17-7 The fiscal year for Saldana, Inc., ends on December 31. On January 2, Year 10, Saldana established a compensatory stock option plan for its key executives who had been employed at least five years. The number of shares of common stock initially included in the plan was approximately 100,000, at an estimated exercise price of $40 a share. The final determination of the number of shares to be offered and the exercise price were to be made on December 31, Year 11, based on a predetermined formula. The formula was designed to adjust the number of shares to be optioned and the exercise price by taking into account the earnings of Saldana and the market price of its common stock during Years 10 and 11.

Options were granted for services to be performed through the end of Year 11, and were exercisable at any time after January 2, Year 12. The estimated number of shares of common stock to be included in the stock option plan, the estimated exercise price, and the market price of the common stock on January 2, Year 10, and on December 31, Year 10, were as follows:

	Jan. 2, Year 10	Dec. 31, Year 10
Estimated number of shares of common stock to be included in stock option plan	100,000	100,000
Estimated exercise price	$40	$40
Market price of common stock	$38	$45

The final contractual provisions of the stock option plan and the market price of Saldana's common stock were determined on December 31, Year 11, as follows:

Number of shares of common stock included in stock option plan	95,000
Exercise price	$41
Market price	$52

On April 20, Year 12, employees exercised options for 30,000 shares of common stock. Saldana had 3,500,000 shares of $5 par common stock outstanding on December 31, Year 11.

Instructions

a What is the measurement date for Saldana, Inc.'s, stock option plan? Explain.

b Compute the total compensation cost to be recognized by Saldana, Inc., under the stock option plan. How is total compensation cost allocated among accounting periods? Show supporting computations and disregard income taxes.

c Prepare journal entries for Saldana, Inc., to record all transactions and events relating to the stock option plan for Year 10 through Year 12. Disregard income taxes.

17-8 Tully Corporation had the following amounts in the stockholders' equity section of its balance sheet on May 31, Year 3:

TULLY CORPORATION
Stockholders' Equity Section of Balance Sheet
May 31, Year 3

Common stock, $10 par, authorized 6,000,000 shares, issued and outstanding 2,500,000 shares	$25,000,000
Additional paid-in capital.	12,500,000
Total paid-in capital	$37,500,000
Retained earnings.	15,775,000
Total stockholders' equity	$53,275,000

Tully's operations had been profitable, but management had decided that additional capital was needed. Therefore, authorization was obtained for the issuance of 250,000 shares of $5 preferred stock with a par of $50 a share. To help assure success of this financing, Tully offered with each share of preferred stock a detachable stock warrant that entitled the holder to acquire one share of Tully's common stock at $40 a share at any time within the next 10 years. The common stock was trading at $35 a share. As soon as the terms of the offering were announced, the warrants began trading at a price of $6 each.

The issuance of 250,000 shares of the $5 preferred stock with detachable stock warrants attached was completed on June 1, Year 3, at $60 a share (including the stock warrant). The market price of the common stock increased during the next several months. On December 1, Year 3, when the common stock was trading at $65 a share, 25,000 warrants were exercised, and Tully issued 25,000 shares of common stock.

Instructions

a Prepare journal entries for Tully Corporation to record the issuance of the preferred stock and the detachable common stock warrants on June 1, Year 3, and the issuance of common stock on December 1, Year 3, when 25,000 warrants were exercised. (Journal entries are not required for dividends on the preferred stock.)

b Prepare the stockholders' equity section of Tully Corporation's balance sheet on December 31, Year 3, assuming that net income since May 31, Year 3, was

$8,400,000, and that dividend action on the preferred stock since that date had been as follows:

Sept. 1   Declared quarterly dividend of $1.25 a share on preferred stock.
Oct. 1   Paid quarterly dividend on preferred stock.
Dec. 1   Declared quarterly dividend of $1.25 a share on preferred stock, payable January 10, Year 4, to stockholders of record December 15, Year 3.

17-9   Roper Company had outstanding two issues of securities: $5 par common stock, and 9% convertible bonds in the face amount of $20,000,000. Interest payment dates of the bond issue were April 1 and October 1. The conversion option in the bond indenture entitled the bondholders to receive 30 shares of Roper's common stock in exchange for each $1,000 bond.

On March 15, Year 4, the annual dividend rate on the common stock was increased from $1.50 to $2 a share. On April 1, Year 4, the holders of $2 million face amount of bonds exercised the conversion option. The market price of the 9% convertible bonds on that date was $122 for each $100 face amount; the market price of Roper's common stock was $40 a share. The ledger account balances pertaining to the convertible bonds and the common stock were as follows on April 1, Year 4, prior to the conversion:

9% convertible bonds payable (maturing in 10 years)................	$20,000,000
Discount on 9% convertible bonds payable (amortized by interest method at 10% yield rate)..	1,246,221
Common stock, $5 par; authorized 2 million shares, issued and outstanding 750,000 shares	3,750,000
Additional paid-in capital..	11,830,500

Instructions

a Prepare a journal entry for Roper Company to record the conversion of bonds on April 1, Year 4, under the carrying amount (book value) method.

b Evaluate the effects of the conversion on income of Roper Company for the year ended March 31, Year 5, with respect to:
   (1) Income before income taxes. (Consider amortization of bond discount.)
   (2) The amounts of income taxes expense and net income. (Assume an income tax rate of 45%)
   (3) The total annual amount of payments to security holders.

c What effect would the conversion have on the annual cash receipts of an investor who converted 100 bonds to common stock on April 1, Year 4?

d Prepare a journal entry for Roper Company to record the conversion of bonds on April 1, Year 4, under the market value method.

17-10   On December 31, Year 5, under a stock option plan that had been approved by stockholders in November, Year 5, Ingle Corporation granted stock options for 40,000 shares of $1 par common stock at an exercise price of $16 a share to officers and key employees. The plan included stock appreciation rights that were exercisable only if the stock options were forfeited; exercise of the stock options required forfeiture of the stock appreciation rights. The options were exercisable in full beginning on December 31, Year 9. No service period was specified for the grantees. Market prices of Ingle's common stock were as follows:

Dec. 31, Year 5 .... *$16*
Dec. 31, Year 6 .... *20*
Dec. 31, Year 7 .... *24*
Dec. 31, Year 8 .... *22*
Dec. 31, Year 9 .... *28*

On December 31, Year 9, grantees exercised their stock appreciation rights and stock options as follows:

Stock appreciation rights exercised:

Grantees of options for 20,000 shares elected to receive cash.

Grantees of options for 15,400 shares elected to receive shares of Ingle's common stock.

Stock options exercised: 4,600 shares of Ingle's common stock.

Instructions

Prepare all journal entries for Ingle Corporation's stock option plan for Year 6 through Year 9. Show supporting computations in explanations for the journal entries. Round computations to the nearest dollar and disregard income taxes.

Treasury Stock and Earnings Per Share

18

Additional topics dealing with stockholders' equity not discussed in the preceding two chapters are (1) the acquisition and retirement or reissuance by a corporation of its capital stock, (2) the preparation of statements of retained earnings and stockholders' equity, and (3) the computation of earnings per share of common stock. A corporation's acquisition of its capital stock reduces its stockholders' equity and affects the computation of earnings per share. Earnings per share is the amount of net income earned on each share of common stock and is considered by many investors as probably the most important financial measurement.

TREASURY STOCK

Treasury stock is the capital stock of a corporation that has been issued, fully paid for, and subsequently acquired by the corporation but not formally retired. When a corporation acquires shares of its capital stock, certain stockholders surrender their ownership interest in the corporation. Thus, the acquisition of treasury stock by a corporation may be viewed as a partial liquidation of the corporation, and the reissuance of treasury stock is a financing transaction. No gain or loss is realized from such transactions, because gains and losses result from disposals of assets and extinguishments of debt, not from issuances or acquisitions of capital stock.

Treasury stock may be acquired by corporations for a variety of reasons, including the following: (1) to buy out a particular stockholder, (2) for use in connection with stock option plans or business combinations, (3) to settle claims against debtors who are also stockholders, (4) to increase earnings per share by reducing the number of shares of common stock outstanding, and (5) to support the market price of the common stock.[1] There is little justification for a corporation's attempting to influence the market price of its common stock through the acquisition and reissuance of treasury stock; such efforts may create a conflict of interest between the corporation and its stockholders and may be illegal in some circumstances. The laws of some states prohibit or severely restrict a corporation's acquisition of its common stock.

In recent years there have been several highly publicized treasury stock acquisitions by corporations fighting threatened takeovers by hostile investor groups. For example, Walt Disney Productions paid nearly $328 million to an investor for the investor's 12.2% interest (4.2 million shares) of Disney's outstanding common stock (see pages 224–225 and 232). The investor had announced a plan to acquire a nearly controlling interest in Disney; that company's acquisition of the investor's common stock resulted in a substantial profit to the investor in an activity that is termed *greenmail* (a reference to *blackmail*).

Another example is the acquisition of 43% of its outstanding common stock by Teledyne, Inc., in May 1984, at a total cost of $1.75 billion. Initially, Teledyne had made a $1 billion *tender offer* to acquire up to 5 million shares at $200 a share. As a result of the tender offer, the market price of Teledyne's common stock promptly rose to $193 from $156 a share in active trading on the New York Stock Exchange. Later in 1984, the market price of Teledyne's common stock increased to over $300 a share before settling back to the $250 to $260 range in the early months of 1985. (Previously, Teledyne had acquired approximately 25 million shares of its outstanding common stock through tender offers over an eight-year period, and another 3 million shares by open-market acquisitions; all 28 million shares of common stock had been retired after some had been carried in the treasury.)

Treasury Stock and Stated (or Legal) Capital

Stated (or *legal*) capital, as explained in Chapter 16, is a statutory definition of the amount of capital to be retained in a corporation for protection of creditors; it is not available for withdrawal by stockholders. Legal capital generally consists of the total par or stated value of capital stock (preferred and common) issued. The acquisition of treasury stock is not regarded as a reduction in legal capital; however, such an acquisition involves an outflow of assets to stockholders, and therefore certain legal restrictions are necessary to protect the corporation's creditors. Generally, a corporation is not permitted to acquire treasury stock if the acquisition would cause total stockholders' equity to be reduced below legal capital. Furthermore, a portion of retained earnings equal to the amount paid for treasury stock generally is restricted and unavailable for dividends.

It should be emphasized that the ***retirement of capital stock*** reduces legal capital, but the ***acquisition of treasury stock*** does not. In terms of economic significance, the retirement of capital stock and the acquisition of treasury stock are similar, because both transactions consist of a return of assets to stockholders and a corresponding reduction in the amount of capital invested in the corporation.

---

[1]In the 38th edition of *Accounting Trends & Techniques* issued by the AICPA in 1984, 408 of the 600 companies included in the survey reported treasury stock, either common or preferred, in their balance sheets.

Treasury Stock Is Not an Asset

A corporation may not own a portion of itself; for this reason, treasury stock is not considered an asset. The ownership of treasury stock does not give a corporation the right to receive cash dividends, to vote, to exercise preemptive rights as a stockholder, or to receive assets when the corporation is liquidated. Corporations may, and sometimes do, formally cancel treasury stock; this action would not be taken if the cancellation actually destroyed an asset. If a corporation were to dissolve, any treasury stock owned by the corporation would contribute nothing in the process of converting assets to cash for distribution to shareholders.

The view that treasury stock is not an asset is strengthened by recognition that treasury stock essentially is the same as unissued capital stock, and no one advocates that unissued stock be classified as an asset in the balance sheet.

Treasury stock sometimes is acquired for subsequent reissuance under employee stock purchase or incentive plans.[2] A corporation may have a liability to employees under such plans. To meet this liability the corporation expends cash to acquire treasury stock and soon thereafter discharges the liability by delivery of the treasury stock to employees. Because the treasury stock will be used to liquidate the liability, it may be viewed as being similar to an investment in securities of any other corporation. The Accounting Principles Board has given recognition to this situation as follows:[3]

> When a corporation's stock is acquired for purposes other than retirement (formal or constructive), or when ultimate disposition has not yet been decided, the cost of acquired stock may be shown separately as a deduction from the total of capital stock, capital surplus, and retained earnings, or may be accorded the accounting treatment appropriate for retired stock, or in some circumstances may be shown as an asset. . . .

The reasons for refusing to view treasury stock as an asset are many and generally are recognized as valid, yet the issue is kept alive by the policy of a few corporations that continue to list treasury stock as an asset.

Alternative Accounting Methods for Treasury Stock

The two alternative accounting methods for treasury stock are (1) the *cost method,* and (2) the *par* or *stated value method.* Although the par or stated value method still receives some theoretical support in accounting literature, large corporations have turned increasingly to the cost method in recent years.[4] Both methods are acceptable under generally accepted accounting principles.

Under the cost method, the acquisition of treasury stock is regarded as a first step in a financial move that is completed by the reissuance of the treasury stock.

---

[2]At the end of 1984, for example, General Motors Corporation reported as an asset approximately 2,054,000 shares of its common stocks, $144 million, as "Common Stocks Held for the Incentive Program."

[3]*APB Opinion No. 6,* "Status of Accounting Research Bulletins," AICPA (New York: 1965), p. 40.

[4]In the 38th edition of *Accounting Trends & Techniques* issued by the AICPA in 1984, common stock held in treasury was carried at cost by 361 companies and at par or stated value by 38 companies; preferred stock held in treasury was carried at cost by 14 companies and at par or stated value by four companies.

Treasury stock thus is viewed as a "suspense" item of stockholders' equity, with the corporation acting as an intermediary between the former stockholders and the new stockholders. When the cost method is used, the Treasury Stock ledger account is debited for the cost of the capital stock acquired; this account is reported in the balance sheet as a deduction from the **total** stockholders' equity. With this arrangement of the stockholders' equity section of the balance sheet, there is no reduction in the legal or stated capital. Because the laws of most states indicate that the acquisition of treasury stock does not reduce legal capital, this balance sheet presentation reflects the prevailing legal concept of treasury stock.

Under the par or stated value method, the possibility of reissuance of the treasury stock is not given much weight. The relationship between the corporation and the former owners of shares of common stock, for example, now held in the treasury has ended; therefore, the ledger account showing paid-in capital in excess of par or stated value relating to the treasury stock is reduced. If the corporation decides to retire the common stock, the Common Stock ledger account also is reduced; the reissuance of treasury stock is recorded as an original issuance of common stock.

Illustration of Accounting for Treasury Stock—Cost Method   To illustrate the cost method of accounting for treasury stock transactions, assume that the balance sheet for Mix Corporation includes the following stockholders' equity section:

Balance sheet stockholders' equity section for treasury stock illustration

MIX CORPORATION
Stockholders' Equity Section of Balance Sheet

Stockholders' equity:

Common stock, $100 par, authorized, issued, and outstanding 10,000 shares.	$1,000,000
Paid-in capital in excess of par	200,000
Total paid-in capital.	$1,200,000
Retained earnings	500,000
Total stockholders' equity	$1,700,000

At this time, Mix acquired in the open market 300 shares of its common stock for the treasury at $115 a share. The acquisition of treasury stock was recorded at cost as illustrated below:

Journal entry for acquisition of treasury stock—cost method

Treasury Stock (300 × $115)	34,500	
Cash		34,500
To record acquisition of 300 shares of common stock for the		
treasury at $115 a share.		

The stockholders' equity section of the balance sheet of Mix Corporation appears as follows when treasury stock was recorded at cost:

Balance sheet stock-
holders' equity section
showing acquisition of
treasury stock—cost
method

MIX CORPORATION
Stockholders' Equity Section of Balance Sheet

Stockholders' equity:

Common stock, $100 par, authorized and issued 10,000 shares, of which 300 shares are in treasury	$1,000,000
Paid-in capital in excess of par	200,000
Total paid-in capital	$1,200,000
Retained earnings (**Note 1**)	500,000
Total paid-in capital and retained earnings	$1,700,000
Less: Treasury stock, 300 shares at cost	34,500
Total stockholders' equity	$1,665,500

Note 1: The declaration of dividends and the acquisition of treasury stock are restricted to $465,500, the amount of the retained earnings reduced by the cost of treasury stock.

The presentation of stockholders' equity when treasury stock is recorded at cost does not show the net amount of capital invested by stockholders; thus, it does not achieve one of the objectives in the classification of corporate capital. However, the cost approach to treasury stock does have the merit of showing as capital stock an amount equal to the legal capital of the corporation.

Let us assume that Mix Corporation *canceled* the 300 shares of treasury stock recorded at cost. This action caused a reduction in legal capital and in additional paid-in capital by the amount paid for treasury stock. The journal entry to record the cancellation of the treasury stock is as follows:

Journal entry for
cancellation of
treasury stock—cost
method

Common Stock (300 × $100)	30,000	
Paid-in Capital in Excess of Par	4,500	
Treasury Stock		34,500
To record cancellation of 300 shares of treasury stock carried at cost.		

The 300 shares of treasury stock were issued originally at $120 each ($1,200,000 ÷ 10,000 = $120), or for a total of $36,000. The shares were acquired at a cost of $34,500, or $1,500 *less* than the paid-in capital relating to these shares. Therefore, the cancellation of the treasury stock requires a reduction of only $34,500 in the paid-in capital ledger accounts; the excess of the amount originally paid in by stockholders over the cost of the treasury stock, $1,500 ($36,000 − $34,500 = $1,500), remains in the Paid-in Capital in Excess of Par ledger account.

If, instead of canceling the 300 shares of treasury stock as previously illustrated, Mix Corporation had reissued these shares at a price of $108 a share, or $2,100 *below cost,* the journal entry would have been as follows:

Journal entry for
reissuance of treasury
stock at a price below
cost—cost method

Cash (300 × $108)	*32,400*	
Paid-in Capital in Excess of Par	*2,100*	
Treasury Stock		*34,500*
To record reissuance of 300 shares of treasury stock at $108 a		
share, or $2,100 below cost.		

Under the cost method, the Treasury Stock ledger account is credited for the cost of the shares of treasury stock that are reissued. Cost may be computed on a weighted-average basis, on a first-in, first-out basis, or by specific identification. When the reissuance price is less than cost, as in the foregoing illustration, the excess of cost over the proceeds from reissuance is debited to Paid-in Capital in Excess of Par. This ledger account was credited at the time the common stock originally was issued; however, if such paid-in capital is insufficient, paid-in capital from previous treasury stock transactions or Retained Earnings is debited for the excess of the cost over the proceeds from reissuance.

When treasury stock is reissued at a price ***above cost,*** the excess of the proceeds over cost of the treasury stock is credited to Paid-in Capital in Excess of Par, as illustrated below:

Journal entry for
reissuance of treasury
stock at a price above
cost—cost method

Cash (300 × $125)	*37,500*	
Treasury Stock		*34,500*
Paid-in Capital in Excess of Par		*3,000*
To record reissuance of 300 shares of treasury stock at $125		
a share, or $3,000 above cost.		

Illustration of Accounting for Treasury Stock—Par or Stated Value Method

To facilitate a comparison between the cost method and the par or stated value method of accounting for treasury stock, we use the same transactions illustrated above for Mix Corporation. Under the par value method, the journal entry to record the acquisition of treasury stock by Mix Corporation is shown below:

Journal entry for
acquisition of treasury
stock—par value
method

Treasury Stock (300 × $100)	*30,000*	
Paid-in Capital in Excess of Par	*4,500*	
Cash (300 × $115)		*34,500*
To record acquisition of 300 shares of common stock for the		
treasury at $115 a share.		

In this journal entry, the reduction in the stockholders' equity is $34,500, or $1,500 less than the $36,000 (300 × $120 = $36,000) originally paid by stockholders. Thus, $1,500 of the capital originally invested by those stockholders who have sold their stock to the corporation remains in the corporation.[5]

After the acquisition of treasury stock, the stockholders' equity section of Mix Corporation's balance sheet is as follows:

Balance sheet stock-holders' equity section showing acquisition of treasury stock—par value method

MIX CORPORATION
Stockholders' Equity Section of Balance Sheet

Stockholders' equity:

Common stock, $100 par, authorized and issued		
10,000 shares	$1,000,000	
Less: Treasury stock, 300 shares at par	30,000	$ 970,000
Paid-in capital in excess of par		195,500
Total paid-in capital		$1,165,500
Retained earnings **(Note 1)**		500,000
Total stockholders' equity		$1,665,500

Note 1: The declaration of dividends and the acquisition of treasury stock are restricted to $465,500, the amount of the retained earnings reduced by the cost of treasury stock.

This form for reporting the stockholders' equity section has the merit of showing the net amount for paid-in capital after the treasury stock acquisitions. However, it may be criticized on the grounds that the net amount shown for common stock ($970,000) may be interpreted erroneously as the legal capital; the legal capital of $1,000,000 was not reduced by the acquisition of treasury stock.

If Mix Corporation should **cancel** all 300 shares of treasury stock, the cancellation is recorded by a debit to Common Stock and a credit to Treasury Stock for $30,000. After cancellation of the treasury stock, the stockholders' equity section would not include treasury stock and there would be no restriction on retained earnings. The cancellation, in effect, has reduced legal capital permanently to $970,000.

---

[5]If the amount paid for treasury stock is more than the amount originally invested by stockholders, the excess is recorded as a debit to the Retained Earnings ledger account. For example, if Mix Corporation paid $39,000 to acquire 300 shares of its common stock originally issued for $36,000, the transaction would be recorded under the par value method as follows:

Treasury Stock (300 × $100)	30,000	
Paid-in Capital in Excess of Par (300 × $20)	6,000	
Retained Earnings (300 × $10)	3,000	
Cash (300 × $130)		39,000

If treasury stock is acquired at a price below par value, the excess of par value over cost of treasury stock is credited to Paid-in Capital in Excess of Par. For example, if Mix Corporation paid only $25,000 for the 300 shares of common stock, the journal entry to record the acquisition would be as follows:

Treasury Stock (300 × $100)	30,000	
Paid-in Capital in Excess of Par		5,000
Cash		25,000

If Mix Corporation, instead of canceling the 300 shares of treasury stock, reissued the shares at a price *above par,* say $108 each, the journal entry is as follows:

Cash (300 × $108)	32,400	
Treasury Stock		30,000
Paid-in Capital in Excess of Par		2,400
To record reissuance of 300 shares of treasury stock at $108		
a share, or $2,400 above carrying amount (par).		

Note that the foregoing journal entry for reissuance of treasury stock is similar to an entry for original issuance of capital stock. The difference between the issuance price of the treasury stock and the par of the treasury stock, as recorded in the Treasury Stock ledger account, is credited to the Paid-in Capital in Excess of Par ledger account. Under the par value approach, the acquisition of treasury stock is viewed as a temporary retirement of the stock; thus, the reissuance of treasury stock logically is recorded in the same manner as an original issuance of capital stock.

In the event that the treasury stock were reissued at *less than par,* it would not be appropriate to debit a Discount on Common Stock ledger account because no "discount liability" attaches to treasury stock reissued below par. Instead, the deficiency is recorded by a debit to Paid-in Capital in Excess of Par if such paid-in capital is available. In the absence of sufficient paid-in capital in excess of par to absorb the deficiency, it should be debited to Retained Earnings.

Summary of Accounting for Treasury Stock

The foregoing discussion suggests the following key points relative to accounting for treasury stock:

1   Treasury stock is not an asset and is not entitled to receive cash dividends, to vote, or to receive assets on liquidation of the corporation.

2   No gain or loss is recognized on treasury stock transactions, either for financial accounting or for income tax purposes.

3   The balance of retained earnings never is increased by treasury stock transactions; however, retained earnings may be reduced by such transactions.

4   The total stockholders' equity is the same, regardless of the method used to record treasury stock; however, the amounts of paid-in capital and retained earnings may vary, depending on the method used.

5   Retained earnings in an amount equal to the cost of treasury stock usually is unavailable for declaration of cash dividends.

6   The laws of some states and contracts with creditors may prohibit the acquisition of treasury stock or may prescribe special accounting treatment for treasury stock.

Redemption of Preferred Stock

Most corporations that issue preferred stock include in the contract a provision that all or any part of the preferred stock may be called for redemption (retirement) at any time desired by the issuer. The call price usually exceeds the issuance price; it may be an unchanging amount or it may be a series of amounts on a sliding scale relating to specified time periods and eventually decreasing to par. When preferred stock is called for redemption, the stock is canceled and is not available for reissuance. Redemption may be effected by a *call* of the stock pursuant to the call provision, by acquisition in the open market, or by a special offer to preferred stockholders to *tender* their stock to the corporation at a price that exceeds the current market price of the stock.

The redemption of preferred stock should not be confused with the acquisition of treasury stock, because *redemption* signifies both acquisition and cancellation of the stock. Preferred stock also may be acquired for subsequent reissuance and held in treasury. However, acquisitions of preferred stock generally are made with the intent to cancel the stock.

To illustrate the redemption of preferred stock, assume that Winters Corporation had issued 10,000 shares of $100 par preferred stock at $102 a share. The call price was $105 a share. If Winters redeemed the entire issue at the call price of $105 a share, the journal entry to record the redemption is as follows:

Journal entry for redemption of preferred stock at a premium

Preferred Stock, $100 par (10,000 × $100)	1,000,000	
Paid-in Capital in Excess of Par: Preferred Stock		
(10,000 × $2)	20,000	
Retained Earnings	30,000	
Cash		1,050,000
To record redemption of 10,000 shares of preferred stock		
for $30,000 in excess of the original issuance price.		

This journal entry eliminates both the Preferred Stock and the Paid-in Capital in Excess of Par: Preferred Stock ledger accounts, because the capital invested by the preferred stockholders has been returned in full, and these investors no longer have any ownership equity in the corporation. The $30,000 paid to the preferred stockholders in excess of their original investment, referred to as *premium paid on retirement of preferred stock,* is debited to Retained Earnings and not to any additional paid-in capital ledger accounts applicable to other classes of capital stock.

When the preferred stock is selling at a market price less than call price, the issuer may redeem a portion of the stock by acquisition in the open market. Returning to the previous example, assume that Winters Corporation acquired 1,000 shares of preferred stock in the open market at $90 a share. The journal entry to record the redemption is shown on page 902.

By a payment of $90,000, Winters has eliminated 1,000 shares of preferred stock representing $102,000 of paid-in capital. Recording the $12,000 excess of the original investment by preferred stockholders over the amount paid to redeem the 1,000 shares of preferred stock in the manner shown on page 902 results in an

Journal entry for re-
demption of preferred
stock at a discount

Preferred Stock, $100 par (1,000 × $100)	100,000	
Paid-in Capital in Excess of Par: Preferred Stock		
(1,000 × $2)	2,000	
Cash (1,000 × $90)		90,000
Paid-in Capital from Redemption of Preferred Stock ...		12,000
To record redemption of 1,000 shares of preferred stock at a		
price $12,000 below the original issuance price.		

increase in the equity of the common stockholders. However, this increase is not a realized gain to be reported in the income statement. It also is improper to credit the $12,000 excess to Retained Earnings, because it originally was recorded as paid-in capital and continues in that category with an appropriate descriptive title.

The two foregoing examples illustrate the following general rules for interpreting the redemption of preferred stock:

1   When preferred stock is redeemed at a cost in excess of the original issuance price, the excess is recorded as a reduction of retained earnings. The excess should *not* be recognized as a loss or debited to additional paid-in capital relating to any other class of capital stock.

2   When preferred stock is redeemed for an amount less than the issuance price, the difference is recorded as a paid-in capital item and *not* as a gain or as an increase in retained earnings.

The disclosure requirements for redeemable preferred stock are described in Chapter 16 (pages 802–803).

STATEMENTS OF RETAINED EARNINGS AND STOCKHOLDERS' EQUITY

Because users of financial statements are interested in all changes in the various components of stockholders' equity, a complete set of financial statements includes:

1   A statement of retained earnings accompanied by a statement of paid-in capital, or alternatively,

2   A statement of stockholders' equity

Currently, most corporations include a statement of stockholders' equity in their annual reports to shareholders. In the 38th edition of *Accounting Trends & Techniques* (1984), the AICPA reported that 371 of 600 surveyed companies presented such a statement.

Statement of Retained Earnings

As explained in Chapter 4 (pages 165–167), a *statement of retained earnings* shows the changes in retained earnings during an accounting period, thus reconciling the beginning and ending balances of retained earnings.

The content and relative importance of the statement of retained earnings in portraying the financial developments during an accounting period have been reduced by the movement to the all-inclusive concept of income reporting. *FASB Statement No. 16,* "Prior Period Adjustments," requires that all items of profit and loss recognized during a period be included in the measurement of net income, except for *prior period adjustments.* Currently, only corrections of material prior period errors and certain changes in accounting principle meet the requirements for classification as prior period adjustments to be recorded in the Retained Earnings ledger account. Thus, when a separate statement of retained earnings is prepared, it is short and consists of the following:

1 The beginning balance of retained earnings (adjusted for any prior period adjustments)

2 An addition of net income (or deduction of net loss) for the accounting period

3 A deduction for any dividends declared during the period

4 The ending balance of retained earnings

A two-year comparative statement of retained earnings for Torrance Company, Inc., that includes a prior period adjustment, is shown below. (Note that, as discussed in Chapter 4, the SEC requires companies subject to its jurisdiction to issue comparative retained earnings statements for *three years*.)

TORRANCE COMPANY, INC.
Statements of Retained Earnings
For Years Ended June 30, Year 10 and Year 9

	Year 10	Year 9
Retained earnings, beginning of year, as originally reported		$850,000
Less: Prior period adjustment: Correction of error (net of income tax effect of $250,000)		280,000
Retained earnings, beginning of year (as restated for Year 9)	$675,000	$570,000
Add (deduct): Net income (loss)	(85,000)	205,000
Subtotals	$590,000	$775,000
Less: Dividends declared ($0.25 and $1.00 a share)	25,000	100,000
Retained earnings, end of year	$565,000	$675,000

Instead of a separate statement of retained earnings, some corporations prepare a *combined statement of income and retained earnings* such as the one for Levant Corporation below:

LEVANT CORPORATION
Combined Statements of Income and Retained Earnings
For Years Ended December 31, Year 10 and Year 9
(dollars in thousands except per-share amounts)

	Year 10	Year 9
Revenue:		
Sales	$1,317,683	$1,140,485
Other revenue	18,886	15,753
Total revenue	$1,336,569	$1,156,238
Costs and expenses:		
Cost of goods sold	$ 650,275	$ 567,206
Selling and administrative expenses	416,699	362,968
Depreciation and amortization expense	41,597	35,862
Income taxes expense	103,339	83,747
Other expenses	3,953	4,634
Total costs and expenses	$1,215,863	$1,054,417
Net income (per share: Year 10, $2.15; Year 9, $1.82)	$ 120,706	$ 101,821
Add: Retained earnings, beginning of year	469,647	391,850
Less: Cash dividends declared ($0.45 and $0.43 a share)	(25,136)	(24,024)
Retained earnings, end of year	$ 565,217	$ 469,647

Reporting Changes in Total Paid-in Capital or Stockholders' Equity

Reporting changes in capital stock and additional paid-in capital is required by *APB Opinion No. 12*, ''Omnibus Opinion—1967.'' The Accounting Principles Board stated[6]

> When both financial position and results of operations are presented, disclosure of changes in the separate accounts comprising stockholders' equity (in addition to retained earnings) and of the changes in the number of shares of equity securities during at least the most recent annual fiscal period and any subsequent interim period presented is required to make the financial statements sufficiently informative. Disclosure of such changes may take the form of separate statements or may be made in the basic financial statements or notes thereto.

---

[6]*APB Opinion No. 12*, ''Omnibus Opinion—1967,'' AICPA (New York: 1967), p. 190.

CANTOR CORPORATION
Statements of Stockholders' Equity
For Years Ended December 31, Year 4 and Year 5

	Capital stock	Additional paid-in capital	Retained earnings
Balances, Dec. 31, Year 3	$ 5,966,000	$21,419,000	$16,161,000
Net income			9,938,000
Cash dividends on common stock ($0.10 a share)			(1,229,000)
Transfer to common stock of amount equal to par value of common stock issued as a 100% stock dividend	6,266,000		(6,266,000)
Exercise of common stock options and warrants	355,000	4,891,000	
Conversion of 12% bonds payable	144,000	3,667,000	
Business combination with Butler Company (preferred stock, $13,527,000; common stock, $1,465,000)	14,992,000	35,723,000	
Balances, Dec. 31, Year 4	$27,723,000	$65,700,000	$18,604,000
Net income			19,518,000
Cash dividends:			
Preferred ($1.50 a share)			(676,000)
Common ($0.12 a share)			(1,741,000)
Exercise of common stock options and warrants	525,000	5,171,000	
Conversion of 12% bonds payable and preferred stock ...	1,260,000	27,558,000	
Balances, Dec. 31, Year 5	$29,508,000	$98,429,000	$35,705,000

Note: Stockholders' Equity: The authorized capital stock of the company consists of 25 million shares of common stock and 2 million shares of preferred stock. The preferred stock outstanding on December 31, Year 5, is convertible to 315,561 shares of common stock and has liquidation preference of $13,524,000.

On December 31, Year 5, the company had reserved 710,000 shares of its common stock for issuance under outstanding common stock warrants. The warrants are exercisable prior to May 31, Year 6, at $12.10 a share. The company also had reserved 525,000 shares of common stock for issuance on conversion of the 12% bonds payable and the convertible preferred stock, and 640,000 shares for issuance under stock option plans.

Common stock shares issued on exercise of stock options during Year 4 and Year 5 amounted to 99,939 and 109,846, respectively. There were options outstanding on December 31, Year 4 and Year 5, for 280,561 and 383,053 shares of common stock, respectively, and the aggregate exercise price of all outstanding stock options was $6,037,000 and $6,067,000, respectively.

Retained earnings of approximately $15,500,000 are available on December 31, Year 5, for payment of cash dividends under the most restrictive provisions of the company's indebtedness contracts.

One approach for compliance with **APB Opinion No. 12** is to prepare a statement of paid-in capital *in addition to the statement of retained earnings*. A more popular approach is to prepare a statement of stockholders' equity, as illustrated on page 905 for Cantor Corporation. In this example, the amounts for preferred stock and common stock are combined in one column headed "capital stock," and a note to the financial statements describes in more detail the events of the two years presented in the statement of stockholders' equity. A statement of stockholders' equity included in a note to the financial statements of Walt Disney Productions is illustrated on page 232.

EARNINGS PER SHARE

Because of the complexities of business activities and the need for a small number of comparative measurements to highlight financial analysis, earnings per share has become perhaps the most important computation for many investors. Probably no financial statistic is cited more widely than earnings per share. In the opinion of many investors, market prices of common stocks are closely related to earnings per share.

Earnings per share is the amount of net income earned on each share of common stock during an accounting period. *Earnings per share is meaningful only with respect to common stock; it should not be computed for preferred stock because the participation in earnings by preferred stockholders is limited by contract.* Assuming that *only common stock is outstanding* and that there was no change in the number of shares outstanding during the accounting period, earnings per share is computed as follows:

$$\frac{\text{Net income}}{\text{Number of shares of common stock outstanding}} = \text{earnings per share}$$

When cumulative, nonconvertible preferred stock also is outstanding, the current dividend requirement on the preferred stock (whether or not declared by the board of directors) is deducted from net income to compute the amount of net income available for the common stock. Dividends on noncumulative, nonconvertible preferred stock are deducted only if *declared.*

Investors in common stocks make extensive use of earnings per share data in the evaluation of the profitability of corporations. By computing the *price-earnings ratio* (market price of a share of common stock divided by earnings per share), investors also attempt to determine whether the market price of the common stock is reasonable or whether it might be too high or too low. However, financial statements are only one part of the total information that may be used to evaluate a corporation's past earnings and to predict its future earnings performance, and the earnings per share amount is a small piece of the total information available in financial statements. Excessive reliance on earnings per share data may result in failure to consider the totality of a corporation's operations, including a wide range of nonfinancial data that may be far more important to investors.

Historical Perspective

The inclusion of earnings per share in the income statement became a generally accepted accounting principle with the issuance of *APB Opinion No. 9,* ''Reporting the Results of Operations,'' in 1966.[7] Three years later, the Accounting Principles Board issued *Opinion No. 15,* ''Earnings per Share,'' to: (1) recognize the importance of the increasingly complex capital structures of many corporations in which the distinctions between common stockholders' equity and other forms of corporate capital were not clearly apparent; (2) provide guidelines and procedures for the computation of earnings per share in a consistent manner that would be meaningful to investors; and (3) specify procedures for reporting the potential dilution in earnings per share.[8] The Accounting Principles Board recognized that it is difficult to identify all conditions that may be encountered in the computation of earnings per share.[9] Although *APB Opinion No. 15* has been widely criticized on the grounds that it deals with financial analysis rather than accounting principles, that it is overly complex, and that it contains some illogical assumptions, it has eliminated the wide diversity of practices previously followed in the computation and reporting of earnings per share data.

In 1978, the Financial Accounting Standards Board suspended earnings per share disclosure requirements for nonpublic enterprises. A *nonpublic enterprise* was defined as an enterprise (1) whose equity and debt securities are not publicly traded on a stock exchange or in the over-the-counter market, or (2) that is not required to file financial statements with the SEC. The FASB took this action pending completion of a study to consider whether certain types of business enterprises should be exempt from some disclosures required by generally accepted accounting principles.[10]

Computation of Weighted-Average Number of Shares of Common Stock Outstanding; Stock Splits and Stock Dividends

The first procedure in the computation of earnings per share is to determine the number of shares of common stock outstanding in each accounting period for which earnings data are to be presented. Earnings per share amounts are based on the *weighted-average* number of shares of common stock outstanding during each period. (At this point of our discussion we are not concerned with common stock equivalents or other complexities discussed later in this chapter.)

Computation of Weighted-Average Number of Shares Outstanding The weighted-average number of shares of common stock outstanding is computed by relating the portion of time during an accounting period that a specific number of shares of common stock was outstanding to the length of that period. For example,

---

[7]*APB Opinion No. 9,* ''Reporting the Results of Operations,'' AICPA (New York: 1966).

[8]*APB Opinion No. 15,* ''Earnings per Share,'' AICPA (New York: 1969).

[9]Shortly after the issuance of *APB Opinion No. 15,* the AICPA published a 189-page monograph by J. T. Ball, ''Computing Earnings per Share—Unofficial Accounting Interpretations of APB Opinion No. 15'' (New York: 1970).

[10]*FASB Statement No. 21,* ''Suspension of the Reporting of Earnings per Share . . . by Nonpublic Enterprises,'' FASB (Stamford: 1978).

if 1,000 shares of common stock were outstanding during the first nine months of Year 1 and 1,400 shares were outstanding during the last three months of Year 1, as a result of the issuance for cash of 400 additional shares of common stock on September 30, Year 1, the weighted-average number of shares of common stock outstanding during Year 1 is 1,100, computed as follows:

Computation of
weighted-average
number of shares of
common stock
outstanding

1,000 shares × ¾ of a year	750
1,400 shares × ¼ of a year	350
Weighted-average number of shares of common stock outstanding during Year 1	1,100

ANSON CORPORATION
Computation of Weighted-Average Number of Shares of Common Stock Outstanding
For Year 3, Year 2, and Year 1

		Year ended Dec. 31,		
		Year 3	**Year 2**	**Year 1**
Analysis of actual changes in the number of shares of common stock outstanding:				
Year 1				
Jan. 1	Number of shares outstanding, beginning of year	840,000	700,000	500,000
Apr. 1	Issuance for cash			200,000
Year 2				
Aug. 5	20% stock dividend		140,000	
Year 3				
Mar. 16	3 for 1 stock split (200% increase)	1,680,000		
Dec. 31	Number of shares outstanding, end of year	2,520,000	840,000	700,000
Computation of weighted-average number of shares of common stock outstanding (giving retroactive recognition to stock dividend and stock split):				
Year 1				
Jan. 1	Number of shares outstanding, beginning of year	840,000	700,000	500,000
Apr. 1	Issuance for cash (200,000 shares × ¾)			150,000
	Subtotals	840,000	700,000	650,000
Year 2				
Aug. 5	20% stock dividend (applied retroactively)		140,000	130,000
	Subtotals	840,000	840,000	780,000
Year 3				
Mar. 16	3 for 1 stock split (applied retroactively)	1,680,000	1,680,000	1,560,000
	Weighted-average number of shares outstanding	2,520,000	2,520,000	2,340,000

The use of the weighted-average number of shares outstanding is necessary when additional shares of common stock are issued for cash or other assets in order to compute a more meaningful earnings per share amount. In the foregoing example, the 400 shares of common stock issued on September 30, Year 1, provided cash that was available to generate earnings only during the last three months of Year 1. These 400 shares were outstanding for one-fourth of a year, or an equivalent of 100 ($400 \times \frac{1}{4} = 100$) shares outstanding for the full year. In other words, the weighted-average number of shares of common stock outstanding consists of 1,000 shares outstanding during the entire year plus 100 full-year-equivalent shares issued on September 30, Year 1.

Effect of Stock Split or Stock Dividend When the number of shares of common stock outstanding changes as a result of a stock split, stock dividend, or reverse split, the computation of the weighted-average number of shares common stock outstanding is adjusted *retroactively*. This is necessary to report earnings per share that are fully comparable in terms of the latest capital structure. If a stock split, stock dividend, or reverse split is to become effective after the close of the latest accounting period *but before financial statements are issued,* the per-share computations should be made on the basis of the *new capitalization*. When earnings per share data are computed on this basis, the method of computation is disclosed in a note to the financial statements.

The computation of the weighted-average number of shares of common stock outstanding, showing retroactive adjustment for a stock dividend and a stock split, is illustrated on page 908 for Anson Corporation.

Net income and earnings per share data as originally reported	**ANSON CORPORATION** **Net Income and Earnings per Share (as Originally Reported)** **For Years Ended December 31, Year 2 and Year 1**	

	From income statement for Year 2	*From income statement for Year 1*
Net income	$3,780,000	$2,574,000
Earnings per share of common stock:		
Year 1: $2,574,000 ÷ 650,000 (weighted-average number of shares outstanding in Year 1, before retroactive adjustment for 20% stock dividend and 3 for 1 stock split)		$ 3.96
Year 2: $3,780,000 ÷ 840,000 (weighted-average number of shares outstanding in Year 2, before retroactive adjustment for 3 for 1 stock split)	$ 4.50	

In the computation of the retroactive weighted-average number of shares of common stock outstanding in Year 1 for Anson Corporation, the 20% stock dividend declared in Year 2 was applied to the 650,000 weighted-average number of shares of common stock outstanding in Year 1; and the 3 for 1 stock split in Year 3 was applied to the 780,000 weighted-average number of shares of common stock after adjustment for the 20% stock dividend.

To continue the example, assume that the net income of Anson Corporation for Year 3 was $5,040,000, and that net income and earnings per share were *originally reported* for Year 2 and Year 1 as shown at the bottom of page 909.

A two-year comparative income statement at the end of Year 2 would show earnings per share for Year 1 of $3.30 ($2,574,000 ÷ 780,000 shares outstanding after giving effect to the 20% stock dividend in Year 2 = $3.30). The three-year comparative net income and earnings per share amounts for Anson Corporation, giving effect to the 20% stock dividend in Year 2 and the 3 for 1 stock split in Year 3, are presented *at the end of Year 3* as follows:

ANSON CORPORATION
Earnings per Share (Reflecting Retroactive Application of 20% Stock Dividend and 3 for 1 Stock Split)
For Years Ended December 31, Year 3, Year 2, and Year 1

	Year 3	Year 2	Year 1
Net income	$5,040,000	$3,780,000	$2,574,000
Earnings per share of common stock:			
Year 1: $2,574,000 ÷ 2,340,000			
shares (adjusted)			$ 1.10
Year 2: $3,780,000 ÷ 2,520,000			
shares (adjusted)		$ 1.50	
Year 3: $5,040,000 ÷ 2,520,000			
shares (adjusted)	$ 2.00		

Earnings per share data thus are reported on a fully comparable basis in terms of the capital structure at the end of Year 3. For example, because one share of common stock outstanding in Year 1 is equal to 3.6 shares at the end of Year 3 as a result of the 20% stock dividend and the 3 for 1 stock split, the earnings for Year 1 are restated retroactively at $1.10 per share ($3.96, as originally reported in the income statement for Year 1, divided by 3.6 = $1.10).

The difficulties encountered in the computation of earnings per share do not end with the computation of the weighted-average number of shares of common stock outstanding. For example: How are earnings per share computed for a corporation that has convertible preferred stock or convertible bonds outstanding? How do outstanding stock options and stock warrants affect the computation of earnings per share? To answer these questions, our discussion focuses on two types of corporate capital structure as follows:

1 Corporations that have a *simple capital structure*

2 Corporations that have a *complex capital structure*

a *Primary* earnings per share, which takes into account the potential dilutive effect of *common stock equivalents* outstanding

b *Fully diluted* earnings per share, which takes into account the **maximum potential dilutive effect** of convertible securities, stock options, and stock warrants outstanding (whether or not common stock equivalents)

Simple Capital Structure

The capital structure of a corporation may consist only of common stock; or the capital structure may include nonconvertible preferred stock, and immaterial amounts of or no potentially dilutive convertible securities, stock options, and stock

Single presentation
of earnings per share
data for corporation
with simple capital
structure and
extraordinary item

SIMPLEX CORPORATION
Earnings per Share Data and Computations
For Years Ended December 31, Year 2 and Year 1

	Year 2	Year 1
Data required to compute earnings per share of common stock:		
Income before extraordinary item (loss)	$810,000	$750,000
Extraordinary item (loss), (net of income tax effect) . . .	$140,000	
Dividend requirement on cumulative, nonconvertible preferred stock	$ 50,000	$ 50,000
Shares of common stock outstanding:		
Beginning of year	400,000	300,000
Issued for cash, July 1, Year 1		100,000
End of year	400,000	400,000
Shares of common stock reserved for employee stock options (option price is $20 and current market price of common stock is $18)	10,000 (1)	10,000 (1)
Weighted-average number of shares of common stock outstanding during year	400,000	350,000 (2)
Presentation in income statement:		
Earnings per share of common stock:		
Income before extraordinary item	$ 1.90 (3)	$ 2.00 (4)
Extraordinary item (loss)	(0.35) (5)	
Net income	$ 1.55	$ 2.00

(1) Excluded from weighted-average number of shares of common stock because options are **antidilutive,** as explained on page 917.
(2) 300,000 shares for the full year, plus 100,000 shares for one-half year (equivalent to 50,000 for a full year) = 350,000 shares.
(3) ($810,000 − $50,000) ÷ 400,000 weighted-average number of shares = $1.90.
(4) ($750,000 − $50,000) ÷ 350,000 weighted-average number of shares = $2.00.
(5) $140,000 ÷ 400,000 weighted-average number of shares = $0.35.

warrants. In such cases, the corporation is said to have a *simple capital structure.* The potential reduction in earnings per share that would occur if convertible securities were converted or if outstanding stock options and stock warrants were exercised is called *dilution.* If the total potential dilution in earnings per share is *less than 3%,* potentially dilutive securities, stock options, and stock warrants need not be considered in the computation of earnings per share. The Accounting Principles Board established the 3% minimum for materiality of potential dilution of earnings per share to achieve a uniform standard in earnings per share computations.

For corporations having a simple capital structure, a *single presentation* of earnings per share in the income statement is appropriate. This single presentation may include an extraordinary item, as on page 911 for Simplex Corporation.

The example for Simplex Corporation shows that the earnings per share before the extraordinary item decreased from $2.00 a share in Year 1 to $1.90 a share in Year 2, despite the fact that the same number of shares of common stock was outstanding on December 31 of each year (400,000 shares) and that the income before the extraordinary item actually increased from $750,000 in Year 1 to $810,000 in Year 2. This is attributed to the increase in the *weighted-average* number of shares outstanding from 350,000 in Year 1 to 400,000 in Year 2. The 100,000 shares issued on July 1, Year 1, were outstanding for only six months in Year 1, but for all 12 months in Year 2. In the absence of extraordinary items, only a single earnings per share amount appears in the income statement for a corporation with a simple capital structure. If the income statement includes the results of a discontinued business segment, extraordinary items, and the cumulative effect of a change in accounting principle, the presentation of earnings per share is more detailed (see page 164 in Chapter 4).

Complex Capital Structure

If a corporation has convertible securities, stock options, stock warrants, or other potentially dilutive securities outstanding, its capital stock structure is classified as *complex* for purposes of earnings per share computations. The Accounting Principles Board took the position that earnings per share should reflect potential dilution if securities that in substance are equivalent to common stock are outstanding. As a result, corporations with a complex capital structure must report with equal prominence in the income statement *primary* earnings per share (which include the dilutive effect of common stock equivalents) and *fully diluted* earnings per share (which include the maximum potential dilutive effect of all convertible securities, stock options, and stock warrants outstanding, regardless of whether they are common stock equivalents); this is referred to as a *dual presentation* of earnings per share. (See page 922 for an example.) These reporting requirements for earnings per share do not change the legal rights of the various security holders or the presentation of other information in the financial statements. The computation of primary earnings per share is explained below; the explanation of fully diluted earnings per share begins on page 918.

Primary Earnings per Share and Common Stock Equivalents   *Primary earnings per share* is the amount of earnings applicable to each share of common stock. The number of shares of common stock consists of the weighted-average number of shares of common stock actually outstanding plus any dilutive common stock equivalents. A ***common stock equivalent*** is a security such as convertible preferred stock that contains provisions enabling its owner to exchange the security for common stock.[11] Such a security is considered equivalent to common stock because its holders have a right to participate in the appreciation of the market price of the common stock. This participation is essentially the same as that of a common stockholder, except that convertible preferred stock and all except zero-coupon convertible bonds carry a specified dividend or interest rate. The market price of a security that is a common stock equivalent is dependent to a considerable degree on the market price of the common stock. Neither actual conversion nor the assumption that conversion is likely to take place is necessary before a security is classified as a common stock equivalent. ***Common stock equivalency is determined at the time the security is issued*** and does not change as long as the security remains outstanding.[12]

In a complex capital structure case, potentially dilutive securities may or may not qualify as common stock equivalents for the computation of primary earnings per share. However, common stock equivalents are not used to compute primary earnings per share if they would be ***antidilutive,*** that is, they would have the effect of ***increasing earnings per share*** or ***reducing a loss per share***. Common stock equivalents may include convertible bonds, convertible preferred stock, stock options, and stock warrants.

Convertible Securities   A convertible bond or preferred stock that at the time of issuance is substantially equivalent to common stock is treated as a common stock equivalent. Convertible preferred stocks and bonds are considered common stock equivalents if ***at the time of issuance*** the ***effective yield,*** based on the market price, is less than 66⅔% of the average **Aa** corporate bond yield for a brief period of time that includes or immediately precedes the issuance date of the convertible security.[13] The effective yield of a convertible bond is measured by its effective interest rate (see Chapter 15, pages 747–750); the effective yield of a convertible preferred stock is its stated annual dividend per share divided by the issuance price per share. The designation **Aa** is assigned by bond rating agencies to bonds that are of high quality and have a strong possibility of paying interest and principal.[14] Only **Aaa** bonds are rated higher than **Aa** bonds.

If convertible ***senior securities*** (bonds payable and preferred stock) do not meet the test of common stock equivalency at the time of issuance, they are not used in the computation of primary earnings per share, but are used (if dilutive) in the computation of fully diluted earnings per share.

A convertible security that is a common stock equivalent is assumed to have been converted to common stock at the beginning of the earliest accounting period for which earnings per share data are reported or at the time of issuance, whichever

---

[11]*APB Opinion No. 15*, p. 225.
[12]Ibid., p. 227.
[13]*FASB Statement No. 55*, "Determining Whether a Convertible Security Is a Common Stock Equivalent," FASB (Stamford: 1982), pp. 2–3; *FASB Statement No. 85*, "Yield Test for Determining Whether a Convertible Security Is a Common Stock Equivalent," FASB (Stamford: 1985), p. 2.
[14]*FASB Statement No. 55*, p. 3.

is the more recent date. For example, if convertible preferred stock were issued on April 1, Year 1, the equivalent number of shares of common stock (including any shares issued pursuant to the conversion of any of the preferred stock) for Year 1 is considered to be outstanding for nine months of Year 1.

In the computation of primary earnings per share, net income is adjusted (increased) by the amount of interest (net of income taxes) on convertible bonds that are dilutive common stock equivalents. (This technique is termed the *if converted method.*) In the determination of net income available for common stock, *net income is not reduced by the amount of the dividend requirement on convertible preferred stock that is a dilutive common stock equivalent.* These procedures are necessary because it is assumed that both the bonds and the preferred stock had been converted to common stock and are no longer outstanding.

Example 1: Convertible Preferred Stock Is a Common Stock Equivalent   At the beginning of Year 1, Wagner Corporation issued at $100 a share, 50,000 shares of $6 convertible preferred stock. At the time the preferred stock was issued, the average **Aa** corporate bond yield was 12%. Each share of preferred stock is convertible to two share of common stock; no shares have yet been converted. If Wagner has net income of $1,900,000 in Year 2 and 400,000 shares of common stock outstanding throughout Year 2, compute the primary earnings per share for Year 2.

Solution: The convertible preferred stock qualifies as a common stock equivalent because its effective yield of 6% ($6 ÷ $100 = 0.06) is less than 8% (66⅔% of the 12% average **Aa** corporate bond yield when the convertible preferred stock was issued). A convertible preferred stock is dilutive if the dividend per share paid on the stock (computed on the basis of the number of shares of common stock that would be issued on conversion) is less than the earnings per share of common stock before the hypothetical conversion is considered. In this case the convertible preferred stock is *dilutive,* because the equivalent converted dividend on the preferred stock is $3 ($6 ÷ 2 shares of common stock = $3), which is less than the earnings per share of common stock before the conversion is assumed, $4 ($1,900,000 net income − $300,000 preferred stock dividend ÷ 400,000 shares of common stock outstanding = $4). The amount of primary earnings per share for Year 2 is computed below:

Computation of primary earnings per share: Convertible preferred stock is a *dilutive* common stock equivalent

$$\frac{\text{Net income (before preferred dividends)}}{\text{Common stock outstanding} + \text{dilutive common stock equivalents outstanding}}$$

$$= \frac{\$1,900,000}{400,000 + (50,000 \times 2)} = \underline{\underline{\$3.80}}$$

The $3.80 amount is reported as primary earnings per share for Year 2 by Wagner Corporation because it is 5% less [($4.00 − $3.80) ÷ $4.00 = 0.05] than the $4.00 amount computed without the common stock equivalent and thus meets the *3% minimum* test for dilution described on page 912.

The conversion of a common stock equivalent, if dilutive, also is assumed for the computation of fully diluted earnings per share; this is illustrated in Example 6 on pages 919–922.

Example 2: Common Stock Equivalent Is Antidilutive   Assume the same facts as in Example 1 for Wagner Corporation, except that net income for Year 2 is only $700,000. Compute primary earnings per share for Year 2.

Solution: Although the convertible preferred stock is a common stock equivalent, conversion is not assumed for the computation of primary earnings per share because the effect would be *antidilutive*. This is illustrated below:

Conversion of
antidilutive convert-
ible preferred stock
is not assumed

> *Earnings per share of common stock:*
>   *Conversion not assumed ($700,000 net income − $300,000 preferred*
>   *stock dividends = $400,000 ÷ 400,000 shares)* *$1,00*
>
>   *Conversion assumed ($700,000 net income ÷ 500,000 shares)* *$1.40*

Because earnings per share would be *increased* if the common stock equivalent were used in the computation, primary earnings per share is reported at $1.00 a share, not $1.40 a share. The assumed conversion of the preferred stock is *antidilutive* (increases earnings per share); therefore, conversion also is not assumed in the computation of fully diluted earnings per share.

Example 3: Convertible Bonds Are Not Common Stock Equivalents   On December 31, Year 1, Catalina Corporation issued at face amount $1 million of 12% convertible bonds when the average **Aa** corporate bond yield was 15%. Each $1,000 bond was convertible to 25 shares of Catalina's common stock. In Year 2, Catalina had a $450,000 net income. The income tax rate is 45% of pre-tax income. During Year 2, no bonds had been converted, and 75,000 shares of common stock were outstanding throughout the year. Compute the primary earnings per share for Year 2.

Solution: The effective yield of 12% ($120 ÷ $1,000 = 0.12) on the convertible bonds *exceeded* 10% (66⅔% of 15% average **Aa** corporate bond yield when the bonds were issued); therefore, the convertible bonds are not common stock equivalents for the computation of primary earnings per share for Year 2. The amount of primary earnings per share is $6 ($450,000 ÷ 75,000 shares = $6). However, conversion of the bonds is assumed for the computation of fully diluted earnings per share, unless the assumed conversion would be antidilutive.

Example 4: Convertible Bonds Are Common Stock Equivalents   Assume the same facts as in Example 3 for Catalina Corporation, except that the interest rate on the convertible bonds is 9% rather than 12%. Compute primary earnings per share for Year 2 if net income is $450,000.

Solution: In this case, the convertible bonds are common stock equivalents because the effective yield of 9% ($90 ÷ $1,000 = 0.09) was *less* than 10% (66⅔% of 15% average **Aa** corporate bond yield when the bonds were issued). The primary earnings per share for Year 2 is $5.00, as computed below:

An example of the *if converted* method for dilutive common stock equivalent

CATALINA CORPORATION
Computation of Primary Earnings per Share
(Convertible Bonds Are a Dilutive Common Stock Equivalent)
For Year 2

Earnings to be used in computation of primary earnings per share:

Net income		$450,000
Add: Interest on convertible bonds, net of income taxes:		
Interest ($1,000,000 × 0.09)	$90,000	
Less: Income taxes ($90,000 × 0.45)	40,500	49,500
Earnings to be used in computation of primary earnings per share		$499,500

Number of shares of common stock to be used in computation of primary earnings per share:

Number of shares of common stock outstanding throughout Year 2	75,000
Add: Number of shares of common stock to be issued, assuming conversion of bonds (1,000 bonds × 25 shares of common stock)	25,000
Number of shares of common stock to be used in computation of primary earnings per share	100,000
Primary earnings per share of common stock ($499,500 ÷ 100,000 shares = $4.995, rounded to $5.00) ..	$ 5.00

If conversion of the bonds were not assumed, the earnings per share would be reported improperly at $6 a share ($450,000 ÷ 75,000 shares = $6). Conversion also is assumed (if dilutive) in the computation of fully diluted earnings per share.

Stock Options and Stock Warrants A corporation may issue stock options (including stock appreciation rights) and stock warrants that give grantees the right to acquire common stock at a stated price. Such options or warrants should be regarded as common stock equivalents *at all times;*[15] however, dilution is disregarded if it is less than 3% in the aggregate. Therefore, primary earnings per share should reflect the impact of the assumed exercise of stock options and stock warrants, including the possible *use of the proceeds* that would be received on the exercise of the stock options and stock warrants. In the computation of primary earnings per

---

[15]*APB Opinion No. 15*, p. 230.

share, exercise of the stock options and stock warrants is assumed *only if such exercise would result in a dilution of earnings per share.*

When the exercise of stock options and stock warrants is assumed, any proceeds that would be received are assumed to be used to acquire common stock for the treasury at the average market price during the accounting period. This is known as the *treasury stock method.* For example, if options to acquire 10,000 shares of common stock at $5 a share are outstanding, and the average market price during the accounting period was $20 a share, the $50,000 that would be received by the corporation from assumed exercise of the stock options and the issuance of 10,000 additional shares of common stock would be sufficient to acquire 2,500 shares of common stock ($50,000 ÷ $20 = 2,500). Thus, 7,500 (10,000 − 2,500 = 7,500) shares are added to the number of shares of common stock already outstanding to compute primary earnings per share. The exercise of the stock options and stock warrants is assumed to have taken place at the *beginning of the accounting period* or *at the time* the stock options and stock warrants were issued, whichever is the more recent date.

The Accounting Principles Board recommended that the exercise of stock options and stock warrants should not be assumed until the common stock traded in excess of the exercise price for "substantially all of three consecutive months ending with the last month of the period to which earnings per share data relate."[16] Under the treasury stock method, stock options and stock warrants have a dilutive effect on earnings per share *only when the average market price of the common stock exceeds the exercise price of the options and warrants.* The computation of primary earnings per share under the treasury stock method is illustrated in the example below. For simplicity, we illustrate the computation for a *fiscal year;* in practice, the computation is required for *each quarter* of the year.[17]

Example 5: Stock Options Are Outstanding   Rawlins Corporation has 200,000 shares of common stock and stock options to acquire 30,000 shares of common stock at $10 a share outstanding throughout Year 2. The stock options were granted to employees several years ago. The average market price of the common stock during Year 2 was $30 a share. Compute primary earnings per share for Year 2 if the net income for Year 2 is $550,000.

Solution: The amount of primary earnings per share for Rawlins Corporation for Year 2 is $2.50 a share, as computed at the top of page 918.

Rawlins Corporation reports primary earnings per share of $2.50 because that amount is 9% less [($2.75 − $2.50) ÷ $2.75 = 0.09] than the earnings per share computation of $2.75 ($550,000 ÷ 200,000 shares = $2.75) that excludes the dilutive effect of the stock options. The 9% dilution meets the *3% minimum* test for dilution described on page 912.

The procedures described for stock options are equally applicable to stock warrants.

---

[16]Ibid., pp. 230–231.
[17]J. T. Ball, *Computing Earnings per Share: Unofficial Accounting Interpretations of APB Opinion No. 15,* AICPA (New York: 1970), pp. 50, 56, and 57.

RAWLINS CORPORATION
Computation of Primary Earnings per Share
(Stock Options Are Dilutive)
For Year 2

Computation of number of shares of common stock to be used in
determination of primary earnings per share:

Number of shares of common stock outstanding throughout Year 2		200,000
Add: Number of shares of common stock to be issued on exercise of stock options	30,000	
Less: Assumed acquisition of common stock for treasury with the proceeds received on exercise of stock options [(30,000 × $10) ÷ $30]	10,000*	20,000
Number of shares of common stock to be used in computation of primary earnings per share		220,000
Primary earnings per share of common stock ($550,000 ÷ 220,000 shares)		$ 2.50

Does not exceed 20% (200,000 × 0.20 = 40,000) of the shares of common stock outstanding at end of Year 2 (see next section).

Limitation on Treasury Stock Method   A departure from the procedure illustrated for Rawlins Corporation is required when the number of shares of common stock assumed to be acquired exceeds 20% of the number of shares of common stock actually outstanding at the end of the accounting period. In such cases, it is assumed that **all** stock options and stock warrants were exercised and the proceeds first were used to acquire 20% of the outstanding common stock, with the balance used to retire outstanding debt. However, if all debt is thus eliminated, it is assumed that the remaining proceeds are used to acquire interest-yielding short-term investments. Appropriate recognition is given to the income tax effects of the assumed use of the potential proceeds from the exercise of stock options and stock warrants.

Computation of fully diluted earnings per share when stock options are outstanding is illustrated in Example 6 beginning on page 919.

It is impractical to cover all situations that may arise in the computation of primary earnings per share; our objective has been to describe the basic issues involved. We now turn our attention to the second part of the **dual presentation** of earnings per share for a complex capital structure—the computation of fully diluted earnings per share.

Fully Diluted Earnings per Share   It is apparent from the foregoing discussion that primary earnings per share may include some potential dilution and that certain potentially dilutive securities are not considered common stock equivalents. However, in the computation of fully diluted earnings per share, **all** dilutive convertible securities, stock options, and stock warrants are assumed to have been converted or exercised in order to reflect the maximum potential dilution, *assuming it exceeds 3%* in the aggregate. As in the computation of primary earnings per share, conversion of securities or the exercise of stock options and stock warrants *should not be assumed if the effect is antidilutive* (would have the effect of increasing earnings per share or reducing a loss per share).

The computation of fully diluted earnings per share differs from the computation of primary earnings per share in the following two respects:

1   All convertible securities and other potentially dilutive securities, whether or not they qualify as common stock equivalents, that *individually* would decrease earnings per share if conversion had taken place, are included in the computation of fully diluted earnings per share. All such conversions are assumed to have taken place at the beginning of the accounting period (or at the time of issuance of the convertible security, if later).

2   To recognize the maximum potential dilution, the market price of the common stock at the end of the accounting period, *if it exceeds* the average market price during the period, is used to determine the number of shares of common stock that could be acquired with the proceeds received on the assumed exercise of stock options and stock warrants. This procedure reduces the number of shares of common stock that could be acquired with the proceeds, and thus has the effect of increasing the number of outstanding shares of common stock on a pro forma basis.

The computation of primary and fully diluted earnings per share when stock options and convertible preferred stock are outstanding is illustrated below:

Example 6: Stock Options and Convertible Preferred Stock Are Outstanding
Primary and fully diluted earnings per share for Year 10 are computed on page 920 from the information presented below for Largo Corporation:

Information for computation of primary and fully diluted earnings per share

Net income for Year 10	$330,000
Number of shares of common stock outstanding throughout Year 10	95,000
Number of shares of $4 cumulative, convertible preferred stock outstanding throughout Year 10; each share of preferred stock is convertible to three shares of common stock; the preferred stock **is not a common stock equivalent, but is dilutive**	3,000
Outstanding stock options (issued in Year 6) to acquire common stock at $20 a share; average market price of common stock during Year 10 was $40 a share, and the market price at the end of Year 10 was $50 a share (because exercise price is **less than** both market prices, the stock options are dilutive)	10,000
Earnings per share, disregarding common stock equivalents and other potentially dilutive securities [($330,000 − $12,000 preferred dividend requirement) ÷ 95,000]	$ 3.35

In the computation of fully diluted earnings per share for Largo Corporation, the assumed proceeds of $200,000 (10,000 × $20 = $200,000) from the issuance of 10,000 additional shares of common stock on the assumed exercise of stock

LARGO CORPORATION
Computation of Primary and Fully Diluted Earnings per Share
For Year 10

	Number of shares	
	Primary	Fully diluted
Computation of number of shares of common stock outstanding to be used in computation of earnings per share for Year 10:		
Number of shares of common stock outstanding throughout Year 10	95,000	95,000
For computation of primary earnings per share:		
Add: Shares of common stock assumed to be issued on exercise of stock options at $20 a share	10,000	
Less: Assumed acquisition of common stock at average market price during Year 10 with proceeds received from assumed exercise of stock options [(10,000 × $20) ÷ $40]	(5,000) (1)	
For computation of fully diluted earnings per share:		
Add: Shares of common stock to be issued on assumed exercise of stock options at $20 a share		10,000
Less: Assumed acquisition of common stock at market price at end of Year 10 with proceeds received from assumed exercise of stock options [(10,000 × $20) ÷ $50]		(4,000)(1)
Add: Assumed conversion of 3,000 shares of preferred stock to common stock (3 for 1)		9,000
Number of shares of common stock outstanding to be used in computation of earnings per share for Year 10	100,000	110,000
Earnings per share of common stock for Year 10:		
Primary ($318,000 ÷ 100,000 shares) (2)	$ 3.18 (3)	
Fully diluted ($330,000 ÷ 110,000 shares)		$ 3.00 (4)

(1) Less than 20% of shares outstanding at end of Year 10 (95,000 × 0.20 = 19,000).
(2) Net income of $330,000 less preferred dividend requirement of $12,000 = $318,000.
(3) 5% less [($3.35 − $3:18) ÷ $3.35 = 0.05] than earnings per share disregarding common stock equivalents; therefore, meets the **3% minimum** test for dilution.
(4) 6% less [($3.18 − $3.00) ÷ $3.18 = 0.06] than primary earnings per share; therefore, meets the **3% minimum** test for dilution.

options is assumed to be used to acquire common stock at $50 a share, the market price of the common stock at the end of Year 10. Because only 4,000 shares ($200,000 ÷ $50 = 4,000) are assumed to be acquired with the proceeds of $200,000, the number of shares of common stock to be used in the computation of fully diluted earnings per share is increased by 6,000 (10,000 − 4,000 = 6,000). In

Summary of earnings per share computations

Capital structure	Earnings per share in income statement	Explanation
1 Simple	Single presentation	Divide net income available for common stock by the weighted-average number of shares of common stock outstanding during the accounting period. Dilutive common stock equivalents are disregarded when the potential dilution **in the aggregate is less than 3% of earnings.**
2 Complex	Dual presentation: **a** Primary	Divide net income (increased by the after-tax effect of assumed conversion of bonds, if any) by the weighted-average number of shares of common stock and common stock equivalents outstanding during the accounting period. Convertible securities may or may not be common stock equivalents on date of issue; stock options and stock warrants always are common stock equivalents. In no case are common stock equivalents included in the computation of primary earnings per share if inclusion is antidilutive. Potential earnings dilution of **less than 3% (in the aggregate)** is disregarded.
	b Fully diluted	Essentially the same procedure as above, except that all convertible securities are assumed to have been converted (at the beginning of the accounting period or issue date, if later) if the effect of the assumed conversion is dilutive. The proceeds from the assumed exercise of stock options and stock warrants are applied to acquire common stock at end-of-period market price if such price is higher than the average market price during the period covered. Potential earnings dilution of **less than 3% (in the aggregate)** is disregarded.

addition, the 3,000 shares of convertible preferred stock that are not common stock equivalents for the computation of primary earnings per share are assumed to be converted to 9,000 (3,000 × 3 = 9,000) shares of common stock for the computation of fully diluted earnings per share. *These adjustments recognize the maximum potential dilution in earnings per share.*

It should be emphasized that in the computation of primary earnings per share, the amount of the dividend requirement on the cumulative, convertible preferred stock (3,000 × $4 = $12,000) was deducted from net income to compute the income available for common stock. However, when fully diluted earnings per share were computed, net income was *not* reduced by the preferred dividend requirement *because the preferred stock was assumed to have been eliminated through conversion to common stock.*

Summary of Earnings per Share Computations

The foregoing discussion of the computation of earnings per share is summarized on page 921.

Presentation of Earnings per Share in the Income Statement

Shown below is an actual two-year presentation of earnings per share (including the accompanying note to the financial statements) by a company with a complex capital structure:[18]

	Year ended December 31,	
	Year 7	**Year 6**
Net income	$342,936,000	$314,149,000
Less: Dividends on preferred stock	29,387,000	35,549,000
Net income available for common stock	$313,549,000	$278,600,000
Earnings per share of common stock **(Note 1):**		
Primary..	$ 4.15	$ 3.98
Fully diluted	$ 3.63	$ 3.30

Note 1: *Earnings per share of common stock are based on the average number of shares of common stock outstanding during each year. Such average shares outstanding were 75,608,800 and 70,079,891 shares for Year 7 and Year 6, respectively. Earnings per share computations, assuming full dilution, include the average common shares issuable for convertible or exchangeable securities and stock options and stock warrants during each year and the elimination of the related dividend and interest requirements, less applicable income taxes. Such average shares, assuming full dilution, were 92,583,448 and 91,964,825 shares for Year 7 and Year 6, respectively.*

Additional examples of presentation of earnings per share are in Chapter 4. The presentation of earnings per share following a change in accounting principle is illustrated in Chapter 22.

---

[18]The SEC requires a three-year presentation of earnings per share data by companies subject to its jurisdiction.

Evaluation of Standards for Earnings per Share

The establishment of uniform standards for the computation and presentation of earnings per share in the income statement of publicly owned corporations has achieved a degree of reliability for this important financial ratio. However, many accountants have reservations about the computational techniques and other assumptions established in *APB Opinion No. 15*, ''Earnings per Share.'' Among these reservations are the following:

1   The primary earnings per share computation supposedly is based on historical data, in contrast to the fully diluted amount, which is a pro forma computation. However, the computation of primary earnings per share involves pro forma assumptions such as those underlying the *treasury stock method* for dilutive stock options and stock warrants.

2   The decision as to whether a convertible security is a common stock equivalent is made only at the *issuance date* of the security. This method disregards subsequent changes in the market price of the convertible security and of the related common stock that might affect the *probability of conversion.* Thus, the *permanent status* assigned to a convertible security on its issuance date may be criticized.

3   Accountants acknowledge that accounting is an art, not an exact science. The measurement of net income involves numerous *assumptions and estimates.* The inclusion of net income in the computation of earnings per share brings the same imprecision to earnings per share data that is present in net income.

4   A corporation may distort its earnings per share amounts by the acquisition and reissuance of treasury stock. Because treasury stock is not outstanding, it is excluded from the weighted-average number of shares of common stock outstanding in the denominator of the earnings per share computation.

In view of the foregoing discussion, it is appropriate to stress once again that many factors other than earnings per share should be considered in the appraisal of the earnings performance of corporations.

REVIEW QUESTIONS

1   Define *treasury stock* and explain how it typically is shown in the balance sheet.

2   For what reasons do corporations acquire their outstanding capital stock?

3   The president of Lawson Corporation stated, ''We seek to acquire 8.4% of our outstanding common stock in order to secure a safe and profitable short-term investment for our excess cash.'' Comment on this quotation.

4   Does the acquisition and reissuance of its outstanding capital stock by a corporation result in a realized gain or a loss to the corporation? Explain.

5   In reviewing the Miscellaneous Revenue ledger account of Roddy Corporation, you find a credit for $200 representing a dividend of $1 a share on 200 shares of treasury stock. You determine that the dividend declaration covered the entire 10,000 shares of common stock originally issued, that the Retained Earnings ledger account was debited for $10,000, and that $9,800 cash was paid to stockholders. Discuss the propriety of Roddy Corporation's accounting for dividends.

6   **a** Discuss the propriety of declaring stock dividends on treasury stock.
     b Should treasury stock be split?
     c How is the issuance of treasury stock (carried at cost) pursuant to a 2% stock dividend recorded?

7   The Treasury Stock ledger account of Tipton Corporation had a debit balance of $108,000, representing the cost of 6,000 shares of its outstanding common stock acquired by Tipton. Later, Tipton exchanged the treasury stock for land that is now listed in its balance sheet as ''Land, at cost . . . $108,000.'' Do you approve of this accounting treatment? Explain.

8   Most states place some restriction on the acquisition by a corporation of its outstanding capital stock. What is the usual nature of such a restriction? What is the purpose of such a restriction?

9   The majority stockholder in Calla Company, a closely held corporation, had an option to acquire all the common stock of a minority stockholder at equity (book value) per share at any time during the first 10 years of operation. After four years, the method of valuing inventories was changed from first-in, first-out to last-in, first-out. At the end of the tenth year, the majority stockholder exercised the option. The minority stockholder objected, arguing that ''the change in the valuation of inventories reduced the option price by thousands of dollars.'' Discuss.

10   What is the appropriate accounting treatment of the difference between original issuance price and the price paid to retire preferred stock?

11   Define *earnings per share* and indicate how this statistic is used by investors.

12   **a** How is the weighted-average number of shares of common stock outstanding during a year computed?
     b What effect do stock dividends and stock splits have on the presentation of earnings per share of common stock for two or more years?

13   Differentiate between the following:
     a *Simple* and *complex* capital structures
     b *Primary* and *fully diluted* earnings per share
     c *Single* and *dual* presentations of earnings per share

14   Discuss the reasons why securities other than common stock may be considered *common stock equivalents* in the computation of primary earnings per share.

15   Explain how convertible securities are determined to be common stock equivalents and how convertible senior securities that are not common stock equivalents affect the computation of earnings per share.

16 Explain the *treasury stock method* as it applies to stock options and stock warrants in the computation of primary earnings per share.

17 For the year ended April 30, Year 6, Sark Corporation reported primary earnings per share of $4.50 and fully diluted earnings per share of $2. What factors may cause such a large difference between the two earnings per share amounts? If the common stock of Sark trades for $36 a share, what is the price-earnings ratio?

18 In an article in the *Financial Analysts' Journal,* an executive of a large bank observed that ''any evaluation of corporate policies in terms of their impact on earnings per share (EPS) is fraught with danger. . . . If the leverage idea is sound, management may increase EPS without making any investment whatever, merely by borrowing cash to retire common stock.'' Do you agree with this observation? Explain.

19 What are some shortcomings of earnings per share computations as required by *APB Opinion No. 15,* ''Earnings per Share''?

EXERCISES

Ex. 18-1 Select the best answer for each of the following multiple-choice questions:

1 When treasury stock accounted for by the cost method is reissued for more than its carrying amount, the excess is recorded as:
a An extraordinary gain
b Income from continuing operations
c An increase in additional paid-in capital
d An increase in retained earnings

2 In the application of the ''treasury stock method'' of computing the dilutive effect of outstanding stock options for fully diluted earnings per share, when is the end-of-period market price of common stock used as the assumed acquisition price of treasury stock?
a Always
b Never
c When the end-of-period market price exceeds both the average market price for the period and the exercise price
d When the end-of-period market price is less than the average market price for the period and exceeds the exercise price

3 Which of the following is included in the computation of earnings per share for a corporation with a simple capital structure?
a Dividends (whether declared or not) on cumulative, nonconvertible preferred stock
b Dividends on common stock
c Common stock equivalents
d Number of shares of nonconvertible preferred stock
e None of the foregoing

4   Are antidilutive common stock equivalents generally used in the computation of:

	Primary earnings per share?	Fully diluted earnings per share?
a	Yes	Yes
b	No	Yes
c	No	No
d	Yes	No

5   A convertible preferred stock is a common stock equivalent if at time of issuance its effective yield:

a Exceeds 66⅔% of the current average **Aa** corporate bond yield
b Equals 66⅔% of the current average **Aa** corporate bond yield
c Is less than 66⅔% of the current average **Aa** corporate bond yield
d Equals or is less than 66⅔% of the current average **Aa** corporate bond yield

6   The general rule for the balance sheet presentation and disclosure of treasury stock accounted for by the cost method is:

a Disclosure of number of shares of treasury stock and deduction of cost of treasury stock from total paid-in capital and retained earnings
b Disclosure of number of shares of treasury stock and deduction of cost of treasury stock from total paid-in capital
c Disclosure of restriction on declaration of cash dividends
d Both **a** and **c**
e None of the foregoing

7   Riggs Company had 1,000 shares of $10 par, 8% cumulative, convertible preferred stock and 10,000 shares of $1 par common stock outstanding throughout the year ended September 30, Year 3. The preferred stock was a common stock equivalent, and each share was convertible to one share common stock. Net income of Riggs for the year ended September 30, Year 3, was $11,000. Primary earnings per share for Riggs Company for the year ended September 30, Year 3, is:
a $1.10   **b** $1.02   **c** $1.00   **d** $0.93   **e** Some other amount

8   In the computation of primary earnings per share, dividends on noncumulative, nonconvertible preferred stock are:
a Deducted from net income whether declared or not
b Deducted from net income only if declared
c Added to net income whether declared or not
d Disregarded

Ex. 18-2   Elizar, Inc., which had 1,000,000 authorized shares of $5 par common stock, completed the following common stock transactions during Year 1, its first year of operations:

Jan. 4   Issued 200,000 shares at $5 a share
Apr. 8   Issued 100,000 shares at $7 a share
June 9   Issued 30,000 shares at $10 a share

July 29   Acquired in the open market for the treasury 50,000 shares at $5 a share

Dec. 31   Reissued 50,000 treasury shares at $9 a share

Assuming Elizar uses the cost method of accounting for treasury stock transactions, compute the balance of Elizar, Inc.'s, Paid-in Capital in Excess of Par ledger account on December 31, Year 1.

Ex. 18-3   Vinci Company, which was organized on October 1, Year 2, with 100,000 authorized shares of $10 par common stock, uses the par value method to account for treasury stock transactions. During the year ended September 30, Year 3, Vinci had the following common stock transactions:

(1) Issued 75,000 shares at $14 a share
(2) Acquired in the open market for the treasury 5,000 shares at $11 a share

Compute the balance of Vinci Company's Paid-in Capital in Excess of Par ledger account on September 30, Year 3.

Ex. 18-4   Narco, Inc., began business on January 2, Year 7, by issuing 200,000 shares of its 400,000 shares of authorized $10 par common stock at $15 a share. During the three-year period ended December 31, Year 9, Narco had total net income of $750,000 and declared dividends totaling $380,000. On January 5, Year 9, Narco acquired from a dissident shareholder 12,000 shares of its common stock for the treasury at $12 a share. On December 31, Year 9, Narco reissued 8,000 shares of treasury stock at $8 a share. Narco uses the cost method of accounting for treasury stock transactions.

Compute total stockholders' equity of Narco, Inc., on December 31, Year 9.

Ex. 18-5   The stockholders' equity section of Lane Company's balance sheet on September 30, Year 5, was as follows:

Stockholders' equity:

Common stock, $10 par, authorized 1,000,000 shares, issued and outstanding 900,000 shares	*$ 9,000,000*
Paid-in capital in excess of par	*2,700,000*
Retained earnings	*1,300,000*
Total stockholders' equity	*$13,000,000*

On October 1, Year 5, Lane acquired from a stockholder and retired 100,000 shares of its common stock for $1,800,000.

Compute the balances of Lane Company's Paid-in Capital in Excess of Par and Retained Earnings ledger accounts after the retirement of the common stock on October 1, Year 5.

Ex. 18-6   The stockholders' equity items of Nance Corporation on January 1, Year 4, were as follows:

Common stock, $20 par, authorized 100,000 shares, issued and outstanding 60,000 shares $1,200,000
Paid-in capital in excess of par 180,000
Retained earnings 760,000

Nance uses the cost method of accounting for treasury stock, and during Year 4 completed the following transactions:

(1) Acquired 1,000 shares of its common stock for the treasury for $34,000
(2) Reissued 600 shares of treasury stock at $38 a share
(3) Retired the remaining 400 shares of treasury stock

Nance had no other stockholders' equity transactions during Year 4.

Compute the amount that Nance Corporation includes in its balance sheet on December 31, Year 4, as paid-in capital in excess of par.

Ex. 18-7 The stockholders' equity section of Edgar Corporation's balance sheet on December 31, Year 5, was as follows:

Stockholders' equity:
Common stock, $100 par, authorized 50,000 shares, issued and outstanding 10,000 shares $1,000,000
Paid-in capital in excess of par 500,000
Total paid-in capital $1,500,000
Retained earnings 800,000
Total stockholders' equity $2,300,000

Early in Year 6, Edgar acquired for the treasury 400 shares of its common stock for $50,000. During Year 6, it reissued 100 shares of treasury stock at $140 a share, reissued 100 shares at $110 a share, and retired the remaining 200 shares of treasury stock. Edgar records treasury stock at cost.

Prepare journal entries for Edgar Corporation to record the acquisition, the reissuance, and the retirement of the treasury stock.

Ex. 18-8 On the retirement of a key employee, the board of directors of Burke Corporation authorized the presentation to the employee of a certificate for 100 shares of Burke's $50 par common stock ''in appreciation of past services.'' The shares were part of Burke's holding of treasury stock, acquired and carried at cost of $75 a share. Equity (book value) per share of common stock was $140, and market value was $125 a share.

Prepare a journal entry for the foregoing transaction of Burke Corporation.

Ex. 18-9 The stockholders' equity section of Toley Company's balance sheet on December 31, Year 2, was as follows:

Stockholders' equity:
Common stock, $10 par, authorized 500,000 shares, issued 90,000 shares, of which 1,210 shares are in treasury . . . . $ 900,000
Paid-in capital in excess of par 20,250
Total paid-in capital . . . . $ 920,250

(continued)

Retained earnings	$ 424,680
Total paid-in capital and retained earnings	$1,344,930
Less: Cost of 1,210 shares of treasury stock	36,300
Total stockholders' equity	$1,308,630

On January 5, Year 3, 650 shares of treasury stock were reissued, and on January 20, Year 3, a 5% stock dividend was declared. The dividend shares were issued on March 10. The market price of the common stock was $22 a share on January 20.

Prepare separate journal entries for Toley Company to record the declaration and distribution of the 5% stock dividend.

Ex. 18-10 Masters Corporation decided that because its $100 par, 10% cumulative preferred stock (which originally was issued at $98 a share) was trading in the stock market at $85 a share, it would acquire and retire as many shares of the preferred stock as possible in an effort to improve earnings per share of common stock. On March 2, Year 6, Masters acquired 5,000 shares of the preferred stock at $86 a share and immediately retired the shares.

Prepare a journal entry for Masters Corporation on March 2, Year 6, to record the acquisition and retirement of the 5,000 shares of the 10% cumulative preferred stock.

Ex. 18-11 Solo Company had the following stockholders' equity ledger account balances on September 30, Year 7:

10% cumulative preferred stock, $100 par, authorized 10,000 shares	$500,000
Common stock, $1 par, authorized 100,000 shares	80,000
Paid-in capital in excess of par: common stock	120,000
Retained earnings..	640,000
Treasury stock: common (6,000 shares), at cost......................	30,000

Prepare the stockholders' equity section of Solo Company's September 30, year 7, balance sheet, with all appropriate disclosures.

Ex. 18-12 The stockholders' equity section of Neman Corporation's December 31, Year 6, balance sheet included the following:

9% cumulative, nonconvertible preferred stock, $100 par, authorized	
10,000 shares, issued and outstanding 1,000 shares	$100,000
Common stock, $10 par, authorized 300,000 shares, issued and	
outstanding 45,000 shares	450,0000

On May 1, Year 7, Neman issued 3,000 shares of common stock for $25 a share.

Compute the weighted-average number of shares of stock to be used in the computation of Neman Corporation's earnings per share for the year ended December 31, Year 7.

Ex. 18-13 On December 31, Year 4, Gammage, Inc., had 500,000 shares of no-par common stock outstanding. On October 1, Year 5, 120,000 shares of common stock were issued for cash. Throughout Year 5, Gammage had $4,000,000 face amount of 8% convertible bonds outstanding. The bonds, which were dilutive common stock equivalents, were convertible to 100,000 shares of Gammage's common stock.

Compute the weighted-average number of shares of common stock and common stock equivalents to be used in the computation of primary earnings per share for Gammage, Inc., for the year ended December 31, Year 5.

Ex. 18-14 Sybil Corporation began operations on January 2, Year 1, by issuing 2,000 shares of common stock for plant assets. On July 1, Year 2, an additional 1,000 shares of common stock were issued for cash. On April 1, Year 3, a 10% common stock dividend was distributed. On July 1, Year 4, the common stock was split 3 for 1. Earnings and dividends per share of common stock for each of the first four years of operations are to be reported on a comparable basis in the annual report to shareholders for Year 4.

Compute the weighted-average number of shares outstanding at the end of each of the four years, Year 1 through Year 4, to be used in the computation of earnings per share of common stock for Sybil Corporation.

Ex. 18-15 Mamey Corporation had 5,000,000 shares of common stock outstanding on December 31, Year 6. An additional 1,000,000 shares of common stock were issued on April 1, Year 7, and 500,000 more on July 1, Year 7. On October 1, Year 7, Mamey issued 10,000, $1,000 face amount, 10% convertible bonds. Each bond is convertible to 50 shares of common stock. The bonds were not common stock equivalents at the time of their issuance, and no bonds were converted to common stock in Year 7.

Compute the weighted-average number of shares of common stock to be used in the computation of primary earnings per share and fully diluted earnings per share, respectively, for Mamey Corporation for Year 7. Assume that the 10% convertible bonds are dilutive.

Ex. 18-16 On December 31, Year 7, Dealey, Inc., had 20,000 shares of nonconvertible preferred stock and 100,000 shares of common stock outstanding. On July 1, Year 8, Dealey paid a cash dividend of $2 a share (the full dividend for Year 8) on the preferred stock and distributed a 10% common stock dividend. Dealey's net income for Year 8 was $777,000.

Compute Dealey, Inc.'s earnings per share for Year 8.

Ex. 18-17 Sandrac Company had 10,000 shares of 6%, $100 par convertible preferred stock and 200,000 shares of no-par, $5 stated value per share common stock outstanding on both December 31, Year 4, and December 31, Year 5. The preferred stock, each share of which was convertible to three shares of common stock, had been issued at par on July 1, Year 4, when the average **Aa** corporate bond yield was 9½%. During Year 5, Sandrac declared the annual preferred stock dividend of $6 a share and had net income of $862,500.

Compute Sandrac Company's primary earnings per share for Year 5.

Ex. 18-18 Olivera Corporation had 100,000 shares of no-par, no stated value common stock outstanding on December 31, Year 6. On July 1, Year 7, Olivera distributed a 10%

common stock dividend. Stock options to acquire 20,000 shares of common stock (adjusted for the Year 7 common stock dividend) at $20 a share were outstanding throughout Year 7. The average market price of Olivera's common stock (which was not affected by the common stock dividend) was $25 a share during Year 7, and the market price was $30 a share on December 31, Year 7. Olivera's net income for Year 7 was $550,000.

Compute Olivera Corporation's primary earnings per share for Year 7.

Ex. 18-19 On December 31, Year 6, Gross Corporation had 400,000 shares of common stock outstanding. On October 1, Year 7, an additional 100,000 shares of common stock were issued. In addition, Gross had $10,000,000 of 8% convertible bonds outstanding on December 31, Year 6, that were convertible to 225,000 shares of common stock. The bonds were dilutive common stock equivalents at the time of their issuance. No bonds were converted to common stock in Year 7. The net income of Gross for the year ended December 31, Year 7, was $3,500,000. The income tax rate was 45%.

Compute the primary earnings per share of Gross Corporation for the year ended December 31, Year 7, rounded to the nearest cent.

Ex. 18-20 Stock warrants exercisable at $20 each to acquire 12,000 shares of Liddy Corporation's common stock were outstanding during an accounting period when the average market price of the common stock was $25 and the ending market price was $30.

Determine the ***increase*** in the weighted-average number of shares of outstanding common stock of Liddy Corporation resulting from application of the "treasury stock method" for the assumed exercise of the stock warrants for the computation of **(a)** primary earnings per share, and **(b)** fully diluted earnings per share. Disregard the 20% test of the "treasury stock method."

Ex. 18-21 Information relating to the capital structure of Cortez Company is as follows:

	Dec. 31, Year 8	Dec. 31, Year 9
9% convertible bonds........................	$1,000,000	$1,000,000
Outstanding shares of:		
Convertible preferred stock................	10,000	10,000
Common stock	90,000	90,000

During Year 9, Cortez paid the current annual dividend of $2.50 a share on its preferred stock. The preferred stock is convertible to 20,000 shares of common stock and is a common stock equivalent. The 9% convertible bonds are convertible to 30,000 shares of common stock, but are not common stock equivalents. The net income of Cortez for the year ended December 31, Year 9, was $485,000. The income tax rate is 45%.

Compute primary earnings per share and fully diluted earnings per share for Cortez Company for Year 9, rounded to the nearest cent.

Ex. 18-22 On January 1, Year 4, Rudolfo Company had 10,000 shares of $4 cumulative, nonconvertible preferred stock, no-par, callable at $55 a share, and 100,000 shares of $5 par common stock outstanding. There was no long-term debt outstanding. On January 2, Year 5, Rudolfo called and retired the preferred stock, and on January 2, Year 6, Rudolfo issued at face amount $1,000,000 of 12% bonds and used the proceeds to acquire in the open market and retire 30,000 shares of common stock. Rudolfo had income before interest and income taxes expense of $800,000 for Year 4, $750,000 for Year 5, and $700,000 for Year 6. Rudolfo's income tax rate is 45%.

Compute Rudolfo Company's earnings per share for Year 4, Year 5, and Year 6, rounded to the nearest cent. Comment on, and explain the significance of, the trend of earnings per share compared with the decreasing income before interest and income taxes expense.

CASES

Case 18-1   For various reasons a corporation may acquire shares of its outstanding common stock for the treasury. When a corporation acquires treasury stock, it has two options as to accounting for the stock: (1) cost method, and (2) par or stated value method.

Instructions

Compare and contrast the cost method with the par or stated value method for each of the following:
a Acquisition of treasury stock at a price less than par or stated value
b Acquisition of treasury stock at a price more than par or stated value
c Subsequent reissuance of treasury stock at a price less than cost but more than par or stated value
d Subsequent reissuance of treasury stock at a price more than either cost or par or stated value
e Effect on net income

Case 18-2   The earnings per share data required for a publicly owned corporation depend on the nature of its capital structure. A corporation may have a simple capital structure and compute only a single earnings per share amount, or it may have a complex capital structure and compute both primary earnings per share and fully diluted earnings per share.

Instructions

a Define the term *common stock equivalent* and describe what securities are considered to be common stock equivalents in the computation of earnings per share.
b Define the term *complex capital structure* and discuss the disclosures (both financial and explanatory) necessary for earnings per share when a corporation has a complex capital structure.

Case 18-3   Dixie Corporation acquired equipment costing $180,000 for $120,000 cash and a promise to deliver an indeterminate number of treasury shares of its $10 par common stock, with a market value of $15,000, on January 2 of each year for the next five years. Hence, $75,000 in "market value" of treasury stock will be required to discharge the $60,000 balance due on the equipment note payable.

Dixie immediately acquired for the treasury 3,000 shares of its common stock in the open market for $48,000 with the expectation that the market price of the stock would increase substantially before the scheduled delivery dates. A total of 2,500 shares of the treasury stock subsequently was issued in payment of the $60,000 balance due on the equipment note payable.

Instructions

a Discuss the propriety of recording the equipment acquired by Dixie Corporation at each of the following amounts:

(1) $120,000 (the cash payment)

(2) $180,000 (the cash price of the equipment)

(3) $195,000 (the $120,0000 cash payment plus the $75,000 market value of the treasury stock that must be transferred to the vendor to settle the obligation in accordance with the terms of the contract)

(4) $160,000 (the $120,000 cash payment plus the $40,000 cost of the 2,500 shares of treasury stock reissued in payment for the equipment)

b Discuss the arguments for classifying the balance on the equipment note payable as:

(1) A liability

(2) Treasury stock subscribed

c Assuming that legal requirements do not affect the decision, discuss the arguments for classifying Dixie Corporation's treasury stock as:

(1) An asset awaiting ultimate disposition

(2) An element of stockholders' equity awaiting ultimate disposition

Case 18-4 Publicly owned corporations are required to present earnings per share data in their income statements.

Instructions

Compare and contrast primary earnings per share with fully diluted earnings per share for each of the following:

a The effect of common stock equivalents on the number of shares used in the computation of earnings per share data.

b The effect of convertible securities that are not common stock equivalents on the number of shares used in the computation of earnings per share data.

c The effect of antidilutive securities.

Case 18-5 Victor Corporation had the following ledger account titles in its December 31, Year 4, trial balance:

12% cumulative, convertible preferred stock, $100 par

Paid-in capital in excess of par: preferred stock

Common stock, $1 stated value

Paid-in capital in excess of stated value: common stock

Retained earnings

Additional Information

(1) There were 2,000,000 shares of preferred stock authorized, of which 1,000,000 were outstanding. All 1,000,000 shares outstanding were issued on January 2, Year 1, for $120 a share. The average **Aa** corporate bond yield was 17% on January 2, Year 1, and was 20% on December 31, Year 4. The preferred stock was convertible to common stock on a 1 for 1 basis until December 31, Year 10; thereafter, the preferred stock was no longer convertible and was callable at $100 by Victor. No preferred stock had been converted to common stock, and there were no dividends in arrears on December 31, Year 4.

(2) The common stock had been issued at amounts in excess of stated value a share since incorporation. Of the 5,000,000 shares authorized, there were 3,500,000 shares outstanding on January 1, Year 4. The market price of the outstanding common stock had increased consistently for the last four years.

(3) Victor had an employee stock option plan under which certain employees and officers might acquire shares of common stock at 100% of the market price on the grant date. All options were exercisable in installments of one-third each year, commencing one year after the grant date, and expired if not exercised within four years of the grant date. On January 1, Year 4, options for 70,000 shares were outstanding at prices ranging from $47 to $83 a share. Options for 20,000 shares were exercised at $47 to $79 a share during Year 4. No options expired during Year 4, and additional options for 15,000 shares were granted at $86 a share during Year 4. The 65,000 options outstanding on December 31, Year 4, had option prices ranging from $54 to $86 a share; of these, 30,000 were exercisable on that date at prices ranging from $54 to $79 a share.

(4) Victor also had an employee stock purchase plan under which Victor paid one-half and the employee paid one-half of the market price of the common stock on the date of the subscription. During Year 4, employees subscribed to 60,000 shares of common stock at an average price of $87 a share. All 60,000 shares were paid for and issued in September, Year 4.

(5) On December 31, Year 4, there was a total of 355,000 shares of common stock set aside for the granting of future employee stock options and for future issuances under the employee stock purchase plan. The only changes in Victor's stockholders' equity for Year 4 were those described above, net income, and cash dividends declared.

Instructions

a Prepare the stockholders' equity section of the balance sheet of Victor Corporation on December 31, Year 4; substitute, where appropriate, Xs for unknown dollar amounts. Also prepare appropriate notes to Victor's financial statements.

b Explain how the amount of the denominator should be determined to compute primary earnings per share for presentation in Victor Corporation's income statement for Year 4. Be specific as to the treatment of each item. If additional information is needed to determine whether an item should be included or excluded, or the extent to which an item should be included, identify the information needed and how the item would be handled if the information were known. Assume that Victor Corporation had substantial net income for the year ended December 31, Year 4.

PROBLEMS

18-1 The stockholders' equity section of Benjamin Corporation's balance sheet was as follows on September 30, Year 7:

> *Stockholders' equity:*
> *Common stock, $20 par, authorized 200,000 shares, issued and*
> *outstanding 120,000 shares* $2,400,000
> *Paid-in capital in excess of par* 2,280,000
> *Retained earnings* 1,540,000
> *Total stockholders' equity* $6,220,000

Benjamin uses the cost method of accounting for treasury stock, and during the year ended September 30, Year 8, had the following transactions or events:

Jan. 6 Acquired for the treasury 2,000 shares of outstanding common stock for $70,000

  14 Reissued 1,200 shares of treasury stock at $40 a share

June 18 Retired 300 shares of treasury stock

Sept. 30 Reported net income of $200,000 for the year ended Sept. 30, Year 8 (no dividends were declared)

Instructions

a Prepare journal entries for the foregoing transactions and events of Benjamin Corporation.

b Prepare the stockholders' equity section of Benjamin Corporation's balance sheet on September 30, Year 8, with related disclosures in a note to the financial statements.

18-2 Erbert Company had the following long-term debt and capital stock outstanding on September 30, Year 3:

> *8% convertible bonds payable due Sept. 30, Year 13, interest payable*
> *Mar. 30 and Sept. 30, issued at face amount, each $1,000 bond con-*
> *vertible to 10 shares of common stock through Sept. 30, Year 8* $100,000
> *6% cumulative, convertible preferred stock, $1 par, 10,000 shares issued*
> *and outstanding, each share convertible to one share of common stock*
> *through Sept. 30, Year 8* 10,000
> *Common stock, $1 par, 11,000 shares issued and outstanding* 11,000

There were no changes in the 8% convertible bonds and 6% cumulative preferred stock outstanding during the year ended September 30, Year 3. The only change in common stock during that year was the issuance of 2,000 shares for cash on March 31, Year 3. The preferred stock is a common stock equivalent, but the convertible bonds are not. Erbert had net income of $25,000 for the year ended September 30, Year 3, net of income taxes expense at a 45% rate.

Instructions

a Compute primary earnings per share and fully diluted earnings per share, rounded to the nearest cent, for Erbert Company for the year ended September 30, Year 3.

b Prepare the bottom portion of Erbert Company's income statement for the year ended September 30, Year 3, beginning with income before income taxes. Show supporting computations. Disregard disclosures required in a note to the financial statements.

18-3   Nolan Corporation's capital structure for the first two years of its operations was as follows:

	Dec. 31, Year 2	Dec. 31, Year 1
8% convertible bonds......................	$1,000,000	$1,000,000
Outstanding shares of:		
Nonconvertible $3 preferred stock	10,000	10,000
Common stock	336,000	300,000

Additional Information

(1) On September 1, Year 2, Nolan issued 36,000 shares of common stock for cash.

(2) Net income of Nolan for the year ended December 31, Year 2, was $750,000.

(3) During Year 2 Nolan declared dividends of $3 a share on its nonconvertible preferred stock.

(4) The 8% convertible bonds were convertible to 40 shares of common stock for each $1,000 bond, and were not common stock equivalents on the date of issuance.

(5) Stock options to acquire 30,000 shares of common stock at $22.50 a share were outstanding at the beginning and end of Year 2. The average market price of Nolan's common stock was $36 a share during Year 2. The market price was $33 a share on December 31, Year 2.

(6) Stock warrants to acquire 20,000 shares of common stock at $38 a share were attached to the preferred stock at the time of issuance. The warrants, which expire on December 31, Year 7, were outstanding on December 31, Year 2.

(7) Nolan's income tax rate was 45% for both Year 1 and Year 2.

Instructions

a Compute the number of shares to be used for the computation of Nolan Corporation's primary earnings per share for the year ended December 31, Year 2.

b Compute Nolan Corporation's primary earnings per share for the year ended December 31, Year 2, rounded to the nearest cent.

c Compute the number of shares to be used for the computation of Nolan Corporation's fully diluted earnings per share for the year ended December 31, Year 2.

d Compute Nolan Corporation's fully diluted earnings per share for the year ended December 31, Year 2, rounded to the nearest cent.

18-4   The stockholders' equity section of Luigi Company's balance sheet on December 31, Year 7, is shown on page 937.

Stockholders' equity:

10% preferred stock, $100 par, callable at $104, authorized 50,000 shares, issued and outstanding 20,000 shares	*$2,000,000*
Common stock, $5 par, authorized 500,000 shares, issued and outstanding 300,000 shares	*1,500,000*
Paid-in capital in excess of par: preferred stock....................	*70,000*
Paid-in capital in excess of par: common stock	*2,200,000*
Total paid-in capital...	*$5,770,000*
Retained earnings	*4,200,000*
Total stockholders' equity	*$9,970,000*

In Year 8, Luigi acquired in the open market and retired 3,000 shares of its preferred stock at $99 a share. Shortly thereafter, the remaining 17,000 shares of preferred stock were called for redemption and retired at the call price of $104 a share. Net income for Year 8 was $863,000; cash dividends of $2 a share were declared and paid on the common stock in Year 8. No dividends were declared or paid on the preferred stock in Year 8.

Instructions

a Prepare journal entries for Luigi Company to record the acquisition and retirement of the preferred stock.

b Prepare the stockholders' equity section of Luigi Company's balance sheet on December 31, Year 8.

18-5 In Year 8, Lasky Corporation issued all shares of its outstanding common stock at a price of $25 a share. On December 31, Year 11, Lasky's balance sheet included the following stockholders' equity section:

Stockholders' equity:

Common stock, $10 par, authorized 500,000 shares, issued and outstanding 200,000 shares	*$2,000,000*
Paid-in capital in excess of par	*3,000,000*
Total paid-in capital...	*$5,000,000*
Retained earnings	*1,950,000*
Total stockholders' equity	*$6,950,000*

On February 15, Year 12, Lasky acquired for the treasury 10,000 shares of its common stock at $48 a share. On December 9, Year 12, Lasky reissued 5,000 shares of treasury stock for $284,000.

Instructions

a Prepare journal entries to record Lasky Corporation's transactions on February 15 and December 9, Year 12, assuming that treasury stock is recorded at cost.

b Prepare journal entries to record Lasky Corporation's transactions on February 15 and December 9, Year 12, assuming that treasury stock is recorded at par.

18-6 A comparative summary of the stockholders' equity of Burbage Corporation, together with additional information, is given below:

	Dec. 31, Year 5		Jan. 1, Year 5
Stockholders' equity:			
Common stock, authorized 250,000 shares; issued:			
On Dec. 31, Year 5, 70,000 shares, $8 par (1,000 shares in treasury)	$560,000		
On Jan. 1, Year 5, 40,000 shares, $10 par			$ 400,000
Common stock dividend to be distributed (6,900 shares)	55,200	$ 615,200	
Paid-in capital in excess of par:			
From issuance of common stock (including $8,000 on Dec. 31, Year 5, from treasury stock transactions)	$808,700		200,000
From common stock dividend (to be distributed Jan. 25, Year 6	276,000	1,084,700	
Total paid-in capital		$1,699,900	$ 600,000
Retained earnings		1,372,440	1,420,200
Total paid-in capital and retained earnings		$3,072,340	$2,020,200
Less: Treasury stock, 1,000 shares at cost		37,000	
Total stockholders' equity		$3,035,340	$2,020,200

Additional Information

(1) In February, Year 5, Burbage's board of directors approved a 5 for 4 stock split, which reduced the par of the common stock from $10 to $8 a share. The split was approved by stockholders on March 1 and distributed on March 25. A memorandum entry was used to record the stock split.

(2) On April 1, Year 5, Burbage acquired for the treasury 2,000 shares of its common stock at $37 a share.

(3) On June 30, Year 5, 1,000 shares of treasury stock were reissued at $45 a share.

(4) On July 1, Year 5, 20,000 shares of $8 par common stock were issued in exchange for certain assets of Holland Company. The current fair value of the 20,000 shares issued was $760,700.

(5) A cash dividend of $2 a share was declared on December 2, Year 5, payable on December 29, to stockholders of record on December 15; a 10% common stock dividend was declared on December 20, to be distributed on January 25, Year 6. The market price of the common stock on December 20 was $48 a share. (The Year 5 financial statements were issued on January 18, Year 6.)

(6) The net income for Year 5 was $421,440, which included an extraordinary item (gain) of $124,490, net of income tax effect.

■■■■■■■■■■ **Instructions**

a Prepare journal entries to record Burbage Corporation's transactions relating to stockholders' equity that took place during the year ended December 31, Year 5. (Debit Income Summary and credit Retained Earnings to record net income for Year 5.)

b Prepare the lower section of Burbage Corporation's income statement for the year ended December 31, Year 5, showing operating income and the extraordinary item (gain). Include earnings per share (rounded to nearest cent) in the income statement.

c Prepare Burbage Corporation's statement of retained earnings for the year ended December 31, Year 5.

18-7 Tucker Corporation is a publicly owned enterprise. On December 31, Year 7, Tucker had 25,000,000 shares of $10 par common stock authorized, of which 15,000,000 shares were issued and 14,000,000 shares were outstanding.

The stockholders' equity ledger accounts on December 31, Year 7, had the following balances:

Common stock, $10 par	$150,000,000
Paid-in capital in excess of par: common.........................	80,000,000
Retained earnings..	50,000,000
Treasury stock: common, 1,000,000 shares	18,000,000

During Year 8, Tucker completed the following transactions:

(1) On February 1, Year 8, 2,000,000 shares of common stock were issued at $18 a share, net of issuance costs.

(2) On February 15, Year 8, Tucker issued at $110 a share, 100,000 shares of $100 par, 8% cumulative preferred stock with 100,000 detachable stock warrants. Each stock warrant contained one right that with $20 could be exchanged for one share of Tucker's common stock. On February 15, Year 8, the market price for one warrant was $1.

(3) On March 1, Year 8, Tucker acquired for the treasury 20,000 shares of its common stock for $18 a share. Tucker uses the cost method to account for treasury stock.

(4) On March 15, Year 8, when the common stock was trading for $21 a share, a stockholder donated to Tucker 10,000 shares of common stock, which appropriately was recorded as treasury stock.

(5) On March 31, Year 8, Tucker declared a cash dividend on common stock of $0.10 a share, payable on April 30, Year 8, to stockholders of record on April 10, Year 8.

(6) On April 15, Year 8, when the market price of the stock warrants was $2 each and the market price of the common stock was $22 a share, 30,000 warrants were exercised. Tucker used unissued shares of common stock to complete this transaction.

(7) On April 30, Year 8, employees exercised 100,000 options that had been granted in Year 6 under a noncompensatory stock option plan. Each option entitled the employee to acquire one share of the common stock for $20 a share. On April 30, Year 8, the market price of the common stock was $23 a

share. Tucker used unissued shares of common stock to complete this transaction.

(8) On May 31, Year 8, when the market price of the common stock was $20 a share, Tucker declared a 5% common stock dividend, distributable on July 1, Year 8, to stockholders of record on June 1, Year 8. The applicable state law prohibits stock dividends on treasury stock. (Credit the Common Stock ledger account on date of declaration of the stock dividend.)

(9) On June 30, Year 8, Tucker reissued the 20,000 shares of treasury stock acquired on March 1, Year 8, and an additional 280,000 treasury shares costing $5,600,000 that were on hand at the beginning of the year. The reissuance price was $25 a share.

(10) On September 30, Year 8, Tucker declared a cash dividend on common stock of $0.10 a share and the yearly dividend on preferred stock, both payable on October 30, Year 8, to stockholders of record on October 10, Year 8.

(11) On December 31, Year 8, the remaining outstanding stock warrants expired.

(12) Net income for Year 8 was $25,000,000.

Instructions

Prepare a working paper to summarize, for each transaction, the changes in Tucker Corporation's stockholders' equity ledger accounts for Year 8. Show supporting computations and use the following headings in the working paper:

Date
Preferred Stock—Number of Shares
Preferred Stock—Amount
Common Stock—Number of Shares
Common Stock—Amount
Common Stock Warrants—Number of Rights
Common Stock Warrants—Amount
Paid-in Capital in Excess of Par: Preferred Stock
Paid-in Capital in Excess of Par: Common Stock
Retained Earnings
Treasury Stock: Common—Number of Shares
Treasury Stock: Common—Amount

18-8   Selected data summarizing the earnings performance of Johnson Corporation for a five-year period are presented on page 941 (all dollar amounts and the number of shares are in thousands).

Late in December of each of the five years, Johnson called 10,000 shares of its preferred stock, paying the call price of 102 plus the final quarter's dividends. During Year 2, Johnson split its common stock 2 for 1, and in Year 4 issued a 20% common stock dividend. On October 1, Year 3, an additional 2,500,000 shares of common stock were issued for cash. On July 1, Year 5, Johnson acquired 5,000,000 shares of common stock from a stockholder who planned to retire. Johnson plans to use the treasury stock for business combinations. There were no common stock equivalents or other potentially dilutive securities outstanding during the five-year period.

	Year 5	Year 4	Year 3	Year 2	Year 1
Income before interest and income taxes expense	$64,120	$38,680	$84,480	$69,940	$47,200
Interest expense	5,200	5,200	9,100	10,400	10,400
Income before income taxes	$58,920	$33,480	$75,380	$59,540	$36,800
Income taxes expense	26,514	15,066	33,921	26,793	16,560
Net income	$32,406	$18,414	$41,459	$32,747	$20,240
Number of shares of common stock outstanding at end of year........................	13,000	18,000	15,000	12,500	6,250
Number of shares of 12%, $100 par preferred stock outstanding at end of year.................	60	70	80	90	100

Instructions

Earnings per share of common stock for the five-year period are to be reported on a comparable basis in Johnson Corporation's annual report to shareholders for Year 5. Compute the earnings per share data to be reported in the Year 5 annual report to stockholders for each of the five years, rounded to the nearest cent.

18-9 Meeker, Inc., was organized on May 1, Year 7, with 3,000,000 authorized shares of $10 par common stock, and 300,000 shares of its common stock were issued for $3,300,000 on May 15, Year 7. Net income through December 31, Year 7, was $125,000.

On July 3, Year 8, Meeker issued 500,000 shares of common stock for $6,250,000. A 5% common stock dividend was declared on October 2, Year 8, and distributed on November 6, Year 8, to stockholders of record on October 23, Year 8. The market price of the common stock was $11 a share on October 2, Year 8. Meeker's net income for the year ended December 31, Year 8, was $350,000.

During Year 9, Meeker completed the following transactions:

(1) In February, Meeker acquired 30,000 shares of its common stock for the treasury for $9 a share. Meeker uses the cost method to account for treasury stock.

(2) In June, Meeker reissued 15,000 shares of treasury stock for $12 a share.

(3) In September, common stockholders were issued stock warrants (for each share owned) for one right to acquire two additional shares of common stock for $13 a share. The rights expire on December 31, Year 9.

(4) In October, stock warrants for 250,000 rights were exercised when the market price of the common stock was $14 a share.

(5) In November, stock warrants for 400,000 rights were exercised when the market price of the common stock was $15 a share.

(6) On December 15, Year 9, Meeker declared its first cash dividend, $0.10 a share, payable on January 10, Year 10, to common stockholders of record on December 31, Year 9.

(7) On December 21, Year 9, in accordance with the applicable state law, Meeker

retired 10,000 shares of treasury stock and restored it to the status of unissued common stock. The market price of the common stock was $16 a share on that date.

Net income for Year 9 was $750,000.

Instructions

Prepare a working paper to summarize all transactions affecting the Common Stock (shares and dollar amounts), Paid-in Capital in Excess of Par, Retained Earnings, and Treasury Stock (shares and dollar amounts) ledger accounts, and the amounts that would be included in Meeker, Inc.'s balance sheet on December 31, Year 9, as a result of the foregoing information. Show supporting computations.

18-10   On February 1, Year 6, the financial vice president of Omeron Company, a small publicly owned enterprise, requested you to compute comparative earnings per share data for its first two years of operations ended December 31, Year 5, for inclusion in Omeron's annual report for Year 5.

Additional Information

(1) Income statements show net income as follows: Year 4, $5,760,000; Year 5, $4,800,000.

(2) On January 1, Year 4, there were outstanding 200,000 shares of $5 par common stock and 20,000 shares of $100 par, 12% convertible preferred stock. The 12% preferred stock had been issued at par. Each share of preferred stock was initially convertible to 2.5 shares of common stock, to be adjusted for any stock dividends and stock splits. The market price of common stock has ranged from $45 to $60 a share during the past two years. The average **Aa** corporate bond yield was 11% at the time the preferred stock was issued.

(3) On December 31, Year 4, a 20% stock dividend was distributed on the common stock. On that date, the market price of the common stock was $50 a share.

(4) In June, Year 5, the common stock was split 2 for 1.

(5) Cash dividends were payable on the preferred stock on June 30 and December 31. Preferred stock dividends were paid in each year; none of the preferred stock had been converted to common stock.

Instructions

a (1) Prepare a working paper to compute the number of shares of Omeron Company's common stock outstanding on December 31, Year 4 and Year 5.

(2) Prepare a working paper to compute the equivalent number of shares of Omeron Company's common stock outstanding for Year 4 and Year 5 for the computation of primary earnings per share. *Equivalent shares* means the number of shares outstanding in Year 4 and Year 5 in terms of the December 31, Year 5, capital structure.

(3) Prepare a working paper to compute the equivalent number of shares of Omeron Company's common stock outstanding for Year 4 and Year 5 for the computation of fully diluted earnings per share.

b Prepare the bottom portion of Omeron Company's income statement, showing primary and fully diluted earnings per share for Year 4 and Year 5.

18-11   The controller of Lido Corporation has requested your assistance in the determination of net income, primary earnings per share, and fully diluted earnings per share
for presentation in Lido's income statement for the year ended September 30, Year
5. As currently determined, Lido's net income was $2,100,000 for the year ended
September 30, Year 5. The controller has indicated that the net income amount
might be adjusted for the following transactions that were recorded directly in the
Retained Earnings ledger account. (The amounts are net of applicable income
taxes.)

(1) The amount of $1,875,000, applicable to a breached Year 1 contract, was
received as a result of a lawsuit. Prior to the award, legal counsel was uncertain
as to the outcome of the suit.

(2) A gain of $1,500,000 was recognized on the sale of Lido's only subsidiary.

(3) A special inventory write-off of $750,000 was made, of which $625,000 applied to goods manufactured prior to October 1, Year 4.

Your working papers include the following data for the year ended September
30, Year 5:

(1) Common stock (on October 1, Year 4, stated value $10, authorized 300,000
shares; effective December 1, Year 4 (following a 2 for 1 stock split), stated
value $5, authorized 600,000 shares):
   Balance, Oct. 1, Year 4:   Issued and outstanding, 60,000 shares
   Dec. 1, Year 4:   60,000 shares issued in a 2 for 1 stock split
   Dec. 1, Year 4:   280,000 shares (stated value $5) issued for cash at $39 a
   share

(2) Treasury stock:
   Mar. 1, Year 5:   Acquired 40,000 shares at $37 a share
   Apr. 1, Year 5:   Reissued 40,000 shares at $40 a share

(3) Series A stock warrants (each warrant was exchangeable at any time with $60
for one share of common stock; effective December 1, Year 4, when the stock
was split 2 for 1, each stock warrant became exchangeable for two shares of
common stock at $30 a share):
   Oct. 1, Year 4:   25,000 stock warrants issued at $6 each

(4) Series B stock warrants (each stock warrant is exchangeable with $40 for one
share of common stock):
   Apr. 1, Year 5:   20,000 stock warrants authorized and issued at $10 each

(5) First mortgage bonds, 11%, due Year 20 (nonconvertible; priced to yield 10%
when issued):
   Balance Oct. 1, Year 4:   Authorized, issued and outstanding, face amount
   of $1,400,000

(6) Convertible debentures, 13.6%, issued in Year 4 and due in Year 24 (each
$1,000 debenture was convertible at any time until maturity to 15 shares of
common stock; effective December 1, Year 4, the conversion ratio became 30
shares of common stock for each debenture as a result of the 2 for 1 stock split):
   Oct. 1, Year 4:   Issued at face amount of $12,000,000.

The following table shows market prices for Lido's securities and the average
Aa corporate bond yield for selected dates:

	Price (or rate) on			Average for year ended Sept. 30, Year 5
	Oct. 1, Year 4	Apr. 1, Year 5	Sept. 30, Year 5	
Common stock	$60	$40*	$36¼*	$37½*
First mortgage bonds, 11%	88½	87	86	87
Convertible debentures, 13.6% . . .	100	120	110	115
Series A warrants	$6	$22	$19½	$15
Series B warrants		$10	$9	$9½
Average **Aa** corporate bond yield .	15%	15½%	16%	15½%

*After 2 for 1 stock split.

Instructions

a Compute the correct net income to be presented in Lido Corporation's income statement for the year ended September 30, Year 5.

b Assuming that the correct net income of Lido Corporation for the year ended September 30, Year 5, was $2,800,000 and that there were no extraordinary items, prepare a working paper to compute (1) the primary earnings per share, and (2) the fully diluted earnings per share that should be presented in Lido's income statement for the year ended September 30, Year 5. A supporting working paper showing the numbers of shares to be used in these computations also should be prepared. (Because of the relative stability of the market price of the common stock, the annual average market price may be used where appropriate in your computations. Assume an income tax rate of 45%. Round earnings per share amounts to the nearest cent.)

18-12 The stockholders' equity section of Misto Company's balance sheet on December 31, Year 5, was as follows:

Stockholders' equity:

$2 cumulative, convertible preferred stock, $25 par, authorized 1,600,000 shares, issued 1,400,000 shares, converted to common 750,000 shares, and outstanding 650,000 shares; involuntary liquidation value, $30 a share, aggregating $19,500,000	$16,250,000
Common stock, $0.25 par, authorized 15,000,000 shares, issued and outstanding 8,800,000 shares	2,200,000
Additional paid-in capital	32,750,000
Total paid-in capital	$51,200,000
Retained earnings	40,595,000
Total stockholders' equity	$91,795,000

Included among the liabilities of Misto were 11% convertible debentures issued at the face amount of $20,000,000 in Year 4. The debentures are due in Year 24, and until then are convertible to the common stock of Misto at the rate of 50 shares of common stock for each $1,000 debenture. To date, none of the debentures has been converted.

On April 2, Year 5, Misto issued 1,400,000 shares of convertible preferred stock at $40 a share. Quarterly dividends to December 31, Year 5, were declared and paid on the preferred stock. The preferred stock is convertible to common stock at the rate of two shares of common for each share of preferred. On October 1, Year 5, 150,000 shares and on November 1, Year 5, 600,000 shares of the preferred stock were converted to common stock.

On July 2, Year 4, Misto granted stock options to its officers and key employees to acquire 500,000 shares of Misto's common stock at $20 a share.

During Year 5, dividend payments and average market prices of Misto's common stock were as follows:

	Dividends a share	Average market price a share	Closing market price at end of quarter
First quarter	$0.10	$28	$30
Second quarter	0.15	24	27
Third quarter	0.10	22	23
Fourth quarter	0.15	26	25
Average for the year		25	

Assume that the average **Aa** corporate bond yield was 14% throughout Year 4 and Year 5, that Misto's net income for the year ended December 31, Year 5, was $48,500,000, and that the income tax rate was 45%.

Instructions

a Prepare a working paper to show the common stock equivalency status of the (1) convertible debentures, (2) convertible preferred stock, and (3) stock options of Misto Company.

b Prepare a working paper to show for Year 5 the computation of:
   (1) The weighted-average number of shares of common stock for the computation of Misto Company's primary earnings per share
   (2) The weighted-average number of shares of common stock for the computation of Misto Company's fully diluted earnings per share

c Prepare a working paper to show for Misto Company for Year 5 the computation to the nearest cent of:
   (1) Primary earnings per share
   (2) Fully diluted earnings per share

18-13 Jersey Corporation was organized on July 3, Year 4. It was authorized to issue 500,000 shares of $5 par common stock and 100,000 shares of $10 par, 10% cumulative, nonparticipating preferred stock. Jersey adopted a June 30 fiscal year.

The following information relates to the stockholders' equity ledger accounts of Jersey:

30,000 shares of preferred stock were issued at $10 a share on June 30, Year 5.

Prior to the year ended June 30, Year 7, Jersey had 160,000 shares of outstanding common stock, issued as follows:

(1) 145,000 shares were issued for cash on July 5, Year 4, at $20 a share.

(2) 10,000 shares were exchanged on August 1, Year 4, for land that had cost the seller $70,000 in Year 1 and which had a current fair value of $130,000 on August 1, Year 4.

(3) 5,000 shares were issued on March 1, Year 6; the shares had been subscribed at $32 a share on October 31, Year 5.

During the year ended June 30, Year 7, the following transactions involving common stock were completed:

October 1, Year 6 Subscriptions were received for 10,000 shares at $40 a share. Cash of $80,000 was received in full payment for 2,000 shares, and stock certificates were issued. The remaining subscriptions for 8,000 shares were to be paid in full by September 30, Year 7, at which time the certificates were to be issued.

December 1, Year 6 Jersey acquired for the treasury 5,000 shares of its common stock in the open market at $37 a share. Jersey uses the cost method of accounting for treasury stock.

December 15, Year 6 Jersey declared a 5% common stock dividend for stockholders of record on January 10, Year 7, to be issued on January 31, Year 7. Jersey's common stock was trading at $45 a share on December 15, Year 6. (Disregard the effect of the stock dividend on subscribed stock.)

June 24, Year 7 Jersey reissued for $108,000, one-half (2,500 shares) of the treasury stock that it had acquired on December 1, Year 6.

Jersey has followed a program of declaring cash dividends in June and December, with payments being made to stockholders of record in the following month. The cash dividends that had been declared since organization of Jersey Corporation are summarized below:

Declaration date	Preferred stock	Common stock
Dec. 15, Year 5	$0.50 a share	$0.10 a share
June 15, Year 6	0.50 a share	0.10 a share
Dec. 15, Year 6	0.50 a share	None
June 15, Year 7	0.50 a share	None

On June 30, Year 6, Jersey's Retained Earnings ledger account had a credit balance of $1,260,000. For the year ended June 30, Year 7, Jersey had net income of $465,000.

Instructions

a Prepare journal entries to record all transactions of Jersey Corporation affecting stockholders' equity completed during the year ended June 30, Year 7.

b Prepare the stockholders' equity section of Jersey Corporation's balance sheet on June 30, Year 7. Show supporting computations.

More Complex Accounting Topics

More Complex Accounting Topics

5

Probably the most controversial and complex topics in financial accounting deal with pension plans, long-term leases, income taxes, and accounting changes. Accountants and rule-making bodies have been searching for solutions to the measurement of periodic pension costs, the presentation of capital leases in the balance sheet, income tax allocation procedures, and the presentation of the effect of accounting changes in the income statement. Although the current body of accounting principles in these areas have been perceived as both practical and theoretically sound, considerable pressure has been mounting in recent years for major changes in such principles.

The final chapter in this part includes a discussion of accounting errors and the preparation of financial statements from incomplete accounting records.

Employers Accounting for Pensions

19

Most publicly owned business enterprises (employers), and many nonpublic enterprises, have pension plans in effect for their employees. In a survey of annual reports of 600 large publicly owned companies, the American Institute of Certified Public Accountants found that 549 companies disclosed the amount of pension expense.[1] Assets of all *private* (nongovernmental) and public pension funds amount to more than one trillion dollars and are expected to increase at a rapid rate. Assets of private pension funds have been increasing much more rapidly than total assets of employers, and pension expense has been increasing faster than employers' earnings. As a result, accounting for pension cost is one of the most important topics in financial accounting.

In this chapter we discuss the nature of pension plans, the theoretical issues involved in accounting for pension plans, and employers' accounting standards for pension plans (*FASB Statement No. 87*). Then, we discuss accounting standards for employers' settlements or curtailments of pension plans (*FASB Statement No. 88*).

NATURE OF PENSION PLANS

A *pension plan* is a contract between a business enterprise (employer) and its employees whereby the enterprise agrees to pay benefits to employees after their retirement. Ordinarily, pension benefits consist of monthly payments to employees after their retirement and additional payments on death or disability of retirees. Under a *noncontributory pension plan,* the employer assumes responsibility for the full cost of pensions; under a *contributory pension plan,* employees bear a portion of the cost of pensions through payroll deductions. Under a *defined benefit pension plan,* the basis of computation of pension benefits for retired employees usually

---

[1]*Accounting Trends & Techniques,* 39th ed., AICPA (New York: 1985), p. 249.

involves employee compensation, years of service, and age on date of retirement. In contrast, benefits to retired employees under a *defined contribution pension plan* depend on the amount of the employer's annual contributions to the plan.

Pension plans generally are *formal;* however, a pension plan's existence may be implied from a well-defined, although perhaps unwritten, practice of paying postretirement benefits.[2]

A *qualified pension plan* under the Internal Revenue Code has the following features: (1) The employer's contributions to the pension fund (within specified limits) are deductible in the computation of federal income taxes; (2) earnings on pension fund assets are not subject to federal income taxes; and (3) only the benefits received by retired employees generally are taxable income to them.

Funded and Unfunded Pension Plans

A *funded pension plan* requires a business enterprise (employer) to make periodic payments to a funding agency (a designated trustee or an outside agency such as a commercial bank or an insurance company). The process of making payments to the funding agency is known as *funding.* Funding may be accomplished through an *insured plan* with a life insurance company or through a *trust fund plan.* Under an insured plan, individual annuities providing retirement and death benefits may be acquired for each employee. Alternatively, a group annuity contract may be acquired by the employer. Under a trust fund plan, the employer makes periodic contributions to a trustee that invests the fund assets in, and pays benefits to retired employees from, a separate legal and accounting entity (pension plan). If a pension plan is not administered by a funding agency, or if employer assets are informally set aside for the payment of pensions, the plan is designated as *unfunded.* Most pension plans today are either fully or partially funded.

Prior to the Pension Reform Act of 1974, also known as the Employee Retirement Income Security Act (ERISA), an employer could assume the obligation for pension benefits without establishing a pension fund. However, under ERISA, all current pension costs must be funded. For pension plans that existed on January 1, 1974, prior service cost must be fully funded in 40 years or less, and prior service cost that arises after that date must be funded in 30 years or less. (*Prior service cost* is defined on page 954.)

Actuaries' Role in Pension Plans

The amounts involved in funding and accounting for pension plans are to a considerable extent determined by actuaries. An *actuary* is an expert in the mathematics of insurance. By applying mortality tables, compound interest formulas, and expectations regarding employee turnover, years of service, and compensation rates, actuaries compute the present value of amounts required to fund defined benefit pension plans; such amounts are said to be on an *actuarial basis.* Actuaries use several methods, termed *actuarial funding methods,* for estimating pension funding under a defined benefit pension plan.

---

[2]*FASB Statement No. 87,* ''Employers' Accounting for Pensions,'' FASB (Stamford: 1985), p. 3.

THEORETICAL ISSUES

Accountants are faced with three significant issues relating to employers' accounting for pension plans. These are listed below:

1   *Timing* the recognition of pension cost *as an expense* in the measurement of net income, particularly when a pension plan covers employees who have already worked a number of years at the time the plan is adopted by the employer

2   *Measuring the amount* of pension expense and any related prepaid pension cost or accrued pension cost that is included in the balance sheet

3   *Presenting* significant information relating to pension plans in a note to the financial statements of the employer

The measurement of periodic pension cost (expense) for defined benefit pension plans involves numerous complexities, including the application of compound interest concepts, estimation of the life expectancy of employees, determination of the age of employees at retirement, future level of interest rates, future price-level changes, probable employee turnover, gains and losses on pension fund investments, future salary levels of employees, pension benefits to be paid, and vesting provisions under pension plans. These complexities, combined with the long-range nature of pension plans, cause significant uncertainties as to the amount of pension benefits utlimately to be paid and the amount of periodic pension expense to be recognized currently by employers under defined benefit pension plans.

Differing Views on Liability under Defined Benefit Pension Plans

It is generally agreed that a pension plan is an *executory contract,* under which the employer promises to pay retirement benefits to its employees in return for their services during their term of employment. However, accountants disagree on the precise nature of the employer's commitment. Some accountants believe the employer's commitment is to the *individual employees or to a group of employees covered by the pension plan.* Other accountants consider the enterprise's obligations to be to the *pension plan itself*—a separate legal and accounting entity. Resolution of these contradictory views is critical for the development of a sound theoretical basis for employers' pension plan accounting because the existence of a liability for unfunded pension cost is dependent on which view prevails.

The accountants who hold that the employer enterprise's obligation is to *individual employees or the employees as a group* would record a liability for the present value of all unfunded pension benefits attributable to employees on a specific balance sheet date, regardless of the requirement that employees continue to render services to the employer prior to their retirement. In contrast, accountants who consider the employer enterprise's obligation to be to the *pension plan* would record no such liability; they insist that the employer has a liability only for unfunded amounts of pension cost not yet paid to the funding agency for the pension plan. In the view of these accountants, pension benefits accrue in much the same fashion as do salaries and wages during the periods that employees render services to the employer. The differences between these two points of view are magnified by the many actuarial estimates that underlie the computations of pension cost and by the long time periods over which services are rendered by employees.

Illustration of Differing Views

To illustrate the difference in accounting between the two opposing views, assume that Wayland Company established a noncontributory defined benefit pension plan for its 20 employees on January 2, Year 10. The pension plan provided for annual pension benefits to each employee who retired at age 65 after at least five years of service to Wayland computed as follows: 1% of the final annual salary multiplied by the total years of service. On January 2, Year 10, ages of Wayland's employees ranged from 27 to 63, and all except six employees had served more than five years. The actuary retained by Wayland computed the present value of *prior service cost* (the estimated cost of prospective retirement benefits earned by employees during their years of service prior to the establishment of the pension plan) at $82,500. Accountants who attribute Wayland's obligation under the pension plan to the group of 20 employees would require Wayland to record a liability for the $82,500 present value of prior service cost on January 2, Year 10, regardless of Wayland's plans for funding that amount. Views on the offsetting debit vary; some accountants would debit an *expense* ledger account, others would debit a *deferred charge* account to be recognized as expense over the employees' future years of service, and another group would debit a Deferred Compensation contra-stockholders' equity account similar to that illustrated in Chapter 17 for compensatory stock option plans.

Accountants who hold that Wayland is obligated to the pension plan rather than the employee group would require no journal entry on January 2, Year 10. The $82,500 present value of prior service cost would be allocated to pension expense in subsequent accounting periods in which the 20 employees rendered services to Wayland. Such a *prospective* allocation of prior service cost is founded on the premise that future accounting periods benefit from increased productivity of employees motivated by the new pension plan.

The concept of prior service cost and other issues underlying accounting for pension plans are discussed in the next section. It is important to keep in mind the divergent views on the existence of a liability with respect to prior service cost in considering accounting standards for defined benefit pension plans.

ACCOUNTING STANDARDS FOR PENSION PLANS

AICPA and FASB Pronouncements on Pension Plans

In 1965 the Accounting Principles Board of the American Institute of Certified Public Accountants published *Accounting Research Study No. 8,* "Accounting for the Cost of Pension Plans."[3] A year later, *APB Opinion No. 8,* "Accounting for the Cost of Pension Plans," was issued to provide guidelines for the measurement

---

[3]Ernest L. Hicks, *Accounting Research Study No. 8,* "Accounting for the Cost of Pension Plans," AICPA (New York: 1965).

of periodic pension cost and for reporting relevant pension plan information in financial statements.

The enactment of ERISA led to the Financial Accounting Standards Board's issuance of *FASB Interpretation No. 3*, "Accounting for the Cost of Pension Plans Subject to the Employee Retirement Income Security Act of 1974." Later, concerned about the increased uncertainties in the pension environment caused by high interest rates, persistent inflation, and the aging United States population, the FASB undertook a study of accounting for defined benefit pension plans themselves and accounting by employers for pensions. *FASB Statement No. 35*, "Accounting and Reporting by Defined Benefit Pension Plans," and *FASB Statement No. 36*, "Disclosure of Pension Information," were issued in 1980 as a result of the FASB's study. Finally, in December of 1985, the FASB issued *FASB Statement No. 87*, "Employers' Accounting for Pensions," which superseded *APB Opinion No. 8*, *FASB Statement No. 36*, and *FASB Interpretation No. 3*. In the remainder of this section we consider the principal provision of *FASB Statement No. 87*.

In accordance with *FASB Statement No. 87*, pension cost of an employer is allocated to expense under the accrual basis of accounting. Thus, the amount of the employer's periodic pension expense is not related to funding policy or left to the whims of management of the employer. Ideally, the total pension cost relating to a particular employee is recognized as expense during the service years of the employee. All employees who may be expected to receive benefits under a pension plan are included in the computation of the employer's periodic pension expense, with appropriate recognition of employee turnover rates.

Employer's Basic Accounting for Pension Plans

To illustrate the employer's basic accounting for pension plans, assume that the pension expense for Napier Corporation for Year 7 amounted to $200,000, Napier paid $200,000 to the funding agency (under the funded plan assumption), and retired employees were paid $50,000. Journal entries required to record this information, assuming (1) a *funded plan*, and (2) an *unfunded plan*, are illustrated below:

Journal entries to record pension expense and payments for funded pension plan and unfunded pension plan

Transactions	(1) Funded pension plan	(2) Unfunded pension plan

Recognition of pension expense for Year 7	Pension Expense 200,000
	    Cash 200,000
		Pension Expense 200,000
		    Accrued
		    Pension
		      Cost...... 200,000

Payment of benefits to retired employees during Year 7	None (Funding agency for pension plan makes payment directly to retired employees)	Accrued Pension Cost.... 50,000 Cash 50,000

The periodic contributions to the pension fund (or funding agency) made by an employer may not equal the amount currently recognized as pension expense. If the contribution to the pension fund is less than the amount recognized as pension expense, the unpaid balance is included in the Accrued Pension Cost ledger account; if the contribution exceeds the amount recognized as pension expense, the difference is debited to the Prepaid Pension Cost account.

Employer's Accounting for Defined Contribution Pension Plan

Under a ***defined contribution pension plan,*** the employer's contribution to the plan typically is measured as a percentage of employer earnings or employees' salaries, and benefits to be received by retired employees depend primarily on the amount contributed by the employer and, if a funded plan, the pension plan's earnings on employer contributions. Generally, the employer's periodic pension expense under a defined contribution pension plan is measured by the employer's required contributions to the plan.[4]

To illustrate the employer's accounting for a defined contribution pension plan, assume that on May 31, Year 6, Regis Company made a required $256,000 contribution to its newly adopted defined contribution pension plan for the year ended on that date. The journal entry for Regis is as follows:

Basic journal entry for defined contribution pension plan

Pension Expense	256,000	
Cash		256,000
To record amount paid to trustee for defined contribution		
pension plan.		

The foregoing journal entry reflects the assumption that Regis Company's required contributions to the pension plan on behalf of a specific employee terminate when that employee retires. If the terms of the defined contribution pension plan require contributions to the plan on behalf of retired employees as well as active employees, the employer must accrue the estimated cost of the post-retirement contributions (presumably on a present-value basis) during the years of employee service.[5] For example, if $42,000 represented the actuaries' estimate of the present value of Regis Company's required post-retirement contributions to the defined contribution pension plan attributable to the year ended May 31, Year 6, the foregoing journal entry for Regis would be modified as follows:

Journal entry for defined contribution pension plan that requires post-retirement contributions

Pension Expense ($256,000 + $42,000)	298,000	
Cash		256,000
Accrued Pension Cost		42,000
To record amount paid to trustee for defined contribution		
pension plan and amount accrued for present value of		
estimated post-retirement contributions.		

---

[4]*FASB Statement No. 87,* p. 18.
[5]Ibid.

If for the year ended May 31, Year 7, Regis Company's required contribution to the defined contribution pension plan was \$273,000, the actuaries' estimate of the present value of required post-retirement contributions was \$47,000, and the appropriate *discount rate* for the time value of money was 10%, Regis Company's journal entry on May 31, Year 7, would be as follows:

Journal entry for defined contribution pension plan that includes interest on unfunded amount

Pension Expense [\$273,000 + \$47,000 + (\$42,000 × 0.10)]...	324,200	
Cash		273,000
Accrued Pension Cost (\$47,000 + \$4,200)		51,200

To record amount paid to trustee for defined contribution pension plan, amount accrued for present value of estimated post-retirement contributions, and interest on unfunded amount from prior years.

Employer's Accounting for Multiemployer Pension Plan

A multiemployer pension plan is one involving two or more unrelated employers in the same industry who contribute to the plan typically in accordance with a collective-bargaining contract. Contributions to such a plan are not segregated by employer; thus, one employer's contributions to the pension plan may be used to pay benefits to retired former employees of another employer participating in the plan.

The Financial Accounting Standards Board defined *pension cost* for an employer that participates in a multiemployer pension plan as the amount of the employer's required contribution to the plan for the accounting period.[6] Thus, accounting for pension expense for a multiemployer pension plan is identical to accounting for pension expense for a defined contribution pension plan that does not require post-retirement contributions.

Employer's Accounting for Insured Pension Plan

Insured pension plans generally involve the acquisition of individual annuity contracts for each employee, or a group annuity contract for all employees covered by the pension plan. Under a *nonparticipating annuity contract,* the employer does not participate in the investment performance or in other experience of the insurance company; thus, Pension Expense is debited and Cash or Accrued Pension Cost is credited for the cost of the nonparticipating annuity contracts attributable to an accounting period.[7] In contrast, a *participating annuity contract* permits the employer to share in the investment performance and perhaps the mortality experience of the insurance company. Because the *participation right* to receive future dividends or retroactive rate credits makes the cost of a participating annuity contract greater than the cost of a nonparticipating contract, a portion of the cost of a participating contract is allocated to an asset ledger account, as in the following example:[8]

---

[6]Ibid., p. 19.
[7]Ibid., p. 17.
[8]Ibid.

Journal entry for
insured pension plan
with participating
annuity contracts

Pension Expense	241,000	
Investment in Annuity Contract Participation Right	62,800	
Cash		303,800

To record acquisition of participating annuity contracts
under insured pension plan and the investment in
participation right.

Thus, accounting for the participation right in an annuity contract resembles accounting for cash surrender value of life insurance illustrated on pages 722–723.

If the current fair value of the participation right is determinable in future accounting periods, the investment ledger account balance is adjusted to reflect the current fair value, with the difference included in the computation of pension expense for the period. Otherwise the cost of the investment is amortized to pension expense over the expected *dividend period* of the participating annuity contract.[9]

Employer's Accounting for Defined Benefit Pension Plan

Most of *FASB Statement No. 87* is devoted to the complex accounting standards for defined benefit pension plans, which, because of the numerous assumptions that underly the computation of pension cost, are subjected to far more uncertainties than are defined contribution pension plans or insured pension plans.

In establishing standards for defined benefit pension plans, the Financial Accounting Standards Board drew on the following fundamental concepts:[10]

1   Pension cost for an accounting period is a single net amount consisting of as many as five components (discussed below).

2   Changes in the pension obligation of an employer and in the value of assets in a funded pension plan are recognized systematically in the computation of pension cost for accounting periods *subsequent to the period in which the changes occur.*

3   Pension plan assets and liabilities for pensions that were recognized as pension cost in past accounting periods are presented at a single net amount in the employer's balance sheet.

The following sections of this chapter discuss and illustrate the foregoing concepts.

Components of Pension Cost for an Accounting Period   The Financial Accounting Standards Board identified the following five components of pension cost (expense) under a defined benefit pension plan:[11]

> *Service cost*—the actuarial present value of benefits attributable to services rendered by employees during the accounting period

---

[9]Ibid.
[10]Ibid., p. ii.
[11]Ibid., pp. 5–6.

Interest cost—interest on the *projected benefit obligation* under the pension plan, which is the actuarial present value on a specific date of all pension benefits attributable to employee services prior to that date

Actual return on plan assets—a reduction in pension cost resulting from the difference between the end-of-period and beginning-of-period current fair values of the assets of a funded defined benefit pension plan, net of employer and employee contributions and benefits paid to retirees

Amortization of unrecognized prior service cost—an apportioned amount of prior service cost of retroactive plan benefits resulting from the adoption or amendment of a pension plan

Gain or loss—An apportionment of a change in value of the projected benefit obligation or of pension plan assets resulting either from actual experience different from assumed experience or from a change in assumptions made by the actuaries for the plan (A gain reduces pension cost and a loss increases pension cost.)

The foregoing components of pension cost are illustrated in the sections that follow. First, we discuss and illustrate the accounting for pension cost of an unfunded defined benefit pension plan, which does not have actual return on plan assets as an element of pension cost. Next, accounting for a funded defined benefit pension plan is considered. Our discussion and illustrations in this area include the basic technique for amortization of unrecognized prior service cost, the test to determine whether any unrecognized gain or loss is to be included in pension cost, accounting for an unfunded accumulated benefit obligation, and disclosure of pension plan information by employers. Finally, we consider six other aspects of accounting for defined benefit pension plans: legal aspects, actuarial funding methods, alternative amortization technique for prior service cost, market-related value for plan assets, limitation on intangible asset for prior service cost, and the transition period for *FASB Statement No. 87.*

Pension Cost for Unfunded Defined Benefit Pension Plan An unfunded defined benefit pension plan initiated on the date that the employer enterprise began operations would first incur only two of the foregoing components—service cost and interest cost. For illustration, we assume that Darien Company established an unfunded noncontributory defined benefit pension plan for its 25 employees on January 2, Year 1, the date it began operations. Because the pension plan became effective on the date Darien began operations, there was no prior service cost.

Assume that Darien's actuaries computed service cost under the pension plan at $40,000 and $45,000, respectively, for Year 1 and Year 2, at an assumed discount rate of 10%. (Actuaries may base their discount rate assumptions on rates implicit in current prices of annuity contracts available for insured pension plans.[12]) Journal entries for Darien Company on December 31, Year 1 and Year 2, are as follows:

---

[12]Ibid., p. 12.

```
Year 1
Dec. 31   Pension Expense.................................    40,000
                  Accrued Pension Cost ....................              40,000
          To record service cost of unfunded defined
          benefit pension plan.


Year 2
Dec. 31   Pension Expense.................................    49,000
                  Accrued Pension Cost ....................              49,000
          To record pension cost as follows:
              Service cost ......................   $45,000
              Interest cost ($40,000 × 0.10) ......    4,000
              Total pension cost ................   $49,000
```

On December 31, Year 2, the balance of Darien Company's Accrued Pension
Cost is $89,000 ($40,000 + $49,000 = $89,000). This amount, which is equal to
the projected benefit obligation under Darien's unfunded noncontributory defined
benefit pension plan, is included with long-term liabilities in Darien's balance sheet
on December 31, Year 2, under the assumption that no benefits are payable because
there are as yet no retired employees. (The current portion of any benefits payable to
retired employees would be included with current liabilities.)

Let us now assume that, as of January 1, Year 3, because of an overall decline
in interest rates, the actuaries for Darien Company's unfunded defined benefit pension plan changed the discount rate to 9% from 10%. As pointed out in Chapter 5
(page 246), the present value of a future amount increases when the interest rate
decreases. Assuming that the actuaries' revised computation of the projected benefit
obligation as of January 1, Year 3, was $101,000, there is an *unrecognized net loss*
of $12,000 ($101,000 − $89,000 = $12,000) for Darien Company's unfunded
noncontributory defined benefit pension plan on that date. In accordance with the
second fundamental concept described on page 958, the Financial Accounting
Standards Board provided that, as a minimum, amortization of *beginning-of-year*
unrecognized net gains and losses should be included in pension cost to the extent
that they exceed 10% of the greater of the projected benefit obligation or the current
fair value of pension plan assets *at the beginning of the year.* The amortization
period is to be the average remaining service period of employees expected to
receive benefits under the pension plan.[13] This *delayed recognition* of unrecognized
net gains and losses was provided by the Financial Accounting Standards Board to
reduce volatility of periodic pension expense that would result from immediate
recognition in full of all gains and losses in the accounting periods in which they
occurred.

In accordance with the foregoing, because Darien Company's pension plan is
unfunded and it has no plan assets, the amount of the January 1, Year 3, unrecognized net loss to be amortized in subsequent periods is $1,900, computed as fol-
lows:

---

[13]Ibid., p. 9.

Computation of unrecgonized loss to be amortized	*Unrecognized net loss, Jan. 1, Year 3 ($101,000 − $89,000)*	*$12,000*
	Less: 10% of projected benefit obligation, Jan. 1, Year 3	
	($101,000 × 0.10)	*10,100*
	Minimum amount of unrecognized net loss to be amortized as part of	
	pension cost beginning in Year 3	*$ 1,900*

Assuming that the average remaining service period for Darien's employees is 10 years[14] and that the actuaries' computation of service cost for Year 3 is $62,000, Darien Company's journal entry on December 31, Year 3, is as follows:

Journal entry for unfunded defined benefit pension plan with service cost, interest cost, and amortized loss	*Year 3*		
	Dec. 31 Pension Expense	*71,280*	
	Accrued Pension Cost		*71,280*
	To record pension cost as follows:		
	Service cost *$62,000*		
	Interest cost ($101,000 × 0.09) *9,090*		
	(Gain) or loss ($1,900 ÷ 10) *190*		
	Total pension cost *$71,280*		

Following the foregoing journal entry, the balance of the Accrued Pension Cost ledger account, $160,280 ($89,000 + $71,280 = $160,280) is $11,810 less than the projected benefit obligation under the unfunded defined benefit pension plan, as computed below:

Computation of excess of projected benefit obligation over accrued pension cost	*Balance of projected benefit obligation, Jan. 1, Year 3*	
	(as revised by actuaries)	*$101,000*
	Add: Service cost and interest cost ($62,000 + $9,090)	*71,090*
	Subtotal	*$172,090*
	Less: Benefits paid	*0*
	Balance of projected benefit obligation, Dec. 31, Year 3	*$172,090*
	Less: Balance of Accrued Pension Cost ledger account,	
	Dec. 31, Year 3	*160,280*
	Excess of projected benefit obligation over accrued pension	
	cost liability	*$ 11,810*

The difference of $11,810 is the unamortized balance of the unrecognized net loss on December 31, Year 3 ($12,000 − $190 = $11,810). In accordance with provisions of *FASB Statement No. 87,* Darien Company might be required to record an additional liability in the amount of $11,810, with a debit to a contra-stockholders' equity ledger account. This situation is described further in a subsequent section of this chapter (pages 974–975).

---

[14]Computation of average service period of employees is illustrated on page 974.

Pension Cost for Funded Defined Benefit Pension Plan   To illustrate accounting for pension cost under a funded defined benefit pension plan, assume that Rimmer Corporation, which had been operating for 10 years, adopted a funded noncontributory defined benefit pension plan on January 2, Year 11. Under provision of the plan, Rimmer's 42 employees were entitled to retroactive benefits (representing prior service cost) valued on January 2, Year 11, by Rimmer's actuaries at $2,000,000, at a discount rate of 11%. Under **FASB Statement No. 87,** the prior service cost must be amortized to each period's pension cost over the expected future period of service of the 42 employees, in accordance with the second fundamental concept on page 958.[15] Accordingly, the appropriate amortization schedule for Rimmer's prior service cost of $2,000,000 was computed as illustrated in the two exhibits below and at the top of page 963.

RIMMER CORPORATION
Computation of Expected Years of Service by 42 Employees
(Service Years Rendered in Each Year)
Year 11 through Year 20

No. of employees	Expected future years of service	\multicolumn{10}{Year ended Dec. 31, Year:}
		11	12	13	14	15	16	17	18	19	20
1	1	1									
2	2	2	2								
4	3	4	4	4							
2	4	2	2	2	2						
3	5	3	3	3	3	3					
7	6	7	7	7	7	7	7				
9	7	9	9	9	9	9	9	9			
7	8	7	7	7	7	7	7	7	7		
5	9	5	5	5	5	5	5	5	5	5	
2	10	2	2	2	2	2	2	2	2	2	2
42	Serv. years rendered	42	41	39	35	33	30	23	14	7	2
	Amortization fraction	$42/266$	$41/266$	$39/266$	$35/266$	$33/266$	$30/266$	$23/266$	$14/266$	$7/266$	$2/266$

Source: Adapted from *FASB Statement No. 87*, "Employers' Accounting for Pensions," FASB (Stamford: 1985), p. 85.

The $2,000,000 prior service cost on January 2, Year 11, the date that Rimmer Corporation's funded noncontributory defined benefit pension plan was adopted, represents the projected benefit obligation of the pension plan on that date and is subject to interest cost at the 11% discount rate for the year ended December 31, Year 11. To complete this illustration, we assume the following additional facts for Rimmer's pension plan for Year 11:

---

[15]Ibid., p. 7.

RIMMER CORPORATION
Amortization of Unrecognized Prior Service Cost of $2,000,000
Year 11 through Year 20

Year ended Dec. 31,	Amortization fraction (p. 962)	Amortization to pension cost
Year 11	42/266	$ 315,790
Year 12	41/266	308,271
Year 13	39/266	293,233
Year 14	35/266	263,158
Year 15	33/266	248,120
Year 16	30/266	225,564
Year 17	23/266	172,932
Year 18	14/266	105,263
Year 19	7/266	52,632
Year 20	2/266	15,037
Totals	266/266	$2,000,000

1 Rimmer funded the entire $2,000,000 prior service cost on January 2, Year 11. The pension plan trustee assumed an 11½% *expected long-term rate of return on plan assets* to be invested to provide for the ultimate payment of benefits included in the pension plan's projected benefit obligation.

2 Rimmer funded service cost of $213,000 and 11% interest cost of $220,000 ($2,000,000 × 0.11 = $220,000) on December 31, Year 11.

3 The *actual return on plan assets* was $240,000, computed as follows:

Current fair value of plan assets, Dec. 31, Year 11		$2,673,000
Less: Employer contributions		
($2,000,000 + $213,000 + $220,000)	$2,433,000	
Employee contributions	0	
Benefits paid to retirees	0	2,433,000
Actual return on plan assets...........................		$ 240,000

The $240,000 actual return on plan assets represents a 12% return on the $2,000,000 employer's contribution that was available for investment throughout Year 11 ($240,000 ÷ $2,000,000 = 0.12). The actual return on plan assets of 12% exceeded the 11½% expected long-term rate of return on plan assets; accordingly, there is a *deferred gain* of $10,000 [$2,000,000 × (0.12 − 0.115) = $10,000] that must be considered in the computation of Rimmer Corporation's pension cost for Year 11. The deferral of the gain is in accordance with the second fundamental concept on page 958; the gain may be amortized to reduce pension cost in future years.

Rimmer Corporation's journal entries for its funded noncontributory defined benefit pension plan for Year 11 are as follows:

Year 11			
Jan. 2	Prepaid Pension Cost............................	2,000,000	
	Cash		2,000,000
	To record funding and deferral of entire prior		
	service cost of pension plan adopted this date.		
Dec. 31	Pension Expense	518,790	
	Cash ($213,000 + $220,000)		433,000
	Prepaid Pension Cost ($315,790 − $230,000)		85,790
	To record pension cost as follows:		
	Service cost	$213,000	
	Interest cost	220,000	
	Actual return on		
	plan assets $240,000		
	Less: Deferred gain 10,000	(230,000*)	
	Amortization of unrecog-		
	nized prior service		
	cost (see page 963)	315,790	
	Total pension cost	$518,790	

*This amount represents the **expected return on plan assets** ($2,000,000 × 0.115 = $230,000).

In the second of the foregoing journal entries, prepaid pension cost is *decreased* by the amortization of prepaid prior service cost, $315,790, and *increased* by the $230,000 excess of Rimmer's $433,000 funding payment to the pension plan trustee over the $203,000 net amount of the pension expense components other than prior service cost amortization ($213,000 + $220,000 − $230,000 = $203,000).

It is important to note that the *discount rate* used by Rimmer's actuaries to compute the projected benefit obligation (11%) differed from the *expected long-term rate of return on plan assets* (11½%). Even though both rates are estimated, the fact that they differ is not unusual, because the discount rate is based on *current prices of annuity contracts* (see page 959) while the expected rate of return is a *long-term projection*.

On December 31, Year 11, the projected benefit obligation of Rimmer Corporation's pension plan totals $2,433,000, computed as follows:

Balance, Jan. 2, Year 11 (prior service cost)	$2,000,000
Add: Service cost for Year 11	213,000
Interest cost for Year 11 ($2,000,000 × 0.11)....................	220,000
Subtotal	$2,433,000
Less: Benefits paid to retirees	0
Balance, Dec. 31, Year 11	$2,433,000

As shown on page 963, the current fair value of plan assets on December 31, Year 11, was $2,673,000; thus, Rimmer's pension plan is overfunded by $240,000 ($2,673,000 − $2,433,000 = $240,000). This overfunding was the result of Rimmer's having disregarded the $240,000 actual return on plan assets for Year 11 (see page 963) in its funding of pension cost for Year 11.

To continue our illustration of Rimmer Corporation's noncontributory funded defined benefit pension plan for Year 12, we assume the following:

1   One employee retired on December 31, Year 11 (see page 962) and was paid an annual pension of $40,000 by the pension plan on December 31, Year 12.

2   The actuaries for Rimmer's pension plan made no changes in the discount rate or other assumptions for Year 12.

3   The actual return on plan assets was $307,395, the same amount as the expected return on plan assets ($2,673,000 × 0.115 = $307,395).

4   Service cost was $224,000, and interest cost was $267,630 ($2,433,000 × 0.11 = $267,630).

5   Rimmer funded $184,235 of total pension cost on December 31, Year 12, representing the net of service cost, interest cost, and actual return on plan assets ($224,000 + $267,630 − $307,395 = $184,235).

Before pension cost for Year 12 may be measured for Rimmer Corporation's pension plan, a computation must be made to determine whether any portion of the $10,000 deferred gain as of January 1, Year 12 (see page 963) must be included in pension cost for Year 12. As indicated on page 960, amortization of beginning-of-year unrecognized net gains and losses is included in pension cost to the extent that they exceed 10% of the greater of the projected benefit obligation or the current fair value of pension plan assets at the beginning of the year. As indicated above, the $2,673,000 current fair value of pension plan assets on December 31, Year 11, exceeded the projected benefit obligation on that date. $2,673,000 × 0.10 = $267,300, which is substantially larger than the $10,000 beginning-of-year deferred gain. Thus, *no amortized gain is included in the computation of pension cost of Rimmer Corporation for Year 12*. Accordingly, Rimmer's journal entry for pension expense on December 31, Year 12, is as follows:

Journal entry for funded defined benefit pension plan with service cost, interest cost, return on plan assets, and amortized prior service cost

Pension Expense	492,506	
Cash		184,235
Prepaid Pension Cost..................		308,271
To record pension cost as follows:		
Service cost	$224,000	
Interest cost	267,630	
Actual return on plan assets (no		
deferred gain or loss)	(307,395)	
Amortization of unrecognized prior		
service cost (see page 963)	308,271	
Amortization of (gain) or loss	0	
Total pension cost	$492,506	

Rimmer Corporation's pension plan remains overfunded $240,000 on December 31, Year 12, as shown below:

Current fair value of plan assets:

Balance, Dec. 31, Year 11 (page 963)		$2,673,000
Add: Actual return on plan assets (same as expected		
return) ($2,673,000 × 0.115).................		307,395
Employer contribution.........................		184,235
Subtotal		$3,164,630
Less: Benefits paid to retirees		40,000
Balance, Dec. 31, Year 12		$3,124,630

Less: Projected benefit obligation:

Balance, Dec. 31, Year 11 (page 964)	$2,433,000	
Add: Service cost for Year 12	224,000	
Interest cost for Year 12		
($2,433,000 × 0.11)	267,630	
Subtotal	$2,924,630	
Less: Benefits paid to retirees	40,000	
Balance, Dec. 31, Year 12		2,884,630
Overfunding of pension plan		$ 240,000

The overfunded status of the pension plan is disclosed in a note to the December 31, Year 12, financial statements of Rimmer Corporation, as explained in a subsequent section of this chapter. Rimmer's pension expense of $492,506 is included in its income statement for Year 12, appropriately allocated among cost of goods sold, selling expenses, and general and administrative expenses (a portion allocable to direct labor and factory overhead may be included in inventories in Rimmer's December 31, Year 12, balance sheet). $293,233 (see page 963) of the $1,605,939 balance ($2,000,000 − $85,790 − $308,271 = $1,605,939) of Rimmer's Prepaid Pension Cost ledger account is included with current assets in Rimmer's December 31, Year 12, balance sheeet because it will be amortized to pension expense in Year 13. The $1,312,706 ($1,605,939 − $293,233 = $1,312,706) balance of the account is included in the Other Noncurrent Assets section of the balance sheet.

Summary of Accounting for Pension Cost of Defined Benefit Pension Plans
The principal features of accounting for the employer's pension cost of defined benefit pension plans may be summarized as follows:

1   Pension cost of both funded and unfunded defined benefit pension plans includes *service cost* and *interest cost,* which are computed by actuaries based on an assumed *discount rate.*

2   Only funded defined benefit pension plans include *actual return on plan assets* in the computation of net pension cost.

3 *Prior service cost* resulting from the adoption or amendment of a defined benefit pension plan is amortized as pension cost over the average service life of employees expected to receive benefits under the plan.

4 *Gains and losses* resulting from differences between expected and actual returns on plan assets or changes in assumptions underlying actuaries' computations for the projected benefit obligation of the pension plan are deferred in the period that they occur and amortized to pension cost over the average remaining service life of employees to the extent that they exceed 10% of the greater of the beginning-of-year current fair value of pension plan assets or the projected benefit obligation under the pension plan.

5 Pension cost of an accounting period is apportioned among cost of goods sold (to the extent that it is not included in inventories) and to operating expense. The amount of prepaid pension cost or accrued pension cost, representing differences between pension cost of an accounting period and amounts funded, if any, is included with assets or liabilities, respectively, in the balance sheet, appropriately classified as current or long-term.

6 The current fair value of plan assets and the projected benefit obligation of a funded defined benefit pension plan are accounted for in the accounting records of the pension plan, which is a legal and accounting entity separate from the employer.

Liability for Unfunded Accumulated Benefit Obligation   If there is an unfunded accumulated benefit obligation for a defined benefit pension plan, the Financial Accounting Standards Board required the recording of a liability.[16] The *accumulated benefit obligation* for a defined benefit pension plan that is a *flat-benefit plan* that does not base pension benefits on future compensation levels is the same as the projected benefit obligation. For a *final-pay plan,* which bases pension benefits on future compensation levels, the accumulated benefit obligation, which is the actuarial present value of benefits attributable to employee services based on *current and past compensation levels,* is less than the projected benefit obligation, which is the actuarial present value of benefits attributable to employee services based on *assumptions as to future compensation levels.*

To the extent that an unfunded accumulated benefit obligation under a defined benefit pension plan does not exceed the amount of unrecognized prior service cost, the offsetting debit for the liability amount is to an intangible asset ledger account. Any excess is debited to a contra-stockholders' equity account.[17]

Illustration of Liability for Unfunded Accumulated Benefit Obligation Offset by Intangible Asset   To illustrate the recording of an intangible asset and an offsetting liability for unfunded accumulated benefit obligation, we return to the Rimmer Corporation example on pages 962–966 and assumed that Rimmer's noncontributory funded defined benefit pension plan was a flat-benefit plan for which the accumulated benefit obligation is the same as the projected benefit obligation. In

---

[16]Ibid., p. 10
[17]Ibid.

addition, we change the assumption as to Rimmer's funding of the $2,000,000 prior service cost existing on January 2, Year 11 (date of adoption of the pension plan) to the following:

1    $500,000 of the prior service cost was funded on January 2, Year 11.

2    $1,500,000 of the prior service cost was funded on January 2, Year 12.

In accordance with the foregoing, Rimmer Corporation's journal entries for the pension plan for Year 11 are as follows:

Journal entries for funded defined benefit pension plan with service cost, interest cost, return on plan assets, deferred gain, and amortized prior service cost

Year 11			
Jan. 2	*Prepaid Pension Cost.............................*	*500,000*	
	Cash		*500,000*
	To record funding and deferral of portion of prior		
	service cost of pension plan adopted this date.		
Dec. 31	*Pension Expense...................................*	*691,290*	
	Cash ($213,000 + $220,000)		*433,000*
	Prepaid Pension Cost		
	($315,790 − $57,500)		*258,290*
	To recognize pension cost as follows:		
	Service cost	*$213,000*	
	Interest cost	*220,000*	
	Actual return on plan assets		
	($500,000 × 0.12)	*$60,000*	
	Less: Deferred gain		
	($500,000 × 0.005)	*2,500*	*(57,500*)*
	Amortization of unrecognized		
	prior service cost....................	*315,790*	
	Total pension cost	*$691,290*	

This amount represents the **expected return on plan assets ($500,000 × 0.115 = $57,500).*

Following the foregoing journal entries, Rimmer Corporation's pension plan has an unfunded accumulated benefit obligation of $1,440,000, computed as follows:

Computation of unfunded accumulated benefit obligation under pension plan

Accumulated benefit obligation, Dec. 31, Year 11 (same as	
projected benefit obligation as computed on page 964 because	
pension plan is a flat-benefit plan)	*$2,433,000*
Less: Current fair value of plan assets, Dec. 31, Year 1	
($500,000 + $60,000 + $433,000).................................	*993,000*
Unfunded accumulated benefit obligation...........................	*$1,440,000*

Under **FASB Statement No. 87,** pension plan assets and liabilities are presented as a single net amount in the employer enterprise's balance sheet (see third fundamental concept on page 958). Because Rimmer Corporation has a Prepaid Pension Cost ledger account with a balance of $241,710 ($500,000 − $258,290 = $241,710) on December 31, Year 11, it must credit a liability account for $1,681,710 ($1,440,000 + $241,710 = $1,681,710) to provide for a **net** liability of $1,440,000 in its December 31, Year 11, balance sheet. The required credit of $1,681,710 to the liability account is less than the $1,684,210 ($2,000,000 − $315,790 = $1,684,210) unrecognized prior service cost on December 31, Year 11, by $2,500 (which is equal to the deferred gain on plan assets that was not included in Rimmer's Year 11 computation of pension cost). Accordingly, Rimmer prepares an additional journal entry for Year 11 as follows:

Journal entry for liability for unfunded accumulated benefit obligation

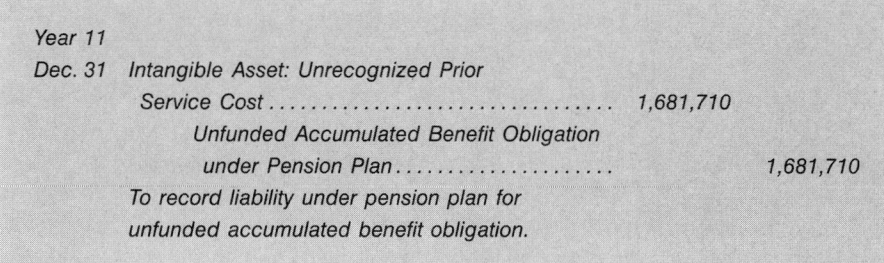

```
Year 11
Dec. 31   Intangible Asset: Unrecognized Prior
              Service Cost ................................   1,681,710
                  Unfunded Accumulated Benefit Obligation
                      under Pension Plan .....................              1,681,710
          To record liability under pension plan for
          unfunded accumulated benefit obligation.
```

In requiring the recording of a liability for unfunded accumulated benefit obligation under a pension plan, the Financial Accounting Standards Board attempted to reach a compromise position between the two differing views on pension plan liabilities described on pages 953–954. The offsetting debit presented a conceptual problem because of the FASB's position that changes in the pension obligation of an employer, such as for prior service cost, are to be recognized in the computation of pension cost for accounting periods **subsequent to the change** (see page 958). A debit to a deferred charge ledger account would not be appropriate because, unlike amounts recorded in a Prepaid Pension Cost ledger account, the unfunded accumulated benefit obligation has not been **paid.** Debiting an intangible asset ledger account to the extent of unrecognized prior service cost may be supported by the assumption that intangible benefits in the form of increased employee productivity and higher morale result from the adoption or amendment (for increased benefits) of a pension plan.

In determining the amount of pension cost to be recognized for Year 12, Rimmer Corporation must ascertain whether any of the $2,500 deferred gain on December 31, Year 11, is to be included in pension cost for Year 12. The minimum amount to be amortized is 10% of the projected benefit obligation on December 31, Year 12, which exceeds the current fair value of plan assets on that date. $2,433,000 × 0.10 = $243,300, which substantially exceeds $2,500; thus, **pension cost for Year 12 does not include amortization of the deferred gain existing on January 1, Year 12.** Accordingly, the first two journal entries for Rimmer Corporation's Year 12 pension cost are as follows:

Journal entries for
funded defined benefit
pension plan with
service cost, interest
cost, return on plan
assets, and amortized
prior service cost

Year 12

Jan. 2   Prepaid Pension Cost.   1,500,000

           Cash 1,500,000

        *To record funding and deferral of remainder
of prior service cost of pension plan adopted
Jan. 2, Year 11.*

Dec. 31   Pension Expense   513,206

          Cash 204,935

          Prepaid Pension Cost. 308,271

        To record pension cost as follows:

Service cost	$224,000	
Interest cost		
($2,433,000 × 0.11).	267,630	
Actual return on plan assets		
(no deferred gain or loss)		
[($993,000 + $1,500,000)		
×0.115]	(286,695)	
Total funded	$204,935	
Amortization of unrecognized		
prior service cost.	308,271	
Amortization of (gain)		
or loss	0	
Total pension cost	$513,206	

On December 31, Year 12, the current fair value of plan assets of Rimmer Corporation's pension plan is $2,944,630, computed as follows:

Computation of current
fair value of plan
assets

Balance, Dec. 31, Year 11 (p. 968)	$ 993,000
Add: Actual return on plan assets (same as expected return)	
($2,493,000 × 0.115)	286,695
Employer contributions ($1,500,000 + $204,935)	1,704,935
Subtotal	$2,984,630
Less: Benefits paid	40,000
Balance, Dec. 31, Year 12	$2,944,630

The $2,944,630 current fair value of plan assets on December 31, Year 12, exceeds the accumulated benefit obligation (equal to the projected benefit obligation) of $2,884,630 (see page 966) by $60,000 ($2,944,630 − $2,884,630 = $60,000); thus, the liability for unfunded accumulated benefit obligation established by Rimmer Corporation on December 31, Year 11, is not required on December 31, Year 12. In accordance with *FASB Statement No. 87,*[18] Rimmer eliminates the unneeded liability with the following journal entry:

---

[18]Ibid.

Journal entry to
eliminate unneeded
liability for unfunded
accumulated benefit
obligation

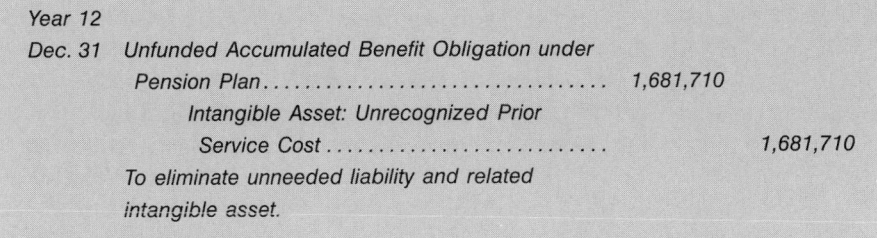

Year 12

Dec. 31 Unfunded Accumulated Benefit Obligation under

Pension Plan................................. 1,681,710

Intangible Asset: Unrecognized Prior

Service Cost 1,681,710

To eliminate unneeded liability and related

intangible asset.

The foregoing illustration demonstrates that the accounting for the liability for unfunded accumulated benefit obligation and the related intangible asset account resembles the accounting for long-term investments in marketable equity securities (see pages 697–700). In both accounting situations, end-of-period journal entries are prepared to adjust the ending balances of—or to eliminate if unneeded—the affected ledger accounts.

Disclosure of Pension Plan Information by Employers

For defined contribution and multiemployer pension plans, the Financial Accounting Standards Board required disclosure in a note to the employer's financial statements of a description of the plan (including employees covered, basis for determining required contributions, and nature and effect of significant matters affecting comparability among accounting periods) and the amount of pension cost recognized during the accounting period or periods covered by the financial statements.[19] The many disclosures for defined benefit pension plans required by the FASB[20] are illustrated on page 972 by reference to the Rimmer Corporation pension plan described on pages 967–969 for the year ended December 31, Year 11.

The "net amortization and deferral" portion of pension cost in the note to financial statements on page 972 is computed as follows:

Computation of "Net
amortization and
deferral"

Amortization of unrecognized prior service cost $315,790

Add: Deferred gain on plan assets.................................... 2,500

Net amortization and deferral portion of pension cost.................. $318,290

Other Aspects of Accounting for Pensions

In this section we describe the following additional features of employers' accounting for pension plans: legal aspects of pension plans, actuarial funding methods, alternative amortization technique for prior service cost, market-related values for pension plan assets, limitation on intangible asset for unrecognized prior service cost, and the transition period for *FASB Statement No. 87.*

Legal Aspects of Pension Plans In order to give more protection to employees covered by private pension plans and to eliminate certain abuses in the management

---

[19]Ibid., pp. 18–19.
[20]Ibid., pp. 15–16.

Note xx The company has a noncontributory defined benefit pension plan covering all its employees. The benefits are based on years of service and the employee's compensation during the current year of employment. The company's funding policy generally is to fund service cost and interest cost. In addition, the company has funded $500,000 of prior service cost during Year 11 and anticipates funding the remainder of prior service cost, $1,500,000, during the year ended December 31, Year 12. Amounts funded are intended to provide not only for benefits attributable to services to date but also for those expected to be earned in the future.

The following table sets forth the pension plan's funded status and amounts included in the company's balance sheet on December 31, Year 11:

Actuarial present value of benefit obligations:	
Accumulated benefit obligation (including vested benefits[21]	
of $1,122,000)	($2,433,000)
Projected benefit obligation for services rendered to date	($2,433,000)
Plan assets at current fair value (primarily United States	
Treasury and corporate bonds)	993,000
Projected benefit obligation in excess of plan assets	($1,440,000)
Unrecognized net gain	(2,500)
Unrecognized prior service cost	1,684,210
Provision for unfunded accumulated benefit obligation	(1,681,710)
Net pension liability included in balance sheet	($1,440,000)

Net pension cost for Year 11 included the following components:	
Service cost—benefits earned during Year 11	$ 213,000
Interest on projected benefit obligation	220,000
Actual return on plan assets	(60,000)
Net amortization and deferral	318,290
Net pension cost for Year 11	$ 691,290

The weighted average discount rate used to compute the actuarial present value of the projected benefit obligation was 11%. The expected long-term rate of return on plan assets was 11½%.

of such plans, Congress enacted ERISA. The major goal of ERISA was to protect employee pension rights through rigid minimum requirements for funding pension benefits, participation in a pension plan by employees, vesting of pension benefits, and detailed disclosure of pension plan activities. Under ERISA administrators of private pension plans must file with the Department of Labor annual reports that include a description of the pension plan, financial statements, and supplementary

---

[21]**Vested benefits** are pension benefits that are not contingent on the employee's continued services to the employer. The $1,122,000 amount is assumed.

exhibits. Some examples of the type of information that must be included in the annual report filed with the Department of Labor by a pension plan are listed below:

1   Statements of plan assets and liabilities and changes in net assets available for the payment of benefits

2   Exhibits of (a) plan investments, (b) transactions involving ''parties in interest'' such as officers and plan fiduciaries, (c) loans in default or exceeding 3% of the value of plan assets, and (d) transactions involving amounts exceeding 3% of the value of plan assets

3   A statement of the assets and liabilities of the trustee, if pension fund assets are held in trust by a bank or an insurance company

4   Statements of salaries, fees, and commissions paid by the plan

5   The number of employees covered by the plan, a periodic actuarial report, and an explanation of any changes of trustee, actuary, independent accountant, administrator, investment advisor, custodian, or insurance company

The Multiemployer Pension Plan Amendments Act of 1980 amended ERISA by requiring employers that withdraw from a multiemployer pension plan to fund a share of the plan's unfunded liabilities when they withdraw, and by increasing minimum funding requirements for such plans.

Actuarial Funding Methods   The annual amount of pension *funding* is based on one of several acceptable actuarial funding methods. The factors used in tentatively resolving uncertainties concerning future events affecting pension funding, such as mortality rates, employee turnover, compensation levels, and the return on pension fund assets, are referred to as *actuarial assumptions.* Actuaries use these assumptions to determine the amounts an employer is to contribute to a pension fund. The first procedure is to determine on the funding date the present value of future pension benefits to be paid to employees. An acceptable actuarial funding method then is applied to the present value of the future pension benefits to determine the current contributions to be made by the employer.

Although actuarial techniques are used primarily to determine the periodic payments to be made to the pension fund (or funding agency), the same techniques may be used to measure periodic pension expense. The amount of the pension cost recognized currently is the present value of future pension benefits that are estimated to have accrued during the current accounting period. Acceptable actuarial methods for measuring pension cost are the *unit-credit method* for flat-benefit plans and the *projected-unit-credit method* for final-pay plans. Under the unit-credit method, the amount of pension cost of the current accounting period usually is equal to the present value of the increase in the employees' retirement benefits resulting from the services performed in the current period. Thus, the pension cost under this method is the present value of the *units* of future pension benefits credited to employees for current services. Under the projected-unit-credit method, the amount of pension cost of the current accounting period usually represents a level amount that will provide for the total projected retirement benefits over the periods of active service of employees.

Alternative Amortization Technique for Prior Service Cost   In recognition of the complexity and detail of the computations of amortization of prior service cost illustrated on pages 962–963, the Financial Accounting Standards Board authorized the use of an alternative method, such as the straight-line method, that results in more rapid amortization of prior service cost. Use of the alternative method must be disclosed in the note to the financial statements that describes the pension plan.[22]

For example, if Rimmer Corporation had adopted the straight-line method of amortization of the $2,000,000 prior service cost, using the data on page 962, it would have computed the average remaining service life of the 42 employees by dividing the denominator of the amortization fraction, 266, by 42 to obtain an average remaining service life of 6⅓ years (266 ÷ 42 = 6⅓). Amortization for each of six years would be $315,789 ($2,000,000 ÷ 6⅓ = $315,789) and for the seventh year would be $105,266 [$2,000,000 − ($315,789 × 6) = $105,266]. Amortization by the straight-line technique results in a larger charge to pension cost in each year except the first, when it is essentially identical to amortization under the conventional method.

Market-Related Value for Pension Plan Assets   In an effort to reduce further the volatility of pension cost resulting from differences between actual returns and expected long-term rates of return on plan assets, the Financial Accounting Standards Board permitted use of a market-related value, rather than current fair value, to compute the expected return on pension plan assets used in the measurement of pension cost and gain or loss from differences between expected return and actual return on plan assets. The *market-related value of plan assets* is a computed value that recognizes changes in current fair value of plan assets over not more than five years.[23] To avoid needless complexities in our discussion of accounting for funded defined benefit pension plans, we do not illustrate the computation of market-related values of plan assets.

Limitation on Intangible Asset for Prior Service Cost   If an employer has a liability for unfunded accumulated benefit obligation of a defined benefit pension plan, and the credit required to establish that liability exceeds the amount of unrecognized prior service cost (which is debited to an intangible asset ledger account), the excess is debited to a contra-stockholders' equity account, net of applicable interperiod tax allocation.[24] To illustrate, return to the Darien Company example on pages 959–961. Assuming that Darien's unfunded noncontributory defined benefit pension plan is a flat-benefit plan, and thus the accumulated benefit obligation on January 1, Year 3, is equal to the projected benefit obligation on that date, as illustrated on page 961, Darien has a $11,810 liability for unfunded accumulated benefit obligation on December 31, Year 3. Because Darien had no unrecognized prior service cost (see page 959), it prepares the following additional journal entry on December 31, Year 3 (disregarding income tax effects):

---

[22]Ibid., pp. 7–8.
[23]Ibid., pp. 8–9.
[24]Ibid., p. 10.

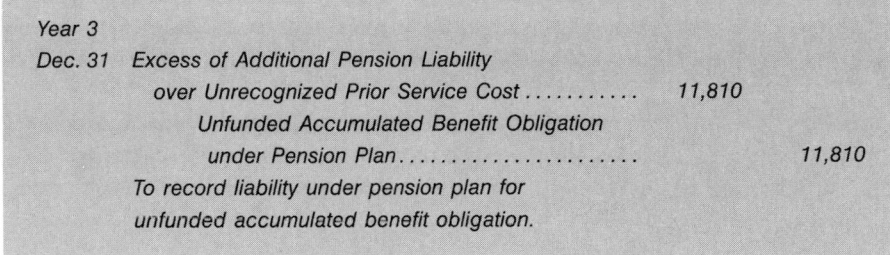

Journal entry for
unfunded accumulated
benefit obligation

Year 3

Dec. 31 *Excess of Additional Pension Liability*
over Unrecognized Prior Service Cost 11,810
Unfunded Accumulated Benefit Obligation
under Pension Plan 11,810
To record liability under pension plan for
unfunded accumulated benefit obligation.

The $11,810 debit amount in the foregoing journal entry is subtracted from the total
paid-in capital and retained earnings in Darien Company's December 31, Year 3,
balance sheet. As stated on page 971, in subsequent years the contra-stockholders'
equity account and related liability are increased, decreased, or eliminated depending on the status of Darien's unfunded accumulated benefit obligation.

Transition Period for *FASB Statement No. 87*   Although the Financial Accounting Standards Board encouraged early application of the provisions of *FASB Statement No. 87,* it permitted a delay until years beginning after December 31, 1988, in
some cases. Further, the FASB permitted an amortization period as long as 15 years
for employers having defined benefit pension plans to record a date-of-application
unrecognized net gain and related excess of pension plan assets over projected
benefit obligation or to record an unrecognized net loss in the converse situation.
The amortization of the unrecognized net gain or net loss is included in the measurement of net pension cost of each accounting period.[25]

Evaluation of Accounting Standards for Pension Plans

FASB Statement No. 87 represents the culmination of more than 10 years of effort
by the Financial Accounting Standards Board to develop improved standards for
employer accounting for pension plans. Despite the long development period for the
Statement, it was adopted by a bare 4 to 3 majority of the FASB. The dissenters
objected to several provisions of the *Statement,* including its inflexibility regarding
acceptable actuarial funding methods, its arbitrariness, its complexity, the questionable intangible asset established to offset an unfunded accumulated benefit obligation, and the use of a market-related value for plan assets. These objections appear
warranted, especially when one considers that *APB Opinion No. 8,* "Accounting
for the Cost of Pension Plans," which was in effect for 20 years prior to the
adoption of *FASB Statement No. 87,* had none of the shortcomings alleged by the
dissenters. For example, *APB Opinion No. 8* permitted the use of many actuarial
funding methods to compute pension cost and had no requirement for recording an
intangible asset or a liability for unfunded accumulated benefit obligation. Pension
cost under *APB Opinion No. 8* generally consisted only of service cost, interest cost
(or contra-cost), and amortization of prior service cost. The only asset or liability
associated with defined benefit pension plans under *APB Opinion No. 8* was

[25]Ibid., p. 21.

prepaid pension cost or accrued pension cost. Far less complex disclosure was required in a note to financial statements under *APB Opinion No. 8* than the disclosure illustrated on pages 971–972. Further, although the Financial Accounting Standards Board stated that footnote disclosure is not an adequate substitute for recognition of items in the body of financial statements,[26] it also acknowledged that the delayed recognition of unrecognized prior service cost, for example, results in excluding the most current and most relevant information from the balance sheet, but that such information is included in required disclosures in a note to the financial statements.[27]

Probably the most disturbing features of *FASB Statement No. 87* are the intangible asset and contra-stockholders' equity ledger accounts established to offset a liability for unfunded accumulated benefit obligation. As explained in Chapter 13, intangible assets—especially unidentifiable intangible assets—are recorded at *cost,* typically in a business transaction with an independent party. In contrast, the intangible asset for unrecognized prior service cost illustrated on page 969 is literally created by a ''stroke of the accountant's pen''; it has no *cost* in terms of a business transaction. The contra-stockholders' equity account illustrated on page 975 is even more unusual; it represents a balance sheet item that does not fit the conventional accounting equation Assets = Liabilities + Owners' Equity.

The Financial Accounting Standards Board acknowledged that *FASB Statement No. 87* continued the evolutionary search for more meaningful and more useful pension accounting by employers, but that the final step in the evolution has not been reached.[28] It is desirable for the FASB to monitor closely pension plan accounting and disclosure in subsequent years and to strive for improvements in a presently questionable accounting model.

EMPLOYERS' SETTLEMENTS OR CURTAILMENTS OF PENSION PLANS

In *FASB Statement No. 88,* ''Employers' Accounting for Settlements and Curtailments of Defined Benefit Pension Plans . . . ,'' the Financial Accounting Standards Board addressed issues involved in radical changes in the ''going-concern'' nature of defined benefit pension plans. A *settlement* of a defined benefit pension plan results from transactions such as lump-sum cash payments to employees in exchange for their rights to receive specified plan benefits or acquisition of nonparticipating annuity contracts to cover vested benefits under the plan. Thus, settlements are irrevocable actions that relieve the employer or the pension plan of primary responsibility for pension benefits and eliminate significant risks related to the obligation and the assets used to accomplish the settlements.[29] A *curtailment* of a

---

[26]Ibid., p. 38
[27]Ibid., p. iv.
[28]Ibid., p. 2
[29]*FASB Statement no. 88,* ''Employers' Accounting for Settlement and Curtailments of Defined Benefit Pension Plans . . . ,'' FASB (Stamford: 1985), p. 2.

defined benefit pension plan takes place when, for example, employee services are terminated earlier than anticipated or a pension plan is terminated or suspended so that employees do not earn benefits for future services. The outcome of a curtailment is a reduction of expected years of future services of present employees or elimination of numerous employees from the accrual of defined benefits for future services.[30]

Both a settlement and a curtailment may occur with respect to a single employer act regarding a defined benefit pension plan. For example, the termination of a defined benefit pension plan involves a curtailment and a settlement because the termination itself constitutes a curtailment and the employees typically receive nonparticipating annuity contracts or lump-sum payments in a settlement in conjunction with the termination of the plan.

Illustration of Accounting for Termination of Defined Benefit Pension Plan

Accounting for a settlement and a curtailment may be illustrated by an example involving a termination of a defined benefit pension plan without adoption of a replacement plan. *FASB Statement No. 88* provides that the maximum gain or loss to be recognized from settlement of a pension obligation is the amount of an unrecognized net gain or loss excluded from the computation of pension cost in prior accounting periods (see pages 960–961) plus any unrecognized net asset existing on the date of initial application of *FASB Statement No. 87* (see page 975). Only a pro rata portion of the maximum gain or loss is recognized if the entire projected benefit obligation is not settled.[31] In a curtailment, the unrecognized prior service cost associated with years of service no longer expected to be rendered is a loss, as is any remaining unrecognized net obligation existing on the date of initial application of *FASB Statement No. 87.*[32]

For example, assume that Rimmer Corporation terminated its funded noncontributory defined benefit pension plan on January 2, Year 12, by acquiring nonparticipating annuity contracts in the amount of the accumulated benefit obligation (identical to the projected benefit obligation) amounting to $2,433,000 (see page 972). The trustee of the pension plan liquidated the plan assets at their current fair value of $993,000, and that amount, plus $1,440,000 cash from Rimmer, was used to acquire the annuity contracts. In accordance with *FASB Statement No. 88,* the $2,500 gain from settlement of the pension plan, which is the amount of the unrecognized net gain on December 31, Year 11, is a gain from settlement; the $1,684,210 unrecognized prior service cost, which we assume is equal to the amount associated with years of service no longer expected to be rendered as illustrated in the exhibit on page 962, is a loss from curtailment of the pension plan. Rimmer Corporation prepares the following journal entry for termination of the pension plan:

---

[30]Ibid.
[31]Ibid., p. 3.
[32]Ibid., p. 4.

```
Year 12
Jan. 2   Unfunded Accumulated Benefit Obligation under
           Pension Plan (p. 969) ........................   1,681,710
         Loss from Termination of Pension Plan .........   1,681,710
               Prepaid Pension Cost (p. 969) ...........                 241,710
               Cash .................................                  1,440,000
               Intangible Asset: Unrecognized Prior
                 Service Cost (p. 969) .................                1,681,710
         To record termination of pension plan and
         acquisition of nonparticipating annuity
         contracts for accumulated benefit
         obligation. Loss from termination of plan
         consists of the following:
             Loss from curtailment ............   $1,684,210
             Less: Gain from settlement .......        2,500
             Loss from termination ...........   $1,681,710
```

The foregoing example of settlement and curtailment of a defined benefit pension plan is simplified. Many complexities result from partial settlements or curtailments **only;** they are beyond the scope of this discussion.

Accounting Standards for Deferred Compensation Contracts

The accrual basis of accounting applicable to pension plans also is applicable to other deferred compensation contracts. Such contracts generally stipulate that employees eligible for benefits must be employed for a specified period and that they should be available for consultation after retirement. The principle for the accrual of deferred compensation expense was formulated by the Accounting Principles Board as follows:[33]

> The estimated amounts to be paid under each contract should be accrued in a systematic and rational manner over the period of active employment from the time the contract is entered into, unless it is evident that future services expected to be received by the employer are commensurate with the payments or a portion of the payments to be made. If elements of both current and future services are present, only the portion applicable to the current services should be accrued.

Disclosure of Postretirement Health and Life Insurance Benefits

In *FASB Statement No. 81,* "Disclosure of Postretirement Health Care and Life Insurance Benefits," the Financial Accounting Standards Board required disclosure of the following information regarding life insurance benefits and health care bene-

---

[33]*APB Opinion No. 12,* "Omnibus Opinion—1967." AICPA (New York: 1967), p. 189.

fits such as dental, hearing, and vision benefits paid to retired employees of a business enterprise:[34]

a A description of the benefits provided, the employee groups covered, and the accounting and funding policies for the benefits

b The cost of the foregoing benefits recognized in the accounting period or periods

c The effects of significant matters affecting comparability of costs recognized for all accounting periods presented

The FASB required the foregoing disclosures as an interim measure pending completion of its study of accounting and reporting for postemployment benefits other than pensions.

REVIEW QUESTIONS

1 Distinguish between the following:
a *Noncontributory pension plan* and *contributory pension plan*
b *Defined benefit pension plan* and *defined contribution pension plan*
c *Unfunded pension plan* and *funded pension plan*
d *Actuary* and *actuarial funding method*

2 What are three significant issues related to accounting for pension plans?

3 Do accountants who maintain that an employer's obligation under a pension plan is to the plan itself advocate the recording of a liability for the present value of all unfunded benefits attributable to employees on a specific balance sheet date? Explain.

4 What are the components of net pension cost of a defined benefit pension plan, as established by *FASB Statement No. 87,* "Employers' Accounting for Pensions"?

5 Define the following
a *Service cost*
b *Actual return on plan assets*
c *Interest cost*
d *Prior service cost*
e *Flat-benefit pension plan*

6 Under what circumstances is the Prepaid Pension Cost ledger account used in accounting for a defined benefit pension plan?

7 How does the *discount rate* differ from the *expected long-term rate of return on plan assets* for a funded defined benefit pension plan?

8 Under what circumstances is a liability for unfunded accumulated benefit obligation recorded for an employer's defined benefit pension plan?

---

[34]*FASB Statement No. 81,* "Disclosure of Postretirement Health Care and Life Insurance Benefits," FASB (Stamford: 1984), p. 2.

9 Explain the nature and purpose of the Unrecognized Prior Service Cost ledger account attributable to an employer's defined benefit pension plan.

10 What were the major objectives of the Employee Retirement Income Security Act of 1974 (ERISA)?

11 List some examples of information required to be disclosed in the annual report of a pension plan under the Employee Retirement Income Security Act of 1974 (ERISA).

12 What are the two actuarial funding methods that are acceptable for the employer's accounting for the cost of a defined benefit pension plan?

13 Explain why the use of *market-related value for pension plan assets* is permitted in the measurement of pension cost.

14 What transition period for the application of *FASB Statement No. 87,* "Employers' Accounting for Pensions," was established by the Financial Accounting Standards Board?

15 What are some criticisms of accounting standards for employers' accounting for pension plans, established by *FASB Statement No. 87,* "Employers' Accounting for Pensions"?

16 Briefly describe the accounting treatment of an employer's *settlement* or *curtailment* of a defined benefit pension plan.

EXERCISES

Ex. 19-1 Select the best answer for each of the following multiple-choice questions:

1 Ideally, the total pension cost relating to a particular employee is recognized as expense:
a Over the expected service lives of all employees active on the date the pension plan is adopted
b Over the specified term of the pension plan
c During the service years of the particular employee
d Over the period specified by ERISA

2 Is periodic pension expense measured by the employer's required contributions to a:

	Defined contribution pension plan?	Defined benefit pension plan?
a	Yes	Yes
b	Yes	No
c	No	Yes
d	No	No

3 Is a portion of the cost of an annuity acquired by the employer under an insured pension plan allocated to an asset ledger account under a:

	Participating annuity contract?	Nonparticipating annuity contract?
a	Yes	No
b	No	Yes
c	Yes	Yes
d	No	No

4   For a defined benefit pension plan, pension cost for an accounting period is a single net amount consisting of as many as:

a Two components
b Three components
c Four components
d Five components

5   An unfunded defined benefit pension plan initiated on the date that the employer began operations would first incur:

a Service cost only
b Service cost and interest cost only
c Service cost, interest cost, and amortization of unrecognized prior service cost
d Service cost and gain or loss only

6   For a defined benefit pension plan, amortization of beginning-of-year unrecognized net gains and losses should be included in pension cost to the extent that they exceed 10% of the:

a Projected benefit obligation
b Current fair value of pension plan assets
c Greater of the projected benefit obligation or current fair value of pension plan assets
d Lesser of the projected benefit obligation or current fair value of pension plan assets

7   The discount rate for a defined benefit pension plan is used by actuaries to compute:

a The projected benefit obligation only
b The expected return on plan assets only
c Both the projected benefit obligation and the expected return on plan assets
d Neither the projected benefit obligation nor the expected return on plan assets

8   Is the accumulated benefit obligation the same as the projected benefit obligation under a defined benefit pension plan that is a:

	Flat-benefit plan?	Final-pay plan?
a	Yes	No
b	No	No
c	No	Yes
d	Yes	Yes

Ex. 19-2   Under the terms of Olive Company's defined contribution pension plan adopted on January 2, Year 1, Olive is obligated to contribute to the plan on behalf of retired employees as well as active employees. For the first two years, Olive's pension plan had the following contributions:

	Year 1	Year 2
For active employees (required)	$123,000	$135,000
For estimated present value of future required		
contributions for retired employees	24,000	31,000

The discount rate is 8%

Prepare journal entries for Olive Company on December 31, Year 1 and Year 2, to record Olive's required contributions to the pension plan on those dates, including interest on unfunded amounts.

Ex. 19-3 On December 31, Year 5, Rupert Corporation acquired participating annuity contracts under its insured pension plan (adopted on January 2, Year 5) at a total cost of $358,000, including $86,000 attributable to the participation right. On December 31, Year 6, when the current fair value of the Year 5 participation right was $93,000, Rupert acquired additional participating annuity contracts at a total cost of $392,000, including $102,000 attributable to the participation right.

Prepare journal entries for Rupert Corporation on December 31, Year 5 and Year 6.

Ex. 19-4 On January 2, Year 1, Crump Company adopted a noncontributory, unfunded defined benefit pension plan. Actuaries computed the service cost under the plan at $86,500 and $91,800, respectively, for Year 1 and Year 2, at a discount rate of 9%.

Compute (**a**) pension expense for Year 2, and (**b**) the balance of the projected benefit obligation on December 31, Year 2, for Crump Company's pension plan.

Ex. 19-5 On January 1, Year 4, actuaries revised the amount of Lubeck Corporation's projected benefit obligation under its noncontributory, unfunded defined benefit pension plan to $347,800 from $284,600, because of a revision in the discount rate to 10% from 12%. The average remaining service period for Lubeck's employees on January 1, Year 4, was eight years.

Compute the minimum amount of unrecognized net gain or loss to be amortized as part of Lubeck Corporation's pension cost for Year 4.

Ex. 19-6 The expected years of service of the 10 employees of Lou Company, which adopted a noncontributory, funded defined benefit pension plan on January 2, Year 6, its sixth year of operation, were as follows:

Number of employees	Expected future years of service
3	8
4	9
3	10

Compute the amortization fractions for each of the 10 years, Year 6 through Year 15, that Lou Company should use to amortize unrecognized prior service cost of $900,000 on January 2, Year 6, the date the pension plan was adopted. (Hint: The amortization fractions for Year 6 through Year 13 are identical.)

Ex. 19-7 The amortization fractions for Kenny Company's unrecognized prior service cost of $520,000 on January 2, Year 4 (the date Kenny's noncontributory, funded defined benefit pension plan was adopted), were based on the following service years expected to be rendered by Kenny's 64 employees during Year 4 through Year 11:

Year 4	64	Year 8	56
Year 5	64	Year 9	48
Year 6	64	Year 10	36
Year 7	64	Year 11	20

Compute the amortization of Kenny Company's unrecognized prior service cost of $520,000 for the eight years ended December 31, Year 11, based on expected years of service of Kenny's employees active on January 2, Year 4.

Ex. 19-8 On December 31, Year 4, following its funding of pension cost for Year 4, Waller Company's unfunded accumulated benefit obligation under its noncontributory, funded, defined benefit (flat-benefit) pension plan was computed as follows:

Accumulated benefit obligation	$6,420,000
Less: Current fair value of plan assets	5,670,000
Unfunded accumulated benefit obligation	$ 750,000

Waller's Prepaid Pension Cost ledger account had a balance of $180,000 on December 31, Year 4, and its unrecognized prior service cost on that date was $840,000.

Prepare a journal entry for Waller Company on December 31, Year 4, to record its liability for unfunded accumulated benefit obligation on that date. Disregard income taxes.

Ex. 19-9 On January 2, Year 6, Weston Company terminated its noncontributory, funded defined benefit (flat-benefit) pension plan by paying $652,000 cash to the plan's trustee, who used that amount plus the $3,577,000 cash from liquidation of plan assets at current fair value to acquire nonparticipating annuity contracts for employees covered by the plan. On December 31, Year 5, ledger account balances related to the pension plan were as follows:

Intangible asset: Unrecognized prior service cost	$2,083,700
Prepaid pension cost	1,431,700
Unfunded accumulated benefit obligation under pension plan	2,083,700

In addition, Weston had an unrecognized net gain of $6,400 under its pension plan on December 31, Year 5.

Prepare a journal entry for Weston Company on January 2, Year 6, to record the termination of its pension plan. Show gain or loss from curtailment and settlement in the explanation for the journal entry.

CASES

Case 19-1   Many business enterprises have pension plans for their employees. Accounting for the cost of defined benefit pension plans is a complex subject in which many technical terms are encountered.

Instructions

a Define *service cost.*

b Define *vested benefits.*

c How are net gains and losses related to the operation of a defined benefit pension plan accounted for?

d What disclosures concerning pension plans are made in a note to the financial statements of employers?

Case 19-2   The board of directors of Oxford Steel Corporation is meeting to discuss the possibility of closing Oxford's outmoded plant in Clay City and concentrating production in modern facilities in Bryanville. In a discussion of costs to be incurred in such a shutdown, a director asked the controller how Oxford's defined benefit pension plan's unrecognized prior service cost attributable to employees terminated as a result of the plant closing would be reported in Oxford's financial statements for the year of the plant closing. The controller replied that the unrecognized prior service cost could be amortized and funded over the time periods originally established for such cost, because the same pension plan covered employees at both the Clay City and the Bryanville plants. The director commented that generally accepted accounting principles should not be so flexible that undepreciated cost of the abandoned Clay City plant assets would have to be written off as a loss, while the unrecognized prior service cost for terminated employees could be recognized as expense over future years.

Instructions

Do you agree with the controller of Oxford Steel Corporation? Alternatively, do you believe that unrecognized prior service cost attributable to employees terminated as a result of the plant closing should be recognized as a loss? Explain.

Case 19-3   Cleary Products, Inc., established a defined benefit pension plan on January 2, Year 1, to provide retirement benefits for all of its employees. The plan was noncontributory and was funded through a trustee, which invested all funds and paid all benefits as they became due. Vesting occurred when an employee retired at age 70. Prior service cost of $110,000 was being amortized by the straight-line method over 15 years and funded over 10 years on a discount rate of 5%. Cleary also funded an amount equal to service cost, net of gains and losses. There have been no amendments to the plan since inception.

The actuary's report on June 30, Year 4, follows:

CLEARY PRODUCTS, INC.
Defined Benefit Pension Plan
Actuary's Report
June 30, Year 4

Funding and pension cost for Year 4

Service cost (before adjustment for gains) computed by the unit-credit method		$ 34,150
Net gains:		
Investment gains (losses):		
Excess of expected dividend revenue over actual dividend revenue		$ (350)
Gain on disposal of investments		4,050
Gains in actuarial assumptions for:		
Mortality		3,400
Employee turnover		5,050
Reduction in pension cost from closing of plant		8,000
Net gains		$ 20,150
Service cost (funded currently)	$14,000	$ 14,000
Prior service cost:		
Funding	14,245	
Amortization		10,597
Total pension cost funded	$28,245	
Total pension expense in income statement		$ 24,597

Pension fund assets, June 30, Year 4

Cash	$ 4,200
Dividends receivable	1,525
Investment in common stocks, at current fair value	162,750
Total pension fund assets	$168,475

Projected benefit obligation, June 30, Year 4

Number of employees	46
Number of employees retired	none
Yearly earnings of employees	$598,000
Projected benefit obligation	$145,000

Actuarial assumptions

Discount rate	5%
Mortality (Year 1 Group Annuity Tables)	
Retirement	Age 70

Instructions

On the basis of generally accepted accounting principles for the cost of defined benefit pension plans, evaluate the (**a**) treatment of gains and losses, and (**b**) computation of pension expense for Cleary Products, Inc.'s income statement. Disregard income tax considerations and requirements of ERISA.

19-1 This problem consists of two unrelated parts.

a On January 2, Year 1, Wessel Corporation adopted a defined contribution pension plan that required Wessel to make contributions to the plan on behalf of retired employees as well as active employees. Information with respect to the first three years that the pension plan was in effect follows:

Year ended Dec. 31,	Required contribution for year	Present value of estimated cost of post-retirement contributions
Year 1	$126,000	$84,000
Year 2	143,000	92,000
Year 3	157,000	98,000

The appropriate discount rate for Wessel was 8%.

Instructions

Prepare journal entries for Wessel Corporation to record payment of required contributions on December 31, Year 1, Year 2, and Year 3, and accrual of pension cost for post-retirement contributions and applicable interest.

b On January 2, Year 1, LaCrosse Company adopted an insured pension plan that required LaCrosse to acquire participating annuity contracts for its active employees at the end of each year. Information with respect to the first three years that the insured pension plan was in effect follows:

Year ended Dec. 31,	Cost of annuity contracts Total	Amount assignable to participation right	Current fair value of all participation rights at end of year
Year 1	$123,000	$28,000	$ 28,000
Year 2	146,000	32,000	63,000
Year 3	154,000	43,000	114,000

Instructions

Prepare journal entries for LaCrosse Company to record acquisition of annuity contracts and related pension expense on December 31, Year 1, Year 2, and Year 3.

19-2 Carrie Company adopted an unfunded noncontributory defined benefit (flat-benefit) pension plan on January 2, Year 1, the date it began operations. Service cost for Year 1 and Year 2 was $63,000 and $68,000, respectively, at a discount rate of 8%. As of January 1, Year 3, the actuaries for Carrie's pension plan changed the discount rate to 9% from 8%, resulting in a $9,800 increase in the projected benefit obligation as of that date. Service cost for Year 3 was $87,000. No benefits were paid to retired employees during the three-year period ended December 31, Year 3.

Instructions

Prepare journal entries for Carrie Company on December 31, Year 1, Year 2, and Year 3, to record pension expense under its unfunded noncontributory defined benefit (flat-benefit) pension plan, and the unfunded accumulated benefit obligation under the pension plan on December 31, Year 3.

19-3 Yuen Corporation adopted a noncontributory funded defined benefit pension plan on January 2, Year 6, with unrecognized prior service cost of $813,000. Expected future years of service of Yuen's 100 employees covered by the pension plan were as follows on January 2, Year 6:

Number of employees	Expected future years of service
3	2
7	3
17	4
21	5
22	6
30	7
100	

Yuen's actuaries established a discount rate of 10% and an expected long-term rate of return on plan assets of 10½%. Service cost was $192,000 for Year 6, the actual return on plan assets was 10½%, and Yuen funded the $813,000 prior service cost in full on January 2, Year 6, and the service cost and interest cost, net of actual return on plan assets, on December 31, Year 6.

Instructions

a Prepare a working paper to compute the expected years of service (service years rendered in each year) by Yuen Corporation's 100 employees on January 2, Year 6.

b Prepare journal entries for Yuen Corporation on January 2, Year 6, to record the funding of the prior service cost, and on December 31, Year 6, to record the funding of net pension cost.

19-4 On January 2, Year 7, Lucinda Corporation's accountant computed the following amortization fractions for prior service cost of $4,240,000 attributable to the 56 employees covered by its noncontributory funded defined benefit (flat-benefit) pension plan adopted on that date:

Year 7	$56/448$	Year 13	$42/448$
Year 8	$56/448$	Year 14	$30/448$
Year 9	$48/448$	Year 15	$30/448$
Year 10	$47/448$	Year 16	$28/448$
Year 11	$46/448$	Year 17	$21/448$
Year 12	$44/448$		

Lucinda elected to fund the $4,240,000 prior service cost in two equal installments on January 2, Year 7, and January 2, Year 8, and to fund net pension cost, exclusive of amortization of prior service cost, in full each December 31, beginning Year 7. Lucinda also decided to amortize unrecognized prior service cost by the straight-line method. Lucinda's actuaries established a discount rate of 7¼% and an expected long-term rate of return on plan assets of 8½%.

The service cost for Year 7 was $422,000 and for Year 8 was $486,000. The actual return on plant assets was 9% for Year 7 and 8½% for Year 8.

Instructions

Compute the following for Lucinda Corporation for Year 7 and Year 8 (no employees retired during those years):
a Total pension cost for year
b Projected benefit obligation at end of year
c Current fair value of plan assets at end of year
d Liability for unfunded accumulated benefit obligation at end of year

19-5 On December 31, Year 5, information regarding the noncontributory funded defined benefit (flat-benefit) pension plan of Campo Company, included the following:

Accrued pension cost	$ 24,000
Current fair value of plan assets	$1,587,000
Deferred gain (from difference between actual return and	
expected return on plan assets in Year 5)	$ 245,900
Discount rate	7%
Expected long-term rate of return on plan assets	8%
Projected benefit obligation	$1,234,000
Unrecognized prior service cost (fully funded)........................	$ 720,000

For Year 6, the following were relevant to the Campo's pension plan:

Actual rate of return on plan assets	8%
Amortization fraction for prior service cost	45/360
Benefits paid to retirees, Dec. 31	$ 86,000
Service cost	$ 134,000

On December 31, Year 6, Campo funded net pension cost for Year 6 plus the accrued pension cost on December 31, Year 5.

Instructions

a Prepare a journal entry for Campo Company on December 31, Year 6, to record its payment to the funding agency and net pension cost.
b Compute the following for Campo Company on December 31, Year 6:
   (1) Current fair value of plan assets
   (2) Deferred net gain
   (3) Projected benefit obligation

19-6 On December 31, Year 8, following funding of a portion of net pension cost for Year 8, Mercedes Company's Prepaid Pension Cost ledger account had a balance of $136,000 attributable to its noncontributory funded defined benefit (flat-benefit) pension plan. Other information with respect to the pension plan follows:

Accumulated benefit obligation (including vested benefits of $843,200) .	$1,325,000
Current fair value of plan assets (primarily corporate bonds).	1,023,000
Unrecognized net gain or loss	0
Unrecognized prior service cost (fully funded).	432,000
Benefits expected to be paid to retirees in Year 9	82,000

Instructions

a Prepare a journal entry for Mercedes Company on December 31, Year 8, to record the liability for unfunded accumulated benefit obligation on that date.

b Prepare a partial balance sheet for Mercedes Company on December 31, Year 8, to present information regarding its pension plan.

c Prepare a partial note to financial statements for Mercedes Company on December 31, Year 8, to disclose the information illustrated in the first two paragraphs of the note to financial statements on page 972.

19-7 Following is a note to the December 31, Year 5, financial statements of Harder Company:

> **Note 7** The company has a noncontributory defined benefit pension plan covering all its employees. The benefits are based on years of service and the employee's compensation during the current year of employment. The company's funding policy generally is to fund service cost and interest cost. In addition, the company has funded $426,400 prior service cost in its entirety. Amounts funded are intended to provide not only for benefits attributable to services to date but also for those expected to be earned in the future.
>
> The following table sets forth the pension plan's funded status and amounts included in the company's balance sheet on December 31, Year 5:
>
> Actuarial present value of benefit obligations:

Accumulated benefit obligation (including vested benefits, $461,000) .	($934,000)
Projected benefit obligation for services rendered to date	($934,000)
Plan assets at current fair value (primarily corporate bonds)	978,000
Plan assets in excess of projected benefit obligation.	$ 44,000
Unrecognized net loss	6,000
Unrecognized prior service cost	213,000
Net pension asset included in balance sheet.	$263,000

> Net pension cost for Year 5 included the following components:

Service cost—benefits earned during Year 5	$ 63,000
Interest on projected benefit obligation	51,000
Actual return on plan assets	(59,000)
Net amortization and deferral	36,600
Net pension cost for Year 5	$ 91,600

> The weighted average discount rate used to compute the actuarial present value of the projected benefit obligation was 6%. The expected long-term rate of return on plan assets was 7%.

Additional Information

(1) "Net amortization and deferral" in the foregoing note consisted of:

Amortization of unrecognized prior service cost (straight-line method) $42,600
Less: Deferred loss on plan assets 6,000
Net amortization and deferral $36,600

(2) Service cost for Year 6 was $68,000.
(3) The actual return on plan assets for Year 6 was 7½%.
(4) Harder funded service cost and interest cost for Year 6 on December 31, Year 6.

Instructions

a Prepare a journal entry for Harder Company on December 31, Year 6, to record the funding of pension cost for Year 6.
b Prepare Harder Company's note to its December 31, Year 6, financial statements for its pension plan. (There were no benefits paid to retirees during Year 6.)

19-8 Selected ledger balances for Rado Corporation's noncontributory, funded defined benefit (flat-benefit) pension plan on December 31, Year 8, were as follows:

Excess of additional pension liability over unrecognized prior
  service cost .... $ 42,300
Intangible asset: Unrecognized prior service cost 362,700
Prepaid pension cost 21,500
Unfunded accumulated benefit obligation under pension plan 405,000

Rado's December 31, Year 9, journal entry for funding of pension cost was:

Year 9
Dec. 31 Pension Expense 163,190
           Prepaid Pension Cost 50,000
             Cash 213,190
         To recognize pension cost as follows:
         Service cost .... $ 82,500
         Interest cost ($905,500 × 0.08) 72,440
         Actual return on plan assets (same as
           expected return)($522,000 × 0.10)... (52,200)
         Net gain or loss 0
         Amortization of unrecognized prior
           service cost ($362,700 ÷ 6) 60,450
         Total pension cost $163,190

Pension benefits paid to retirees on December 31, Year 9, totaled $34,600. There was no unrecognized net gain or loss.

Instructions

a Prepare a journal entry for Rado Corporation on December 31, Year 9, to adjust the Unfunded Accumulated Benefit Obligation and related ledger accounts.
b Assuming that Rado Corporation terminated its defined benefit pension plan on January 2, Year 10, by paying sufficient cash ($273,050) to the pension plan trustee to enable the trustee to acquire annuity contracts with the cash and the proceeds from realization of the pension plan assets at carrying amount (December 31, Year 9, current fair value), prepare a journal entry for Rado Corporation to record the termination.

Accounting for Leases

20

Accounting for leasing transactions is a challenging problem for accountants. Leasing as a means of acquiring the services of plant assets has grown in popularity and complexity as a result of capital shortages and income tax considerations.

Plant assets may be acquired outright or by rental of the assets under a lease contract. Lease contracts are an important means of obtaining the use or financing the acquisition of almost any kind of property, ranging from office machines to factory buildings.[1]

In some cases, a business enterprise constructs or acquires property, sells it to an investor, and simultaneously leases the property from the investor in a **sale-leaseback transaction.** In other cases, an enterprise leases existing property or property constructed to its specifications. An enterprise that leases property for use in its operations may agree to pay certain **executory costs** (such as property taxes, insurance, and maintenance) incident to use of the property.

Numerous standards were developed by the Accounting Principles Board to enable accountants to identify leases of similar economic substance so that they would be reported in a consistent and meaningful manner.[2] The Financial Accounting Standards Board issued **Statement No. 13,** "Accounting for Leases," which superseded all previous pronouncements on lease accounting. Subsequently, the FASB amended **Statement No. 13** through numerous statements and interpretations. All these pronouncements then were integrated in **Accounting for Leases: FASB Statement No. 13 as amended and interpreted through May 1980.**[3] More recently, the FASB authorized separate (and simplified) accounting pronouncements for lessors and lessees.

---

[1]In the 38th edition of *Accounting Trends & Techniques* published by the AICPA in 1984, 546 of the 600 surveyed companies disclosed lease transactions.

[2]See *APB Opinion No. 5,* "Reporting of Leases in Financial Statements of Lessee," AICPA (New York: 1964); *APB Opinion No. 7,* "Accounting for Leases in Financial Statements of Lessors," AICPA (New York: 1966); *APB Opinion No. 27,* "Accounting for Lease Transactions by Manufacturer or Dealer Lessors," AICPA (New York: 1972); *APB Opinion No. 31,* "Disclosure of Lease Commitments by Lessees," AICPA (New York: 1973).

[3]*Accounting for Leases: FASB Statement No. 13 as Amended and Interpreted through May 1980,* FASB (Stamford; 1980).

Nature of Leases

A *lease* is a contract conveying the right to use tangible property, usually for a stated period of time. The owner of the property for which the right is transferred is the *lessor,* and the party to whom the right is transferred is the *lessee.* A further transfer of the right to use an asset from a lessee to another party during the term of the lease is a *sublease.*

The accounting for leases may be divided into two parts—accounting by lessors and accounting by lessees. Lessors report the transfer of rights to use property that they own, and lessees account for and disclose payments for rights to use property that they do not own. If all lease contracts were identical, the accounting for leases would be simple. However, lease accounting is complicated because contracts that are in essence sales transactions may be structured as leases, and other contracts may provide for the lease to be converted to a sale transaction on a later date, usually at the option of the lessee. Although there is no simple model for identifying a specific transaction as a lease or a sale of property, guidelines have been developed by the Financial Accounting Standards Board for analyzing each transaction and determining the appropriate accounting for it. The remainder of this chapter is devoted to a discussion and illustration of these guidelines.

Terminology for Leases

As do many other specialized areas, leasing has its own language. The following summary of the terminology used for leases underlies the accounting and reporting issues involved in leasing transactions:[4]

1   *Bargain purchase option* A provision giving the lessee the right to acquire leased property at a price so favorable that exercise of the option appears reasonably assured at the inception of the lease.

2   *Bargain renewal option* A provision giving the lessee the right to renew a lease at a rental so favorable that exercise of the option appears reasonably assured at the inception of the lease.

3   *Contingent rentals* Increases or decreases in lease payments after the inception of a lease that result from changes in factors on which lease payments are based.

4   *Economic life of leased property* The remaining period during which the leased property is expected to be usable for the purpose for which it was designed, with normal repairs and maintenance, without being limited by the lease term.

5   *Estimated residual value of leased property* The estimated fair value of the leased property at the end of the lease term. The portion of the estimated residual value that is not guaranteed by the lessee or by a third party unrelated to the lessor is known as the *unguaranteed residual value.*

6   *Fair value of leased property* In a sales-type lease (see page 1003), the fair value is the normal selling price of the leased property adjusted for any unusual

[4]Adapted from *Accounting for Leases,* pp. 219–226.

market conditions. In a direct financing-type lease (see page 1003), the cost or carrying amount of the property and the fair value usually are the same at the inception of a lease, unless substantial time has passed since the lessor acquired the property.

7 *Inception of lease* Date of the lease contract (or commitment, if earlier).

8 *Incremental borrowing rate* Rate that, at the inception of the lease, the lessee would have incurred to borrow funds necessary to acquire the leased property.

9 *Initial direct costs* The costs (such as commissions, legal fees, and costs of processing documents) incurred by a lessor that are directly associated with negotiating and completing a lease contract.

10 *Interest rate implicit in the lease (lessor's implicit interest rate)* The discount rate (applied to the minimum lease payments and any *unguaranteed residual value*) that causes the aggregate present value to be equal to the fair value of leased property to the lessor, minus any investment tax credit retained by the lessor.

11 *Lease term* The fixed noncancelable term of a lease plus (1) any periods covered by bargain renewal options, (2) any periods for which failure to renew a lease places a heavy penalty on the lessee, (3) any periods covered by renewal options during which a guarantee by the lessee of the lessor's debt related to leased property is expected to be in effect, (4) any periods covered by renewal options that precede the exercise date of a bargain purchase option, and (5) any periods during which the lessor has a right to renew or extend a lease. However, in no case shall the lease term extend beyond the date on which a bargain purchase option becomes exercisable.

12 *Minimum lease payments* The payments that the lessee is obligated to make or may be required to make; such payments include (1) the minimum periodic rentals up to the date of a bargain purchase option, (2) any *guarantee by the lessee of residual value,* (3) any payment on failure to renew or extend a lease, and (4) the payment required by a bargain purchase option. Executory costs (such as insurance, maintenance, and property taxes in connection with the leased property) are excluded from minimum lease payments.

13 *Renewal or extension of lease* The continuation of a lease contract beyond the original lease term, including a new lease for the same property with the same lessee.

The terms *unguaranteed residual value* in definitions **5** and **10** and *guarantee by the lessee of residual value* in definition **12** warrant further comment. In some leases, the lessee guarantees a stated residual value for the leased property. The purpose of such a guarantee is to assure the lessor that the leased property will be cared for adequately by the lessee and will not be worthless at the end of the lease term. All or part of a guaranteed residual value must be paid to the lessor by the lessee unless the lessor disposes of the leased property at the end of the lease term at an amount equal to or in excess of the guaranteed value.

An unguaranteed residual value is the responsibility of the lessor. In substance, the lessor does not ''sell'' the unguaranteed residual value of the leased property to the lessee. Thus, the lessor accounts for the unguaranteed residual value as part of the *gross investment in the lease,* as illustrated in subsequent sections of this chapter.

ACCOUNTING BY LESSEES

Leases are classified for accounting purposes by lessees as either capital leases or operating leases. *Capital leases* have characteristics of an acquisition, and *operating leases* cover the use of an asset for a portion of its economic life. The concept of the capital lease is derived from the view that a lease that transfers to the lessee most of the risks and benefits of property ownership should be accounted for by the lessee as the acquisition of an asset and the incurrence of a liability.[5] Thus, the *economic substance* of the leasing transaction is given greater weight than its *legal form.*

Criteria for Capital Lease

If a lease meets any *one* of the following criteria at its inception, it must be capitalized by the lessee:[6]

1   The lease transfers ownership of the leased property to the lessee by the end of the lease term.

2   The lease contains a bargain purchase option.

3   The lease term is equal to 75% or more of the economic life of the leased property.

4   The present value of the minimum lease payments is at least 90% of the excess of the fair value of the leased property over any investment tax credit retained by the lessor.

If the beginning of the lease term falls within the last 25% of the total estimated economic life of the leased property, the last two criteria are not used, and the lease must be tested against the first two criteria only. To compute the present value of the minimum lease payments, the lessee uses its incremental borrowing rate, unless (a) the lessee can learn the lessor's implicit interest rate, and (b) the lessor's implicit interest rate is less than the lessee's incremental borrowing rate. If both these conditions are met, the lessee uses the lessor's implicit interest rate.

Computation of Amount Capitalized by Lessee

The lessee records a capital lease as both an asset and a liability in an amount equal to the present value of the minimum lease payments during the lease term. However, if the computed present value exceeds the fair value of the leased asset at the inception of the lease, the *amount capitalized is the fair value of the asset.*[7] A

---

[5]*Accounting for Leases,* p. 67.
[6]Ibid., pp. 10–11.
[7]Ibid., pp. 12–13.

leased asset should never be capitalized at an amount in excess of its fair value at the inception of the lease. The lease payments capitalized exclude any executory costs such as property taxes, insurance, and maintenance, which are expensed by the lessee. If the capital lease transfers ownership of the asset to the lessee or if the lease contains a bargain purchase option, the leased asset is depreciated over its economic life in the same manner as other assets owned by the lessee. Assets under other capital leases also are depreciated, but over the lease term. At the end of the lease term, an amount equal to any residual value to the *lessee* (because the lessee acquired ownership of the leased property) remains in the leased asset ledger account.

Periodic payments other than contingent rentals made by the lessee are allocated between a reduction of the lease liability and interest expense. This allocation produces a constant periodic rate of interest expense on the carrying amount of the lease liability. Contingent rentals are included in the lessee's expenses as they accrue. Assets and liabilities recorded under capital leases are reported as separate items in the lessee's balance sheet, and the liabilities are segregated between current and noncurrent amounts.

Illustration of Lessee's Accounting for a Capital Lease

Data for Illustration   On January 2, Year 1, Lee Company, the lessee, entered into an equipment lease with Lore Corporation, the lessor, having the following provisions:

(1) The lease has a fixed noncancelable term of 30 months, with rent of $270, exclusive of executory costs, payable at the beginning of each month, starting January 2, Year 1. There are no contingent rental provisions.
(2) The lessee guarantees a residual value of $4,000 at the end of 30 months, when the equipment is returned to Lore Corporation.
(3) The lessee pays executory costs separately to the lessor, and is to receive any excess of selling price of the equipment over the guaranteed residual value at the end of the lease term.
(4) The lease is renewable periodically based on a schedule of rentals and guarantees of the residual values, which decrease over time.

Other relevant information is as follows:

(1) Lore Corporation's interest rate implicit in the lease is 12% a year (1% a month); Lore has informed Lee Company of this rate. Lee's incremental borrowing rate is 15% a year (1¼% a month).
(2) The lessor's cost of the leased equipment is $10,200 (net of the investment tax credit retained by the lessor); this is also the lessor's fair value at the inception of the lease, January 2, Year 1.
(3) The economic life of the equipment is 60 months; the lessee depreciates owned equipment on a straight-line basis.
(4) The residual value at the end of the lease term is estimated to be $4,000, the amount guaranteed by the lessee.
(5) On July 2, Year 3, the end of the lease term, the equipment is sold by the lessor for $4,200 to an independent third party. The lessor paid the lessee the $200

excess ($4,200 − $4,000 = $200) of the proceeds over the guaranteed residual value.

(6) The fiscal years for the lessee and the lessor end on December 31.

Computations and Classification of the Lease The minimum lease payments for the lessee are computed as follows:

Minimum lease payments by lessee

Minimum rental payments over the lease term ($270 × 30)	$ 8,100
Add: Lessee's guarantee of the residual value at end of lease term	4,000
Total minimum lease payments	$12,100

The lease *does not meet* the first three criteria on page 994: The lease does not transfer ownership to the lessee by the end of the lease term; the lease does not contain a bargain purchase option; and the lease term (30 months) is not equal to 75% or more of the estimated economic life of the equipment (60 months). However, the fourth criterion *is met*.

The present value of the minimum lease payments, computed with the lessor's implicit interest rate (because it is less than the lessee's incremental borrowing rate and is known to the lessee), exceeds 90% of the fair value of the equipment at the inception of the lease. Thus, the *lessee classifies the lease as a capital lease*. The present value computations by the lessee, using the lessor's implicit interest rate of 1% a month because it is *known to the lessee and is less than the lessee's incremental borrowing rate,* are shown below:

Computation of present value of minimum lease payments: Lee Company (lessee) lease with Lore Corporation (lessor)

Monthly lease rentals ($270 × present value of annuity due of 30 rents of 1 at 1% = $270 × 26.065785*)	$ 7,038
Add: Residual value guaranteed by lessee ($4,000 × present value of 1 discounted for 30 periods at 1% = $4,000 × 0.741923*)	2,968
Total present value of minimum lease payments	$10,006
Fair value (cost) of equipment at inception of lease	$10,200
Present value of minimum lease payments as a percentage of fair value of equipment ($10,006 ÷ $10,200)	98%

*See Appendix at end of Chapter 5

Journal Entries of Lessee The journal entries for Lee Company (lessee) for the first two monthly payments, depreciation expense at the end of the first year, and the disposal of the leased equipment by the lessor at the end of the lease term (July 2, Year 3) are illustrated on page 997. The related ledger accounts (except Cash), showing all journal entries for the lease during Year 1, appear on pages 998 and 999. (The lessor records this lease as a *direct financing lease,* which is discussed on pages 1010–1014.)

Lessee's journal
entries for capital
lease

LEE COMPANY (lessee)
Journal Entries

Year 1

Jan.   2   Leased Equipment—Capital Lease   10,006
                    Liability under Capital Lease (net)   10,006
            To record capital lease at inception of lease.

         2   Liability under Capital Lease (net)   270
                    Cash   270
            To record lease payment for first month.

Feb.   2   Interest Expense [($10,006 − $270) × 0.01]   97
            Liability under Capital Lease (net) ($270 − $97)   173
                    Cash   270
            To record lease payment for second month.

Dec. 31   Depreciation Expense [($10,006 − $4,000) × ¹²⁄₃₀] . .   2,402
                    Leased Equipment—Capital Lease   2,402
            *To record depreciation expense (straight-line
            method) for first year of lease. (Thirty-month term of
            lease is used for depreciation expense because the
            lease does not transfer ownership of the equipment
            to the lessee and does not contain a bargain
            purchase option.)*

        31   Interest Expense ($7,739 × 0.01)   77
                    Interest Payable   77
            *To record accrued interest on lease obligation on
            Dec. 31, Year 1. (See page 998 for computation of
            $7,739 balance in Liability under Capital Lease
            ledger account.)*

Year 3

July   2   Cash   200
            Liability under Capital Lease (net)   4,000
                    Leased Equipment—Capital Lease   4,000
                    Gain on Disposal of Leased Equipment   200
            *To record lessor's sale of leased equipment at
            amount $200 in excess of guaranteed residual
            value and liquidation of liability under capital lease.*

Leased Equipment—Capital Lease

Date	Explanation	Debit	Credit	Balance
Year 1				
Jan. 2	Capital lease at inception	10,006		10,006 dr
Dec. 31	Depreciation for Year 1		2,402	7,604 dr

Liability under Capital Lease (net)

Date	Explanation	Debit	Credit	Balance
Year 1				
Jan. 2	Capital lease at inception		10,006	10,006 cr
2	First lease payment	270		9,736 cr
Feb. 2	($270 − $97 interest)	173		9,563 cr
Mar. 2	($270 − $96 interest)	174		9,389 cr
Apr. 2	($270 − $94 interest)	176		9,213 cr
May 2	($270 − $92 interest)	178		9,035 cr
June 2	($270 − $90 interest)	180		8,855 cr
July 2	($270 − $89 interest)	181		8,674 cr
Aug. 2	($270 − $87 interest)	183		8,491 cr
Sept. 2	($270 − $85 interest)	185		8,306 cr
Oct. 2	($270 − $83 interest)	187		8,119 cr
Nov. 2	($270 − $81 interest)	189		7,930 cr
Dec. 2	($270 − $79 interest)	191		7,739 cr

In the January 2, Year 1, journal entry to record the lease, the Liability under Capital Lease ledger account was credited with the ***present value*** of the minimum lease payments during the lease term. This ***net method*** of accounting by lessees was illustrated in ***FASB Statement No. 13,*** "Accounting for Leases."[8] As an alternative, the Liability under Capital Lease account might be credited for the $12,100 total of the minimum lease payments, as follows:

```
Year 1
Jan. 2  Leased Equipment—Capital Lease ................     10,006
        Discount on Liability under Capital Lease .........      2,094
              Liability under Capital Lease (gross) ........             12,100
        To record capital lease at inception of lease.
```

This ***gross method*** is consistent with the accounting for deferred payment contracts illustrated in Chapter 11 (page 559). If the lease obligation were recorded in this manner, the journal entry for the ***second month's*** lease payment would be as shown on page 999.

---

[8]Ibid., p. 84.

Interest Payable

Date	Explanation	Debit	Credit	Balance
Year 1				
Dec. 31	Accrued interest for Dec.		77	77 cr

Depreciation Expense

Date	Explanation	Debit	Credit	Balance
Year 1				
Dec. 31	[($10,006 − $4,000) × $^{12}/_{30}$]	2,402		2,402 dr

Interest Expense

Date	Explanation	Debit	Credit	Balance
Year 1				
Feb. 2	($9,736 × 0.01)	97		97 dr
Mar. 2	($9,563 × 0.01)	96		193 dr
Apr. 2	($9,389 × 0.01)	94		287 dr
May 2	($9,213 × 0.01)	92		379 dr
June 2	($9,035 × 0.01)	90		469 dr
July 2	($8,855 × 0.01)	89		558 dr
Aug. 2	($8,674 × 0.01)	87		645 dr
Sept. 2	($8,491 × 0.01)	85		730 dr
Oct. 2	($8,306 × 0.01)	83		813 dr
Nov. 2	($8,119 × 0.01)	81		894 dr
Dec. 2	($7,930 × 0.01)	79		973 dr
31	($7,739 × 0.01)	77		1,050 dr

Lessee's journal entry to record lease payment under the **gross method**

Year 1

Feb. 2   Interest Expense   97

       Liability under Capital Lease (gross)   270

           Discount on Liability under Capital Lease   97

           Cash   270

       To record lease payment for second month.

The credit to the Leased Equipment—Capital Lease ledger account in the December 31, Year 1, journal entry for depreciation is in accordance with the illustration in *FASB Statement No. 13,* "Accounting for Leases." Alternatively, an Accumulated Depreciation ledger account might be used, as for owned equipment.

Had the lessee elected on July 2, Year 3, to renew the lease, the renewal would be treated as a new lease extending to the date of the next renewal option. The lessee would compare the present value of the minimum lease payments (rent and guarantee of any residual value) over the renewal period with the $4,000 fair value of the equipment to the lessor at the inception of the new lease. Although the fair value of the equipment on July 2, Year 3, is $4,200, the proceeds from sale of the equipment, the value accruing to the lessor is limited to $4,000, the amount guaranteed by the lessee.

Lessee's Accounting for Operating Leases

Leases that do not qualify as capital leases are accounted for as *operating leases* by the lessee; that is, the lease is *not capitalized,* and periodic lease payments usually are recorded by debits to the Rent Expense ledger account. If an operating lease requires rent to be paid other than in equal periodic amounts, Rent Expense is debited on a straight-line basis unless another method is considered to be more representative of the benefits derived from use of the leased property.[9] Executory costs under operating leases are recognized as expenses in the period incurred, as they are for capital leases.

Sale-Leaseback Transactions

An owner of an asset may sell it and immediately lease it back from the acquirer. Such *sale-leaseback transactions* give lessees use of assets without a large investment of capital and provide lessors with profitable investments. In addition, both lessors and lessees may derive significant income tax advantages from sale-leaseback transactions.

Because the sale of the asset and the leaseback represent in effect a single transaction, neither the selling price of the asset nor the periodic rental payments may be evaluated separately from the other. Consequently, the Financial Accounting Standards Board suggested the following standard to be used in accounting for most sale-leaseback transactions:[10]

> If the lease meets one of the criteria for treatment as a capital lease . . . , the seller-lessee shall account for the lease as a capital lease; otherwise, as an operating lease. Any profit or loss on the sale shall be deferred and amortized in proportion to the amortization of the leased asset, if a capital lease, or in proportion to the related gross rental charged to expense over the lease term, if an operating lease, ...

To illustrate the accounting for a sale-leaseback transaction, assume that on May 1, Year 1, Cree Company sold land and a building for $1,540,000, and immediately leased the property from its owner on a 10-year operating lease for monthly rent of $15,000, beginning May 1, Year 1. On that date, the carrying amounts of the land and building in Cree's accounting records were $400,000 and $900,000, respectively, and the building had a remaining economic life of 15 years. Accumulated depreciation on the building totaled $300,000 on May 1, Year 1.

---

[9]Ibid., p. 17.
[10]Ibid., pp. 33–34.

Journal entries for Cree Company for the sale-leaseback transaction are as follows for the first month:

Lessee's journal entries for sale-leaseback transaction (operating lease)

CREE COMPANY
Journal Entries

Year 1

May 1	*Cash*		*1,540,000*	
	Accumulated Depreciation of Building		*300,000*	
	Land			*400,000*
	Building ($900,000 + $300,000)			*1,200,000*
	Deferred Gain on Disposal of Plant Assets			*240,000*

To record sale of land and building, and de-
ferral of gain for amortization over term of
related operating lease. Deferred gain is
computed as follows:

Proceeds on sale	*$1,540,000*	
Less: Carrying amount of land		
and building ($400,000 +		
$900,000)	*1,300,000*	
Deferred gain	*$ 240,000*	

1	*Rent Expense ($15,000 − $2,000)*		*13,000*	
	Deferred Gain on Disposal of Plant Assets			
	($240,000 ÷ 120)		*2,000*	
	Cash			*15,000*

To record payment of first month's rent of land
and building under operating lease, and amorti-
zation of deferred gain over the lease term.

The journal entry to record the payment of each month's rent is the same during the lease term. As a result of the deferral of the gain and its amortization over the lease term, total rent expense over the 10-year lease term is $1,560,000, computed as follows:

Total rent expense over the lease term

Gross rent payments over the lease term ($15,000 × 120)	*$1,800,000*
Less: Deferred gain amortized over the lease term	*240,000*
Total rent expense over the lease term ($13,000 × 120)	*$1,560,000*

Disclosure of Leases in Financial Statements of Lessee

The following information with respect to leases is disclosed in a note to the lessee's financial statements:[11]

---

[11]Adapted from *Accounting for Leases*, pp. 17–18.

1 For capital leases:

   a The gross amount of assets recorded under capital leases as of the date of each balance sheet presented by major classes. This information may be combined with the comparable information for owned assets.

   b Future minimum lease payments as of the latest balance sheet date, in the aggregate and for each of the five succeeding fiscal years, with separate deductions from the total for the amount representing executory costs, including any profit thereon, included in the minimum lease payments and for the amount of the imputed interest necessary to reduce the net minimum lease payments to present value.

   c The total of minimum sublease rentals to be received in the future under noncancelable subleases as of the latest balance sheet date.

   d Total contingent rentals actually incurred for each accounting period for which an income statement is presented.

   e Assets recorded under capital leases and the accumulated depreciation thereon are separately identified in the lessee's balance sheet or in a note thereto. Similarly, the related liabilities are separately identified in the balance sheet and are subject to the same considerations as other liabilities in classifying them as current and noncurrent. The amount of depreciation on assets recorded under capital leases is disclosed.

2 For operating leases having initial or remaining noncancelable terms in excess of one year:

Disclosure of leases by lessee

Note: Leases

Leased properties under capital leases presented in the accompanying balance sheet on December 31, Year 11, represent the present value of future rental payments at the inception of the leases of $48.5 million, less accumulated depreciation of $19.6 million computed on a straight-line basis over the terms of the related leases. Liabilities under capital leases of $34.7 million represent the present value of future rental payments after deduction of $3.1 million classified as a current liability.

   A summary of capital lease arrangements and the aggregate future lease payments on December 31, Year 11, follows:

Year of lease	Term, years	Units leased	Future lease payments (in millions)		
			Present value	*Imputed interest*	*Total*
Year 1	15	90 locomotives	$ 8.2	$ 2.0	$10.2
Year 6	18	54 locomotives	17.1	9.7	26.8
Years 9–10	8	900 trailers	5.7	1.6	7.3
Various other capital leases			6.8	4.0	10.8
Totals			$37.8	$17.3	$55.1

   Required payments under capital leases during the next five years (Year 12 through Year 16) are $5.3 million; $6.9 million; $6.9 million; $6.9 million; and $5.8 million, respectively. Total rental expense for all operating leases was $28.4 million in Year 11 and $21.1 million in Year 10.

     a Future minimum rental payments required as of the latest balance sheet date, in the aggregate and for each of the five succeeding fiscal years.

     b The total of minimum rentals to be received in the future under noncancelable subleases as of the latest balance sheet date.

3 For all operating leases, rental expense for each period for which an income statement is presented, with separate amounts for minimum rentals, contingent rentals, and sublease rentals. Rental payments under leases with terms of a month or less that were not renewed need not be included.

4 A general description of lease contracts, including, but not limited to, the following:

     a The basis on which contingent rental payments are determined.

     b The existence and terms of renewal or purchase options and rental escalation clauses.

     c Restrictions imposed by the lease contracts, such as those concerning dividends, additional debt, and further leasing.

A note (shown at the bottom of page 1002) to the financial statements of a large railroad company provides an illustration of disclosure of leases by the lessee.

ACCOUNTING BY LESSORS

Leases are classified for financial accounting by lessors as *sales-type leases, direct financing leases, leveraged leases,* or *operating leases.* Normally, sales-type leases arise when manufacturers or dealers use leasing as a means of marketing their products and require the recognition of a profit or loss by the lessor at the inception of the lease. A sales-type lease must meet *one or more* of the criteria for a capital lease (see page 994 under accounting by lessees) *as well as the following two additional criteria:*

1   The collectibility of the lease payments is reasonably predictable.

2   No important uncertainties surround the amount of unreimbursable costs yet to be incurred by the lessor under the lease.

Important uncertainties might include commitments by the lessor to protect the lessee from obsolescence of the leased property.[12]

Leases that do not give rise to a profit or loss to the lessor at the inception of the lease, but otherwise qualify as sales-type leases, are treated as *direct financing leases* by lessors. Such leases are typically financing arrangements by lessor enterprises that normally are not involved in the direct sale of the assets leased. In direct financing leases, the carrying amount and the fair value of the leased property generally are the same at the inception of the lease.

A *leveraged lease* is an arrangement whereby a long-term creditor provides the *nonrecourse financing* to the lessor for a leasing transaction between the lessee and

---

[12]Ibid., p. 11.

the lessor. A leveraged lease generally is designed to provide maximum income tax benefits to the three parties (lessor, lessee, and long-term creditor) involved in the transaction.

Leases that are not sales-type, direct financing, or leveraged leases are accounted for by lessors as *operating leases*.

Sales-Type Leases

Because sales-type leases are used by manufacturers or dealers to market their products, they resemble sales of products in exchange for long-term promissory notes. Thus, the accounting for sales-type leases is similar to the accounting for a sale of merchandise under the perpetual inventory system. For example, a sale in exchange for a note receivable bearing a fair rate of interest is recorded with a debit to Notes Receivable and a credit to Sales for the face amount of the note (and selling price of the product), and a debit to Cost of Goods Sold and a credit to Inventories for the cost of the product.

The comparable journal entries for a sales-type lease are complicated by three features not found in the typical sale of merchandise in exchange for a promissory note. One feature that is always present in a sales-type lease is the interest implicit in the minimum lease payments, which are receivable by the lessor over an extended period. Two other possible features of a sales-type lease transaction are an *unguaranteed* residual value (a *guaranteed* residual value is a component of minimum lease payments) and *initial direct costs,* such as commissions, legal fees, and document processing costs incurred by the lessor in negotiating and completing the lease contract.

To illustrate the journal entries for a sales-type lease that includes the foregoing features, we provide the following schematic:

Elements of accounting for sales-type lease

Lease Receivables	*(1)*	
Cost of Goods Sold	*(2)*	
Unearned Interest Revenue		*(3)*
Sales		*(4)*
Inventories		*(5)*

To record sales-type lease at inception and cost of leased property.

Cost of Goods Sold	*(6)*	
Cash		*(6)*

To record payment of initial direct costs incurred under sales-type lease.

(1) **Gross investment in the lease:** *The total of the minimum lease payments (which includes any* **guaranteed residual value** *of the property but excludes any* **executory costs***), plus any* **unguaranteed residual value**

(2) *Cost (or carrying amount) of leased property, less present value of any* **unguaranteed residual value** *(which is not "sold" by the lessor)*

(3) *Gross investment in the lease less the* **net investment in the lease,** *which is the present value (at the lessor's implicit rate) of the items comprising the gross investment in the lease*

(4) *Present value (at the lessor's implicit rate) of the minimum lease payments only (because any* **unguaranteed residual value** *is not "sold" by the lessor)*

(5) *Cost (or carrying amount) of leased property*

(6) *Amount of initial direct costs*

The key amounts in the foregoing schematic are the ***gross investment in the lease*** and the ***net investment in the lease.*** Once these amounts have been computed, completion of the two journal entries at the inception of a sales-type lease that includes initial direct costs is a matter of supplying the amounts for the components of the journal entries. It should be noted that the net investment in the lease (gross investment in the lease less unearned interest revenue) is the amount that appears in the lessor's balance sheet, segregated between current and noncurrent assets. The unearned interest revenue is recognized as interest revenue over the lease term at the lessor's implicit rate under the ***interest method.***

Accounting for a Sales-Type Lease Illustrated

To illustrate the accounting for a sales-type lease, assume that on December 31, Year 1, Orr Company leased equipment (which had a cost of $11,500 and a fair value of $14,000) to LSE, Inc., for four years on the following terms:

(1) LSE agreed to make four annual rental payments of $4,000 (excluding executory costs) starting on December 31, Year 1.[13] The economic life of the equipment is six years with an ***unguaranteed*** residual value of $2,500; LSE uses the straight-line method of depreciation.

(2) LSE agreed to absorb all maintenance costs, insurance, and property taxes; $800 of initial direct costs were incurred by Orr.

(3) LSE was required to return the equipment to Orr at the end of the lease term, December 31, Year 5.

(4) Orr's implicit interest rate on December 31, Year 1, for this transaction was 10% a year. LSE had an incremental borrowing rate of 12% a year on December 31, Year 1, and could not learn Orr's implicit interest rate.

Orr Company's ability to collect the minimum lease payments is reasonably predictable, and there are no important uncertainties surrounding the amount of any additional costs to be incurred by Orr.

Because the fair value of the equipment ($14,000) exceeds its cost ($11,500); because the present value of the minimum lease payments, $13,947 (see page 1006), is at least 90% of the fair value of the leased property ($14,000 × 0.90 = $12,600); and because of the conditions described in the preceding paragraph, Orr (the lessor) records the lease as a sales-type lease. LSE (the lessee), records the lease as a capital lease because the present value of the minimum lease payments to LSE, $13,607 (see page 1006), meets the 90% of fair value test.

Computation of Lessor's Gross Investment in the Lease   Orr Company's gross investment in the lease with LSE, Inc., is computed as follows:

Computation of lessor's gross investment in sales-type lease

Annual rental payments ($4,000 × 4)	*$16,000*
Add: Unguaranteed residual value	*2,500*
Gross investment in lease	*$18,500*

[13]Lease payments generally are made monthly; we assume annual payments to minimize computations in the illustration.

The computation of the gross investment in the lease provides the amount for the debit to the Lease Receivables ledger account in the journal entry on page 1007.

Computation of Lessor's Net Investment in the Lease By application of the lessor's implicit rate of 10%, the net investment in the lease is computed below:

Computation of lessor's net investment in sales-type lease

Present value of annual rental payments (minimum lease payments) ($4,000 × 3.486852*)	$13,947
Add: Present value of unguaranteed residual value ($2,500 × 0.683013†)	1,708
Net investment in lease	$15,655

*From Table 4 of Appendix at end of Chapter 5, adjusted for **annuity due**
†From Table 2 of Appendix at end of Chapter 5

The computation of the net investment in the lease provides the remaining amounts necessary to complete the lessor's journal entry at the inception of the lease, as indicated on page 1004.

Computation of Amount to Be Capitalized by Lessee Because the lessee cannot learn the lessor's implicit interest rate, the lessee uses its incremental borrowing rate, 12% a year, to compute the present value of the minimum lease payments, as follows:

Computation of lessee's present value of minimum lease payments

Present value of annual rental payments (minimum lease payments) ($4,000 × 3.401831*)	$13,607

*From Table 4 of Appendix at end of Chapter 5, adjusted for **annuity due**

Journal Entries and Ledger Accounts The journal entries for both the lessor and the lessee for Years 1 and 2 are presented on page 1007. (The lessee's journal entries are shown for comparative purposes.) The lessor's ledger accounts for Lease Receivables, Unearned Interest Revenue, and Interest Revenue for the term of the lease are shown on page 1008.

On December 31, Year 5, the end of the lease term, the lessor's net investment in the lease is $2,500, computed as follows:

Net investment in sales-type lease at end of lease term

Balance of Lease Receivables ledger account	$2,500
Less: Balance of Unearned Interest Revenue ledger account	–0–
Net investment in lease, Dec. 31, Year 5	$2,500

The $2,500 is the *unguaranteed residual value* that was estimated at the inception of the lease. Had the estimate of the unguaranteed residual value been found to be excessive as a result of periodic reviews during the lease term, a loss would have

	ORR COMPANY (lessor) Journal Entries (sales-type lease)			LSE, INC., (lessee) Journal Entries (capital lease)		
Year 1 Dec. 31	Lease Receivables	18,500		Leased Equipment—Capital Lease	13,607	
	Cost of Goods sold ($11,500 − $1,708)	9,792		Liability under Capital Lease (net)		13,607
	Unearned Interest Revenue ($18,500 −		2,845	To record capital lease at inception. (See page		
	$15,655)		13,947	1006 for computation.)		
	Sales		13,947			
	Inventories		11,500			
	To record sales-type lease at inception and cost of leased equipment.					
31	Cost of Goods Sold	800		No entry.		
	Cash		800			
	To record payment of initial direct costs incurred under sales-type lease.					
31	Cash	4,000		Liability under Capital Lease (net)	4,000	
	Lease Receivables		4,000	Cash		4,000
	To record receipt of first lease payment.			To record lease payment for first year.		
Year 2 Dec. 31	Cash	4,000		Interest Expense [($13,607 − $4,000) × 0.12] ...	1,153	
	Unearned Interest Revenue [($18,500 −			Liability under Capital Lease (net) ($4,000 −		
	$2,845) − $4,000] × 0.10	1,166		$1,153)	2,847	
	Lease Receivables		4,000	Cash		4,000
	Interest Revenue		1,166	To record lease payment for second year.		
	To record receipt of second lease payment, and interest earned during Year 2.			Depreciation Expense ($13,607 ÷ 4)	3,402	
				Leased Equipment—Capital Lease		3,402
				To record depreciation expense (straight-line method) for first year of lease. Four-year term of the lease is used because the lease does not contain a bargain purchase option and does not transfer ownership of the leased property to the lessee.		

Selected ledger
accounts of lessor
for sales-type lease

Lease Receivables

Date	Explanation	Debit	Credit	Balance
12/31/1	Inception of lease	18,500		18,500 dr
12/31/1	Receipt of first payment		4,000	14,500 dr
12/31/2	Receipt of second payment		4,000	10,500 dr
12/31/3	Receipt of third payment		4,000	6,500 dr
12/31/4	Receipt of fourth payment		4,000	2,500 dr

Unearned Interest Revenue

Date	Explanation	Debit	Credit	Balance
12/31/1	Inception of Lease ($18,500 − $15,655)		2,845	2,845 cr
12/31/2	Interest for Year 2 {[($18,500 − $2,845) − $4,000] ×0.10}	1,166		1,679 cr
12/31/3	Interest for Year 3 {[($14,500 − $1,679) − $4,000] × 0.10}	882		797 cr
12/31/4	Interest for Year 4 {[($10,500 − $797) − $4,000] × 0.10}	570		227 cr
12/31/5	Interest for Year 5 {[($6,500 − $227) − $4,000] × 0.10}	227		−0−

Interest Revenue

Date	Explanation	Debit	Credit	Balance
12/31/2	Interest for Year 2		1,166	1,166 cr
12/31/2	Closing entry	1,166		−0−
12/31/3	Interest for Year 3		882	882 cr
12/31/3	Closing entry	882		−0−
12/31/4	Interest for Year 4		570	570 cr
12/31/4	Closing entry	570		−0−
12/31/5	Interest for Year 5		227	227 cr
12/31/5	Closing entry	227		−0−

been recognized by the lessor and the Lease Receivables account would have been credited for the amount of the loss. An *upward* revision of unguaranteed residual value is not made during the lease term; to do so would result in the recognition of an unrealized gain. Only if the lessor sells the leased property for more than $2,500 at the end of the lease term is a realized gain recognized.

Termination of Sales-Type Lease   If a sales-type lease is terminated before the end of the lease term by mutual consent without penalty, the lessee recognizes a gain or a loss.[14] For example, assume that the lease in the foregoing illustration is

[14]Ibid., p. 15.

terminated on December 31, Year 3 (the end of the second year of the lease term), prior to the rental payment due on the date and prior to the recognition of interest expense and depreciation expense for Year 3. The journal entry to record the termination in the accounting records of LSE, Inc. (the lessee), is as follows:

Lessee's journal entry for termination of capital lease

Interest Expense [($13,607 − $6,847) × 0.12]	811	
Liability under Capital Lease (net) ($13,607 − $6,847)	6,760	
Depreciation Expense ($13,607 ÷ 4)	3,402	
Gain on Termination of Capital Lease		768
Leased Equipment—Capital Lease ($13,607 − $3,402)		10,205
To record termination of capital lease through mutual consent and depreciation and interest expense for second year of lease.		

The gain recognized by the lessee on termination of the lease results from the lessee's having extinguished a lease liability with a carrying amount of $7,571, including accrued interest ($6,760 + $811 = $7,571) by returning to the lessor the leased equipment with a carrying amount of $6,803 ($10,205 − $3,402 = $6,803). The difference between the two amounts is the $768 realized gain ($7,571 − $6,803 = $768).

On termination of the sales-type lease, the lessor records the equipment at the *lowest* of its original cost, present fair value, or present carrying amount, and recognizes any loss represented by the difference from the net investment in the terminated lease. The lessor does not recognize a gain on an early termination of a lease, because the gain has not been realized.[15]

Sales-Type Lease with Guaranteed Residual Value   A sales-type lease having a *guaranteed residual value* requires a slightly different journal entry at the inception of the lease because the guaranteed residual value is part of the *minimum lease payments,* rather than a separate item, in the computation of the gross investment and the net investment in the lease. For example, if the Orr Company-LSE, Inc., lease described on page 1005 had provided for a *guaranteed,* rather than an *unguaranteed,* residual value of $2,500, the journal entry on December 31, Year 1, for Orr (the lessor) would have been as follows:

Journal entry for sales-type lease with **guaranteed** residual value

Lease Receivables	18,500	
Cost of Goods Sold	11,500	
Unearned Interest Revenue		2,845
Sales		15,655
Inventories		11,500
To record sales-type lease at inception and cost of leased equipment.		

[15]Ibid., p. 22.

In the foregoing journal entry, both cost of goods sold and sales are $1,708 larger than in the journal entry on page 1007 under the unguaranteed residual value illustration ($11,500 − $9,792 = $1,708; $15,655 − $13,947 = $1,708). The $1,708 difference is the present value of the residual value ($2,500 × 0.683013 = $1,708) which *is considered to have been sold by the lessor* to the lessee when it is guaranteed by the lessee under a sales-type lease.

In sales-type leases in which the lessee guarantees a minimum residual value of the property at the end of the lease term, or in which there is a penalty for failure to renew, the lessor's lease receivables at the end of the lease term will be equal to the amount of the guarantee or penalty that becomes effective that date. At the termination of the existing term of a lease being renewed, the net investment in the lease is adjusted to the fair value of the leased property to the lessor on that date, and the net adjustment is debited or credited to Unearned Interest Revenue, which is recognized as interest revenue over the renewal term.

Direct Financing Leases

In direct financing leases, the gross investment in the lease is computed in the same way as for sales-type leases, but the net investment in the lease equals the difference between the gross investment in the lease and the unearned interest revenue.[16] Unearned interest revenue is the difference between the gross investment in the lease and the cost or carrying amount of the leased property. *Any initial direct costs are expensed, and an equal portion of the unearned interest revenue is recognized as interest revenue in the same accounting period.* The net investment in the lease currently recoverable is classified as a current asset, and any contingent rentals are recognized as revenue when such rentals become receivable.

In direct financing leases containing a residual value guarantee or a penalty for failure to renew, the lessor follows the same procedure described for sales-type leases. Similarly, any estimated unguaranteed residual value should be reviewed periodically and, if necessary, adjusted as described for sales-type leases. Because the lessor in a direct financing lease is not selling a product, Sales and Cost of Goods Sold ledger accounts are not used.

Illustration of Accounting for a Direct Financing Lease with Initial Direct Costs To illustrate the accounting for a direct financing lease with initial direct costs, assume that on July 31, Year 1, Lessor Corporation leased to Lessee Company equipment with a cost and fair value of $11,127. The initial direct costs incurred by the lessor were $200. The lease was for seven years at an annual rent (excluding executory costs) of $2,000 payable at the beginning of each year. The economic life of the equipment was nine years, and the estimated *unguaranteed* residual value at the end of seven years was $1,200. Lessee uses the straight-line method of depreciation. Lease payments were determined at an amount that will give Lessor a 10% annual rate of return on its net investment in the lease, including initial direct costs of $200.

Lessee Company knows Lessor Corporation's 10% implicit interest rate, which is less than Lessee's 13% incremental borrowing rate. Lessee agreed to pay

---

[16]Ibid., p. 23.

LESSOR CORPORATION
Journal Entries (direct financing lease)

Year 1
July 31

Lease Receivables [($2,000 × 7) + $1,200]	15,200	
Unearned Interest Revenue ($4,073 − $200)		3,873
Equipment Held for Lease		11,127
Interest Revenue		200

To record direct financing lease at inception, and to record interest revenue equal to initial direct costs of lease.

31

Operating Expenses	200	
Cash		200

To record payment of initial direct costs of lease.

31

Cash	2,000	
Lease Receivables		2,000

To record receipt of first lease payment.

Year 2
July 31

Cash	2,000	
Unearned Interest Revenue [($15,200 − $3,873) − $2,000] × 0.10	933	
Lease Receivables		2,000
Interest Revenue		933

To record receipt of second lease payment, and interest earned during the year ended July 31, Year 2.

LESSEE COMPANY
Journal Entries (capital lease)

Leased Equipment—Capital Lease ($2,000 × 5.355261*)	10,711	
Liability under Capital Lease (net)		10,711

To record capital lease at inception.
*From Table 4 of Appendix at end of Chapter 5, adjusted for **annuity due**

No entry.

Liability under Capital Lease (net)	2,000	
Cash		2,000

To record lease payment for first year.

Interest Expense [($10,711 − $2,000) × 0.10]	871	
Liability under Capital Lease (net) ($2,000 − $871)	1,129	
Cash		2,000

To record lease payment for second year.

Depreciation Expense ($10,711 ÷ 7)	1,530	
Leased Equipment—Capital Lease		1,530

To record depreciation expense (straight-line method) for first year of lease. Seven-year term of lease is used for depreciation because the lease does not transfer ownership of the equipment to the lessee and does not contain a bargain purchase option.

all executory costs, the collectibility of the lease payments was reasonably predictable, and no additional costs were expected to be incurred by Lessor. An Equipment Held for Lease ledger account is used by Lessor.

This lease meets the criteria for classification as a sales-type lease, *but because there is no element of profit at the inception of the lease*, it is recorded as a *direct financing lease* by Lessor Corporation and a *capital lease* by Lessee Company. This accounting treatment is appropriate because (1) the lease term exceeds 75% of the economic life of the equipment ($7 \div 9 = 0.778$); (2) the present value of the minimum lease payments ($\$2,000 \times 5.355261^* = \$10,711$) is more than 90% of the fair value of the equipment at the inception of the lease ($\$11,127 \times 0.90 = \$10,014$); (3) the collectibility of the lease payments is reasonably assured, and no additional costs were expected to be incurred by the lessor; and (4) there is no profit for the lessor at the inception of the lease.

The gross investment in the lease, unearned interest revenue, and the net investment in the lease are computed for the lessor as follows:

Computation of gross investment, unearned interest, and net investment in direct financing lease

Gross investment in lease [($2,000 minimum lease payments × 7) + $1,200 unguaranteed residual value]	$15,200
Unearned interest revenue ($15,200 gross investment in lease − $11,127 cost of leased equipment)	$ 4,073
Net investment in lease ($15,200 gross investment in lease − $4,073 unearned interest revenue)	$11,127

Because the lessee does not obtain rights to the equipment at the end of the lease term and the residual value of the equipment is not guaranteed, only the present value of the minimum lease payments ($10,711) is recorded by the lessee. The journal entries to record this lease in the accounting records of both lessee and lessor for the first two years of the lease term are shown on page 1011 (both the lessor and the lessee have a July 31 fiscal year), and the lessor's ledger accounts for Lease Receivables, Unearned Interest Revenue, and Interest Revenue are shown below and on page 1013.

Selected ledger accounts of lessor for direct financing lease

		Lease Receivables			
Date	**Explanation**		**Debit**	**Credit**	**Balance**
7/31/1	Inception of lease		15,200		15,200 dr
7/31/1	Receipt of first payment			2,000	13,200 dr
7/31/2	Receipt of second payment			2,000	11,200 dr
7/31/3	Receipt of third payment			2,000	9,200 dr
7/31/4	Receipt of fourth payment			2,000	7,200 dr
7/31/5	Receipt of fifth payment			2,000	5,200 dr
7/31/6	Receipt of sixth payment			2,000	3,200 dr
7/31/7	Receipt of seventh payment			2,000	1,200 dr

*From Table 4 of Appendix at end of Chapter 5, adjusted for *annuity due*.

Unearned Interest Revenue

Date	Explanation	Debit	Credit	Balance
7/31/1	Inception of lease [($15,200 − $11,127) − $200]		3,873	3,873 cr
7/31/2	Interest for Year 2 {[($15,200 − $3,873) − $2,000] × 0.10}	933		2,940 cr
7/31/3	Interest for Year 3 {[($13,200 − $2,940) − $2,000] × 0.10}	826		2,114 cr
7/31/4	Interest for Year 4 {[($11,200 − $2,114) − $2,000] × 0.10}	709		1,405 cr
7/31/5	Interest for Year 5 {[($(9,200 − $1,405) − $2,000] × 0.10}	580		825 cr
7/31/6	Interest for Year 6 {[($7,200 − $825) − $2,000] × 0.10}	437		388 cr
7/31/7	Interest for Year 7 {[($5,200 − $388) − $2,000] × 0.10}	281		107 cr
7/31/8	Interest for Year 8 {[($3,200 − $107) − $2,000] × 0.10}	107*		−0−

Interest Revenue

Date	Explanation	Debit	Credit	Balance
7/31/1	Revenue to offset initial direct costs		200	200 cr
7/31/1	Closing entry	200		−0−
7/31/2	Interest for Year 2		933	933 cr
7/31/2	Closing entry	933		−0−
7/31/3	Interest for Year 3		826	826 cr
7/31/3	Closing entry	826		−0−
7/31/4	Interest for Year 4		709	709 cr
7/31/4	Closing entry	709		−0−
7/31/5	Interest for Year 5		580	580 cr
7/31/5	Closing entry	580		−0−
7/31/6	Interest for Year 6		437	437 cr
7/31/6	Closing entry	437		−0−
7/31/7	Interest for Year 7		281	281 cr
7/31/7	Closing entry	281		−0−
7/31/8	Interest for Year 8		107*	107 cr
7/31/8	Closing entry	107		−0−

*Adjusted $2 for rounding error

Note that the initial direct costs of $200 are recognized as operating expenses at the inception of the lease and that an equal amount of interest revenue is recognized in the same accounting period. This procedure is explicitly required by *FASB Statement No. 13*, ''Accounting for Leases.'' After the $200 reduction of the unearned interest revenue, the $3,873 balance, when subtracted from the $15,200 gross investment in the lease, yields the $11,327 present value of the lease for the lessor at the lessor's implicit interest rate of 10%, as illustrated below:

Computation of
lessor's present value
of direct financing
lease

Present value of annuity due of 7 rents of $2,000 at 10% (present value of minimum lease payments) ($2,000 × 5.355261*)	$10,711
Add: Present value of unguaranteed residual value ($1,200 × 0.513158†). .	616
Present value of lease	$11,327

*From Table 4 of Appendix at end of Chapter 5, adjusted for **annuity due.**
†From Table 2 of Appendix at end of Chapter 5

Leveraged Leases

From the standpoint of the lessee, leveraged leases are classified and accounted for the same as nonleveraged leases. From the standpoint of the lessor, leveraged leases are classified as direct financing leases; sales-type leases may not be classified as leveraged leases, according to *FASB Statement No. 13,* ''Accounting for Leases.''[17] The lessor records the investment in a leveraged lease *net of the nonrecourse debt.* The amount recorded generally consists of (1) rent receivable (net of portion applicable to principal and interest on the nonrecourse debt), (2) the amount of the investment tax credit to be realized in the transaction, (3) any estimated residual value of the leased asset, and (4) a reduction for any unearned revenue items. Because the lease receivables are recorded net of the nonrecourse debt, interest revenue is not recognized by the lessor. Instead, a Revenue from Leveraged Leases ledger account is credited for net positive cash flows not allocated to the recovery of the lessor's net investment in the lease.

Accounting procedures for the various aspects of leveraged leases in the accounting records of the lessor are quite complex and therefore are not illustrated in this general discussion of leasing.[18] An illustration of a leveraged lease appears in the Appendix at the end of this chapter.

Operating Leases

Rent is recognized as revenue by lessors over the lease term of an operating lease as it becomes receivable according to the provisions in the lease. However, if the rent payments are not received in level amounts, rent revenue is recognized on a straight-line basis, unless another basis is considered more appropriate. An example of a basis that may be more appropriate than straight-line is hours of usage for a machine. Any initial direct costs, if material in amount, relating to an operating lease are deferred and recognized as expenses over the lease term in the same manner as rent revenue is recognized.

Leased property under operating leases is included by the lessor with or near plant assets in the balance sheet.[19] The leased property is depreciated in accordance with the lessor's normal depreciation policy, and in the balance sheet the accumulated depreciation is deducted from the investment in the leased property.

---

[17]Ibid., p. 41.
[18]Appendix E of *FASB Statement No. 13,* ''Accounting for Leases'' (as amended) contains extensive illustrations of accounting and financial statement presentation for leveraged leases.
[19]*Accounting for Leases,* p. 24.

Disclosure of Leases in Financial Statements of Lessor

When leasing (except leveraged leasing) is a significant part of the lessor's business activities in terms of revenue, net income, or assets, the information set forth below and on page 1016 with respect to leases is disclosed in the financial statements or in a note to the financial statements.[20]

1 For sales-type leases and direct financing leases:

    a The components of the net investment in sales-type and direct financing leases as of the date of each balance sheet presented. The components include (1) the future minimum lease payments to be received, with separate deductions for amounts representing executory costs included in the

Disclosure of leases by lessor

> **Note: Leasing Arrangements with Company as Lessor**—*The company leases computer equipment under various contracts with terms ranging from one to seven years. Substantially all leases are accounted for under the operating method or as leases equivalent to sales in accordance with* **FASB Statement Nos. 13** *and* **17.** *The company's cost of equipment under operating leases on December 31, Year 2, was $476,540,000, less accumulated depreciation of $269,851,000. The net investment in sales-type leases on December 31, Year 2, was as follows:*
>
> | | *(in thousands)* |
> |---|---:|
> | *Total minimum lease payments receivable* | *$44,909* |
> | *Estimated residual value of equipment* | *50* |
> | *Less: Unearned interest revenue* | *(5,775)* |
> | *Net investment in sales-type leases* | *$39,184* |
>
>   *Minimum lease payments, including amounts representing executory costs and any related profit, to be received in each of the next five years under the above lease contracts are as follows:*
>
> | | *Sales-type leases* | *Operating leases* |
> |---|---:|---:|
> | | *(in thousands)* | |
> | *Year 3* | *$17,848* | *$223,483* |
> | *Year 4* | *12,701* | *163,643* |
> | *Year 5* | *9,589* | *107,877* |
> | *Year 6* | *3,107* | *62,073* |
> | *Year 7* | *1,183* | *23,226* |
> | *Later years* | *481* | |
> | *Totals* | *$44,909* | *$580,302* |
>
>   *The company retains title to all of its leased computer equipment, pays taxes, licenses and insurance on such equipment, and provides for its general maintenance. At the end of the lease term, the equipment generally is returned to the company.*

---

[20]Adapted from *Accounting for Leases*, p. 24.

minimum lease payments, and the allowance for doubtful lease payments receivable; (2) the unguaranteed residual values reverting to the lessor; and (3) the unearned interest revenue.

b Future minimum lease payments to be received for each of the five succeeding fiscal years as of the latest balance sheet date.

c The amount of unearned interest revenue included in income to offset initial direct costs recorded as expenses for each accounting period for which an income statement is presented. (For direct financing leases only.)

d Total contingent rentals included in income for each accounting period for which an income statement is presented.

2 For operating leases:

a The cost and carrying amount, if different, of property on lease or held for leasing by major classes of property, and the total amount of accumulated depreciation as of the latest balance sheet date.

b Minimum future rentals on noncancelable leases as of the latest balance sheet date, in the aggregate and for each of the five succeeding fiscal years.

c Total contingent rentals included in income for each accounting period for which an income statement is presented.

3 A general description of lease contracts.

The note to the financial statements of a computer company at the bottom of page 1015 provides an illustration of disclosure of leases by the lessor.

OTHER ASPECTS OF ACCOUNTING FOR LEASES

In the preceding pages we discuss and illustrate the principal aspects of lease accounting. In this section, we consider the following topics: leases involving real estate, leases between related parties, computation of the lessor's implicit interest rate, computation of the current portion of lease liabilities and receivables, and accounting for the investment tax credit.

Leases Involving Real Estate

Leases involving land only are accounted for as capital leases by the lessee if the lease contract includes either of the first two criteria on page 994. Otherwise, a lease for land is accounted for as an operating lease. Generally, the amount capitalized in the Leased Land—Capital Lease ledger account is not depreciated.

The accounting for leases involving both land and buildings depends on (1) which of the criteria on page 994 are met by the lease, and (2) the ratio of the fair values of the land and buildings. *Accounting for Leases* specifies the conditions under which the land and building elements are accounted for as a single unit or as separate units, and whether the leases are accounted for as capital leases or operating leases by lessees and as sales-type leases, direct financing leases, or operating leases by lessors.[21]

---

[21]Ibid., pp. 28–30.

If only part of a building is leased, the accounting procedures for both the lessee and the lessor depend on whether the cost and the fair value of the leased part of the building may be determined objectively.

Leases between Related Parties

Leases in which the lessor and the lessee are related parties are accounted for according to the *economic substance rather than their legal form* if the terms of the lease contract are affected significantly by the relationship. *Related parties* include the following:[22]

1   A parent company and its subsidiaries

2   An owner enterprise and its partnerships or joint ventures

3   An investor and its influenced investees

4   Two or more entities subject to significant influence of a parent company, owner enterprise, or investor

The nature and extent of leasing transactions between related parties are disclosed in notes to the financial statements of both the lessor and the lessee.

Computation of Lessor's Implicit Interest Rate

We have simplified our illustrations of accounting for leases by providing the interest rate implicit in the lease. In practice, this rate must be computed by a process of *iteration* (trial and error) involving computers, electronic calculators, or present value tables. Simplification of this process has been a research objective of several accountants.[23]

Computation of Current Portion of Lease Liabilities and Receivables

The current portion of lease liabilities is included in the current liabilities section of the lessee's balance sheet, and the current portion of lease receivables appears in the current asset section of the lessor's balance sheet. Without the assistance of a computer, electronic calculator, or present value tables, determination of the current portion of a lease with monthly payments requires separate computations of the principal portion of the next 12 lease payments or receipts.

A short-cut approximation of the current portion is possible by use of the "Rule of 78." (The sum of the digits for 12 consecutive months is 78.) This technique recognizes that the principal portion of each successive monthly lease payment or receipt increases by a nearly uniform amount. For example, the Liability under Capital Lease ledger account of Lee Company on page 998 indicates that almost every monthly principal payment after the first one (which was not affected by interest) was $2 larger than the previous month's payment. Thus, if we multiply this $2 increment by 78 and add the product to 12 times the $191 principal portion

---

[22]Ibid., p. 2.
[23]See Erich Obersteiner and Paul J. Jalics, "Determining Implicit Interest," and Michael Masoner and Jackson A. White, "Implicit Interest Rate Table," *Journal of Accountancy* (May 1980), pp. 34–44.

of the December 2, Year 1, lease payment, we have an approximation of the current portion of the lease liability on December 31, Year 1, as follows:

Computation of current portion of lease liability by "Rule of 78"

$2 × 78	$ 156
$191 × 12	2,292
Estimated current portion of lease liability on Dec. 31, Year 1..............	$2,448

This estimate is a reasonably close approximation of the actual current portion of the principal payments (applicable to Year 2), which is $2,442.

Accounting for the Investment Tax Credit

A lessor under a direct financing lease may retain the investment tax credit on assets held for lease, or it may pass through the credit to the lessee. (A lessor under a sales-type lease is not entitled to an investment tax credit because assets that it leases are included in inventories.) If the direct-financing lessor uses the investment tax credit, the cost of the assets held for lease must be reduced by the investment tax credit to determine the carrying amounts of the assets. A lessee to which the investment tax credit is passed through by the lessor (which then generally would require larger minimum lease payments) may use either the *deferral method* or the *flow-through method* (see Chapter 11, page 564) to account for the investment tax credit.

Appraisal of Accounting Standards for Leases

Prior to the issuance of *FASB Statement No. 13,* "Accounting for Leases," lessees were required to capitalize only leases that were considered the equivalent to an acquisition of property. Leases often were designed to enable the lessor to record the lease as a sale but at the same time allow the lessee to account for the lease as an operating lease. Thus, billions of dollars of leased assets were not included in the balance sheet of either the lessee or the lessor. Many lessees viewed leasing as an attractive source of "off-balance-sheet financing," because the lease liability appeared in a note to the financial statements rather than in the liabilities section of the balance sheet. However, users of financial statements and the Securities and Exchange Commission considered such accounting practices unsatisfactory. *FASB Statement No. 13* changed all this. Under current accounting standards, financial statements are more consistent with the conceptual framework of accounting, more informative, and more comparable among business enterprises that lease and those that acquire assets outright.

However, *FASB Statement No. 13* and related pronouncements may be faulted in some respects. The fact that to date the Financial Accounting Standards Board has issued eight statements and six interpretations on lease accounting indicates that the FASB's accounting standards for leases had flaws requiring correction. Further, in view of the FASB's emphasis on the economic substance of capital leases (acquisition of assets) over their legal form (rental of assets), the requirement for separate classifications of assets held under capital leases and the related liabilities in the lessee's balance sheet (see page 1002) is questionable. If a capital lease is in fact an acquisition of an asset and an incurring of a liability, such separate classifications appear unwarranted. Finally, the FASB's use of the **net method** of accounting by lessees for liabilities under capital leases, but the **gross method** of accounting by lessors for lease receivables, appears inconsistent.

Some critics have characterized the accounting standards for leases as unnecessarily complicated, especially for small, nonpublic business enterprises. In response, the Financial Accounting Standards Board has undertaken a project to publish separate accounting standards for lessees and for lessors, while not making any substantive changes in the standards enacted in **FASB Statement No. 13,** "Accounting for Leases," and the other pronouncements summarized on page 991. Whether this action will silence the critics is doubtful, because advocates of less-complicated accounting rules for small business enterprises view accounting standards required for leases as needlessly cumbersome.

APPENDIX: ILLUSTRATION OF A LEVERAGED LEASE

The following illustration of the lessor's accounting for a leveraged lease is adapted from **Accounting for Leases: FASB Statement No. 13 as amended and interpreted through May 1980** (pages 90–105):

On January 2, Year 1, Lessor, Inc., acquired equipment for leasing at a cost of $1,000,000. To pay for the equipment, Lessor used $400,000 cash and the proceeds of a $600,000, 9%, nonrecourse bank loan payable in 15 annual installments of $74,435 [$600,000 ÷ 8.060688* = $74,435], beginning on December 31, Year 1. Also on January 2, Year 1, Lessor leased the equipment to Lessee Corporation on a 15-year lease requiring Lessee to pay $90,000 annually, beginning on December 31, Year 1. The unguaranteed residual value of the equipment was estimated at $200,000, to be realized on December 31, Year 16 (one year after the termination of the lease). For depreciation of the equipment, Lessor adopted the following:

1 Seven-year economic life

2 Double-declining-balance method for first two years; sum-of-the-years'-digits method for remaining five years, with $100,000 residual value

Lessor, Inc., is entitled to a $100,000 investment tax credit (realizable on December 31, Year 1). There were no initial direct costs of the lease. Lessor classifies the leveraged lease as a direct financing lease.

Lessor's Journal Entries on January 2, Year 1

The journal entries for Lessor, Inc., on January 2, Year 1, are as follows:

---

*Present value of ordinary annuity of 15 rents of 1 at 9%, from Table 4 of the Appendix at the end of Chapter 5.

LESSOR, INC.
Journal Entries (leveraged lease)
January 2, Year 1

Equipment Held for Lease	*1,000,000*	
Cash		*400,000*
Notes Payable to Bank		*600,000*

To record acquisition of equipment for cash and 9%, 15-year note, payable $74,435 annually, beginning on Dec. 31, Year 1.

Lease Receivables [($90,000 × 15) − ($74,435 × 15)]	*233,475*	
Notes Payable to Bank	*600,000*	
Income Taxes Payable	*100,000*	
Equipment Held for Lease ($1,000,000 − $200,000) . .		*800,000*
Unearned and Deferred Revenue		*133,475*

To record lease of equipment on a 15-year lease with annual rent of $90,000 payable beginning on Dec. 31, Year 1. Gross lease receivable of $1,350,000 ($90,000 × 15 = $1,350,000) is reduced by total principal and interest payments of $1,116,525 ($74,435 × 15 = $1,116,525) on related nonrecourse debt. Income taxes liability is reduced by amount of investment tax credit to be realized on the leased equipment. Equipment Held for Lease ledger account is reduced to amount of unguaranteed residual value.

Lessor's Journal Entries on December 31, Year 1

On December 31, Year 1 (and on subsequent year-ends), Lessor prepares journal entries for the leveraged lease as follows:

(1) Collection of lease payment ($90,000) for first year
(2) Payment on nonrecourse note ($74,435) for first year
(3) Apportionment of realized portion of unearned and deferred revenue to Revenue from Leveraged Leases ledger account
(4) Income tax effects of timing difference between financial accounting and income tax accounting for the leveraged lease

Journal entries 1 and 2 involve only the Cash and Lease Receivables ledger accounts, because the amount originally recorded in the latter account is net of the total payments required on the nonrecourse note payable. Determination of the amounts for journal entries 3 and 4 requires a detailed analysis of the cash flows for each of the 15 years of the lease and a ''trial and error'' computation of the lessor's implicit interest rate. Because of the complexity of these computations, they are not illustrated here.

REVIEW QUESTIONS

1   Define each of the following terms:

a *Lease*
b *Sublease*
c *Sale-leaseback transaction*
d *Operating lease*
e *Leveraged lease*

2   Listed below are some terms used in accounting for leases. Give a short definition of each term.

a *Inception of lease*
b *Bargain purchase option*
c *Unguaranteed residual value*
d *Lessor's implicit interest rate*
e *Initial direct costs*

3   What are the components of the *minimum lease payments* of a typical capital lease of the lessee?

4   To be classified as a *capital lease* by the lessee, a lease must meet one of four criteria at its inception. List these four criteria.

5   Briefly describe the accounting procedures that are followed by the lessor and by the lessee for an *operating lease*.

6   Summarize the procedures followed by the lessee to account for a *capital lease*.

7   A *sales-type lease* (from the standpoint of the lessor) must meet one or more of the criteria of a capital lease as well as two additional criteria. What are these two additional criteria?

8   Differentiate between the accounting procedures used by lessors to account for a *sales-type lease* and for a *direct financing lease*.

9   What disclosures are required for various types of leases in the financial statements or a note to the financial statements of lessees?

10   What disclosures are required for various types of leases in the financial statements or a note to the financial statements of lessors?

11   Marv Company leased a computer for three years at $25,000 a month, with an option to renew the lease for five years at $1,500 a month or to acquire the computer for $20,000 after the lease term of three years. How is this transaction recorded by Marv Company? Explain.

12   Ko Corporation leased an asset under a lease requiring the payment of $24,000 a year in rent. At the end of the current year, when the lease had a remaining term of 10 years, Ko subleased the asset for rent of $36,000 a year for 10 years. When is the gain from this transaction recognized by Ko Corporation? Explain.

13   A lessee's incremental borrowing rate is 18% a year. Unknown to the lessee, the lessor's implicit interest rate is 15%. How do these facts affect the lessee's accounting for a capital lease? Explain.

14   The economic life of leased equipment under a capital lease is 10 years, and the lease term is eight years. How do these facts affect the depreciation of the leased equipment by the lessee? Explain.

15   How does a lessor account for contingent rentals under a direct financing lease?

16   What major reforms in lease accounting were made by the Financial Accounting Standards Board in *FASB Statement No. 13*, "Accounting for Leases" and related pronouncements?

EXERCISES

Ex. 20-1   Select the best answer for each of the following multiple-choice questions:

1   On November 1, Year 2, Lessee Company entered into a 10-year noncancelable lease with Lessor Company for a machine owned by Lessor. The machine had a fair value of $200,000 at inception of the lease, and an economic life of 13 years. Present value of the minimum lease payments is $120,000, and executory costs amounted to $3,000 a year. Lessee is obligated to return the machine to Lessor on expiration of the lease. No bargain purchase option is provided. How much should Lessee record as an asset and corresponding liability at the inception of this lease?
a $0   **b** $120,000   **c** $123,000   **d** $200,000   **e** Some other amount

2   On July 1, Year 5, Lessee Company sold a machine to Lessor Company, and simultaneously leased it back for three years. Pertinent data are:

Economic life, July 1, Year 5.	10 years
Sales price	$120,000
Carrying amount, July 1, Year 5	$ 20,000
Monthly rent under leaseback	$ 1,266
Interest rate implicit in lease	12%
Present value of lease rentals ($1,266 for 36 months at 12%)	$ 38,116

How much gain should Lessee recognize on July 1, Year 5, on the sale of the machine?
a $0   **b** $33,333   **c** $61,884   **d** $100,000   **e** Some other amount

3   For an operating lease, the lessee records equal monthly rental payments as:
a Part interest expense and part depreciation expense
b Part interest expense and part reduction of lease liability
c Entirely a reduction of lease liability
d Rent expense

4   On January 2, Year 1, Lessee, Inc., entered into a 10-year noncancelable lease requiring payments of $100,000 a year, beginning January 2, Year 1. Lessee's incremental borrowing rate is 12%, but the lessor's implicit interest rate, which is known to Lessee, is 10%. Present value factors for an annuity due of 10 rents are 6.75902 at 10% and 6.32825 at 12%. The economic life of the leased property is 12 years, and ownership of the leased property remains with the lessor at expiration of the lease. The amount that Lessee, Inc., capitalizes for the leased property on January 2, Year 1, is:

a $0   **b** $632,825   **c** $675,902   **d** $1,000,000   **e** Some other amount

5   In a lease that is recorded as a sales-type lease by the lessor, the difference between the gross investment in the lease and the sum of the present values of the components of the gross investment is recognized as revenue:

a In full at the lease's expiration
b In full at the lease's inception
c Over the lease term, under the interest method of amortization
d Over the lease term, under the straight-line method of amortization

6   The excess of the fair value of leased property at the inception of the lease over its cost or carrying amount is recorded by the lessor as:

a Unearned revenue from a sales-type lease
b Unearned revenue from a direct-financing lease
c Manufacturer's or dealer's profit from a sales type lease
d Manufacturer's or dealer's profit from a direct-financing lease

7   On May 1, Year 3, See Company sold machinery to an unaffiliated enterprise for its current fair value of $275,000. Simultaneously, See leased back the machinery at $750 a month for five years, with no option to renew the lease or to reacquire the machinery. On May 1, Year 3, the machinery had a carrying amount of $250,000 and a remaining economic life of 10 years. See's rent expense for the machinery for the year ended October 31, Year 3, is:

a $0   **b** $2,000   **c** $2,500   **d** $4,500   **e** Some other amount

8   For a capital lease, an amount equal to the present value at the beginning of the lease term of the minimum lease payments during the lease term, excluding the portion of the payments representing executory costs, is recorded by the lessee as a/an:

a Expense
b Liability but not as an asset
c Asset but not as a liability
d Asset and a liability

9   For a six-year capital lease, the portion of the minimum lease payment in the third year applicable to the reduction of the lessee's lease liability is:

a Less than in the second year
b More than in the second year
c The same as in the fourth year
d More than in the fourth year

Ex. 20-2   Wing Company leased a new machine from Buck Company on October 31, Year 5, under a lease with the following pertinent information:

Lease term	10 years
Annual rent payable each Oct. 31, beginning Oct. 31, Year 5	$200,000
Economic life of machine...	15 years
Lessor's implicit interest rate (unknown to lessee)	10%
Lessee's incremental borrowing rate	12%

Wing has an option to acquire the machine on October 31, Year 15, by paying $250,000, which is significantly less than the $500,000 expected current fair value of the machine on the option exercise date. At the inception of the lease, the exercise of the option appears to be reasonably assured.

Compute the amount that Wing Company debits to the Leased Equipment—Capital Lease ledger account on October 31, Year 5. Use the Appendix at the end of Chapter 5 and round all amounts to the nearest dollar.

Ex. 20-3 On November 1, Year 4, Lessee Company signed a ten-year noncancelable lease for equipment. The lease required annual payments of $15,000 starting November 1, Year 4, with title to the equipment passing to Lessee at the expiration of the lease term. Lessee treated this transaction as a capital lease. The equipment had an economic life of 15 years, with no residual value. Lessee uses the straight-line method of depreciation for its plant assets. Aggregate lease payments were determined to have a present value of $101,385, based on the lessor's implicit interest of 10%, which was known to Lessee.

Compute Lessee Company's interest expense and depreciation expense for the year ended October 31, Year 5, rounded to the nearest dollar.

Ex. 20-4 Arbo Company leased equipment from Blake Corporation on December 31, Year 6, for a 10-year term (equal to the economic life of the leased property). Payments of $100,000 were due annually, beginning December 31, Year 6, and Arbo guaranteed a residual value of $2,000 for the equipment. Arbo's incremental borrowing rate was 12%; Blake's implicit interest rate, which was unknown to Arbo, was 10%. Arbo made the $100,000 lease payments on December 31, Year 6, and December 31, Year 7.

Compute the balance of Arbo Company's Liability under Capital Lease (net) ledger account on December 31, Year 7, after the lease payment made on that date. Use the Appendix at the end of Chapter 5 and round all amounts to the nearest dollar.

Ex. 20-5 On March 1, Year 4, Lessee Company entered into a five-year capital lease for equipment with Lessor Company, with the following details:

Annual rental due each Mar. 1, beginning Year 4	$10,000
Bargain purchase option, Mar. 1, Year 9	$ 1,000
Economic life of leased equipment	8 years
Executory costs (maintenance) payable each Mar. 1, beginning Year 4....	$ 500
Lessee's incremental borrowing rate	15%
Lessor's implicit interest rate (known to Lessee)	12%
Estimated residual value of equipment at end of lease term	$ 1,500

Prepare all journal entries for Lessee Company's capital lease for the year ended February 28, Year 5, assuming Lessee made all payments to Lessor when due. Use the Appendix at the end of Chapter 5 and round all amounts to the nearest dollar.

Ex. 20-6 In its equipment lease with Roddy Company that expired on July 31, Year 8, Tovar Corporation guaranteed a residual value of $5,000 for the equipment. On July 31, Year 8, Roddy notified Tovar that it had sold the equipment to a third party for $4,600.

Prepare a journal entry for Tovar Corporation on July 31, Year 8, to record its payment of cash to Roddy Company in settlement of its residual value guarantee.

Ex. 20-7 On January 2, Year 7, Lessee Corporation signed a 10-year noncancelable lease for machinery. The terms of the lease required Lessee to make annual payments of $30,000 for 10 years beginning January 2, Year 7, with title to the machinery to pass to Lessee at the end of this period. The machinery has an economic life of 15 years and no residual value. Lessee uses the straight-line method of depreciation for all its plant assets. Lessee appropriately accounted for the lease transaction as a capital lease, using its incremental borrowing rate of 12% a year.

Compute the following for Lessee Corporation for Year 7 (use the Appendix at the end of Chapter 5 and round all amounts to the nearest dollar):

a Present value of minimum lease payments, January 2, Year 7

b Interest expense for Year 7

c Depreciation expense for Year 7

Ex. 20-8 On June 30, Year 4, Day Company sold equipment for $560,000. The equipment had a carrying amount of $500,000 and a remaining economic life of 10 years. That same day, Day leased back the equipment at $11,000 a month for five years, with no option to renew the lease or reacquire the equipment.

Compute Day Company's rent expense for the equipment for the year ended December 31, Year 4.

Ex. 20-9 Widden Corporation leased equipment to Colby, Inc., on January 2, Year 1, for an eight-year term requiring annual payments of $800,000 each January 2, beginning Year 1. The economic life of the equipment was eight years, with no residual value. The equipment was carried in Widden's Inventories ledger account at a cost of $4,200,000. Widden appropriately accounted for the lease as a sales-type lease, using an implicit interest rate of 10%.

Compute Widden Corporation's interest revenue for each of the years ended December 31, Year 1 and Year 2. Use the Appendix at the end of Chapter 5 and round all amounts to the nearest dollar.

Ex. 20-10 Leasing, Inc., leased equipment to Macco Company on July 1, Year 5, for an eight-year term and annual payments of $600,000 each July 1, beginning Year 5. The equipment was carried in Leasing's Inventories ledger account at a cost of $2,800,000, and Leasing appropriately accounted for the lease as a sales-type lease, using an implicit interest rate of 12%.

Compute the gross profit and interest revenue to be recognized by Leasing, Inc., for the year ended June 30, Year 6. Use the Appendix at the end of Chapter 5 and round all amounts to the nearest dollar.

Ex. 20-11 On January 2, Year 7, Lessor, Inc., entered into a five-year sales-type lease for equipment with Lessee Company with the following details:

Annual payment due each Jan. 2, beginning Year 7	$10,000
Bargain purchase option, Jan. 2, Year 12.	$ 1,000
Cost of equipment in Lessor's Inventories ledger account	$32,000
Economic life of equipment	8 years
Initial direct costs paid by Lessor, Jan. 2, Year 7	$ 800
Executory costs (insurance and maintenance) to be paid to Lessor by	
Lessee each Jan. 2, beginning Year 7	$ 1,500
Lessee's incremental borrowing rate	15%
Lessor's implicit interest rate (known to Lessee).	12%
Residual value of equipment	none

Lessor uses the perpetual inventory system.

Prepare journal entries for Lessor, Inc., for the year ended December 31, Year 7, assuming Lessee Company made all lease payments when due. Use the Appendix at the end of Chapter 5 and round all amounts to the nearest dollar.

Ex. 20-12 On January 2, Year 6, Tracy, Inc., leased equipment to Rue Company at an annual rent of $100,000 receivable at the beginning of each year for 10 years. The first payment was received immediately. The equipment cost $650,000 and had an economic life of 13 years and no residual value. The interest rate implicit in the lease was 12%. Tracy had no other costs associated with the lease. Tracy should have accounted for the lease as a sales-type lease but mistakenly accounted for it as an operating lease.

Compute the effect on income before income taxes during Year 6 as a result of Tracy, Inc.'s, (lessor's) incorrect classification of the lease as an operating lease rather than as a sales-type lease. Use the Appendix at the end of Chapter 5 and round all amounts to the nearest dollar.

Ex. 20-13 Cedar Company retired a machine from production on January 2, Year 5, for the purpose of leasing it. The machine had a carrying amount of $900,000 after 15 years of use and was expected to have four more years of economic life and no residual value. The machine was being depreciated on a straight-line basis. On March 1, Year 5, Cedar leased the machine to Lew Company for $330,000 a year for a four-year period ending February 28, Year 9. Cedar incurred total maintenance and other related costs under the lease contract of $45,000 relating to the year ended December 31, Year 5. Lew paid $330,000 to Cedar on March 1, Year 5. The lease was classified properly as an operating lease by both Cedar and Lew.

a Compute the income before income taxes derived by Cedar Company from the lease for the year ended December 31, Year 5.

b Compute the amount of rent expense incurred by Lew Company under the lease for the year ended December 31, Year 5.

Ex. 20-14 Lessor Company leased equipment to Lessee Company on May 1, Year 6. At that time the collectibility of the minimum lease payments was not reasonably predictable. The lease expires on May 1, Year 8. Lessee could have acquired the equipment from Lessor for $900,000 instead of leasing it. Lessor's accounting records showed a carrying amount of $800,000 for the equipment on May 1, Year 6. Lessor's depreciation on the equipment in Year 6 was $200,000. During Year 6, Lessee paid $240,000 rent to Lessor. Lessor incurred maintenance and other related costs of $22,000 under the terms of the lease in Year 6. After the lease with Lessee expires, Lessor will lease the equipment to another party for two years.

a Compute Lessor Company's pre-tax income derived from its operating lease with Lessee Company during Year 6.

b Compute Lessee Company's pre-tax expense incurred under its operating lease with Lessor Company during Year 6.

Ex. 20-15 Logo Company, a dealer in equipment, leased equipment to Mann, Inc., on July 1, Year 6. The lease was appropriately accounted for as a sales-type lease by Logo and as a capital lease by Mann. The lease was for a 10-year term (the economic life of the equipment) expiring June 30, Year 16. The first of 10 equal annual payments of $500,000 was made on July 1, Year 6. Logo had acquired the equipment for $2,675,000 on January 2, Year 6, and established a selling price of $3,375,000 for the equipment. The present value on July 1, Year 6, of the rent payments over the lease term discounted at 12% (Logo's implicit interest rate, which was known to Mann and was less than Mann's incremental borrowing rate) was $3,164,125.

a Compute the amount of (1) gross profit and (2) interest revenue that Logo Company (lessor) recognizes for the year ended December 31, Year 6. Round all amounts to the nearest dollar.

b Compute the amount of (1) depreciation expense (straight-line method, with no residual value) and (2) interest expense that Mann (lessee) recognizes for the year ended December 31, Year 6. Round all amounts to the nearest dollar.

Ex. 20-16 The following information is available for a lease of a machine that is classified as a sales-type lease by Blunt Company, the lessor, and a capital lease by Easton, Inc., the lessee:

Cost of machine to lessor	$31,000
Initial payment by lessee at inception of lease	1,000
Present value of remaining 47 monthly payments of $1,000 each discounted at 1% a month	37,354

a Record the lease (including the initial receipt of $1,000) and the receipt of the second installment of $1,000 in the accounting records of Blunt Company, the lessor. Round all amounts to the nearest dollar.

b Record the lease (including the initial payment of $1,000) and the payment of the second installment of $1,000 in the accounting records of Easton, Inc., the lessee. Round all amounts to the nearest dollar.

Ex. 20-17 Mell Corporation leased a heavy crane to Canby Company on July 1, Year 10, on the following terms:

(1) 48 payments of $1,500 at the end of each month were to be paid by Canby.

(2) The cost of the crane to Mell was $51,064.

Mell appropriately accounted for the lease as a direct financing lease; the difference between total rent receipts, $72,000 ($1,500 × 48 = $72,000), and the cost of the crane, $51,064, was computed to yield a return of 1½% a month over the lease term.

  Prepare journal entries for Mell Corporation to record the lease contract and the receipt of the first payment on July 31, Year 10. Record unearned interest revenue of $20,936 ($72,000 − $51,064 = $20,936) and round all amounts to the nearest dollar. Disregard initial direct costs and residual value.

Ex. 20-18   On March 1, Year 1, Lessor, Inc., entered into a direct financing lease with Lessee Company for a four-year term with annual payments of $10,000 beginning March 1, Year 1. The lease was for equipment carried in Lessor's Equipment Held for Lease ledger account at its cost (and fair value) of $33,239; the equipment had an unguaranteed residual value of $1,500. Lessor's implicit interest rate was 15%, after allowance for initial direct costs of $450 paid by Lessor on March 1, Year 1.

  a Compute Lessor, Inc.'s, gross investment in the lease, unearned interest revenue, and net investment in the lease. Round all amounts to the nearest dollar.

  b Prepare three-column ledger accounts for Lessor, Inc.'s, Lease Receivables and Unearned Interest Revenue ledger accounts, and post the journal entries for the four-year term of the lease to the accounts. Round all amounts to the nearest dollar.

Ex. 20-19   On October 1, Year 6, Miller Corporation leased equipment carried in its Equipment Held for Lease ledger account at a cost (and fair value) of $20,434 to Naylor Company on a five-year lease with annual payments of $5,000 beginning on October 1, Year 6, and a guaranteed residual value of $1,000. Miller's implicit interest rate was 12%, after allowance for initial direct costs of $320 paid by Miller on October 1, Year 6.

  a Compute Miller Corporation's gross investment in the lease, unearned interest revenue, and net investment in the lease.

  b Prepare journal entries for Miller Corporation on October 1, Year 6, to record the inception of the lease, the payment of initial direct costs, and the receipt of the first lease payment from Naylor Company.

  c Compute Miller Corporation's interest revenue (rounded to the nearest dollar) under the lease for the year ended September 30, Year 7.

CASES

Case 20-1   Reuben Company leased equipment from Traynor Company. The classification of the lease makes a difference in the amounts included in the balance sheets and income statements of both Reuben and Traynor.

Instructions

  a What criteria must be met by the lease in order that Reuben Company (lessee) classify it as a capital lease?

b What criteria must be met by the lease in order that Traynor Company (lessor) classify it as a sales-type lease or a direct financing lease?

c Contrast a sales-type lease with a direct financing lease.

Case 20-2   On January 2, Year 7, Nickell Company, a lessee, entered into three noncancelable leases for equipment, Lease 1, Lease 2, and Lease 3. None of the three leases transfers ownership of the equipment to Nickell at the end of the lease term. For each of the three leases, the present value at the beginning of the lease term of the minimum lease payments, excluding the portion representing executory costs, is 75% of the excess of the fair value of the equipment to the lessor at the inception of the lease over any related investment tax credit retained by the lessor and expected to be realized by the lessor.

Additional Information

(1) Lease 1 does not contain a bargain purchase option; the lease term is equal to 80% of the economic life of the equipment.

(2) Lease 2 contains a bargain purchase option; the lease term is equal to 50% of the economic life of the equipment.

(3) Lease 3 does not contain a bargain purchase option; the lease term is equal to 50% of the economic life of the equipment.

Instructions

a How does Nickell Company (lessee) classify each of the three leases, and why? Discuss the rationale for your answer.

b What amount, if any, does Nickell Company record as a liability at the inception of the lease for each of the three leases?

c Assuming that the minimum lease payments are made on a straight-line basis, how does Nickell Company record each minimum lease payment for each of the three leases?

Case 20-3   Lindy Corporation entered into a lease contract with Lenore Leasing Corporation for a machine. Lenore's primary business is leasing, and it is not a manufacturer or dealer. Lindy leased the machine for a period of three years, which is 50% of the machine's economic life. Lenore was to take possession of the machine at the end of the initial three-year lease and lease it to an unrelated enterprise. Lindy did not guarantee any residual value for the machine, and the lease did not contain a bargain purchase option.

Lindy's incremental borrowing rate is 10%, and the lessor's implicit interest rate in the lease, 8½%, was not known to Lindy. With either rate, the present value of the minimum lease payments was between 90 and 100% of the fair value of the machine on the date of the lease contract.

Lindy agreed to pay all executory costs directly, and no allowance for these costs was included in the lease payments.

Lenore was reasonably certain that Lindy would pay all lease payments, and, because Lindy had agreed to pay all executory costs, there were no important uncertainties regarding costs to be incurred by Lenore.

Instructions

a With respect to Lindy Corporation (lessee), answer the following questions:

(1) What type of lease has been entered into? Explain.

(2) How does Lindy compute the amount to be recorded for the lease or asset acquired?

(3) What ledger accounts are created or affected by this transaction and how are the lease costs related to the transaction matched with revenue?

(4) What disclosures does Lindy make in a note to the financial statements regarding this lease or asset?

b With respect to Lenore Leasing Corporation (the lessor), answer the following questions:

(1) What type of lease has been entered into? Explain.

(2) How is this lease recorded by Lenore, and how are the amounts determined?

(3) How does Lenore determine the amount of revenue to be recognized on receipt of each lease payment?

(4) What disclosures does Lenore make in a note to the financial statements regarding this lease?

Case 20-4   **a** Capital leases and operating leases are the two classifications of leases described in pronouncements of the Financial Accounting Standards Board, from the standpoint of the lessee.

Instructions

(1) Describe how a capital lease is accounted for by a lessee, both at the inception of the lease and during the first year of the lease, assuming that the lease transfers ownership of the property to the lessee at the end of the lease term, and that equal monthly payments are made by the lessee at the beginning of each month.

(2) Describe how an operating lease is accounted for by a lessee, both at the inception of the lease and during the first year of the lease, assuming that equal monthly payments are made by the lessee at the beginning of each month.

Do not discuss the criteria for distinguishing between capital leases and operating leases.

b Sales-type leases and direct financing leases are two of the classifications of leases described in pronouncements of the Financial Accounting Standards Board, from the standpoint of the lessor.

Instructions

Compare and contrast a sales-type lease with a direct financing lease as follows:

(1) Gross investment in the lease

(2) Recognition of interest revenue

(3) Manufacturer's or dealer's profit

Do not discuss the criteria for distinguishing between the leases described above and operating leases.

Case 20-5   Wingo Aircraft Company manufactures small single- and multiple-engine aircraft primarily for sale to individuals, flying clubs, and corporations. Wingo is one of the pioneers in the industry and has developed a reputation as a leader in small-craft engineering and marketing innovations.

During the last few years, Wingo has leased profitably an increasing number of aircraft to flying clubs. The leasing activity currently represents a significant portion of Wingo's annual volume. Details of a typical lease contract with flying clubs follow:

(1) The flying club signs a long-term lease with Wingo for the aircraft.

(2) The lease has a noncancelable term of 6 to 18 years, depending on the aircraft's economic life. The lease term is set at 75% of the economic life of the aircraft leased.

(3) The club is required to deposit with Wingo an amount equal to 10% of the total lease rent for the lease term. The deposit is not refundable, but it is used in lieu of rent during the last one-tenth of the lease term.

(4) A bank lends Wingo an amount equal to the remaining 90% of the total lease rent after deducting a discount of 14% a year. The net discounted amount is paid immediately to Wingo. The bank-loan contract requires Wingo to use the lease payments from the flying club to repay the loan to the bank.

(5) As a condition for the loan, the bank requires Wingo to insure the leased aircraft for an amount equal to the loan.

(6) The flying club indorses Wingo's bank-loan contract as a surety, thus obligating itself if Wingo should default on the loan.

(7) When the bank loan is paid in full at the end of the lease term, the flying club may acquire the aircraft and receive title to it by paying Wingo $100.

Instructions

Discuss the criteria and other aspects of Wingo Aircraft Company's leasing activities that it should consider in determining whether to account for its flying club leases as operating leases or as sales-type leases. In your discussion, identify criteria that are clearly met from the facts presented. For criteria that are not clearly met, indicate what additional information is needed to reach a conclusion with respect to each criterion.

Case 20-6   Apollo Airlines recently acquired eight jetliners for a total cost of $180 million. It plans to depreciate the jets by the sum-of-the-years'-digits method over a 12-year economic life. It is estimated that the jets will have a resale value of $24 million at the end of 12 years. To finance the acquisition of the jets, Apollo borrowed $180 million, payable at the rate of $20 million a year plus interest at 8% on the unpaid balance. The first payment is due one year after the loan is arranged.

Solo Airlines leased from Execucraft, Inc., eight jetliners of the same type acquired by Apollo for a 12-year term. Solo does not have an option to acquire the jets at the end of the lease term, and it classified the lease as an operating lease. Lease payments are $22 million a year, payable at the end of each year. The lease payments do not include property taxes, insurance, and maintenance of the jetliners; Solo pays all such expenses. The annual rent was computed to give Execucraft, Inc.

(lessor), slightly less than 8% return on investment, taking into account the $24 million resale value of the jets at the end of the 12-year lease term. The lease is noncancelable.

Instructions

a Prepare a working paper to compute annual expenses (depreciation and interest) for Apollo Airlines in connection with the ownership of the eight jetliners. How do annual expenses for Apollo compare with the annual lease rental expense incurred by Solo Airlines? What is the significance of the difference?

b Show the amounts relating to the jets and the related loan that appear in the balance sheet of Apollo Airlines at the end of the first year. In what respect is the balance sheet for Solo Airlines different?

c Do you believe that the classification of the lease as an operating lease by Solo Airlines was in conformity with the provisions of *FASB Statement No. 13,* "Accounting for Leases"? State reasons for your conclusion. (Use the Appendix at the end of Chapter 5 if necessary.)

PROBLEMS

20-1 Albany Corporation leases equipment to several lessees. All its leases in effect during Year 5 were operating leases except for a sales-type lease entered into on January 2, Year 5.

Rent revenue from Albany's operating leases totaled $800,000 for Year 5. The cost of the leased equipment was $3,700,000, which was being depreciated by the straight-line method over an estimated economic life of five years with an estimated residual value of $200,000. No equipment leased under operating leases was acquired or constructed during Year 5. Maintenance and repair costs for the equipment leased under operating leases totaled $70,000 during Year 5.

The January 2, Year 5, sales-type lease was for a six-year term expiring on December 31, Year 10. The cost of the leased equipment was $3,500,000, and it had no estimated residual value. Executory costs under the sales-type lease totaling $120,000 were paid by the lessee during Year 5. The first of six equal annual payments of $750,000 under the lease was received by Albany from the lessee on January 2, Year 5. Albany's implicit interest rate under the lease was 10%.

Additional Information

(1) Other revenue of Albany for Year 5, exclusive of amounts described in the foregoing paragraphs, totaled $50,000.

(2) Other operating expenses of Albany for Year 5, exclusive of amounts described in the foregoing paragraphs, totaled $400,000.

(3) Albany's income tax rate is 45%.

Instructions

Prepare a single-step income statement for Albany Corporation (lessor) for Year 5. Show supporting computations. (Use the Appendix at the end of Chapter 5 and round all amounts to the nearest dollar.) Disregard earnings per share.

20-2   Coville Corporation had the following leases in effect during Year 7:

(1) An operating lease with Wellfry Company for equipment, dated July 1, Year 7, with monthly rent of $115,000 for the three-year lease term payable beginning at the inception of the lease. The equipment, which had an eight-year economic life with no residual value, had been carried in the finished goods inventory at cost of $7,000,000 from January 2, Year 7, when it was completed, until it was leased to Wellfry. Maintenance and repair costs paid by Coville for the equipment during the last six months of Year 7 totaled $8,300.

(2) A sales-type lease with Yamaki Company dated January 2, Year 7, for an eight-year term, with annual payments of $600,000 payable beginning on January 2, Year 7. The equipment, which had an economic life of eight years with no residual value, had been carried in Coville's finished goods inventory at cost of $3,000,000. Coville's implicit interest rate under the lease was 10%, which was known to Yamaki and was less than Yamaki's incremental borrowing rate of 12%. Coville paid initial direct costs of $2,300 on October 1, Year 7. Executory costs may be disregarded.

Coville, Wellfry, and Yamaki use the straight-line method of depreciation.

Instructions

(Use the Appendix at the end of Chapter 5 and round all amounts to the nearest dollar.)

a (1) Compute Coville Corporation's (lessor's) revenue and expenses related to the operating lease with Wellfry Company for the year ended December 31, Year 7.

(2) Compute Wellfry Company's (lessee's) expenses related to the operating lease with Coville Corporation for the year ended December 31, Year 7.

b (1) Compute Coville Corporation's (lessor's) revenue, costs, and expenses related to the sales-type lease with Yamaki Company for the year ended December 31, Year 7.

(2) Compute Yamaki Company's (lessee's) expenses related to the capital lease with Coville Corporation for the year ended December 31, Year 7.

20-3   During your examination of the financial statements of Dixon Enterprises for the year ended December 31, Year 6, you find that Dixon had erroneously debited two monthly payments of $5,000 each (November 1 and December 1) under a capital lease dated November 1, Year 6, to the Rent Expense ledger account. Your examination of the lease disclosed that it was for a four-year term, included a bargain purchase option of $8,000, and provided that $1,200 of the $5,000 monthly payment was for insurance, $300; maintenance, $400; and property taxes, $500. You are unable to learn the lessor's implicit interest rate, but you do learn that Dixon's incremental borrowing rate is 12%. The leased equipment under the capital lease had an economic life of six years with a residual value of $6,000. Dixon uses the straight-line method of depreciation for plant assets and recognizes depreciation expense monthly.

Instructions

Prepare a correcting journal entry for Dixon Enterprises (lessee) on December 31, Year 6, to correct the accounting for the capital lease. Use the Appendix at the end of Chapter 5 and round all amounts to the nearest dollar. Disregard income taxes.

20-4   On September 30, Year 3, the end of a fiscal year, Lessee Company entered into a five-year capital lease with Lessor Corporation for equipment with a six-year economic life and a residual value of $2,500. Payments under the lease, excluding executory costs, were $60,000 a year, beginning on September 30, Year 3. Title to the equipment was to be transferred to Lessee on September 30, Year 8. Lessor's implicit interest rate is 12%; Lessee had an incremental borrowing rate of 15% and did not know Lessor's implicit interest rate. On September 30, Year 5, before Lessee made the lease payment due on that date or prepared year-end adjusting entries, the sales-type lease (from the viewpoint of Lessor) was terminated by mutual consent with no penalties.

Instructions

Prepare journal entries related to the capital lease for Lessee Company on September 30, Year 3, Year 4, and Year 5. Compute depreciation expense by the straight-line method. Use the Appendix at the end of Chapter 5 and round all amounts to the nearest dollar. Disregard executory costs.

20-5   On December 31, Year 4, Lido Company leased equipment from Rodeo, Inc., for four annual payments (excluding executory costs) of $10,000, beginning December 31, Year 4. The lease contained a bargain purchase option exercisable by Lido on December 31, Year 8, in the amount of $2,000. The equipment had a five-year economic life with a residual value of $1,000. Because Lido did not know Rodeo's implicit interest rate, Lido used its incremental borrowing rate of 15% to account for the capital lease. Lido depreciates plant assets by the straight-line method.

Instructions

Prepare three-column ledger accounts for Lido Company's (lessee's) Leased Equipment—Capital Lease and Liability under Capital Lease (net) ledger accounts, and post thereto all journal entries related to the capital lease for the five years ended December 31, Year 9. Use the Appendix at the end of Chapter 5 and round all amounts to the nearest dollar. Disregard executory costs.

20-6   On July 1, Year 4, Ramer Corporation leased equipment to Gamble Company. The equipment had been carried in Ramer's Inventories ledger account at a cost of $220,000. Both companies have a June 30 fiscal year. There were no other significant costs associated with the lease and no residual value guarantee by the lessee. The lease was for a noncancelable term of eight years, with $50,000 rent payable by Gamble on each July 1; title to the equipment passes to Gamble at the end of the lease term. Gamble made the first lease payment on July 1, Year 4. Ramer's implicit interest rate, which was known to Gamble and was less than Gamble's incremental borrowing rate of 13%, was 10%, and the present value of an annuity due of eight rents of 1 at 10% is 5.868419. The equipment had an economic life of 12 years with no residual value, and was to be depreciated under the straight-line method.

Instructions

(Round all computations to nearest dollar.)

a Prepare journal entries for Ramer Corporation (lessor) on July 1, Year 4, to record the lease transaction as a sales-type lease and receipt of $50,000 from Gamble Company for the first lease payment.

b Prepare a journal entry for Ramer Corporation (lessor) on June 30, Year 5, to recognize interest revenue for one year.

c Prepare a journal entry for Ramer Corporation (lessor) on July 1, Year 4, to record the lease transaction, but for this part of the problem *assume that the lease was classified as an operating lease.*

d Compute the expenses relative to the lease for Gamble Company (lessee) for the year ended June 30, Year 5, assuming that it classified the lease (1) as an operating lease, and (2) as a capital lease.

20-7 Prado, Inc., was incorporated in Year 1 with a fiscal year ending July 31. Prado's primary product is a sophisticated on-line inventory control system. Its customers pay a fixed fee plus a usage charge for using the system.

Prado leased a large, BIG-I computer system from the manufacturer. The lease required rent of $372,000 a year for the 12-year lease term. The economic life of the computer was 15 years.

Each $372,000 payment included $72,000 for the maintenance on the computer to be performed by the manufacturer. Lease payments were payable beginning on August 1, Year 2, the date the computer was installed and the lease contract was signed.

The lease was noncancelable for its 12-year term and was collateralized only by the manufacturer's security interest in the BIG-I system. On August 1, Year 14, Prado was to acquire title to the BIG-I system under the lease contract.

The lease was accounted for as a capital lease by Prado, and the computer was to be depreciated by the straight-line method with a $140,000 residual value. Borrowed funds for this type of transaction would have cost Prado 12% a year. The lessor's implicit interest rate was unknown to Prado.

Instructions

Prepare journal entries for Prado, Inc. (lessee), for the year ended July 31, Year 3, relating to the lease. Show supporting computations in the explanation for each journal entry. Use the Appendix at the end of Chapter 5 and round all amounts to the nearest dollar.

20-8 On January 2, Year 1, Speeders, Inc., leased a racing car from Seabring Leasing Company. The fixed noncancelable term of the lease was 24 months, with an option to renew month by month based on a schedule of rents and guarantees of the residual value that decreased over time. The cost, fair value, and economic life of the racing car were as follows:

Cost (carried in Racing Equipment ledger account of Seabring Leasing)	$116,200
Fair value at inception of lease (Jan. 2, Year 1)	$116,200
Economic life	36 months

The lease specified that Speeders was to pay $4,125 on the first day of each month and that it guaranteed a residual value of $36,000 to Seabring Leasing at the end of 24 months (December 31, Year 2).

Speeders was to receive any excess over the guaranteed amount at the end of the lease term. Collectibility of lease rent was reasonably predictable, and no unreimbursable costs were expected to be incurred by Seabring Leasing, which paid $657 initial direct costs of the lease on January 2, Year 1, representing commissions. The rent was deemed to be fair, and the residual value guarantee was expected to approximate actual realizable value. Speeders depreciates other racing cars it owns by the straight-line method, and its incremental borrowing rate generally was 1% a month, which also was the interest rate implicit in the lease. At the end of the lease term, December 31, Year 2, the racing car was sold to a third party by Seabring Leasing for $40,000. The excess of proceeds received over the guaranteed residual value was paid by Seabring Leasing to Speeders.

Instructions

a How is the lease classified by Seabring Leasing Company (lessor) and Speeders, Inc. (lessee)? Explain in terms of criteria required by *FASB Statement No. 13*, "Accounting for Leases." Use the Appendix at the end of Chapter 5 to compute the present value of minimum lease payments and round all amounts to the nearest dollar.

b Prepare journal entries at the inception of the lease (including the first lease payment) in the accounting records of (1) Seabring Leasing Company (lessor), and (2) Speeders, Inc. (lessee).

c Prepare journal entries at the end of the lease term in the accounting records of (1) Seabring Leasing Company (lessor), and (2) Speeders, Inc. (lessee). Assume that entries to recognize depreciation expense, interest revenue, or interest expense have been recorded on December 31, Year 2.

20-9 Breakers Ballroom entered into a lease on April 1, Year 1, for a sound system from Sound Equipment Leasing Co. The fixed noncancelable term of the lease was four years with an option to renew at terms that represented expected fair value on the option date. The following data relate to the sound system:

Cost to Sound Equipment Leasing Co. (carried in Equipment Held for Lease ledger account)	$19,142
Fair value at inception of lease	$19,142
Economic life	4 years

The lease contract specified that Breakers was to pay $489 on the first day of each month, and that it guaranteed a residual value of $2,000 to Sound Equipment Leasing Co. at the end of 48 months. Breakers was to receive any excess over the $2,000 guarantee at the end of the lease term.

The collectibility of the lease rentals was reasonably predictable, and no unreimbursable costs were to be incurred. Initial direct costs of the lease (commissions) paid by Sound Equipment Leasing on April 1, Year 1, totaled $854. The rent was deemed to be fair, and the residual value guarantee was expected to approximate the sound system's realizable value at the end of the lease term. Breakers depreciated other plant assets by the straight-line method and had an incremental borrowing rate of 15% compounded monthly. The interest rate implicit in the lease was 1% a month and was known to Breakers.

At the end of the lease term, the sound system was sold by Sound Equipment Leasing to a third party for $1,800, and the excess of the residual value guarantee over the sales proceeds was paid by Breakers to Sound Equipment Leasing.

Instructions

a How is the lease classified by the lessor and the lessee? Explain your conclusion in terms of the classification criteria required by *FASB Statement No. 13*, "Accounting for Leases." Use the Appendix at the end of Chapter 5 to compute the present value of minimum lease payments and round all amounts to the nearest dollar.

b Prepare the journal entries required at the inception of the lease for (1) Sound Equipment Leasing Co. (lessor), and (2) Breakers Ballroom (lessee).

c Prepare the journal entries required at the termination of the lease for (1) Sound Equipment Leasing Co. (lessor), and (2) Breakers Ballroom (lessee). Assume that entries to recognize depreciation expense, interest revenue, or interest expense had been recorded on March 31, Year 5.

20-10 Craig Company leased equipment with an economic life of 12 years to Mim Company on January 2, Year 1, for a period of 10 years. The selling price of the equipment was $288,258, and the unguaranteed residual value at the end of the lease term was estimated at $20,000. Mim was to pay annual rent of $40,000 at the beginning of each year and was responsible for all maintenance, insurance, and property taxes. Craig incurred costs of $197,200 in manufacturing the equipment and $5,000 in negotiating and closing the lease contract. The collectibility of the lease payments was reasonably predictable, and no additional costs were expected to be incurred by Craig. The implicit interest rate for Craig was 9% a year and was known to Mim, which had an incremental borrowing rate of 12%.

Instructions

(Use the Appendix at the end of Chapter 5 and round all amounts to the nearest dollar.)

a How is the lease classified by Craig Company (lessor)? Explain.

b Assuming that Craig Company (lessor) classified the lease as a sales-type lease, compute the following at the inception of the lease:

(1) Gross investment in lease
(2) Net investment in lease
(3) Unearned interest revenue
(4) Sales proceeds under the lease

(5) Cost of goods sold (cost of equipment plus initial direct costs less present value of the unguaranteed residual value)

c Prepare a working paper summarizing the amortization of the net investment in the lease and the recognition of interest revenue over the lease term for Craig Company (lessor).

d Prepare the journal entries for the first year of the lease for Craig Company (lessor).

20-11 On December 31, Year 1, Maladay, Inc., leased equipment to Fairview Company. The equipment had a cost and fair value of $278,158. The term of the lease was for seven years, with a $50,000 payment due each December 31 starting in Year 1. The unguaranteed residual value was estimated at $30,000 at the end of the lease term, and the economic life of the equipment was nine years. The terms were designed to give Maladay a 10% annual rate of return on its net investment (including initial direct costs), which had a present value of $283,158.

Fairview was to pay all property taxes, insurance, and maintenance; Maladay paid a commission of $5,000 to a broker for arranging the lease. Collectibility of the lease payments was reasonably predictable, and there were no additional costs to be incurred by Maladay.

Instructions

(Use the Appendix at the end of Chapter 5 and round all amounts to the nearest dollar.)

a How is the lease classified by Maladay, Inc. (lessor)? Explain.

b Assuming that Maladay, Inc. (lessor), classified the lease as a direct financing lease, compute the following at the inception of the lease:

(1) Gross investment in lease

(2) Unearned interest revenue

(3) Net investment in lease

c Prepare a working paper summarizing the amortization of the $283,158 present value of the lease and the recognition of interest revenue over the lease term for Maladay, Inc. (lessor).

d Prepare the journal entries for Maladay, Inc. (lessor), on December 31, Year 1, and on December 31, Year 2, relating to the lease.

20-12 On April 1, Year 5, Keel Corporation entered into a five-year, noncancelable equipment lease with Nora Corporation. Annual rent of $10,000 (excluding executory costs) was payable in advance, starting on April 1, Year 5. The lease gave Keel an option to acquire the equipment on March 31, Year 10, for $1,000, and the lease was classified appropriately as a sales-type lease by Nora and as a capital lease by Keel.

The economic life of the equipment was 10 years, and management of Keel estimated that the residual value of the equipment at the end of its economic life would approximate the dismantling and removal costs. The straight-line method of depreciation is used by Keel, and its fiscal year ends on March 31.

The incremental borrowing rate for Keel on April 1, Year 5, was 10% a year. Nora's implicit interest rate also was 10%.

Instructions

(Use the Appendix at the end of Chapter 5 and round all amounts to the nearest dollar.)

a Prepare a summary of Keel Corporation's (lessee's) minimum lease payments and interest expense for each of the five years of the lease (April 1, Year 5, through March 31, Year 10).

b Prepare journal entries for Keel Corporation (lessee) relating to the lease for the year ended March 31, Year 6.

c Assuming that the equipment was carried in Nora Corporation's (lessor's) Inventory of Equipment ledger account at $37,000 and that initial direct costs paid by Nora Corporation totaled $1,200, prepare journal entries for Nora Corporation to record the lease, payment of initial direct costs, and receipt of first lease payment.

20-13 In Year 1, Expro Company negotiated and closed a long-term lease for truck terminals. The terminals had been constructed to Expro's specifications on land owned by Expro. On January 2, Year 2, Expro took possession of the truck terminals.

Although the truck terminals had a composite economic life of 40 years, the noncancelable lease term was for 20 years from January 2, Year 2, with a bargain purchase option available on the expiration of the lease. Expro had an option to acquire the truck terminals for $1,000 on December 31, Year 21. You have determined that the truck terminals and related liability were to be accounted for as a capital lease by Expro.

The 20-year lease was effective for the period January 2, Year 2, through December 31, Year 21. Rent payments of $1,000,000 were payable to the lessor on January 2 of each of the first 10 years of the lease term. Rent payments of $300,000 were due on January 2 for each of the last 10 years of the lease. Expro also was obligated to make annual payments to the lessor of $95,000 for property taxes and $155,000 for insurance; these payments also were due on January 2. The lease was structured to give the lessor a 10% rate of return, which was known to Expro. The incremental borrowing rate of Expro was 12%.

Instructions

(Use the Appendix at the end of Chapter 5 and round all amounts to the nearest dollar.)

a Prepare a working paper to compute for Expro Company (lessee) the present value of the minimum lease payments on January 2, Year 2.

b Prepare journal entries for Expro Company (lessee) to record the:

    (1) Lease transaction and the payment to the lessor on January 2, Year 2 (separate entries).

    (2) Depreciation of the truck terminals for Year 2, using the straight-line method with a $200,000 residual value.

(3) Interest expense for the year ended December 31, Year 2.

(4) Payment to the lessor on January 2, Year 3.

20-14 Macco Corporation, a lessor of office machines, acquired for $500,000 on December 31, Year 9, a new machine that was delivered the same day to Ranger Company under a direct financing lease.

Additional Information

(1) The lease term was seven years, which was the same as the economic life of the machine, which had an unguaranteed residual value of $60,000.

(2) The 10% investment tax credit on the cost of the machine was retained by Macco, which expected to use the credit in its income tax returns for Year 9 and thus to reduce its income taxes payable on December 31, Year 9, by the amount of the credit.

(3) Macco's implicit interest rate of 12% was known to Ranger.

(4) Ranger's incremental borrowing rate was 14% on December 31, Year 9.

(5) Seven equal annual lease payments were payable each December 31, Year 9 through Year 15.

(6) There were no initial direct costs associated with the lease.

(7) Ranger appropriately accounted for the lease as a capital lease. Both Macco and Ranger use the calendar year and the straight-line method of depreciation for plant assets.

Instructions

(Use the Appendix at the end of Chapter 5 and round all amounts to the nearest dollar.)

a Compute the annual lease payments under the lease.

b Compute the gross investment in the lease and unearned interest revenue for Macco Corporation (lessor) on December 31, Year 9.

c Compute the expenses of Ranger Company (lessee) under the lease for the year ended December 31, Year 10.

d Prepare journal entries for Macco Corporation (lessor) on December 31, Year 9, to record the inception of the lease and the first lease payment.

Accounting for Income Taxes

21

OVERVIEW OF THE ISSUES

One of the more challenging areas of accounting is the problem created when a corporation's pre-tax accounting income differs materially from taxable income reported in its income tax return. A major objective of the financial reporting system is to measure and disclose income and financial position in accordance with generally accepted accounting principles. The tax law, through the Internal Revenue Code, has several objectives. Raising revenue for the federal government and providing incentives for certain types of economic behavior are two of these objectives.

Many provisions of the tax code create comparative advantages for certain taxpayers. ACRS (Accelerated Cost Recovery System) depreciation is an example. The tax law allows larger depreciation deductions (a "deduction" is an "expense" for income tax purposes) to be taken early in the economic life of business assets and smaller deductions later in their life. This provision creates earlier, and therefore more valuable, tax savings, which is an incentive for investment in such assets.

Because the measurement of pre-tax accounting income and taxable income (the difference between taxable revenues and tax deductions) reflect these different objectives, it is not surprising that the results are often materially different.

The differences between the Internal Revenue Code and generally accepted accounting principles are numerous. In general, accounting principles recognize revenue and expenses on the accrual basis, whereas the tax code uses a mix of the accrual and cash bases of accounting. Specific differences include (1) the recognition of most income tax effects in the period the events occur for accounting and on the cash basis for income tax purposes; (2) the tax system's provision for carryback and carryforward of operating losses; (3) accounting's separate disclosure of the tax effect on extraordinary items, cumulative effects, and other items; (4) differences in the way investment tax credits and other tax credits are recognized; and (5) the accounting for tax in interim reports. This chapter discusses these issues from both a theoretical and a practical perspective.

The yearly tax liability of a corporation can be a significant percentage of total expenses. It is an obligation that must be measured and reported. *FASB Statement No. 96,* ''Accounting for Income Taxes,'' is the main pronouncement governing the measurement and reporting of the economic effects of income taxes in financial statements,[1] and the accounting for differences between the two systems.

CAUSES OF DIFFERENCES BETWEEN TAX AND FINANCIAL REPORTING SYSTEMS

The major differences between the two systems can be classified as (1) temporary differences, (2) permanent differences, (3) different treatment of operating loss carrybacks and carryforwards, (4) results of intraperiod tax allocation, and (5) results of tax credits.[2]

Temporary Differences

Temporary differences include differences between revenues, expenses, gains, and losses recognized in specific years for accounting and tax purposes. They arise from differences between the tax basis of an asset or liability and its reported amount, which will cause ''taxable'' or ''deductible'' amounts in future years. Taxable future temporary differences will cause taxable income to exceed pre-tax accounting income in the future. Deductible future temporary differences will have the opposite effect.

For example, if the ACRS depreciation deduction is expected to be $40,000 in a future year, and accounting depreciation is expected to be $25,000, the $15,000 difference is a deductible temporary difference. The term ''deductible difference'' is used because the tax law will allow $15,000 more depreciation to be deducted for tax purposes than will be recognized for financial statement purposes, in the future.

Temporary differences ''reverse'' in future years. If tax depreciation in the first year of an asset's useful life exceeds accounting depreciation, in future years the situation will be reversed. The reversal aspect of temporary differences plays an important role in accounting for income taxes.

Major categories of temporary differences include: (1) revenues or gains that are taxable before or after recognition in the financial statements; (2) expenses or losses that are deductible before or after recognition in the financial statements; (3) a reduction in the tax basis of assets arising from tax credits; and (4) increases in the tax basis of assets from inflation indexing (allowed by certain tax jurisdictions). The first two are of primary concern in this chapter.[3]

---

[1] *FASB Statement No. 96,* ''*Accounting for Income Taxes,''* FASB (Stamford: 1987). The *Statement* is effective for fiscal years ending after December 15, 1988, although earlier application is encouraged. Retroactive application in the first year of applying *FASB Statement No. 96* is encouraged but not required. If no prior year is restated, then the cumulative effect of initially applying the *Statement* is included in that year's income and the effect on net income from continuing operations, net income, and related per-share disclosures are required. The *Statement* applies to all domestic and foreign income taxes affecting U.S. corporations. The *Statement* supercedes much of the prior governing pronouncement, *APB Opinion No. 11,* ''Accounting for Income Taxes,'' AICPA (New York, 1967).

[2] These definitions derive from *FASB Statement No. 96,* and from *APB Opinion No. 11.*

[3] The others are: investment tax credits reported under the deferral method; foreign operations for which the reporting currency is the functional currency; and business combinations reported under the purchase method (*FASB Statement No. 96,* par. 10).

Examples of items that cause temporary differences are: warranties (expensed in year of sale, deducted in year of claim), rent expense and revenue (recognized in year of occupancy, taxed or deducted in year of payment), and installment revenue (recognized in year of sale, taxed in year of receipt). *Interperiod income tax allocation* (as opposed to *intra*period tax allocation) is the process of accounting for temporary differences.

Permanent Differences

Permanent differences refer to income items that are reported for tax but not for financial statement purposes, or vice versa. The two systems are simply always different. These differences do not "reverse." Generally accepted accounting principles require that income tax expense reflect the tax law for these items. The tax law determines the ultimate tax liability. Interperiod tax allocation is not required for permanent differences.

Following is a list of important permanent differences.

1   Insurance premiums on policies for corporate officers, for which the corporation is beneficiary, are not tax deductible, and the proceeds on such policies are not taxable. Both the premiums and the proceeds are recognized in accounting income.

2   Amortization of goodwill is not deductible but is a financial accounting expense. The indefinite nature and term of goodwill are the reasons for its nondeductibility.

3   Many fines and penalties are not deductible, yet are expenses for income reporting. Congress did not wish to reduce the penalty by making them tax deductible.

4   The difference between cost depletion and tax or "percentage" depletion is a permanent difference. The tax code allows a deduction equal to a percentage of taxable revenues from the exploitation of certain natural resources. This deduction is often much greater than cost depletion, and thus this provision of the tax code is an example of the "economic incentive" aspect of the tax laws. Accounting recognizes the tax depletion amount in computing income tax expense.

5   Dividends received by corporations on investments in capital stock are often not fully taxed, yet they represent income for financial accounting purposes. Also, the equity method of accounting recognizes income of investees, yet is often not fully taxed due to the dividends received deduction.

6   Interest received on state and local bonds represents accounting revenue but is not taxable. The relevant tax code provision effectively lowers the cost of financing for local governments. A lower interest rate on their bonds makes them competitive with higher yields on taxable bonds.

Income tax expense and the tax liability reflect the same amount of tax effect for items that represent permanent differences.

Operating Loss Carrybacks and Carryforwards

The tax law allows a corporation with negative taxable income (an operating loss) to carry back the loss three years. The tax paid in those years is refunded to the extent of the loss or the last three years' taxable income, whichever is less. If the last three years' taxable income is insufficient to absorb the loss, the corporation carries the remaining loss forward 15 years to absorb future taxable income. The law also allows corporations with operating losses to choose the carryforward option only and bypass the carryback option.

These options effectively reduce the operating loss by refunding taxes already paid, or reducing future taxes that would otherwise have been due. Financial accounting has no similar provision, but the benefits of the operating loss carrybacks and carryforwards must be measured and reported in the financial statements.

Consider the following information for Thomas Company:

THOMAS COMPANY
Taxable Income History

Year	Taxable income
A	$ 1,000
B	2,000
C	3,500
D	4,000
E	(11,000)
F	500
G	2,500

Assuming a 30% tax rate, Thomas Company would have paid tax equal to 30% of its taxable income in each of Years A–D. Then, for tax Year E, assuming it chooses the carryback and carryforward option, it would receive a refund of $2,850 [= 0.30($2,000 + $3,500 + $4,000)]. Year A is not considered, because it is outside the three-year carryback period. The $1,500 remaining Year E loss is left to carry forward. In Year F the company would pay no tax, because the $500 income in that year would be absorbed by the remaining loss, leaving a $1,000 loss to carry forward. In Year G the tax liability would be $450 = [0.30($2,500 − $1,000 remaining loss)]. At this point, no remaining carryforward benefit remains.

Had the loss in Year E been $3,000 rather than $11,000, the refund for that year would have been only $900 [= 0.30($3,000)]. The loss would absorb all of Year B's taxable income and $1,000 of Year C's taxable income.

The company could have chosen not to carry back the loss of $11,000 incurred in Year E. In that case, no refund would be received for Year E, and no tax would be paid in Years F and G, leaving $8,000 of loss to carry forward.

Operating loss carrybacks and carryforwards are subject to the following rules: (1) the loss carryback and carryforward represents negative taxable income and therefore absorbs past or future taxable income, not tax; (2) both carrybacks and carryforwards must absorb the earliest years' taxable income completely, before moving ahead; and (3) the earliest tax operating loss must be used completely before a subsequent operating loss can be carried back or forward.

Intraperiod Tax Allocation

Generally accepted accounting principles require that the tax effects of certain items be associated directly with those items in the income statement or statement of retained earnings. As discussed in Chapters 3 and 4, these items include: extraordinary items, gains and losses on disposal of discontinued operations, income and loss from discontinued operations, cumulative effects of changes in accounting principle, and prior period adjustments. The period's total tax effect is distributed to several different accounts *within one accounting period.*

Income Tax Expense relates only to income from continuing operations. The tax effects of the above items are reported as offsets to their gross amount. The income statement (or retained earnings statement for prior period adjustments) reports the item net of tax with parenthetical disclosure of the tax effect.

Intraperiod tax allocation is consistent with the segregation of these items on the income statement and in the retained earnings statement. Inclusion of the tax effects on these items in the income tax expense on ordinary income would distort the relationship between ordinary income and its tax effect.

Tax Credits

The tax code includes provisions for direct tax credits for specific expenditures that Congress wishes to encourage. These credits are often a percentage of the expenditure made and reduce the tax liability in the amount of the credit. The investment tax credit (discussed later in the chapter) is a popular example. Such credits may cause a difference between the tax liability and income tax expense for financial accounting purposes.

INTERPERIOD TAX ALLOCATION

The Basic Issue

Interperiod tax allocation is the process of allocating income tax expense to *several accounting periods.* Temporary differences necessitate this process. The major problems in this area are the measurement of income tax expense, and related deferred tax assets and liabilities.

For example, assume the following facts for Valley Corporation:

VALLEY CORPORATION

Depreciable asset acquired Jan. 1, Year A: cost $80, useful life 2 years, annual revenues $100. The only expenses for Valley Corporation are depreciation and taxes (at 30%).

Year	Tax depreciation	Accounting depreciation	Tax liability	Pre-tax accounting income
A	$50	$40	$15.00*	$60
B	30	40	21.00†	60

*[$15.00 = 0.30(taxable income) = 0.30($100 − $50)]
†[$21.00 = 0.30(taxable income) = 0.30($100 − $30)]

The $10 difference in depreciation between the two systems of accounting is a *temporary* difference. For Valley, should income tax expense for Years A and B be

$15 and $21, respectively, or 0.30($60) = $18 in both years? In other words, should income tax expense be based on taxable income or pre-tax accounting income?

FASB Statement No. 96 answered this and other questions concerning *how financial accounting should measure and report income tax effects in the income statement and the balance sheet*. The tax *liability* is $15 in Year A and $21 in Year B, since the liability is defined by the tax law. Accounting principles have nothing to say about this.

In this simple example, interperiod tax allocation requires $18 of income tax expense to be *recognized* in both years. The $3 difference between income tax expense and liability in Year A is a temporary one that will reverse. In Year B, $21 will be paid in taxes, yet only $18 of income tax expense will be recognized. The total depreciation deduction of $80 is therefore *allocated* to each year in accordance with generally accepted accounting principles. As a result, the total tax for the two years ($36) also is *allocated* to the two periods. Thus the interperiod tax allocation *matches* the income tax expense to the periods in which the underlying events, as measured by the financial accounting system, *occurred*.

An added benefit of this allocation process is that reported income tax expense is a constant rate of pre-tax accounting income (= $18/$60) *equalling* the 30% statutory income tax rate.

In Year A for Valley, $3 of tax is said to be "deferred." A firm cannot legally *defer* its taxes. "Deferred" in this context refers to the faster recognition of income tax expense ($18) than payment ($15). The $3 is deferred relative to the tax that would be due if it were based on accounting income. This deferral is reversed in Year B, when $21 is paid but only $18 expense is recognized. The following journal entries reflect interperiod tax allocation applied to Valley and represent current accounting practice, assuming that other criteria (to be discussed later) are met:

12/31/A	Income Taxes Expense 18		
	Deferred Income Taxes		3
	Income Taxes Payable		15
12/31/B	Income Taxes Expense 18		
	Deferred Income Taxes 3		
	Income Taxes Payable		21

The Deferred Income Taxes account at 12/31/A represents the $3 liability for tax that was recognized in Year A but that is not expected to be paid until Year B.

If interperiod tax allocation were not applied to the events affecting Valley Corporation, Income Tax Expense would be a fluctuating amount, based on *constant* pre-tax accounting income, and would not reflect the legal tax rate.

Interperiod tax allocation has long been a controversial topic. A brief discussion of the theory and alternative accounting treatments of differences between tax and accounting income caused by temporary differences will highlight the more important theoretical considerations and provide a context for understanding current accounting principles in this area.

Conceptual Issues Surrounding Interperiod Tax Allocation

There are three major issues or areas of controversy. (1) Should income taxes be allocated across periods? If not, income tax expense would equal the tax liability on income from continuing operations. (2) If income taxes are to be allocated, should *all* temporary differences be considered (*comprehensive* allocation) or only a subset (*partial* allocation)? (3) If income taxes are to be allocated, what tax rates should be used to calculate future tax effects, and how should the tax effects be disclosed?

Issue 1: Allocation or No Allocation of Income Taxes Those arguing *for* interperiod tax allocation maintain the following. (1) Income taxes result from earning income. The tax expense should be the tax caused by each period's earnings, independent of the time of payment. (2) Failure to match income taxes with pre-tax accounting income causes misleading fluctuations in final net income. (3) A tax "saving" attributable to a temporary difference is only a postponement of the income tax and therefore should not reduce income tax *expense*. (4) Furthermore, interperiod tax allocation provides a more appropriate measure of long-term earnings potential as it reflects the tax ultimately payable on the events of the reporting year, as measured by the financial accounting system. (5) The going-concern assumption also supports interperiod tax allocation. Taxes accrued will ultimately be paid.

Opposition to interperiod tax allocation is based primarily on the nature of income taxes and the possibility that temporary differences may, in fact, be "permanent." There are several arguments. (1) Income tax expense should be based on taxable income that *causes* the tax. The expense should be the legal liability for the period because income taxes are based on the legal concept of taxable income rather than on accounting income. (2) The shifting of income taxes in time tends to be permanent for many business entities. For example, adoption of ACRS depreciation by an entity acquiring a constant or increasing amount of depreciable equipment each year realizes a permanent postponement in the year of adoption. (3) The cost of interperiod tax allocation procedures exceeds its benefit.

The first issue is the most crucial one for the accounting profession. Many accountants feel that neither set of arguments is persuasive. Consider the following: X Company and Y Company acquire identical plant assets. Both use straight-line depreciation and the same economic lives for financial accounting, but X Company uses ACRS depreciation and Y Company uses straight-line depreciation for income tax purposes. Barring unusual circumstances, X Company is clearly "better off" than Y Company because X Company owes less income taxes *now* and will enjoy interest-free use of the funds arising from this tax postponement until the temporary differences reverse. This advantage exists regardless of whether the plant assets are replaced or whether the total investment in plant assets increases. Yet present income tax allocation requirements produce identical net incomes for both companies, and X Company's economic gain is disregarded.

However, this problem would not be resolved by not allocating income taxes. Nonallocation would show the entire deferral as income for X Company. However, in future years Y Company is able to deduct more depreciation than X Company from its taxable income with respect to these assets. To the extent that these future deductions have economic value, Y Company is "better off" than X Company; yet without income tax allocation this economic gain would be disregarded.

There is no easy solution. Clearly in this tax deferral example, X Company has gained an advantage of using "tax dollars" without paying interest. A reasonable measure of X Company's economic gain would at first seem to be the difference between the gross income tax deferral and its *discounted value*. This would be consistent with viewing the tax deferral as a long-term liability. But if the tax deferral is a liability, it is indeed a most unusual one. The "liability" is paid only if future taxable income is earned; it may be postponed indefinitely through the acquisition of more depreciable plant assets, or it may increase or decrease as Congress changes income tax rates. As a result, both the estimate of the amount to be paid and the selection of an appropriate interest rate for discounting this type of liability might be viewed as highly speculative.

From a standpoint of traditional financial accounting, whereby net income is viewed as the critical measure of management performance, discounting the deferred tax items might achieve greater "fairness" than do present interperiod tax allocation procedures. However, from a standpoint of stock market evaluation of earnings potential, there is increasing evidence that the critical factors are the *timeliness* and *completeness* of financial statement disclosures. Thus, the present interperiod tax allocation procedures may represent the best practical solution because they are simpler and more objective than discounting.

Issue 2: Comprehensive Allocation or Partial Allocation Assuming that interperiod tax allocation is to be required, should all or only a subset of temporary differences be considered? In an effort to find a compromise position in the arguments for and against interperiod tax allocation, some accountants have recommended *partial allocation* of timing differences. Supporters of partial interperiod tax allocation argue that when recurring differences between pre-tax accounting income and taxable income appear to cause an indefinite postponement of income tax payments, tax allocation is not required for such differences. For example, assume that Z Company, which has a growing investment in plant assets, uses straight-line depreciation for financial accounting and ACRS depreciation for income tax purposes. Under the partial allocation approach, the annual income taxes expense for Z Company would be the income tax actually paid each year.

Advocates of partial allocation thus assume that income taxes expense for financial accounting should be the income tax payable for each year, except for cases in which nonrecurring temporary differences between taxable income and pre-tax accounting income cause material misstatement of income taxes expense and net income. Such an exception is illustrated by the installment sale of an asset at a gain, which is recognized for financial accounting in the current year but is not taxable until future years when the cash proceeds are received.

The more widely accepted position is that all temporary differences between pre-tax accounting income and taxable income require *comprehensive allocation* of income taxes. Under comprehensive allocation, income taxes expense for a specific year includes all accruals, deferrals, and estimates necessary to adjust the income taxes actually payable for the year in order to recognize the tax effects of transactions included in pre-tax accounting income for that year. Tax effects of initial temporary differences are recognized and allocated to those years in which the initial differences *reverse*. Comprehensive allocation thus associates tax effects with related transactions as they are reported in the income statement.

Issue 3: Tax Rates and Disclosure Whether comprehensive allocation or partial allocation is required, the tax rates used in the allocation process and the method of disclosure of tax effects must be decided. Three approaches have been suggested:

1 *The deferred method* is an "income statement approach," and uses *tax rates in effect when the deferral of tax takes place* to compute the income tax effects of current temporary differences. Under this approach, the change in the deferred tax account is the product of the current tax rate and the temporary difference. For Valley Corporation, that tax effect in Year A is \$3 [= \$(50 − \$40)(0.30)]. No adjustment is made to the deferred tax account for subsequent changes in income tax rates.

The deferred method maintains that current tax rates are objective, emphasizes the income statement and the matching concept, and deemphasizes consideration of the true value of liabilities.

2 *The liability method* is a "balance sheet" approach and uses currently enacted tax rates and rates in effect when the temporary differences reverse to compute the income tax effect of temporary differences. When tax rates change, the deferred tax account is adjusted to reflect the current tax rate. For example, if the tax rate were increased to 40% during Year B, Valley Corporation would increase the deferred income tax account to \$4 [= (0.40 − 0.30) (\$10 temporary difference)]. The advantage of the liability method is that the deferred tax liability is a better measure of the future liability as it reflects the tax rate in effect at the time of reversal.

3 *The net-of-tax method* views the income tax effects of temporary differences as *valuation* accounts associated with the related assets and liabilities causing the temporary differences. In Valley's case, the \$3 deferral of tax in Year A would be deducted from the property being depreciated, in the form of a valuation account, on the balance sheet. Income tax expense in Year A exceeds the tax liability by \$3 because of the extra amount of depreciation deducted for tax purposes. Therefore the \$3 represents the reduction in *future* tax deductibility of the asset, and therefore its value. Hence the reduction from the asset account. The advantage of this approach is to associate tax effects with the assets and liabilities that produce them. This is somewhat similar to intraperiod tax allocation of tax effects.

Current Generally Accepted Accounting Principles and Rationale

The above discussion of issues and their possible outcomes represents a sample of the questions the FASB considered in its deliberations on *Statement of Financial Accounting Standards No. 96*. It chose to require *comprehensive interperiod tax allocation,* applied through the use of the *liability* method. In essence, the matching concept is to be applied to the measurement of income tax consequences, subject to the constraints of the *Statement of Financial Accounting Concepts No. 6* definitions of asset and liability.[4] Adjustments to the deferred tax accounts are required when tax rates change.

The objective of accounting for income taxes in *Statement No. 96* is to recognize the current tax payable, and the deferred taxes payable or refundable in future periods, as of the date of the balance sheet, which resulted from events recognized in the financial statements. The tax effects are measured by enacted tax laws.

All temporary differences are considered, and current tax rates and rates in effect when differences reverse are used to calculate the deferred tax accounts. In this way the income tax consequences of events are recognized in the same reporting period as the underlying events that caused them, as measured by the financial accounting system. The assumption is made that there will be future recovery and settlement of the reported amounts of tax assets and tax liabilities, respectively.

The tax consequences of temporary differences that will result in net *taxable* amounts in future years meet the three aspects of the *Statement of Financial Accounting Concepts No. 6* definition of a liability (*probable, future sacrifice, resulting from past transactions or events*). They are probable future sacrifices because the tax will have to be paid in the future, and are the result of past events creating the temporary differences. In these cases, a deferred tax *liability* will be recognized to record these future tax consequences in the current period.

The tax consequences of temporary differences that will result in net *deductible* amounts in the future and *that may be carried back* to the current or prior periods resulting in a refund of taxes meet the three aspects of the *Statement No. 6* definition of an asset (*probable future benefit, controlled by entity, resulting from past transactions or events*). They are probable benefits exclusively controlled by the entity that must have earned taxable income in the current or past periods for the benefit to exist. In these cases a deferred tax asset is recorded to reflect the future tax consequences.

However, net deductible amounts that must be carried forward to obtain a future benefit do not establish deferred tax assets in the current period because future income must be assumed. Future income is not a past event or transaction. It may contribute, however, to the recording of tax assets in future years.

In no case is future income assumed in the measurement of deferred tax assets and liabilities. The future taxable and deductible items resulting from temporary differences are assumed to be the only items affecting tax liability in future years.

Some accountants consider the *FASB Statement No. 96* limitation of tax asset recognition to net deductible amounts that can be carried back to prior or current years inconsistent with the measurement of deferred tax liabilities. The FASB's rationale for their position is that net taxable amounts always result in tax payments under the tax law, but deductible amounts result in tax benefits only if they reduce present or past taxable amounts. Deductible amounts that do not reduce taxes other-

---

[4] *Statement of Financial Accounting Concepts No. 6,* "Elements of Financial Statements," FASB (Stamford: 1985), par. 25: "Assets are probable future economic benefits obtained or controlled by a particular entity as a result of past transactions or events"; and par. 35: "Liabilities are probable future sacrifices of economic benefits arising from present obligations of a particular entity to transfer assets or provide services to other entities in the future as a result of past transactions or events."

wise paid or payable are a loss carryforward. Without future income, there is no benefit for these deductible amounts.

The current distinction between the measurement of deferred tax assets and liabilities is a major departure from previous accounting rules. Under *APB Opinion No. 11,* the deferred tax account change could be calculated from the current year's aggregate temporary difference, and the beginning balance of the account. Now, under *FASB Statement No. 96, future* temporary differences are analyzed to determine the account change. In certain cases, assets that would have been recognized under the old rules are not recognized under the new rules.

For example, assume that in Year A a company's only temporary difference is warranty expense. Accounting recognizes $2,000 warranty expense in Year A, and the tax return will recognize no expense until Year E, the year the claim is expected. Under *APB Opinion No. 11,* a $600 deferred tax asset would be recognized assuming a 30% tax rate. This asset represented accounting's recognition of the tax deduction in Year A, the year the expense is recognized. The asset would be extinguished in Year E when the tax law recognizes the deduction. *Now, under FASB Statement No. 96,* no deferred tax asset would be recognized in Year A because the deductible amount from Year E cannot be carried back to Year A. The law allows at most a three-year carryback period. Interperiod tax allocation is therefore more constrained by the currently accepted definitions of assets and liabilities.

The assumption that the future revenues, expenses, gains, and losses contributing to the future temporary differences are the *only* taxable or deductible items in those years is important. For example, at the end of Year B for a company, the only temporary difference that remains is a revenue item expected in Year C. Accounting revenue is expected to be $2,000, and taxable revenue is expected to be $3,000. With a 30% tax rate, the end-of-year deferred tax liability is therefore $300. *If no other* transactions occur in Year C, the Year C tax return will reflect a $900 tax liability whereas the income tax expense would be $600, and the $300 deferred tax "liability" is therefore extinguished.

If the situation were reversed ($3,000 accounting revenue and $2,000 tax revenue expected), and no other transactions occurred in Year C, the tax return would reflect a $600 tax liability and income tax expense would be $900. The deferred tax asset is therefore extinguished. In both these examples, no assumptions of positive future income (beyond the expected temporary differences) were made.

Balance Sheet Classification, Income Tax Expense, and Tax Rate Changes

The deferred tax asset and liability are classified as current or long term according to the expected year in which net deductible or net taxable amounts will be realized. In Valley Corporation's case, the $3 deferred tax liability would be classified as a current liability at the end of Year A, as the entire balance is expected to be reversed the next year. Had a portion of the $3 not been expected to reverse until after the end of Year B, that part would have been classified in the long-term category. If the temporary difference is related to an asset or liability classified as current due to an operating cycle exceeding a year, the portion of the deferred tax attributable to this item is also classified as current.[5] At most, four different deferred tax accounts are possible: current and long-term assets and liabilities.

Once deferred tax assets or liabilities are measured, *income tax expense* is determined by the necessary change in deferred tax asset or liability, and the tax liability (or refund) for the period. This expense must be allocated among income from continuing operations, discontinued operations, extraordinary items, prior period adjustments, and cumulative effects of accounting principles.

The most current tax rates and laws are used to measure deferred tax liabilities and assets. These tax rates are the best estimates of the tax rates in effect during the reversal periods. As tax rates and laws change in the future, the change in estimate is recorded as an adjustment to the beginning balance of the deferred tax asset or liability. The adjustment is the amount necessary to restate the tax assets or liabilities to the balance computed under the new rates. An ordinary gain or loss is recognized on the adjustment.

Steps in Measuring Deferred Assets and Liabilities, and Disclosure

FASB Statement No. 96 requires that the deferred tax amounts be determined as if a tax return were prepared for the net amount of temporary differences resulting in net taxable or net deductible amounts in future years. The deferred account at the close of the reporting period will indicate the tax payable or refundable in future years as a result of tax consequences of events recognized in current or preceding years. The following are the general steps for determining income tax expense and the change in the deferred account(s) at the end of a fiscal year. These steps do not include consideration of tax loss carryforwards and carrybacks. The latter are discussed in a later section.

1   Determine the temporary differences expected in each *future* year.

2   Determine whether there is a net *taxable* amount from temporary differences (taxable income exceeds pre-tax accounting income) or a net *deductible* amount (taxable income is less than pre-tax accounting income) in each future year.

3   Carry back (three years at most) or forward (15 years at most) net deductible amounts in those future years to offset net taxable amounts in the following order: (a) current or previous years, (b) years previous to the year of the net deductible amount, and then (c) years after the year of the net deductible amount.

4   The required ending balance of a deferred tax asset is the tax benefit of any net deductible amounts that can be carried back to the current or previous years. If a balance exists in the deferred tax account, adjust it to this required ending balance.

---

[5] If a temporary difference cannot be attributable to a particular asset or liability but other related assets and liabilities are classified as current because of an operating cycle exceeding one year, then the tax effect of that temporary difference is also classified as current. Examples are financial accounting's use of percentage of completion for long-term construction contracts when the completed-contract method is used for tax purposes. Also, organization costs may create a deferred tax liability or asset. In both of these examples, there may be no related asset or liability for financial accounting.

5   Net deductible amounts that remain after step 3 that cannot be brought back to current or prior years do not become tax assets but rather must wait to be used in future years.

6   Calculate the amount of tax on any remaining net taxable amounts using present tax rates. The resulting future payable is the required ending balance of the deferred tax liability. If a balance exists in the deferred tax account, adjust it to this required ending balance.

7   The income tax expense account (or income tax benefit account) is the balancing value given the required adjustments in the deferred tax asset and/or liability account, and the current tax payable or receivable.

The following must be disclosed for each set of financial statements:

1   Current income tax expense or benefit (penalties and interest are not components of income tax expense)

2   The deferred income tax balance

3   Investment tax credits

4   Government grants to the extent recognized as a reduction of income tax expense

5   The benefits of operating loss carryforwards

6   Adjustments of a deferred tax asset or liability or asset for enacted changes in tax laws[6]

In addition, the reported amount of income tax from continuing operations should be reconciled to the amount of income tax expense that would have resulted from the statutory tax rate applied to income from continuing operations before tax. The difference between these two figures results mainly from permanent differences and tax credits. An example is provided in the next section.

The basic accounting principles and sequence of steps for interperiod tax allocation are best illustrated with numerical examples. The following examples build progressively more complex situations to characterize the currently accepted interperiod tax allocation process.

Examples to Illustrate Current Accounting Principles, and Further Discussion

The examples in this chapter employ a short tax-planning horizon for ease of illustration. Although longer horizons are common in practice, because of longer depreciation schedules and other financial accounting and tax code provisions, the measurement and disclosure principles are independent of the length of the planning horizon. The tax rate in all examples is 0.30.

---

[6]*FASB Statement of Financial Accounting Standards No. 96*, par. 27.

Example 1: One Temporary Difference, Deferred Liability Nicole Corporation began operations in Year A and purchased a $16,000 asset to be depreciated over the next four years for tax and accounting purposes as follows:

Year	A	B	C	D
Accounting	$ 4,000	$4,000	$4,000	$4,000
Tax	10,000	3,000	2,000	1,000

The tax depreciation pattern is exaggerated for purposes of the example. Nicole's taxable income is $20,000 in Years A–D. Depreciation is the only difference between the two systems. The future temporary difference schedule follows.

Year A schedule of future taxable amounts

Year	B	C	D
Accounting depreciation	$4,000	$4,000	$4,000
Tax depreciation	3,000	2,000	1,000
Taxable amount	$1,000	$2,000	$3,000
Tax rate	0.30	0.30	0.30
Deferred tax liability	$ 300	$ 600	$ 900

Sum of deferred tax liability amounts: $1,800

Tax accrual entry for Dec. 31, Year A

```
Income Taxes Expense ....................  7,800
    Deferred Income Taxes ..............        1,800
    Income Taxes Payable ..............        6,000   [= ($20,000)(0.30)]
```

Only years *after* Year A are presented in the table, as those are the only temporary differences that will cause *future* tax consequences. The deferred tax liability represents $1,800 of taxes payable in future years, in excess of the income tax expense that will be recognized by accounting. In Year A, accounting recognized $1,800 income tax in excess of the amount payable. This excess is the "deferred" amount payable in future years.

The taxable amount row in the schedule represents the amount by which taxable income will exceed pre-tax accounting income in future years. Tax payments in excess of Income Taxes Expense will be required in those years. Although Year A resulted in lower tax payments than Income Taxes Expense, this difference will reverse in the remaining three years of the example. An amount $300 of the $1,800 is a current liability since it is expected to reverse within one year. The remainder is classified as a long-term liability.

The Year A income statement shows the following:

NICOLE CORPORATION
Partial Income Statement
For the Year Ended December 31, Year A

Net income before tax		$26,000*
Income taxes expense		
Payable currently...	$6,000	
Deferred...	1,800	7,800
Net income		$18,200

*Taxable income ($20,000) + depreciation difference ($6,000)

The entry for Year B would be derived using the same analysis. The schedule would be the same except that Year B would not be present. The new sum of Deferred Liability amounts would be only $1,500. That is the necessary balance at the end of Year B. Therefore, the Deferred Income Taxes account should be reduced by $300 to adjust it to the new amount of expected future tax payments. This is the "reversal" aspect of interperiod tax allocation.

Tax accrual entry for Dec. 31, Year B		
Income Taxes Expense 5,700		
Deferred Income Taxes 300		
Income Taxes Payable	6,000	

Continuing the process would result in four years of $6,000 Income Taxes Payable ($24,000) and the following four amounts of Income Taxes Expense: $7,800 + $5,700 + $5,400 + $5,100 = $24,000.

The tax code requires that installment payments of the estimated annual tax liability be paid during the year. For ease of illustration, we assume that taxes are paid in one installment after the end of each tax year. This assumption does not affect the measurement of the deferred tax accounts or income tax expense. In addition, the above examples and those that follow employ a single tax rate. The tax code imposes a graduated rate schedule with rates that increase with taxable income. However, large corporations quickly reach the highest tax bracket and may use the highest marginal rate for the measurement of deferred tax accounts. Other corporations that do not reach the highest the rate quickly may use an average tax rate expected to be applicable to each future year in the schedule.

Management must make certain estimates of the future events that will affect the measurement of deferred tax accounts. These events include the timing of receipts and payments of revenues and expenses, and the timing of asset dispositions.

These tax-planning strategies structure future years' schedules of tax consequences. In general, strategies will attempt to reduce taxes payable or increase the benefit of net deductible amounts. For example, a tax-planning strategy could attempt to accelerate taxable amounts to years of a tax loss carryforward. Reasonable estimates are allowed. However, *FASB Statement No. 96* requires that any tax-planning strategy should (1) be within the control of management, (2) be in agreement with existing tax laws, (3) not involve significant implementation cost, and (4) be in agreement with financial accounting assumptions critical to the underlying asset or liability. These requirements constrain the measurement of deferred tax accounts to reasonable expectations of future events. Future income is not an event that may be assumed.

Example 2: Multiple Temporary Differences, and a Permanent Difference
Assume the same facts as in Example 1 and two additional considerations. (a) Nicole performed consulting services in Year A for a client who will pay on the following installment basis:

Year	Installment Payment
A	$ 0
B	500
C	1,000
D	1,500

The revenue from the consulting contract is recognized as accounting income in Year A, since the work is finished and receipt of billing is reasonably assured. (b) Nicole also recognized $3,000 of cost depletion in accounting income and $8,000 percentage depletion on its tax return. The temporary difference schedule follows.

Year A schedule of future taxable amounts

Year	B	C	D
Accounting depreciation	$4,000	$4,000	$4,000
Accounting consulting revenue	-0-	-0-	-0-
Net decrease in accounting income	$4,000	$4,000	$4,000
Tax depreciation	$3,000	$2,000	$1,000
Tax consulting revenue	500	1,000	1,500
Net decrease in taxable income	$2,500	$1,000	$ (500)
Net taxable amount	$1,500	$3,000	$4,500
Tax rate	0.30	0.30	0.30
Deferred tax liability	$ 450	$ 900	$1,350

Sum of deferred tax liability amounts: $2,700

Note that the net taxable amount is similar to that in Example 1 except that two temporary differences must be considered. These are netted to determine the net taxable amount expected in the future. In Year B, for example, the accounting items result in a net ($4,000) effect on pre-tax accounting income whereas the tax items result in a net ($2,500) effect on taxable income. Therefore a net taxable amount of

$1,500 is expected, since taxable income will be reduced by a smaller amount than pre-tax accounting income. Considering all three years, there is a net taxable amount of $9,000 to be expected.

The $5,000 depletion difference is a permanent difference. Both the taxes payable and income taxes expense reflect the same tax consequence for this item, which in this case is $8,000 depletion. Income Taxes Expense will be determined by the Taxes Payable amount and the change in the Deferred Taxes account. Therefore Income Taxes Expense will automatically reflect tax depletion. Year A's pre-tax accounting income is $34,000 (= $20,000 + $6,000 depreciation difference + $3,000 consulting revenue difference + $5,000 depletion difference).

Tax accrual entry for Dec. 31, Year A

Income Taxes Expense 8,700		
Deferred Income Taxes		2,700
Income Taxes Payable		6,000

Here $450 of the $2,700 liability is classified as short-term and the remainder as long-term.

FASB Statement No. 96 (par. 62) allows the calculation of the required deferred taxes account balance to be based on the aggregate accumulated temporary differences on the balance sheet date, if such results are not materially different from those based on a complete schedule of future years' differences. For instance, the net temporary difference for Year A above is $9,000 (= $6,000 depreciation difference + $3,000 consulting revenue difference). This is equal to the sum of all future net temporary differences in the schedule ($9,000 = $1,500 + $3,000 + $4,500), which served as the basis for the required deferred taxes liability balance. For comprehensiveness, the remaining examples will continue to illustrate the entire future schedule. The end-of-chapter problems occasionally rely on the quicker aggregate calculation.

The reported income taxes expense on pre-tax accounting income from continuing operations must be reconciled to the amount *that would have resulted* from applying the tax rate to pre-tax income from continuing operations. Either percentages or dollar amounts may be used in the reconciliation. A major source of differences between these two amounts is permanent differences. In Example 2, the permanent difference (excess of percentage depletion over accounting depletion) caused the effective tax rate to decrease relative to the tax based solely on pre-tax accounting income. One possible footnote disclosure for this reconciliation follows.

NICOLE CORPORATION
Year A Reconciliation of Statutory and Effective Tax Rates

Statutory tax rate	0.30
Effect of excess of tax over accounting depletion..........................	(0.044)
Effective tax rate	0.256

[0.044 = $5,000(0.30)/$34,000]

The permanent difference effectively reduced the tax rate applicable to the $34,000 pre-tax accounting income because of the additional deduction not reflected in pre-tax accounting income. The effective tax rate is the ratio of reported income tax expense to pre-tax accounting income (in this case $8,700/$34,000 = 25.6%) and represents the tax rate recognized by the financial accounting system.

As mentioned previously, if tax rates change, the deferred taxes account must be adjusted and a gain or loss recognized. To illustrate the accounting for tax rate changes, assume that during Year B the rate was increased to 35%. The deferred taxes account is restated, as of January 1, Year B, to the amount reflecting the new tax rate. Using the Year A schedule of temporary differences, the required ending deferred account balance would be $3,150 [= (0.35)($1,500 + $3,000 + $4,500)]. A $450 (= $3,150 − $2,700) increase is therefore required. The original tax rate (0.30) was an estimate of the tax rate to be in effect at the time of the reversal. The adjustment is a change in estimate and requires current and prospective treatment. The required entry is:

As of Jan. 1, Year B

Loss on Adjustment of Deferred Income Taxes 450	
Deferred Income Taxes	450

The loss is ordinary and included in income from continuing operations. The Year B tax accrual entry would employ the new tax rate.

Example 3: Gain on Sale of Fully Tax-Depreciated Asset To illustrate another type of temporary difference, assume that Susan Corporation purchased a depreciable asset costing $100 with an estimated $10 salvage value at the beginning of Year C. The asset will be depreciated over its three-year useful life as follows:

Year	C	D	E
Accounting depreciation	$30	$30	$30
Tax depreciation	50	30	20

In this example there is no salvage value assumed for tax purposes. Any proceeds on the sale of a fully tax-depreciated asset is a taxable gain. No other tempo-

Year C schedule of future taxable amounts

Year	D	E
Accounting depreciation	$30	$30
Net decrease to accounting income	30	30
Tax depreciation	$30	$20
Tax gain on sale		10
Net decrease to taxable income	30	$10
Net taxable amount	-0-	$20
Tax rate		0.30
Deferred tax liability		$ 6

rary differences are expected, and there is no beginning deferred tax balance. Susan earned $200 of pre-tax accounting and taxable income before the depreciation amounts in Years C–E.

In Year E, taxable income will exceed pre-tax accounting income by $20, the sum of the $10 depreciation difference and the $10 gain on sale of the asset. The tax accrual entries follow.

Tax accrual entry for Dec. 31, Year C

Income Taxes Expense 51		
Deferred Income Taxes	6	
Income Taxes Payable	45	[= ($200 − $50)(0.30)]

Tax accrual entry for Dec. 31, Year D

Income Taxes Expense 51		
Income Taxes Payable	51	[=($200 − $30)(0.30)]

Tax accrual entry for Dec. 31, Year E

Income Taxes Expense 51		
Deferred Income Taxes 6		
Income Taxes Payable	57	[= ($200 − $20 + $10)(0.30)]

The long-term deferred income taxes liability on December 31, Year C, represents the excess of tax payments over the tax based on accounting income in years after Year C, and would be reclassified as a current liability on December 31, Year D.

Example 4. Net Deductible Amount That Cannot Be Carried Back to Current or Previous Years In the previous examples, each year in the future schedule was expected to produce a net taxable amount (taxable income > pre-tax accounting income). In this example, a future year produces a deductible amount (pre-tax accounting income > taxable income in a future year), which is treated as an ''operating loss'' for interperiod tax allocation purposes. The net deductible amount is first carried back to absorb earlier taxable amounts in the future year schedule, and then any excess is carried forward to absorb later taxable amounts in the future year schedule. Since future income cannot be assumed, no asset is recognized for unused portions of the ''carryforward.''

Marie Company was organized in Year A. It entered into two transactions that created temporary differences: (1) it extended a four-year warranty on a major sale during the year ($2,600 warranty expense was recognized for accounting); and (2) it purchased an asset costing $19,200 with a six-year life and no salvage value ($3,200 and $6,700 depreciation for accounting and tax, respectively, in Year A). The claim on the warranty is expected in Year E, the last year of warranty coverage, at which time it will be tax deductible. The estimated expenses for accounting and tax purposes for the remaining years are reflected in the following schedule:

Year A
schedule
of future
taxable
and
deductible
amounts

Year	B	C	D	E	F
Accounting warranty expense	-0-	-0-	-0-	-0-	-0-
Accounting depreciation	$3,200	$3,200	$3,200	$ 3,200	$3,200
Net decrease to accounting income	$3,200	$3,200	$3,200	$ 3,200	$3,200
Tax warranty deduction	-0-	-0-	-0-	$ 2,600	-0-
Tax depreciation	$3,000	$2,800	$2,500	$ 2,200	$2,000
Net decrease to taxable income	$3,000	$2,800	$2,500	$ 4,800	$2,000
Taxable amount	$ 200	$ 400	$ 700		$1,200
Deductible amount				$(1,600)	
"Loss" carryback	(200)	(400)	(700)	1,300	
"Loss" carryforward				300	(300)
Net taxable amount...................	0	0	0	0	900
Tax rate					0.30
Deferred tax liability					$ 270

The Year A tax accrual entry would include a $270 credit to the Deferred Income Taxes account, classified as a long-term liability. The $1,600 net deductible amount in Year E is the excess of pre-tax accounting income over taxable income resulting from $2,600 more warranty deduction for taxes and $1,000 less depreciation for taxes. Using the assumption that the future temporary differences are the only future taxable items, and the three-year carryback of operating loss provision, the $1,600 may be carried back to absorb the Years B–D taxable amounts. This leaves $300 to carry forward to absorb $300 of the $1,200 taxable amount in Year F. Had the carryforward amount been in excess of $1,200, there would be no deferred liability recognized in Year A, and the unused portion of the carryforward would not cause any further recognition in the accounts for Year A. This unused amount would be disclosed in the footnotes. It could, however, absorb new taxable amounts from temporary differences created after Year A.

Example 5: Deferred Tax Asset   This example is similar to Example 4 except that a deductible amount can be carried back to the current year. In Year A, Virginia Company reported $800 of taxable income, and the following expenses for accounting and tax:

	Accounting	Tax
Warranty (3-year) expense or deduction	$5,000	-0-
Depreciation expense or deduction	3,200	$6,700

The estimated future expense amounts for accounting and tax purposes are reflected in the following schedule:

Year A
schedule
of future
taxable
and
deductible
amounts

Year	A	B	C	D	E	F
Taxable income	$800					
Accounting warranty expense		-0-	-0-	-0-	-0-	-0-
Accounting depreciation		$3,200	$3,200	$ 3,200	$3,200	$3,200
Net decrease to accounting income		$3,200	$3,200	$ 3,200	$3,200	$3,200
Tax warranty expense		-0-	-0-	$ 5,000	-0-	-0-
Tax depreciation		$3,000	$2,800	2,500	$2,200	$2,000
Net decrease to taxable income		$3,000	$2,800	$ 7,500	$2,200	$2,000
Taxable amount		$ 200	$ 400		$1,000	$1,200
Deductible amount				$(4,300)		
"Loss" carryback	(800)	(200)	(400)	1,400		
"Loss" carryforward				2,900	(1,000)	(1,200)
Remaining "loss" carryforward						700

In this example the net deductible amount in Year D may be carried back to the current period. The three-year carryback period includes Year A and therefore creates a benefit to be realized after Year A but to be recognized in Year A. If depreciation and warranty expense are the only items reported for tax purposes in Year D, the resulting tax loss can be carried back to Year A and produce a refund. The $800 benefit of the carryback fulfills the *FASB Statement No. 6* definition of an asset as it is probable, under the control of the company, and solely a result of past transactions. The remaining $700 of the carryforward is not recognized in the accounts since future income is needed to secure benefit.

Tax accrual entry for
Dec. 31, Year A

Deferred Tax Benefit (Asset).... 240
    Income Taxes Payable ...   240   [= 0.30(800)]

This benefit will be reduced in future years when the warranty deduction is taken for tax purposes. Deferred Taxes (Asset) is classified as a long-term asset until December 31, Year C.

Example 6: Deferred Tax Asset and Liability This example illustrates a deferred asset and liability recognized in the same year, and their changes over three years. The Morris Corporation began Year B with no deferred taxes account. It purchased an asset that will be depreciated over five years according to the following schedule:

Year	B	C	D	E	F
Tax depreciation	$3,000	$2,000	$1,000	$ 800	$ 700
Accounting depreciation	1,500	1,500	1,500	1,500	1,500

During Years B through D, Morris earned $18,000 of taxable income. The Year B schedule of temporary differences follows.

Year B schedule of future taxable and deductible amounts

Year	B	C	D	E	F
Taxable income $18,000					
Taxable amount (depreciation difference) ...			$ 500	$ 700	$ 800
Deductible amount (depreciation difference) ...		$(500)			
"Loss" carryback	(500)	500			
Net taxable amounts		-0-	$ 500	$ 700	$ 800
Tax rate			0.30	0.30	0.30
Deferred tax liability			$ 150	$ 210	$ 240

Tax accrual entry for Dec. 31, Year B

Income Taxes Expense 5,850			
Deferred Tax Benefit.................. 150		[= $500(0.30)]	
Deferred Income Taxes	600	[= $150 + $210 + $240]	
Income Taxes Payable	5,400	[= $18,000(0.30)]	

Tax accrual entry for Dec. 31, Year C

Income Taxes Expense 5,550			
Deferred Tax Benefit...................	150	[to close]	
Income Taxes Payable	5,400	[= $18,000(0.30)]	

Tax accrual entry for Dec. 31, Year D

Income Taxes Expense 5,250			
Deferred Income Taxes 150		[= $600 − ($210 + $240)]	
Income Taxes Payable	5,400	[= $18,000(0.30)]	

The deferred tax asset recognized in Year B represents the "prepayment" of $150 tax in Year B relative to the accounting income tax expense recognized (accounting depreciation in Year C will be less than tax depreciation). At the end of Year C the benefit is exhausted, as there are no future years for which accounting pre-tax income exceeds taxable income because of expected temporary differences. The deferred tax liability reflects any future taxable amounts remaining after the net deductible amounts have been exhausted.

Recapitulation: Steps in Interperiod Tax Allocation

The previous six examples show that the net deductible amounts in any future year first should be carried back (three years at most) and then any unused portion carried forward, before net taxable amounts are considered. Any carryforward of a net deductible amount unused after exhausting all future taxable amounts causes no further recognition of benefits in the accounts for the current year. Any taxable amounts remaining after all net deductible amounts have been exhausted support the recognition of a deferred tax liability.

Federal tax law subjects corporations to an "alternative minimum tax" (AMT). The corporation pays the higher of the AMT and the normally computed tax. The measurement of deferred tax accounts and income tax expense is based on the two tax computations. The pattern of temporary differences may be different between the two systems, but the same assumptions and tax strategies are used. Because knowledge of the AMT is not assumed, it is not discussed further in this chapter.

The general steps discussed previously for the measurement of deferred tax accounts and income tax expense do not consider *tax loss operating carrybacks and carryforwards.* The next section discusses this problem, the measurement of benefits from these items, and financial accounting disclosure.

TAX LOSS OPERATING CARRYBACKS AND CARRYFORWARDS: GENERALLY ACCEPTED ACCOUNTING PRINCIPLES

As previously discussed, a corporation with negative taxable income can apply that loss to previous and future years to reduce taxes paid or a future tax liability. The major accounting questions in this area concern the timing and measurement of benefit recognition. The generally accepted accounting principles for these issues follow.

1 A loss *carryback* creates a benefit in the year of the loss if taxes in the previous three years have been paid. The benefit is not contingent on any future event. This benefit is recognized in the loss year as a current receivable and a gain that increases pre-tax accounting income (which is not necessarily a loss). The amount of the benefit to be recorded is limited by the taxes paid in the previous three years. If the operating loss exceeds total taxable income in the previous three years, the remaining unused loss is carried forward.

A loss carryback does not interact with future temporary differences, as no benefit exists beyond the year of loss. Therefore the deferred tax accounts are not affected by the loss carryback.

2 **a** A loss *carryforward* creates a benefit recognized in the loss year *only to the extent of future taxable amounts* in the future year schedule. The loss carryforward is similar to a net deductible amount that cannot be carried back to current or previous years. It reduces future taxable amounts. As such, it reduces the required deferred tax liability and the accounting loss (or increases accounting income). The amount of the carryforward in excess of such taxable amounts (such as remaining net deductible amounts that cannot be carried back to current or previous years) is not recognized until it can be used to offset future taxable amounts.

b The benefit of the carryforward is *realized* in profitable years after the loss.

In those years, the carryforward reduces the tax liability and income tax expense by the tax reduction it provides.

The amounts and expiration dates of unused carrybacks and carryforwards should be disclosed in the footnotes.

The accounting for operating loss carrybacks and carryforwards is based on the same underlying concepts used in interperiod tax allocation. The nature of the resulting benefits, and their measurement, is similar for both types of tax consequences. The assumption of future income is not employed in the measurement of those benefits. Benefits can be recognized only when assured. The next three examples illustrate current accounting principles for tax operating loss carrybacks and carryforwards, and their interaction with future temporary differences.

Example 7: Operating Loss Carryback Refer back to the discussion of the Thomas Company, whose taxable income history is repeated below:

THOMAS COMPANY
Taxable Income History

Year	Taxable income
A	$ 1,000
B	2,000
C	3,500
D	4,000
E	(11,000)
F	500
G	2,500

Assume that Thomas anticipates no temporary differences and chooses the carryback-carryforward option in Year E, the year of the loss. The entry to recognize the refund is:

Tax accrual entry for Dec. 31, Year E

Income Tax Refund Receivable 2,850		
Income Tax Operating Loss Carryback Credit	2,850	

The receivable is a current asset, and the income tax operating loss carryback credit is a gain. Year A is not considered because it is outside the three-year carryback period. Of the loss, $1,500 remains to carry forward to Year F. The $2,850 is a refund of taxes paid in previous years. The latter portion of the Year E income statement would appear as follows:

THOMAS COMPANY
Partial Income Statement
For Year Ended December 31, E

Income from continuing operations before taxes .... $(11,000)
Income tax operating loss carryback credit   2,850
Net loss .... $ 8,150

Example 8: Operating Loss Carryforward, No Temporary Differences In this case, no benefit can be recognized for accounting purposes until the future income is recognized. Continuing from Example 7, in Year F the remaining $1,500 loss is carried forward to absorb the $500 income. The Year F entry is:

Income Tax Expense 150   [= $500(0.30)]
    Income Tax Operating Loss Carryforward Credit...   150

The Income Tax Operating Loss Carryforward Credit account is a gain and is treated as a reduction of income tax expense on the income statement. The latter portion of the Year F income statement would appear as follows:

Income from continuing operations before taxes $500
Income taxes expense .... $ 150
Income tax operating loss carryforward credit ....   (150)   -0-
Net income $500

In Year G, only $1,000 of the loss remains to carry forward. The Year G entry is:

Income Taxes Expense 750
    Income Tax Operating Loss Carryforward Credit.................   300
    Income Taxes Payable   450
    [$750 = 0.30($2,500)]
    [$300 = 0.30($1,000)]
    [$450 = ($2,500 − $1,000)(0.30)]

The latter portion of the Year G income statement would appear as follows:

Income from continuing operations before taxes $2,500
Income taxes expense .... $ 750
Income tax operating loss carryforward credit ....   (300)   (450)
Net income $2,050

Example 9: Tax Operating Losses and Temporary Differences   The previous two examples illustrated the basic accounting for tax operating losses. When future taxable differences exist, an operating loss carryforward creates a benefit by absorbing some or all of those future taxable amounts, reducing the necessary deferred tax liability balance. This example illustrates the interaction of temporary differences and operating losses.

Patricia Corporation began operations in Year A. Following is its taxable income history and a schedule of net temporary differences (all causing taxable differences).

PATRICIA CORPORATION
Taxable Income History and Temporary Differences

Year	Taxable income	Net temporary difference (causing future taxable income to exceed pre-tax accounting income)*
A	$ 70,000	$ 3,000
B	30,000	8,000
C	(120,000)	10,000
D	10,000	4,000
E	30,000	6,000

*For example, the temporary difference in Year A will cause future taxable income to exceed pre-tax accounting income. This means that Year A pre-tax accounting income exceeds taxable income by $3,000.

For simplicity, the deferred tax account will be calculated from the aggregate temporary difference on each balance sheet date. Following is Patricia Corporation's schedule of income taxes payable and schedule of deferred tax liability.

PATRICIA CORPORATION
Schedule of Income Taxes Payable

Year	Amount of operating loss carried: Back	Amount of operating loss carried: Forward	Income taxes payable (receivable)
A			$ 21,000*
B			9,000*
C	$100,000		(30,000)†
D		$10,000	-0-‡
E		10,000	6,000§

*30% (taxable income)
†Refund of taxes paid in Years A and B from operating loss carryforward.
‡No taxes are paid due to the carryforward of $10,000 loss to absorb Year D taxable income.
§Carryforward of remaining $10,000 loss leaves $20,000 income to be taxed [$6,000 = 0.30($20,000)].

PATRICIA CORPORATION
Schedule of Deferred Tax Liability

Year	Aggregate temporary difference (future taxable amount) Beginning	Increase	Ending	Future operating loss carryforward	Deferred tax liability ending balance
A	-0-	$ 3,000	$ 3,000		$ 900*
B	$ 3,000	8,000	11,000		3,300*
C	11,000	10,000	21,000	$20,000†	300‡
D	21,000	4,000	25,000	10,000†	4,500§
E	25,000	6,000	31,000		9,300*

*30% (ending aggregate temporary difference)
† The amount of the remaining operating loss carryforward at the end of the year (see the schedule of income taxes payable)
‡30% ($21,000 future taxable amount − $20,000 future deductible amount)
§30% ($25,000 future taxable amount − $10,000 future deductible amount)

Operating loss carrybacks do not interact with future temporary differences, because no benefit exists beyond the loss year. Operating loss carryforwards, on the other hand, do not provide benefit *until future income occurs,* and therefore interact with future taxable amounts. At the end of Year C, $20,000 remains of the operating loss carryforward after carrying back $10,000 of the loss. This is used to offset $20,000 of the future taxable amount resulting from the aggregate temporary difference. Had the remaining loss carryforward exceeded $21,000, there would be no further recognition of benefit at December 31, Year C. A current deferred tax *benefit* cannot be generated from carryforwards.

At the end of Year D, only $10,000 of the loss remains to carry forward, as $10,000 was used to absorb Year D's taxable income. *Then,* at the end of Year E, no more loss remains, because it was used to absorb *taxable* income. Therefore the operating loss disappears from the schedule.

The following entries would be made for Years A–E and reflect the previous schedules:

Entry on Dec. 31, Year A

Income Taxes Expense 21,900		
Deferred Income Taxes		900
Income Taxes Payable....................................		21,000

Entry on Dec. 31, Year B

Income Taxes Expense 11,400		
Deferred Income Taxes		2,400
Income Taxes Payable....................................		9,000

Entry on Dec. 31,
Year C

Income Tax Refund Receivable 30,000	
Deferred Income Taxes 3,000	
Income Tax Operating Loss Carryback Credit	30,000
Income Tax Operating Loss Carryforward Credit..........	3,000

Entry on Dec. 31,
Year D

Income Taxes Expense 7,200	
Deferred Income Taxes	4,200
Income Tax Operating Loss Carryforward Credit.............	3,000

Entry on Dec. 31,
Year E

Income Taxes Expense 13,800	
Deferred Income Taxes	4,800
Income Tax Operating Loss Carryforward Credit............	3,000
Income Taxes Payable	6,000

The changes in the Deferred Income Taxes account are derived from the schedule of deferred tax liability. For example, the $3,000 reduction (debit) in Year C is the difference between the beginning balance ($3,300) and the required ending balance ($300). The Year C income statement would reflect the following.

PATRICIA CORPORATION
Partial Income Statement
For Year Ended December 31, Year C

Income from continuing operations before taxes		$(110,000)*
Income tax operating loss carryback credit	30,000	
Income tax operating loss carryforward credit	3,000	33,000
Net Loss		77,000

*Year C created a temporary difference causing future taxable income to exceed pre-tax accounting income. Therefore, in Year C, pre-tax accounting income must exceed taxable income by that amount.

INTRAPERIOD TAX ALLOCATION

The need for tax allocation within an accounting period (also known as *intraperiod tax allocation*) arises, for example, when extraordinary items are included in net income or a prior period adjustment is recorded in the current period. If extraordinary items and prior period adjustments are taxable or are deductible for income tax purposes, income taxes (or tax refunds) are apportioned among income before extraordinary items and prior period adjustments. Income taxes applicable to income before extraordinary items are based on the difference between revenue and expenses before giving effect to the income tax consequences of extraordinary items. Extraordinary items and prior period adjustments are reported *net* of the income tax effect in the income statement and the statement of retained earnings, respectively.

Extraordinary Gain and Prior Period Adjustment

To illustrate a situation involving an extraordinary gain and a prior period adjustment, assume that Marvin Company reported the following for Year 4:

Data for illustration

Income before income taxes (fully taxable at 45%)	*$300,000*
Extraordinary gain (taxable at 30%)	*800,000*
Prior period adjustment—increase in earnings for Year 1 as a result of an error (fully taxable at 45%)	*200,000*

The presentation of these items by Marvin Company in its Year 4 income statement and statement of retained earnings with and without intraperiod tax allocation is shown below.

Presentation of extraordinary gain and prior period adjustment with and without intraperiod tax allocation

	With intraperiod tax allocation	*Without intraperiod tax allocation*
Income statement:		
Income before income taxes	$300,000	$ 300,000
Income taxes expense	135,000	465,000*
Income (loss) before extraordinary item	$165,000	$(165,000)
Extraordinary item (gain):		
With tax allocation [$800,000 −		
($800,000 × 0.30)]	560,000	
Without tax allocation		800,000
Net income	$725,000	$ 635,000
Statement of retained earnings:		
Increase in beginning balance of retained earnings (prior period adjustment)	$110,000†	$ 200,000

*Income taxes expense ($300,000 × 0.45)	$135,000
Tax on extraordinary gain ($800,000 × 0.30)	240,000
Tax on prior period adjustment ($200,000 × 0.45)	90,000
Income taxes payable currently	$465,000
†$200,000 − ($200,000 × 0.45)	$110,000

Failure to apply intraperiod tax allocation procedures by Marvin Company distorts its income statement and also understates its net income by $90,000

($725,000 − $635,000 = $90,000), the income tax effect of the prior period adjustment, which is included in the statement of retained earnings.

Assuming that the extraordinary gain and the prior period adjustment already had been recorded in appropriate ledger accounts (before recognition of the income tax effects), income taxes for Year 4, with intraperiod tax allocation, are recorded by Marvin Company as illustrated below:

<table>
<tr><td>*Income Taxes Expense* ....</td><td>*135,000*</td><td></td></tr>
<tr><td>*Extraordinary Item—Gain (income tax effect)* ....</td><td>*240,000*</td><td></td></tr>
<tr><td>*Retained Earnings (income tax effect of prior*</td><td></td><td></td></tr>
<tr><td>   *period adjustment)* ....</td><td>*90,000*</td><td></td></tr>
<tr><td>   *Income Taxes Payable* ....</td><td></td><td>*465,000*</td></tr>
<tr><td colspan="3">*To record income tax effects of operating income, extra-*</td></tr>
<tr><td colspan="3">*ordinary item (gain), and prior period adjustment (correction*</td></tr>
<tr><td colspan="3">*of error).*</td></tr>
</table>

Journal entry for intraperiod tax allocation to extraordinary gain and to prior period adjustment

Extraordinary Loss

To illustrate a situation involving an extraordinary loss, assume that in Year 5 Marvin Company reported pre-tax accounting income of $600,000 and incurred a fully deductible extraordinary loss of $500,000. The income tax rate is 45%, and the liability for income taxes is $45,000 ($100,000 × 0.45 = $45,000). The comparative summary below shows how Marvin's income statement appears with and without intraperiod tax allocation:

Presentation of extraordinary loss with and without intraperiod tax allocation

	With intraperiod tax allocation	Without intraperiod tax allocation
Income before income taxes...............	$600,000	$600,000
Income taxes expense	270,000	45,000
Income before extraordinary item	$330,000	$555,000
Extraordinary item (loss):		
With intraperiod tax allocation		
[$500,000 − ($500,000 × 0.45)]	275,000	
Without intraperiod tax allocation		500,000
Net income	$ 55,000	$ 55,000

The greater clarity obtained with intraperiod tax allocation is apparent. This presentation shows the after-tax effect of the extraordinary loss and the normal impact of income taxes on income before income taxes. If intraperiod tax allocation is not used, users of the income statement will question the relationship between the pre-tax accounting income of $600,000 and the disproportionately low income taxes expense of $45,000. Without intraperiod tax allocation, both the amount of income before extraordinary item and the amount of the extraordinary item (loss) are overstated by $225,000 ($500,000 × 0.45 = $225,000), the tax effect of the extraordinary item (loss). With intraperiod tax allocation, income taxes are recorded as follows:

Journal entry for
intraperiod tax
allocation to
extraordinary loss

Income Taxes Expense ($600,000 × 0.45) 270,000		
Extraordinary Item—Loss (income tax effect)		225,000
Income Taxes Payable		45,000
To record income tax effects on pre-tax income and extra-		
ordinary item (loss).		

Because we have assumed that the loss of $500,000 had already been recorded in the Extraordinary Item–Loss ledger account, the income tax effect of $225,000 is recorded as a credit (an offset) in the Extraordinary Item–Loss account. It would be possible to record the income tax effect in a separate ledger account. In either case, the extraordinary loss is reported in the income statement net of income taxes, that is, at $275,000, with appropriate disclosure of the current income tax liability and the income tax effect of the loss.

Intraperiod tax allocation is an effort to match income taxes (or tax credits) with special items such as extraordinary gains and losses and prior period adjustments. In this way, such items are reported net of income taxes; that is, at amounts representing the net *economic impact* of such items. Other situations requiring intraperiod income tax allocation include recognition of the cumulative effect of a change in accounting principle and reporting the results (including any gain or loss on disposal) if a discontinued business segment. Treatment of these items is similar to the treatment of extraordinary items and is discussed in Chapters 3 and 22.

Temporary differences do not complicate intraperiod tax allocation unless an item requiring intraperiod allocation causes a temporary difference. In this case, the temporary difference is grouped with the others in the determination of the deferred tax account change. Otherwise, the change in the deferred account is calculated in the normal fashion, as is the income tax payable. The highest marginal rate applicable to the firm is generally used to calculate the tax effects of the items that require intraperiod allocation. Income tax expense is the final value and is determined by the others in the tax accrual entry. The lower marginal rates are generally applied to income from continuing operations.

For example, the following information was derived from Griswold Corporation for Year F:

GRISWOLD CORPORATION
Income Statement Information
For Year Ended December 31, Year F

Before-tax items (all credit balances)

Income from continuing operations	$100,000
Extraordinary gain	10,000
Cumulative effect of change in accounting	20,000
Prior period adjustment	30,000
Deferred tax liability, Jan. 1, Year F	10,000
Deferred tax liability, Dec. 31, Year F	14,000

Tax rates:

15% on first $25,000 of taxable income

30% on taxable income in excess of $25,000

Griswold's tax accrual entry follows.

Income Taxes Expense 30,250		
Extraordinary Gain. 3,000		[$10,000(0.30)]
Cumulative Effect. 6,000		[$20,000(0.30)]
Retained Earnings 9,000		[$30,000(0.30)]
Deferred Income Taxes	4,000	[$14,000 − $10,000]
Income Taxes Payable	44,250	

[$44,250 = 0.15($25,000) + 0.30($100,000 + $10,000 + $20,000 + $30,000 − $25,000)]

OTHER TAX ACCOUNTING TOPICS

The primary focus of our discussion thus far has been on accounting for interperiod and intraperiod income tax allocation. Accounting for income taxes is complicated by the need to measure income taxes expense for interim periods and by many technical tax laws relating to tax credits designed, for example, to stimulate domestic and foreign investments, to create jobs, and to encourage common stock ownership by employees. Also, the purchase and sale of income tax benefits (investment tax credits and depreciation deductions, for example) may create difficult financial accounting problems.

The accounting for the investment tax credit and the allocation of income taxes to interim periods are discussed in the remaining pages of this chapter.

Investment Tax Credit

As stated in Chapter 11, either the *flow-through method* or the *deferral method* may be used to account for the investment tax credit (ITC).[7] Prior to the 1986 Tax Reform Act, tax law permitted taxpayers to reduce their current year's income tax liability by up to 10% of the cost of eligible plant assets acquired during the year. The 1986 Tax Reform Act eliminated the ITC, but the accounting issues are still relevant to ITCs granted prior to 1986. Under the flow-through method, the entire ITC is considered a reduction in the current year's income taxes expense; under the deferral method, the ITC is viewed as a deferred credit and is amortized as a reduction of income taxes expense over the economic life of the plant asset acquired.

To illustrate the two methods of accounting for the ITC, assume that on January 2, Year 1, Dean Company acquired at a cost of $500,000 a machine that is eligible for a 10% ITC of $50,000 ($500,000 × 0.10 = $50,000). The machine had an economic life of five years. Income taxes expense before the ITC was $300,000 in Year 1 and $200,000 in Year 2. The journal entries under each method of accounting for the ITC are illustrated on page 1073 for Years 1 and 2.

---

[7] The 1984 edition of *Accounting Trends & Techniques* indicates that 541 of the 600 companies surveyed used the flow-through method, 50 companies used the deferral method, and nine companies made no reference to investment tax credits.

The accounting for the ITC may be complicated by carryback and carryforward provisions of income tax laws, as well as rules for the *recapture* of the ITC on disposal of qualifying plant assets before the expiration of a specified holding period. The amount of any ITC lost as a result of the recapture provision of tax law is added to income taxes payable in the year the ITC is lost. When the flow-through method is used, the Income Taxes Expense ledger account is debited for the ITC lost. Under the deferral method, the ITC lost is debited to the Deferred Investment Tax Credit ledger account (and to the Income Taxes Expense account if the amount of the ITC lost exceeds the unamortized balance).

DEAN COMPANY
Journal Entries for Investment Tax Credit (ITC)

Flow-through method	*Deferral method*
Year 1	Year 2
Income Taxes Expense 250,000	Income Taxes Expense 290,000
Income Taxes Payable 250,000	Deferred Investment Tax
To record income taxes	Credit 40,000
expense net of ITC	Income Taxes Payable... 250,000
($300,000 − $50,000 =	To record income taxes
$250,000).	expense [$300,000 −
	($50,000 ÷ 5) = $290,000];
	deferred ITC ($50,000 ×
	⅘ = $40,000); and income
	taxes payable ($300,000 −
	$50,000 = $250,000).
Year 2	Year 2
Income Taxes Expense 200,000	Income Taxes Expense 190,000
Income Taxes Payable 200,000	Deferred Investment Tax
To record income taxes	Credit 10,000
expense.	Income Taxes Payable... 200,000
	To record income taxes
	expense ($200,000 −
	$10,000 = $190,000) and
	amortization of ITC
	($50,000 ÷ 5 = $10,000).

Allocation of Income Taxes to Interim Periods

When interim earnings reports are prepared, an estimate of income taxes expense for each quarter must be made before the actual income tax liability for the year is known. If income taxes were assessed at a flat rate, it would be a relatively simple matter to compute the tax on the income to date. However, the progressive feature of the corporate income tax raises the question whether the income to date should be *annualized* and proportionate income tax accrued for the period to date, or whether the *marginal approach* should be used so that the first amount of income is taxed at lower rates.

A similar question arises when a corporation has a seasonal income pattern. For example, high income experienced early in a year may be offset by losses later in the year. If the marginal approach were adopted, the income tax liability (in terms of the actual amount ultimately to be paid) would be overstated during the early part of the year and would have to be adjusted downward during the latter part of the year when losses were incurred.

The Accounting Principles Board provided the following answers to these questions.[8]

> At the end of each interim period the company should make its best estimate of the effective tax rate expected to be applicable for the full fiscal year. The rate so determined should be used in providing for income taxes on a current year-to-date basis. The effective tax rate should reflect anticipated investment tax credits, foreign tax rates, percentage depletion, capital gains rates, and other available tax planning alternatives. However, in arriving at this effective tax rate no effect should be included for the tax related to significant unusual or extraordinary items that will be separately reported or reported net of their related tax effect in reports for the interim period or for the fiscal year.
>
> The tax effects of losses that arise in the early portion of a fiscal year (in the event carryback of such losses is not possible) should be recognized only when realization is assured beyond any reasonable doubt . . . An established seasonal pattern of loss in early interim periods offset by income in later interim periods should constitute evidence that realization is assured beyond reasonable doubt, unless other evidence indicates the established seasonal pattern will not prevail. The tax effects of losses incurred in early interim periods may be recognized in a later interim period of a fiscal year if their realization, although initially uncertain, later becomes assured beyond reasonable doubt. When the tax effects of losses that arise in the early portions of a fiscal year are not recognized in that interim period, no tax provision should be made for income that arises in later interim periods until the tax effects of the previous interim losses are utilized. Changes resulting from new tax legislation should be reflected after the effective dates prescribed in the statutes.

Thus, the estimate of the income tax rate to be applied to interim periods should include: (1) consideration of the effect of rate differentials, permanent differences between pre-tax accounting income and taxable income, anticipated investment tax credits and other items; (2) selection of rates to be applied to ordinary income, extraordinary items, etc.; and (3) adjustment of income tax rates for legislation enacted during the fiscal year.[9]

For example, assume that Remo Company is subject to income taxes at 20% on the first $50,000 of taxable income and at 45% on taxable income in excess of

---

[8]*APB Opinion No. 28,* ''Interim Financial Reporting,'' AICPA (New York: 1973), pp. 527–528.
[9]*FASB Interpretation No. 18,* ''Accounting for Income Taxes in Interim Periods,'' FASB (Stamford: 1977), pp. 4–5; *APB Opinion No. 28,* pp. 527–528.

$50,000. Capital expenditures yielding a $15,500 investment tax credit were planned for Year 5. Actual pre-tax income for the first quarter of Year 5 was $100,000, and at the time the income statement for the first quarter of Year 5 was being prepared, pre-tax income for Year 5 was expected to be $400,000. There were no extraordinary items or temporary differences. Income taxes expense for the first quarter of Year 5 is computed as follows:

Computation of income taxes expense for first quarter of fiscal year

Estimated income taxes expense for Year 5:

[($50,000 × 0.20) + ($350,000 × 0.45)] *$167,500*

Less: Anticipated investment tax credit *15,500*

   Net estimated income taxes expense for Year 5 .... *$152,000*

Estimated effective income tax rate for Year 5:

$152,000 ÷ $400,000 .... *38%*

Income taxes expense for the first quarter of Year 5 ($100,000 × 0.38) .... *$ 38,000*

For subsequent quarters, the year-to-date income taxes expense is computed with a current estimate of the effective tax rate. The income taxes expense for each quarter is the difference between the new year-to-date income taxes expense and the income taxes expense previously recognized up to the beginning of the quarter. Assume, for example, Remo Company had pre-tax income of $130,000 for the second quarter of Year 5 and now expected pre-tax income for Year 5 of $500,000 instead of $400,000; if the investment tax credit is now estimated at $12,500 instead of $15,500, the income taxes expense for the second quarter of Year 5 would be computed as follows:

Computation of income taxes expense for second quarter of fiscal year

Estimated income taxes expense for Year 5:

($50,000 × 0.20) + ($450,000 × 0.45) *$212,500*

Less: Anticipated investment tax credit *12,500*

   Net estimated income taxes expense for Year 5 .... *$200,000*

Estimated effective income tax rate for Year 5:

$200,000 ÷ $500,000 .... *40%*

Income taxes expense for the second quarter of Year 5:

   Year-to-date income taxes expense [($100,000 + $130,000) × 0.40] ..... *$ 92,000*

   Less: Income taxes expense for the first quarter of Year 5 (see above) .. *38,000*

Income taxes expense for the second quarter of Year 5 .... *$ 54,000*

If the estimated income tax rates fluctuate among interim periods, the income taxes expense for each quarter may be quite disproportionate to the quarterly pre-tax income. To illustrate, assume the following pre-tax income and quarterly estimated income tax rates for Tyrone Company for Year 10:

	Pre-tax income	Estimated income tax rate
First quarter	$200,000	45%
Second quarter	300,000	39%
Third quarter	100,000	44%
Fourth quarter	150,000	43%

The estimated income taxes expense for each quarter of Year 10 is computed below.

First quarter ($200,000 × 0.45)	$ 90,000
Second quarter [($500,000 × 0.39) − $90,000]	$105,000
Third quarter [($600,000 × 0.44) − ($500,000 × 0.39)]	$ 69,000
Fourth quarter [($750,000 × 0.43) − ($600,000 × 0.44)]	$ 58,500

Because of the fluctuations in the quarterly income tax rates for Year 10, the *effective quarterly income tax rate* ranges from 35% to 69%, as demonstrated in the table below.

	Pre-tax income	Income taxes expense	Effective quarterly income tax rate
First quarter	$200,000	$ 90,000	45%
Second quarter	300,000	105,000	35%
Third quarter	100,000	69,000	69%
Fourth quarter	150,000	58,500	39%
Total for Year 10	$750,000	$322,500	43%

The income taxes expense of $105,000 for the second quarter equals $117,000 (the estimated income tax rate of 39% for Year 10 applied to the pre-tax income of $300,000 for the second quarter) less $12,000, the reduction in income taxes expense for the first quarter because of the decrease in the estimated tax rate from 45% to 39% [($300,000 × 0.39) − ($200,000 × 0.06) = $105,000].

Extraordinary items and other items not included in pre-tax income are treated as marginal items for purposes of interim income tax allocation. Income taxes expense is computed both with and without the extraordinary item, and the difference is the tax applicable to the extraordinary item.

■■■■■■■■ REVIEW QUESTIONS

1   What is the objective of generally accepted accounting principles in their application to the income statement? What are the objectives of income tax laws?

2   Define *interperiod tax allocation, intraperiod tax allocation,* and *interimperiod tax computation.*

3   What assumptions are necessary in the implementation of income tax allocation for financial accounting?

4   What are three sources of differences between pre-tax accounting income and taxable income?

5   Describe two situations that result, under interperiod tax allocation procedures, in deferred income tax credits for financial accounting.

6   Describe two situations that result, under interperiod tax allocation procedures, in a recognized deferred tax benefit.

7   Explain the following interperiod tax allocation approaches:
a *Deferred method*
b *Liability method*
c *Net-of-tax method*

8   Briefly describe when future net deductible amounts from temporary differences result in recognized assets, and when they do not.

9   What is meant by an *operating loss carryback* and an *operating loss carryforward?*

10   Explain the different accounting problems that arise in accounting for an operating loss carryback and for an operating loss carryforward.

11   Describe three situations that produce a permanent difference between taxable income and pre-tax accounting income. Give an example of each.

12   Briefly summarize the arguments for and against interperiod income tax allocation.

13   Explain how each of the following ledger accounts is classified (for example, current asset or current liability) in the balance sheet:
a Deferred Income Taxes
b Deferred Income Tax Benefit
c Income Tax Refund Receivable
d Income Tax Operating Loss Carryforward Credit

14   What information regarding income taxes is included in a note to the financial statements?

15   What two approaches may be used to account for the *investment tax credit* (ITC)? Briefly describe each method and indicate which one is more widely used.

16   Identify and briefly explain some of the problems involved in the estimate of income taxes expense for interim accounting periods.

17 Explain why the effective income tax rate for each quarter of a fiscal year may differ significantly from the actual income tax rate for the year.

EXERCISES

Ex. 21-1 Select the best answer for each of the following multiple-choice questions:

1 At the most recent year-end, Lane Company's deferred tax benefit related to a noncurrent liability exceeded a deferred income tax related to a current asset. Which of the following is reported in Lane's most recent year-end balance sheet?
a The deferred tax benefit as a current asset
b The excess of the deferred tax benefit over the deferred income tax as a current asset
c The deferred tax benefit as a noncurrent asset and the deferred income tax as a current liability
d The excess of the deferred tax benefit over the deferred income tax as a noncurrent asset

2 The amount of income taxes applicable to transactions that are reported with intraperiod income tax allocation is computed:
a By multiplying the item by the effective income tax rate
b As the difference between the income taxes computed based on taxable income excluding the item and the taxes computed based on taxable income including the item
c As the difference between the income taxes computed on the item based on the amount used for financial accounting and the amount used in the computation of taxable income
d By multiplying the item by the difference between the effective income tax rate and the statutory income tax rate

3 An example of an item requiring intraperiod income tax allocation is:
a Interest revenue on municipal bonds
b Estimated expenses for major repairs accrued for financial accounting in one year, but deducted for income tax purposes when paid in a subsequent year
c Rent revenue included in income for income tax purposes when collected, but deferred for financial accounting until realized in a subsequent year
d Reporting a prior period adjustment in the statement of retained earnings

4 Which of the following requires intraperiod income tax allocation?
a The portion of dividends reduced by the dividends-received deduction available to corporations under federal income tax law
b The excess of Accelerated Cost Recovery System depreciation for income tax purposes over straight-line depreciation for financial accounting
c Extraordinary gains and losses
d All differences between taxable income and pre-tax accounting income

5 An Income Tax Operating Loss Carryback Credit is presented in a corporation's:
a Income statement as a reduction of pre-tax operating loss

b Balance sheet as a current asset

c Income statement as an extraordinary item

d Balance sheet as a contra to deferred income taxes

6 Rollo Corporation had interest revenue on municipal bonds of $200,000 in Year 2. For financial accounting, Rollo included the $200,000 in its income statement. For income tax reporting, the $200,000 was exempt income. Assuming an income tax rate of 45%, what is reported in the provision for deferred income taxes relative to the interest revenue in Rollo's income statement for the year ended December 31, Year 2?

a $0 **b** $90,000 credit **c** $90,000 debit **d** $200,000 debit

e Some other amount

7 Agard Company's effective income tax rate is 45%. For the year ended December 31, Year 1, Agard's income statement included depletion of $1,000,000 in cost of goods sold, based on the cost of natural resource assets being depleted. However, Agard properly deducted $4,000,000 for percentage depletion in its Year 1 income tax return. What amount is reported as provision for deferred income tax credits in Agard's Year 1 financial statements?

a $0 **b** $450,000 **c** $1,350,000 **d** $1,800,000 **e** Some other amount

8 On December 31, Year 3, Tower Corporation reported a $10,000 deferred tax liability in its balance sheet. One year previous, the account had a balance of $8,000. Taxable income for Year 3 was $50,000, and the tax rate was 30%. What is income taxes expense for Year 3?

a $17,000 **b** $15,000 **c** $13,000 **d** Another amount

9 Bishop Corporation began operations in Year 1 and had operating losses of $200,000 in Year 1 and $150,000 in Year 2. For the year ended December 31, Year 3, Bishop had pre-tax accounting income and taxable income of $300,000. For the three-year period Year 1 through Year 3, assume an income tax rate of 45% and no permanent or timing differences between pre-tax accounting income and taxable income. In Bishop's Year 3 income statement, what amount is reported as income taxes expense?

a $0 **b** $45,000 **c** $67,500 **d** $135,000 **e** Some other amount

10 On January 2, Year 5, Clark Company acquired equipment at a cost of $150,000 that will be depreciated as follows:

Year	5	6	7	8	9
Accounting	$30,000	$30,000	$30,000	$30,000	$30,000
Tax	60,000	45,000	30,000	15,000	-0-

Assuming that the tax rate is 30%, what is the balance of the deferred tax benefit on December 31, Year 5?

a $4,500 **b** $15,000 **c** $30,000 **d** -0-

Ex. 21-2 Martin Company began operations on January 3, Year 1, and a substantial part of its sales were made on the installment plan. For financial accounting Martin recognized revenue from all sales on the accrual basis. However, in its income tax returns, Martin reported revenue from installment sales on the installment method. Information concerning pre-tax income from installment sales under each method is as follows:

Year	Accrual basis	Installment method
1	$400,000	$150,000
2	650,000	600,000
3	500,000	800,000

The effective income tax rate for all years was 45%, and there were no other timing differences.

Prepare journal entries for Martin Company to record income taxes expense for each year (omit explanations).

Ex. 21-3 For the year ended December 31, Year 1, Rex Corporation reported pre-tax accounting income of $1,000,000. The following information is available for Year 1:

Interest revenue on municipal bonds .... $ 80,000
Depreciation deduction claimed in tax return in excess of depreciation
  expense in income statement...................................... 140,000
Warranty expense on the accrual basis of accounting................ 65,000
Actual warranty expenditures 35,000

Rex's effective income tax rate is 45% for Year 1.

Prepare a journal entry for Rex Corporation to record income taxes expense for the year ended December 31, Year 1 (omit explanation). Assume that Rex computes the change in deferred taxes accounts from the aggregate temporary difference on the balance sheet date.

Ex. 21-4 Sunrise Company uses the deferral method of accounting for the investment tax credit. In Year 5, Sunrise had a $37,800 investment tax credit as a result of acquisitions early in Year 5 of plant assets with a 10-year economic life. On December 31, Year 5, Sunrise's accountant recorded an income tax liability of $160,000 before recognition of the investment tax credit.

Prepare journal entries for Sunrise Company on December 31, Year 5, and on December 31, Year 6, to adjust income taxes expense for the effect of the investment tax credit.

Ex. 21-5 Samore Corporation began Year D with a $10,000 deferred tax liability. During Year D, Samore earned $200,000 of taxable income. The remaining future temporary differences at the end of Year D are:

Year	E	F	G	H
Taxable amounts $4,000	$8,000	$3,000	$ 5,000
Deductible amounts				16,000

The tax rate is 30%. Provide the Year D tax accrual entry.

Ex. 21-6   Assume the facts in Exercise 21-5 except that during Year D, the tax rate was changed to 35%. Provide any necessary adjusting entry in Year D and the tax accrual entry for Year D.

Ex. 21-7   Acosta Corporation's accounting records for the year ended December 31, Year 9, showed pre-tax accounting income of $400,000. In the computation of taxable income, the following timing differences were taken into account:

Depreciation deducted for income tax purposes in excess of depreciation recognized in income statement $80,000
Income from installment sale reported for income tax purposes in excess of income recognized in income statement...................... 60,000

The income tax rate is 45%.

Compute Acosta's current income tax liability on December 31, Year 9.

Ex. 21-8   In Year 5, Kane Company reported $300,000 of pre-tax accounting income, but only $80,000 in its income tax return. In Year 6, pre-tax accounting income was $350,000 and taxable income was $450,000.

Prepare Kane Company's journal entry to record income taxes expense and income taxes payable for Year 6, assuming that the reversal of temporary differences was responsible for the disparity between pre-tax accounting income and taxable income. The income tax rate is 45%.

Ex. 21-9   Mejia Company began operations in Year A and purchased an asset costing $100,000 that was to be depreciated as follows:

Year	A	B	C	D	E
Tax	$40,000	$30,000	$20,000	$ 5,000	$ 5,000
Accounting	20,000	20,000	20,000	20,000	20,000

Assuming a taxable income of $150,000 and a 30% tax rate in Year A, provide the Year A tax accrual entry.

Ex. 21-10   The pre-tax accounting income and taxable income for Otake Corporation over a three-year period are presented below:

Year	Pre-tax accounting income	Taxable income
1	$100,000	$140,000
2	100,000	95,000
3	100,000	95,000

The differences between pre-tax accounting income and taxable income are explained as follows:

(1) Taxable income in Year 1 included $45,000 of rent revenue that was recognized in the accounting records at the rate of $15,000 a year.

(2) Amortization of goodwill at the rate of $10,000 a year was recognized in the accounting records but was not deductible in the computation of taxable income. (Amortization of goodwill does not create a temporary difference for income tax allocation purposes.)

Prepare journal entries for Years 1, 2, and 3 to record Otake Corporation's income taxes. Assume that income taxes are 45% of taxable income.

Ex. 21-11 Income statements for Peter Corporation show the following pre-tax results for the first three years of its operations:

Year 1: Operating loss .... $(100,000)
Year 2: Operating income 240,000
Year 3: Operating loss .... (200,000)

Peter operates in a cyclical and highly competitive capital goods industry.

Prepare Peter Corporation's journal entries for each year to record the tax effects of operating loss carryforwards or carrybacks. Assume that operating losses as reported in the income statements are allowable in full for income tax purposes and that the income tax rate is 45%.

Ex. 21-12 Lui Corporation reported pre-tax accounting income of $300,000 and an extraordinary gain of $1.2 million for the year ended March 31, Year 4.

Prepare a journal entry to record the tax effect of the pre-tax accounting income and of the extraordinary gain. (Record the tax effect of the gain as a debit to the Extraordinary Gain ledger account.) Show how the foregoing information is presented in the income statement for the year ended March 31, Year 4. (The income tax rate is 45% on income before income taxes and 30% on the extraordinary gain.)

Ex. 21-13 Aki Corporation issues financial statements on a quarterly basis. During Year 1, its actual quarterly results and its expectations were as follows:

	Pre-tax accounting income		Expected for year	
	Quarter	Year to date	Pre-tax accounting income	Investment tax credit
End of 1st quarter	$20,000	$ 20,000	$ 80,000	$5,100
End of 2d quarter	10,000	30,000	60,000	2,500
End of 3d quarter	40,000	70,000	90,000	5,500
End of year	30,000	100,000	100,000	6,500

Assuming that Aki's income tax rate is 20% on the first $50,000 of taxable income and 45% on taxable income above $50,000, and that taxable income is the same as pre-tax accounting income, compute the (a) estimated effective income tax rate for each quarter, (b) year-to-date income taxes expense at the end of each quarter, and (c) income taxes expense for each quarter.

■■■■■■■■■■■■■ **CASES**

Case 21-1   Plaga Company was organized on January 2, Year 1, and adopted the accrual basis of accounting for financial accounting. For income tax purposes, Plaga adopted the cash basis of accounting because accounts receivable were expected to exceed accounts payable by a significant amount each year. Thus, Plaga could defer the payment of income taxes through the use of the cash basis of accounting for income tax purposes.

You were engaged to examine the financial statements of Plaga for the year ended December 31, Year 1. In a discussion of interperiod tax allocation procedures with you, Laura Dykes, controller, objected to the use of comprehensive tax allocation for all differences between Plaga's pre-tax accounting income and taxable income. She stressed that forecasts of Plaga's future operations indicated an ever-increasing deferred income tax liability from comprehensive tax allocation because of the growth of accounts receivable in relation to accounts payable.

Instructions

How would you respond to the controller's objections? Explain.

Case 21-2   Discuss the similarities between the generally accepted accounting principles for interperiod tax allocation and those for tax operating loss carrybacks and carryforwards.

Case 21-3   Nelson Construction Corporation was organized early in Year 1 after Rick Nelson was awarded a contract to build a major section of a highway in Alaska. The completion of the contract will take four years, and Nelson does not plan to bid on additional contracts. All costs incurred by Nelson are chargeable to the highway contract; thus, Nelson will not record any selling and administrative expenses. Assume that the income tax rate is 20% on the first $50,000 and 45% on any excess.

The pre-tax profit on the construction-type contract is estimated at $200,000. Under the percentage-of-completion method of accounting, $50,000 of the profit will be recognized in each of the four years. Income taxes of $10,000 ($50,000 × 0.20 = $10,000) will be paid on March 15 of each year starting in Year 2 if the percentage-of-completion method is adopted for income tax purposes. If the completed-contract method is adopted for income tax purposes, income taxes in the amount of $77,500 [($200,000 × 0.45) − ($50,000 × 0.25) = $77,500] will be paid on March 15, Year 5.

Instructions

a Assume that Nelson Construction Corporation considers 8% a fair rate of return after income taxes. Prepare a working paper to show whether Nelson should use the completed-contract method or the percentage-of-completion method of accounting for income tax purposes. Compute the net advantage of the method you recommend, in terms of dollar savings as of March 15, Year 5. (The amount of an ordinary annuity of four rents of 1 at 8% is 4.5061.)

b Assume that Nelson Construction Corporation had a large amount of income each year from other sources and that the entire profit on the construction-type contract is taxed at the marginal rate of 45%. What method of accounting do you recommend for income tax purposes? What is the net advantage for Nelson Construction as of March 15, Year 5, if money is worth 8%?

Case 21-4   In Year 10, Utah Company received $50,000 as an advance rental on one of its mining properties. The rent advance was subject to income taxes in Year 10, although Utah did not recognize rent revenue for financial accounting until Year 11.

In Year 10, Utah reported taxable income of $250,000, paying income taxes of $100,000 (20% on the first $50,000 of taxable income and 45% on the balance of $200,000). The controller reported $200,000 as Utah's pre-tax accounting income for Year 10 and $22,500 of income taxes applicable to the rent advance ($50,000 × 0.45 = $22,500) as an asset (deferred tax benefit) in the balance sheet.

In Year 11, Utah suffered a decline in income as a result of declining metal prices, and its operations resulted in pre-tax accounting income of only $50,000, including the rent advance received in Year 10. When the controller presented Utah's Year 11 income statement to the president, the latter commented, ''I thought you said the effect of interperiod tax allocation was to show in each year a tax expense that bore a normal relationship to pre-tax accounting income. You report pre-tax accounting income of $50,000 and show income taxes of $22,500. If we had taxable income of only $50,000 we would pay only $10,000 in income taxes. I realize we broke even in the income tax return this year and won't actually pay any income tax, but I think your tax allocation procedure is incorrect.''

Instructions

a Prepare partial comparative income statements for Utah Company for Years 10 and 11, starting with income before income taxes and following the controller's approach.

b What is the issue implicit in the president's comment? How would you reply if you were the controller?

PROBLEMS

21-1   This problem consists of three independent parts.

a Turley Corporation's income statement for the year ended December 31, Year 10, showed pre-tax accounting income of $500,000. The following items for Year 10 were treated differently in the income tax return from the way they were treated in the accounting records:

	Income tax return	Accounting records
Rent revenue	$ 60,000	$ 40,000
Depreciation expense....................................	160,000	100,000
Amortization of goodwill*		30,000
Interest revenue*	30,000	40,000

*Permanent differences between pre-tax accounting income and taxable income

Assume that Turley's effective income tax rate is 45% for Year 10, and that the two temporary differences will reverse in different years, with the rent difference reversing within three years.

Instructions

Prepare a journal entry for Turley Corporation to record income taxes expense for the year ended December 31, Year 10.

b Dugan Corporation began operations on January 5, Year 8. Dugan recognized income on construction-type contracts under the percentage-of-completion method in its financial statements but used the completed-contract method for income tax purposes. Income before income taxes under each method was as follows:

Year	Percentage-of-completion	Completed-contract
8	$400,000	$100,000
9	650,000	350,000
10	800,000	1,400,000

For all years, Dugan's effective income tax rate was 45%, and there were no other timing differences.

Instructions

Prepare a journal entry for each year to record income taxes expense for Dugan Corporation.

c The income statement for Yamamura Corporation for the year ended June 30, Year 5, included the following pre-tax amounts:

Income from continuing operations $1,750,000
Depreciation expense, which was $100,000 less than the amount
  reported in the income tax return   600,000
Insurance expense (premiums on life insurance policies on which
  Yamamura was the beneficiary)   50,000
Loss from operations and disposal of a discontinued business
  segment   800,000
Extraordinary gain (extinguishment of long-term debt)   500,000

Yamamura recorded payments of $480,000 on estimated income taxes in the Income Taxes Expense ledger account during the year ended June 30, Year 5. The effective income tax rate for Yamamura was 45%.

Instructions

Prepare a journal entry to adjust Yamamura Corporation's Income Taxes Expense ledger account for the year ended June 30, Year 5.

21-2 Pre-tax accounting income of Westlake Corporation, after all adjustments and corrections, was $280,000 for Year 1, $212,000 for Year 2, and $252,000 for Year 3. The income tax rate was 45% in each of the three years. Depreciation expense, rent revenue, and interest revenue have been included in pre-tax accounting income and taxable income for Years 1, 2, and 3, as follows:

	Pre-tax accounting income	Taxable income
Depreciation expense:		
Year 1	$50,000	$70,000
Year 2	54,000	71,000
Year 3	58,000	68,000
Rent revenue:		
Year 1	9,000	9,500
Year 2	9,000	8,500
Interest revenue (tax-free municipal bonds):		
Year 1	8,000	
Year 2	4,000	
Year 3	3,800	

Westlake computes its deferred tax accounts on the aggregate temporary difference on the balance sheet date.

Instructions

a Compute the amount of income taxes payable for Westlake Corporation on December 31, Years 1, 2, and 3

b Compute the amount of income taxes expense for Westlake Corporation for Years 1, 2, and 3

c Prepare a journal entry to record income taxes of Westlake Corporation for each year (omit explanations)

21-3   Lake Corporation had pre-tax accounting income of $400,000 for Year 1 and was subject to income taxes of 45%. The following items were treated in one way in the computation of the $400,000 pre-tax accounting income but were treated differently in the computation of taxable income:

(1) Lake recorded $70,000 in product warranty expense; for income tax purposes only $44,000 of warranty costs actually incurred was deductible. The remaining warranty claim is expected in Year 2.

(2) $80,000 of profits on construction-type contracts was included by Lake in pre-tax accounting income on the percentage-of-completion basis. Only one-fourth of this amount was taxable in Year 1; the balance was to be taxed in Year 2 when the remaining construction-type contracts were completed.

(3) A lease deposit of $40,000 was received by Lake and credited to a long-term liability ledger account. It was taxable in Year 1 but would not be realized for financial accounting until Year 5.

(4) Lake recorded $130,000 depreciation expense in its accounting records by the straight-line method. Accelerated Cost Recovery System depreciation of $150,000 was taken in the income tax return. This difference is expected to completely reverse in Year 2.

Instructions

a Compute the income taxes expense to be included in Lake Corporation's Year 1 income statement, and the amount of income taxes currently payable.

b Prepare a journal entry to record Lake Corporation's income taxes expense and related deferred income tax debits and credits on December 31, Year 1. Prepare a schedule of future temporary differences.

c Prepare a partial income statement for Lake Corporation on December 31, Year 1, beginning with income before income taxes.

d Indicate the amount and classification of any income tax items in Lake Corporation's balance sheet on December 31, Year 1.

21-4 Zeno Corporation was subject to income taxes at 45% of taxable income and had made estimated income tax payments of $310,000 during Year 4. No computation of taxable income had been made for Year 4, but the pre-tax accounting income for Year 4 was stated correctly at $900,000. The following items required consideration in the reconciliation of pre-tax accounting income and taxable income for the year ended December 31, Year 4. Zeno began Year 4 with no deferred tax accounts.

(1) Zeno acquired another business enterprise at the beginning of Year 2, and recorded $300,000 of goodwill, which was being amortized over 20 years.

(2) Gross profit on installment sales had been recognized in the amount of $250,000 in the accounting records. For income tax purposes, only $150,000 of gross profit was reportable in Year 4. The remaining $100,000 is expected to be reported in Year 5.

(3) Pension expense accrued during Year 4 amounted to $44,000; only the $30,000 cash deposited in a pension trust fund was deductible in the Year 4 income tax return. The related pension plan liability was to be paid in Year 5.

(4) Straight-line depreciation of $190,000 had been recognized in the accounting records; however, $240,000 Accelerated Cost Recovery System (ACRS) depreciation will be claimed in the income tax return. This difference is expected to reverse in Year 5.

Instructions

a Compute the additional income taxes to be paid by Zeno Corporation for the year ended December 31, Year 4.

b Prepare a journal entry to record Zeno Corporation's remaining income taxes expense for Year 4, assuming that the estimated tax payments were debited to the Income Taxes Expense ledger account during the year. Prepare a schedule of future temporary differences.

c Prepare a partial income statement for Zeno Corporation for the year ended December 31, Year 4. Start with the $900,000 income before income taxes.

d Show Zeno Corporation's balance sheet presentation of all income tax items on December 31, Year 4.

21-5 Roadman Company began operations in Year 1. During Years 1 and 2, it purchased assets that are expected to be depreciated in the following fashion for accounting and tax purposes:

Year	1	2	3	4	5	6	Total
Accounting	$3,000	$7,000	$6,500	$6,000	$5,000	$3,000	$30,500
Tax (ACRS).....	5,000	9,000	6,000	5,000	4,000	3,000	32,000

The difference in total depreciation is due to a residual value expected in Year 6. ACRS depreciation assumes zero salvage value. The tax rate is 30%. Roadman earned $20,000 taxable income in Years 1 and 2.

Instructions

a Prepare a schedule of future temporary differences for Year 1.

b Prepare the Year 1 and Year 2 tax accrual entries and indicate the balance sheet classification of each deferred account.

c Prepare partial income statements for Years 1 and 2.

21-6 Gerald Finnell is president and sole shareholder of Jerry's, Inc., a successful restaurant. During the year ended December 31, Year 8, confident in the competence and integrity of the assistant manager, Finnell left for a six-month trip to Africa. On returning he found that the manager had been stealing from the restaurant to cover gambling losses and that the quality (and patronage) of the restaurant had suffered. As a result, a pre-tax operating loss of $300,000 was incurred in Year 8. On the basis of prior success, Finnell was confident that under his personal direction the restaurant would be restored to profitability immediately. The pre-tax operating income for Year 9 was $220,000. The income tax rate for all years involved was 45%.

Instructions

a Prepare journal entries to record income taxes of Jerry's, Inc., for the years ended December 31, Year 8 and Year 9. Assume that of the $300,000 operating loss for Year 8, only $200,000 could be carried back to preceding years.

b Prepare partial comparative income statements for Jerry's, Inc., for the years ended December 31, Year 8 and Year 9.

21-7 The following comparative income statements were presented to Kay Park, president of Park Corporation:

PARK CORPORATION
Comparative Income Statements
For Years Ended December 31, Year 6 and Year 5

	Year 6	Year 5
Net sales	$1,090,000	$1,000,000
Cost of goods sold	690,000	630,000
Gross profit on sales	$ 400,000	$ 370,000
Operating expenses	250,000	280,000
Income before income taxes	$ 150,000	$ 90,000
Income taxes expense	92,000	10,000
Net income	$ 58,000	$ 80,000

After examining the statements, Park frowned, "When I send these statements to my father, who owns 30% of the common stock, he will never understand why net income fell in the face of a substantial increase in income before income taxes."

"There are two reasons," commented the controller. "You will remember that last year we took a $40,000 fully deductible earthquake loss on the East Bend warehouse, and this year we had a gain of $120,000 (taxed at 30%) when we sold our Cable Company common stock, our only investment, and used the proceeds to build a new warehouse. Both these transactions were reported in the statement of retained earnings, but their tax effects were included in income taxes expense for the year ended December 31, Year 6."

"I'll have trouble getting that across to my father," Park replied. "He knows we're subject to federal taxes of 46% on all income over $50,000 and 20% on the first $50,000. An 820% increase in income taxes in the income statement is going to be confusing. Can't you revise the income statement so that the reasons for these odd tax amounts will be apparent?"

Instructions

a Prepare revised comparative income statements for Park Corporation that will, in your opinion, meet the objections raised by Kay Park. Assume that both the earthquake loss and the gain on the sale of Cable Company common stock are extraordinary items.

b Prepare a correcting entry for Park Corporation on December 31, Year 6, to restate the ledger account balances (assume that the accounting records for the year ended December 31, Year 6, have not been closed).

21-8 Kenneth Helwig, controller of Ken Corporation, has summarized the following data with respect to Ken's operations for the year ended December 31, Year 5:

Sales	$1,500,000
Extraordinary gain resulting from a successful antitrust suit for treble damages (taxable at ordinary income tax rates)	300,000
Cost of goods sold	1,000,000
Operating expenses (includes $20,000 amortization of goodwill)	285,000
Correction of error resulting form double-counting items in inventories on Dec. 31, Year 4	60,000

Because Helwig is busy with problems arising in connection with a newly installed computer system, he has asked you, as an independent consultant, to assist him in the preparation of the income statement for Year 5. There were no temporary differences in Year 5.

Instructions

a Compute the income taxes of Ken Corporation for Year 5 applicable to current operations, to the extraordinary gain, and to the prior period adjustment. The income tax rate for Year 5 is 45%; for Year 4 it was 42%.

b Prepare Ken Corporation's condensed income statement for Year 5. Disregard earnings per share.

c Prepare Ken Corporation's statement of retained earnings for Year 5. The balance of retained earnings reported on December 31, Year 4 (without correction for the error in inventories), was $720,000, and cash dividends of $110,000 were declared in Year 5.

21-9 Keith Renken, the controller of Sells Company, handed an assistant a sheet of paper on which appeared the information shown below, saying, "Here's the story on our accounting and taxable income for the current year; I'd like you to put these amounts together in an income statement and a statement of retained earnings."

SELLS COMPANY
Computation of Pre-Tax Accounting Income
For Year Ended March 31, Year 8

	Debit	Credit
Sales (net)...		$869,000
Interest revenue on municipal bonds (nontaxable)		10,000
Prior period adjustment—refund of income taxes as a		
result of error discovered by Internal Revenue agents.......		30,000
Cost of goods sold	$519,000	
Operating expenses	128,000	
Earthquake loss (not covered by insurance), before		
income tax effect.......................................	142,000	
Gain on extinguishment of debt, before income tax effect		90,000
Subtotals	$789,000	$999,000
Prior period adjustment (see above).......................	30,000	
Income taxes payable (see below)	51,750	
Net income	128,250	
Totals	$999,000	$999,000

SELLS COMPANY
Computation of Income Taxes Payable
For Year Ended March 31, Year 8

Sales (net)...		$869,000
Gain on extinguishment of debt (fully taxable)		90,000
Total revenue		$959,000
Less: Cost of goods sold.................................	$519,000	
Operating expenses	128,000	
Earthquake loss (fully deductible)	142,000	
Excess of ACRS depreciation over straight-line		
depreciation used for financial accounting	55,000	844,000
Taxable income		$115,000
Income tax rate		0.45
Income taxes payable		$ 51,750

The amount of income taxes payable for the year ended March 31, Year 8, was computed correctly.

Instructions

a Prepare a journal entry for Sells Company to record income taxes expense, deferred income tax credits, and intraperiod allocation of taxes. Assume that the earthquake loss and the gain on extinguishment of debt qualify as extraordinary items for financial accounting.

b On the basis of this information, and assuming an income tax rate of 45%, prepare an income statement and a statement of retained earnings for Sells Company for the year ended March 31, Year 8. Sells reported a retained earnings balance of $1,917,200 on March 31, Year 7, and declared cash dividends of $75,000 during the year ended March 31, Year 8. Disregard earnings per share.

21-10 In Year 5, Queen Company had sales of $800,000 and pre-tax accounting income of $300,000. Straight-line depreciation expense of $80,000 was recorded for financial accounting, but Accelerated Cost Recovery System depreciation for income tax purposes amounted to $124,000. Cost depletion of $100,000 was deducted to compute pre-tax accounting income, but a deduction for depletion equal to 22% of sales was allowed in the income tax return.

Pre-tax accounting income did not include a gain of $440,000 from the disposal of land on the installment basis, which was reported as an extraordinary item. The gain from the disposal of the land was reported as an extraordinary item because it resulted from the only disposable parcel of land that Queen owned and because the land had been owned for more than 30 years. Only one-fourth of the selling price was collected in Year 5; therefore, only $110,000 of the gain was taxable at 30% in Year 5.

Pre-tax accounting income was taxed at 20% of the first $50,000 and 46% of the balance. An operating loss of $50,000 and a capital loss of $8,000 were carried forward from Year 4, and are available to reduce the income tax liability for Year 5; the capital loss carryforward was to be offset against the gain from the disposal of land in Year 5.

Instructions

a Prepare a journal entry for Queen Company to record income taxes for Year 5.

b Prepare Queen Company's income statement for Year 5. Disregard earnings per share.

21-11 Juan Cortez, controller of Madera Corporation, was injured in an accident shortly after the end of Year 5. In his absence, the accountant for Madera prepared the following income statement for use in connection with the Year 5 audit:

MADERA CORPORATION
Income Statement
For Year Ended December 31, Year 5

Sales	$2,000,000
Rent revenue (an additional $5,000 advance rent was received and is taxable in Year 5 but will not be recognized as revenue until Year 6)	45,000
Interest revenue (including $6,000 tax-free municipal bond interest)	14,000
Total revenue	$2,059,000

(continued)

▮▮▮▮▮▮▮ Cost of goods sold $1,400,000
Operating expenses (including straight-line depreciation
  of $45,000; Accelerated Cost Recovery System de-
  preciation for income tax purposes is $60,000)   500,000
Extraordinary loss: Seizure of shipment of goods by
  foreign terrorists (fully deductible for income tax
  purposes)   250,000
Additional depreciation expense recognized this year
  attributable to error in computation of depreciation for
  Year 4 (same error was included in the income tax
  return for Year 4)   49,000
      Total costs and expenses   2,199,000
      Loss before income tax effect .... $ (140,000)

The income tax rate in effect for Years 1 through 5 was 45%; taxable income amounted to more than $200,000 each year in Years 2, 3, and 4.

Instructions

a Compute all essential income tax amounts in connection with Madera Corporation's income statement for the year ended December 31, Year 5.

b Prepare Madera Corporation's journal entry to record income taxes on December 31, Year 5. Assume that the operating loss for Year 5 is carried back to Year 2, and that an amended income tax return is filed for Year 4 because of the error in the computation of depreciation.

c Prepare Madera Corporation's combined statement of income and retained earnings for the year ended December 31, Year 5. The retained earnings balance as previously reported on December 31, Year 4, was $1,543,000; cash dividends of $85,000 were declared on December 10, Year 5.

21-12 Climber Corporation's complete schedule of temporary differences (actual and expected) appears below:

Year	A	B	C	D	E	F
Tax depreciation	$12,000	$7,000	$6,000	$4,000	$3,000	$3,000
Accounting depreciation ...	6,000	6,000	6,000	6,000	6,000	5,000
Tax rental revenue.........	4,500	-0-	4,500	-0-	9,000	-0-
Accounting rental revenue..	3,000	3,000	3,000	3,000	3,000	3,000

Climber used the above data for its tax accrual entry at the end of each year A–D. No estimate changes were found to be necessary. Climber's taxable income in Years A–D follow:

Year	Taxable income
A	$ 20,000
B	10,000
C	(35,000)
D	10,000

Instructions

a Prepare a schedule to determine the balance of the deferred tax accounts at the end of each of the years A–D. Remember that the operating loss could not be predicted.

b Prepare a schedule to determine the tax liability for each year A–D.

c Prepare the Year A–D tax accrual entries for Climber Corporation.

Accounting Changes, Errors, and Incomplete Records

22

As generally accepted accounting principles change in response to changes in the economic and social environment, accountants must find ways to implement the new principles in financial reporting. Placing new principles and new accounting estimates into the stream of financial statements may make current period statements inconsistent with those of prior accounting periods. However, new and improved principles and estimates should not be ignored simply to maintain consistency with the financial reporting of the past. In this chapter we explore some approaches to the adoption of new accounting principles and estimates with the goal of maintaining the maximum degree of comparability and, at the same time, gaining the advantages inherent in a change to improved or preferable accounting principles and estimates.

Also in this chapter we discuss methods of correcting and reporting errors that are discovered in previously issued financial statements. Finally, we consider ways in which accountants may develop financial statements from incomplete accounting records.

ACCOUNTING CHANGES

In the past, questions often were raised as to how certain accounting changes should be reported in the financial statements while at the same time preserving the consistency and comparability of the statements. By changing its accounting practices, a business enterprise might affect significantly the presentation of its financial position and results of operations. The change also might distort the earnings trend reported in income statements for earlier years.

For example, suppose that Romm Company acquired equipment early in Year 1 for $500,000. The equipment had an economic life of eight years and a net residual value of $50,000. For two years the equipment was depreciated by the straight-line method. Early in Year 3, Romm revised its original estimates and concluded that the equipment had a remaining economic life of 10 years and a revised net residual value of $100,000. During Year 3, Romm also changed from the straight-line method to an accelerated method of depreciation and merged with Poo Ling Company in a business combination accounted for as a pooling of interests. It is evident that the financial statements prepared by Romm at the end of Year 3 would not be comparable with the financial statements issued in Years 1 and 2, unless the changes that took place were reported in a manner designed to preserve comparability.

The foregoing illustration has examples of (1) a *change in accounting estimate* (the revisions of estimated economic life and net residual value of the equipment), (2) a *change in accounting principle* (the change from the straight-line method to an accelerated method of depreciation), and (3) a *change in reporting entity* (the inclusion of Poo Ling Company in the financial statements for Year 3). Thus, accountants must find appropriate methods of reporting these accounting changes to users of financial statements so that the statements are not misleading and so that a meaningful comparison of earnings for the three-year period may be made.

For many years, the disclosures of accounting changes often were incomplete and obscure and resulted in suggestions by some critics that such changes were used by management to manipulate reported earnings. Many users of financial statements not only misunderstood the reasons for accounting changes but also failed to grasp their full impact. In an effort to establish principles for measuring and reporting the effects of accounting changes on financial statements, the Accounting Principles Board defined the different types of accounting changes and established guidelines for reporting such changes in financial statements.[1]

Types of Accounting Changes

In *Opinion No. 20,* ''Accounting Changes,'' the Accounting Principles Board was concerned with two issues: (1) the reporting of accounting changes, and (2) the accounting for corrections of errors in previously issued financial statements. The

---

[1]*APB Opinion No. 20,* ''Accounting Changes,'' AICPA (New York: 1971).

APB classified accounting changes in the three categories illustrated in the preceding section, that is, changes in accounting principle, changes in accounting estimate, and changes in reporting entity.

A *change in accounting principle* may occur in two ways. The first results from the adoption of a generally accepted accounting principle different from one used previously for financial accounting. For example, the issuance of a new accounting principle by the FASB is sufficient support for a change in accounting principle. The second type of change in accounting principle involves a change in the method used to measure assets and liabilities. Examples of "method" changes in accounting principle include a change in the method of computing depreciation, such as a change to an accelerated depreciation method from the straight-line method; and a change in the method of valuing inventories such as a change from last-in, first-out to first-in, first-out.

A *change in accounting estimate* may be required as new events occur and as better information becomes available about the probable outcome of future events. Examples of changes in accounting estimates include: An increase in the percentage used to estimate doubtful accounts expense from 2% to 5% of sales; a major write-down of inventories because of obsolescence; a change in the economic lives of plant assets; a change in the recoverable units of natural resources; and a revision in the estimated liability for outstanding product warranties.

A *change in reporting entity* takes place when the group of companies comprising the reporting entity changes. For example, if one company combines with another company in a pooling of interests, the financial statements (which combine the revenue, expenses, assets, liabilities, and stockholders' equity of the combining companies) of the current year are not comparable with those of previous years without adequate disclosure of the change in reporting entity and the impact on the financial statements caused by the change.

A *correction of an error* is not considered an accounting change and is required when errors are discovered in previously issued financial statements. Errors may result from mathematical computations, mistakes in the application of accounting principles, or oversight or misuse of facts that existed at the time the financial statements were prepared. Examples of corrections of errors include the discovery that material amounts of depreciation expense were not recorded in prior accounting periods, and *a change from an accounting principle that is not generally accepted to one that is generally accepted.*

Change in Accounting Principle

A change in accounting principle leads to a departure from the standard auditors' assurance that financial statements are prepared "in conformity with generally accepted accounting principles applied on a basis *consistent with that of the preceding year*." In the preparation of financial statements there is a presumption that accounting principles once adopted should not be changed, so that meaningful comparisons of successive financial statements may be made. Consequently, a change in accounting principle is appropriate only when a business enterprise adopts an *alternative* generally accepted accounting principle that *clearly is preferable*. A change *from an unacceptable accounting principle to an accepted accounting principle is a correction of an error* rather than a change in accounting principle.

As stated earlier, a change in accounting principle generally is appropriate in two situations. The first is a change to a different method of applying a generally accepted accounting principle. For example, a change from the first-in, first-out method to the last-in, first-out method of inventories valuation would qualify. However, a business enterprise is permitted to change to a new method only if it can demonstrate that the new method is *preferable* in that it *more fairly presents the enterprise's financial position and results of operations.* The second situation in which a change in accounting principle is appropriate is the issuance of a pronouncement by the Financial Accounting Standards Board that creates a new accounting principle, expresses a preference for an accounting principle, or rejects a specific accounting principle. In either situation, the reason for the change in accounting principle and the effect of the change on net income are disclosed in a note to the financial statements of the accounting period in which the change is made.

In *Opinion No. 20,* "Accounting Changes," the Accounting Principles Board specifically excluded two events from being considered a change in accounting principle. These are (1) the initial adoption of an accounting principle to report transactions occurring for the first time, and (2) the adoption of a principle to report transactions that are substantially different from those previously occurring.

How should a change to a preferable accounting principle (or the selection of a different method of applying an accounting principle) be reported in order to preserve the comparability among current and future financial statements and those issued in the past? The answer to this question depends on the type of change in accounting principle and the magnitude of its effect. A change that has a material effect on net income is reported more completely than a change that has little effect on net income. Also, the effects of certain types of changes on financial statements of prior accounting periods may be more difficult to analyze than the effects caused by other types of changes. For this reason, the Accounting Principles Board stated that changes in accounting principle that have a material effect on net income should be classified into one of the following categories (1) those for which the *cumulative effect* of the change applicable to prior periods is included in the income statement for the period in which the change is made, and (2) those which require the *restatement* of the financial statements previously issued.

Cumulative Effect of Change Reported in Current Accounting Period   The Accounting Principles Board concluded that "most changes in accounting should be recognized by including the cumulative effect, based on a *retroactive computation,* of changing to a new accounting principle in net income of the period of the change. . . ."[2] The possibility that public confidence in financial statements would be reduced if the statements of prior accounting periods were restated retroactively was a major factor in the APB's conclusion. Examples of changes in accounting principle in this category are a change in the method of computing depreciation expense for

---

[2]Ibid., pp. 391–392.

previously recorded plant assets (for example, a change from the sum-of-the-years'-digits method to the straight-line method),[3] and a change from the first-in, first-out method to the last-in, first-out method of inventory valuation. The following guidelines should be followed for changes in accounting principle that require recognition of the cumulative effect of the change in the current year's income statement:

1 Financial statements for prior accounting periods included for comparative purposes are presented as previously reported.

2 The *cumulative effect* of the change in accounting principle on the retained earnings balance at the beginning of the accounting period in which the change is made is included in the net income of the period of the change. The amount of the cumulative effect is the difference between **(a)** *the actual amount of retained earnings at the beginning of the period of the change,* and **(b)** *the amount of retained earnings that would have been reported on that date if the new accounting principle had been applied retroactively for all prior periods.* In the computation of the cumulative effect, appropriate consideration is given to income taxes. The total and per-share amount of the cumulative effect is included in the income statement *below any extraordinary items.*

3 The total and per-share effects of the change in accounting principle on the income before extraordinary items and on the net income of the accounting period in which the change is made are disclosed.

4 Income before extraordinary items and net income computed on a *pro forma basis* are included in the income statement for all prior accounting periods presented as if the newly adopted accounting principle had been used in prior periods. Thus, *pro forma* means "on the assumption that a different accounting principle is used" to prepare the financial statements. If an income statement is presented for the current period only, the actual and pro forma amounts (including earnings per share) for the immediately preceding period are disclosed.

Let us examine how a change in depreciation method would be reported. Suppose that Alta Company, which owns and operates office buildings, decided at the beginning of Year 5 to change from the straight-line method to an accelerated method of depreciation. The accelerated method, which had been used appropriately for income tax purposes, now was *considered preferable* for financial accounting for the following reasons: (1) The revenue-producing capability of the office buildings tended to decline as the buildings became older, and (2) because most competitors used accelerated methods of depreciation, the change would make the income statements of Alta more comparable with other companies in the office rental business.

---

[3]A change to the straight-line method at a specified point in the economic life of an asset may be planned at the time the accelerated depreciation method is adopted to depreciate the cost fully over the economic life of the asset. Consistent application of such a policy is not a change in accounting principle under *APB Opinion No. 20,* "Accounting Changes."

If the accelerated method of depreciation had been used by Alta in past years for financial accounting, total depreciation would have been $600,000 more. Therefore, income before income taxes would have been $600,000 less. Assuming an income tax rate of 45%, the journal entry in Year 5 to record the change in accounting principle is:

Journal entry to record change in depreciation method

Cumulative Effect of Change in Accounting Principle		
($600,000 − $270,000)	330,000	
Deferred Income Tax Credits ($600,000 × 0.45)	270,000	
Accumulated Depreciation of Office Buildings		600,000
To record effect of change in accounting principle (a		
change from straight-line method to accelerated method of		
depreciation).		

The debit of $270,000 to the Deferred Income Tax Credits ledger account is the amount of income taxes Alta Company deferred in the past as a result of using the straight-line method of depreciation for financial accounting while using an accelerated method for income tax purposes. The cumulative effect of the change in accounting principle, $330,000, is the net amount by which retained earnings would have been ***decreased*** had the accelerated method of depreciation also been used for financial accounting. The cumulative effect is reported in the income statement after any extraordinary items, as illustrated in the two-year partial income statements of Alta Company on page 1101.

As stated in ***Note 1*** accompanying the income statements of Alta Company, the pro forma income before extraordinary item for Year 4 was decreased by $140,000 ($2,600,000 − $2,460,000 = $140,000), or $0.14 a share. Thus, the pro forma amounts for Years 4 and 5 are fully comparable because both are stated in terms of the newly adopted accelerated depreciation method.

In some situations, the determination of the cumulative effect of a change in accounting principle may be impossible. An example of this type of change is a change in inventories pricing method from the first-in, first-out method to the last-in, first-out method. In such situations, the disclosure is limited to showing the effect of the change on the net income and earnings per share of the accounting period in which the change is made. In such situations, the reason for not showing the cumulative effect of the change in accounting principle should be stated.

Cumulative Effect in Interim Periods   In ***Opinion No. 28,*** "Interim Financial Reporting," the Accounting Principles Board stated that a cumulative-effect-type change in accounting principle adopted in an interim period "should be reported in the interim period in a manner similar to that to be followed in the annual report."[4] Subsequently, the Financial Accounting Standards Board amended this rather general guideline in two important respects as follows:[5]

---

[4]*APB Opinion No. 28,* "Interim Financial Reporting," AICPA (New York: 1973), p. 530.
[5]*FASB Statement No. 3,* "Reporting Accounting Changes in Interim Financial Statements . . . ," FASB (Stamford: 1974), p. 4.

1 When a cumulative-effect-type accounting change is made during the *first* interim period of a fiscal year, the cumulative effect of the change on retained earnings at the *beginning of that fiscal year* is included in net income of the first interim period.

2 When a cumulative-effect-type accounting change is made in *other than the first* interim period of a fiscal year, *no* cumulative effect of the change is included in

Cumulative effect of change in accounting principle in the income statements

ALTA COMPANY
Partial Income Statements
For Years Ended December 31, Year 5 and Year 4

	Year 5	Year 4
Income before extraordinary item and cumulative effect of change in accounting principle	$3,000,000	$2,600,000
Add: Extraordinary item—income tax benefit of operating loss carryforward		60,000
Less: Cumulative effect (to end of Year 4) of change in accounting principle **(Note 1)**.	(330,000)	
Net income	$2,670,000	$2,660,000
Earnings per share of common stock:		
Income before extraordinary item and cumulative effect of change in accounting principle	$ 3.00	$ 2.60
Add: Extraordinary item—income tax benefit of operating loss carryforward		0.06
Less: Cumulative effect (to end of Year 4) of change in accounting principle **(Note 1)**	(0.33)	
Earnings per share of common stock (100,000 shares) . . .	$ 2.67	$ 2.66
Pro forma amounts, assuming the change in accounting principle is applied retroactively (Note 1):		
Income before extraordinary item	$3,000,000	$2,460,000
Earnings per share before extraordinary item	$ 3.00	$ 2.46
Net income	$3,000,000	$2,520,000
Earnings per share of common stock	$ 3.00	$ 2.52

Note 1: *During the year ended December 31, Year 5, the company changed its accounting for depreciation from the straight-line method to an accelerated method. The new method is a generally accepted method used in the industry, and it is believed the new method will cause the company's operating results to be more comparable with operating results of other companies in the industry. The effect of the change for the year ended December 31, Year 5, was to decrease income before extraordinary item by $120,000 (or $0.12 per share). The adjustment of $330,000 (after reduction of $270,000 for deferred income tax credits) to apply retroactively the new method is included in net income of Year 5. The pro forma amounts for Year 4 have been adjusted for the effect of retroactive application of the change of depreciation expense and related income taxes. The effect of the change for the year ended December 31, Year 4, was to decrease income before extraordinary item by $140,000 (or $0.14 per share).*

net income of the period of change. Instead, financial information for the pre-change interim periods of the fiscal year in which the change is made is restated by application of the newly adopted accounting principle to the pre-change interim periods. The cumulative effect of the change on retained earnings at the *beginning of that fiscal year* is included in restated net income of the first interim period of the fiscal year in which the change is made. Whenever financial information that includes those pre-change interim periods is presented, it is presented on the restated basis.

The Financial Accounting Standards Board also required extensive disclosure of a cumulative-effect-type accounting change in interim reports, including the nature and justification for the change and the effect of the change on net income and related per-share amounts for all interim periods presented.

Changes Requiring Restatement of Prior Periods' Financial Statements   Some changes in accounting principle are reported through restatement of the financial statements of prior accounting periods, including the following:

1   A change from the last-in, first-out method of pricing inventories to another method of pricing inventories

2   A change in the method of accounting for construction-type contracts

3   A change in accounting for development costs in extractive industries

4   A change from retirement-replacement-betterment accounting to depreciation accounting for railroad track structures[6]

5   A change in reporting entity (see pages 1107–1109)

6   A change from an acceptable accounting principle to another acceptable accounting principle for a closely held corporation issuing financial statements to the public for the first time (see page 1109)

Why is restatement of prior periods' financial statements appropriate for the foregoing accounting changes? Although a number of reasons might be cited, the main reason for the restatement of prior periods' financial statements is that the amount of the cumulative effect of the accounting change might be so large as to render the income statement potentially misleading. Imagine the effect on a business enterprise changing from the last-in, first-out to the first-in, first-out method of pricing inventories in, say, 1986. If the enterprise had been operating for 30 years and had priced inventories at the original base layer, the beginning inventories in 1986 would approximate 1956 prices. Thus, a change from the last-in, first-out method to first-in, first-out method of pricing inventories could have such a material effect on net income that the cumulative-effect approach would distort the net income of the enterprise for 1986.

When prior period financial statements are restated, the *nature of the change*

---

[6]*FASB Statement No. 73,* ''Reporting a Change in Accounting for Railroad Track Structures (an amendment of *APB Opinion No. 20*),'' FASB (Stamford: 1983), p. 1.

in accounting principle, as well as the justification for the change, are disclosed for the accounting period in which the change is made. Disclosure of the effect of the accounting change on income before extraordinary item, net income, and the related per-share amounts is made for all periods presented. This disclosure may be in the income statement or in a note to the financial statements, and need not be repeated in subsequent periods.[7]

To illustrate the restatement of an income statement for a prior period as a result of a change in accounting principle, assume the following: Lasky Company adopted the completed-contract method of accounting for construction-type contracts when it was incorporated in Year 1. Lasky reported net income of $137,500 in Year 1 and $330,000 in Year 2. At the beginning of Year 3, because of improvements in its estimating procedures, Lasky changed to the percentage-of-completion method of accounting for construction-type contracts. The effect of this change in accounting principle, assuming an income tax rate of 45%, is summarized below:

Effect of change from completed-contract method to percentage-of-completion method of accounting for construction-type contracts

Year	Income before income taxes		Differences		
	Completed-contract method	**Percentage-of-completion method**	**Before income tax effect**	**Income tax effect, 45%**	**Increase in net income**
1	$250,000	$550,000	$300,000	$135,000	$165,000
2	600,000	700,000	100,000	45,000	55,000
3	700,000	850,000	150,000	67,500	82,500

Lasky Company's journal entry in Year 3 to record the change in accounting principle is as follows:

Journal entry to record change in accounting for construction-type contracts

```
Estimated Earnings on Contracts in Progress
  ($300,000 + $100,000) .....................................  400,000
       Deferred Income Tax Credits ($135,000 + $45,000) ....              180,000
       Retained Earnings ($165,000 + $55,000) .............              220,000
  To record effect of change in accounting principle (a change
  from completed-contract method to percentage-of-completion
  method of accounting for construction-type contracts).
```

As indicated in Chapter 9 (page 469), the Estimated Earnings on Contracts in Progress ledger account is a positive valuation account that increases the carrying amount of the contracts in progress (asset) to cost plus accrued earnings. The Deferred Income Tax Credits account is credited because the income taxes attributable to the estimated earnings on contracts in progress will not be paid by Lasky until the contracts are completed.

---

[7]*APB Opinion 20*, p. 396.

The partial two-year comparative income statements for Lasky Company at the end of Year 3, giving retroactive effect to the change in accounting principle, are shown below:

Reporting the effect
of retroactive change
in the income
statements

LASKY COMPANY
Partial Income Statements
For Year 3 and Year 2

	Year 3	Year 2 (restated— Note 1)
Income before income taxes	$850,000	$700,000
Income taxes expense:		
Payable currently	$315,000	$270,000
Deferred	67,500	45,000
Total income taxes expense	$382,500	$315,000
Net income	$467,500	$385,000
Earnings per share of common stock (100,000 shares)	$ 4.68	$ 3.85

Note 1: *The company accounted for construction-type contracts by the percentage-of-completion method in Year 3, whereas in all prior years the completed-contract method was used. The new method of accounting was adopted to report the results of operations in a manner that more closely portrays the economic activity of the company. The company's management is of the opinion that it has the expertise to make reasonably accurate estimates of costs to compute the percentage of completion on contracts. Financial statements of prior years have been restated to apply the new method of accounting retroactively. For income tax purposes, the completed-contract method will be continued. The effects of the accounting change on net income and earnings per share of Year 3, and on net income and earnings per share previously reported for Year 2, follow:*

	Year 3	Year 2
Increase in:		
Net income	$82,500	$55,000
Earnings per share of common stock	$ 0.83	$ 0.55

The balances of retained earnings for Year 2 and Year 3 have been adjusted for the effect (net of income taxes) of retroactive restatement of the new method of accounting.

To illustrate the effect of the change in the presentation of retained earnings, the two-year comparative statements of retained earnings for Lasky Company are illustrated at the top of page 1105. In this illustration we assume that Lasky has not declared any dividends since it was incorporated in Year 1.

In some situations, the pro forma effect on the net income of individual prior accounting periods cannot be computed or reasonably estimated (because the information may not be available), although the cumulative effect on retained earnings at the beginning of the period of change can be determined. The cumulative effect in such cases is reported in the income statement of the period of change and the reason for not restating prior periods' results is disclosed.[8]

---

[8]Ibid., p. 395.

Statements of retained earnings with restatement of beginning balances	**LASKY COMPANY** **Statements of Retained Earnings** **For Year 3 and Year 2**	

	Year 3	Year 2
Retained earnings, beginning of year, as previously reported	$ 467,500	$137,500
Add: Cumulative effect of retroactive restatement of new method of accounting for construction-type contracts ...	220,000	165,000
Retained earnings, beginning of year, as restated	$ 687,500	$302,500
Net income	467,500	385,000
Retained earnings, end of year, as restated	$1,155,000	$687,500

Change in Accounting Estimate

Much of accountants' work involves the use of subjective judgment. That is, accountants often must estimate the economic life and residual value of plant assets, the amount of probable uncollectible accounts receivable, and inventories obsolescence, and make other decisions that require the estimate of the effects of future events. As time passes, new events and better information may require that the original estimate of amounts such as economic life or net residual value of plant assets be revised to reflect the events and information.

For example, assume that management had estimated the economic life of a plant asset at 10 years, with no net residual value at the end of 10 years. The cost of the asset, $20,000, has been depreciated $2,000 a year for seven years. At the end of the eighth year, management determined that the asset had a remaining economic life of four years and that its net residual value would be $500 at the end of 12 years of use. The revised annual depreciation expense over the remaining economic life of the asset is computed as follows:

Computation of revised annual depreciation for plant asset with changed estimates of economic life and net residual value	Cost of plant asset	$20,000
	Less: Depreciation for Years 1 through 7 at $2,000 a year ($2,000 × 7) ...	14,000
	Undepreciated cost at beginning of Year 8 (carrying amount)	$ 6,000
	Less: Estimated net residual value at end of Year 12	500
	Amount to be depreciated in Years 8 through 12 (5 years)	$ 5,500
	Revised annual depreciation for Years 8 through 12 ($5,500 ÷ 5 years of remaining economic life)	$ 1,100

The changes in estimated economic life and net residual value affect only the remaining five years of economic life (Years 8 through 12); *no correction of the previously reported earnings for Years 1 through 7 is required.* Because accounting measurements based on estimates are imperfect, and some disparity between past and subsequent estimates cannot be avoided, retroactive restatements of previously reported earnings as a result of changes in accounting estimates may cast suspicion on both the original and the revised earnings amounts. The information used to revise the service potential of the plant asset could not have been anticipated at the time the asset was acquired. Revised estimates are based on present conditions and management policies. Therefore, a reasonable approach is to allocate the unexpired service potential of the plant asset over its remaining economic life based on the latest information.

A change in an accounting estimate occurs because new or better information became available in the current accounting period. Thus, it follows that the resulting change in accounting estimate should affect the computation of net income of the period in which the change is made; if the change has a continuing effect, it should be consistently applied to all periods following the period of the change. *A change in accounting estimate does not require (as does a change in accounting principle) the recording of the cumulative effect of the change in the current period or the retroactive restatement of financial statements for prior periods.* Although disclosure of the effects on prior financial statement amounts is not necessary for estimates that are made in the ordinary course of accounting for items such as doubtful accounts expense or obsolescence of inventories, any change in estimate that has a significant effect on net income and earnings per share is disclosed in a note to the financial statements, as illustrated below for a publicly owned steel manufacturer:

Disclosure of change
in accounting estimate

> *In connection with a review of depreciation methods, the company determined that its steel production equipment would continue in service beyond the economic lives over which it was being depreciated. Accordingly, the company revised the economic lives of the equipment to 25 years from 18 years. The change in accounting estimate, which was applied effective January 1, Year 6, reduced depreciation expense and net loss for Year 6 by approximately $1,900,000, or $0.20 per share of common stock.*

A revision of the estimated economic life or net residual value of a plant asset, as described above, is a change in accounting estimate. A change in the method of computing depreciation on a previously acquired plant asset is a change in accounting principle. But what if a business enterprise acquired a new plant asset and decided that the output method of depreciation is the most appropriate method for the asset? As long as it continued to depreciate its previously acquired plant assets under the same method as before, there is no need for a cumulative-effect adjustment in the income statement, because there was no change in accounting principle for those assets. However, the effect of the new method of depreciation for *newly acquired plant assets* on the net income of the accounting period in which the change is made is disclosed.

In certain instances, a change in accounting principle may be accompanied by a change in accounting estimate. In such cases *it is difficult to separate the effect of the change in principle from the effect of the change in estimate.* For example, a business enterprise that has been deferring and amortizing certain costs might decide to change to a policy of recognizing such costs as expenses because the future benefits of the costs have become doubtful. This type of change often is related to the process of obtaining additional information that calls for a revision of the original judgment that the costs will provide future benefits. Because the new accounting method was adopted as a result of the change in estimated future benefits, *such a change is accounted for as a change in accounting estimate.*[9]

Change in Reporting Entity

Certain events, such as a business combination of two or more companies accounted for as a *pooling of interests* (see Chapter 16, page 820), result in financial statements that are in effect the statements of a *different reporting entity.* A change in reporting entity is viewed as a special type of change in accounting principle that *requires the restatement of the financial statements of all prior accounting periods as though the combined enterprise had existed all along.*

The following condensed two-year financial statements of Combinor Corporation and Combinee Company are used to illustrate a change in reporting entity resulting from a business combination accounted for as a pooling of interests. The financial statements were prepared immediately prior to a pooling-type business combination of the two enterprises on December 31, Year 2.

COMBINOR CORPORATION AND COMBINEE COMPANY
Condensed Financial Statements Prior to Business Combination
For Years Ended December 31, Year 2 and Year 1

	Combinor Corporation Year ended Dec. 31,		Combinee Company Year ended Dec. 31,	
	Year 2	*Year 1*	*Year 2*	*Year 1*
	Income Statements			
Revenue	$ 800,000	$ 600,000	$400,000	$300,000
Costs and expenses	600,000	500,000	250,000	200,000
Net income	$ 200,000	$ 100,000	$150,000	$100,000
	Statements of Retained Earnings			
Retained earnings, beginning of year	$ 400,000	$ 300,000	$250,000	$150,000
Net income	200,000	100,000	150,000	100,000
Retained earnings, end of year	$ 600,000	$ 400,000	$400,000	$250,000
	Balance Sheets			
Total assets	$1,600,000	$1,300,000	$800,000	$600,000
Liabilities	$ 900,000	$ 800,000	$350,000	$300,000
Common stock, $1 par	100,000	100,000	50,000	50,000
Retained earnings	600,000	400,000	400,000	250,000
Total liabilities & stockholders' equity	$1,600,000	$1,300,000	$800,000	$600,000

---

[9]Ibid., p. 388.

On December 31, Year 2, Combinor Corporation issued 40,000 shares of its $1 par common stock to shareholders of Combinee Company for all 50,000 shares of Combinee's outstanding $1 par common stock. (Out-of-pocket costs of the business combination are disregarded in this illustration.) As a result of this combination, which was accounted for as a pooling of interests, Combinee was liquidated and Combinor acquired Combinee's net assets. Combinor Corporation issues the following restated financial statements of the *new reporting entity* for Year 2 and Year 1:

Illustration of change
in reporting entity

COMBINOR CORPORATION
Condensed Financial Statements
(restated for effects of pooling-of-interests business combination)
For Years Ended December 31, Year 2 and Year 1

	December 31,	
	Year 2	Year 1
Income Statements		
Revenue	$1,200,000	$ 900,000
Costs and expenses	850,000	700,000
Net income	$ 350,000	$ 200,000
Statements of Retained Earnings		
Retained earnings, beginning of year:		
As previously reported	$ 400,000	$ 300,000
Add: Adjustment to reflect pooling of interests with		
Combinee Company	250,000	150,000
As restated	$ 650,000	$ 450,000
Net income	350,000	200,000
Retained earnings, end of year	$1,000,000	$ 650,000
Balance Sheets		
Total assets	$2,400,000	$1,900,000
Liabilities	$1,250,000	$1,100,000
Common stock, $1 par	140,000	140,000
Additional paid-in capital	10,000	10,000
Retained earnings	1,000,000	650,000
Total liabilities & stockholders' equity	$2,400,000	$1,900,000

Under pooling-of-interests accounting, the business combination of Combinor Corporation and Combinee Company is considered to have taken place on January 1, Year 1, the beginning of the earliest accounting period covered by Combinor's financial statements on page 1107, rather than on December 31, Year 2. Accordingly, the income statement and balance sheet show *combined amounts* for all elements—revenue, expenses, assets, liabilities, and stockholders' equity. Combinor Corporation's statements of retained earnings show the *retroactive adjustment* of beginning retained earnings amounts to include comparable amounts for Combinee Company. As a result of issuing common stock with a par value of $40,000 (40,000 × $1 = $40,000) for Combinee's total paid-in capital of $50,000, Combinor recorded additional paid-in capital of $10,000 ($50,000 − $40,000 = $10,000).

Pooling-of-interests accounting for business combinations is discussed further in *Modern Advanced Accounting* of this series.

Initial Public Issuance of Financial Statements

As pointed out on page 1098, most changes from one acceptable accounting principle to another acceptable principle do not require the restatement of financial statements of prior accounting periods. An exception is made for a closely held company *issuing securities to the public for the first time.* Potential investors in the securities of a company "going public" are better served by earnings summaries for a period of years prepared on the basis of the newly adopted accounting principle. Comparisons of operating results are more meaningful because the newly adopted accounting principle also will be used in future periods. Therefore, the *financial statements issued in connection with an initial public offering of securities are restated retroactively for all periods for which financial statements are presented.*[10]

CORRECTION OF ERRORS

In previous chapters we note the difficulties inherent in the measurement of periodic net income of a business enterprise. At best, accountants measure only the impact of past transactions and events and make informed estimates of the present effect of probable future events. In addition, *errors* in financial statements may result from mathematical mistakes, mistakes in the application of accounting principles, or the oversight or misuse of facts that existed at the time the financial statements were prepared. An example of a correction of an error is a *change from an accounting principle that is not generally accepted to one that is generally accepted.*

Correction of an Error in Previously Issued Financial Statements

When a material error is discovered in previously issued financial statements, the correction of the error is reported as a *prior period adjustment.*[11] The nature of the error and the effect of its correction on net income and earnings per share are disclosed in the financial statements of the accounting period in which the error is corrected. An example of such disclosure, generally presented in a note to the financial statements, is shown at the top of page 1110.

---

[10]Ibid., pp. 396–397.
[11]*FASB Statement No. 16*, "Prior Period Adjustments," FASB (Stamford: 1977), p. 5.

Illustration of note
describing correction
of error

> **Note—Correction of error:** *A major revision of labor standards in February, Year 3, resulted in a charge to Year 2 earnings of $2,500,000 because of reduced labor and factory overhead costs included in inventories on December 31, Year 2. In connection with the pricing of the December 31, Year 2, inventories in February, Year 3, the company determined that* **an error** *had been made in the application of factory overhead to the December 31, Year 1, inventories. The correction resulted in a reduction of the December 31, Year 1, inventories by $450,000. Earnings before income taxes for Year 1 were reduced from $1,500,000 to $1,050,000; net income was reduced from $816,000 to $600,000; and earnings were reduced from $0.41 to $0.30 per share of common stock.*

If an error has a material effect on previously issued financial statements, retroactive revision of the statements for prior periods may be required. Whenever users of financial statements analyze the financial affairs of a business enterprise, they want to see comparative income statement data for a number of years. When such comparative income statements are prepared, it generally is desirable to revise prior years' income statements to correct material errors discovered after the original financial statements were issued. The Auditing Standards Division of the AICPA has made the following recommendation on this point:[12]

> If the effect on the financial statements or auditor's report of the subsequently discovered information can promptly be determined, disclosure should consist of issuing, as soon as practicable, revised financial statements and auditor's report. . . . Generally, only the most recently issued audited financial statements would need to be revised, even though the revision resulted from events that had occurred in prior years.

Correction of Previously Issued Financial Statements Illustrated

To illustrate the correction of a material error, assume that Trevor Corporation acquired a machine on January 2, Year 1 for $100,000. The machine had an economic life of 10 years with no net residual value, and was being depreciated by the straight-line method. The accountant incorrectly recorded (for financial accounting and in income tax returns) annual depreciation expense for Year 1 through Year 4 at $1,000 a year rather than at the correct amount of $10,000 a year ($100,000 ÷ 10 = $10,000) because of a computation error. Thus, depreciation expense was understated by $9,000 a year ($10,000 − $1,000 = $9,000), or $36,000 for the four-year period ($9,000 × 4 = $36,000). The error was discovered early in Year 5, after the following condensed financial statements *had been issued:*

---

[12]*Statement on Auditing Standards No. 1,* "Codification of Auditing Standards and Procedures," AICPA (New York: 1973), p. 129.

TREVOR CORPORATION
Comparative Income Statements (before correction)
For Year 4 and Year 3

	Year 4	Year 3
Sales	$300,000	$280,000
Costs and expenses	270,000	260,000
Net income	$ 30,000	$ 20,000
Earnings per share of common stock (10,000 shares)	$ 3.00	$ 2.00

TREVOR CORPORATION
Comparative Balance Sheets (before correction)
End of Year 4 and Year 3

	Year 4	Year 3
Assets		
Other assets	$260,000	$225,000
Machinery	320,000	290,000
Less: Accumulated depreciation	(80,000)	(65,000)
Total assets	$500,000	$450,000
Liabilities & Stockholders' Equity		
Liabilities	$170,000	$150,000
Common stock, $10 par	100,000	100,000
Retained earnings	230,000	200,000
Total liabilities & stockholders' equity	$500,000	$450,000

Assuming an income tax rate of 45%, the following correcting journal entry is required for Trevor Corporation early in Year 5:

Journal entry to
correct computational
error of prior periods

Income Tax Refund Receivable ($36,000 × 0.45)	16,200	
Retained Earnings ($36,000 − $16,200).....................	19,800	
Accumulated Depreciation of Machinery		36,000
To correct error in computation of depreciation expense for		
Year 1 through Year 4, and to establish receivable for income		
taxes overpaid for those years.		

If corrected financial statements for prior years are not issued in Year 5, the ***prior period adjustment*** of $19,800 is reported in the statement of retained earnings for Year 5 as a correction to retained earnings at the beginning of Year 5. When corrected financial statements for prior years are issued in Year 5, the beginning and ending balances for retained earnings are ***corrected retroactively*** for each prior year for which corrected financial statements are issued. As an example, the corrected comparative financial statements of Trevor Corporation for Year 4 and Year 3 are presented below:

TREVOR CORPORATION
Comparative Income Statements (after correction)
For Year 4 and Year 3

	Year 4	Year 3
Sales	$300,000	$280,000
Costs and expenses	274,950	264,950
Net income	$ 25,050	$ 15,050
Earnings per share of common stock (10,000 shares)	$ 2.51	$ 1.51

TREVOR CORPORATION
Comparative Balance Sheets (after correction)
End of Year 4 and Year 3

	Year 4	Year 3
Assets		
Other assets	$276,200	$237,150
Machinery	320,000	290,000
Less: Accumulated depreciation	(116,000)	(92,000)
Total assets	$480,200	$435,150
Liabilities & Stockholders' Equity		
Liabilities	$170,000	$150,000
Common stock, $10 par	100,000	100,000
Retained earnings	210,200	185,150
Total liabilities & stockholders' equity	$480,200	$435,150

In the corrected income statements, costs and expenses of each year are increased retroactively by the $9,000 understatement in annual depreciation expense net of $4,050 income taxes ($9,000 × 0.45 = $4,050). Thus, net income for each year is decreased by $4,950 ($9,000 − $4,050 = $4,950).

The balance sheet items requiring correction at the end of Year 4 and Year 3 are other assets, accumulated depreciation, and retained earnings. Because depreciation expense was understated by $9,000 a year, the cumulative effect is $36,000 at the end of Year 4 ($9,000 × 4 = $36,000), and $27,000 at the end of Year 3 ($9,000 × 3 = $27,000). The corrected balance of accumulated depreciation at the end of Year 4 is $116,000 ($80,000 as originally reported plus $36,000 correction = $116,000), and at the end of Year 3 it is $92,000 ($65,000 as originally reported plus $27,000 correction = $92,000). Other assets are increased $4,050 a year for the income tax refunds receivable resulting from the understatement of depreciation expense in the income tax returns of each year. Thus, other assets total $276,200 at the end of Year 4 [$260,000 + ($4,050 × 4) = $276,200] and $237,150 at the end of Year 3 [$225,000 + ($4,050 × 3) = $237,150]. The amount of retained earnings is restated to $210,200 ($230,000 − $19,800 = $210,200) at the end of Year 4, and to $185,150 [$200,000 − ($4,950 × 3) = $185,150] at the end of Year 3.

Types of Errors

Many accounting errors are brought to light by the controls in the double-entry accounting system. Independent accountants, internal auditors, and Internal Revenue agents may uncover errors during an examination of the accounting records. The installation of an improved accounting system may uncover material errors resulting from the inadequacies of the previous system. Thus, the necessity of correcting errors is more likely to occur in a small business enterprise than in a large publicly owned corporation.

The problem of dealing with errors of the same type may be generalized to some extent. Once the nature of the distortion created by a class of error is understood, it is possible to determine the effect of similar errors.

Errors Affecting Only Balance Sheet Amounts An error that affects only balance sheet amounts may arise because (1) journal entries were made to the wrong ledger account, (2) transactions were omitted from the journal, or (3) the amounts of certain journal entries were wrong. For example, if Accounts Payable is debited instead of Accounts Receivable, total assets and total liabilities are understated by the same amount. When the error is discovered, only balance sheet amounts require correction.

Errors Affecting Only Income Statement Amounts An error that is confined to income statement amounts has no effect on net income. Such errors generally arise through misclassification; for example, an expense or revenue item may be debited or credited to the wrong ledger account.

Errors Affecting both the Balance Sheet and the Income Statement Errors that affect both the balance sheet and the income statement fall into two categories: (1) Errors that will be counterbalanced in the next accounting period, and (2) errors that will not be counterbalanced in the next period.

Some errors, if not discovered, *will be counterbalanced* in the course of the next period's accounting. The typical counterbalancing error causes a misstatement of the net income of one accounting period and the balance sheet at the end of that period, which is offset by a misstatement of income in the *opposite direction* in the following period. The balance sheet at the end of the second period and the net income of subsequent periods are not affected by the error, which has in a sense "corrected itself" over the two periods.

An example of a counterbalancing error is the failure to record accrued wages at the end of an accounting period. The liability wages payable is understated at the end of the period, and because wages expense is understated, net income is overstated in the period the error is made. In the following period, the payment of the unrecorded accrued wages is debited to expense; thus, wages expense for the second period is overstated. As a result, net income of the second period is understated by an amount equal to the overstatement of the previous period. If proper wage accruals are made at the end of the second period, the wages payable in the balance sheet on that date is correct. The balance of retained earnings also is correctly stated at the end of the second period.

Other errors affect both the balance sheet and the income statement, but *are not counterbalanced* in the next accounting period. For example, suppose an acquisition of equipment is debited to expense by mistake. Because an expense is overstated in the period the error is made, net income for that period is understated by an amount equal to the cost of the equipment less the depreciation expense that should have been recognized. Net income also is overstated in subsequent periods by the amount of unrecorded depreciation expense on the equipment while it is in service. Equipment in the balance sheet is understated throughout its economic life.

Analyzing the Effect of Errors

When an error is discovered, the accountant must analyze the effect of the error on financial data for prior, current, and subsequent accounting periods. Because it is not feasible to discuss every possible error that might occur, we illustrate in this section the reasoning used in the determination of the effect of errors. The illustrations are designed to show corrections required to produce revised income statements of prior periods, and do not purport to illustrate the application of any Financial Accounting Standards Board pronouncement. In other words, we are concerned primarily with omissions and other errors that may occur in a *small business enterprise that does not issue financial statements to the public.*

Analysis of effect of overstatement of inventories at end of Year 4

Income Statement

Year 4	Year 5	Year 6
Net income is overstated by $3,400. (Cost of goods sold is understated, because ending inventories were overstated.)	Net income is understated by $3,400 (Cost of goods sold is overstated, because beginning inventories were overstated.)	Error has fully counterbalanced; no correction is required.

Balance Sheet

Year 4	Year 5	Year 6
Assets are overstated by $3,400. (Ending inventories are overstated.) Retained earnings is overstated by $3,400. (Net income was overstated.)	Balance sheet items are properly stated, because Dec. 31, Year 5, inventories are correct, and overstatement of retained earnings in Year 4 has been offset by understatement of net income in Year 5.	No correction is required.

As an example, let us trace the effect of an error in the determination of the amount of inventories at the end of an accounting period. Assume that we discover that the inventories on December 31, Year 4, are overstated by $3,400, and that the *periodic inventory system is used.* We may analyze the effect of this error (disregarding income taxes) as illustrated at the bottom of page 1114.

The action to be taken on discovery of this error depends on when the error is discovered and the extent of the revision of financial statements that is desired.

Discovery in Year 4 If the error is discovered in Year 4 before the ledger accounts are closed, a separate correcting journal entry is not necessary. The ending inventories under the *periodic inventory system* are recorded at the time closing entries are made, and it is a simple matter to use the revised inventories amount in the closing (or adjusting) entries. The ending inventories in the income statement for Year 4 are decreased by $3,400, and net income is decreased by this amount.

Discovery in Year 5 If the error is discovered at any time prior to the closing of the ledger accounts for Year 5, the correcting entry is:

Journal entry to correct error in ending inventories of prior accounting period

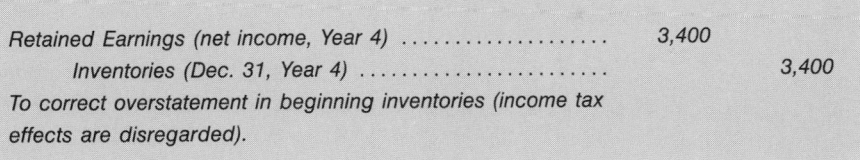

Retained Earnings (net income, Year 4) 3,400
    Inventories (Dec. 31, Year 4) 3,400
To correct overstatement in beginning inventories (income tax effects are disregarded).

The purpose of this entry is to correct the financial statements for Year 5. Both the net income for Year 5 and the balance sheet at the end of Year 5 are stated correctly after the prior period adjustment of $3,400 (correction of net income for Year 4) is recorded in the Retained Earnings ledger account. In the statement of retained earnings for Year 5, the prior period adjustment is reported as a correction of the beginning balance of retained earnings.

Discovery in Year 6 If the error in the inventories at the end of Year 4 were not discovered until Year 6, no correcting entry would be required, because the error has been fully counterbalanced. If the Year 4 and Year 5 financial statements were to be corrected retroactively, this could be accomplished by changing the inventories and retained earnings amounts in these statements or by the use of a working paper. As of the beginning of Year 6, however, all balance sheet ledger accounts are free of this error.

Working Paper for Analysis of Errors

The first procedure in the correction of errors is to analyze the effect of the errors on financial data. The next procedure is to prepare the necessary correcting journal entries. In the course of an audit or when an accountant is assigned to correct accounting records that had not been maintained correctly, a substantial number of errors, affecting several accounting periods, may be discovered. In such cases it may be helpful to use a working paper to analyze the errors and their effects on financial statements. The working paper also serves as the underlying support for a single correcting journal entry to bring the accounting records up to date. There is no standard form of working paper; one form that has proved useful for this purpose is illustrated in the following example:

Illustration An audit of the accounting records of Lamm Trading Company early in Year 8 disclosed the following errors affecting the financial statements for Year 6 and Year 7:

(1) Unexpired insurance was omitted from the accounting records; insurance premiums were debited to Insurance Expense at the time of payment. The correct amount of unexpired insurance at the end of Year 6 was $550, and at the end of Year 7 it was $980.

(2) No journal entry had been made to accrue interest on notes payable at the end of the year. Interest was debited to Interest Expense at the time of payment. Interest payable at the end of Year 6 was $1,700, and at the end of Year 7 it was $480.

(3) Interest on notes receivable was credited to Interest Revenue when received. At the end of Year 6, interest receivable amounted to $450, and at the end of Year 7 it was $840.

(4) Lamm rented part of its land, receiving rent in advance; receipts were credited to Rent Revenue. Unearned rent at the end of Year 6 was $1,800, and at the end of Year 7 it was $740.

(5) Lamm is subject to state and federal income taxes at a rate of 45% of taxable income. There are no differences between taxable income and pre-tax accounting income. It is assumed that Year 6 income tax returns will be amended to reflect corrections of the foregoing errors, and that Lamm will claim a refund for excess income taxes paid in Year 6, or will pay any tax deficiency.

Lamm Trading Company reported net income of $20,000 for Year 6, and $16,000 for Year 7. We wish to determine the extent of the errors in the net income for Year 6 and Year 7, and to correct the accounting records as of December 31, Year 7. The working paper on page 1117 illustrates a procedure that may be followed.

Let us assume that the ledger accounts *have been closed* at the end of Year 7. On the basis of our working paper analysis, the following journal entry corrects the ledger accounts as of December 31, Year 7:

Journal entry to correct ledger accounts for errors *after* accounts are closed	Unexpired Insurance...	980	
	Interest Receivable	840	
	Income Tax Refund Receivable	1,125	
	Retained Earnings (net income, Years 6 and 7)		330
	Interest Payable...		480
	Unearned Rent..		740
	Income Taxes Payable		1,395
	To correct errors revealed by audit in Year 8 after the ledger accounts had been closed for Year 7.		

LAMM TRADING COMPANY
Working Paper for Analysis of Errors
December 31, Year 7

Explanation	Net income for Year 6 (Dr) Cr*	Net income for Year 7 (Dr) Cr*	Balance sheet ledger accounts requiring correction Dec. 31, Year 7 (Dr) Cr*	Ledger accounts
(1) Unexpired insurance omitted:				
Dec. 31, Year 6	$ 550	$ (550)		
Dec. 31, Year 7		980	$(980)	Unexpired Insurance
(2) Accrued interest on notes payable omitted:				
Dec. 31, Year 6	(1,700)	1,700		
Dec. 31, Year 7		(480)	480	Interest Payable
(3) Accrued interest on notes receivable omitted:				
Dec. 31, Year 6	450	(450)		
Dec. 31, Year 7		840	(840)	Interest Receivable
(4) Unearned rent omitted:				
Dec. 31, Year 6	(1,800)	1,800		
Dec. 31, Year 7		(740)	740	Unearned Rent
Increase (or decrease) in income before income taxes	$ (2,500)	$ 3,100		
(5) Revision of income taxes (45%):				
Year 6 income taxes expense overstated	1,125		(1,125)	Income Tax Refund Receivable
Year 7 income taxes expense understated		(1,395)	1,395	Income Taxes Payable
Increase (or decrease) in net income	$(1,375)	$ 1,705	330	Retained Earnings
Net income, as originally reported	20,000	16,000		
Corrected net income	$18,625	$17,705		

*Separate columns for debit and credit amounts may be used.

Trace the amounts in this journal entry to the working paper and you will see that all the data necessary for the entry were developed in the working paper. To prepare a corrected income statement for Year 7, it is necessary to revise the specific expense and revenue ledger accounts to reflect the total increase of $1,705 in Year 7 net income. If the ledger accounts *had not been closed* at the time the correcting entry was made, it would be necessary to expand the correcting journal entry to include corrections to revenue and expense accounts for Year 7, as shown on page 1118.

The analysis of errors in the working paper indicates that net income for Year 7 was understated by $1,705. If Year 7 revenue and expense ledger accounts are to be

Journal entry to
correct ledger
accounts for errors
before accounts are
closed

Unexpired Insurance........................	980	
Interest Receivable	840	
Income Tax Refund Receivable	1,125	
Retained Earnings (net income, Year 6)	1,375	
Income Taxes Expense (Year 7)	1,395	⎫ Correction of
Insurance Expense ($980 − $550)		430 ⎪ revenue and
Interest Expense ($1,700 − $480)		1,220 ⎬ expense ledger
Interest Revenue ($840 − $450)		390 ⎪ accounts to
Rent Revenue ($1,800 − $740)		1,060 ⎭ reflect $1,705
Interest Payable		480 increase in net
Unearned Rent........................		740 income for Year 7
Income Taxes Payable		1,395

To correct errors revealed by audit in Year 8.
Ledger accounts had not been closed on
Dec. 31, Year 7.

corrected, it is necessary to look at the details in the column headed "Net income for Year 7" and determine the specific revenue and expense accounts that require correction. All the necessary amounts appear in this column, but the working paper does not show the ledger accounts involved. It is possible to add a column or two to the working paper and enter the account titles at the time the working paper is prepared. However, it usually is easier to determine the appropriate revenue or expense account by noting the description of the error in the explanation column. For example, when we see that unexpired insurance was omitted at the end of both Year 6 and Year 7, it is apparent that the correction involves insurance expense. Unexpired insurance increased from $550 to $980 during Year 7; therefore, it is clear that insurance expense was overstated by $430 ($980 − $550 = $430) because an increase in assets in this amount was incorrectly recognized as an expense. This reasoning is used to determine the credit of $430 to Insurance Expense in the correcting journal entry above.

The working paper for analysis of errors illustrated on page 1117 is helpful in tracing the effect of errors on net income for several years and in providing the basis for the necessary journal entry or entries to correct ledger account balances at the end of the latest year. Once the necessary journal entries have been recorded, the balance sheet and income statement for the latest year may be prepared.

If comparative financial statements are to be prepared, there remains the problem of revising the financial statements of prior years to reflect the correction of errors. A correcting entry always revises balance sheet ledger accounts to their corrected balances at the end of the current year, but it does not correct account balances on any prior date. Similarly, once the revenue and expense accounts for a year have been closed, a journal entry to correct errors has no effect on any revenue and expense accounts for that year.

If there are few errors affecting data for prior years, it is usually a simple matter to make the necessary changes in amounts appearing in financial statements for prior years. However, when there are numerous errors, or when the correcting entries are complex, it may be desirable to use a working paper to correct the financial statements for prior years. A working paper that provides two columns for the original ledger account balances, two columns for the correcting entries, and two columns each for the corrected income statement and balance sheet amounts serves this purpose, and also serves as a permanent record for the accounting files.

FINANCIAL STATEMENTS FROM INCOMPLETE RECORDS

The heart of the double-entry accounting system is the analysis of the effect of each business transaction or event on the accounting equation: Assets = liabilities + owners' equity. Many small business enterprises operate with varying degrees of success with only minimal accounting records and without the benefit of a complete accounting system. A system (or lack of system) in which transactions are not analyzed and recorded in the double-entry framework sometimes is called a *single-entry accounting system.* The accounting records of social clubs, civic organizations, and small business enterprises often are maintained on a single-entry basis.

At some time after the data have been well muddled, an accountant is likely to be called on to sift through the accounting records and gather enough information to complete an income tax return and to prepare financial statements. Thus, the process of recasting single-entry accounting information into the double-entry framework is a practical analytical exercise.

Balance Sheet from Incomplete Accounting Records

A business enterprise having no formal accounting system still must record certain basic information. For example, a record of cash received and checks written and a record of amounts receivable from customers and amounts payable to creditors is essential. It is possible to prepare a balance sheet on any date for such an enterprise from various sources of information. Cash may be determined by count and by reconciliation of bank statements. Amounts receivable from customers may be summarized from unpaid sales invoices. Inventories may be counted, weighed, or measured, and their cost determined from suppliers' invoices. The cost of plant assets owned similarly may be established. Amounts payable to creditors may be determined from invoices and monthly statements. Ownership equity is the difference between the amounts assigned to assets and to liabilities.

Computation of Net Income from Single-Entry Accounting Records

One way to measure net income from single-entry accounting records is to analyze the change in owners' equity during an accounting period. We know that owners' equity is the residual interest in the net assets of a business enterprise and that it is increased by net income and additional investments, and decreased by net losses and withdrawals by owners. By the process of elimination, if we know the beginning and ending balance of owners' equity and the amount of any additional investments or withdrawals by owners, we may compute the change in owners' equity attributable to the net income or loss during an accounting period as follows:

Computation of net
income or net loss by
analysis of changes
in owners' equity

	Example A (net income)	Example B (net loss)
Owners' equity at end of accounting period	$22,000	$20,000
Less: Owners' equity at beginning of period	18,500	25,000
Total increase (decrease) in owners' equity	$ 3,500	$ (5,000)
Add: Amounts withdrawn by owners	4,800	2,600
Less: Additional investments by owners	(1,000)	(500)
Net income (loss) for period	$ 7,300	$ (2,900)

For most purposes, a more complete picture of operations is needed than that conveyed by the net income amount. The Internal Revenue Service requires detail of revenue and expenses in income tax returns. For even the most elementary budgeting and managerial control purposes, information is required as to how net income was computed. The objective, then, is to develop revenue and expenses from single-entry accounting records. Because cash transactions are of major importance in any business enterprise, a detailed record of cash receipts and payments is a valuable source of information. This is demonstrated below:

From a detailed list of cash receipts we may determine:	From a detailed list of cash payments we may determine:
Cash receipts from sales and other revenue	Cash paid for purchases of merchandise and operating expenses
Collections on customers' accounts	Payments to trade creditors
Proceeds from disposal of plant assets	Cash paid to acquire plant assets
Amounts borrowed	Payments on loans
Cash investments by owners	Cash withdrawals by owners

If, in addition to cash receipts and payments data, we have (1) a list of assets at the beginning and end of the accounting period, and (2) a list of liabilities at the beginning and end of the period, we may compute the owners' equity at the beginning and end of the period, and prepare comparative balance sheets. From this information, plus some help from miscellaneous sources, we may reconstruct the major components of the income statement. In the sections that follow are some examples to illustrate how the various revenue and expense items may be derived from information available in single-entry accounting records.

Illustration: Income Statement from Incomplete Accounting Records   To illustrate the preparation of an income statement, we assume a relatively simple situation. The balance sheet on December 31, Year 1, summary of operations for Year 2, ledger account balances on December 31, Year 2, and additional information for Joe's Place, a single proprietorship, presented on pages 1121–1122, serve as a basis for our illustration.

JOE'S PLACE
Balance Sheet
December 31, Year 1
(prepared from incomplete accounting records)

Assets		*Liabilities & Proprietor's Capital*	
Cash.....................	$ 4,680	Accounts payable..........	$ 9,400
Notes receivable	12,000	Salaries payable...........	1,100
Accounts receivable.......	4,000	Unearned rent.............	600
Interest receivable........	320	Total liabilities	$ 11,100
Inventories	18,000		
Unexpired insurance	500		
Land....................	50,000		
Building and equipment ...	140,000		
Less: Accumulated			
depreciation	(62,500)	Joe Palermo, capital	155,900
Total assets	$167,000	Total liabilities & capital ..	$167,000

JOE'S PLACE
Summary of Operations
For Year Ended December 31, Year 2
(from cash and supplementary records)

Cash receipts:		
Collections on accounts receivable........................	$35,000	
Sales for cash	42,000	
Interest revenue	540	
Rent revenue	3,600	$81,140
Cash payments:		
Accounts payable for merchandise (including freight-in)	$53,400	
Insurance premiums	940	
Salaries	10,700	
Other operating expenses	3,000	
Drawings by owner......................................	6,000	74,040
Sales returns and allowances (all applicable to Year 2 sales) ..		1,800
Cash discounts taken by customers (sales discounts).........		600
Accounts receivable written off as uncollectible during		
Year 2..		300
Cash discounts taken on purchases (purchases discounts)....		1,100
Purchases returns and allowances (all applicable to Year 2		
purchases)		970

JOE'S PLACE
Ledger Account Balances
December 31, Year 2
(from supplementary analysis)

Cash (verified through count and bank reconciliations)	*$11,780*
Notes receivable (no change during Year 2)	*12,000*
Accounts receivable	*7,600*
Interest receivable	*530*
Inventories	*25,000*
Unexpired insurance	*700*
Accounts payable	*8,500*
Salaries payable	*1,900*
Unearned rent	*450*

Additional Information

(1) No acquisitions or disposals of plant assets were made in Year 2.
(2) Depreciation expense is computed at $12,800 for Year 2.
(3) Payroll taxes and income tax withholdings are disregarded.
(4) The direct write-off method is used to record doubtful accounts expense.

Computation of Gross Sales   Sales are from two sources, cash receipts from customers and gross increases in accounts receivable. Because accounts receivable on December 31, Year 1, reflect revenue collected in prior years, cash collections of these receivables during Year 2 have no connection with the revenue of that year. Therefore, the beginning balance of accounts receivable must be deducted from the total cash collections to compute sales for Year 2 that were collected in cash. Conversely, accounts receivable on December 31, Year 2, represent sales that were not included in cash receipts of Year 2 and therefore must be added to cash receipts

JOE'S PLACE
Computation of Gross Sales
For Year Ended December 31, Year 2

Sales on credit for Year 2:		
Collections on accounts receivable	*$35,000*	
Accounts receivable written off as uncollectible	*300*	
Sales returns and allowances (all applicable to		
Year 2 sales)	*1,800*	
Cash discounts taken by customers	*600*	
Accounts receivable, Dec. 31, Year 2	*7,600*	
Less: Accounts receivable, Dec. 31, Year 1	*(4,000)*	*$41,300*
Add: Sales for cash		*42,000*
Gross sales		*$83,300*

to compute the sales for that year. Accounts receivable included in this computation should include only accounts arising from the sale of goods and services.

Sales returns and allowances, sales discounts, and accounts receivable written off during Year 2 represent sales during that year that were not collected in cash and are not included in accounts receivable on December 31, Year 2. However, these amounts should be included in the computation of gross sales for Year 2. Applying this reasoning, the computation of gross sales for Joe's Place is shown at the bottom of page 1122.

Computation of Other Revenue The amount of other revenue, such as interest revenue and rent revenue, may be computed from comparative balance sheets and cash receipts data as illustrated below:

JOE'S PLACE
Computation of Other Revenue
For Year Ended December 31, Year 2

	Interest revenue	Rent revenue
Revenue received in cash in Year 2	$540	$3,600
Less: Revenue received in cash but not realized in Year 2:		
Unearned rent, Dec. 31, Year 2		450
Interest receivable, Dec. 31, Year 1	320	
Cash receipts representing revenue for Year 2	$220	$3,150
Add: Revenue realized in Year 2 but not included in cash receipts:		
Unearned rent, Dec. 31, Year 1		600
Interest receivable, Dec. 31, Year 2	530	
Revenue	$750	$3,750

Computation of Cost of Goods Sold The cost of goods sold is derived from information about purchases and inventories. The amount of ending inventories may be determined by counting, weighing, or measuring. Presumably, the amount of beginning inventories was determined comparably; if not, an estimated amount must be used.

The amount of purchases may be computed from cash payments and accounts payable at the beginning and end of Year 2. The balance of accounts payable on December 31, Year 1, includes purchases during prior years that were not a part of the operating results of Year 2. Therefore, from total cash payments to suppliers we must deduct the December 31, Year 1, balance of accounts payable to compute the cash outlays for purchases applicable to Year 2. Accounts payable on December 31, Year 2, represent credit purchases during Year 2 that must be added to compute the total amount of purchases for that year. An analysis of invoices provides information as to the cash discounts taken and the credits received for purchases returns and allowances during Year 2.

The following illustration for Joe's Place demonstrates how reasoning and a systematic organization of the available data are used to compute the cost of goods sold. The first step is to compute the amount of gross purchases for Year 2, as shown below:

JOE'S PLACE
Computation of Gross Purchases
For Year Ended December 31, Year 2

Payments on accounts payable during Year 2 (including freight-in)	$53,400
Add: Cash discounts taken on purchases	1,100
Purchases returns and allowances (all applicable to Year 2 purchases)	970
Accounts payable, Dec. 31, Year 2	8,500
Less: Accounts payable, Dec. 31, Year 1	(9,400)
Gross purchases	$54,570

In the computation of gross purchases, only liabilities relating to merchandise purchases should be included. This analysis, together with the amounts for inventories, provides the information necessary to compute cost of goods sold as shown below:

JOE'S PLACE
Computation of Cost of Goods Sold
For Year Ended December 31, Year 2

Inventories, Dec. 31, Year 1		$18,000
Add: Gross purchases (see above)	$54,570	
Less: Cash discounts taken on purchases	(1,100)	
Purchases returns and allowances	(970)	
Net purchases		52,500
Cost of goods available for sale		$70,500
Less: Inventories, Dec. 31, Year 2		25,000
Cost of goods sold		$45,500

Computation of Operating Expenses Expenses arise from cash payments, from purchases of goods and services on credit, and from the consumption of assets. Because cash payments during an accounting period may involve the acquisition of assets or the payment of liabilities that relate to expenses of prior periods, computation of expenses of the current period requires an analysis of both asset and liability ledger account balances, as well as of cash payments.

The balance of any asset account that is subject to amortization increases as a result of the acquisition of additional assets, and decreases as the assets are used up. The normal process for the computation of the ending balance of such an asset account is: Beginning account balance, plus acquisitions of assets, less assets consumed, equals ending account balance. In the computation of expenses, we usually are able to compute the beginning and ending balance of the related asset account and the cost of new acquisitions during the accounting period (through an analysis of cash payments and credit transactions). We may convert this information to the amount of expense for the period as follows:

Reconstruction of expense through analysis of related asset account

Assets acquired during accounting period...............................	$ XX
Less: Asset account balance at end of period	(XX)
Add: Asset account balance at beginning of period	XX
Expense for period..	$XXX

The computation of expenses by analysis of accrued liability balances and related cash payments is a similar process. The beginning balance of the accrued liability account is deducted from the total cash payments during the current period to compute the cash payments relating to the current period's expense. Adding to this amount the balance of the accrued liability account at the end of the period produces the expense for the current period.

Computation of operating expenses for Joe's Place is illustrated below:

JOE'S PLACE
Computation of Operating Expenses
For Year Ended December 31, Year 2

	Insurance expense	Salaries expense	Other operating expenses	Depreciation expense
Cash payments during Year 2 ..	$940	$10,700	$3,000	
Less: Amounts included in cash payments but not expenses of Year 2:				
Prepayments, Dec. 31, Year 2	(700)			
Accrued liability, Dec. 31, Year 1		(1,100)		
Add: Amounts not included in cash payments but allocable to operations of Year 2:				
Prepayments, Dec. 31, Year 1	500			
Accrued liability, Dec. 31, Year 2		1,900		
Depreciation expense (as computed)				$12,800
Operating expenses	$740	$11,500	$3,000	$12,800

JOE'S PLACE
Working Paper for Preparation of Financial Statements from Incomplete Accounting Records
For Year Ended December 31, Year 2

Accounts	Balance sheet, Dec. 31, Year 1 Debit	Balance sheet, Dec. 31, Year 1 Credit	Transactions for Year 2 Debit	Transactions for Year 2 Credit	Income statement for Year 2 Debit	Income statement for Year 2 Credit	Balance sheet, Dec. 31, Year 2 Debit	Balance sheet, Dec. 31, Year 2 Credit
Cash	4,680		(1) 42,000	(5) 53,400			11,780	
			(2) 35,000	(6) 14,640				
			(3) 4,140	(8) 6,000				
Notes receivable	12,000						12,000	
Accounts receivable	4,000		(1) 41,300	(2) 37,700			7,600	
Interest receivable	320		(3) 210				530	
Inventories, Dec. 31,								
Year 1	18,000				18,000			
Unexpired insurance	500		(6) 200				700	
Land	50,000						50,000	
Building and equipment	140,000						140,000	
Accumulated depreciation		62,500		(7) 12,800				75,300
Accounts payable		9,400	(5) 55,470	(4) 54,570				8,500
Salaries payable		1,100		(6) 800				1,900
Unearned rent		600	(3) 150					450
J. Palermo, capital		155,900						155,900
J. Palermo, drawings			(8) 6,000				6,000	
Sales				(1) 83,300		83,300		
Sales ret. and allow.			(2) 1,800		1,800			
Sales discounts			(2) 600		600			
Doubtful accounts expense			(2) 300		300			
Interest revenue				(3) 750		750		
Rent revenue				(3) 3,750		3,750		
Purchases			(4) 54,570		54,570			
Purchases ret. and allow.				(5) 970		970		
Purchases discounts				(5) 1,100		1,100		
Insurance expense			(6) 740		740			
Salaries expense			(6) 11,500		11,500			
Other operating expenses			(6) 3,000		3,000			
Depreciation expense			(7) 12,800		12,800			
Inventories, Dec. 31,								
Year 2						25,000	25,000	
Subtotals					103,310	114,870	253,610	242,050
Net income					11,560			11,560
Totals	229,500	229,500	269,780	269,780	114,870	114,870	253,610	253,610

Explanation of transactions and events for Year 2:
(1) Gross sales, $42,000 in cash and $41,300 on credit
(2) Collections on accounts receivable; sales returns and allowances, sales discounts, and doubtful accounts expense
(3) Collection of interest and rent revenue; adjustment of interest receivable and unearned rent
(4) Gross purchases
(5) Payments on accounts payable; purchases returns and allowances and purchases discounts
(6) Payments for expenses; adjustment of unexpired insurance and salaries payable
(7) Depreciation expense
(8) Owner's drawings

■■■■■■■■■■ **Working Paper for Preparation of Financial Statements from Incomplete Accounting Records** The foregoing computations and other information derived from incomplete accounting records may be used to prepare financial statements. Many accountants prefer to summarize the information in a working paper, as illustrated on page 1126 for Joe's Place. Financial statements may be prepared from the information in the last four columns of the working paper. Alternative forms of the working paper may be used; for example, a pair of columns for a trial balance on December 31, Year 2 may be added following the "Transactions for Year 2" columns in the working paper illustrated on page 1126.

The income statement and the balance sheet prepared for Joe's Place from the working paper on page 1126 have no unusual features and are not illustrated here; the statement of changes in proprietor's capital for the year ended December 31, Year 2, follows:

JOE'S PLACE
Statement of Proprietor's Capital
For Year Ended December 31, Year 2

Proprietor's capital, beginning of year................................	$155,900
Add: Net income...	11,560
Subtotal...	$167,460
Less: Drawings	6,000
Proprietor's capital, end of year	$161,460

REVIEW QUESTIONS

1 Describe the purpose of *APB Opinion No. 20,* "Accounting Changes."

2 What are two types of *accounting changes?* Briefly describe each type.

3 Describe a situation in which a *change in accounting principle* is considered appropriate.

4 How is the *cumulative effect* of a change in accounting principle computed and reported in the income statement for the accounting period in which the change is made?

5 List six examples of changes in accounting principle that require the retroactive restatement of financial statements for prior periods.

6 Lundy Company wrote down the carrying amount of its plant assets by $15 million in Year 2. The reasons given were: "To reduce excess capacity by closing inefficient plants and to recognize obsolescence attributed to new technological developments and a shift in the demand for our products."

How should the write-down be reported in Lundy Company's financial statements?

7   Seafaring Corporation debited $87.9 million to operating expense as a result of a write-down of the carrying amount of its tanker fleet. Included in this amount was $65 million ''for possible losses in the future.'' Evaluate the accounting treatment of this write-down.

8   How is a material error in previously issued financial statements reported in the accounting period the error is discovered?

9   What is the basis for distinguishing between an error in the measurement of net income of a prior period that should be treated as a prior period adjustment, and an error whose correction should be considered a part of the measurement of net income in the accounting period in which it is discovered?

10   Which of the following material errors should be treated as a prior period adjustment?

a A depreciable plant asset that originally was estimated to have an economic life of four years is now estimated to have an economic life of six years.

b A substantial deficiency in income taxes relating to the income of two years ago is assessed by the Internal Revenue Service as a result of an error in the interpretation of tax laws.

c An analysis of credit experience indicates that actual doubtful accounts expense over the past three years has exceeded the provision for such expense made at the rate of 1% of net credit sales.

d A substantial amount of merchandise in transit at the close of the previous year was included in purchases but was not included in the ending inventories.

e An audit reveals that the cost of a depreciable plant asset was inadvertently recognized as expense last year.

11   Errors affecting both the balance sheet and the income statement may be classified into two types. Identify and define each type.

12   Why is it important to correct material errors even after they have counterbalanced?

13   Explain what is meant by the term *single-entry accounting system.*

14   Briefly describe two methods that may be used to compute the amounts required to prepare financial statements from incomplete accounting records.

EXERCISES

Ex. 22-1   Select the best answer for each of the following multiple-choice questions:

1   On November 1, Year 3, Tom Company acquired machinery at a cost of $150,000. The machinery was being depreciated by the double-declining-balance method over an economic life of 10 years, with no residual value. On November 1, Year 5, Tom decided to change to the straight-line method of depreciation. Disregarding income taxes, the cumulative effect of this accounting change is:
a $0   **b** $24,000   **c** $28,200   **d** $54,000   **e** Some other amount

2   Pro forma effects of retroactive application usually are reported in the income statement for a change:

a In the economic lives of depreciable plant assets

b In the residual values of depreciable plant assets

c From the straight-line method of depreciation to the double-declining-balance method of depreciation for previously recorded plant assets

d From presenting financial statements for individual companies to presenting consolidated financial statements

3   A business enterprise changed from the double-declining-balance method of depreciation for previously recorded plant assets to the straight-line method. The cumulative effect of the change on the amount of retained earnings at the beginning of the accounting period in which the change is made is reported separately as a (an):

a Extraordinary item

b Component of income after any extraordinary items

c Component of income from continuing operations

d Prior period adjustment

4   The correction of a material error in the financial statements of a prior accounting period is included, net of applicable income taxes, in the current period's:

a Income statement after income from continuing operations and before any extraordinary items

b Income statement after income from continuing operations and after any extraordinary items

c Statement of retained earnings as an adjustment of the beginning balance

d Statement of retained earnings after net income but before dividends

5   The typical counterbalancing error that affects both the income statement and the balance sheet of an accounting period:

a Is offset by a misstatement, in the opposite direction, of net income of the succeeding period

b Also misstates net income of several succeeding accounting periods

c Is offset by a misstatement, in the opposite direction, of total owners' equity in the balance sheet of the succeeding period

d Is offset by a misstatement, in the opposite direction, of both net income and total owners' equity in the financial statements of the succeeding period

6   During the year ended October 31, Year 8, Lou Company, which uses the periodic inventory system, discovered a $50,000 understatement of the inventory of October 31, Year 6. No other errors were found. The accounting records have not been closed for the year ended October 31, Year 8. Disregarding income taxes, Lou Company's appropriate action is to prepare:

a A journal entry debiting Retained Earnings and crediting Prior Period Adjustment (net income, fiscal Year 6) for $50,000

b A journal entry debiting Prior Period Adjustment (net income, fiscal Year 7) and crediting Prior Period Adjustment (net income, fiscal Year 6) for $50,000

c A journal entry debiting Cost of Goods Sold (fiscal Year 7) and crediting Cost of Goods Sold (fiscal Year 6) for $50,000

d No journal entry

7   A change in the net residual value of a plant asset, depreciated by the straight-line method, that was made because additional information had been obtained is:

a An accounting change reported in both the accounting period of the change and future periods, if the change affects future periods

b An accounting change reported by restatement of the financial statements of all prior accounting periods presented

c A correction of an error of prior accounting periods

d Not an accounting change

8 Webster Company acquired a machine on January 2, Year 4, for $480,000. On the date of acquisition the machine had an economic life of six years with no residual value. The machine was being depreciated under the straight-line method. On January 2, Year 7, Webster determined, as a result of additional information, that the machine had an economic life of eight years from the date of acquisition, with no residual value. An accounting change was made for the year ended December 31, Year 7, to reflect this additional information. What is the amount of depreciation expense for the machine for the year ended December 31, Year 7?

a $0   **b** $30,000   **c** $48,000   **d** $60,000   **e** Some other amount

9 When a cumulative-effect-type change in accounting principle is made during a year, the cumulative effect on retained earnings is computed:

a During the year using a weighted-average method

b As of the date of the change

c As of the beginning of the year in which the change is made

d As of the end of the year in which the change is made

e In some other manner

Ex. 22-2 Corb Company, which began operations on January 2, Year 3, used an accelerated method of depreciation for machinery until January 2, Year 5. On that date, Corb adopted the straight-line method of depreciation for both newly acquired and previously acquired machinery. Information concerning depreciation expense under each method follows:

Year ended Dec. 31,	Depreciation expense	
	Accelerated method	Straight-line method
Year 3	$400,000	$300,000
Year 4	530,000	375,000
Year 5	600,000	400,000

The direct effects of Corb's accounting change are on depreciation expense and income taxes expense only. The income tax rate for Year 3 through Year 5 was 45%.

Compute the cumulative effect of Corb Company's change in accounting principle for its income statement for Year 5.

Ex. 22-3 Naomi Company began operations on January 2, Year 6, and used the first-in, first-out method to value its inventories. Management is contemplating a change to the last-in, first-out method in Year 7 and is interested in determining what effect such a change will have on net income. Accordingly, the following information has been accumulated:

	Year 6	Year 7
Ending inventories:		
First-in, first-out method	$240,000	$270,000
Last-in, first-out method	200,000	210,000
Net income (computed under the first-in, first-out-method) . .	120,000	170,000

Compute net income of Naomi Company for Year 7, assuming that the change to the last-in, first-out method of inventory valuation was effected in Year 7. The income tax rate was 45% in both Year 6 and Year 7.

Ex. 22-4 Remo Company included the following assets in its balance sheet on December 31, Year 5:

Equipment	$3,780,000	
Less: Accumulated depreciation	1,260,000	$2,520,000
Goodwill (net)		1,225,000

Both assets were acquired early in Year 1. The equipment had been depreciated over an economic life of 15 years with no residual value, and the goodwill had been amortized over a period of 20 years. Late in Year 6, Remo decided that the total economic life of the equipment should be reduced to 12 years and that goodwill should be amortized over a period of 30 years from the date of acquisition.

Compute Remo Company's annual depreciation expense on the equipment and amortization of goodwill for Year 6, assuming that the net residual value of the equipment was estimated at $210,000 late in Year 6.

Ex. 22-5 During the year ended October 31, Year 13, the following occurred for Hardy Company, which uses the periodic inventory system:

(1) A change in the estimated economic life of Hardy's building to 30 years from 40 years (the estimated net residual value of the building remained unchanged at $40,000). The building had been acquired on October 31, Year 2, at a cost of $840,000. Hardy used the straight-line method of depreciation for the building.

(2) The discovery on March 18, Year 13, of a $60,000 understatement of Hardy's inventories of October 31, Year 12. This error resulted in a $27,000 understatement of Hardy's income tax liability for the year ended October 31, Year 12.

Prepare journal entries for Hardy Company (1) on March 18, Year 13, to correct the error in the October 31, Year 12, inventories, and (2) on October 31, Year 13, to reflect the accounting change. Hardy's income tax rate is 45%, and it will file an amended income tax return for the year ended October 31, Year 12.

Ex. 22-6 On December 31, Year 1, Trace Company's accountant recorded the cost of patents acquired from an inventor, intending to amortize the cost over five years. At the end of Year 3, it was discovered that the sales manager's Year 1 salary of $40,000 had been recorded in the Patents ledger account on December 31, Year 1. Trace is subject to a 45% income tax rate and intends to file amended income tax returns for Year 1 and Year 2.

Prepare a journal entry for Trace Company to correct this error on December 31, Year 3, after adjusting entries have been made but before the ledger accounts have been closed for Year 3.

Ex. 22-7   The following errors in the accounting records of the Foss & Grable Partnership were discovered on January 18, Year 4:

Year of error	Ending inventories overstated	Depreciation understated	Accrued rent revenue not recorded	Accrued interest expense not recorded
Year 1	$10,000		$ 3,000	
Year 2		$2,500	11,000	
Year 3	14,000			$1,500

The partners share net income and losses equally.
a Prepare a correcting journal entry on January 18, Year 4, assuming that the ledger accounts were closed for Year 3.
b Prepare a correcting journal entry on January 18, Year 4, assuming that the ledger accounts are still open for Year 3 and that the partnership uses the perpetual inventory system.

Ex. 22-8   Rio Company's financial statements contained the following errors:

	Dec. 31, Year 3	Dec. 31, Year 4
Ending inventories (periodic system)	$2,000 understated	$1,800 overstated
Depreciation expense.................	400 understated	No error

Net income as determined by Rio was $25,000 in Year 3 and $30,000 in Year 4. An insurance premium of $1,500 was prepaid in Year 3 covering Year 3, Year 4, and Year 5. The entire amount was debited to Insurance Expense. In addition, on December 31, Year 4, a fully depreciated machine was sold for $3,400, but the disposal was not recorded until January 5, Year 5. There were no other errors during Year 3 or Year 4, and no corrections have been made for any of the errors. Income taxes may be disregarded.
a Compute Rio Company's corrected net income under the accrual basis of accounting for Year 4.
b Compute the total effect of the errors on Rio Company's working capital on December 31, Year 4.
c Prepare a journal entry to correct Rio Company's accounting records on January 15, Year 5. Assume that ledger accounts have been closed for Year 4. (The gain on the disposal of the fully depreciated machine was recognized, but in the wrong year.)

Ex. 22-9   The cash records of Zwick Corporation show that $28,400 was collected in July, Year 7, from credit customers and $12,400 was received from cash sales. The amount due from credit customers increased from $7,300 at the beginning of July to $9,150 at the end of July. In July the credit manager had written off $1,090 of trade accounts receivable as uncollectible.

From the foregoing information, compute the gross sales of Zwick Corporation for July, Year 7.

Ex. 22-10   Placer Company sells television cable services to customers, who may choose to pay $25 a month for the service or may pay in advance a yearly charge of $250 for 12 months of service. During Year 8, Placer collected $160,700 from customers. Additional information for Year 8 follows:

	Jan. 1, Year 8	Dec. 31, Year 8
Advance payments by customers	$3,500	$5,700
Accounts receivable from customers	6,820	6,970

From the information given, compute the total cable revenue of Placer Company for Year 8.

Ex. 22-11   The inventories of Moll Company increased by $18,500 during Year 4, and the accounts payable to merchandise suppliers increased by $9,600. During Year 4, Moll paid $130,200 to suppliers and $7,200 freight-in charges on merchandise. Moll also purchased $5,800 of merchandise for cash.

Compute Moll Company's cost of goods sold for Year 4.

Ex. 22-12   The following information was taken from the accounting records of Toma Company for Year 1:

	Jan. 1	Dec. 31
Stockholders' equity (no capital stock was issued or retired). .	$98,000	$117,000
Cash	6,000	12,400
Inventories	20,000	14,000
Payable to merchandise suppliers	8,000	8,500
Trade accounts receivable	14,200	18,200
Cash paid to merchandise suppliers		70,000
Operating expenses and income taxes paid (including $800 prepaid on December 31)		32,000
Year 1 sales written off as uncollectible (an additional allowance of $750 is required on Dec. 31)		500
Dividends declared and paid		20,000
Depreciation expense		6,200
Other assets	77,800	82,350
Other liabilities	12,000	22,000

Prepare an income statement for Toma Company for Year 1 on the accrual basis of accounting. Show supporting computations for sales, cost of goods sold, and total operating expenses and income taxes. (Hint: First compute net income and work back to sales.)

CASES

Case 22-1 It is important to differentiate among the various types of accounting changes and to report such changes in the financial statements in conformity with generally accepted accounting principles.

Instructions

a What type of accounting change is a change from an accelerated method of depreciation to the straight-line method of depreciation for plant assets? Discuss the propriety of such a change.

b How are pro forma amounts required to be disclosed for certain types of accounting changes computed?

c What type of accounting change is a change in the economic lives of plant assets? Include in your discussion how such a change is reported in the income statement for the accounting period in which the change is made and disclosed in a note to the financial statements for that period.

d A business combination accounted for as a pooling of interests results in an accounting change. Describe the accounting change and the means by which it is reported in the financial statements.

Case 22-2 A business enterprise may change its method of accounting for certain items. The change may be classified as a change in accounting principle, a change in accounting estimate, or a change in reporting entity. Listed below are two independent situations relating to accounting changes:

a Wister, Inc., determined that the economic lives of its plant assets were too long to match the cost of the plant assets with the revenue produced. Therefore, Wister decided in January, Year 7, to reduce the economic lives of all of its existing plant assets by five years.

b Lorraine Company decided in January, Year 4, to adopt the straight-line method of depreciation for plant assets. The straight-line method would be used for new acquisitions as well as for previously acquired plant assets for which depreciation had been computed by an accelerated method.

Instructions

For each situation that is described above, provide the information indicated below. Complete your discussion of the first situation before discussing the second situation.

(1) Type of accounting change

(2) Manner of reporting the change under generally accepted accounting principles, including a discussion, where applicable, of how amounts are computed

(3) Effect of the change on the balance sheet and on the income statement

(4) Additional disclosure required in a note to the financial statements

Case 22-3 Some accounting changes may affect the second reporting standard of generally accepted auditing standards, which states, ''The report shall state whether (accounting) principles have been consistently observed in the current period in relation to the preceding period.''

Assume that the following list describes changes that *have a material effect* on a corporation's financial statements for the current accounting period:

(1) A change from the completed-contract method to the percentage-of-completion method of accounting for construction-type contracts.

(2) A change in the estimated economic life of previously acquired plant assets based on newly acquired information.

(3) Correction of a material error in inventory pricing made in a prior period.

(4) A change from prime costing to full absorption costing method of inventory valuation.

(5) A change from presentation of financial statements of individual corporations to presentation of consolidated financial statements for all affiliated corporations.

(6) A change from deferring and amortizing preproduction costs to recognizing such costs as expenses when incurred because future benefits of the costs have become doubtful. The new accounting method was adopted in recognition of the change in estimated future benefits.

(7) A change to including the employer's share of FICA taxes with "retirement benefits" in the income statement from including it with "other taxes."

(8) A change from the first-in, first-out method to the last-in, first-out method of inventory valuation.

(9) A change from the last-in, first-out method to the first-in, first-out method of inventory valuation.

Instructions

Identify the type of change described in each item above and state whether the prior period's financial statements should be restated when presented in comparative form with the current period's statements.

Case 22-4 Vitale Corporation, which is closely held, plans to issue additional shares of common stock to the public to finance an expansion program. Vitale has operated for five years and has never had an audit. To meet the requirements of the Securities and Exchange Commission, Vitale has hired CPAs to audit its financial statements for Year 10.

In its financial statements for the past five years, Vitale has reported the following earnings and stockholders' equity:

	Net income	Earnings per share of common stock	Stockholders' equity
Year 6	$368,000	$1.84	$4,945,000
Year 7	390,000	1.95	5,195,000
Year 8	435,000	2.18	5,350,000
Year 9	470,000	2.35	5,620,000
Year 10	510,000	2.55	5,870,000

The auditors discovered in the course of their examination that Vitale consistently had omitted from its ending inventories in each of the five years merchandise in a warehouse in Ohio. This warehouse operation had not proved successful and had been discontinued in Year 10; therefore, the inventories at the end of Year 10 were not affected by the error. Warehouse records showed that the inventory of merchandise in the warehouse at the end of each year, stated at lower of average cost or market, was as follows: Year 6, $190,000; Year 7, $90,000; Year 8, $220,000; Year 9, $115,000. The auditors also discovered that because the sales report from the warehouse was late in arriving at the end of Year 7, $80,000 of sales applicable to Year 7 operations were not recorded until Year 8.

When the auditors insisted that these errors be corrected retroactively in the presentation of income data for the five-year period in the SEC registration statement, Vitale's controller objected. ''The warehouse has been discontinued. There is no inventory there now. All these errors have washed themselves out in the accounting records, and there is no point in going back and raking over the dead coals of past history. There's nothing wrong with our balance sheet at the end of Year 10 or our income statement for Year 10, and that's what the people who acquire our common stock are interested in.''

Instructions

Compute the effect of the errors discovered by the auditors on the financial statements of Vitale Corporation. Disregard income taxes. What position would you take with respect to the controller's objection?

PROBLEMS

22-1   On January 2, Year 5, prior to the enactment of the Accelerated Cost Recovery System for income tax depreciation, Maxey Corporation acquired for $240,000 a machine with an economic life of 10 years and a net residual value of $20,000. Maxey used the straight-line method of depreciation for Year 5 through Year 7. On January 2, Year 8, Maxey appropriately changed to the sum-of-the-years'-digits method of depreciation for the machine. Maxey will file amended income tax returns for Year 5, Year 6, and Year 7 to reflect the change.

Instructions

a Compute the carrying amount of Maxey Corporation's machine on December 31, Year 8.

b Compute the cumulative effect of Maxey Corporation's accounting change for the year ended December 31, Year 8, assuming the direct effects of the change are on depreciation expense and income taxes expense only. The income tax rate is 45%.

c Prepare a journal entry for Maxey Corporation on January 2, Year 8, to record the accounting change. Disregard deferred income tax credits.

22-2   The financial statements of Kirby Company, which began operations on January 2, Year 4, showed pre-tax accounting income of $4,030,000 for Year 5 and $3,330,000 for Year 4.

Additional Information

(1) Expenditures for plant assets were $2,800,000 in Year 5 and $4,000,000 in Year 4. Included in the Year 5 expenditures was $1,000,000 for equipment acquired on January 2, Year 5, with no residual value. Kirby used the straight-line method of depreciation and a 10-year economic life for the equipment in

Year 5. On December 31, Year 5, Kirby determined that the equipment had only an eight-year economic life when acquired.

(2) On January 2, Year 5, Kirby paid $180,000 for insurance premiums and debited the entire amount to Insurance Expense. The premiums applied entirely to Year 4, and the amount is material.

(3) Kirby's Allowance for Doubtful Accounts ledger account had a credit balance of $7,000 on December 31, Year 5, and a credit balance of $97,000 on December 31, Year 4. During Year 5, trade accounts receivable totaling $90,000 had been written off to the allowance account as uncollectible. Kirby had used 0.2% of net credit sales to compute doubtful accounts expense in prior years, but had not yet made the computation for Year 5. Kirby's net credit sales were $58,500,000 for Year 5 and $49,230,000 for Year 4.

(4) Kirby's Liability under Product Warranty ledger account had a credit balance of $230,000 on December 31, Year 5. An analysis indicated that the balance should be $400,000 on that date.

(5) Prior to Year 5, Kirby had debited the cost of relining its blast furnaces to Maintenance and Repairs Expense. In Year 5, Kirby changed to a policy of capitalizing and depreciating relining costs over a five-year economic life, with no residual value. This accounting change met the requirements for a change in accounting principle. Prior to the accounting change, Kirby had expensed relining costs of $280,000 on January 2, Year 4, and $300,000 on January 2, Year 5.

Instructions

a Prepare a working paper to compute Kirby Company's correct pre-tax accounting income for Year 5 and Year 4. Show supporting computations, and disregard income taxes. The final amount in your working paper is to be labeled ''Income before income taxes and cumulative effect of change in accounting principle, as corrected.''

b Compute the cumulative effect, disregarding income taxes, of Kirby Company's accounting change for Year 5.

22-3 During the year ended December 31, Year 3, Joliet Company, which had been organized in Year 1, changed its method of accounting for property taxes during construction of plant assets from expensing property taxes to capitalizing them as building costs. The data below were taken from Joliet's accounting records:

	Year 3	Year 2	Year 1
Income before cumulative effect of accounting change in Year 3	$400,000	$270,000	$150,000
Property taxes during construction	125,000	75,000	24,500
Depreciation of buildings—based on expensing all property taxes	50,000	35,000	30,000
Depreciation of buildings—based on capitalizing all property taxes	59,000	39,000	30,980
Earnings per share as reported, before cumulative effect of accounting change in Year 3	2.00	1.35	0.75

The income for Year 3 was measured under the newly adopted accounting principle. The number of shares of common stock outstanding during the entire three-year period was 200,000.

Instructions

a Compute the cumulative effect of the change in accounting principle to be included in Joliet Company's income statement for Year 3. Assume a 45% income tax rate. Round all amounts to the nearest dollar.

b Compute the effect of the change in accounting principle on earnings per share of Joliet Company for each of the three years, rounded to the nearest cent.

c Prepare partial comparative income statements for Joliet Company for Year 2 and Year 3. The income statements should include the cumulative effect of the change in accounting principle, the earnings per share, and pro forma amounts for Year 2, as illustrated on page 1101.

22-4 The following fragmentary information relates to the financial position of May's Shop, a single proprietorship, at the beginning and at the end of Year 6:

	Jan. 1, Year 6	Dec. 31, Year 6
Owner's equity (May Day, capital)	$81,900	$97,800
Inventories	15,800	27,320
Accounts payable (to suppliers)	40,000	25,000
Short-term prepayments	1,800	2,400
Accrued liabilities	3,150	2,850

A summary of checks written shows that $200,000 was paid to suppliers during Year 6, $67,000 was paid for operating expenses, and $17,400 cash was withdrawn by May Day. Depreciation expense for Year 6 is $8,400, and the provision for doubtful accounts expense is 2% of gross sales.

Instructions

On the basis of the foregoing information, prepare an income statement for May's Shop for Year 6. Show supporting computations, rounded to the nearest dollar.

22-5 Kinder, Inc., has used the completed-contract method of accounting for its construction-type contracts for 10 years. In Year 11, Kinder decided to change to the percentage-of-completion method to achieve a better matching of contract costs and contract revenue in its income statements. Kinder had recently hired an expert in cost estimation, and management believed that it would be possible to make reasonably accurate estimates of costs to be used in the determination of the percentage of completion on each contact. In addition, management decided that it would be unfair to stockholders to report a decrease in earnings for Year 11, which was attributed to the following two factors:

(1) Several major contracts were completed in Year 10, which resulted in an unusually large net income.

(2) Few contracts were completed in Year 11, although Kinder had 40% more work under construction in Year 11 than it did in Year 10, and had 30% more employees on the payroll.

A summary of results for the last two years under the completed-contract method follows:

	Year 11	Year 10
Contract revenue	$6,000,000	$18,600,000
Cost of contract revenue	4,500,000	14,700,000
Operating expenses	1,050,000	900,000
Income taxes expense (45%)	202,500	1,350,000
Net income	247,500	1,650,000

Application of the percentage-of-completion method to the operations of the last two years would have given the following results:

	Year 11	Year 10
Contract revenue	$17,400,000	$9,300,000
Cost of contract revenue	14,100,000	7,500,000

Operating expenses under the percentage-of-completion method are the same as reported under the completed-contract method. The completed-contract method will continue to be used for income tax purposes. Income tax allocation procedures for timing differences will be used in the preparation of revised financial statements, giving retroactive effect to the change in accounting principles. Assume that income taxes are 45% of pre-tax accounting income.

Instructions

Restate the comparative income statements for Kinder, Inc., for Year 10 and Year 11, giving retroactive recognition to the change in accounting principle. Assume that 300,000 shares of common stock were outstanding during the two-year period. Prepare a note to the financial statements that explains the reason for the change in accounting principle and the effect of the change on net income and earnings per share. (See illustrative note on page 1104 describing this type of accounting change.) Disregard deferred income credits.

22-6   Condensed statements of income and retained earnings of Nubo Corporation for the years ended December 31, Year 4, and December 31, Year 3, are as follows:

NUBO CORPORATION
Condensed Statements of Income and Retained Earnings
For Years Ended December 31, Year 4 and Year 3

	Year 4	Year 3
Sales	$3,000,000	$2,400,000
Cost of goods sold	1,300,000	1,150,000
Gross profit on sales	$1,700,000	$1,250,000
Operating expenses	$ 450,000	$ 500,000
Income taxes expense (45%)	562,500	337,500
Total expenses	$1,012,500	$ 837,500
Income before extraordinary item (loss)	$ 687,500	$ 412,500
Extraordinary item (loss) (net of income tax credit $450,000)	(550,000)	

(continued)

Net income	$ 137,500	$ 412,500
Retained earnings, beginning of year................	862,500	450,000
Retained earnings, end of year	$1,000,000	$ 862,500

Following are three *unrelated situations* involving accounting changes and classification of certain items as ordinary or extraordinary. Each situation is based on the condensed statements of income and retained earnings of Nubo Corporation shown on page 1139 and above and requires revisions to the statements.

Situation A

On January 2, Year 2, Nubo acquire machinery at a cost of $150,000. Nubo adopted the double-declining-balance method of depreciation for this machinery for both financial accounting and income taxes, and had been recording depreciation over an estimated economic life of 10 years, with no residual value. At the beginning of Year 4, the straight-line method of depreciation was adopted for both financial accounting and income taxes. Due to an oversight, however, the double-declining-balance method was used for Year 4. For financial accounting, depreciation expense is included in operating expenses.

The extraordinary item for Year 4 related to shutdown expenses incurred during a labor strike during Year 4.

Situation B

At the end of Year 4, Nubo's management decided that the estimated rate of doubtful accounts expense was too low. The rate used for Years 3 and 4 was 1% of total sales, and due to an increase in the write-off of uncollectible accounts, the rate for Year 4 was increased to 3% of total sales. The amount recorded as doubtful accounts expense (included in operating expenses) was $30,000 for Year 4 and $24,000 for Year 3.

The extraordinary item for Year 4 related to a loss incurred in the abandonment of obsolete equipment.

Situation C

The extraordinary item for Year 4 represented a correction of a material error (after income taxes) in the computation of cost of goods sold. Of the total amount, $467,500 related to Years 1 and 2 and $82,500 related to Year 3.

Instructions

For each of the three *unrelated situations,* prepare revised condensed statements of income and retained earnings of Nubo Corporation for the years ended December 31, Year 4, and December 31, Year 3. Each answer should recognize the appropriate accounting changes and other items outlined in the situation. Disregard earnings per share computations.

22-7   Mona Meadows started a single proprietorship, Mona's Boutique, on July 10, Year 1, by investing $75,000 in cash and merchandise. Net income for the remainder of Year 1 was $30,000, and for Year 2 it was $56,250. Meadows made no additional investments and made no withdrawals since July 10, Year 1. Comparative balance sheets prepared by Meadows are as follows:

MONA'S BOUTIQUE
Balance Sheets
December 31, Year 2 and Year 1

Assets

	Year 2	Year 1
Cash	$ 22,650	$ 16,650
Accounts receivable	67,500	48,750
Inventory	60,000	42,600
Equipment	55,000	45,000
Total assets	$205,150	$153,000

Liabilities & Owner's Equity

	Year 2	Year 1
Notes payable to bank	$ 10,000	$ 15,000
Accounts payable	33,900	33,000
Mona Meadows, capital	161,250	105,000
Total liabilities & owner's equity	$205,150	$153,000

The following errors were discovered by the auditor who was engaged on January 20, Year 3, to examine the financial statements of Mona's Boutique:

(1) Inventory was overstated by $4,500 on December 31, Year 1.
(2) Interest payable of $1,800 was not recorded on December 31, Year 1, and interest payable of $1,200 was not recorded on December 31, Year 2.
(3) Inventory of supplies of $1,050 was not recorded as an asset on December 31, Year 1, and inventory of supplies of $450 on December 31, Year 2, had been expensed.
(4) A credit sale of $1,200 on December 31, Year 2 was not recorded in Year 2.
(5) Accounts receivable of $2,500 resulting from sales in Year 1 were uncollectible on December 31, Year 2, but there had been no write-offs of accounts receivable in either Year 1 or Year 2. An allowance for doubtful accounts equal to 6% of the corrected amount of accounts receivable (after the write-off of $2,500 on December 31, Year 2) should have been established at the end of each year.
(6) Depreciation expense of $1,500 was not recorded in Year 1 and depreciation expense of $3,000 was not recorded in Year 2.

Instructions

a Prepare a working paper for analysis of errors to correct the net income of Mona's Boutique for Year 1 and for Year 2.

b Prepare a correcting journal entry for Mona's Boutique on January 20, Year 3, assuming that the ledger accounts are closed for Year 2.

c Prepare corrected comparative balance sheets for Mona's Boutique on December 31, Year 1 and Year 2. (*Note to student:* Be sure that capital for Meadows on December 31, Year 1 is equal to the original investment plus the corrected net income for Year 1; similarly, the capital for Meadows on December 31, Year 2, should equal the original investment plus the total corrected net income for Years 1 and 2.)

22-8 The office manager of Cue Corporation, a closely held corporation, prepared the following balance sheet on December 31, Year 3:

CUE CORPORATION
Balance Sheet
December 31, Year 3

Assets		Liabilities & Stockholders' Equity	
Cash	$ 9,800	Accounts payable..........	$ 25,600
Accounts receivable (net)...	37,000	Income taxes payable......	2,700
Inventory.................	45,000	Common stock, $1 par	40,000
Furniture and equipment		Retained earnings	61,500
(net)....................	38,000	Total liabilities & stock-	
Total assets	$129,800	holders' equity..........	$129,800

Cue began operations early in Year 1, and income statements prepared by the office manager showed the following net income for the three-year period: Year 1, $26,000; Year 2, $19,200; Year 3, $16,300.

Carl Cue, the president of Cue Corporation, was concerned about this income trend, and asked a CPA firm to examine Cue's financial statements. This review disclosed that the following errors and omissions had not been corrected during the applicable years:

End of	Inventory over-stated	Inventory under-stated	Prepaid rent omitted	Unearned revenue omitted	Accrued expenses (misc. pay-ables) omitted	Accrued revenue (misc. receiv-ables) omitted
Year 1	$8,700		$ 950		$1,400	
Year 2	6,500		1,100	$ 800	1,200	$ 400
Year 3		$4,900	1,300	1,250	900	2,700

Combined federal and state income taxes were 45% of pre-tax accounting income. Cue Corporation will file amended income tax returns for Years 1 and 2; the income tax return for Year 3 had not been filed at the time the foregoing errors were discovered. No dividends had been declared by Cue during the first three years of its operations.

Instructions

a Prepare a working paper for analysis of errors to correct Cue Corporation's net income for Year 1, Year 2, and Year 3. Round all amounts to the nearest dollar.

b Assuming that the ledger accounts have been closed on December 31, Year 3, prepare a journal entry for Cue Corporation to correct the accounting records as of December 31, Year 3.

c Prepare a corrected balance sheet for Cue Corporation on December 31, Year 3.

d If you were presented with revised income statements for Cue Corporation for the past three years, would your conclusions regarding its earnings trend be changed substantially? Comment.

22-9   Robert Lin began RL Company, a single proprietorship, several years ago. For a number of years Lin's wife maintained the accounting records, but early in Year 5, she became seriously ill. Lin consulted a bookkeeping service whose manager told him, "You keep a record of your cash receipts and payments, and a list of your assets and liabilities at the beginning and end of the year, and I'll prepare financial statements for you at the end of the year."

At the close of Year 5, Lin presented the following data to the manager of the bookkeeping service:

RL COMPANY
Analysis of Cash Receipts and Cash Payments for Year 5

Cash receipts:		*Cash payments:*	
Jan. 1, Year 5, cash		*Accounts payable (net of*	
balance	*$ 18,460*	*$6,480 cash discounts)*	*$225,650*
Proceeds of bank loan	*40,000*	*Acquisition of equipment*	*25,000*
Cash sales	*87,300*	*Operating expenses*	*47,610*
Interest received	*1,590*	*Insurance policy premium*	*980*
Notes receivable	*13,000*	*Freight-in on purchases*	*12,400*
Equipment rental	*7,000*	*Notes payable (including*	
Accounts receivable (net of		*interest of $600)*	*15,600*
$4,130 cash discounts)	*177,690*	*Dec. 31, Year 5, cash*	
		balance	*17,800*
Total cash receipts	*$345,040*	*Total cash payments*	*$345,040*

RL COMPANY
List of Assets and Liabilities on January 1 and December 31, Year 5

	Jan. 1	*Dec. 31*
Cash	*$ 18,460*	*$ 17,800*
Notes receivable	*15,000*	*2,000*
Interest receivable	*900*	*500*
Accounts receivable	*43,560*	*64,320*
Inventory	*38,900*	*43,400*
Unexpired insurance	*1,900*	*1,500*
Equipment (net of accumulated depreciation)	*124,000*	*136,000*
Total assets	*$242,720*	*$265,520*
Notes payable	*$ 10,000*	*$ 35,000*
Interest payable	*500*	*1,750*
Accounts payable	*47,500*	*52,300*
Other liabilities	*3,400*	*6,300*
Unearned rent	*1,200*	*1,800*
Total liabilities	*$ 62,600*	*$ 97,150*

Lin reported that all accounts and notes receivable were from merchandise sales and that $1,400 of accounts receivable had been written off during Year 5, of which $850 was from sales prior to Year 5. Lin estimated that $1,420 of the December 31 receivable may be uncollectible. Only purchases of merchandise were recorded in accounts payable.

Instructions

a On the basis of the foregoing information, prepare an income statement for RL Company for Year 5. Prepare exhibits in support of the revenue and expenses included in the income statement.

b Prepare a statement of changes in proprietor's capital for RL Company for Year 5.

22-10 Panich Corporation was organized on July 1, Year 1, with authorized stock of 200,000 shares of $5 par common stock and 10,000 shares of $100 par, 12% preferred stock. John Panich was given 200 shares of preferred stock and 2,000 shares of common stock for services and expenses totaling $30,000 incurred in organizing and promoting Panich Corporation. Attorneys' fees of $1,800, incurred in connection with the formation of Panich Corporation had not been paid as of September 30, Year 1.

Additional Information

(1) On July 15, Year 1, John Panich transferred assets from his single proprietorship to Panich Corporation in exchange for 6,000 shares of preferred stock. The current fair values of the assets were as follows: notes receivable, $360,000; inventories, $60,000; equipment, $180,000. Panich Corporation did not begin operations until August 1, Year 1, but interest of $900 accrued on the notes receivable between the time they were transferred to Panich Corporation and July 31, Year 1. This amount was debited to Interest Receivable on July 31.

(2) On July 31, Year 1, 160,000 shares of common stock were issued at par for cash, of which $150,000 was used to acquire land and $600,000 was applied to the cost of a building on the land. The building cost $1,340,000; the unpaid balance was represented by a 15% mortgage note payable due in 10 years. Interest on the mortgage note payable did not begin accruing until August 1, Year 1, and was payable monthly.

(3) On September 30, Year 1, the accountant for Panich Corporation prepared a summary of all transactions completed by Panich Corporation during August and September, Year 1, in the form of "net" debit and credit *changes in ledger account balances.* This information, which includes all adjusting entries, except for ending inventories (periodic inventory system) and income taxes, is shown below and on page 1145.

	Net changes in ledger account balances, Aug. 1 to Sept. 30, Year 1	
	Debits	**Credits**
Cash		$ 28,300
Accounts receivable	$ 76,285	
Allowance for doubtful accounts		1,250
Interest receivable	3,600	
Accumulated depreciation of building		8,375
Accumulated depreciation of equipment		6,500
Organization costs		1,060
Accounts payable		18,500
		(continued)

Sales		$164,800
Purchases	$110,000	
Operating expenses (including depreciation, amortiza-		
tion of organization costs, and doubtful accounts		
expense)	24,000	
Interest expense	18,500	
Interest revenue (does not include $900 earned in		
July, Year 1)		3,600
Totals	$232,385	$232,385

The organization costs (an asset) was being amortized over 60 months, starting August 1, Year 1. The inventories on September 30, Year 1, amounted to $68,200.

Instructions
a Prepare the balance sheet of Panich Corporation on July 31, Year 1. Income taxes expense should be provided at the rate of 45% on the interest revenue recognized in July. This was the only item of revenue or expense through July 31, Year 1.
b Prepare an income statement for Panich Corporation for the two months ended September 30, Year 1. Income taxes expense is 45% of pre-tax accounting income. Do not compute earnings per share.
c Prepare the balance sheet of Panich Corporation on September 30, Year 1.
d Prepare an analysis of cash receipts and cash payments of Panich Corporation to reconcile the decrease of $28,300 in the Cash ledger account during the two-month period ended September 30, Year 1.

22-11 Yolo Corporation decided that in the preparation of its Year 3 financial statements two accounting changes would be made from the methods used in prior years:

(1) **Depreciation** For plant assets acquired prior to the enactment of the Accelerated Cost Recovery System, Yolo previously had used the declining-balance method for both income taxes and financial accounting, but decided to change during Year 3 to the straight-line method for financial accounting only. The excess of accelerated depreciation over straight-line depreciation is summarized below:

Prior to Year 2	$1,300,000
Year 2..	101,000
Year 3..	99,000
Total	$1,500,000

Depreciation expense is allocated to cost of goods sold and to selling and administrative expenses in the ratio of 75% and 25%, respectively.

(2) **Doubtful accounts expense** In the past Yolo had recorded doubtful accounts expense equal to 1.5% of net sales. After a careful analysis, Yolo decided that a rate of 2% was more appropriate for Year 3. Doubtful accounts expense is included in operating expenses.

The financial statements on page 1146 are preliminary, prepared before giving effect to the two accounting changes.

YOLO CORPORATION
Income Statements
For Years Ended December 31, Year 3 and Year 2

	Year 3	Year 2
Net sales	$80,520,000	$78,920,000
Cost of goods sold	54,847,000	53,074,000
Gross profit on sales	$25,673,000	$25,846,000
Operating expenses	19,540,000	18,411,000
Income from operations	$ 6,133,000	$ 7,435,000
Other revenue (expense), net	(1,198,000)	(1,079,000)
Income before income taxes	$ 4,935,000	$ 6,356,000
Income taxes expense	2,220,750	2,860,200
Net income	$ 2,714,250	$ 3,495,800

YOLO CORPORATION
Balance Sheets
December 31, Year 3 and Year 2

	Year 3	Year 2
Assets		
Current assets	$43,561,000	$43,900,000
Plant assets, at cost	45,792,000	43,974,000
Less: Accumulated depreciation	(23,761,000)	(22,946,000)
Total assets	$65,592,000	$64,928,000
Liabilities & Stockholders' Equity		
Current liabilities	$21,124,000	$23,650,000
Long-term debt	15,154,000	14,097,000
Common stock, $10 par	11,620,000	11,620,000
Retained earnings	17,694,000	15,561,000
Total liabilities & stockholders' equity	$65,592,000	$64,928,000

There have been no timing differences between pre-tax accounting income and taxable income prior to the two accounting changes. The income tax rate is 45%.

Instructions

Compute for the items listed below the amounts to be included in the Year 3 and Year 2 financial statements of Yolo Corporation after adjustment for the two accounting changes. Show amounts for both Year 3 and Year 2, and include supporting computations.

a Accumulated depreciation
b Deferred income tax credits
c Operating expenses
d Current portion of income taxes expense
e Deferred portion of income taxes expense
f Retained earnings
g Pro forma net income (disregard effect on earnings per share)

22-12 You have been engaged to examine the financial statements of Bart Corporation for the year ended December 31, Year 6. In the course of your examination you ascertained the following information:

(1) A check for $1,500 representing the repayment of an unused employee expense advance was received on December 29, Year 6, but was not recorded until January 2, Year 7.

(2) Bart used the allowance method of accounting for doubtful accounts expense. The allowance was based on 3% of past-due accounts receivable (over 120 days) and 1% of current accounts at the close of each month. Because of changing economic conditions, the amount of past-due accounts increased significantly, and management decided to increase the percentage based on past-due accounts to 5%. The following balances were available:

	Nov. 30, Year 6 Dr (Cr)	Dec. 31, Year 6 Dr (Cr)
Accounts receivable.................................	$390,000	$430,000
Past-due accounts included in accounts receivable	12,000	30,000
Allowance for doubtful accounts......................	(28,000)	9,000

(3) The inventory on December 31, Year 5 did not include merchandise costing $7,000 that was stored in a public warehouse. Merchandise costing $3,000 was erroneously counted twice and included twice in the inventory on December 31, Year 6. Bart used the periodic inventory system.

(4) On January 2, Year 6, Bart acquired a new machine costing $97,000. The machine was being depreciated by the straight-line method over an economic life of 10 years, with no residual value. When the machine was installed, Bart paid for the following items, which were not included in the cost of the machine, but were debited to Repairs and Maintenance Expense:

Delivery costs	$ 2,500
Installation costs...	8,000
Rearrangement of related equipment	4,000
Total...	$14,500

(5) On January 2, Year 5, Bart leased a building for 10 years under an operating lease at a monthly rent of $12,000. On that date, Bart paid the lessor the following amounts:

Rent deposit	$ 6,000
First month's rent...	12,000
Last month's rent...	12,000
Installation of new walls and offices	80,000
Total...	$110,000

The entire amount of $110,000 was debited to Rent Expense in Year 5.

(6) In January, Year 5, Bart issued $200,000 of 8%, 10-year bonds at 97 (97% of face amount). The discount was debited to Interest Expense in Year 5. Interest on the bonds was payable on December 31 of each year. Bart recognized

interest expense of $22,000 for Year 5 and $16,000 for Year 6. Bart planned to amortize the discount on bonds payable by the straight-line method.

(7) On May 3, Year 6, Bart exchanged 500 shares of treasury stock (its $50 par common stock) for land to be used as a site for a new factory. The treasury stock had cost $70 a share when it was acquired, and on May 3, Year 6, it had a current fair value of $80 a share. Bart received $2,000 when an existing building on the land was sold for scrap. The land was recorded at $40,000, the $2,000 received for scrap was credited to Other Revenue, and Bart recognized a gain of $5,000 on the reissuance of the treasury stock.

(8) The Advertising and Promotion Expense ledger account included an amount of $75,000, which represented the cost of printing sales catalogs for a special promotional campaign in January, Year 7.

(9) Bart adopted a funded defined benefit pension plan on January 2, Year 6. Based on actuarial computations, the service cost for Year 6 was $70,000, and the prior service cost on January 2, Year 6, was $900,000. Bart adopted the straight-line basis for amortization of prior service cost over the 10-year average remaining service period of employees. On December 31, Year 6, Bart remitted $970,000 to the trustee and debited the entire amount to Pension Expense.

(10) Bart was a defendant in a lawsuit by a former customer. Bart's legal counsel advised management that Bart had a good defense. Bart's counsel did not anticipate any impairment of Bart's assets or that any significant liabilities would be incurred as a result of the lawsuit. However, management established a loss contingency of $100,000 by a debit to an expense ledger account.

Instructions

Prepare a working paper to show the effect of errors on Bart Corporation's financial statements for Year 6. The items in the working paper are to be presented in the same sequence as the facts are given with corresponding numbers (1) through (10). Use the following columnar headings for the working paper:

No.	Explanation	Income statement Dr (Cr)	Balance sheet, Dec. 31, Year 6 Dr (Cr)	Ledger accounts
(1)				

22-13 Following are financial statements of Helena Corporation for the end of its first year of operations:

HELENA CORPORATION
Statement of Income and Retained Earnings
For Year Ended December 31, Year 1

Net sales		$2,950,000
Costs and expenses:		
Cost of goods sold	$1,670,000	
Depreciation expense	40,000	

(continued)

Research and development expense . . . .$	30,000	
Other operating expenses	650,000	
Total costs and expenses		$2,390,000
Income before income taxes		$ 560,000
Income taxes expense		252,000
Net income and retained earnings, end of year		$ 308,000

HELENA CORPORATION
Balance Sheet
December 31, Year 1

Assets

Current assets:

Cash	$ 150,000
Short-term investments, at cost	60,000
Accounts receivable, less allowance for doubtful accounts	
of $59,000	391,000
Inventories	430,000
Unexpired insurance	15,000
Total current assets	$1,046,000
Plant assets, less accumulated depreciation of $40,000	386,000
Research and development costs	120,000
Total assets	$1,552,000

Liabilities & Stockholders' Equity

Current liabilities:

Accounts payable and accrued liabilities	$ 592,000
Income taxes payable	252,000
Total current liabilities	$ 844,000
Stockholders' equity:	
Common stock, $10 par, authorized, issued, and outstanding	
40,000 shares	$ 400,000
Retained earnings	308,000
Total stockholders' equity	$ 708,000
Total liabilities & stockholders' equity	$1,552,000

Additional Information

(1) The short-term investments are marketable equity securities with an aggregate market value of $55,000 on December 31, Year 1.

(2) An aging of accounts receivable on December 31, Year 1, indicated that accounts totaling $36,000 were doubtful of collection.

(3) Merchandise costing $12,000 that was out on consignment had been omitted from the physical inventory on December 31, Year 1.

(4) A $3,000 insurance premium paid on December 31, Year 1, and debited to Insurance Expense applied to a policy that expired on December 31, Year 2.

(5) Helena had adopted a funded defined benefit pension plan on July 1, Year 1. Service cost for the first year of the plan, which had not been funded as of December 31, Year 1, was estimated at $45,000.

(6) The cost of a machine acquired for $24,000 on July 1, Year 1, had been debited to Repairs and Maintenance Expense and closed to Cost of Goods Sold. Helena uses the straight-line method of depreciation, no net residual value, and a five-year economic life for machines of this type.

(7) Helena incurred research and development costs of $150,000 during Year 1 in the development of an invention that Helena expects to be patented in Year 2. Helena initiated a five-year amortization period for the research and development costs, beginning in Year 1.

(8) During January, Year 2, a competing business enterprise filed a patent infringement suit against Helena, claiming $200,000 damages. Helena's legal counsel considers it probable that Helena will be held liable for $50,000 damages by the court.

(9) Helena's income tax rate is 45%.

Instructions

Prepare a working paper, with accounts listed in ledger sequence, to correct Helena Corporation's ledger account balances on December 31, Year 1. Explain corrections at the bottom of the working paper. Show supporting computations. Disregard deferred income tax credits.

Analytical Procedures and Statements

Analytical Procedures and Statements

6

The purpose and the preparation of the statement of cash flows, analysis of financial statements, and accounting for the effects of changing prices constitute the subject matter of the final part of the textbook. The statement of cash flows is now a major financial statement. Because the statement of cash flows may be prepared under either the direct or the indirect method, both approaches are discussed and illustrated. Analysis of financial statements provides an opportunity to integrate much of the subject matter of the textbook and to develop relationships useful for business and investment decisions. Despite the abatement in the level of inflation in recent years, the effect of changing prices on net income and on financial statements generally continues to be a topic of considerable importance to accountants and users of financial statements.

Statement of Cash Flows

23

INTRODUCTION

This chapter considers the nature and preparation of the statement of cash flows (SCF). The Financial Accounting Standards Board requires all profit-oriented enterprises to present a SCF when an income statement and balance sheet are presented in financial reports.[1] *FASB Statement of Accounting Standards No. 95* supersedes *APB Opinion No. 19,* which required the statement of changes in financial position. That statement could be constructed using "funds" of several definitions, including working capital (current assets less current liabilities) and others.

The requirement of a *cash* statement reflects the growing demand for cash flow disclosures to supplement the traditional accrual accounting information present in the other financial statements, and represents an important departure from previous accounting principles.

The increasing number of firms declaring bankruptcy while disclosing positive income illustrates the relevance of cash flow information. The W. T. Grant Corporation case was a striking example. This firm's net income was positive for several years prior to its 1973 bankruptcy, and its stock was selling at healthy multiples of earnings per share. However, its cash flow from operations during the years 1966–1973 was negative for six of those eight years. The firm encountered severe problems with increasing inventory and accounts receivable levels. A close look at the trend in operating cash flow would have signaled problems well before bankruptcy. Information about past cash flows provides information relevant to the prediction of future cash flows for the reporting entity.

---

[1] "Statement of Cash Flows," *Statement of Financial Accounting Standards No. 95,* FASB (Stamford: 1987). This statement is effective for fiscal years ending after July 15, 1988, and for all profit-oriented enterprises. The statement does not require the SCF for not-for-profit enterprises. Restatement of prior years is encouraged.

This chapter discusses (1) the development of the current requirement of the statement of cash flows, (2) the SCF's general usefulness, (3) the specific accounting principle requirements and disclosure choices available, and (4) how to prepare the SCF.

HISTORICAL BACKGROUND

For many years, the basic financial statements of business enterprises were the balance sheet and the income statement. Creditors often requested an explanation for the difference between net income and changes in cash or working capital. To fill this need, many enterprises voluntarily prepared a statement of sources and applications of funds, or *funds* statement.

In 1961, the AICPA issued its *Accounting Research Study No. 2,*[2] which considered the need to increase cash and other "funds" flow reporting in annual reports, and contributed to the first official pronouncement, *APB Opinion No. 3,*[3] regarding funds flows. This opinion was issued in 1963 and encouraged but did not require the presentation of a funds statement.

Eight years later, in 1971, *APB Opinion No. 19*[4] was issued, which officially required a funds statement and recommended it be titled "The Statement of Changes in Financial Position." This statement was generally prepared under a "working capital" concept and supplied information about sources and uses of working capital.

In the early 1980s, the "cash" version of the statement became more popular. In addition, many firms began to use a format that summarized the cash flow activities into *operating, investing,* and *financing* categories.[5] The increasing emphasis on cash reflected the need to provide information useful to cash flow prediction, and to supplement information already present in the financial statements. During this time, the FASB issued a Discussion Memorandum[6] that considered the need to become more focused on cash flow reporting and to require greater disclosure uniformity in the statement of changes in financial position. A majority of respondents to the Memorandum favored the cash concept, indicating their preference for cash as the most accurate measure of short-term liquidity.

In 1984, the FASB published its *Concepts Statement No. 5* as part of its Conceptual Framework Project, which sets guidelines for future generally accepted

---

[2]*Accounting Research Study No. 2,* "Cash Flow Analysis and the Funds Statement," Perry Mason, AICPA, (New York: 1961).

[3]*APB Opinion No. 3,* "The Statement of Sources and Application of Funds," AICPA (New York: 1963).

[4]*APB Opinion No. 19,* "Reporting Changes in Financial Position," AICPA (New York: 1971).

[5]The 38th edition of *Accounting Trends & Techniques* (1984), showed a more than 400% increase in a three-year period in the number of surveyed firms using the cash concept for their statements of changes in financial position. Further, the number of companies showing operating, investing, and financing activities in these changes more than trebled in a two-year period.

[6]Discussion Memorandum, "Reporting Funds Flow, Liquidity, and Financial Flexibility," FASB (Stamford: 1980).

accounting principles. It called for financial statements that disclose the cash flows for the reporting period.[7] Furthermore, paragraph 37 of *Concepts Statement No. 1* stated:

> Financial reporting should provide information to help present and potential investors and creditors and other users in assessing the amounts, timing, and uncertainty of prospective cash receipts from dividends or interest and the proceeds from the sale, redemption, or maturity of securities or loans. The prospects for those cash receipts are affected by an enterprise's ability to generate enough cash to meet its obligations when due and its other cash operating needs, to reinvest in operations, and to pay cash dividends.[8]

Many general reasons have been cited for the historic decision to require a *cash flow statement* rather than a statement based on working capital or another definition of funds. Working capital includes items that may not contribute to the short-term ability to pay debts. Inventory and prepaid expenses are two examples. The complexity of net income measured under GAAP rules had been blamed for reduced confidence in earnings per share figures. Many financial statement users are unable to derive cash flow from income.[9] Many accounting principles contribute to this problem. For example, net income includes long-term asset cost allocations and other noncash expenses that have no effect on liquidity. The equity method of accounting for long-term investments recognizes income of subsidiaries on the parent's books without requiring cash flow to support it. A trend of positive net income is not necessarily a guarantee of corporate survival.

The demand for cash flow disclosure, the need for uniformity in this important area, and the FASB's mandate for cash flow disclosure all contributed to the many significant changes in the required third financial statement.

Figure 1 is an example statement of cash flows following the ***direct format*** permitted by ***FASB Statement No. 95***. The other format choice, the indirect format, is illustrated later in the chapter. The SCF is divided into the three major categories of activities causing cash flows: operating, investing, and financing activities. The statement explains, in noncash terms, the change in cash and cash equivalents (investments in securities that are similar to cash) for the period, as a result that reconciles the beginning and ending balances of cash and cash equivalents. A supplemental schedule lists significant noncash investing and financing transactions that represent major changes in financial position. The schedule reconciling net income and cash flow from operating activities, and the accounting policy footnote, provide further information of relevance to cash flows. The preparation of this statement is discussed later in the chapter.

---

[7] *Statement of Financial Accounting Concepts No. 5*, "Recognition and Measurement in Financial Statements of Business Enterprises, FASB (Stamford: 1984), par. 13.

[8] *Statement of Financial Accounting Concepts No. 1*, "Objectives of Financial Reporting by Business Enterprises," FASB (Stamford: 1978).

[9] "Are More Chryslers in the Offing?," *Forbes*, February 2, 1981.

ELECTRA CORPORATION
Statement of Cash Flows
For Year Ended December 31, Year 3

Operating activities

Collections from customers	$150,000	
Interest received on loans	20,000	
Dividends received on investments	15,000	
Cash provided by operating activities	$185,000	
Payments to suppliers and employees	$110,000	
Interest payments	15,000	
Tax payments	15,000	
Cash used by operating activities	$140,000	
Net cash flow from operating activities		$ 45,000

Investing activities

Purchase of equity securities	$(60,000)	
Purchase of debt securities	(40,000)	
Proceeds from sale of property	20,000	
Acquisition of property	(30,000)	
Proceeds from sale of investments	35,000	
Collections on loans	10,000	
Net cash used by investing activities		$(65,000)

Financing activities

Dividends paid . . . . , .	$(25,000)	
Proceeds from stock issuance	80,000	
Proceeds from short-term debt	5,000	
Proceeds from bond issuance	30,000	
Payments on capital leases	(5,000)	
Payments to retire long-term debt	(40,000)	
Purchase of treasury stock	(10,000)	
Net cash provided by financing activities		$ 35,000
Net increase in cash and cash equivalents		$ 15,000
Cash and cash equivalents, Jan. 1, Year 3		40,000
Cash and cash equivalents, Dec. 31, Year 3		$ 55,000

Reconciliation of net income to net cash flow from
operating activities

Net income	$ 70,000	
Adjustments to reconcile net income to net cash		
provided by operating activities		
Depreciation and amortization	30,000	
Net accounts receivable decrease	10,000	
Inventory increase	(5,000)	

(continued)

Accounts payable decrease	(20,000)
Gain on sale of property	(40,000)
Net cash flow from operating activities	$ 45,000

Schedule of noncash investing and financing activities

Capital lease obligations incurred for equipment.	$ 50,000
Common stock issued to acquire land	$ 65,000
Conversion of bonds to common stock	$ 80,000

Disclosure of accounting policy

For purposes of the Statement of Cash Flows, Electra considers all highly liquid debt securities purchased with a maturity of three months or less to be cash equivalents.

THE PURPOSE AND GENERAL USEFULNESS OF THE STATEMENT OF CASH FLOWS

The main purpose of the SCF is to provide investors, creditors, and other financial statement users with information about the cash flows of an enterprise for a reporting period. This information is intended to help users assess: (1) a business entity's ability to generate future positive net cash inflows; (2) its ability to pay its debts, dividends, and interest; (3) the reasons for differences between income and cash flows; and (4) the effects of cash and noncash transactions on the entity's financial position.

The SCF discloses specific cash flow "event" information and provides a link between the beginning and ending balance sheets. For example, there are any number of explanations for a $2,000,000 change in gross Property, Plant, and Equipment. The balance sheet merely lists the account balances at different points in time. It does not explain *why* the changes occurred.

The SCF is an itemization of all changes in cash in terms other than cash. The double-entry accounting system guarantees that the change in cash and cash equivalents must equal the aggregate change in all other accounts. The SCF, through its disclosure of all transactions affecting cash and cash equivalents, discloses the reasons underlying the change in cash and cash equivalents during the reporting period.

The following are examples of specific disclosures found on the SCF: acquisitions of property and investments; disposals of property and investments; loans made to other organizations and collections on loans; major borrowings and stock issuances; extinguishment of debt and purchases of treasury stock; the disposition of profits; capital investment; and research and development.

Many decisions and evaluations made by financial statement users require cash flow information. A business entity's ability to generate positive cash flow constrains its ability to meet obligations and pay dividends, and is therefore an important consideration to potential creditors and investors. The relationship of net income and cash flow from operations is also important to financial statement users. The "quality" of net income indicates the degree to which net distributable assets have been generated. The nature and pattern of a business entity's cash and noncash investing and financing activities also impacts decisions.

Information concerning "financial flexibility," the ability of a business entity to adapt to favorable and unfavorable changes in operating conditions, is also valued by investors and creditors. Greater financial flexibility implies easier entrance into new markets and greater ability to withstand difficult economic conditions. Ability to generate positive cash flow is a source of financial flexibility. The decision whether to extend credit to a company is influenced by financial flexibility and the historical trend of cash flows from operations. Disclosure of cash flow information should assist financial statement users to make the evaluations and decisions in these and other related areas.

The SCF adds to the financial description of a business entity when used in conjunction with the income statement and balance sheet, and particularly if the *trend* of cash flows over several years is considered. The SCF presents the pure cash flow information that often cannot be derived from the other statements. The net cash flow from operations, however, should not be viewed as a substitute for net income. Decisions that may not be indicative of the longer-run ability of a business entity to provide a positive cash flow on a continuing basis may affect the cash flow information disclosed for a particular period. Both the cash and accrual descriptions of events are important, and the requirement of an SCF now ensures that both will be available for the assessment of future cash flow and income potential of enterprises.

SPECIFIC REQUIREMENTS OF *FASB STATEMENT NO. 95*

This section considers the major disclosure requirements and provisions of *FASB Statement No. 95*. These include: (1) cash and cash equivalents as the reporting basis for the SCF, (2) the three categories of cash flows, (3) significant noncash investing and financing transactions, and (4) statement formats permitted.

Cash and Cash Equivalents: The Reporting Basis of the SCF

FASB Statement No. 95 requires that the SCF explain the change in "cash and cash equivalents" for the reporting period, thus eliminating the ambiguity caused by different "funds" definitions prior to *Statement No. 95*. The SCF reports the net change in cash and cash equivalents as a result that reconciles the beginning and ending balances of cash and cash equivalents (see Figure 1). The change in cash and cash equivalents reported in the SCF will equal the net change over the period in all accounts comprising cash and cash equivalents.

"Cash" includes all accounts for which cash deposits and withdrawals can be made at any time without prior notice or penalty. "Cash equivalents" are short-term, highly liquid investments that are: (1) readily converted into a known amount of cash, and (2) with an original maturity (to the purchasing entity) of three months or less. The intent of the three-month maturity rule is to include only investments that were made for the purpose of earning interest on temporarily idle funds and to exclude investments that place capital at significant risk of price fluctuation. Cash equivalents are so near maturity that there is immaterial risk of change in principal value from interest rate changes.

Examples of cash equivalents include Treasury notes, commercial paper, and money market funds. A two-year U.S. Treasury note purchased three months prior to maturity would be a cash equivalent, but a two-year Treasury note purchased four months prior to maturity would not become a cash equivalent a month after purchase.

Cash management practices require an adequate return on temporarily unused cash balances. Business entities routinely employ banks and other financial institutions to invest their excess cash in government securities and money market funds. These investments have essentially the same liquidity as cash. The assessment of future cash flows by financial statement users will therefore consider all items that are essentially cash.

FASB Statement No. 95 does not require cash equivalency status to be applied to all securities that fulfill the definition. Many companies, including financial institutions and insurance companies, consider many of these securities to be longer-term investments. Therefore, each company must disclose its accounting policy relative to the classification of cash equivalents. Any change in the policy is treated as a change in accounting principle, with retroactive application to all comparative financial statements disclosed. For simplicity, all the examples in this chapter assume that securities meeting the definition are classified as cash equivalents.

The Three Classifications of Cash Flows

All cash inflows and outflows are classified into one of three categories in the SCF: financing cash flows, investing cash flows, and operating cash flows. Figure 1 illustrates each of the three types of cash flows. There are both cash inflows and outflows in each category.

The separation of cash flows into the three functional categories facilitates prediction of specific cash flows. Operating cash flows are listed first in the SCF, and are defined as those cash flows that are not investing or financing.

Cash Flows from Investing Activities Investing activities include purchases and sales of productive assets, other companys' debt and equity securities (which are not cash equivalents), and other investment activities. Capitalized interest (to the extent paid) is also included in the investing category, as the cash paid for interest capitalized increases the account of the property under construction. Insurance proceeds for property involved in a casualty is an investing cash inflow.

Cash Flows from Financing Activities Financing activities include issuance of capital stock and debt securities, dividend payments to the company's shareholders, repayment of debt, and purchase and retirement of treasury stock. All principal payments on debt incurred to acquire productive assets are financing outflows, whether seller-financed or third party-financed. Loans from financial institutions are generally considered financing activities, whereas loans from suppliers for the purchase of materials are operational activities.

The SCF disclosure for extraordinary items depends on whether the underlying transaction is financing or investing. For example, the extraordinary gain or loss from early retirement of bonds is associated with a financing transaction (the bond retirement). Therefore the cash outflow to retire the bonds is a financing cash outflow. The "extraordinary" nature of the gain or loss does not affect the cash flow classification. An extraordinary casualty loss on property, for example, stems from an investing transaction.

Most extraordinary items are not cash flows and therefore are not listed on the SCF. However, the related tax effect *is* a cash flow and is treated as an adjustment to the cash flow associated with the extraordinary item. For example, the tax savings from the extraordinary casualty loss above increase the investing cash inflow. The SCF would list the tax effect as an addition to the insurance proceeds, in the investing category. The comprehensive example later in the chapter provides a numerical illustration.

Cash Flows from Operating Activities   Operating cash flows result mainly from the day-to-day income-producing activities of the enterprise and include all transactions affecting cash that do not belong in the investing or financing category. Cash inflows in this category include collections on accounts receivable, and interest and dividends received on investments. Cash outflows include payments to suppliers for inventory and supplies, payments for interest on debt, and payments for other costs of doing business. Note that dividends received from investments are operating cash inflows, but dividends paid by the company to its shareholders are financing cash outflows. Interest paid *and* received are operating cash flows. Interest paid and received, and dividends received, affect net income and therefore are operational flows.

Other examples of operational cash flows are: amounts received and paid from lawsuits; payments and receipts of principal amounts on long-term and short-term loans to and from suppliers; insurance proceeds from health and life insurance policies; and payments to suppliers for installment purchases and receipts from customers on installment sales, regardless of the time period involved.

The distinction between the operating and the longer-term financing and investing categories is an important segregation of (1) the repetitive activities that create the primary value added for the firm, from (2) the more discrete events that represent basic changes in the enterprise's financial structure. The operating/nonoperating distinction is a critical one for financial statement users interested in predicting an enterprise's ability to generate cash flow in the future. The ability of an enterprise to generate cash from operations is an important factor in maintaining liquidity and solvency on an ongoing basis. A business enterprise that must resort to sales of its investments or productive capacity to generate a positive cash flow cannot do so indefinitely.

It is the fundamental nature of the transaction that determines whether a cash flow should be included in operations or in one of the other two categories. The FASB used "association with net income" as a major criterion for determining whether a cash flow should be included in the operating category. For example, although interest payments are a cost of financing, interest expense is a component of net income. The FASB reasoned that the close association of "operating" activities and the income-generating process favored the classification of interest payments within the operating category. In addition, many enterprises maintain a line of credit with a financial institution for short-term operational loans. Interest on these funds is thus closely linked to the operating activities of the enterprise.

Certain transactions may appear to stem from financing or investing activities but should appear in the operating section of the SCF when the transactions are clearly related to the main-line income-producing activities of the enterprise. An enterprise that invests and sells long-term assets as a direct source of income would report the associated cash flows in the operations section. If the enterprise leased the assets rather than sold them, the lease payments would be classified as investing inflows (and the lessee would classify the outflows as financing).

Significant Noncash Financing and Investing Activities

To supplement the cash flow information and to complete the disclosure of changes in financial position, significant noncash financing and investing transactions are disclosed. These transactions must be disclosed in a supplemental schedule or reported in the footnotes to the SCF. They should be identified clearly as noncash transactions. The cash portion of transactions that have both cash and noncash components is disclosed in the SCF, with the noncash portion disclosed in the notes or schedule.

The acquisition of land valued at $100,000 through the issuance of bonds is an example. The land acquisition is an investing activity and the issuance of bonds is the means of financing. If disclosed in a schedule, the one-line disclosure would be:

Acquisition of land through bond issue............................ $100,000

This noncash transaction is economically equivalent to first issuing bonds for cash and then using the proceeds for the land purchase. This additional reporting requirement ensures that all major financing and investing activities are disclosed. If the value of the land had been $150,000 and $50,000 cash had been paid in addition to the bonds, a $50,000 investing cash flow would be disclosed in the SCF (land purchase) in addition to the above disclosure.

Other examples of transactions in this category are: conversions of debt to equity; exchanges of assets for other assets; exchanges of liabilities for other liabilities; contracts for capital leases (*payments* on capital leases are financing cash outflows); and receipt of donated property.

Certain other events are generally not considered significant noncash financing or investing transactions. These include stock dividends issued and received, stock splits, and appropriations of retained earnings. These are not considered exchange transactions or significant changes in capital structure and would not be disclosed in the SCF or in supplemental schedules.

SCF Format Alternatives: The Direct and Indirect Methods

FASB Statement No. 95 allows two alternative formats for disclosure of cash flow from operating activities: the *direct* and *indirect* methods. The FASB recommends the direct format. The reported subtotal, net cash flow from operating activities, is the same for either format alternative, as are the entire investing and financing sections of the SCF.

The direct format computes net cash flow from operating activities *directly,* by listing all operating cash receipts and payments in the body of the statement. Figure 1 is an example of a SCF prepared under the direct format. The direct format must disclose, at a minimum, the following categories of cash flows:

1   Cash collected from customers

2   Interest and dividends received

3   Other operating receipts

4   Cash paid to employees and suppliers

5   Interest payments

6   Income tax payments

Enterprises that choose the direct method must also disclose the reconciliation of net income and net cash flow from operating activities in a supplemental schedule. This is the same reconciliation used by the indirect method. See Figure 1.

The *indirect* format reconciles net income and net cash flow from operating activities by adjusting net income for noncash revenues, expenses, gains, losses, and changes in operational working capital accounts during the reporting period. It does *not* list the operating cash flows. The reconciliation may appear in the body of the SCF or in a supplemental schedule. If the latter approach is chosen, only the net cash flow from operations appears in the body of the statement. The reconciling items should be clearly identified as such to avoid any inference that they are cash flows.

The minimum breakdown of the reconciling items is:

1   Deferrals of past operating receipts and payments

2   Accruals of expected future operating receipts and payments

3   Changes in receivables, inventories, payables, and other operating current assets and liabilities

4   Other classes of reconciling items including depreciation and amortization

5   Noncash gains and losses

Furthermore, the indirect format must disclose interest payments (net of interest capitalized) and income tax payments in a supplemental schedule or in the notes. Given the required reconciling items and income statement accounts, users may be able to approximate the direct method disclosures from the indirect format.

Figure 2 is an illustration of the indirect format applied to the Electra Corporation. The reconciliation appears in a separate schedule and is the same reconciliation found in Figure 1. Note the separate disclosure of changes in the relevant working capital accounts. The supplemental disclosure of interest and tax payments is necessary for the indirect format, as they do not appear in the reconciliation. The direct format automatically discloses these items in the body of the SCF.

Figure 2
Indirect format

ELECTRA CORPORATION
Statement of Cash Flows
For Year Ended December 31, Year 3

Net cash flow from operating activities		$ 45,000
Investing activities		
Purchase of equity securities	$(60,000)	
Purchase of debt securities	(40,000)	
Proceeds from sale of property	20,000	
Acquisition of property	(30,000)	
Proceeds from sale of investments	35,000	
Collections on loans	10,000	
Net cash used by investing activities		$(65,000)
Financing activities		
Dividends paid	$(25,000)	
Proceeds from stock issuance	80,000	
Proceeds from short-term debt	5,000	
Proceeds from bond issuance	30,000	
Payments on capital leases	(5,000)	
Payments to retire long-term debt	(40,000)	
Purchase of treasury stock	(10,000)	
Net cash provided by financing activities		$ 35,000
Net increase in cash and cash equivalents		$ 15,000
Cash equivalents, Jan. 1, Year 3		40,000
Cash equivalents, Dec. 31, Year 3		$ 55,000
Supplemental disclosure of cash flow information		
Interest payments		$ 15,000
Income tax payments		$ 15,000
Reconciliation of net income to net cash provided		
from operating activities *(all amounts assumed)*		
Net income	$ 70,000	
Adjustments to reconcile net income to net cash		
provided by operating activities		
Depreciation and amortization	$ 30,000	
Net accounts receivable decrease	10,000	

(continued)

Inventory increase	(5,000)
Accounts payable decrease	(20,000)
Gain on sale of property	(40,000)
Net cash flow from operating activities	$45,000

Schedule of noncash investing and financing activities

Capital lease obligations incurred for equipment.	$ 50,000
Common stock issued to acquire land	$ 65,000
Conversion of bonds to common stock	$ 80,000

Disclosure of accounting policy

For purposes of the Statement of Cash Flows, Electra considers all highly liquid debt securities purchased with a maturity of three months or less to be cash equivalents.

The indirect and direct formats were also allowed by *APB Opinion No. 19* for the statement of changes in financial position. The indirect format predominated in published statements. The majority of respondents to the FASB's Discussion Memorandum on cash flows favored the indirect format, stating that the information required to present the direct format is more expensive to provide.[10]

The reconciliation highlights the differences between net income and operating cash flow and is therefore useful in assessing the degree to which net income represents changes in liquid resources. The main advantage of the direct format is the disclosure of the actual cash flows contributing to net cash flow from operations. Financial analysts may be better able to predict the components of operating cash flow from knowledge of the past components. Since the reconciliation of net income and operating cash flows is present in both formats, the direct format supplies the user with more information.

The Appendix to this chapter discusses the preparation of the reconciliation and its underlying logic. It also provides a lengthy example.

Gross and Net Disclosure: Data Aggregation

The FASB considered the issue of data aggregation in the SCF. Generally, gross cash flows should be disclosed. Netting cash flows reduces the information content of the statement. In situations with large numbers of similar transactions of large amounts, with quick turnover and short maturities, some netting of flows is allowed. Examples are cash flows from investments, loans, and debt.

Cash flows are grouped by similar type within the three categories. For example, all cash received from customers is grouped together into one cash inflow disclosure in the operating category, and is reported separately from all proceeds from common stock issuance within the financing activity. This requirement ensures that different classes of cash flows are disclosed separately to avoid the loss of "event" information.

---

[10]Discussion Memorandum, "Reporting Funds Flow, Liquidity, and Financial Flexibility."

''Cash flow per share'' is an aggregated statistic that is often computed by financial analysts and is the ratio of net cash flow from operations to the number of common stock shares outstanding. *FASB Statement No. 95* specifically prohibits the reporting of cash flow information on a per-share basis.

The FASB cited the following reasons for this position: potential confusion between cash flow and earnings, per share; disagreement about the components of the numerator and denominator; and concern that users might assume that the statistic represents the amount available for dividends. However, contractually determined cash flow per unit values (as required by an agreement between the company and its owners) are not precluded.

Summary Table: Format Considerations

The following table provides a checklist for the important format aspects of *FASB Statement No. 95* and distinctions between the direct and indirect methods.

	Format	
	Direct	*Indirect*
Cash flows are segregated into operating, investing, and financing activities.	Yes	Yes
The change in cash and cash equivalents reconciles the beginning and ending balances of cash and cash equivalents.	Yes	Yes
Schedule reconciling net income and operating cash flow.	Supporting schedule	In body of SCF or in supporting schedule
Significant noncash investing and financing activities in supporting schedule or notes referencing the SCF.	Yes	Yes
Supplemental disclosure of interest payments, net of capitalized interest, and income tax payments.	No (reported in body of SCF)	Yes
Cash equivalent policy disclosure in note to SCF.	Yes	Yes

PREPARATION OF THE STATEMENT OF CASH FLOWS

This section illustrates the SCF preparation process. Two examples are provided: first a basic example to illustrate the process, and then a more comprehensive example to illustrate a work sheet and a more involved situation. The two examples in the chapter use the direct format. The Appendix to the chapter illustrates the indirect format by highlighting the preparation of the reconciliation of net income and operating cash flows found in both formats.

There are many methods of preparing the SCF. The objectives of any method are to identify all cash flow transactions and significant noncash investing and financing transactions, and to disclose them correctly on the SCF.

The approach illustrated in this chapter is a **transactions analysis method.** It searches the accounting system for transactions that affected cash and cash equivalents. Entries are reconstructed to isolate those that contain cash or significant noncash investing or financing activities. These entries are **not** recorded or posted to accounts again. Rather they serve as an analysis tool to "discover" the cash flows that occurred during the period.

The information search is performed in this order: (1) income statement; (2) changes in retained earnings (through the owners' equity statement, retained earning statement, or other information); (3) "additional" information; and (4) the remaining unexplained balance sheet account changes (other than cash and cash equivalents). The first three sources will generally uncover most of the transactions that require SCF disclosure. The process is complete when all account changes have been explained.

A Basic Example of SCF Preparation (Direct Format)

Figure 3 provides Kings Corporation's financial statement data to illustrate the preparation of its SCF (direct method).

Figure 3
Financial statements and additional information

KINGS CORPORATION
Comparative Balance Sheets
December 31, Year 4 and Year 5

	Year 4	Year 5
Assets		
Cash and cash equivalents.............................	$ 14,000	$ 68,000
Accounts receivable	21,000	31,000
Allowance for doubtful accounts	(1,000)	(1,000)
Inventories...	100,000	80,000
Property, plant, and equipment	350,000	460,000
Accumulated depreciation.............................	(180,000)	(260,000)
Investment in Thor Corporation		50,000
Intangibles, net......................................	80,000	75,000
Total assets	$ 384,000	$ 503,000
Liabilities		
Accounts payable	$ 10,000	$ 17,000
Bonds payable.......................................	100,000	140,000
Convertible bonds payable		50,000
Total liabilities	$ 110,000	$ 207,000
Owners' equity		
Common stock.......................................	$ 191,000	$ 212,000
Retained earnings	83,000	84,000
Total owners' equity	$ 274,000	$ 296,000
Total liabilities & owners' equity....................	$ 384,000	$ 503,000

(continued)

KINGS CORPORATION
Income Statement
For Year Ended December 31, Year 5

Sales...		$ 675,000
Cost of goods sold		(405,000)
Gross margin		$ 270,000
Other expenses		
Interest expense	$ 20,000	
Depreciation	120,000	
Amortization of intangibles	5,000	
Marketing and administrative expense..................	80,000	
Total other expenses...................................		(225,000)
Net income		$ 45,000

Additional information for Year 5

1. Assume that all sales were on credit, and there are no income taxes expense.
2. Equipment was acquired for $100,000.
3. Land was acquired for cash.
4. A building was sold for its carrying amount (original cost, $120,000; accumulated depreciation, $40,000).
5. Doubtful accounts expense for Year 5 was $1,000 and is included in marketing and administrative costs.
6. The convertible bonds were issued Dec. 31 for Thor Corporation common stock.

The information in Figure 3 indicates that cash and cash equivalents has increased $54,000. Most of the balance sheet accounts have changed, but it is not possible to determine immediately all the specific cash flows that ultimately explain the $54,000 change in cash from the information sources available. This is a major purpose of the SCF. The SCF is not prepared to determine the change in cash and cash equivalents. That change is already known. Rather, it provides the specific reasons *why* these accounts have changed, in terms of noncash accounts.

Analysis of Transactions This example illustrates the logic behind the account analysis resulting in the completed SCF for Kings Corporation appearing in Figure 4. Refer to that figure after each account is analyzed. The Appendix explains the reconciliation process.

1 Analysis of Income Statement Accounts

Sales The accounts associated with sales are: Accounts Receivable, which increased $10,000 during the year; Allowance for Doubtful Accounts, which experienced no net change; and Doubtful Accounts Expense which was $1,000 (from additional information). The reconstructed summary entries are:

```
    (1) Accounts Receivable .............................. 675,000
            Sales....................................              675,000

    (2) Marketing and Administrative Expense.................   1,000
            Allowance For Doubtful Accounts ..............            1,000

    (3) Allowance for Doubtful Accounts.....................   1,000
            Accounts Receivable ..........................            1,000

(a) (4) Cash ............................................... 664,000
            Accounts Receivable ..........................            664,000
```

Entries (1) and (2) are implied directly from the Sales account in the income statement and additional information item 5. Note that entry (2) debits Marketing and Administrative Expense, as Kings Corporation groups doubtful accounts expense into that account. The zero change in the Allowance account implies entry (3), which is a specific account write-off. Entries (1) and (3) cause a net positive $674,000 change in Accounts Receivable. This information, and the $10,000 net increase in Accounts Receivable, imply entry (4). The $664,000 cash collection on Accounts Receivable is operating cash flow (*a*) on the completed SCF in Figure 4.

Cost of Goods Sold   The accounts related to this expense are Inventories, which decreased $20,000; and Accounts Payable, which increased $7,000. No additional information is relevant to this account. The reconstructed summary entries are:

```
    (5) Cost of Goods Sold ................................... 405,000
            Inventories.....................................            405,000

    (6) Inventories.......................................... 385,000
            Accounts Payable .............................            385,000

(b) (7) Accounts Payable ................................... 378,000
            Cash..........................................            378,000
```

Entry (5) is implied directly from the Cost of Goods Sold account. Entry (6) is implied by the $20,000 net decrease in Inventories for the year and entry (5), which decreased Inventories $405,000. Therefore, purchases of inventories must have been $385,000. Finally, if purchases were $385,000 (an Accounts Payable increase), and Accounts Payable increased a net of $7,000, then Kings must have paid $378,000 on account. The cash flow in (7) is an operating cash flow and is item (*b*) on the completed SCF.

Interest Expense   Because no interest was payable at the beginning or end of Year 5, it may be assumed that the entire expense was paid in cash. The reconstructed entry is:

```
(c) (8) Interest Expense ....................................... 20,000
            Cash..........................................            20,000
```

This is operating cash flow (*c*) on the completed SCF.

Depreciation and Amortization   Both Depreciation Expense and Amortization of Intangibles are noncash expenses and therefore are not listed in the SCF using the direct format.

Marketing and Administrative Expense   There are no accounts related to this expense, but additional information item 5 is relevant. Entry (2) above has already accounted for $1,000 of this expense, therefore the reconstructed entry is:

(d) (9) Marketing and Administrative Expense 79,000		
Cash		79,000

The cash flow in (9) is operating cash flow (*d*) on the completed SCF.

At this point, all income statement accounts have been explained with the associated cash flows disclosed in the SCF. All operating working capital account changes (Accounts Receivable, Inventories, and Accounts Payable) have been explained, as well as Intangibles. As each information source is analyzed, there are fewer account changes to explain in the remaining information sources.

2   Analysis of Retained Earnings
Kings Corporation did not present a separate owners' equity statement or retained earnings statement, but there is sufficient information present to analyze retained earnings. Retained earnings increased $1,000 during Year 5. Since net income was $45,000, $44,000 of declared dividends is implied. Therefore, the reconstructed entries are:

(10) Income Summary..................................... 45,000		
Retained Earnings		45,000
(e) (11) Retained Earnings 44,000		
Cash		44,000

The cash flow in entry (11) is defined by *FASB Statement No. 95* as a financing cash outflow and is item (*e*) in the completed SCF. The Retained Earnings account has been completely explained.

3   Analysis of Additional Information
Items 1 and 5 of additional information have been incorporated into disclosures in the SCF. The remainder of the additional information items are analyzed at this point.
Items 2, 3, and 4 pertain to Property, Plant, and Equipment and to Accumulated Depreciation. A T account is a useful tool to analyze an account with several relevant transactions. The T account below analyzes the two accounts affected by the remaining additional information. All known information pertaining to the two accounts has been entered into the T accounts.

Property, plant, and equipment				
Balance, Jan. 1, Yr. 5	350,000		120,000	(G) Building sold
Equipment acquired	100,000	(G)		
Land acquired	130,000	(I)		
Subtotals	580,000		120,000	
Balance, Dec. 31, Yr. 5	460,000			

Accumulated depreciation				
Accumulated deprec- iation: building	40,000	(G)	180,000	Balance, Jan. 1, Yr. 5
			120,000	(G) Depreciation exp.
Subtotals	40,000		300,000	
			260,000	Balance, Dec. 31, Yr. 5

(G) Signifies a given or known transaction
(I) Signifies an implied transaction

The $130,000 land acquisition was implied by the known transactions affecting the gross Property, Plant, and Equipment account. The $130,000 debit caused the account to balance, and the additional information indicated an acquisition of land. No transaction was implied by the analysis of Accumulated Depreciation. The account balanced by considering all known events affecting that account. The reconstructed entries for these two accounts are:

(f) (12)	Property, Plant, and Equipment		100,000	
	Cash			100,000
(13)	Depreciation Expense		120,000	
	Accumulated Depreciation			120,000
(g) (14)	Property, Plant, and Equipment		130,000	
	Cash			130,000
(h) (15)	Cash		80,000	
	Accumulated Depreciation		40,000	
	Property, Plant, and Equipment			120,000

The cash flows in entries (12), (14), and (15) are investing cash flows and are indicated by letter in the SCF. The changes in Property, Plant, and Equipment and in Accumulated Depreciation have been explained.

The remaining additional information item (6) refers to a noncash transaction. There are no other accounts or additional information relevant to this transaction, and no cash is involved. The reconstructed entry is:

(i) (16)	Investment in Thor Corporation		50,000	
	Convertible Bonds			50,000

This entry explains the changes in the respective balance sheet accounts and requires disclosure (*i*) in a schedule to the SCF.

4   Analysis of Remaining Unexplained Balance Sheet Accounts
Generally, only a few balance sheet account changes remain unexplained at this point. For Kings Corporation these are Bonds Payable and Common Stock. Bonds Payable and Common Stock do not generally appear together in entries, the amounts of their changes are not the same, and no other information indicates that they are related in this instance. Therefore it is assumed that they are independent and that cash was involved in their changes.

Bonds Payable increased $40,000 in Year 5, indicating that bonds in that amount were sold. This cash flow is a financing cash flow and appears in the SCF as item (*j*). The reconstructed entry is:

(j) (17) Cash.. 40,000
                     Bonds Payable   40,000

The Bonds Payable account balance is now completely explained.
The Common Stock account increased $21,000. The reconstructed entry is:

(k) (18) Cash 21,000
                     Common Stock...................................   21,000

The cash flow in entry (18) is a financing cash flow and is item (*k*) in the completed SCF.

Completing the SCF   At this point, all account changes have been explained and all transactions affecting cash have been isolated. The three subtotals, net cash flow from operating activities, net cash flow used by investing activities, and net cash flow provided by financing activities, are calculated to provide summary information for the three categories of cash flows. The change in cash and cash equivalents for Year 5 reconciles the beginning and ending balances. The schedule of noncash investing and financing activities does not affect the change in cash and cash equivalents and does not have a meaningful total.

Figure 4
Direct format

KINGS CORPORATION
Statement of Cash Flows
For Year Ended December 31, Year 5

Operating activities

Collections from customers	$ 664,000	(a)
Payments to suppliers	(378,000)	(b)
Interest payments	(20,000)	(c)
Marketing and administrative payments............	(79,000)	(d)
Net cash flow from operating activities	$ 187,000	

(continued)

Investing activities

Equipment acquisition	$(100,000)	(f)
Land acquisition.................................	(130,000)	(g)
Building sale proceeds	80,000	(h)
Net cash used by investing activities		$(150,000)

Financing activities

Dividends paid	$ (44,000)	(e)
Bond issuance	40,000	(j)
Common stock issuance	21,000	(k)
Net cash provided by financing activities		$ 17,000
Net increase in cash and cash equivalents		$ 54,000
Cash and cash equivalents, Jan. 1, Year 5...........		14,000
Cash and cash equivalents, Dec. 31, Year 5		$ 68,000

**Reconciliation of net income to net cash flow
provided by operating activities**

Net income	$ 45,000
Adjustments to reconcile net income to net cash provided by operating activities	
Depreciation expense..........................	120,000
Intangible amortization	5,000
Net accounts receivable increase	(10,000)
Inventory decrease	20,000
Accounts payable increase....................	7,000
Net cash provided by operating activities	$ 187,000

**Schedule of noncash investing and financing
activities**

Acquisition of Thor Corporation common stock through issuance of convertible bonds	$ 50,000	(i)

Disclosure of accounting policy

For purposes of the Statement of Cash Flows, Kings considers all highly liquid debt securities purchased with a maturity of three months or less to be cash equivalents.

The SCF in Figure 4 indicates that operating activities were the main source of cash for the period. Healthy sales and cash collections, and low costs relative to sales, contributed to the operating cash flow. Net flow from financing activities contributed only a small portion of the total. The company paid almost all of its net income as dividends in Year 5. If Year 5 results are representative of the last several years, it appears that Kings Corporation is retaining a material amount of cash for the ultimate replacement of productive assets, since dividends did not exceed income. Without the SCF, financial statement users would find reconstructing the cash flow information very difficult or impossible. The Appendix discusses the reconciliation.

The next example uses a more complex set of facts and provides an example of work sheet preparation.

A Comprehensive Example (Direct Format): The Work Sheet

A work sheet enables professional accountants to organize and record their work. It is an organized and structured document and provides evidence used in litigation and other proceedings. A work sheet also helps to ensure that all balance sheet changes have been explained by the end of the preparation process.

A work sheet is an optional procedure. Some accountants find it easier to prepare a SCF without one. Furthermore, there are many different approaches to their construction. The one featured in this chapter relies exclusively on reconstructed entries to determine cash flows and noncash investing and financing activities.

Figure 5 provides Classic Stores Corporation's financial statement data to illustrate the preparation of its SCF (direct method).

Figure 5
Financial statements and additional information

CLASSIC STORES CORPORATION
Comparative Balance Sheets
December 31, Years 1 and 2

	Year 1	Year 2
Assets		
Cash	$125,000	$ 159,000
Short-term investments	60,000	40,000
Accounts receivable, net	30,000	15,000
Inventories	25,000	20,000
Land	80,000	241,000
Buildings, net	200,000	553,889
Equipment, net	100,000	60,000
Leased equipment under capital lease, net		56,955
Investment in Baldwin Corporation	80,000	88,000
Total assets	$700,000	$1,233,844
Liabilities		
Accounts payable	$ 20,000	$ 10,000
Dividends payable...................................	80,000	30,000
Taxes payable	10,000	8,000
Current portion, liability under capital lease		4,039
10% Convertible bonds payable	100,000	
12% Bonds payable	100,000	100,000
Unamortized premium on 12% bonds payable	12,000	11,000
Liability under capital lease........................		45,638
Deferred taxes	20,000	85,000
Owners' equity		
Common stock, $10 par..............................	100,000	176,000
Paid-in capital in excess of par	100,000	420,000
Retained earnings, appropriated	25,000	40,000
Retained earnings, unappropriated...................	145,000	324,167
Treasury stock, at cost	(12,000)	(20,000)
Total liabilities & owners' equity	$700,000	$1,233,844

(continued)

CLASSIC STORES CORPORATION
Income Statement
For Year Ended December 31, Year 2

Sales..		$ 2,452,000
Cost of goods sold		(1,610,000)
Gross margin		$ 842,000
Other expenses	$137,000	
Interest expense	9,394	
Depreciation expense..................................	126,328	
Doubtful accounts expense............................	49,000	(321,722)
		$ 520,278
Net realized gain on sale of		
short-term investments	$ 18,000	
Investment income	32,000	
Gain on sale of land	50,000	100,000
Net income before extraordinary		
item and taxes		$ 620,278
Income tax expense		(248,111)
Net income before extraordinary		
item...		$ 372,167
Extraordinary casualty loss, net of $28,000 tax savings....		(42,000)
Net income		$ 330,167

Additional information for Classic Stores Corporation, Year 2

1. All sales are on credit.
2. Classic Stores is taxed at an average rate of 40%.
3. The short-term investments are considered cash equivalents.
4. The 12% bonds pay interest annually on Dec. 31.
5. On Jan. 2, the corporation acquired equipment through a capital lease requiring a $10,000 down payment and nine annual payments of $10,000 each Dec. 31 through Year 10. Classic Stores' incremental borrowing rate is 12%. The leased equipment is expected to last 10 years.
6. The convertible bonds were converted on Jan. 2. Each $1,000 bond was converted into 20 shares of common stock. The book value method was used to record the conversion.
7. In February, Classic Stores purchased a building and land parcel by paying $100,000 down and issuing 4,000 shares of common stock whose market value on that date was $50 per share. The fair market value of the land was an estimated $120,000.
8. In March, a 10% common stock dividend was issued. The stock price at the date of declaration was $60 per share.
9. $8,000 of interest was capitalized on a self-constructed building started and completed in Year 2. There were no remaining construction-related payables at

(continued)

the end of Year 2. The total capitalized cost of the building was $80,000, which was $10,000 under appraised value for property tax purposes.

10. $40,000 of dividends were declared.

11. The investment in Baldwin Corporation represents ownership of 40% of Baldwin's outstanding common stock. The original purchase price of the stock equaled book value. There was no change in Classic Stores' ownership percentage during Year 2, and no shares of Baldwin were bought or sold. Baldwin earned $80,000 during Year 2.

12. Land with an original cost of $60,000 was sold for $110,000.

13. A building suffered an extraordinary casualty loss from unusual storm damage. The reduction in net book value was $150,000 and insurance proceeds covered only $80,000 of the loss, which reduced taxes at the average tax rate applicable to the company.

14. Depreciation expense included $80,000 on buildings and $40,000 on equipment.

15. Late in the year, Classic Stores invested most of its increase in cash in buildings ($323,889) and land ($101,000).

16. Accounts payable relate only to inventory purchases.

Analysis of Transactions The objective is the same whether or not a work sheet is used: to explain the change in cash and cash equivalents in terms of all the other accounts, and to disclose all significant noncash investing and financing transactions. The change in cash and cash equivalents for Classic Stores is $14,000 (the net of $34,000 Cash increase, and $20,000 decrease in Short-Term Investments, which are considered cash equivalents in this example).

The work sheet has two sections: (1) the listing of the balance sheet and income statement accounts; and (2) the listing of items that are transferred to the SCF (the SCF section). The beginning-of-year balances appear on the left and end-of-year balances on the right. The middle two columns are used to account for all account changes. The reconstructed entries explaining each balance sheet account except cash and cash equivalent accounts are transferred to these middle columns. The changes in cash and cash equivalents are listed in these center columns, and they are also used as balancing figures.

Those components of reconstructed entries affecting cash, or that are considered noncash transactions, are listed in the SCF section. Cash inflows are debits; outflows are credits. The net change in cash and cash equivalents is a balancing figure. The noncash disclosures in the work sheet are *in addition* to the transfers from reconstructed entries, as no cash flow appears in these entries. This section ends the work sheet.

The numbers in parentheses indicate the reconstructed entry number; the letters in parentheses indicate items appearing in the SCF section. Two different arithmetic checks are provided by the work sheet format after its completion. *First,* the sum of all debit changes in balance sheet accounts must equal the sum of all credit changes plus or minus the change in cash and cash equivalents. Also, net income must equal the difference between the sum of the credit and debit changes for the income statement accounts. Likewise, the sum of all debit entries in the SCF section of the work sheet must equal the sum of all credit entries, plus or minus the change in cash and cash equivalents. *Second,* each balance sheet account must be explained. The sum of beginning-of-year balance and all changes listed in the work sheet must equal the end-of-year balance.

As each SCF disclosure item is determined, refer to Figure 6. The completed SCF, taken from the work sheet, appears in Figure 7.

Figure 6

CLASSIC STORES CORPORATION
Work Sheet for the Statement of Cash Flows
For Year Ended December 31, Year 2

Balance sheet accounts	Balances 12/31/1	Transactions for Year 2 Debit	Transactions for Year 2 Credit	Balances 12/31/2
Cash	125,000	(X)		159,000
Short-term investments, net	60,000		(X)	40,000
Accounts receivable, net	30,000	(1) 2,452,000	49,000 (2)	15,000
			2,418,000 (3)	
Inventories	25,000	(5) 1,605,000	1,610,000 (4)	20,000
Land	80,000	(3) 120,000	60,000 (20)	241,000
		(32) 101,000		
Buildings, net	200,000	(14) 8,000	80,000 (16)	553,889
		(15) 72,000	150,000 (21)	
		(31) 180,000		
		(32) 323,889		
Equipment, net	100,000		40,000 (16)	60,000
Leased equipment under capital lease, net investment		(9) 63,283	6,328 (13)	56,955
in Baldwin	80,000	(18) 32,000	24,000 (19)	88,000
Totals	700,000			1,233,844
Accounts payable	20,000	(6) 1,615,000	1,605,000 (5)	10,000
Dividends payable	80,000	(27) 90,000	40,000 (26)	30,000
Taxes payable	10,000	(22) 28,000	183,111 (23)	8,000
		(24) 157,111		
Current portion, liability under capital lease			4,039 (12)	4,039
10% Convertible bonds payable	100,000	(30) 100,000		
12% Bonds payable	100,000			100,000
Unamortized premium	12,000	(8) 1,000		11,000
Liability under capital lease		(10) 10,000	63,283 (9)	45,638
		(11) 3,606		
		(12) 4,039		
Deferred taxes	20,000		65,000 (23)	85,000
Common stock	100,000		16,000 (25)	176,000
			20,000 (30)	
			40,000 (31)	
Paid-in capital in excess of par	100,000		80,000 (25)	420,000
			80,000 (30)	
			160,000 (31)	

(continued)

Retained earnings, appropriated	25,000		15,000 (29)	40,000
Retained earnings, unappropriated	145,000	(25) 96,000 (26) 40,000 (29) 15,000	330,167 (28)	324,167
Treasury stock, at cost	(12,000)	(33) 8,000		(20,000)
Subtotal		7,124,928		
Change in cash and cash equivalents		(x) 14,000		
Totals	700,000	7,138,928	7,138,928	1,233,844

Income statement accounts				
Sales			2,452,000 (1)	2,452,000
Cost of goods sold		(4) 1,610,000		1,610,000
Other expenses		(7) 137,000		137,000
Interest expense		(8) 11,000 (11) 6,394	8,000 (14)	9,394
Depreciation expense		(13) 6,328 (16) 120,000		126,328
Doubtful accounts expense		(2) 49,000		49,000
Net realized gain			18,000 (7)	18,000
Investment income			32,000 (18)	32,000
Gain on land sale			50,000 (20)	50,000
Income tax expense		(23) 248,111		248,111
Extraordinary loss, net		(21) 70,000	28,000 (22)	42,000
Net income		(28) 330,167		330,167
Totals		2,588,000	2,588,000	

Operating activities	**Cash inflows**		**Cash outflows**	
Collections from customers	(3) (a) 2,418,000			
Payments to suppliers			1,615,000 (6)	(b)
Payments for other operating costs			137,000 (7)	(c)
Interest payments			12,000 (8) 6,394 (11) (8,000) (14)	(h) 10,394
Net gain from sale of investments	(17) (i) 18,000			
Dividends from investments	(19) (j) 24,000			
Tax payments on income before extraordinary item			185,111 (22)	(24) (n)
Investing activities				
Cash payments on self-constructed building including capitalized interest			8,000 (14) 72,000 (15)	(g) 80,000

(continued)

Proceeds on land sale	(20) (l) 110,000		
Proceeds from insurance on extra. loss, including $28,000 tax savings	(21) (22) (m) 108,000		
Acquisition of land and building		100,000 (31)	(r)
Acquisition of land and buildings		424,889 (32)	(t)
Financing activities			
Payments on liability under capital lease		10,000 (10) 3,606 (11)	(e) 13,606
Dividend payments		90,000 (27)	(o)
Treasury stock purchase		8,000 (33)	(u)
		2,664,000	
Net increase in cash and cash equivalents		14,000 (x)	
Totals	2,678,000	2,678,000	
Noncash investing and financing activities			
Acquisition of equipment under capital lease			(d) 63,283
Reclassification of long-term lease liability to current liability			(f) 4,039
Increase in equity investment: excess of share of earnings over dividends received			(k) 8,000
Dividends declared in Year 2 but not paid			(p) 30,000
Conversion of 10% convertible bonds			(q) 100,000
Acquisition of land and building through common stock issuance			(s) 200,000

1   Analysis of Income Statement Accounts

The accounts related to Sales in this example are Accounts Receivable, net, and Doubtful Accounts Expense. Additional information item 1 states that all sales are on credit. The reconstructed entries are:

(1)	Accounts Receivable, net	2,452,000	
	Sales..		2,452,000
(2)	Doubtful Accounts Expense	49,000	
	Accounts Receivable, net		49,000
(a) (3)	Cash	2,418,000	
	Accounts Receivable, net		2,418,000

Entry (3) is the first operating cash flow and is listed in the operating activities section of the work sheet, item (*a*). The amount in entry (3) is the balancing value for Accounts Receivable, net, after recording entries (1) and (2) into the work sheet. Accounts Receivable, net, Doubtful Accounts Expense, and Sales accounts are now explained, and the relevant cash flow has been "extracted." The work sheet is a device that structures the process of recording those entries that will ultimately explain the change in all account balances.

Cost of Goods Sold The accounts relevant to this expense are Inventories and Accounts Payable. No additional information is applicable. Entries (4)–(6) reconstruct the events leading to the determination of cash payments to suppliers.

(4)	Cost of Goods Sold	1,610,000	
	Inventories.................................		1,610,000
(5)	Inventories	1,605,000	
	Accounts Payable		1,605,000
(b) (6)	Accounts Payable	1,615,000	
	Cash		1,615,000

Entry (5) holds the amount that explains the Inventories balance change once entry (4) has been entered into the work sheet. Then entry (6) explains the Accounts Payable change after recording the previous two entries. (Accounts Payable relate only to inventory purchases.) The cash flow in entry (6) is operating cash outflow (*b*) in the work sheet.

Other Expenses An examination of the information in Figure 5 reveals no accounts or additional information pertaining to Other Expenses. Therefore, the reconstructed entry is:

(c) (7)	Other Expenses	137,000	
	Cash		137,000

The cash credit is cash outflow (*c*) in the operating activities section of the work sheet.

Interest Expense   In general, this account may be affected by interest payables, bond premium and discount amortization, and capitalization of interest. For Classic Stores, the relevant additional information items are 4, 5, and 9. Item 4 indicates the timing of expense recognition and cash payment on the 12% bonds. Entry (8) illustrates the December 31 cash payment:

> (8) Interest Expense 11,000
>   Premium on 12% Bonds Payable 1,000
>   Cash   12,000

This entry explains the change in Unamortized Premiums. The $12,000 cash flow is entered into the operating activities section of the work sheet, but given the other information relevant to Interest Expense, a letter is not yet assigned as there may be other cash payments for interest.

Additional information item 5 concerns a capital lease that will affect Interest Expense. The present value of the lease payments at January 2, Year 2, is $63,283 [= $10,000 + $10,000(5.32825)]. The January 2 reconstructed entries are:

> (d)   (9) Leased Equipment under Capital Lease 63,283
>   Liability under Capital Lease   63,283
> (e) (10) Liability under Capital Lease 10,000
>   Cash   10,000

Entry (9) records a significant noncash investing and financing transaction and therefore appears in the noncash section of the work sheet [item (*d*)]. This disclosure is in addition to the debit and credit transfer of entry (9) to the work sheet. The cash outflow in entry (10) is a financing outflow, as the lease is the means of financing the equipment acquisition. The lease requires December 31 payments for the remainder of the lease term; therefore the financing activities cash flow is left incomplete until the December 31, Year 2, payment is analyzed. Letter (*e*) indicates the position of the financing outflow in the work sheet.

The end-of-Year 2 reconstructed entries are:

> (e) (11) Interest Expense ($63,283 − $10,000)(0.12) 6,394
>   Liability under Capital Lease........................... 3,606

(continued)

	Cash		3,606
	Cash		6,394
(f) (12)	Liability under Capital Lease...........................	4,039	
	Current Portion, Liability under Capital Lease		4,039
(12/31/3)	Interest Expense ($53,283 − $3,606)(0.12)	5,961	
	Current Portion, Liability under Capital Lease	4,039	
	Cash		10,000
(13)	Depreciation Expense ($63,283/10)	6,328	
	Leased Asset under Capital Lease		6,328

Entry (11) recognizes the interest expense for Year 2 on the lease, and the reduction of the lease liability. The entry is written with two cash credits to emphasize the very different nature of the two cash flow components. The $3,606 is a financing cash flow, as it reduced a liability incurred for financing purposes. This is added to the cash flow in entry (10) for a total $13,606 cash payment on lease liability, as indicated in the financing activities section of the work sheet [item (e)]. The $6,394 portion is an operating cash flow, since it is an interest payment. This is added to the $12,000 previous interest payment from (8), as indicated in the operating activities section of the work sheet [item (h)]. The cash interest payment total must be adjusted for capitalized interest before the final total is entered into the work sheet. The work sheet item (11) for interest expense adds to the $11,000 from item (8). The debit to Liability under Capital Lease in (11) adds to the $10,000 debit from (10) already listed.

Entry (12) and the unnumbered entry dated 12/31/3 illustrate the reclassification of that portion of the long-term lease liability to be paid in Year 3, to current liability status. The Year 3 entry is presented to illustrate the derivation of the $4,039 credit to the current liability. This reclassification is considered by many accountants to be a significant change in financial position, as it contributes to the change in current and long-term liabilities. See item (f) in the noncash portion of the work sheet. Entry (12) completes the explanation of the Liability under Capital Lease and the current portion.

Entry (13) is the required depreciation expense recognition entry, has no effect on the SCF, and explains the change in the Leased Equipment balance.

The remaining reconstructed entries implied by additional information item 9 complete the explanation of Interest Expense:

(g) (14)	Buildings	8,000	
	Interest Expense		8,000
(g) (15)	Buildings	72,000	
(h)	Cash		72,000

The $8,000 of interest payments capitalized in Year 2 are classified under investing activities, as they contribute to the acquisition of property. In this example, the $8,000 is added to the cash construction costs in (15) to yield item (g), the total $80,000 financing cash outflow. Note that entry (14) appears in the operating activities section of the work sheet as a negative interest payment. This adjusts the operating interest cash outflow by the capitalized interest included in the previous cash outflows [(8) and (11)]. Item (h) is the total cash outflow for operating interest ($10,394). Entry (14) also appears as a positive figure along with (15) in the investing activities section. Entry (14) is therefore used four times in the work sheet, but the last two occurrences "cancel out." This work sheet treatment facilitates full disclosure of the adjustment to interest payments and cash building costs. Also, the total capitalized cost is less than the "ceiling" appraisal value. Therefore, under generally accepted accounting principles, no adjustment is needed to the recorded building cost.

At this point, interest has been explained. In so doing, the current portions of Liability under Capital Lease, Liability under Capital Lease, Unamortized Premium on 12% Bonds, and Leased Asset under Capital Lease were explained. In addition, five items that appear on the SCF [(d)–(h)] were triggered by the analysis of all accounts related to interest expense. This is a natural consequence of the interaction of many accounts and the search for all transactions relevant to each account.

Depreciation Expense $6,328 of this expense has been recorded on the work sheet in item (13). Additional information item 14 reveals the remaining $120,000, and entry (16) reconstructs the expense recognition.

(16) Depreciation Expense 120,000		
Buildings, net		80,000
Equipment, net		40,000

There is no cash flow involved with this operating expense.

Doubtful Accounts Expense   This expense was explained by entry (2) in the work sheet. No further accounts or additional information is relevant.

Net Realized Gain on Sale of Short-Term Investments   From additional information item 3, short-term investments are cash equivalents for Classic Stores. The net gain represents the net increase in cash from sales of these securities. Gains and losses on these securities are not expected to be common given their short maturity. The reconstructed entry is:

(i) (17) Cash.. 38,000		
Short-term Investments		20,000
Net Gain on Sale		18,000

Item (*i*) reflects the net cash inflow (the gain) in the operating activities section. No other entry is made to the work sheet, as the other remaining accounts in (17) are cash or cash equivalents. The (x) indicates balancing quantities that net to the $14,000 change in these two accounts.

Investment Income Additional information item 11 provides the necessary data to reconstruct entries (18) and (19) relevant to investment income. The equity method is used to account for the 40% investment in Baldwin Corporation:

(18) Investment in Baldwin Corporation	32,000	
Investment Income		32,000
(*j*) (19) Cash	24,000	
Investment in Baldwin Corporation		24,000

The investment account has increased by a net of $8,000; given the investment income information, entry (19) is implied. The cash flow in (19) is operating inflow (*j*) in the work sheet. The two entries may be considered a related system. Classic's investment income ($32,000) is represented by a $24,000 cash inflow and an $8,000 increase in its investment account. This latter increase is a noncash investing item representing the unrealized increase in asset value from Baldwin's profits in Year 2. It is a financial position change not explained by a cash flow, and appears as item (*k*) in the noncash portion of the work sheet. The Investment in Baldwin Corporation account change has been explained.

Gain on Land Sale Reconstructed entry (20) relies on the income statement and additional information item 12:

(*l*) (20) Cash	110,000	
Land		60,000
Gain on Land Sale		50,000

The cash inflow is an investing cash inflow, item (*l*).

Income Tax Expense and Extraordinary Item The treatment of income tax expense in the SCF becomes more complex with extraordinary items. The tax effects of the latter are an adjustment to any cash flow from the event causing the extraordinary item and therefore are categorized with the cash flow. However, the total cash outflow for taxes usually cannot be segregated into ordinary and extraordinary components.

Historically, firms have grouped the change in tax liability (Taxes Payable) with the cash flow associated with the extraordinary items in their statements of changes in financial position. We continue this approach. This assumption implies that the portion of tax liability change caused by the extraordinary item affected cash in the reporting period. The cash flow for taxes on income *before* extraordinary items will therefore be a "plug" or assumed value.

Classic Store's income tax entries provide an example. Additional information items 2 and 13 are relevant to the Income Tax account, as are the Taxes Payable, Extraordinary Loss, and Deferred Taxes accounts. Entries (21) and (22) reconstruct the events pertaining to the extraordinary loss:

```
(m) (21)  Cash .............................................. 80,000
          Extraordinary Loss ................................. 70,000
               Building.......................................      150,000

(m) (22)  Taxes Payable (70,000) (.40)........................ 28,000
               Extraordinary Loss .............................      28,000
```

The traditional disclosure is illustrated in work sheet item (*m*). This is an investing cash inflow, as it is a property disposal. $108,000 is ultimately the sum to be realized.

Reconstructed entries (23) and (24) complete the recognition of income tax in Year 2:

```
    (23)  Income Tax Expense ................................ 248,111
              Deferred Taxes................................       65,000
              Taxes Payable ................................      183,111

(n) (24)  Taxes Payable ..................................... 157,111
              Cash ........................................      157,111
```

Entry (23) reflects the income tax expense on the income before extraordinary item and explains the change in deferred taxes. Entry (24) contains the actual cash payment that occurred in Year 2 and the debit to Taxes Payable required to complete the explanation of that account. The assumption that realization of the tax savings from the extraordinary item occurred in Year 2 comes into play here. The tax savings of $28,000 implies a tax payment on income before extraordinary items of $28,000 + $157,111(= $185,111) for there to be a *net* cash payment of $157,111. Item (*n*) in the operating section of the work sheet discloses this cash outflow ($185,111). Note that together with the $28,000 tax *savings* (*m*), a net $157,111 cash outflow is disclosed, which agrees with the true cash outflow.

2   Analysis of Retained Earnings

Items 8 and 10 of additional information are relevant to Retained Earnings, as well as the Retained Earnings, Appropriated and Dividends Payable accounts. The reconstruction of the stock dividend entry (item 8) requires knowledge of the number of shares of common stock outstanding just prior to the dividend. A perusal of the remaining additional information items reveals that:

(1) The event in item 6 resulted in the issuance of 2,000 shares of common stock (20 shares for each of 100 convertible bonds) prior to the stock dividend; and

(2) The event in item 7 resulted in the issuance of 4,000 shares of common stock prior to the stock dividend.

At the beginning of the year, 10,000 shares of common stock were outstanding. Therefore, 16,000 shares were outstanding prior to the stock dividend. Reconstructed entry (25) illustrates the recording of the stock dividend:

(25) Retained Earnings 96,000		
Common Stock [16,000(0.10)($10)]		*16,000*
Paid-in Capital in Excess of Par [16,000(0.10)($50)] ...		*80,000*

The stock dividend is not considered a significant noncash transaction and is not listed in the SCF section of the work sheet.

Item 10 of additional information reveals the declared dividends for Year 2. The $40,000 declaration represents an equal increase to Dividends Payable. However, that account decreased $50,000 during the year, implying $90,000 of paid dividends. Reconstructed entries (26) and (27) illustrate the dividend declaration and payment:

(26) Retained Earnings 40,000		
Dividends Payable		*40,000*
(o) (27) Dividends Payable 90,000		
Cash		*90,000*

We may assume the $80,000 beginning balance in Dividends Payable was paid first, and then $10,000 of those declared in Year 2. The $90,000 cash payment is item (*o*) in the financing activities section, and the $30,000 declared but unpaid dividends is listed as noncash financing activity (*p*). This item represents the commitment to transfer resources to owners in Year 3. The Dividends Payable account change has been explained.

The transfer of net income to Retained Earnings is illustrated in entry (28):

(28) Income Summary 330,167		
Retained Earnings		*330,167*

Transferring entry (28) to the work sheet leaves a $15,000 decrease in Retained Earnings yet to be explained. The only remaining related unexplained account is Retained Earnings, Appropriated, which has increased $15,000 during the year. Entry (29) is the reconstructed entry:

(29) Retained Earnings *15,000*
  Retained Earnings, Appropriated *15,000*

The above entry completes the explanation of Retained Earnings and does not require any disclosure in the SCF, as appropriations of Retained Earnings are not considered a significant noncash transaction or change in financial position.

3 Analysis of Additional Information

The analysis of the first two information sources leaves only items 6, 7, and 15 to be considered. Entries (30)–(32) reconstruct the accounting for the events described in those items.

(q) (30) 10% Convertible Bonds Payable *100,000*
  Common Stock [$100(20)($10)] *20,000*
  Paid-in Capital in Excess of Par *80,000*

The bond conversion is a significant change in financial position and is item (q) in the noncash section of the work sheet.

(r) (31) Buildings *180,000*
(s)   Land *120,000*
  Cash *100,000*
  Common Stock [(4,000)($10)] *40,000*
  Paid-in Capital in Excess of Par *160,000*

The acquisition of land and buildings through cash and stock issuance is a mixed transaction. The cash outflow is investing cash outflow (r), and the $200,000 noncash portion of the acquisition is noncash investing item (s). Reconstructed entry (32) exhausts the remaining information:

(t) (32) Buildings *323,889*
  Land *101,000*
  Cash *424,889*

Classic Stores experienced a large net cash inflow from operations in Year 2 and reinvested much of it into new facilities. Entry (32) results in item (t), an investing cash outflow, and completes the explanation of the Buildings, net and Land account changes.

4 Analysis of Remaining Unexplained Balance Sheet Accounts

The only unexplained account is Treasury Stock, which increased $8,000. Entry (33) reconstructs the transaction:

> *(u) (33) Treasury Stock* *8,000*
> *Cash* *8,000*

The $8,000 cash flow is financing cash outflow (*u*). At this point, all balance sheet and income statement account changes have been explained, and all cash flows and noncash transactions have been isolated in the work sheet.

Completion of the Work Sheet and Transfer to the SCF   The various totals discussed previously are calculated and placed into the work sheet, which now lists the three types of cash flows and the noncash transactions. These individual cash flows and transactions may be transferred directly to the SCF, which appears in Figure 7. The reconciliation is explained in the Appendix to the chapter.

The major source of cash for Classic Stores was operations. Classic was very successful in Year 2, with net cash flow exceeding net income by a substantial margin. Classic did not pay much of this cash flow in dividends, but rather reinvested it in what appears to be a prosperous growth market. Expansion appears wise for Classic. The Appendix discusses the indirect format applied to Classic Stores for Year 2.

Figure 7
Direct
format

CLASSIC STORES CORPORATION
Statement of Cash Flows
For Year Ended December 31, Year 2

Operating activities

Collections from customers	$ 2,418,000	(a)
Payments to suppliers	(1,615,000)	(b)
Payments for other operating costs	(137,000)	(c)
Interest payments	(10,394)	(h)
Net gain from sale of cash equivalents	18,000	(i)
Dividends from investments	24,000	(j)
Tax payments on income before extraordinary items	$ (185,111)	(n)
Net cash flow from operating activities		$ 512,495

Investing activities

Cash payments on self-constructed building including capitalized interest	$ (80,000)	(g)
Proceeds from land sale	110,000	(l)
Proceeds from insurance on extraordinary casualty loss, including $28,000 tax savings	108,000	(m)

(continued)

Acquisition of land and building	(100,000) *(r)*	
Acquisition of land and buildings	(424,889) *(t)*	
Net cash flow used by financing activities		$(386,889)

Financing activities

Payments on liability under capital lease.......................$	(13,606) *(e)*	
Dividend payments	(90,000) *(o)*	
Treasury stock purchase	(8,000) *(u)*	
Net cash flow used by financing activities		$(111,606)
Net increase in cash and cash equivalents		$ 14,000
Cash and cash equivalents, Jan. 1, Year 2.....................		185,000
Cash and cash equivalents, Dec. 31, Year 2		$ 199,000

**Reconciliation of net income to net cash flow from
operating activities**

Net income before extraordinary items.........................		$ 372,167
Adjustments to reconcile net income to net		
cash provided by operating activities		
Accounts receivable decrease	15,000	
Inventories decrease......................................	5,000	
Accounts payable decrease	(10,000)	
Amortization of bond payable premium	(1,000)	
Depreciation expense.....................................	126,328	
Investment income	(32,000)	
Dividends received on investments........................	24,000	
Gain on land sale	(50,000)	
Deferred taxes increase..................................	65,000	
Taxes payable decrease	(2,000)	
Net cash flow from operating activities ....$	512,495	

Schedule of noncash investing and financing activities

Acquisition of equipment under capital		
lease...$	63,283 *(d)*	
Reclassification of long-term capital lease		
liability to current liability ....$	4,039 *(f)*	
Increase in equity investment: excess of		
share of earnings over dividends		
received...$	8,000 *(k)*	
Dividends declared in Year 2 but not paid ....$	30,000 *(p)*	
Conversion of 10% convertible bonds ....$	100,000 *(q)*	
Acquisition of land and building through		
issuance of common stock ....$	200,000 *(s)*	

Disclosure of accounting policy

For purposes of the Statement of Cash Flows, Classic Stores considers all highly liquid debt securities purchased with a maturity of three months or less to be cash equivalents.

CONCLUSION

This chapter has discussed the purpose, usefulness, and preparation of the statement of cash flows. The FASB voted to require a *cash flow statement* and end the previous choice of the cash, working capital, or other "fund" definitions. This requirement is a reflection of the demand and potential usefulness of cash flow information. Together with the balance sheet and income statement, the three basic statements now provide a more complete picture of a business entity's past activities and more varied information useful for prediction.

Although business entities have a choice between the direct and indirect methods, there is likely to be an increased uniformity of disclosure relative to the previous statement of changes in financial position. The ability to compare firms should be enhanced by the statement of cash flows.

APPENDIX: THE INDIRECT FORMAT, AND PREPARING THE RECONCILIATION OF NET INCOME AND NET CASH FLOW FROM OPERATIONS

The two examples of SCF preparation in this chapter emphasized the direct method. If the indirect format is chosen, the operating activities section discloses **only** the reconciling items, and the operating cash flows are not disclosed. This Appendix extends the discussion of the reconciliation of net income and net cash flow from operations and focuses on its preparation. The preparation of the reconciliation in the comprehensive example is explained.

To prepare the reconciliation, one step is added to the transaction analysis approach. If a reconstructed entry's effect on cash or cash equivalents is different from its effect on net income, a reconciling item is necessary in the amount of the difference. The reconciling item will cause the net income effect (after adjustment by the reconciling item) to equal the effect on cash and cash equivalents.

For example, in the following reconstructed entry,

Interest Expense	98,000	
Premium on Bonds Payable	2,000	
Cash		100,000

the cash effect is −$100,000 while the net income effect is only −$98,000. Therefore the $2,000 amortization is subtracted from net income as a reconciling item, making the total income effect a negative $100,000.

Depreciation expense of $30,000 is another example. Net income is reduced by $30,000, yet there is no cash effect. Therefore, to correct net income with respect to its contribution to cash, the $30,000 is added back to net income in the reconciliation. Now the income effect equals the cash effect.

Changes in operational working capital accounts are also reconciling items. For example, a $20,000 increase in Accounts Receivable over the reporting period is subtracted from net income. In this case, credit sales must have exceeded cash collections by $20,000, as credit sales increase Accounts Receivable and cash collections decrease it. Yet net income reflects the credit sales, not the cash collections. The $20,000 subtraction "corrects" net income's contribution to operating cash flow.

All changes in working capital accounts relating to operations must be disclosed in a similar manner. In general, current asset increases are subtracted, and decreases are added. Current liability increases are added to net income, and decreases are subtracted. Dividends Payable is an example of a nonoperating working capital account. Such accounts are not treated in the manner just described, but rather are analyzed as investing or financing cash flows.

Another category of reconciling items is gains and losses on financing and investing transactions. For example, a $40,000 gain from the sale of property for $200,000 is included in net income, yet the transaction itself is an investing transaction. The $40,000 gain is subtracted from net income, as it did not provide cash. The $200,000 proceeds is an investing cash inflow and is disclosed the same way under either format. Some accountants argue that these items may imply to users that these gains and losses are operating items, since they appear in the reconciliation. This potential confusion must be weighed against the advantages of the reconciliation.

FASB Statement No. 95 did not indicate which specific income value should be used to begin the reconciliation. The authors favor income from continuing operations, as most extraordinary items are not operational. No adjustment for extraordinary items is required under this approach.

The Comprehensive Example (Indirect Format)

This section discusses the comprehensive example (Classic Stores) assuming the indirect format. The same reconstructed entries are considered, and only the operating activities section will differ between the two formats.

References to the 33 reconstructed entries are made by number. As each entry is considered, any reconciling items are placed directly into the supplementary reconciliation schedule of the indirect format SCF in Figure 8.

Entries (1)–(3) concern Sales and related accounts. These three entries cause a combined $2,418,000 cash increase and $2,403,000 income increase. The $15,000 difference equals the net Accounts Receivable decrease. This necessitates item (*a*) in the reconciliation: a $15,000 addition adjustment to net income. Now, collections on receivables are reflected by net income.

Entries (4)–(6) relate to Cost of Goods Sold and related accounts. The three entries cause a combined $1,615,000 cash decrease and $1,610,000 net income decrease. Therefore, $5,000 must be subtracted from net income to achieve agreement with the cash change. Together, the $5,000 Inventory decrease and $10,000 Accounts Payable decrease provide the needed $5,000 subtraction adjustment, and both are listed as item (*b*). Normally, the preparer can proceed directly to the operating working capital account changes.

Entry (7) features an operating transaction whose cash change equals its net income change. Other Expenses were paid fully in cash by the end of Year 2. No adjustment is needed for the indirect SCF, but note the difference in disclosure between the two formats. The *direct* format listed the $137,000 cash outflow in the SCF. The *indirect* format does not disclose the item.

The analysis of Interest Expense requires considering all relevant entries, which in Classic's case are entries (8) through (15). Only those having an impact on operating activities need be considered. The income effect relevant to interest expense is computed from entries (8), (11), and (14). The net income change is a $9,394 decrease, the interest expense recognized in Year 2 (= −$11,000 − $6,394 + $8,000). Note that entry (14) capitalized interest, which increases net income. To determine the *operating* cash flow from transactions related to Interest Expense, entries (8), (11), and (14) must again be considered. Note that entry (10), the down payment on the lease, is a *financing* cash outflow and is therefore not considered here. Entry (8) caused a $12,000 negative operating cash change, and entry (11) caused a $6,394 negative operating cash change. However, entry (14) *capitalizes* and converts $8,000 of those operating interest cash payments into an *investing* cash flow. Therefore, the net *operating* cash decrease caused by interest is −$10,394 (= −$12,000 − $6,394 + $8,000). We now have the operating cash change (−$10,394), and the net income change (−$9,394). A $1,000 subtraction adjustment is therefore necessary and is represented by the amortization of bond premium. The interest expense simply overstates the cash outflow by the amortization amount. This adjustment is item (c) in the reconciliation.

In the course of analyzing entries (8)–(15), entry (13), the depreciation of Leased Equipment under Capital Lease was encountered. Treating similar accounts together, this amount is added to entry (16) for depreciation expense. These two entries combine to produce a $126,328 total depreciation expense. This requires an addition adjustment, and is item (d) in the reconciliation.

Entry (17) records the net gain on sales of cash equivalent securities. No adjustment is needed in the indirect SCF as the operating cash change ($18,000) equals the gain included in net income.

Entry (18) records a $32,000 net income increase without corresponding cash inflow. Therefore, item (e) subtracts the $32,000 from net income. Related entry (19) provides the opposite effect. A $24,000 operating cash inflow occurs without related income change, therefore item (f) adds $24,000 to net income. A disclosure alternative to (e) and (f) is a single $8,000 subtraction adjustment from net income representing the excess of Classic's share of Baldwin income over dividends received.

Entry (20) represents a $50,000 income increase without cash inflow. The $110,000 cash inflow is an investing cash inflow. Item (g) is the necessary subtraction adjustment from net income before extraordinary items.

Entries (21) and (22) record the extraordinary item and are not related to operations. They do affect entries (23) and (24) however, which record the operational tax effects for Year 2. Recall that we assumed that the entire tax savings on the extraordinary item was realized in Year 2, implying the tax payments on income before extraordinary income (operating income) were $185,111. This negative cash change is to be compared to Income Tax Expense (an operating account) of $248,111, necessitating a $63,000 addition adjustment. This equals the Deferred Taxes balance change ($65,000) less the Taxes Payable decrease. The latter balance change would cause a subtraction adjustment. Together, the Deferred Taxes and

Taxes Payable change combine to account for the needed $63,000 addition adjustment. These are listed as items (*h*) and (*i*) in the reconciliation.

The remaining entries, (25) through (33), do not affect income or provide operational cash flows. Therefore, no further entries are considered. Of course, if we had not already prepared the *direct* SCF, we would analyze these entries also. Figure 8 illustrates the completed SCF under the indirect format.

Figure 8
Indirect
format

CLASSIC STORES CORPORATION
Statement of Cash Flows
For Year Ended December 31, Year 2

Net cash flow from operating activities		$ 512,495
Investing activities		
Cash payments on self-constructed building including capitalized interest	$ (80,000) (g)	
Proceeds from land sale	110,000 (l)	
Proceeds from insurance on extraordinary casualty loss, including $28,000 tax savings...	108,000 (m)	
Acquisition of land and building	(100,000) (r)	
Acquisition of land and buildings	(424,889) (t)	
Net cash flow used by financing activities		$(386,889)
Financing activities		
Payments on liability under capital lease......................	$ (13,606) (e)	
Dividend payments	(90,000) (o)	
Treasury stock purchase	(8,000) (u)	
Net cash flow used by financing activities		$(111,606)
Net increase in cash and cash equivalents		$ 14,000
Cash and cash equivalents, Jan. 1, Year 2.....................		185,000
Cash and cash equivalents, Dec. 31, Year 2		$ 199,000
Supplemental disclosure of cash flow information		
Interest payments (net of interest capitalized)		$ 10,394
Income tax payments		$ 185,111
Reconciliation of net income to net cash provided by operating activities		
Net income before extraordinary items......................	$ 372,167	
Adjustments to reconcile net income to net cash provided by operating activities		
Accounts receivable decrease............................	15,000 (a)	
Inventories decrease....................................	5,000 (b)	
Accounts payable decrease	(10,000) (b)	
Amortization of bond payable premium	(1,000) (c)	

(continued)

Depreciation expense.......................................	126,328	(d)
Investment income	(32,000)	(e)
Dividends received on investments.........................	24,000	(f)
Gain on land sale	(50,000)	(g)
Deferred taxes increase....................................	65,000	(h)
Taxes payable decrease	(2,000)	(i)
Net cash flow from operating activities		**$ 512,495**

Schedule of noncash investing and financing activities

Acquisition of equipment under capital lease...	$ 63,283	(d)
Reclassification of long-term capital lease liability to current liability	$ 4,039	(f)
Increase in equity investment: excess of share of earnings over dividends received..	$ 8,000	(k)
Dividends declared in Year 2 but not paid	$ 30,000	(p)
Conversion of 10% convertible bonds	$ 100,000	(q)
Acquisition of land and building through issuance of common stock	$ 200,000	(s)

Disclosure of accounting policy

For purposes of the Statement of Cash Flows, Classic Stores considers all highly liquid debt securities purchased with a maturity of three months or less to be cash equivalents.

REVIEW QUESTIONS

1 What are the major purposes of the statement of cash flows? How does it fulfill them?

2 What types of disclosures generally would not be available to the financial statement user without the statement of cash flows?

3 What factors resulted in the requirement of a *cash* statement, rather than a statement based on other "fund" definitions?

4 What are *cash equivalents,* and why is the SCF based on cash and cash equivalents rather than simply cash?

5 Give examples of each of the three major categories of cash flows.

6 Why is cash flow per share disclosure not permitted in financial statements?

7 Why is net income often not a good measure of the increase in a firm's ability to pay its debts? Provide examples of specific transactions and accounts in your answer.

8 Why are many noncash transactions listed in the statement of cash flows? Give examples.

9   Give examples of transactions and events that are not disclosed in the statement of cash flows, and why.

10   How would the purchase of land through a cash down payment and incurrence of a mortgage liability be disclosed in the statement of cash flows?

11   In general, how are extraordinary items treated in the statement of cash flows? Provide an example with tax effects.

12   Explain why a $10,000 net reduction in Prepaid Rent during a reporting period would be added to net income in the reconciliation of net income and cash flows from operating activities.

13   Explain why an Accounts Payable decrease and Inventories increase would result in two subtraction adjustments from net income in the reconciliation of net income and cash flows from operating activities.

14   When would negative net income be accompanied by a positive cash flow from operating activities on the statement of cash flows?

15   Why are the proceeds from the *sale* of property disclosed in the investing activities section of the statement of cash flows?

16   Discuss all the effects on the statement of cash flows of the sale of a building at less than book value.

17   How is capitalized interest treated in the statement of cash flows?

18   Under the indirect format, why is the gain on sale of equipment subtracted from net income in the statement of cash flows yet is not listed in the body of the statement under the direct format?

19   Explain how dividends *declared but not paid* in the reporting period, and dividends *declared and paid* in the reporting period, are disclosed in the statement of cash flows.

20   How would the recognition of doubtful accounts expense be handled in the statement of cash flows under the two formats permitted by the FASB?

EXERCISES

Ex. 23-1   Select the best answer for each of the following multiple-choice questions:

1   Which of the following is not disclosed in a statement of cash flows?
a Acquisition of plant assets in exchange for common stock
b Distribution of common stock dividend
c Refunding of a bond issue
d Conversion of convertible bonds to common stock
e All of the above are disclosed
2   How is the amortization of discount on bonds payable disclosed in a statement of cash flows using the indirect format?
a It is not disclosed

b As a financing outflow

c As an addition to net income

d As a subtraction from net income

3   In the preparation of a statement of cash flows using the indirect format, an increase in inventories is an adjustment to net income because:

a Cash was increased, inventories being a current asset.

b Inventories are an expense in the measurement of income, but do not require the use of cash.

c The increase in inventories resulted from purchases in excess of cost of goods sold, and thus is an assumed use of cash.

d All changes in noncash ledger accounts are disclosed under the mandate to disclose all significant noncash financing and investing activities.

4   In a statement of cash flows using the indirect format, is doubtful accounts expense added to net income if it relates to

	Current accounts receivable	Long-term accounts receivable
a	Yes	Yes
b	Yes	No
c	No	Yes
d	No	No

5   How is patents amortization expense presented in a statement of cash flows using the indirect format?

a It is not disclosed

b As an investing outflow

c As an addition to net income

d As a subtraction from net income

6   How is a loss on the disposal of machinery presented in a statement of cash flows using the indirect format?

a It is not disclosed

b As an investing outflow

c As an addition to net income

d As a subtraction from net income

7   Corpus Corporation sold a computer in Year 2 for $140,000. The cost of the computer was $500,000, and the accumulated depreciation on the date of sale was $400,000. How should this transaction be disclosed on the statement of cash flows using the indirect format?

a A deduction from net income of $40,000 and an investing inflow of $140,000

b An addition to net income of $40,000 and an investing inflow of $140,000

c An investing inflow of $140,000

d A financing inflow of $140,000

8   Which of the following is included in a statement of cash flows only because of the mandate to disclose significant noncash investing and financing activities?

a Conversion of preferred stock to common stock

b Acquisition of treasury stock for cash

c Issuance of common stock for cash

d Declaration and payment of cash dividends

9   An example of an addition to net income in a statement of cash flows using the indirect format is:

a Increase in accounts receivable

b Decrease in accounts payable

c Decrease in short-term prepayments

d Increase in inventories

Ex. 23-2   From the following data for Johnson, Inc., compute the amount of cash provided from operating activities during Year 5:

	Dec. 31, Year 5	Jan. 1, Year 5
Accounts receivable (net)	$40,400	$30,400
Accounts payable	30,000	48,000
Accumulated depreciation (no plant assets were retired during the year)........................	64,000	52,000
Inventories..	60,000	55,000
Other current liabilities	7,200	3,200
Short-term prepayments....................................	4,400	6,000
Net income	82,600	

Ex. 23-3   Mars Corporation reported net income of $100,000 and declared and paid dividends of $50,000 in Year 2. Balance sheets on December 31, Year 2 and Year 1, follow:

MARS CORPORATION
Balance Sheets
December 31, Year 2 and Year 1

	Year 2	Year 1
Assets		
Cash	$ 165,000	$ 25,000
Accounts receivable (net)	135,000	75,000
Inventories..	160,000	200,000
Equipment (net)	760,000	600,000
Total assets	$1,220,000	$900,000
Liabilities & Stockholders' Equity		
Accounts payable	$ 80,000	$ 50,000
Bonds payable (due in Year 15)	160,000	200,000
Common stock, no par or stated value	580,000	300,000
Retained earnings	400,000	350,000
Total liabilities & stockholders' equity	$1,220,000	$900,000

Equipment was acquired for $150,000 cash; common stock with a current fair value of $80,000 was issued in exchange for equipment; and additional common stock was issued for cash.

Prepare Mars Corporation's statement of cash flows under the indirect format.

Ex. 23-4 Following are condensed comparative balance sheets of Gisselle Company for the years ended December 31, Year 7 and Year 6:

GISSELLE COMPANY
Balance Sheet
December 31, Year 7 and Year 6

	Year 7	Year 6
Assets		
Cash	$ 150,000	$ 100,000
Other current assets	798,000	540,000
Equipment	2,460,000	2,400,000
Accumulated depreciation of equipment	(872,000)	(840,000)
Goodwill (net)	960,000	1,000,000
Total assets	$3,496,000	$3,200,000
Liabilities & Stockholders' Equity		
Current liabilities	$ 720,000	$ 322,000
Bonds payable	800,000	1,200,000
Discount on bonds payable	(24,000)	(42,000)
Common stock, no par or stated value	2,224,000	2,224,000
Retained earnings (deficit)	(224,000)	(504,000)
Total liabilities & stockholders' equity	$3,496,000	$3,200,000

During Year 7, Gisselle sold, at no gain or loss, equipment with a carrying amount of $152,000 and acquired equipment for $300,000 cash. On January 2, Year 7, Gisselle extinguished, at no gain or loss, long-term bonds payable with a face amount of $400,000. No dividends were declared or paid in Year 7.

Prepare the Year 7 statement of cash flows for Gisselle using the indirect format.

Ex. 23-5 Explain how each of the following transactions is shown in a statement of cash flows for Year 10.

a Cash dividends of $400,000 were declared on December 11, Year 10, payable on January 14, Year 11.

b A 5% common stock dividend was distributed; the market value of the dividend shares, $2,040,000, was transferred from Retained Earnings to paid-in capital ledger accounts.

c Mining properties valued at $760,000 were acquired on January 2, Year 10, in exchange for bonds payable with a face amount of $800,000. The bonds were to mature on December 31, Year 19. The straight-line method is used for amortization of bond discount.

d An additional income tax assessment of $196,000 was debited to the Retained Earnings ledger account as a prior period adjustment. The assessment resulted from a material error in the preparation of prior years' income tax returns.

Ex. 23-6 Jasper Company had net income of $161,200 for Year 5. The following items were included in the measurement of net income:

Amortization of premium on bonds payable	$ 10,000
Investment loss from 25% owned investee	240,000
Depreciation expense	90,000
Doubtful accounts expense (current accounts receivable)	22,400
Unrealized loss in value of marketable equity securities (current portfolio)	50,000
Amortization of organizational costs	6,000
Write-down of obsolete inventories to cost of goods sold	36,000
Extraordinary item (gain), net of income tax effect of $67,500	82,500

Compute the amount of cash provided from operating activities for Jasper Company in Year 5.

Ex. 23-7 Comparative balance sheets for Reed Company on December 31, Year 2, and Year 1, follow:

REED COMPANY
Comparative Balance Sheets
December 31, Year 2 and Year 1

	Year 2	Year 1
Assets		
Cash	$ 105,000	$ 130,000
Accounts receivable (net)	200,000	180,000
Inventories	195,000	80,000
Plant assets	520,000	310,000
Less: Accumulated depreciation of plant assets	(160,000)	(100,000)
Total assets	$ 860,000	$ 600,000
Liabilities & Stockholders' Equity		
Accounts payable	$ 140,000	$ 110,000
Common stock, $10 par	560,000	400,000
Paid-in capital in excess of par	50,000	
Retained earnings	110,000	90,000
Total liabilities and stockholders' equity	$ 860,000	$ 600,000

On June 15, Year 2, Reed issued 16,000 shares of common stock in exchange for equipment. There were no disposals of plant assets in Year 2. Dividends of $50,000 were declared and paid to stockholders during Year 2. The allowance for doubtful accounts was reduced by $6,000 during Year 2 as a result of writing off accounts receivable known to be uncollectible, and increased by $10,000 on December 31, Year 2, to record doubtful accounts expense.

Prepare Reed Company's statement of cash flows for Year 2, under the indirect format.

Ex. 23-8 A summary of the financial position of Houck Company on February 28, Year 10 and Year 9, is shown below:

	Feb. 28, Year 10	Feb. 28, Year 9
Cash	$ 60,000	$ 40,000
Other working capital accounts	115,000	152,000
Noncurrent assets:		
Investment in Nulty, Inc., common stock (equity method) ...	165,000	150,000
Land	120,000	90,000
Buildings	240,000	200,000
Less: Accumulated depreciation of buildings	(100,000)	(92,000)
Totals	$ 600,000	$540,000
Long-term debt & stockholders' equity:		
Notes payable, due Feb. 28, Year 15......................	$ 40,000	
Common stock, $1 par....................................	400,000	$400,000
Retained earnings	160,000	140,000
Totals	$600,000	$540,000

The net income of $50,000 (after depreciation expense of $8,000) included investment income (equity method) of $15,000 from Nulty, Inc. A cash dividend was declared and paid during the year ended February 28, Year 10.

Prepare Houck Company's statement of cash flows for Year 10 under the indirect format.

Ex. 23-9 Information selected from the financial statements of Datamax Corporation for Year 8 follows:

Net income	$ 20,000
Depreciation expense..	30,000
Income tax expense	15,000
Increase (cr.) in Deferred Taxes	3,000
Accounts Receivable increase	8,000
Sales..	300,000

Prepare the operating activities section of the statement of cash flows for Datamax using the direct format.

Ex. 23-10 Prepare the Operating Activities of the statement of cash flows for Datamax, in Exercise 23-9, using the indirect format.

Ex. 23-11 The comparative balance sheets for Random Access Corporation follow:

	Year 5	Year 4
Assets		
Cash	$ 20,000	$ 30,000
Accounts receivable, net	60,000	50,000
Inventories...	12,000	8,000
Property, plant, and equipment, net	140,000	80,000
Intangibles, net.......................................	60,000	70,000
Total assets	$292,000	$238,000

(continued)

Liabilities & Owners' Equity

Current liabilities	$ 40,000	$ 10,000
Long-term liabilities	60,000	30,000
Common stock	200,000	180,000
Retained earnings	(8,000)	18,000
Total liabilities & owners' equity	$292,000	$238,000

The company has requested that you prepare their statement of cash flows for Year 5, and has provided the following information for Year 5:

(1) No property, plant, or equipment was sold.
(2) Depreciation expense was $30,000.
(3) $30,000 of dividends were declared and paid.
(4) No intangibles were purchased or sold.

Prepare the statement of cash flows, using the indirect format, for Year 5.

Ex. 23-12   The comparative balance sheets for Macro Corporation follow:

	Year 7	Year 6
Assets		
Cash	$ 40,000	$ 80,000
Other current assets	60,000	40,000
Property, plant, and equipment, net	250,000	300,000
Investment in land	100,000	
Total assets	$450,000	$420,000
Liabilities & Owners' Equity		
Current liabilities	$ 40,000	$ 70,000
Dividends payable	20,000	80,000
Bonds payable		50,000
Mortgage payable on land	80,000	
Common stock	120,000	100,000
Paid-in capital in excess of par	40,000	20,000
Retained earnings	150,000	100,000
Total liabilities & owners' equity	$450,000	$420,000

Additional Information for Year 7:
(1) No property, plant or equipment was purchased or sold.
(2) Dividends declared were $60,000.

Prepare Macro's statement of cash flows using the indirect format.

Ex. 23-13   Describe the statement of cash flows disclosure for the following items, assuming the direct format. Answer in terms of the body of the SCF, not the supporting schedules.

(1) Sale of $40,000 of cash equivalents for a $30,000 gain.
(2) Write off $10,000 of Accounts Receivable.
(3) Declare and distribute stock dividend; $100,000 debit to Retained Earnings.

(4) Capitalize $20,000 of interest to Buildings.

(5) Recognize $15,000 of uncollectible accounts expense.

(6) Depletion of $150,000 is recognized.

(7) Recognize $25,000 equity in income of investee.

(8) Recognize unrealized $10,000 loss, as an adjusting journal entry, on long-term marketable securities.

(9) Recognize, as an adjusting journal entry, a $30,000 unrealized loss on short-term marketable equity securities.

Ex. 23-14 Assume the indirect format in the previous exercise and describe the disclosure in the statement of cash flows for each item. Include any disclosure necessary on supporting schedules.

Ex. 23-15 Determine into which of the three categories of cash flows in the SCF each of the following would be disclosed:

(1) Proceeds from sale of building

(2) Collection on a lawsuit

(3) Collections from customers on accounts receivable

(4) Proceeds from a note payable to the bank

(5) Payments on a note payable to a supplier for inventory purchases

(6) Collection of ordinary dividends from common stock investments

(7) Collection of liquidating dividends from common stock investments

(8) Purchase of cash equivalents that are not treated by the purchaser as cash equivalents for the purpose of SCF disclosures

Ex. 23-16 Determine into which of the three categories of cash flows in the SCF each of the following would be disclosed:

(1) Mortgage payment that includes principal and interest

(2) Purchase of treasury stock

(3) Payment of dividends to shareholders

(4) Retirement of debt

(5) Insurance proceeds on the death of corporate executive; corporation is beneficiary

(6) Insurance proceeds on involuntary destruction of property

(7) Payment of interest on notes payable to suppliers

(8) Excise tax payments

CASES

Case 23-1 Schein Engineering Company is a growing manufacturer of electronic instruments and technical equipment. You have been retained by Schein to advise it in the preparation of a statement of cash flows. For the year ended October 31, Year 2, you obtained the following information concerning certain transactions and events of Schein:

(1) Net income for the year was $1,600,000, which included a deduction for an extraordinary loss of $186,000 [see item (5) below].

(2) Depreciation expense of $480,000 was included in the income statement.

(3) Uncollectible accounts receivable of $60,000 were written off against the allowance for doubtful accounts. Also, $74,000 of doubtful accounts expense was included in the measurement of net income for the year, and the same amount was added to the allowance for doubtful accounts.

(4) A gain of $9,400 was recognized on the disposal of a machine having a cost of $150,000, of which $50,000 was undepreciated on the date of sale.

(5) On April 1, Year 2, a freak lightning storm caused an uninsured inventories loss of $186,000 ($360,000 loss, less reduction in income taxes of $174,000). This extraordinary loss was included in net income as indicated in (1) above.

(6) On July 3, Year 2, land and building were acquired for $1,200,000; Schein gave in payment $200,000 cash, $400,000 current fair value of its unissued common stock, and a $600,000 mortgage note payable due in three years.

(7) On August 3, Year 2, $1,400,000 face amount of Schein's 10% convertible debentures were converted under the carrying amount (book value) method to $280,000 par value of its common stock. The bonds had been issued at face amount.

(8) Schein's board of directors declared a $640,000 cash dividend on October 20, Year 2, payable on November 15, Year 2, to stockholders of record on November 5, Year 2.

Instructions

Explain how each of the above items would be handled in the preparation of Schein's statement of cash flows, for the year ended October 31, Year 2. Assume the direct format.

Case 23-2   Two financial statements of the Killow Corporation follow:

KILLOW CORPORATION
Balance Sheet
January 1, Year 6

Assets

Cash	$ 20,000
Other current assets	54,000
Equipment	96,000
Accumulated depreciation	(30,000)
Net intangibles	10,000
Total assets	$150,000

Liabilities & Owners' Equity

Current liabilities	$ 24,000
Common stock, no par	54,000
Retained earnings	72,000
Total liabilities & owners' equity	$150,000

KILLOW CORPORATION
Statement of Cash Flows
For Year Ended December 31, Year 6

Operating activities

Net cash flow from operating activities	$ 62,000

Investing activities

Proceeds from sale of equipment	$ 14,000
Land acquisition	(28,000)
Equipment acquisition	(60,000)
Net cash used in investing activities	$(74,000)

Financing activities

Common stock issuance	$ 26,000
Dividends paid	(24,000)
Net cash flow from financing activities	$ 2,000
Net decrease in cash	$ 10,000

**Schedule to reconcile net income and net cash flow
from operating activities**

Net income	$ 48,000
Depreciation expense	20,000
Amortization of intangibles	2,000
Gain on equipment sale	(8,000)
Net cash flow from operating activities	$ 62,000

Additional Information

(1) Accumulated depreciation on equipment sold: $12,000.

(2) On December 31, Year 6, total current liabilities were $11,000.

Instructions

From the financial statements and other information, prepare the December 31, Year 6, balance sheet for Killow.

Case 23-3 The accountant for Mega Corporation prepared the following tentative ''funds'' statement and was unaware of the specific reporting requirements for the statement of cash flows.

MEGA CORPORATION
Cash Funds Statement
For Year Ended December 31, Year 4

Cash provided

Net income	$240,000
Issuance of long-term note payable	70,000
Depreciation and amortization	60,000

(continued)

Loss on equipment disposal	10,000
Proceeds on equipment disposal	80,000
Stock dividend distributed	30,000
Amortization of bond premium	4,000
Deferred tax increase	20,000
Total cash provided	$514,000

Cash applied

Acquisition of land	$ 50,000
Acquisition of equipment	25,000
Accounts receivable decrease	10,000
Inventories increase	5,000
Equity in income of investee	12,000
Retirement of bonds	250,000
Dividends declared	100,000
Total cash applied	$452,000

Net increase in cash for Year 4	$ 62,000

The accountant discovered that cash actually increased $124,000 and has requested your assistance in correcting the funds statement. Other information pertaining to Year 4 made available by the accountant includes:

(1) Common stock was issued for land with a market value of $200,000.
(2) Prepaids decreased $10,000.
(3) A $20,000 appropriation of Retained Earnings was created.
(4) The declared dividends are payable in Year 5.

Instructions

a Discuss the disclosure errors in the accountant's attempted cash flow statement.
b Prepare a revised statement of cash flows in compliance with current accounting standards.

Case 23-4 The statement of cash flows for Lomax Corporation for Year 6 follows. Lomax is a regional, general-purpose retailer. The corporate president is very pleased with the large increase in liquidity during Year 6. The president has delegated most operating authority to the financial vice president and has requested your advise on the strategic planning for the corporation. He has advised you that the Year 6 statement of cash flows is typical of Year 4 and Year 5 results.

LOMAX CORPORATION
Statement of Cash Flows
For Year Ended December 31, Year 6

Operating activities

Net cash flow from operating activities	$150,000

Investing activities

Proceeds from land sale	$ 60,000

(continued)

Proceeds from insurance on
casualty loss including
$40,000 tax savings 100,000
Proceeds from equipment sale 150,000
Net cash provided by investing activities $310,000

Financing activities

Payments on liability under
capital lease ....$ (28,000)
Net cash used by financing activities...........................$ (28,000)

Net increase in cash...$432,000
Cash, Jan. 1, Year 6.. 178,000
Cash, Dec. 31, Year 6 ....$610,000

Schedule to reconcile net income to net cash flow from operating activities

Net income before extraordinary items..........................$ (50,000)
Accounts receivable increase................................... (20,000)
Inventories increase .... (10,000)
Prepaids increase .... (15,000)
Accounts payable increase......................................   50,000
Equity in income of investee................................... (65,000)
Depreciation 195,000
Amortization   20,000
Loss on equipment disposal.....................................   45,000
Net cash from operating activities.............................$150,000

Schedule of noncash investing and financing activities

Acquisition of equipment under capital
lease $312,000
Reclassification of long-term liability
under capital lease to current
liability ....$ 12,818
Acquisition of property through bond
issue $160,000

Additional Information for Year 2
(1) Lomax appropriated $25,000 of Retained Earnings.
(2) A stock dividend was distributed. The market value of shares issued was $200,000.

Instructions
Draft a report advising the president of Lomax on both long- and short-run financial strategies. Consider operating, investing, and financing activities in your report.

Case 23-5 Prepare the relevant sections of the direct format statement of cash flows required for the disclosure of the following items for both format options available. Be sure to indicate the relevant section of the statement affected by each item. All items refer to Year 12 of the Champaign Corporation.

(1) $25,000 of interest was capitalized to Buildings. Total interest expense before capitalization was $175,000, and total capitalized building costs through December 31 were $350,000, including the capitalized interest.

(2) A computer was traded for another computer. The recognized gain on exchange was $30,000. "Boot" of $100,000 was received on exchange.

(3) Equity in income of investee recognized was $16,000. This consisted of the following:

The company's share of investee net income $24,000
Amortization of excess of market value over
  book value of depreciable assets of
  investee .... (6,000)
Amortization of goodwill .... (2,000)

In addition, $20,000 of dividends were received from the investee during the year.

(4) A $25,000 permanent loss was recognized on a short-term investment in equity securities of another corporation. The lower-of-cost-or-market method has been used to account for this investment.

(5) $50,000 of research and development expense was incurred.

(6) The change in Taxes Payable for the year was a decrease of $30,000 resulting in an ending balance of $50,000; and deferred taxes increased (credit) $20,000.

Case 23-6   Prepare the relevant sections of the direct format statement of cash flows required for the disclosure of the following items for both format options available. Be sure to indicate the relevant section of the statement affected by each item. All items refer to Year 3 of Springfield Corporation.

(1) The corporation enjoyed a tax loss carryforward from the previous year that reduced current taxes payable $40,000.

(2) A $25,000 overstatement of previous years' book depreciation was discovered in the current year. The corporation is taxed at a 40% average rate.

(3) Equipment was leased on January 1. The lease required a $20,000 down payment, and five yearly $50,000 payments due each December 31. The lease qualified as a capital lease, and the incremental borrowing rate was 12%. Assume straight-line depreciation of the leased asset and a five-year useful life.

(4) $200,000 (face) of convertible bonds were converted on January 2. The book value of the bonds at conversion was $198,000 and the market value of stock issued was $250,000. Total par of stock issued on conversion was $100,000. The "market value" method was used to account for the conversion.

(5) The corporation was involved in a troubled-debt restructure. As the creditor, the corporation accepted land worth $200,000 as full settlement of a debt whose book value was $260,000.

(6) A property dividend consisting of investments in stock of other corporations was distributed. The book value of the stock was $250,000 and its market value $300,000, at dates of declaration and distribution.

PROBLEMS

23-1 Financial statements of Polished Apple Company for the year ended November 30, Year 3, its first year of operations, are presented:

POLISHED APPLE COMPANY
Statement of Income and Retained Earnings
For Year Ended November 30, Year 3

Net sales		$1,400,000
Costs and expenses:		
Costs of goods sold	$700,000	
Operating expenses	320,000	
Interest expense	40,000	1,060,000
Income before income taxes		$ 340,000
Income taxes expense:		
Current	$144,000	
Deferred	9,000	153,000
Net income		$ 187,000
Less: Cash dividends declared and		
paid ($1.20 a share)		60,000
Retained earnings, end of year		$ 127,000

POLISHED APPLE COMPANY
Balance Sheet
November 30, Year 3

Assets

Current assets:		
Cash		$ 50,000
Accounts receivable (net)		120,000
Inventories		190,000
Short term prepayments		3,000
Total current assets		$ 363,000
Plant assets (net of $120,000 accumulated depr)		960,000
Total assets		$1,323,000
Current liabilities:		
Accounts payable		$ 60,000
Income taxes payable		144,000
Current portion of long-term debt		80,000
Total current liabilities		$ 284,000
Long-term debt:		
10% note payable, due $80,000 a year		
with interest on unpaid balance	$240,000	
Deferred income tax credits	9,000	249,000
Total liabilities		$ 533,000
Stockholders' equity:		
Common stock, no par or stated value,		

(continued)

authorized 100,000 shares, issued and outstanding 50,000 shares	$663,000	
Retained earnings	127,000	790,000
Total liabilities & stockholders' equity		$1,323,000

Additional Information for Year Ended November 30, Year 3

(1) On December 1, Year 2, Polished Apple (*a*) issued 50,000 shares of common stock at $13.26 a share; (*b*) borrowed $400,000 from a bank on a 10% promissory note payable, which was due $80,000 a year plus interest on the unpaid balance, beginning November 30, Year 3; and (*c*) acquired plant assets costing $1,080,000 for cash of $1,062,000 and an account payable of $18,000. There were no other acquisitions or disposals of plant assets during the year ended November 30, Year 3. Polished Apple began operations on December 1, Year 2.

(2) On November 30, Year 3, Polished Apple (*a*) declared and paid a cash dividend of $1.20 a share to common stockholders; and (*b*) paid $80,000 principle and $40,000 interest ($400,000 × 0.10 = $40,000) to the bank.

(3) Deferred income taxes resulted from Polished Apple's use of straight-line method of depreciation for financial accounting and the Accelerated Cost Recovery System for income taxes.

Instructions

Prepare a statement of cash flows for Polished Apple Company for the year ended November 30, Year 3, under the direct format.

23-2   Financial statements of Bopeep Corporation for the year ended December 31, Year 4, were as follows:

BOPEEP CORPORATION
Income Statement
For Year Ended December 31, Year 4

Revenue...	$854,000
Cost and expenses (including depreciation expense, $60,000)...	714,000
Net income	$140,000

BOPEEP CORPORATION
Statement of Stockholders' Equity
For Year Ended December 31, Year 4

	Common stock, no par	Retained earnings (deficit)	Total
Balances, beginning	$1,100,000	$(252,000)	$ 848,000
Issuance of common stock in exchange for equipment	250,000		250,000
Net income		140,000	140,000
Balances, end	$1,350,000	$(112,000)	$1,238,000

BOPEEP CORPORATION
Balance Sheets
December 31, Year 4 and Year 3

	Year 4	Year 3
Assets		
Cash	$ 130,000	$ 110,000
Other current assets	331,200	194,000
Equipment	1,480,000	1,200,000
Accumulated depreciation............................	(436,000)	(420,000)
Goodwill (net)	480,000	500,000
Total assets	$1,985,200	$1,584,000
Liabilities & Stockholders' Equity		
Current liabilities	$ 360,000	$ 160,000
Bonds payable (due Dec. 31, Year 8)	400,000	600,000
Discount on bonds payable	(12,800)	(24,000)
Common stock, no par or stated value	1,350,000	1,100,000
Retained earnings (deficit)	(112,000)	(252,000)
Total liabilities & stockholders' equity	$1,985,200	$1,584,000

Additional Information for Year 4

(1) Equipment was sold at its carrying amount of $76,000 and equipment was acquired for $150,000 cash.
(2) On January 2, bonds with a face amount of $200,000 were extinguished at 101. Discount on bonds payable is amortized by the straight-line method.

Instructions

Prepare Bopeep Corporation's statement of cash flows for the year ended December 31, Year 4, under the indirect format.

23-3 Comparative income statements and balance sheets and a statement of stockholders' equity of Whale Company are shown below:

WHALE COMPANY
Income Statements
For Years Ended December 31, Year 5 and Year 4

	Year 5	Year 4
Net sales	$6,500,000	$4,000,000
Cost of goods sold	5,000,000	3,200,000
Gross profit on sales..................................	$1,500,000	$ 800,000
Operating expenses including tax......................	1,080,000	520,000
Net income	$ 420,000	$ 280,000

WHALE COMPANY
Statement of Stockholders' Equity
For Year Ended December 31, Year 5

	Common stock, no par	Retained earnings	Total
Balances, beginning of year..........	$ 900,000	$ 330,000	$1,230,000
Issuance of common stock for cash ...	300,000		300,000
Net income		420,000	420,000
Cash dividends declared.............		(240,000)	(240,000)
Balances, end of year	$1,200,000	$ 510,000	$1,710,000

WHALE COMPANY
Balance Sheets
December 31, Year 5 and Year 4

	Year 5	Year 4
Assets		
Current assets:		
Cash	$ 240,000	$ 200,000
Short-term investments............................	80,000	
Accounts receivable (net)	840,000	580,000
Inventories......................................	660,000	420,000
Short-term prepayments...........................	100,000	50,000
Total current assets...........................	$1,920,000	$1,250,000
Plant assets	1,130,000	$ 600,000
Accumulated depreciation...........................	(110,000)	(50,000)
Total assets...................................	$2,940,000	$1,800,000

Liabilities & Stockholders' Equity		
Current liabilities:		
Accounts payable	$ 530,000	$ 440,000
Dividends payable................................	60,000	
Other current liabilities	140,000	130,000
Total current liabilities	$ 730,000	$ 570,000
Notes payable, due June 30, Year 8	500,000	
Total liabilities	$1,230,000	$ 570,000
Stockholders' equity:		
Common stock, no par.............................	1,200,000	900,000
Retained earnings	510,000	330,000
Total liabilities & stockholders' equity	$2,940,000	$1,800,000

Additional Information for Year 5

(1) The note payable due June 30, Year 8, was issued in exchange for equipment.

(2) There were no disposals of plant assets.

(3) Short-term prepayments of $500,000 were made in Year 5.

Instructions

Prepare a statement of cash flows for Whale Company under the direct format for the year ended December 31, Year 5. Preparation of a work sheet is recommended.

23-4   Shown below are the financial statements for Major, Inc.:

MAJOR, INC.
Income Statement
For the Year Ended December 31, Year 5

Net sales		$3,233,836
Cost and expenses:		
Cost of goods sold	$841,200	
Depreciation expense...............................	450,000	
Amortization expense	20,000	
Other operating expenses	430,000	
Interest expense	29,000	
Income taxes expense	658,636	
Total costs and expenses		2,428,836
Net income		$ 805,000

MAJOR, INC.
Statement of Stockholders' Equity
For Year ended December 31, Year 5

	Preferred stock, $100 par	Common stock, no par	Retained earnings	Total
Balances, beg., as previously reported	$ 480,000	$2,940,000	$6,600,000	$10,020,000
Prior period adjustment:				
Claim for refund of				
Year 3 income taxes			25,000	25,000
Balances, beg. as adjusted	$ 480,000	$2,940,000	$6,625,000	$10,045,000
Redemption of preferred stock				
at 104¾	(480,000)		(22,800)	(502,800)
Net income			805,000	805,000
Dividends:				
Cash			(420,000)	(420,000)
5% common stock...............		210,000	(210,000)	
Balances, end of year	$ 0	$3,150,000	$6,777,200	$9,927,200

MAJOR, INC.
Balance Sheets
December 31, Year 5 and Year 4

	Year 5	Year 4
Assets		
Cash	$ 157,000	$ 120,900
Accounts receivable	560,400	520,400

(continued)

Allowance for doubtful accounts	(85,000)	(80,000)
Income tax refund receivable	25,000	
Inventories	2,898,900	2,853,800
Equipment	7,963,200	7,663,200
Accumulated depreciation	(616,400)	(486,400)
Goodwill (net)	500,000	520,000
Total assets	$11,403,100	$11,111,900

Liabilities & Stockholders' Equity

Accounts payable	$ 483,264	$ 596,700
Income taxes payable	658,636	495,200
Interest payable	15,000	
10% Bonds payable, due 1/2/25	300,000	
Premium on bonds payable	19,000	
Preferred stock, $100 par		480,000
Common stock, no par	3,150,000	2,940,000
Retained earnings	6,777,200	6,600,000
Total liabilities & stockholders' equity	$11,403,100	$11,111,900

Additional Information for Year 5

(1) Uncollectible accounts receivable of $40,000 were written off.
(2) Equipment costing $400,000 that had accumulated depreciation of $320,000 was sold at carrying amount. New equipment was acquired for cash and in exchange for the 10% bonds payable, which were issued for $320,000 on January 2, Year 5, with interest payable annually.
(3) Premium on bonds payable was amortized by the straight-line method.

Instructions

Prepare a statement of cash flows, using the direct format, for Major, Inc., for the year ended December 31, Year 5.

23-5 Following are financial statements of Volk Corporation:

VOLK CORPORATION
Income Statement
For the Year Ended December 31, Year 2

Revenue	$760,000
Costs and expenses	630,000
Net income	$130,000

VOLK CORPORATION
Statement of Stockholders' Equity
For Year Ended December 31, Year 2

	Common stock, $25 par	Paid-in capital in excess of par	Retained earnings	Total
Balances, beg............	$400,000	$ 80,000	$190,000	$670,000
Issuance of 800 shares of common stock in exchange for land	40,000	60,000		100,000
Net income			130,000	130,000
Dividends:				
Cash			(88,000)	(88,000)
5% stock, 800 shares ...	20,000	30,000	(50,000)	
Balances, end	$460,000	$170,000	$182,000	$812,000

VOLK CORPORATION
Balance Sheets
December 31, Year 2 and Year 1

	Year 2	Year 1
Assets		
Cash	$ 88,440	$ 71,600
Accounts receivable (net)	80,800	48,000
Inventories	75,200	73,600
Short-term prepayments..............................	8,360	8,800
Land	138,000	38,000
Buildings	552,000	500,000
Accumulated depreciation: buildings	(184,000)	(160,000)
Equipment	763,200	720,000
Accumulated depreciation: equipment..................	(476,000)	(440,000)
Patents (net)	64,000	80,000
Total assets	$1,110,000	$ 940,000
Liabilities & Stockholders' Equity		
Accounts payable	$ 128,000	60,000
Other current liabilities	40,000	20,000
Long-term debt, due Dec. 31, Year 10.................	130,000	190,000
Common stock, $25 par..............................	460,000	400,000
Paid-in capital in excess of par	170,000	80,000
Retained earnings	182,000	190,000
Total liabilities & stockholders' equity	$1,110,000	$ 940,000

Additional Information for Year 2
(1) There were no disposals of building or equipment.
(2) No patents were acquired or sold.

Instructions

Prepare Volk Corporation's statement of cash flows for Year 2 under the indirect format.

23-6   Following are financial statements for Boggess Company:

BOGGESS COMPANY
Income Statement
For Year Ended December 31, Year 7

Net sales		$1,892,400
Costs and expenses:		
Cost of goods sold	$788,030	
Depreciation expense.	178,000	
Amortization expense	26,400	
Loss on disposal of machinery.	26,000	
Other operating expenses	164,880	
Income taxes expense	319,090	
Total costs and expenses		1,502,400
Net income		$ 390,000

BOGGESS COMPANY
Statement of Stockholders' Equity
For Year Ended December 31, Year 7

	Preferred stock, $100 par	Common stock, $5 par	Retained earnings	Total
Balances, beg.	$200,000	$1,000,000	$536,000	$1,736,000
Redemption of preferred				
stock	(20,000)		(2,000)	(22,000)
Net income			390,000	390,000
Cash dividends			(80,000)	(80,000)
Balances, end	$180,000	$1,000,000	$844,000	$2,024,000

BOGGESS COMPANY
Balance Sheets
December 31, Year 7 and Year 6

	Year 7	Year 6
Assets		
Cash	$ 290,000	$ 372,000
Accounts receivable	506,000	546,000
Allowance for doubtful accounts	(28,000)	(34,000)
Inventories	966,000	1,076,000
Long-term investments	300,000	

(continued)

Leasehold improvements (net)	58,000	76,000
Machinery and equipment............................	1,854,000	1,294,000
Accumulated depreciation............................	(832,000)	(744,000)
Patents (net)	55,600	60,000
Total assets	$3,169,600	$2,646,000

Liabilities & Stockholders' Equity

Accounts payable	$ 465,600	$ 210,000
Dividends payable..................................	80,000	
Current portion of 10% serial bonds payable	100,000	100,000
10% serial bonds payable, less current portion	500,000	600,000
Preferred stock, $100 par	180,000	200,000
Common stock, $5 par.............................	1,000,000	1,000,000
Retained earnings	844,000	536,000
Total liabilities & stockholders' equity	$3,169,600	$2,646,000

Additional Information for Year 7

(1) New machinery and equipment were acquired for $792,000. In addition, machinery with a carrying amount of $122,000 was sold for $96,000.

(2) Legal costs of $4,000 were incurred in the successful defense of a patent.

(3) Income taxes for Year 7 and bond interest were paid on December 31, Year 7.

Instructions

Prepare Boggess Company's statement of cash flows for the year ended December 31, Year 7, under the indirect format.

23-7 Financial statements of Postum Corporation are shown below:

POSTUM CORPORATION
Income Statement
For Three Months Ended March 31, Year 4

Revenue:		
Sales..	$490,414	
Investment income	11,760	
Gain on disposal of land	21,400	
Total revenue		$523,574
Costs and expenses:		
Cost of goods sold	$276,814	
Depreciation expense...............................	2,500	
Other operating expenses	44,020	
Interest expense	2,300	
Income taxes expense ($672 deferred)	69,904	
Total costs and expenses		395,538
Net income		$128,036

POSTUM CORPORATION
Statement of Stockholders' Equity
For Three Months Ended March 31, Year 4

	Convertible preferred stock, $2 par	Common stock, $1 par	Retained earnings	Total
Balances, beg..............	$ 60,000	$160,000	$166,200	$386,200
Conversion of				
preferred stock.............	(60,000)	60,000		
Net income			128,036	128,036
Cash dividends			(16,000)	(16,000)
declared..................				
Balances, end				
of period	$ 0	$220,000	$278,236	$498,236

POSTUM CORPORATION
Balance Sheets
March 31, Year 4 and December 31, Year 3

	Mar. 31, Year 4	Dec. 31, Year 3
Assets		
Current Assets:		
Cash	$ 174,800	$ 50,600
Short-term investments.............................	14,600	33,000
Accounts receivable (net)	98,640	48,640
Inventories.......................................	97,180	62,180
Total current assets................................	$ 385,220	$194,420
Investment in Mecca Company common stock,		
at equity..	134,200	122,440
Land	37,400	80,000
Building	500,000	500,000
Equipment	163,000	
Accumulated depreciation: building and		
equipment	(32,500)	(30,000)
Other assets	30,200	30,200
Total assets	$1,217,520	$897,060

Liabilities & Stockholders' Equity		
Current liabilities:		
Accounts payable	34,660	$ 42,440
Dividends payable.................................	16,000	
Income taxes payable	69,232	
Total current liabilities.............................	$ 119,892	$ 42,440
Bonds payable.....................................	230,000	100,000

(continued)

Discount on bonds payable	(4,300)	(4,600)
Deferred income taxes credit	1,692	1,020
Other long-term liabilities	372,000	372,000
Convertible preferred stock, par $2		60,000
Common stock, par $1	220,000	160,000
Retained earnings	278,236	166,200
Total liabilities & stockholders' equity	$1,217,520	$897,060

Additional Information for Three Months Ended March 31, Year 4

(1) On January 8, Year 4, Postum sold short-term investments for cash at their carrying amount. The investments had been owned for less than two months and are considered cash equivalents.

(2) On January 17, Year 4, land was sold for $64,000 cash.

(3) On March 25, Year 4, Postum acquired equipment for cash.

(4) On March 31, Year 4, additional bonds payable were issued at face amount for cash. Discount on bonds payable was amortized by the straight-line method.

(5) The carrying amount of the investment in Mecca Company common stock included an amount attributable to goodwill of $6,440 on December 31, Year 3. Goodwill was being amortized at an annual rate of $960.

Instructions

Prepare Postum Corporation's statement of cash flows for the three months ended March 31, Year 4, under the direct format.

23-8 Shown below are financial statements of Zero Company:

ZERO COMPANY
Income Statement
For Year Ended December 31, Year 2

Revenue:		
Net sales	$3,900,000	
Investment income	26,000	
Total revenue		$3,926,000
Costs and expenses:		
Cost of goods sold	$2,300,000	
Depreciation expense	106,000	
Amortization expense	8,000	
Other operating expenses	1,010,000	
Interest expense	30,000	
Loss on disposal of equipment	10,000	
Income tax expense		
($22,000 deferred)	180,000	
Total costs and expenses		$3,644,000
Net income		$ 282,000

ZERO COMPANY
Statement of Stockholders' Equity
For Year Ended December 31, Year 2

	Common stock, $10 par	Additional paid-in capital	Retained earnings	Treasury stock	Total
Balances, beg. year	$800,000	$350,000	$668,000	$(34,000)	$1,784,000
Issuance of common stock for cash	20,000	26,000			46,000
Conversion of $100,000 face amount of convertible bonds	40,000	60,000			100,000
Reissuance of Treasury stock		16,000		34,000	50,000
Net income			282,000		282,000
Cash dividends declared and paid			(86,000)		(86,000)
Balances, end of year	$860,000	$452,000	$864,000	$ -0-	$2,176,000

ZERO COMPANY
Balance Sheets
December 31, Year 2 and Year 1

	Year 2	Year 1
Assets		
Cash	$ 550,000	$ 360,000
Accounts receivable (net)	590,000	610,000
Inventories	1,098,000	862,000
Investment in Track Company common stock at equity	146,000	120,000
Land	700,000	400,000
Other plant assets	1,248,000	1,212,000
Accumulated depreciation	(278,000)	(214,000)
Goodwill (net)	32,000	40,000
Total assets	$4,086,000	$3,390,000
Liabilities & Stockholders' Equity		
Accounts payable and accrued liabilities	$1,208,000	$1,126,000
Notes payable (long-term)	300,000	
Bonds payable	320,000	420,000
Deferred income tax credits	82,000	60,000
Common stock, $10 par	860,000	800,000
Additional paid-in capital	452,000	350,000
Retained earnings	864,000	668,000
Treasury stock (at cost)		(34,000)
Total liabilities & stockholders' equity	$4,086,000	$3,390,000

Additional Information for Year 2

(1) On January 2, Year 2, Zero sold equipment costing $90,000, with a carrying amount of $48,000, for $38,000 cash.

(2) On July 1, Year 2, Zero acquired equipment for $126,000 cash.

(3) On December 31, Year 2, land with a current fair value of $300,000 was acquired through the issuance of a long-term promissory note in the amount of $300,000. The note called for 15% interest and was due on December 31, Year 7.

(4) Deferred income tax credits represented temporary differences relating primarily to the use of the Accelerated Cost Recovery System for income taxes and the straight-line method of depreciation for financial accounting.

Instructions

Prepare Zero Company's statement of cash flows for the year ended December 31, under the direct format.

23-9 Financial statements of Bates Company are shown below:

BATES COMPANY
Income Statement
For Year Ended December 31, Year 6

Revenue:		
Net sales	$1,884,600	
Dividends..	11,000	
Gain on disposal of long-term investments	40,000	
Gain on disposal of equipment	10,000	
Total revenue		$1,945,600
Costs and expenses:		
Cost of goods sold	$ 396,400	
Depreciation expense...............................	298,000	
Other operating expenses	143,200	
Interest expense	96,000	
Income taxes expense		
($30,000 deferred).................................	506,000	
Total costs and expenses		$1,439,600
Net income		$ 506,000

BATES COMPANY
Statement of Stockholders' Equity
For Year Ended December 31, Year 6

	Common stock, $20 par	Additional paid-in capital	Retained earnings	Total
Balances, beg. as previously recorded	$1,200,000	$488,000	$ 816,000	$2,504,000

(continued)

Prior period adjustment: Additional income tax assessment for Year 4		(40,000)	(40,000)
Balances, beg. year as adjusted........................... 1,200,000	488,000	776,000	2,464,000
Issuance of 4,000 shares common stock in exchange for land............................ 80,000	120,000		200,000
Net income		506,000	506,000
Cash dividends declared and paid................................		(60,000)	(60,000)
Balances, end $1,280,000	$608,000	$1,222,000	$3,110,000

BATES COMPANY
Balance Sheets
December 31, Year 6

	Year 6	Year 5
Assets		
Cash	$1,082,000	$ 616,000
Accounts receivable (net)	1,170,000	990,000
Inventories..	1,790,000	1,560,000
Long-term investments, at cost	360,000	510,000
Land	700,000	500,000
Building and equipment.............................	2,120,000	1,440,000
Accumulated depreciation...........................	(590,000)	(340,000)
Leased equipment under capital lease	316,000	
Total assets......................................	$6,948,000	$5,276,000
Liabilities & Stockholders' Equity		
Accounts payable and accrued liabilities	$1,520,000	$1,646,000
Current portion of long-term debt	318,000	
Notes payable, long-term	600,000	
10% Bonds payable	1,000,000	1,000,000
Premium on bonds payable	32,000	36,000
Liability under capital lease..........................	248,000	
Deferred income tax credits	120,000	90,000
Common stock, $20 par.............................	1,280,000	1,200,000
Additional paid-in capital	608,000	488,000
Retained earning	1,222,000	816,000
Total liabilities & stockholders' equity	$6,948,000	$5,276,000

Additional Information for Year 6

(1) On December 31, Year 6, Bates borrowed $900,000 on a 15% promissory note payable $300,000 a year beginning December 31, Year 7.

(2) On June 15, Year 6, Bates acquired equipment costing $784,000 cash. On July 1, Year 6, Bates sold for $66,000 cash equipment costing $104,000 that had a carrying amount of $56,000.

(3) On December 31, Year 6, Bates leased equipment under a 10-year capital lease with equal annual payments of $50,000 due each December 31, beginning in Year 6. The $50,000 lease payment due on December 31, Year 7, will consist of $32,000 interest and $18,000 principal.

Instructions

Prepare a statement of cash flows for Bates Company for the year ended December 31, Year 6, assuming the direct format.

23-10 Selected financial statements of Millcreek Company for Year 2 follow:

MILLCREEK COMPANY
Income Statement
For Year Ended December 31, Year 2

Sales...		$53,500
Cost of goods sold:		
Inventories, Jan. 1.......................................	$ 20,000	
Purchases	25,000	
Goods available...	$ 45,000	
Inventories, Dec. 31	(15,000)	
Cost of goods sold		30,000
Gross profit on sales.......................................		$23,500
Expenses:		
Operating..	$ 5,000	
Depreciation	3,750	
Interest	750	9,500
Income before income taxes...............................		$14,000
Income taxes expense		3,500
Net income		$10,500

MILLCREEK COMPANY
Statement of Stockholders' Equity
For Year Ended December 31, Year 2

	Common stock, $10 par	Paid-in capital in excess of par	Retained earnings	Total
Balances, beg..................	$50,000	$5,000	$15,000	$70,000

(continued)

Issuance of 500 shares common stock in exchange for equipment	5,000	1,000		6,000
Net income			10,500	10,500
Cash dividends declared.			(2,500)	(2,500)
Balances, ending.	$55,000	$6,000	$23,000	$84,000

MILLCREEK COMPANY
Comparative Balance Sheets
December 31, Year 2 and Year 1

	Year 2	Year 1
Assets		
Cash	$ 14,950	$ 7,000
Accounts receivable (net)	16,500	13,500
Inventories	15,000	20,000
Short-term prepayments.	800	500
Equipment	65,000	50,000
Accumulated depreciation.	(9,750)	(6,000)
Total assets	$102,500	$85,000
Liabilities & stockholders' equity		
Accounts payable	$ 7,750	$11,700
Interest payable	750	
Income taxes payable	3,500	3,300
Dividends payable.	2,500	
Long-term notes payable	4,000	
Common stock, $10 par.	55,000	50,000
Paid-in capital in excess of par	6,000	5,000
Retained earnings	23,000	15,000
Total liabilities & stockholders' equity	$102,500	$85,000

Additional Information for Year 2

(1) Equipment was acquired for $9,000 cash.

(2) Cash of $4,000 was borrowed from a bank on a long-term promissory note due in Year 5.

Instructions

Prepare Millcreek's Year 2 statement of cash flows under the direct format.

23-11   Following are the financial statements of Hilo Company for Year 2:

HILO COMPANY
Income Statement
For Year Ended December 31, Year 2

Revenue:		
Net sales		*$430,200*
Gain on disposal of long-term		
investments		*40,000*
Total revenue		*$470,200*
Costs and expenses:		
Cost of goods sold	*$340,400*	
Depreciation expense	*60,000*	
Interest expense	*49,500*	
Other operating expenses	*70,245*	
Loss on disposal of short-term		
investments	*1,055*	
Total costs and expenses		*$521,200*
Net income before extraordinary item		*(51,000)*
Extraordinary loss on bond retirement		*(4,000)*
Net loss		*$ (55,000)*

HILO COMPANY
Statement of Stockholders' Equity
For Year Ended December 31, Year 2

	Convertible preferred stock, $100 par	Common stock, $5 par	Paid-in capital in excess of par	Retained earnings	Total
Balances, beginning	$150,000	$250,000	$170,000	$362,500	$932,500
Issuance of 3,500 shares					
of common stock		17,500	136,500		154,000
Conversion of 250 shares of					
preferred stock to 750					
shares of common stock	(25,000)	3,750	21,250		
Net loss				(55,000)	(55,000)
Cash dividends declared and					
paid on preferred stock				(20,000)	(20,000)
Balances, ending	$125,000	$271,250	$327,750	$287,500	$1,011,500

HILO COMPANY
Balance Sheets
December 31, Year 2 and Year 1

	Year 2	Year 1
Assets		
Cash	$ 38,000	$ 85,000
Short-term investments		15,000
Accounts receivable, net	217,500	130,000
Inventories	246,500	200,000
Long-term investments, at cost	260,000	305,000
Equipment, net	976,500	850,000
Total assets	$1,738,500	$1,585,000
Liabilities & Stockholders' Equity		
Bank overdraft	$ 500	
Notes payable to suppliers	175,000	$ 20,000
Accounts payable	157,500	145,000
10% bonds payable	400,000	500,000
Discount on bonds payable	(6,000)	(12,500)
Convertible preferred stock,		
$100 par	125,000	150,000
Common stock, $5 par	271,250	250,000
Paid-in capital in excess of		
par, common	327,750	170,000
Retained earnings	287,500	362,500
Total liabilities & owners' equity	$1,738,500	$1,585,000

Additional Information for Year 2

(1) Equipment costing $30,000 was sold for its carrying amount of $15,000. Additional equipment was acquired for cash.

(2) On July 1, Year 2, 10% bonds payable with a face amount of $100,000 were called at 102 and extinguished. The bonds were due June 30, Year 4.

Instructions

Prepare Hilo's statement of cash flows for Year 2, assuming the direct format.

Analysis of Financial Statements

24

Many groups outside a business enterprise—creditors, investors, regulatory agencies, financial analysts, labor union leaders—are interested in its financial affairs. This is particularly true for publicly owned corporations. Management also is interested in the results and relationships reported in financial statements. Outsiders do not have access to the detailed data available to management and must rely on published information in making business decisions. In this chapter we consider the analysis of financial statements as a basis for decision making by outsiders.

Management makes operating and financial decisions based on a wide variety of reports that are either generated by the enterprise's own information system or available from other sources. Management's use of financial information is mentioned in many of the preceding chapters. More sophisticated analyses of profit-volume relationships, make-or-buy decisions, differential costs, financial forecasts, product line profitability, gross profits, distribution costs, and rates of return on investments usually are covered in cost and management accounting courses and for that reason are not discussed in this chapter.

Sources of Financial Information Available to Outsiders

The first procedure in financial analysis is to obtain useful information, at least cost, including some information not found in financial statements. The major sources of financial information for publicly owned corporations are described in the following sections.

Published Reports   As stated in Chapter 4, corporations whose stock is publicly owned issue annual and quarterly reports. Annual reports of public corporations contain comparative financial statements and notes to the financial statements, supplementary financial information, and management's discussion and analysis of the comparative years' operations and prospects for the future. Annual reports are made available to the public as well as to stockholders.

Securities and Exchange Commission (SEC)   Public corporations are required to file annual reports with the SEC. These reports (*Form 10-K*) are particularly valuable sources of financial information because the SEC prescribes a standard format and terminology and because they typically contain information not included in reports to stockholders. Public corporations generally indicate in their annual reports to stockholders that a copy of the *Form 10-K* filed with the Securities and Exchange Commission may be obtained free of charge by writing to the corporation. Quarterly reports filed with the SEC (*Form 10-Q*) also are a valuable source of information.

Credit and Investment Advisory Services   Organizations such as Moody's Investors Service and Standard & Poor's Corporation compile financial information for investors in annual volumes and periodic supplements. A wide variety of data relating to business enterprises, particularly small and medium-sized enterprises, is published by such organizations as Dun & Bradstreet, Inc., and Robert Morris Associates. Many trade associations collect and publish financial ratios for enterprises in various industries. Major brokerage firms and investment advisory services compile financial information about public corporations and make it available to their customers. In addition, most brokerage firms maintain a staff of analysts who study business conditions and review published financial statements; visit plants and meet with executives to obtain information on new products, industry trends, and management changes; and interpret all this information for investors.

Audit Reports   When an independent CPA firm performs an audit, its report is addressed to the board of directors, and frequently to the stockholders, of the audited enterprise. The CPA firm's opinion on financial statements is included in annual reports. Frequently, the audit report consists only of the opinion; however, in auditing smaller clients, the CPA firm may prepare a *long-form report,* which contains detailed financial information and comments. Banks and other lending institutions often rely on long-form audit reports for financial information about small business enterprises applying for loans.

What Is Financial Analysis?

Knowing what to look for and how to interpret it is the essence of the art of financial analysis. Financial analysis is a process of *selection, relation, and evaluation.* The first procedure is to select from the total information available about a business enterprise the information relevant to the decision under consideration. The second procedure is to arrange the information in a way that will bring out significant relationships. The final procedure is to study these relationships and interpret the results.

Financial statements themselves are organized summaries of detailed information, and are thus a form of analysis. The types of financial statements accountants prepare, the way they arrange items in the statements, and their standards of disclosure are influenced by a desire to provide information in convenient and useful form. In using financial statements, analysts focus their attention on key amounts and relationships, then extend their investigation to ascertain why the conditions revealed by the financial statements exist.

Procedure of Analysis

Financial analysis is not primarily a matter of making computations. The important part of the analytical process begins when the computational task is finished. However, there are some analytical procedures that are useful in highlighting important relationships and reducing masses of detail to convenient numerical form so that the essential facts may be grasped quickly.

Ratios Ratios may be expressed as percentages, as fractions, or as a stated comparison between two amounts. For example, we might describe the relationship between $120 million of sales and $24 million of operating income as: (1) operating income is 20% of sales; (2) operating income is ⅕ of sales; (3) the ratio of sales to operating income is 5 to 1; (4) for every dollar of sales the enterprise earned 20 cents in operating income. Each of these ratios describes the relationship between sales and operating income. The computation of a ratio does not add any information not already inherent in the amounts under study. A useful ratio may be computed only when a significant relationship exists between two amounts; a ratio of two unrelated amounts is meaningless.

A ratio, once computed, is best interpreted by comparing it with the same ratio for recent accounting periods and for other business enterprises, and with an appropriate industry standard. Such comparisons are discussed on pages 1249–1251.

Component Percentages: Common-Size Financial Statements The ratio of one amount in a financial statement to the total that includes that amount is called a *component percentage*. Reducing data to component percentages helps the analyst to visualize both the relative importance of the amounts in the financial statements and the changes from period to period.

Financial statements expressed in component percentages are sometimes called *common-size financial statements.* Two examples, one for Ara Company and one for Ali Company and Bry Company, are presented below and on page 1230.

Each item in the income statements is reported as a percentage of net sales

ARA COMPANY
Common-Size Income Statements
For Years Ended December 31, Year 2 and Year 1

	Year 2	Year 1
Net sales	100.0%	100.0%
Cost of goods sold	63.2	66.4
Gross profit on sales	36.8%	33.6%
Operating expenses	23.2	24.2
Income before income taxes	13.6%	9.4%
Income taxes expense	5.0	3.2
Net income	8.6%	6.2%

In the first example for Ara Company, reducing the operating data to component percentages helps the analyst to see the major factors that brought about an increase in the rate of earnings per dollar of sales. In the second example, compo-

Items in the balance
sheets are reported
as a percentage
of total assets

ALI COMPANY and BRY COMPANY
Common-Size Balance Sheets
December 31, Year 1

	Ali Company	Bry Company
Assets		
Current assets	56.4%	43.2%
Plant assets (net)	38.7	50.1
Other assets	4.9	6.7
Total assets	100.0%	100.0%
Liabilities & Stockholders' Equity		
Current liabilities	36.2%	20.5%
Long-term debt	24.0	12.6
Total liabilities	60.2%	33.1%
Stockholders' equity	39.8	66.9
Total liabilities & stockholders' equity	100.0%	100.0%

nent percentages highlight the difference in the asset and capital structures; Ali Company has a larger proportion of debt and a relatively larger amount of current assets; Bry Company is financed to a larger degree by use of equity capital and has a relatively larger investment in plant assets.

When information is reduced to simple terms, there may be some loss of completeness, but there may be some gains. Component percentages emphasize relative size rather than absolute amounts. For example, if Ara Company has managed to increase its net income from 6.2% to 8.6% of sales only by reducing sales volume in half, there is no hint of this in the common-size income statements. Similarly, the common-size balance sheets will not reveal, for example, that Ali Company may be ten times as large as Bry Company.

Changes over Time   The analytical information that may be gleaned from the financial statements of only one year is limited. Previous chapters describe the

Example of a 5-year
summary

WALT DISNEY PRODUCTIONS
Revenues, Net Income, and Dividends
For Years Ended September 30, 1980 through 1984

	1984	1983	1982	1981	1980
Revenues (millions)	$1,656	$1,307	$1,030	$1,005	$915
Net income (millions)	98*	93	100	121	135
Earnings per share (dollars)	2.73	2.70	3.01	3.72	4.16
Cash dividends per share (dollars)	1.20	1.20	1.20	1.00	0.72

*Includes $76 million from change in accounting for investment tax credit.

difficulty of measuring income and financial position accurately. Furthermore, an enterprise's experience in a single year may not be typical. Investigating performance over a reasonable number of years is a useful form of financial analysis.

Public corporations' annual reports include a five-year summary of selected financial data. For example, the data at the bottom of page 1216 are taken from the annual report of Walt Disney Productions on page 237 of Chapter 4. We note that the revenues and cash dividends per share of Walt Disney Productions generally have been growing steadily, but that net income and earnings per share generally have declined.

There are a number of ways this five-year record may be presented to facilitate analysis. In the summary below relating to sales and net income, the dollar change each year from the previous year, the percentage change from the previous year, and the *trend percentage* in relation to the first year in the series are shown for Walt Disney Productions:

Summary of increases and trend percentages revenues and net income

	WALT DISNEY PRODUCTIONS Analysis of Changes For Years Ended September 30, 1980 through 1984					
	Dollar change from previous year (in millions of dollars)		**Percentage change from previous year**		**Trend percentage in relation to 1980**	
Year	**Revenues**	**Net income**	**Revenues**	**Net income**	**Revenues**	**Net income**
1980					100.0%	100.0%
1981	+ 90	−14	+ 9.8	−10.4	109.8	89.6
1982	+ 25	−21	+ 2.5	−17.4	112.6	74.1
1983	+277	− 7	+26.9	− 7.0	142.8	68.9
1984	+349	+ 5	+26.7	+ 5.4	181.0	72.6

Each of these computations points out the change in revenues and net income over the five-year period in a slightly different way. If the analyst is primarily interested in absolute change, the dollar changes tell the story. The percentage of increase or decrease year by year expresses growth or decline in comparison with the prior year's performance. Trend percentages (computed by dividing the amount for each year by the amount for the base year) reveal a total growth of 81.0% (181.0% − 100.0% = 81.0%) in revenues and a decline of 27.4% (100.0% − 72.6% = 27.4%) in net income over a period of four years for Walt Disney Productions.

Analytical Objectives

The outcome of business decisions (to acquire or dispose of a company's securities or to extend or refuse to extend credit, for example) naturally depends on future events. Financial statements are essentially a record of the past. Therefore, analysts study financial statements as evidence of past performance that may be useful in making predictions of future performance. The management of a company is responsible for earning as large a return as possible on the resources invested in the company consistent with the objectives of maintaining a sound financial condition, meeting social responsibilities, and doing business in accordance with high ethical standards. Insofar as the attainment of these objectives may be measured quantitatively (and quantitative information usually is only a part of the basis for any business decision), financial statements provide useful information.

In looking at past performance and present position, the financial analyst seeks answers to two primary questions: (1) What is the company's earnings performance, and (2) is the company in sound financial condition? We may examine the process of analysis within the framework of these two questions.

ANALYSIS OF EARNINGS PERFORMANCE

Unfortunately, an outside analyst usually does not have access to many of the important details that underlie reported net income. Most published income statements are highly condensed, and the outsider must be satisfied with a general review of the relationship between revenue, cost of goods sold, total operating expenses, and net income. This requires a careful analysis of gross profit percentages and *operating expense ratios* (total operating expenses divided by net sales) over a number of years. Also, the analyst will review any items of nonoperating revenue and expense, extraordinary items, accounting changes, and disposals of business segments, in order to predict the likely normal earning power of a business enterprise.

Net Income and Accounting Practices

The point is made throughout this book that the amount of net income reported in an accounting period may be affected by the accounting practices followed. These practices are selected by management; independent auditors merely inform users that the financial statements were prepared "in conformity with generally accepted accounting principles consistently applied." Unfortunately, a wide variety of accounting principles may be considered "generally accepted," and financial analysts must determine the accounting practices and principles used, especially for the recognition of revenue and expenses, and then evaluate their impact on reported net income. In other words, financial analysts are concerned with the *quality of reported earnings.*

In recent years significant progress has been made in reducing areas of differences in financial accounting and reporting, and additional reforms are contemplated by authoritative bodies. The required inclusion in annual reports of a description of the accounting policies used in the preparation of financial statements was an important development.[1] The accounting policies for revenue recognition, depreciation, inventories, leases, pension plans, consolidation of subsidiaries, business combinations, and income taxes, for example, are especially significant to financial analysts. In addition, the notes to the financial statements provide useful information on these and other financial accounting and reporting matters.

---

[1] *APB Opinion No. 22,* "Disclosure of Accounting Policies," AICPA (New York: 1972).

Trend in Earnings

The analysis of earnings always should cover several years, not only because of the difficulty of measuring income year by year but also because it is important to know how a company performs in periods of prosperity and adversity. Net income may be satisfactory in one year and decline substantially in the following year, because of unfavorable business conditions.

One of the first things an analyst looks for is the trend of revenue (sales) over a number of years. A rising trend of revenue usually is a sign of expansion. Obviously, the revenue trend is not the whole story, because a growth in revenue is not always accompanied by a corresponding increase in net income, as evidenced by the revenues and net income data for Walt Disney Productions on page 1230. The ideal situation is to find a company maintaining a constant or increasing *rate* of net income on a rapidly growing revenue.

The pattern of revenue and net income throughout the business cycle is also an important factor. There is obviously greater risk in investing in (or lending to) a company whose net income fluctuates widely with changes in business conditions than in an enterprise able to show *stability* of earnings throughout all phases of the business cycle. An enterprise that must reduce operations severely during recessions inevitably suffers in terms of such factors as effective product planning and employee morale, and may find it difficult to cover its fixed expenses. Furthermore, earnings tend to decline faster than revenue because some expenses are fixed. Investors are interested in identifying a *cyclical* company, not only because the risk of investment is higher, but also because the timing of their investment will depend on the company's performance in relation to cyclical trends. A shift by investors to *defensive stocks* (common stocks of companies that perform well in all phases of the business cycle) when a recession is in the offing and a shift to stocks of cyclical companies at the first sign of an economic upturn are popular investment strategies.

Return on Investment

Business executives invest capital with the objective of earning a satisfactory rate of return. The rate of return depends on numerous factors, including the nature of competition and the risks inherent in an industry. Management often is evaluated in terms of the rate of return it is able to earn on invested capital. Although outsiders cannot determine the rate of return on the investment for particular divisions or segments of a business enterprise, they may make some overall estimates of the rate. This rate may serve as a valuable index in evaluating the relative profitability of a particular company and the quality of its management.

The *rate of return on investment* for any period is determined by dividing ''income'' by average investment. The appropriate income amount to be used depends on the related concept of *investment.* This is at the top of page 1234.

In each case net income excludes any extraordinary items, discontinued operations, or cumulative effect of change in accounting principle; and the investment is computed as an average for the period. Ratio **1** is a measure of the earnings (after interest and income taxes) that relate to the total economic resources employed by a company. It is possible to add interest expense to net income to compute an approximation of earnings before payment of interest to creditors but after income taxes.

Three different rates
of return

Appropriate income amount	Concept of investment (in all cases an average for the period covered by the income amount)
1 *Return on total assets:*	
Net income	*÷ total assets*
2 *Return on total stockholders' equity:*	
Net income	*÷ total stockholders' equity*
3 *Return on common stockholders' equity:*	
Net income applicable to common stock ÷ common stockholders' equity	

Some analysts prefer to compute return on total assets *before interest and income taxes,* in which case a ratio of operating income to total assets is used. If total assets include some idle plant assets, bond sinking funds, or long-term investments, such assets and the related earnings generated by the assets are excluded from rate of return computations.

Ratios **2** and **3** are computed from the viewpoint of stockholders, and the approach used depends on whether the analyst is interested in the rate of return on total stockholders' equity or on common stockholders' equity. In the computation of the rate of return on common stockholders' equity, dividends on cumulative preferred stock for each period are deducted from net income to obtain *net income applicable to common stock.* The data for Barker Company shown below (in millions of dollars) are used to compute the three rate-of-return ratios:

Rates of return
computed on page
1235 are based on
these data

BARKER COMPANY
Data for Analysis
(in millions of dollars)

Income statement data			Balance sheet data			
	Year 2	Year 1		Year 2	Year 1	Year 0
Net sales	$130	$ 95	Current assets...	$19	$20	$18
Other revenue.....	10	5	Noncurrent assets	61	60	56
Total revenue ...	$140	$100	Total assets ...	$80	$80	$74
Cost of goods sold	$ 95	$ 65				
Operating expenses	26	20	Current liabilities	$ 6	$10	$ 9
Interest expense ..	1	1	Long-term debt .	19	20	21
Income taxes expense (50%) ...	9	7	Preferred stock..	16	16	16
Total expenses ..	$131	$ 93	Common stock-holders' equity	39	34	28
Net income	$ 9	$ 7	Total liabilities & stockholders'			
Less: Preferred stock dividends ..	1	1	equity........	$80	$80	$74
Available for common stock ...	$ 8	$ 6				

The rates of return described in the outline on page 1234 are computed below for Barker Company (all dollar amounts are stated in millions):

Computation of rates of return

Measurement	Computation		
	Year 2		**Year 1**
1 Return on total assets..	$\dfrac{\$9}{\frac{1}{2}(\$80 + \$80)} = \dfrac{\$9}{\$80} = 11.2\%$		$\dfrac{\$7}{\frac{1}{2}(\$80 + \$74)} = \dfrac{\$7}{\$77} = 9.1\%$
2 Return on total stockholders' equity.......	$\dfrac{\$9}{\frac{1}{2}(\$55 + \$50)} = \dfrac{\$9}{\$52.5} = 17.1\%$		$\dfrac{\$7}{\frac{1}{2}(\$50 + \$44)} = \dfrac{\$7}{\$47} = 14.9\%$
3 Return on common stockholders' equity.......	$\dfrac{\$8}{\frac{1}{2}(\$39 + \$34)} = \dfrac{\$8}{\$36.5} = 21.9\%$		$\dfrac{\$6}{\frac{1}{2}(\$34 + \$28)} = \dfrac{\$6}{\$31} = 19.4\%$

Interpreting Return on Investment Each of the measures of return on investment for Barker Company shows an improved performance in Year 2. If we consider the underlying factors—the revenue generated per dollar of investment (*asset turnover rate*) and the net income per dollar of revenue—we obtain some additional insight:

Asset turnover rate × percentage earned on total revenue equals . . .

	Year 2	Year 1
Revenue generated per dollar of assets:		
$\dfrac{\text{Total revenue}}{\text{Average investment (total assets)}}$	$\dfrac{\$140}{\$80} = \$1.75$	$\dfrac{\$100}{\$77} = \$1.30$
Net income per dollar of revenue:		
$\dfrac{\text{Net income}}{\text{Total revenue}}$	$\dfrac{\$9}{\$140} = 6.4\%$	$\dfrac{\$7}{\$100} = 7.0\%$

Although Barker earned a smaller margin of income per dollar of total revenue in Year 2, it was able to improve its volume of revenue per dollar of investment from $1.30 to $1.75. This ratio may be viewed as the *number of times total assets are turned over* and may be used to verify the rates of return on total assets as follows:

. . . rate of return on total assets

Year 2: $1.75 × 6.4% = 11.2 cents per dollar of assets, or 11.2%
Year 1: $1.30 × 7.0% = 9.1 cents per dollar of assets, or 9.1%

What we have done here is simply multiply the rate earned on revenue by the asset turnover rate to measure the earnings rate on assets. This concept is really a truism: If a profit of 3%, for example, is earned on sales, and $10 of sales is generated by each $1 of assets, then the rate earned on assets is $10 \times 3\%$, or 30%.

Trading on the Equity   When a business enterprise borrows money for long-term purposes, it is *trading on the equity,* or *using financial leverage.* The results from trading on the equity may be favorable or unfavorable to common stockholders. If the rate earned before interest and income taxes on total assets is higher than the interest rate paid for the use of money, the common stockholders will gain; if the interest rate is higher than the earnings rate on assets, then a loss to common stockholders results from trading on the equity. Issuance of preferred stock produces similar results but is more ''expensive'' to the common stockholders, because dividends paid on preferred stock are not deductible in the computation of taxable income.

The fact that the return on common stockholders' equity for Barker Company is higher than the return on total assets is significant. Barker is successfully trading on the equity; that is, the total of interest on bonds and dividends on preferred stock is less than the earnings on capital raised through these *senior securities.* Barker has about $20 million in long-term debt at an interest cost of about 5% before income taxes ($1 million $\div$ $20 million = 0.05) and 2½% after income taxes at 50%, and it has $16 million in preferred stock paying dividends of approximately 6.3% ($1 $\div$ $16 = 0.063). Barker earned 11.2% after income taxes on its total assets during Year 2. Therefore, the funds raised through the issuance of senior securities earned a much higher rate than the fixed interest and dividends paid by Barker. This excess accrued to Barker's common stockholders, resulting in a 21.9% rate earned on common stockholders' equity in Year 2 and 19.4% in Year 1.

Earnings, Dividends, and Equity (Book Value) per Share

Because stockholders think in terms of the number of shares they own or plan to acquire or dispose of, reducing corporate financial information to per-share terms puts it in a useful perspective for stockholders. Perhaps the most commonly used statistics relating to common stocks are *earnings* (or *loss*) *per share* and *dividends per share.* These appear widely in financial press releases, prospectuses, proxy materials, and various reports to stockholders.

Comparative earnings per share data, supported by complete financial statements, are useful in evaluating the performance of a company from the common stockholders' point of view. There is little doubt that earnings (or loss) per share is a highly significant summary amount, but it has some serious limitations; and there are dangers in focusing too much attention on it.

The manner of computing and reporting of earnings per share has been a major concern not only of the accounting profession but also of the Securities and Exchange Commission and the major stock exchanges. The technical aspects of computing and reporting *primary* and *fully diluted* earnings per share are discussed and illustrated in Chapter 18.

Dividends on common stock represent historical facts and should be reported at amounts actually paid, except in cases following stock splits or stock dividends. In such cases, ''the presentation of dividends per share should be in terms of the current equivalent number of shares outstanding at the time of the dividend, so that the earnings and dividends per share will be reported on a comparable basis. When dividends per share are presented on other than a historical basis, the basis of presentation should be disclosed.''[2]

Dividend Payout Ratio, Dividend Yield, and Price-Earnings Ratio Investors in common stock are more interested in earnings and dividends in relation to the *market price* of their shares than in relation to the equity (book value) of their shares, because market price measures the amount of money they forgo at any specific time by a decision to continue owning the common stock. To illustrate, suppose that Jane Adams owns one share of common stock of Solo Company that currently earns $5 a share and pays a dividend of $2 a share. The equity (book value) is $40 a share and the current market price of Solo's common stock is $50. The fact that Solo is earning a return of 12½% on stockholders' equity ($5 ÷ $40 = 0.125) is of secondary interest to Adams, because she gives up the use of $50 by the decision to own this share. Thus, Adams views this investment as one producing an *earnings yield* of 10% ($5 ÷ $50 = 0.10), a *dividend payout ratio* of 40% ($2 ÷ $5 = 0.40), and a *dividend yield* of only 4% ($2 ÷ $50 = 0.04). In investment circles the earnings yield usually is expressed in reverse as a *price-earnings ratio*[3] of *ten times earnings* or simply 10 to 1 ($50 ÷ $5 = 10).

Serious investors monitor the relationships among earnings, dividends, and the market prices of common stock and seek to evaluate such relationships by analyzing the financial data available to them. The table below shows these relationships for three hypothetical companies:

Note differences in dividend payout ratios, yields, and price-earnings ratios

	Coy Company	Day Company	Elm Company
Earnings per share in Year 5	$1.00	$2.50	$5.00
Dividends per share in Year 5	$0.60	$2.00	$2.00
Market price per share during Year 5:			
High	$7	$50	$110
Low......................................	$3	$35	$ 96
Ending	$5	$40	$100
Dividend payout ratio	60%	80%	40%
Dividend yield on market price, Dec. 31, Year 5	12%	5%	2%
Price-earnings ratio, Dec. 31, Year 5	5 to 1	16 to 1	20 to 1

---

[2]*APB Opinion No. 9,* ''Reporting the Results of Operations,'' AICPA (New York: 1966), p. 126.
[3]The price-earnings ratios generally are determined using primary earnings per share for the latest 12 months, excluding extraordinary items. The price earnings ratios for stocks traded on the New York and American Stock Exchanges are reported in most daily newspapers, along with the annual price range, the daily high and low prices, the closing price, and the net price change from the previous day's closing price.

This divergence in price-earnings and yield ratios (an even wider spread often exists among listed common stocks) suggests that investors assess the risks and future prospects of these three investments in quite different terms. Coy Company, for example, may be a marginal producer in its industry, with highly volatile earnings and low growth prospects. As a result, its common stock trades at a low price-earnings ratio of *five times earnings* and yields 12%. The common stock of Day Company trades at a much higher multiple of earnings and yields 5%. In contrast, Elm Company appears to be a "growth company"; the price-earnings ratio for its common stock is *twenty times earnings* and the yield is 2% because only 40% of its net income is distributed to stockholders.

An investor who tries to determine whether the market price of a common stock is reasonable must consider a variety of factors. All, however, relate to an estimate of the ultimate return on investment; this return depends on the dividends received during the period the common stock is held and the price obtained when the stock is sold, both of which are difficult to project with any degree of precision.

Earnings and Fixed Charges   A company that finances its operations with long-term debt or preferred stock is committed to pay a fixed return to the holders of these securities. The commitment on long-term debt is stronger than on preferred stock, because in the latter case the obligation is only that preferred dividends will be paid before any dividends on common stock are declared. A company that *passes* a preferred dividend has impaired its financial reputation to some degree, but a company that cannot pay interest on its debt is in serious financial trouble.

Bondholders and preferred stockholders have learned from experience that the relationships between earnings and fixed charges are useful measures of the safety of their investment. The data below for Foy Company and Glo Company are used to illustrate two ratios that measure these relationships:

	Foy Company	Glo Company
Operating income	$600,000	$900,000
Less: Interest on long-term debt	200,000	100,000
Income before income taxes	$400,000	$800,000
Less: Income taxes expense	200,000	400,000
Net income	$200,000	$400,000
Less: Preferred stock dividends	50,000	200,000
Net income available for common stock	$150,000	$200,000

Data used to compute times fixed charges are earned

Times Interest Earned   The times interest earned ratio may be computed in two ways as shown at the top of page 1239.

Because interest expense is deductible for income taxes, logic would seem to support *method 1*. Business executives and investors are strongly conditioned to an after-tax view of corporate affairs, however, which may explain why *method 2* generally is used in practice. The after-tax computation always results in a more conservative measurement for coverage of interest expense.

Alternative methods
for computing times
interest earned

	Foy Company	Glo Company
Method 1: *Times interest earned before income taxes:*		
(a) Operating income	$600,000	$900,000
(b) Interest expense	$200,000	$100,000
Times interest earned (a ÷ b)	3 times	9 times
Method 2: *Times interest earned after income taxes:*		
Net income	$200,000	$400,000
(a) Add: Interest expense	200,000	100,000
(b) Income before interest charges	$400,000	$500,000
Times interest earned (b ÷ a)	2 times	5 times

Times Preferred Stock Dividends Earned The computation of the number of times preferred stock dividends are earned also may be made in two ways, as illustrated below:

Are the dividends on
the preferred stock
of Foy Company more
assured?

	Foy Company	Glo Company
Method 1: *Net income available for preferred stock dividends:*		
(a) Net income	$200,000	$400,000
(b) Preferred stock dividend requirement	$ 50,000	$200,000
Times preferred stock dividends earned (a ÷ b)	4 times	2 times

These ratios make it appear that preferred stock dividends of Foy Company are better protected by earnings than its interest expense; yet interest obviously has a prior claim. To overcome this objection, the test of preferred stock dividend safety most often used is the ***number of times combined interest expense and preferred stock dividends are earned.*** This is illustrated for Foy Company and Glo Company below:

No, based on this
computation!

	Foy Company	Glo Company
Method 2: *Times interest expense and preferred stock dividends are earned:*		
Interest expense	$200,000	$100,000
Preferred stock dividend requirement	50,000	200,000
(a) Total interest expense and preferred stock dividend requirement	$250,000	$300,000
(b) Net income (after taxes) plus interest expense	$400,000	$500,000
Number of times interest expense and preferred stock dividends are earned (b ÷ a)	1.6 times	1.7 times

''Times-earned'' ratios are useful not only to creditors and preferred stockholders but also to common stockholders. Common stockholders know that a company that has to forgo paying either interest or preferred stock dividends will suffer financial embarrassment at the least; furthermore, they are concerned about a sufficiency of earnings and cash to allow for common stock dividends. There is little mystery in interpreting times-earned ratios—the higher the ratio the more favorable for bondholders and preferred stockholders. The more difficult question is: How large should the ratios be to satisfy these two groups without being detrimental to the common stockholders? In general, the answer to this question depends on the stability of past and potential earnings over the business cycle; if earnings are stable, lower times-earned ratios may be viewed as satisfactory.

In the analysis of financial statements, the coverage of fixed charges logically should be expanded to include **_all_** fixed obligations of a company. For example, a company must make regular payments on long-term operating leases, property taxes, and other fixed commitments, in addition to interest on debt, before dividends may be declared. The ability of a company to generate sufficient revenue in excess of variable expenses to cover fixed charges is one of the most important considerations to the analyst.

Equity (Book Value) per Share   The term **_equity_** (or **_book value_**) **_per share_** often is used in negotiations for the sale of a business enterprise. In closely held corporations, it is not unusual for one common stockholder to have a contractual right to acquire the common stock of other stockholders at a price equal to the equity per share of the common stock. Computation of equity per share generally is based on going-concern value, not on the assumption of liquidation. **_Equity per share is the amount of net assets applicable to each share of outstanding capital stock._** When a corporation has only common stock outstanding, equity per share is computed by dividing the total stockholders' equity by the number of shares of stock outstanding, as illustrated below:

Equity (book value) per share of common stock

$$\frac{\text{Total stockholders' equity}}{\text{Number of shares outstanding}} = \frac{\$2,500,000}{100,000} = \$25 \text{ equity per share}$$

If a corporation has treasury stock, the debit balance in the Treasury Stock ledger account is deducted to measure the total stockholders' equity, and the number of shares outstanding does not include the shares of treasury stock.

Equity per share is used to some extent as a guide for investors, but usually with recognition that other measurements, such as earnings per share, are more important determinants of market prices for common stocks. The equity per share as traditionally computed may be far different from the per-share **_current fair value_** of net assets. Even though common stocks often trade at prices far above or far below the equity per share, some investors feel that the equity per share should be considered, along with other information, in making investment decisions.

The concept of ''equity per share'' is more meaningful and more widely used for common stock than for preferred stock; however, if a corporation has both types of stock outstanding, the total equity of the preferred stock must be determined as a preliminary step in the computation of the equity per share of the common stock, as illustrated in the example below:

Equity (book value) per share—two classes of capital stock outstanding

> *Equity (book value) per share of common stock—two classes of capital stock outstanding:*
>
> *Total stockholders' equity (net of cost of treasury stock)*............. $9,280,000
>
> *Less: Amount applicable to 10%, $100 par preferred stock: 10,000*
> *shares outstanding (callable at 108)*.......................... 1,080,000
>
> *Equity applicable to $1 par common stock: 1,000,000 shares*
> *outstanding (not including treasury stock)*...................... $8,200,000
>
> *Equity (book value) per share of common stock: $8,200,000 ÷*
> *1,000,000 shares*.. $ 8.20

The equity of the preferred stock in this example is $108 a share. In the computation of the equity of the preferred stock, consideration must be given to any *cumulative dividends in arrears* and other contractual limitations on the equity of preferred stockholders in the net assets of the corporation. On a going-concern basis, is it (1) par or stated value, (2) call price, or (3) liquidation price that is most significant in measuring the equity of the preferred stock? Nearly all preferred stocks contain a call provision; this call price usually is the maximum claim against net assets under the preferred stock contract. Although there may be no immediate prospect that the preferred stock will be called, the call price probably is more significant from the viewpoint of the going concern than is the liquidation price. Therefore, the authors favor using the call price of the preferred stock as the most appropriate measure of the equity applicable to preferred stock.

Significant changes in the equity per share of common stock may result from transactions such as conversions of bonds payable or preferred stock to common stock, issuances of additional shares of common stock, business combinations, and quasi-reorganizations. Some examples of events that change the equity per share of common stock are listed below:

Increases in equity per share: Net income, reverse splits, issuance of additional common stock at prices in excess of the present equity per share, acquisition of common stock for the treasury at prices less than the present equity per share, and redemption of preferred stock at prices less than the present equity per share of the preferred stock.

Decreases in equity per share: Net loss, cash dividends (including any dividends in arrears on cumulative preferred stock), stock dividends, stock splits, issuance of additional common stock at prices less than the present equity per share, acquisition of common stock for the treasury at prices in excess of the present equity per share, and redemption of preferred stock at prices in excess of the present equity per share of the preferred stock.

ANALYSIS OF FINANCIAL STRENGTH

A strong earnings record usually accompanies a strong financial position. Furthermore, an unsatisfactory financial position appears much less unfavorable in the presence of a good earnings record; a company with proved earning power usually works out its financial problems. However, a good earnings record is not the whole story. A company's ability to meet its obligations, to cope with economic adversity, to shift resources to meet changing conditions—in short, its financial strength—is an important factor to continuing survival and growth. In seeking evidence of financial strength, analysts consider first the relationship between assets and liabilities. They ask questions such as: Will the company be able to pay its liabilities when they are due? Does the company have the resources to meet current commitments and future demands for cash necessary to conduct its business successfully?

Data used to analyze working capital position

HOM COMPANY
Selected Financial Data
For Year 1 through Year 3
(in thousands of dollars)

	Year 3	Year 2	Year 1
Current assets:			
Cash	$ 50	$ 80	$ 60
Short-term investments		50	150
Accounts receivable (net)	500	400	300
Inventories (first-in, first-out cost)	1,100	700	500
Short-term prepayments	70	60	50
Total current assets	$ 1,720	$ 1,290	$ 1,060
Current liabilities:			
Notes payable	$ 120	$ 100	
Accounts payable	680	330	$ 170
Other current liabilities	220	170	140
Current portion of long-term debt	180	200	200
Total current liabilities	$ 1,200	$ 800	$ 510
Net sales	$ 3,500	$ 3,000	$ 2,600
Cost of goods sold	(2,600)	(2,000)	(1,900)
Operating expenses	(600)	(500)	(400)
Interest expense	(48)	(49)	(50)
Income before income taxes	$ 252	$ 451	$ 250
Income taxes expense	122	231	125
Net income	$ 130	$ 220	$ 125

Ability to Pay Short-Term Debt

A company's short-term financial strength (or *liquidity*) is dependent on two primary factors: its working capital position and the speed with which it generates liquid assets. We provide the selected financial data for Hom Company on page 1242 as a basis for discussion of these factors.

Working Capital Position   The amount by which current assets exceed current liabilities is the *working capital* of a business enterprise. Changes in the amount of working capital from one accounting period to another are significant, because the amount of working capital is a useful indicator of short-term debt-paying ability.

In addition to the dollar amount of working capital, two analytical ratios of working capital position often are computed. The *current ratio* (current assets divided by current liabilities) helps put the amount of working capital in perspective by showing the relationship between current resources and short-term debt. The *quick ratio* (sometimes called the *acid-test ratio*) focuses on immediate liquidity. Inventories and short-term prepayments, the least liquid current assets, are excluded in the computation of the quick ratio. *Quick assets* consist of cash, short-term investments, and short-term receivables; and the quick ratio is computed by dividing quick assets by current liabilities. The working capital position of Hom Company is summarized below:

Current ratio and quick ratio

HOM COMPANY
Analysis of Working Capital Position
For Year 1 through Year 3
(in thousands of dollars)

	Year 3	Year 2	Year 1
(a) Current assets	$1,720	$1,290	$1,060
(b) Current liabilities	1,200	800	510
Working capital (a − b)	$ 520	$ 490	$ 550
Current ratio (a ÷ b)	1.4	1.6	2.1
(c) Total quick assets (cash, short-term investments, and accounts receivable)	$ 550	$ 530	$ 510
Quick ratio (c ÷ b)	0.5	0.7	1.0

Each measurement presented above contributes something to the analysis of Hom Company's working capital position. Hom has maintained its working capital at about $500,000 during the three-year period. However, its relative short-term liquidity has worsened, as indicated by the steady decline in the current ratio from 2.1 to 1.4 and in the quick ratio from 1.0 to 0.5 from Year 1 to Year 3. This is a picture of a company that may be heading toward financial difficulty, unless these trends are reversed. The increase in accounts payable from $170,000 to $680,000 during the last two years suggests that payments to creditors may be falling behind schedule. Thus, the analysis has brought to light a potential trouble spot in Hom's financial position. However, if the increase in accounts payable is the result of large current expenditures for research and development, or for inventories in anticipation of a significant increase in sales, then the trend must be evaluated in a more favorable light.

Need for Working Capital   A business enterprise generates working capital through a series of events called the *operating cycle*. The operating cycle refers to the process of investing cash in inventories, converting the inventories to accounts receivable through sales, and collecting the receivables in cash, which in turn is used to pay current liabilities incurred in operations and to replace inventories. The average length of time necessary to complete this cycle is important in determining an enterprise's working capital needs. An enterprise with a short operating cycle may manage comfortably on a relatively small amount of working capital and with relatively small quick and current ratios. A long operating cycle requires a larger margin of current assets and larger quick and current ratios unless the credit terms of suppliers can be extended accordingly. The average length of the operating cycle may be estimated by adding the number of days' sales in average inventories to the average age of accounts receivable.

Inventories Turnover   The total cost of all goods that have been moved out of inventories during a year is represented by the cost of goods sold amount in the income statement. Therefore, the ratio of cost of goods sold to the average inventories during an accounting period is a measure of the number of times that inventories turn over on the average and must be replaced. The larger this turnover, the shorter the average time between investment in inventories and sales transactions.

Average inventories generally are determined by averaging monthly or quarterly inventory amounts. This information usually is not available to external analysts, however, and therefore only an average of the inventories at the beginning and end of the year is used. Because many companies adopt a fiscal year that ends when inventories are at a minimum, inventories turnover computed in this manner may appear larger than it really is.

Dividing the annual cost of goods sold by average inventories produces a "times per year" turnover rate. Turnover may be expressed in days by dividing 365 by the number of turnovers per year. An additional useful measure is the *number of days' sales in ending inventories,* computed by multiplying 365 days by the fraction of which the ending inventories is the numerator and cost of goods sold is the denominator. The three-year analysis of inventories for Hom Company is shown at the top of page 1245.

These computations show that inventories turnover has slowed during the three-year period from a little over three months to about four months, and that there are enough inventories on hand at the end of Year 3 to meet sales requirements at current levels for approximately five months (154 days).

For a manufacturing enterprise, the overall inventories turnover may be estimated by dividing cost of goods sold by the average amount of the three inventories: material, goods in process, and finished goods. Alternatively, three separate turnover rates may be computed: (1) cost of goods sold divided by average finished goods inventory, (2) cost of goods manufactured divided by average goods in process inventory, and (3) material used divided by average material inventory.

Inventories turnover and days' sales in inventories

HOM COMPANY
Analysis of Inventories
For Year 1 through Year 3
(in thousands of dollars)

	Year 3	Year 2	Year 1
(a) Cost of goods sold	$2,600	$2,000	$1,900
Inventories, beginning of year .	$ 700	$ 500	$ 540*
Inventories, end of year	1,100	700	500
(b) Average inventories	$ 900	$ 600	$ 520
(c) Turnover per year (a ÷ b)	2.9 times	3.3 times	3.7 times
Number of days' sales in **average** inventories (365 ÷ c)	126 days	111 days	99 days
Number of days' sales in **ending** inventories.............	154 days†	128 days	96 days

*Assumed
†365 × $1,100/$2,600 = 154

It should be pointed out that the foregoing computations would be misleading if the current cost of inventories were substantially higher than historical cost. In such cases, alternative measurements should be used to analyze inventories.

Receivables turnover and days' sales in receivables

HOM COMPANY
Analysis of Accounts Receivable
For Year 1 through Year 3
(in thousands of dollars)

	Year 3	Year 2	Year 1
(a) Net sales	$3,500	$3,000	$2,600
Accounts receivable, beginning of year	$ 400	$ 300	$ 280*
Accounts receivable, end of year	500	400	300
(b) Average accounts receivable .	$ 450	$ 350	$ 290
(c) Accounts receivable turnover (a ÷ b)	7.8 times	8.6 times	9.0 times
Number of days' sales in **average** accounts receivable (365 ÷ c)	47 days	42 days	41 days
Number of days' sales in **ending** accounts receivable .	52 days†	49 days	42 days

*Assumed
†365 × $500/$3,500 = 52

Accounts Receivable Turnover The turnover of accounts receivable may be computed in a manner comparable to that for inventories. Unless a business enterprise has a large amount of cash sales, sales for an accounting period produce inflows of accounts receivable. When net sales is divided by the average balance of accounts receivable during the period, the result is a rough indication of the average length of time necessary to convert accounts receivable to cash. Ideally, only credit sales should be included in the sales amount, and an average monthly balance of *gross* accounts receivable should be used. However, these refinements may not be possible in external analysis, and a less exact computation may serve the purpose of indicating favorable or unfavorable trends. The reasonableness of the ending balance of accounts receivable may be evaluated by computing the ***number of days' sales in ending accounts receivable***. The accounts receivable of Hom Company are analyzed at the bottom of page 1245 (dollar amounts are in thousands).

It is evident that, absent a change in credit terms, collections have slowed down over the three-year period. The trend is unfavorable; interpretation of the absolute amounts depends on the credit terms and policies of Hom Company.

Length of Operating Cycle As stated on page 1244, an estimate of the average length of the operating cycle may be computed by adding the average days' sales in inventories and in accounts receivable. This is illustrated below for Hom Company:

Length of operating cycle for Hom Company

	Year 3	Year 2	Year 1
Average days to dispose of inventories	126	111	99
Average days to collect accounts receivable	47	42	41
Average days in operating cycle	173	153	140

The operating cycle of Hom has increased by more than a full month (33 days) from Year 1 to Year 3. If this has happened inadvertently, it may explain the unfavorable trend in the current and quick ratios. If the change is the result of company policy, it indicates the need for a larger amount of working capital to finance current operations.

Number of Days' Operations to Cover Negative Working Capital When current liabilities exceed current assets, management may estimate the length of time it will take to eliminate the negative working capital as a result of generating liquid assets from operations. For example, assume that the current liabilities of Lomax Corporation on March 31, Year 6, exceeded its current assets by $20,000. Assume further that Lomax's operations are relatively stable during a calendar year and normally generate working capital as follows:

Working capital provided from operations . . .		
Net income		$ 75,000
Add: Depreciation expense and other expenses that do not require		
use of working capital		45,000
Working capital normally provided from operations over 12-month		
period		$120,000

From the foregoing information we may estimate that the negative working capital of $20,000 will be eliminated in approximately two months:

. . . will eliminate
the working capital
deficit in two months

$$\frac{\$20,000 \text{ (negative working capital)}}{\$120,000 \text{ (annual working capital provided from operations)}}$$
$$\times 365 \text{ days} = 61 \text{ days}$$

Interpreting the Analysis of Liquidity

The following factors should be considered in interpreting the liquidity of a company as shown by the analytical procedures just described:

1 Creditors tend to believe that the larger the current and quick ratios and the shorter the operating cycle, the better. From the viewpoint of company performance, there are limits. It is possible for a company to accumulate working capital in excess of the amount that may be employed profitably. Thus, excessive current and quick ratios are unfavorable indicators. Similarly, an unusually high rate of inventories turnover may indicate that a company is losing business by failing to maintain adequate inventories to serve customers' needs. A rapid turnover of accounts receivable may indicate overly severe credit policies that reduce revenue below levels that could be achieved by more liberal credit terms.

2 Because creditors and other outsiders emphasize a company's working capital position as evidence of short-run solvency, there is a temptation for managers to take action just before the end of an accounting period to make the working capital relationships appear more favorable than they are. This process is called *window dressing.* By postponing purchases, allowing inventories to decrease below normal levels, using all available cash to pay current liabilities, and pressing collections on accounts receivable, a company may artificially improve its current and quick ratios, as well as its inventories and accounts receivable turnover rates. Decreases in accounts receivable and inventories will increase turnover rates. Any equal decrease in both current assets and current liabilities will improve a current ratio that already is more than 1 to 1.

3 Even when no deliberate attempt has been made to present an artificially favorable picture, the working capital position shown by year-end financial statements is probably more favorable than at any other time of the year. This is particularly true when a company has adopted a *natural business year* that ends during an ebb in the seasonal swing of business activity. At times of peak activity, accounts receivable, inventories, and current liabilities tend to be at higher levels. There are many reasons why a natural business year is desirable, and accountants generally encourage companies to adopt such an accounting period.

Analysis of Capital Structure

The way in which a business enterprise meets its financing needs, as reflected in its *capital structure,* is an important factor in assessing its financial strength and the use of *financial leverage.* The most common approach for this purpose is to restate the major elements of the liabilities and stockholders' equity to component percentages of total assets, as shown below:

Three ways to measure relationship between debt and equity

	Component percentages			*Debt and equity ratios*	
Total assets		100%			
Sources of financing:					
Current liabilities		10%			
Long-term debt		18%			
Total liabilities		28%	→ Debt ratio		28%
Preferred stock	9%				
Common stockholders'					
equity	63%	72%	→ Equity ratio		72%
Total liabilities & stock-					
holders' equity		100%		Debt to equity ratio (28 ÷ 72) . . .	39%

Debt and Equity Ratios   Analysts often condense the essence of the capital structure of a company into one or more of three ratios. The *debt ratio* is the ratio of total liabilities to total assets; the *equity ratio* is the ratio of stockholders' equity to total assets; and the *debt-to-equity ratio* is the ratio of total liabilities to stockholders' equity. Any one of these ratios tells the essential story about the debt-equity relationship for a company.

Financial analysts compute other ratios to aid in evaluating capital structure. For example, the ratio of total plant assets to stockholders' equity sometimes is used as a test of the adequacy of equity capital. If the investment in plant assets is substantial relative to stockholders' equity, this indicates that a company has borrowed heavily to invest in nonliquid assets, which may lead to difficulties should earnings not prove satisfactory.

Evaluating Capital Structure

What factors should be considered in evaluating the capital structure of a company? The answer to this question depends on the concerns of creditors and stockholders.

Creditors' View   Creditors are primarily concerned with the safety of their claims. They view a relatively low debt ratio as a favorable factor because it indicates a substantial cushion of protection against a shrinkage in asset values. Because the source for payment of debt is either new borrowing or internal cash flow, all creditors are interested in long-run financial strength and a healthy earnings record. The debt ratio and the times-interest-earned ratio are the prime indicators of financial strength from the creditor's viewpoint.

Stockholders' View   Present or prospective stockholders are concerned with a company's ability to meet its long-term debt obligations, because failure to pay interest or current maturities of debt is a serious matter affecting adversely both the credit standing of the company and the position of stockholders. A low debt ratio, or the absence of long-term debt, is not necessarily to the stockholders' advantage. To the extent that a company is able to earn a return in excess of the interest rate on its long-term debt, its stockholders' benefit from the *leverage factor.* However, this benefit may be more than offset by the increased risks and costs of the various restrictive covenants included in the borrowing contract by the lender, which may limit management's freedom of action.

It has been argued that the existence of long-term debt or other senior securities increases the risk borne by common stockholders and causes the common stock to trade at a lower price-earnings ratio. In a well-managed and profitable company, it is doubtful whether a reasonable amount of debt increases the common stockholders' risk sufficiently to be reflected in the price-earnings ratio of the common stock. If the amount of long-term debt is excessive and earnings are not increasing, it is likely that the advantage of *trading on the equity* will be offset by the dampening effect of the large debt on the market price of the company's common stock.

Capacity for Additional Investment and Growth in Earnings

A business enterprise seldom is able to maintain a stable position over a long period of time; it either changes and grows, or stagnates and dies. A healthy company must be able to finance the development of new products as old ones lose their profit potential, and to move in new directions as demand and technology change. An important element of financial strength is the ability to generate additional cash when needed.

In part, this means the ability to borrow or to obtain new capital from owners. Another major source of investment capital is earnings retained for use in business operations. Many enterprises typically generate more cash or working capital each period than the amount of net income (see Chapter 23). The amount of cash or working capital provided from operations, less dividend and sinking-fund requirements, offers a rough indicator of the internally generated funds available to expand the level of operations (expand plant capacity, develop new products, enter new markets, undertake business combinations) or to retire long-term debt.

Standards for Comparison

When analysts have computed the significant dollar and percentage changes and ratios and have reduced the mass of financial data to digestible form, they need some criteria as a guide in evaluating these findings and in making business and investment decisions. Three possibilities are discussed in the following sections.

Past Record of the Company   A comparison of analytical data over time (sometimes called *horizontal analysis,* in contrast to *vertical analysis,* which deals with single-year financial statements) may reveal trends in performance and position that will aid in determining progress or lack of progress and may help in assessing future prospects. Many companies present trends in sales, earnings, and other data in graphic form. (For examples, see pages 219, 221, 223, and 225 of Chapter 4.) As a basis for forecasting, the projecting of past trends into the future has serious limitations, because changes may reverse direction at any time. However, knowing that the trend is favorable or unfavorable leads to further inquiry as to the underlying reasons.

Another limitation of horizontal analysis is that the past record of a company does not afford a basis for comparison with similarly situated companies. For example, if the sales of a company have increased 10%, but industry sales have increased 50%, the 10% increase may appear to be favorable, but the company's sales performance in its industry is poor.

Comparison with Competitors or Industry as a Whole   Perhaps the best way to put a company's performance in perspective is to compare its position and operating results with those of competitors. For example, a study by Dun & Bradstreet, Inc., of the financial statements of drug companies showed the following:

Example of financial statistics for an industry

	Current ratio	Net profits on net sales	Return on owners' investment	Total debt to owners' equity	Net sales to inventories (times)
Upper quartile	3.5	11.3%	20.4%	35.8%	9.1
Median	2.6	6.8	15.4	43.5	6.3
Lower quartile	1.8	2.9	5.5	63.6	4.6

On the basis of this kind of information, an analyst examining the financial statements of a drug company obtains some idea of the position of the company in relation to others in the industry. Note that Dun & Bradstreet, Inc., apparently computes "inventories turnover" by dividing net sales by the amount of average inventories. Although this procedure often is used by financial analysts as a matter of convenience, it does not measure "turnover," but simply relates the average level of inventories (at cost) to the sales volume for the year (at selling prices).

One of the difficulties in making comparisons among business enterprises is that some companies that appear to be in the same industry are not comparable because industries are difficult to define. For example, many companies have diversified their activities by moving into new fields or acquiring other companies whose business activities are not closely related, with the result that companies falling roughly within the same industry are no longer comparable in many respects. When *diversified enterprises* report industry segment sales and profitability figures, it is much easier to analyze their financial statements.

In *FASB Statement No. 14,* "Financial Reporting for Segments of a Business Enterprise," the Financial Accounting Standards Board established standards for disclosure of information about the reporting company's operations in different industries, its foreign operations and export sales, and its major customers.[4] This *Statement* also required that a company operating predominantly or exclusively in a single industry identify that industry. The information to be reported for each significant industry segment includes: revenue, profitability, identifiable assets, and other related disclosures such as depreciation expense and capital expenditures. A *significant industry segment* is one that: (1) includes 10% or more of the combined identifiable assets of the company; or (2) generates 10% or more of the company's revenue; or (3) generates 10% or more of the company's operating income or loss. The purpose of disclosure of segment information is to assist users of financial statements to analyze and understand the company's past performance and future prospects.[5] (See *Note 11* on page 233 for Walt Disney Productions.)

Comparison with Independent Statistical Measures It often is useful to relate certain financial indexes for a business enterprise to statistical measures. For example, a comparison of the trend of sales or net income with an *index of industrial production* may show whether the enterprise is growing more slowly or faster than the economy. Similarly, indexes may be developed for sales and net income, for example, comparing the performance of a single enterprise with the industry performance index during the same period. Price indexes may be used to deflate sales in dollars to determine whether the growth in sales is a growth in physical volume or the result of inflation. It also may be possible to relate financial data to physical measures of production or output. For example, statistics such as the average freight haul in miles per ton, or the average revenue per ton-mile, give a useful basis for comparing the operating performance of different railroad companies.

Inflation and Analysis of Financial Statements

Financial statements prepared on the basis of historical cost do not reflect fully the economic resources or the *real* income (in terms of purchasing power) of a business enterprise. Financial analysts must attempt to evaluate the impact of inflation on the financial position and results of operations of the enterprise they are evaluating. They should raise questions such as: How much of the income is attributable to price increases? Are expenses (such as depreciation) understated in terms of current price levels? Is the enterprise gaining or losing from inflation because of the composition of its assets and the amount of its liabilities? Financial statements adjusted for price-level changes are illustrated in Chapter 25.

Summary of Ratios and Other Analytical Measurements

The more widely used ratios and other measurements discussed in this chapter and their significance are summarized on pages 1252–1253.

The relevance of any of the foregoing measurements depends on the direction of its trend and on its comparison with a predetermined standard. The information

---

[4]*FASB Statement No. 14,* "Financial Reporting for Segments of a Business Enterprise," FASB (Stamford: 1976), p. 1

[5]Ibid., p. 2.

available in financial statements may be useful in appraising a company's financial position, in predicting its earnings, and in making other predictive judgments about the company. Relationships among reported data may be quite informative. However, we must remember that financial statements have limitations and that qualitative factors may be far more important than "cold figures." For example, factors such as the following should be considered by analysts in predicting the likely earnings performance of a company: (1) source of markets for the company's products and services; (2) growth potential for its products and services; (3) market share in its industry; (4) patent protection, if any, for its major products; (5) sensitivity of its earnings to economic fluctuations; (6) effect of technological and environmental changes on its business activities; and (7), perhaps the most important factor, the quality of its management.

	Ratio or other measurement	Method of computation	What it shows
Summary of ratios and other analytical measurements	**1** Return on total assets	$\dfrac{\text{Net income} + \text{interest expense}}{\text{Average investment in assets}}$	Productivity of assets
	2 Return on common stockholders' equity	$\dfrac{\text{Net income} - \text{preferred stock dividends}}{\text{Average common stockholders' equity}}$	Earning power on residual owners' equity
	3 Earnings per share of common stock	$\dfrac{\text{Net income} - \text{preferred dividends}}{\substack{\text{Average number of shares} \\ \text{of common stock outstanding}}}$	Amount earned on each share of common stock
	4 Price-earnings ratio for common stock	$\dfrac{\text{Market price per share}}{\text{Earnings per share}}$	Whether market price of common stock is in line with earnings
Earnings performance	**5** Dividend yield on common stock	$\dfrac{\text{Dividends per share}}{\text{Market price per share}}$	Return to common stockholders based on current market price of common stock
	6 Dividend payout ratio for common stock	$\dfrac{\text{Dividends per share}}{\text{Earnings per share}}$	Percentage of earnings distributed as dividends
	7 Number of times interest earned (before income taxes)	$\dfrac{\text{Operating income}}{\text{Annual interest expense}}$	Coverage of interest expense (particularly on long-term debt)
	8 Times preferred stock dividends earned	$\dfrac{\text{Net income}}{\text{Annual preferred stock dividends}}$	Adequacy of earnings to pay preferred stock dividends

(continued)

9 Equity (book value) per share of common stock	$$\frac{\text{Common stockholders' equity}}{\text{Number of shares of common stock outstanding}}$$	Amount of net assets allocable to each share of common stock
10 Current ratio	$$\frac{\text{Current assets}}{\text{Current liabilities}}$$	Short-run debt-paying ability
11 Quick (acid-test) ratio	$$\frac{\text{Quick assets}}{\text{Current liabilities}}$$	Short-term liquidity
12 Inventories turnover	$$\frac{\text{Cost of goods sold}}{\text{Average inventories}}$$	Ability to control investment in inventories
13 Accounts receivable turnover	$$\frac{\text{Net sales on credit}}{\text{Average accounts receivable}}$$	Possible excessive accounts receivable; effectiveness of collection policy
14 Debt ratio	$$\frac{\text{Total liabilities}}{\text{Total assets}}$$	Extent of borrowing and trading on the equity (financial leverage)
15 Equity ratio	$$\frac{\text{Total stockholders' equity}}{\text{Total assets}}$$	Protection to creditors and extent of trading on the equity (financial leverage)
16 Debt-to-equity ratio	$$\frac{\text{Total liabilities}}{\text{Total stockholders' equity}}$$	Relationship between borrowed capital and equity capital

Financial strength— liquidity and leverage

Analysts should keep in mind that, although a balance sheet is a statement of assets and claims against these assets, most assets are stated at historical cost, and not all elements of value are included in the balance sheet (for example, capable management, good credit standing, potential new products, internally developed goodwill, and the appreciation in the value of assets, especially natural resources). Furthermore, the *quality of assets and earnings* must be carefully evaluated. An income statement is a product of matching expired costs with realized revenue and covers only a brief period of a company's life. Consequently, the income statement does not necessarily measure the *improvement in the company's economic wealth* during the accounting period. The dangers of attaching too much significance to either the balance sheet or the income statement should be recognized by those undertaking an analysis of financial statements.

REVIEW QUESTIONS

1 Describe four sources from which an outsider might obtain financial information about a business enterprise.

2 Explain what is meant by the following terms:
a *Trend percentage*   **d** *Capital structure*
b *Common-size statements*   **e** *Dividend payout ratio*
c *Trading on the equity*   **f** *Price-earnings ratio*

3 **a** Discuss some limitations of single-year financial statements for purposes of analysis and interpretation.
  b To what extent are these limitations overcome by the use of comparative financial statements?
  c In what ways may a five-year summary of financial data be misleading?

4 Describe the effect of each of the following transactions on the indicated ratios. Will the ratio increase, decrease, or remain unchanged?

Transactions	*Ratios*
a *Purchase of merchandise for cash*	**a** *Current ratio of 2 to 1*
b *Payment of accounts payable*	**b** *Quick ratio of 0.6 to 1*
c *Accounts receivable written off against Allowance for Doubtful Accounts ledger account*	**c** *Average age of accounts receivable of 60 days*
d *Declaration of cash dividend on pre-ferred stock*	**d** *Equity ratio of 60%*
e *Distribution of a 10% common stock div-idend*	**e** *Loss per share of common stock, $1.20*
f *Conversion of long-term debt to common stock*	**f** *Return on total long-term capital*
g *Change from fifo to lifo method of inven-tories valuation during period of rising prices*	**g** *Inventories turnover*

5 The following ratios have been used at times by financial analysts. Explain what each ratio indicates, and why it is (or is not) significant.
a Ratio of plant assets to long-term debt
b Ratio of net sales to working capital (working capital turnover)
c Ratio of current liabilities to inventories
d Ratio of total operating expenses to current liabilities
e Ratio of plant assets to stockholders' equity
f Ratio of long-term debt to working capital
g Ratio of net sales to stockholders' equity
h Ratio of net income to current assets

6 In an analysis of the financial position and operations of a business enterprise, it is necessary to have some standards or criteria for comparison. Suggest several standards that may be employed for this purpose.

7 An estimate of inventories turnover sometimes is made by dividing net sales by average inventories. Evaluate this method of computing inventories turnover.

8 What procedures are required to compute the equity (book value) per share of common stock in each of the following cases?

a Both preferred stock and common stock are outstanding

b Treasury stock (common) has been acquired

9 The equity (book value) of 100,000 shares of common stock is $40 a share. Indicate the effect of each of the following four transactions on the equity per share:

a Issuance of additional shares of common stock at $10 a share pursuant to stock option contract

b Issuance of additional shares of common stock at $60 a share through rights offering

c Acquisition of common stock for treasury at $75 a share

d Conversion of bonds at 20 shares of common stock for every $1,000 bond

10 Two companies have the same amount of working capital. The current debt-paying ability of one company is much weaker than the other. Explain how this could occur.

11 Explain how you would evaluate the ability of a business enterprise to make required payments on long-term debt or to finance replacements of plant assets, assuming that you had available financial statements of the enterprise for the last five years.

12 If you were asked to make three analytical computations (ratios, percentages, etc.) that would be most useful in appraising the financial statements of a corporation from the viewpoint of the following parties, which computations would you make, and why do you feel these are of prime importance?

a Short-term creditor

b Long-term creditor

c Prospective investor in the corporation's preferred stock

d Prospective investor in the corporation's common stock

13 In response to a request that its *profit margins on different products* be disclosed, the management of Raines Company responded, ''Public disclosure would cause us to suffer at the hands of our competitors, particularly in regard to a product that accounts for 90% of our sales.'' In what ways would the disclosure of this information possibly be detrimental to Raines?

14 The following comments by an oil company executive appeared in an article in a financial journal:

> In seeking textbook ratios between current assets and current liabilities, some companies may be going overboard on building up cash. These ratios may not mean much any more. In the old days, when these ratios were established, credit facilities weren't so readily available as they are today. There are elements of liquidity that don't show up in the balance sheet, such as a contractual line of bank credit, which may be just as solid as a savings account. But to some extent, we're stuck with archaic ratios that the investment community likes to see.

15 *FASB Statement No. 14,* "Financial Reporting for Segments of a Business Enterprise," established standards for disclosure of information about the reporting enterprise's operations in different industries, its foreign operations and export sales, and its major customers. Define a ***significant industry segment*** and indicate the type of information that is reported for each such segment.

EXERCISES

Ex. 24-1   Select the best answer for each of the following multiple-choice questions:

1   Are inventories included in the computation of the:

	Quick (acid-test) ratio?	Current ratio?
a	Yes	Yes
b	Yes	No
c	No	Yes
d	No	No

2   How are the following used in the computation of the dividend payout ratio for a corporation with only common stock outstanding?

	Dividends per share	Earnings per share	Equity per share
a	Denominator	Numerator	Not used
b	Denominator	Not used	Numerator
c	Numerator	Denominator	Not used
d	Numerator	Not used	Denominator

3   A corporation's dividend yield for an accounting period is computed by dividing:
a Dividends declared per share by earnings per share
b Dividends declared per share by equity (book value) per share
c Dividends declared per share by end-of-period market price per share
d Earnings per share by dividends per share

4   The number of days' sales in average accounts receivable is computed by:
a Multiplying the accounts receivable turnover by 30
b Dividing the accounts receivable turnover by 30
c Multiplying the accounts receivable turnover by 365
d Dividing 365 by the accounts receivable turnover

5   Sato Company has total liabilities of $600,000 and total stockholders' equity of $900,000. Sato's equity ratio is:
a 150.0%   **b** 66.7%   **c** 60.0%   **d** 40.0%   **e** Some other percentage

6   The ratio of an amount in a financial statement to the total that includes the amount is a:
a Component percentage
b Common-size percentage
c Trend percentage
d Turnover percentage

7   In comparing the current ratios of two companies, why is it inappropriate for the analyst to assume that the company with the larger current ratio is more successful than the other company?

a The current ratio includes assets other than cash

b A large current ratio may indicate inadequate inventories

c A large current ratio may indicate inefficient management of current assets and current liabilities

d The two companies may define **working capital** differently

8   Which of the following transactions increases a current ratio of at least 1:1?

a Disposal of short-term investments at a loss

b Use of the equity method of accounting for an influenced investee

c Borrowing cash on a short-term promissory note

d Paying the principal of a short-term promissory note

9   Ander Company was organized on January 2, Year 1, with the following capital structure:

> 10% cumulative preferred stock, par and liquidation value $100,
>   callable at 110, authorized, issued, and outstanding 1,000 shares $100,000
> Common stock, $5 par, authorized 20,000 shares, issued and outstanding
>   10,000 shares   50,000

Ander's net income for the year ended December 31, Year 1, was $450,000, but no dividends were declared. How much was Ander's common stockholders' equity (book value) per share on December 31, Year 1?

a $44   **b** $45   **c** $49   **d** $50   **e** Some other amount

Ex. 24-2   Trend percentages and common-size percentages for Westward Company for the years ended December 31, Year 2 and Year 1, are shown below:

	Year 2	Year 1
Trend percentages:		
Net sales	120%	100%
Cost of goods sold	?	100
Gross profit on sales	?	100
Operating expenses and income taxes expense..............	?	100
Net income	?	100
Common-size percentages:		
Net sales	100%	100%
Cost of goods sold	?	?
Gross profit on sales	45%	?%
Operating expenses and income taxes expense..............	27.5	30
Net income	?%	10%

a Compute the missing trend percentages and common-size percentages for Westward Company.

b If the net income for Year 1 amounted to $10,000, compute the net income of Westward Company for Year 2.

Ex. 24-3   The following common-size income statements are available for Lewis Corporation for the two years ended December 31, Year 5 and Year 4:

	Year 5	Year 4
Net sales	100%	100%
Cost of goods sold	55	70
Gross profit on sales	45%	30%
Operating expenses (including income taxes expense).........	20	18
Net income	25%	12%

The trend percentages for sales are as follows:

Year 5...	125%
Year 4...	100%

Compute the trend percentage for gross profit on sales of Lewis Corporation for Year 5, rounded to the nearest tenth.

Ex. 24-4   The information below (in thousands of dollars) for three companies is presented to you on December 31, Year 10:

	Alb Company	Bur Company	Con Company
Total assets	$140,000	$140,000	$140,000
Current liabilities	$ 20,000	$ 50,000	$ 20,000
10% bonds payable, due in Year 15	40,000		
12% bonds payable, due in Year 20		10,000	
10% bonds payable, due in Year 22			80,000
Stockholders' equity	80,000	80,000	40,000
Total liabilities & stockholders' equity	$140,000	$140,000	$140,000
Net income	$ 14,025	$ 12,650	$ 9,790

Compute the following for each company for Year 10:
a Number of times interest was earned (before income taxes), to the nearest hundredth. The income tax rate is 45%.
b Rate earned on ending stockholders' equity, to the nearest tenth
c Rate earned on total assets on December 31, Year 10 (before interest expense and income taxes of 45%), to the nearest tenth

Ex. 24-5   Quigley, Inc., has the following capital structure (in millions): 10% bonds, $12.5; 11% preferred stock, $30.0; common stock (paid-in capital and retained earnings), $50.0. Income before interest and income taxes at 45% for Year 6 was $15 million.
Compute the amount of Year 6 earnings of Quigley, Inc., available for common stock.

Ex. 24-6   Exeter Corporation reported earnings per share for Year 4 of $4.20 on 100,000 shares of common stock outstanding during the entire year. On April 1, Year 5, Exeter declared a 50% common stock dividend, and on October 1 it issued 60,000 shares of common stock for cash. Net income for Year 5 was $528,000. No preferred stock was outstanding.

   Compute the increase or decrease in earnings per share of common stock of Exeter Corporation in Year 5.

Ex. 24-7   Silvio Corporation had total stockholders' equity of $35,500,000, including $10,750,000 of additional paid-in capital and retained earnings. The capital stock included in stockholders' equity on April 30, Year 5, follows:

> 12% preferred stock, $50 par, callable at $53 a share, 200,000 shares
> issued and outstanding (no dividends in arrears) $10,000,000
> Common stock, $10 par, 5,000,000 shares authorized, 1,550,000 shares
> issued, 1,500,000 shares outstanding (50,000 shares, cost
> $750,000, in treasury)   15,500,000

   Compute the equity (book value) per share of common stock of Silvio Corporation on April 30, Year 5

Ex. 24-8   Comparative balance sheets and other financial information for Winsett Company, a retail enterprise, are presented below. Dollar amounts are in thousands.

WINSETT COMPANY
Comparative Balance Sheets
December 31, Year 2 and Year 1
(in thousands of dollars)

	Year 2	Year 1
Assets		
Cash	$ 7,000	$ 4,000
Short-term investments	2,000	4,000
Accounts receivable (net)	13,000	9,000
Inventories	9,000	7,000
Plant assets (net)	69,000	66,000
Total assets	$100,000	$90,000
Liabilities & Stockholders' Equity		
Current liabilities	$ 14,000	$16,000
Bonds payable, due in Year 15	24,000	20,000
Common stock, $10 par	30,000	30,000
Retained earnings	32,000	24,000
Total liabilities & stockholders' equity	$100,000	$90,000

Sales for Year 2 were $100 million, and cost of goods sold amounted to $58 million. Other items from the income statement for Year 2 were: Interest expense, $2 million; income taxes expense, $9.9 million; and net income, $12.1 million.

Show how you would compute the following ratios (or measurements) for Winsett Company for Year 2 by listing the appropriate dollar or other amounts to be used in computing each item. For example: debt ratio, $38,000 ÷ $100,000.

a Current ratio
b Quick (acid-test) ratio
c Times interest earned (before income taxes)
d Rate of gross profit on sales
e Earnings per share of common stock

Ex. 24-9   Information for Hovack Company is presented below for the two years ended December 31, Year 2 and Year 1:

	Year 2	Year 1
Cash	$ 30,000	$ 30,000
Accounts receivable	60,000	40,000
Less: Allowance for doubtful accounts	(5,000)	(4,000)
Inventories	45,000	35,000
Plant assets (net)	230,000	189,000
Totals	$360,000	$290,000
Accounts payable	$ 50,000	$ 40,000
12% bonds payable	100,000	100,000
Common stock, $5 par	130,000	100,000
Retained earnings	80,000	50,000
Totals	$360,000	$290,000
Sales (all on credit)	$180,000	$120,000
Cost of goods sold	100,000	70,000
Gross profits on sales	$ 80,000	$ 50,000
Operating expenses and income taxes expense	50,000	30,000
Net income	$ 30,000	$ 20,000

Compute each of the following for Hovack Company for Year 2 (show computations):

a Quick (acid-test) ratio
b Number of days' sales in gross accounts receivable at year-end
c Inventories turnover
d Equity (book value) per share of common stock at year-end
e Number of days' sales in inventories at year-end

Ex. 24-10   Selected amounts from the comparative balance sheets of Ohio Corporation are as follows:

	Dec. 31, Year 2	Dec. 31, Year 1
Current assets	$4,224,000	$3,500,000
Other assets	5,376,000	6,500,000
Current liabilities	1,920,000	2,500,000
Bonds payable, due in Year 7	1,680,000	2,000,000
Common stock, $10 par	3,600,000	3,600,000
Retained earnings	2,400,000	1,900,000

Dividends of $220,000 were declared in Year 2. Dividends and net income accounted for the change in retained earnings. There was no preferred stock outstanding.

Compute the following for Ohio Corporation (show computations):

a Current ratio, December 31, Year 1
b Working capital, December 31, Year 2
c Equity ratio, December 31, Year 1
d Debt ratio, December 31, Year 2
e Earnings per share of common stock for Year 2
f Equity (book value) per share, December 31, Year 2

Ex. 24-11   Selected financial data for Menzies Corporation follow:

	Dec. 31, Year 2	Dec. 31, Year 1
Cash	$ 10,000	$ 80,000
Short-term investments	30,000	10,000
Accounts receivable (net)	50,000	150,000
Inventories	90,000	150,000
Plant assets (net)	340,000	360,000
Notes payable (current)	20,000	40,000
Accounts payable	70,000	110,000
Mortgage note payable (due in Year 5)	280,000	280,000
Cash sales	1,800,000	1,600,000
Credit sales	500,000	800,000
Cost of goods sold	1,000,000	1,400,000

Compute the following for Menzies Corporation for Year 2 (show supporting computations):

a Quick (acid-test) ratio
b Accounts receivable turnover
c Inventories turnover
d Current ratio

Ex. 24-12   **a** Lopar Corporation's net accounts receivable totaled $250,000 on December 31, Year 1, and $300,000 on December 31, Year 2. Net cash sales for Year 2 totaled $100,000, and the accounts receivable turnover for Year 2 was 5.

Compute Lopar Corporation's total net sales for Year 2.

b Selected financial information for Capper Company follows:

	Year 2	Year 1
8% noncumulative, nonconvertible preferred stock, $100 par and liquidation value	$125,000	$125,000
Common stock	400,000	300,000
Retained earnings	185,000	75,000
Dividends declared and paid on preferred stock	10,000	10,000
Net income	120,000	60,000

Compute Capper Company's return on common stockholders' equity for Year 2.

c Proteus Company's stockholders' equity on December 31, Year 7, was as follows:

6% cumulative preferred stock, $100 par, 1,000 shares authorized, issued, and outstanding (dividends in arrears for Year 3 through Year 7) $100,000
Common stock, $10 par, 300,000 shares authorized, 50,000 shares issued and outstanding 500,000
Retained earnings 90,000

Compute Proteus Company's equity (book value) per share of common stock on December 31, Year 7.

d Vance Corporation had 100,000 shares of $10 par common stock issued and outstanding throughout Year 8. Total stockholders' equity on December 31, Year 8, was $2,800,000, and net income for the year ended December 31, Year 8, was $800,000. During Year 8 Vance declared and paid dividends of $3 a share on the common stock. Market price of Vance's common stock was $24 on December 31, Year 8.

Compute the price-earnings ratio of Vance Corporation's common stock for the year ended December 31, Year 8.

CASES

Case 24-1 Financial statements and notes to the financial statements prepared by the accountant of Romo Company for the year ended October 31, Year 8, follow:

ROMO COMPANY
Income Statement
For Year Ended October 31, Year 8

Sales		$1,000,000
Cost of goods sold		750,000
Gross profit on sales		$ 250,000
Expenses:		
Doubtful accounts expense	$ 7,000	
Insurance	13,000	
Lease expenses (Note 1)	40,000	
Repairs and maintenance	30,000	
Pensions (Note 2)	12,000	
Salaries	60,000	162,000
Earnings before income taxes		$ 88,000
Income taxes expense		28,740
Net income		$ 59,260
Earnings per share		$ 0.5926

ROMO COMPANY
Statement of Retained Earnings
For Year Ended October 31, Year 8

Retained earnings, beginning of year	$150,000
Add: Extraordinary item (gain), net of income tax effect	25,000
Net income	59,260
Subtotal	$234,260
Less: Dividends ($0.3426 a share)	34,260
Retained earnings, end of year	$200,000

ROMO COMPANY
Balance Sheet
October 31, Year 8

Assets

Cash		$ 15,000
Accounts receivable (net)		150,000
Inventories		120,000
Total current assets		$285,000
Land		125,000
Trademark **(Note 3)**		250,000
Total assets		$660,000

Liabilities & Stockholders' Equity

Accounts payable		$ 80,000
Other current liabilities		20,000
Deferred income tax credits **(Note 4)**		80,000
Common stock, $1 par **(Note 5)**	$100,000	
Paid-in capital in excess of par	180,000	
Retained earnings	200,000	480,000
Total liabilities & stockholders' equity		$660,000

Note 1—Long-Term Lease Under the terms of a five-year noncancelable lease for buildings and equipment, the company is obligated to make annual rental payments of $40,000 in each of the next four fiscal years. At the conclusion of the lease term, the company has an option to acquire the leased assets for $20,000 (a bargain purchase option) or to renew the lease for another five-year term at an annual rental of $5,000.

Note 2—Pension Plan Substantially all employees are covered by the company's pension plan. Pension expense is equal to the total of pension benefits paid to retired employees during the year.

Note 3—Trademark The company's trademark was acquired from Apex Corporation on January 2, Year 6, for $250,000.

██████████   **Note 4—Deferred Income Tax Credits**   The entire amount of the deferred income tax credits resulted from tax-exempt municipal bonds that were held during the previous fiscal year, giving rise to a difference between taxable income and reported net income for the year ended October 31, Year 7. The deferred income tax credits amount was computed on the basis of expected tax rates in future years.

Note 5—Warrants   On January 2, Year 7, one common stock warrant was issued to stockholders of record for each share of common stock owned. An additional share of common stock is to be issued on exercise of 10 stock warrants and receipt of an amount equal to par value. For the six months ended October 31, Year 8, the average market price for the company's common stock was $5 a share, and no warrants were exercised.

Note 6—Contingency   On October 31, Year 8, the company was contingently liable for product warranties in an amount estimated to aggregate $75,000. This loss contingency was not recognized in the accounting records.

Instructions

Review the foregoing financial statements of Romo Company for the year ended October 31, Year 8, and the notes to the financial statements. Identify any inclusions or exclusions from them that are in violation of generally accepted accounting principles, and indicate corrective action to be taken. Do not comment as to format or style. Respond in the following order:

> Income statement
> Statement of retained earnings
> Balance sheet
> Notes to the financial statements
> General

Case 24-2   Lindell Corporation needs additional capital for plant expansion. The board of directors is considering obtaining the funds by issuing additional short-term promissory notes, long-term bonds, preferred stock, or common stock.

Instructions

a What primary factors should the board of directors of Lindell Corporation consider in selecting the best method of financing plant expansion?

b One member of the board of directors suggests that Lindell should maximize trading on the equity, that is, using stockholders' equity as a basis for borrowing additional funds at a lower rate of interest than the expected earnings rate from the use of the borrowed funds.

   (1) Explain how trading on the equity affects earnings per share of common stock.

   (2) Explain how a change in income tax rates affects trading on the equity.

   (3) Under what circumstances should a corporation seek to trade on the equity to a substantial degree?

c Two specific proposals under consideration by the board of directors are to issue 14% subordinated income bonds, or to issue 14% cumulative, nonparticipating, nonvoting preferred stock, callable at par. In discussing the impact of the two proposals on the debt to equity ratio, one member of the board of directors stated that the resulting debt to equity ratio would be the same under either alternative because the income bonds and preferred stock should be included in the same balance sheet classification. What are the arguments (1) for, and (2) against inclusion of the subordinated income bonds and the preferred stock in the same balance sheet classification?

Case 24–3   The following information was extracted from annual reports to stockholders of three large corporations:

(1) Revenue has increased steadily for the past few years and last year rose 10% over that for the previous year to a record $1.6 billion. Earnings from operations rose 19% to $134.2 million, or $3.95 per common share after preferred dividends. Our profits have grown steadily for the last five years and have exceeded industry growth; the 19% increase in profits compares with 12% for the gas industry and 9% for all industries. (Local Gas Company)

(2) Income reinvested in the business, which also is to the benefit of stockholders, was $130.1 million, or $2.40 per common share. (Won Steel Corporation)

(3) The information below relates to Lick Company (dollar amounts are in millions):

	Year 3	Year 2	Year 1
Gross revenue	$133	$ 99	$70
Net income	$ 28	$ 18	$12
Working capital.................................	$ 34	$ 52	$87
Current ratio	2 to 1	5 to 1	10 to 1
Plant assets (net)	$275	$145	$92

Instructions

a Do you consider the information regarding the company's growth compared with industry growth presented by Local Gas Company useful to stockholders? Is there a possibility that the information may be misleading?

b Comment on the information taken from the annual report of Won Steel Corporation in view of the following additional facts for the latest year:

(1) Earnings amounted to $4.60 per share compared with an average of $6.59 per share 8 to 10 years ago.

(2) The rate earned on stockholders' equity amounted to less than 8%.

(3) The balance sheet included over $1.28 billion of short-term investments and over $268 million in cash.

c As a stockholder, would you be concerned about the decrease in the current ratio of Lick Company? Explain.

Case 24–4   As the consultant to the president of Coleman Corporation, you are asked to compute some key ratios based on the information in the comparative financial statements. These key ratios will be used by the president to convince creditors that Coleman is solvent and to support the use of going-concern valuation procedures in the financial statements. The president wants to save time by concentrating on only these key ratios.

The data requested and the computations taken from the financial statements follow:

	Year 7	Year 6
Current ratio	2.5:1	2.0:1
Quick (acid-test) ratio	0.7:1	1.2:1
Plant assets to stockholders' equity	2.6:1	2.3:1
Sales to stockholders' equity	2.5:1	2.8:1
Net income	Up 30%	Down 10%
Earnings per share of common stock	$3.12	$2.40
Equity (book value) per share of common stock	Up 5%	Up 8%

Instructions

a The president asks that you prepare a list of brief comments stating how each of these items supports the solvency and going-concern status of Coleman Corporation. These comments are to be used in the presentation of data to creditors. Prepare the comments requested, giving the implications and the limitations of each item separately and then the collective inference one may draw from them about the solvency and going-concern status of Coleman.

b Having done as the president requested in part **a,** prepare a list of additional ratio-analysis-type data for the president that you think the creditors will request to supplement the data provided in part **a.** Explain why you consider the additional data to be helpful to creditors in evaluating the solvency of Coleman Corporation.

c What warnings would you offer creditors of Coleman Corporation about the limitations of using ratio analysis to evaluate solvency and the going-concern valuations of assets?

Case 24–5 Doris Simpson, executive vice president of Cannon Corporation, was having lunch with three students who were being considered for a position as her assistant. Simpson pointed out that many of her clients were active in acquiring other companies and that ''the person who will be hired should be able to make effective overall analyses of the financial position and operating results of companies that are for sale.'' In order to get a better line on the business and financial acumen of the three students, she posed the following question to them:

Suppose that I called one of you at 10 P.M. one evening and asked you to fly to Houston the next morning to investigate the operations and financial position of Todd Corporation, which is for sale at a price of $5 million. I would like to have a preliminary report by phone before 5 P.M. on that same day and a final report within a week. Arrangements have been made for you to visit the corporate offices of Todd. What approach would you take in preparing these reports?

The three students then proceeded to summarize their approach to this hypothetical assignment.

Instructions

Assuming that you are one of the three students being considered for the position as assistant to the executive vice president of Cannon Corporation, write a brief report summarizing the areas you would evaluate and the approach you would take in preparing the preliminary and the final reports.

Case 24–6 The complete set of financial statements and notes to the financial statements for Le Bow Corporation is shown below and on pages 1268–1269.

LE BOW CORPORATION
Statement of Income and Retained Earnings
For Year Ended August 31, Year 6

Sales		$3,500,000
Less: Returns and allowances		35,000
Net sales		$3,465,000
Less: Cost of goods sold...........................		1,039,000
Gross profit on sales		$2,426,000
Less: Selling expenses	$1,000,000	
General and administrative expenses **(Note 1)** ...	1,079,000	2,079,000
Operating earnings		$ 347,000
Other revenue:		
Purchases discounts..............................	$ 10,000	
Gain from increase in value of investments in real estate	100,000	
Gain on reissuance of treasury stock	200,000	
Correction of error in prior year's income statement...	90,000	400,000
Ordinary earnings		$ 747,000
Add: Extraordinary item (gain on disposal of plant assets)		53,000
Income before income taxes		$ 800,000
Less: Income taxes expense		380,000
Net income		$ 420,000
Add: Retained earnings, beginning of year		2,750,000
Subtotal		$3,170,000
Less: Dividends (12% stock dividend declared but not distributed)	$ 120,000	
Appropriated for contingency **(Note 4)**	300,000	420,000
Unappropriated retained earnings, end of year		$2,750,000

LE BOW CORPORATION
Balance Sheet
August 31, Year 6

Assets

Current assets:

Cash	$ 80,000
Accounts receivable (net)	110,000
Inventories	130,000
Total current assets	$ 320,000

Other assets:

Investments in real estate (current fair value)	$1,508,000	
Investment in Cobb Company, at cost **(Note 2)**	160,000	
Plant assets (net)................................	4,000,000	
Goodwill **(Note 3)**	250,000	
Discount on bonds payable	42,000	
Total other assets		5,960,000
Total assets		$6,280,000

Liabilities & Stockholders' Equity

Current liabilities:

Accounts payable		$ 140,000
Income taxes payable		320,000
Stock dividend payable		120,000
Total current liabilities		$ 580,000

Other liabilities:

Payable to Oldham Company **(Note 4)**	$ 300,000	
Liability under employee pension plan...............	450,000	
Bonds payable (including portion due in one year) ...	1,000,000	
Deferred income tax credits	58,000	
Total other liabilities.............................		1,808,000
Total liabilities		$2,388,000

Stockholders' equity:

Common stock	$1,000,000	
Paid-in capital in excess of par	142,000	
Unappropriated retained earnings..................	2,750,000	
Total stockholders' equity		3,892,000
Total liabilities & stockholders' equity		$6,280,000

Notes to Financial Statements

1 Depreciation expense is included in general and administrative expenses. During the year, the company changed from the straight-line method of depreciation to the sum-of-the-years'-digits method.

2 The company owns 40% of the outstanding common stock of Cobb Company. Because the ownership is less than 50%, consolidated financial statements with Cobb are not presented.

3 As per federal income tax laws, goodwill is not amortized. The goodwill was acquired in Year 3.

4 The amount payable to Oldham Company is contingent on the outcome of a lawsuit that is currently pending. No loss is expected; however, the maximum loss would not exceed $300,000, and that amount was appropriated by a debit to the Retained Earnings ledger account.

Instructions

Identify and explain the deficiencies in the presentation of Le Bow Corporation's financial statements for the year ended August 31, Year 6. If an item appears in both financial statements, identify the deficiencies for each financial statement separately. There are no arithmetical errors in the statements. Organize your answer as follows:

a Deficiencies in the statement of income and retained earnings
b Deficiencies in the balance sheet
c Other deficiencies

PROBLEMS

24-1 Financial statements of Braley Corporation for the two years ended December 31, Year 2, follow:

BRALEY CORPORATION
Income Statements
For Years Ended December 31, Year 2 and Year 1

	Year 2	*Year 1*
Net sales	*$6,300,000*	*$4,000,000*
Costs and expenses:		
Cost of goods sold	*$4,900,000*	*$3,200,000*
Loss on disposal of plant assets	*10,000*	
Operating expenses and income taxes expense	*690,000*	*630,000*
Total costs and expenses	*$5,600,000*	*$3,830,000*
Net income	*$ 700,000*	*$ 170,000*

BRALEY CORPORATION
Statements of Stockholders' Equity
For Years Ended December 31, Year 1 and Year 2

	Common stock, $10 par	*Additional paid-in capital*	*Retained earnings*	*Total*
Balances, Jan. 1, Year 1	*$ 900,000*	*$100,000*	*$250,000*	*$1,250,000*
Net income			*170,000*	*170,000*
Cash dividends ($1 a share)			*(90,000)*	*(90,000)*
Balances, Dec. 31, Year 1	*$ 900,000*	*$100,000*	*$330,000*	*$1,330,000*

(continued)

Issuance of 10,000 shares of common stock for cash, Apr. 1, Year 2	$ 100,000	$ 25,000		$ 125,000
Net income			$ 700,000	700,000
Dividends:				
Cash ($1.25 a share)			(125,000)	(125,000)
Stock (20,000 shares)	200,000	75,000	(275,000)	
Balances, Dec. 31, Year 2	$1,200,000	$200,000	$ 630,000	$2,030,000

BRALEY CORPORATION
Balance Sheets
December 31, Year 2 and Year 1

	Year 2	Year 1
Assets		
Current assets:		
Cash	$ 480,000	$ 220,000
Accounts receivable (net)	840,000	560,000
Inventories	760,000	470,000
Total current assets	$2,080,000	$1,250,000
Plant assets	$1,330,000	$ 800,000
Less: Accumulated depreciation of plant assets	210,000	150,000
Total plant assets	$1,120,000	$ 650,000
Total assets	$3,200,000	$1,900,000
Liabilities & Stockholders' Equity		
Current liabilities:		
Accounts payable	$ 830,000	$ 440,000
Dividends payable................................	40,000	
Other current liabilities	300,000	130,000
Total current liabilities	$1,170,000	$ 570,000
Stockholders' equity:		
Common stock, $10 par	$1,200,000	$ 900,000
Additional paid-in capital	200,000	100,000
Retained earnings	630,000	330,000
Total stockholders' equity	$2,030,000	$1,330,000
Total liabilities & stockholders' equity	$3,200,000	$1,900,000

Additional Information for Year 2
(1) Braley disposed of plant assets with a cost of $100,000 and a carrying amount of $30,000.
(2) Braley acquired for cash plant assets costing $630,000.

Instructions
Compute the following for Braley Corporation for the year ended December 31, Year 2 (show computations):

a Cash provided from operations

b Earnings per share of common stock (round to the nearest cent)

c Cash dividends payout ratio for common stock (round to the nearest percent)

d Accounts receivable turnover (round to the nearest whole number)

e Inventories turnover (round to the nearest whole number)

f Quick (acid-test) ratio (round to the nearest tenth)

24-2 The stockholders' equity section of Ramo Company's December 31, Year 7, balance sheet follows:

RAMO COMPANY
Stockholders' Equity Section of Balance Sheet
December 31, Year 7

Stockholders' equity:

Common stock, $1 par, authorized 40,000,000 shares, issued and outstanding 20,000,000 shares	$ 20,000,000
Additional paid-in capital	222,000,000
Retained earnings	280,000,000
Total stockholders' equity	$522,000,000

Additional Information for Year 8

(1) On January 15, Year 8, Ramo declared a 10% common stock dividend; the market price of Ramo's common stock was $10 a share on that date.

(2) On July 1, Year 8, Ramo acquired 500,000 shares of its common stock for the treasury for $12 a share. Ramo uses the cost method of accounting for treasury stock.

(3) On October 22, Year 8, Ramo discovered a $24,000,000 understatement of its December 31. Year 7, inventories. Ramo's income tax rate is 45%.

(4) On December 15, Year 8, Ramo declared a cash dividend of $1 a share on the common stock outstanding.

(5) Ramo's net income for the year ended December 31, Year 8, was $55,000,000, after giving effect to the error in item (3) above.

Instructions

a Prepare Ramo Company's statement of stockholders' equity for the year ended December 31, Year 8, in thousands of dollars.

b Compute the following for Ramo Company for Year 8 (show computations):

(1) Earnings per share of common stock, rounded to the nearest cent

(2) Dividend payout ratio, rounded to the nearest tenth of a percent

(3) Equity (book value) per share, rounded to the nearest cent

(4) Return on common stockholders' equity, rounded to the nearest tenth of a percent

24-3 The principal stockholders of Oregon Corporation are concerned about Oregon's current financial position and return on investment. They requested your assistance in analyzing the following financial statements:

OREGON CORPORATION
Statement of Working Capital Deficit
December 31, Year 2

Current liabilities		$223,050
Less: Current assets:		
Cash	$ 5,973	
Accounts receivable (net)	70,952	
Inventories	113,125	190,050
Working capital deficit		$ 33,000

OREGON CORPORATION
Income Statement
For Year Ended December 31, Year 2

Sales	$760,200
Cost of goods sold	452,500
Gross profit on sales	$307,700
Operating expenses (including $27,980 depreciation expense)	155,660
Income before income taxes	$152,040
Income taxes expense	68,418
Net income	$ 83,622

Assets other than current assets consisted of plant assets with a carrying amount of $443,450 on December 31, Year 2.

Instructions

Compute the following for Oregon Corporation for the year ended December 31, Year 2 (show computations):

a Number of days' sales uncollected [Accounts receivable (net) on December 31, Year 1, were $66,456.]

b Inventories turnover (The inventories on December 31, Year 1, were $126,273.)

c Number of days' operations required to cover the working capital deficit

d Return on total assets as a product of assets turnover rate and net income per dollar of revenue (Total assets on December 31, Year 1, amounted to $648,220.)

24-4   Comparative balance sheets of Naylor Corporation follow:

NAYLOR CORPORATION
Comparative Balance Sheets
December 31, Year 2 and Year 1

	Year 2	Year 1
Assets		
Cash	$ 18,000	$ 12,000
Short-term investments (at cost, which is less than market value)	6,000	12,000
Accounts receivable	42,000	30,000
Less: Allowance for doubtful accounts...................	(12,000)	(6,000)

(continued)

Inventories	$ 27,000	$ 21,000
Plant assets	270,000	261,000
Less: Accumulated depreciation of plant assets	(69,000)	(60,000)
Total assets	$282,000	$270,000

Liabilities & Stockholders' Equity

Accounts payable	$ 12,000	$ 15,000
Other current liabilities	9,000	3,000
8% long-term note payable, due in Year 12	60,000	60,000
$9 preferred stock, $100 par	15,000	30,000
Common stock, $10 par	30,000	30,000
Additional paid-in capital	90,000	90,000
Retained earnings	66,000	42,000
Total liabilities & stockholders' equity	$282,000	$270,000

All sales were made on credit and amounted to $450,000 in Year 2. Gross profit on sales was 40% of sales, and net income was 10% of sales. Income taxes expense was 45% of pre-tax income.

Instructions

Compute the following for Year 2:

a Return (before income taxes expense and interest expense on the 8% long-term note payable) on total assets, December 31, Year 2

b Accounts receivable turnover (gross basis)

c Inventories turnover

d Current ratio

e Quick ratio

f Times interest earned on the 8% long-term note payable (before income taxes)

24-5 Selected statistics for Widd Company, Inc., for the three most recent years appear below:

	Year 3	Year 2	Year 1
Gross profit percentage	36%	33⅓%	30%
Inventories turnover........................	20 times	25 times	14 times
Average inventories.........................	$ 19,200	$18,000	$35,000
Average accounts receivable (net)	$100,000	$84,375	$43,750
Income tax rate	45%	45%	45%
Net income as percentage of sales	12%	7%	6%
Maximum credit period allowed to customers .	60 days	60 days	30 days

Instructions

a Prepare income statements for Widd Company, Inc., for Year 1, Year 2, and Year 3.

b Comment on the trend in sales volume, the gross profit percentage, and the net income percentage.

c Compute the accounts receivable turnover rates and comment on the trend in view of the change in credit terms in Year 2. All sales were made on credit.

24-6 You have been assigned by the acquisitions committee of a diversified enterprise to examine a potential acquisition, Ginger Company. Ginger is a merchandiser that was offered for sale because of the death of its founder and principal stockholder. Recent financial statements of Ginger are shown below and on page 1275.

GINGER COMPANY
Income Statements
For Years Ended January 31, Year 3 and Year 2

	Year 3	Year 2
Sales	$3,000,000	$2,600,000
Less: Costs and expenses:		
Cost of goods sold	$2,256,000	$2,002,000
Wages	360,000	271,000
Supplies	43,600	34,600
Depreciation	100,000	75,000
Interest	22,400	22,400
Loss on disposal of plant assets	65,000	105,000
Total costs and expenses	$2,847,000	$2,510,000
Income before income taxes	$ 153,000	$ 90,000
Income taxes expense	68,000	40,000
Net income	$ 85,000	$ 50,000
Earnings per share of common stock	$ 3.08	$ 1.81

GINGER COMPANY
Balance Sheets
January 31, Year 3, Year 2, and Year 1

	Year 3	Year 2	Year 1
Assets			
Cash	$ 130,000	$ 120,000	$ 100,000
Accounts receivable (net)	430,000	470,000	300,000
Inventories	400,000	300,000	200,000
Plant assets	900,000	800,000	700,000
Less: Accumulated depreciation	(325,000)	(250,000)	(200,000)
Total assets	$1,535,000	$1,440,000	$1,100,000
Liabilities & Stockholders' Equity			
Accounts payable	$ 300,000	$ 260,000	$ 220,000
8% notes payable, due Jan. 31,			
Year 11	280,000	280,000	
Common stock, $25 par	690,000	690,000	690,000
Retained earnings	265,000	210,000	190,000
Total liabilities & stockholders' equity	$1,535,000	$1,440,000	$1,100,000

GINGER COMPANY
Statements of Changes in Financial Position (Working Capital Concept)
For Years Ended January 31, Year 3 and Year 2

	Year 3	Year 2
Financial resources provided:		
Net income	$ 85,000	$ 50,000
Add: Depreciation expense..........................	100,000	75,000
Loss on disposal of plant assets	65,000	105,000
Working capital provided from operations	$250,000	$230,000
Notes payable issued for cash......................		280,000
Disposal of plant assets............................	10,000	
Total financial resources provided	$260,000	$510,000
Financial resources applied:		
Plant assets acquired...............................	$200,000	$230,000
Dividends declared and paid	30,000	30,000
Total financial resources applied	$230,000	$260,000
Increase in financial resources (working capital)	$ 30,000	$250,000

Composition of working capital (disregard)

Instructions

For Ginger Company for the years ended January 31, Year 3 and Year 2:

a Compute the inventories turnover rates for Year 2 and for Year 3.

b Compute the current ratio on January 31, Year 3.

c Compute the rate of return on average stockholders' equity for Year 3.

d Summarize the cash flow for Year 3 by restating the statement of changes in financial position on the cash concept. Disregard composition of working capital.

e Comment on the operating results of Ginger Company for Year 3.

24-7 Carr Company has asked for a line of trade credit from Ball Company. It is estimated that sales to Carr by Ball will amount to $2,000,000 each year. Ball is a wholesaler that sells nationally, and Carr is a retailer that has a number of stores in Oregon. Ball has had a gross profit of 60% in recent years and expects to have a similar gross profit on sales to Carr. The sales to Carr will be approximately 15% of Ball's present sales volume. Recent financial statements of Carr are presented below and on pages 1276–1277.

CARR COMPANY
Income Statements
For Years Ended December 31, Years 10, 9, and 8
(in thousands of dollars)

	Year 10	Year 9	Year 8
Net sales	$24,900	$24,500	$24,200
Cost of goods sold	18,000	17,200	16,900
Gross profit on sales	$ 6,900	$ 7,300	$ 7,300
Selling expenses	$ 4,600	$ 4,400	$ 4,300
Administrative expenses	2,700	2,400	2,300
Total expenses	$ 7,300	$ 6,800	$ 6,600

(continued)

Income (loss) before income taxes expense or			
credit	$ (400)	$ 500	$ 700
Income taxes expense (credit)	(180)	225	315
Net income (loss)	$ (220)	$ 275	$ 385

CARR COMPANY
Balance Sheets
December 31, Years 10, 9, and 8
(in thousands of dollars)

	Year 10	Year 9	Year 8
Assets			
Current assets:			
Cash	$ 1,600	$ 1,800	$ 2,600
Short-term investments (at cost)		200	400
Accounts receivable (net)	8,480	8,500	8,000
Inventories	2,800	3,200	2,800
Short-term prepayments......................	600	600	700
Total current assets	$13,480	$14,300	$14,500
Plant assets (net)............................	5,900	5,400	4,300
Total assets	$19,380	$19,700	$18,800
Liabilities & Stockholders' Equity			
Current liabilities:			
Notes payable	$ 4,200	$ 3,700	$ 3,200
Accounts payable	4,100	3,700	2,800
Other	1,000	1,125	915
Total current liabilities	$ 9,300	$ 8,525	$ 6,915
Long-term debt, 8% ($1 million extinguished on			
Dec. 31, Year 9 and Year 10)..................	1,000	2,000	3,000
Total liabilities	$10,300	$10,525	$ 9,915
Stockholders' equity	9,080	9,175	8,885
Total liabilities & stockholders' equity	$19,380	$19,700	$18,800

CARR COMPANY
Statements of Changes in Financial Position (Working Capital Concept)
For Years Ended December 31, Years, 10, 9, and 8
(in thousands of dollars)

	Year 10	Year 9	Year 8
Financial resources provided			
Net income (loss)	$ (220)	$ 275	$ 385
Add: Depreciation expense...................	500	500	400
Working capital provided from operations	$ 280	$ 775	$ 785
Disposal of plant assets.....................			200
Reissuance of treasury stock	125	115	
Total financial resources provided	$ 405	$ 890	$ 985

(continued)

Financial resources applied

Acquisition of plant assets	$ 1,000	$ 1,600	$1,200
Dividends declared		100	100
Extinguishment of long-term debt	1,000	1,000	
Total financial resources applied	$ 2,000	$ 2,700	$1,300
Increase (decrease) in working capital	$(1,595)	$(1,810)	$ (315)

Instructions

a Compute the following ratios or other measurements for Carr Company for Year 10:

(1) Rate of return on average total assets (before interest expense on long-term debt and income taxes credit)

(2) Rate of return on sales

(3) Quick (acid-test) ratio

(4) Current ratio

(5) Inventories turnover

b As part of the analysis to determine whether or not Ball Company should extend credit to Carr Company, *assume* that the ratios below were computed from Carr's financial statements. For each ratio indicate whether it is favorable, unfavorable, or neutral in the decision to grant credit to Carr. Briefly explain your choice for each ratio.

	Year 10	Year 9	Year 8
(1) Rate of return on total assets	(0.87)%	1.12%	1.96%
(2) Rate of return on sales	(0.69)%	0.99%	1.69%
(3) Quick (acid-test) ratio	1.19 to 1	1.36 to 1	1.73 to 1
(4) Current ratio	1.67 to 1	1.92 to 1	2.39 to 1
(5) Inventories turnover (times)	4.52	4.32	4.41
(6) Equity relationships:			
Current liabilities	48.0%	43.0%	36.0%
Long-term liabilities	5.0	10.5	16.0
Stockholders' equity..................	47.0	46.5	48.0
Totals	100.0%	100.0%	100.0%
(7) Asset relationships:			
Current assets	69.5%	72.5%	77.0%
Plant assets	30.5	27.5	23.0
Totals	100.0%	100.0%	100.0%

c Should Ball Company grant credit to Carr Company? Support your answer with facts given in the problem.

d What additional information, if any, should Ball Company obtain before making a final decision on Carr Company's request for credit?

24-8 Selected information taken from the financial statements for Barstow Corporation for the past four years is shown at the top of page 1278.

	Year 10	Year 9	Year 8	Year 7
Net sales	$800,000	$642,000	$624,000	$580,000
Cost of goods sold	560,000	417,300	411,840	400,200
Gross profit on sales	240,000	224,700	212,160	179,800
Net income	56,000	25,680	30,000	34,500
Accounts receivable (net)	88,000	45,000	50,000	40,000
Inventories (first-in, first-out)	80,000	125,000	82,400	102,000
Industry sales index (Year 7 = 100)	118	112	110	100

All sales were on credit terms of 2/10, n/30.

Instructions

a For each of Years 7 through 10, compute the following for Barstow Corporation and present in tabular form:

(1) Gross profit percentage

(2) Net income percentage

(3) Expenses (including income taxes but excluding cost of goods sold) as percentage of net sales

(4) Number of days' sales in ending inventories (nearest day)

(5) Number of days' sales in ending accounts receivable (nearest day)

(6) Index of Barstow Corporation's sales to industry sales index

b Briefly comment on the trend in each item (1) through (6) in part **a.**

24-9 The preferred and common stocks of Mexicali Company are listed on the New York Stock Exchange. The market price of the common stock was $19¾ a share on both December 31, Year 5 and Year 4. Mexicali's financial statements for the years ended December 31, Year 5 and Year 4, are presented below and on page 1279.

MEXICALI COMPANY
Statements of Income and Retained Earnings
For Years Ended December 31, Year 5 and Year 4
(in thousands of dollars)

	Year 5	Year 4
Net sales	$600,000	$500,000
Costs and expenses:		
Cost of goods sold	$490,000	$400,000
Operating expenses	66,000	60,000
Other expenses	7,000	6,000
Total costs and expenses	$563,000	$466,000
Income before income taxes	$ 37,000	$ 34,000
Income taxes expense	16,650	15,300
Net income	$ 20,350	$ 18,700
Retained earnings, beginning of year....................	134,500	126,200
Dividends: Preferred stock	(400)	(400)
Common stock............................	(11,800)	(10,000)
Retained earnings, end of year	$142,650	$134,500

MEXICALI COMPANY
Balance Sheets
December 31, Year 5 and Year 4
(in thousands of dollars)

	Year 5	Year 4
Assets		
Current assets:		
Cash	$ 3,500	$ 3,600
Short-term investments (at cost, which approximates market value)	13,000	11,000
Accounts receivable (net)	105,000	95,000
Inventories (at lower of first-in, first-out cost or market)	126,000	154,000
Short-term prepayments	2,500	2,400
Total current assets	$250,000	$266,000
Investments in common stock (at equity)	2,000	3,000
Plant assets (net)	311,000	308,000
Goodwill and patents (net)	6,000	6,500
Other assets	21,000	24,500
Total assets	$590,000	$608,000
Liabilities & Stockholders' Equity		
Current liabilities:		
Notes payable	$ 5,000	$ 15,000
Accounts payable	38,000	48,000
Income taxes payable	350	500
Other current liabilities	24,500	27,000
Payments due within one year on long-term debt	6,500	7,000
Total current liabilities	$ 74,350	$ 97,500
Long-term debt	169,000	180,000
Deferred income tax credits	74,000	67,000
Other liabilities	9,000	8,000
Total liabilities	$326,350	$352,500
Stockholders' equity:		
10% cumulative, nonparticipating preferred stock, $100 par and call price, authorized 50,000 shares, issued and outstanding 40,000 shares	$ 4,000	$ 4,000
Common stock, $1 par, authorized 20,000,000 shares, issued and outstanding 10,000,000 shares	10,000	10,000
Paid-in capital in excess of par: common stock	107,000	107,000
Retained earnings	142,650	134,500
Total stockholders' equity	$263,650	$255,500
Total liabilities & stockholders' equity	$590,000	$608,000

Instructions

From the foregoing information, compute items **a** through **h** (listed at the top of page 1280) for Mexicali Company for Year 5 (show supporting computations).

a Current ratio
b Quick (acid-test) ratio
c Number of days' sales in average net accounts receivable, assuming all sales were on credit
d Inventories turnover rate
e Equity (book value) per share of common stock
f Earnings per share of common stock
g Price-earnings ratio for common stock
h Dividend payout ratio (for preferred stock and common stock combined)

24-10   The income statement, unclassified balance sheet, and additional information for Maddox Company are shown below and on page 1281.

MADDOX COMPANY
Income Statement
For Year Ended December 31, Year 1

Net sales	$1,500,000
Cost of goods sold	900,000
Gross profit on sales	$ 600,000
Operating expenses and interest expense	498,000
Income before income taxes	$ 102,000
Income taxes expense	45,900
Net income	$ 56,100
Earnings per share of common stock	$ 0.90

MADDOX COMPANY
Balance Sheet
December 31, Year 1

Assets

Cash	$ 174,000
Accounts receivable (net)	566,000
Inventories	320,000
Plant assets (net)	740,000
Patents (net)	26,000
Other intangible assets (net)	14,000
Total assets	$1,840,000

Liabilities & Stockholders' Equity

Accounts payable	$ 194,000
Income taxes payable	32,000
Miscellaneous liabilities	38,000
10% bonds payable, due Year 18	300,000
7% cumulative, nonparticipating preferred stock, $100 par, callable at $110	200,000

(continued)

Common stock, no-par, 50,000 shares authorized, issued, and		
outstanding	$	400,000
Retained earnings		720,000
Treasury stock, 400 shares of preferred stock		(44,000)
Total liabilities & stockholders' equity		$1,840,000

Additional Information for Year 1

(1) There were no preferred dividends in arrears, and the balances in the Accounts Receivable and Inventories ledger accounts were unchanged.

(2) There were no changes in the Bonds Payable, Preferred Stock, Treasury Stock, or Common Stock ledger accounts.

(3) All sales were on credit.

Instructions

From the foregoing information, compute the following for Maddox Company to the nearest tenth:

a The current ratio on December 31, Year 1

b The number of times bond interest was earned during Year 1, using the theoretically preferable method

c The number of days' sales in inventories on December 31, Year 1

d The average number of days in the operating cycle during Year 1

e The equity (book value) per share of common stock on December 31, Year 1

f The rate of return on year-end common stockholders' equity for Year 1

g The debt ratio on December 31, Year 1

h The equity ratio on December 31, Year 1

24-11 Ratio analysis often is applied to test the reasonableness of the relationships among current financial data against those of prior-year financial data. Given prior financial relationships and a few key amounts, a CPA may prepare estimates of current financial data to test the reasonableness of data furnished by a client.

Carlson Corporation has in recent years maintained the following relationships among the data in its financial statements:

(1) Gross profit rate on net sales	40%
(2) Net income rate on net sales	10%
(3) Selling expenses as a percentage of net sales	15%
(4) Accounts receivable turnover	8 per year
(5) Inventories turnover	6 per year
(6) Quick (acid-test) ratio	2 to 1
(7) Current ratio...	3 to 1
(8) Quick-asset composition—8% cash, 32% short-term investments, 60% accounts receivable (net)	
(9) Assets turnover	2 per year
(10) Ratio of total assets to intangible assets	20 to 1
(11) Ratio of accumulated depreciation to cost of plant assets	1 to 3

(continued)

Carlson had net income of $120,000 for Year 15, after income taxes at the rate of 45%, which resulted in earnings of $2.60 per share of common stock.

Additional Information

(1) Capital stock authorized, issued (all in Year 2), and outstanding:
Preferred, 6% cumulative, nonparticipating, $50 par, issued at 10% in excess of par
Common, $5 par, issued at 10% in excess of par
(2) Market price of common stock on December 31, Year 15, $31.25 a share.
(3) Preferred dividends declared in Year 15, $3,000.
(4) Times interest earned in Year 15, 16 times (after interest and income taxes).
(5) The amounts of the following were the same on December 31, Year 15, as on January 1, Year 15: inventories, accounts receivable, 10% bonds payable—due Year 27, and total stockholders' equity.
(6) All purchases and sales were on credit.

Instructions

a Prepare a condensed income statement and a balance sheet for the year ended December 31, Year 15, presenting the amounts that should appear in Carlson Corporation's financial statements. Captions appearing in the balance sheet are: Current Assets, Plant Assets, Intangible Assets, Current Liabilities, Long-Term Debt, and Stockholders' Equity. In addition to the ledger accounts given in the problem, you should include accounts for Short-Term Prepayments, Other Current Liabilities, and Administrative Expenses. Show supporting computations.
b Compute the following for Year 15 (show computations): (1) rate of return on stockholders' equity, (2) price-earnings ratio for common stock, (3) dividends declared per share of common stock, and (4) dividends declared per share of preferred stock.

24-12   The stockholders' equity of Ramon Company on December 31, Year 1, was as follows:

9% cumulative, convertible preferred stock, $50 par and liquidation value, 600,000 shares authorized, no shares issued	
Common stock, $10 par, 6,000,000 shares authorized, 2,000,000 shares issued and outstanding	*$20,000,000*
Paid-in capital in excess of par: common	*7,500,000*
Retained earnings	*6,500,000*
Total stockholders' equity	*$34,000,000*

Additional Information

(1) On January 2, Year 2, Ramon issued 100,000 shares of the 9% cumulative, convertible preferred stock for $54 a share. Each share of the preferred stock, which was a common stock equivalent, was convertible to four shares of Ramon's common stock.

(2) On February 1, Year 2, Ramon acquired for the treasury 20,000 shares of its outstanding common stock at $16 a share. Ramon uses the cost method of accounting for treasury stock.

(3) On May 1, Year 2, Ramon issued 500,000 shares of previously unissued common stock at $17 a share.

(4) On November 1, Year 2, Ramon reissued 10,000 shares of treasury stock at $21 a share.

(5) On December 14, Year 2, Ramon declared the yearly cash dividend on the 9% preferred stock and a $1 per share dividend on the common stock, both payable January 14, Year 3, to stockholders of record on December 31, Year 2.

(6) On January 20, Year 3, before the nominal ledger accounts were closed for Year 2, Ramon discovered that the inventories for December 31, Year 1, had been understated by $300,000 (after-income taxes effect on Year 1 net income was $165,000). An appropriate correcting journal entry was recorded.

(7) After correction of the beginning inventories, net income of Ramon for Year 2 was $4,500,000.

Instructions

a Prepare a statement of stockholders' equity for Ramon Company for the year ended December 31, Year 2.

b Prepare the stockholders' equity section of Ramon Company's balance sheet on December 31, Year 2.

c Compute the following for Ramon Company for Year 2 (show computations):

(1) Equity (book value) per share of common stock, December 31, Year 2

(2) Return on average common stockholders' equity for Year 2

(3) Earnings per share of common stock for Year 2 (There were no other common stock equivalents or other potentially dilutive securities.)

Accounting for the Effects of Changing Prices

25

One of the primary purposes of financial statements is to provide information for decision making. Decision makers such as investors, creditors, and management realize that financial statements prepared under generally accepted accounting principles may not reflect current economic values. As a result, it has been suggested that financial statements would be more useful if historical costs were adjusted for the changing value of the dollar, or if historical costs were abandoned entirely and replaced with current fair values or with current costs.

In this chapter we describe some conceptual issues that are faced by accountants and users of financial statements when changes in the general price level or changes in the current costs of assets are incorporated in the accounting model. The final section of this chapter includes a discussion of *FASB Statement No. 89,* "Financial Reporting and Changing Prices" which encourages disclosure of *current-cost* and *inflation-adjusted* information.

FINANCIAL STATEMENTS RESTATED FOR CHANGES IN THE GENERAL PRICE LEVEL

Needed: A Stable Measurement Unit

Money is the measuring unit used in the preparation of financial statements. The dollar, or any other monetary unit, represents a unit of value; it measures the amount of purchasing power available to acquire goods and services. Implicit in the use of money as a measuring unit is the assumption that the dollar is a stable unit of value, just as the mile is a stable unit of distance and an acre is a stable unit of area. But unlike the mile and the acre, the dollar is not a stable measurement unit.

For many years the prices of goods and services in the United States economy have been rising. When the general price level rises, the value of money decreases. The *general price level* is the weighted average of the prices of goods and services in the economy and is measured by an *index* with a base year assigned a value of 100. The reciprocal of the general price-level index represents the *purchasing power* of the dollar. Thus, if the general price-level index in Year 1 is 100 and in Year 5 is 125, the current (Year 5) purchasing power of the dollar amounts to only 80% (100 ÷ 125 = 0.80) of the base-year dollar; in other words, prices have risen 25%, and the purchasing power of the dollar has decreased by 20%. The most common measurements of the general price level are: *Consumer Price Index, Producer Price Index,* and *Gross National Product Implicit Price Deflator.* The Financial Accounting Standards Board selected the Consumer Price Index for All Urban Consumers (CPI-U) for the computation of information on a constant-dollar basis.[1] Based on this index, the purchasing power of the dollar at the end of 1988 was significantly less than one-half of its purchasing power at the end of 1974.

Despite the steady erosion in the purchasing power of the dollar in the United States for more than 50 years, accountants generally have continued to assume that the value of the dollar is stable. Until recently, income tax laws have ignored changes in the purchasing power of the dollar. This unrealistic assumption is one of the reasons why traditional financial statements are considered by many users to be potentially misleading. Consequently, proposals have been made to restate the *historical-cost/nominal-dollar* financial statements to *constant purchasing power* by use of an appropriate general price-level index.

Historical Cost versus Current Fair Value

Even if the historical-cost/nominal-dollar financial statements were restated to reflect the changing value of the dollar, the resulting statements would still be presented in terms of historical costs and would not reflect the current fair values of assets. For example, a tract of land that cost $1 million would be restated at $1.5 million if the general price level had risen by 50%. However, the current fair value of the land might be $5 million because the price of land had risen more than the general price level. Historical cost reflects the current fair value of a plant asset on the date of acquisition; but a significant change in the current fair value of the asset after acquisition tends to make historical cost misleading for decision-making purposes. As a result, some users of financial statements have argued that current fair values of assets should replace historical costs as a valuation basis used in the preparation of general-purpose financial statements.

Effects of Inflation on Financial Statements

As stated earlier, the United States economy has experienced persistent inflation (increase in the general level of prices) for many years. Stated another way, the

---

[1] *FASB Statement No. 89,* "Financial Reporting and Changing Prices," FASB (Stamford: 1986), par. 8.

value of the dollar has been falling. How does inflation affect the measurement of income and the presentation of financial position for a business enterprise? Suppose that Reyes Company acquired a building for $1 million early in Year 1 when the general price-level index was 100. The building had an estimated economic life of 20 years with no residual value and had been depreciated at the rate of $50,000 a year. Assume that the general price-level index at the end of Year 5 is 200; thus, the cost of the building in constant (end-of-Year 5) purchasing power is $2 million. *The higher constant-purchasing-power cost of the building is attributed entirely to the decrease in the purchasing power of the dollar;* a doubling in the general price-level index means that a dollar at the end of Year 5 can buy only half as much as in Year 1. Financial statements prepared in accordance with generally accepted accounting principles at the end of Year 5 would include the following information relating to the building:

Data from historical-cost/nominal-dollar financial statements

REYES COMPANY
Data from Historical-Cost/Nominal-Dollar Financial Statements
For Year 5

In balance sheet		*In income statement*	
Building	$1,000,000	Depreciation expense . . .	$50,000
Less: Accumulated de-			
preciation	250,000		
Carrying amount of			
building	$ 750,000		

Is this a meaningful portrayal of economic facts? Clearly it is not. Giving effect to the 50% reduction in the purchasing power of the dollar (100% increase in the general price-level index), the information may be presented more meaningfully in constant purchasing power as follows:

Data from historical-cost/constant-purchasing-power financial statements

REYES COMPANY
Data from Historical-Cost/Constant-Purchasing-Power Financial Statements
For Year 5

In balance sheet		*In income statement*	
Building	$2,000,000	Depreciation expense . .	$100,000
Less: Accumulated de-			
preciation	500,000		
Carrying amount of			
building	$1,500,000		

Both presentations are stated in terms of historical cost; however, in the latter the historical cost is adjusted to reflect the current general price-level index. The increase of $750,000 in the carrying amount of the building would be reflected in the stockholders' equity section of the balance sheet. When financial statements are not adjusted for increases in the general price-level index, carrying amounts of depreciable plant assets and depreciation expense may be significantly understated; similarly, inventories, cost of goods sold, other nonmonetary assets, and various other expenses also may be understated. When the effects of changes in the general price-level index are ignored, net income is measured by matching costs and revenue expressed in *nominal dollars* having *different purchasing power*.

Income Measurement and Maintenance of Capital   Suppose that you purchase 1,000 pounds of sugar for $4,000 when the general price level is 100 and sell the sugar for $4,300 when the general price level is 110. How much gross profit did you realize on the transaction? By comparing your cost of $4,000 with the sales proceeds of $4,300, you conclude that you realized a gross profit of $300. However, in reaching this conclusion you are using different types of dollars. It would be more logical to say that your investment of $4,000 is now equivalent to $4,400 in terms of current purchasing power ($4,000 × 1.10 = $4,400) and that you actually lost $100 ($4,400 − $4,300 = $100) on the transaction because you cannot purchase another 1,000 pounds of sugar for $4,000 today to restock your inventory. In other words, you failed to recover your investment and thus incurred an *economic loss* (loss in purchasing power) of $100 on the transaction.

To illustrate this point with another example, suppose that a business enterprise acquired land in Year 1 for $100,000 and sold it for $200,000 in Year 11. If the general price-level index doubled during that 10-year period, thus cutting the value of money in half, the enterprise is not ''better off'' as a result of these two transactions; the $200,000 received for the land in Year 11 is equal to the $100,000 invested in Year 1. In terms of the dollar as a measuring unit, however, accountants recognize a gain of $100,000 ($200,000 − $100,000) in Year 11 under historical-cost/nominal-dollar accounting, and the government may levy a tax on the ''gain.'' Thus, by combining the Year 1 and Year 11 transactions in dollar terms, accountants conclude that the enterprise is ''better off'' (by recognizing a gain) if it recovers more than the original *number of dollars* invested in the land.

Failure to consider the changing value of money in the preparation of financial statements in a period of inflation means that what is reported as income may be, in part, a *recovery of capital*. The amount of *original capital invested in the business enterprise would not be maintained,* and taxable income, income taxes expense, and net income may be overstated. Taxable income may be overstated because depreciation expense is not large enough to offset the inflation in the prices of plant assets. This characteristic of traditional financial statements is perhaps the major argument in favor of *constant-purchasing-power* accounting. However, failure to recognize the effect of price-level changes during a period of inflation does not necessarily result in an overstatement of net income, because there may be an offsetting purchasing power gain from borrowing. This point is explained in the following section.

Monetary Items and Purchasing Power Gains and Losses   In discussions of the changing value of the dollar, balance sheet items are classified either as monetary or as nonmonetary items. Cash, certificates of deposit, notes receivable, accounts receivable, investments in nonconvertible bonds that will be held to maturity, and most liabilities are examples of *monetary items* because they represent current purchasing power or obligations to pay a fixed number of dollars. All other balance sheet items (inventories, investments in common stocks, plant assets, intangible assets, and stockholders' equity) are examples of **nonmonetary items.** A complete list of monetary and nonmonetary items is presented in the Appendix at the end of this chapter (pages 1314–1316).

Changes in the general price level give rise to **purchasing power gains and losses** as a result of an enterprise's holding monetary items. The ownership of cash or claims to cash in the form of notes receivable and accounts receivable result in a loss of purchasing power when the general price level is rising; in contrast, owing money during a period when the general price level is rising results in a gain of purchasing power because the monetary liabilities may be paid with cheaper dollars. We may summarize this point as follows: When the general price level is rising, it is advantageous to be in a **negative monetary position,** that is, to hold an excess of monetary liabilities over monetary assets; a **positive monetary position** (excess of monetary assets over monetary liabilities) results in a loss of purchasing power when the general price level is rising. To illustrate, assume the following balance sheets (in millions of dollars) for two companies at the end of Year 1:

Comparative balance sheets: historical-cost/ nominal-dollar accounting

	X Company	Y Company
Cash and notes and accounts receivable	$600	$100
Inventories and plant assets (net)	300	800
Total assets	$900	$900
Liabilities (current and long-term)	$200	$650
Stockholders' equity	700	250
Total liabilities & stockholders' equity	$900	$900

If at the end of Year 2 the general price-level index had increased by 10% (from 120 to 132, for example) and the foregoing **balance sheets remained unchanged,** the balance sheets would be restated to constant purchasing power as follows:

Comparative balance sheets: historical-cost/ constant-purchasing-power accounting

	X Company	Y Company
Cash and notes and accounts receivable . . .	$600	$100
Inventories and plant assets (net)	330 ($300 × 1.1)	880 ($800 × 1.1)
Total assets	$930	$980
Liabilities (current and long-term)	$200	$650
Stockholders' equity	770 ($700 × 1.1)	275 ($250 × 1.1)
Purchasing power gain or (loss)	(40)*	55†
Total liabilities & stockholders' equity	$930	$980

* Loss from holding cash and receivables, $60 ($600 × 0.10 = $60), reduced by the gain from borrowing, $20 ($200 × 0.10 − $20) − $40. X Company has a positive monetary position.
† Gain from borrowing, $65 ($650 × 0.10 = $65), reduced by the loss from holding cash and receivables, $10 ($100 × 0.10 = $10) = $55. Y Company has a negative monetary position.

The nonmonetary items (inventories, plant assets, and stockholders' equity) are restated to constant purchasing power by use of a **conversion factor** of 1.1 (132 ÷ 120 = 1.1).[2] Stated another way, the current general price-level index is equal to 110% of the index on the date when inventories and plant assets were acquired. **Monetary items are not restated because these items are stated in terms of constant purchasing power.**

To illustrate the fundamental effects of inflation on the financial statements of the two companies we used a static and admittedly oversimplified example; we assumed that all assets and liabilities remained unchanged while the general price-level index was rising by 10%. A later example provides a more complex illustration.

FAIR-VALUE ACCOUNTING

Significance of Changes in Value

The restatement of historical-cost/nominal-dollar financial statements for price-level changes recognizes the fact that the value of the dollar is not stable. Such financial statements require no other departures from generally accepted accounting principles. Many accountants believe that an additional departure is needed to add relevance and usefulness to financial statements. In their view, historical costs and completed transactions should be replaced by **fair-value accounting.** They argue that financial statements showing current fair values of assets and the changes in such values convey a more meaningful picture of the financial position and earning power of business enterprises.

To illustrate, suppose that a business enterprise acquired land for $100,000 and a factory building for $600,000. The building is being depreciated over a 30-year economic life with no residual value, or $20,000 a year. During the first 10 years the current fair values of the land and building increased substantially. At the end of the 10-year period (during which the general price level remained stable), it was apparent that the land and building were worth considerably more than their carrying amounts. As a result, the financial statements for the enterprise in the eleventh year showed: (1) assets and stockholders' equity that were substantially below current fair value; (2) net income that was overstated because the full economic cost of using the building was not recognized in annual depreciation expense; and (3) rates of return (on assets and stockholders' equity) that were overstated, because what essentially was capital recovery in terms of current prices was being reported as a part of net income and because assets and stockholders' equity were understated.

Assuming that at the beginning of the eleventh year the current fair value of the land was $180,000 and the current fair value of the building was $1,000,000 (cost if new of $1,500,000 less depreciation to date on such cost of $500,000), the appraisal **might** be recorded as illustrated at the top of page 1291.

The annual depreciation expense on the building would be $50,000

---

[2]The adjustment of financial statements for changes in the general price-level index generally is facilitated by computing the relationship between the current index and the base-year index as a **conversion factor** in decimal form. For example, a current index of 126.9 and a base-year (or date-of-transaction) index of 90 gives a conversion factor of 1.41 (126.9 ÷ 90 = 1.41).

($1,500,000 ÷ 30 years = $50,000) to reflect the current cost of building services consumed each year. The balance sheet would show land and building at amounts approximating current fair value, and net income would represent the amount by which the enterprise was "better off" after recovering the current fair value of the remaining building services over the next 20 years, assuming that no further value changes occurred during that period.

Possible journal entry to record current fair values of plant assets

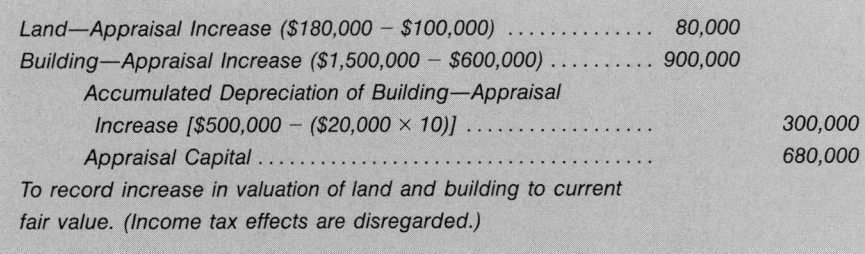

Land—Appraisal Increase ($180,000 − $100,000)	80,000	
Building—Appraisal Increase ($1,500,000 − $600,000)	900,000	
Accumulated Depreciation of Building—Appraisal		
Increase [$500,000 − ($20,000 × 10)]		300,000
Appraisal Capital		680,000
To record increase in valuation of land and building to current		
fair value. (Income tax effects are disregarded.)		

Relationship between Constant-Purchasing-Power Accounting and Fair-Value Accounting

The use of fair-value accounting does not mean that changes in the general price level would be ignored. Constant-purchasing-power accounting and fair-value accounting are complementary responses to different measurement problems. *The two approaches are not mutually exclusive alternatives.* Dealing with one is not a substitute for dealing with the other, and either or both approaches may be adopted in financial statements. Restatement of financial statements for general price-level changes does not deal with specific price changes, and fair-value accounting does not deal specifically with inflation. The different alternatives that may be followed in the preparation of financial statements are:

1   Historical cost/nominal dollars

2   Historical cost/constant purchasing power

3   Current fair value, without separate identification of the effects of general price-level changes

4   Current fair value, with the effects of general price-level changes shown separately

Financial statements adjusted for changes in the general price level are based on historical cost; however, the unit of measurement (the dollar) is adjusted to reflect changes in its general purchasing power. In contrast, *fair-value accounting is a departure from historical cost* because the current fair values for assets are derived from appraisals that reflect both changes in the general price level and changes in the relative price levels of specific goods. Thus, fair-value accounting represents a clear break from historical cost for a particular business enterprise. For example, if M Company and N Company acquired identical assets on different dates and at different prices, historical-cost/constant-purchasing-power accounting would give different adjusted values for the assets of each enterprise. However, fair-value accounting would give the *same value* for the assets of both enterprises because fair-value accounting is not tied to historical costs.

If changes in the general price level *are not* incorporated in fair-value financial statements, the difference between historical costs and current fair values of assets is referred to as an *unrealized holding gain or loss;* the unrealized holding gain or loss, net of the tax effect, is reported as a separate item in the income statement. If changes in the general price level *are* incorporated in fair-value financial statements, the unrealized holding gain or loss (difference between historical costs and current fair values of assets) consists of (1) a net purchasing power gain or loss, and (2) the net gain or loss resulting from changes in the relative values of specific assets. These two distinct types of net gains or losses would be reported separately in the income statement.

Use of Current Fair Values in Financial Statements of Business Enterprises

Proposals to incorporate current fair values in accounting measurements are not new. For example, fair values are used in the application of the lower-of-cost-or-market rule to the valuation of inventories and marketable equity securities, and assets may be written down to current fair value in a quasi-reorganization. In such cases the use of current fair values results in a reduction in the carrying amounts of assets *below* cost (or carrying amount in terms of historical cost). However, current fair values also are used when such values exceed historical cost. For example, marketable securities held by mutual funds and inventories of certain metals and agricultural products frequently are reported at current fair (or market) value.

Use of Current Fair Values in Personal Financial Statements

Personal financial statements are issued for individuals or families to organize and plan their financial affairs or for obtaining credit, estate planning, and similar purposes. In *Statement of Position 82-1,* "Accounting and Financial Reporting for Personal Financial Statements," the Accounting Standards Division of the American Institute of Certified Public Accountants supported the use of current fair values in personal financial statements as follows:[3]

> The primary focus of personal financial statements is a person's assets and liabilities, and the primary users of personal financial statements normally consider estimated current value information to be more relevant for their decisions than historical cost information. Lenders require estimated current value information to assess collateral, and most personal loan applications require estimated current value information. Estimated current values are required for estate, gift, and income tax planning, and estimated current value information about assets is often required in federal and state filings of candidates for public office.
>
> The Accounting Standards Division therefore believes personal financial statements should present assets at their estimated current values and liabilities

---

[3]*Statement of Position 82-1,* "Accounting and Reporting for Personal Financial Statements," AICPA (New York: 1982), par. 3–4.

at their estimated current amounts at the date of the financial statements. . . . This Statement of Position explains how the estimated current values of assets and the estimated current amounts of liabilities should be determined and applied in the preparation and presentation of personal financial statements.

Estimates of Current Fair Value

Thus far, we have mentioned the possibility of replacing historical costs of assets with current fair values without specifying how these values might be determined. The concept of current fair value most widely referred to in legal proceedings is "an exchange price that a willing and informed purchaser and an equally willing and informed seller would reach through negotiation." This should not be confused with *market value,* which is the price obtainable currently for any asset. No single method of estimating current fair value is entirely satisfactory; therefore, in order to be able to evaluate intelligently the arguments for and against fair-value accounting, it may be helpful to identify some of the methods used to estimate current fair value.

Capitalization of Net Cash Inflows In theory, the ideal way to estimate the current fair value or *economic value* of an asset is to compute the present discounted amount of the probable future net cash inflows expected to result from the use of the asset. This is known as *direct valuation.* A limitation of the direct valuation approach is that estimates of future net cash inflows are likely to be highly subjective. More important, the earnings and cash inflows of a business enterprise are a joint product of all its resources, and it is virtually impossible to identify the contribution to earnings and cash inflows of a particular asset. The concept of direct valuation, although somewhat impractical for the valuation of specific assets, is useful for appraising the merits of two *indirect valuation* methods discussed below.

Exit Values The *current exit value* of an asset is the amount that could be realized from its current sale; the *expected exit value* of an asset is the amount of cash to which the asset is expected to be converted in the course of operations. Exist values may be viewed as current fair values only for assets that are in fact offered for sale, and as minimum values for assets that are continued in use. However, in some cases the current fair values of assets may be materially above exit values. Exit values are related to, but are not identical to, market values because exit values may imply an urgent need to sell. Although reasonable estimates of exit values may be made for assets such as investments in marketable equity securities and inventories, estimates of exit values for plant assets and intangible assets, for example, may be quite difficult to obtain.

Current Cost The *current cost* of an asset is the estimated cost of acquiring the same service potential provided by the asset, adjusted for estimated depreciation since acquisition.[4] Current cost may be approximated by applying an appropriate *specific-price index* to the historical cost of assets, particularly plant assets. Alternatively, direct pricing (for example, vendors' invoices) may be used to determine current cost. Specific-price indexes are available for broad categories of plant as-

---

[4]*FASB Statement No. 89,* par. 18.

sets. The application of specific-price indexes to estimate the current cost of plant assets is illustrated as follows:

Estimates of current cost of plant assets by use of specific price indexes

Assets	Historical cost	Specific-price indexes on date of acquisition	Current specific-price indexes	Conversion factors	Current cost
Building	$200,000	100	125	125/100	$250,000
Less: Accumulated depreciation	60,000	100	125	125/100	75,000
Carrying amount of building	$140,000				$175,000
Land	400,000	120	168	168/120	560,000

The building was acquired for $200,000 when the specific-price index for building construction in this industry was 100. Because the index now is 125, the historical cost of the building is restated to current cost of $250,000 ($200,000 × 1.25 = $250,000); accumulated depreciation is similarly adjusted. The specific-price index of land costs in the geographic area where the land is located increased from 120 to 168 since the land was acquired; therefore, the historical cost of the land, $400,000 is multiplied by 1.40 (168 ÷ 120 = 1.40) to estimate the current cost of $560,000 ($400,000 × 1.40 = $560,000).

HISTORICAL DEVELOPMENT OF ACCOUNTING PRINCIPLES FOR EFFECTS OF CHANGING PRICES

The issues of whether and how to reflect price changes in financial statements have been among the major questions facing the accounting profession. In the academic literature alone, an enormous literature has developed concerning these issues. Accounting policy makers have been reluctant to require formal disclosures of the effects of price changes in the financial statements, and have never required the restated amounts to be disclosed in the primary statements.[5]

Accounting Principles Board *Statement No. 3* indicated that historical-cost financial statements adjusted for inflation may provide useful information not available in the primary statements. APB *Statements* are not recognized formally as GAAP, and *Statement No. 3* did not require restatement but allowed general price-level financial statements as long as they were not presented as the primary statements.[6]

In the 1970s, both the Financial Accounting Standards Board and the Securi-

---

[5]Write-downs of assets, the lower-of-cost-or-market method, and other required accounting measurements *do* incorporate price-level changes, but there has been no pronouncement requiring systematic restatement of accounts for price changes in the primary financial statements.

[6]*APB Statement No. 3,* ''Financial Statements Restated for General Price-Level Changes,'' AICPA (New York: 1969).

ties and Exchange Commission considered proposed requirements for disclosing the effects of changing prices. The FASB decided that the costs of such disclosures would exceed their benefits, and that many users would be unprepared to interpret them in a meaningful way.

During the late 1970s, inflation increased significantly in the United States. The SEC began to require certain large firms to disclose the replacement cost of selected income statement and balance sheet items. When the FASB issued *Statement No. 33,* the SEC's requirement was revoked.

FASB Statement No. 33, issued in 1979, was a major departure from previous accounting principles and reflected the FASB's concern about the major effects of price changes on financial statements. For many business entities in the 1970s, income adjusted for inflation was a small fraction of reported income. The *Statement* required supplementary information on price changes to be included in annual reports of corporations with total assets exceeding $1 billion, or with inventories and gross property, plant, and equipment exceeding $125 million. For the first time, the accounting profession had mandated formal recognition of price changes in financial statements. These supplementary disclosures appeared in the footnotes.

The disclosures included both constant purchasing power adjustments and current-cost (specific-price) adjustments. The disclosures involved restating the following items: sales; income from continuing operations; net assets; inventories; property, plant, and equipment; and other items. The purchasing power gain or loss was also required to be disclosed. Many of the provisions in *FASB Statement No. 33* continue on in the present governing pronouncement *(FASB Statement No. 89).* Between *Statement No. 33* and *Statement No. 89,* the FASB issued a number of statements revising and amending *Statement No. 33.*[7]

FASB Statement No. 82 was the most significant of these because it revoked certain constant purchasing power disclosure requirements. This reflected the greater importance attached to specific-price changes relative to inflation adjustments.

CURRENT GENERALLY ACCEPTED ACCOUNTING PRINCIPLES

Current accounting principles in this area are embodied in *FASB Statement No. 89.*[8] The *Statement removes* the *Statement No. 33* reporting requirements for the

---

[7]*FASB Statement No. 39,* "Financial Reporting and Changing Prices: Specialized Assets—Mining and Oil and Gas," FASB (Stamford: 1980); *FASB Statement No. 40,* "Financial Reporting and Changing Prices: Specialized Assets—Timberlands and Growing Timber," FASB (Stamford: 1980); *FASB Statement No. 41,* "Financial Reporting and Changing Prices: Specialized Assets—Income Producing Real Estate," FASB (Stamford: 1980); *FASB Statement No. 46,* "Financial Reporting and Changing Prices: Motion Picture Films," FASB (Stamford: 1981); *FASB Statement No. 54,* "Financial Reporting and Changing Prices: Investment Companies," FASB (Stamford: 1982); *FASB Statement No. 69,* "Disclosures about Oil and Gas Producing Activities," FASB (Stamford: 1982); *FASB Statement No. 70,* "Financial Reporting and Changing Prices: Foreign Currency Translation," FASB (Stamford: 1982); *FASB Statement No. 82,* "Financial Reporting and Changing Prices: Elimination of Certain Disclosures," FASB (Stamford: 1984).

[8]This *Statement* is effective for all financial statements issued after December 2, 1986, applies to all business enterprises, and supercedes all previous FASB *Statements* on accounting for changing prices.

supplementary disclosure of the effects of price changes, but continues to *encourage* the disclosure. Should an enterprise choose to disclose such information, *FASB Statement No. 89* provides recommended guidelines for measurement and presentation of that information, and suggests certain minimum disclosures.[9]

The FASB combined the previous *Statements* into a recommended set of disclosures. Other forms of presentation are not discouraged. For example, a business entity may choose to *comprehensively restate* all financial statement accounts for general and specific price changes. The example to follow illustrates the minimum disclosures, but the procedures can be expanded to the entire set of accounts in much the same fashion.

Given the indefinite nature of current-cost estimates, the lack of general applicability of the inflation rate to specific resources, and the lack of agreement on the usefulness of the disclosures in general, the FASB does not hold these disclosures to the same degree of accuracy required in the primary financial statements.[10] The major disclosures fall into two groups: (1) a five-year summary, and (2) current-year disclosures. Both include current-cost and inflation adjustments. The major provisions follow.[11]

I. Five-Year Summary of Selected Financial Data

The five-year summary allows meaningful comparisons of important financial statistics across several years. The data provided in the summary are stated in terms of constant dollars at the same point in time.

For each of the five most recent years, including the current reporting year, the following nine amounts are disclosed, restated to dollars of constant purchasing power:

1   Net sales and other operating revenues

2   Income from continuing operations, on a current-cost basis. Only cost of goods sold, depreciation, depletion, and amortization expense require restatement in this calculation

3   Purchasing power gain or loss on net monetary items

4   Change in current cost (or recoverable amount if lower) of inventory and property, plant, and equipment, net of inflation

5   Aggregate foreign currency translation adjustment[12]

6   Net assets on a current-cost basis

7   Income from continuing operations per common share, on a current-cost basis

8   Cash dividends declared, per common share

9   Market price per common share, at year-end

---

[9]*Ibid.*, par. 3.
[10]*Ibid.*, par. 48.
[11]*Ibid.*, par. 7–11.
[12]Foreign currency translation adjustments are discussed in advanced accounting courses and are not discussed further in this chapter.

Any one of the following bases may be used for restating the above disclosures to dollars of constant purchasing power:

a. Average-of-current-year constant purchasing power.

b. End-of-current-year constant purchasing power.

c. Base-period constant purchasing power. (The base period presently used is 1967, for which the CPI-U is 100.)

The relevant CPI-U for each of five years in the summary is also disclosed.

II. Disclosures for the Current Year

If income from continuing operations on a current-cost/constant purchasing power basis is significantly different from income from continuing operations reported in the primary income statement, the following five amounts are required disclosures:[13]

1   Income from continuing operations on a current-cost basis. Only cost of goods sold, depreciation, depletion, and amortization expense require restatement in this calculation

2   Purchasing power gain or loss on net monetary items

3   Ending current cost (or recoverable amount if lower) of inventory and property, plant, and equipment

4   Change in current cost (or recoverable amount if lower) of inventory and property, plant, and equipment, net of inflation

5   Aggregate foreign currency translation adjustment

Most of current-year disclosures are also present in the five-year summary. The methods of restatement to constant purchasing power allowed for the five-year summary apply to the current-year disclosures as well. Items 2 and 4 of the current disclosures are affected by this choice.

Income from continuing operations on a current-cost basis is reported exclusive of the other items of required disclosure. Although these items are separate, they may appear in the same statement, may be presented in a reconciliation format, or may appear in footnotes.

III. Additional Disclosures

Beyond the five-year summary and current-year disclosures, *FASB Statement No. 89* requires disclosure of information concerning the basis for the above calculations. This additional information is intended to assist users to understand the effects of changing prices on the enterprise. Specifically, the following are required:

---

[13]*Ibid.*, par. 11.

1   An explanation of the disclosures included and a discussion of their significance in terms of the enterprise

2   The principal types of information used to calculate the current-cost information

3   Any difference in depreciation methods, useful lives, and salvage values used in depreciation calculations between the primary financial statements and the supplementary disclosures.

The FASB's minimum supplementary disclosure guidelines focus on those accounts most susceptible to the effects of changing prices. Cost of goods sold, amortizations, depreciation, and depletion often represent large dollar amounts and are the result of expense recognition of expenditures occurring in previous years. Many other expenses represent cash outflows in the current year and are therefore not affected by price changes to the same degree.

Property, plant, and equipment is also sensitive to price changes. It is often a very substantial percentage of total assets and represents older dollars. Intangibles are often of lesser amount and less certain benefit. Many long-term liabilities are monetary and are therefore not subject to adjustment.

Further Measurement and Disclosure Guidelines

Within the above disclosure guidelines, several choices remain for the reporting enterprise. The method of restatement to constant purchasing power was one. Other measurement and disclosure choices and guidelines follow.

1   The estimate of current inventory cost is either the purchase or production cost to replace existing inventory.

2   The estimate of current cost of property, plant, and equipment may be any one of the following: (*a*) cost of a new asset with the service potential of the original asset (when new), reduced by depreciation; (*b*) cost of a used asset of the same condition and age as the present asset; or (*c*) the cost of a new asset with different service potential, adjusted for the difference in service value between the new and the present asset, reduced by depreciation.

3   In developing the current costs of inventory and property, plant, and equipment, either direct pricing (for example, vendors' invoices and standard manufacturing costs) or indexation may be used. Indexation is the application of internal or external *specific* price indexes to the assets in question. These specific indexes apply to broad categories of plant assets.

4   If income from continuing operations adjusted for inflation is not significantly different from income from continuing operations on a current-cost basis, inflation adjustments may be substituted for current-cost information. In this case, income from continuing operations may be restated on a constant-dollar basis (through adjustment of cost of goods sold, amortizations, depreciation, and depletion). The other disclosures continue to be required except for the change in current cost of inventory and property, plant, and equipment, net of inflation.

5   Last-in, first-out (lifo) inventory amounts from the primary financial statements provide acceptable approximations of cost of goods sold on a current-cost basis. An adjustment for the effect of changing prices on any lifo layer liquidations must be made.

6   The recoverable amount of inventory and property, plant, and equipment is the cash amount expected to be received from *sale* or *use* of the asset. The market value (from sale) is employed only if the asset is to be sold in the near future. If the recoverable amount is permanently lower than current cost, the recoverable amount is to be used in the supplementary disclosures in place of current cost. In ongoing business enterprises it is expected that the recoverable amount (in use) will exceed the current cost, otherwise the asset would not have been purchased.

7   The supplementary disclosures encouraged by the FASB need not be present in interim reports or presented on a segmental basis (although the latter is recommended).

8   Income taxes expense is specifically exempt from adjustment for changing prices.

9   Additional disclosures are required for entities with significant investments in natural resources (not discussed further in this chapter).

The next section illustrates these disclosure guidelines with a comprehensive example.

ILLUSTRATION OF *FASB STATEMENT NO. 89* DISCLOSURES

A relatively simple set of financial statements and other information for Baker Company is used to illustrate the application of the *FASB Statement No. 89* measurement and disclosure guidelines.

Background Information

BAKER COMPANY
Balance Sheets (Historical-Cost/Nominal-Dollar Basis)
December 31, Year 4 and Year 5

Assets	Year 4	Year 5
Monetary assets (cash and receivables)	$200,000	$260,000
Inventories (first-in, first-out cost)	150,000	130,000
Land	40,000	40,000
Equipment	200,000	200,000
Less: Accumulated depreciation	(80,000)	(100,000)
Total assets	$510,000	$530,000

(continued)

Liabilities & Stockholders' Equity

Current liabilities	$ 80,000	$ 34,000
Long-term liabilities	100,000	116,000
Common stock, $1.40 par	140,000	140,000
Additional paid-in capital	160,000	160,000
Retained earnings	30,000	80,000
Total liabilities & stockholders' equity	$510,000	$530,000

BAKER COMPANY
Statement of Income and Retained Earnings
(Historical-Cost/Nominal-Dollar Basis)
For Year Ended December 31, Year 5

Sales (14,000 units)		$800,000
Cost of goods sold:		
Beginning inventories (first-in, first-out cost − 3,750 units)	$150,000	
Purchases	500,000	
Cost of goods available for sale	$650,000	
Less: Ending inventories (first-in, first-out cost − 3,000 units)	130,000	
Cost of goods sold		520,000
Gross profit on sales......................................		$280,000
Operating expenses (excluding depreciation)	$ 96,000	
Depreciation expense	20,000	116,000
Income before income taxes...............................		$164,000
Income taxes expense		74,000
Income from continuing operations		$ 90,000
Retained earnings, Jan. 1, Year 5		30,000
Less: Dividends (paid Dec. 31, Year 5)		(40,000)
Retained earnings, Dec. 31, Year 5		$ 80,000

(1) Year 5 beginning inventory was purchased at the end of Year 4.
(2) The land and equipment were acquired at the beginning of Year 1. The equipment has a 10-year useful life and zero residual value, and is depreciated on the straight-line basis.
(3) 100,000 shares of common stock were outstanding throughout Year 5.
(4) Sales, purchases, and operating expenses (excluding depreciation) took place evenly throughout the year. Inventories are priced on a first-in, first-out (fifo) basis. Goods in ending inventory were acquired evenly during the year.
(5) The dividend was declared and paid on December 31, Year 5.
(6) The current and long-term liabilities are monetary items.

Selected CPI-U Indexes

	Average	End-of-year
Year 5...	157.5	163.8
Year 4...	148.0	150.0
Year 3...	136.0	142.0
Year 2...	128.0	131.0
Year 1...	110.0	118.0

BAKER COMPANY
Current-Cost Information

	Dec. 31, Year 4	Dec. 31, Year 5
Inventory	$150,000	$144,000
Land	70,000	80,000
Equipment	360,000	380,000

(1) The current cost of equipment as shown represents the cost of a new asset with similar service potential to that of Baker Company's equipment when new.
(2) In all cases, the recoverable amounts exceeded the current cost amounts.
(3) Baker Company used specific-price-level indexes and vendors' invoices to estimate the current-cost amounts.

BAKER COMPANY
Data for Five-Year Summary
As Originally Reported
At Average-of-Year CPI-U

Year	1	2	3	4	5*
Sales (000s)	$300	$450	$650	$700	$800
Common stock shares outstanding (000s)	100	100	100	100	100
Income from continuing operations, current-cost basis	$10,000	$12,000	$ 8,000	$ (4,000)	
Purchasing power gain (loss)	1,500	(2,000)	(2,200)	2,800	
Excess of increase in specific prices of inventory over inflation	12,600	39,210	37,640	48,110	
Excess of increase in specific prices of property, plant, and equipment over inflation	10,680	2,200	6,000	12,800	
Ending net assets, current-cost basis (000s)	$280	$310	$330	$426	
Per-share information: Income from continuing operations, current-cost basis	0.10	0.12	0.08	(0.04)	
Cash dividend declared	0.10	0.10	0.30	0.30	0.40
Market price, year-end	6.00	8.25	10.50	12.00	13.30

*The omitted Year 5 values are determined in the analysis to follow.

FASB Statement No. 89 Supplementary Disclosures for Year 5

The Year 5 disclosures are illustrated first as the current year affects the five-year summary. Baker Company chooses the average-year CPI-U purchasing power option for all constant-dollar restatements. All constant-dollar amounts therefore reflect the average Year 5 general price level.

1   *Income from continuing operations* for Baker Company requires two accounts to be adjusted to the current-cost basis: Cost of Goods Sold and Depreciation. Baker Company uses fifo. 14,000 units were sold in Year 5. The average current cost per unit is applied to the units sold because sales were assumed to occur evenly throughout the year.

$$\frac{\text{Cost of goods sold}}{\text{on current-cost basis}} = \text{(units sold)(average current cost per unit)}$$
$$= (14,000)(\$150,000/\$3,750 + \$144,000/\$3,000)/2$$
$$= 14,000(\$40 + \$48)/2$$
$$= 14,000(\$44) = \$616,000$$

The $616,000 adjusted cost of goods sold may be interpreted as an estimate of the cost of goods sold on a replacement-cost basis. Some accountants argue that this value is a better representation of the true expense on a going-concern basis. The difference between the current cost and historical cost ($96,000 = $616,000 − $520,000) is the amount of *reported* income that must be retained for replacement of inventory sold in Year 5 for Baker Company to maintain its capital. If Baker Company distributed all its reported income in Year 5, it would have *divested* itself of $96,000 capital that will be required to replenish inventory.

Baker Company uses the same depreciation method for the supplemental disclosures and the primary statements. Depreciation expense on a current-cost basis is the product of average current cost (reduced by residual value) and the fraction appropriate to the depreciation method used. In Baker Company's case:

$$\frac{\text{Depreciation expense on}}{\text{a current-cost basis}} = \text{(average current equipment cost)}/10$$
$$= [(\$360,000 + \$380,000)/2]/10$$
$$= [\$370,000]/10$$
$$= \$37,000$$

The current-cost depreciation expense is based on the cost of a *new* asset (with a service potential similar to that of the original asset when new). The assumption is that the company will eventually *replace* the equipment. The $37,000 represents the depreciation that would have been recognized by Baker Company in Year 5 had the equipment been restated to average current cost. It reflects the reduction from net income needed to avoid disinvestment, on a going-concern basis. Other methods of depreciation would be applied in their usual fashion, to the average current cost ($370,000) rather than the gross historical cost ($200,000).

The effect of specific price changes on the two expenses requiring adjustment has been considerable, as shown below.

BAKER COMPANY
Effect of Specific Price Changes on Cost of Goods Sold and Depreciation
Income before Continuing Operations on a Current-Cost Basis

	As reported in primary income statement	Current-cost basis	Excess of current cost over reported amount
Cost of goods sold	$520,000	$616,000	$96,000
Depreciation expense	20,000	37,000	17,000
Increase in expenses from current-cost restatement			$(113,000)
Income from continuing operations as reported			90,000
Income from continuing operations, current cost			$ (23,000)

On a going-concern basis, using current costs as an estimate of the replacement cost of inventories and equipment, Baker Company failed to earn income in Year 5 sufficient to cover capital needs in the future.

2 *The purchasing power gain or loss on net monetary items* may be computed several different ways. Through its examples, *FASB Statement No. 89* recommends restating the beginning and ending net monetary balances to the average CPI-U. Specific changes in net monetary items are assumed to have occurred at the average CPI-U.[14] The same logic used in the earlier examples of purchasing power gains and losses is employed in this example. The difference is that changes in net monetary items occurred during Year 5. The computation of the purchasing power loss for Baker Company appears below.

---

[14]A more precise calculation would apply the daily CPI-U to each change in net monetary items.

BAKER COMPANY
Computation of Purchasing Power Loss
For Year Ended December 31, Year 5

	Historical-cost/ nominal-dollar basis	Conversion factors	Historical-cost/ constant-purchasing-power basis
Net monetary items, Jan. 1, Year 5:			
Monetary assets (cash and receivables)	$ 200,000		
Less: Current liabilities	(80,000)		
Long-term liabilities	(100,000)		
Net monetary items, Jan. 1, Year 5	$ 20,000	1.05 (A)	$ 21,000

(continued)

Add: Sources of net monetary items during Year 5:			
Sales..........................		800,000	1.00 (B)	800,000
Subtotals		$820,000		$821,000
Less: Uses of net monetary items during Year 5:			
Purchases	$ 500,000		1.00 (B)	$500,000
Operating expenses (excluding depreciation expense)	96,000		1.00 (B)	96,000
Income taxes expense	74,000		1.00 (B)	74,000
Dividends.....................	40,000		0.962 (C)	38,480
Total uses of net monetary items during Year 5...........		710,000		$708,480
Net monetary items as restated, Dec. 31, Year 5, if there were no purchasing power gain or loss				$112,520
Net monetary items on hand, Dec. 31, Year 5:			
Monetary assets (cash and receivables)	$ 260,000			
Less: Current liabilities	(34,000)			
Long-term liabilities	(116,000)	$110,000	0.962 (D)	105,820
Purchasing power loss for Year 5 ...				$ 6,700

(A) The amount of net monetary items on Jan. 1, Year 5, is rolled forward by multiplying $20,000 by the conversion factor of 1.05, which is the ratio of the Year 5 average price index to the price index on Jan. 1, Year 5 (157.5 ÷ 150.0 = 1.05).
(B) Sales, purchases, operating expenses, and income taxes expense are assumed to occur at the average CPI-U.
(C) Dividends were paid on Dec. 31, Year 5, and therefore are restated to average CPI-U. The conversion factor is 157.5/163.8 = 0.962.
(D) 0.962 = 157.5/163.8

Baker Company maintained a net monetary *asset* position throughout Year 5, a year in which the general price level increased. For Baker Company to have experienced no loss in general purchasing power, it would have had to own $112,520 of net monetary items (in average Year 5 dollars) at the close of Year 5. However, its net monetary asset balance on December 31, Year 5, was only $105,820 in average Year 5 dollars. The loss occurred because it increased its net monetary asset position in a time of rising prices.

In general, during inflation, a purchasing power gain occurs if the restated ending net monetary liability balance exceeds the actual ending balance, or if the restated ending net monetary asset balance is less than the actual ending balance. On the other hand, a loss occurs if the restated ending net monetary asset balance exceeds the actual balance, or if the restated ending net monetary liability balance is less than the actual ending balance.

3 *The ending current cost of inventory and property, plant, and equipment* will reflect the present cost to replace the current service potential of these assets. Current cost depreciation (in item 1 above) reflected the assumption of replacement of service potential equivalent to the original asset when new. However, the *balance sheet* value for property, plant, and equipment at current cost must reflect the *present* service potential, at current cost. In general, this is the ending current cost of a new asset of service potential similar to that of the original asset when new, less accumulated depreciation to the balance sheet date based on that ending current cost. The accumulated depreciation to date would reflect the depreciation method, useful life, and residual value.

The ending current cost of inventory is given ($144,000). The ending cost of equipment is $190,000 [= $380,000 − 0.5($380,000)], as the asset has been employed by Baker Company for one-half its useful life at the end of Year 5. This current cost represents an estimate of the replacement cost of the current service potential of the original asset. The current cost of equipment *at the end of Year 4* was $216,000 [= $360,000(0.60)], as only 40% of the useful life had been consumed by that time. The current cost at the end of each year is used in this calculation.

The ending current cost of land is given ($80,000). Land is not depreciated and therefore requires no adjustment.

4 *The change in current cost of inventory, and property, plant, and equipment, net of inflation,* recognizes the effect of both types of price changes on important asset holdings. The change in current cost is affected by physical quantity changes. For example, the *quantity* of inventory was reduced 750 units during Year 5.

The change in current cost for the year is determined before the inflation adjustment is applied. The calculations for Baker Company follow.

BAKER COMPANY
Year 5 Change in Current Costs, Net of Inflation

	Current cost	Conversion factor	Current cost at average CPI-U
Inventory			
Beginning balance	$ 150,000[1]	1.05[a]	$ 157,500
Purchases	500,000[2]	1.00[b]	500,000
Cost of goods sold	(616,000)[3]	1.00[b]	(616,000)
	$ 34,000		$ 41,500
Ending balance	144,000[1]	0.962[c]	138,528
Increase before inflation	$ 110,000		
Increase net of inflation	97,028		$ 97,028
Inflation effect	$ 12,972		

(continued)

Land

Beginning balance	$ 70,000[1]	1.05[a]	$ 73,500
Ending balance	80,000[1]	0.962[c]	76,960
Increase before inflation	$ 10,000		
Increase net of inflation	3,460		$ 3,460
Inflation effect	$ 6,540		

Equipment

Beginning balance	$ 216,000[4]	1.05[a]	$ 226,800
Depreciation	(37,000)[3]	1.00[b]	(37,000)
	$ 179,000		$ 189,800
Ending balance	190,000[4]	0.962[c]	182,780
Increase before inflation	$ 11,000		
Decrease net of inflation	(7,020)		$ (7,020)
Inflation effect	$ 18,020		

[1] Given information.
[2] The historical cost of purchases was the current cost at time of purchase.
[3] From item 1, income from continuing operations on a current-cost basis.
[4] From item 2, ending current cost of inventory and property, plant, and equipment.
[a] $157.5/150 = 1.05$
[b] Assumed to occur evenly throughout the year.
[c] $157.5/163.8 = 0.962$

The above calculations remove the effect of inflation from the total increase in current cost (a holding gain measured in current-cost nominal dollars), leaving the increase in current cost measured in dollars of constant purchasing power. The calculation is similar to the purchasing power gain or loss. Consider the inventory current-cost column. Had there been no change in current cost of inventories, Baker Company would have ended Year 5 with $34,000 inventory at current cost. The cost to replace or reproduce inventory increased dramatically, however, and the company ended Year 5 with $144,000 at current cost, an increase of $110,000 in nominal current-cost dollars.

The application of the inflation adjustment allows measurement of all current-cost amounts at the same point in time. Had the current-cost amounts kept pace with inflation, Baker Company would have ended Year 5 with $41,500 of inventory at current cost. But the company ended Year 5 with $138,528 in inflation-adjusted current-cost dollars of inventory. The difference represents a $97,028 increase in current cost net of inflation. Therefore, inflation represented $12,972 of the total increase in current cost measured in nominal dollars. If inventory price changes had exactly followed inflation, the increase in current cost would have been only $12,972.

The denominator of the conversion factors for the beginning balances is the index at the beginning of Year 5, not the index on the date of acquisition. The beginning current-cost values have already been *rolled forward* to January 1, Year 5.

Completed Year 5 Disclosures

The results from items 1–4 are combined in the following statement, which meets the requirements for the voluntary supplemental disclosures on effects of price changes.

BAKER COMPANY
Statement of Income from Continuing Operations
Adjusted for Changing Prices
For Year Ended December 31, Year 5
(number in parentheses indicates previous section source)

Income from continuing operations, as reported
in the primary income statement .... $ 90,000
Adjustments to reflect current costs
  Cost of goods sold .... (96,000) (1)
  Depreciation .... (17,000) (1)
Income (loss) from continuing operations adjusted for
changes in specific prices .... $ (23,000)
Loss from decline in purchasing power of net
monetary assets .... $ (6,700) (2)
Current cost on Dec. 31, Year 5
  Inventories $144,000 (3)
  Property, plant, and equipment .... 270,000 (3)*

	Inventory	Property, plant, and equipment
Increase in specific prices	$110,000 (4)	$21,000 (4)†
Effect of increase in general price level......................	12,972 (4)	24,560 (4)‡
Excess of increases in specific prices over increase in general price level	$ 97,028	$ (3,560) (4)§

*$270,000 = $80,000 (land) + $190,000 (equipment)
†$21,000 = $10,000 (land) + $11,000 (equipment)
‡$24,560 = $6,540 (land) + $18,020 (equipment)
§($3,560) = $3,460 (land) + ($7,020) (equipment)

FASB Statement No. 89 Supplementary Disclosures: The Five-Year Summary

The five-year summary restates the selected financial statement and market information to dollars of constant purchasing power. It therefore allows financial statement users to compare results of several periods measured with a stable monetary denomination.

Baker Company chooses to restate all values to the average Year 5 CPI-U. Each new year's summary will drop the earliest year in the previous year's summary and add the current year. Assuming inflation over all years affected, the values in the summary will continue to increase each year. For example, the Year 3 values in the Year 4 summary will be less than the Year 3 values in the Year 5 summary.

The five-year summary builds on calculations from earlier years. The calculations in the schedule that follows may appear less complex than those illustrated for Year 5 alone because they build on amounts already restated to current-cost dollars from previous years. In addition, the calculations for Year 5 have already been completed. The following schedule presents Baker Company's Year 5 five-year

BAKER COMPANY
Five-Year Comparison of Selected Financial Data
Adjusted for Effects of Changing Prices
In Average Year 5 Dollars

Year	For Year Ended December 31, Year				
	1[a]	2[b]	3[c]	4[d]	5
Sales (000s)	$430	$554	$753	$745	$800
Income from continuing operations, current-cost basis	$14,318	$14,766	$ 9,265	$ (4,257)	$(23,000)[e]
Purchasing power gain (loss)	2,148	(2,461)	(2,548)	2,980	(6,700)[e]
Excess of increase in specific prices of inventory over inflation	18,041	48,247	43,590	51,198	97,028[e]
Excess of increase in specific prices of property, plant, and equipment over inflation	15,292	2,707	6,949	13,622	(3,560)[e]
Ending net assets, current cost basis (000s)	$401	$381	$382	$453	$524[f]
Per-share information: Income from continuing operations, current-cost basis	$0.14	$ 0.15	$ 0.09	$ (0.04)	$ (0.23)
Cash dividend declared	0.14	0.12	0.35	0.32	0.40
Market price, year-end	8.59	10.15	12.16	12.77	13.30

[a](Corresponding value from originally reported data) (157.5/110)
[b](Corresponding value from originally reported data) (157.5/128)
[c](Corresponding value from originally reported data) (157.5/136)
[d](Corresponding value from originally reported data) (157.5/148)
[e]From Year 5 supplementary disclosures
[f]Primary net assets + excess of current cost over historical cost for inventory and property, plant, and equipment:
$380,000 + ($144,000 − $130,000) + ($270,000 − ($40,000 + $100,000)) = $524,000

summary and relies on the earlier schedule, ''Data for Five-Year Summary as Originally Reported.''

The values in the five-year summary for Years 1 through 4 are the product of the originally reported values and the relevant conversion factor. This factor is the ratio of average CPI-U for Year 5 to the average CPI-U for the particular year. The ''originally'' reported data is taken from the particular year's annual report, which would have reported values restated to the average CPI-U for that year. Had the original data already been rolled forward to the end of Year 4, all restatements would have used the 157.5/148 = 1.064 conversion factor.

Although several of the amounts, including market price per share and others, are listed in the originally reported data as ''end-of-year'' values, they too had been restated to the average CPI-U for the particular year.

Net assets at year-end, on a current-cost basis, is the sum of the net assets reported in the primary statements plus the excess of current cost over historical cost amounts for inventory and property, plant, and equipment. These were the only two amounts requiring adjustment for price changes.

FASB Statement No. 89 Supplementary Disclosures: Further Discussion

Inflation Adjustments in Lieu of Current Cost   As mentioned earlier, if Baker Company's income from continuing operations adjusted for inflation is not materially different from the current-cost-adjusted value, inflation adjustments may be substituted for current-cost amounts. For Baker Company, Year 5 income from continuing operations adjusted for inflation would be computed as follows:

BAKER COMPANY
Income from Continuing Operations
Adjusted to Average Year 5 Dollars
For Year Ended December 31, Year 5

			Average Year 5 dollars	
Cost of goods sold adjustment				
Beginning balance $150,000	(157.5/150)		$ 157,500	
Purchases 500,000			500,000	
Ending inventory .... (130,000)			(130,000)*	
Cost of goods sold 520,000			$ 527,500	
Increase in cost of goods sold due to inflation adjustment				$ 7,500
Depreciation adjustment				
Depreciation adjusted for inflation since				
acquisition $200,000(0.10)(157.5/105)†			$ 30,000	
Historical-cost depreciation			20,000	
Increase in depreciation due to inflation adjustment				10,000
Total adjustment for inflation				$(17,500)
Income from continuing operations as reported				90,000
Income from continuing operations adjusted for inflation				$ 72,500

*It is assumed that ending inventory is already stated on an average-cost basis, as it represents purchases during the year on a fifo basis
†Assume that CPI-U was 105 on the date of equipment purchase.

As illustrated in the calculation, the adjustment to constant dollars uses the ratio of the price-level index into which the amounts are to be adjusted (average Year 5 dollars) to the index on the date of acquisition. The $72,500 income represents the income remaining after providing for capacity replacement as measured in constant dollars.

The inflation-adjusted income is materially different from the earlier current-cost version of income (negative $23,000). Therefore, Baker Company would not report the inflation-adjusted income in lieu of the recommended current-cost income. The FASB has expressed a strong preference for current cost over inflation adjustments. Specific price changes are more *relevant* to the firm than are general price changes. It is apparent that *specific* price changes have affected Baker Company to a much greater degree than has inflation.

Other Inventory Valuation Methods   Business entities may use inventory methods other than first-in, first-out. If Baker Company had used the *average* cost flow assumption, there would be no difference in the supplementary disclosures, as there would be no change in the current-cost information. The *difference* between current-cost income and reported income would be different between the fifo and lifo assumptions, however.

Had Baker Company used lifo, and no lifo inventory layer liquidations had taken place, reported cost of goods sold would be an acceptable estimate of cost of goods sold at current cost. Last-in, first-out assumes the sale of the most recently purchased items. There would be no need to calculate the cost of goods sold adjustment in the calculation of current-cost income.

The portion of cost of goods sold represented by a prior period lifo layer liquidation should be assigned a current-cost value by using a specific-price index for the period in which those ''liquidated'' units were purchased. The difference between current cost and historical cost for this portion of cost of goods sold could be considerably larger than for the other portion of cost of goods sold.

Comprehensive Restatement of Financial Statements for Changing Prices
Some business entities chose to restate their financial statements *comprehensively* to comply with the supplementary disclosure requirements of *FASB Statement No. 33.* All accounts are restated using this approach. The supplementary disclosures under *FASB Statement No. 89* may also be presented in a comprehensive manner, provided that the suggested disclosures are present. A business entity choosing this alternative has considerable latitude in disclosure format. Often, the purchasing power gain or loss is included in inflation-adjusted income, and holding gains or losses (increases or decreases in current cost) are included in current-cost income. The following are general guidelines for a comprehensive restatement.

Inflation-Adjusted Financial Statements
1   Most *sales and revenues* are assumed to occur uniformly throughout the year. Therefore, if end-of-year constant dollars are the preferred measure, the ratio of ending to average CPI-U is used for restatement. If year-average dollars are preferred, no adjustment is necessary. Any material revenues that are not recognized evenly throughout the year should be restated from the date of recognition.

2   *Cost of goods sold* requires adjustments to beginning inventories (the denominator of the conversion factor is the CPI-U on the date of acquisition—there may be several separate calculations required for different acquisition dates), purchases, and ending inventories. Purchases are generally assumed to take place evenly throughout the year. The adjustment for ending inventories must consider the cost flow assumption used, to ascertain the assumed date of acquisition.

3   *Operating expenses* other than depreciation, amortization, and depletion typically require no adjustment if year-average dollars is the preferred measure, as they are assumed to occur evenly throughout the year.

4   *Depreciation, depletion, and amortization* is adjusted from the date of acquisition (see earlier illustration in the discussion of inflation adjustments in lieu of constant cost).

5   *Dividends* are adjusted from the date of declaration.

6   *Nonmonetary assets, and contributed capital* accounts are adjusted from the date of acquisition or issuance. Accumulated depreciation is treated as a ''negative'' asset and receives the same adjustment as the corresponding asset. Monetary items require no restatement to end-of-year dollars, as their amount of purchasing power or claim on purchasing power is equal to their stated value. However, a restatement *from* (denominator) ending *to* (numerator) average is required if year-average dollars are the preferred measure. In addition, when prior years' balance sheets are shown in comparison with the current year's balance sheet, the prior years' monetary items are restated to the current year's CPI-U (average or end-of-year).

7   *Retained earnings* may be computed separately from the adjusted income and purchasing power gains and losses, but is more often computed as a balancing amount.

Current-Cost Financial Statements

1   *Sales and other revenues* generally require no restatement, as they are assumed to represent current cost at time of recognition.

2   *Cost of goods sold* is calculated as discussed earlier in the recommended disclosures.

3   *Operating expenses* other than depreciation, depletion, and amortization are measured at current cost upon recognition, and no adjustment is required.

4   *Depreciation, depletion, and amortization* are calculated as discussed earlier in the recommended disclosures.

5   *Dividends* declared at year-end require no adjustment. Those declared at other times may be adjusted for the effect of inflation since their declaration. It is at declaration that a monetary item is created.

6   *Nonmonetary assets* are adjusted in a fashion similar to the earlier illustration of inventory, land, and equipment for Baker Company.

7   *Monetary items* are generally considered to represent current costs and therefore require no adjustment. It may be desirable, however, to use a current interest rate to discount remaining payments on long-term debt if the original interest rate is no longer representative of current interest rates.

8 *Contributed capital* accounts represent the current cost of dollars invested and therefore require no adjustment.

9 *Retained earnings* may be computed directly by considering current-cost income and holding gains and losses. However, it is often computed as a balancing amount.

10 *Holding gains and losses* are the increases or decreases in current cost during the period that assets are held. For example, on December 31, Year 5, Baker Company has experienced a $40,000 total holding gain on land (= $80,000 − $40,000) since acquisition. These gains and losses may be separated into realized and unrealized components. Inventory sold in Year 3 causes any relevant holding gain to be realized in Year 3. Furthermore, if an asset has been held several years, the portion of the holding gain or loss attributable to the current year is often identified.

The lack of guidelines and requirements for comprehensively restated financial statements allows great flexibility in disclosure. This flexibility, however, may have been a contributing factor to the present lack of requirement for disclosure of price-level changes.

APPRAISAL OF FASB REQUIREMENTS

The debate on accounting for the effects of changing prices continues in the profession. The FASB considered the three approaches to measuring price-level changes discussed earlier. The advantage of the first, the historical-cost/constant-dollar system, is that all disclosures are measured with a constant measuring unit—a significant improvement over historical-cost statements alone. Increases in the cost of productive capacity and inventories due to inflation are measured in the income-determination process. All accounts in such statements can be meaningfully compared. The main disadvantage of this system is that the inflation rate is an *average* of many *specific* prices and often does not equal the specific price changes of resources that a particular entity must replace. Holding gains, income adjusted for inflation, and balance sheet account adjustments may be materially different from the changes in specific prices of the entity's resources.

The second alternative, current fair value or current cost without adjustment for inflation, has similar advantages to the first. Income measures adjusted for changes in specific prices provide better long-term measures of wealth increase than historical-cost accounting, as they consider the cost to replace resources. Many argue that current cost is superior to constant-dollar adjustments in this respect because specific prices are more directly relevant to future commitments of resources. However, current costs are less reliable than inflation adjustments that employ published statistics, used by many enterprises. Current-cost nominal dollars are not adjusted for inflation, making comparisons across periods difficult.

The third alternative, current-cost/constant-dollar, is the most complex. It combines the advantages of the first two and removes their major disadvantages. Returns *of* and *on* capital are separated and measured in constant dollars. The effects of both types of price changes are considered. Income measured under this approach is a better measure of the wealth increase (after a provision for replacement of existing operating capacity) than the other two approaches. Further, balance sheet values across different periods may readily be compared.

In *FASB Statement No. 33,* the Financial Accounting Standards Board took a compromise position between two opposing views on accounting for inflation. One view, favored by the FASB itself in an earlier exposure draft of a proposed Statement, is that historical-cost/constant-purchasing-power financial statements are the most meaningful indicators of the effects of inflation on a business enterprise. Proponents of this view argue that constant-purchasing-power data are more reliable than current-cost data, because constant-purchasing-power amounts are computed with a uniform measure—the Consumer Price Index for All Urban Consumers.

Another view, favored at one time by the Securities and Exchange Commission, is that constant-purchasing-power data are not as meaningful as current-cost data because of shortcomings of general price-level indexes such as the Consumer Price Index for All Urban Consumers. Such indexes are misleading, critics claim, because of their assumption of a "mix" of goods and services in the computation of the indexes. Supporters of current-cost measures of inflation argue that current-cost amounts of the resources of a business enterprise provide more relevant data for decision makers than do constant-dollar data.

From an accounting principles standpoint, the arguments are presently moot, given that *FASB Statement No. 89* has lifted the disclosure requirement. The FASB expressed many reasons for rescinding the requirement to disclose the effects of price-level changes in financial reports. The respondents to the Exposure Draft that preceded *FASB Statement No. 89*[15] were predominantly in favor of rescinding the requirement.

Responses to the Exposure Draft, and other research, indicated that the *FASB Statement No. 33* disclosures were not widely used and that few financial statement users were considering them. A serious concern was raised that the cost to provide the disclosures was greater than their benefit. This concern was consistent with the general lack of interest in the disclosures. Furthermore, there was evidence that users were developing their own analyses to measure price-change effects in financial statements. Many considered the formal disclosures complex and confusing. There was little protest to the elimination of the historical-cost/constant-dollar requirements *(FASB Statement No. 33).*

Concerns arose about the comparability and quality of information provided by reporting entities. Given the flexibility of the guidelines provided in *FASB Statement No. 33,* users experienced difficulties interpreting the data across business entities. The placement of the supplementary disclosures at the end of the annual report, and its unaudited nature, did not increase the incentive to use the data.

A few years after *FASB Statement No. 33* became effective, the inflation rate in the United States declined significantly, further reducing the perceived impor-

---

[15]*Proposed Statement of Financial Accounting Standards,* "Financial Reporting and Changing Prices: Current Cost Information," FASB (Stamford: 1984).

tance of the supplementary data. Coupled with this macroeconomic change, some users reported a greater interest in information concerning the effect of interest-rate changes on business entities, and the ability of these entities to raise capital.

Other respondents criticized the reliability of current-cost disclosures. These disclosures are inherently inaccurate, and business entities are allowed a variety of approaches to estimate them. Further, the present current-cost concept is based on the replacement of *existing* service potential. Business entities have expressed a lack of intent to replace existing capacity. The assumption ignores expected contraction or growth in the business. The "experimental" nature of *FASB Statement No. 33* (the FASB was committed to review the project within five years of its inception), and the potential that the data would not be available for an extended period, discouraged use of the disclosures.

The Board has acknowledged the many problems with disclosures on price changes. However, it will continue to consider the issue of price changes as part of its deliberations on major accounting issues.[16] The contention that price increases cause historical-cost financial statements to disclose illusory profits and hide the erosion of capital is not disputed. Inflation rates can increase as they have in the past.

Certain Board members expressed the concern that should inflation increase, the process of developing new accounting standards for price changes could be hurt by the elimination of *Statement No. 33* requirements. Business entities may not maintain data bases and systems for this purpose and will be faced with increased costs of compliance in the future should a new standard again require the disclosures.

---

[16]*FASB Statement No. 89,* par. 127.

APPENDIX: MONETARY AND NONMONETARY ITEMS

Assets	Monetary	Nonmonetary
Cash on hand and demand bank deposits	X	
Time deposits	X	
Securities investments:		
Common stock (not accounted for by the equity method)		X
Preferred stock (convertible or participating)	Circumstances may indicate that such stock is either monetary or nonmonetary. See convertible bonds.	
Preferred stock (nonconvertible, nonparticipating)	X	
Convertible bonds	If the market values the security primarily as a bond, it is monetary; if it	

(continued)

	Monetary	Nonmonetary
	values the security primarily as a common stock, it is nonmonetary.	
Bonds (other than convertibles)	X	
Notes and accounts receivable	X	
Allowance for doubtful notes and accounts receivable	X	
Inventories used on contracts	*They are, in substance, rights to receive amounts of money if the future cash receipts on the contracts will not vary because of future changes in specific prices. Goods used on contracts to be priced at market on delivery are nonmonetary.*	
Inventories (other than inventories used on contracts)		X
Short-term prepayments	*Claims to future services are nonmonetary. Prepayments that are deposits, advance payments, or receivables are monetary because the prepayment does not obtain a specific quantity of future services, but rather is a fixed money offset.*	
Long-term receivables	X	
Refundable deposits	X	
Advances to unconsolidated subsidiaries	X	
Equity investment in unconsolidated subsidiaries or other investees		X
Pension, sinking, and other funds under an enterprise's control	*The specific assets in the fund should be classified as monetary or nonmonetary. See listings under securities investments on page 1314.*	
Cash surrender value of life insurance policies	X	
Plant assets		X
Accumulated depreciation of plant assets		X
Intangible assets		X
Prepaid income taxes†	X	

Liabilities

	Monetary	Nonmonetary
Notes and accounts payable	X	
Accrued liabilities	X	

(continued)

	Monetary	Nonmonetary
Accrued vacation pay		Nonmonetary if it is paid at the wage rates as of the vacation dates and if those rates may vary.
Cash dividends payable	X	
Deferred revenue		Nonmonetary if an obligation to furnish goods or services is involved.
Refundable deposits	X	
Bonds payable and other long-term debt	X	
Unamortized premium or discount and prepaid interest	X	
Convertible bonds payable	X	
Accrued pension obligations		Fixed amounts payable to a fund are monetary; all other amounts are non-monetary.
Obligations under warranties		X
Deferred income tax credits*	X	
Deferred investment tax credits		X

*Although classification of this item as nonmonetary may be technically preferable, the monetary classification provides a more practical solution for the purposes of constant purchasing power accounting.

Source: Adapted from **FASB Statement No. 89,** "Financial Reporting and Changing Prices," par. 96.

REVIEW QUESTIONS

1   What evidence can you provide in support of the assertion that "the dollar is not a stable unit of value"?

2   List three indexes of the general price level in the United States. Which index was selected by the Financial Accounting Standards Board as a measure of the general movement in prices?

3   Evaluate the following quotation: "If historical-cost/nominal-dollar financial statements were restated to reflect the changing purchasing power of the dollar, assets would be stated at current fair value and net income would not be measured by matching expired costs with realized revenue."

4   Explain how the use of generally accepted accounting principles may result in reporting as a part of net income what may be a recovery of capital.

5   Explain each of the following:
a *Monetary items*   **c** *Negative monetary position*
b *Positive monetary position*   **d** *Purchasing power gains and losses*

6   What is meant by the expression *conversion factor?* Compute the conversion factor for land if the general price-level index was 80 on the date the land was acquired and is 144 today.

7   To what extent have current fair values been used by accountants in the preparation of financial statements?

8   Why did the Accounting Standards Division of the American Institute of Certified Public Accountants recommend the use of current fair values in personal financial statements?

9   What is a *holding gain or loss?* How is it measured?

10   The basic method of valuation used in accounting for plant assets is historical cost (nominal dollars), less depreciation. At various times during their economic life it is possible to estimate the current fair value of such assets by use of one of the following methods:
a *Capitalization of net cash inflows* (or *direct valuation*)
b *Exit values* (both current and expected)
c *Current cost*
   Explain the meaning of the term *current fair value* and define each of the foregoing methods of estimating current fair value.

11   Evaluate the following quotation: ''Accounting is no more than the recording and reporting of transactions; incorporation of current fair values of assets in the financial statements is neither feasible nor useful; besides, it lacks reliability.''

12   List the Financial Accounting Standards Board's recommended supplementary information disclosure requirements regarding changing prices in the annual reports of corporations.

13   Define *income from continuing operations.*

14   What is meant by ''change in current cost, net of inflation?''

15   May a business enterprise elect to use the average, the end-of-year, or base-period Consumer Price Index for All Urban Consumers to compute the constant-purchasing-power information authorized by the Financial Accounting Standards Board? Explain.

16   Define *recoverable amount.*

17   Explain how income from continuing operations is adjusted to current cost for the recommended current-year disclosures.

18   Explain how historical-cost/constant-purchasing-power balance sheet data of a prior year are *rolled forward* for comparative balance sheets.

19   The recoverable amount of Wight Company's land on March 31, Year 6, is $1,482,000. Current cost of the land on that date is $1,843,000. How do these facts affect the preparation of current-cost supplementary information for Wight's annual report for the year ended March 31, Year 6? Explain.

EXERCISES

Ex. 25-1   Select the best answer for each of the following multiple-choice questions:

1   The Financial Accounting Standards Board requires that the current cost of inventories be measured as the:
a Recoverable amount, regardless of the current cost
b Current cost, regardless of the recoverable amount

c Higher of current cost or recoverable amount

d Lower of current cost or recoverable amount

2   In the computation of information on a historical-cost/constant-purchasing-power basis, which of the following is classified as *nonmonetary?*

a Cash surrender value of life insurance

b Long-term accounts receivable

c Allowance for doubtful accounts

d Inventories, other than inventories used on contracts

3   Do purchasing power gains and losses result from:

	Monetary assets and liabilities?	Nonmonetary assets and liabilities?
a	Yes	Yes
b	Yes	No
c	No	No
d	No	Yes

4   The Consumer Price Index for All Urban Consumers is used to compute information on a:

a Historical-cost basis

b Current-cost basis

c Constant-purchasing-power basis

d Nominal-dollar basis

5   In the computation of information on a historical-cost/constant-purchasing-power basis, which of the following is classified as *monetary?*

a Obligations under product warranties

b Inventories, other than inventories used on contracts

c Trademarks

d Short-term investments in common stocks

e None of the foregoing

6   A method of accounting based on measures of current cost or lower recoverable amount, without restatement to units of the same general purchasing power, is:

a Historical-cost/constant-purchasing-power accounting

b Historical-cost/nominal-dollar accounting

c Current-cost/constant-purchasing-power accounting

d Current-cost/nominal-dollar accounting

Ex. 25-2   LeMons Company's plant assets on December 31, Year 6, were composed of the following:

Year acquired	Percent depreciated	Historical cost
Year 4	30%	$30,000
Year 5	20	20,000
Year 6	10	10,000
Total plant assets		$60,000

LeMons uses the straight-line method, no residual values, and a 10-year economic life for depreciation of all plant assets, and takes a full year's depreciation in the year of acquisition of plant assets. There were no disposals of plant assets in Year 6. Average Consumer Price Indexes for All Urban Consumers were as follows: Year 4, 100; Year 5, 120; Year 6, 150.

Compute the amount of depreciation expense for LeMons Company's historical-cost/constant-purchasing-power income statement for the year ended December 31, Year 6.

Ex. 25-3 Reno Corporation prepared the following nominal-dollar data for the computation of its purchasing power gain or loss on net monetary items for inclusion in its supplementary information for Year 4:

	Dec. 31, Year 3	Dec. 31, Year 4
Monetary liabilities	$1,566,000	$2,449,000
Less: Monetary assets	600,000	1,000,000
Net monetary liabilities	$ 966,000	$1,449,000

Average Consumer Price Indexes for All Urban Consumers were as follows: December 31, Year 3, 210; December 31, Year 4, 230; average for Year 4, 220.

Compute Reno Corporation's purchasing power gain or loss (expressed in average Year 4 constant purchasing power) on net monetary items for the year ended December 31, Year 4. (Hint: Compare the *nominal-dollars* increase in net monetary liabilities with the increase expressed in *constant purchasing power.*)

Ex. 25-4 Lexx Company acquired a machine in Year 8 when the average Consumer Price Index for all Urban Consumers (CPI-U) was 180. The average CPI-U was 190 for Year 9 and 200 for Year 10. Depreciation expense for the machine was $200,000 a year.

Compute historical-cost/constant-purchasing-power depreciation expense for Lexx Company's machine for Year 10.

Ex. 25-5 Mono Company was organized on January 2, Year 7. Selected balances from the historical-cost/nominal-dollar balance sheet on December 31, Year 7, were as follows:

Cash	$50,000
Short-term investments, common stocks (acquired on Jan. 2, Year 7)	70,000
Short-term investments, bonds (acquired on Jan. 2, Year 7, and held for speculation)	80,000
Long-term note receivable	90,000

The Consumer Price Index for All Urban Consumers was 100 on December 31, Year 6 (and January 2, Year 7), and 110 on December 31, Year 7.

Compute the amounts at which the foregoing items would be presented in Mono Company's historical-cost/constant-purchasing-power balance sheet on December 31, Year 7.

Ex. 25-6   Oro, Inc., was organized on January 2, Year 3, when common stock was issued for cash of $50,000 and land with a current fair value of $200,000. Oro did not begin operations until Year 4, and no transactions occurred in Year 3, except the issuance of the common stock. The Consumer Price Index for All Urban Consumers was 100 on December 31, Year 2, and 110 on December 31, Year 3.

Compute the purchasing power gain or loss to be included in a historical-cost/constant-purchasing-power income statement for Oro, Inc., for Year 3.

Ex. 25-7   For each independent situation below, compute the purchasing power gain or loss, assuming that assets and liabilities remained unchanged during the entire accounting period. The Consumer Price Index for All Urban Consumers rose by 7% during the period:

a Monetary assets $220,000
   Monetary liabilities... 60,000

b Monetary assets $260,000
   Current monetary liabilities 100,000
   Long-term monetary liabilities 300,000

c Cash $140,000
   Short-term investments in common stocks 200,000
   Notes receivable 90,000
   Accounts receivable 60,000
   Inventories.. 100,000
   Plant assets (net of accumulated depreciation)......................... 600,000
   Monetary liabilities... 475,000
   Stockholders' equity 625,000

Ex. 25-8   Amador Company was organized and began operations in Year 1. Amador adopted the last-in, first-out method of inventory pricing and has consistently used this method. On December 31, Year 15, the composition of the inventory and the average Consumer Price Index for All Urban Consumers in the year of purchase were as follows:

Purchased in Year 1 (index = 90) $380,000
Year 3 layer (index = 100)... 20,000
Year 10 layer (index = 120) 15,000
Year 15 layer (index = 135) 45,000
   Total inventory at last-in, first-out cost, as shown in historical-
   cost/nominal-dollar balance sheet on Dec. 31, Year 15 .... $460,000

Prepare a working paper to restate Amador Company's inventory on December 31, Year 15, to reflect changes in the average Consumer Price Index for All Urban Consumers.

Ex. 25-9   Pak Corporation paid $1,200,000 in December, Year 6, for certain items of its inventory. In December, Year 7, one-half of the items were sold for $1,100,000 when the current fair value of the entire group of items was $1,400,000.

Compute the amount to be shown as the total gain resulting from the above facts in Pak Corporation's current fair value income statement for Year 7. Disregard income taxes.

Ex. 25-10 Duran Corporation acquired a machine for $2,000,000 in Year 4 when the specific-price index was 180. The applicable specific-price index was 190 on December 31, Year 5, and 200 on December 31, Year 6. Depreciation expense on a historical-cost/nominal-dollar basis was $200,000 a year.

Compute Duran Corporation's average current cost of depreciation expense for Year 6.

Ex. 25-11 Toland Company acquired a machine on December 31, Year 7, for $200,000. The machine was being depreciated on the straight-line basis with no residual value and a five-year economic life. There was an increase in current cost of the machine of 10% during Year 8 and 10% during Year 9 (based on the December 31, Year 8, current cost).

Compute accumulated depreciation on a current-cost basis for inclusion in Toland Company's supplementary current-cost information for Year 9.

Ex. 25-12 Villar Company's plant assets on December 31, Year 8, were composed of the following:

Year acquired	Percent depreciated	Historical cost	Current cost
Year 6	30%	$50,000	$ 70,000
Year 7	20	15,000	19,000
Year 8	10	20,000	22,000
Total plant assets		$85,000	$111,000

Villar uses the straight-line method, no residual values, and a 10-year economic life for depreciation of all plant assets, and takes a full-year's depreciation in the year of acquisition of plant assets.

Compute the net current cost (after accumulated depreciation) of Villar Company's plant assets on December 31, Year 8.

Ex. 25-13 Details of Windsor Corporation's cost of goods sold for Year 3 were as follows:

	Units	Historical costs
Finished goods inventory, Jan. 1, Year 3	10,000	$ 530,000
Add: Cost of goods manufactured	45,000	2,790,000
Cost of goods available for sale	55,000	$3,320,000
Less: Finished goods inventory, Dec. 31, Year 3	15,000	945,000
Cost of goods sold	40,000	$2,375,000

Estimated current cost of Windsor's finished goods inventory was $58 a unit on January 1, Year 3, and $72 a unit on December 31, Year 3.

Compute the average current cost of Windsor Corporation's cost of goods sold for Year 3.

Ex. 25-14   Valuation to reflect constant purchasing power, as opposed to current cost, yields differing amounts for a business enterprise's financial statements. Several transactions concerning one asset of Roebuck Corporation, a calendar-year enterprise, are summarized below:

Year 4: Acquired land for $400,000 cash on December 31; current cost at year-end was $400,000.

Year 5: Owned this land all year; current cost at year-end was $520,000.

Year 6: Sold this land for $690,000 on October 31.

The average Consumer Price Index for All Urban Consumers for each year was as follows:

Year 4	*100*
Year 5	*110*
Year 6	*120*

On your working paper, set up the format below and complete the information based on the transactions described above for Roebuck Corporation. Assume that holding gains and losses are included in current-cost data.

	Historical-cost/ constant-purchasing-power	**Current-cost**
Valuation of land in balance sheet:		
Dec. 31, Year 4	$	$
Dec. 31, Year 5		
Gain in income statement:		
Year 4	$	$
Year 5		
Year 6		
Totals	$	$

CASES

Case 25-1   Financial reporting should provide information to help investors, creditors, and other users of financial statements. The Financial Accounting Standards Board recommends that corporations disclose certain supplementary information.

Instructions

a Describe the historical-cost/constant-purchasing-power method of accounting. Include in your discussion how historical-cost amounts are used to make historical-cost/constant-purchasing-power measurements.

b Describe the principal advantage of the historical-cost/constant-purchasing-power method of accounting over the historical-cost/nominal-dollar method of accounting.

c Describe the current-cost method of accounting.

d Why would depreciation expense for a specific year differ under the current-cost method of accounting as compared with the historical-cost method of accounting? Include in your discussion whether depreciation expense is likely to be higher or lower under the current-cost method of accounting as compared with the historical-cost/nominal-dollar method of accounting in a period of rising prices, and why.

Case 25-2   Advocates of fair-value accounting propose several methods for estimating the approximate current fair values of assets. Two of the methods proposed are *current cost* and *present value of future cash inflows.*

Instructions

Describe each of the two methods cited and discuss the advantages and disadvantages of the various procedures used to estimate the valuation of assets for each method.

Case 25-3   Jean Daily, the controller of Exeter Company, is discussing a comment you made in the course of presenting your audit report.

"... and frankly," Daily continued, "I agree that we, too, are responsible for finding ways to produce more relevant financial statements that are as reliable as the ones we now produce.

"For example, suppose we acquired an item of inventory for $400 when the general price-level index was 110. And, later, the item was sold for $750 when the general price-level index was 121 and the current cost was $540. We could compute and report a 'holding gain' of $100."

Instructions

a Explain to what extent and how current costs are used under generally accepted accounting principles to value inventories.
b Explain how Jean Daily computed the holding gain of $100.

Case 25-4   Valuation of assets is an important topic in accounting theory. Suggested valuation methods include the following:

> *Historical-cost/nominal-dollar*
> *Historical-cost/constant-purchasing-power*
> *Discounted cash inflows*
> *Market price* (current selling prices)
> *Current cost* (current purchase prices)

Instructions

a Why is the valuation of assets a significant issue?
b Explain the basic theory underlying each of the valuation methods listed above. Do not discuss advantages and disadvantages of each method.

Case 25-5   A common objective of accountants is to prepare useful financial statements. To attain this objective many accountants maintain that the financial statements must be adjusted for changes in the general price level. Other accountants believe that financial statements should continue to be prepared on the basis of unadjusted historical cost.

Instructions

a List arguments for adjusting financial statements for changes in the general price level.

b List arguments for preparing financial statements only on the basis of unadjusted historical cost.

c In their discussions about accounting for changes in the general price level and the methods of measuring them, uninformed individuals frequently have failed to distinguish between adjustments for changes in the price levels of specific goods and services and adjustments for changes in the purchasing power of the dollar. What is the distinction? Discuss.

Case 25-6   Financial statements are tools for the communication of quantifiable economic information to users as one of the factors for a variety of management and investment decisions. To fulfill this function, accounting data should be quantifiable and relevant for the kinds of decisions to be made. They should be reliable and free from bias. Many accountants believe that for some purposes current cost is a more useful measure than historical cost and recommend that dual financial statements be prepared showing both historical costs and current costs.

Instructions

a Discuss the ways in which historical costs and current costs conform to the standards of *reliability* and *freedom from bias.*

b Describe briefly how the current cost of the following assets might be determined:

(1) Inventories

(2) Investments in marketable securities

(3) Equipment

(4) Natural resources

Case 25-7   Discuss the factors that led to the FASB's removal of the requirement to disclose the effects of price changes in financial statements.

PROBLEMS

25-1   Select the best answer for each of the following multiple-choice questions relating to historical-cost/constant-purchasing-power accounting:

1   Roy Company reported sales of $2,000,000 in Year 3 and $3,000,000 in Year 4. Sales were made evenly throughout each year. The general price-level index during Year 2 remained constant at 100, and at the end of Year 3 and Year 4 it was 102 and 104, respectively. What amount does Roy Company report as sales for Year 4 in terms of end-of-Year 4 purchasing power?
a $3,000,000   **b** $3,029,126   **c** $3,058,821   **d** $3,120,000

2   On January 2, Year 5, Noone Corporation mortgaged one of its properties as collateral for a $1,000,000, 15%, five-year loan. During Year 5, the general price level increased evenly, resulting in a 5% increase for the year.

In a historical-cost/constant-purchasing-power balance sheet on December 31, Year 5, at what amount does Noone Corporation report its mortgage note payable?

a $950,000   **b** $1,000,000   **c** $1,025,000   **d** $1,050,000

3   If land was acquired in Year 10 for $150,000 when the general price-level index was 100 and sold on December 31, Year 19, for $240,000 when the index was 170, the historical-cost/constant-purchasing-power income statement for Year 19 shows:

a A purchasing power gain of $105,000 and a loss on disposal of land of $15,000
b A gain on disposal of land of $90,000
c A purchasing power loss of $15,000
d A loss on disposal of land of $15,000
e None of the foregoing

4   A business enterprise was organized on January 2, Year 2. Selected items from the historical-cost/nominal-dollar balance sheet on December 31, Year 2, had the following amounts:

Accounts receivable (net) .... $ 70,000
Accounts payable 60,000
Long-term debt 110,000
Common stock 100,000

At what amounts are these selected items shown in a historical-cost/constant-purchasing power balance sheet on December 31, Year 2, if the general price-level index was 100 on December 31, Year 1, and 110 on December 31, Year 2?

	Accounts receivable	Accounts payable	Long-term debt	Common stock
a	$70,000	$60,000	$110,000	$100,000
b	$70,000	$60,000	$110,000	$110,000
c	$70,000	$60,000	$121,000	$110,000
d	$77,000	$66,000	$121,000	$110,000

5   If the base year is Year 1 (when the general price-level index was 100) and land is acquired for $50,000 in Year 5 when the general price-level index is 108.5, the cost of the land restated to Year 1 purchasing power (rounded to the nearest dollar) is:

a $54,250   **b** $50,000   **c** $46,083   **d** $45,750   **e** Some other amount

6   Assume the same facts as in question **5** above. The cost of the land restated to December 31, Year 10, purchasing power when the general price-level index is 119.2 (rounded to the nearest dollar) is:

a $59,600   **b** $54,931   **c** $46,083   **d** $45,512   **e** Some other amount

7   If land is acquired at a cost of $120,000 in January, Year 13, when the general price-level index was 120 and is sold in December, Year 19, when the index was 150, the selling price that results in no gain or loss in historical-cost/constant-purchasing-power financial statements is:

a $180,000   **b** $144,000   **c** $120,000   **d** $150,000   **e** Some other amount

Use the following information to answer questions **8** through **10:**

Equipment acquired for $120,000 on January 2, Year 1, when the general price-level index was 100, was sold on December 31, Year 3, at a price of $85,000. The equipment had an economic life of six years, with no residual value, and was depreciated by the straight-line method. The general price-level index on December 31, Year 1, was 120, on December 31, Year 2, was 150, and on December 31, Year 3, was 175.

8   In historical-cost/constant-purchasing-power comparative financial statements for Year 1 and Year 2, the Year 1 financial statements show equipment (net of accumulated depreciation) at:

a $150,000   **b** $125,000   **c** $100,000   **d** $80,000   **e** Some other amount

9   The historical-cost/constant-purchasing-power financial statements for Year 2 include depreciation expense of:

a $35,000   **b** $30,000   **c** $25,000   **d** $20,000   **e** Some other amount

10   The historical-cost/constant-purchasing-power income statement for Year 3 includes:

a A gain of $35,000   **d** A loss of $20,000
b A gain of $25,000   **e** Some other amount
c No gain or loss

25-2   Daniel Company elected to disclose the minimum current-cost data required by the Financial Accounting Standards Board. Daniel sells a single product, which it values at first-in, first-out cost in historical-cost/nominal-dollar financial statements. Daniel's perpetual inventory records showed the following information for Year 6:

	Units	Amount
Balance, Dec. 31, Year 5	10,000	$ 60,000
Add: Purchases during Year 6	510,000	4,472,000
Subtotals	520,000	$4,532,000
Less: Sales during Year 6	502,000	4,391,600
Balance, Dec. 31, Year 6	18,000	$ 140,400

Unit price quotations from three of Daniel's vendors were as follows:

Dec. 31, Year 5	$6.70, $6.80, $7.00
Dec. 31, Year 6	$8.10, $8.30, $8.35

Daniel generally purchases from the vendor quoting the lowest unit cost.

Daniel's selling expenses generally amount to 10% of net sales. Expected unit selling prices of Daniel's product were as follows:

Dec. 31, Year 5	$10.40
Dec. 31, Year 6	12.60

Instructions

Prepare a working paper to compute Daniel Company's average current cost of goods sold for Year 6, and the current cost of its inventory on December 31, Year 6.

25-3 The historical-cost/nominal-dollar income statement for Gish Corporation is shown below:

GISH CORPORATION
Income Statement (Historical-Cost/Nominal-Dollar Basis)
For Year Ended December 31, Year 4

Net sales		$700,000
Cost of goods sold:		
Inventories, Jan. 1, Year 4 (last-in, first-out cost)	$ 80,000	
Net purchases	450,000	
Cost of goods available for sale	$530,000	
Less: Inventories, Dec. 31, Year 4 (last-in, first-out cost)	95,000	435,000
Gross profit on sales		$265,000
Operating expenses:		
Selling (reducing net monetary assets)	$ 30,000	
General and administrative (reducing net monetary assets)	25,000	
Depreciation	35,000	90,000
Income before income taxes		$175,000
Income taxes expense		78,750
Net income		$ 96,250

All items in the income statement were recorded at a fairly uniform rate throughout Year 4. Beginning inventories and depreciable plant assets were acquired when the Consumer Price Index for All Urban Consumers was 125. The lifo layer of $15,000 added to inventories during Year 4 consists of goods acquired throughout the year. Changes in the Consumer Price Index for All Urban Consumers during Year 4 are summarized below:

Jan. 1, Year 4 (conversion factor = 1.200) 150
Average for Year 4 (conversion factor = 1.078) 167
Dec. 31, Year 4 (conversion factor = 1.000) 180

Instructions

Prepare a working paper to restate Gish Corporation's Year 4 income statement to historical-cost/constant-purchasing-power at the *end* of Year 4. Assume that the purchasing power loss as a result of holding net monetary assets during Year 4 was $10,460.

25-4 Nikko Company was organized and began operations on June 1, Year 1, and adopted a fiscal year ending May 31. Nikko rented land and a building under an operating lease on June 1, Year 1. Nikko's equipment acquisitions and related specific-price indexes during the year ended May 31, Year 2, were as follows:

	Cost	Specific-price index
June 1, Year 1	$ 48,000	120
Dec. 1, Year 1	39,000	130
Mar. 1, Year 2	50,000	150
Total	$137,000	

Nikko depreciates equipment to the nearest month by the straight-line method over a 10-year economic life with no residual value.

The specific-price index for Nikko's equipment on May 31, Year 2, was 160. Nikko computed value in use for its equipment as follows:

June 1, Year 1	$ 70,000
May 31, Year 2	175,000

Instructions

Prepare a working paper to compute the current cost of Nikko Company's equipment and related accumulated depreciation on May 31, Year 2, and the average current cost of its depreciation expense for the year ended May 31, Year 2. Round conversion factors to the nearest thousandth and other computations to the nearest dollar.

25-5   Financial statements of Langer Company for the year ended June 30, Year 3, its first year of operations, are presented below and on page 1329.

LANGER COMPANY
Statement of Income and Retained Earnings
For Year Ended June 30, Year 3

Net sales		$1,400,000
Costs and expenses:		
Cost of goods sold	$700,000	
Operating expenses	320,000	
Interest expense	40,000	1,060,000
Income before income taxes		$ 340,000
Income taxes expense:		
Current	$144,000	
Deferred	9,000	153,000
Net income		$ 187,000
Less: Dividends ($0.60 a share)		60,000
Retained earnings, end of year		$ 127,000

LANGER COMPANY
Balance Sheet
June 30, Year 3

Assets

Current assets:		
Cash	$	50,000
Accounts receivable (net)		120,000
Inventories (first-in, first-out cost)		190,000
Short-term prepayments		3,000
Total current assets	$	363,000
Plant assets (net of $120,000 accumulated depreciation)		960,000
Total assets		$1,323,000

(continued)

Liabilities & Stockholders' Equity

Current liabilities:

Accounts payable	$ 60,000
Income taxes payable	144,000
Current portion of long-term debt	80,000
Total current liabilities	$ 284,000

10% note payable, due $80,000 a year with interest

on unpaid balance	240,000
Deferred income tax credits	9,000
Total liabilities	$ 533,000

Stockholders' equity:

Common stock, no par or stated value, authorized

200,000 shares, issued and outstanding 100,000 shares	$ 663,000
Retained earnings	127,000
Total stockholders' equity	$ 790,000
Total liabilities & stockholders' equity	$1,323,000

Additional Information

(1) On June 30, Year 2, Langer completed the following transactions:

Issued 100,000 shares of common stock to the public at $6.63 a share

Borrowed $400,000 from a bank on a 10% promissory note, which was due $80,000 a year plus interest on the unpaid balance, beginning on June 30, Year 3, and was guaranteed by an affiliated enterprise

Acquired plant assets costing $1,080,000 for cash of $1,000,000 and an account payable of $80,000

(2) Langer began operations on July 1, Year 2.

(3) There were no other plant asset acquisitions or disposals during the year ended June 30, Year 3.

(4) On June 30, Year 3, Langer completed the following transactions:

Declared and paid a cash dividend of $0.60 a share to common stockholders

Paid $80,000 principal and $40,000 interest ($400,000 × 0.10 = $40,000) to the bank

(5) The deferred income tax credits resulted from Langer's use of the straight-line method of depreciation for financial accounting and the Accelerated Cost Recovery System for income taxes.

(6) The Consumer Price Index for All Urban Consumers was as follows for the year ended June 30, Year 3:

July 1, Year 2	100
June 30, Year 3	120
Average for year	110

Instructions

Prepare for Langer Company a working paper to compute Langer's purchasing power gain or loss on net monetary items for the year ended June 30, Year 3. Round all conversion factors to the nearest thousandth, and round all amounts to the nearest dollar.

25-6   The Tilton Company provided the following data stated in terms of the average CPI-U for each year shown:

Year	3	4	5	6	7
Sales.....................	$30,000	$45,000	$48,000	$70,000	$65,000
Income from continuing operations, current- cost basis	2,000	3,150	2,950	5,700	3,900
Purchasing power gain (loss)	800	(1,600)	3,100	2,900	(1,700)
Excess of increase in specific prices of inventory over inflation..................	20,000	22,000	18,000	34,000	19,000
Excess of increase in specific prices of property, plant, and equipment over inflation..................	42,000	38,000	42,180	16,900	32,000
Ending net assets, current-cost basis....................	65,000	60,000	52,000	63,000	57,500
Per-share information: Income from continuing operations, current- cost basis	$100	$157.50	$147.50	$285	$195
Cash dividend declared...	80	80	100	150	200
Market price, year-end	26	23	20	22	23

Selected CPI-U indexes for each year were as follows:

Year	CPI-U
3	120
4	130
5	150
6	160
7	180

Instructions

Prepare the five-year summary as part of the FASB-recommended supplementary disclosures on the effects of changing prices, for Tilton's Year 7 annual report. Assume that Tilton chooses the average-of-year purchasing-power option.

25-7   Selected current-cost data for Lucinda Corporation's inventories and net plant assets during Year 8 are presented below:

	Inventories	Net plant assets
Balances, Dec. 31, Year 7	$120,000	$1,240,000
Purchases or additions (at average Year 8 purchasing power)	870,000	70,000
Cost of goods sold or depreciation expense	920,000	120,000
Balances, Dec. 31, Year 8	180,000	1,650,000

Consumer Price Indexes for All Urban Consumers were as follows:

Dec. 31, Year 7	120
Average for Year 8	140
Dec. 31, Year 8	150

Instructions

Prepare working papers to compute the following for Lucinda Corporation (assume that the current cost of merchandise purchases, costs of goods sold, additions to plant assets, and depreciation expense are stated in average Year 8 purchasing power):

a Increase in current cost of inventories, net of inflation, measured in average Year 8 purchasing power.

b Increase in current cost of net plant assets, net of inflation, measured in average Year 8 purchasing power.

25-8 Ozawa Company was organized on December 31, Year 9. Ozawa's management has decided to supplement its Year 12 historical-cost/nominal-dollar financial statements with historical-cost/constant-purchasing-power financial statements. The following general ledger trial balance (historical-cost/nominal-dollar basis) and additional information are available:

OZAWA COMPANY
Trial Balance
December 31, Year 12

	Debit	Credit
Cash and accounts receivable (net)	$ 540,000	
Short-term investments (common stock)	500,000	
Inventories	440,000	
Equipment	650,000	
Accumulated depreciation of equipment		$ 164,000
Accounts payable		400,000
15% bonds payable, due in Year 30		500,000
Common stock, $10 par...............................		1,000,000
Retained earnings, Dec. 31, Year 11	46,000	
Sales...		1,900,000
Cost of goods sold	1,508,000	
Depreciation expense..................................	65,000	
Other operating expenses, interest expense, and income taxes expense	215,000	
Totals	$3,964,000	$3,964,000

Additional Information

(1) Monetary assets (cash and accounts receivable) exceeded monetary liabilities (accounts payable and bonds payable) by $445,000 on December 31, Year 11. The amounts of monetary items are fixed in terms of numbers of dollars, regardless of changes in specific prices or in the Consumer Price Index for All Urban Consumers.

(2) Purchases ($1,840,000 in Year 12) and sales were made evenly during Year 12.

(3) Depreciation expense was computed by the straight-line method, with a full year's depreciation taken in the year of acquisition and none in the year of retirement. The depreciation rate is 10%, and no residual value of plant assets is anticipated. Acquisitions and retirements of plant assets have been made evenly during each year, and the retirements in Year 12 consisted of assets acquired during Year 10. An analysis of the Equipment ledger account follows:

Year	Beginning balance	Acquisitions	Retirements	Ending balance
10		$550,000		$550,000
11	$550,000	10,000		560,000
12	560,000	150,000	$60,000	650,000

(4) The 15% bonds payable were issued in Year 10, and the short-term investments were acquired at regular intervals during Year 12. Other operating expenses and interest expense were incurred evenly during Year 12.

(5) Assume that Consumer Price Indexes for All Urban Consumers (Year 4 = 100) were as follows:

Annual averages	CPI-U	Conversion factors*
Year 9	113.9	1.128
Year 10	116.8	1.100
Year 11	121.8	1.055
Year 12	126.7	1.014

Quarterly averages		CPI-U	Conversion factors
Year 11	4th	123.5	1.040
Year 12	1st	124.9	1.029
	2d	126.1	1.019
	3d	127.3	1.009
	4th	128.5	1.000

*Average index for 4th quarter of Year 12 (128.5) divided by the index for any preceding period. For example, the conversion factor for Year 9 is 1.128 (128.5 ÷ 113.9 = 1.128).

Instructions

a Prepare a working paper to restate Ozawa Company's Equipment ledger account balance on December 31, Year 12, from historical-cost/nominal-dollars to historical-cost/constant-purchasing-power.

b Prepare a working paper to analyze in historical-cost/nominal-dollars Ozawa Company's Accumulated Depreciation of Equipment ledger account for Year 12.

■■■■■■■■■■ **c** Prepare a working paper to analyze (in historical-cost/constant-purchasing-power) Ozawa Company's Accumulated Depreciation of Equipment ledger account for Year 12.

d Prepare a working paper to compute Ozawa Company's purchasing power gain or loss on its net monetary items for Year 12 (disregard income taxes). The working paper should give consideration to appropriate items in (or related to) the balance sheet and the income statement.

25-9 Yolie Corporation was organized on December 31, Year 4, and issued 100,000 shares of $1 par common stock for $500,000. On January 2, Year 5, Yolie completed the following transaction:

Land	80,000	
Buildings	200,000	
Equipment	150,000	
Cash		300,000
Long-Term Notes Payable		130,000
To record acquisition of assets valued at current fair value		
in exchange for cash and long-term notes payable.		

The changes in the Consumer Price Index for All Urban Consumers during Year 5 are summarized below:

	CPI-U	Conversion factor to restate to end-of-Year 5 purchasing power
Dec. 31, Year 4 (also for Jan. 1, Year 5)	110	1.232
July 1, Year 5 (also the average for Year 5)	110	1.120
Sept. 30, Year 5	115.5	1.067
Dec. 31, Year 5	123.2	1.000

On September 30, Year 5, Yolie paid a cash dividend of 50 cents a share and issued 10,000 additional shares of common stock at $8 a share.

The balance sheet on December 31, Year 5, and the statement of income and retained earnings for Year 5, on the historical-cost/nominal-dollar basis, are as follows:

YOLIE CORPORATION
Balance Sheet
December 31, Year 5

Assets		Liabilities & Stockholders' Equity	
Monetary assets	$390,000	Current liabilities	$110,000
Inventories	100,000	Long-term notes payable	130,000
Land	80,000	Common stock, $1 par	110,000
Buildings (net)	192,000	Additional paid-in capital	470,000
Equipment (net)	138,000	Retained earnings	80,000
		Total liabilities & stock-	
Total assets	$900,000	holders' equity	$900,000

YOLIE CORPORATION
Statement of Income and Retained Earnings
For Year Ended December 31, Year 5

Net sales		$1,260,000
Cost of goods sold		920,000
Gross profit on sales		$ 340,000
Expenses:		
Depreciation	$ 20,000	
Other (including interest and income taxes)	190,000	210,000
Net income		$ 130,000
Less: Dividends ($0.50 a share)		50,000
Retained earnings, end of year		$ 80,000

Sales amounted to approximately $105,000 a month, and expenses accrued at the rate of $17,500 a month. Both the cost of goods sold and the ending inventories consist of a representative cross section of merchandise purchased throughout Year 5. All liabilities are monetary liabilities.

Instructions

a Prepare a working paper to restate Yolie Corporation's statement of income and retained earnings for Year 5 to a historical-cost/constant-purchasing-power basis. Compute the purchasing power gain or loss in a supporting exhibit.

b Prepare a working paper to restate Yolie Corporation's December 31, Year 5, balance sheet to a historical-cost/constant-purchasing-power basis.

25-10 Financial statements and other relevant information for Nick Corporation follow:

NICK CORPORATION
Balance Sheets
December 31, Year 6 and 7

	Year 6	Year 7
Assets		
Monetary assets	$ 20,000	$ 25,000
Inventories (first-in, first-out)	18,000	28,500
Equipment	50,000	80,000
Accumulated depreciation	(20,000)	(30,000)
Intangibles (net)	10,000	8,000
Total assets	$ 78,000	$111,500
Liabilities & Stockholders' Equity		
Current liabilities	$ 10,000	$ 15,000
Long term liabilities	30,000	30,000
Common stock, $1 par	20,000	20,000
Additional paid-in capital	20,000	20,000
Retained earnings	(2,000)	26,500
Total liabilities & stockholders' equity	$ 78,000	$111,500

NICK CORPORATION
Statement of Income and Retained Earnings
For Year Ended December 31, Year 7

Sales...		$700,000
Cost of goods sold		
Beginning inventories (fifo, 200 units)...................	$ 18,000	
Purchases (5,100 units)	474,300	
Ending inventories (fifo, 300 units)	(28,500)	
Cost of goods sold		463,800
Gross profit on sales....................................		$236,200
Operating expenses excluding depreciation		
and amortization	$ 44,000	
Depreciation expense...................................	10,000	
Amortization expense	2,000	56,000
Income before income taxes.............................		$180,200
Income taxes expense		54,060
Net income		$126,140
Retained earnings, Jan. 1, Year 7		(2,000)
Dividends (paid Dec. 31, Year 7)		(97,640)
Retained earnings, Dec. 31, Year 7		$ 26,500

Additional Information

(1) The current cost per unit of inventory on January 1, Year 7, was $110, and on December 31, Year 7, it was $120. Both amounts were less than associated recoverable amounts. The current cost of purchases is the average current cost for the year.

(2) Equipment was purchased December 31, Year 7. The straight-line method is used, and no salvage value is assumed. A patent was purchased at the end of Year 6, has no salvage value, and has a five-year useful life.

(3) Sales and operating expenses occurred evenly throughout the year.

(4) All liabilities are monetary.

(5) The total current costs of equipment were $55,000 and $100,000 at the end of Years 6 and 7, respectively. The Year 7 acquisition represents current cost. The current cost of the patent was $15,000 and $19,000 at the end of Years 6 and 7, respectively. The current-cost amounts represent the cost of service potential equivalent to new assets, and are less than recoverable amounts.

(6) Selected CPI-U indices:

Year	Average	Ending
7	300	320
6	260	275
4	220	240

Nick Corporation chose to provide supplementary disclosures of the effects of price changes, and uses the average CPI-U for restatement to dollars of constant purchasing power.

Instructions

Provide the supplementary disclosures as recommended by *FASB Statement No. 89*. Omit the five-year summary of the effects of changing prices.

25-11   Bradberry Company prepared its Year 4 financial statements, which follow, according to generally accepted accounting principles.

BRADBERRY COMPANY
Income Statement
For Year Ended December 31, Year 4

Sales		$260,000
Cost of goods sold		
Beginning inventories (first-in, first-out)	$ 40,000	
Purchases	110,000	
Ending inventories (first-in, first-out)	(26,000)	
Cost of goods sold		124,000
Gross profit on sales		$136,000
Operating expenses excluding		
depreciation	$ 30,000	
Depreciation expense	47,200	
Total operating expenses		77,200
Income before income taxes		$ 58,800
Income taxes expense		17,640
Net income		$ 41,160

BRADBERRY COMPANY
Balance Sheets
December 31, Year 3 and Year 4

	Year 3	Year 4
Assets		
Cash	$ 40,000	$ 80,000
Accounts receivable	30,000	65,000
Inventory	40,000	26,000
Property, plant, and equipment		
Income before income tax	300,000	300,000
Accumulated depreciation	(104,600)	(151,800)
Total assets	$ 305,400	$ 319,200
Liabilities & Stockholders' Equity		
Accounts payable	$ 32,000	$ 27,000
Bonds payable	100,000	120,000
Common stock, no par	80,000	100,000
Retained earnings	93,400	72,200
Total liabilities & stockholders' equity	$305,400	$319,200

Additional Information

(1) Property, plant, and equipment consists of a building and equipment. The building was purchased January 2, Year 2, for $200,000, is depreciated over 10 years under the sum-of-the-years'-digits method, and has a $13,000 salvage value. The salvage value is an estimate of current cost to be received at the end of the building's useful life. The equipment was purchased late in December, Year 1, for $100,000, has no salvage value, has a five-year useful life, and is depreciated under the straight-line method.

(2) 8,000 units purchased December 1, Year 3, comprise the beginning inventory. 5,000 units purchased December 1, Year 4, comprise the ending inventory. 22,000 units were purchased during Year 4.

(3) Current-cost information:

	Jan. 1, Year 4	Dec. 31, Year 4
Inventory/unit	$ 5.50	$ 5.70
Building	250,000	280,000
Equipment	120,000	150,000

The building and equipment current-cost amounts represent the cost to replace service potential equivalent to new buildings and equipment. In all cases, recoverable amounts exceed current cost.

(4) Selected CPI-U indices

Jan. 1, Year 2	120
Dec. 1, Year 3	150
Dec. 31, Year 3	155
Average, Year 4	160
Dec. 1, Year 4	170
Dec. 31, Year 4	175

Instructions

Bradberry Company has asked you to prepare the supplementary disclosures for Year 4 for the effects of price changes, in accordance with *FASB Statement No. 89.* Assume that all changes in monetary items occurred evenly throughout the year, and Bradberry Company chooses to use average-Year 4 dollars for restatement to constant purchasing power. Omit the five-year summary.

Index

13-5 *b* Amort. for first 40 weeks, $4,200 per telecast.
13-6 *b* Total intangible assets, $41,560.
13-7 *a* $13,000; *c* $71,475; *d* $32,359.
13-8 *a* Prior period adjustment (debit), $209,410.
13-9 *a* (1) $94,700; (2) $56,800; (3) $40,500; (4) $81,800.

14-1 Pre-tax income: Year 9, $43,109; Year 10, $67,591.
14-3 *a* $9,000; *b* Year 3, $728,500; Year 4, $3,069,125.
14-4 Goodwill, $930,000; amortization for Year 8, $23,250.
14-5 *a* $3,018,000; *b* $277,000.
14-6 *a* Total gain, $37,210; *b* debit investment account, $1,610.
14-7 *b* Net long-term investment: Year 1, $258,000; Year 2, $215,000.
14-9 *a* Imputed goodwill, $120,000; *c* net investment income, $65,250.
14-10 *a* $450,909.
14-11 *a* Imputed goodwill, $950,000; *c* Year 3 amort., $12,250; *d* write-off, $182,875.
14-12 *a* Gain: (1) $565; (2) $528; (3) $525; *b* total, 4,740 shares at cost of $135,185.
14-14 *b* Total investments, $624,775.
14-15 *a* $1,096,505; *b* $538,800, and interest receivable, $60,000; *c* interest revenue, $156,705; total gains, $87,600.

15-1 Aug. 31 bond interest expense, $89,503.
15-2 *a* Sept. 30 bond interest expense, $177,683; *b* loss, $359,878.
15-3 *a* $975,815; *b* discount amort. for year ended 1/2/9, $1,818.
15-4 *c* Gain, $34,400.
15-5 *a* $885,301; *b* amortization, $3,118 and $3,305.
15-6 *a* $2,448,800; *b* loss, $297,600; *c* bond issue costs, $35,200; net bonds payable, $15,840,000.
15-7 *c* Amort. of discount, $500; gain, $21,250.
15-8 *a* Mar. 1, Year 2: amort. of premium, $14,327; *b* amort. of discount, $9,789.
15-9 *b* Amort. of discount, $240; *c* credit Paid-in Capital in Excess of Par, $554,480.
15-10 *a* Interest expense: Year 1, $196,000; Year 5, $39,200; *b* gain, $4,000.
15-11 *a* $3,898,485; *b* amort. of discount, $14,924 and $19,049.
15-12 *c* Credit Paid-in Capital in Excess of Par, $1,896,280; *d* loss, $4,600.
15-13 *a* (1) loss, $18,236; (2) gain, $26,433; (3) proceeds, $955,140.

16-1 Total stockholders' equity, $2,666,000.
16-2 Available for dividends on common stock, $184,000.
16-3 *b* Total stockholders' equity, $6,230,000.
16-4 *b* Total stockholders' equity, $4,514,510.
16-5 *b* Total stockholders' equity, $1,137,500.
16-6 *b* Total stockholders' equity, $6,073,500.
16-7 *b* Retained earnings, $13,743,200; *c* total stockholders' equity, $17,430,700.

16-8 *b* Total stockholders' equity, $2,850,000.
16-9 *a* $25.75 a share; *b* $5.25 a share; *c* total stockholders' equity, $10,091,300.
16-11 *b* Common stock, $1,042,600, paid-in capital in excess of par, $10,017,800; retained earnings, $4,764,900.
16-12 *b* Paid-in capital: preferred stock, $4,832,000 and common stock, $2,880,000; stated capital, $950,000.

17-1 *b* Net common stock options, Dec. 31: Year 8, $80,000; Year 9, $160,000.
17-2 *b* Total stockholders' equity, $2,824,700.
17-3 *b* Total stockholders' equity, $5,212,000.
17-4 *a* Compensation expense, Year 5, $280,000; *b* Total stockholders' equity, $163,350,000.
17-5 Jan. 2, Year 16, gain, $27,000,000.
17-6 *b* Total stockholders' equity, $77,800,000.
17-7 *b* Compensation cost, $1,045,000.
17-8 *b* Total stockholders' equity, $77,050,000.
17-9 *a* Credit Paid-in Capital in Excess of Par, $1,575,378; *b* pre-tax income will increase by $187,726; *d* loss, $524,622.
17-10 Compensation expense: Year 8, $20,000; Year 9, $300,000.

18-1 *b* Total stockholders' equity, $4,398,000.
18-2 *a* (1) $1.25; (2) antidilutive.
18-3 *a* 323,250; *b* $2.23; *c* 363,250; *d* $2.50.
18-4 *b* Total stockholders' equity, $8,168,000.
18-6 *b* Net income per share, $7.14.
18-7 Dec. 31 balances: common stock, $179,350,000; paid-in capital in excess of par: common stock, $107,200,000; retained earnings, $54,782,500.
18-8 Earnings per share: Year 1, $1.25; Year 5, $2.04.
18-9 Dec. 31 balances: common stock, $21,300,000; paid-in capital in excess of par, $5,545,000; retained earnings, $572,500.
18-10 *b* Earnings per share: Year 4, $11.50 and $9.60: Year 5, $9.50 and $8.00.
18-11 *a* Net income, $4,725,000; *b* earnings per share, $8.00 and $5.14.
18-12 *c* Earnings per share: (1) $5.11; (2) $4.73.
18-13 *b* Total stockholders' equity, $5,508,000.

19-1 *a* Pension expense: Year 2, $241,720; *b* Pension expense: Year 2, $111,000.
19-2 Pension expense: Year 1, $63,000; Year 2, $73,040.
19-3 Pension expense: Year 6, $337,935.
19-4 Total pension cost: Year 8, $952,982.
19-5 *b* Projected benefit obligation: Dec. 31, Year 6, $1,368,380.
19-6 *a* Intangible asset dr., $432,000.
19-7 Pension expense, $98,180.
19-8 Dr. unfunded accum., Dec. 31, Year 9, $60,450.

20-1 Net income, $31,569.
20-2 *a* (1) Total expenses, $445,800; (2) $690,000; *b* (1) total revenue, $3,813,156; (2) total expenses, $732,236.
20-3 Debit Leased Eqpt.—Capital Lease, $146,686; credit Liability under Capital Lease (net), $144,575.
20-4 Sept. 30, Year 5, gain on termination, $2,510.